OSSA LATINITATIS SOLA

I

OSSA LATINITATIS SOLA

AD MENTEM REGINALDI RATIONEMQUE

THE MERE BONES OF LATIN

ACCORDING TO THE THOUGHT AND SYSTEM OF REGINALD

Reginaldus Thomas Foster and
Daniel Patricius McCarthy

THE CATHOLIC UNIVERSITY OF AMERICA PRESS
Washington, DC

Superiorum cum permissu

Every effort has been given to determining the exact source of each of the texts reproduced in the reading sheets, and if the source of the few uncredited texts becomes available, it will be acknowledged in subsequent printings.

The paper used in this publication meets the minimum requirements of American National Standards for Information Science—Permanence of Paper for Printed Library Materials, ANSI Z39.48-1984.
∞

Library of Congress Cataloging-in-Publication Data
Foster, Reginaldus Thomas, 1939– author.
Ossa Latinitatis sola ad mentem Reginaldi rationemque = The mere bones of Latin according to the thought and system of Reginald / Reginaldus Thomas Foster and Daniel Patricius McCarthy.
pages cm
Includes bibliographical references and indexes.
ISBN 978-0-8132-2832-7 (pbk. : alk. paper) 1. Latin language—Textbooks. I. McCarthy, Daniel P. (Daniel Patrick), author. II. Title. III. Title: Mere bones of Latin according to the thought and system of Reginald.
PA2087.5.F67 2015
478.2421—dc23
2015023750

"LATINITATIS CORPUS"

REGINALDO PROCURATORE

ADIUTORE DANIELE

QUINQUE IN VOLUMINIBUS

"LATIN'S BODY"

REGINALD BEING THE OVERSEER

DANIEL THE ASSISTANT

IN FIVE VOLUMES

Latinitatis Corpus: The "Body of Latin" is a way of speaking about an appreciation of the Latin language and through it an engagement with Latin writers and speakers throughout the history of western civilization. Through personal interaction with authors of every era and branch of knowledge and type of human experience, our own knowledge of western religions, sciences, and arts has increased, and the full range of human experience is made available.

As an appreciation of Latinity has grown within, the mingling with Latinity grows without. It includes decades of teaching the Latin language in our present day to anyone interested in learning, from the first session-class-meeting to the most fully developed association with authors of every age.

Teaching Latin during the academic term has given an opportunity to develop and test a proper method of drawing others into and guiding them in their dealing with the language. This method of teaching has been recorded in this volume I, *Ossa Latinitatis Sola: The Mere Bones of Latin,* which presents the mere bones or skeletal structure of the language through one hundred and five encounters over three academic years. The reading sheets included in this volume consist of a collection of real Latin texts taken from sources of every age who become our guide and textbook. They contain innumerable examples to illustrate every aspect of the Latin language. In these Latin texts teachers are encouraged to seek and find examples in order to illustrate each aspect of the language and eventually to compose their own fresh collections of reading sheets annually.

To help teachers with this task of finding examples, there is projected an accompanying volume II entitled, *Ossium Carnes Multae*: *The Bones' Meats Abundant*, which will provide numerous, complete letters written by Cicero in their beautiful, functional fullness along with our commentary on nearly every phrase in which we illustrate specific examples of Latin usage present in these letters and cross-referenced to their corresponding encounters in the *Ossa* teaching book. To accompanying these examples, we have also recorded recitations of the letters of Cicero. We call this collection volume III: *Os Praesens Ciceronis Epistularis*: *The Immediate Mouth of Cicero in his Letters*.

Another offering we are making is a collection of worksheets or exercises that direct the student in the learning of the language. We call these projects *ludi domestici* or "home games." The production of new *ludi* yearly for classes taught in Rome over several decades means that all we need to do now is collect them and arrange them according to their corresponding encounters of the Five Experiences. That volume IV of *Ludi* we call: *Ossibus Ludi Exercendis: Games for Exercising the Bones*.

The school work at Rome for decades provided the opportunity of visiting geographical and historical places where the events of western history unfolded while we were using original Latin texts as our guide. These texts have been collected, and we provide them in volume V under the title: *Ossibus Revisenda Migrantibus*: *Things—Places—Events to be Revisited, As Bones Roam About*.

We hope these our own five volumes of *Latinitatis Corpus*: *The Body of Latin* may appeal both to an academic community and more broadly to all those who are engaged in study, research, and teaching Latin, and may inspire them to produce similar works.

Besides these volumes, teaching Latin during the *Schola Latinitatis Aestiva,* "Summer School of Latin," is intended for more advanced study. The long summer evenings give particular opportunity to sit in the garden *sub arboribus,* "under the trees," to experience without end, *sine fine,* how the language was and is spoken.

Libraries will gain invaluable tools, and Latin teachers will find in this series the resources needed to fulfill their mission of drawing others into the documentation of human realities of western civilization expressed in Latin.

flagranti paulatim exorta prius
ex audientium participum studentium Latine
consortio et auxilio ipsa haec
~Latinitatis Corporis~ volumina
ferventem dehinc aliorum similium
ad sodalium affinium sectantium Latine
eruditionem atque conformationem
optato sane auspicato
proficiunto valentoque
XVIII Kal. Dec. MMXIV

THESE VERY BOOKS "OF THE BODY OF LATINITY"
HAVING GRADUALLY ARISEN PREVIOUSLY
FROM THE FERVENT ASSOCIATION AND HELP
OF CLASSROOM-LISTENERS, PARTICIPANTS
AND PEOPLE ZEALOUS ABOUT LATIN,
AS IS WISHED OF COURSE UNDER A GOOD OMEN
MUST PROFIT AND BE EFFECTIVE IN THE FUTURE
FOR THE ARDENT EDUCATION AND PREPARATION
OF OTHER SIMILAR ASSOCIATES, COMPANIONS
AND ONES PURSUING LATIN

14 NOVEMBER 2014

CONTINENTUR

contents

TERTIA EXPERIENTIA 251
Third Experience

IMAGINES

illustrations

EXORDIUM

foreword

Iamdudum exspectas, optime sodalis, librum qui fundamenta de modo Fosteriano docendi unum in locum conferat. Quo facto editores a me petierunt ut Exordium scribam quo animus tuus, ut opinor, ardentius excitetur ad hanc viam Latinae docendae et discendae linguae sequendam. Etenim si ego, qui nullis in aliis studiis nisi scientificis versatus sum, lingua Latina institui et aliqua antiquarum litterarum cognitione erudiri potui, nemo est quin, consilia Reginaldi secutus, facultatem legendi, scribendi, et loquendi Latine adipiscatur.

Quodsi nihil magis valet ad linguam Latinam ediscendam quam diligentissime et accuratissime cuiusque verbi formam necnon totius sententiae significationem observare ac omnino perscrutari, insipientis est hunc onerosum laborem defugere et vagam significationis sententiae notionem satis habere. Minime mirum nobis videri debet eos meliores et fortiores vigere qui cautiores et attentiores singula elementa curaverint. Hoc enimvero Reginaldus docet, hoc praecellit.

Qua de re spero fore ut magis disciplinam quam methodum ex hoc libro colligas, optime sodalis, magis indicationem quam praescriptionem. Ne dubites quin, Reginaldi "ossibus" instructus, gravitati cuiusque muneris quo fungeris convenias. Nihilominus memor esto: "nil sine magno vita labore dedit mortalibus" (Horatius, *Serm.* I, 9, 59–60).

Quod ad me attinet, testificari velim quibus Reginaldi consiliis nunc valeam ad bene beateque operandum apud Officum pro Litteris Pontificiis expediendis. Haec quidem profecto necessaria esse opinor, neque iis praeditus essem nisi Reginaldus ipse ea suppeditavisset.

I. Unum necessarium

Cum Reginaldus lexicon extolleret tamquam unum instrumentum necessarium, non possum non confiteri eum mihi insanire visum. Cum autem conclave Reginaldi in aedibus Vaticanis occupavissem et nihil omnino repperissem nisi mensam, telephonum, Pontificis imaginem, ac densum dictionarium quod *Lewis and Short* appellatur—nullum scilicet instrumentum computatorium, nullum graphium, nullum calamum, nullam chartam (Reginaldus, ut videtur, omnia dictabat)—liquido patuit eum fidem servare. Ego vero, verens ne qua regula grammatica me fugeret, plurimos alios libros in officinam attuli quibus citius dubia de usu linguae solvere possem. Sed cotidiana exercitatione scriptorumque optimorum exempla acute ac subtiliter inspiciendo, certior factus sum verissimum esse facilius ad Latini sermonis usum antiquaeque Latinitatis imitationem nos pervenire si optimum lexicon super omnia usurpemus, non solum quia partes principales necnon significationes omnium verborum contineat, sed etiam cum fons sit inexhaustus linguae Latinae vivae.

Re vera minime hoc est mirandum, quandoquidem, rudimentis linguae habitis, necesse est nativum et incorruptum Romani sermonis odorem spirare qui tantummodo ex ampliore lexico sentiri potest. Alioqui sermo noster, verbis insolitis barbarisque infectus, quasi fictus ac immundus evadit atque sententias Romanorum in dictiones nostras neglegenter convertimus; quod impedimentum superamus si oculis Romanorum mundum conspicimus, cerebris Romanorum cogitamus et cogitata dicimus eodem modo quo Romani ea dicerent si nostris temporibis viverent. Qua de causa ad paginas optimi lexici recurremus et, eloquentiam et optimam scribendi rationem in illo reperientes, paulatim nulloque paene negotio ad Terentii proprietatem ac Ciceronianam facilitatem appropinquabimus. Neque enim dubitandum est quin non solum vocabula maiorum nostrorum, sed etiam humanitatem et sapientiam unico ex hoc instrumento necessario effodiemus.

II. Copia fontium

Lectione multa sermonem latinum optime capi posse Reginaldus semper dicit et ideo studentibus tradit ingentem turbam scriptorum. Sollertia quam maxima curat ut discipuli copiam locorum ante oculos unoquoque die habeant; in quos legendos ita studiose operam navent, ut iam etiam modos scribendi omnium aetatum more experiantur. Primum Ioannis XXIII deinde Ovidii, tum Plauti tum Erasmi, modo Pii II modo Quintiliani, semper autem Ciceronis: locupletissimas sententias ruminantur ut tam componendi quam intellegendi facultatem paulatim adquirant. Hoc modo demum cognovi nihil utilius esse cupientibus sollertiam Latinitatis adipisci quam litterarum tum recentium tum antiquarum, tum classicarum tum ecclesiasticarum pariter exempla perscrutari. Praeterea nullus torpor, nulla neglegentia, nullus hebes sensus memoriam obtundet si mentes exacuemus auctores iugiter alternantes, ita ut in dolore solacium, in labore quietem, in paupertate divitias fidelissime e diversis litteris mutuemur. Equidem hodie alium atque alium scriptorem summo mane lego in officina priusquam animum ad scribendum convertam, praecipue quod, saepe ad eadem genera documentorum scribenda me conferens, praeprimis instandum est ne in molestam repetitionem vocabulorum incidam.

III. Sonoritas linguae

Gloriam Latinitatis e consonantia verborum effluere atque nihil neque dulcius neque suavius modulatione sentantiarum latinarum esse, valde

Reginaldo assentior. Nam si quis absolutum verae amoenitatis requirat exemplar, ad nihil rectius se verterit quam ad Latinitatem. Nihil enim in quopiam genere litterarum praesto est unde nos non possimus venari voluptatem. Reginaldus quidem poetas non praetermittit, quorum carminibus studentes prosam orationem molliorem reddere possunt.

Insuper—quod quidem maioris momenti videtur—intellectus Latinarum rerum ex auditu venit. Nam antequam venustas et pulchritudo Latinitatis percipiatur, non solum necesse est cuique auditori intellegere ea quae aures eius percutiunt, sed intellegere *solum* per aures quae dicuntur intellegi posse. Ea est hominum natura, ut cum quis aliquid mente vult capere, dat operam ut id capiatur aliquo sono qui ore proferri potest. Iustissimum ergo est sermonem “lingua” potius quam “manu” designari. Tametsi scripta manent, tamen, oribus auribusque deficientibus, scripta numquam exsisterent.

Qua re sapientissimus scriptor iocosus Americanus Marcus Twain quondam dixit se nil morari hominem qui uno tantum modo quodque verbum scribere posset. Quisnam porro non meminerit iudicium Socratis contra scripta in dialogo cum Phaedro relatum? Ipse enim non solum verebatur ut memoria teneremus quae promptissima in libris vel in Tela Totius Terrae reperiuntur, sed ne in adrogantiam, qua nihil est peius, recideremus, aestimantes nos ea sapere quae non magis quam leviter nota sunt nobis.

Intellegentiam ex auditu oriri Reginaldus iterum iterumque monstrat, quatenus numquam scriptiones discipulos tractare sinit nisi quis ante clara voce recitaverit. Quamobrem etiamnunc, cum quodlibet opusculum in officina confeci, antequam id superioribus tradam, bis aut ter clara voce perlego ut errores corrigantur, aspera molliantur, supervacua deleantur.

Nihil mihi restat nisi ut multis nominibus gratias agam humanissimo et benignissimo Patri Danieli McCarthy, O.S.B., qui diligentissime hoc volumen exaravit quo tibi, optime sodalis, ossa praebentur, quibus efficaci, vivaci necnon diuturna experientia linguae Latinae fruaris.

Vale.

Rev.dus Dominus Daniel B. Gallagher
Scriptor
Ex Aedibus Vaticanis, Kalendis Iuniis, anno MMXI

IDEM EXORDIUM
the same foreword

Here at last is a book that brings together the basic elements of Foster's teaching method into one place. Perhaps you have been waiting for such a book as long as I have. Now that it is done, I would like to offer a word of encouragement to you, the reader, to follow Foster's unique way of teaching and learning Latin. Indeed, my lack of training in the classics prior to taking Foster's course is itself a testimony to the effectiveness of his method. Thus I am convinced that anyone who patiently follows his path will acquire the ability to read, write, and speak Latin.

Above all, Reggie insists that nothing is more conducive to learning Latin than recognizing the form of every word and analyzing the meaning of every sentence with utmost diligence and precision. It would be a shame to avoid this kind of hard work and settle for a vague "general idea" of what the sentence means. Accordingly, we should not be surprised to discover that those who emerge the strongest and most prepared in Latin are those who took the greatest pains to understand the littlest things from the beginning. This is what Reggie teaches and excels at.

My hope is that you take away from this book more a discipline than a method, more an approach than a recipe. I have little doubt that once you have built a strong skeleton out of these "bones," you will be able to tackle any Latin task you wish. But never forget what Horace said: "Life has given nothing to us without hard work."

I simply would like to mention three aspects of Reggie's approach to Latin that I use daily in continuing his work at the Vatican. I think these aspects are absolutely necessary, and I never would have acquired them if it were not for him.

The One Thing Necessary

I used to think that Reggie's high estimation of the dictionary as the one tool necessary for doing Latin well was rather crazy. But when I moved into his office at the Vatican Secretariat of State and found nothing but a desk, a telephone, a picture of the pope, and a thick dictionary by Lewis and Short—no computer, no pencil, no pen, no paper (apparently he dictated everything)—I realized how serious he was. Nevertheless, out of fear that I might forget some obscure grammatical rule, I hauled in a load of reference books all the same, thinking I might need them to resolve any doubts I had about correct Latin usage whenever composing texts. With daily practice, however, and a close, attentive study of the best writers, I discovered that a facility with the language and the ability to imitate classical authors can be ours if we allow ourselves to rely *primarily* on a first-rate dictionary, not only insofar as it contains the principal parts and meanings of every Latin word, but insofar as it is an inexhaustible thesaurus of examples taken from living Latin.

This really should come as no surprise since, once we have learned how the language works, we need only breathe the pure, fresh air of authentic Roman discourse that can be acquired by consulting a comprehensive dictionary. If we do not, our way of expressing things in Latin becomes liable to strange, barbaric imports and starts to sound artificial and contrived; this is a problem we can avoid if we take the trouble to look at the world through Roman eyes, think with a Roman mind, and express our thoughts the way the Romans would express them if they were around today. This is why we must constantly make use of a superb Latin dictionary, for in its pages we find true eloquence and the best ways of expressing our thoughts, so that we can gradually assimilate the naturalness of Terence and the smoothness of Cicero. Moreover, with this one necessary tool we mine not only the words of those who have gone before us but their culture and wisdom as well.

An Abundance of Sources

Reggie always says that in order to understand Latin we need to read a variety of sources, and he accordingly introduces his students to a wide range of different authors. He takes great pains to expose his students to many different types of Latin each day. By applying themselves to a close study of these different authors, they quickly get a taste of the various styles of Latin spanning the centuries: first John XXIII, then Ovid; now Plautus, now Erasmus; a little Pius II, a little Quintilian, and always some Cicero. Reggie's students sink their teeth into the juicy sentences of a range of authors for the purpose of both comprehension and composition. Reggie has convinced me that nothing is more conducive to a mastery of the language than giving equal time to a careful study of examples taken from both ancient and neo-Latin, classical and ecclesiastical sources. Moreover, if we continue to sharpen our minds by alternating between these different authors, our memories will never grow dull, groggy, weak, or numb, and in times of sadness we find consolation, in weariness rest, and in want riches. That is why I begin each day by reading one and then another author before turning my thoughts to writing. These authors help me to avoid falling into the trap of recycling the same words over and over again, especially when writing the same kinds of documents.

The Sound of the Latin

I now agree wholeheartedly with Reggie that the glory of Latin comes from its mellifluous harmony, and that nothing is sweeter or more pleasing than the rhythm of Latin sentences. If we want a foolproof example of true beauty, we need only to turn to Latin. Indeed, there is nothing that cannot be found in every sort of writing from which we cannot draw some pleasure. Reggie also dedicates time to the poets, for by reading good poetry his students learn how to smooth out their prose.

More importantly, an understanding of Latin comes from hearing it. In order to relish the gorgeous sound of Latin, one must first understand that it is *only* through the ears that we can understand a spoken language at all. It is of the very nature of oral communication that, whenever we want to wrap our minds around something, we first try to encapsulate it into some kind of sound that we can produce with our mouths. Consequently, it is for good reason that we use the word for tongue (*lingua*) to designate a language rather than the word for hand (*manus*). While it may be true that *scripta manent*—"written things endure"—it is equally true that writing would never have existed if it were not for our mouths and ears.

That is why the great American humorist Mark Twain once quipped that he couldn't care less about a man who could spell a word in only one way. And who can forget Socrates' censure against writing in his dialogue with Phaedrus? Not only was the philosopher afraid that we would neglect to commit anything to memory that was readily available in books or on the World Wide Web, but that we would also become haughty by thinking we knew things with which we were only vaguely familiar.

Reggie demonstrates again and again that the comprehension of a spoken language comes only through hearing, whenever he refuses to move on to a new passage until someone first reads the passage at hand out loud. That is why even today, before turning some piece of writing over to the superiors in the office, I read it two or three times aloud so that errors may be corrected, rough spots smoothed out, and anything superfluous deleted.

In closing, I must thank the distinguished Father Daniel McCarthy, OSB, for collaborating assiduously with Reggie to give you these "bare bones" for an effective, stimulating, and enduring experience of the Latin language.

Be well.

Msgr. Daniel B. Gallagher
Writer
From the Vatican, 1 June 2011

PRAEFATIO

prologue

Practical Teaching Advice

"You could read this on the beach!" says Fr. Reginald when surveying the first drafts of this text dictated by him and edited by Daniel McCarthy. A novel of the inner workings and expression of the Latin language, this narrative account could teach Latin as if by reading a novel on the beach. Our teacher's expletive reminds us that the style of this presentation is discursive and is simply not a grammar. It is not a list of rules and texts to be learned by heart. It is, rather, the voice of the teacher giving an oral account of the living Latin language.

The method and style that Reginald has developed and used over the years helps the teacher of the Latin language carefully to observe the students' progress, to encourage them to experience the Latin language, and to make it their own: thus the narrative account is its own pedagogical style. Each of the one hundred and five encounters presented here develops from the previous one, and there is plenty of opportunity given for repetition, revision, and consolidation of what has been learned thus far. Learning and teaching the Latin language in this way will not, however, dispense us from thinking clearly or applying ourselves and our intellect to discovery. This method demands a commitment on the part of both teacher and student, so much so that a written "contract" is recommended to clarify what is essential in these encounters.

The book provides *the mere bones of Latin* along with the living flesh of real Latin literature of authors of every age. The teacher introduces the living voice of these Latin authors and helps the students to see the bones or the structure of the language in these real Latin authors.

It can be done: it has been done

Mary Oliver, recent Pulitzer Prize-winning poet, sums up her approach to poetry, life, and faith in a section within the poem "Sometimes." They are instructions that are applicable to us as we prepare to learn and teach the Latin language in a new way.

Instructions for living a life:
Pay attention.
Be astonished.
Tell about it.

Latin requires attention, wonder, and communication. Learning and teaching Latin in a new way requires those same disciplines.

Instructions for teaching Latin:
Pay attention.
Be astonished.
Tell about it.

Departing from the familiar manual style

Fear of leaving familiar methods behind is like leaving behind familiar territory for the new. This fear can be a block to the progress of teachers and students alike.

We have met teachers of Latin who are simply not prepared to let go of the Latin grammar they first used as a child or in college. But if teachers wish to continue learning from their ongoing encounter with Latin authors, then we can encourage them to let it go and set out for deeper waters.

Fearing to use another method

Fear of adopting a new pedagogy can be a further block to teachers and students alike, and so we do not suggest replacing one set of rote-learning of tables and grammar with another set of rote-learning. We encourage teachers, rather, to leave that behind in favor of understanding the language and meeting its authors in personal encounter. Indeed, the numbering system for the times of verbs clears the deck of technical verbiage and helps the student to learn the logical sequence of human thought shaped and formed by the Latin expression. We offer every encouragement to be cautiously fearless.

Incorporating a company of voices

As a person returns from the beach refreshed, so too this narrative account of the Latin language provides the insights that will refresh every teacher using whatever method of instruction. But just as time at the beach is not spent alone, this novel introduces teachers to many people and helps the student to join this new company of friends. So, this volume helps the diligent teacher to introduce real Latin authors to students in each personal encounter at every level of experience. In this way the teacher provides flesh to the bones and makes teaching Latin a personal expression developed from the teacher' patient conversation with this company of voices. It will indeed be a challenge to the teacher to make this introduction to the Language a series of personal encounters rather than mechanical calculations.

Supplementing tried methods

One way of transitioning to the pedagogy of this book is first to supplement accustomed methods of teaching with new material. I suggest first introducing the range of meanings for each verb time in the indicative and subjunctive. In this way students will have direct access to the many English expressions corresponding to the Latin forms to which we then easily assign a number just as an easy reminder; then the teacher and students will be free of the misleading technical terminology. I also suggest that, as the noun and adjective and pronoun functions are introduced, from the beginning it is far easier to speak about the subject and object, rather than nominative and accusative case, and to say the function "of-possession" for the genitive, "to-for-from" for the dative, "by-with-from-in" for the ablative; this gives everyone direct access to the meanings of words without the encumbering technical terminology that ends up filtering the thought process. Once these two simple steps have been mastered by the teacher, further transitions to the method of the book are seamless.

Weaning oneself from grammatical style

This book and the pedagogical method behind it has no lists and tables as in a grammar. Such a style blocks the learning of any language; just think of the way we learned and practiced and perfected our mother tongue. This method follows that pedagogy of our childhood and invites us to play at the beach and to meet new friends there. When we are refreshed by this new company of friends, we will want to introduce them to our students in refreshing ways.

Adopting a narrative account of the Latin language

Just as this book can be "read on the beach," the lesson plan for each encounter should be well prepared and thought-out for oral delivery in conversational style. This will help the teacher make the encounter more human in style as it introduces the students to the ongoing voice of Latin literature.

To conclude, I turn to the words of Reginald himself:

Why study Latin at all?

"Well," says Reginald, "it is about three-fourths of our western civilization, for one, and all of our thoughts and ideas and prayers have come to us through Latin. The Enlightenment, Science, the Reformation, it all happened in Latin."

How to save Latin?

"Latin is saved by teaching well," Reginald continues. "If you teach music well, you will be converted to the best composers, and you will turn to the most inspiring artists. If Latin is taught well, you will have not ten seconds of boredom, and you will convert your students to this adventure."

James G. Leachman
Institutum Liturgicum, London
Ealing Abbey, London
KU Leuven, Belgium

PROOEMIVM SCRIPTORVM

authors' introduction

Today we join ourselves to millions of people who in history knew Latin and used Latin, to millions of people who throughout the ages studied Latin, mastered Latin and taught Latin, and to people who have left innumerable monuments and eternal creations of Latin for the past twenty-three hundred years.

Latin and its literature are human creations and consequently are learnable and workable by people on planet earth. Latin did not drop down from heaven but was born and grew and evolved and changed for all these centuries.

Latin is not dead, and it will never die, just as Bach or Handel on their harpsichords will never die.

If we want to get into the continuity and stream of human thought until our very own age—you could almost say until 1945—the vehicle of and the key to the whole of western civilization is hidden and buried in the Latin language and Latin literature. And whether we like it or not, that is how things happened and that is how things are. Even if we vote them out, they are still here.

In history, some very wise people immediately saw the value of this tool of human communication, of this mental monument. They were willing to spend time and energy on mastering it. Our library shows us that very many people did master Latin, and that it is quite possible for normal humans to do the same. Those who are studying Latin, and will continue to do so, belong to a very special category, if you wish, of people who share these convictions and have had this experience. Most of them, of course, will vehemently witness to the fact that Latin has changed their lives and has some mystical or magic element which has fascinated and sustained, which has educated and guided people in history for ages.

The saddest thing to see is not so much a decline in the number of those working on this challenging and super-rewarding enterprise, but to see that in very many cases Latin and the whole reality and world of Latin is being presented in a way which cannot help but alienate people from this noble undertaking. There are many teaching methods around the world. Some are ingenious, others are foolish, because the originators of the methods perhaps never understood or learned Latin correctly themselves.

The following pages are the meager result of over forty years of helping people to grow fast and solidly in the knowledge and use and appreciation of Latin. These forty years have been spent with not one minute of boredom or idleness, because the business of learning Latin is a long one that demands not superior intelligence, but a certain kind of character, of seriousness and mature thoroughness that some people do not have.

Therefore, the objective of these pages is to get people into immediate contact with and understanding, love, and use of the entire Latin language in all its literary types and periods of time and authors. Personal practice has been that, by eliminating terminology and all kinds of preambles to the language and literature, people can have access immediately to real solid, natural Latin, which they can then imitate and use and find in these infinite authors and works of Latin in the world.

So the emphasis will be on what things mean, not on what they are called; on how the language functions, not on some sort of artificial rules it allegedly follows. Concentration will be directed to the immediate practice of Latin and the natural learning of it by means of a self-teaching approach which maintains contact with real solid Latin that has existed in this world for all this time.

Some approaches to Latin are far too slow because the learner is held back from genuine Latin for too long a time, because the learner is burdened with the baggage of terminology and irrelevant questions and subtitles, because the impression given is that of schemas, forms, and regulations that you need to master before you see the real language. And that is why any method which does not take on the language from the very first day is in all probability a tremendous waste of time, and, what is worse, it creates a false idea or perception of what Latin actually is.

On the other hand there are programs which are too fast in the sense that teachers or proponents of Latin think that by jamming in patterns of nouns and verbs and anything else you want, and by memorizing nonsense syllables quickly and blindly and superficially, the language is being learned or absorbed or lived out with joy and pleasure.

So on the one hand some people are going too slowly, because they are not dealing with true Latin but with stories, made-up sentences, false examples of Latin. On the other side some are being pushed through a nightmare of grammar talk and lists and forms, and so forth.

What we are trying to do in the following pages provides a certain answer to both of those approaches, which certainly does not promise mountains of gold and certainly does not promise to solve all the problems that there are in Latin learning, but maybe these pages will help some people to get into this adventure story faster and stay in it longer and appreciate it more.

The matter presented here has been the fruit of some personal reflection and especially of much cooperation with studious people who are beginning to learn Latin, who are advancing in Latin, who are finally perfecting their own knowledge and command of Latin. So it has been a common effort which certainly has produced some effect or some benefit in the past and maybe through these pages may continue to do so in the future.

The book is clearly divided into "Experiences" large and small, not lessons, because we are not going to be working with a dead substance but sensing Latin grow inside of us, as we ourselves grow in our mastery and love of it. They are Experiences because, as we move along, it all just gets richer and fuller and more magnificent with time. No one ever decided or could determine what a first or second or third lesson is supposed to do in Latin, but people might want to say that they just have come to know Latin and to love it and to have had this living experience of this human language without breaking it down into artificial lessons.

We have here five bigger "Experiences," which include various degrees or levels of learning.

The First Experience	is the initial exposure to the nature and workings of Latin, especially in word position, verbs, and nouns through daily contact with genuine Latin texts.
The Second Experience	is the immediate application of preliminary training *through speaking activities,* which run concurrently with all other experiences.
The Third Experience	is the second grade of immersion into Latin realities.
The Fourth Experience	is the final, third cycle of Latin assimilation and the end of the systematic language treatment.
The Fifth Experience	is the open-ended, limitless familiarization and further enjoyment of Latin fine points and literary pieces of all times in all fullness.

All five of these bigger Experiences are composed of smaller episodes, which we call "encounters," because they are personal "encounters" between the teacher together with the learner, between the self-teacher or reader and Latin literature. So it is just a variation on a personal encounter of Latin-language people with its masters and creators for centuries.

But, consideration having been made for the realities of human learning, generous time has been distributed throughout the individual parts of the Experiences in order that repetition may be possible and provided, in order that forgetting and relearning may naturally happen, in order that a most natural absorption of Latin elements may be offered. Consequently, nothing is squeezed into a short period, but rather all is extended over an arc of several school-calendar years. The various Experiences will permit this gradual growth as the encounters are allowed time during the week and vacation intervals as they appear on the calendar. In this book there will be frequent repetitions of things which every teacher will recognize and appreciate as necessary parts of human learning. Inasmuch as this is a pedagogical help or guide, the repetitions are intended and hopefully will be tolerated by users and also eventual critics.

The objective is to touch on the whole Latin language in its uses and transformations during the various periods of literature. Every year, be it in the summer sessions or the annual ones, a different packet of Latin authors representing every age of Latin literature is supplied in the classroom to each participant. They are nothing but photocopies of real Latin texts as they exist in books and libraries, which are used by the teacher or self-instructor to find examples to use for filling out the skeleton presentation given in these pages. In addition, the teacher or self-instructor can get his or her own readings. The teacher is advised to find different authors each year so that the encounter with the Latin language may remain fresh and challenging. Collections of readings from past years remain in circulation among class participants, and one year's edition is added partly at the end of each Experience in this book.

As the emphasis in classroom teaching is placed on the student's own practical self-teaching, exercises or personal projects called *ludi domestici* are given twice a week to confirm the learning of new material and repetition of old material. These assignments are corrected and reviewed in class together. Suggestions are always welcome and accepted and discussed with the students.

The ideal of this present publication is not to create or provide a class manual to teach Latin. That would immediately kill the spontaneity which is desired and required. Instead the various elements of the Latin language are gradually presented in a skeleton form—*OSSA*—leaving the choice of concrete texts and examples up to the teacher personally, as some will prefer examples of Latin uses from the poets or prose, from classic authors, from medieval authors, from the Renaissance, from church Latin, from any source. So freedom is left and also the responsibility is left to the individual using this book to personalize it to their own spontaneous way of presenting the different parts of the Latin language, and the examples will be discovered and used by the individual.

Consequently, this book is one-third of a certain kind of method, because it gives the theory. It also provides a second third, the original Latin sources so that the teacher can directly implement the theory in his or her classroom. The final third, the *ludi domestici* are not provided here, because we encourage the teachers to compose these. With the *ludi* the students teach themselves the Latin language, and they review them together in class. Collections of reading sources with *ludi* are already in informal circulation and our own collection of *Ludi* are in preparation for an accompanying volume number four to this one.

Our approach here to the Latin language deals with the essence or *OSSA* of the same language and is directed toward the essentials. There is only one essential reference book which the students must have in class and at home as a companion to everything presented here. That essential reference book is a complete Latin dictionary for the simple reason that, as we shall see, the language is presented and taught out of the dictionary, not out of any grammar book or manual textbook. The nouns, adjectives and pronouns, prepositions, adverbs and conjunctions, and especially the various verb groups are consulted and learned immediately from the dictionary, which for sure provides all the essential building blocks of the language. From this dictionary begins the teaching and practice and understanding of the language. For the beginning Experiences, an available dictionary like Cassell's, Smith, Oxford, or Langenscheidt is sufficient, but not for example, a little pocket book.

For the higher Experiences and summer school the smaller dictionaries are not sufficient because they do not embrace a big enough expanse of the Latin language whereas the only one available today that does this is Lewis and Short's *A Latin Dictionary*, published under the Oxford name. This is the only dictionary today that practically goes from 200 BCE to 500 CE The *Oxford Latin Dictionary* ends at about 160 CE and does not contain material from the patristic and biblical and late-antiquity authors. So a dictionary suitable to the level is to be brought to class and used there for regular consultation, and used at home as the *ludi* direct.

Because our training involves composing simple Latin sentences both in class and for the *ludi*, a small English-to-Latin dictionary is practically necessary. Because the "Lewis and Short" does not have such, we recommend any dictionary that has a vernacular-to-Latin section for use in the First Experience and beyond.

Individuals learning Latin might get a good idea of the attitude and atmosphere of our friendly encounters from the "academic contract" immediately following, which in past years the annual participants in the five Experiences have had to submit with their signature to show that they understand how we are going to do things. The "academic contract" looks atrocious, but in fact it is not, and it is quite possible and it shows how happy and serious we are about mastering Latin.

In this publication as in class we composed our own Latin examples, but where we cite another author, for consistency we have adapted the text to the formatting of this book, especially the Latin citations which typically appear here italicized regardless of their original style.

The explanations of the Experiences and the encounters given in this book are practically a transcription or dictation taken from the classroom oral dialogue. For that reason its language may appear on the lighter side, but should be more lively and accessible, and, as our colleague James Leachman said in his own introduction, it makes for good reading on the beach, while being deadly serious about the fullness and subtleties, the richness and glories of our perennial Latin language.

Reginaldus Thomas Foster and Daniel Patricius McCarthy

PACTVM ACADEMICVM

academic contract

Reginald Foster developed this "academic contract" for his students in Rome and has used it since for people approaching the Experiences presented in this book. It is provided for your consideration. It defines for the reader the methods and approaches of teachers and also the attitude and mindset of students or self-teachers with regard to studying Latin in our particular system.

I, the undersigned party of this academic contract:

____________________________________ ,

have maturely determined to study and progressively to master the Latin Language and Latin Literature in the Foster "Experiences":

ONLY IF I take Latin as an independent, sovereign subject of study and in no way a false addition, special course, appendix, sideline of any faculty, school, program, or plan of education;

ONLY IF I am totally free in my decision to dedicate myself to Latin according to the particular method and system, presented in class—without any outside pressures or obligations coming from advisers, institutional rules, faculty deans, Vatican offices, intimate friends, blood relatives, marriage spouses, or spiritual directors-confessors;

ONLY IF I carefully complete my own personal projects both inside and outside the classroom, with no external assistance, guidance, or counseling—which prove to be useless and harmful;

ONLY IF I am present in person actively at all school encounters, as consistently and regularly as the human condition allows;

ONLY IF I find in my daily life a reasonable, workable, tolerable home and school activity schedule which—even leaving room for other theoretically more pressing and important studies—will assure me of a tranquil and deep application and growth in Latin without any nervous frustration or mental anguish;

ONLY IF I pursue my chosen "Experience" to the very end, finishing all the assigned *Ludi Domestici* up to the final one, on time;

ONLY IF I personally ask and answer pertinent questions, before, during, after classes, with genuine interest and honest enthusiasm;

ONLY IF I destine a fitting amount of time and have peace every week to think and reason, to resolve Latin problems and teach myself, and consequently to assimilate this fundamental language gradually—not to hurry carelessly nor to try to memorize blindly any type of forms-paradigms-schemas;

ONLY IF I refuse all sorts of foolish joint-study arrangements, group consultations, copying sessions with others, as well as aids from external texts, tutors or books;

ONLY IF I absorb this heavenly language and literature on its own merit, apart from empty credits or records, and eventual letters of confirmation.

signature: ____ *(date)* ____________.

LECTIONUM RATIONES

rationale of the reading sheets

On just about every page of the encounters of our five Experiences, the reader or teacher alone or in the classroom has been advised to consult real Latin literature from every period and there find infinite examples of the matter treated in the encounters. Many sincere and studious individuals are paralyzed and wonder where they are going to find all this literature. In fact it is found in the Latin-language section of any substantial library or on the bookshelves of Latin scholars and enthusiasts around the world.

We are very conscious of this concrete difficulty, and in response we are producing our volume number two of numerous letters of Cicero where nearly every sentence is an example of many Latin usages, each cross-referenced to the encounters of this book. Individual usages will be understood in the full expression of an entire letter so that we may learn from his vibrant, living language.

But more immediately we have decided to include in this volume a certain mass of Latin literature to which we also refer throughout the course of this work. These are pages of Latin writings from about 200 BCE to our present day. Some people will be surprised at the boldness of this project, so we ought to explain here the nature of these reading sheets.

As an appendix to each experience we have chosen completely at random a collection of readings with a mixture of poetry and prose, of sacred and secular literature, of good and bad writers, of ancient and middle and modern literature. No attempt has been made to collect easier texts for the earlier experiences and more difficult texts for the later experiences for this precise reason: because Latin is what it is, there is no such thing as easy Latin or difficult Latin. Cicero can be very easy and immediately understandable, whereas a Bible text may be obscure and difficult; classical poetry can be simple, but medieval poetry can be very challenging; Thomas Aquinas and the other scholastics can be very demanding, whereas Erasmus can be child's play. So, the sheets do not correspond to any calculation of difficulty or ease in usage. Rather, the readings are presented as just a part of the whole history of Latin literature. In preparation for class the teacher is invited to identify in these reading sheets specific examples appropriate to each encounter to illustrate the matter of the Latin language under discussion.

These five collections of reading sheets were originally used during a particular academic year, one of many collections we could have chosen. We are ready to admit publicly that the readings are not the best or the most ideal or, even less likely, the perfect selections of Latinity, as there is no such thing, just as there is no such bar of music which is the best in the world. The fact is that for thirty-five years, as many different packets of readings were made up and given to the students, so there was no strict repetition of anything. This makes every year's Experiences new ones, although the basic teaching of the Latin language remains according to our system.

Method of producing sheets

Our method of producing reading sheets is for the teacher to photocopy texts from the inexhaustible supply of Latin books available in libraries and anywhere else. We were sure to select texts of many different authors from every era of Latin literature and genre. These photocopied pages were cut up so that the essential elements of the Latin text could be arranged and pasted onto a single sheet of paper or at most two sheets. By essential elements we mean the title and the text without the critical apparatus, because our task is not the critical reconstruction of the text, but rather the understanding of the text as it appears in the printed volume or manuscript edition in a library personal or communal. We added to each sheet of paper the name and dates of the author and arranged them in chronological order according to the dates of each writer. Then we assigned our own numbering system typically from the letter A to M, omitting the letter "J." Each packet of sheets was compiled for one of the Five Experiences, others for the different groups of summer school. There are fewer sheets for the second experience, but the fourth experience has two pages for each author. These sheets of paper were then photocopied and distributed free of charge to the students as the packet of reading sheets for each Experience.

The texts are found as they are in this world; they have not been doctored or manipulated or, we hate to use the word, "dumbed-down." As a consequence of our method, some pages are clearly legible, some are more difficult to read corresponding to the condition of the source and so provide opportunity for students to learn how to read these texts as they exist in the library. The idea is to get the students as close as we can to the books that they may find on bookshelves everywhere as they are printed in different styles, without computerized enhancing or even correction of mistakes; this is all part of our naturalized learning and absorption of the Latin language. In this way students learn how to approach books.

The production of this book

For the production of this book, our method has been followed on the following reading sheets indicated first with the number of the Experience in Arabic numerals, followed by the letter of the sheet in its packet: 1-L, 2-F, 4-B, 5-H.

Our original idea and ideal was to present here the reading sheets as photocopies of texts as they are found in library books on the shelf and consequently available to everyone with all of their errors, blots and typographical peculiarities in order to avoid any impression of manipulating or changing the text for any given reason. However, certain external conditions were made to prevail which resulted in presenting library book editions and copies of Latin authors in a different way in the majority of the reading sheets in this volume.

Many of these texts are taken from older editions, to be honest, with the intent of avoiding onerous copyright difficulties. Although we are quite conscious that newer editions may and do exist, nevertheless in our pedagogical intention super-critical texts are not necessary. We are conscious of more recent Latin composition which is noted on occasion.

Sentence structure

Among the readings are found sheets entitled *Sententiarum Structura Latinarum*, "Structure of Latin Sentences," sheets 1-D, 3-D, 3-I; *Latinarum Compages Sententiarum*, "Formation of Latin Sentences," sheet 1-I; *Latinarum Compositio Scriptionum*, "Arranging of Latin Sentences," sheets 4-D, 4-I. These each have a number of short texts chosen from another random selection of authors. Different personal or conventional systems are used to point out the connections and functions of words. The system used here is our own convention. In the following key you can see that subjects are underlined with a solid line, objects with a dashed line and verbs with a dotted line. The connection between separated words is indicated by a wavy underscore. Larger clauses are set off by square brackets, while smaller ones are set in rounded parentheses. Conjunctions such as *et* and *–que* are set apart in a box.

KEY:

Subjects

Objects

Verbs

Distant connections

[Larger clauses]

(Lesser clauses)

et and -que

Not every such instance is indicated and the teacher may use and adapt these as is spontaneously helpful in revealing the structure of each sentence by connecting nouns and adjectives, by showing the subject and verb and objects, and by marking off clauses within clauses within a whole paragraph with brackets and parentheses. While these marks may look confusing, closer observation will show the pedagogical intention in presenting these complete texts with their essential parts in this way.

Keep it fresh and lively

These reading sheets are intended to inspire other teachers to do the same and to find their own texts and supply them to students fresh and new every year. The user can find short phrases, long sentences, or whole paragraphs to analyze on any level of Latin learning from the first day to the top of the mountain. This demands time and patience, but is part of the vocation of a teacher and a learner. The fact is, the reading sheets contained in this volume, and in the next volume the letters of Cicero, will supply more than enough consultation matter for a long, long time.

We wish much success and enjoyment and full learning of Latin by means of the teaching that has gone before and the reading helps which have been provided here as a taste of other possible adventures.

COMPENDIARIA AVCTORVM OPERVMQVE NOMINA

abbreviated names of works and authors

Ambros. Ambrosius Mediolanensis (333–397 CE)
de Paen., de Paenitentia
Ep., Epistulae
in Luc., Expositio Evangelii secundum Lucam, Libri X

Aug. Aurelius Augustinus Hipponensis (354–430 CE)
de Gratia, de Gratia et libero arbitrio
Enar. in psal., Enarrationes in psalmos.
Ep., Epistulae

Caes. Gaius Iulius Caesar (c. 100–44 BCE)
B. C., Bellum Civile
B. G., Bellum Gallicum

Cat. Gaius Valerius Catullus (c. 84–c. 54 BCE)
Carm., Carmina

Cic. Marcus Tullius Cicero (106–43 BCE)
Ac., Academicae Quaestiones
Att., Epistulae ad Atticum
De Div., De Divinatione
Fam., Epistulae ad Familiares
Imp. Pomp., Oratio de Imperio Gnaei Pompei, or *Pro Lege Manilia*
Rosc. Am., Oratio pro Quinto Roscio Amerino
Rosc. Com., Oratio pro Sexto Roscio Comoedo

Cod. Iur. *Codex Iuris Canonici* (1983)

Cypr. Thascius Caecilius Cyprianus Carthaginiensis (c. 200–258 CE)
de Lapsis
Ep., Epistulae

Dante Dantes Alagherius (1265–1321)
de Mon., de Monarchia

Enc. Pat. *Enchiridion Patristicum*

Eras. Desiderius Erasmus Roterodamus (1466–1536)
Stult. Laus, Stultitiae Laus

GL Gildersleeve and Lodge
Gildersleeve's Latin Grammar

Hier. Eusebius Hieronymus (c. 342–420 CE)
ad Eph., in Epistulam ad Ephesios commentarii
contra Vigil., contra Vigilantium
Eccles., in Ecclesiasten commentarius
Hab., in Habacuc commentarii
Isa., in Isaiam commentarii

Hor. Quintus Horatius Flaccus (65–8 BCE)
Ep., Epistulae
Serm., Sermones

Isid. Isidorus Hispalensis (560–636 CE)
Etym., Etymologiae

Leo Leo Magnus (440–461 CE)
Tract., Tractatus

Liv. Titus Livius (59 BCE–17 CE)
ab Vrbe condita

Lucr. Titus Lucretius Carus (c. 99–c. 55 BCE)
de Rerum natura

Mart. Marcus Valerius Martialis (c. 40–c. 103 CE)

Morus Thomas Morus (1478–1535)
Epigram., Epigrammata

Nep. Cornelius Nepos (c. 100–c. 25 BCE)
Vitae

Ov. Publius Ovidius Naso (43 BCE–17 CE)
Am., Amores
Pont., Epistulae ex Ponto

Picco. Aeneas Sylvius Piccolomini (1405–1464), Pius II (1458–1464)
Comm., Commentarii Rerum Memorabilium

Plaut. Titus Maccius Plautus (c. 254–184 BCE)
Men., Menaechmi
Poen., Poenulus
Stich., Stichus
Rud., Rudens

Plin. Gaius Plinius Caecilius Secundus (minor; 61/62–113 CE)
Ep., Epistulae

Polit. Angelus Politianus (1454–1494)
Ep., Epistulae

Quint. Marcus Fabius Quintilianus (c. 35–c. 95 CE)
Inst., Institutiones Oratoriae

Sall. Gaius Sallustius Crispus (86–c. 35 BCE)
Iug., Iugurtha
B. Cat., Bellum Catilinae or *De coniuratione Catilinae*

Sen. Lucius Annaeus Seneca (c. 4 BCE–65 CE)
Ep., Epistulae
Vit. Beat., de Vita beata

Tac. Gaius Publius Cornelius Tacitus (c. 55–c. 119 CE)
Germ., Germania

Ter. Publius Terentius Afer (195/185–c. 159 BCE)
And., Andria
Eun., Eunuchus
Heaut., Heautontimorumenos
Phorm., Phormio

Tert. Quintus Septimius Florens Tertullianus (c. 150/170–c. 230 CE)
adver. Hermo., adversus Hermogenem
de Carnis res., de Carnis resurrectione
Paen., de Paenetentia

Tib. Albius Tibullus (c. 60–19 BCE)
Carm., Carmina

Verg. Publius Vergilius Maro (70–19 BCE)
Aen., Aeneis
Georg., Georgica

Vulg. Nov. Nova Vulgata Bibliorum Sacrorum editio, 1998
II Sam., Liber secundus Samuelis
Prov., Liber Proverbiorum
Matt., Evangelium secundum Matthaeum
Luke, Evangelium secundum Lucam

VOCABVLORVM COMPENDIA

abbreviations of words

abl.	ablative, form or function by-with-from-in
abl. abs.	ablative absolute
acc.	object, object form or function
ACI	*Accusativus Cum Infinitivo,* accusative with the infinitive
adj.	adjective
adv.	adverb
BCE	before the Common Era
Bk.I	noun and adjective Block 1
Bk.II	noun and adjective Block 2
c.	common gender
CE	of the Common Era
cf.	*confer,* "compare"
dat.	dative, form or function to-for-from
dep.	*deponens*, deponent
e.g.	*exempli gratia*, for the sake of an example
eccl.	ecclesiastical Latin
f.	feminine gender
gen.	genitive, form or function of-possession
Gp.I	verb Group 1
Gp.II	verb Group 2
Gp.III	verb Group 3
Gp.IV	verb Group 4
loc.	locative, form or function of place where
M & M	expressions of Mind and Mouth
m.	masculine gender
MA	Modal Attraction
n.	neuter gender

nº	number
nom.	nominative, subject form or function
OCD	*Ordo Carmelitarum Discalceatorum*, Order of Discalced Carmelites (Carmelite)
OO	*Oratio Obliqua*, indirect discourse
OSB	*Ordo Sancti Benedicti*, Order of Saint Benedict (Benedictine)
p.	page
pass.	passive
subj.	subject, subject form or function (subjunctive is spelled out)
T.1, T.1i	Time 1 indicative
T.1s	Time 1 subjunctive
T.2s	Time 2 subjunctive
T.2, T.2i	Time 2 indicative
T.3s	Time 3 subjunctive
T.3, T.3i	Time 3 indicative
T.4s	Time 4 subjunctive
T.4a, T.4ai	Time 4a indicative
T.4b, T.4bi	Time 4b indicative
T.5, T.5i	Time 5 indicative
T.6, T.6i	Time 6 indicative
Track I	Primary sequence of tenses
Track II	Secondary (historical) sequence of tenses
v.	*vide*, "see"
v. a.	active verb, transitive verb
v. dep.	*verbum deponens*, deponent verb
v. n.	neuter verb, intransitive
voc.	vocative, form or function of direct address

PRIMA EXPERIENTIA

first experience

ET·HIC·EPISCOPVS:CIBV:ET:
POTV: BE NE DIC IT·

ENCOUNTER 1

OSSIUM GLUTEN: SENTENTIARUM LATINARUM ORDO = EXITUS ET VOCABULA. SIGNA PERSONARUM IN VERBIS

the bones' glue: the structure of Latin sentences = terminations and vocabulary. signs of persons in verbs

Introduction

As you begin this Latin adventure, we are speaking to you after having revised this book, *Ossa Latinitatis Sola*, and having written the initial draft of the second book in this series, *Ossium Carnes Multae*. The working of the Latin language, we wish to impress upon you, must be perceived and emphasized from the first encounter and illustrated with numerous examples. A thorough understanding and appreciation of the following principles will be your salvation in approaching Latin. These principles will save you an infinity of time in redoing and correcting your understanding or renderings into any language on earth. The following considerations, unfortunately, are not noticed or observed by many people when learning Latin, and yet they are essential and demanding.

These principles of the Latin language serve these first two books and all of our work as the glue that holds the whole enterprise together. So, we call these principles the *Ossium gluten*, "the bones' glue." It may take hours for this glue to be absorbed totally, and days, months, if not years, for this glue to set fully until these principles hold your Latin experience together. We present the eleven principles in the following list and then in the subsequent commentary.

OSSIUM GLUTEN: *the bones' glue*

1. Word order in itself never essentially reveals the meaning of the Latin sentence.
2. The position of the words is not fixed.
3. Only the ending-termination of the word tells you its function-role in the sentence.
4. Functions produce true meaning, rather than empty jargon.
5. Literature will teach you.
6. Read the entire sentence, because you will not know what is where: the subject may be last, the object first.
7. Never begin blindly with the first word.

8. Know your vocabulary and how it appears in the dictionary.
9. Each Latin sentence has a trap; every sentence is an adventure.
10. One letter of variation in a word can totally change your understanding.
11. Learn Latin from the dictionary and literature, not from a grammar.
12. Enjoy the Architecture of Latin.

1. Word order in itself never essentially reveals the meaning of the Latin sentence

Most other languages produce their meaning from the physical order of words, one after another. Change the order of the words and you change their meaning, as in, "Mary sees Robert" and "Robert sees Mary." Here, changing the order of two words reverses the meaning of the sentence.

We must convince ourselves that Latin is totally different, that the words can be scattered, and the order in itself never *essentially* reveals the meaning and notion of the sentence. Every real Latin sentence can illustrate this fact of the language. Two Latin sentences can have the same word order but with opposite meanings. We can say *Robertus Mariam videt*, "Robert sees Mary," or *Robertum Maria videt*, "Mary sees Robert." We can also change their word order and both of these Latin sentences still produce the same meaning.

2. The position of the words is not fixed

The disposition of words in a Latin sentence is extremely free, but is neither irrational nor foolish. Any logical element can be anywhere, within the limits of a phrase or clause, depending on the inspiration and style of the author. The verb may be first, the subject last, the object in between, as will be illustrated by the teacher through numerous examples from any readings.

The word order varies because of each author's impulse or inspiration, sense of beauty, harmony, music or the rhythm of the Latin sentence. So, while word order may be elegant or clumsy, clear or obscure, smooth or crude, obvious or difficult to decipher, still we must never rely on word order alone or the placement of words to produce the meaning of a Latin sentence.

The word order may follow every possible arrangement, and it will never have to reflect the same order of words in contemporary languages.

3. Only the ending-termination of the word tells you its function-role in the sentence

Most Latin words have variable endings, which are flags telling the reader what the word is doing in the sentence, what its task is, or what we call its function in the sentence. The human mind, when noting this fact, will put all these messages together and produce meaning. This can be pointed out by any text on any page of genuine Latin in this world and must be made clear from the very beginning.

Every language has a different system for determining the function of a word in a sentence. English depends mostly on word order and to almost no degree on endings. German has four functions of nouns, pronouns, and adjectives, plus the verb; Greek has five; Slavic languages have many more. Latin is moderate with seven functions. They include besides the verb:

function: subject
function: object
function: of-possession
function: by-with-from-in
function: to-for-from
function: direct address
function: place.

One of the challenges and joys for everyone learning Latin is to know what ending has what function in the sentence. This is a delicate and lengthy task.

4. Functions produce true meaning, rather than empty jargon

You can see in the above presentation of the functions that we wish to cut out terminology and move directly from the function of a word in a sentence to its meaning. That is why we refer to the function "by-with-from-in," because almost every use of that function means one of those four words. We refer to the function "to-for-from," which has these three meanings.

Learning and teaching Latin must not be encumbered by terminology that intrudes in this direct expression of meaning. Foolishly parroting memorized lists of word endings means nothing, because they are outside of a human expression.

The mental analysis of the endings of words to determine their function in the sentence will be slower in the beginning but will speed up naturally with practice and repetition of this mental process. Cicero and his wife Terentia and their children, Tulliola and Marcus, had the same learning curve!

5. Literature will teach you

Continuous reading and familiarity with real Latin literature will permit the recognition of the functions and their meaning. This operation becomes easier when it considers and understands a complete human thought expressed in genuine Latin. The Latin language did not come down from the skies, but was generated by humans speaking and developing their communication on earth. Some people may be tempted by the apparent security of memorization charts, which never lead to understanding this full human communication.

6. Read the entire sentence, because you will not know what is where: the subject may be last, the object first

Because of the free and unpredictable disposition of words in the Latin sentence, the ending—that is to say the function of every single word—must be mentally seen, registered, catalogued, and analyzed. That means that the whole Latin sentence must be read, heard, viewed in its entirety in order to see the functions and the connections among all the elements.

Words that go together like a noun and its adjective or a verb and its subject and object may be separated by ten or fifteen other words, but the function of each will show their interrelationship and contribution to the whole expression. Reading a sentence quickly as if the word order were sufficient, and guessing the general meaning of a sentence will not lead to any clear understanding or genuine encounter with the author, but may create the impression of Latin competence and experience, which in fact are empty and false.

7. Never begin blindly with the first word

Never begin understanding with the first word of the Latin sentence, because people have this temptation to pounce on that first word and start babbling from there. Some eloquent Latin sentences begin with a lesser element and gradually build until at last the whole sentence comes together; but to understand the function of the lesser elements or any element, you must consider the whole sentence.

8. Know your vocabulary and how it appears in the dictionary

It is not enough to know sterile endings alone, because in Latin the same letters of an ending can have different functions in different words, contrary to Esperanto. You must learn the ending and its function together with the vocabulary. Namely, you must know where the word comes from, how it is found in the dictionary, what its place is in the language. Once that is clear, the function of that word in a sentence will be nearly certain.

All the words in the following example have the same ending *–IS* presented in capital letters, although they have different presentations in the dictionary. Only by knowing the vocabulary notation in the dictionary can you understand what the ending is doing and thereby discern the function of the word in the sentence:

*aud**IS***	you hear
*patr**IS***	of the father
*mir**IS** mod**IS***	in wonderful ways
*omn**IS** voc**IS***	of every word.

Many Latin sentences can be taken in many different ways, because the endings of different words may be the same. For example, the Latin word *vis* means "force" if it is a noun, but if it is a verb it means "you wish." Only the dictionary origin of each word will tell you how to interpret its ending and thus its function in the sentence.

9. Each Latin sentence has a trap; every sentence is an adventure

Every Latin sentence hides some sort of trap, and part of the Latin adventure is to sort out the various possibilities and come to a conclusion. Even after you have mastered the entire Latin language, it will never yield automatic results, and after you have read and analyzed every syllable, you will still have to reason and think to find the most logical and acceptable meaning. Latin is precise and infallible, if you are observing, combining and deducing, concluding.

In the expression *cives nunc vocamus*, the word *cives*, "citizens," as we shall learn, can function either as the subject or as the object. The sentence, then, can mean either "now we are calling the citizens" or "we the citizens are calling now." So, the endings are essential, but even after you understand every word, you still have to think it out. The question *cur portas portas*? ("Why are you carrying the doors?") plays on the two different functions of the word *portas*, which can act as a verb meaning "you are carrying" or can be the object meaning "the doors." The amazing thing is that neither you nor spirits can tell which instance of *portas* is functioning as the verb and which as the object, yet the meaning is infallible. But the question remains, "Which is the verb?"

All this requires attention and thought and may be tiring, but in the end it is rewarding, because it opens the door to the essence of Latin.

10. One letter of variation in a word can totally change your understanding

The difference of one letter of the alphabet in a word can change or upturn the whole story in Latin as in other languages. We recently came across a form of the verb *dispicio*, which is a perfectly fine verb meaning "I discern." There is another word, however, *despicio*, which means "I despise." Because of the similarity of these two words, only one letter different, formal writing today may avoid the use of *dispicio* to avoid confusion with *despicio*.

The confusion of forms is exacerbated in Latin because so many forms differ by only one letter, and often an internal letter. This happens in every language, but in Latin this happens in every sentence.

11. Learn Latin from the dictionary and literature, not from a grammar

The way through the confusion of a Latin sentence is to learn how the word appears in the dictionary and that will then nail down the possible forms of the word and their functions in a sentence, which we shall gradually learn. For example, *canes* can mean three things in Latin, each with a different dictionary entry. It can mean "dogs" in the plural. It can mean "you will sing" from one verb, and from a different verb it can mean "you are grey-haired." Consulting a good dictionary in the classroom and at home is essential for distinguishing these different words that can have the same form but function in different ways in a sentence.

The four words in the following expression all end in the same way, *auxilium civium omnium egregium*, "the outstanding assistance of all the citizens." It is not sufficient to associate one meaning with each word, because that will not tell you how it functions in this expression. Only by knowing the vocabulary and the dictionary entry for each word can we distinguish the different functions of each word in the expression.

Thus, our whole method of learning Latin consists in 1) knowing the vocabulary from the dictionary and, based on the dictionary entry, 2) we must know the possible forms and their functions in the sentence 3) as exemplified by the literature. Without these, the student floats around aimlessly forever.

12. Enjoy the Architecture of Latin

One architectonic trick that was used by Latin writers and occupies much of our attention both here and especially in our second book, *Ossium Carnes Multae*, on the letters of Cicero, is "subordination," namely a clause depending on a clause on various levels and often placed one within the other. This architecture of the Latin sentence we liken to Chinese boxes or Russian dolls where a clause is nestled within a larger one and by layers within the full sentence—as an inner court is surrounded by a *porticus*, surrounded by a walkway, and enclosed by the outer walls of a building. As in the construction of a building, this produces symmetry in the architecture of a Latin sentence. The student's task is to keep the boxes together and to see the whole sentence growing into this full construction.

The beauty of the architecture of Latin is well expressed by L. P. Wilkinson in the first words of introduction to his book, *Golden Latin Artistry:*

> Ever since I have been able to read Latin, it has been the sound and movement and architectonics of the language that have fascinated me, at least as much as the substance of anything most Romans had to say ... and of course form and content are really indissoluble. But there are literatures in which the formal element plays a far greater part than in others, and when we are not absorbed in reading them, we can sit back and obtain an intellectual pleasure, perhaps even increase our appreciation at the next reading, by examining how the writer, consciously or unconsciously, has obtained his effects. And one of the pioneers of this practice was, in fact, Cicero (p. XI).

An appreciation of the beauty of Latin may take hold right away and inspire students as they absorb and digest, assimilate and realize these twelve principles; this is humanly possible and totally rewarding.

The signs of persons in verbs

We prefer to begin our discussion with the verb, which is the soul of any human sentence. The ending of the Latin verb tells you what the nature and number of the subject is. The actual subject may be expressed by a word in the subject form or must be known from the contents of the whole story. The personal endings of Latin verbs have been the same for twenty-three hundred years and are found in every sentence and can be learned on the spot with absolutely no difficulty; this can be done from the very first day of Latin if it is presented correctly and effectively.

We are dealing here with the basic, active meaning of the verbs and their forms. The passive will be treated later in our adventure.

If the subject of the sentence is "you" in the singular, then the ending of the verb will be *–s*. (Do not worry about this now, but on one occasion the ending for "you" in the singular will not be *–s*, but *–sti**, something that is pointed out by us in the beginning and for a while indicated by an asterisk until the verbs are treated.) Innumerable examples of all this can be found in the readings at random.

If the subject is "I," then the ending can be either *–o*, *–m*, or *–i*. Subsequent learning will tell which of these three endings applies and when.

If the subject is "we," then the ending will be *–mus*.

If the subject is "he, she, it," then the ending indiscriminately will be *–t*. This ending does not define the subject better, but leaves it "he, she, it." The precise subject is revealed only by an expressed subject or the entire story.

If the subject is "they," then the ending must be *–nt*

If the subject is "you" (plural, which will be for the rest of our study "you all"), then the ending will be *–tis*. (As indicated above, even here on one occasion instead of *–tis* the ending will be *–stis***. You will learn subsequently when this happens in the language.)

Thus for twenty-three hundred years:

you (singular)	= *–s* (*–sti**)
I	= *–o*, *–m*, *–i*
we	= *–mus*
he, she, it	= *–t*
they	= *–nt*
you (plural)	= *–tis* (*–stis***).

Examples from the teacher or reading sheets could be like the following:

feci, "I did"	*fecerunt*, "they did"	*fecisti*, "you did"
amas, "you love"	*amant*, "they love"	*amo*, "I love."
amabam, "I was loving"	*amabatis*, "you all were loving"	
amabo, "I shall love"	*amabit*, "he, she, it will love"	
	amabimus, "we shall love"	

As the teacher points out the verbs on any reading sheet, you can now finally state the meaning of the personal endings.

ENCOUNTER 2

ASINUS – CAPRA – VEHICULUM. DUPLEX PRINCIPIUM IN NEUTRIS SUPREMUM

Block I nouns. super double principle in neuters

Introduction

After surveying the verbs and their personal endings in the first encounter, in this encounter we shall present some nouns to get the language working actively within us and working passively in our reading.

For a definite pedagogical reason and contrary to traditional Latin grammars and texts, we present two huge Blocks of nouns with their corresponding Blocks of adjectives, employing a distinction that also occurs in Greek, one Block or the other Block. This method facilitates the comprehension of the nouns and adjectives in one block and the nouns and adjectives in the other, and it really works and avoids all confusion and meaningless memorizing. There were no declensions for the Romans.

1. Block I nouns: *Asinus – capra – vehiculum*

We gather three families of nouns together in the First Block along with the adjectives. The nouns of each of these three families are distinguished by their entry in the dictionary. The dictionary will be our guide.

Consult your dictionary to find the entry:

asinus, *i*, m., a donkey.

The four elements of this dictionary entry tell us first the singular subject form of the noun, here *asinus*. Second, the sign of the noun family, here the letter *–i*. Third, the grammatical—not natural—gender of the noun as happens in many languages, but only as a rare exception in English, here "m." for "masculine." Fourth, its meaning in English, here "a donkey." Let us look at each of these elements for several nouns.

In the above example, the first word given, *asinus*, we call the "dictionary entry" for this noun. In this case, *asinus* is the form when the noun functions as the subject of a sentence. The second part of the dictionary entry, *–i*, is the sign of the noun's family; by no means is it the plural, as is so often erroneously understood. The third part is the grammatical—not natural—gender of the noun. In this case "m." means that *asinus* is a masculine noun, as are most of the nouns of this family, and refers to a donkey regardless of the sex of the thing it names. Listed fourth is the English meaning of the noun, "a donkey."

Let us take another noun, say:

capra, *ae*, f., a she-goat.

From this we already know, first, that the "dictionary entry" of the noun is *capra*. This is the form when the word functions as the singular subject of a sentence. Second, the ending *–ae* is the sign of the noun's family. Third, the grammatical gender of the noun is "f." for "feminine," as are most of the nouns in this family, with some notable exceptions. In this case *capra* happens to refer to "a she-goat." So, although at first glance the grammatical gender happens to coincide with the sex of the animal described, this connection is not intrinsic. Finally, we see that *capra* means "a she-goat."

The third family of nouns in our First Block is represented by the noun:

vehiculum, *i*, n., a vehicle.

Again, the dictionary entry is *vehiculum*, which is the form when the noun is used as the singular subject of a sentence. Second, the ending *–i* is the sign of the noun's family, not its plural. Third, the grammatical gender of the noun is "n." for "neuter." All of the nouns ending in *–um*, *–i* are neuter. Fourth, in English *vehiculum* means, "a vehicle."

Thus, we have seen three families of nouns with endings that will correspond to the First Block of adjectives which have the endings *–us –a –um*. The three families of nouns in this First Block have the endings:

–us, *–i*
–a, *–ae*
–um, *–i*.

2. Object forms

We want to point out immediately what happens in Latin when these nouns of Block I have a different function in the sentence. We have already seen the form of these nouns when they function as a subject in the sentence:

asinus *capra* *vehiculum*.

When these three and all the innumerable nouns of the First Block function as the direct object in the sentence, the endings of the nouns change.

This presumes that we can identify the subject and object in the vernacular. Our Latin approach here takes for granted basic human language uses and concepts such as singular, plural, subject, and object. In this regard, for English speakers there is a very useful guide by Norma Goldman, *English Grammar for Students of Latin*.

Subjects like *asinus* ending in *–us*, as objects become *asinum* ending in *–um*. Subjects like *capra* ending in *–a* are changed to the object *capram* ending in *–am*. Subjects like *vehiculum* ending in *–um* remain the same even though their function in the sentence has changed to the object. Thus, we have seen:

asinus	*capra*	*vehiculum*	subject function
asinum	*capram*	*vehiculum*	object function.

What must be stressed is that the ending of the noun indicates the function no matter where the noun is in the sentence. It can be anywhere, the first word, the last word, and its ending will indicate its function.

3. Plural subjects

We can immediately see the plural forms of these and all the nouns of these three families when they function as the plural subject of a sentence. Again, their endings change to indicate their function as plural subjects. The singular subject *asinus* ending in *–us* becomes the plural *asini* ending in *–i*. Singular nouns like *capra* ending in *–a* are changed in the plural to *caprae* ending in *–ae*. Singular nouns like *vehiculum* ending in *–um* are changed to the plural *vehicula* ending in *–a*. Thus, we have seen:

asinus	*capra*	*vehiculum*	singular subject function
asini	*caprae*	*vehicula*	plural subject function.

The neuter singular and plural you may recognize from English. We say "one millennium," "two millennia"; "a single criterion," "several criteria"; "a football stadium," and "many stadia."

4. Plural objects

The plural object forms of these three nouns, representative of their noun families, will now be added. Once again the endings are changed to indicate this specific function in the sentence. This time, rather than beginning with the dictionary entry, we shall begin with the singular object form of each noun and then give its plural object form. This practice we call "reversing" whereby we make the singular word plural, or the plural word singular. Reversing words will prove an important way of learning them and of showing that we have a correct understanding of the word and of its function in the sentence.

We have already seen that when a noun like *asinus, –i*, functions as the singular object in a sentence, its form is *asinum* ending in *–um*. When we reverse *asinum*, that is to say when we make it the plural object of the sentence, it has the form *asinos* ending in *–os*. If a word belongs to the family of nouns like *capra, –ae*, its singular object *capram* ending in *–am* is reversed to its plural form *capras* ending in *–as*. If a word belongs to the family of nouns like *vehiculum, –i*, its singular object *vehiculum* ending in *–um* has the plural form *vehicula* ending in *–a*. Thus, we have seen:

asinum	*capram*	*vehiculum*	singular object function
asinos	*capras*	*vehicula*	plural object function.

So, you have the subject and the object both plural and singular of these three families of nouns, which are cousins and belong to the same general block corresponding below to adjectives that end similarly in *–us –a –um*.

It will be a great consolation for first learners to know that with this matter we already are introduced to roughly 40% of the nouns in the Latin language and 50% of the adjectives—and all this in our second encounter.

5. Ambiguities

You will notice immediately several things which are going to warn you from the very beginning about the nature and pitfalls and traps of the Latin language. You will notice that the ending *–a* can indicate several functions in a sentence. It can function as a singular subject feminine or as a plural subject or object neuter. You will notice that the ending *–um* can function as a singular object masculine or as a singular subject or object neuter. The only way to decide how nouns ending in *–a* or *–um* function in a sentence is to know your vocabulary. If you know your vocabulary, then the dictionary entry will tell you to which family a noun belongs. Only knowing which family a noun belongs to will allow you to decide how the noun is functioning in the sentence.

For example, the dictionary entry gives *capra, –ae,* f., and from this entry we know that the form *capra* cannot be a neuter plural subject or object; we know that this is the form when it functions as the subject in the sentence. Similarly the dictionary gives the entry *asinus, –i,* m., and from this entry we know that the form *asinum,* which may appear as a neuter, is in fact a masculine object. The dictionary entry will tell you which block the noun is from and then you will be able to recognize and create the different forms of the noun according to its different functions in the sentence. Again much class time can and should be spent on identifying these nouns—subjects and objects—on any reading sheet you want. These noun Blocks and families must be reviewed and inculcated by looking at examples on reading sheets or at real Latin examples provided by the teacher.

6. The super principle in neuters

Another rule for many languages is that in the neuter the subject and the object form are identical. We call this the "super principle," because it hovers over all other principles and is completely immobile and no exception exists. In the Latin language this ambiguity produces immediate confusion and work for human thought. If we say:

Vehiculum indicat aurum

inasmuch as both *Vehiculum* and *aurum* are neuters, the sentence can mean both:

The vehicle points out the gold
The gold points out the vehicle,

because, as we have stressed in the first encounter, the word order does not produce the meaning; rather, the endings do. In this sentence both nouns are identical, and we start our Latin adventure.

The example:

Asinum vehiculum portat

must mean

The vehicle is carrying the donkey.

We know that *vehiculum* can be the object or subject because it is neuter and comes from *vehiculum, –i*. But we also know that *asinum* must be the object because it comes from *asinus, –i*, which leaves *vehiculum* as the subject.

But if we have the sentence:

Instrumentum vehiculum portat

we are lost, because with two neuters we do not know which the sentence means:

The instrument is carrying the vehicle
The vehicle is carrying the instrument.

This super principle for the neuters works both in the singular and in the plural. Lots of thinking is involved, but also a mental triumph and intellectual pleasure.

We can profitably play with these little things for a long time in very many examples from Latin literature. The important matter is to realize that the endings are still our salvation. Ambiguity is unavoidable, but the dictionary entry will help us know what the endings mean for each word and how it functions in the sentence. Even after we have learned all the elements and usages of the language, thinking is still necessary.

7. Observations

Looking at the dictionary entry once again, we said that the second element tells us the family that a noun belongs to. You may have noticed that for the entry *asinus, –i*, m., the second element, *–i*, looks like the ending for the plural subject *asini*. However coincidental, this is not the case. The second element does not indicate the subject plural form of the noun. Rather, it tells me what family the noun belongs to. At this point, this second element indicates the block and family the noun belongs to, but later in our training we shall see that it has its own specific function and meaning.

Again, for the entry *capra, –ae*, f., the second element, *–ae*, seems to indicate the subject plural form *caprae*. Likewise, this is not the case. The second element does not give the plural form of the noun, but, rather, tells me what family the noun belongs to.

This is seen more clearly with *vehiculum, i*, n., where the second element *–i* does not indicate the plural form, which in the neuter is *vehicula*. Rather the *–i* tells me to which family the noun belongs.

At this point we want to look at our reading sheets or Latin literature to see all the subjects and objects coming from these three families of nouns, which for us constitute Block One. We can spot them and want to watch the word order and the freedom of the word order and the fluid mobility of the Latin sentence.

We shall also notice later on, not today, that there are adjectives with exactly the same endings and exactly the same functions. For example, you can find in your dictionary the entry:

parvus –a –um.

Here we see the masculine singular subject *parvus*, the feminine singular subject *parva*, and the neuter singular subject *parvum*. We shall talk about this type of adjective on another day.

8. Note on our method

Some people might be interested to know why here you will not find paradigms or charts that give all the forms for nouns, adjectives, or verbs. If you wish to learn in that manner, you may consult an almost infinite number of Latin grammar books which teach the language in that way, a way we carefully avoid here for several reasons. First, paradigms and word charts are usually presented as some sort of essence of the Latin language, which they are not. Second, the Romans did not have them; they had the language. Third, we do not want students to memorize lists of word forms extracted from whole sentences, because the word forms have meaning only in a full human expression. Fourth, worse yet is to reduce these schemas of words to a list of endings only. We do not want students to memorize nonsense syllables *–a –ae –ae –am –a* like a parrot presentation. They may think that by doing so they know Latin. Fifth, we wish to break the bad habit and bad pedagogy and the whole futile approach which has nothing to do with the Latin language.

We insist that students from their First Latin Experience learn the function of the word in its sentence. So far we have summarily presented seven functions for nouns together with their precise forms for the subject and object functions of Block I. We shall present the functions essentially and progress gradually through our First Experience to an understanding of all the functions, rather than recite some meaningless exercise with no understanding or appreciation of the content.

ENCOUNTER 3

PERSONARUM PRONOMINA. ET – AC – ATQUE; ET . . . ET; –QUE . . . –QUE

pronouns of persons. conjunctions: and, also, even; both . . . and; both . . . and

Introduction

With our verbs and nouns moving ahead in our developing Latin art, we can easily begin the pronouns by looking at their subject and object forms. The pronouns, like the nouns, are connected with the verbs.

1. Pronouns of persons

The singular subject for "you" is *tu*, and its plural is *vos*. The singular object for "you" is *te*, and its plural is also *vos*. You are now trained to note and maybe to expect that the same form *vos* is ambiguous, because it functions both as the subject and object plural. What will resolve this ambiguity is naturally the verb. If the verb, for example, ends in *–t*, then its subject is "he, she, it" and *vos* will be the object. If, however, the verb ends in *–tis* (*–stis***), then *vos* can be its natural subject and object, so:

vos bene videtis in speculo

can mean both:

you all see well in the mirror
you all see yourselves well in the mirror.

The subject pronoun for "I" is *ego*, and its plural is *nos*. The object pronoun for "me" is *me* and its plural is *nos*, where we have the same phenomenon as with *vos*, namely that *nos* can function as the subject or object, and the verb will save us there.

The subject pronoun for "he" is *is;* the one for "she" is *ea*; the one for "it" is *id*. When these pronouns function as the object, then *is* becomes *eum*, "him," and *ea* becomes *eam*, "her," and *id* remains *id*, "it," according to the super principle for neuters. When these pronouns are reversed and made plural, then *is* becomes *ei* or *ii*, "they, people, men," and *eum* becomes *eos*, "them, people, men"; the plural of *ea* "the woman" is *eae* "the women" and of *eam* is *eas*, "the women"; the reverse of *id* is *ea* "those things, the things," which functions as both subject and object according to the super principle for neuters.

Here we notice by our growing sense of the nature of the Latin language many things. First, the endings of the pronouns *eum* and *eam* and *eos* and *eas* are the same as previously seen for the nouns, as are *ea* and *eae*. There is a consistency here which you must notice and which will help you overcome many Latin difficulties.

Second, you will also notice that *ea* can mean "she," which functions as the singular subject, and it can also mean "those things" and function as the subject or object in the neuter plural. This means that the sentence

Ea ea nominat

is going to produce an interesting thing in Latin. One of the two pronouns *ea* must be the feminine subject, and the other must be the plural object in the neuter. The sentence must mean:

She names the things.

Because the word order is not essential for meaning in Latin, I do not know which *ea* is which. This is one of the mysteries which no person can solve, but which will make you very smart. That is Latin.

We learned in our first encounter that the verbs of themselves indicate the subjects, and we can remind people that in Latin, contrary to English and German, for example, the pronoun subject does not have to be expressed. So I can say *canto* or *canto ego*, "I sing"; *vos cantatis* or *cantatis*, "you all sing." I can say *cantat* or *is, ea, id cantat*, "he, she, it sings." However, the declaration of that pronoun subject is in general rather rare in Latin; it is there mostly for emphasis or importance, because the verb itself indicates the subject clearly enough.

2. *Et – ac – atque*: and, also, even

As an extra piece of new Latin material in our third encounter we can briefly say that the idea "and" is expressible in three general ways in Latin.

1. The word *et* is the normal and simple connector of two equal parts which are not specially related.
2. The word *ac*, also written *atque*, joins things which are closer together by nature like mothers and fathers, sisters and brothers.

Both *et* and *ac*, *atque* mean "and." The dictionary will also give *et* with an emphatic meaning "even," as in *et ego intellego*, "even I understand," or *et eos laudamus*, "we praise even them." They must both be carefully distinguished from another Latin word *at* also written *atqui*, which means "but, however." This suggests another principle for Latinists, as we say: one letter in Latin can kill you: *interficere te Latine una potest dumtaxat littera*.

3. The third and, among the Romans super-favorite, way of expressing "and" is by the suffix *–que*, which by definition is added to the end of a word toward the beginning of the second element.

This word for "and, also," *–que*, does not occur between words but is attached to the end of a second word which is being joined, or, if we are dealing with a longer sentence or paragraph, *–que* will be joined to the end of one of the first words of the second element or the second clause or the second sentence. That means that when *–que* is observed, a connection has to be seen between two equal parts that may be divided at a distance. In theory the use of *–que* indicates a closer connection yet, but many times all of these forms of saying "and, also" are just interchangeable and a matter of style or variation of the Latin text. Examples include:

mater et pater
mater ac pater
mater paterque.

To join two phrases you could say:

Nostra pulsamus instrumenta hymnosque cantamus vestros
We sound our instruments, and we sing your hymns.

In the above example, note that the *–que* joins two equal elements, namely the two verbs, *pulsamus*, "we sound," and *cantamus*, "we sing." The *–que* is not joined to the second of these verbs, but to the first word of the second element, that is to the plural object *hymnos*, "hymns." Here ... *hymnosque* ... does not mean "and hymns," but "and [we sing] hymns."

Finally, there are a number of other elegant and useful combinations such as *et ... et* in the following:

Et filii et canes adstabant
Both children and dogs were standing nearby.

Et formicas observamus et elephantos
We respect both ants and elephants.

In the above example, *et ... et* means "both ... and." The use of *–que ... –que* is similar:

Noctesque diesque cantavimus
We sang both days and nights.

Epistolaeque advenerunt sarcinaeque
Both letters and packages arrived.

Again, all of these common elements in the Latin language will be confirmed by a simple glance on a sheet of real Latin, as found at the end of this experience or provided by the teacher, where *et ...* , *ac ...* , and *–que* will appear elegantly and naturally in every other sentence.

ENCOUNTER 4

TRAPEZITA, AE; SOCER, ERI; HONESTUS, A, UM; LIBER, ERA, ERUM

variations in Block I nouns. adjectives of Block I

Introduction

Once we have become acquainted with our First Block of masculine, feminine, and neuter nouns, we want to point out some very slight dictionary variations that will cause no confusion, because now we know how to use the dictionary.

1. The varying reality of Latin words

One variation is a word like *nauta, –ae*, m., "a sailor," which is masculine. Many people presume it is feminine, because they think all the nouns ending in *–a –ae* are feminine. But we know we will get the gender from the dictionary, and it is masculine for *nauta, –ae*. Another example is *trapezita, –ae*, m., "a banker," which belongs to the family of nouns ending in *–a –ae* and is also masculine in gender according to the dictionary. When one of these nouns is accompanied by an adjective, it will be masculine, which will cause a little disturbance but not for long.

Another variation occurs in the singular subject of certain words. For example, if we see the plural subjects *soceri* or *arbitri*, we might expect that their reverse, the singular subjects, would be *socerus* and *arbitrus*. But, when we consult the dictionary, we find instead *socer, eri*, m., "a father-in-law," and *arbiter, tri*, m., "a judge." Your dictionary tells you that *socer* and *arbiter* belong to this First Block of nouns, because the second part ends in *–i*, while the singular subjects are slight variations on the ending. The dictionary also tells you that *socer* and *arbiter* are masculine. From the dictionary entry you can already construct the plural objects *soceros* and *arbitros* and then reverse them to the singular objects *socerum* and *arbitrum*. These are small variations; they are not many, and they are noticed and absorbed easily.

2. *Honestus, a, um*

Part of our pedagogy is to introduce 50% of all Latin adjectives in the same block as 40% of nouns. So, as hinted above, let us consult an adjective in the dictionary. The dictionary entry is:

honestus, a, um, honorable, noble.

This tells us that *honestus* is masculine, *honesta* feminine, and *honestum* neuter. Adjectives of this type, *–us, –a, –um*, follow the First Block of nouns, with its endings and functions.

Thousands of these adjectives are going to have exactly the same modification of their endings as the nouns of the same type. In Latin 50% of adjectives are going to follow this particular pattern, and it is a consolation to know that already in the beginning with our Block I nouns and cousin Block I adjectives we are practically dealing with half of them all.

3. *Liber, era, erum*

As you have already seen for the noun *arbiter*, a slight variation occurs in certain adjectives like:

liber, era, erum, free, unfettered.

Here, we might have expected the masculine form *liber* to have been *liberus*, but instead, the dictionary gives us *liber, era, erum.*
Putting all this together, we have the examples:

Honestus et liber nauta currit
A noble and free sailor runs

Honestum et liberum nautam dilaudant
They praise a noble and free sailor.

In both of these examples all the endings are different, but in fact they all agree in gender, number, and function. The Latin poets from Plautus to our present day are good guides to this connection between nouns and adjectives that go together, even though they do not have the same endings, because of the loose positioning of the words in their verses, and so again the use of reading sheets with poets is recommended at this point to show the distances but connections between nouns and their proper adjectives scattered about in the sentence.

ENCOUNTER 5

ADIECTIVA VELUT SUBSTANTIVA; BREVITAS ET AMBIGUITAS

adjectives used as nouns according to their gender; brevity and ambiguity

Introduction

When people say in contemporary languages, "The good do this" or "The good conquer the evil," and they say "die Guten und die Schlechten" or "i buoni e i cattivi," what they are doing is what the Latins and the Greeks have been doing for ages: using adjectives as nouns.

1. Adjectives used as nouns according to their gender

This is very popular and extremely frequent in Latin. To do this, the Romans use the adjective that corresponds to the gender and number of the missing noun. For example:

Boni bona faciunt

which expanded out to its whole ramification means:

Good people do good things.

In this case, *bona* is a neuter plural adjective meaning "good things," and *boni* is the masculine plural adjective meaning "the good people, good men." You might also note that *boni*, "good people," serves as the subject of *faciunt*, ending in *–nt*, which, as you already know from our first encounter, means "they."

If the same sentence refers to a number of women doing good things, then you simply change *boni*, which is masculine, to *bonae*, which is feminine plural, and we have the sentence:

Bonae bona faciunt
Good women do good things.

Here the adjective has the same gender and number as the noun, which is not expressed, so that the adjective takes over as a full-fledged noun.

The use of an adjective as a noun is extremely important, especially in the neuter, for example:

universa	all things
singula	individual things
parva	small things.

In all of these the noun idea is contained in the adjective that is used.

2. Brevity and ambiguity

Because in so many instances throughout all of Latin literature the noun is not expressed, but is thus contained in the adjective, you are going to have extremely pithy, short, and effective Latin sentences that use this phenomenon, as in:

Bonos boni laudant
Good people praise good people.

These Latin sentences will be so pithy that they will produce a certain ambiguity, as in the following:

Bona bona facit
A good woman does good things.

This expression has a certain ambiguity, because *bona* can mean at least two things in the Latin language. Here, one *bona* is the feminine singular subject, "a good woman," agreeing with the subject of the verb *facit*. Because *facit* ends in –*t*, you know that its subject is indiscriminately "he, she, it." The other *bona* is the neuter plural object meaning "good things." The problem is that, because the word order does not produce the meaning of the Latin sentence, you can not know which *bona* is the subject, "a good woman," and which is the object, "good things." Good luck!

Now it is up to the teacher to look around and find in any source or any monument of Latin literature examples of these things which are very frequent and which will allow the students to master this idea immediately. At the same time the teacher will be repeating everything we have said so far about verbs, pronouns, and the whole real Latin language learned up to now.

ENCOUNTER 6

CASUUM DEMONSTRATIO + SIGNIFICATIO. PRAEPOSITIONES + ACCUSATIVUS – QUATTUOR CUM MOTU

indication and meaning of the functions.
prepositions with the object form
– four with motion

Introduction

From all of Latin literature we have seen that the language at its highest development produced seven possible functions for nouns and adjectives and pronouns. This puts Latin more or less in the middle of languages where some, like German and Greek, have four functions and others have twelve or thirteen functions. So Latin is not the most developed or the most underdeveloped language. It is in the middle.

1. Indication and meaning of the functions

Here the functions will be pointed out and their technical names given, not because the technical names are essential but because the technical names are found everywhere in the world and in other Latin textbooks and grammars. So we shall give the names out of courtesy and necessity, not out of any enthusiasm for or support of them.

The list of the seven functions already touched on in Encounter One begins with the "subject" function, technically called the nominative case, because it is used to name people and things.

The next function we have seen is the "object" function, also called the accusative case because it is used most of the time when someone accuses someone else as the object of the accusation.

The third function is of origin and possession, and so we call it the function "of-possession." This function is usually expressed in English either by "of," as in "a picture of the father" or "friends mindful of us," or by an apostrophe and "s," as in "the mother's money," meaning "the money of the mother." This is called the genitive case because natural generation points out the origin of something, as in "They are the children of John and Dianne" or "Michael and Eleanor's daughter is Kathryn."

The fourth function will have a very broad application and very many smaller functions in it, but they can all come down and be reduced more or less to the ideas of "by-with-from-in." This is an abbreviated way of saying instrument (by), accompaniment (with), separation (from), place wherein (in). The natural meaning of this function is separation "from" although it includes many others. This is called the ablative case because its basic idea is expressed by the participle *ablatum*, meaning "a thing having been taken away."

The fifth function is that of the general idea "to" or "for" or "from," and so we call it the function "to-for-from." Its uses will have the natural meaning of "to" or "for," but it will also be used in connection with very many Latin verbs whose indirect object is going to fall into the category "from." Because *dare* in Latin means "to give" this function is generally called the dative case because it is the case of the one to whom something is given.

The sixth function is used to express direct address, when someone is called upon or named, as in "*O my dear friend*, where were you?" or "Mr. Bender, please close the door." We call this the function of "address," but, because the Latin verb meaning "to call" is *vocare*, the case of calling or naming is also called the vocative case.

The last function in Latin is a remnant of a larger use, and it is used with proper names of towns and small islands to designate "location." For example, one may say, "I was born in Florence" in Latin as, *Natus sum Florentiae*. Here the one word *Florentiae* all by itself means "in Florence." We call this the location function, and others call it the locative case from the Latin word for "a place," *locus*.

The uses of the seven functions will gradually be explained slowly over a period of our three Experiences.

At this point the teacher will bring out reading sheets or will produce examples and, understanding whole sentences, will point out the function of every single word and give the general idea of the seven functions as they are found in real literature without any emphasis on the technical term but rather on the idea behind each function ending. Students will provide the meaning, once the teacher has designated the function. For example, the teacher may simply tell the students, "This is an example of by-with-from-in," and the students will directly, exactly, clearly, immediately understand the concept without technical talk.

2. Prepositions with the object form

Now then, after mentioning the functions, we can pick up one function and start illustrating it. The object function as given above is used on two occasions: 1) to designate the direct object of the verb in the sentence and 2) to designate the direct object of one half of the prepositions in the Latin language. To anticipate things coming later, we can say now that half of the prepositions will take the object form and half will take this other form that we call the function by-with-from-in. In this regard the teacher just once in the student's life will want to list all of the prepositions as given in B. L. Gildersleeve and Gonzalez Lodge, *Gildersleeve's Latin Grammar*, n° 415, or in any Latin manual. Write the prepositions on the board or screen with their general meanings. The learners will be encouraged to consult the dictionary to learn the vast richness of each preposition beyond appearances, which are much broader than any restricted translation, or any short vocabulary list to be memorized for school quizzes. The prepositions that take the object form are:

ad toward, to, at (the window), according to, up to (time), in order to, for (our consolation)

adversus (adversum) toward, in the direction of, against, toward (as in "love toward your parents")

ante with place and time: in front of, before (not to be confused with the Greek *anti*, which means "against"; so "anti-war" is "against the war," but "ante-bellum" is "before the war")

apud with persons: beside, by, with, at the house of, among, in the time of, near, at, in the writings of

circa, circum, circiter around (place or time)

cis, citra on this side of, short of, without

clam unbeknownst to (*clam me*: unknown to me)

contra against, opposite

erga toward (in moral relationships, similar to *adversum*), against (Be careful because *ergo* means "therefore, for the sake of," and *erga* means "toward, against." One letter in Latin!)

extra outside (as in *extra ordinem*: out of the ordinary, extraordinary)

infra below (as in *infra* red: below the red rays on the spectrum)

inter between (two), among (many); *inter nos*: among us (inter-mural sports are between schools)

intra within (*intra venas*: within the veins) (Intra-mural sports are within the walls of one school.)

iuxta classical meaning: next door to, next to (something) (*iuxta positus*: having been placed next to, in juxtaposition); an important, frequent later meaning found in the Bible, patristic writing, canonical use: according to

ob in the sight of, in front of, for, because of, on account of, for the sake of (*ob viam*: in front of the road. The English word "obvious" means that you are face-to-face on the road.)

penes in the possession of, in the authority of, in the hand of

per through, with the help of, with the mediation of, by, over (*Per* never, ever means "for," as in, *per eos* means "through them" but never "for them.")

pone behind (in the poets)

post (like *ante*) behind, after (*post partum*, after childbirth; *ante meridiem*, A.M.; *post meridiem*, P.M.)

praeter beyond, except, beside, outside of (it is inclusive and exclusive, for example *praeter eum*: exclusively, "everyone except him"; inclusively, "everyone beside him," meaning to start with him and add others)

propter nearby, next to; on account of, because of

secundum according to (The phrase *Evangelium secundum Marcum* does not mean "the second gospel.")

supra above

trans over, beyond (in numerous English applications)

ultra beyond (Ultra-violet light is beyond violet in the spectrum.)

usque up to.

The purpose of this list of prepositions is not to have anyone memorize them all, but it is to give students or curious people a look once in their life at the whole number of prepositions, to see them once and then to be advised that each one can be studied in the dictionary in order to discover the richness and multiple uses of every preposition. The learner will also notice with joy and exultation now a fuller meaning of innumerable English words derived or compounded with the same Latin prepositions.

3. Four prepositions with motion

We have said that half of all the Latin prepositions will take the object form and the other half will take the form by-with-from-in. There are, however, only four prepositions that are on the fence between those two collections of prepositions; these are "in a special box." These four can take either the object form or the form by-with-from-in. These four are *in*, *sub*, *super*, and *subter*. Consulting your dictionary again and again, you will learn that these four are used with the object function when the idea of motion—geographical or moral—is expressed in the sentence. So the preposition *in* followed by the object form implies motion "into, onto, toward, against, for," and the preposition *sub* followed by the object form implies motion "below, underneath"; *super* and *subter* are obvious and on the rare side. Here is their list:

in (with the object form) into, onto, toward, against, for; (with the form by-with-from-in; no motion) in, place where, location or rest in a place

sub under, below, underneath (with the object form: under which a thing comes, goes, extends; in temporal relations it means closely before or after something); under (with the form by-with-from-in: under which a thing is situated or takes place)

subter beneath

super over, above.

ENCOUNTER 7

MODI INDICATIVI TEMPORA EORUMQUE INTELLECTUS VERNACULI

times-tenses of the indicative mode and their vernacular meanings

Introduction

The verb has always been considered the heart of any sentence in any language and the same is especially true of Latin. A word of caution is necessary to make people aware that the Romans or Latins are by far more precise and more exacting in their use and in their understanding of the Latin verb than is customary in rather careless modern languages. At this moment it is important that we see the general possibilities of the Latin verb in the mode of direct declaration and of direct questions, sometimes called the indicative or indicating mode. A previous general language experience in any tongue would and could help us immensely to grasp Latin. Poor preparation in the schooling of Latin students slows, complicates, and impedes the Latin process sadly and painfully. Sorry!

Times-tenses of the indicative mode and their vernacular meaning

The mode of direct declaration and question, as in many other languages, has six logical verb times in Latin. In keeping with our general approach of direct contact with the essence and the meaning of things and the avoidance of unnecessary terminology, which impedes learning and slows down a whole spontaneous process, we in this school will give various English meanings for each Latin verb form to which we assign a simple number. The student will find out that the reference to a number will recall certain meanings, and terminology can be avoided. Because the technical names are found in other pedagogical systems which cause and perpetuate confusion, we shall give the technical names out of courtesy and not out of enthusiasm for them. In this encounter we shall give the meanings in English contained in each Latin time. In a later encounter we shall see how to produce, to construct, the forms themselves of the verbs in each of these times.

Time 1

The meanings contained in Time 1 are given by the example:

diligimus
we love
we are loving (*progressive*)
we do love (*intensive or emphatic*).

All three of these concepts are contained in the simple Latin form. Other systems call Time 1 the present tense. The point is not that the two names are interchangeable with each other, Time 1 with the present tense, but that we prefer to associate the Latin verb in Time 1 directly with the three concepts that it expresses in English. This immediacy between Latin and the range of expression in English will cut through obscure terminology and give the student direct access to the meanings of the times in English.

Time 2

Time 2 denotes a continual or habitual or repeated or frustrated action in the past. The meanings of Time 2 are given with the example:

Agros colebat
He was cultivating the fields
He used to cultivate the fields
He always cultivated the fields
He continued to cultivate the fields
He tried to cultivate the fields
He was cultivating and continued to cultivate the fields
He would cultivate the fields (*whenever it happened*).

All of these concepts are contained in the simple Latin form. This time and its meanings are usually compared to the moving film of a movie camera. The film itself has numerous photos of the action taken in rapid-fire sequence so that, when passed through a movie projector, we see that the film records a continuous action repeated over time in the past. This time is rather rare in Latin because of the precise kind of action it is indicating, namely repeated or continuous action in the past, not any simple previous reality whatsoever. Other systems call Time 2 the imperfect tense. Again this terminology creates a stumbling block for students desiring to learn as directly as possible the full range of meaning contained in the Latin verb.

By the way, Michelangelo signed his immortal Pietà in the Basilica of St. Peter with *Michaelangelus faciebat*, "Michelangelo was making [this]," which hints that perhaps he never considered it finished.

Time 3

The meanings contained in Time 3 are given through this example:

cantabunt	*cantabimus*
they will sing	we shall sing
they will be singing	we shall be singing.

In other systems this time is called the simple future. Note that these are not to be confused with the command forms in correct English, which are just the opposite, as we shall see. For example, "I shall" and "we shall" express the simple future, whereas "I will" and "we will" are command forms. These are reversed for "you shall," "he, she, it shall," "they shall," which are command forms, but "you will," "he, she, it will," "they will" express the simple future.

These are standard, traditional, high English usages, which obviously are not being observed everywhere today. Most people do not make these distinctions, but they shall be observed here for clarity.

Time 4

Time 4 is the dominating verb of the past. The history of the world is really written in Time 4, as it narrates individual history, events. The Latin language has a great, lamentable deficiency here, because the one verbal form must express two distinct time frames. In English we must choose between the two different time concepts that are expressed by one verbal form. So we must make a distinction between Time 4a and Time 4b. Both Time 4a and Time 4b have the same verb form in Latin, but they express different time values.

Time 4a

Time 4a describes an action in the past which somehow affects or touches the present or comes up to the present or continues into the present. The meanings of Time 4a are given here with the fuller expression contained in the time of this verb:

scripsistis
you all have written (and I have the letter here)
you all have been writing (up until the present time).

Time 4b

Time 4b is the most used historical-narration time with which we narrate individual past events that have no necessary connection to the present moment. Whether these past events occurred a minute ago or a thousand years ago does not make any difference. They all are considered without a necessary connection to the present, as in the example:

imperavit

he commanded (this morning or last year or referring to Julius Caesar or two minutes ago)

he did command.

In contrast to Time 2 describing a motion picture, both Time 4a and Time 4b can be compared to single photographs. Time 4a is a photograph that reaches into the present, and Time 4b is a photograph of a past event that does not touch on the present.

The difference between Time 4a and Time 4b can be heard in the descriptions of a building completed in 1930. The construction and completion of this building may be described in Time 4a, Time 4b, and Time 2 in the following examples that supply an implied statement:

Aedificium perfecerunt idque ante me video hac inaugurationis die

They have completed the building and I see it in front of me on this dedication day (Time 4a)

Aedificium perfecerunt anno millesimo nongentesimo trigesimo

They completed the building in 1930 (said in 1931 or 2014; Time 4b)

Aedificium perficiebant octo annos

They were constructing this building for eight years (from 1922–1930; Time 2).

The top two above present a photograph of the completion of the building, but with different references to the present. Time 4a considers the completion of the building with its reference to the present, and Time 4b considers the completion of the building as a completed action in the past without a necessary reference to the present.

What we call Time 4a is called the pure or present perfect in Gildersleeve and Lodge n° 235–38. What we call Time 4b is called the historical perfect or the Greek aorist in Gildersleeve and Lodge n° 239–240. Their difference is explained in Gildersleeve and Lodge n° 235:

1. The Pure Perfect differs from the Historical Perfect, in that the Pure Perfect gives from the point of view of the Present an instantaneous view of the development of an action from its origin in the Past to its completion in the Present; that is, it looks at both ends of an action, and the time between is regarded as a Present. The Historical Perfect obliterates the intervening time and contracts beginning and end into one point in the Past.
2. An intermediate usage is that in which the Perfect denotes an action in the Past (Historical), whose effect is still in force (Pure).

Our Time 4a is otherwise called the present perfect or the pure perfect, and our Time 4b is called the historical perfect. Some people will know this distinction from Greek, which has totally different verbal forms for the perfect (Time 4a) and the aorist (Time 4b), but the Latinist is stuck with one, which multiplies, not lessens, the difficulties.

Time 5

Time 5 describes a past action that precedes another past action. The meanings of Time 5 are given in the example:

petiveras
you had asked
you had been asking.

What we call Time 5 is commonly called in other systems the pluperfect tense from the Latin, *plus quam perfectum*, which means "more than perfect."

Time 6

The last one, Time 6, describes a future action that is completed before another future action takes place. The meanings contained in Time 6 are given with the example:

respondero
I shall have answered
I shall have been answering.

Time 6 is very common in Latin, more so than in English, especially in conjunction with Time 3. The Romans are very precise on its use in ways that we are not. What we call Time 6 is known in other systems as the future perfect tense. The Romans will say:

> *Dabo quodcumque voluerint*
> I shall give whatever they will have wanted.

The mode of direct declarations and questions has these six possible times in the Latin language. We have presented each time in direct correlation with the possible English equivalents contained within the time of the Latin verb. By making such a direct correlation between each time and its range of meaning in English—to which we assign a number—we hope to facilitate the spontaneous and natural learning of the Latin language.

Examples pointed out in class on every page of Latin literature, at the same time in the same breath as all of the above theory, will confirm the teaching, begin the natural learning of the verbs, and console the learner to a very great degree. Latin will be learned immediately.

ENCOUNTER 8

PRINCIPALES VERBORUM PARTES. TEMPORA 4, 5, 6 OMNIUM VERBORUM: COMPOSITIO FACILIS

principal parts of verbs.
times 4, 5, 6 of all verbs:
easy construction

Introduction

In most languages like Latin or English or German or Italian, the verbs have different forms to express different times and functions. In English we have the forms "do, did, done"; in German, "tun, tat, getan"; in Italian, "faccio, fare, feci, fatto"; and in French, "fais, faire, fait, fait." The principal forms of the Latin verb are presented in every dictionary. In Greek there are six principal forms of the verb, in German and English three, in Latin four. The principal elements of the Latin verb give us all the possible and necessary information needed to form or construct every conceivable expression with that verb in the Latin language and literature.

1. The principal parts of verbs

For Latin the principal parts of each verb are given in the dictionary, usually four in number. If they are not all there, then either the principal parts are so obvious that the dictionary indicates only the pattern so that you can supply all the parts yourself, or the missing form of the verb does not appear in Latin literature.

We open the dictionary and consult at random several words; we find these entries:

pario, párĕre, peperi, partum, 3, to give birth to
cano, cánĕre, cecini, cantum, 3, to sing
aedifico, aedificáre, aedificavi, aedificatum, 1, to build
sentio, sentíre, sensi, sensum, 4, to think, feel
ardeo, ardére, arsi, arsum, 2, to burn.

These entries tell you the four principal parts of these verbs. Let's look at each of them essentially. The first principal part is *pario*, "I give birth to," and *cano*, "I sing." These are the forms of Time 1 in the mode of direct discourse and question.

The second principal part is *párĕre* and *cánĕre*. This form can be called the gerund (a gerund in its subject or object form), or some people prefer to call it the infinitive. As such, *párĕre* means "giving birth to, to give birth to," and *cánĕre*, means "singing, to sing," and *aedificáre* means "building, to build." This principal part tells you to what group the verb belongs. We shall look more carefully at the verb groups in another encounter.

The third principal part is *peperi*, meaning "I have given birth to, I gave birth to," and *cecini*, meaning "I have sung, I sang," and *arsi*, meaning "I have burned, I burnt." The third principal part gives the form for Time 4, which is the same for Time 4a and Time 4b, as you now know.

The fourth principal part, which does not exist for some verbs, is so common in Latin that you will find it in practically every other sentence and its meaning is very clear in English. For example the fourth principal part from the verb *pingo, pingere, pinxi, pictus –a –um*, is the participle *pictus, picta, pictum*, meaning as a participle, "one having been painted," or simply "painted." Notice that it sounds passive and describes previous action. In some manuals of Latin it is called the perfect passive participle, which can be a misleading term as we shall see. Another example is, *deleo, delere, delevi, deletus –a –um*, where *deletus deleta deletum* mean as a participle, "one having been destroyed," or simply "destroyed," which is both antecedent and passive.

To form all the variations of a verb, we need all four of its principal parts. Some words are missing their third or fourth principal part, which means that we do not have examples of that part of the verb in Latin literature. Otherwise, normally these four parts are essential and all we need to understand and use the verb.

We shall learn how to form the times of verbs gradually, and we shall learn what every one means and how every one is used. The first thing to know is the four principal forms of the verb from the dictionary.

2. Times 4, 5, 6 and their easy formation

Now, with a little flip of the hand and almost unbelievable ease we are going to learn one-half of the whole verb in the mode of direct discourse and question. We must remember what we did on the first day with the personal endings of the verbs in order to master this quickly.

If you take any verb in your dictionary as teacher or student, any crazy verb you want, take for example:

venio, venire, veni, ventum, 4, to come
video, videre, vidi, visum, 2, to see

you know that third principal part is going to end in *–i*, in this case *veni* and *vidi*. Consider the third principal part as the form for Time 4; then you already know what *veni* means in Time 4a, "I have come," and in Time 4b, "I came," and therefore *vidi* means "I have seen, I saw." The ending *–i* is the personal ending you learned on the first day to mean "I." Likewise, *peperi* means "I have given birth to, I gave birth to," and *cecini* means "I have sung, I sang."

Finally we shall form all the other forms of the verb in Time 4 without any conjugations or any memorizing. You simply recall what you learned from the first day. The plural of *vidi* is *vidimus*, and the others are *cecinimus* and *venimus*. The form for "she has given birth" is *peperit*, and the others are *vidit* and *venit*.

Because Time 4 is used so often in the Latin language to narrate the whole history of the world and because typically the most common forms are the most irregular, there are several irregular forms to see in Time 4.

Time 4 has a special form that the Romans use when referring to "they." The personal ending is not going to be a simple *–nt* but the fuller form *–érunt*. Thus we have *venérunt* and its singular *venit* and we have *cecinérunt* and its singular *cecinit* and we have *sensérunt* and its singular *sensit*. If you compare the plural form with its singular forms here, you will notice that the vowel *–i–* drops out of the forms meaning "they," *venérunt*, *sensérunt*, and *cecinérunt*. This is because the personal ending *–érunt* has a long *–é–*, which we have indicated in the above examples. This accented long *–é–* phonetically swallows up the *–i–*. Some students do not learn that long *–é–* accent for many years and vocalize Latin as uneducated people, but you will not make that mistake. You can spot this form on every page of Latin literature and in almost every sentence that you will read. With a little experience you will become familiar with these special forms and recognize them from a distance, and the teacher will insist on the correct accent as Latin sentences are read out loud frequently instead of being accepted as dead matter for reading alone.

Another thing perhaps to put in brackets and remember is that the historians such as Caesar, Sallustius, Renaissance writers, and many others use another alternative for the ending *–érunt*. Instead of *–érunt*, they will write *–ére*. This means that "they have given birth to" is *peperére*, and "they did sing" is *cecinére*. These forms are not to be confused with the second principal part, the gerund or infinitive of these verbs, and are typically easy to spot because you can see the third principal part of the verb. This is simply an alternative form, and the authors switch back and forth as they please, but it is always difficult to distinguish this from the infinitive-gerund; thus: *venire* is "to come"; *venére* is "they came." But *vĭdére* is "to see"; *vīdére* is "they saw." That's Latin!

Two other special forms in Time 4 are those for "you" and "you all." You simply have to recall now those special forms that we learned in our first encounter and that we marked with an asterisk or two for this one special use. In Time 4 the personal ending for "you" is *–sti**and for "you all" is *–stis***. The form for "you gave birth to" is *peperisti* and for "you all gave birth to" is *peperistis*. The same forms for the other verbs are *cecinisti* and its plural *cecinistis*, and *venisti* and its plural *venistis*. From today on you will no longer bother with the asterisk because you know that this special ending appears only in Time 4.

That is all you have to say about Time 4 for every verb in the Latin language. You do not have so-called conjugations but one pattern, and you do not have to memorize anything. These forms can be found on every reading sheet and page of 2,300 years of Latin literature, and you and your teacher can come up with an infinite number of your own examples by consulting the principal parts in your dictionary. There are no other exceptions in Time 4 in the entire language.

Time 5 is the easiest thing in the world. You have the meanings already from a previous encounter. Once you have the third principal part of the verb, which is Time 4, the fastest maneuver is to write one word to establish the entire pattern for Time 5. Instead of *peperi* you write *pepereram* ... Instead of the final *–i*, you have the ending *–eram*. The same holds for *veni*, which becomes *veneram* ... and for *cecini*, which becomes *cecineram* ... Each of these three dots remind you that you already know from our first encounter how to do the rest for every Latin Time 5 verb.

Time 6 is much the same story. Take the third principal part, and instead of the final *–i*, make it *–ero*. Thus you have *venero*, *cecinero*, and *peperero*. Then you have to be very careful because that final *o* is difficult to work with. The *o* switches to *i* and "you will have given birth" is *pepereris* ... and "you will have sung *cecineris* ... and "you will have come" is *veneris* ... Once you have these forms, you have the entire system, if you follow the three dots and use the personal endings from the first encounter. Thus, you will have *pepererint*, *cecinerimus*, and *venerit*.

Therefore, with a little bit of observation and a flip of the pen you have in one encounter the entire system for Times 4, 5, and 6 for every single verb in the Latin language in the active mode of direct discourse and question. This ready achievement is very encouraging for beginners to accomplish without verb charts and memorizing forms and reciting nonsense syllables for the ends of words. Do not write out conjugations because it is a waste of time that could be spent profitably looking at reading sheets of literature from every age and pointing out examples of each of these forms in the living Latin language.

But you do have to be careful with every letter of a word because *pepererat* is Time 5 and means "she had given birth," and *pepererit* is Time 6, meaning "she will have given birth"; "we had sung" is *cecineramus*, and "we shall have sung" is *cecinerimus;* "you had come" is *veneras*, whereas "you will have come" is *veneris*. One letter can make all the difference in Latin, so you have to account for every letter. One letter can kill your understanding of the Latin word and sentence, idea, and thought. Do not be fooled by the super-easy forms, because the whole thing is rather delicate.

ENCOUNTER 9

VERBUM "ESSE" TOTO IN INDICATIVO. NULLUM OBIECTUM + "ESSE"

the verb "to be" in the whole indicative.
no object with the verb "to be"

Introduction

Because "to be" is such a frequently used verb, its forms are irregular in all languages. In English we say, "I am," "you are," "she is." In Latin too the forms are irregular, but you already know from our previous encounters most of what you need to construct all the forms for this verb in all the times of the indicative in a few short steps.

1. The verb "to be" in the whole indicative

The Latin word meaning "to be" or "to exist" is, in its four principal parts:

sum, esse, fui, futurus –a –um.

These mean:

sum:	I am, I am being
esse:	to be, being
fui:	I have been, I was
futurus –a –um:	about to be, going to be, fixing to be.

The usual fourth principal part of this verb does not exist, because the idea of "being" does not allow the passive participle, as if one could say "I am existed" or "having been existed," which is clearly impossible in English as in Latin. Therefore, in place of the usual fourth principal part, we have given another form which will tell you how to make certain forms of the verb, as we shall see in another encounter.

Following the same system we have used thus far, you can construct all the forms of this verb for Times 4, 5, and 6, because they are the same forms for every verb in the language, as said previously.

From the third principal part, *fui,* you can change the personal endings presented in our first encounter to create easily all the indicative forms for Time 4. Simply recall everything we said in our previous encounter about Time 4 and apply it here, including the two forms with the special endings, *fuisti,* meaning "you were, you have been," and its plural *fuistis,* "you all were, have been." The other special form is *fuérunt,* meaning, "they were, they existed." The teacher can open up any reading material and point this verb out on every page.

Time 5 is formed in the same way as we have already seen for *veneram.* If we begin with *fui*, then in place of that *–i* we have the ending *–eram* ... Thus, we begin with the form *fueram* ... "I had been," and from that form we can supply all the personal endings from our first encounter.

Time 6 is formed just as for *cecineris*. Begin with *fui* and change the *–i* to *–ero* to make the form *fuero,* meaning "I shall have been." Again, the final *–o* changes in the other forms to *–i* and the personal endings are added. So we say *fuerint*, "they will have been," and *fuerit*, "he, she, it will have been."

That concludes Times 4, 5, and 6 of the verb "to be" in direct discourse and question. We have seen that it is completely regular with all the same special forms as all other verbs of the Latin language. All we have to do now, then, is to give a little bit of attention to Times 1, 2, and 3 for the verb *sum, esse, fui, futurus –a –um*.

Time 1 is irregular in Latin as in other languages. We have already seen the dictionary entry *sum*, which means, "I am, I exist." Consequently, its plural is *sumus*. The form for "they are" is *sunt* and in the singular *est*. The form for "you are, you exist" is *es,* and, according to our endings on the first day, its plural is *estis*. These are all the forms for Time 1 in direct discourse and question.

Time 2 is the easiest, because you say "I was being, I used to be, I tried to be, I continued to be," all of which are contained in the one verbal form *eram*. Then you take the endings from the first encounter to supply all of the other forms such as *erant*, *eramus*, and *erat*.

Time 3 has the same phenomenon as we saw in our last encounter for Time 6; that is, we begin with *ero*, which means "I shall be." To create the other forms, as for Time 6, the final *–o* changes to *–i*, and you add the personal endings you already know to form *erit*, *erimus*. According to this pattern, you would expect the form *erint*, but the form is rather *erunt*, and means "they will be." You simply have to notice this several times in the literature to recognize it, and then you will see it on every page.

That completes the whole verb "to be" in the mode of direct discourse and question. Nothing else is necessary.

2. No object with the verb "to be"

One caution is becoming more urgent as we go along, namely that the verb "to be" and similar verbs like "to remain," "to appear," and "to stay" do not have an object. People who speak English throughout this world have difficulty with this in their own language when they erroneously say, "It is me." In this case the word "me" has been presupposed to be the object of "it is," but this expression is incorrect English, because the verb "it is" does not take the object "me"; the sentence should be "It is I." Similarly, rather than saying "it is us," we say in good English, "It is we"; not "it is them," but "it is they." Learning this in Latin is going to be difficult for the student because of the influence of modern faulty English. But even if you can get away with these poor expressions in English heard from the mouths of famous, influential people, politicians, philosophers, happily in Latin you cannot get away with this corruption.

Thus, in Latin we say:

Ego sum	It is I
Ea est amica	[My] friend is she (not her).

Technically speaking, these verbs of being, remaining, appearing, and staying are called intransitive verbs, that is verbs that do not take an object, or copulative verbs because they simply connect the two parts of the sentence but do not produce objects. The predicate of these verbs is in the subject form and not in the object form, regardless of how poorly people use modern languages.

Again, look on your reading sheets and prepare examples of this. Everywhere you will see sentences with "to be" without an object form.

ENCOUNTER 10

PRONOMEN RELATIVUM: SUBIECTUM + OBIECTUM. QUATTUOR PRINCIPIA

the relative pronoun
as subject and object.
four principles

Introduction

Just to review our concepts, a pronoun stands in the place of a noun. Pronouns include "he, she, it" and "who" and "what," in as much as they stand in place of nouns in the story.

Relative pronouns in English include "who, whom, which, what, whose." A relative pronoun, likewise, is a pronoun in as much as it stands in place of a noun. It is relative in as much as it relates one part of the discourse to someone or something in the other part of the discourse. By its definition the relative pronoun "relates," and thus by its nature its own clause does not stand on its own, but relates to something outside of its own clause. In English we say:

The book which ...
The children who ...
The policeman whom ...
The citizens whose ...

In the above examples, the relative pronoun "which" refers to the book, "who" refers to the children, "whom" refers to the policeman, "whose" refers to the citizens. In these cases we call the book, the children, the policeman, and the citizens the antecedent because each precedes its corresponding relative pronoun logically and most often geographically, and stands outside the relative clause.

Many things follow from the basic idea that the relative pronoun refers to something outside of its own clause, especially the following four principles, unusual and difficult for beginners but essential for Latinists.

1. Four principles

The four principles to consider for every relative pronoun are:

- relative pronouns are either masculine, feminine, or neuter
- relative pronouns are either singular or plural
- relative pronouns will have their own forms that point out their different functions in the clause, which we have seen: subject, object, of-possession, by-with-from-in, to-for-from

- relative pronouns refer to something—some idea—outside of their own clause, which is going to be either expressed or understood.

This last item, about understood antecedents, points up a huge problem that will be with us for our whole life in Latin, but we shall talk about that in our next encounter.

The rule for choosing or understanding the relative pronoun is that its gender and number come from outside its own clause, but its function comes from inside its own clause.

One consequence of this rule is that the antecedent gives only its gender and number to the relative pronoun, and the antecedent's function in its own sentence does not have any influence on the form, and consequently the function of, the relative pronoun itself.

Another consequence is that the function of the relative pronoun has to be determined by its use in its own clause. Take for example the clear distinction between the subject function and the object function in the following sentences:

The money, which bought the election, was secret
The money, which the election bought, disappeared.

In the first example the relative pronoun "which" functions as the subject of its own clause, that is the subject of the verb "bought." In the second example "which" functions as the object of its clause, that is the object of "bought." In both examples, the relative pronoun "which" refers outside of the relative clause to the money, no matter what the function is. These examples indicate the difficulty and subtlety of using the relative pronoun in English.

2. Forms

In this encounter we shall point out the forms of the relative pronoun, but the problem here immediately becomes apparent. As usual, Latin has not so many forms but so few, and as a consequence too many forms do too many different things. So, this is going to demand much attention.

If the relative pronoun functions as the subject in its own clause and refers to something outside of its own clause that is masculine and singular, then the relative pronoun is: *qui*. If that relative pronoun becomes the object of its own clause, then its form is *quem*. The plural of both of these are *qui* as subject, and *quos* as object respectively.

As you can see, you already have two different uses of the relative pronoun *qui*. Both function as the subject in their own clauses, and both refer to a masculine antecedent. One is singular and the other plural. Because the *qui* functions as the subject in its own clause, the verb that goes with it will tell you whether the *qui* is singular or plural.

If the relative pronoun functions as the subject in its own clause and refers to something outside its own clause that is feminine and singular, then the relative pronoun is *quae*. If that relative pronoun becomes the object of its own clause, then its form is *quam*. The plural of these are *quae* and *quas* respectively.

If the relative pronoun functions as the subject in its own clause and refers to something outside its own clause that is neuter and singular, then the relative pronoun is *quod*. The super principle in the neuter tells us that the object function will look the same. The plural of both of these is *quae*, again according to the super principle.

As is evident once again, you have two different uses of the relative pronoun *quae*. Both function as the subject in their own clauses. One is singular and feminine, and the other is plural and neuter. Because the *quae* functions as the subject in its own clause, the verb that goes with it will tell you whether the *quae* is singular or plural. A great amount of analysis and reflection is necessary here, because otherwise you get the whole thing mixed up and understand nothing.

Four of these relative pronouns have the same form, *quae*. They are the feminine singular and plural subject and the neuter plural subject and object. This means you will have a lot of necessary observation and thinking to do. The verbs will help you a bit, but they will not tell you everything. Only reading Latin literature to see a multitude of these relative pronouns will help you to spot the antecedent and the function of the relative pronoun in its own concrete sentence.

Romans absolutely loved to hear and to use the relative pronoun, far more than one does in English. There is hardly a sentence on any reading sheet where it is not found or any page of Latin literature where it occurs less than 20 times. If you observe any reading sheet more closely, you will notice that the Romans loved the sound *qu–* as in: *quoniam*, *quando*, *quam*, *cuius*, *qui*, *quibus*, *quicumque*. In just about every sentence you will have the *qu–* sound. This sound and pronoun are infinitely more common in Latin than in English. In fact, sometimes in English you cannot hear the relative pronoun anymore, and it is discouraged in writing.

ENCOUNTER 11

PRONOMEN RELATIVUM: BREVITAS, ANTECEDENTIS OMISSIO, ORDO

relative pronoun:
brevity, the omission of the antecedent, position

Introduction

Contact with Latin literature will convince anyone and everyone of how the Romans loved to deal with and to hear the relative pronoun. We want to be honest about this and get to the essentials and put our teeth into the language.

1. The location of the relative pronoun out in front

After reading out loud several paragraphs of Latin literature from all ages, the first thing that must strike the reader is the location of both the relative pronoun and the relative clause within the overall discourse. Namely, the Romans, because of the freedom of their sentence structure and style, loved to put the relative clause locally in front of the word it describes, which it anticipates. While this is nearly impossible to do in English, the Romans love it, and you can't count the number of sentences that begin with *qui* and *quos* and *quarum* as the first word. This practice is elegant and very beautiful and clear. This is a matter of style and is not confusing at all, but you had better be ready for it with a little help.

Going back to our principle discussed on the first day, you cannot start with the first word of the Latin sentence, because in this case the sentence starts with the relative expression, which depends on its antecedent coming later in the sentence. The teacher can point out a few examples and help the student to see the whole sentence with the relative statement at its beginning, for example:

Quem misisti perutilis est liber
The book, which you sent, is very useful

Quae venerant nos salutaverunt
The women who had come greeted us.

2. The omission of the pronoun antecedent

The next part of this very common relative phenomenon is the omission of the "pronoun antecedent," that is to say the antecedent of the relative pronoun that stands outside of the relative clause. This is going to cause trouble and confusion and desperation for the rest of your life. But it is a fact of

Latin life, and whether you compose or try to read Latin literature, you must be acquainted with the omission of the pronoun antecedent.

We say in English: "They who do this will be rewarded." Here, the relative pronoun is "who," and its antecedent "They." The Romans are going to omit entirely the word "They" and begin the sentence with "Who," as in "Who do this, will be rewarded." This does not sound good in English, but the Romans love to do it, as in:

> *Quae audivisti falsa sunt*
> [The things] which you have heard are false
>
> *Qui hoc faciunt praemium accipient*
> [They, the people, the men] who do this will receive a prize

This sentence of five words begins with the relative pronoun *Qui*, and its antecedent is not expressed. To understand this sentence, we will not begin with the first word but with the main verb, *accipient*, "they will receive." The relative *Qui* functions as the subject of the verb *faciunt*, "Who do this." Therefore, the antecedent of *Qui* is "they," written in Latin as either *ei* or *ii*, which is the implied subject of the verb *accipient*, "they, who do this, will receive ..." The Romans with great delight will simply leave out the *ei* or *ii*.

Take the example of only three words:

> *Quos laudas honoro*
> Whom you praise, I honor.

What is the *Quos* doing in the sentence and what does it refer to outside of its relative clause? To find out we do not begin with the first word of the sentence, but with its independent verb *honoro*, "I honor." The relative pronoun *Quos*, "whom," can only be the object of the verb *laudas*, "whom you praise." Because *Quos* is masculine and plural it refers to something masculine and plural in the main sentence. The only thing that is missing is the object of *honoro*, namely *eos*, "the ones, them, the men." In English you have to draw this sentence out and make the antecedent explicit and say:

> I honor them (the people, the men), whom you are praising.

This phenomenon may look mysterious but is simple and most effective. The trick is that here the pronoun antecedent *eos* is omitted, and the sentence begins with *Quos*. Coincidentally both *Quos* and *eos* are objects of their respective sentences.

Take the expression:

> *Quae hoc faciunt praemia accipient*
> The women who do this will receive prizes.

We do not begin with the first word here but with the independent verb *accipient*, "they will receive." Because of the super principle, *praemia*, "prizes," can function as the subject of *accipient*, "the prizes will receive," but we take it as the object, "they will receive prizes." Because *faciunt*, "they do," already has an object, *hoc*, "they do this," the relative *Quae* functions as the subject of *faciunt* and means either "[The women] who do this," or "[the things] which do this." In the former case, the missing antecedent is *eae*; the women both do this and receive prizes. In the latter case the missing antecedent is *ea*, "the things"; perhaps computers are playing chess and winning prizes.

This phenomenon is an essential part of the Latin language and will cause confusion and suffering until an individual masters the trick; that is all it is. To help you master this trick, examples are drawn from every sheet of Latin literature, and the teacher can supply many more, such as the following:

> *Quas laudas, honoro*
> I honor the women whom you are praising
> (*eas* is the missing object of *honoro*.)
>
> *Quod laudas, honoro*
> I honor that which you praise
> (*id*, "it, the thing," is the understood object of *honoro*)
>
> *Qui tibi scribo benevolentiam significo*
> I, who am writing to you, make known [my] good will.

In the above example, *Qui* is the subject of *scribo* and so implies the antecedent *ego*. Outside the relative clause the implied subject of *significo* is *ego*, "I"; the missing antecedent. Take the example:

> *Qui tibi scribo laudant*
> They praise me who am writing to you
> (*me* is the implied object of *laudant*).

This sentence begins with the relative clause which depends on the last word of the sentence. So the first word of the sentence, *Qui*, really starts off the second part of the sentence, the relative clause. Those who reject this structure will miss the whole message.

This phenomenon has been a mystery for many people for a long time. You might as well just accept it as a neat part of the Latin language, because the Romans love to do this, as their genuine literature will confirm and prove.

3. Brevity

The above examples show the extreme economy of Latin because of what they omit from the sentence. Here is another example of the same:

> *Quos laudas honoro quem amant.*

These five Latin words require eleven English words to express fully:

> I, whom they love, honor the people, whom you are praising.

We begin here with the governing verb *honoro*, "I honor." The relatives *Quos* and *quem* must both function as the objects of their respective verbs; *Quos laudas* means "whom you are praising," and *quem amant* means "whom they love." Although you cannot hear it in English, *Quos* is masculine plural, and *quem* masculine singular. Here the antecedent of *Quos* is *eos*, the plural object of *honoro*, "I honor the ones, the people, the men, whom you are praising," and the antecedent of *quem* is *ego*, the subject of the main verb, "I, whom they love, honor ..."

All those words are necessary in English, but the Latin draws this expression so close and tight as almost to strangle you because it is so compressed. You have to get used to this especially with examples in Latin literature, where there are surely a hundred examples on every page. The teacher can also propose his or her own examples in addition to consulting the reading sheets at the end of this Experience. It will also keep you from beginning with the first word or simply following the words in their order in the hope for meaning.

4. Relative box

At the beginning of this our First Experience we carefully stated that word order is not essential to produce the meaning in Latin. We never said, however, that Latin word order is irrational or completely arbitrary or whimsical. You cannot put 1,000 Latin words into a mixer and pull them out at random and have them make sense, and even if the first and last word of the Latin Bible were to agree grammatically with each other, this does not mean that the author intended them to go together. The Romans have the same kind of brain and mind as we do. The way they keep ideas together that belong together while preserving greater freedom in word order is challenging and surprising, but not foolish.

We can liken the structure of a Latin sentence often to a series of Chinese boxes within boxes, or to the well-known Russian artistic practice of nestling dolls and Easter eggs. Each of these artistic examples points to the physical necessity of containing one box entirely within another. Nestling boxes do not allow one box to be partly inside and partly outside another box. If you break up the boxes, then they no longer contain each other, and you have a broken and confused mess.

In Latin literature there is a system of style and composition, which creates literary boxes within boxes, that is clauses within clauses. One of the more practical and fundamental principles that govern the use of the relative pronoun in Latin literature is what we lightly designate as "the relative box." This idea of the relative box can help us determine especially which verb goes with which relative pronoun. The verb that goes with the relative pronoun must appear geographically before the sentence returns to the larger clause. Sometimes the relative pronoun is separated from its verb by yet another relative clause lying within. Each dependent clause must be fully accounted for in all of its elements before or behind its verb.

The overall sentence is likened to the outermost box. Within the overall sentence numerous clauses can hide within one another, but each subordinate clause must be complete, wherever it is in the main clause. Clauses can follow one another, each clause ending before the next one begins. Sentences can also begin with a dependent clause which is followed eventually by the verb it depends on, or a sentence may end with a subordinate clause. A subordinate clause may be surrounded both before and after by words from the larger clause on which it depends. What Latin literature does not allow is for a bigger box to be contained in a smaller box, or, in literary terms, for a subordinate clause to contain the sentence on which it depends.

The absolutely infallible and no-exception rule here for composing and understanding Latin is that the clauses may not be torn apart; that would be the equivalent of busting up the containing boxes. You cannot switch the verb, subject, object, or other elements from one clause to another.

This phenomenon can result in a rather comic situation in which you have three verbs in a row at the end of the sentence, each one connecting with its own clause. Take this simple example:

> *Librum quem heri tu qui meus amicus es misisti legi*
> I read the book, which you, who are my friend, sent yesterday.

Here you end up with three verbs in a row: *es misisti legi*. The verb *es* must go with *qui*. The verb *misisti* must go with *quem*, because it is the next verb that follows after you have omitted the intervening clause. The verb *legi* is the independent verb of the sentence and goes with the first word, *Librum*. We can put brackets in this sentence to help us see the boxes:

> *Librum [quem heri tu (qui meus amicus es) misisti] legi.*

Another way of saying this is that the clause *qui ... es* depends on the clause *quem ... misisti*, which in turn depends on the main sentence *Librum ... legi*.

In the above extreme example we have for the first time included parentheses and square brackets to highlight the clauses within clauses. Students and teachers everywhere will benefit from marking and analyzing this phenomenon. To show this more clearly in very many sentences, we have indicated this structure in examples from every author with conventional signs. These can be found on the reading sheets entitled *Sententiarum Latinarum Structura* following each Experience.

Nota bene

A warning or counsel is necessary at this point for users of the English language with regard to the relative pronoun. The fact is that today the relative pronoun in English is many times omitted completely or understood and felt somewhere in the sentence. There are many examples of this, where you say simply:

> We received the money you sent last week
> *Argentum quod transmisisti priore hebdomada excepimus.*

Users of Latin and every other language have to add the word "which" or "that" to introduce the clause "you sent ..."

We mention this only because some people might wish to put the English sentence into acceptable Latin. We wish to spare them from the mistake of making both sides of the expression independent sentences, not realizing that the "which" or "that" understood in the English has to be expressed in Latin. Another example is:

> This is a picture of the robber they arrested last night
> *Haec latronis imago est quem superiore nocte comprehenderunt.*

To put this into standard Latin you must say "whom they arrested last night." This is a serious warning especially intended to those who might not realize what is implied or felt in the English. Again, we say:

> These are singers we all admire
> *Cantores hi sunt quos admiramur omnes.*

Again the word "whom" is understood here. People conversant in every other language have to say something like, "whom we admire."

All of the above technical talk will be understood by "hands-on" dealing with genuine Latin examples. Familiarity with principles will be acquired only by practice, only by reading, only by correct and corrected analyzing for a long time. This is the way in which a new pianist slowly grows in acquaintance with notes, keys, combinations, harmonies, rhythms, scales—the whole reality.

ENCOUNTER 12

RELIQUA INDICATIVI TEMPORA 1, 2, 3 SECUNDUM VERBI GENUS. DIFFICULTATES FUTURI

remaining times of the indicative 1, 2, 3 according to verb type. difficulties of Time 3

Introduction

We are reminded once again that for the expression of direct talk and question, we have already covered and learned and mastered Time 4, Time 5, and Time 6. Repeatedly in every text of Latin literature and in every *ludus domesticus* we have identified and understood and confirmed that Times 4, 5, and 6 are the same for all verbs in the whole Latin language. We have mastered half of the verbal times without resorting to conjugations or tables.

Today in one lesson we will finish off the verbal times by looking at Time 1 and Time 2 and Time 3. As in the case of the other times, or so-called tenses, also these will be presented and done very quickly and effectively with a "sleight of hand." We shall add to the personal endings, which we know from our first day of class, a few additional touches, and then everything will be done very quickly.

1. The four verb types—Groups

When it comes to Times 1, 2, and 3, the Latin dictionary definitely gives us verb types—Groups, as is obvious on inspection of any edition of that same book. We say verb Groups to distinguish them from noun and adjective Blocks. The verb Groups are characterized in Latin, as even in English, by the vowel that is predominant in the verb. We cannot avoid this, but it is quite workable. It pertains to the structure of the human voice and evolution of human languages.

When we examine the verbs of Latin, we see four different predominant vowels, which establish four different patterns or Groups of verbs. The vowels are:

ā the long *a*
ē the long *e*
ĕ the short *e*, phonetically sounding like a short *i* to the Roman ear
ī the long *i*.

In the second principal part of each verb given in today's dictionaries, these predominant vowels will be seen clearly, in the infinitive or gerund as stated previously.

We shall learn these verb Groups by looking up specific words in the dictionary at home or in class to examine the second principal part of each. For example, we have a word like:

confírmo, confirmāre, confirmávi, confirmátum, 1.

In the second principal part you see the ending *–āre*, which means that the predominant vowel is *–ā–*, the long *–a–*. Because there is no verb group with a short *–ă–* vowel, the long *–ā–* is sometimes written without the bar over it. Verbs like this one belong to what we call Group I. Some dictionaries indicate this verb Group with the number 1 without giving the infinitive.

When we flip through the dictionary again, we see a word like:

móneo, monēre, mónui, mónitum, 2.

Verbs like this one belong to what we call Group II. Some dictionaries indicate this verb Group with the number 2 following the principal forms. In the second principal part you see the ending *–ēre*, which means that the predominant vowel is *–ē–*, the long *–e–*. The length of this vowel is typically indicated in some way in the dictionary to distinguish it from the following verb group. The distinction between the second and third verb group is so essential that in our book we will mark by exception the infinitive of this group with the long *–ē–*, because people constantly confuse this group of verbs with the next.

Look in the dictionary again, for a word like:

péllo, péllĕre, pépuli, púlsum, 3.

In the second principal part you see the ending *–ĕre*, which means that the predominant vowel is *–ĕ–*, the short *–e–*, which in certain forms of that same verb will change to *–ĭ–*, a short *–i–* vowel, for phonetic reasons. The length of the short *–ĕ–* vowel in the second principal part is typically indicated in some way in the dictionary to distinguish it from the previous verb group. Verbs like this one belong to what we call Group III. Some dictionaries indicate this verb Group with the number 3 following the principal forms.

Finally, look up a verb such as:

séntio, sentīre, sénsi, sénsum, 4.

In the second principal part you see the ending *–īre*, which means that the predominant vowel is *–ī–*, the long *–i–*. Because there is no verb group with a short *–ĭ–* vowel, the long *–ī–* is sometimes written without the bar over it. Verbs like this one belong to what we call Group IV. Some dictionaries indicate this verb Group with the number 4 following the principal forms, as above.

These four groups of verbs have been developed by the use of the human voice and the human tongue, and we end up with four verb groups distinguished according to their predominant vowel sounds. You will see these four verb groups referred to as conjugations 1, 2, 3, 4 with the same numbering system we use above to talk about verb Groups I, II, III, IV.

2. Times 2 and 1 of the indicative

The remaining times of the indicative can be quickly presented and readily understood. Again, rather than resorting to verb charts and paradigms, we shall use our practice of reversing verbs from singular to plural and from plural to singular and so learn all the forms of Times 1, 2, 3. Just for kicks we shall start with Time 2.

2.1 *Time 2*

The marker for Time 2 is the syllable *–ba–* followed by the personal endings. The predominant vowel of each verb group will appear in some form immediately before that *–ba–*.

Group I verbs in Time 2 will look like the following example with the full range of its meanings in English:

confirmábam
I was strengthening
I used to strengthen ...

Notice that the *–a–* is predominant. The personal ending given above is *–m*, and you know the other personal endings from our first encounter, such as *confirmabamus* and *confirmabant*, so there is no need to repeat them here.

Group II verbs in Time 2 will look like:

monébam
I used to advise
I was admonishing ...

Again, the predominant vowel appears, in this case the long *–ē–*. You already know the other forms.

Group III verbs in Time 2 follow the example:

pellébam
I was pushing, driving ...

We know that the predominant vowel for this Third Group of verbs is the short *–ĕ–*. This vowel appears as lengthened to *ē* in the forms of Time 2. This means that the endings of Group II and Group III verbs are identical and can cause trouble if you do not know your vocabulary.

Group IV verbs in Time 2 are like the form:

sentiébam
I was thinking, feeling ...

Originally this form was *sentíbam*, but already before Cicero the form changed phonetically to *sentiébam*. The rest you know from the first encounter, and that takes care of Time 2 in all four verb groups. You have thousands of verbs at your disposal that you can now deal with in Time 2, scanning your Latin library or the reading sheets following each experience.

2.2 *Time 1*

Time 1 requires a knowledge of the predominant vowels, and these are clearly evident and essential to the formation and meaning of each verb.

Group I verbs in Time 1 are like *confirmare*:

confírmo	*confírmat . . .*
I strengthen	she strengthens.

In the dictionary entry of the verb, here *confirmo*, the predominant vowel *–a–* does not appear, but is found in the second dictionary element *confirmare*, and consequently it does appear in the other forms of Time 1, as here *confirmat*. You already know all the other forms from our first encounter.

Group II verbs in Time 1 are like *monēre:*

móneo	*mónent . . .*
I warn	they warn.

The predominant vowel *–ē–*, appears in the dictionary entry. It also appears in the other forms of the verb in Time 1. You know the other personal endings, so there is no need to repeat them here.

Group III verbs in Time 1 follow the example of *pellĕre*:

péllo	*péllimus*	*péllunt . . .*
I drive	we drive	they drive.

The predominant vowel does not appear in the dictionary entry. This is the case with the forms of Group III verbs in Time 1, as in the above example and others such as *pellit, pellis, pellitis*. You might expect the plural of *pellit* to be *pellint*, but it is a bit different, *pellunt*, "they drive," which you already had before when the plural of *erit* was *erunt*. So, it is not so crazy that this happens in the language.

Group IV verbs in Time 1 are like *sentio*:

séntio	*sentítis . . .*
I feel	you all feel.

The predominant vowel is *–ī–*, which appears in the dictionary form of the verb and in the other forms, which you know. Again, you might expect the plural of *sentit* to be *sentint*, but it is *sentiunt*, "they feel," which is similar to *pellunt*.

Those are the four groups of verbs in Time 1. Confusion easily arises when forms look like one another. For example, *sentit* may look like a verb of the Third Group, but, knowing your vocabulary, you recognize that it belongs to the fourth. The accents follow the normal rules, which require knowing the vocabulary. For example, "we drive" is *péllimus*, but "we feel" is *sentímus*.

In the next class we shall immediately review everything we have learned thus far until it becomes familiar and second nature. As we have said, learning a human language such as Latin should not be reduced to memorizing nonsense syllables, schemas, and conjugations, because languages and the human expression of thought do not work that way naturally.

3. Time 3 and its difficulties

When we come to Time 3, we have a very strange phenomenon that occurs only in the Latin language, as far as we know. In Time 3 we have two completely different systems or patterns for our verbs. We do not have to argue now whether this came about from Greek or Indo-European or Italian dialects. However it came about, Latin has two totally distinct systems in Time 3. You will learn them very quickly and that will be the end of Times 1, 2, 3, 4, 5, and 6 for the verb in direct discourse and question.

3.1 *Time 3 in Groups I, II*

In Time 3, verb Groups I and II are cousins using one system, and Groups III and IV are cousins using another system. This will cause confusion until it is clear to you and you know your vocabulary.

Group I verbs like *memoro, memorāre, memoravi, memoratum*, 1, "to mention," form Time 3 in this way:

memorábo	*memorábimus*	*memorábunt*
I shall mention	we shall mention	they will mention.

You can see the predominant vowel *–ā–*. As we have seen several times before, that final *–o* in *memorabo* turns immediately to *–i–* in the remaining forms of this verb, and then the personal endings are added as in *memorabimus*.

Group II verbs such as *noceo, nocēre*, "to harm, hurt," form their future in the same way:

nocébo	*nocébitis*	*nocébunt*
I shall harm	you all will harm	they will harm.

You already know all the other forms. We have seen in Time 6 that the complete verbal form for "he, she, it" ending in *–it* becomes plural in an ordinary way, namely with the ending *–int*. Here in Time 3 the ending becomes *–unt*, with no further discussion. The reversed form of *nocebit* is *nocebunt*, not *nocebint*, as *memorabunt* is the reversed of *memorabit*. We will have to ask the Romans why this happened.

3.2 *Time 3 in Groups III, IV*

We have said that verb Groups III and IV have a completely different system, one not recognizable from and having nothing to do with the system of Groups I and II. Time 3 for Group III *pello* is not *pellabo*, but *pellam*. You can see how far away these are from one another. Time 3 for Group IV *sentio* is *sentiam*. Then, in Groups III and IV the ending *–am* immediately changes to *–e–* followed by the personal endings:

péllam	*pélles*
I shall drive	you will drive
séntiam	*sentiétis*
I shall feel	you all will feel.

The other personal endings are all from our first encounter.

That is the end of Times 1, 2, 3, 4, 5, and 6 in the mode of direct discourse and question. Learning these forms does not require memorizing charts in an arbitrary order, but practice spotting the forms of the verbs in Latin literature and moving from one form to another, from one time to another, from singular to plural and back again.

You must know your vocabulary to see the difference between the endings of *cantabit* and *sentit*. Both end in *–it*, but *cantabit* is from Group I and means "he, she, it will sing," and *sentit* is from Group IV and means "he, she, it feels." Thus, the ending *–it* is no indication of the verbal times. Only when you know the second principal part of a verb, the gerund or infinitive, will you know to which of the four groups of verbs a word belongs, and then you can decide what that ending *–it* means. Similarly *ducet* from Group III means "he, she will lead," but *docet* from Group II is "she, he teaches."

The same trap that catches people all the time, but is just a part of learning Latin, is the difference between, on the one hand, *nocemus* and, on the other, *pellemus* and *sentiemus*. The difficulty here is that *nocemus* is from Group II, and so is Time 1, whereas *pellemus* and *sentiemus* are from Groups III and IV respectively, and so are Time 3. Students will continue to confuse these forms because they do not know their vocabulary and which group each verb belongs to.

This looks like a mass of stuff, but it is not that difficult, if students or teachers move around and pull out of their memories and minds these forms of the different times at random: *cantant*, "they sing"; *sentient*, "they will feel"; *nocebimus*, "we shall harm." If students construct in their minds, not in their memories, the times of the verbs, then they can run through all the 6 times of the indicative for a verb in one and one-half minutes. Let us note finally that *scribam* is "I shall write"; *scripseram*, "I had written"; *scribebam*, "I was writing."

We have reached the end of the treatment of the indicative mode, expressing direct discourse and questions. Learn how to work with the verbs gradually, how to recognize them in literature, and how to construct them on your own, if you know the vocabulary.

Hereafter in our book we will express the six times with the abbreviations T.1, T.2, T.3, T.4, T.5, T.6, and likewise for the four groups of verbs we will say Gp.I, Gp.II, Gp.III, Gp.IV, and we might as well at this point also introduce the abbreviation for the two Blocks of nouns and adjectives: Bk.I, Bk.II.

ENCOUNTER 13

OMNIA ITERANTUR MODI INDICATIVI TEMPORA. INTERROGANDI FORMULAE; ALIA QUAESITA SIMILIA

all the times-tenses of the indicative mode are repeated.
ways of asking;
other similar questions

Spend a whole class on the reading sheets or teacher's examples, a book from the Bible or from Virgil or Caesar or Cicero or Thomas Aquinas or the liturgy or whatsoever text you want, and identify the verbs. The teacher will give the principal parts of the verb, and the student will identify the time of each verb by number and will say what the word means. That will be the end of the whole story.

The teacher and student will jump around from one time to another. If you find on a reading sheet a verb that you identify as T.2, and you say what the verb means in English, then give the form of the verb for T.5, T.6, T.4, T.3, T.1, and for each state what the verb means in English. As soon as the students start dealing with the verb in this way, they will feel very much at home and be able to move around from one time to another, just as they are free to do in other known languages.

The verbs in all the times of direct discourse and question may look like a disorganized, vast forest of various growth, but it is not so. It is very simple. It is learned not by memorizing tables and charts and nonsense syllables, but by getting into practice dealing with the language as an integral and complex human phenomenon, by learning it naturally with joy and pleasure, and not artificially by pounding in or spurting out nonsense forms with pain and hatred: *cum dolore et odio.*

1. Question particles *nonne, num, –ne*

Perhaps it will be useful here to show how the Romans, besides statements and declarations, also asked questions with these same indicative times as above. There are three ways to ask questions which conveniently anticipate the answer. First, if the answer anticipated is "yes," then the question particle is *nonne*, for example:

Nonne placet tibi lingua Latina?

Because the expected response is clear in the Latin expression, it is important to formulate this also in good English, as in:

"Certainly the Latin language pleases you, doesn't it?"
Response: "Of course it does."

You can see that the English question obviously provokes the affirmative answer, "Yes, it does." The second of these question particles, *num*, anticipates a negative answer, for example:

Num defodiebas rosas in horto?
"Certainly you did not bury the roses in the garden, did you?"
Response: "Of course not."

Again, you can hear in the English the negative anticipated response, "No, I did not." Third, when the answer can go both ways, an uncertain negative or positive, then the question particle *–ne*, known technically as an enclitic, is added to some word, for example:

Vidistine aquilam in tecto?
"Did you see the eagle on the roof?"
Response: "Yes, I did" or "No, I did not."

The question does not anticipate a positive or negative response, but leaves the response open and ambiguous.

These three question particles do not necessarily begin their sentences, because they can be placed further along in the sentence. We can state the same three above questions in these ways with no difference in meaning:

Lingua nonne latina tibi placet?
Rosas num in horto defodiebas?
Aquilam in tectone vidisti?

Finally, what we have said of these three particles will be true later as well in the third experience when we get to indirect questions.

2. Other similar questions

For the curious and diligent student we can make a list of other common interrogative words to round out our treatment of the indicative in some short phrases. You may notice that several of them are the same forms as the relative pronouns, but here used to ask questions as interrogative pronouns. Your Latin dictionary will confirm the existence of *qui, quae, quod* both as relative and interrogative, a fact unknown to many people, for example:

Quis umquam hoc dicet?
"Who will ever say this?"

Quem in scholam misisti?
"Whom did you send to school?"

Ubi latitabo?
"Where shall I hide?"

Quibus auxiliis montem scandis?
"With what helps do you climb the mountain?"

Cur obmutescimus?
"Why are we falling silent?"

Quo modo illam linguam didicisti?
"How did you learn that language?"

Quando revenit mater tua?
"When did your mother come back?"

Ut vales?
"How are you doing?"

Quod argumentum vobis heri praeceptor explicavit?
"What subject matter did the teacher explain to you-all yesterday?"

ENCOUNTER 14

PECULIARES VERBORUM FORMAE: CONTENDO, ERE; –IO, ERE

special forms of the verbs: contendo, ere; –io, ere

Introduction

After we have made ourselves acquainted thoroughly with the whole vision and working of the Latin verb in six times of direct discourse and question, we are mature enough to add or take in some special linguistic peculiarities which occur in every human language, and which we have to know in Latin too.

1. Special forms of verbs: *contendo, ere*

We will start things out with the verb:

> *contendo, conténdĕre, contendi, contentum,* 3, to hasten, strive.

We would just like to point out that the principal parts of this verb produce several forms which are identical. In this case, the second principal part, *conténdĕre*, tells us that this verb is in verb Gp.III. Both T.1 and T.4 of this verb will produce the forms *contendimus* and *contendit*. Each of these forms can have at least seven meanings, which increases the difficulties and requires that you distinguish them precisely and exclude the ones that are not in the story. Thus, *contendit* means in T.1:

> he hastens
> she does hasten
> it is hastening

and in T.4a *contendit* means:

> she has hastened
> he has been hastening

and in T.4b *contendit* means:

> it did hasten
> she hastened.

This again brings out the nature of the Latin language. It is not that we have so much to learn, but we have so little material with which to express our thoughts. Most other languages are going to distinguish all these meanings and bring them out in their vernacular. In Greek you have many more forms to express each of these different times. It may seem to the student that learning all of the Greek forms is an insurmountable task, but a greater number of forms help the speaker to communicate more rapidly and precisely and with less ambiguity. In Latin all of these forms are contained in that one verb, and that is what makes Latin so demanding and satisfying for mature people.

2. Special forms of verbs: *capio, ere*

There is a cluster of verbs, perhaps about 8 or 9 with almost numberless compounds, which appear in the dictionary in a strange way. Again the dictionary helps us. For example:

capio, *cápĕre*, *cepi*, *captum*, 3, to take in hand
rapio, *rápĕre*, *rapui*, *raptum*, 3, to seize, snatch
sapio, *sápĕre*, *sapivi* or *sapii*, —, 3, to taste
facio, *fácĕre*, *feci*, *factum*, 3, to do, make.

In each of these examples above, the first entry ends in *–io*, which would normally indicate verb Gp.IV, but the infinitives all indicate Gp.III with the short *–ĕ–*. In T.4, 5, 6 these verbs are the same as for all verbs, but in T.1, 2, 3 they have a mixture of forms, some forms from Gp.III and others from Gp.IV.

This small Group of verbs has an importance well beyond their number, because they are the basis of so many compound verbs. From *rapio* we have, for example, *arripio* (to snatch), *diripio* (to plunder); and we have *sapio* (to taste, to be wise), *desipio* (to be foolish); and we have *capio*, *accipio*, *recipio*. In the end you finish with almost 100 compound verbs that straddle this fence.

Working with this Group of verbs is not so difficult, because when possible they have an *–i–*. This means that in T.1, 2, and 3, the Romans want to express the letter *–i–*, which usually doesn't appear in Gp.III. This means that in T.1, 2, and 3 they tend to stay on the side of Gp.IV even though the infinitive is of Gp.III.

T.1 includes the *–i–* and follows the pattern of *capiunt*, *rapiunt*, *sapiunt*, and all the compounds will have an *–iunt*, which is a sign of Gp.IV.

T.3 includes the *–i–* and follows a pattern like *accipiam*, *decipiam*, *arripiam* and then continues as usual with forms like *arripies*. There is one special case in which the *–i–* does not appear in Gp.III. We shall see that shortly.

T.2 includes the *–i–* and follows the pattern *capiebam*, *rapiebam*, *sapiebam*. These too look as though they belong to the fourth Group.

With a little bit of Latin reading and training, after a while you will be able to recognize these verbal forms that appear in the dictionary as *–io*, *ĕre*. Some books call this small Group of verbs and their compounds the *–io* verbs of Gp.III, others the *–ĕre* verbs of Gp.IV. Enough!

3. Special contracted forms of verbs

Contracted forms occur in every language, as in:

> We're going.
> Wha'da ya' want?

There are contractions in Latin too. The important ones for us to know and recognize are going to come especially in Gp.I. Take for example the verb:

> *demonstro, demonstrare, demonstravi, demonstratum*, 1, to point out.

The dictionary tells you that T.4 is *demonstravi*, "I have demonstrated." During the classical era this form was pronounced with a *–u–* sound in place of the *–v–*. The sound *–aui–* was fairly weak and tended to be abbreviated. This happens especially in the "you" form of this verb, *demonstravisti*. Here the classical pronunciation was *–uisti*, not *–visti*. The contraction involved the omission of the sound *–ui–*, that is, the letters *–vi–*. Thus, *demonstra(vi) sti* becomes *demonstrasti*. In the plural, the same phenomenon occurs with the resulting contraction, *demonstrastis*.

This same contraction also occurs in the "they" form. Again, instead of pronouncing *demonstraverunt*, they pronounced *–uerunt* or simply abbreviated the form by omitting the sound *–ue–*, that is the letters *–ve–*, and *demonstra(ve)runt* became *demonstrarunt*. This contraction is not a new form but is very important and frequent in all of Latin literature. It is simply the result of the frequency and speed with which this form was pronounced.

T.5 has similar cases of contraction. Instead of *demonstraveram* pronounced, *–ueram*, the contracted form is *demonstraram*. Instead of *demonstraveramus* you will see the contraction *demonstraramus*. Cicero often says *putarant*, a contraction for *putaverant*, "they had thought." These contractions do not look like the full forms given in any list or book. They are due to on-the-street pronunciation.

T.6 provides similar contractions. The weak vowel *–ve–* in the verb *putavero* will result in the contraction *putaro*, and *putaverimus* will contract to *putarimus*. *Putarint* is therefore T.6; *putarant* T.5; *putarunt* T.4.

These contractions are all due to the fact that the letter *v* was pronounced *u*. Today we tend to pounce on the *v* in the Italian, Church pronunciation, but it is not correct, and the Romans would probably have laughed to hear such later Latin talk.

In all languages contractions are part of living, colloquial speech, and the same is true of Latin. Obviously contractions are more frequent in the comedians and in examples of colloquial Latin rather than in super literature. Yet we have to know them, because when you least expect it, they are going to pop up. Even Virgil and others say *noro*, and people go crazy because they don't know that it is a contraction of *novero* in T.6i which means "I shall know." Another common one is *nosti*, a contraction of *novisti*, "you have come to know." Another one very common in the historians is *aedificarunt*, a contraction of *aedificaverunt*, "they constructed." Once you are aware of the contractions, they are less of a surprise when you see one, but if you are innocent of them, then you will not know what is causing that form.

4. Other special forms of verbs

Any other peculiarities are found in comprehensive Latin language books, as Gildersleeve and Lodge, where you will also find defective verbs, which do not have certain times, and other strange phenomena. The important thing is to become familiar with the pattern of the whole Latin verb in four groups of them. Rather than memorizing anything, once you begin to move from one time to another with any given form, then you will become more fluid and natural with the whole system, and these peculiar contractions won't disturb you at all. These are not new things to learn at all; they are just little variations.

With these contractions, we have established and understood rather quickly the whole pattern of the Latin verb in direct statements and questions, that is, in the active indicative mode.

ENCOUNTER 15

VOCABULA IN –IS: M, F, N, IN LEXICO CUM EXEMPLIS

Block II nouns in –is: masculine, feminine, neuter, in dictionary with examples

Introduction

We have said that most nouns in the Latin language can be divided into two big Blocks (40% each), as in Greek. We have also been dealing with the corresponding (50%) block of adjectives that ends with *–us*, *–a*, *–um* as found in your dictionary.

The sign of Bk.I nouns is given in the second part of the dictionary entry for each noun. The three families of nouns in this block have as their second part in the dictionary either *–i* (masculine), *–ae* (feminine), or *–i* (neuter), but with some variations or exceptions of the genders. We have been dealing with these nouns and their adjectives in our lessons and *ludi* and readings, and have seen how they have similar patterns in their subjects and objects, singular and plural.

In the present encounter we shall see Bk.II of nouns, that is, practically the other half of the nouns in the language, and after that the corresponding block of adjectives.

If 40% of all nouns are part of Bk.I and 40% of Bk.II, the other 20% we usually see during the last half hour of our First Experience. We don't have to bother with them now because there are no adjectives with that block of nouns.

Nouns in *–is*

We begin with the nouns as they appear in the dictionary. The teacher is free as a bird to pull out any examples she or he wants to use. As before, the essential element in the dictionary entry is the second part given for these nouns, which later will have its own meaning and function, and which indicates the block to which the noun belongs.

This second element in the dictionary is going to have the ending *–is*. You will have no difficulty distinguishing Bk.II nouns by the ending *–is* from Bk.I nouns, which are marked by the endings *–i*, *–ae*, *–i*. A note to the wise: numberless words in the Latin language end in *–is*!

Once you have found a noun whose second part ends in *–is*, then you will see that its first part, the dictionary entry itself, very often has an unexpected form. We call this first part the "crazy form" of the noun. As always, the first part of the dictionary entry gives the subject form of the noun, but, because this form of the noun is crazy, we will write it with a long dash like this: ——, to indicate that it cannot be used to determine the other forms of the noun (except for neuter nouns, because they follow the super principle, where the crazy form is the same as the singular object). Then, after that long dash, we are going to indicate the second part of the dictionary entry like this: *–is*, to indicate that the second part ends in *–is*. This second part of the noun often is something very different from the crazy form. Thus, we indicate this noun block like this:

——, *–is*.

Because the dictionary entry is the crazy form and unexpected, the second part of the dictionary entry gives you the word you can deal with to determine all the other forms of the noun.

Another difficulty with this block of nouns is that the gender of each noun has to be learned with the noun, and there is little discussion about this. The ending of the noun in the dictionary entry will not help you determine the gender of the noun. It simply must be learned or looked up in the dictionary repeatedly until you do learn the gender with each noun.

We can check ten words right away, and you will see what we are talking about. Look up for example the word for "king." You will find it in the dictionary under the crazy form *rex*. Because this is the crazy form, we cannot use it to determine the other forms of the noun. The second part of the noun is *regis*. When we see that *–is*, we know that the noun *rex, regis* belongs to Bk.II nouns. The dictionary has to give us the form *regis*, so that we can work with that form, not with *rex*. The dictionary also tells us that *rex, regis*, m., "a ruler, a king" is a masculine noun.

Take another example, say, *homo, hominis*, c., "a human being." The dictionary entry is the crazy form *homo*. The second entry, *hominis*, tells us that this noun belongs to Bk.II, and it gives us the form from which we can create all the other forms of this noun. The dictionary also tells us that the gender of this noun is "c." sometimes written as "comm.," meaning "common." This means that the same form serves for both masculine and feminine. The adjectives that modify *homo, hominis*, have to agree with the intended gender of this noun and may tell you whether this noun is understood as masculine or feminine.

Let us see the word for "earth." The dictionary entry, *tellus*, of course, does not tell us to which block this noun belongs. You might assume that it is a noun of Bk.I, as in *tellus, –i*, m. Only when you see the second entry *telluris* do you realize that this is a noun of Bk.II. With the second part, *telluris*, you now have the form with which you can create all the other forms of the noun. The dictionary also tells us that *tellus, telluris*, f., "the earth," is a feminine noun. Here is a noun that ends in *–us* but is feminine and belongs not to Bk.I but to Bk.II.

There are innumerable nouns of Bk.II in the Latin language. We shall see the adjectives of Bk.II in another encounter, but for now we have to be clear about these nouns.

Let us take a neuter noun. The dictionary entry gives us *flumen*, *fluminis*, n., "a flowing of water." The crazy form is followed by the second part, which tells us that this noun is of Bk.II. From the crazy form we cannot form any of the other forms of this noun (except the singular object form), but from the second form we can.

A few other crazy forms will help us to practice our understanding of Bk.II nouns. Take the word for the priest who blessed the bridges and so forth, *pontifex*, *pontificis*, m., "a Roman high-priest." The ending of the crazy form, *–fex*, is impossible to work with in Latin. Only the second part, ending in *–is*, gives us a workable form. In this case the noun is masculine.

Let us take the noun *sacerdos*, *sacerdotis*, c., "a priest, a priestess." The Romans had both male and female priests, and they used this noun to refer to priests of either sex, making this a noun of common gender.

When reading literature, if we come across a Bk. II noun used as the singular subject in its sentence, then we can easily find its entry in the dictionary, because it will be the crazy form. The crazy form of a neuter noun may also function as the singular object in the sentence, because of the super principle. If we come across any other form of these nouns on our sheets, then we may have some difficulty finding its entry in the dictionary because its form comes from the second part in the dictionary, not from the dictionary entry itself.

If you find on a sheet, for example, the form *pontificis*, you now know to look up in the dictionary the crazy form *pontifex*. If you find *telluris*, you now know to look up *tellus*. The form *fluminis* will lead you to the entry *flumen*, and *hominis* to the crazy form *homo*, and *regis* to *rex*.

The difference between the crazy form and the second form in the dictionary creates a problem with this block of nouns. If you come across the word *pedis*, you may need to spend a Saturday afternoon with the dictionary to locate the crazy form *pes*. This practice will teach you how this system works and encourage you to learn the full dictionary expression for each of these nouns along with its gender.

Upon further reflection, you may recall that in English, bicycles still have *pedals* and streets have *pedestrian* crossings and humans are *bi-pedal*. In all of these words the letter "d" comes not from the Latin crazy form but from the second form, which is the basis for all other forms of the noun. In English we also say *regal* and *regicide*, both from the second form *regis* and not from the crazy form *rex*.

These nouns of Bk.II are not going to follow the same pattern as the nouns of Bk.I. Let us look now to see how to recognize and produce the different forms of these nouns so that you will know how each word functions in its sentence.

The dictionary entry tells you the form of these nouns when they are used as the singular subject of a sentence. This is the case regardless of whether the noun is masculine, feminine, or neuter.

If the noun is masculine or feminine, then the ending for the object is *–em*. The problem is that this ending has nothing to do with the crazy form of the noun. To recognize or produce the object form for these nouns, you must begin with the second form in the dictionary. Instead of the ending *–is*, the object form has the ending *–em*. For example, if you have the word *rex, regis*, you cannot create the object form from the crazy form, *rex*. You must use the second form, *regis*, to form the object form, *regem*. The object form for *homo, hominis* is not *homem* based on the crazy form, but *hominem* based on the second form. Similarly, *pontifex, pontificis* has the object form *pontificem*.

As a side note, a certain number of nouns, about 15 to 20 of them, can have the object ending not in *–em* but in *–im* for a certain phonetic reason. For example, look up the word *turris, turris*, f., "a tower." In this case, both the crazy form and the second form happen to be the same. The second form ends in *–is*, telling you that this noun belongs to Bk.II. A good dictionary will also tell you that the singular object form in Latin literature may be either *turrim* or *turrem*. You just might find this special ending in the writings of Augustus or Iulius Caesar.

In the plural, the masculine and feminine subject forms of these nouns will end in *–es*. That is to say that the plural of *rex* is *reges*, because the plural is formed not from the crazy form but from the second form in the dictionary. The plural of *homo* is *homines* in both the masculine and feminine because this noun is of common gender, and the plural of *sacerdos* is *sacerdotes* for both sexes because of the common gender. The plural of *tellus* is *tellures*, of *pes* is *pedes*, of *turris* is *turres*.

The plural object of those same nouns, both masculine and feminine and common gender, also ends in *–es*, and your troubles have just begun. Because the subject and object forms in the plural both end in *–es*, you cannot tell them apart. Perhaps the verb will help you, but not always. There will be ambiguity all over the place because you cannot tell which this sentence means:

Matres patres amant
Mothers love fathers
Fathers love mothers.

Unfortunately we are hopelessly stuck. You can argue for one meaning, but the other will always be possible.

Sometimes, if you go on with Latin literature, especially with the Oxford edition of Latin classics, you will often see the object plural ending in *–īs* with a very long *–ī–*, rather than ending in *–es*. St. Thomas will never do this, but the editions of Cicero, Horace, Virgil, depending on the printer and publisher, may have the object ending in *–is*, not *–es*.

If the noun is neuter, the super principle tells us that the form found in the dictionary is not only the subject but also the singular object. You may think that this makes things easier, but it causes no end of trouble for people, because, when you see that form in a sentence, the form itself will not tell you whether it functions as the subject or as the object of the sentence. For example, some people will see the dictionary entry for *corpus*, "a body," and think that it is a noun of Bk.I with the object singular *corpum*. If you read further, you see that *corpus, corporis*, belongs to Bk.II nouns. You might then think that the object form is *corporem*. Only if you read further will you see that *corpus, corporis*, n., "a body," is a neuter noun, and because of the super principle its object singular is the same as the crazy form *corpus*.

Most neuter plurals of Bk.II form their subject and object form ending in *–a*. For example, the plural of *corpus* is *corpora*. Again, the plural form is not based on the crazy form, but on the second form in your dictionary. Only if you begin with *corporis* will you produce *corpora*. Likewise, the plural of *tempus* is *tempora*, which is produced from the second form, *temporis;* of *flumen* is *flumina*, which is based on the second form, *fluminis*. If you have the entry *litus, litoris*, n., "the sea-shore," then the plural of *litus* is *litora*. Again, this covers most of the neuter plurals, say, 85% of them.

Because of the super principle, the subject and the object of the neuter plurals will have the same form ending in *–a*.

While 85% of all neuter nouns of Bk.II end in *–a* in the subject and object plural, about 15% of them will end in *–ia* because of a hidden *–i–* in their nature and pattern; for example, the plural of *animal* is *animalia*, and the reverse of *mare* is *maria*, and *insigne* becomes *insignia*, and the plural of *altar* is *altaria*.

Look at examples of these Bk.II nouns in your reading sheets, and with a bit of trial and error and a few mistakes and a lot of dictionary work these nouns will come naturally to you, and the ambiguities will become more familiar. You must know the crazy form and construct the other forms from the second form of these nouns and learn the gender with each noun.

In systems other than ours Bk.II is called the third declension, which we do not do because we divide our nouns on the basis of the two big Blocks of nouns and adjectives that cover the entire language, as in Latin's predecessor: Greek.

ENCOUNTER 16

NOMINA RURSUS IN –IS

again nouns in –is

Turn to your reading sheets and to your dictionary to discover these words occurring naturally in every sentence and paragraph and on every page. Practice reversing the nouns from the singular to the plural, subject to object, and vice versa, and you will get a feel for these nouns and their ambiguities right away with no memorizing at all. You will just know it nicely from the Latin language.

ENCOUNTER 17

EADEM NOMINA
NECNON FORMAE DUPLICIS IMPERATIVI
+ "ESSE"

the same nouns
as well as the forms of the double command
including the verb "to be"

Introduction

Once again students need continual repetition with the nouns as they appear in the reading sheets and with their identification as subjects and objects. Finding words in the dictionary is particularly difficult, because the dictionary entries are often far from the forms you would expect. Becoming familiar with the forms of the nouns will take time; in the meantime, the teacher will review all of the 6 times of verbs to keep the whole language moving at once.

Our next step is to finish the verb construction now with the command forms, also known as imperatives. If you know Greek, the command forms are all based on the Greek or Indo-European forms.

The command forms in Latin are very simple. One form of command is the simple, straight, present imperative of a command on the spot. The other form of command is used in formulae, especially in laws and decrees, and also in very familiar language at home; it is sometimes called the "second imperative" or the "future imperative" because it contains a more general or distant command. The big distinction is between these two.

You should have no problem with the forms except that many forms are deceptive because they look like or are identical to many other forms in the Latin language. So you have to know the vocabulary and the verb origin in the dictionary. If you know the verb's origin, you will know the command form and recognize it in the reading sheets.

We shall learn the imperatives according to the four groups of verbs distinguished by their predominant vowels. In this way we will keep the vowels distinct and the accents distinct.

1. *–are*

The predominant vowel of verb Gp.I is the long *–ā–*, and the second principal part in the dictionary ends with *–are*, as in:

nego, negāre, negavi, negatus, 1, to deny, negate; say no.

The simple command has forms only for "you" and "you all." In the singular "you must deny!" or "deny!" is *nega*, and in the plural *negate* means "you all must deny!" or "you all deny!"

When we come to the second or future command form, the Latins make a distinction between you and he, she, it, which really doesn't occur in our modern languages, but it occurs in Greek.

The second command of *nega* is *negato*. To make a distinction between these two, we render *nega* as "you must deny!" and *negato* as "you shall-must deny!" or we might speak in the language of the Ten Commandments of Moses and say, "thou shalt deny!" as if it were a command or a precept of the law. With some intuition we could image Charlton Heston giving the Ten Commandments in the second command form. The plural form of *negato* is *negatote,* meaning "you-all must deny!"

To say "he, she, it must deny!" it just so happens that the form is the same as "thou shalt deny!" Thus, *negato* means either "he, she, it shall-must deny!" or "you shall-must deny!" The plural meaning "they shall-must deny!" is *neganto*. This form is simply the form for T.1, *negant*, "they are denying," with an *–o* attached to the end of it. Thus, *negant*, "they are denying," becomes *neganto,* "they shall-must deny!" You will not find these forms that often, but they do appear more often in the Latin Bible and in all ordinary Latin authors. Although these are not the most important forms of the verbs, you will find these forms everywhere in the works of Plautus and Terentius and Cicero's letters to friends and courtroom debates.

2. *–ēre*

The predominant vowel of verb Gp.II is the long *–ē–*, and the second principal part in the dictionary ends with *–ēre*, as in:

> *valeo, valēre, valui, valitum*, 2, to be strong, to be well, to be in good health.

The simple command for "you must be in good health!" is *vale*, and in the plural *valēte* has an accent on the long *–ḗ–* and means "all you people take care!" or simply "good-bye."

The second command form meaning "thou shalt be in good health!" is *valéto*, and its plural is *valetote*.

To say "he, she, it must be in good health" is also *valéto*, and its plural is *valento*. These forms are the same as for verb Gp.I.

3. *–ĕre*

The predominant vowel of verb Gp.III is the short *–ĕ–*, and the second principal part in the dictionary ends with *–ĕre*. The forms for this group of verbs follow the Latin and Greek system and are normal and will cause you no problem, unless you think in Italian. There is a big mix-up here, and the accents will not be the same between Latin and Italian or other modern languages. What gives rise to the problem with this group of verbs is the short *–ĕ–* vowel, which affects the accents of the verbal forms in Latin in predictable and normal ways. You have to be very clear about the accents in this group of verbs. Our example is:

promitto, promíttĕre, promisi, promissum, 3, to put forth, to promise.

The simple command for "you must promise!" is *promítte*, which is the same as Gp.II verbs such as *vale* above. The plural "you all must promise" is *promíttĭte*. This form contrasts with the same form in Gp.II verbs such as *valéte* where a short *–ĕ–* becomes a short *–ĭ–*. Here the accent falls on the previous syllable *promíttĭte*. That is about the only difficulty with the simple command forms.

The second command "thou shalt promise!" is *promíttĭto*. Its plural is *promittitóte*, meaning, "you-all must promise!"

Again, you say "he, she, it shall-must promise!" with the same form as "thou shalt promise!" namely *promíttĭto*, and its plural is *promittúnto*.

The only problem with this group of verbs is with the accent of the form *promíttĭto*. There is no problem with the Latin, which is normal and predictable. The problem occurs only when you confuse these forms with the accents of modern Italian. The only solution is diligence and clarity.

4. *–ire*

The predominant vowel of Gp.IV verbs is the long *–ī–*, and the second principal part in the dictionary ends with *–ire*, as in:

audio, audīre, audivi or *audii, auditum*, 4, to hear, to listen to.

The simple command for "you must hear!" is *audi*, and the plural "you all must hear!" is *audíte*. Because the *–ī–* is long, it is naturally accented. The scriptures say *Aperíte portas*, "Open, you-all, the doors!"

The second command form meaning "thou shalt hear!" is *audíto*, and its plural is *auditote*.

To say "he, she, it must hear" is also *audíto*, and its plural is *audiunto*, which is the same as the form of the verb in T.1 with a final *–o*. These forms follow the same pattern.

5. *–io, ĕre*

The small Group of verbs that are mixed between Gp.III and Gp.IV are half in the Group of *–ĕre* verbs and half in the Group of *–ire* verbs, as in the example:

rapio, rapĕre, rapui, raptum, 3, to snatch, to grab, to take away.

The simple commands follow the pattern for verb Gp.III; namely, "you must seize!" is *rape*, and the plural "you all must seize!" is *rápite*.

For the second imperatives, the verb follows the pattern of Gp.IV verbs. The second command form meaning "thou shalt seize!" is *rápito*, and its plural is *rapitóte*.

To say "he, she, it must seize" is also *rápito*, and its plural is *rapiúnto*, again following the pattern of verb Gp.IV.

Up to this point we have seen the two main Blocks of nouns and half of the adjectives corresponding to Bk.I nouns. We have seen all six times of the verb in the indicative. Now we have seen the imperatives, which are simple transcriptions from the Greek. We have done this without any paradigms, charts, or memorizing nonsense syllables. You might just look at all the different uses of the letter "i" and the letters "to" scattered throughout. Many of these forms end with *–i* and with *–o*, now including the imperatives. This poses no problem, if you know the origin of the word or if you know the verb group or the noun block it belongs to.

6. *esse*

The imperatives of the verb "to be" are easy and do not cause any difficulty. The dictionary entry is:

sum, esse, fui, futurus

The simple command "you must be!" is *es*, which is very rare, but it does appear a few times in Plautus. This is the same form as T.1 "you are." Its plural "you all must be!" is *este* as in the Christmas hymn *Adeste fideles*, "Be present, you faithful!"

The second command form meaning "thou shalt be!" is *esto*, and its plural is *estote*, which appears often in the scriptures, as in the passage, *estote perfecti*, "Be ye perfect!" (*v.* Vulg. Nov. *Matt.* 5.48).

To say "he, she, it must be" is also *esto*, which we sometimes use to mean "OK." Its plural is *sunto*, which is the same as the form of the verb in T.1, *sunt*, with a final *–o*.

Other examples at hand include this expression of Marcus Tullius Cicero (106–43 BCE), which Cicero writes in a letter to Trebatius:

Verum illud esto (Cic. *Fam.* VII, 18, 4)
That must be true.

In a letter from Marcus Caelius to Cicero, he quotes Roman law:

in quo ita erat: quod eorum iudicum maior pars iudicarit, id ius ratumque esto (Cic. *Fam.* VIII, 8, 3)

in which it was thus: "what the majority of those judges will have decided, that must be the law and confirmed."

The reading sheets of the fifth experience in this volume include a letter of Ambrosius Mediolanensis (333–397 CE) to Titianus (Sheet 5-E), in which Ambrose says:

Ideoque promptior esto decisioni, cuius et spes potior et fructus est (Ambros. *Ep. Titiano*, 2)

And therefore you must be more ready for a decision, whose both hope and outcome is more valuable.

The comedy *Poenulus*, by Titus Maccius Plautus (c. 254–184 BCE), provides this example, in which Plautus says:

bonam dedistis, aduocati, operam mihi.
cras mane, quaeso, in comitio estote obuiam. (Plaut. *Poen*, 806–807)
Lawyers, you have given good attention to me.
Please, tomorrow morning you all must be present in the forum.

In a letter Cicero wrote to Atticus, he says:

habeo Iunium et Quinctilem in metu. Esto, duos quidem mensis sustinebit Bibulus (Cic. *Att*. VI, 1, 14)

I am fearful of Iunius and Quinctilius. Let it be; indeed Bibulus will endure two months.

In another letter to Atticus, Cicero says:

age, esto: hoc commune est (Cic. *Att*. IX, 9, 3)
come on! OK: this is a common expression.

ENCOUNTER 18

ADIECTIVA IN –IS. TRES MODI IN LEXICO. IUNCTIO I + II

Block II adjectives in –is. three ways in the dictionary. joining Blocks I and II

Introduction

In our fourth encounter we saw Bk.I adjectives presented in the dictionary according to their endings *–us*, *–a*, *–um*. Corresponding to each of these endings we had already seen three families of nouns that comprise Bk.I nouns. More recently we have seen Bk.II nouns. Now we will study the adjectives that correspond to Bk.II nouns. For your consolation remember that all the adjectives of the Latin language are divided into two big Blocks, each comprising 50% of the adjectives. So, we are half done, and after this second half nothing will remain of the adjectives.

1. Adjectives in *–is*

We have already presented the nouns of Bk.II in a special way from the dictionary. The dictionary entry may be a crazy form, unexpected, given the other forms of the noun. The crazy form is followed by a form that ends in *–is*. This is followed by the noun's gender. We then worked with the second form in the dictionary to recognize and produce the object form, and next the plural object and subject forms. We also saw that the masculine and feminine nouns have one system, and the neuters have their system, which follows the super principle.

Now the adjectives of Bk.II will have the same endings and functions as the respective nouns of Bk.II. The adjectives, however, are presented in three different ways in the dictionary, and we have to be careful about how they are presented. Again, all the adjectives presented in these three ways belong to Bk.II and will have the same endings as their corresponding nouns in this block.

1.1 *First way in the dictionary*

Many adjectives in Bk.II are presented with three special forms, one for each gender. For example, the adjective meaning "quick" is *celer, celeris, celere*, where *celer* is the masculine form, *celeris* the feminine, and *celere* the neuter form. The way these words are presented in the dictionary:

celer, *celeris*, *celere*, adj., swift

is sufficient to indicate the entry is an adjective of Bk.II, with three different forms for the singular subjects corresponding to the three genders.

The masculine and feminine forms will follow the same pattern as the masculine and feminine nouns of Bk.II; namely, the singular object will end in –*em*, as in *celerem*, and the plural subject and object will end in –*es*, as in *celeres*. Like the nouns of Bk.II, the same phenomenon occurs in the object plural in that the ending –*es* is frequently replaced by –*is* with a long –*i*–. Thus, instead of the object plural *celeres*, you may see *celeris* with the same meaning and function in the sentence.

The neuter form *celere* will have the same form in the singular subject and object according to the super principle.

Remember, the nouns of this block in their neuter plural subject and object forms end in –*a* 85% of the time, and 15% of the time they end in –*ia*. The adjectives of this block are just the opposite, where 85% of the time they end in –*ia*, and only 15% of the time in –*a*. Here the neuter plural subject and object form is *celeria*.

Take for example the adjective of three endings meaning "sharp":

acer, *acris*, *acre*, adj., sharp.

The way the entry is presented indicates that this is a Bk.II adjective of three endings. The plural of *acer* and *acris* is *acres*, their object singular is *acrem*, and its plural is also *acres* or frequently *acris* with a long –*i*–. The plural of the neuter *acre* is *acria*, and the super principle tells us that the object form is the same as each subject form. Adjectives of Bk.II in three endings are not that common; about thirty such words in the language appear so in the dictionary.

1.2 *Second way in the dictionary*

The second way in which adjectives of Bk.II are presented in the dictionary is infinitely more common. These adjectives have the same form for the masculine and feminine, and a special form for the neuter. Take as example the adjective meaning "well-known, noble":

nobilis, *nobile*, adj., well-known.

The first word, *nobilis*, is the masculine and feminine form, and the second, *nobile*, is the neuter form.

The same well-known phenomenon is going to happen with these adjectives. For the masculine and feminine, the singular object ends in –*em*, as in *nobilem*. The plural of *nobilis* is *nobiles*, and the plural of *nobilem* is also *nobiles* or very commonly *nobilis*, with a long –*i*–.

The plural of the neuter *nobile* is *nobilia*, which is an example of 85% of the neuter adjectives of this block. The super principle tells us that the object form in the singular is *nobile* and in the plural *nobilia*, as expected.

Be careful! All of these forms are extremely misleading because the ending –*is* is all over the language as are the endings –*e* and –*ae*. Vocabulary is our only salvation.

1.3 *Third way in the dictionary*

The third way in which the adjectives of Bk.II are often presented in the dictionary and literature is with one form for all three genders. If you look in your dictionary at this point, it will give you the entry for *velox*. Then it will give you the form *velocis*, and the entry will look like a noun. Some dictionaries give the second form in parentheses such as (*velocis*), and some simply state "adj." for "adjective." So the entry:

velox, *velocis*, adj., swift

looks exactly like the noun, except that it says that it is an adjective. The dictionary entry *velox* is the form for the masculine, feminine, and neuter when it is used as a singular subject. The second form given, *velocis*, is not the form for another gender. Rather, exactly like the noun, the second form tells you how to recognize and produce all the other forms of the adjective, because you cannot use the form *velox* to produce the other forms. The other forms of this adjective are all predictable. The masculine and feminine have the singular object form *velocem*, their subject plural *veloces*, and their object plural *veloces*, which is often *velocis* with a long *–i–*. The super principle means that the singular object in the neuter is also *velox*, and the subject plural in the neuter is *velocia*, which follows the pattern of 85% of these adjectives and serves as the plural object as well.

That is how the adjectives of Bk.II are presented. A textbook may talk about adjectives of three terminations, of two terminations, or of one termination.

We wish to point out that *velocia*, ending in *–ia*, is a neuter plural following the pattern of 85% of the adjectives in Bk.II. Do not forget there are thousands of feminine nouns ending in *–ia*. That is why you have to be extremely careful and know your vocabulary. Take the example:

Amicitia velocia officia poscit
Friendship demands quick services.

The verb here is *poscit*, meaning "it demands." The noun *amicitia* functions as the subject and has the dictionary entry *amicitia, amicitiae*, f., "friendship." The noun *officia* functions as the object; it is a neuter plural from *officium, officii*, n., "service," in the dictionary and means "services." The services are described by the adjective *velocia*, which is also a neuter plural from *velox, velocis*, adj., "quick" in the dictionary. The only way to make sense of this sentence is to know your vocabulary because all the words end in *–ia* except the verb. One is a singular noun, one is a neuter plural noun, and one is a plural adjective. There is no guess work if you know your vocabulary.

In subsequent encounters we shall learn the endings of the other functions of the nouns and adjectives, but for now the subject and object functions are necessary to grasp immediately and clearly. We have intentionally presented alternatively verbs and nouns and adjectives to keep them all mixed up as if in a big bowl and moving together. You will distinguish and understand—something which we can say in clear and concise Latin: *distingues intellegesque.*

2. Joining Blocks I and II

As we progress, remember to review everything we have already encountered because that is how we are made and that is how the mind functions. Thus far we have seen Bk.I nouns and Bk.I adjectives, Bk. II nouns and Bk.II adjectives. At this point you can have a lot of fun mixing them up by taking an adjective of Bk.I and a noun of the other Block and making them agree, although the endings are not going to appear the same. This is one of the fascinating points to learn about Latin.

We will find words in the Latin sentence that all agree, although they do not have the same endings. If the teacher emphasizes these things, the students will be fascinated. Take the example:

canis bonus et velox
a good and swift dog.

All three Latin words agree because they are all singular masculine subjects. Other languages simplify this and often have the same endings for all three words. Take an example in the plural:

Bonos veloces canes videmus
We see good swift dogs.

The first three words are all masculine plural objects.

What is worse, as in poetry, so in prose, the adjective and the noun will be separated, very often by several words. The ideas belong together even though the words are separated geographically in the sentence and can belong to either block, and their endings may not look the same, but they will agree with one another. You have to know enough vocabulary and be observant enough to connect the nouns and adjectives that go together but are separated. Take the example:

Bonus et velox ante nos ludit canis
A good and swift dog is playing in front of us.

Here the adjectives *bonus* and *velox* agree with *canis* although they are not written together and their endings do not look as if they agree, but they are all masculine singular and subject form. You could even have the very elegant sentence:

Bonus ante nos veloxque ludit canis.

The meaning is the same as previously, but the word order is open and free and does not essentially determine the meaning of the sentence but enhances its elegant style. All the words tie in together, although they are not in the places we would expect. The elegance of this sentence can make it difficult to decipher unless you know your vocabulary. You must immediately consult, read, and analyze especially examples of poetry in the reading sheets following each experience.

To summarize some of these difficulties of the Latin language, we would say first that the adjectives and nouns ending in *–ia* will be neuter plural in Bk.II and feminine singular in Bk.I. To discern which they are and to distinguish one from another, you have to know your vocabulary.

Second, you will see nouns and adjectives of the two different Blocks that go together even though they will not be placed next to each other or look as if they agree with one another.

Third, we have seen verbs for the "you" form that end in *–is* or *–as*, as do many nouns and adjectives. We have also seen imperative verbs that end in *–e* or *–a*, just like many neuter nouns or adjectives of Bk.II.

I am still amazed after fifty years by how the Romans did it. In some of the poets, the adjectives are two lines away, yet they still hold together. The Romans did it and were used to it and not disturbed, upset, or in desperation.

I hate to say it but at the end of eight weeks of summer school or several Experiences, some people are still trying to tie words together that look as if they go together but really do not, because these people were never trained correctly. You cannot and will not rely on looks; that is just out. You will turn to the dictionary forms until you know your vocabulary and then apply your training.

ENCOUNTER 19

SINGULARUM ADHUC TRADITARUM REPETITIO RERUM

repetition of all elements explained thus far

This encounter is dedicated to examining the reading sheets or the examples of the teacher slowly and patiently and calmly to review the whole language presented thus far. The verbs are to be identified and constructed by the students up and down the six times and in the imperative. Examples of adjectives and nouns of Bk.I and II, mixed together, are to be discovered and created. This class encounter will allow everything we have learned and forgotten to breathe a bit.

Of course the students will have *ludi* every step of the way, and the *ludi* will be created anew each year to keep the teacher fresh and supple in her or his use and knowledge of the Latin language.

We have seen a mass of material here, but we are going actually very slowly to let Latin grow within us. Patience with ourselves helps as we encounter this language together in the classroom—or on the beach: *in aula aut in ora*!

ENCOUNTER 20

POSSESSIONIS CASUS IN NOMINIBUS + ADIECTIVIS; BINI USUS

the of-possession function in nouns and adjectives; two usages

Introduction

We left our last encounter to a review of everything, just to let ourselves breathe a little and let the whole language work in us with a little patience.

So far we have been talking about just two functions in the language out of the seven indicated in the first encounter, namely the subject and object. Now is the time to introduce another essential function of the language, namely the double function "of-possession" with its proper endings.

One big usage of this function is to express the idea "of." Different forms of the word "of" exist in the English language, including:

a picture *of her*
the love *of them*
the desire *of honesty*
the avoidance *of fraud*
fond *of us*.

The other big usage of this function is to show possession, which is expressed in English in two ways: again, either "of" or the addition at the end of a word of an apostrophe followed by the letter "s," or the letter "s" followed by an apostrophe. For example, we say:

the gift *of the child*
the *child's* gift

the education *of the students*
the *students'* education

the gift of the Jacksons
the Jacksons' gift.

These are the two main uses of the Latin function of-possession. We shall eventually learn a few others, which, although not the same, work in this same form and can be reduced practically to those two ideas.

The manuals will call this function the "genitive" from the verb:

gigno, gignere, genui, genitum, 3, to beget, bear, bring forth, produce

because you are generated as the child *of someone*. So, you are the son *of Mary* or *Mary's* son. This is the main use of this function beside the general expression "of." We desire to keep the two main usages of this function ever present in the students' minds, and so we call this the function of-possession. In this way the uses of this function are known and understood directly without any encumbering technical terminology.

1. First Block of nouns

The forms are extremely simple, and you already know them because the second form of the nouns of Bk.I and II in the dictionary is in fact the of-possessive form; now you will know its natural meaning. In most dictionaries today, after the dictionary entry, the second form given for nouns, the form that indicates to which block a noun belongs, is in fact the form of-possession.

This means that when you had:

> *asinus*, *asini*, m., a donkey

the second form given means:

> *asini*
> of the donkey
> the donkey's.

For a noun like:

> *porta*, *portae*, f., a door

the second form means:

> *portae*
> of the door
> the door's.

It is the same story for neuter nouns, to complete Bk.I. For a noun like:

> *documentum*, *documenti*, n., a lesson, an example

the second form means:

> *documenti*
> of the document
> the document's [value, length, . . .].

In Bk.I nouns you can see that the form of-possession for the feminine *portae* ends in *–ae*, but that the form for both the masculine and neuter are the same, for example *asini* and *documenti*, both ending in *–i*. The most confusing and disturbing thing is that today the masculine *asini* is identical in form with its plural subject. These were and sounded different to the Romans. Besides that, the potential ambiguity is great, for example:

> *Filii libros possident*

could mean:

They possess the books of the son
The sons possess books.

2. Second Block of nouns

The same thing is true for Bk.II nouns. The second part in the dictionary is the form of-possession, which ends in –*is*. This second part in the dictionary distinguishes Bk.II nouns from the first. Take the example:

senator, *senatoris*, m., a senator.

First is the crazy form, *senator*, followed by the form of-possession:

senatoris
of the senator
the senator's [qualities, stature, . . .].

Take the example:

corpus, *corporis*, n., a body.

After the crazy form, *corpus*, the form of-possession means:

corporis
of the body
the body's [mass, sickness, . . .].

Today most dictionaries are the same and give the form of-possession as the second entry. From the dictionary we learn that the final vowels for the form of-possession for nouns of Bk.I are, –*i*, –*ae*, and of Bk.II is –*is*. The only thing yet to learn about these is what happens to those vowels when the forms become plural.

3. Plural forms of Block I nouns

The plural of *asini* is *asinorum*, which means "of the donkeys" or "the donkeys'." Here the singular ending –*i* becomes the plural ending –*orum*, thus:

asini	*asinorum*
of a donkey	of the donkeys
a donkey's	the donkeys'.

Take for example:

Repetitio est mater studiorum vel asinorum
Repetition is the mother of studies or of blockheads.

The plural of *portae* is *portarum*, meaning "of the doors" or "the doors'." Here the singular ending –*ae* is reversed to the plural ending –*arum*. Take for example:

fenestra portae	*fenestrae portarum*
the window of a door	the windows of the doors
a door's window	the doors' windows

salus animae	*salus animarum*
the salvation of the soul	the salvation of souls.

You can see a consistency between the masculine ending *–orum* and the feminine ending *–arum*. Everyone recognizes these clear and heavy plural forms *asinorum, portarum, animarum* to be very Latin forms and words. They are heavy and famously characteristic of Latin and not so nice as the Greek, which is much smoother. As a joke we used to accentuate that characteristic Latin ending *–orum*, as representative of the whole Latin language, when we used to say, "I'm studying *Latinórum*," as if to say, "I'm studying the embodiment of the whole Latin language."

Turning to the neuter of Bk.I, the plural of *documenti* is *documentorum*, which means "of the documents" or "the documents'." Here, as for the masculine, the singular ending *–i* becomes the plural ending *–orum*. There really are no exceptions, perhaps a few in early Latin; for example *mater familias*, "mother of a family," where the genitive *familias* follows the Greek.

4. Plural forms of Block II nouns

We are dealing with nouns like *hominis, fluminis, regis, corporis, virtutis*, or any other of infinitely numerous examples on your reading sheets. We have said that the form ending in *–is* is given second in the dictionary. The plural form is going to be very tricky, because 85% of these nouns in Bk.II have in the plural the ending *–um*, a simple *–um*. Thus we have:

hominis	*hominum*
fluminis	*fluminum*
regis	*regum*
corporis	*corporum*
virtutis	*virtutum*.

But for a definite reason, which should not slow us down right now (see Gildersleeve and Lodge n° 56), 15% of these nouns are going to have the plural ending *–ium*. Take for example the nouns:

navis, navis, f., a ship
civis, civis, c., a citizen
animal, animalis, n., an animal.

The dictionary entry gives the singular form of-possession as *navis, civis, animalis*. The plural of the form of-possession is not *navum, civum, animalum*, but *navium, civium, animalium:*

navis rostrum	*navium rostra*
the prow of the ship	*prows of ships*.

Other examples include the nouns:

turris, turris, f., a tower
gens, gentis, f., a race, clan
cor, cordis, n., the heart.

They are among the 15% of nouns that form the plural of-possession ending in –*ium*, as in the examples:

turris constructio the construction of the tower	*turrium constructio* the construction of towers
gentis imperator the commander of the nation	*gentium imperator* the commander of peoples
cordis stupor numbness of heart	*cordium stupor* the amazement of hearts.

What has to be pointed out right away here are the practical difficulties that are going to cause problems if you are not awake. In Bk.I nouns *portae, documenti, asini* can be either the singular form of-possession or the plural subject form. These sentences can be eternally ambiguous. This is never going to go away, and you simply have to sit down and analyze what you are doing and what the sentence is saying.

In Bk.II the big massive trap and hole-in-the-ground is the form *hominum, fluminum, regum, corporum, virtutum*, which will be confused with singular neuters of Bk.I such as *vehiculum, verbum, elementum*, which function as both subjects and objects, and they will be confused with singular objects of the type –*us*, –*i*, such as *equum, digitum, calamum*. Now the same letters can function as the plural form of-possession, in Bk.II. Take the example:

Virtutum computo numerum
I count the number of virtues.

Here *Virtutum* is the plural form of-possession of *virtus, virtutis*, f., "virtue"; the other noun is the object singular of *numerus, numeri*, m., "a number." The only way to distinguish the plural of-possession from the singular object is to know the vocabulary. Also note: one letter distinguishes *virtutem* from *virtutum*.

Another possible trap is the thousand neuter nouns of Bk.I ending in –*ium* functioning as both subjects and objects, which look like 15% of Bk.II nouns ending in –*ium* and functioning as the plural form of-possession, as in:

auxilium navium
the assistance of the ships

civium proelium
the battle of citizens.

The dictionary gives you the entries *auxilium, auxilii*, n., "a help," and *proelium, proelii*, n., "a battle," which tells you that *auxilium* and *proelium* are singular and function as subjects or objects of a sentence. You already know the dictionary entry *navis, navis*, f., "a ship," and *civis, civis*, c., "a citizen," which tells you that *navium, civium* is the plural form of-possession. Vocabulary, calm and precise reading, and sharp thinking are your only salvation always and everywhere in Latin, or we may say: *in vocabulis ac lectionibus tranquillis et accuratis necnon acri cogitatione unica est salus semper ubique latinitatis posita.*

5. Adjectives in *–us, –a, –um*

We can dispose of the adjectives in a moment because in Bk.I the adjectives are identical with the nouns. The only trouble here is that the dictionary entry for the adjectives does not give the form of-possession as it does for the nouns. Rather, the dictionary entry points out the block to which the adjectives belong. The sign of Bk.I is an entry like *honestus, a, um*, and from this you put into practice what you know of the nouns of Bk.I. For example the forms of-possession in the singular and plural are:

honesti	*honestorum*
honestae	*honestarum*
honesti	*honestorum.*

The endings of those adjectives are identical with the endings of the nouns, and that is the end of the story.

Be careful with the few masculine nouns of the family *–a, –ae*, such as *nauta, nautae*, m., "a sailor," and *trapezita, ae*, m., "a banker." You might one day wish to say:

honesti trapezitae officia
the services of an honest banker

honestorum officium nautarum
the service of honest sailors.

In both cases the adjective agrees with its noun, *honesti trapezitae* and *honestorum nautarum*, whereas *officium* is a neuter singular functioning as either the subject or the object, as we warned you. We only have to observe and be very careful, because otherwise the language itself will win and destroy us, that is to say in Latin, *alioquin lingua vincet ipsa nosque extinguet.* We shall never learn Latin unless we pinpoint things accurately.

6. Adjectives in ——, *–is*

Bk.II of adjectives again presents no problem. The dictionary entry typically gives you only the singular subject form of these adjectives, for example, *celer, celeris, celere*, "swift." All the nouns and all the adjectives of Bk.II form the singular form of-possession in the same way, with the ending *–is*. Here, the adjective *celeris* is the form both for the feminine subject and the form of-possession in the masculine, feminine, and neuter singular. If we have the noun *hirundo, hirundinis*, f., "a swallow," then we can say:

celeris hirundo effugit
a swift swallow escapes

celeris hirundinis volatus
the flight of a swift swallow.

In these examples you can see that the same form *celeris* describes the subject in the first sentence and is the form of-possession in the second.

In the plural, these adjectives will have the inverse phenomenon as the nouns. We have seen that 85% of the nouns form their plural ending of-possession in –*um*, and only 15% end in –*ium*. The adjectives are absolutely the inverse for a definite reason (see Gildersleeve and Lodge nº 83). For 85% of the adjectives the plural form of-possession will end in –*ium* and 15% in –*um*. Many people do not know how to deal with this. You just have to be very careful.

One letter makes all the difference. If you notice that the object singular (masculine and feminine) of Bk.II nouns and adjectives ends in –*em* and the plural form of-possession ends in –*um*, then you will see that the difference is one letter. The singular form of-possession of Bk.II nouns and adjectives ends in –*is*, and these same words have the subject and object plurals (masculine and feminine) ending in –*es* where the object plural is sometimes written with a long –*īs*, as we have seen. You must train yourself to be very careful and notice the difference of one letter.

We do not want schemas. Rather, we want to turn immediately to the reading sheets and look for these forms and note the ambiguity that you are going to have unless you are attentive to every letter. The most common type of Bk.II adjectives is: *facilis*, *facile*, "easy." Logic will give you *facilis* as of-possession for all genders: masculine, feminine, and neuter. This will also shock you into realizing that *facilis* can have seven functions in Latin: singular subject masculine and feminine, whose reverse is *faciles*; plural object masculine and feminine as a substitute for *faciles*, whose reverse is *facilem*; singular of-possession masculine, feminine, and neuter, whose reverse is *facilium*, producing the headache mentioned above. This is why we continually reverse expressions from singular to plural or from plural to singular, to reveal how we understand any given text. The solution is complete mastery of vocabulary and disciplined reasoning. After you have learned all the possibilities in Latin, you still have to think.

7. Genitive in front

An element of style that every Latinist in the world knows and is very dear to the Romans is the practice of placing the form of-possession out in front of the word it describes. In English we say, "a mother's patience"; so too the Romans do this all the time. Take the example:

> *Meam ad matrum honorem dirigo orationem*
> I direct my speech to the honor of the mothers.

In this example the preposition *ad*, "to, unto," does not go with *matrum*, which is the plural form of-possession "of mothers" placed out in front of the word it describes, *honorem*, "the honor." Many students start with the first word of the sentence without considering the whole sentence and seeing this connection. Sometimes the form of-possession is placed even before the preposition as in the example:

familiarum contra omnes difficultates
against all difficulties of the families.

Here, the form of-possession *familiarum*, "of families," goes with *difficultates*, "difficulties," at the other end of the expression, but it is placed out even in front of the preposition *contra*, "against." The position of the form of-possession out in front is going to cause trouble and ambiguity because there is no indication of whether it goes with the words to the right or to the left, with what follows or what precedes. Given the example:

Filii magistrorum honorem augent,

which does it mean:

The sons of teachers increase honor
Children increase the honor of teachers?

Here the question is whether *magistrorum*, "of teachers," goes with *filii*, "sons," or with *honorem*, "honor." The problem is that the sentence does not tell you and you have to sit down and figure it out. This illustrates one of our principles from the first day: after you understand the whole sentence, you still have to think and figure it out. Its understanding will never be obvious unless to a thinker.

The use of examples from reading sheets will clarify or alleviate the difficulties right away. But you have to know the problems that will come up, and these are the problems that make Latin such an adventure and fun.

ENCOUNTER 21

VOCIS PASSIVAE INDICATIO IN TEMPORIBUS 1, 2, 3. PHONETICAE EXCEPTIONES

demonstration of the passive voice in Times 1, 2, 3. phonetic exceptions

Introduction

When we presented the active voice we began with T.4, 5, 6 for the definite reason that they are all identical everywhere in the dictionary and in literature. In this encounter, however, we shall present the passive beginning with T.1, 2, 3, for another definite intention that will become clear a little later, and you will understand why.

1. Full English meaning of Times 1, 2, 3 passive

Just to be sure that we all know what we are talking about, and to clarify something that is slipping into oblivion more every day, we should give the full English meaning of these passive times. Take the example in T.2:

extollebatur
he, she, it was being extolled
he, she, it continued to be extolled
he, she, it used to be extolled
he, she, it would be extolled (whenever it was possible).

In English those are about all the different meanings contained in that T.2 passive.

In T.1, let us say:

removemur
we are removed
we are being removed.

It is important to understand these meanings of T.1 in the passive, because the English expression "we are removed" may come up again as a false rendering of another Latin time, as we shall see.

In T.3 we have the example:

regentur
they will be ruled
they will continue to be ruled.

You really can't say much more than that in English.

2. Formation of Times 1, 2, 3 in Latin

The formation of these verbs is child's play, if we have learned carefully the formation of the active of T.1, 2, 3, because in about twenty seconds of learning we are going to take the active forms of T.1, 2, 3 and flip them over into the passive. We shall do this without conjugations and without memorizing schemas. But this presumes that first we have mastered the active meanings and forms; otherwise, there is going to be double-trouble.

The forms of the verbs will not change fundamentally between the active and the passive, as you will see. All the vowels and the entire construction for the composition of the verbs in T.1, 2, 3 remain exactly the same with the few exceptions that will be mentioned.

We start with the active form of the verb. This is for all verbs of the Latin language, and it is going to be important, because later on we are going to get a set of verbs that look passive but are really active and make up a big part of the Latin language, and so we have to know how these active ones function passively.

A long time ago, in our first encounter, we learned that for all verb groups the personal ending *–t* means "he, she, it." In T.1, 2, 3 we flip the active form of all verbs ending in *–t* into its passive form, which is *–tur*. So, if you know the active form *movebit*, "she will move," now you can flip it into the passive by saying *movebitur*, "she will be moved," in T.3. The final *–t* simply becomes *–tur*. The same thing happens for all verb groups in T.1 and 2 as well; for example, *laudat* becomes *laudatur*, "he is praised," and *dirigebat* becomes *dirigebatur*, "it was being directed." Nothing can be simpler than this: *nihil hoc facilius*.

We also learned that for all verb groups the personal ending that means "we" is *–mus*. In T.1, 2, 3 we shall flip the active form ending in *–mus* into its passive form, which is *–mur*. So, if you wish, the verb *extollimus* becomes *extollimur*, "we are extolled," and *extollemus* becomes *extollemur*, "we shall be extolled," and *extollebamus* becomes *extollebamur*, which contains the various meanings given above such as, "we were being extolled." The important thing is that we know how to form the active; then we can flip it over to the passive in a moment.

Likewise we learned that the personal ending that means "you" in the singular is *–s*. In T.1, 2, 3 we shall flip this active form ending in *–s* into its passive form, which is *–ris*. So, if you wish, the verb *adiuvabas* becomes *adiuvabaris*, "you were being helped," and *dices* becomes *diceris*, "you will be called," and *extollebas* becomes *extollebaris* with the multiple meanings given above, including, "you were being extolled." It is essential that we know how to form the active and then go over to the passive in a moment. To do this, you only have to know the active form first.

The personal ending that means "they" we learned is *–nt*. In T.1, 2, 3 we flip this active form from *–nt* into its passive form *–ntur*, which looks much like the passive form for "he, she, it." So, the verb *regunt* becomes *reguntur* "they are ruled," and *laudabunt* becomes *laudabuntur*, "they will be praised," and *removebant*, becomes *removebantur*, "they were being removed."

When you come to the subject "I," remember that in the active you learned that the personal endings were either –*o* or –*m* or –*i*, but we have recently seen that –*i* belongs only in T.4 and therefore is out of consideration here. To make the ending –*o* passive, it simply becomes –*or*, but the ending –*m* is changed to a simple –*r*. Thus, *adiuvabo*, "I shall help," becomes *adiuvabor*, "I shall be helped." Taking our other pattern for the future, as we learned so nicely, *dirigam*, "I shall direct," becomes *dirigar*, "I shall be directed," where the personal ending –*m* becomes a simple –*r*. In T.1, *moveo* becomes *moveor*, "I am moved." In T.2, *rapiebam* becomes *rapiebar*, "I was being seized."

That leaves us with one more personal ending, "you" in the plural, which has a very curious form in the passive and has been explained in many ways because of the example of Greek or of other Indo-European influences. In the active we learned the personal ending for "you all" is –*tis*. In the passive this becomes –*mini*. So, the active for "you all call," *vocatis*, becomes *vocamini*, "you all are being called." Very simply, "you will write," *scribetis*, becomes *scribemini*, "you will be written" (say, in the book of life). In T.2 we have the same story where *laudabatis* in the passive is *laudabamini*, "you were being praised." In T.1 we have *auditis*, which becomes *audimini*, "you all are being heard."

Those are the endings for the passive. According to our system, the important thing is that we first know the active forms of all 3 times in the whole Latin language, and then we can flip the active into the passive in a millisecond. With this we already have three-fourths of the whole verb in the indicative: the active T.4, 5, 6 and 1, 2, 3, and now the passive T.1, 2, 3. We shall see the passive forms for T.4, 5, 6 in another encounter.

3. Phonetic exceptions

Students do not have trouble with two phenomena we wish to note here. These are simply phonetic exceptions, not tricks or traps of the Romans for future generations. You have learned the active ending –*s* for "you" and its passive counterpart –*ris*. There are two cases in Latin where the vowel before that final –*s* is modified because the accent falls back and the vowels lose their strength.

The first exception occurs in T.3 of verb Gp.I and Gp.II. You already have the form *adiuvábĭs*, "you will help." If you flip this to make it passive, you would expect the form to be *adiuvabiris*. But, because of a shift in accent, the phonetic change occurs and the resulting form is *adiuváběris*, "you will be helped." Similarly, from *delēre* "to destroy," *delēbis*, "you will destroy," in the passive becomes *delēběris*, "you will be destroyed," instead of *delebiris*, which does not exist. Their plurals are normal. So the plural of *adiuváběris*, "you will be helped," with that exceptional –*ě*–, is normal, *adiuvabimini*, "you all will be helped," and *delēběris* is reversed as *delebimini*.

The other case of this same phonetic change occurs in T.1 of verb Gp.III, where a short vowel forces the accent to move back a syllable. Again the same thing happens as above, where the active form has an *–ĭ–* and the passive form substitutes an *–ĕ–*. Take the example *dirigis*, "you are directing," which in the passive is not *dirigĭris*, but *dirígĕris*. Its plural is normal, and *dirígitis* becomes *dirigimini*, "you all are directed." Students, for some reason, have no problem with this.

One confusing consequence of this phonetic change is that verbs in Gp.III have the same letters for the "you" form in T.1 passive as in T.3 passive. Take for example the verb:

ago, agere, egi, actum, 3, to drive.

In T.1 the form for "you drive" is *agis*, and its passive you have just learned is the exceptional *ágĕris*, "you are driven." In T.3 the form for "you will drive" is *ages* and its passive is *agéris*, "you will be driven." The difference between the two forms is the accent and their meaning:

ágeris	you are driven
agéris	you will be driven.

That in brief is the whole story of the Latin passive in T.1, 2, 3, which is not that bad if you know the active. If you don't know the active, then in our system the passive is a double trouble, because you must have the active to change it over to the passive.

Here again we need a lot of practice, but in a few minutes the students will spot the passives right away in the reading sheets, and you will notice that the general sign of the passive in the Latin language is *–r*. The only strange thing is the passive form for "you" in the plural, which ends in *–mini*.

ENCOUNTER 22

PASSIVARUM FORMARUM EXERCITATIO

exercise of the passive forms

Continual familiarity with the passive endings in the reading sheets will get people familiar with these forms. Now would be the time to note that some verbs have passive endings with active meanings; these are the deponent verbs, but don't worry about that now.

What is important now is to see how slight changes, difficult to spot inside in the verb, alter the meaning. For example:

intellegitur	it is understood	T.1 passive
intellegetur	it will be understood	T.3 passive.

The difference between the two forms is one letter. In the first word you have to see that the *–i–* internal to the word indicates T.1, and in the second the internal *–e–* indicates the future, T.3. The endings are easily recognizable as passive, but it will take time to see the internal vowel that indicates the time of the verb, depending on vocabulary and one's training.

Once the subtle difference of one letter no longer frightens, it becomes natural and can be spotted right away. Just review slowly, and play around by jumping around the times from 2 to 3 and then to 1 in the singular and the plural, and point out the above exceptions in the vowels, and review them all.

ENCOUNTER 23

POSSESSIO – GEN. IN RELATIVIS: LATINE + ANGLICE

function of-possession in relatives: in Latin and English

Introduction

A while ago we saw the relative pronoun and its governing principles so far, namely its position, brevity, and the omission of the antecedent. The next step after our nouns and adjectives is to add to the relative pronoun a detail that is not that difficult at all, namely the form of-possession of the relative pronoun.

Function of-possession in relatives in Latin and English

In English the form of-possession of the relative pronoun appears as "of whom, of which; whose." These are all that we have in English. You cannot see in these words the gender or number of these English forms, but you must see them in Latin.

The Latin is very simple. First the form of-possession connects two sentences. For example, the sentences:

> This is a picture
> The artist *of the picture* is unknown to us

become:

> This is a picture *whose* artist is unknown to us.

Other examples:

> The lions have beautiful manes
> The lions will be guarded

become:

> The lions *whose* manes are beautiful will be guarded.

We can say:

> The couple are now engaged
> We possess the rings of the couple

which become:

> The couple, whose rings we possess, are now engaged
> The couple, the rings of whom we possess, are now engaged.

We have said that for the relative pronoun, the gender and number come from outside its own clause and its function comes from within its own clause. Here we are talking about the function of-possession. Instead of saying "of him," the relative pronoun will say "of whom" or "whose"; instead of saying "of the books," it will say "of which" or even "whose."

It has only three forms in Latin corresponding to the gender and number of the antecedent. If the antecedent is singular, whether masculine, feminine, or neuter, then the relative pronoun is *cuius*, meaning "of which, of whom, whose." The form *cuius* just sits there and does not change, regardless of the gender of its antecedent. If the antecedent is masculine or neuter plural, then the relative pronoun is *quorum*. If the antecedent is feminine plural, then the relative pronoun is *quarum*. That is all there is to say. Here is an example:

> *Linguam, cuius amor me tot annos tenet, Latinam adhuc quotidie adhibeo*
>
> I am still using to this very day the Latin language, *whose love* holds me for so many years
>
> I am still using to this very day the Latin language, *the love of which* holds me for so many years.

Without great disturbance or confusion the word order may move a bit in the example above in Latin, for example:

> *Linguam, amor cuius me tot annos tenet, Latinam adhuc quotidie adhibeo.*

Examples are available and worthy of study in every reading sheet or in the teacher's examples.

ENCOUNTER 24

POSSESSIO: IS – EA – ID + EIUS – EORUM – EARUM; MEUS + MEI; NOSTER + NOSTRI, NOSTRUM

of-possession; he, she, it; of him, her, it; his, hers, its, of them (men), of them (women); their; my, of me; our, of us

Introduction

The matter of this encounter is essential, as always, and delicate, as always. At first sight this may look very confusing, but there is no reason to be troubled. If we keep a few ideas straight and clear, we will be safe for ever in the Latin language. We are talking about the form of-possession, that is, the so-called genitive forms of the personal pronouns.

We have already seen the form of-possession for the relative and for nouns of both groups and adjectives of both groups. Now we want to spend a little time carefully and not rapidly noting the of-possession forms of the personal pronouns.

It will help to go back to our initial understanding of this function in the Latin language, where it had two meanings: "of" and also possession. We say "of" as in "the love *of* study" and "avoidance *of* hatred" and "desirous *of* good weather," and possession as in "a son *of* the father," "the father's son," "the mother's brother."

1. Of me – my

We will divide our presentation into two rows, without any interest in schemas or graphs. Two separate rows will keep our ideas clear forever. The forms in the top row express, "of," which in fact hint at an object, as in, "love of some art," "hatred of all things," "mindful of it," "forgetful of them." Some manuals call this an objective genitive. The forms in the bottom of our presentation express possession, as in "my book," "the book of the brother," "the sister's money." If we keep these two rows and their respective ideas clear—"of" with an object on the top row and on the bottom row "possession"—then without schemas and without graphs you will see personal pronouns function in Latin in very special and intricate and demanding ways.

Now let us turn to the personal pronouns. On the top row, if you want to say "of me," as in "mindful of me," "forgetful of me," "love of me," then the form for "of me" is *mei*.

If we come down to the bottom row, when you want to say "my book" or "the writings of me" or even "the efforts of me," meaning possession, the Romans do not use the above of-possession form as in our nouns and adjectives presented thus far, but they use the adjective *meus, a, um*, "my, mine." So, let us distinguish our two rows:

of:	*mei*
possession:	*meus, mea, meum.*

Here you can clearly see the distinctions the Romans make between the pronoun "of me," *mei*, and the possessive "my, mine" which is expressed by *meus –a –um*.

2. Of us – our

On the top row, to say "of us," as in "the esteem of us" or "the praise of us," you use the form *nostri**. In a moment we shall catch up with that asterisk. If we come down to the second row to express possession as in "our work," "our praises," or even "the accomplishments of us" meaning possession, then the Romans do not use the form on the top row, but the possessive Bk.I adjective *noster, nostra, nostrum*. So, our vision becomes:

of:	*mei*	*nostri**
possession:	*meus . . .*	*noster, nostra, nostrum.*

You will note that this is not what we did with our nouns and adjectives where there is only one form of-possession. Now we see that in the case of personal pronouns, "of" has one form, and possession is expressed by an adjective.

3. Of you – your

On the top row, if you want to say "of you" in the singular, as in "he has a great idea of you," or "neglectful of you," then the form for "of you" is *tui*, which is unchangeable, of course, because the forms on the top row are pronouns, not adjectives. Furthermore, the one form *tui* contains the masculine, feminine, neuter. On the second row, if you want to express the possession "your," then the Romans again use the possessive adjective *tuus, a, um*, as shown:

of:	*mei*	*nostri**	*tui*
possession:	*meus . . .*	*noster . . .*	*tuus, tua, tuum.*

If you make the distinction between the two rows "of" and possession, which we have been doing from the very beginning, you will have no problems at all.

4. Of you all – your

On the top row, if you want to say "of you all" as in "a photo of you all," then the form is *vestri**. The form *vestri*, "of you all," is the plural "of"-form of *vos*, "you all." On the second row, if you want to express the possession "your" in the plural, as in "the common property of you all," or "your common property," then the Romans use the possessive adjective as above, and the form is *vester, vestra, vestrum*. Again, we shall see to that asterisk shortly. Thus far we have seen:

of:	*mei*	*nostri**	*tui*	*vestri**
possession:	*meus . . .*	*noster . . .*	*tuus . . .*	*vester, vestra, vestrum.*

5. Of him, her, it – his, her, its

When we consider the form for "he, she, it," we must be very, very careful, because what happens in Latin does not happen in other languages, period. On the top row, if we want to say "forgetful of her," "mindful of it," the form for "of her" and "of it" and "of him" is *eius*. There is already a problem here, because you cannot see the gender of *eius*, which is masculine, feminine, and neuter: the meaning comes from the story.

Staying on the top row, but turning to the plural of *eius*, we see that for "of them," as in "mindful of them" and "considerate of them" in the masculine and neuter, the form is *eorum* and the feminine form is *earum*, as in *amans earum* meaning, "fond of these women." Our two rows, then, look like this:

of:	*mei*	*nostri**	*tui*	*vestri**	*eius*	*eorum, earum*
possession:	*meus . . .*	*noster . . .*	*tuus . . .*	*vester . . .*		

Now the next step is important, as we turn to the bottom row corresponding to *eius* and *eorum*, *earum*, thus far left blank. You had better highlight these forms and be careful. When the Romans come to say "his, hers, its" and "theirs," in normal, straight talk their Latin language does not have a possessive adjective corresponding to "my" and "your" and "ours," as in other languages. They do not have an adjective to do this. On the bottom row, therefore, the Latin language has to use the same form, that is to say, *eius*. Thus, *eius* on the top row means "of her," "of him," "of it," and on the bottom row *eius* means the possessive "his," "hers," "its." This is because the Romans do not have a possessive adjective to distinguish one from the other as *meus*, *noster*, *tuus*, *vester* do above, which is clear in the following:

of:	*mei*	*nostri**	*tui*	*vestri**	*eius*	*eorum, earum*
possession:	*meus . . .*	*noster . . .*	*tuus . . .*	*vester . . .*	*eius*	*eorum, earum*

To say, for example:

Their money was stolen

you have to rethink the sentence and say in Latin:

The money of them was stolen.

In very many other languages in this world there is a possessive adjective meaning "their," but in Latin you have to fall back on saying "of them," whether masculine and neuter as *eorum* or feminine as *earum*, thus:

Their [of the women] money was stolen
Earum pecunia est surrepta.

This is the system you simply have to get used to: for the first and second person we have an adjective to express possession, but when we come to the third person, as in "his," "her," "its," "theirs," Latin does not have a possessive adjective, so you have to fall back on the genitive "of her," "of him," "of it." The problem is that the genitive *eius* is the same for masculine, feminine, and neuter, so the meaning comes from the entire thought expressed, but in the plural we have *eorum* for the masculine and neuter and *earum* for the feminine.

At this point it is important to flip open our reading sheets or turn to any Latin author, and, on any page you want, you will see the words *eius* and *eorum* and *earum* dozens of times, and you will see *meus* and *noster* all over the place. For example, it is strange that "our father" is *pater noster*, where *noster* is a possessive adjective. But if you say "their father," you have to say *pater eorum*, "the father of those men, people," or *pater earum*, "the father of those women," because Latin does not have a possessive adjective to do this. So you will find pages of Latin jumping back and forth for the possessive form, as in:

He brought my and her books
Attulit libros meos et eius.

In this example you have to say, "He brought my books and the books of her."

If you keep the two-row distinction in this way, you will also keep clear the distinction that *eius* means "of him, her, it," but *eius* also means "his, hers, its." But we are stuck in seeing the gender of *eius*, because we cannot. To decide the gender of *eius*, you have to read the whole story, and it will tell you what *eius* means; you have to see what the story is about. So the magic word with *eius* and *eorum* is the "story line." This is also our dear Latin!

6. *Nostri*, vestri**

Now let us note two things. The first one concerns the two asterisks we mentioned above. We have already seen the two forms *nostri* and *vestri* when they mean "of us" and "of you-all," as in the expressions, "forgetful *of you-all*," "mindful *of us*," "fond of *us*," "considerate *of you-all*." When these words are used in numerical expressions such as "many of us," "some of you," "no one of you," "ten of you," then they refer to part of a number, and the form is *nostrum* and *vestrum*. So when you see *vestrum* and *nostrum*, they look like possessive adjectives, *noster*, *nostra*, *nostrum* and *vester*, *vestra*, *vestrum*, but they may in fact be the genitive plural of *nos* and *vos* in a numerical kind of expression. Some people call this a partitive genitive because it refers to part of a whole, but that term is not important other than to have seen it once. Here are some examples:

Amantes sunt nostri
They are fond of us

Plures nostrum faciunt hoc
Many of us do this

Quis nostrum hoc dicet?
Who of us will say this?

Nemo eorum et nostrum erit vestri memor
No one of them and of us will be mindful of you.

In the top example, *nostri* is the personal pronoun "of us," but in the next two examples *nostrum* looks like the adjective but is the alternate form of the genitive plural for numbers used with "of us." In the third example, *vestri memor* has the objective genitive we saw previously and means "mindful of you-all," where *vestri*, "of you-all," is the object of *memor*, "mindful." But *nostrum* is a partitive genitive, going with *nemo*, "not one person," and means "not one person of us [out of 100 people]." The distinction between objective and partitive genitive is made only with the words *nostrum*, *vestrum* and *nostri*, *vestri*. Thus, both "mindful of them" and "no one of them" is expressed necessarily as *eorum* and *earum*. The problem is that in English you cannot hear this difference, for example, "fond of us" and "ten of us."

The second note concerns a word that you and all students have noticed in your dictionary and will scream out, *suus, a, um*, which means "his, her, its, their, one's own." For now we will keep this word out of the picture so that we may learn *eius* and *eorum, earum* and their functions for a while. We must not confuse the special consideration and later discussion about *suus, a, um* and how it is used in a special circumstance with what we have said so far about *eius* and *eorum, earum*.

Now is the time to open up your reading sheets and see 150 examples of all this material explained and illustrated by the teacher or by the individual to oneself, so it doesn't remain theoretical or up in the air, because any page of Latin literature will have all of this matter all over the place.

ENCOUNTER 25

ITERATIO POSSESSIONIS IN PRONOMINIBUS

repetition of-possession in the pronouns

The nice, calm repetition and investigation of examples with *meus, eius, noster, eorum* and the whole story of their functions will afford a much-appreciated review of the entire subject with concrete examples.

ENCOUNTER 26

CETERAE PASSIVI VERBI FORMULAE: 4, 5, 6. COLLOCATIO PARTIUM

remaining forms of the passive verb in Times 4, 5, 6.
the placing of the verbal parts

Introduction

After having presented T.1, 2, 3 passive first, now we finish with T.4, 5, 6 passive. The passive forms of T.4, 5, 6 in absolutely no way follow the same system as the passive forms of T.1, 2, 3. The passive forms of T.4, 5, 6 for all children of Adam and Eve will certainly look like and come to be confused with the active T.1, 2, 3 of the verb "to be": everybody makes this mistake. In what follows now, all confusion will be eliminated drastically and definitively, if it is grasped and absorbed with open minds and hearts and if looks or appearances are disregarded.

1. Meaning of Times 4, 5, 6 passive

Let us get some examples of these times with their meaning in English so that we know what we are talking about:

T.4 passive:

salutati sunt
T.4a: they have been greeted
T.4b: they were greeted

T.6 passive:

recepta erit
she will have been received

T.5 passive:

repulsi eratis
you all had been rejected.

Now is the time to talk about these examples with their meanings. The language presents these three times as compound verbs, composed of two elements: a form of the verb "to be" with the fourth principal part of the verb in question.

The worst thing that can possibly happen, yet the most common thing you can possibly do, is to take those verb parts and start translating them as they appear alone, because these verb forms look as if they mean one thing, but in fact they mean something else. This problem will never go away, and even super Latin students continually fall and make mistakes forever because these verb forms are very deceptive.

You simply have to discipline yourself to get this into your head. The passive forms of these verbs mean what they do not initially look like. That is to say, *salutati sunt* looks as if it means "they are greeted," but "they are greeted" is T.1 passive, and *salutati sunt* is T.4 passive and means "they have been greeted" (T.4a) or "they were greeted" (T.4b).

Likewise, the compound form *recepta erit* looks as if it means "she will be received," but "she will be received" is T.3 passive, and *recepta erit* is T.6 passive and means "she will have been received." You simply have to have mental rigor and retrain yourselves to understand this.

Similarly, the compound form *repulsi eratis* looks as if it means "you were repulsed-rejected," but that would be T.4 passive. Instead, *repulsi eratis* is T.5 passive and means "you had been rejected." So the first problem is that the appearance misleads you to think one thing, but the solid facts of the Latin language indicate something else.

2. Forming Times 4, 5, 6 passive

The next problem is how you form T.4, 5, 6 in the passive with the meanings you have learned.

T.4 passive is a compound of T.1 of the verb "to be" such as *sumus, estis, sunt*... and the fourth principal part of the verb in question. This combination produces T.4a and 4b in the passive.

T.6 passive is a compound of T.3 of the verb "to be" such as *ero, erit*... and the fourth principal part of the verb in question. This combination produces the meaning proper to T.6 passive.

T.5 passive is a compound of T.2 of the verb "to be" such as *eram, erant*... and the fourth principal part of the verb in question. This combination produces T.5 passive, although it looks as if it means something else.

3. The placing of the verbal parts

Another thing to shock and disturb you is that the word order is not essential, as we have been saying from the beginning of our study; whether you say *repulsi eratis* or the other way around, *eratis repulsi*, is not essential to the meaning of the verb. This also goes for T.6 passive, for example *erit recepta* or *recepta erit*, and for T.4 as in *repulsi estis* and *estis repulsi*. The two parts of these compound verbs that produce these passive forms may be and on many occasions are in fact separated by a number of other words coming between them. That produces the strange phenomenon whereby you can have the fourth principal part *salutati* on one end of the sentence and *sunt* on the other end, and it still functions as one compound verb and produces T.4 passive. Take the example:

Sunt amici nostri a nobis salutati
Our friends have been greeted by us.

The worst mistake you can make is to begin translating with the first word without reading the whole sentence to the end. When you see that first word, *sunt*, you might think you have a verb in T.1, "they are," but you have to read to the last word in the sentence to realize that *Sunt* ... *salutati* form a compound verb in a completely different time, and the meaning switches around to "they were greeted." So, the problem is that T.4, 5, 6 in the passive are easily confused with the active T.1, 2, 3 of the verb "to be" because they look like one thing, but mean something else. Latin is demanding at any age of literature. We must grow up and not act as infants.

4. Observations

Another thing to note: the fourth principal part of these verbs will agree with its own subject. In T.4 we have this example with its plural:

Salutatus, a, um sum
I (a man, woman, thing) have been greeted

Salutati, ae, a sumus
We (men, women, things) have been greeted

Sunt fratres (sorores) heri hic salutati (salutatae)
The brothers (sisters) were greeted here yesterday

and in T.6:

Receptum erit aurum
The gold will have been brought back

Repudiata erunt praemia
The prizes will have been rejected

and in T.5:

Repulsus eras latro
You the thief had been driven away

Discipuli eratis non repulsi
You the students had not been driven away.

These expressions tell us that those verb forms, as adjectives *repulsus, a, um,* and *salutatus, a, um,* and *receptus, a, um,* have to agree with the subject of the sentence and get their gender and number from the subject of the sentence. They are going to vary depending on the subject.

The difficulties we have seen are that the two parts of the one compound form may be separated, inverted. Worse yet, they look as if they mean one thing, but in fact they mean something else. Take the pain, suffering, and discipline to keep yourself from falling into the eternal trap of misunderstanding these verb times.

Here, you must go to any reading sheet you want or to your own examples, to the Bible or to Cicero's letters, which are out of this world, or to Caesar, Virgil, Plautus, Augustine, and you will see these forms functioning as T.4, 5, 6, and you will get used to this and notice these forms all over the literature.

ENCOUNTER 27

ABLATIVI CASUS VIS AC FORMAE IN NOMINIBUS ET ADIECTIVIS

the meaning and forms of the function by-with-from-in in nouns and adjectives

Introduction

As we progress in comprehending and absorbing the various functions of nouns, adjectives, and pronouns in the Latin language, after the three previous functions of subject, object, and of-possession, we now take up in fact the richest and the most frequently used function in the Latin language, which in the books goes by the title ablative, *ablativus*, written in the dictionary as *abl.* This technical word describes the natural and basic use of this function. The term is derived from the verb *aufero, auferre, abstuli, ablatus*, meaning, "to take away," where the fourth principal part *ablatus* means, "having been taken away." The ablative case basically is the case of taking away or of separation in every possible turn or nuance or application imaginable.

No matter how many special or individual uses of the ablative we may want to point out and learn, they are all reduced to four concepts: *by, with, from, in*. We are not interested in technical terminology or in the names of things, but we want to know the meanings and the forces of the various uses of the ablative, which are reducible to those four ideas: *by, with, from, in*. So, in our system, to avoid the word "ablative," we will call this the function by-with-from-in, and everyone understands clearly and immediately and directly the meanings that we are talking about, which the books call the ablative.

It is interesting to see that this form does not exist in Greek or modern German, but that in Latin it is a catch-all for very many ideas expressed by the four concepts *by, with, from, in*.

In this encounter we shall also see that the function by-with-from-in is used with the second half of the prepositions. Remember that one-half of all prepositions in Latin take the object form; now we wish to see the other half, which take the form by-with-from-in. Although this half numbers fewer prepositions, their use is just as common as the other half, as we shall see in the next encounter.

While introducing the form by-with-from-in and the prepositions that take this form, we will definitely turn to our reading sheets and examples to see and understand how this function is used in Latin literature. The teacher or individual student can find the various meanings and uses of the ablative in concrete examples on reading sheets. Finding these examples is a worthwhile experience, because they are abundant and available in just about every Latin sentence.

Recognizing and constructing the form by-with-from-in is easy to do if we look at all of these forms at once, rather than presenting them piecemeal in different charts and schemas. Looking across one row of writing at all the endings that signify this function, we shall learn to identify them right away. Immediately we will warn ourselves that these forms are going to look like so many other forms and uses and functions in the Latin language ending in *–a*, *–o*, *–i*, *–e*, *–is*. We shall soon realize the importance and necessity of being precise and exact with our words and uses and with the vocabulary in the dictionary, so that we shall have no difficulty.

So that we do not have floating nonsensical endings of words to memorize or forms of words that are extracted from their broader function in the sentence and from human thought, we shall look with linear succession at all the forms by-with-from-in using the preposition *pro*, "in place of, on behalf of, according to, for," or *de*, "down from, away from, concerning, about."

1. Block I nouns and adjectives

For Bk.I nouns and adjectives the masculine singular ends in *–o*, as in *pro amico* meaning, among other things, "on behalf of a friend," or as in *de animo* or *ex animo,* whose meanings include, "from the heart." Its plural ends in *–is*, as in *pro amicis*, whose meanings include "for friends," and *ex libris*, which could mean "from books."

Immediately we recognize this problem, that these forms are going to look like the form of-possession of Bk.II nouns, which ends in *–is*, as in *rex*, *regis* and *corpus*, *corporis* and *homo*, *hominis*.

Accordingly, in the same line with Bk.I nouns and adjectives, the ending for the feminine singular is *–a*, and its plural ends in *–is*. We can add, right away, that the singular form looks the same as the subject form of these nouns. However, when the Romans spoke Latin, they heard a difference between the subject form and the form by-with-from-in. The subject form ends in a short *–ă*, and the form by-with-from-in ends in a long *–ā*. In the written text, however, the two forms look the same. This is going to create infinite problems as in the example:

Pecunia me servavit.

The form *pecunia* in appearance can function either as the subject or as by-with-from-in. If it is taken as the subject, then the *–a* is short, *pecuniă*, and the sentence means:

Money saved me.

If the *–a* is long, then *Pecuniā* is the form by-with-from-in, and the sentence means:

She, he, it saved me with money.

You can argue for an eternity over this. Unless the length of that final *–a* is discoverable, then you cannot tell the difference. Most often the length of the vowel is discoverable in poetry, where the shorts and longs are fixed and infallible. This is the problem and the challenge of Latin. Some book publishers will mark the ablative with a long mark or a little sign, as in *pecuniā* or *pecuniâ*, as a favor to tell students that this form is intended, but not every publisher does this. Thus, *gratiă* is "grace" as a subject, but *gratiā* means "with, by grace."

Finishing Bk.I nouns and adjectives, the neuter is the same as the masculine. The singular ends in *–o* and the plural in *–is*. For example, *pro bello* can mean, "on behalf of the war," and *ex documentis* can mean, "according to the documents." The feminine singular is distinguished in its ending in *–a*.

2. Block II nouns and adjectives

Coming to Bk.II nouns, we really have a problem because of the nature of the vowels and how they sound, long and short. We can make a broad principle about the ablatives to recognize and use them. The principle is linguistically very confusing and subject to disputes, but we could say the masculine, feminine, and neuter nouns of Bk.II have a singular form by-with-from-in that ends 85% of the time in the letter *–e* and only 15% of the time in the letter *–i*. The plural of both of these ends in *–ibus*.

When we come to the adjectives of Bk.II, as we have seen before, the percentages are reversed. The adjectives of Bk.II end in the letter *–i* 85% of the time and only 15% in the letter *–e*. The plural of both forms is the same as for the nouns and ends in *–ibus*.

That is all you need in order to recognize and use the nouns and adjectives of Bk.I and II. That said, there is going to be a continual inconsistency in the readings and also in composition, with regard to whether the ablative of the nouns is going to end in *–e* or *–i*. Some words jump back and forth. If you consult Gildersleeve and Lodge nº 56, you will see the ablative with an alternative *–e* or *–i* in parentheses to indicate this possibility.

Some words are very consistent. As an example, for the phrase "in the ship" you will consistently find *in navi*, following the minority of 15% for nouns, but even then you might find *in nave* according to the majority of 85% for nouns. An example from the adjectives is the phrase *in vetere testamento*, where *vetere* follows the minority of 15% of the adjectives, but some people are insistent in following the majority of 85% of the adjectives and writing *in veteri testamento*. That you cannot resolve.

The difficulty is due to the difference between the long or short *–i* and how the Romans heard the word. Authors did not agree in the second or third century, and they jumped back and forth between the endings. Centuries later, the copyists of the seventh and eighth centuries were also inconsistent. Even today we have variant readings and you just have to accept the fact that we have texts on both sides, and it is impossible to decide because of the spelling used in the manuscripts.

Therefore, another difficulty of this second block is that the nouns and the adjectives in this function will not always have the same ending, according to our percentages. When these words are separated in a text, seeing their connection will be difficult for readers or hearers of Latin. You have to know your vocabulary perfectly and you must be thinking to see the connection between the two forms by-with-from-in, when you find them, one an adjective ending in *–i* in one part of the sentence and in another part of the sentence a noun ending in *–e*, both following their respective 85% rules. An instance comes to mind from the Christmas homily given in 440 CE by Leo Magnus (440–461) in which Leo has three examples of this almost in the same breath. Even at that late Latin age, 500 years after Cicero, Leo says:

> *magno et mirabili aequitatis iure certatum est* (Leo, *Tract.* XXI, 2)
> by a great and wonderful law of justice the battle was had.

The problem here is that *mirabili* looks as if it goes with *aequitatis*, but it does not. Rather, both *magno* and *mirabili* agree with *iure*, all in the form by-with-from-in, but each of the three endings is different, the latter two following their respective 85% incidence of these endings in the ablative. In encounter 33 we shall also see that *mirabili* is the same as the form to-for-from, which prompts a word to the wise and vigilant: Latin is never automatic and demands continual analysis, which we can say in Latin: *Verbum sat sapienti vigilantique: Lingua Latina numquam sua sponte intellegitur, verum perpetuam quandam pervestigationem poscit.*

The second example is from the same text where Leo says:

> *inenarrabili divinae pietatis opere* (Leo, *Tract.* XXI, 1)
> by an unspeakable work of divine goodness.

Again, as you approach the text, you might think that *inenarrabili* goes with *pietatis*, but it does not. Rather, *inenarrabili* goes with *opere*, each following the 85% rule which ends in *–i* for adjectives, here *inenarrabili*, and in *–e* for nouns, here *opere*, of Bk.II. Again in encounter 33 you will see that *inenarrabili* can also be the form to-for-from. These are very fine distinctions of one letter, and you must be extremely precise and careful.

We have the same problem again in the third example given to us by Leo:

> *noli in veterem vilitatem degeneri conversatione recidere*
> (Leo, *Tract.* XXI, 3)
> do not fall back into the old worthlessness by degenerate behavior.

Likewise *degeneri* goes with *conversatione*, each following their respective 85% rules. Again, we shall see in encounter 33 that *degeneri* is the same form as to-for-from. You might also note that the verb *noli* also ends with the letter *–i*, where it is the sign of the imperative. The reading sheets provide abundant examples of this on every page.

These three examples show how the similarities of different forms and the connections between words with different endings often separated by other words can produce a linguistic mess, if you are not super-cautious. Once again, you have to know your vocabulary, but even after you know the whole language, still you must think because that is the nature of Latin. Beginners may have difficulty accommodating themselves to this and even the experienced Latinist may be caught off-guard, because Latin has a trap in every sentence, and so demands careful attention. While this may at first be tiring, students do catch on and soon come to see how fascinating and beautiful the nature of the Latin language is.

The teacher will wisely take any reading sheet and from top to bottom will identify or help the students to identify the forms by-with-from-in as they appear in concrete Latin sentences together with varying meanings.

ENCOUNTER 28

ABLATIVI ITEM FORMAE IN PRONOMINIBUS ET RELATIVIS. PRAEPOSITIONES CUM ABLATIVO

likewise the forms by-with-from-in used in pronouns and relatives. prepositions with the ablative

Introduction

In this encounter we continue our discussion of the form by-with-from-in with regard to pronouns and a listing of the prepositions with the same function.

1. Pronoun forms by-with-from-in

The pronouns logically follow the same pattern as the nouns; namely, "for him" is *pro eo*, and in the plural "for the men" is *pro eis* or *pro iis*. In the feminine, "for her" is *pro ea*, and in the plural "for the women" is *pro eis* or *pro iis*. Note that in the plural you cannot see the difference in gender. In the neuter, "from it" is *de eo*, with the same form as the masculine, and in the plural "from the things" is *de eis* or *de iis*. Again in the plural you cannot see the gender, whether masculine, feminine, or neuter.

The other pronouns are *me, te, nobis, vobis*; namely, we can say *pro me*, "for me"; *pro te*, "for you"; *pro nobis*, "for us"; and *pro vobis*, "for you all." For example, during the liturgy we say *ora pro nobis*, "pray for us."

2. Relative pronoun forms by-with-from-in

Turning to the relative pronouns, we begin with the masculine "concerning which man," *de quo*, and the feminine "about what woman," *de qua*, and the neuter "from what thing," *de quo*, just like the masculine. The plural for all three is *quibus*, as in "about what women," *de quibus*. (Note: rarely, but often enough, for example in the poets, instead of *quibus* you will find *queis*, which sounded like *quis*, with a long *–is*, as it was originally, but in prose you will not really find that.)

3. Comments

Those are the forms by-with-from-in and the general usage of this function. You will need continual practice in recognizing and using them. Take the example:

I lived in the ship of my friend
In amici mei navi vixi.

Besides the preposition, all the words end in *–i*. The preposition *in* goes with *navi*, and the pair *amici mei* are of-possession singular. The verb *vixi* means "I lived." That is Latin at its best, and you had just better be ready for it to appreciate it.

It would be better to spend time now on the reading sheets identifying the forms by-with-from-in, especially when you have nouns and adjectives from two different Blocks agreeing with one another but not ending with the same letters and often separated by several other words. Ovid has five or six words between two ablatives, each with a different ending. He will say:

In magna fui duos dies navi
For two days I was in a big ship

and place *navi* at the end of the verse. He expects you to be very observant and cautious. This phenomenon is not easy if you think you can run through it and carelessly deal with any text, word after word, because Latin does not work that way, but it is workable.

4. Prepositions with the function by-with-from-in

In encounter six we presented the prepositions that take the object function along with four prepositions that are on the fence and take both the object function and the function by-with-from-in with differences in meaning. Here we present the prepositions that take only the function by-with-from-in, and, now that you have learned about this function, for the sake of completeness we can repeat the four prepositions that are on the fence taking both functions. You can find a few more listed in Gildersleeve and Lodge nº 417. You are encouraged to consult your dictionary because there you will find the full range of meaning for each one. Each dictionary entry indicates something like this: "prep. with abl.," meaning "preposition with the ablative." Here are the prepositions that take the form by-with-from-in:

a, ab (abs)	from, away from, by (a personal agent, not an instrument)
absque	*without*
coram	before, in the presence of
cum	with (accompaniment, not instrumentality) ("He walked with a dog" is accompaniment; instrumentality would be "He hit the thief with a stick," which is not expressed with *cum*.)
de	(geographical) from, down from (reference) concerning, about, of, in respect to
e (ex)	out of, from, according to
prae	before, in front of, because of, for (thousands of English derivatives such as "predate," "premeditated")

pro (geographical) before, in front of, in the presence of, for, on behalf of, in favor of, in the service of, on the side of, instead of, for the sake of, in proportion to, in keeping with

sine without (the normal word for "without")

tenus up to (as in "up to his belly button").

Thinking of our cousin language Greek, where things are infinitely more complicated than in Latin, the prepositions in Latin happen to be simpler. Greek presents many possibilities: the preposition takes the object or the form to-for-from or the form of-possession.

We ought briefly to review what we have learned in another encounter about prepositions on the fence between the object form and the form by-with-from-in. There are four of them which are listed here again. Consulting your dictionary again and again, you will learn that these four are used with the object function when the idea of motion—geographical or moral—is expressed in the sentence. So the preposition *in* followed by the object form implies motion "into, onto, toward, against, for," and the preposition *sub* followed by the object implies motion "below, underneath"; *super* and *subter* are obvious and on the rare side. Here is their list:

in (with the object form) into, onto, toward, against, for; (with the form by-with-from-in; no motion) in, place where, location or rest in a place

sub under, below, underneath (with the object form: under which a thing comes, goes, extends; in temporal relations it means closely before or after something); under (with the form by-with-from-in: under which a thing is situated or takes place)

subter beneath

super over, above.

One example of the distinction in meaning the different forms produce, an example which people are not going to get right, is the sentence:

In viam salutis nos perduxit
He has led us *onto* (*unto*, *into*, *towards*) the way of health-salvation.

This means that we are not on the way of health-salvation and that he leads us onto the way. On the other hand, you have the sentence:

In via salutis nos perduxit
He has led us ahead *on* the road of salvation.

This example indicates that we were on the road of salvation when he led us ahead. Another example is the sentence:

Resurrexerunt in vitam aeternam

which does not mean, "They arose in eternal life," but:

They arose *unto* (*for*, *up to*) eternal life.

5. Prepositions *a, ab, abs,* and *cum* in finer detail

Thus far we have in the proper place and time presented on the one hand the natural meanings of the forms by-with-from-in, and on the other hand we have considered the list of prepositions which either always take the form by-with-from-in or, as one of the four in the box, can take either that same form or the object. Considering the natural difficulty of the matter and the frequent misunderstanding and misuse of the preposition, here we would like to spend some time on the nature and ramifications of the one preposition *a, ab, abs*, and to distinguish its use from another preposition, *cum*.

5.1 *Forms*

This preposition is found in three ways: *a, ab, abs*. The form *abs,* however, was apparently becoming obsolete during the time of the great Cicero himself, because in his youthful orations and letters he does use *abs*, but at perhaps 30 or 35 years of age he abandoned *abs*, and we do not find it in his extant writings for the rest of his life. It will turn up again in the Renaissance at the hands of people who want to be, as Erasmus said, *Ciceronis simii*, "monkeys of Cicero," trying to super-imitate the master.

Be careful; another trap in Latin is the word *absque*, which means "without." Although some superficial scholars may think it is a variation of *a, ab, abs*, nevertheless it has nothing to do with *a, ab, abs*, as a good dictionary will tell.

Manuscript tradition seems to suggest that the form *a* was used before consonants and *ab* was used before vowels so that you would distinguish the two words when you say, for example, *ab agricolis*, "from farmers," rather than keeping the mouth open and so eliding the two words into one as happens if you say quickly *a agricolis*. Knowing how iron-fast that was observed would require a study of all the literature and how often it was used, but to be honest, some authors do not observe this distinction. Many times *a* and *ab* are used indiscriminately: *a nobis, ab nobis*. You can read a discussion about this with examples in a complete dictionary.

5.2. *Scrutinizing the dictionary*

Here we have a revelation that some people do not notice, that there are really two distinct and opposite meanings for *a, ab*. One is close to the natural meaning by-with-from-in, namely "from," "away from," indicating separation. The opposite meaning is "by," indicating an agent. You can produce in Latin seriously ambiguous sentences, playing on this double meaning, for example:

> *magno in tumultu publicis a custodibus sumus feliciter erepti servatique*
>
> in a big riot we were fortunately snatched away and saved from the police men
>
> in a big riot we were fortunately snatched away and saved by the police men.

The choice between one meaning or the other, this ambiguity is attributed to the natural double force of *a, ab* according to the dictionary. To choose between these two meanings, you have to follow the story because the dictionary will not help you.

5.3. *Instrument or personal agent*

We are next faced with another hurdle in Latin, namely with the different concepts of using an instrument to do something or of an agent doing something itself. Here we have a fundamental separation of ideas and usages in Latin between instrumentality and agency.

For example, you can say, "The geography was devastated by the hurricane," where we would consider the hurricane as a non-thinking or impersonal force, and we could add, "by the water, flooding, clouds, wind."

We can take a similar sentence and say, "The neighborhood was destroyed by worthless politicians," where we are definitely speaking about personal agency, but we could also refer to living agency and say "by the forest animals" or to moral agency and say "by the bank" as a corporate person. In each case we are talking about the agent doing something itself.

In both examples the English construction is the same, whether we say "by the hurricane" or "by the politicians," but in Latin these different concepts are expressed differently.

In Latin we have a firm principle about instrumentality and agency: that instrumentality or means is expressed with the use of the form by-with-from-in with no preposition, whereas agency is expressed by the preposition *a* or *ab* with the form by-with-from-in. We can give the above examples in Latin:

The geography was devastated by the hurricane
Loca sunt turbine devasta

The neighborhood was destroyed by worthless politicians
Loca sunt a perditis politicis devastata

We can distinguish between the two concepts of instrumentality and agency in the following examples:

He was hit with a stick
Baculo est percussus

He was hit by a robber
A latrone est percussus.

This distinction is based on the different concepts and not on the English words, which may be very much the same. Understanding Latin and creating Latin demand that we think of what is happening in the Latin sentence. This is confirmed by a million examples from any type of Latinity you want.

5.4. *"Cum" with the form by-with-from-in*

The expression "with a stick" immediately suggests that we are faced with a third concept in addition to instrumentality and agency. We mentioned this in our catalogue of the prepositions, when we said that *cum* followed by the form by-with-from-in is used to express accompaniment or association, not instrumentality or agency. The problem is that the expression in English can be just about the same for each of these, so we must distinguish the concepts so that we will use the correct expression in Latin. We can see this ambiguity in the sentence:

> In the morning he was walking with a stick.

If we mean that a person is holding the stick as he walks along, then the idea is accompaniment or association:

> *Mane cum baculo inambulabat.*

Or we may mean that a man uses a cane as an instrument to help him walk in the morning, as in:

> *Mane baculo nisus inambulabat*
>
> He was walking supported by a stick.

In the following sentence you can see the difference between the two instances of "with a stick." First the stick is an instrument for playing a game. Second the stick accompanies or is associated with the dog walking home:

> He and his dog were playing with a stick,
> but the dog walked home with the stick in his mouth.
>
> *Ipse canisque eius ramulo ludebant,*
> *at canis domum remigravit cum ramulo suo in ore.*

Staying with the canine example, we can see all three usages in the following sentence:

> My good will was won over by him with the dog so friendly
> *Mea benevolentia est ab illo cum blandissimo cane conciliata*
>
> My good will was won over by him with the tricks of the dog so friendly
> *Mea benevolentia est ab illo blandissimi canis artificiis conciliata.*

In both Latin renderings above a man was the agent winning over the good will of the speaker. In the first Latin rendering the man was accompanied by his dog so friendly. In the second the man used the tricks of the dog as an instrument to win over the good will of someone.

Sometimes the English is ambiguous and so the translator has to decide which meaning is intended to render the appropriate expression in Latin, as in the example:

> The hay was brought to the market by a farmer walking with a horse.

If the hay is piled up on the back of the horse, then the horse is the instrument the farmer uses, and you can say:

> The hay was brought to the market with (by means of) a horse by a farmer walking
>
> *Faenum equo ad mercatum est ab agricola ambulante delatum.*

If the hay is on the farmer's back, and the farmer is leading a horse to town, then the horse accompanies the farmer, and you can say:

> The hay was brought to the market by a farmer walking with a horse
>
> *Faenum ad mercatum est ab agricola cum equo ambulante delatum.*

You can see three distinct concepts: instrumentality, personal agency, accompaniment. Instrumentality is expressed by the simple form by-with-from-in without a preposition. Personal agency is expressed by the preposition *a* or *ab* followed by the form by-with-from-in. Accompaniment is expressed by the preposition *cum* followed by the form by-with-from-in. These three concepts will help you determine which Latin expression to use or is used, but the English will be no help to you at all.

ENCOUNTER 29

VERBA DEPONENTIA

deponent verbs

Introduction

One of the more interesting phenomena of the Latin language, which, by the way, pre-existed in Greek, is a large mass of verbs that are passive in their verbal form but have active meanings. In other languages this is a kind of reflexive verb. For example, in the sentence, "She built a house for herself," the reflexive idea is "to build for oneself," which may appear in Greek, for example, in the middle voice, which can look like the passive. In any case, these verbs are very beloved to the Romans, and they are very frequent; maybe so much as a quarter or a third of all the verbs in the Latin language belongs to this category.

1. Deponent verbs

If we look in the dictionary, we see that some verbs in their dictionary entry are presented immediately in the passive form. For example, in the first place you have:

gratulor	ending in *-or*
patior	ending in *-or*
largior	ending in *-or*
sequor	ending in *-or*
venor	ending in *-or*
fateor	ending in *-or.*

Setting aside their meanings for the moment, these forms are the dictionary entries for each of these words, and an observant person will notice that each one ends in the letter *-r*, which is the sign that they are passive from the start.

The dictionary entry then will follow with the abbreviation "v. dep.," which in Latin means *verbum deponens*. Now, the verb

depono, depónere, deposui, depositum, 3

means "to put down" or "to put away." Therefore, a massive category of verbs—*verba deponentia*—by their form, definition, and use "put away" most of their active forms but keep the passive forms. They "put away" most of their passive meanings but keep their active meanings. That is what a deponent verb is. It is half of a normal Latin verb that combines its remaining passive forms with its remaining active meanings. Thus, we say a deponent verb is passive in form and active in meaning.

That means if I come across the example *sequitur*, the ending *–tur* is passive in form, and so the verb looks as if it is also passive in meaning. But if you know from your vocabulary and dictionary that *sequitur* is from a deponent verb, then you know it is active in meaning: "he, she, it follows" or "he, she, it is following."

At this point, people naturally ask how to say "he, she, it is being followed." The response is that you cannot use the verb *sequor*. Rather, you have to find another verb that is not deponent to express the passive meaning. The form *sequitur* is already passive and cannot be made any more passive in form, but its meaning is active and cannot be made passive. Thus, *sequitur* means "he, she, it is following."

The problem is in most cases you are not going to be able even to guess from the context whether any given verb passive in form is also passive in meaning or active in meaning, because it is a deponent verb, as in the example:

Praemia largiuntur.

This sentence looks as if it means "Prizes are given out," but the verb is deponent, and therefore the sentence means "they give out prizes." With the same verb I cannot say in Latin "prizes are given out," because the deponent nature of this verb requires an active meaning.

When you come to dealing with Latin literature, sooner or later you are going to have to know which verbs are deponent, and if you talk to a Latinist with any experience, they know in fact which verbs are deponent and which verbs are not deponent.

There are certain indications that will help you spot a deponent verb when you come across one in the literature. One is already mentioned. In the dictionary the first entry of a deponent verb is passive in form. The dictionary entry starts out passive, which means that the verb is deponent. The second way to know whether a verb is deponent is the indication in the dictionary: "v. dep." The third indication, which might be some people's salvation, is this: if you have a sentence in Latin with a verb passive in form followed by a noun or a pronoun in the object form, this is a clear indication that the verb is deponent, because passive verbs do not have objects, but deponent verbs with passive forms do have objects. For example, if you come across the sentence:

Benevolentiam consequitur

you know the verb is deponent because it is passive in form and yet it has an object. Thus, this sentence means:

He, she, it attains good-will.

These three indications will help you decide whether a verb passive in form is deponent and thus active in meaning when you meet it in a sentence.

There is no need for panic with deponent verbs, no fright and no terror here. All that you know about the formation of passive verbs from a long time ago applies right now. All you learned about the passive in T.1, 2, 3, 4, 5, and 6 is simply applied here, and all you will learn later on when studying the passive of the subjunctive times. The only thing is that the meaning of a deponent verb is active.

Deponent verbs belong to all the four groups of Latin verbs. Just as the verbs we have already seen, the groups of deponent verbs are determined by the second part of each entry in the dictionary. As in the other verbs this second part is the gerund, also called the infinitive. For deponent verbs the infinitive forms will be passive. You have not yet seen the passive infinitive forms, so we can point them out below as we identify each of the verb groups.

1.1 *verb Group I*

Take, for example, the verb:

> *laetor, laetari, laetatus sum*, 1, v. dep., to rejoice, feel joy.

First of all, we notice that there are not four principal parts, so let us now look at the three parts that are left. As we learned before, the dictionary entry *laetor* is T.1 meaning "I rejoice" or "I am rejoicing." I know this verb is deponent because from the beginning it is passive in form. The second principal part is the gerund or infinitive: *laetari*. The final *–i* of the ending *–ari* tells me that this form in Latin is passive and this verb is deponent. Here we see the form of the passive infinitive of Gp.I. The third principal part is *laetatus sum*, which is the form for T.4a and b: "I have rejoiced, I did rejoice." This third principal part is misleading because it looks like the fourth principal part of normal verbs. With a normal verb, the fourth part meant, for example, "having been done" or "having been constructed," which is passive in meaning and therefore impossible in a deponent verb, because its meaning is active. Here *laetatus* means "having rejoiced," which is active in meaning.

Once you know these three principal parts of the deponent verb, whatever you learned about the passive form will apply here. If you want to say "they are happy," the active form would be *laetant*, but you make it passive in form to get *laetantur*, which has active meaning. Or, to say "they will rejoice," you take the active form, which would have been *laetabunt*, and make it passive to get *laetabuntur*, which has active meaning. Or, to say "we were happy," the active form would be *laetabamus*. The passive deponent form is *laetabamur*, since *laetabamus*, and *laetabunt*, and *laetant* no longer exist in Latin.

1.2 *verb Group II*

Take, for example, the verb:

> *mereor, merēri, meritus sum*, 2, v. dep., to deserve.

The dictionary entry *mereor* is passive in form, telling us that this verb is deponent, so its meaning is active: "I deserve." The second principal part is the gerund or infinitive *merēri*. Here we see that the *–ē–* is long and so accented, telling us this is a verb of Gp.II. The *–i* in the ending *–eri* is a sign that the form is passive, the passive infinitive. The third principal part is *meritus sum*. This tells us the form of the verb in T.4a and b.

Whatever you learned about verb Gp.II in any of the tenses applies here. The form *meremur* (not *meremus*) means "we do merit"; *merebimini* (not *merebitis*) means "you all will deserve"; the form *merebar* (not *merebam*) means "I was worthy of something"; the form *meriti sunt* as T.4a means "they have merited," because it is deponent.

Just as the first two groups are identified by the endings of their active infinitives, *–are* and *–ēre*, so too the endings of the passive infinitives identify the first two groups of the deponent verbs, as *–ari* for Gp.I and *–ēri* for Gp.II. Everything we learned about the passive forms of Times one through six applies here but with active meanings.

1.3 *verb Group III*

Moving to Gp.III, the entry for *loquor* in your dictionary and the one for *sequor* is going to give one of the most confusing and hardest forms in the language:

> *loquor, loqui, locutus sum*, 3, v. dep., to speak
> *sequor, sequi, secutus sum*, 3, v. dep., to follow.

The second principal part here is the infinitive that ends in a simple *–i*, and what is so deceiving is that it does not look like an infinitive at all. It is very confusing to have in the middle of a Latin sentence the infinitive *loqui*, which looks like some verb in T.4, meaning "I have spoken," but it is not. Because it is deponent, *loqui* consequently has the active meaning "to speak." There are hundreds of these verbs, so you have to get used to seeing this form. The rest of this verb group functions as the others do and will cause you no difficulty; *lóqueris* is "you speak," *loquéris* is "you will speak," their plurals being *loquimini* and *loquemini*.

1.4 *verb Group IV*

Verb Gp.IV returns to a more recognizable pattern, as in the example:

> *orior, oriri, ortus sum*, 4, v. dep., to arise.

From the infinitive *oriri* you can recognize the passive infinitive of verb Gp.IV, but because the verb is deponent it means "to arise" or "to get up."

1.5 *verb Group –io, ĕre*

We even have some deponents that belong to the on-the-fence Group, which mixes the endings *–io* and *–ĕre*. This Group causes no confusion because we shall treat them just as we did the verbs in *–io, ĕre*, but we are going to keep their forms passive, as in the example:

> *patior, pati, passus sum*, 3, v. dep., to bear, suffer.

The dictionary entry for this Group in the active ends in *–io*, but here we see the passive form ending in *–ior*, as you would expect. The infinitive is *pati*, as you now expect from verb Gp.III. From this verb we get the forms *patimini*, meaning "you people are suffering," and *passus sum* in T.4a, meaning "I have suffered," and in T.4b meaning "I suffered." The problem here is that the form for T.4 looks like something else.

The sentence:

Dolores patientur

might look as if it means "pains will be suffered," but because the verb is deponent, *dolores* has to be the direct object, not the subject, and the sentence means "they will be suffering pains."

That is the story of the deponent. We shall talk later on in our Latin training about the participles of deponent verbs, but for now we want to recognize the deponent form and use it carefully.

To summarize, the endings of the deponent infinitives are: *–ari*, *–eri*, *–i*, *–iri*, and for the mixed Group *–i*. We can talk about many other details later, but they will not be difficult. Now you have to be conscious of the fact that a mass of verbs belongs to this collection of deponents.

2. Observations

Most people say deponents in Latin developed under the influence of the Greek middle voice, which is passive in form but has an active meaning with the nuance that something is done for oneself. There are only a handful of deponent verbs in Latin that are passive in form with the active meaning akin to the original Greek idea that I do something for myself. Take for example the verb:

utor, uti, usus sum, 3, v. dep., to make use of.

You can see from the second principal part, *uti*, that this verb belongs to verb Gp.III. Perhaps the Greek equivalent would mean "I get usefulness for myself," and it would be a middle-voice verb, which most of the time looks like the passive.

Or take the example from the dictionary

fruor, frui, fructus sum, 3, v. dep., to enjoy.

Again, you can see that this is a deponent verb of Gp.III; the infinitive *frui* tells you that. Perhaps the underlying Greek idea is to procure enjoyment for myself. That is the reflexive force of the middle voice, which overflowed into Latin.

There are only a few deponent verbs in Latin that preserve to some extent the original force of the Greek middle voice with reference to oneself. Rather, the Romans developed the great majority of deponent verbs, which are outright passive in form and active in meaning, without maintaining the reflexive force meaning "for oneself." If you know to look out for these, then you will learn them from the literature itself as you encounter them in the thought of real Latin authors. Consulting a dictionary will clarify any doubts.

Another phenomenon occurs with some words that in the dictionary have at the same time a deponent form and a form that is not deponent. One example, of course, is:

mereor, merēri, meritus sum, 2, v. dep., to merit
mereo, merēre, merui, meritum, 2, v. a., to merit

fabricor, fabricari, fabricatus sum, 1, v. dep., to build
fabrico, fabricare, fabricavi, fabricatum, 1, v. a., to build.

The deponent form of these verbs is clear from the three passive parts and the abbreviation "v. dep." The non-deponent verbs are indicated by the four active forms and the abbreviation "v. a.," which means *verbum activum*, meaning that the verb is active. The active form of this verb may have a passive form with a passive meaning, and you must carefully distinguish it from the deponent verb, which also has a passive form but is active in meaning. One author will use such a verb as a deponent, and another author will use it normally.

Another such verb is:

oscito, oscitare, oscitavi, oscitatum 1, v. a., to yawn
oscitor, oscitari, oscitatus sum 1, v. dep., to yawn.

This verb is both deponent and non-deponent. We know this from a careful observation of Latin literature, not from a golden box sent down from heaven.

Another example concerns the papal blessing. There are two forms for the verb *impertio, impertire*:

impertio, impertire, impertivi or impertii, impertitum, 4, v. a., to impart
impertior, impertiri, impertitus sum, 4, v. dep., to impart.

One author of papal documents would use the deponent form of the verb:

Sanctus Pater impertitur benedictionem

while another would use the active form:

Sanctus Pater impertit benedictionem.

There are about twenty verbs in the Latin language that jump back and forth between deponent and non-deponent forms. This is part of the Latin adventure.

We do not give a comprehensive list of these verbs here or elsewhere, because it is more helpful to treat specific cases as they occur in the Latin text and then, consulting our standard Latin dictionary by Lewis and Short, to discover with the student how specific words are used. As the student and teacher encounter such words in Latin texts, their full meaning will be learned with ease from the dictionary, which is in turn based on Latin literature.

A note on the method of learning is suggested here. It is better to know that a phenomenon exists in the language so that you will recognize it when it appears in literature, than to be deceived by the brevity of lists whose each word requires a thorough review of its meanings and usages in the dictionary. For example, a vocabulary list will state that the verb *imponere* means, "to place on, on top of," from its component parts *in* and *ponere*. Students who stop there do not realize that it also means "to deceive," as in the English word "an imposter." Another example would be *lego, legere*, which everyone learns in a vocabulary list as meaning "to read," but the first meaning in the dictionary is "to gather, collect," and when your eyes and mind gather and collect words, you are reading.

As a pedagogical tool, we consider vocabulary lists counter-productive, because they bring people to believe that every word has just one meaning to which they are stuck. Then the teacher has to wean them off the lists and to help them develop a facility with using the dictionary, where they will discover the full use of each word from sound literature. We have not learned a word fully until we know all of its meaning; only consulting the full dictionary entry will indicate our progress. This is why from the first day we teach Latin from the dictionary.

Electronic versions of dictionaries, especially when viewed on small screens that restrict our view of the full entry on the page, again are not helping people thoroughly. Such consultation may give ready answers to single questions, but too easily people become lazy and merely notice their answer without learning the word. If people do not consult a dictionary, they will not see all the columns dedicated to small words such as *ut* or *cum;* they will not see words nearby with related or contrary meanings; and they will not understand from the outset the task ahead. If you look and discover the full use of a word and learn it with a certain amount of effort, you just might remember it. If you consult virtual reality, it will come and go. The quick fix today is not to be confused with lasting education.

Again we would open just about any reading sheet that we have at hand among the reading sheets following each experience, and the teacher or someone who knows Latin will point out the deponent verbs, and anyone who studies Latin will slowly learn them and never forget them.

ENCOUNTER 30

REFLEXIVI PRONOMINIS USUS: MEUS – MEI – ME – MIHI; TUUS – TUI – TE – TIBI . . .

use of the reflexive pronoun: my, of me, me, to me, myself; yours, of you, you, to you, yourself . . .

Introduction

Because of its frequent use and important place in the language, we must devote a little special attention today to the pronoun in every language, including Latin, which we call reflexive. The very technical name used indicates its nature. The reflexive pronoun is a pronoun in a sentence that reflects specifically to the subject of its own or its principal clause.

1. Use of reflexive pronouns

Contrary to what many people think, you can have the reflexive use of all the pronouns. In the examples:

I groom myself
I groom my hair
She views herself in the mirror
She views her jewelry

both pronouns "myself" and "my" are reflexive, because they reflect back to the subject of their own sentences, "I." Likewise, "herself" and "her" reflect back to the subject, "She." If you say:

They groom me
The barber grooms my hair

the pronouns "me" and "my" do not reflect back to the subjects, "They" and "he," and therefore are not reflexive.

The same thing occurs with the other pronouns. If I say:

They call them criminals

then I am referring to two different groups of people, but if I say:

They call themselves patriots

then the pronoun "themselves," which is the object of the calling, is in fact referring back to the subject "they" and thus is reflexive. You can tell already that it does not matter how the pronoun sounds in English; what is important is the concept and its function in the sentence, reflecting back upon its subject. It is essential that we distinguish whether the pronoun is reflexive or not because in Latin different pronouns will be used based on this distinction.

The reflexive pronoun has one specific usage we shall point out now by turning to the specific pronouns.

2. *Meus – mei – me – mihi; tuus – tui – te – tibi,* et al.

The reflexive pronouns of "I" and "we" and "you" and "you all" are the same as the normal pronouns. That is to say:

> *Adiuvat te*
> He is helping you
>
> *Adiuvas te*
> You are helping yourself.

In the first example above, the pronoun *te* is not reflexive, but in the second one it is, because it reflects back on the subject of the sentence, the implied *tu* contained in the verb. You can see this is not a new form here, but it is a new function for a form you already know.

The same thing occurs with the possessive adjectives *meus, a, um* and *tuus, a, um*, as in the example:

> *Libros tuos portat Priscilla*
> Priscilla is carrying your books
>
> *Libros tuos portas*
> You are carrying your (own) books.

In the first sentence *tuos* is not reflexive because it does not reflect back to Priscilla, the subject of the verb, but in the second, *tuos* reflects back to the implied pronoun *tu* contained in the verb *portas*. In these cases, the Latin pronouns *tuos* and *te* function in both ways as do the other pronouns for "I," "we," "you," and "you all."

A very useful exercise is to reverse from singular to plural or from plural to singular these various personal pronouns, when you find them in literature. Take, for example, the sentence:

> *Memor eris semper mei*
> You will always be mindful of me.

If the student or Latinist reverses this to say:

> *Memores eritis semper meorum*

then it is clear that the person does not understand the function of that *mei*, which is the personal pronoun meaning "of me" and is not the possessive adjective meaning "of mine." In this example its reverse is:

> *Memores eritis semper nostri*
> You all will always be mindful of us.

ENCOUNTER 31

PRONOMINIS REFLEXIVI USUS: SUUS, A, UM; SE – SUI – SIBI. DIFFICULTATES

use of the reflexive pronoun: his, hers, its, their, one's own; himself, herself, themselves, oneself. difficulties

Introduction

When you come to the persons "he, she, it, they," the Romans and many other languages such as German, Italian, and French have a special pronoun for the reflexive forms of "him, her, it, they." They also have a special reflexive adjective to designate possession, "his, hers, its, theirs, one's own." Although this is very simple, still it is going to take clear analysis.

In the previous encounter we said that the possessive adjectives *meus, a, um*, or *noster, nostra, nostrum*, or *vester, vestra, vestrum*, or *tuus, a, um*, function in two ways. They function as possessive adjectives, and, when they reflect back on the subject of the sentence, they function as reflexive adjectives.

When we turn to the third person, we find in the literature that the Romans had a completely different system. We have seen part of this system already in encounter twenty-four when we said that *eius* can mean "of him, of her, of it" and then "his, hers, its" regardless of gender.

In that same encounter we also said that the Romans do not have a possessive adjective equivalent to *meus, a, um*, or *noster, nostra, nostrum*, or *vester, vestra, vestrum*, or *tuus, a, um*, one that means "his, hers, its." They do not have a possessive adjective equivalent to *eius* and *eorum*. At that point we also said that Latin has one big exception, unlike other languages, to which we turn now.

1. *Suus, a, um*

That exception is *suus, a, um*, which does not mean "his, hers, its, theirs" in a generic, possessive sense, but only in a reflexive sense, reflecting back to the subject. This does not contradict what we said before because the use of *suus, a, um* is not the simple equivalent of the possessive *meus, a, um*, which functions both as a possessive adjective and as a reflexive adjective.

In encounter twenty-four we said that to determine whether *eius* means "his," "hers," or "its," we have to look at the idea expressed in the whole story. When we come to the reflexive pronoun, however, we look not to the idea expressed in the story but to the subject of its sentence. So the magic word for the reflexive pronoun is the "subject of the sentence," whereas the magic word for *eius* is the "story." Thus, *suus, a, um* is not an adjective equivalent to *eius* and *eorum*.

We can check that we have the right meaning of *suus, a, um* in English if we add the word "own," as in "his own, her own, its own," but we cannot rely on this help to solve the question because the word "own" can be omitted easily. We shall give examples soon below.

2. *Se – sui – sibi*

The reflexive pronoun *sui* is the form of-possession. It has three meanings in the following sentence:

> *Imaginem habet sui*
>
> He has an image of himself
> She has an image of herself
> It [e.g., the computer] has an image of itself.

The reflexive pronoun *sui* is the one form of-possession for all three persons: he, she, it. As a reflexive pronoun it follows the principle that the subject tells us whether *sui* means "of himself" or "of herself" or "of itself."

The reflexive pronoun *se* is the object form and sometimes appears as *sese*. Again, it reflects back to the subject of the sentence, for example:

> *Se defendit Marcus*
> Mark defends himself
>
> *Se defendit Maria*
> Mary defends herself
>
> *Se defendit animal*
> The animal defends itself.

In each of these the meaning of *se* depends upon what the subject is. The one form is masculine, feminine, and neuter, and so has all three meanings.

If the subject is not clear or if you have a difficulty with the subject, then the difficulty is not clarified by the reflexive pronoun, which depends on the subject for its meaning.

The reflexive pronoun *se* is also used for the function by-with-from-in. I can say:

> *De se loquitur*
>
> He is speaking about himself
> She is speaking about herself
> It is speaking about itself.

Although the pronoun *se* goes with the preposition *de*, we still have to go back to the subject of the sentence to discover to whom it refers.

If you want to change the above example so that the subject of the sentence is speaking about someone else, then you have to rely upon the normal personal pronouns that are not reflexive, as in:

De eo loquitur Maria

Maria is speaking about him
Maria is speaking about it

De ea loquitur Marcus
Marcus is speaking about her.

Both types of pronouns can be combined as in:

Maria loquitur de eo et se
Maria is speaking about him and herself.

The only pronoun we have not yet seen is the function to-for. It is coming down the line soon enough in encounter thirty-three, but a little peek now will help us. If you say, "I snatch money for myself," then "for myself" is *mihi*, as in:

Pecuniam mihi capio.

If you say, "You grab monkeys for yourself," then "for yourself" is *tibi*, as in:

Simias tibi capis.

The following sentence has several meanings:

Coronam sibi capit

He gets a crown for himself
She gets a crown for herself
It (a business) gets a crown for itself.

Once again *sibi* is masculine, feminine, and neuter, and so its meaning is determined by the subject according to our principle.

Other possibilities do not include the reflexive pronoun, but just the non-reflexive use of the pronoun, as in the following sentences:

Pecuniam ei capio
I get money for him, her, it

Pecuniam tibi capimus
We get money for you

Pecuniam mihi capit
She, He, It gets money for me.

Once again we see the pronouns *mihi*, *tibi* used both reflexively and non-reflexively. We see *ei* used to mean "for him, her, it" without reference to the subject, and *sibi* to refer to the subject's self as in "for itself, for herself, for himself."

Latin is more precise than other languages, even if these precisions are accompanied by their own proper ambiguities, as in the example:

Vocat suos amicos

He calls his own friends
She calls her own friends
It (an animal) calls its own friends.

But if we say:

She calls his friends

we must go back to using *eius*:

Maria vocat eius amicos
Mary calls the friends of him, her, it (not her own).

Some people find this aspect of Latin mysterious and confusing, but it is not. Rather, it is pure logic with consequences.

The meaning of the words *sui, se, sibi; suus, a, um* apply both to the singular "he, she, it" and the plural "they," and the same principles apply with the same clarity, as in:

Sui custodes habent imaginem et eorum
The police have an image of themselves and of those people.

The reflexive pronoun *sui* is the form of-possession both singular and plural, just as *sibi*, the form to-for, as in:

Sibi non parcunt
They do not give concessions to themselves.

If you say:

Eorum favorem habent
They have the support of them

then *eorum* refers to the support of some other people other than the subject, because *sui* would be reflexive.

3. Difficulties

What causes confusion, to talk for a moment about *suus, a, um*, is that the ending of the adjective is going to agree with the word it modifies, not the subject; but its meaning is going to refer back to the subject, not the word it modifies. Take, for example, the sentence:

Priscilla habet libros suos
Priscilla has her books.

Here the adjective *suos* is masculine, not because it means "his," which it does not, but because the word for "books," *libros*, is masculine. The meaning of *suos* comes from the subject, which is Priscilla, and so here the masculine adjective means "her"; that is what causes confusion. Take another sentence:

Robertus habet libros suos
Robert has his own books.

Here *suos* is plural because it agrees with "books," *libros*, but its meaning refers back to Robert, the subject.

We have seen that the adjective can be used as a noun. So, in the sentence:

Laudant suas

the adjective *suas* agrees with a feminine noun that is not there, one such as *feminas*, "the women," but its meaning refers back to the subject of *Laudant*, which contains the pronoun *ei*, "they." So, the two words mean:

They praise their own women.

You can change the sentence to say:

Laudat suos
He, she, it praises his, her, its (own) people.

Again, the meaning of *suos* comes from the subject, but the ending of *suos* agrees with the implied noun, perhaps *viros*, "the men."

Another difficulty concerns identifying the subject, wherever it is. Any book about Latin and any study of the literature will force us to define what we mean by the subject of the sentence, and here we have to be honest about the fact that it can be somewhat broad: which subject? Namely, we can have a direct subject and an indirect subject. The difference between the indirect and direct subject means that you have a chance of infinite ambiguity. That is just the way things are in English as well. If one were to say:

Augustus asked Virgil to sing about his fatherland

you could ask whose fatherland it is. If it is Virgil's fatherland, then "his" refers directly to the subject of the verb "to sing," which is Virgil. But you also must be conscious of the fact that Augustus is ruling the world and could ask Virgil to sing about the fatherland of Augustus himself. In that case "his" refers to the subject controlling the whole sentence and so is an indirect reflexive. Latin literature gives us these indirect and direct subjects, and you cannot deny them, and they are not going to go away. Relax and think! We shall give Latin examples in a minute.

Another problem noted in any book you want is that the reflexive can even refer to the subject of the whole discourse, chapter, or story, and not necessarily to the subject of its own sentence. In that case we can speak about a logical subject.

Say, for example, we are talking about Iulius Caesar for a whole chapter. We can have *suus*, *sui*, *se*, and *sibi*, which refer not to any proximate subject but to the logical subject of the whole story, namely Caesar. A logical reflexive does not refer directly to the grammatical subject of its own sentence or indirectly to that of another sentence, but to the subject of the whole story, and thus the reflexive is logical.

Imagine St. Bernard giving a discourse on the Blessed Virgin Mary; even in sentences where he is the subject, where he is thinking of Mary and singing the praises of Mary, Bernard could use *suus, a, um* to refer to Mary because she is the subject of the whole discourse.

Thus, there are three possible reflexives: direct, indirect, and logical. No teacher can deny or hide this.

One last point, which is no consolation, but again it is almost demanded by our heads: sometimes *suus, a, um* is going to refer to the nearest thing you are talking about. For example, the teacher could say:

I have asked the students their opinions.

The grammatical subject is "I," but the logical subject or the focus of the whole sentence is the "students." Theoretically, because the grammatical subject is "I," the Latin pronoun for "their" should be *eorum*, "of them," referring to people other than the subject. This would mean, "I have asked the students the opinions of them," which looks as if the opinions do not belong to the students but to yet other people. In this case, because the pronoun is standing very close to the object, "students," the focus of the whole sentence, you can possibly end up with a reflexive, "their," that refers to that nearest word. It would almost look foolish to say:

Rogavi discipulos sententias eorum
I asked the students the opinions of them (that is, of other persons).

Technically this would be correct because the subject is "I," but it does not look right in English or Latin, and in the literature on occasion they will say:

Rogavi discipulos suas sententias
I asked the students their own opinions.

A number of examples more illustrate the difficulties here. The first one is from a letter of Cicero to Atticus:

A Caesare valde liberaliter invitor in legationem illam sibi ut sim legatus (Cic. *Att.* II, 18, 3)

I am very generously being invited by Caesar that I be a lieutenant for him for that mission.

The subject of the verbs *invitor*, "I am being invited," and *sim*, "I be," is in both cases "I." In order to refer to Caesar, you technically expect the pronoun *ei*, "for the other one [not the subject]," namely "for Caesar." Yet, Caesar is running both the whole world and this sentence as well in which he is the logical, real subject of the action. Thus, Cicero says *sibi*, "for himself," referring to Caesar.

The next example is from *de Bello Gallico* by Gaius Iulius Caesar (c. 100–44 BCE), in which Caesar says:

neque cognoscendi quid fieret neque sui colligendi hostibus facultatem relinquunt (Caes. *B. G.* III, 6, 1)

neither do [the Romans] leave to the enemies the possibility of getting to know what was happening nor of regrouping themselves.

The subject of the verb *relinquunt*, "[neither] do they leave," is an implied *Romani*, "the Romans," who are the subject of the story here. You would technically expect the reflexive pronoun *sui* to refer to the Romans, as if to say, "neither do the Romans leave to the enemies the possibility ... of regrouping the Romans." Rather, Caesar here uses *sui* in the tightly formed gerundive, *sui colligendi*, to refer to the subject of the gerundive itself, as in "of the enemies regrouping themselves."

Another example is once again from our friend Cicero writing to Atticus:

> *Paetus, ut antea ad te scripsi, omnes libros quos frater suus reliquisset mihi donavit* (Cic. *Att.* II, 1, 12)
>
> as I wrote to you before, Paetus donated all the books to me which his brother had left.

You would correctly expect *suus* to refer to the subject of the verb *reliquisset*, which is *frater*, "... brother had left." Rather, you can see right away that Cicero was using *suus* as an indirect reflexive referring to *Paetus*, the subject of the main clause. *Paetus* is talking in the whole sentence, saying in effect, "my brother left the books." Cicero is reporting the account of Paetus telling that his own brother had done this.

This example is from Titus Livius (59 BCE–17 CE), in which Livy says:

> *His nuntiis prope uno tempore turbati erectique Magonem cum classe sua copiisque in Hispaniam mittunt* (Liv. XXIII, 32)
>
> Almost at one time disturbed and encouraged by these reports, they send Mago with his fleet and troops to Spain.

The *sua* should refer to the subject of *mittunt*, the Roman senators, but it is obvious that *sua* refers to Mago. You would say the logical subject of the sentence is Mago, not the senate.

Plautus gives this touching sentence in which a woman is talking about her friend who is poor.

> *Pam. Placet ille meus mihi mendicus: suo' rex reginae placet.*
> *idem animust in paupertate qui olim in diuitiis fuit*
>
> (Plaut. *Stich.* 133–34)
>
> Pamphilus: That beggar man of mine is pleasing to me: her own king is pleasing to the queen.
>
> the attitude is the same in poverty which existed once upon a time in riches.

The beautiful text points out colloquial street Latin talk where *animust* is a contraction of *animus est* and where *suo'* with the apostrophe shows the final "*s*" was almost silent and therefore *suo'* stands for *suos*, which is the Greek form for *suus*. A woman is talking about a queen, and she says of the Queen, "her king," and the *suus* should refer to the king, the subject of *placet*, but it really refers to the queen, who is the center of attention here. Thus, *suus* agrees grammatically with *rex*, but it refers to the queen. You have to say it this way to avoid saying something that sounds foolish. Otherwise you would say *eius rex placet reginae*, which would mean "someone else's king is pleasing to the queen."

If you consult for example the two volumes *Ausführliche Grammatik der lateinischen Sprache*, by R. Kühner and C. Stegmann, on the reflexive, after reading seventy pages you will not know much more, and you are just stuck with this ambiguity.

Returning to the practice of reversing from the singular to the plural and from the plural to the singular is very useful here, as in the example:

> *Sunt amantissimi sui*
> They are very fond of themselves.

Its reverse is:

> *Est amantissima sui*
> She is very fond of herself

where the *sui* does not change because it means "of him, of her, of it, of them, of oneself."

ENCOUNTER 32

REPETITIONES OMNIUM

review of all things

As always the pace should now be slowed down, and time should be given to relearn slowly and rehear and redo all of the things we have learned thus far, because we are coming to the end of this First Experience. Consulting our reading sheet or examples is absolutely essential here to confirm and stabilize all these different details and principles that have been presented.

We should add just a note here about Latin style. This will not surprise anyone, because we have been talking about this all along. The note is this: the Latins love to put the preposition, whether it be with the accusative or with the ablative, very elegantly between the noun and its adjective. Therefore, we should be ready to see the connections between adjectives and nouns that jump over the preposition. You can find, for example:

Tuis de litteris accepi nuntium
I got the news about your letter.

Sometimes the adjective is separated from its noun by 4, 5, 6 words, with the preposition between them, as in:

Manifestam civium omnium contra voluntatem egit
He acted against the clear will of all the citizens.

Here *manifestam* describes *voluntatem* and *contra* is between them, coming right before *voluntatem*. You are expected to see these connections, because the Romans loved to do this. In the dictionary you might find expressions such as:

qua de causa
for which reason

quam ob rem
on what account.

Here the prepositions come between the adjectives and their nouns. This is a matter of style and not anything new. If we are observant enough and careful enough, we shall see the agreement between the elements of the sentences; it is very common and delightful for people understanding it.

This very elegant style is to be confirmed by reading on any sheet you want. Here the teacher can look ahead and find examples of this on the source sheets which are easily discoverable, because the Romans liked putting the preposition between the adjective and its noun.

ENCOUNTER 33

CASUS DATIVI INTELLECTUS AC FIGURAE IN NOMINIBUS ET ADIECTIVIS ATQUE IN PRONOMINIBUS ET RELATIVIS

meaning and forms of the function to-for-from in nouns and adjectives as well as in pronouns and relatives

Introduction

Of the seven functions in the Latin language pointed out in the beginning, today we have the fifth one. We have seen the subject and object. We have seen the form of-possession. We have seen the form by-with-from-in, and now we want to talk about the fifth of this collection of functions. In technical terms other people "out there" call this function the *casus dativus*, from the verb *do, dare, dedi, datum*, which means "to give." So, it is the case in general for expressing "to give *to someone*," or "to do something *for someone*." So, the natural meaning of this particular function is "to" or "for," as its name indicates. Immediately we should add as a shock that it can also mean "from," because of special usages we shall explain. Because of these meanings, without any technical terminology we call this the form "to-for-from." Some people resist the idea of "from," because it is the opposite of "to" or "for," but the meaning "from" can be explained in a way that is compatible with the meanings "to" or "for," as we shall see.

The initial and perpetual difficulty with many of the forms of the function to-for-from is that they look like and in fact are often the same as the forms for the ablative. Again we come back to the basic principle we gave at the beginning of the First Experience: namely, we have to be conscious of the entire language and, besides that, think and figure things out; otherwise, we shall not understand the Latin language. If we are thinking and analyzing, then the language works marvelously. We present the forms for to-for-from as we did the forms by-with-from-in, namely across the board so that you see their pattern right away.

1. Block I forms

In Bk.I nouns the masculine form for "to my friend" is *amico*, which you will notice is the same as the form by-with-from-in. The feminine form for "to my girlfriend" or "to the girl" or "to the queen" is going to end in *–ae*, as in *amicae, puellae, reginae*. Here again you will notice that this form is identical with the form of-possession in the singular and with the subject plural. So, when you see *reginae*, think "the queens," "of the queen," and now "to-for-from the queen." You then have to read the entire text, the whole sentence, and figure out which meaning fits. Yes, the ending helps, but not as much as you may want. If you see these ambiguities now, you will know how to address problems later on.

Completing Bk.I nouns, the neuter is the same as the masculine, ending in –*o*. For example, "to the institute" is *instituto*, which again is the same as the form by-with-from-in.

Turning now to the adjectives of Bk.I, we see that they are identical to the nouns. There is no distinction in the form to-for-from between the adjectives and nouns of Bk.I.

The plural of the endings –*o* and –*ae* and –*o* is: –*is*. For example, "to the friends," whether the friends are males or females, is *amicis*, "to the queens" is *reginis*, and "to the institutes" is *institutis*. This is no consolation, because the same form is used for the plural form by-with-from-in, and likewise for the of-possession of Bk.II; for example, "of the king" is *regis*, also ending in –*is*. You have to know the similarities between these forms. Students and scholars will fail here because of the multiplication of forms ending in –*is* throughout the Latin language. But once you know where the word comes from, your vocabulary, then you just about know what it means. This is disturbing for the beginners who believe they can whistle and coast along without difficulty, just guessing and faking.

2. Block II forms

Now let us turn to Bk.II nouns indicated in your dictionary by the crazy form and the second entry that ends in –*is*. The form to-for-from is a little clearer here because the masculine, feminine, and neuter singular all end in –*i*. So, in the sentence "I take food that is helpful *for the body*," the expression "for the body" is *corpori*. In the sentence "I give authority *to the common people*," the form is *genti*. This form is easier than the Bk.II form by-with-from-in, which 85% of the time ends in –*e* and only 15% of the time in –*i*. The form to-for-from, however, has no exceptions: always –*i*, which people readily accept. But you can see a ready confusion in Bk.II because the singular form to-for-from is identical to the form by-with-from-in for 15% of the nouns, all ending in –*i*.

In the plural, Bk.II nouns are identical for the form to-for-from and the form by-with-from-in: both end in –*ibus*. For example, a public vehicle "for all people" is *omnibus*, and that is the word you have in modern languages today for a public "bus," previously called even in English an "omnibus." The form is the same for all three genders.

The adjectives of Bk.II are identical to the nouns in the form to-for-from. The only difficulty is that 85% of the time the form by-with-from-in will be the same as the form to-for-from. We shall hold off giving examples for the moment so that we may first present the next section.

3. Pronoun forms to-for-from

The forms of the pronouns are relatively easy and easily recognizable. The form for "to me" is *mihi*. Because the Romans did not hear the letter *h* in *mihi*, they sometimes wrote *mī* with a long *–i*. Its plural, "to us," is *nobis*, which is why we see in the liturgy and symphonic renditions: *Agnus Dei ... dona nobis pacem*, "Lamb of God ... grant *to us* peace." The form for "to you" is *tibi*, and its plural "to you all" is *vobis*. We have already seen the forms *nobis* and *vobis* because they are the same as the forms by-with-from-in. One and the same form is used to mean "to him" and "to her" and "to it"; the form is *ei*. Its plural "to them" is *eis* or *iis*, and again you cannot see the gender.

At this point you must go back to the reading sheets to see these forms in the context of complete human thoughts, because this theory is best put into action immediately.

4. Relative pronoun forms to-for-from

The relative pronoun for "to whom" and "for whom" and "from whom" in the singular is *cui*, which is masculine and feminine and neuter. Some people take it as two syllables *cu-i*, but some others take it as one syllable, *cui* pronounced rapidly. Do not confuse the form *cui* with the subject form *qui*. The plural of *cui* is *quibus*, which is the same as the form by-with-from-in. Some of the poets contract the form *quibus* to *quīs* with a long *–is*.

5. Reflexive pronoun forms to-for-from

As we saw previously, the reflexive forms for "I" and "you" and "we" and "you" in the plural are the same as the non-reflexive forms we had already learned. The same holds true for the reflexive forms to-for-from, so "to-for-from myself" is *mihi;* "to-for-from yourself," *tibi;* "to-for-from ourselves," *nobis;* "to-for-from yourselves," *vobis*. But note well: the form for "to-for-from himself" and "to-for-from herself" and "to-for-from itself" and "to-for-from themselves" is the single form *sibi*, which covers for all of them in the reflexive. For example, "I provide it for them" is *Id provideo eis*, and, "They provide it for them (others) is *Id provident eis*, but "They provide it for themselves" using the reflexive *sibi* is *Id provident sibi*.

As far as the forms are concerned, that is all there is to say, but again you must consult the reading sheets immediately to see examples anywhere you want of the form to-for-from all over the place, because that is how the Romans spoke their language.

6. *Circus Latinitatis maximus*

In this massive Latin circus every word demands laser-sharp analysis plus total dictionary comprehension. To make us grow fast and to prepare us for the whole vision of Latin, some brilliant lines from the recently corrected (1998) Latin Vulgate Bible of the fourth century, from the *Liber Proverbiorum*, the Book of Proverbs, have all these usages and forms mixed together and thrown out there for us. We present these here for recreation, like an optional diversion.

The first proverb is:

In labiis sapientis invenitur sapientia. (Vulg. Nov. *Prov.* 10.13)

Some readers are going to take *labiis* and *sapientis* as going together because they both end in –*is*, and the student will say, "wise lips," which makes sense in English, but if the teacher supplies the Latin for that, *in labiis sapientibus*, then everyone will see the difference in expression. They will see that *labiis* is in the form by-with-from-in and *sapientis* is in the form of-possession, producing the meaning:

Wisdom is found on the lips of the wise person.

Here is a second proverb:

Possidere sapientiam quanto melius est auro [!]
(Vulg. Nov. *Prov.* 16.16)

Here *quanto* does not agree with *auro*, both ending in –*o*. They are there for two different reasons: *quanto* signifies degree and goes with *melius* to produce the statement, "by how much better" or simply "how much better," whereas *auro* is in the form by-with-from-in giving a comparison meaning "than gold." This produces the statement like an exclamation:

Possessing wisdom is how much better than gold.

Yet another proverb is:

Melior est patiens viro forti, et, qui dominatur animo suo, expugnatore urbium. (Vulg. Nov. *Prov.* 16.32)

This proverb looks like a menagerie of forms. The combination *viro forti* could be in the form to-for-from, but here it is in the form by-with-from-in and goes with *melior* to express a comparison meaning "better than a strong man." In contrast, *animo suo* could be in the form by-with-from-in, but it goes with the verb *dominatur*, which we shall see presently is one of the 65 verbs whose complement is in the form to-for-from, which you can almost hear in English if you say "he has dominance over his own spirit." Again, *expugnatore*, is in the form by-with-from-in and goes with *melior* to produce a second comparison meaning "[better] than the destroyer." That is how you get the meaning:

A patient person is better than a strong man, and he who controls his own spirit [is better] than the destroyer of cities.

Take this proverb where many forms could also be dative, but in fact are all ablative:

Unguento et ture delectatur cor et dulcedine amici in consilio ex animo.
(Vulg. Nov. *Prov.* 27.9)

You can also find *ture* in your dictionary under *thus, thuris*, "incense." Here *unguento* is the same form as a dative, but with that passive verb *delectatur*, "[the heart] is delighted," both *unguento* and *ture* and *dulcedine* are in the form by-with-from-in to express instrumentality and so appear without any preposition. Next, *consilio* and *animo* are also in the same form as the dative, but here are objects of their respective prepositions *in* and *ex*.

The heart is delighted by ointment and incense and by the sweetness of a friend in counsel from the heart.

Stay awake to read this proverb:

Fortitudo simplici via Domini et ruina his, qui operantur malum
(Vulg. Nov. *Prov.* 10.29)

because sleepiness might produce the meaning, "a simple way of the Lord" or "a simple fortitude." The word *simplici* standing there in the midst of the sentence may escape the drowsy who do not see the form to-for-from, meaning "for the simple person." This is in addition to the ending –*i* shared by *simplici* and *Domini*, which have nothing to do with each other, because the latter is the form of-possession meaning "of the Lord." If the student says "of the simple Lord" the teacher can immediately produce the Latin *simplicis Domini* to clarify the difference. This is a favorite game we can all play in class, stopping to produce the forms we think we understand until we see them correctly. All these problems are resolved by knowing vocabulary and endings with absolute precision, and you still have to think to produce the following meaning:

Valor is the way of the Lord for the simple person and ruination for these people who work evil.

It is difficult to stop, so here is another proverb:

Misericordia et veritas te non deserant: circumda eas gutturi tuo.
(Vulg. Nov. *Prov.* 3.4)

It is very clear that *gutturi* is not in the form by-with-from-in which would be *gutture*, but it must be in the form to-for-from because of the compound verb *circumda*. Instead of writing *da eas circum guttur tuum*, with the neuter object according to the super principle, they put the *circum* on the verb to produce *circumda* and *guttur tuum* changes from the object of *circum* to the complement of *circumda* in the form to-for-from to produce *gutturi tuo*, as in:

May mercy and truth not abandon you: put them around your throat.

We cannot pass up one final example:

Dominus dat sapientiam, et ex ore eius scientia et prudentia. Thesaurizabit rectis sollertiam et clipeus erit gradientibus simpliciter servans semitas iustitiae et vias sanctorum custodiens. (Vulg. Nov. *Prov.* 2.6–7)

Here both *rectis* and *gradientibus* can be in the form by-with-from-in and the form to-for-from. The meaning demands the natural function to-for-from in the plural. When you come to *semitas iustitiae*, the word *iustitiae* must be the form of-possession in the singular, meaning "paths of justice," or the form to-for-from in the singular, meaning "paths for justice"; however, in no way is *iustitiae* the subject plural. The subject forms *scientia* and *prudentia* are the same as the forms by-with-from-in. The verb *est* is understood. Given these possibilities, we produce the statement:

The Lord gives wisdom and out of his mouth knowledge and prudence. For the righteous he will gather dexterity as a treasure and it will be a shield for the ones walking simply, keeping the paths of justice and guarding the ways of the holy ones.

7. Usages

The uses of the form to-for-from can be collected into three big categories, which are very logical and very intelligible.

7.1. *Natural usage*

The first is the natural usage depending on the main verb and meaning "to" or "for." This usage will never change.

To illustrate the natural use of the form to-for-from, perhaps the reader would be delighted to see examples from Rome's greatest epigrammatist: Marcus Valerius Martialis (c. 40–c. 103 CE). These are all two-line epigrams or poems by Martial that have the whole Latin language in them. Here we meet many of the forms we have seen so far and at the same time see the Latin traps which demand pinpoint analysis and thinking.

Spongia
Haec tibi sorte datur tergendis spongea mensis
utilis, expresso cum levis imbre tumet (Mart. XIV, 144)

Sponge
This sponge useful for wiping off tables is given to you by chance,
When—the water having been squeezed out—it blows up light.

Two subject forms end in *–is*, both *utilis*, "useful," and *levis*, "light," both of which go with *spongea*, the "sponge." The verb *datur*, "[this sponge] is given," gives rise to a natural use of the form to-for-from in the plural, *tergendis mensis*, which you will learn in the Third Experience means "for wiping off tables." Here four words end in *–is*, but there is no confusion, if you know what you are doing.

Another epigram from Martial reinforces this usage:

Hordeum
Mulio quod non det tacituris, accipe, mulis.
haec ego coponi, non tibi, dona dedi. (Mart. XIII, 11)

Barley
Receive such barley which the mule-driver is not giving to mules about to keep silence.
I have given these gifts to the innkeeper, not to you.

Several words look as if they are in the form to-for-from: *mulio, tacituris, mulis, coponi, tibi, dedi*. However, *mulio* is the subject, "the mule-driver." For now we and your teacher can point out that, following the verb *det*, "[the mule-driver] is [not] giving," the natural use of the form to-for-from is seen in *tacituris mulis*, "to mules about to keep silence," all of which you will learn in the Third Experience. By the way, the singular of *tacituris mulis* is *tacituro mulo*, "to the mule about to keep silence." Likewise, *dedi* is not in the form to-for-from, but rather is the same verb in T.4a, "I have given," producing the natural use of the form to-for-from in its two complements *coponi*, also spelled *cauponi*, "to the innkeeper," and in the other part of the sentence *tibi*, "to you"; all three of these end in *–i*: the verb *dedi*, the noun *coponi*, and the pronoun *tibi*, which you will learn below in this same encounter.

7.2. The 65

The second big usage is a real stickler in Latin. The form to-for-from is used with a certain number of verbs, which number about 65; thus we call them simply, "the 65." They are all listed in Gildersleeve and Lodge nº 346 remark 2. The meanings of these 65 verbs include "Advantage or Disadvantage, Yielding and Resisting, Pleasure and Displeasure, Bidding and Forbidding" (Gildersleeve and Lodge nº 346). Your dictionary will tell you that each of these verbs is used with the form to-for-from, that is, with the dative case, abbreviated in your dictionary as "dat." This has ramifications when you make the verb passive, but we shall leave that for the Fourth Experience.

This function to-for-from with these verbs is, perhaps, a phenomenon of the Indo-European mother tongue, because in its modern descendant languages these same ideas are also expressed with the function to-for-from. There must be a "dative mentality" underlying these expressions.

Open your dictionary to the entry for *parco*, *parcĕre*. The dictionary will tell you:

parco, *parcĕre*, *peperci*, *parsum*, 3, to spare; constructed usually with *dat.*

If you have a Latin dictionary like Lewis and Short, you will see this, but even if your dictionary does not specify that *parco* is constructed with the form to-for-from, the dictionary examples will indicate this. The problem here is simply to know whether a verb is one of the 65 or not. In Latin literature these verbs will be accompanied by words in the form to-for-from, but, if you do not know whether a verb is one of the 65, you are not going to understand what those forms are doing in their sentences, because they so often look like the forms by-with-from-in, and many other forms in Latin. You will learn by use, by reading, and by consultation which verbs belong to the 65, much as you did for the deponent verbs; you either know they belong to this group or not. It is not automatic or a guessing game.

Of the 65 verbs, we will mention several here to help you get into the Latin language. The first two are *servio*, "to serve," and *placeo*, "to please." Both take the form to-for-from, as in the example:

I serve my friend.

Here, "my friend" looks like the direct object in English, but when we put the main verb "I serve" into Latin and say *servio*, then the dictionary tells us that what looks like the object form in English must be expressed in Latin by the form to-for-from, as in *meo amico*. Thus, we have:

> *Meo servio amico*
> I serve my friend

The same occurs with the verb *placeo*:

> *Suis placet popularibus*
> He, she, it pleases his, her, its compatriots.

In the dictionary you will also find a similar word:

> *adiuvo, adiuvare, adiuvi, adiutum*, 1, to give aid to, to help *aliquem*.

That word in the object form *aliquem*, "someone," tells you that this verb takes the object form. Thus we say:

> *Meum adiuvo amicum*
> I help my friend.

We simply have to know that *adiuvo* takes the object form, whereas *subvenio* takes the form to-for-from, meaning practically the same thing. Many students in class read a text and see the form to-for-from floating somewhere and will ask whether the verb is one of the 65. When the teacher answers correctly, it is great fun. But if you do not know which verbs are among the 65, you at least must be aware of this possibility and be able to look the verb up in the dictionary to see how it is used. Familiarity with Latin literature will sharpen a certain linguistic suspicion and knowledge of these verbs.

The fact that these verbs take the form to-for-from does not depend so much on their meaning, although that is what caused this phenomenon. For example, there are certain verbs of indulging and forgiving that are going to take the so-called dative case in most languages. But that is not a necessary assumption. For example, the English verb "to spare" takes the object form, just as the German verb *schonen*, "to spare," takes the object form, but the Latin verb *parco* takes the form to-for-from. You just have to know this as part of your Latin training.

The other difficulty is that when these Latin forms to-for-from are rendered into English, they most often do not sound as such at all, but as simple direct objects. Fortunately, in just about every instance you can rework the meaning of each of these 65 verbs so that its complement will sound in English in that precise way, for example:

> *Cur hostibus non pepercisti?*
> Why did you not spare the enemies?

The form to-for-from comes out in English if you say:

> Why were you not merciful, indulgent *to the enemies?*
>
> *Hodie non oboediunt multi legibus*
>
> Today many people do not obey the laws
> People today do not submit *to the laws*
> People do not give obedience *to the laws* today

Studemus linguae diligenter Latinae

We are studying the Latin language
We are zealous *for the Latin language*
We are working *on the Latin language.*

Notice that most alternatives, as quasi-synonyms of the 65, will have their objects in the regular form, as in:

Cur hostes non eripuisti?
Why did you not save the enemies?

Hodie non custodiunt multi leges
Today many people do not keep the laws

Discimus linguam diligenter Latinam
We are learning the Latin language diligently.

Again we turn to Martial for another epigram:

Qui ducis vultus et non legis ista libenter,
omnibus invideas, livide, nemo tibi (Mart. I, 40)

You who make a face and do not read these things willingly,
O jealous man, may you envy all people, but no one you.

Both forms *ducis* and *legis* look like the form of-possession from the nouns *dux* and *lex*, but they are not. Rather here they are T.1 of the verbs *ducere* and *legere*. In the last encounter of this First Experience you will learn how *ducis vultus* can express the idea "to draw a facial expression." Martial uses one of the 65 verbs, *invideas*, "may you envy," whose complement is in the form to-for-from here: both *omnibus*, "all people," and in the other part of the sentence *tibi*, "you." See how much you have to know just for two lines!

The unexpected surprises in content and in Latin form found in the *Codex Iuris Canonici* of 1983 can inspire us to better things. In this *Code of Canon Law* we find:

> *Sodales, ut vocationi suae fideliter respondeant eorumque actio apostolica ex ipsa unione cum Christo procedat, sedulo orationi vacent, sacrarum Scripturarum lectioni apto modo incumbent.* (*Cod. Iur.* 719. 1)
>
> In order that the members [of a religious community] may faithfully answer their calling, and that their apostolic activity may proceed from the association itself with Christ, they should perseveringly spend time on prayer, they should pursue the reading of sacred scriptures in a suitable way.

Three verbs here take the form to-for-from, but just for kicks we made the above rendering so that they would not sound to-for-from at all. First, *respondeant*, "they may answer their calling" or "they may respond to their calling." In your dictionary, *respondeo, respondere* is considered one of the 65, but in the English expression "answer me" you cannot hear the form to-for-from, but you can say, "respond to me."

Second, *vacent*, "they should spend time on prayer" or "they should be free for prayer." The dictionary says for *vaco, vacare*, that it is used both with the form to-for-from as one of the 65 and with the form by-with-from-in. At holiday time we used to say *vacabo scholis et vacabo ludis*, where *vacabo scholis* with the form by-with-from-in means "I shall be free from classes" but *vacabo ludis* in the form to-for-from means "I shall be free for games."

Third, *incumbant*, "they should pursue the reading" or "they should devote themselves to the reading." This verb *incumbo, incumbere*, means "to rest on" or "to sit on top of something" as does a mother hen, or "I devote myself to something." It is a compound verb which we introduce immediately below.

7.3. *Compound verbs*

The third big usage of the form to-for-from is what we call the compound verbs, due partly to what they mean and partly to their construction. Let us begin the explanation with their construction. In the dictionary certain prepositions are often attached as prefixes to certain words. The list of these prepositions is given in Gildersleeve and Lodge nº 347: *ad, ante, con, in, inter, ob, (post,) prae, sub,* and *super*. In literature, these simple verbs are used with prepositions which in turn have their own objects. The phenomenon of compound verbs is explained by taking these prepositions and appending them as prefixes to these verbs, which become compound verbs. When this occurs, the original object of the preposition becomes the complement of the verb in the form to-for-from. A ready example is:

> I am assisting at a public show
> *Sisto ad spectaculum publicum*.

Here the simple verb *sisto* is accompanied by the preposition *ad* with its object form *spectaculum publicum*. But there is another word in your Latin dictionary, *adsisto*, which is composed of the preposition *ad* and the verb *sisto*. The compound *adsisto* means "to assist at," and its meaning is completed with the form to-for-from. So you end up saying:

> *Publico adsisto spectaculo*
> I am assisting at a public show.

Note that this sentence with the compound verb and the form to-for-from means exactly the same as the previous sentence with the simple verb and the prepositional phrase.

The preposition *ante* can be prefixed to the verb *ponere* to make the word *antepono*, which the dictionary tells us takes the dat., as in this idea and its expressions:

> *Pono apes ante aquilas*
> *Apes aquilis antepono*
>
> I put bees before eagles.

Another example is:

There were many merits in his works
Multa merita erant in eius operibus.

But your dictionary gives you the compound verb *insum*, "to be present in," which is a combination of the preposition *in* with the simple verb *sum*. In this case, the form by-with-from-in *operibus* shifts into the form to-for-from, which is also *operibus*, so you say with the same meaning:

Multa merita inerant eius operibus
There were many merits in his works.

You cannot see it, but *operibus* is now the form to-for-from because of the compound verb *insum*. You can see the difference if we reverse both of these examples:

Multum meritum erat in eorum opere
Multum meritum inerat eorum operi

There was much merit in the work of them.

This phenomenon is extremely common. The Latin poets especially like this, because it saves them space and does not require using a whole prepositional phrase.

The phenomenon of compound verbs is a daily occurrence with the prefixes *in*– and *cum*– and *ex*–. For example the simple verb *venio* and the preposition *cum* form the compound verb *convenio*, meaning "to come together with." We can use this compound verb in this way:

Meis veniam cum amicis
Meis conveniam amicis

I shall come together with my friends
I shall agree with my friends.

Some brilliant, natural examples of these compound verbs with the form to-for-from are found in the memorable Renaissance Latin of the autobiography of one of the leaders of that movement, namely Aeneas Sylvius Piccolomini (1405–1464), also known as Pope Pius II (1458–1464). Here Piccolomini is addressing the political parties of his home town, Pienza, who had a civil war going on between them. He threatens that he will depart if they will not stop fighting each other:

> *contra Pius instare et, nisi pareant, patrie iusta neganti benignam subtracturum se manum asserere, atque ob hanc causam inter flexit et dimissa Tuscia per Vmbriam iter habuit, Senensibus interminatus, nisi morem gererent, se patria posthabita per Perusiam, Aretium et Florentiam in Galliam profecturum*
> (Picco. *Comm.* II, 13)

> on the contrary Pius was insisting and was asserting that, if they did not obey, he would withdraw a kind hand from the fatherland denying legitimate things, and for this reason he redirected his journey and, Tuscany having been discarded, made his way through Umbria, having threatened the people of Siena that, if they would not comply, he would head for Gaul through Perugia, Arezzo, and Florence—his fatherland having been put aside.

Here we have three compound verbs whose complements are in the form to-for-from. The first example we highlight with a hyphen between the preposition serving as a prefix and its verb, *patrie ... sub-tracturum*, "[he] will withdraw ... from the fatherland," where *patrie* is the Renaissance spelling for *patriae*, in the form to-for-from, here meaning "from," as explained below. The second one is *Senensibus inter-minatus*, "having threatened the people of Siena," where you cannot hear the form to-for-from in English. The last one is *post-habere*, a compound verb that is used here without an object, but you will learn its function here in the Third Experience.

Turning again to another two-line epigram from Martial, we find this illustration:

> *Quid recitaturus circumdas vellera collo?*
> *conveniunt nostris auribus ista magis* (Mart. IV, 41)

> You, about to recite what, are putting pieces of fleece around your neck?
> those pieces are more suitable for our ears.

Here Martial uses *circumdas* as a compound verb whose complement *collo* is in the form to-for-from. The English rendering makes the prefix *circum*, "around," into a preposition, as if the Latin said, *das vellera circum collum*, "you are putting pieces of fleece around your neck." Likewise, *conveniunt* is a compound verb whose complement *nostris auribus* is in the form to-for-from, which is identical to the form by-with-from-in. You also see that *nostris* ends in *–is*, as does *magis*, which is a comparative adverb meaning "to a greater extent," "more so."

Mixing up authors, eras, and styles of Latin, we return to the autobiography of Piccolomini, who says:

> *Senenses emolumentis carituri curie recessuro presuli mille instare pericula affirmabant* (Picco. *Comm.* II, 25)

> The Sienese about to live without the profits of the curia were affirming that a thousand dangers were threatening the prelate about to leave.

The compound verb *in-stare* means "to hang over" or "to press upon" used here with the form to-for-from, *presuli*, to mean "were threatening the prelate."

Martial gives a final epigram to illustrate the compound verb:

> *Quod clamas semper, quod agentibus obstrepis, Aeli,*
> *non facis hoc gratis: accipis, ut taceas.* (Mart. I, 95)

> O Aelius, the fact that you are always screeching and that you are heckling people pleading cases.
> you do not do this for nothing: you take [money] that you may shut up.

The implied subject *tu*, "you," produces three verbs ending in *–is*, *obstrepis*, "you are screeching," *facis*, "you do," *accipis*, "you take," all three of which are not to be confused with the plural form to-for-from. The verb *obstrepis*, "you are heckling," is a compound verb whose complement is in the form to-for-from, *agentibus*, which you can not hear if you say, "you are heckling people pleading cases." You can hear this in English if you say "you are making noise in face of people pleading cases," or "you are running interference for people pleading cases." We can make the prefix *ob–* into a preposition to produce the sentence *quod ob agentes strepis*, with the meaning, "the fact that you are making noise in front of people pleading cases." The word *gratis* is an abbreviated form of *gratiis*, the plural form by-with-from-in, meaning "with a favor" or "without any price."

These are the three basic usages for the form to-for-from. Experience shows that presenting these three usages in this way is successful and helps many people. The students spot the compound verbs right away and quickly discover the 65 verbs.

8. "From"

People who are not trained in our method may think that the dative can mean only "to" or "for," but they will be happy to know how we get that meaning "from" in the function we have simply called "to-for-from" since its introduction. In the last encounter we said that the meaning "from" can be explained in a way that is consistent with the meanings "to" and "for" due to the two big usages of the form to-for-from with the 65 verbs and with compound verbs. Let us begin with an example from the 65. Look in your dictionary for the entry *adimo, adimere*, meaning "to take away." Whether this verb is compound or one of the 65 does not make much difference, because your dictionary will tell you that "to take away from someone" uses the form to-for-from, as in:

> *Ademit eis libertatem*
> He took freedom away from them.

In this case the pronoun *eis* or *iis* is in the form to-for-from. This is clear when we reverse the singular to plural and plural to singular:

> *Ademerunt ei libertates*
> They took freedoms away from him, her, it.

Here we can clearly distinguish the form *ei*, which is to-for-from, and the form *eo* or *ea*, which is by-with-from-in. Reversing these sentences reveals how you understand the sentence.

A good example using the relative pronoun could be:

> *Adamus Evaque pepererunt liberos quibus abstulerunt integritatem*
> Adam and Eve begot children from whom they took away innocence.

The students may notice that *quibus* has to mean "from whom."

If someone asks, "Since when does the dative case mean 'from'?" since its introduction our students answer that it can always mean "from" besides "to" or "for," and that saves an infinity of misery and confusion and frustration. If the questioner is convinced that it can mean only "to" or "for," you can ask them to look it up in Gildersleeve and Lodge n° 345, where the talk is about this function. There it says that the meaning is "*to, for, from*," and the students will be surprised to see "from" printed there in italics, because they were not fully trained.

There are many compound verbs that take this form to-for-from with the special meaning "from," especially the compounds with the prefix *a* or *ab*, which sometimes becomes the prefix *au*–, for example, *aufero, auferre,* "to take away," as in:

> *Tulit pecuniam ab eis*
> *Abstulit pecuniam eis*
> He took money away from them.

Their reversed sentences are:

> *Tulerunt pecunias ab eo (ea)*
> *Abstulerunt pecunias ei*
> They took monies away from him (her), it.

In these examples, the meaning "from" derives not so much from the natural meaning of the form to-for-from, which is still "to-for," but from these other two principal usages, namely from the 65 and compound verbs.

In the last encounter we said that the meaning "from" can be explained in a way that is consistent with the meanings "to" and "for." The meaning "from" is a form of relationship. Its use does not indicate, in the example, that one is taking away money "from" someone else, but that one is taking away money "with regard to someone else" or money "belonging to someone else" or money "with their concern." This form describes the relationship, in the example, between them and their money, where the form for "them" is in the form to-for-from because of this connection "to them." For example, using the verb *eripio*, "to snatch, we can say:

> *Non eripiam tibi bulgam*
> I shall not snatch the suitcase from you.

But the verb *eripiam* is a compound of the preposition *ex* and *rapiam*, meaning "to snatch from." To get the meaning of the form to-for-from, we might say:

> *Non eripiam tibi bulgam*
> I shall not snatch away the suitcase *with regard to you*
> I shall not snatch-away the suitcase *that belongs to you*
> I shall not snatch-away the suitcase *that concerns you.*

Do not remain with the theory any longer, but investigate concrete examples in the readings provided at the end. This would be a good time to repeat the five functions learned thus far this year so that you have a firmer grasp of them and make them more natural. We shall see the final two functions in a later Experience.

ENCOUNTER 34

IMPERATIVUS PASSIVUS ET DEPONENS

passive and deponent command forms

Introduction

To review what we have learned of the verb, we began by learning the active forms in T.4, 5, 6 and then in T.1, 2, 3. We learned the passive forms in T.1, 2, 3 and then in T.4, 5, 6. We also learned the active imperatives, that is, the command forms. The last element of the Latin verb in this our First Experience, therefore, is to see quickly and rather easily the passive forms of those commands, which more frequently will also be the command forms for deponent verbs. That will leave only the subjunctive and the participles and their usages with the usages of the infinitives for the Third Experience.

1. Passive imperatives

For normal verbs the passive forms have passive meaning, but for the deponents the passive forms have active meaning. Because passive commands in their concepts are on the rare side, the deponent commands with active meaning are much more numerous.

In all four groups of verbs and in the special Group in –*io*, *ere*, the passive imperative of "you" in the singular looks like the active infinitive. This means that the form *laudare* as an imperative means, "be praised!"; this is in addition to what you learned before: that *laudare* means "praising" or "to praise." Now, as a command *laudare* means "be praised!"

Knowing this, we can easily go down the line and see that all the active infinitives now can also be passive commands. An example from Gp.II is *movēre*, which now also means "be moved!" From Gp.III, *imponĕre* now means "be placed!" Virgil uses this form when Aeneas tells his father to get up on his shoulder and says *inponĕre*, "be thou placed [on my shoulder]!" This is immortalized in the statues of Aeneas carrying his father on his shoulder. In Gp.IV we have *erudire*, which now means "be taught!" In regard to the –*io*, *ere* verbs, which straddle Gp.III and Gp.IV, the pattern is the same, and the verb form *capere* means not only "to catch," but now as a passive command means "be caught," "you must be caught." That is the whole list of verbs.

The plural of those forms provides a case where the Latin language is very disappointing, because it runs out of forms. The passive commands for "you all" are the same as the passive forms for T.1 for "you all"; that is to say, *laudamini* means both "you all are praised" and now the command form "you people must be praised!"; *movemini* now also means "you people must be moved!"; *imponimini* means "you people must be imposed, put on top!"; *erudimini*, "you people must be taught!"; and our special Group is normal again in that *capimini* now also means "you must be caught!" These passive commands are very rare, because people do not use passive commands that often in any language.

2. Imperative deponents

The more important aspect for us are the deponent verbs, which have these passive forms with active meaning. These forms are the only command forms for the deponents by definition. We shall explain the forms by means of examples.

In Gp.I, we have already seen that the passive command form of *laudo, laudare, laudavi, laudatus* in the singular is the same form as the active infinitive *laudare*, which means both "to praise" and "you must be praised!" For the deponents, however, the only infinitives we have seen are passive in form and active in meaning. For example, the infinitive of *dignor* is *dignari*, which is passive in form and active in meaning, "to deign, condescend," and *laetor, laetari* is "to rejoice, be happy."

To produce the passive command form, with active meaning for the deponents, we have to create the form that would be the active form of the infinitive, if deponents had one. So, for *dignor, dignari, dignatus*, the active infinitive, if it had one, would be *dignare*. This form, just like the example above, *laudare*, is the passive command form, which for *laudare* is passive in meaning, but for *dignare* is active in meaning because deponent. So, *dignare* means "deign! condescend!" but *dignari* means "to deign," "to condescend." This form comes up frequently in the liturgy when we say *dignare benedicere*, "deign to bless!" Here *dignare* is the passive command form with active meaning, "deign," and the other is the infinitive *benedicere*, "to bless." To catch this you must be very conscious and wide awake. The plural of *dignare* is *dignamini*, which is both the command form, "you all must condescend!" and the form for T.1, "you all are condescending." A challenging formula in Vatican liturgy is *Dignare, Domine, donare*, which means, "Lord, deign to grant!"—one verb an imperative, the other an infinitive.

Another example occurs in the liturgy on the fourth Sunday in Lent, called *Laetare* Sunday, meaning "the "Rejoice! Sunday." The word *laetare* comes from the first word of the liturgy on that day: *Laetare Ierusalem*, "Rejoice, Jerusalem" (*cf.* Isaiah 66:10–11). If you know that the verb *Laetor, laetari, laetatus* is deponent, then you will not confuse this with an active infinitive, which it cannot be. The plural of *laetare* comes up very often, especially in the Psalms: *laetamini*, "you all must rejoice!"

If we turn to Gp.II, your dictionary has the verb *confiteor, confiteri, confessus*, meaning "to confess." The command form looks like the active form of the infinitive, if one existed; namely, *confitēre* as a command means "confess!" Its plural, *confitemini*, means both "you all must confess!" and "you all are confessing." This form, *confitemini Domino*, occurs very often in the

Psalms, meaning "confess, give praise to the Lord!" as you can see in Psalm 66 illustrated on page 252 of this volume.

Gp.III gives the examples *sequor, sequi, secutus*, "to follow," and *loquor, loqui, locutus*, "to speak." Their command forms are *sequĕre*, "follow!" and *loquĕre*, "speak!" and their plurals are the same form as T.1, *sequimini*, "you all must follow!" and *loquimini*, "you all must speak!" The former is used famously in the Bible where Jesus tells the soon-to-be disciple Matthew, *sequere me*, "follow me!" (Vulg. Nov. *Matt.* 9.9).

Gp.IV gives us the verb *largior, largiri, largitus*, "to grant," so you can say:

> *Omnibus tuis dona largire civibus*!
> Grant gifts to all your citizens!

Here, *largire* looks like an infinitive, which it cannot be because it is deponent, so it is a command. This becomes clear if we reverse the sentence to say:

> *Omni tuo* (*tua*) *donum largimini civi*!
> You all must grant a gift to your every citizen!

Here we see the plural *largimini*, which is the same form for both the command "you all must grant!" and T.1 "you all are granting."

Take a deponent verb of that special Group on the fence between Gp.III and Gp.IV, for example *patior, pati, passus*, "to suffer, endure"; the imperative is going to look like the active infinitive of *pati*, which would be *patĕre*, "suffer! endure!" and its plural is *patimini*, "suffer-ye! you all must endure!" Or we can take *morior, mori, mortuus*, where *mori* means "to die" and *morĕre*! means "you must die!"

3. Second imperative

Thus far in this Experience we have considered the simple command form in both "you" and "you all." With a few examples of our own, we can easily present the passive forms of the second or future imperative, which are very rare in Latin literature. The passive forms of the second or future imperative are very simple to make from the active forms of the second imperative, because all you do is change the personal ending of the active form to *–or*.

That is to say, *laudato*, "thou shalt praise!" becomes *laudator*, "thou shalt-must be praised!" As we have seen before, the same form is used for "he, she, it must be praised," *laudator*. The second imperative passive has no form for "you all"; it just does not seem to be found in the literature.

The second command form for "they must be praised!" as you would expect, adds the ending *–or* to the T.1 form, so that *laudant*, "they praise," becomes *laudantor*, "they must be praised." This form looks similar to that for T.1 passive, *laudantur*, "they are praised." If we flip the passive *laudantor* to the active we have *laudanto*, "they must praise."

With that you can logically finish all the other forms for the verb groups. The deponent example, *confitetor* means "you must praise!" and "he, she, it must praise!" and *confitentor culpas* means "they must confess their faults!"

In Gp.III we have the forms *imponitor,* "you must be imposed!" and "he, she, it must be imposed!" and *imponuntor,* "they must be imposed!" These forms are very rare, and you can read Latin for a year or two and never find them, and then in some poet all of a sudden it will pop up.

In Gp.IV the passive command forms will be *eruditor,* "you must be taught!" and "he, she, it must be taught!" and *erudiuntor*, "they must be taught!"

For our special Group we find *capitor*, "you must be grasped!" and "he, she, it must be grasped!" and *capiuntor,* "they must be grasped!" That is all you have to do.

These passive command forms are really very simple, and they follow the Greek pattern. The problem is that they look like so many other forms in the language, and you have to remember or keep in mind the different functions of the same form.

These normal verbs have passive forms with passive meaning. The deponent commands for the second or future imperative are exactly the same in form, but by definition their passive forms have active meanings.

That is the end of the treatment of the verb in our First Experience. We hope that it has not been painful or impossible, because it is not or should not be so, if we just reason things nicely or notice things carefully in solid examples.

ENCOUNTER 35

MANUS, US; SPECIES, IEI: ADIECTIVA NULLA; 20% NOMINUM

hand; appearance: no adjectives; 20% of nouns

Introduction

Let us recall the amount of the language we have already learned: Bk.I nouns and adjectives gave us 40% of all nouns and 50% of all adjectives. Bk.II gave us another 40% of the nouns and the other 50% of all adjectives. The mathematics tells you that no adjectives are left over for our last encounter of the First Experience, because we have finished them in one way or another in two 50% Blocks. The mathematics also tells you that approximately 20% of the nouns of the Latin language remain to be presented. Because these remaining nouns do not have any corresponding block of adjectives, we have waited to present them in this last encounter.

Most of the time the students have no difficulty with these small Blocks of nouns, which we compare to an appendix, a little branch hanging out on the extreme end. These noun Blocks do not exist in Greek, but in Latin they are an outgrowth of Bk.II nouns, just variations that you will see and discover everywhere as everyday words.

Manus, us: no adjectives; 10% of nouns

We can divide the 20% that is left over into two equal Blocks, each representing 10% of all nouns. The first small block of nouns in this appendix is sometimes called the fourth declension by the manuals. These nouns are recognizable, as always, from the second element given in the dictionary. In Bk.I nouns this second element in the dictionary was either *–i* or *–ae* or *–i* and in Bk.II *–is*.

The nouns of this block are indicated by the second element that ends in *–us*. Because the dictionary entry for these nouns also ends in *–us*, we call these the *–us, us* nouns. Most of them are masculine, but a few are feminine and fewer are neuter, but we are dealing with a small number of nouns and for some reason everyone recognizes them.

The first little block of them includes, for example, the dictionary entry *exercitus, exercitus*, "army." Note that the entry is not *exercitus, exerciti*, as in Bk.I, but *exercitus, us*. This block includes the word *senatus, senatus*, "senate." Both *exercitus* and *senatus* are masculine nouns. A feminine example is the word for "hand," *manus, manus*, and the word for "home" is *domus, domus*, which is also feminine.

For the other forms of the masculine and feminine nouns of the Block

–us, us, the problem here again is that the same letters have many functions. Let us look at the other forms of these nouns in the same way we presented the previous Blocks. From the dictionary we know that *manus* is the singular subject. The form *manus* is also the plural subject, not *mani* as you might have expected. The Romans heard those two forms differently: *manus* in the singular with a short ending *–ŭs* and in the plural with a long *–ūs;* and some editions might even mark the long *–ūs* to help you see the plural subject.

The object form is *manum* or *exercitum*, and the plural again ends in a long *–ūs*, as in *manūs* or *exercitūs*. You can see the language is running out of steam.

The form of-possession you have in the dictionary, and, if you look carefully, you find *manūs* again with a long *–ūs* giving that function.

The plural of that ends in *–uum* as in *manuum* or *domuum* or the expression "Lord God of hosts," which is *Dominus Deus exercituum*. Now remember that the singular object is *exercitum*, but the plural form of-possession is *exercituum*. You must observe and be careful.

Quite often you will see the form by-with-from-in, which just happens to end in the simple *–u* as in *manu;* the plural is *manibus*. You will see *manu forti*, as in the phrase "the Lord led us out *with a strong hand*," and its reverse is *manibus fortibus*, "with strong hands." An early Christian greeting, *Dominus vobiscum*, "the Lord be with you," elicits the response *et cum spiritu tuo*, "and with your spirit." So, the noun *spiritus, spiritus* is another masculine noun of this block. Another example is the expression *maior natu* meaning "older by birth."

The form to-for-from ends in *–ui* as in *senátui* or *mánui* or *exercítui* or *spirítui*. A common doxology is, *Gloria patri et filio et spirítui sancto*. The plural is like the plural form by-with-from-in: *manibus, exercitibus, spiritibus*. These forms have existed for ages, and that is the end of it.

There are about 4 or 5 neuter nouns in the Block *–us, us*. It is almost too useless to mention them, but the famous one is *genu, genus*, n., "a knee." The subject form is *genu* in the singular and *genua* in the plural. Because of the super principle the subject form is the same as the object form: *genu* and *genua*. Your dictionary gives the form of-possession as *genus*, and its plural is *genuum*. The form by-with-from-in is *genu*, and its plural *genibus*. The form to-for-from is *genui*, and its plural is also *genibus*. These few neuter *–us, us* nouns are later developments, little bits of stuff that did not go very far. That is the end of that.

Species, iei: no adjectives; 10% of nouns

The last block of nouns in the whole language is what some people call the fifth declension. As a block they are not that many and again are part of our appendix to the language that stands out on a limb without any adjectives; they appear frequently in everyday life. All of these nouns are feminine.

These are identified once again from the second element in the dictionary. If you have, for example, the dictionary entry *spécies*, then the second element is *speciéi*, and the word means "the outward appearance." Another one that is very common is the word for "face": *fácies*. In the dictionary the second element is *faciéi*. Another one is the most famous word in the dictionary, *res*, and its second element is *rei*, meaning "a thing."

We can quickly give other forms. The letter "*i*" will be common. The plural of *species* is *species*. The object is *speciem*, and its plural is *species*. Likewise, the plural of *res* is also *res*. Its object is *rem*, and its plural is also *res*.

The form of-possession is from the dictionary: *speciéi, faciéi, rei*. In the plural these end in *–erum*. We have already seen the endings *–orum, –arum, –uum, –um, –ium*, and now we add *–erum* as in *speciérum, faciérum*. More common is the form *rerum* "of things," which some people know from the beginning of a papal document on social teaching, *Rerum novarum*, "Of New Things," a reference to people interested in new things or revolution.

The form by-with-from-in is *re* and in the plural *rebus;* and *specie* and in the plural *speciébus*. You will find the form *re* very often, for example in the word *re publica*, which comes from *res publica* with *re* in the form by-with-from-in. Cicero wrote a book on the public entity called *De re publica*. That is why you have the English word "re-public."

The form to-for-from in the singular is the same as the form of-possession found in the dictionary, namely *speciéi, fidéi, rei*. Its plural is the same as the plural form by-with-from-in. That is the end of the Latin language.

Concluding comment

If this Experience is extended and repeated over a period of 35 classes with daily repetition, the whole language will appear very simple as it should, because it is. Learning Latin is not a matter of memorizing schemas or nonsensical, meaningless syllables. It is, rather, a matter of seeing examples. We have emphasized and continue to do so as we go merrily along: we must have our reading sheets nearby, and as soon as we do something new in these different encounters, immediately we must flip over to our reading sheets so that we may enjoy reading Latin literature at length.

QVID·MIRARIS·APEM QVAE MEL DE·FLORIBVS·HAVRIT
SI TIBI·MELLITAM·GVTTVRE·FVNDIT·AQVAM

PRIMAE EXPERIENTIAE LECTIONUM PAGINULAE

Reading Sheets—First Experience

READING 1-A

QVINTVS HORATIVS FLACCVS
[65–8 BCE]

EPISTVLARVM LIB. I.

VIII

CELSO gaudere et bene rem gerere Albinovano
Musa rogata refer, comiti scribaeque Neronis.
si quaeret quid agam, dic multa et pulchra minantem
vivere nec recte nec suaviter; haud quia grando
contuderit vitis oleamque momorderit aestus, 5
nec quia longinquis armentum aegrotet in agris;
sed quia mente minus validus quam corpore toto
nil audire velim, nil discere, quod levet aegrum;
fidis offendar medicis, irascar amicis,
cur me funesto properent arcere veterno; 10
quae nocuere sequar, fugiam quae profore credam;
Romae Tibur amem ventosus, Tibure Romam.
post haec, ut valeat, quo pacto rem gerat et se,
ut placeat iuveni percontare, utque cohorti.
si dicet 'recte,' primum gaudere, subinde 15
praeceptum auriculis hoc instillare memento:
ut tu fortunam, sic nos te, Celse, feremus.

IX

SEPTIMIVS, Claudi, nimirum intellegit unus
quanti me facias, nam cum rogat et prece cogit
scilicet ut tibi se laudare et tradere coner,
dignum mente domoque legentis honesta Neronis,
munere cum fungi propioris censet amici, 5
quid possim videt ac novit me valdius ipso.
multa quidem dixi cur excusatus abirem;
sed timui mea ne finxisse minora putarer,

dissimulator opis propriae, mihi commodus uni.
sic ego, maioris fugiens opprobria culpae, 10
frontis ad urbanae descendi praemia. quodsi
depositum laudas ob amici iussa pudorem,
scribe tui gregis hunc et fortem crede bonumque.

X

VRBIS amatorem Fuscum salvere iubemus
ruris amatores, hac in re scilicet una
multum dissimiles, ad cetera paene gemelli
fraternis animis—quidquid negat alter et alter—
adnuimus pariter vetuli notique columbi. 5
tu nidum servas; ego laudo ruris amoeni
rivos et musco circumlita saxa nemusque.
quid quaeris? vivo et regno simul ista reliqui
quae vos ad caelum fertis rumore secundo,
utque sacerdotis fugitivus liba recuso, 10
pane egeo iam mellitis potiore placentis.
vivere naturae si convenienter oportet,
ponendaeque domo quaerenda est area primum,
novistine locum potiorem rure beato?
est ubi plus tepeant hiemes, ubi gratior aura 15
leniat et rabiem Canis et momenta Leonis,
cum semel accepit Solem furibundus acutum?
est ubi divellat somnos minus invida cura?
deterius Libycis olet aut nitet herba lapillis?
purior in vicis aqua tendit rumpere plumbum, 20
quam quae per pronum trepidat cum murmure rivum?
nempe inter varias nutritur silva columnas,
laudaturque domus longos quae prospicit agros.
naturam expelles furca, tamen usque recurret,
et mala perrumpet furtim fastidia victrix. 25
non qui Sidonio contendere callidus ostro
nescit Aquinatem potantia vellera fucum
certius accipiet damnum propiusve medullis,
quam qui non poterit vero distinguere falsum.
quem res plus nimio delectavere secundae, 30
mutatae quatient. si quid mirabere, pones
invitus. fuge magna: licet sub paupere tecto
reges et regum vita praecurrere amicos.
cervus equum pugna melior communibus herbis
pellebat, donec minor in certamine longo 35
imploravit opes hominis frenumque recepit;
sed postquam victor violens discessit ab hoste,
non equitem dorso, non frenum depulit ore.

sic qui pauperiem veritus potiore metallis
libertate caret, dominum vehet improbus atque 40
serviet aeternum, quia parvo nesciet uti.
cui non conveniet sua res, ut calceus olim,
si pede maior erit, subvertet, si minor, uret.
laetus sorte tua vives sapienter, Aristi,
nec me dimittes incastigatum, ubi plura 45
cogere quam satis est ac non cessare videbor.
imperat aut servit collecta pecunia cuique,
tortum digna sequi potius quam ducere funem.
haec tibi dictabam post fanum putre Vacunae,
excepto quod non simul esses cetera laetus. 50

XI

Qvid tibi visa Chios, Bullati, notaque Lesbos,
quid concinna Samos, quid Croesi regia Sardis,
Zmyrna quid et Colophon? maiora minorave fama,
cunctane prae Campo et Tiberino flumine sordent?
an venit in votum Attalicis ex urbibus una, 5
an Lebedum laudas odio maris atque viarum?
scis Lebedus quid sit; Gabiis desertior atque
Fidenis vicus; tamen illic vivere vellem,
oblitusque meorum obliviscendus et illis
Neptunum procul e terra spectare furentem. 10
sed neque qui Capua Romam petit imbre lutoque
aspersus volet in caupona vivere; nec qui
frigus collegit, furnos et balnea laudat
ut fortunatam plene praestantia vitam.
nec si te validus iactaverit Auster in alto, 15
idcirco navem trans Aegaeum mare vendas.
incolumi Rhodos et Mytilene pulchra facit quod
paenula solstitio, campestre nivalibus auris,
per brumam Tiberis, Sextili mense caminus.
dum licet ac vultum servat Fortuna benignum, 20
Romae laudetur Samos et Chios et Rhodos absens.
tu quamcumque deus tibi fortunaverit horam
grata sume manu neu dulcia differ in annum,
ut quocumque loco fueris vixisse libenter
te dicas; nam si ratio et prudentia curas, 25
non locus effusi late maris arbiter aufert,
caelum non animum mutant qui trans mare currunt.
strenua nos exercet inertia: navibus atque
quadrigis petimus bene vivere. quod petis hic est,
est Vlubris, animus si te non deficit, aequus. 30

XII

FRVCTIBVS Agrippae Siculis quos colligis, Icci,
si recte frueris, non est ut copia maior
ab Iove donari possit tibi. tolle querelas:
pauper enim non est cui rerum suppetit usus.
si ventri bene, si lateri est pedibusque tuis, nil 5
divitiae poterunt regales addere maius.
si forte in medio positorum abstemius herbis
vivis et urtica, sic vives protinus ut te
confestim liquidus Fortunae rivus inauret,
vel quia naturam mutare pecunia nescit, 10
vel quia cuncta putas una virtute minora.
miramur, si Democriti pecus edit agellos
cultaque, dum peregre est animus sine corpore velox,
cum tu inter scabiem tantam et contagia lucri
nil parvum sapias et adhuc sublimia cures; 15
quae mare compescant causae, quid temperet annum,
stellae sponte sua iussaene vagentur et errent,
quid premat obscurum lunae, quid proferat orbem,
quid velit et possit rerum concordia discors,
Empedocles an Stertinium deliret acumen? 20
verum seu piscis seu porrum et caepe trucidas,
utere Pompeio Grospho et, si quid petet, ultro
defer; nil Grosphus nisi verum orabit et aequum.
vilis amicorum est annona bonis ubi quid deest.
ne tamen ignores quo sit Romana loco res, 25
Cantaber Agrippae, Claudi virtute Neronis.
Armenius cecidit; ius imperiumque Phraates
Caesaris accepit genibus minor; aurea fruges
Italiae pleno defundit Copia cornu.

READING 1-B

GAIVS VELLEIVS PATERCVLVS

[19 BCE–35 CE]

HISTORIARVM ROMANORVM AD M. VINICIVM COS. LIBRI DVO

... [3] Insigne coronae classicae, quo nemo umquam Romanorum donatus erat, hoc bello Agrippa singulari virtute meruit. Victor deinde Caesar reversus in urbem contractas emptionibus complures domos per procuratores, quo laxior fieret ipsius, publicis se usibus destinare professus est templumque Apollinis et circa porticus facturum promisit, quod ab eo singulari extructum munificentia est.

LXXXII. [1] Qua aestate Caesar tam prospere †Libium in Sicilia Bñ fortuna in Caesare et in re publica militauit† ad Orientem. Quippe Antonius cum xiii legionibus ingressus Armeniam ac deinde Mediam et per eas regiones Parthos petens habuit regem eorum obvium: [2] primoque duas legiones cum omnibus impedimentis tormentisque et Statiano legato amisit, mox saepius ipse cum summo totius exercitus discrimine ea adiit pericula, a quibus servari se posse desperaverat, amissaque non minus quarta parte militum captivi cuisdam sed Romani, consilio ac fide servatus, qui clade Crassiani exercitus captus, cum fortuna non animum mutasset, accessit nocte ad stationem Romanam praedixitque, ne destinatum iter peterent, sed diverso silvestrique pervaderent. [3] Hoc M. Antonio ac tot illis legionibus saluti fuit: de quibus tamen totoque exercitu haud minus pars quarta, ut praediximus, militum, colonum servitiique desiderata tertia est; impedimentorum vix ulla superfuit. Hanc tamen Antonius fugam suam, quia vivus exierat, victoriam vocabat. Qui tertia aestate reversus in Armeniam regem eius Artavasden fraude deceptum catenis, sed, ne quid honori deesset, aureis vinxit. [4] Crescente deinde et amoris in Cleopatram incendio et vitiorum, quae semper facultatibus licentiaque et adsentationibus | aluntur, magnitudine, bellum patriae inferre constituit, cum ante novum se Liberum Patrem appellari iussisset, cum redimitus hederis coronaque velatus aurea et thyrsum tenens cothurnisque succinctus curru velut Liber Pater vectus esset Alexandriae.

LXXXIII. [1] Inter hunc apparatum belli Plancus, non iudicio recta legendi neque amore rei publicae aut Caesaris, quippe haec semper impugnabat, sed morbo proditor, cum fuisset humillimus adsentator reginae et infra servos cliens, cum Antonii librarius, cum obscenissimarum rerum et auctor et minister, [2] cum in omnia et [in] omnibus venalis, cum caeruleatus et nudus caputque redimitus arundine et caudam trahens, genibus innixus Glacum saltasset in convivio, refrigeratus ab Antonio ob manifestarum rapinarum indicia trinsfugit ad Caesarem: et idem postea clementiam victoris pro sua virtute interpretabatur, dictitans id probatum a Caesare, cui ille ignoverat; mox autem hunc avunculum Titius imitatus est. [3] Haud absurde Coponius, vir e praetoriis gravissimus, pater Silii socer, cum recens transfuga multa ac nefanda Plancus absenti Antonio in senatu obiceret, multa, inquit, mehercules fecit Antonius pridie quam tu illum relinqueres.

LXXXIV. [1] Caesare deinde et Messala Corvino consulibus debellatum apud Actium, ubi ante quam dimicaretur, explaratissima Iulianarum partium fuit victoria. Vigebat in hac parte miles atque imperator illa marcebant omnia: hinc remiges firmissimi, illinc inopia adfectissimi: navium haec magnitudo modica nec celeritati adversa, illa specie terribilior: hinc ad Antonium nemo, illinc ad Caesarem cotidie aliquis transfugiebat; [2] rex Amyntas meliora et utiliora secutus; nam Deillius exempli sui tenax ut a Dolabella *ad Cassium, a Cassio ad Antonium, ita ab Antonio transiit* ad Caesarem; virque clarissimus Cn. Domitius, qui solus Antonianarum partium numquam reginam nisi nomine salutavit, maximo et praecipiti periculo transmisit ad Caesarem. Denique in ore atque oculis Antonianae classis per M. Agrippam Leucas expugnata, Patrae captae, Corinthus occupata, bis ante ultimum discrimen classis hostium superata.

LXXXV. [1] Advenit deinde maximi discriminis dies, quo Caesar Antoniusque productis classibus pro salute alter, in ruinam alter terrarum orbis dimicavere. [2] Dextrum navium Iulianarum cornu M. Lurio commissum, laevum Arruntio, Agrippae omne classici certaminis arbitrium; Caesar ei parti destinatus, in quam a fortuna vocaretur, ubique aderat. Classis Antonii regimen Publicolae Sosioque commissum. At in terra locatum exercitum Taurus Caesaris, Antonii regebat Canidius. [3] Ubi initum certamen est, omnia in altera parte fuere, dux, remiges, milites, in altera nihil praeter milites. Prima occupat fugam Cleopatra: Antonius fugientis reginae quam pugnantis militis sui comes esse maluit et imperator, qui in desertores saevire debuerat, desertor exercitus sui factus est. [4] Illis etiam detracto capite in longum fortissime pugnandi duravit constantia et desperata victoria in mortem dimicabatur. Caesar, quos ferro poterat | interimere, verbis mulcere cupiens clamitansque et ostendens fugisse Antonium, quaerebat, pro quo et cum quo pugnarent. [5] At illi cum diu pro absente dimicassent duce, aegre summissis armis cessere victoriam, citiusque vitam veniamque Caesar promisit. Quam illis ut eam precarentur persuasum est; fuitque in confesso milites optimi imperatoris, imperatorem fugacissimi militis fuctum officio, [6] ut dubites, suone an Cleopatrae arbitrio victoriam temperaturus fuerit, qui ad eius arbitrium direxit fugam. Idem locatus in terra fecit exercitus, cum se Canidius praecipiti fuga rapuisset ad Antonium.

LXXXVI. [1] Quid ille dies terrarum orbi praestiterit, ex quo in quem statum pervenerit fortuna publica, quis in hoc transcursu tam artati operis exprimere audeat? [2] Victoria vero fuit clementissima, nec quisquam interemptus est paucissimis exceptis, qui deprecari quidem pro se non sustinerent. Ex qua lenitate ducis colligi potuit, quem aut initio trimviratus sui aut in campis Philippiis, si sic licuisset, victoriae suae facturus fuerit *modum.* At Sosium L. Arruntii prisca gravitate celeberrimi fides, mox diu *cum* clementia luctatus sua Caesar, servavit incolumem. [3] Non praetereatur Asinii Pollionis factum et dictum memorabile: namque cum se post Brudusinam pacem continuisset in Italia neque aut vidisset umquam reginam aut post enevartum amore eius Antonii animum partibus eius se miscuisset, rogante Caesare, ut secum ad bellum proficisceretur Actiacum: mea, inquit, in Antonium maiora merita sunt, illius in me beneficia notiora; itaque discrimini vestro me subtraham et ero praeda victoris.

LXXXVII. [1] Proximo deinde anno persecutus reginam Antoniumque Alexandream, ultimam bellis civilibus imposuit manum. Antonius se ipse non segniter interemit, adeo ut multa desidiae crimina morte redimeret. At Cleopatra frustratis custodibus inlata aspide morsu eius, sane expers muliebris metus, spiritum reddidit. [2] Fuitque et fortuna et clementia Caesaris dignum, quod nemo ex his, qui contra eum arma tulerant, ab eo iussuve eius interemptus. D. Brutum Antonii interemit crudelitas. Sextum Pompeium ab eo devictum idem Antonius, cum dignitatis quoque servandae dedisset fidem, etiam spiritu privavit. [3] Brutus et Cassius ante, quam victorum experirentur animum, voluntaria morte obierunt. Antonii Cleopatraeque quis fuisset exitus narravimus. Canidius timidius decessit, quam professioni eius, qua semper usus erat, congruebat. Ultimus autem ex interfectoribus Caesaris Parmensis Cassius morte poenas dedit, ut dederat Trebonius *primus.*

READING 1-C

MARCVS CORNELIVS FRONTO

[100–166 CE]

EPISTVLAE

Domino meo Caesari.

Niger Censorius diem suum obiit. Quincuncem bonorum suorum nobis reliquit testamento cetera honesto, quod ad verba vero adtinet inconsiderato; in quo irae magis quam decori suo consuluit. Inclementius enim progressus est in Gavium Maximum clarissimum et nobis observandum virum.

Ob eam rem necessarium visum scribere me Domino nostro patri tuo et ipsi Gavio Maximo difficillimae quidem rationis epistulas: in quibus et factum Nigri mei, quod improbabam, non reprehendere nequibam, et tamen amici atque heredis officium, ut par erat, retinere cupiebam. Haec ego te, ut mea omnia cetera, scire volui, conatus mehercules ad te quoque de eadem re prolixiores litteras scribere: sed recordanti cuncta mihi melius visum non obtundere te neque a potioribus avocare.

Domino meo.

Annum novum faustum tibi et ad omnia, quae recte cupis, prosperum cum tibi tum Domino nostro patri tuo et matri et uxori et filiae ceterisque omnibus, quos merito diligis, precor. Metui ego invalido adhuc corpore turbae et impressioni me committere. Si dei iuvabunt, perendie vos vota nuncupantes videbo. Vale mi Domine dulcissime. Dominam saluta.

Domino meo.

Perendie, Domine, te videbo: sum enim adhuc a cubito et cervice infirmus. Fer me, obsecro, nimia et ardua a te postulantem: ita in animum meum induxi posse <te> efficere quantum contenderis. Nec deprecor quin me oderis, nisi quantum postulo perfeceris, si ut facis animum et studium accommodaveris. Vale, Domine, anima mea mihi potior. Dominam matrem saluta.

Domino meo.

Pueri dum e balneis me sellula, ut adsolent, advehunt, imprudentius ad ostium balnei fervens adflixerunt. Ita genum mihi simul abrasum et ambustum est: postea etiam inguen ex ulcere extitit. Visum medicis ut lectulo me tenerem. Hanc causam, si tibi videbitur, etiam Domino patri tuo indicabis, si tamen videbitur. Etiam eras mihi adsistendum erit familiari. Hodierno igitur otio et quiete labori me crastino praeparabo. Victorinus noster aget, ne me acturum putes. Vale, Domine dulcissime. Dominam saluta.

Domino meo.
Quom te salvom et illaesum dei praestiterunt, maximas deis gratias ago. Te certum habeo, quom instituta tua reputo, haud perturbatum: ego, quamlibet vos sapientes me inrideatis, consternatus equidem sum. Vale, Domine dulcissime, et deis curae esto. Dominam saluta.

Domino meo.
Gratia ad me heri nocte venit. Sed pro Gratia mihi fuit quod tu gnomas egregie convertisti, hanc quidem quam hodie accepi prope perfecte, ut poni in libro Sallustii possit, nec discrepet aut quicquam decedat. Ego beatus hilaris sanus iuvenis denique fio, quom tu ita proficis. Est grave quod postulabo; sed quod ipse mihi et profuisse memini non potest quin a te quoque postulem. Bis et ter eandem convertito, ita ut fecisti in illa gnome brevicula. Igitur longiores quoque bis ac ter converte naviter, audacter. Quodcumque ausus fueris cum isto ingenio, perficies: at enim cum labore laboriosum quidem negotium concupisti, sed pulchrum et rectum et paucis impetratum. De ... perfecte absolveris. Plurimum tibi in oratione facienda <proderit hic labor>: tum certe quidem cotidie <aliquas sententias excerpere> ex Iugurtha aut ex Catilina. Diis propitiis, quom Romam reverteris, exigam a te de<nuo ver>sus diurnos. Dominam matrem tuam saluta.

Domino meo.
Omnia nobis prospera sunt, quom tu pro nobis optas, neque enim quisquam dignior alius te, qui a dis quae petiit impetret; nisi quod, ego quom pro te precor, nemo alius te dignior est pro quo impetretur. Vale, domine dulcissime. Dominam saluta.

Domino meo.
Aridelus iste, qui tibi litteras meas reddit, a pueritia me curavit a studio perdicum usque ad seria officia. Libertus vester est; procurabit vobis industrie; est enim homo frugi et sobrius et acer et diligens. Petit nunc procurationem ex forma suo loco ac iusto tempore. Faveto ei, Domine, quod poteris. Si formam non cognosces hominis, ubi ad nomen Arideli ventum fuerit, memento a me tibi Aridelum commendatum. Vale, Domine dulcissime. Dominam saluta.

Domino meo.
Saenius Pompeianus in plurimis causis a me defensus, postquam publicum Africae redemit, plurimis causis rem familiarem nostram adiuvat. Commendo eum tibi, quom ratio eius a Domino nostro patre tuo tractabitur, benignitatem ingenitam tibi, quam omnibus ex more tuo

tribuis, ut huic et mea commendatione et tua consuetudine ductus impertias. Vale, Domine dulcissime.

Domino meo.
Quaecumque mihi precatus es, omnia in tua salute locata sunt. Mihi sanitas, bona valetudo, laetitia, res prosperae meae ibi sunt, quom tu corpore animo rumore tam incolumi uteris, tam carus patri, tam dulcis matri, tam sanctus uxori, tam frater bonus ac benignus. Haec sunt quae me cum hac valetudine tamen cupientem vitae faciunt. Absque te satis superque et aetatis et laboris et artis et gloriae, dolorum vero et aegritudinum aliquanto plusquam satis superque.

Filiae meae iussu tuo osculum dedi. Numquam mihi tam suavis tamque saviata visa est. Dominam saluta, Domine dulcissime. Vale et fer osculum matronae tuae.

Domino meo.
Cholera usque eo adflictus sum ut vocem amitterem, singultirem, suspirio angerer, postremo venae deficerent, sine ullo pulsu venarum animo male fieret; denique conclamatus sum a nostris; neque sensi aliquamdiu: ne balneo quidem aut frigida aut cibo recreandi me ac fovendi medicis tempus aut occasio data, nisi post vesperam micularum minimum cum vino destillatum gluttivi. Ita focilatus totus sum. Postea per continuum triduum vocem non recuperavi. Sed nunc deis iuvantibus commodissime valeo, facilius ambulo, clarius clamito: denique, si dei iuvabunt, cras vehiculo vectari destino. Si facile silicem toleravero, quantum pote ad te curram. Tum vixero quom te videro. Ad VII Kal. Roma proficiscar, si dei iuvabunt, Vale, Domine dulcissime, Desiderantissime, causa optima vitae meae. Dominam saluta.

Domino meo.
In hortis vindemias ago. Commode valeo. Aegre tamen insisto dolore digitorum in sinistro pede. Pro Faustina mane cotidie deos appello. Scis enim me pro tua salute optare ac precari. Vale mi Domine dulcissime. Dominam saluta.

Domino meo.
Plurimos natales dies liberum tuorum prosperis tuis rebus ut celebres parentibus probatus, populo acceptus, amicis pergratus, fortuna et genere et loco tuo dignus, omni vita mea redemisse cupiam, non hac modo exigua vita quae mihi superest, sed illa etiam quam vixi, si quo modo <in> integrum redigi ac pro te tuisque liberum tuorum commodis in solutum dependi potest. Si facile ingredi possem, hie erat dies quo cum primis complecti te cuperem, sed concedendum est pedibus scilicet, quando ipsi parum procedunt. Ego de aquarum usu delibero. Si certius quid statuero, faciam tibi notum. Vale mi Domine dulcissime. Faustinam tuam meis verbis

appella et gratulare, et matronas nostras meo nomine exosculare sed, uti ego soleo, cum plantis illis et manibus. Dominam saluta.

Caesari suo consul.
Meum fratrem beatum, qui vos in isto biduo viderit! At ego Romae haereo compedibus aureis vinctus; nec aliter Kal. Sept. expecto quam superstitiosi stellam, qua visa ieiunium polluant. Vale, Caesar, decus patriae et Romani nominis. Vale, Domine.

READING 1-D

SENTENTIARVM STRVCTVRA LATINARVM

structure of Latin sentences

[200 BCE–420 CE]

Largus item liquidi fons luminis, aetherius sol,
irrigat assidue caelum candore recenti
suppeditatque novo confestim lumine lumen.

TITVS LVCRETIVS CARVS [99–55 BCE]

Nos ab isto eventu diligentissima et fidelissima castitas sepsit, [quantumque ab stupris et ab omni post matrimonium excessu,] tantum et ab incesti casu tuti sumus.

QVINTVS SEPTIMVS FLORENS TERTVLLIANVS [160–220 BCE]

Primus itaque error, (qui de istorum officina tenebrosa prorumpit,) duas fingit ecclesias, unam carnalem, divitiis pressam, effluentem divitiis [al.: deliciis], sceleribus maculatam, (cui Romanum praesulem aliosque inferiores praelatos dominari asserunt,) aliam spiritualem, frugalitate mundam, virtute decoram, paupertate succinctam, (in qua ipsi soli eorumque complices continentur.)

PONTIFEX IOANNES XXII [1318 CE]

[carmina cum primum populo iuvenalia legi,]
barba resecta mihi bisve semelve fuit.
moverat ingenium totam cantata per urbem
nomine non vero dicta Corinna mihi.

PVBLIVS OVIDIVS NASO [43 BCE–18 CE]

In Sanctis enim, (qui Christo se dedicavérunt
propter regnum cælórum)
tuam decet providéntiam celebráre mirábilem,
(qua humánam substántiam
et ad primæ oríginis révocas sanctitátem
et ad experiénda dona,
(quæ in novo sæculo sunt habénda,) perducis.)

MISSALE ROMANVM PAVLI VI [1975 CE]

KEY:

Subjects

Objects

Verbs

Distant connections

[Larger clauses]

(Lesser clauses)

et and -que

Letabundus rediit
avium concentus,
ver iocundum prodiit
gaudeat iuventus,
nova ferens gaudia!
modo vernant omnia;
Phebus serenatur;
redolens temperiem
novo flore faciem
Flora renovatur.

CARMEN BVRANVM – 74 [SAECVLI XIII]

Rufum istum, amicum tuum, (de quo iterum iam ad me scribis) adiuvarem, [quantum possem] [etiamsi ab eo laesus essem] [cum te tantopere viderem eius causa laborare.]

MARCVS TVLLIVS CICERO [106–43 BCE]

Tunc enim perfecte consummabitur in nobis illa nostri Salvatoris oratio, (qua pro suis discipulis oravit ad Patrem dicens: *Ut dilectio qua dilexisti me, in eis sit, et ipsi in nobis* [Io. 17, 26]; et iterum: *Ut omnes unum sint, sicut tu, Pater, in me et ego in te, ut et ipsi in nobis unum sint* [ib. 21]) [quando illa Dei perfecta dilectio (qua *prior nos ille dilexit*) [I Io.4, 10], in nostri quoque transierit cordis affectum.]

IOANNES CASSIANVS [360–435 CE]

Quanto magis nos, (quibus animarum medicina commissa est) omnium christianorum domos debemus amare quasi proprias!

EVSEBIVS HIERONYMVS [342-420 CE]

KEY: Subjects are underlined with a solid line.
Objects are underlined with a broken line.
Verbs are underlined with a line of dots.
Distant connections of words and phrases are underlined with a wavey line.
[Larger clauses are in square brackets,] (lesser ones in rounded parentheses.)
The words et and -que are placed in boxes.
Note: This code is used to illustrate the functions and connections of words as an aid to teaching, and is not intended to appear in absolutely every instance.

READING 1-E

BIBLIA
NOVA VVLGATA LATINA
[1979 CE]

LIBER PRIMUS MACCABAEORUM

1 [1] Et factum est, postquam percussit Alexander Philippi Macedo, qui prius regnavit in Graecia, egressus de terra Cetthim, Darium regem Persarum et Medorum, [2] constituit proelia multa et obtinuit munitiones et interfecit reges terrae; [3] et pertransiit usque ad fines terrae et accepit spolia multitudinis gentium, et siluit terra in conspectu eius, et exaltatum est et elevatum est cor eius. [4] Et congregavit virtutem fortem nimis et obtinuit regiones gentium et tyrannos, et facti sunt illi in tributum. [5] Et post haec decidit in lectum et cognovit quia moreretur; [6] et vocavit pueros suos nobiles, qui secum erant nutriti a iuventute, et divisit illis regnum suum, cum adhuc viveret. [7] Et regnavit Alexander annis duodecim et mortuus est. [8] Et obtinuerunt pueri eius regnum, unusquisque in loco suo; [9] et imposuerunt omnes sibi diademata post mortem eius, et filii eorum post eos annis multis. Et multiplicata sunt mala in terra.

[10] Et exiit ex eis radix peccatrix, Antiochus Epiphanes filius Antiochi regis, qui fuerat Romae obses, et regnavit in anno centesimo tricesimo septimo regni Graecorum. [11] In diebus illis exierunt ex Israel filii iniqui et suaserunt multis dicentes: « Eamus et disponamus testamentum cum gentibus, quae circa nos sunt, quia, ex quo recessimus ab eis, invenerunt nos multa mala » . [12] Et bonus visus est sermo in oculis eorum; [13] et destinaverunt aliqui de populo et abierunt ad regem, et dedit illis potestatem, ut facerent iustitias gentium. [14] Et aedificaverunt gymnasium in Hierosolymis secundum leges nationum; [15] et fecerunt sibi praeputia et recesserunt a testamento sancto et iuncti sunt nationibus et venumdati sunt, ut facerent malum.

[16] Et paratum est regnum in conspectu Antiochi, et coepit regnare in terra Aegypti, ut regnaret super duo regna. [17] Et intravit in Aegyptum in multitudine gravi, in curribus et elephantis et equitibus et navium multitudine; [18] et constituit bellum adversus Ptolemaeum regem Aegypti, et veritus est Ptolemaeus a facie eius et fugit, et ceciderunt vulnerati multi. [19] Et comprehenderunt civitates munitas in terra Aegypti, et accepit spolia terrae Aegypti. [20] Et reversus est Antiochus, postquam percussit Aegyptum in centesimo et quadragesimo tertio anno, et ascendit ad Israel

et ad Hierosolyma in multitudine gravi [21] et intravit in sanctificationem cum superbia et accepit altare aureum et candelabrum luminis et universa vasa eius [22] et mensam propositionis et libatoria et phialas et pateras aureas et velum et coronas et ornamentum aureum, quod in facie templi erat; et comminuit omnia. [23] Et accepit argentum et aurum et vasa concupiscibilia et accepit thesauros occultos, quos invenit; [24] et, sublatis omnibus, abiit in terram suam et fecit caedem hominum et locutus est superbia magna.

[25] Et factus est planctus magnus in Israel et in omni loco eorum; [26] et ingemuerunt principes et seniores, virgines et iuvenes infirmati sunt, et speciositas mulierum immutata est, [27] omnis maritus sumpsit lamentum, et quae sedebat in toro maritali, lugebat; [28] et commota est terra super habitantes in ea, et universa domus Iacob induit confusionem.

[29] Et post duos annos dierum misit rex principem tributorum in civitates Iudae et venit Ierusalem cum turba magna; [30] et locutus est ad eos verba pacifica in dolo, et crediderunt ei. Et irruit super civitatem repente et percussit eam plaga magna et perdidit populum multum ex Israel. [31] Et accepit spolia civitatis et succendit eam igne et destruxit domos eius et muros eius in circuitu; [32] et captivas duxerunt mulieres et natos et pecora possederunt. [33] Et aedificaverunt civitatem David muro magno et firmo et turribus firmis; et facta est illis in arcem. [34] Et posuerunt illic gentem peccatricem, viros iniquos, et convaluerunt in ea; [35] et posuerunt arma et escas et, congregatis spoliis Ierusalem, reposuerunt illic; et facti sunt in laqueum magnum. [36] Et factum est hoc ad insidias sanctificationi et in diabolum malum in Israel semper; [37] et effuderunt sanguinem innocentem per circuitum sanctificationis et contaminaverunt sanctificationem. [38] Et fugerunt habitatores Ierusalem propter eos, et facta est habitatio exterorum et facta est extera semini suo; et nati eius reliquerunt eam. [39] Sanctificatio eius desolata est sicut solitudo, dies festi eius conversi sunt in luctum, sabbata eius in opprobrium, honor eius in nihilum. [40] Secundum gloriam eius multiplicata est ignominia eius, et sublimitas eius conversa est in luctum.

[41] Et scripsit rex Antiochus omni regno suo, ut essent universi populus unus, [42] *et relinqueret unusquisque legem suam. Et receperunt omnes gentes secundum verbum regis Antiochi;* [43] et multi ex Israel consenserunt cultui eius et sacrificaverunt idolis et coinquinaverunt sabbatum. [44] Et misit rex libros per manus nuntiorum in Ierusalem et in civitates Iudae, ut sequerentur leges gentium terrae, [45] et prohibere holocausta et sacrificia et placationes fieri in templo Dei et contaminare sabbata et dies sollemnes [46] et polluere sancta et sanctos, [47] instruere aras et templa et idola et immolare porcina et pecora communia [48] et relinquere filios suos incircumcisos et polluere animas eorum in omni immundo et abominatione, [49] ita ut obliviscerentur legem et immutarent omnes iustificationes; [50] et quicumque non fecerit secundum verbum regis Antiochi, morietur. [51] Secundum omnia verba haec scripsit omni regno

suo et praeposuit consideratores super omnem populum et mandavit civitatibus Iudae immolare per civitatem et civitatem. [52] Et congregate sunt multi de populo ad eos, omnes, qui dereliquerant legem Domini, et fecerunt mala in terra; [53] et posuerunt Israel in abditis et in absconditis fugitivorum locis.

[54] Die quinta decima mensis Casleu, quinto et quadragesimo et centesimo anno, aedificavit abominationem desolationis super altare; et per civitates Iudae in circuitu aedificaverunt aras [55] et ante ianuas domorum et in plateis sacrificabant, [56] Et libros legis, quos invenerunt, combusserunt igne scindentes eos; [57] et ubicumque inveniebatur apud aliquem liber testamenti, et si quis consentiebat legi, constitutio regis interficiebat eum. [58] In virtute sua faciebant haec Israeli, omnibus, qui inveniebantur in omni mense et mense in civitatibus. [59] Et quinta et vicesima die mensis sacrificabant super aram, quae erat super altare; [60] et mulieres, quae circumciderant filios suos, interficiebant secundum iussum [61] — et suspendebant infantes a cervicibus eorum — et domos eorum et eos, qui circumciderant illos. [62] Et multi in Israel obtinuerunt et confortati sunt apud se, ut non manducarent immunda, [63] et elegerunt mori, ut non polluerentur escis et non profanarent testamentum sanctum, et moriebantur. [64] Et facta est ira magna super Israel valde.

2 [1] In diebus illis surrexit Matthathias filius Ioannis filii Simeonis sacerdos ex filiis Ioarib ab Ierusalem et consedit in Modin. [2] Et habebat filios quinque: Ioannem, qui cognominabatur Gaddis, [3] et Simonem, qui vocabatur Thasi, [4] et Iudam, qui vocabatur Maccabaeus, [5] et Eleazarum, qui vocabatur Abaron, et Ionathan, qui vocabatur Apphus.

[6] Et vidit blasphemias, quae fiebant in Iuda et in Ierusalem, [7] et dixit: « Vae mihi! Ut quid natus sum videre contritionem populi mei et contritionem civitatis sanctae? Et sederunt illic, cum daretur ea in manibus inimicorum, sanctificatio in manu extraneorum. [8] Factum est templum eius sicut homo ignobilis, [9] vasa gloriae eius captiva abducta sunt, trucidati sunt parvuli eius in plateis eius, iuvenes eius in gladio inimicorum. [10] Quae gens non hereditavit regnum eius et non obtinuit spolia eius? [11] Omnis ornatus eius ablatus est; quae erat libera, facta est ancilla. [12] Et ecce sancta nostra et pulchritudo nostra et gloria nostra desolata est, et polluerunt ea gentes. [13] Ut quid nobis adhuc vita? » . [14] Et scidit vestimenta sua Matthathias et filii eius et operuerunt se ciliciis et planxerunt valde.

[15] Et venerunt, qui ex rege compellebant discessionem in civitatem Modin, ut sacrificarent. [16] Et multi de Israel accesserunt ad eos, et Matthathias et filii eius congregati sunt. [17] Et responderunt, qui missi erant a rege, et dixerunt Matthathiae: « Princeps et nobilis et magnus es in hac civitate et confirmatus filiis et fratribus. [18] Nunc accede primus et fac iussum regis, sicut fecerunt omnes gentes et viri Iudae et, qui remanserunt in Ierusalem, et eris tu et filii tui inter amicos regis et tu et

filii tui glorificabimini et argento et auro et muneribus multis » . [19] Et respondit Matthathias et dixit magna voce: « Etsi omnes gentes, quae in domo regni sunt, regi oboediunt, ut discedat unusquisque ab officio patrum suorum, et consentiunt mandatis eius, [20] et ego et filii mei et fratres mei ibimus in testamento patrum nostrorum. [21] Propitius sit nobis Dominus, ne derelinquamus legem et iustificationes. [22] Non audiemus verba regis, ut practereamus officium nostrum dextra vel sinistra » . [23] Et, ut cessavit loqui verba haec, accessit quidam Iudaeus in omnium oculis sacrificare super aram in Modin secundum iussum regis. [24] Et vidit Matthathias et zelatus est, et contremuerunt renes eius; et attulit iram secundum iudicium et insiliens trucidavit eum super aram. [25] Et virum regis, qui cogebat immolare, occidit in ipso tempore et aram destruxit; [26] et zelatus est legem, sicut fecit Phinees Zamri filio Salomi. [27] Et exclamavit Matthathias voce magna in civitate dicens: « Omnis, qui zelum habet legis statuens testamentum, exeat post me » . [28] Et fugit ipse et filii eius in montes, et reliquerunt, quaecumque habebant in civitate. [29] Tunc descenderunt multi quaerentes iustitiam et iudicium in desertum, ut sederent ibi, [30] ipsi et filii eorum et mulieres eorum et pecora eorum, quoniam induraverant super eos mala.

[31] Et renuntiatum est viris regis et excrcitui, qui erat in Ierusalem civitate David, quoniam descenderunt viri quidam, qui dissipaverant mandatum regis, in loca occulta in deserto. [32] Et cucurrerunt post illos multi, et deprehendentes eos applicaverunt contra eos et constituerunt adversus eos proelium in die sabbatorum [33] et dixerunt ad cos: « Usque hoc nunc! Exite et facite secundum verbum regis et vivetis » . [34] Et dixerunt: « Non exibimus neque faciemus verbum regis, ut polluamus diem sabbatorum » . [35] Et concitaverunt adversus eos proelium. [36] Et non responderunt eis, nec lapidem miserunt in eos, nec oppilaverunt loca occulta [37] dicentes: « Moriamur omnes in simplicitate nostra, et testes erunt super nos caelum et terra quod iniuste perditis nos » .

READING 1-F

AVRELIVS AVGVSTINVS

[354–430 CE]

ENARRATIONES IN PSALMOS

IN PSALMVM XCI. ENARRATIO.

SERMO.

1. Attendite ad psalmum: det nobis Dominus aperire mysteria quae hic continentur; cum propter fastidium animorum eadem diuerse uarieque tractantur. Nam nullum aliud canticum nos docet Deus, nisi fidei, spei, et caritatis: ut fides
5 nostra firma sit in ipso, quamdiu non illum uidemus, credentes in eum quem non uidemus, ut gaudeamus cum uiderimus, et fidei nostrae succedat species lucis eius, ubi iam non nobis dicetur: Crede quod non uides; sed, gaude quia uides. Spes etiam nostra incommutabilis sit, et figatur in illo, et non nutet
10 et fluctuet, non agitetur; sicut ipse Deus in quo figitur, non potest agitari. Spes enim modo uocatur; tunc non spes, sed res erit. Tamdiu enim uocatur spes, quamdiu non uidetur quod speratur, dicente apostolo: *Spes autem quae uidetur, non est spes: quod enim uidet quis, quid sperat? Si autem quod non*
15 *uidemus speramus, per patientiam exspectamus.* Modo ergo patientia necessaria est, quamdiu ueniat quod promissum est. Nemo autem patiens est in bonis. Quando exigitur de homine patientia, in malis agit; quando dicitur: Patiens esto, tolera, sustine, molestia est, sub qua te Deus uult esse fortem, tole-
20 rantem, longanimem, patientem. Sed numquid decipit qui promisit? Medicus exserit ferrum ad secandum uulnera, et dicit ei quem secturus est: Patiens esto, sustine, tolera; in doloribus exigit patientiam, sed post dolores promittit salutem. Et ille qui tolerat dolores in ferro medici, nisi sibi
25 proponat sanitatem, quam nondum habet, deficit in dolore quem patitur. Multa ergo mala sunt in isto saeculo, intus, foris; prorsus non cessant, abundant scandala; nemo illa sentit, nisi qui graditur uiam Dei. Ei dicitur in omnibus diuinis paginis, ut toleret praesentia, speret futura, amet quem non
30 uidet, ut amplectatur cum uiderit. Caritas enim quae tertia nobis adiungitur ad fidem et spem, maior est supra fidem et

spem: quia fides rerum est quae non uidentur; erit autem species cum uisae fuerint; et spes rei est quae non tenetur; quae adueniente ipsa re, non erit iam spes, quia tenebimus, non
35 sperabimus; caritas autem non nouit nisi crescere magis magisque. Si enim amamus quem non uidemus, quomodo amaturi sumus cum uiderimus? Desiderium ergo nostrum crescat. Christiani non sumus, nisi propter futurum saeculum: nemo praesentia bona speret, nemo sibi promittat feli-
40 citatem mundi, quia christianus est; sed utatur felicitate praesenti, ut potest, quomodo potest, quando potest, quantum potest. Cum adest, consolationi Dei gratias agat; cum deest, iustitiae Dei gratias agat. Vbique sit gratus, nusquam ingratus: et Patri consolanti et blandienti gratus sit; et Patri emen-
45 danti et flagellanti et disciplinam danti gratus sit; amat enim ille semper, siue blandiatur, sine minetur; et dicat quod audistis in psalmo: *Bonum est confiteri Domino et psallere nomini tuo, Altissime.*

2. Titulus psalmi habet: *Psalmus cantici in diem sabbati.* Ecce et hodiernus dies sabbati est: hunc in praesenti tempore otio quodam corporaliter languido et fluxo et luxurioso celebrant Iudaei. Vacant enim ad nugas; et cum
5 Deus praeceperit sabbatum, illi in his quae Deus prohibet exercent sabbatum. Vacatio nostra a malis operibus, uacatio illorum a bonis operibus est. Melius est enim arare, quam saltare. Illi ab opere bono uacant; ab opere nugatorio non uacant. Nobis sabbatum indicit Deus. Quale? Primo ubi sit
10 uidete. Intus est, in corde est sabbatum nostrum. Multi enim uacant membris, ct tumultuantur conscientia. Omnis homo malus, sabbatum habere non potest; nusquam enim illi conquiescit conscientia; necesse est in perturbationibus uiuat. Cui autem bona est conscientia, tranquillus est; et ipsa tran-
15 quillitas sabbatum est cordis. Attendit enim promissorem Dominum; et si laborat in praesenti, extenditur spe futuri, et serenatur omne nubilum tristitiae; sicut dicit apostolus: *Spe gaudentes.* Ipsum autem gaudium in tranquillitate spei nostrae, sabbatum nostrum est. Hoc commendatur, hoc can-
20 tatur in isto psalmo, quomodo sit homo christianus in sabbato cordis sui, id est, in uacatione et tranquillitate et serenitate conscientiae suae non perturbatus. Inde dicit hic, unde solent perturbari homines, et docet te agere sabbatum in corde tuo.

3. Primum est, ut tu ipse, si aliquid profecisti, Deo confitearis ex eo quod profecisti, quia munera ipsius sunt, non merita tua. Hinc incipe sabbatum, non tibi tribuendo quasi non acceperis quod accepisti, neque excusando te ab eo quod facis
5 mali, quia ipsa sunt tua. Peruersi enim homines et perturbati, qui non agunt sabbatum, mala sua Deo tribuunt, bona sua

sibi. Si quid boni fecerit, Ego feci, dicit; si quid mali fecerit, quaerit quem accuset, ne confiteatur Deo. Et quid est: Quaerit quem accuset? Si non est ualde impius, ad manum habet
10 satanam quem accuset; satanas fecit, dicit, ipse mihi persuasit, quasi satanas habeat potestatem cogendi. Astutiam suadendi habet. Sed si satanas loqueretur, et taceret Deus, haberes unde te excusares; modo aures tuae positae sunt inter monentem Deum, et suggerentem serpentem. Quare
15 huc flectuntur, hinc auertuntur? Non cessat satanas suadere malum; sed nec Deus cessat admonere bonum. Satanas autem non cogit inuitum; in tua potestate est consentire, aut non consentire. Si aliquid persuadente satana mali feceris, dimitte satanam, accusa te, ut accusatione tua Dei miseri-
20 cordiam merearis. Expetis illum accusare qui non habet ueniam? Te accusa, et accipis indulgentiam. Deinde multi non accusant satanam, sed accusant fatum. Fatum meum me duxit, dicit. Cum dixeris illi: Quare fecisti? quare peccasti? Et ille: Fato meo malo. Ne dicat: Ego feci, iam manus
25 ad Deum tendit; lingua blasphemat. Nondum quidem hoc aperte dicit, sed tamen attende, et uide quia hoc dicit. Quaeris ab illo quid sit fatum, et dicit: Stellae malae. Quaeris ab illo quis fecit Stellas, quis ordinauit Stellas; non habet quid tibi respondeat, nisi Deus. Restat ergo ut siue per trans-
30 ennam, siue per cannam longam, siue per proximum, Deum accuset; et cum Deus puniat peccata, Deum faciat auctorem peccatorum suorum. Non potest enim fieri ut puniat quod fecit: punit quod facis, ut liberet quod fecit. Aliquando autem, dimissis omnibus, omnino directe eunt in Deum; et quando
35 peccant, dicunt: Deus hoc uoluit; si nollet Deus, non peccarem. Ad hoc monet ut non solum non audiatur ut non pecces, sed accusetur quia peccas? Quid ergo nos docet psalmus iste? *Bonum est confiteri Domino.* Quid est: *confiteri Domino?* In utraque re, et in peccato tuo, quia tu fecisti, et in
40 bono facto, confitere Domino, quia ipse fecit. Tunc psalles nomini Dei altissimi: quaerens gloriam Dei, non tuam; nomen ipsius, non tuum. Si enim tu quaeris nomen Dei, quaerit et ipse nomen tuum; si autem tu neglexeris nomen Dei, delet et ipse nomen tuum. Quomodo autem dixi: Quaerit nomen tuum?
45 Quomodo dixit discipulis suis uenientibus, posteaquam misit eos euangelizare. Cum fecissent multa miracula, et in nomine Christi daemonia eiecissent, redeuntes dixerunt: *Domine, ecce daemonia nobis subiecta sunt.* Dixerunt quidem: *in nomine tuo;* sed ille uidit in eis quia ipsa glorificatione gaudebant, et
50 extollebant se, et ibant inde in superbiam, quia licuit illis expellere daemonia. Vidit illos quaerere gloriam suam, et ait

illis, quaerens ipse, imo conseruans nomina eorum apud se:
Nolite gaudere in hoc; gaudete autem quod nomina uestra scripta
sunt in caelo. Ecce ubi habes nomen, si tu nomen Dei non ne-
55 glegas. Psalle ergo nomini Dei, ut fixum sit apud Deum nomen
tuum. Psallere autem quid est, fratres? Psalterium organi
genus est; chordas habet. Opus nostrum, psalterium nostrum
est; quicumque manibus operatur opera bona, psallit Deo;
quicumque ore confitetur, cantat Deo. Cantat ore, psalle
60 operibus. Ad quam rem?

4. *Ad annuntiandum mane misericordiam tuam,*
et ueritatem tuam per noctem. Quid sibi uult quia
mane annuntianda est misericordia Dei, et per noctem
ueritas Dei? Mane dicitur, quando nobis bene est; nox dici-
5 tur, quando tristitia tribulationis est. Quid ergo dixit breuiter?
Quando tibi bene est, gaude Deo, quia misericordia ipsius est.
Iam tu forte diceres: Si ergo gaudeo Deo, quando mihi bene
est, quia misericordia ipsius est; quando in tristitia, in tribu-
latione sum, quid facio? Misericordia ipsius est, quando mihi
10 bene est; crudelitas ergo ipsius, quando male est? Si laudo
misericordiam, quando bene est; reprehendam ergo crudelitatem, quando male est? Non. Sed quando bene est, lauda
misericordiam; quando male, lauda ueritatem; quia peccata
flagellat, non est iniquus. In nocte erat Daniel, quando ora-
15 bat; erat enim in captiuitate Ierusalem, erat in potestate
hostium. Tunc multa mala sancti patiebantur; tunc ipse in
lacum leonum missus est, tunc tres pueri in ignem praecipitati
sunt. Haec patiebatur in captiuitate populus Israel: nox erat.
Per noctem confitebatur Daniel ueritatem Dei; dicebat in
20 oratione: *Peccauimus, impie egimus, iniquitatem fecimus: tibi,*
Domine, gloria, nobis confusio. Veritatem Dei annuntiabat
per noctem. Quid est ueritatem Dei annuntiare per noctem?
Non accusare Deum, quia pateris aliquid mali, sed tribuere
illud peccatis tuis, emendationi ipsius: *Ad annuntiandum*
25 *mane misericordiam ipsius, et ueritatem per no-*
ctem. Cum misericordiam annuntias mane, et ueritatem per
noctem, semper laudas Deum, semper confiteris Deo, et psal-
lis nomini eius.

5. *In decachordo psalterio, cum cantico in cithara.*
Decachordum psalterium non modo audistis. Decachordum
psalterium significat decem praecepta legis. Sed cantare
in illo opus est, non portare psalterium. Nam et Iudaei habent
5 legem; portant, non psallunt. Qui sunt qui psallunt? Qui
operantur. Parum est: qui operantur cum tristitia, nondum
psallunt. Qui sunt qui psallunt? Qui cum hilaritate faciunt
bene. In psallendo enim hilaritas est. Et quid dicit apostolus?

Hilarem enim datorem diligit Deus. Quidquid facis, cum hilari-
10 tate fac: bonum tunc et bene facis. Si autem cum tristitia facis, fit de te, non facis; et portas magis psalterium, non cantas.
In psalterio decachordo, cum cantico in cithara,
hoc est, uerbo et opere. *Cum cantico,* uerbo; *in cithara,*
opere. Si uerba sola dicis, quasi canticum solum habes, ci-
15 tharam non habes; si operaris, et non loqueris, quasi solam
citharam habes. Propter hoc et loquere bene, et fac bene, si
uis habere canticum cum cithara.

6. *Quia iucundasti me, Domine, in factura tua,*
et in operibus manuum tuarum exsultabo. Videtis
quid dicat. Tu me fecisti bene uiuentem, tu me formasti;
si quid forte boni facio, in factura manuum tuarum exsulta-
5 bo; quomodo dicit apostolus: *Ipsius enim sumus figmentum,*
creati in operibus bonis. Nisi enim te formaret ad opera bona,
non nosses nisi opera tua mala. *Qui* enim *loquitur mendacium,*
de suo loquitur: hoc euangelium dicit. Omne peccatum mendacium est. Contra legem enim et contra ueritatem quidquid
10 est, mendacium dicitur. Ergo quid ait? *Qui loquitur menda-*
cium, de suo loquitur, id est, qui peccat, de suo peccat. Attendite sententiam contra. Si enim qui loquitur mendacium, de
suo loquitur; restat ut qui loquitur ueritatem, de Dei loquatur. Ideo dicitur in alio loco: *Deus solus uerax; omnis autem*
15 *homo mendax.* Non tibi dicitur in hac sententia: Vade, securus
mentire, quia homo es; imo uide te hominem, quia mendax
es; et ut sis uerax, bibe ueritatem, ut de Deo ructes, ut sis
uerax. Quia de tuo illam non potes habere, restat ut inde
illam bibas, unde fluit. Quomodo si a luce recesseris, in tene-
20 bris es; quomodo lapis non de se feruet, sed uel a sole uel ab
igne, si eum calori subtraxeris, frigescit; ibi apparet, quia
quod feruebat, non erat ipsius; sed feruebat uel a sole uel ab
igne; sic et tu si a Deo recesseris, frigesces; si ad Deum accesseris, feruesces; sicut dicit apostolus: *Spiritu feruentes.*
25 Item de luce quid dicit? Si ad eum accesseris, in lumine eris;

READING 1-G

VENANTIVS FORTVNATVS

[535–600 CE]

MISCELLANEA

CAPUT IV.

De basilica sancti Martini.

[Basilicam in honorem sancti Martini a Fausto episcopo erectam, et celebrem religione, hoc carmine illustrat]

Emicat aula decens, venerando in culmine ducta,
Nomine Martini sanctificata Deo.
Cui vitae merito fiducia tanta coruscat,
Ut populís tribuat quod pia vota rogant.
Extulit hanc Faustus devoto corde sacerdos;
Reddidit et Domino prospera dona suo.

CAPUT XV.

Ad eumdem.

Pastor opime gregis, cunctis tua pabula prosunt
Qui satias animas, quam bene membra foves?
Sic avidos reddis convivas nectare lactis,
Ut scutella levet, quod cocleare solet.

CAPUT XVI.

Ad eumdem.

Currit ovis, repetens a te sua pascua, pastor,
Qui cibus esse soles, da mihi panis opem.

CAPUT XVII.

De pictura vitis, in mensa ejus dictum.

[Occasione cujusdam picturæ, in qua ales rostro carpebat uvas, Villici liberalitatem in convivas extollit.]

Vitibus intextis ales sub palmite vernat,
Et leviter pictas carpit ab ore dapes.
Multiplices epulas meruit conviva tenere,
Aspicit hinc uvas, inde falerna bibit.

CAPUT XXXV.

Ad Joannem Diaconum.

[Iter facturus Fortunatus hoc poema, perpetuæ pignus amicitiae, reliquit Joanni Diacono, ac per eum communibus amicis salutem scribit.]

Pignus amicitiae semper memorabile nostrae.
Versibus exiguis, chare Joannes, habe.
Ut cum me rapiunt loca nunc incognita forsan,
Non animo videar dulcis abesse tuo.
Anthemium patrem per te, venerande, saluto,
Cujus in affectu consolidatus agor.
Hilarium pariter nobis in amore tenacem
Insero carminibus, quem mea corda colunt.
Perpetuo maneas meritis felicíbus ævo;
Hæc quoque cum relegis, me memorare velis.

CAPUT XXVI.

Ad eumdem.

[Poetam quemdam a seriis curis ad convívii festivitatem, invitat ita tamen, ut, miscens jocos, honestas item tueatur.]

Quamvis doctiloquax te seria cura fatiget,
Huc veniens festos misce, poeta, jocos.
Sic tamen, ut propriam rationem servet honestas,
Nam solet incautus sermo movere manus.

CAPUT XXVII.

De brevitate vitæ.

[Ex vitæ brevitate et infirmate virtutes animi ac cœlestes delicias commendat.]

Vita brevis hominum, fugiunt præsentia rerum,
Tu cole quae potius non moritura manent.
Erige justitiam, cole pacem, dilige Christum.
Expete delicias, quas sine fine geras.

CAPUT XXVIII.

Ad eumdem.

[A strepitu ac negotiis forensibus ad convivii jucunditatem ac securitatem invitat.]

Pelle Palatinas post multa negotia rixas,
Vivere jucunde mensa benigna monet.
Causae, iræ, strepitus sileant, fora, jurgia, leges,
Hic placeat requies, quam dat amica dies.

CAPUT XIII.

Pro castaneis.

[Vimineam fiscellam, sui ipsius manibus textam, una cum castaneis, ad Agnetem et Radegundem dono mittit Fortunatus.]

Ista meis manibus fiscella est vimine texta,
Credite mi, charæ mater et alma soror.
Et quæ rura ferunt, haec rustica dona ministro,
Castaneas molles, quas dedit arbor agris.

CAPUT XIV.

De calice Leontii episcopi.

[Calicem a Leontio et Placidina ædi sacræ oblatum commemorat.]

Summus in arce Dei pia dona Leontius offert,
Votis juncta sacris, et Placidina simul.
Felices, quorum labor est altaribus aptus,
Tempore qui parvo non peritura ferunt.

CAPUT XXI.

Ad Hilarium episcopum.

[Salutatorias ad Hilarium episcopum litteras mittit, suamque in absentem memoriam et benevolentiam declarant.]

Lux sincera animi, mihi semper dulcis Hilari,
Quamvis absentem quem mea cura videt.
Cujus honestus amor tantum mea corda replevit,
Ut sine te nunquam mente vacante loquar.
Versibus exiguis mandamus vota salutis;
Quæ dedit affectus, sint tibi chara [grata], precor.

CAPUT XXXIV.

Ad archidiaconum Meldensem.

[Archidiacono Meldensi, qui ad se, nondum de facie notum, mustum dono miserat, gratias agit hoc carmine.]

Si mihi vel vestros licuisset cernere vultus,
Munere pro tanto plurima verba darem.
Direxit nobis mustum tua chara voluntas,
Et dulces animos dulcia dona probant.
Quem non vidisti, promptus satiare parasti:
Quid facias illi, qui tibi notus adest?
Det tibi larga Deus, qui curam mente fideli,
De grege pontificis, magne minister, habes.

CAPUT XIII

Ad eumdem pro commendatione mulieris.

[Gregorii virtutem laudat, ac mulierem, quam a Gregorio commendatam acceperat, ad illum revertentem pariter commendat.]

Summe Pater patriæ, specimen pietatis opime,
Dulce caput Turonis, religionis apex.
Jugiter alta sequens, clementi corde Gregori,
Unde animæ decus est, huc ratione petens.
Quam commendasti venientem, celse sacerdos,
Hanc redeuntem ad te, suscipe more patris.
Sis quoque longævus cunctorum care recursus,
Et mihi vel reliquis sit tua vita seges.

CAPUT XX.

Pro ovis et prunis.

[Acceptis ab Agnete et Radegunde prunis et ovis, agit gratias, et earum jussis se narrat paruisse; quae, ut bina ova sumeret ad vesperam, praescripserant.]

Hinc me deliciis, illinc me pascitis herbis,
Hinc ova occurrunt, hinc mihi pruna datur.
Candida dona simul præbentur et inde nigella,
Ventri utinam pax sit, sic variante cibo.
Me geminis ovis jussistis sero cibari,
Vobis vera loquor, quatuor ipse bibi.
Atque utinam merear cunctis parere diebus:
Sic animo ceu nunc hoc gula jussa facit.

CAPUT XXII.

De convivio.

[Radegundem adjurat, ut in convivio aliquid et ipsa cibi sumeret]

Per pietatis opus, per qui pius imperat astris,
Per quod mater amat, frater et ipse cupit:
Ut, dum nos escam capimus, quodcunque ciberis,
Quod si tu facias, bis satiabor ego.

CAPUT XXI.

De absentia sua.

[Pluvio cœlo impeditum se fuisse narrat, quominus ad Agnetem et Radegundem veniret, ne unam quibus horam caeteroquin abfuturus.]

Si me non nimium pluviatilis aura vetaret,
Dum nesciretis, vos repetisset amans.
Nec volo nunc absens una detenter ut hora,
Cum mea tunc lux est, quando videtur amans.

CAPUT XXV.

Ad convivam

[Conviviam, ad domesticas, ac vulgares epulas invitatum, amore laute exceptum fuisse ostendit.]

Qui venis ad charos conviva fidelis amicos,
Quod minus est epulis, plus in amore capis.
Non haec per pelagus peregrinus detulit hospes,
Sume libens patrii quod genuere lares.

READING 1-H

BERNARDVS CLARAVALLENSIS

[1090–1153 CE]

SENTENTIAE

SERIES PRIMA

1. TRES SUNT QUI TESTIMONIUM DANT IN CAELO: PATER ET FILIUS ET SPIRITUS SANCTUS. Tres in terra: spiritus, aqua et sanguis. Similiter tres in inferno; in Isaia legimus: VERMIS EORUM NON MORIETUR, ET IGNIS EORUM NON EXSTINGUETUR. Duo mala sunt vermis et ignis: altero roditur conscientia, altero concremantur corpora. Tertium additur desperatio, quae in eo utique intelligitur quod dicitur: NON MORIETUR, ET NON EXSTINGUETUR. His qui in caelo sunt, datur testimonium beatitudinis; his qui in terra, iustificationis; his qui in inferno sunt, damnationis. Primum testimonium est gloriae, secundum gratiae, tertium irae.

2. De Spiritu Sancto testatur Scriptura, quia procedit, spirat, inhabitat, replet, glorificat. Procedere dicitur duobus modis: unde, et quo. Unde? A Patre et Filio. Quo? Ad creaturam. Procedendo praedestinat; spirando vocat quos praedestinavit; inhabitando iustificat quos vocavit; replendo accumulat meritis, quos iustificavit; glorificando ditat praemiis, quos accumulavit meritis.

3. Spiritus Sanctus arguit mundum de peccato quod dissimulat; de iustitia quam non ordinat, dum sibi non Deo eam dat; de iudicio quod usurpat, dum, tam de se quam de aliis, temere iudicat.

4. Usque hodie in civibus Babylonis aquarum effusio, id est confusio cogitationum, terram facit inanem et vacuam. Dum enim fluitat circa carnem cogitatio universa, nullum ex ea sperare est fructum salutis. Dividantur ergo aquae ab aquis, quatenus anima quoque, ut dignum est, partem sibi vindicet sollicitudinis et meditationis. Sane inferiores certis limitibus coerceantur, certis contineantur alveis, ut necessitatis terminos non excedant, ut proinde superiores copiosius dilatentur. Ex hoc sane dat Dominus benedictionem, ET TERRA NOSTRA DABIT FRUCTUM SUUM.

5. Cum in populo Dei carnales alii sint et alii spirituales: nec illi tamen aeternorum, nec isti carent omnimodis temporalium desiderio. In eo sane distant, quod plus alia appetunt alii, et secundum ea quae praeferunt, aut spirituales, aut carnales iudicantur. Hinc est quod in benedictionibus Iacob et Esau, et ros caeli, et terrae pinguedo nominatur, sed non eodem ordine in utroque. DET TIBI DEUS DE RORE CAELI ET DE PINGUEDINE TERRAE ABUNDANTIAM, ait Isaac ad Iacob. Ad Esau

vero: IN PINGUEDINE TERRAE, inquit, ET IN RORE CAELI DESUPER ERIT BENEDICTIO TUA. Quid autem singuli praeferant, a studiis eorum et sollicitudinibus innotescat.

7. DE STERCORE BOUM LAPIDATUS EST PIGER. Boves sunt qui in opere Dei strenue exercentur, qui seminant in lacrimis, sed in gaudio metent. Isti sane quaecumque sunt huius mundi, arbitrantur ut stercora. Piger vero, cuius sabbata videntes hostes derident, dehonestatur ab hostibus in otio suo, sicut boves strenui in laboribus suis honestantur a Deo. Quem enim maligni spiritus pigrum vident ad spiritualia exercitia, in cogitationibus eius ingerunt importune terrena, velut de stercoribus boum massas coagulantes, et pigrum, sicut dignus est, lapidantes.

8. OSCULETUR ME OSCULO ORIS SUI. Tria sunt oscula, reconciliatorium, remuneratorium, contemplatorium. Primum ad pedes, secundum ad manum, tertium ad os sumitur. In primo accipitur remissio peccatorum, in secundo manus virtutum, in tertio cognitio secretorum. Vel ita: osculum doctrinae, naturae, gratiae.

10. REVERTERE, REVERTERE SUNAMITIS, REVERTERE, REVERTERE, UT INTUEAMUR TE. Revertere primo ab inepta laetitia, revertere secundo ab inutili tristitia, revertere tertio ab inani gloria, quarto revertere a latenti superbia. Inanis gloria est, quae ab ore hominum venit extrinsecus. Superbia latens oritur intrinsecus. Cum haec omnia vitia reliquerit anima, intuebitur eam sponsus eius. Ob hoc autem debet ab illis abstinere, ut digna fiat eius conspectibus. Unde et ad cam dicitur: REVERTERE, REVERTERE, UT INTUEAMUR TE.

11. Pastorum est vigilare super gregem ad tria necessaria: ad disciplinam, ad custodiam, ad preces. Ad disciplinam, propter morum corruptionem, ne grex commissus propria molestia deficiat. Ad custodiam, propter diabolicam suggestionem, ne hostili seducatur calliditate. Ad preces, propter tentationum instantiam, ne vincatur a pusillanimitate. In disciplina rigor iustitiae, in custodia spiritus consilii, in prece affectus compassionis.

12. Duas ad intelligendum se condidit universitatis Auctor creaturas, hominem et angelum. Hominem iustificant fides et memoria, angelum beatificant intellectus et praesentia. Et quia homines quandoque perducendi sunt ad aequalitatem angelorum, necesse est ut interim iustificentur per fidem, et per fidem proficiant ad intellectum. Scriptum est enim: NISI CREDIDERITIS, NON INTELLIGETIS. Itaque fides via est ad intellectum; nam fide mundatur cor, ut intellectus videat Deum. Similiter et memoria Dei, via est ad praesentiam Dei. Qui enim hic habet mandatorum eius, ut ea faciat, memoriam; hic merebitur quandoque ut eius quoque videat praesentiam. Habeant igitur intellectum et praesentiam angeli Dei in caelo; habeamus et nos eius fidem et memoriam in mundo.

13. Pars tua sumus Domine, quam tulisti de manu Amorrhaei in

gladio et arcu tuo. Gladius tuus sermo vivus et efficax, arcus tuus incarnatio tua. Ibi enim, velut curvato sapientiae ligno et pio quodam modo flexa divinitate, nervus carnis vehementer extentus et humanitas ineffabiliter aucta cognoscitur. Pars ergo tua sumus et populus acquisitionis tuae, quem acquisisti verbo praedicationis, et mysterio incarnationis.

14. In circumcisione nec nervus rumpitur, nec os comminuitur, ut robustiora quaeque et firmiora serventur illaesa. Aperitur autem cutis, amputatur caro, sanguis effunditur, ut illecebrosa mollities castigetur. In carne quidem peccatum, quod in ea manet, intellige, porro in cute operimentum eius, in sanguine vero incentivum. Haec igitur vera est circumcisio spiritu, non littera, si velamen excusationis et dissimulationis per compunctionem cordis, et confessionem oris amoveas; si peccati consuetudinem correctione conversationis abscidas; si denique, ut necessarium est, occasiones quoque peccati et fomitem fugias concupiscentiarum.

15. Obtulerunt ei munera aurum, thus, et myrrham. Haec fortassis pro loco et tempore necessaria videbantur. Auri pretium ob paupertatem; myrrhae unguentum ob infantilis, ut assolet, corporis teneritudinem; thuris odoramentum ob sordidam stabuli mansionem. Nos vero, quoniam ilia iam omnia transierunt, offeramus ei acceptabiliora munera: myrrhae unctionem in communione socialis vitae, thuris speciem in suaveolentia bonae famae, auri splendorem in conscientiae puritate, quo videlicet nec de officiosa conversatione familiarem gratiam, nec de laudabili opinione inanem gloriam, sed honorem Dei, et fratrum utilitatem quaerere studeamus.

16. Ante omnia ut sine murmuratione sint fratres. Forte aliqui leve peccatum aestimant murmurare; sed non hic, qui ante omnia monet esse cavendum. Puto autem ne illum quidem leve reputasse, qui murmurantibus aiebat: Non contra nos est murmur vestrum, sed contra Dominum. Nos enim quod sumus? Sed ne eum quoque qui dixit: Neque murmuraveritis, sicut quidam murmuraverunt, et perierunt ab exterminatore. Illo nimirum exterminatore, qui positus est in hoc ipsum, ut a terminis beatae illius civitatis arceat murmurantes, et longe faciat a finibus eius, cui dicitur: Lauda Ierusalem Dominum, lauda Deum tuum Sion, qui posuit fines tuos pacem. Nihil enim commune habent murmur et pax, gratiarum actio et detractio, zelus amaritudinis et vox laudis. Itaque in ore trium et talium testium stet hoc verbum, ut pestem istam murmurationis summopere nobis noverimus esse cavendam.

17. Tres sunt quibus reconciliari debemus, homines, angeli, Deus. Hominibus per aperta opera, angelis per occulta signa, Deo per puritatem cordis.[2] Nam de operibus quae coram hominibus facienda sunt, scriptum est: Luceat lux vestra coram hominibus, ut videant opera vestra bona, et glorificent Patrem vestrum qui in caelis est. De angelis dicit David: In conspectu angelorum

PSALLAM TIBI. Occulta autem signa sunt gemitus, suspiria, usus cilicii, et cetera paenitentiae insignia, quae angelis placent. Unde est illud: GAUDIUM EST ANGELIS DEI SUPER UNO PECCATORE PAENITENTIAM AGENTE. Ut autem Deo reconciliemur, nec operibus, nec signis, sed puritate et simplicitate cordis indigemus. Scriptum est enim: BEATI MUNDO CORDE, QUONIAM IPSI DEUM VIDEBUNT. Et illud: SI OCULUS TUUS FUERIT SIMPLEX, TOTUM CORPUS TUUM LUCIDUM ERIT.

18. TEMPLUM DEI SANCTUM EST, QUOD ESTIS VOS. Templum Dei est claustrum religiosorum. Duo parietes claustri sunt, activi et contemplativi, Maria et Martha, interior et exterior. Interiori necessarii sunt duo ordines lapidum, cavere scilicet vitium voluptatis et curiositatis. Exteriori similiter duo, ne sint fraudulenti, aut turbulenti. Unde Dominus: FIDELIS SERVUS ET PRUDENS. Fidelis, ne sit fraudulentus; prudens, ne sit turbulentus. Paries ex adverso qui hinc inde utrumque coniungit, sunt praelati, et hi qui fideliter ingrediuntur et egrediuntur, sicut de Domino dictum est: A SUMMO CAELO EGRESSIO EIUS, ET OCCURSUS EIUS USQUE AD SUMMUM EIUS, NEC EST QUI SE ABSCONDAT A CALORE EIUS.

19. Quinque de causis addiscit homo, ut sciat, ut sciatur scire, ut vendat, ut aedificet, ut aedificetur. Ut sciat, curiositas est; ut sciatur scire, vanitas; ut vendat, simonia; ut aedificet, caritas; ut aedificetur, humilitas.

19B. QUI NUTRITI ERANT IN CROCEIS, id est deliciis spiritualibus, AMPLEXANTUR STERCORA, id est curam ventris.

20. INITIUM SAPIENTIAE TIMOR DOMINI. Timor primus revocat euntes ad mortem, cui succedit tristitia saecularis; hanc excludit spes aeternitatis. Haec duo, apprehendentes filium prodigum positum super equum desiderii, deducunt per campos fiduciae. Insequitur eos abeuntes Astutia, suadens aut praecipitium aut iter devium. Mundus enim in maligno positus est. Spes praecedit equum; Timor subsequitur. Mittitur Prudentia ut temperet Timorem. Sed minutio timoris est augmentum spei et immoderate post se trahit equum desiderii. Sed, ne incurrant praecipitium aut iter devium, mittitur Temperantia ut equo frenum imponat. Itaque isti quattuor caute deducentes filium regis perveniunt ad quoddam castellum cui nomen est iustitia, ubi et hospitantur. Quod videntes inimici, videlicet eos esse inclusos, obsident arcem.

READING 1-I

LATINARVM COMPAGES SENTENTIARVM

formation of Latin sentences

[200 BCE–2001 CE]

agnos exemit exinde suos[que] redemit,
nos miseros vero simil pietate supremo
patri placavit, miserando reconciliavit.

OTHLOH EMMERAM [1010–1072 CE]

Post longum tempus epistulas tuas sed tres pariter recepi, omnes elegantissimas amantissimas, [et] quales a te venire praesertim desideratas oportebat.

CAIVS PLINIVS SECVNDVS [61–113 CE]

Deus, (qui beátum Dionýsium eiús[que] sócios
ad prædicándam géntibus glóriam tuam misísti
eós[que] virtúte constántiæ in passióne roborásti)
tríbue nobis, quæsumus,
ex eórum imitatióne próspera mundi despícere,
et nulla eius advérsa formidáre.

MISSALE ROMANVM PAVLI VI [1975 CE]

KEY:

Subjects

Objects

Verbs

Distant connections

[Larger clauses]

(Lesser clauses)

[et] and -[que]

saluto te, (uicine Apollo), (qui aedibus
propinquos nostris accolis,) venero[que] te
[ne Nicobulum me sinas nostrum senem
priu' conuenire quam sodalem uiderim
Mnesilochi Pistoclerum,] (quém ad epistulam
Mnesilochus misit super amica Bacchide.)

TITVS MACCVS PLAVTVS [254–184 BCE]

Discant igitur hanc vocem omnes Ecclesiae filii magno pretio redempti, gratis iustificati [et] [cum adversitas violentae alicuius tentationis incuberit] praesidio potentissimae orationis utantur, [ut superato tremore formidinis accipiant tolerantiam passionis.]

PONTIFEX LEO MAGNVS [440–461 CE]

nunc te uocales impellere pollice chordas,
  nunc precor ad laudes, flectere uerba meas.
ipse triumphali deuinctus tempora lauro,
  (dum cumulant aras) ad tua sacra ueni.
sed nitidus pulcherque ueni: nunc indue uestem
  sepositam, longas nunc bene pecte comas.
(Phoebe,) sacras Messalinum sine tangere chartas
  uatis, et ipse precor (quid canat illa) doce.
haec dedit Aeneae sortes, [postquam ille parentem
  dicitur et raptos sustinuisse Lares.]
nec fore credebat Romam, [cum maestus ab alto
  Ilion ardentes respiceretque deos.]

ALBIVS TIBVLLVS [60–19 BCE]

Cetera item omnia a sacris canonibus et oecumenicis conciliis ac praecipue a sacrosancta Tridentina synodo tradita, definita ac declarata indubitanter recipio atque profiteor;

CONCILIUM OECUMENICUM VATICANUM I [1869–1870 CE]

Navigia atque agri culturas moenia leges
arma vias vestis <et> cetera de genere horum,
praemia, delicias quoque vitae funditus omnis,
carmina picturas, et daedala signa polire,
usus et impigrae simul experientia mentis,
paulatim docuit pedetemptim progredientis.

TITVS LVCRETIVS CARVS [99–55 BCE]

KEY: Subjects are underlined with a solid line.
Objects are underlined with a broken line.
Verbs are underlined with a line of dots.
Distant connections of words and phrases are underlined with a wavey line.
[Larger clauses are in square brackets,] (lesser ones in rounded parentheses.)
The words et and -que are placed in boxes.
Note: This code is used to illustrate the functions and connections of words as an aid to teaching, and is not intended to appear in absolutely every instance.

READING 1-K

CONCILIVM OECVMENICVM CONSTANTIENSE

[1414–1418 CE]

[Sententia condemnatoria articulorum Ioannis Wicleff]

1. Substantia panis materialis, et similiter substantia vini materialis, manent in sacramento altaris.

2. Accidentia panis non manent sine subiecto in eodem sacramento.

3. Christus non est in eodem sacramento identice et realiter in propria persona corporali.

4. Si episcopus vel sacerdos est in peccato mortali, non ordinat, non conficit, non consecrat, nec baptizat.

5. Non est fondatum in evangelio, quod Christus missam ordinarit.

6. Deus debet obedire diabolo.

7. Si homo debite fuerit contritus, omnis confessio exterior est sibi superflua et inutilis.

8. Si papa sit praescitus et malus, et per consequens membrum diaboli, non habet potestatem super fideles ab aliquo sibi datam, nisi forte a Caesare.

9. Post Urbanum VI non est aliquis recipiendus in papam, sed vivendum est more Graecorum sub legibus propriis.

10. Contra scripturam sacram est, quod viri ecclesiastici habeant possessiones.

11. Nullus praelatus debet aliquem excommunicare, nisi prius sciat, eum esse excommunicatum a Deo: et qui sic excommunicat, fit haereticus ex hoc, vel excommunicatus.

12. Praelatus excommunicans clericum, qui appellavit ad regem vel ad concilium regni, eo ipso traditor est regis et regni.

13. Illi qui dimittunt praedicare, sive verbum Dei audire propter excommunicationem hominum, sunt excommunicati, et in die iudicii traditores Christi habebuntur.

14. Licet alicui diacono vel presbytero praedicare verbum Dei, absque auctoritate sedis apostolicae vel episcopi catholici.

15. Nullus est dominus civilis, nullus est praelatus, nullus est episcopus, dum est in peccato mortali.

16. Domini temporales possunt ad arbitrium suum auferre bona temporalia ab ecclesia possessionatis habitualiter delinquentibus, id est ex habitu, non solo actu, delinquentibus.

17. Populares possunt ad suum arbitrium dominos delinquentes corrigere.

18. Decimae sunt purae eleemosynae, et parochiani possunt propter peccata suorum praelatorum ad libitum suum eas auferre.

19. Speciales orationes applicatae uni personae per praelatos, vel religiosos, non plus prosunt eidem quam generales, caeteris paribus.

20. Conferens eleemosynam fratribus, est excommunicatus eo facto.

21. Si quis ingreditur religionem privatam qualemcumque, tam possessionatorum, quam mendicantium, redditur ineptior et inhabilior ad observantiam mandatorum Dei.

22. Sancti instituentes religiones privatas, sic instituendo peccaverunt.

23. Religiosi viventes in religionibus privatis, non sunt de religione christiana.

24. Fratres tenentur per labores manuum victum acquirere, et non per mendicitatem.

25. Omnes sunt simoniaci, qui se obligant orare pro aliis, eis in temporalibus subvenientibus.

26. Oratio praesciti nulli valet.

27. Omnia de necessitate absoluta eveniunt.

28. Confirmatio iuvenum, clericorum ordinatio, locorum consecratio, reservantur papae et episcopis propter cupiditatem lucri temporalis et honoris.

29. Universitates, studia, collegia, graduationes, et magisteria in eisdem, sunt vana gentilitate introducta, et tantum prosunt ecclesiae sicut diabolus.

30. Excommunicatio papae vel cuiuscumque praelati non est timenda, quia est censura antichristi.

31. Peccant fundantes claustra, et ingredientes sunt viri diabolici.

32. Ditare clerum, est contra Christi mandatum.

33. Silvester papa et Constantinus imperator erraverunt ecclesiam dotando.

34. Omnes de ordine mendicantium sunt haeretici, et dantes eis eleemosynam sunt excommunicati.

35. Ingredientes religionem aut aliquem ordinem, eo ipso inhabiles sunt ad observandum divina praecepta, et per consequens perveniendi ad regna caelorum, nisi apostataverint ab eisdem.

36. Papa cum omnibus clericis suis possessionem habentibus sunt haeretici, eo quod possessionem habent, et omnes consentientes eis, omnes scilicet domini saeculares, et caeteri laici.

37. Ecclesia Romana est synagoga satanae nec papa est immediatus et proximus vicarius Christi et apostolorum.

38. Decretales epistolae sunt apocryphae, et seducunt a Christi fide: et clerici sunt stulti qui student eas.

39. Imperator et domini saeculares seducti sunt a diabolo, ut ecclesiam dotarent de bonis temporalibus.

40. Electio papae a cardinalibus per diabolum est introducta.

41. Non est de necessitate salutis credere Romanam ecclesiam esse supremam inter alias ecclesias.

42. Fatuum est credere indulgentiis papae et episcoporum.

43. Iuramenta illicita sunt, quae fiunt ad roborandum humanos contractus et commercia civilia.

44. Augustinus, Benedictus, Bernardus damnati sunt, nisi poenituerint de hoc, quod habuerunt possessiones, et instituerunt, et intraverunt religiones: et sic a papa usque ad infimum religiosum omnes sunt haeretici.

45. Omnes religiones indifferenter introductae sunt a diabolo.

[**Articuli damnati I. Huss**]

1. Unica est sancta universalis ecclesia, quae est praedestinatorum universitas. Et infra sequitur: universalis sancta ecclesia tantum est una, sicut tantum unus est numerus omnium praedestinatorum.

2. Paulus numquam fuit membrum diaboli, licet fecerit quosdam actus actibus ecclesiae malignantium consimiles.

3. Praesciti non sunt partes ecclesiae, cum nulla pars eius ab ea finaliter excidat, eo quod praedestinationis charitas, quae ipsam ligat, non excidit.

4. Duae naturae, divinitas et humanitas, sunt unus Christus.

5. Praescitus etsi aliquis sit in gratia secundum praesentem iustitiam tamen numquam est pars sanctae ecclesiae: et praedestinatus semper manet membrum ecclesiae, licet aliquando excidat a gratia adventitia, sed non a gratia praedestinationis.

6. Sumendo ecclesiam pro convocatione praedestinatorum, sive sit in gratia, sive non secundum praesentem iustitiam, isto modo ecclesia est articulus fidei.

7. Petrus non fuit nec est caput sanctae ecclesiae catholicae.

8. Sacerdotes quomodolibet criminose viventes, sacerdotii polluunt potestatem et sicut filii infideles sentiunt infideliter de septem sacramentis ecclesiae, de clavibus, officiis, censuris, moribus, caeremoniis, et sacris rebus ecclesiae, veneratione reliquiarum, indulgentiis, et ordinibus.

9. Papalis dignitas a Caesare inolevit, et papae praefectio et institutio a Caesaris potentia emanavit.

10. Nullus sine revelatione assereret rationabiliter de se, vel de alio, quod esset caput ecclesiae particularis sanctae: nec Romanus pontifex est caput Romanae ecclesiae.

11. Non oportet credere, quod iste quicumque particularis Romanus pontifex, sit caput cuiuscumque particularis ecclesiae sanctae, nisi Deus eum praedestinaverit.

12. Nemo gerit vicem Christi, vel Petri, nisi sequatur eum in moribus; cum nulla alia sequela sit pertinentior, nec aliter recipiat a Deo procuratoriam potestatem: quia ad illud officium vicarii requiritur et morum conformitas, et instituentis auctoritas.

13. Papa non est manifestus et verus successor principis apostolorum, Petri, si vivit moribus contrariis Petro: et si quaerit avaritiam, tunc est vicarius Iudae Iscarioth. Et pari evidentia cardinales non sunt manifesti et veri successores collegii aliorum apostolorum Christi, nisi vixerint more apostolorum, servantes mandata et consilia domini nostri Iesu Christi.

14. Doctores ponentes quod aliquis per censuram ecclesiasticam emendandus, si corrigi noluerit, saeculari iudicio est tradendus, pro certo sequuntur in hoc pontifices, scribas et phariseos, qui Christum nolentem eis oboedire in omnibus, dicentes, *Nobis non licet interficere quemquam,* ipsum saeculari iudicio tradiderunt, eo quod tales sunt homicidae graviores quam Pilatus.

15. Oboedientia ecclesiastica est oboedientia secundum adinventionem sacerdotum ecclesiae, praeter expressam auctoritatem scripturae.

16. Divisio immediata humanorum operum est, quod sint vel virtuosa, vel vitiosa: quia si homo est vitiosus, et agit quicquam, tunc agit vitiose; et si est virtuosus, et agit quicquam, tunc agit virtuose. Quia sicut vitium, quod crimen dicitur, sive mortale peccatum, inficit universaliter actus hominis vitiosi, sic virtus vivificat omnes actus hominis virtuosi.

17. Sacerdos Christi vivens secundum legem eius, et habens scripturae notitiam, et affectum ad aedificandum populum, debet praedicare, non obstante praetensa excommunicatione. Et infra: quod si papa vel aliquis praepositus mandet sacerdoti sic disposito non praedicare, non debet subditus oboedire.

18. Quilibet praedicantis officium de mandato accipit, qui ad sacerdotium accedit: et illud mandatum debet exsequi, praetensa excommunicatione non obstante.

19. Per censuras ecclesiasticas excommunicationis, suspensionis et interdicti, ad suam exaltationem clerus populum laicalem sibi suppeditat, avaritiam multiplicat, malitiam protegit, et viam praeparat antichristo. Signum autem evidens est, quod ab antichristo tales procedant censurae, quas vocant in suis processibus fulminationes, quibus clerus principalissime procedit contra illos qui denudant nequitiam antichristi, quam clerus pro se maxime usurpavit.

20. Si papa est malus, et praesertim si est praescitus, tunc ut Iudas apostolus est diabolus, fur et filius perditionis[1], et non est caput sanctae militantis ecclesiae cum nec sit membrum eius.

21. Gratia praedestinationis est vinculum, quo corpus ecclesiae et quodlibet eius membrum iungitur ipso capiti insolubiliter.

22. Papa, vel praelatus malus et praescitus, est aequivoce pastor, et vere fur et latro.

23. Papa non debet dici sanctissimus etiam secundum officium, quia alias rex etiam deberet dici sanctissimus secundum officium, et tortores et praecones dicerentur sancti: immo etiam diabolus deberet vocari sanctus, cum sit officiarius Dei.

24. Si papa vivit contrarie Christo, etiamsi ascenderet per ritam et legitimam electionem secundum constitutionem humanam vulgatam, tamen aliunde ascenderet, quam per Christum, dato etiam quod intraret per electionem a Deo principaliter factam. Nam Iudas Iscarioth rite et legitime est electus a Deo Iesu Christo ad apostolatum, et tamen *ascendit aliunde in ovile ovium.*

25. Condemnatio quadragintaquinque articulorum Ioannis Wicleff per doctores facta est irrationabilis et iniqua, et male facta, et ficta est causa per eos allegata, videlicet quod[b] nullus ex eis sit catholicus, sed quilibet eorum aut est haereticus, aut erroneus, aut scandalosus.

DESIDERIVS ERASMVS ROTERODAMVS

[1466–1536 CE]

EPISTOLAE

EPISTOLA XXII.

Erasmus Batto suo S. D.

VIDE quantum maledicendo valeas. Unica tantum epistola victus, do manus, arena cedo, in *Angliam* usque profugio: hic certe me à tuis conviciis tutum fore confido. Nam si me persequi voles, alter tibi adeundus erit orbis: & pigritiam probe novi tuam, qui tametsi mediis in fluctibus es natus, nihil tamen pejus odisti fluctibus. Quod si huc quoque tuæ conviciatrices epistolæ penetrabunt, audio in ultima *Britannia Orchadas* esse insulas; in has aufugiam, etiamsi quid est *Orchadibus* remotius, vel ad *Antipodas* usque. I nunc, & de gloriosa victoria magnificum triumphum agito. Bene vale. *Parisiis*, Anno 1497.

EPISTOLA L.

Erasmus cuidam.

VBI nostrum *N.* isthuc iturum intellexissem, nolui inanem venire, præsertim qui me obnixe rogaret, ut sese apud te commendatum facerem. Obsecro itaque, ut eum pro tua veteri consuetudine tractes. Non clam me est, nec ille quidem ignorat, quantum possis, quantumque mea causa velis. Effice ne vel illum sua spes, vel me mea de te opinio fallat. *N.* quidem tibi novum amicum comparaveris, me vero arctius devinxeris. Vale.

EPISTOLA LXVII.

Erasmus Fausto suo S. D.

QVAE, malum, tu mihi objicis ænigmata? Num me *Oedipum* putas, aut *Sphingem* mihi esse domi? Quanquam equidem somnio tuas muscas, aviculas, formicas, cuniculos velle. Verum alias jocabimur, nunc cœna emenda est, quare ænigmatistes esse desinas oportet. Vale.

Epistola LXXXIX.

Erasmus Rot. Antonio Lutzenburgo S. D.

Accepi ſimul & Abbatis munus, & à *Batto* miſſam pecuniolam: qua de re ſi nunc parum accurate gratias ago, ne putes id inde eſſe, quod parum hoc munere ſim lætus, ſed erat negotii quiddam, & valetudo admodum agitata. Cæterum quantum & te, & Abbatem, de hoc dono pro meis meritis, quæ nulla ſunt, deamem, brevi declarabo. Valebis, & tui ſimilis, mi *Antoni*, eſſe perges. Anno 1499.

Epistola XC.

Erasmus Rot. Petro Notho S. D.

Quod tam officioſe res noſtras curas, *Petre* humaniſſime, deamo te, & gratiam habeo plurimam. Jam pridem iſthic me videres, niſi Abbas *Bertinicus*, jamjam abeuntem, jam accinctum remoratus eſſet. *Pſalterium* fac emas, ſi modo caſtigatum eſt, & integrum, & ſi character mediocris: adero iſthic dubio procul ad Paſchales ferias. Pecuniam miſſurus eram, ſed cum has ſcriberem literas, puer haud etiam certus erat, num iſtuc eſſet iturus, quare de pecunia jubeo te ſecurum eſſe. Vale, & nos ama. Anno 1499.

Epistola CLVII.

Erasmus Roterod. Thomæ Linacro, Medico regio, S.D.

Tametsi novum non erat, tamen gratiſſimum fuit, quod ex *Mori* literis cognovi te tam amice nobis favere, licet immerentibus. Novum Teſtamentum adeo placet ubique doctis, etiam ex ordine Theologorum, ut indocti pudore obticeſcant. Febricula ſubito oborta fuit in cauſa, quo minus me navigationi commiſerim, præſertim diſſuadente medico *Ghisberto*. Majorem in modum te rogo, ut pharmacum, quod, quum proxime eſſem *Londini*, ſumpſi te auctore, denuo deſcriptum mihi tranſmittas: nam puer ſchedulam apud pharmacopolam reliquit. Erit id mihi longe gratiſſimum. Cætera ex *Moro* cognoſces. Bene vale. Ex divo *Audomaro* 5. Junii, Anno 1514.

Crocus regnat in Academia *Lipſienſi*, publicitus *Græcas* docens literas. Utinam prodirent tuæ lucubrationes, fidem omnibus facturæ meæ prædicationis, qua nuſquam non utor, vel quod ita res habet, vel quo magis noſtros ad ſtudium inflammem. Si quid erit hujus negotii, in quo tibi queam gratificari, ſenties hominem ad obſequendum promptiſſimum. Rurſum vale. *Grocino* facito me commendatum, quem adeo non odi, ita me Deus amet, ut ex animo venerer etiam ac ſuſpiciam. Rurſum vale. Anno 1514.

EPISTOLA CCXLV.

Erasmus Rot. Marco Laurino S. D.

SCRIPSIT ad me *Batti* fincerissimi quondam amici mei filius *Cornelius Battus*: juvenis bene linguax, satisque doctus, sed loripes: is tenetur hujus regionis desiderio: nam *Gruningæ* agit hypodidascalum. Si forsitan te adierit, expende num tibi possit usui esse: sin minus, remitte illum *Lovanium*. Nolim ut mea causa quicquam agas adversus animi tui sententiam. Bene vale. Scribam alias copiosius. *Lovanio* 29. Aprilis, Anno 1517.

EPISTOLA CCXLII.

Erasmus Gonello suo S. D.

GRATUM erat tuum munusculum, gratior epistola tam amica, gratissimus animus, nihil etiamnum immutatus diutina consuetudinis intermissione. *Clementem* summæ spei juvenem meis verbis admonebis, ut ab intempestivo studio temperet. Memini quam ille sit libro affixus, præsertim ut à nocturna scriptione quantum licet abstineat, & si forsitan ob Cardinalis negotia cogetur scribere, stans & erectus scribere assuescat. Nolim hoc ingenium ante diem perire, malimque servari studiis, quam Cardinaliciis negotiis impendi. Bene vale. *Lovanio* 22. Aprilis, Anno 1517.

EPISTOLA CCXLVI.

Erasmus Rot. Antonio Clavæ S. D.

NUPER videbaris optare *Græcum Herodotum*: eum ad te dono mitto; nam facile mihi reperietur alius in hoc itinere. Bene vale. *Robertum Cæsarem* vix possum salutare, qui nuper nos tam superbe destituerit in cœna. *Lovanio* 29. Aprilis, Anno 1517.

EPISTOLA CCXCVI.

Erasmus Rot. Andreæ Hochstrato S.

DEFLEXI nonnihil ab itinere meo, ut & te veterem amicum meum viderem, & urbis tam celebris conspectu fruerer, verum, utrunque frustra malo quodam meo fato. Nam & tu aberas, & urbs ita placuit, ut à nulla unquam discesserim lubentius. Bene vale. *Leodio*, Anno 1517.

READING 1-M

HORATIVS ANTONIVS BOLOGNA

[2000–2001 CE]

DIARIVM LATINVM

DE CLEOPATRAE FORMA

Omnes qui in antiquas Aegypti res incumbunt hoc incredibile nuntium in quibusdam ephemeridibus mirabundi scriptum invenerunt: Cleopatram, Aegyptiorum reginam, adspectu et corporis forma admodum foedam fuisse.

Cum autem multa eademque fabulosa legamus, quae de Aegyptiorum regina antique Graecorum Latinorumque scriptores tradiderunt, animo statim concipimus Cleopatram mulierum omnium pulcherrimam fuisse. Quod nec immerito fit, quoniam regina, optimis rebus instituta, non solum mulierum sed virorum etiam longe doctissima et callidissima fuit: nam ex compluribus imaginibus, e marmoreo signo, quod apud Museum Capitolinum servatur, nec non ex omnium scriptorium consensu mutuamur Cleopatram, minime ceteris aetatis suae mulieribus dissimilem, haud indecoro fuisse corpore.

Mortuo patre, Cleopatra, XVII annos nata, Pompeio favente, primum Ptolemaeo XIII, tum Ptolemaeo XIV fratribus, ut antiquis illis temporibus apud Aegyptios mos fuit, ut regnum servaret, haud invita nupsit. Puella firmo animo regnum tenuit, insidias vitavit, bellorum imperium sibi vindicavit, regiam domum ampliorem sumptuosioremque fecit, bibliothecam innumeris libris ornavit Museumque novis signis et instrumentis ditavit. Nihilo minus Cleopatrae regnum felix sed breve fuit: nam ingens periculum antiquo et ditissimo Aegyptiorum regno iam diu imminebat, quoniam Romani, ceteris populis subactis, Aegyptum quoque in dicionem suam redigere cupiebant. Ideo ad tantum regnum subigendum nullam occasionem amiserunt.

Pugna Pharsalica confecta, Pompeius, paucis militibus comitantibus, in Aegyptum pervenit, ubi Ptolemaei regis iussu necatur et infelicis imperatoris caput Caesari supervenienti ostenditur. Quod cum vidit, Caesar, ira motus, Ptolemaeo regnum adimit, Aegyptum sub potestatem populi Romani redigit, ingentes divitias Romam mittit, Cleopatram captivam aliquot dies tenet, donec mulier, calliditate usa, ad victoris pedes se proicit et illius viri, ad cuius nutum orbem perhorrescebat, pelex fit et filium, cui Caesario nomen fuit, eidem haud invita gignit. Mortuo Caesare, Antonium quoque deliciis suis devincit, uterque apud Actium contra Octavianum populumque Romanum pugnant. Cum autem recentem quoque victorem muliebribus artibus frustra subigere conetur, Cleopatra per aspidem, ut plerumque narratur, sibi mortem consciscit.

Cum autem apud praeclarum Museum Londiniense antiqua Aegyptiorum artificia exponenda essent, vestigatores et qui rebus antiquis praesunt, Cleopatrae figuram, recentissimis instrumentis auxiliantibus, sunt perficere conati. Instrumentum compulatorium, indiciis et argumentis perpensis, hoc responsum dedit: Cleopatrae, praeter parvum corpus, nasus longus, venter obesus, dentes putridi et exerti, crura valgia, cutis sicca et rimosa, ilia opima fuerunt. Quibus auditis et in actis diurnis perlectis, rerum antiquarum periti nesciunt quomodo Caesar et Antonius, quorum iudicia haud spernenda fuerunt, tam turpem mulierem adamare potuerint. Non desunt tamen qui, reginae signis inspectis, nec immerito haec omnia falsa putent.

PERNICIOSVM AVTOCINETORVM CERTAMEN

Complures nostrae aetatis iuvenes, quibus parentes omnia quae cupiant maxima cum liberalitate donant, in otio disidioso maiorem vitae partem plerumque terunt. Cum nullum magni viri sequantur exemplum et nullum bonae artis incitamentum colant cuius beneficio se in dies meliores efficiant, ut taedium vitae vitent e sibi nomen apud aequales comparent, manifesto periculo corpora obicere non dubitant. Quo factum est ut, ne mentes eorum cessatione torpeant neve maerore conficiantur, novum quoddam autocinetorum certamen, legibus parentumque moribus vetantibus, clam statuere et comparare decreverunt.

Cum autem omnes fere iuvenes, quamvis humili loco nati, se velocissimis autocinetis instruxissent, quomodo clariores inter aequales fieri possent, novum quoddam spiritus et prudentiae certamen constituerunt, ex quo audacissimus quisque non solum nomen, verum pecuniam etiam pareret. Hoc vero certaminis genus, legibus vetitum, noctu peragunt. Ideo hora dicta complures iuvenes, autocinetis ad cursum paratis, in locum constitutum cum amicis et fautoribus conveniunt: intempesta enim nocte civitatum viae vastae plerumque et desertae sunt. Sed haud raro fit, ut illa quoque hora, qua cives probi in lectis iacent, incautus autocineti ductor magno sui detrimento transeat et vitam inscius amittat.

Tales autem iuvenum conventus fiunt in extremis civitatum partibus, ubi viae plerumque ampliores sunt. Qui iis certaminibus intersunt, maiorem noctis partem in tabernis saltatoriis plerumque terunt: vino gravati, acutis sonis obtusi et medicamentis stupefactivis hebetati, alter alterum ad certamen lacessat, in quo ob magnam vehiculorum rapiditatem haud pauci vitam amittunt. Qui victor evasit magnis laudibus afficitur eiusque nomen per hominum ora volitat. Amicis et fautoribus ipse deo similis videtur et veluti terrarum dominus ab aequalibus colitur.

Insequenti die nuntii televisifici et diurnarii nuntium vulgare non dubitant complures iuvenes, maiore noctis parte in tabernis saltatoriis transacta, cum domum redirent, vitam amisisse. Vigiles, interrogati quomodo casus evenerit et quibus de causis tarn multi iuvenes exstincti sint, verum se profiteri dicunt. Nonnullos in carcerem coniciunt, sed iudices, plerumque, brevem post custodiam liberant. Parentum fletus, matrum lacrimae, sponsarum maerores neminem iuvant: insequenti nocte in iisdem viis alii iuvenes, amicorum deperditorum immemores, mortale certamen comparant et quidam inter ignes et cruciatus vita cedunt.

MVLIERES PVGILES FIENT

Mulieres quoque, cum iisdem ac viri iuribus moribusque fruantur, pugilatui studere cupiunt. Hoc nuntium, quamvis incredibile, in actis diurnis mulieres ipsae, quibus aequalitas cordi est, paucos ante menses mirabundae legerunt.

Olim viri tantum in stadiis certabant et bravium accipiebant; nunc vero nullum certamen est, in quo mulieres quoque praemia et gloriam merito et iure non consequantur.

Praeter pugilatum, ut constat, in Italia saltem, mulieres iisdem muneribus et officiis ac viri fungi possunt. Sed in innumeris orbis nationibus, mulieres inter se pugilatu quoque certare valent et magna illa praemia consequi possunt, quorum gratia nomen et gloria a terrarum peritis laudentur et magnificentur. Mulierum certamina magni habentur, propterea quod ludi magistri et apparatores ingentem nummorum summam cumulant et, cruentis imaginibus venditis iisdemque per instrumenta televisifica diffusis, praemiorum divitiarumque spe mulierum animos alliciunt.

Mulierum votis auditis et cognitis, rei publicae senators legem condiderunt, cuius gratia Italicae quoque mulieres tantum ludum colere possunt. Ut viri, qui, pugilatus auxilio, magna nummum vim congerunt et eorum nomina ab omnibus glorificantur, ita mulieres, spe fisae fore ut et ipsae ditissimae celeberrimaeque quam primum fiant, ludum illum exercere poseunt: se minime viris vi vel corporis praestantia cedere.

Attamen non desunt qui, prudentia ac ratione ducti, cum luctuosum ludum damnent et viros, incolumitate amissa, deplorent et mulieres ad pugilatum minime idoneas esse putent: ludum cruentum, quo nullum ferociorem, ne viris quidem licere. Sed nostra aetate nulli viro nullique denique feminae impedimentum est, quo minus cruentum quoque ludum colat et, manibus sanguine contaminatis, dum vulgus furens plaudit, victrix evadat et mulieris casu gaudeat. Verum est nostris temporibus quid rectum aequumque sit homines se nescire dicere.

ANIMALIA HOMINIS VITA POTIORA

Perpaucis abhinc horis per instrumentum televisificum diurnarii magna cum eloquentia nuntium vulgaverunt quondam vigilem, ut canem e morte eriperet, in flammas se immittere non dubitasse; eundem praeterea, cum animal ob gasium mortiferum iam moriturum esset, os suum ad canis os, ut spiritum resumeret, applicare ausum esse; hoc strenuum virum semel atque iterum fecisse, donec animal, viribus refectis, surrexit et abiit. Loci incolae, qui ad incendium exstinguendum convenerant et in tutum inter flammas familiam tantum duxerant, apud armarium ferreum canem reliquerant, quoniam domus tectique pars proruere inciperat.

In tanta trepidatione non desunt qui, omnibus ad vivendum necessariis relictis, in flammis canem relictum esse memorent: is fuit vigil qui animalis pietate affectus, flammarum mortisque vim despiciens, domum ingressus est, accurate vestigavit et paulo post canem secum ferens apparuit. Qui aderant, vigilem redeuntem maximis plausibus persecuti sunt.

Paulo post idem instrumentum televisificum terrificas imagines ostendit et triste nuntium vulgavit: totum fere Mozambicum, claram Africae regionem, aquis esse mersum, incolarum partem perisse, partem magna cum difficultate in viciniora loca salutem petiisse. Tristes cuiusdam mulieris imagines diurnarii ostenderunt, quae in alta arbore, pluvia cadente et aquis regionem inundantibus, nullo auxiliante, filium sola peperat. Milites deinde eam in helicopterum funis traxerunt et in proximum valetudinarium cum filio duxerunt. Quomodo mulieris nuntium narraverint, referens horresco, quoniam desunt apta verba quibus tam inurbanis viris obiurgem. Puer, immo homo, cane minor a quibusdam homunculis habetur.

Fragiles hominum imbecillorum animos callidi diurnarii paucis sed effícacibus verbis nec non imaginibus inflammare solent. Recens est opinio, haud paucos homines animalia humano genere potiora putare. Quae quidem despicienda non sunt, sed nullo modo, ne pueris quidem indigentibus, praeferenda videntur.

SECUNDA EXPERIENTIA

second experience

CATHEDRALEM HANC AEDEM
LITVRGICAS OMNINO AD NORMAS
VATICANO II VENIENTES EX CONCILIO
MAGNA NON SINE DIFFICVLTATE
RENOVATAM
SOLLEMNITER ATQVE FELICITER
IX DIE MENSIS FEBRVARII ANNO MMII
ARCHIEPISCOPVS IPSE ORDINARIVS
INAVGVRAVIT ITERVM DEDICAVIT
REMBERTVS GEORGIVS WEAKLAND O.S.B.

According to our program of five Latin Experiences the interested person must be advised that the Second Experience is not the second level of any kind of systematic treatment of the language. This is because of the nature of the word "language," which comes from the Latin word *lingua*, which means "tongue" or "speech" or "language." Our conviction has always been that as soon as we learn some element of the language, and of course the First Experience gave us ample material, we should start to use it as a language, that is, as a spoken means of communication.

The Second Experience in our program, therefore, is an immediate introduction to living, spoken Latin with no notes and no commentaries, but just the use of the language. We consider these spoken encounters to be a further experience of the language.

Later on you will see that the Third Experience of the language is the second level of systematic treatment of the language's elements. It continues the orderly presentation found in the First Experience. Therefore, the Second Experience of the language is its direct and immediate application in the encounter with the spoken language.

The problem with spoken Latin is we must know some vocabulary and we must know some real expressions of the language. Following this Experience, therefore, we provide reading sheets consisting of numerous texts of real Latin to help you in learning the spoken language.

We provide these original Latin texts to address a third consideration, namely a concern of ours. Many wonderful people, intelligent and brilliant scholars, have mastered the Latin language and are easily able to compose Latin conversations based on what they know. Because Latin is not our native tongue, however, and we were not born into a Latin-speaking community, we are hesitant to use books of Latin conversation written by the contemporaries of our own age. Such compositions introduce the student to the style and word order of a contemporary author, especially in recent examples of conversational Latin still available in book form in which the Latin style of the sentences is consistently the same from page 1 to page 200, and represent the author's own composition of phrases and stories. Such accounts cannot introduce people or students into the feeling and the operating of the whole language naturally.

Original Latin literature including examples of real Latin conversations provided following the Second Experience are drawn from many authors until about the 1600s, the last era in which we can still presume that people spoke Latin more or less naturally and according to the genius of the Latin language, not artificially according to their training.

Our encounters with spoken Latin in this Second Experience require not only native Latin literature but also a teacher able to converse in real Latin correctly.

Examples of native Latin conversation are readily available and include Plautus or letters in which Trajan is talking with Plinius and Plinius with the Emperor. You can hear Cicero talking with his family in his letters to them or to his best friend Atticus. There are infinite examples in Petronius and in Virgil, which include the conversations between Aeneas and Dido. There are conversations in Horace, and Seneca talks with Lucilius in very familiar terms, as if they were talking on the phone. Examples are found in Terentius and in the letters between the teacher Marcus Fronto and his student Marcus Aurelius in which they talk back and forth.

The ancient Christian authors provide examples, especially the epistles of Cyprian to the community in Carthage or at Rome. Augustine of Hippo talks out of his heart when conversing with the Lord in the *Confessions*.

The Renaissance provides an infinity of examples, especially in the letters between Erasmus, Thomas More, and Politianus. They talk back and forth, and their use of the Latin language is still quite natural. Erasmus in his *Colloquia familiaria* wants to teach Latin phraseology and vocabulary and to bring people as close as he can to the natural language. So we must not hesitate to follow Erasmus and other authors of his age. In later generations this native understanding of Latin was somewhat lost, and the language became artificial.

The issue is not simply a matter of adding vocabulary, because we can always develop ways of speaking about space ships, automobiles, cell-phones, and the internet. The greater difficulty for us concerns how to deal with the language, its flow and natural structure. To discover this we must turn to the authors who have a native facility with the language. For most of our careers we should insist on sticking close to these magnificent examples of fine, natural, imitable Latin.

This kind of native Latin conversation is our model and inspiration and the source of our conversation. We shall watch how they use the language in their conversations, their vocabulary and word order and elegant turns of expression, which were quite natural for the Romans but may appear complicated and artificial to us foreigners; and we are foreigners. We must stick close to the examples of native Latin conversations not to show off or to impress, but to teach and to communicate with the real Latin tongue.

We use these authors' examples of native Latin conversation in a definite way. We begin with an example sentence, as a child would imitate parents or teachers, and by imitating we let the language grow. Then we begin to play with this sentence by changing the times of the verbs, reversing the singular to the plural and plural to the singular, reversing the subject and the object, or flipping from the active to the passive and from the passive to the active. In one simple sentence you can work your way through just about the whole language, not by following arbitrary schemas and declensions and verb charts, but by following these human ways of thinking and playing with the language.

You can take a simple sentence of a few words by Cicero in a letter he wrote to his secretary Atticus and see how Cicero is speaking:

> *Duas a te accepi epistulas heri.* (*Att.* XIV, 2, 1)

We might say:

> *Duas a te accipiam epistulas cras*
> *Duas a te acceperam epistulas nudiustertius*
> *Duae a te sunt a me acceptae litterae heri*
> *Dixit heri Cicero duas a te se accepisse epistulas nudiustertius*
> *Dixit heri Cicero duas a te se accepturum epistulas cras.*

When working with the imperative, for example, it is helpful to take a Latin example and express it in the other twelve imperatives in the Latin language, all the while adding several other elements so that as it expands you can work and rework the whole thing in your own mind.

Such imitation and play may be tiring, because we have to set aside our ways of thinking formed by our vernacular language and force ourselves to exercise our minds in forming Latin phrases and sentences. However tiring, this is worthwhile and essential to get moving with the language until it becomes easier, and we become bolder and richer in our expressions both in conversation and in writing.

As the students learn a new element or phenomenon of the language, they can immediately put it into practice by finding an example in the reading sheets, and through imitation and play they can work through the new material until it becomes familiar. They can combine sentences together in innumerable ways, for example with *quod*, *quia*, *quoniam*, or with *cum* and the subjunctive according to the sequence of tenses. All of this play happens naturally on the basis of the original Latin text the authors give you until the language becomes oiled and malleable and functions smoothly for you.

Because the Second Experience consists of imitating and playing with these authors, this Experience is open to everyone from every Experience. Beginners from the first week can imitate and play in basic ways, and Latinists from the top Experience will always find examples from the reading sheets to learn from. This Second Experience, consequently, is open-ended, and you can just go on forever speaking Latin.

Beyond imitating and playing with the language, a couple of other elements can be helpful in learning to speak the language. In our encounters *sub arboribus*, in the park "under the trees," we begin with a real Latin text from which we draw out a definite theme for discussion—not politics or religion—and a moderator for the conversation may ask different people to say something in Latin about the theme. This is especially helpful for the taciturn, because some people do not speak any language voluntarily and do not like to talk, period. A theme can help them to enter into a moderated conversation.

Some clubs have formed around the dining table and meet regularly for a meal of Latin conversation. Others find that written correspondence in Latin is helpful because it gives the opportunity for reflected consideration not to impress but to imitate and play and make the language one's own.

Conversation in any language requires humility because we are going to make mistakes publicly in what we say and in our conversation with others. A club moderator needs the courage to point out the errors of others not to discourage but to encourage, and the humility to accept correction by others. A moderator can help to pace the conversation so that the timid also have a chance to learn by speaking. We should not be afraid of making mistakes and of being corrected in any language.

SECUNDAE EXPERIENTIAE LECTIONUM PAGINULAE

Reading Sheets—Second Experience

READING 2-A

TITVS MACCIVS PLAVTVS

[254–184 BCE]

ASINARIA

LI. Hercle uero tu cauebis ne me attingas, si sapis,
né hodie malo cum auspicio nomen commutaueris.
LE. quaeso, aequo animo patitor. LI. patitor tú item quom ego te referiam. 375
LE. dico ut usust fieri. LI. dico hercle ego quoque ut facturu' sum.
LE. ne nega. LI. quin promitto, inquam, hostire contra ut merueris.
LE. ego abeo, tu iam, scio, patiere. sed quis hic est? is est,
ille est ipsus. iam ego recurro huc. tu hunc interea hic tene.
uolo seni narrare. LI. quin tuom officium facis ergo ac fugis? 380

MERCATOR LIBANVS

ME. Vt demonstratae sunt mihi, hasce aedis esse oportet
Demaenetus ubi dicitur habitare. i, puere, pulta
atque atriensem Sauream, si est intus, euocato huc.
LI. quis nostras sic frangit fores? ohe, inquam, si quid audis.
ME. nemo etiam tetigit. sanun es? LI. at censebam attigisse 385
propterea huc quia habebas iter. nolo ego fores conseruas
meas a te uerberarier. sane ego sum amicus nostris.
ME. pol hau periclum est cardines ne foribus ecfringantur,
si | istoc exemplo omnibus qui quaerunt respondebis.
LI. ita haec morata est ianuá : extemplo ianitorem 390
clamat, procul si quem uidet ire ad se calcitronem.
sed quid uenis? quid quaeritas? ME. Demaenetum uolebam.
LI. si sit domi,dicam tibi. ME. quid eiius atriensis?
LI. nihilo mage intus est. ME. ubi est? LI. ad tonsorem ire dixit.
ME. quom uenisset post non redit? LI. non edepol. quid uolebas? 395
ME. argenti uiginti minas, si adesset, accepisset.
LI. qui pro istuc? ME. asinos uendidit Pellaco mercatori

mercatu. LI. scio. tu id nunc refers? iam hic credo eum adfuturum.
ME. qua facie uoster Saurea est? si is est, iam scire potero.
LI. macilentis malis, rufulus aliquantum, uentriosus, 400
truculentis oculis, commoda statura, tristi fronte.
ME. non potuit pictor rectius describere eiius formam.
LI. atque hercle ipsum adeo contuor, quassanti capite incedit.
quisque obuiam huic occesserit irato, uapulabit.
ME. siquidem hercle Aeacidinis minis animisque expletus cedit. 405
si med iratus tetigerit, iratus uapulabit.

LEONIDA MERCATOR LIBANVS

LI: Quid hoc sit negoti neminem meum dictum magni facere?
Libanum in tostrinam ut iusseram uenire, is nullus uenit.
ne ille edepol tergo et cruribus consuluit hau decore.
ME. nimis imperiosust. LI. uae mihí! LE. hodie saluere iussi 410
Libanum libertum? iam manú emissu's? LI. opsecro te.
LE. ne tú hercle cum magno malo mihi obuiam occessisti.
qur non uenisti, ut iusseram, in tostrinam? LI. hic me moratust.
LE. siquidem hercle nunc summum Iouem te dicas detinuisse

EPIDICVS

domi meae eccam saluam et sanam. nam postquam audiui ilico
e meo séruo illam esse captam, continuo argentum dedi
ùt emeretur. ille eam rem ádeo sobrie et frugaliter 565
accurauit ut—ut ad alias res est inpense inprobus.
PH. fac uideam, sei mea, sei saluam (me) uis. PE. eho! istine, Canthara,
iube Telestidem huc prodire filiam ante aedis meam,
ut suam uídeat matrem. PH. remigrat animus nunc demum mihi.

ACROPOLISTIS PERIPHANES PHILIPPA

AC. Quid est, pater, quod me exciuisti ante aedis? PE. Ut matrem tuam 570
uideas, adeas, aduenienti des salutem atque osculum.
AC. quam meam matrem? PE. quae exanimata exsequitur aspectum tuom.
PH. quis istaec est quam tu osculum mi ferre iubes? PE. tua filia.
PH. haecine? PE. haec. PH. egone osculum huic dem? PE. qur non,
quae ex te nata sit?
PH. tú homo insanis. PE. egone? PH. tune. PE. qur? PH. quia égo 575
hanc quaé siet
neque scio neque noui neque ego hanc oculis uidi ante hunc diem.
PE. scio quid erres: quia uestitum atque ornatum immutabilem
habet haec, *
PH. * aliter catuli longe olent, aliter sues.
né ego me nego nosse hanc quae sit. PE. pro deum atque hominum 580
fidem!

quid? ego lenocinium facio quí habeam álienas domi
atque argentum egurgitem domo prósus? quid tu, quae patrem
tuom uocas me atque osculare, quid stas stupida? quid taces?
AC. quid loquar uis? PE. haec negat se tuam esse matrem. AC. ne fuat
si non uolt: equidem hac inuita tamen ero mátris filia; 585
non med istanc cogere aequom est meam esse matrem si neuolt.
PE. qur me igitur patrem uocabas? AC. tua istaec culpast, non mea.
non patrem ego te nominem, ubi tu tuam me appelles filiam?
hanc quoque etiam, si me appellet filiam, matrem uocem.
negat haec filiam me suam esse: non ergo haec mater mea est. 590
postremo haec mea culpa non est: quae didici dixi omnia;
Epidicus mihi fuit magister. PE. perii! plaustrum perculi.
AC. numquid ego ibi, pater, peccaui? PE. si hercle te umquam audiuero
me patrem uocare, uitam tuam ego interimam. AC. non uoco.
ubi uoles pater esse ibi esto; ubi noles ne fueris pater. 595
PH. quid (si) | ob eam rem hanc emisti quia tuam gnatam ratu's,
quibu' de signis agnoscebas? PE. nullis. PH. qua re filiam
credidisti nostram? PE. seruos Epidicus dixit mihi.
PH. quid si seruo aliter uisum est, non poteras nouisse, opsecro?
PE. quid ego, qui illam ut preimum uidi, numquam uidi postea? 600
PH. perii misera! PE. ne fle, mulier. intro abi, habe animum bonum;
ego illam reperiam. PH. hinc Athenis ciuis eam emit Atticus:
adulescentem equidem dicebant emisse. PE. inueniam, tace.
abi modo intro atque hanc adserua Circam Solis filiam.
ego relictis rebus Epidicum operam quaerendo dabo : 605
si inuenio exitiabilem ego illi faciam hunc ut fiat diem.—

ACTVS V

STRATIPPOCLES EPIDICVS DANISTA
TELESTIS

ST. Male morigerus mihi est danista, quei a me argentum non petit
neque illam adducit quam (emi) ex praeda. sed eccum incedit Epidicus.
quid illuc est quod illí caperrat frons seueritudine?
EP. si undecim deos praéter sese secum adducat Iuppiter, 610
ita non omnes ex cruciatu poterunt eximere Epidicum.
Periphanem emere lora uidi, ibi aderat una Apoecides;
nunc homines me quaeritare credo, senserunt, sciunt
sibi data esse uerba. ST. quid agis, mea Commoditas? EP. quod miser.
ST. quid est tibi? EP. quin tu mihi adornas ad fugam uiaticum 615
priu' quam pereo? nam per urbem duo defloccati senes
quaeritant me, in manibus gestant copulas secum simul.
ST. habe bonum animum.

READING 2-B

EVSEBIVS HIERONYMVS

[342–420 CE]

DIALOGVS ADVERSVS PELAGIANOS

LIBER PRIMVS

1. ATTICVS. Dic mihi, Critobule, uerum est quod a te scriptum audio, posse hominem sine peccato esse, si uelit, et facilia Dei esse praecepta? CRITOBVLVS. Verum, Attice, sed non eodem sensu ab aemulis accipitur, quo a me dictum est. — A. Quid enim ambiguitatis in dicto est, ut diuersae intellegentiae tribuatur occasio? Nec quaero ut de utroque pariter respondeas. Duo enim a te proposita sunt: unum, posse hominem sine peccato esse, si uelit, alterum, facilia Dei esse praecepta. Licet ergo simul dicta sint, tamen per partes singula disserantur, ut quorum una uidetur fides, nulla sit in sententiarum diuersitate contentio. — C. Ego, Attice, dixi hominem posse absque peccato esse, si uelit, non, ut quidam maledici calumniantur, absque Dei gratia (quod etiam cogitasse sacrilegum est), sed simpliciter posse, si uelit, ut subaudiatur "cum Dei gratia". — A. Ergo et malorum in te operum auctor est Dominus? — C. Nequaquam ita ut aestimas, sed si quid in me boni habeo, illo suggerente et adiuuante completur. — A. Non de natura quaero, sed de actu: quis enim dubitat Deum omnium creatorem? Hoc mihi respondeas uelim: quod agis bonum, tuum est an Dei? — C. Meum et Dei, ut ego operer et ille adiuuet. — A. Et quomodo haec omnium opinio est, quod Dei auferas gratiam, et quidquid homines agimus, propriae tantum asseras uoluntatis? — C. Miror, Attice, cur erroris alieni a me causam rationemque flagites, et id quaeras quod scriptum non est, cum perspicuum sit quid scripserim. Dixi hominem posse sine peccato esse, si uelit: numquid addidi "absque Dei gratia"? — A. Sed ex eo quod non addidisti, uideris negare. — C. Immo ex eo quod non negaui, dixisse aestimandus sum: neque enim quidquid non dicimus, negare arbitrandi sumus. — A. Confiteris igitur posse hominem sine peccato esse, si uelit, cum Dei gratia? — C. Non solum fatebor, sed et libere proclamabo. — A. Errat ergo qui Dei gratiam tollit? — C. Errat. Quin potius arbitrandus est impius, cum Dei nutu omnia gubernentur, et hoc quod sumus et habemus appetitum propriae uoluntatis, Dei conditoris sit beneficium. Vt enim liberum possideamus arbitrium et uel ad bonam uel ad malam partem declinemus propria uoluntate, eius est gratiae qui nos ad imaginem et similitudinem sui tales condidit.

3. C. Quid mihi necesse est contra alios dicere, cum meum responsum habeas? — A. Tuum responsum cuiusmodi? Bene eos sentire, an male? —

C. Et quae me cogit necessitas ut contra alios promam sententiam? — A. Disputationis ordo et ratio ueritatis. An ignoras omne quod dicitur aut esse aut non esse et aut inter bona aut inter mala debere numerari? Hoc igitur de quo interrogo, aut bene dici aut male, ingratis tibi fatendum est. — C. Si in singulis rebus quas gerimus Dei utendum est adiutorio, ergo et calamum temperare ad scribendum et temperatum pumice terere, manumque aptare litteris, taccre, loqui, sedere, stare, ambulare, currere, comedere, ieiunare, flere, ridere, et cetera huiusmodi, nisi Deus iuuerit, non poterimus? — A. Iuxta meum sensum non posse perspicuum est. — C. Et in quo liberum habemus arbitrium et Dei in nos gratia custoditur, si ne hoc quidem absque Deo possumus facere?

4. A. Num sic donata est liberi arbitrii gratia, ut Dei per singula tollatur adminiculum? — C. Non tollitur Dei adiutorium, cum creaturae et semel dati liberi arbitrii gratia conseruetur. Si enim absque Deo, et nisi per singula ille me iuuerit, nihil possum agere, nec pro bonis me iuste operibus coronabit nec affliget pro malis, sed in utroque suum uel recipiet uel damnabit auxilium. — A. Dic ergo simpliciter quod Dei auferas gratiam: quidquid enim tollis in partibus, necesse est ut et in genere neges. — C. Non nego gratiam, cum ita me a Deo asseram conditum ut per Dei gratiam meae datum sit uoluntati, uel facere quid uel non facere. — A. Dormitat igitur Deus in operibus nostris, semel data liberi arbitrii potestate, nec orandus est ut in singulis rebus nos iuuet, cum uoluntatis nostrae sit et proprii arbitrii, uel facere si uolumus, uel non facere si nolumus.

7. A. Non me pudet nescire quod nescio, et de quo futura est disputatio, debet inter utrumque conuenire quem sensum habeat. — C. Ego hoc assero, qui potest se uno die abstinere a peccato, posse et altero; qui duobus, posse et tribus; qui tribus, posse et triginta; atque hoc ordine et trecentis, et tribus milibus et quamdiucumque se uoluerit obseruare. — A. Dic ergo simpliciter posse hominem in perpetuum sine peccato esse si uelit. Possumusne omne quod uolumus ? C. Nequaquam. Neque enim possum quidquid uoluero; sed hoc solum dico, posse hominem sine peccato esse, si uelit. — A. Quaeso ut mihi respondeas. Hominem me putas, an beluam? — C. Si de te ambigo utrum homo an belua sis, ipse me beluam confitebor. — A. Si ergo, ut dicis, homo sum, quomodo, cum uelim et satis cupiam non peccare, delinquo? — C. Quia uoluntas imperfecta est. Si enim uere uelles, uere utique non peccares. — A. Ergo tu qui me arguis non uere cupere, sine peccato es, quia uere cupis? — C. Quasi ego de me dicam, quem peccatorem esse confiteor, et non de paucis et raris, si qui uoluerint non peccare.

8. A. Interim ex meo tuoque iudicio, et ego qui interrogo et tu qui respondes peccatores sumus. — C. Sed possumus non esse si uelimus. — A. Dixi uelle me non peccare, te quoque id sentire non dubium est. Quomodo igitur quod uterque uolumus, uterque non possumus? — C. Quia plene

non uolumus. — A. Da ergo qui maiorum nostrorum plene uoluerint et potuerint. — C. Hoc quidem non facile est ostendere. Neque enim quando dico posse hominem sine peccato esse, si uelit, aliquos fuisse contendo; sed simpliciter posse esse, si uelit. Aliud est namque esse posse, quod Graece dicitur τῇ δυνάμει aliud esse, quod illi appellant τῇ ἐνεργείᾳ. Possum esse medicus; sed interim non sum. Possum faber; sed necdum didici. Quidquid igitur possum, licet necdum sim, tamen ero, si uoluero.

11. C. Dum nescis, proprio captus es laqueo. — A. Quonam modo? — C. Ex sententia Domini asseris hominem posse esse perfectum. Quando enim dicit: *Si uis perfectus esse, uende omnia quae habes, et da pauperibus, et ueni, sequere me,* ostendit hominem, si uoluerit et fecerit quae praecepta sunt, posse esse perfectum. — A. Validissimo quidem pugno me percussisti, ita ut caligo mihi ante oculos obuersari coeperit; sed tamen hoc ipsum quod dicit: *si uis esse perfectus,* ei dicitur qui non potuit, immo noluit et idcirco non potuit. Tu autem ostende mihi qui et uoluerit et potuerit quod nunc pollicitus es. — C. Quae enim me cogit necessitas ostendere qui perfecti fuerint, cum perspicuum sit posse esse perfectos ex eo quod uni a Saluatore sit dictum, et per unum omnibus: *si uis esse perfectus?* — A. Tergiuersaris et *in eodem luto haesitas:* aut enim quod potest fieri, aliquando factum est, aut si numquam factum est, fieri non posse concede.

12. C. Quid ultra differo? Scripturarum auctoritate uincendus es. Vt cetera praetermittam, nonne his duobus testimoniis tibi imponetur silentium, in quibus Iob et Zacharias Elisabethque laudantur? Nisi fallor enim in Iob ita scriptum est: *Homo quidam erat in regione Ausitide, nomine Iob, et erat homo ille uerax et sine crimine, uerus Dei cultor, abstinens se ab omni re mala.* Et iterum: *Quis est qui arguit iustum meum sine peccato, et loquitur uerbis suis per ignorantiam?* In Euangelio quoque secundum Lucam: *Fuit in diebus Herodis regis Iudaeae sacerdos quidam nomine Zacharias. de uice Abia, et uxor illi de filiabus Aaron et nomen eius Elisabeth. Erant autem ambo iusti ante Deum, incedentes in omnibus mandatis et iustificationibus Domini, sine querela.* Si uerus Dei cultor est et immaculatus ac sine crimine; et qui ambulant in cunctis iustificationibus Domini iusti sunt in conspectu eius, puto quod peccato careant et nulla re indigeant quae ad iustitiam pertinet. — A. Proposuisti testimonia quae non de alterius Scripturae loco, sed de propriis libris absoluta sunt. Nam et Iob postquam percussus est plaga multa aduersus sententiam Dei, prouocans eum ad iudicium dixisse conuincitur: *Atque utinam sic iudicaretur uir cum Deo, quomodo iudicatur filius hominis cum collega suo.* Et iterum: *Quis mihi tribuat auditorem, ut desiderium meum omnipotens audiat et librum scribat ipse qui iudicat?* Et rursum: *Si fuero iustus, os meum impia loquetur, et si absque crimine, prauus inueniar; et si purificatus niue et lotus mundis manibus, satis me sorde tinxisti et exsecratum est me uestimentum meum.*

20. C. Nullus ergo sanctorum, quamdiu in isto corpusculo est, cunctas potest habere uirtutes? — A. Nullus, quia nunc ex parte prophetamus et ex parte cognoscimus. Nec enim possunt omnia esse in hominibus, quia non est immortalis filius hominis. — C. Et quomodo legimus: qui unam habuerit, omnes habere uirtutes? A. Participatione, non proprietate. Necesse est enim ut singuli excellant in quibusdam, et tamen hoc quod legisse te dicis, ubi scriptum sit nescio. — C. Ignoras hanc philosophorum esse sententiam? — A. Sed non apostolorum. Neque enim curae mihi est quid Aristoteles, sed quid Paulus doceat. — C. Obsecro te, nonne Iacobus apostolus scribit qui in uno offenderit, esse eum omnium reum? — A. Ipse locus se interpretatur. Non enim dixit, unde coeperat disputatio, "qui diuitem pauperi in honore praetulerit, reus est adulterii uel homicidii". In hoc enim delirant Stoici, paria contendentes esse peccata. Sed ita: *Qui dixit "non moechaberis", dixit et "non occides"; quod si non occides, moecharis autem, factus es transgressor legis.* Leuia enim leuibus et grauia grauibus comparantur, nec ferula dignum uitium gladio uindicandum est, nec gladio dignum scelus ferula coercendum. C. Esto ut nullus sanctorum omnes uirtutes habeat; hoc certe dabis, in eo quod potest facere, si fecerit, esse perfectum. — A. Non tenes quid supra dixerim? — C. Quidnam illud est? — A. Perfectum esse in eo quod fecit et imperfectum in eo quod facere non potuit. — C. Sed sicut perfectus est in eo quod fecit, quia facere uoluit, ita et in eo per quod imperfectus est, quia non fecit, perfectum esse potuisse, si facere uoluisset. — A. Quis enim non uult facere quod perfectum est, aut quis non cunctis cupiat florere uirtutibus? Si totum requiris ab omnibus, tollis rerum diuersitatem et gratiarum distantiam et Creatoris artificem uarietatem, cui sacro Propheta sonat carmine: *Omnia in sapientia fecisti.* Indignetur lucifer, quare lunae fulgorem non habeat; luna super suis defectibus et labore causetur cur annuum solis circulum singulis mensibus expleat; sol queratur quid offenderit ut lunae cursu tardior sit. Clamemus et nos homunculi quid causae exstiterit, ut homines et non angeli facti simus.

21. C. Nimius es in una atque eadem quaestione, ut persuadere coneris hominem uniuersa simul habere non posse, quasi aut inuiderit aut non potuerit Deus praestare imagini et similitudini suae ut in omnibus suo respondeat Creatori. — A. Egone nimius, an tu? qui soluta proponis et non intellegis aliud esse similitudinem, aliud aequalitatem: illud picturam, hoc esse corporis ueritatem. Verus equus camporum spatia transuolat, pictus parieti haeret in curru. Arriani Dei Filio non concedunt quod tu omni homini tribuis. Alii non audent perfectum in Christo hominem confiteri, ne suscipere in eo hominis peccata cogantur, quasi potentior sit creatio Creatore et idipsum filius tantum hominis, quod Filius Dei. Aut igitur propone alia, quibus respondeam, aut desine superbire et da gloriam Deo. — C. Immemor es sponsionis tuae, et dum argumentis argumenta con<n>ectis ac per Scripturarum latissimos campos infrenis equi libertate baccharis, super fortissima quaestione, cui pollicitus es te in consequentibus

responsurum, omnino tacuisti, obliuionem simulans ut necessitatem responsionis euaderes. Sed ego stultus ad horam tribui quod petebas, existimans oblaturum sponte quod acceperas et non admonitum reddere quod debebas. — A. Nisi fallor, de possibilibus mandatis dilata responsio est: pone igitur ut uolueris.

READING 2-C

SEVERINVS BOETHIVS

[480–524 CE]

PHILOSOPHIAE CONSOLATIO

3. **1**. Vos quoque, o terrena animalia, tenui licet imagine uestrum tamen principium somniatis uerumque ilium beatitudinis finem licet minime perspicaci qualicumque tamen cogitatione prospicitis, eoque uos et ad uerum bonum naturalis ducit intentio et ab eodem multiplex error abducit. **2**. Considera namque an per ea quibus se homines adepturos beatitudinem putant ad destinatum finem ualeant peruenire. **3**. Si enim uel pecunia uel honores ceteraque tale quid afferunt cui nihil bonorum abesse uideatur, nos quoque fateamur fieri aliquos horum adeptione felices. **4**. Quodsi neque id ualent efficere quod promittunt bonisque pluribus carent, nonne liquido falsa in eis beatitudinis species deprehenditur?

5. Primum igitur te ipsum, qui paulo ante diuitiis affluebas, interrogo: inter illas abundantissimas opes numquamne animum tuum concepta ex qualibet iniuria confudit anxietas? — **6**. Atqui, inquam, libero me fuisse animo quin aliquid semper angerer reminisci non queo. — **7**. Nonne quia uel aberat quod abesse non uelles uel aderat quod adesse noluisses? — Ita est, inquam. — **8**. Illius igitur praesentiam, huius absentiam desiderabas? — Confiteor, inquam. — **9**. Eget uero, inquit, eo quod quisque desiderat? — Eget inquam. — Qui uero eget aliquo non est usquequaque sibi ipse sufficiens. — Minime, inquam. — **10**. Tu itaque hanc insufficientiam plenus, inquit, opibus sustinebas? — Quidni? inquam. — **11**. Opes igitur nihilo indigentem sufficientemque sibi facere nequeunt, et hoc erat quod promittere uidebantur. **12**. Atqui hoc quoque maxime considerandum puto quod nihil habeat suapte natura pecunia ut his a quibus possidetur inuitis nequeat auferri. — Fateor, inquam. — **13**. Quidni fateare, cum eam cotidie ualentior aliquis eripiat inuito? Vnde enim forenses querimoniae, nisi quod uel ui uel fraude nolentibus pecuniae repetuntur ereptae? — Ita est, inquam. — **14**. Egebit igitur, inquit, extrinsecus petito praesidio quo suam pecuniam quisque tueatur. — Quis id, inquam, neget? **15**. Atqui non egeret eo nisi possideret pecuniam, quam possit amittere. — Dubitari, inquam, nequit. — **16**. In contrarium igitur relapsa res est; nam quae sufficientes sibi facere putabantur opes alieno potius praesidio faciunt indigentes. **17**. Quis autem modus est quo pellatur diuitiis indigentia? Num enim diuites esurire nequeunt, num sitire non possunt, num frigus hibernum pecuniosorum membra non sentiunt? **18**. Sed adest, inquies, opulentis quo famem satient, quo sitim frigusque depellant. Sed hoc modo consolari quidem diuitiis indigentia potest, auferri penitus non potest; nam si haec hians semper atque aliquid poscens opibus expletur, maneat necesse est quae possit expleri. **19**. Taceo quod naturae minimum, quod auaritiae nihil satis est. Quare si opes nec summouere indigentiam possunt et ipsae suam faciunt, quid est quod eas sufficientiam praestare credatis?

3. Videsne quantum malis dedecus adiciant dignitates? Atqui minus eorum patebit indignitas si nullis honoribus inclarescant. **4**. Tu quoque num tandem tot periculis adduci potuisti ut cum Decorato gerere magistratum putares, cum in eo mentem nequissimi scurrae delatorisque respiceres? **5**. Non enim possumus ob honores reuerentia dignos iudicare quos ipsis honoribus iudicamus indignos. **6**. At si quem sapientia praeditum uideres, num posses eum uel reuerentia uel ea qua est praeditus sapientia non dignum putare? — Minime. — **7**. Inest enim dignitas propria uirtuti, quam protinus in eos quibus fuerit adiuncta transfundit. **8**. Quod quia populares facere nequeunt honores, liquet eos propriam dignitatis pulchritudinem non habere.

9. In quo illud est animaduertendum magis: nam si eo abiectior est quo magis a pluribus quisque contemnitur, cum reuerendos facere nequeat quos pluribus ostentat, despectiores potius improbos dignitas facit. **10**. Verum non impune; reddunt namque improbi parem dignitatibus uicem, quas sua contagione commaculant.

11. Atque ut agnoscas ueram illam reuerentiam per has umbratiles dignitates non posse contingere: si qui multiplici consulatu functus in barbaras nationes forte deuenerit, uenerandumne barbaris honor faciet? **12**. Atqui si hoc naturale munus dignitatibus foret, ab officio suo quoquo gentium nullo modo cessarent, sicut ignis ubique terrarum numquam tamen calere desisitit. **13**. Sed quoniam id eis non propria uis sed hominum fallax adnectit opinio, uanescunt ilico cum ad eos uenerint qui dignitates eas esse non aestimant.

14. Sed hoc apud exteras nationes: inter eos uero apud quos ortae sunt num perpetuo perdurant? **15**. Atqui praetura magna olim potestas, nunc inane nomen et senatorii census grauis sarcina; si quis quondam populi curasset annonam magnus habebatur, nunc ea praefectura quid abiectius? **16**. Vt enim paulo ante diximus, quod nihil habet proprii decoris, opinione utentium nunc splendorem accipit, nunc amittit.

5. **1**. An uero regna regumque familiaritas efficere potentem ualet? Quidni, quando eorum felicitas perpetuo perdurat? **2**. Atqui plena est exemplorum uetustas, plena etiam praesens aetas, qui reges felicitatem calamitate mutauerint. O praeclara potentia, quae ne ad conseruationem quidem sui satis efficax inuenitur!

3. Quodsi haec regnorum potestas beatitudinis auctor est, nonne, si qua parte defuerit, felicitatem minuat, miseriam importet? **4**. Sed quamuis late humana tendantur imperia, plures necesse est gentes relinqui quibus regum quisque non imperet. **5**. Qua uero parte beatos faciens desinit potestas hac impotentia subintrat, quae miseros facit; hoc igitur modo maiorem regibus inesse necesse est miseriae portionem.

6. Expertus sortis suae periculorum tyrannus regni metus pendentis supra uerticem gladii terrore simulauit. **7.** Quae est igitur haec potestas, quae sollicitudinum morsus expellere, quae formidinum aculeos uitare nequit? Atqui uellent ipsi uixisse securi, sed nequeunt; dehinc de potestate gloriantur. **8.** An tu potentem censes quern uideas uelle quod non possit efficere, potentem censes qui satellite latus ambit, qui quos terret ipse plus metuit, qui ut potens esse uideatur in seruientium manu situm est? **9.** Nam quid ego de regum familiaribus disseram, cum regna ipsa tantae imbecillitatis plena demonstrem? Quos quidem regia potestas saepe incolumis, saepe autem lapsa prosternit. **10.** Nero Senecam familiarem praeceptoremque suum ad eligendae mortis coegit arbitrium, Papinianum diu inter aulicos potentem militum gladiis Antoninus obiecit. **11.** Atqui uterque potentiae suae renuntiare uoluerunt, quorum Seneca opes etiam suas tradere Neroni seque in otium conferre conatus est; sed dum ruituros moles ipsa trahit, neuter quod uoluit effecit. **12.** Quae est igitur ista potentia, quam pertimescunt habentes, quam nec cum habere uelis tutus sis et cum deponere cupias uitare non possis?

13. An praesidio sunt amici quos non uirtus sed fortuna conciliat? Sed quem felicitas amicum fecit infortunium faciet inimicum. **14.** Quae uero pestis efficacior ad nocendum quam familiaris inimicus?

7. **1.** Quid autem de corporis uoluptatibus loquar, quarum appetentia quidem plena est anxietatis, satietas uero paenitentiae? **2.** Quantos illae morbos, quam intolerabiles dolores quasi quendam fructum nequitiae fruentium solent referre corporibus! **3.** Quarum motus quid habeat iucunditatis ignoro; tristes uero esse uoluptatum exitus, quisquis reminisci libidinum suarum uolet intelleget. **4.** Quae si beatos explicare possunt, nihil causae est quin pecudes quoque beatae esse dicantur, quarum omnis ad explendam corporalem lacunam festinat intentio. **5.** Honestissima quidem coniugis foret liberorumque iucunditas; sed nimis e natura dictum est nescio quem filios inuenisse tortores. Quorum quam sit mordax quaecumque condicio neque alias expertum te neque nunc anxium necesse est ammonere. **6.** In quo Euripidis mei sententiam probo, qui carentem liberis infortunio dixit esse felicem.

VII. Habet hoc uoluptas omnis:
stimulis agit fruentes
apiumque par uolantum
ubi grata mella fudit
fugit et nimis tenaci
ferit icta corda morsu.

8. **1.** Nihil igitur dubium est quin hae ad beatitudinem uiae deuia quaedam sint nec perducere quemquam eo ualeant ad quod se perducturas esse promittunt. **2.** Quantis uero implicitae malis sint breuissime monstrabo. **3.** Quid enim? Pecuniamne congregare conaberis? Sed eripies habenti. Dignitatibus fulgere uelis? Danti supplicabis et qui praeire ceteros honore cupis poscendi humilitate uilesces. **4.** Potentiamne desideras? Subiectorum insidiis obnoxius periculis subiacebis. **5.** Gloriam petas? Sed per aspera quaeque distractus securus esse desistis. **6.** Voluptariam uitam degas? Sed quis non spernat atque abiciat uilissimae fragilissimaeque rei, corporis, seruum?

7. Iam uero qui bona prae se corporis ferunt, quam exigua, quam fragili possessione nituntur! Num enim elephantos mole, tauros robore superare poteritis, num tigres uelocitate praeibitis? **8.** Respicite caeli spatium, firmitudinem, celeritatem et aliquando desinite uilia mirari. Quod quidem caelum non his potius est quam sua qua regitur ratione mirandum. **9.** Formae uero nitor ut rapidus est, ut uelox et uernalium florum mutabilitate fugacior! **10.** Quodsi, ut Aristoteles ait, Lyncei oculis homines uterentur, ut eorum uisus obstantia penetraret, nonne introspectis uisceribus illud Alcibiadis superficie pulcherrimum corpus turpissimum uideretur? Igitur te pulchrum uideri non tua natura, sed oculorum spectantium reddit infirmitas. **11.** Sed aestimate quam uultis nimio corporis bona, dum sciatis hoc quodcumque miramini triduanae febris igniculo posse dissolui.

12. Ex quibus omnibus illud redigere in summam licet quod haec quae nec praestare quae pollicentur bona possunt nec omnium bonorum congregatione perfecta sunt, ea nec ad beatitudinem quasi quidam calles ferunt nec beatos ipsa perficiunt.

VIII. Eheu, quae miseros tramite deuios
abducit ignorantia!
Non aurum in uiridi quaeritis arbore
nec uite gemmas carpitis,
non altis laqueos montibus abditis
ut pisce ditetis dapes
nec uobis capreas si libeat sequi
Tyrrhena captatis uada;

READING 2-D

CARMINA BVRANA

[SAEC. XIII CE]

196

1. In taberna quando sumus,
non curamus, quid sit humus,
sed ad ludum properamus,
cui semper insudamus.
quid agatur in taberna,
ubi nummus est pincerna,
hoc est opus, ut queratur,
sed quid loquar, audiatur.

2. Quidam ludunt, quidam bibunt,
quidam indiscrete vivunt.
sed in ludo qui morantur,
ex his quidam denudantur;
quidam ibi vestiuntur,
quidam saccis induuntur.
ibi nullus timet mortem,
sed pro Baccho mittunt sortem.

3. Primo pro nummata vini;
ex hac bibunt libertini.
semel bibunt pro captivis,
post hec bibunt ter pro vivis,
quater pro Christianis cunctis,
quinquies pro fidelibus defunctis,
sexies pro sororibus vanis,
septies pro militibus silvanis.

4. Octies pro fratribus perversis,
novies pro monachis dispersis,
decies pro navigantibus,
undecies pro discordantibus,
duodecies pro penitentibus,
tredecies pro iter agentibus.
tam pro papa quam pro rege
bibunt omnes sine lege.

5. Bibit hera, bibit herus,
bibit miles, bibit clerus,

bibit ille, bibit illa,
bibit servus cum ancilla,
bibit velox, bibit piger,
bibit albus, bibit niger,
bibit constans, bibit vagus,
bibit rudis, bibit magus,

6. Bibit pauper et egrotus,
bibit exul et ignotus,
bibit puer, bibit canus,
bibit presul et decanus,
bibit soror, bibit frater,
bibit anus, bibit mater,
bibit ista, bibit ille,
bibunt centum, bibunt mille.

7. Parum durant sex nummate,
† ubi ipsi immoderate
bibunt omnes sine meta,
quamvis bibant mente leta.
sic nos rodunt omnes gentes,
et sic erimus egentes.
qui nos rodunt, confundantur
et cum iustis non scribantur.

199

1. Puri Bacchi meritum
licitat illicitum:
    pocula festiva
    non sunt consumptiva.
        Bacchum colo
        sine dolo,
        quia volo,
    quod os meum bibat.

2. Hac in plana tabula
mora detur sedula.
    pares nostri, sortes,
    pugnant sicut fortes;
        nam per ludum
        fero dudum
        dorsum nudum
    ut mei consortes.

200

1. Bacche, bene venies gratus et optatus,
per quem noster animus fit letificatus.
Refl. Istud vinum, bonum vinum, vinum generosum,
reddit virum curialem, probum, animosum.

2. Bacchus forte superans pectora virorum
in amorem concitat animos eorum.
Refl. Istud vinum, bonum vinum, vinum generosum,
reddit virum curialem, probum, animosum.

3. Bacchus sepe visitans mulierum genus
facit eas subditas tibi, o tu Venus.
Refl. Istud vinum, bonum vinum, vinum generosum,
reddit virum curialem, probum, animosum.

4. Bacchus venas penetrans calido liquore
facit eas igneas Veneris ardore.
Refl. Istud vinum, bonum vinum, vinum generosum,
reddit virum curialem, probum, animosum.

5. Bacchus lenis leniens curas et dolores
confert iocum, gaudia, risus et amores.
Refl. Istud vinum, bonum vinum, vinum generosum,
reddit virum curialem, probum, animosum.

6. Bacchus mentem femine solet hic lenire
cogit eam citius viro consentire.
Refl. Istud vinum, bonum vinum, vinum generosum,
reddit virum curialem, probum, animosum.

7. Bacchus illam facile solet expugnare,
a qua prorsus coitum nequit impetrare.
Refl. Istud vinum, bonum vinum, vinum generosum,
reddit virum curialem, probum, animosum.

8. Bacchus numen faciens hominem iocundum,
reddit cum pariter doctum et facundum.
Refl. Istud vinum, bonum vinum, vinum generosum,
reddit virum curialem, probum, animosum.

9. Bacche, deus inclite, omnes hic astantes
leti sumus munera tua prelibantes.
Refl. Istud vinum, bonum vinum, vinum generosum,
reddit virum curialem, probum, animosum.

10. Omnes tibi canimus maxima preconia,
te laudantes merito tempora per omnia.

201

I.

Tu das, Bacche, loqui, tu comprimis ora loquacis,
Ditas, deditas, tristia leta facis.
Concilias hostes, tu rumpis federa pacis,
Et qui nulla sciunt, omnia scire facis.
Multis clausa seris tibi panditur arca tenacis;
Tu das, ut detur, nil dare posse facis.
Das ceco visum, das claudo crura salacis:
Crederis esse deus, hec quia cuncta facis.

II.

Ergo bibamus, ne sitiamus, vas repleamus.
Quisque suorum posteriorum sive priorum
Sit sine cura morte futura re peritura.

III.

Pone merum et talos, pereat, qui crastina curat.

IV.

Bacchus erat captus vinclisque tenacibus aptus;
Noluit ergo deus carceris esse reus.
Ast in conclavi dirupit vincula suavi
Et fractis foribus prodiit e laribus.

202

1. O potores exquisiti,
licet sitis sine siti,
en bibatis expediti
et scyphorum inobliti!
scyphi crebro repetiti
non dormiant,
et sermones inauditi
prosiliant.

2. Qui potare non potestis,
ite procul ab his festis!
procul ite! quid hic estis?
non est locus hic modestis.
inter letos mos agrestis
modestie
index est et certus testis
ignavie.

3. Si quis latitat hic forte,
qui recusat vinum forte,
ostendantur ei porte!
exeat hac de cohorte!
plus est nobis gravis morte,
si maneat;
sic recedat a consorte,
ne redeat.

4. Vina qui non gustat pura,
miser vivat et in cura!
vino sors lenitur dura,
procul ergo sit mixtura!
multum enim contra iura
delinquitur,
cum hec dei creatura
corrumpitur.

5. Dea deo ne iungatur!
deam deus aspernatur;
nam qui Liber appellatur,
libertate gloriatur.
virtus eius adnullatur
ad pocula,
et ad mortem infirmatur
ex copula.

6. Cum regina sit in mari,
dea potest appellari,
sed indigna tanto pari,
quem presumat osculari.
numquam Bacchus adaquari
se voluit,
neque libens baptizari
sustinuit.

7. Pure sequor tam purarum
puritatem personarum,
quia constat omne rarum
raritate magis carum.
ut in vino vis aquarum
non proficit,
sic in aqua vini parum
non sufficit.

8. Cura Bacchus et sopore
corda pio solvit more,
sumpto Baccho meliore
dulcis sapor est in ore;
vini constat ex sapore
 letitia,
recalescit in amore
 mens saucia.

203

1. Hiemali tempore,
dum prata marcent frigore
 et aque congelescunt,
concurrunt in estuario,
 qui regnant cum Decio
 et postquam concalescunt,
socius a socio ludens irretitur.
qui vestitus venerat, nudus reperitur.
 hei, trepidant divitie,
cum paupertas semper servit libere.

READING 2-E

ANTONIVS GALATEVS

[1444–1517 CE]

EREMITA

CACODAEMON. Quoniam peccasti, quoniam sceleste vitam egisti; et cum maxima feceris peccata tu tibi sanctus videbaris.

CALODAEMON. Quaenam sunt ista peccata?

CACODAEMON. Tu, qui semper aderas, haec ignoras?

CALODAEMON. Ignoro equidem.

CACODAEMON. Ignoras?

CALODAEMON. Ignoro; sed quae sunt?

CACODAEMON. Sine, expediam libellum.

CALODAEMON. Expedias, sed interim dimitte hunc.

CACODAEMON. Non dimittam. Sed vide in prima fronte paginae; hic, cum adolescens cremum ingrederetur, videns senem fessum oratione ct ieiuniis stertentem, maximum addidit cachinnum.

CALODAEMON. Perge, grande est hoc apud Deum facinus!

CACODAEMON. Dicam et maius; hic dum per arenas incursantes vidisset Saracenos, ne comprehenderetur et ut vitam servaret, aufugit et se in crepidine quadam abscondit.

CALODAEMON. Haec infirmitas est, non peccatum; perge quidem in secundam paginam.

CACODAEMON. Cum contemplaretur et oraret, inter orandum gravi somno correptus est.

CALODAEMON. Quin perge?

CACODAEMON. Mittamus cetera, dicam peccatum gravissimum: cum sacerdos quidam conficeret Sacramentum Eucharistiae, maximum in Ecclesia Dei, screatum coniecit.

CALODAEMON. **Hoc** naturae est, non hominis vitium.

CACODAEMON. Rides? Ista tibi levia videntur; dicam maximum. Cum videret senem eremitam fustibus a Saracenis caedi (quingenti enim illum comprehenderant equites), ipse, qui armatus erat palmeo baculo, non succurrit opem imploranti.

CALODAEMON. Quingentos ne equites ut solus et imbecillis aggrederetur?

CACODAEMON. Quingentos. Non fas est timere mortem virum Deo dicatum.

CALODAEMON. Ego metum, qui cadere possit in constantem virum, nunquam statuerem cuiquam in peccatum. Vidi quamplurimos, qui se ad moriendum paratos praedicabant, cum mors prope admota fuit excussitque magnanima illa verba, flebiliter et muliebriter ab hoste mortem deprecari! Invenies nonnullos qui pro amico periculis se exponant, qui vero certae morti neminem. Nefas est dicere, sed dicam quia verum est: Dei filius, vitae auctor et mortis domitor, tergiversari visus est, quando abscondit se et exivit de templo et cum dixit: "transeat a me calix iste." Quin potius dimitte hunc miserum; nihil enim peccavit; non sunt haec crimina, sed calumniae; sicophanta es.

CACODAEMON. Vide ne conviciis agamus; mihi commissum est explorare hominum maledicta et malefacta; haec est divina iustitia, punire sontes ac bonos tutari. Mihi si eripiatur accusandi potestas, en officium et libellum abicio. Tutare tu malos viros, ut si forte Deus irascatur, in te saeviat; quomodo viri boni vivere possent, si mali non punirentur?

CALODAEMON. Esto bono animo.

EREMITA. Iturusne ad inferos?

CALODAEMON. Deus ipse tibi opem ferat, et innocentia tua, quandoquidem ego non possum tibi opitulari.

EREMITA. At tu, Cacodaemon, si unquam inferorum pectora tetigit misericordia, hoc abs te peto, ut liceat mihi semel videre quem semper optavi paradisum, et pro quo tot lacrymas fudi, tot labores prodidi, et famem, sitim, calores et frigora perpessus sum.

CACODAEMON. Faciam, ac lubens, ut cum paradisum videris et beatam vitam quam tibi ademptam tuis peccatis prospexeris, maiori moerore angaris, cum in infernum demersus fueris. Eamus, sequere; sed porrige brachium, ut te arctissime comprehendam; nam fugitivus mihi videris.

EREMITA. Non sum.

CACODAEMON. Mirum est; nam quis me non fugeret?

EREMITA. Heu! Sentio suaves auras, spirantes zephyros.

CACODAEMON. Haec est aura paradisi.

EREMITA. Qui dulcis cantus complet aures meas! Audio murmura praeterlabentium aquarum et avium concentus.

CACODAEMON. Haec sunt beatorum spirituum gaudia, quae mihi negavit Deus.

EREMITA. Beata video illa nemora, olfacio, miser, redolentium herbarum flores et pomorum flagrantium odores.

CACODAEMON. Ut rumparis invidia et perpetuo doleas.

EREMITA. Muri illi argentei quid sibi volunt?

CACODAEMON. Sunt claustra paradisi, unde contra ius nos deturbati fuimus.

EREMITA. Porta illa adamantina aliisque gemmis ornata?

CACODAEMON. Paradisi porta est.

EREMITA. Estne alia?

CACODAEMON. Nulla.

EREMITA. Quare, cum ampla sit regio?

CACODAEMON. Quoniam una est ad beatam vitam via: virtus ipsa.

EREMITA. Sed cur tam angusta est?

CACODAEMON. Quoniam arcta est via quae ducit ad vitam; quae vero ad nos latissima: certe "noctu atque diu patet atri ianua Ditis."

Eremita. Cur clausa est porta?

CACODAEMON. Quoniam difficilis est aditus ad beatitudinem, et paucis quos Deus amavit patet.

EREMITA. Precor te, quoniam exorabilem inveni, ut moremur paulum, donec aliquis ingrediatur aut exeat, ut quae intus gerantur videam.

CACODAEMON. Et hoc quoque faciam, ut te maiori dolore afficiam. Sed, crede mihi, frustra morabimur. Vide ut hic nulla sint vestigia; non sunt attrita limina; raris patent fores; rara virtus; raro aperitur haec ianua. Certum est, praeter nos miseros, hinc exivisse neminem; et quandoque multa volvuntur saecula, antequam quisquam introcat. Nos accedamus ad limina, observemus!

EREMITA. Dic, quaeso, quaenam est turba haec, quae nos sequitur? O candidas, o beatas animas! O sanctos mores! O iucundos sermones! O graves incessus!

CACODAEMON. Tu, o senex, fortunatus es.

... alloquamur hominem: Exi foras.

EREMITA. Non exibo, etiamsi me gladio isto percusseris.

PAULUS. Exi, sceleste.

EREMITA. Exi tu, pharisaee, sycofanta, qui codicillos a praeside impetrasti, ut Christianos vinctos duceres in Hierusalem, o boni viri, o carnificis officium! Ego te, Paule, recte novi.

PAULUS. Persequutus sum Christianos, fateor; sed postea evasi doctor gentium, et mortem pro Christo obii.

EREMITA. Verum est; sed postquam te luminibus orbatum sensisti, quasi coactus et invitus credidisti.

PAULUS. Tandem pro Christo mortuus sum.

EREMITA. Tu et hic claviger, dum potuistis pericula in mari, pericula in terra, pericula in falsis fratribus evitastis; tu te civem romanum asseruisti; tu per sportam demissus es; quid plura? Tandem, cum Deo placuit, ad fata vestra pervenistis; cum non potuistis amplius declinare pericula, romano gladio extincti fuistis.

PAULUS. Non bene nosti Paulum Tarsensem, Doctorem gentium, Vas electionis.

EREMITA. Quinimmo et gladiatorem optimum et Christianorum insectatorem.

PAULUS. Satis est. Ego abeo.

PETRUS APOSTOLUS. Data est mihi potestas etiam angelis imperare. Venite, beati spiritus, pellite hunc et praecipitem ad Tartara mittito.

ANGELI. Certe mitis vir ingenii videtur, nec vires tentabit nostras; exi.

EREMITA. Exire vos omnes iubeo.

ANGELI. Nosne?

EREMITA. Vos, ne iterum in vestrum Creatorem bella moveatis, exemplo fratris vestri Luciferi.

ANGELI. Tu insanis; nos partes Creatoris nostri secuti sumus; nos bella gessimus, nos arma contra Dei hostes induimus, nos hoc caelum tutati sumus, nos denique Deo coronam regni huius dedimus.

... Homo sum ingenui pudoris, nec novi unquam veritatem inficiari. Sanctissima sunt instituta tua, et unum est quod maxime miror: cur docuisti recutiri homines?

ABRAAM. Ut distingueretur ab Ethnicis nobile et antiquum Iudaeorum genus.

EREMITA. Cur non iussisti potius incidi patentem aliquam partem corporis, ut palpebram scilicet, nasum aut aurem? Hoc enim modo facilius cognosci posset et Iudaeus et Ethnicus.

ABRAAM. Non ipse novi causam; Deus sic iussit.

EREMITA. Nil plus interrogo. Sed aliud est propter quod, si ego vellem, accusare possem.

ABRAAM. Tune me?

EREMITA. Ego te; an ignoras quam maximas virtutes plerumque comitantur maxima vitia?

ABRAAM. Tune Abraam arguere patriarcham potes?

EREMITA. Minime, sed illum qui propter ancillae amorem tam molestus fuit uxori, ut Deum offenderet; qui sororem accepit uxorem, qui deinde ancillam cum filio repulit, ut iratae uxori placeret; qua mortua senex habuit concubinarum gregem.

ABRAAM. Quid ais, fatue senex? Concessa erant haec eo tempore.

READING 2-F

DESIDERIVS ERASMVS ROTERODAMVS
[1466–1536 CE]

COLLOQVIA FAMILIARIA

SYRUS, GETA.

SY. OPto tibi multam felicitatem. GE. Et ego tibi conduplicatum opto, quicquid optas mihi. SY. Quid agis rei? GE. Confabulor. SY. Quid? confabulare solus? GE. Ut vides. SY. Fortasse tecum. Proinde tibi videndum, ut cum homine probo fabuleris. GE. Imo cum lepidissimo congerrone confabulor. SY. Quo? GE. Apulejo. SY. Istud quidem nunquam non facis. Sed 3 amant alterna Camœnæ. Tu perpetuo studes. GE. Non est ulla studiorum satietas. SY. Verum, sed 4 est tamen modus quidam. Non omittenda quidem sunt studia, sed tamen intermittenda nonnunquam. Non abjicienda sunt, sed relaxanda. Nihil suave quod perpetuum. 5 Voluptates commendat rarior usus. Tu nihil aliud quam studes. Perpetuo studes. Continenter incumbis literis. Indesinenter inhæres chartis. Studes noctes ac dies. Nunquam non studes. Assiduus es in studio. Jugiter intentus es libris. Nullum facis studendi finem, neque modum. Nullam studiis tuis requiem intermisces. Nunquam studendi laborem nec intermittis, nec remittis. GE. Age, tuo more facis. Rides me ut soles. Nunc ludis tu quidem me. Salse me rides. Satyricum agis. 6 Naso me suspendis adunco. Non me fallit tuum scemma. Nunc plane joco mecum agis. Sum tibi risui. Rideor abs te. Pro delectamento me habes. Nunc me ludos deliciasque facis. Eadem opera assue mihi auriculas asini. Ipsi codices pulvere situque obducti loquuntur, quam sim immodicus in studio. SY. Emoriar, ni loquor ex animo. Disperеam, si quid fingo. Ne vivam, si quid simulo. Loquor id quod sentio. Quod res est dico. Serio loquor. Ex animo loquor. Non secus sentio, quam loquor.

Cur non visis?

GE. Quid causæ est, quod tam diu nos non inviseris? Quid rei est, quod nos tam raro visis? Quid accidit, quod tanto tempore nos non adieris? Quare tam rarus es salutator? Quid sibi vult, quod nos tam diu non conveneris? Quid obstitit quo minus visas nos frequentius? Quid impedimento fuit, quo minus jam diu feceris nobis tui videndi copiam?

Succeſſus.

SA. Res ſucceſſit opinione melius. Fortuna votis utriuſque favit. Si fortuna tibi nupſiſſet, non potuiſſet eſſe obſequentior. Res tua & ventis, & amne ſecundo proceſſit. Vicit etiam vota noſtra fortunæ faventis afflatus. Opinor te litaſſe Rhamnuſiæ, cui ſic ex ſententia cadunt omnia. Plus impetravi quam fuiſſem auſus optare. Ventis per omnia ſecundis hic curſus nobis peractus eſt. Res omnis cecidit ex ſententia. Pulchre nobis cecidit hæc alea. Opinor volaſſe noctuam, adeo feliciter exiit nobis parum ſapienter inſtitutum.

Gratiarum actio.

JA. Equidem & gratiam habeo, & habiturus ſum, quoad vivam, maximam. Pro iſto tuo in me officio pares agere gratias vix poſſim, referre nequaquam. Video quantum debeam tuo in me ſtudio. Nihil miror, neque enim tu quicquam novi feciſti, & hoc magis debeo. De iſthoc tuo in me officio, amo te mi Sapide, ut par eſt, maxime Quod hac in cauſa præſtiteris amicum minime aulicum, & habetur a me gratia, & ſemper habebitur. Quod meum negocium tibi cordi fuerit, amo te, & habeo gratiam. Iſthoc officio gratiam iniſti apud me maximam. Pergratum eſt, quod cauſam meam egeris bona fide. Ex omnibus officiis, quæ tu plurima in me contuliſti, hoc eſt longe gratiſſimum. Referre gratiam parem nequaquam poſſum: agere accuratius inter nos ſupervacaneum ſit: quod unum poſſum, habebo dum vixero. Iſthoc beneficio fateor tibi me magnopere devinctum eſſe. Hoc nomine plus tibi debeo, quam unquam ſolvendo eſſe queam. Hoc beneficio arctius me tibi devinxiſti, quam ut poſſim diſſolvere. Obligatiorem me tibi reddidiſti, quam ut nomen meum e tuo diario poſſim unquam expungere. Hoc officio me ſic tuum reddidiſti, ut nullum mancipium æque ſit in rebus heri ſui. Hac re me tibi devinctiorem reddidiſti, quam ut unquam æs alienum poſſim reſolvere. Plurimis nominibus tibi debeo, ſed non alio plus quam hoc. Pro mediocribus beneficiis agendæ ſunt gratiæ: hoc majus eſt, quam ut conveniat verbis gratias agere.

An accepisti literas? Formula.

PE. Nihilne literarum accepisti? Num aliquas e patria recepisti literas? Nullæ tibi sunt redditæ literæ? Num quid scriptorum accepisti? Num quas accepisti epistolas? Ecquas ab amiculis accepisti literas? Nihil epistolarum advolavit e Gallia?

Responsio.

CH. Literarum nihil accepi. Ne pilum quidem literarum accepi. Ne tantulum quidem adfertur literarum. Nemo literam ad me. Ne verbum quidem a quoquam redditur. Tantum literarum accepi jam diu, quantum vides in oculo meo. Equidem pecunias, quam literas malim. Argentum accipere malim, quam epistolas. Nummos recipere malim, quam epistolia. Nihil moror literas; modo veniat argentum. Equidem numerari malo mihi, quam scribi.

Percontandi Forma in primo congressu.

GEORGIVS, LIVINVS.

GE. EX qua tandem corte aut cavea nobis ades? LI. Quid ita? GE. Quia male saginatus. Quia macie pelluces totus, ariditate crepitas. Unde prodis? LI. E collegio 4 Montis acuti. GE. Ergo ades nobis onustus literis. LI. Imo pediculis. GE. Pulchre comitatus advenis. LI. Sane, nec tutum est nunc viatorem ire incomitatum. GE. Agnosco sodalitium scholasticum. Ecquid novarum rerum adfers e Lutetia? LI. Illud in primis, quod scio, tibi videbitur incredibile: Lutetiæ Beta sapit, & Quercus concionatur. GE. Quid tu narras? LI. Hoc quod audis. GE. Quid ego audio? LI. Hoc quod narro. GE. Monstri simile. Oportet illic fungos & lapides esse auditores, ubi tales concionentur. LI. Atqui sic res habet. Nec audita narro, sed comperta. GE. Oportet igitur illic plurimum sapere homines, si sapit Beta & Quercus. LI. Recte conjectas.

Alia.

GE. Valesne? LI. Contemplare vultum. GE. Quin potius lotium jubes? An me putas medicum? Non rogo, quid valeas, nam facies ipsa loquitur te belle valere, sed quomodo tibi placeas. LI. Corpus quidem belle habet, sed animo male est. GE. At non valet, qui isthac parte laborat. LI. Sic res habent meæ: Corpus valet, sed ægrotat crumena. GE. Facile isti morbo medebitur mater. Ut valuisti usque? LI. Varie, ut sunt res mortalium. GE. Satin' recte vales? Salvane res? Satin' salvæ res? Fuistine semper prospera valetudine? LI. Prosperrima, gratia superis. Ego Dei beneficio perpetuo bellissime valui. Semper prospera valetudine sum usus. Hactenus bona valetudine fui, fausta, incolumi, felici, prospera, secunda, integra, 5 basilica, athletica, pancratica valetudine. GE. Faxint superi ut isthuc sit perpetuum ac proprium. Lætus isthuc audio. Voluptatem mihi nuncias. Est isthuc mihi auditu perquam jucundum. Sermonem istum ex te audire supra modum gaudeo. Isthuc haud invitus audio. Oppido lætor isthuc audire ex te. Ut idem semper facias, opto. Ut ad istum modum quam diutissime valeas, opto. Tibi gratulor, mihi gaudeo. Gratia superis. Gratiam habeo superis. LI. Equidem pulchre valeo, si tu vales. GE. Nihil interim molestiæ fuit? LI. Nihil, nisi quod vestra consuetudine frui non licuit. GE. Quo pacto vales? LI. Recte, pulchre, belle, perbelle, bellissime, perpulchre, feliciter, commode, minime male. Valeo ut volo potius, quam ut mereor: 6 basilice, pancratice, athletice. GE. Exspectabam ut diceres etiam, taurice.

Male valere.

GE. Rectene vales? LI. Vellem quidem. Non admodum ex sententia. Equidem utcunque valeo. Sic satis. Valeo ut possum, quando ut volo non licet. Ut soleo. Ita ut superis visum est. Non optime sane. Sic ut antehac pejus nunquam. Valeo ut solitus sum. Valeo ut solent, quibus cum medicis res est. GE. Ut vales? LI. Secus quam vellem. GE. Qua valetudine es? LI. Haud sane commoda, incommoda, perquam incommoda, infelici, parum prospera, parum secunda, mala, adversa, infausta, imbecilli, dubia, mediocri, vix mediocri, longe alia quam vellem, tolerabili, qualem optem hostibus meis. GE. Rem mihi sane quam acerbam narras. Prohibeant superi. Avertat Deus. Bona verba. Hic cupiam te vanum esse. Bono sis animo oportet. Forti infractoque sis animo. Multum juvat animus in re mala bonus. Fulciendus est animus spe fortunæ secundioris. Quid morbi est? Quod mali genus est? Quis te morbus habet? Quo morbo teneris? Quid habes morbi? Quis te tenet morbus? LI. Nescio, & hoc laboro periculosius. GE. Verum. Nam ad sanitatem gradus est, novisse morbum. Nullosne consuluisti medicos? LI. Equidem permultos. GE. Quid respondent? LI. Id quod 7 advocati Demiphoni apud Comicum, alius negat, alius ait, alius deliberandum censet. In hoc consentiunt omnes, me miserum esse. GE. Quam pridem habet te hoc mali? Diu est quod teneris isto morbo? Quantum temporis est quod te malum hoc corripuit? LI. Dies plus minus viginti. Ferme mensis est. Jam tertius est mensis. Mihi quidem seculum videtur, quod ægrotare cœpi. GE.

Credo, Formula.

PE. Facile credo. Haud difficile creditu est. Credi istud perfacile potest. Istud tibi quis non credat? Admodum incredulus fuerit, qui hoc non tibi credat. Profecto habeo tibi fidem. Istius rei mihi facile fidem facis. Credo tibi vel injurato. Verisimile dicis. Adferunt tamen nonnihil solatii literæ. At ego alterutrum malim, quam neutrum.

Utilitatis, Formula.

CH. Quorsum spectant literæ sine pecunia? Ad quid tandem inanes conducunt literæ? Quorsum valent, ad quid conferunt, faciunt, prosunt, proficiunt literæ vacuæ? Cui gratæ, cui acceptæ literæ sine nummis? Quid emolumenti adferunt literæ inanes? Cui bono sunt ociosæ literæ? Quid juvant? Cui sunt usui? Ad quid conducibiles sunt? Quid secum adferunt momenti? Cui rei sunt utiles inanes epistolæ?

READING 2-G

GEORGIVS SCHWEIDER

[1962 CE]

LATINE LOQUOR

Míchael, Norbértus

Mich. Visne mihi commodáre tuum Horátium? *Norb.* Volo équidem, modo illum répetas a Conrádo, cui uténdum dedi. *Mich.* Quo signo vis répetam? *Norb.* Nempe hoc, quod eius hábeo epístulas. *Mich.* Id mihi satis est. *Norb.* Sed quando reddes? *Mich.* Cum descrípsero contéxtum in tres aut quattuor praelectiónes. *Norb.* Matúra ígitur: ne meo stúdio incómmodes. *Mich.* Maturábo. *Norb.* Sed heus tu, cave mácules: alióquin aegre commodábo posthac. *Mich.* Nempe indígnus essem benefício.

Robértus, Patrícius

Rob. Unde nunc redis? *Patri.* Foris. *Rob.* Cur prodiísti? *Patri.* Ut irem domum. *Rob.* Quid eo? *Patri.* Petítum libros meos. *Rob.* Eho, cur non attulísti? *Patri.* Oblítus eram. *Rob.* Síccine soles ieutáculum aut meréndam oblivísci? *Patri.* Raríssime. *Rob.* Profécto, magna fuit neglegéntia. *Patri.* Immo máxima: sed quid agas? Scholástici sumus. *Rob.* Quid si praecéptor tuum factum sciret? *Patri.* Fortásse poenas darem. *Rob.* Ain tu, fortásse? procul dubio vapuláres. Non te pudet sine libris in scholam veníre? *Patri.* Non solum pudet, sed etiam piget: verúmtamen ne me accúses óbsecro. *Rob.* Nihil minus cógito: sed non possum dissimuláre, quin ego te reprehéndam. *Patri.* Istud, credo équidem, amíce facis: ítaque boni cónsulo. *Rob.* Id satis est mihi. Eámus intro in auditórium. *Patr.* Tempus est.

Iacóbus, Iúlius.

Iacob. Ubi nunc est pater tuus? *Iul.* Puto eum esse Antvérpiae. *Iacob.* Quid illic agit? *Iul.* Negotiátur. *Iacob.* Ex quo témpore? *Iul.* Ab ipso inítio mercátus. *Iacob.* Valde miror, qui aúdeat illic commorári tot dies, cum pituíta tanta sit per totam urbem. *Iul.* Non est adeo mirándum. *Iacob.* Ítane tibi vidétur? *Iul.* Ita profécto. Fuit enim álias in maióre perículo, sed Dóminus Deus semper eum custodívit. *Iacob.* Credo équidem, et adhuc custódiet. Sed quando est reversúrus? *Iul.* Néscio. In horas exspectámus. *Iacob.* Redúcat eum Deus! *Iul.* Ita precor.

Adólphus, Praecéptor.

Adolph. Salvus sis, praecéptor. *Praec.* Auspicáto ádvenis: quid núntias? *Adolph.* Orat te pater meus, ut ánimi causa eámus una in hortos suos suburbános. *Praec.* Ad eam rem nos invítat serénitas, et nunc sumus feriáti. Sed quid illic aspéctu iucúndum vidébimus? *Adolph.* Várias et pulchras árbores cum suis frúctibus, item herbárum et florum miram varietátem. *Praec.* Nihil est illis rebus hoc témpore iucúndius. *Adolph.* Ea est Dei erga nos beneficéntia. *Praec.* Quam quidem assíduis laúdibus prósequi debémus. *Adolph,* Sed véreor, ne patri in mora simus. *Praec.* Tantísper exspécta, dum togam muto, ut sim ad ambulándum expedítior. Iam parátus sum: nunc eámus. Sed estne domi pater? *Adolph.* Prae fóribus nos exspéctat. *Praec.* Bene res habet: vide, ut eum decénter salútes. *Adolph.* De hoc, te docénte, saepe admóniti fúimus.

Lucas, Lambértus.

Luc. Quid ita laetus es? *Lambert.* Quia venit pater. *Luc.* Ain'tu? unde venit? *Lambert.* Lutétia. *Luc.* Quando advénit? *Lambert.* Modo. *Luc.* Iamne salutásti? *Lambert.* Salutávi, cum ex vehículo descénderet. *Luc.* Quid ámplius illi fecísti? *Lambert,* Calceaménta detráxi. *Luc.* Miror, te non mansísse domi, propter eius advéntum. *Lambert.* Nec ille permisísset, nec ego vellem, praesértim nunc, cum audiénda est praeléctio. *Luc.* Bene tibi cónsulis, qui témporis ratiónem hábeas. Sed quid pater? valétne? *Lambert.* Recte, Dei benefício. *Luc.* Équidem gaúdeo plúrimum tua et eius causa, quod salvus péregre redíerit. *Lambert.* Facis, ut amícum decet: sed cras plúribus verbis colloquémur. Vide praeceptórem, qui iam ingréditur auditórium. *Luc.* Eámus audítum praelectiónem.

Albértus, Magíster.

Alb. Praecéptor, pater te invítat ad prándium, si tibi placet. *Mag.* Estne solus? *Alb.* Solus, opínor, praeter domésticos. *Mag.* Excúsa me illi, iam enim aliúnde invitátus sum. Age tamen illi meis verbis grátias. *Alb.* Numquid vis áliud? *Mag.* Nihil, nisi ut matúre ad scholam rédeas. *Alb.* Matúre, iuvánte Deo.

Praecéptor, Vincéntius.

Praec. Ubi est Martínus? *Vinc.* Ivit ad forum. *Praec.* Quid eo? *Vine.* Emptum, ut dixit, cíngulum. *Praec.* Iniússu meo non exíre débuit: sed hoc nihil ad te. Quis dabit vobis meréndam? *Vinc.* Dixit se hora secúnda reversúrum, ut daret nobis. *Praec.* Quid si fallat? *Vine.* Id non est moris eius. *Praec.* Nisi ad horam affúerit, ádmone uxórem de vestra meránda, habet enim clavem álteram cellae penáriae.

Paulus, ioánnes

Paul. Estne domi frater tuus? *Ioan.* Cur istud rogas? *Paul.* Pater meus vóluit eum convenire. *Ioan.* Non est in hac urbe. *Paul.* Ubi ígitur? *Ioan.* Péregre proféctus est. *Paul.* Quando? *Ioan.* Núdius tértius. *Paul.* Quonam ivit? *Ioan.* Lutétiam. *Paul.* Qua iter factúrus est? *Ioan.* Lugdúno. *Paul.* Utrum pedes an eques ivit? *Ioan.* Ivit in equo. *Paul.* Quando redíbit? *Ioan.* Néscio. *Paul.* Sed quem diem constítuit illi pater? *Ioan.* Iussit, ut hic adesset ad vigésimum huius mensis diem. *Paul.* Ducat illum Deus, ac redúcat! *Ioan.* Ita precor.

NORBÉRTUS, MAXIMILIÁNUS.

Norbert. Ubi fuísti his diebus? *Maximil.* Ruri. *Norbert.* Quo in loco? *Maximil.* In villa nostra. *Norbert.* Quid agébas illic? *Maximil.* Ministrábam patri. *Norbert.* Quid vero ille? *Maximil.* Pastinábat vites nostras. *Norbert.* Quando illinc rediísti? *Maximil.* Heri tantum. *Norbert.* Quid pater? *Maximil.* Una mecum revértit. *Norbert.* Bene factum: sed quo nunc is? *Maximil.* Recta domum. *Norbert.* Quando répetes ludum litterárum? *Maximil.*Cras, iuvánte Deo, aut summum peréndie. *Norbert.* Ergo ínterim vale. *Maximil.* Et tu vale, mi Norbérte.

PRAECÉPTOR, TERÉNTIUS

Praec. Demíror, unde nunc vénias? *Ter.* Domo rédeo, praecéptor. *Praec.* Cur íveras domum? *Ter.* Petítum meréndam. *Praec.* Quam ob rem non attulísti? *Ter.* Mater erat occupáta. *Praec.* Quid tum? debuísti exíre iniússu meo? *Ter.* Non débui, fáteor. *Praec.* Quid ígitur meruísti? *Ter.* Plagas accípere: sed ignósce mihi, quaeso, praecéptor. *Praec.* Cur non petivísti exeúndi potestátem? *Ter.* Quia nou audébam te interpelláre. *Praec.* Quid agébam? *Ter.* Tenébas libéllum quemdam, et legébas áliquid. *Praec.* Fíeri pótuit, sed vos tamen saepe me interpellátis ob rem leviórem. Nunc ígitur para te ad vapulándum. *Ter.* Parce mihi, óbsecro, praecéptor. *Praec.* Sine, ut prius cógitem aliquantísper. Age, parco: tum quia ingenue confitéris, tum quod satis studiósus mihi vidéris. *Ter.* Grátias ago máximas, praecéptor humaníssime.

NORBÉRTUS, OTTO.

Norb. Unde veniébas modo? *Ot.* E culína. *Norb.* Quid illuc íveras? *Ot.* Ut me calefácerem. *Norb.* Tu, credo, libéntius es in culína, quam in schola, nonne? *Ot.* Nihil mirum: in schola non est ignis, sicut in culína. *Norb.* Abi, si sapis. *Ot.* Útinam tam sáperem in divínis rebus, quam in cura córporis! *Norb.* Fac sápias. *Ot.* Quómodo? *Norb.* Stúdio, cura, labóre, diligéntia. *Ot.* Non parco labóri. *Norb.* Recte facis: sed est tempus exspectándum, cuius progréssu fiunt ómnia: intérea precándus est Deus assídue. *Ot.* Bene mones: útinam ille stúdia nostra promóveat in glóriam sui nóminis. *Norb.* Id fáciet, si pergámus eum cólere diligénter.

LUDOVÍCUS, MAXIMILIÁNUS.

Ludo. Habésne multos libros? *Max.* Non ádmodum. *Ludo.* Sed quos habes? *Max.* Rudiménta grammáticae, collóquia scholástica, Teréntium, Vergilium, Horátium, epístulas Cicerónis cum vernácula interpretatióne, Catónem, Léxicon, Testamentum Novum et Catechéseos librum, praetérea librum chartáceum ad scribéndum dictáta praeceptóris. *Ludo.* Tu vero quos habes? *Max.* Omnes hábeo, quos enumerásti, praeter Catónem, Teréntium et Cicerónis epístulas. Cur enim libros hábeam, qui non praelegúntur in schola nostra? At ego, dum sumus otiósi, lego intérdum illos: ut semper áliquid addíscam novi, praesértim in lingua latína, et honestátis móribus. *Ludo.* Prudénter facis, mi Maximiliáne. O me míserum! qui numquam dídici, quid sit studiósum esse! *Max.* Disce ígitur. Praestat enim sero, quam numquam díscere.

Paulus, Renátus.

Paul. Quid rides? *Ren.* Néscio. *Paul.* Nescis? Magnum signum stultítiae. *Ren.* Me ígitur stultum vocas? *Paul.* Mínime vero: sed dico tibi, arguméntum esse stultítiae, cum quis ridet, et ridéndi causam nescit. *Ren.* Quid est stultítia? *Paul.* Si diligénter evólvis Catónem tuum, istud quod quaeris, invénies. *Ren.* Nunc non hábeo meum Catónem, et volo áliam rem ágere. *Paul.* Quod habes negótium? *Ren.* Est mihi ediscéndum áliquid de Lógica.

READING 2-H

ANDREAS FRITSCH BEROLINENSIS

[1996 CE]

INDEX SENTENTIARVM AC LOCVTIONVM

(*variis ibidem in paginis*)

belli peritus: Nep. Reg. 2,2.
bellica laus: Caes. Gall. 6,24.3; Cic. Marcell. 6 (bellicas laudes)
bellissimus ille pusio: Apvl. met. 9.7,4 *(dieser hübsche Knabe)*
bello Helvetiorum confecto. Caes. Gall. 1,30.1
bello Punico primo: Cic. nat. 2,7
bello Punico secundo: Cic. off. 3,47; Sall. Iug. 5,4
bellona, si hodie nobis victoriam duis, ast ego tibi templum voveo.: Liv. 10,19,17
bellum autem ita suscipiatur, ut nihil aliud nisi pax quaesita videatur.: Cic. off. 1,80
bellum est enim sua vitia nosse.: Cic. Att. 2,17,2
bellum gerere: ≈ Cic. off. 2,45; Liv. 9,8,8; Sen. epist. 5l,8(→ fortuna mecum b. gerit)
bellum inferre finitimis: Caes. Gall. 1,2,4 (his rebus fiebat, ut et minus late vagarentur et minus facile finitimis b. i. possent)
bellum inferre: ≈ Caes. Gall. 1,36,5; Nep. Milt. 3.1
bellum iustum: ≈ Cic. off. 1,36
bellum parare: Caes. Gall. 3,9,3; 5,3.4; 6.2,3
bellum peractum est.: Sen. Tro. 1168
bellum pomum: Petron. 57,3 *(ein sauberes Früchtchen)*
bellum renovare: Nep. Ham. 1,4
bellum se ipsum alet.: ≈ Cato ap. Liv. 34,9,12
bellum subito exarsit: Cic. Lig. 3
bellum tertium Punicum: Cic. off. 1.79
bellumque inter eos gerebatur et mari el terra: Nep. Hann. 10.2
belua: Plavt. Most 569 *(Tier, Rindvieh, Schafskopf:* cfr Brix ad Plavt. Trin. 952)
bene ac feliciter eveniret: Liv. 21,17,4 (ut b. ac f. eveniret quod bellum populus Romanus iussisset): 31,5,4 (→ ea res uti populo Romano sociisque ac nomini Latino bene ac f. c.); →bene et feliciter
bene admones: Avg. mag. 5.4
bene adtendisti.: Avg. mag. I I.I
bene ais.: Cic. Quinct. 79bene ambula et redambula!: Plavt. Capt. 900
bene ambula!: Plavt. Asin. 108; Capt. 900; Mil. 936
bene ambula, bene rem geras!: Plavt. Mil. 936

bene ambuletis et sit Deus in itinere vestro et angelus eius comitetur vobiscum: VVLG. Tob. 5.21
bene atque amice dicis. di dent, quae velis.: PLAVT. Stich. 469
bene atque feliciter evenire: ≈ CIC. Mur. I (→ quod precatus ...); LIV. 36.1,2 (→ ut ea res senatui populoque Romano b. atque f. eveniret); → bene ac feliciter; → bene et feliciter
bene autem mori est libenter mori.: SEN. epist. 61,2 (→ hoc animo tibi hanc epistulam scribo ...)
bene cedere: Ov. met. 8,862; cfr HOR. sat. 2,1,31 s. (si male cesserat, ... si bene)
bene cenare: ≈ CATVLL. 13,1 (→ cenabis bene, mi Fabulle ...)
bene cenare: ≈ CIC. fin. 2,24
bene cogitata, si excidunt, non occidunt.: PVBLIL. sent. B 28
bene commemorasti; recordor prorsus ac libentissime: AVG. soliloq. 2,32,8
bene convenit: SEN. epist. 4,11 (cui cum paupertate b. c., dives est.)
bene cubes!: cfr GÜTHLING, Dt.-lat. Wörterb., s.v. *Nacht (Gute Nacht!)*
bene de re publica meriti: NEP. Phoc. 2,2
bene de re publica meritum: CAES. civ. 1,13,1
bene dicendi scientia: QVINT. inst. 2,15,38 (→ his adprobatis simul manifestum est illud quoque. quem finem vel quid summum et ultimum habeat rhetorice, quod τέλος dicitur, ad quod omnis ars tendit: nam si est ipsa bene dicendi scientia, finis eius et summum est bene dicere)
bene dicere: SALL. Catil. 3,1 *(hier: gewandt reden)*
bene dixisti, quia non habeo virum.: VVLG. 1011. 4.17 (NEOVVLG.: hoc vere dixisti)
bene docet loqui, qui bene docet facere.: Ps.SEN. mor. 2

erant eo tempore Athenis duae factiones, quarum una populi causam agebat, altera optimatium: NEP. Phoc. 3,2
erant hae difficultates belli gerendi, quas supra ostendimus: CAES. Gall. 3,10,1
erant illis omnia communia: VVLG. Act. 4,32; cfr 2,44
erant in quadam civitate rex et regina. hi tres numero filias forma conspicuas habuere.: APVL. Met. 4, 28,1
erant omnino itinera duo, quibus itineribus domo exire possent: unum per Sequanos...alterum per provinciam nostrum ... : CAES. Gall. 1,6,1-2
erant plena laetitia et gratulatione omnia: CAES. Civ. 1,74,7
erant, qui dicerent, Sisyphum diu laturam fecisse, Tantalum siti periturum, nisi illi succerreretur, aliquando Ixionis miseri rotam sufflaminandam.: SEN. apocol. 14,3
erant, qui metu mortis mortem precarentur: PLIN. epist. 6,20,15
erat autem difficile rem tantam tamque praeclaram inchoatam relinquere.: CIC. nat. 1,56
erat autem fere hora sexta.: VVLG. Luc. 23,44
erat autem mane.: VVLG. Ioh. 18,28

erat autem Parasceve Paschae hora quasi sexta et dicit Iudaeis: "ecce rex vester!": VVLG. Ioh. 19,14
erat enim cum institutus optime, tum etiam perfecte planeque eruditus: CIC. Brut. 282
erat enim historia nihil aliud nisi annalium confectio, cuius rei memoriaeque publicae retinendae causa ab initio rerum Romanarum usque ad P. Mucium pontificem maximum res omnis singulorum annorum mandabat litteris pontifex maximus referebatque in album et proponebat tabulam domi ...)
erat enim iam vespera: VVLG. Act. 4.3
erat hiems summa, tempestas ... perfrigida, imber maximus.: CIC. Verr. II 4,86
erat in desiderio civitatis, in ore, in sermone omnium.: CIC. Phil. 10,14
erat mihi in animo recta proficisci ad exercitum, aestivos menses reliquos rei militari dare, hibernos iuris dictioni.: CIC. Att. 5,14,2
erat nemo, in quem ea suspicio conveniret.: CIC. S. Rosc. 64
erat praeterea cum eo adulescens illustris, formosus, Hasdrubal, quem nonnulli diligi turpius, quam par erat, ab Hamilcare loquebantur: non enim maledici tanto viro deesse poterant.: NEP. Ham. 3.2
erat sane somni paratissimi.: PLIN. epist. 3,5,8
erat sine dubio caelum grave sordidis nubibus, quae fere aut in aquam aut in ventum resolvuntur SEN. epist. 53,1
erat structura muri eius ex lapide iaspide: VVLG. Apoc. 21,18
eratque in terris magna exspectatio: PHAEDR. 4,24,2
ere, ne me species! me inpulsore haec non facit.: TER. Eun. 988
erectos ad sidera tollere vultus: OV. met. 1,86
ereptis opibus noli maerere dolendo, / sed gaude potius, tibi si contingat habere: Ps. CATO dist. 4,35
ergo accipite disciplinam per sermones meos, et proderit vobis.: VVLG. Sap. 6,25
ergo adcura, sed propere opust.: PLAVT. Mil. 805 (accura; opus est)
ergo arbores seret diligens agricola, quarum aspiciet bacam ipse numquam.: CIC . Tusc. 1,31
ergo attende pauca, quae restant!: AVG. soliloq. 2,22,1
ergo attende! - istic sum.: AVG. soliloq. 1,28,5
ergo contenti munere invicti Iovis / fatalis annos decurramus temporis, / nec plus conemur quam sinit mortalitas.: PHAEDR. app.3,12-14
ergo edepol palles. si sapias, eas ac decumbas domi.: PLAVT. Merc. 373
ergo etiam stultis acuit ingenium fames: PHAEDR. app. 22,7
ergo exeundum ad libertatem est.: SEN. dial. 7,4,4
ergo haec quoque hactenus.: CIC. Att. 5,13,2 *(Also auch das wäre erledigt.)*; → atque haec quidem hactenus
ergo hoc proprium est animi bene constituti et laetari bonis rebus et dolere contrariis.: CIC. Lael. 47

ergo hinc abesto, livor!: PHAEDR. 3 prol. 60
ergo hominum genus in cassum frustraque laborat / semper et in curis consumit inanibus aevom.: LVCR. 5,1430
ergo incipe quaerere!: AVG. soliloq. 1,7,2
ergo infigi debet persuasio ad totam pertinens vitam: hoc est, quod decretum voco.: SEN. epist.
95,44
ergo non levitas mihi, / sed certa ratio causam scribendi dedit.: PHAEDR. 4 prol. 8 s.
ergo opifex plus sibi proponet ad formarum quam civis excellens ad factorum pulchritudinem?: CIC. fin. 2,115
ergo quid refert mea, / cui serviam, clitellas dum portem meas?: PHAEDR. 1,15,9 s.
ergo quin legis?: PLAVT. Pseud. 40
ergo tu Tyrius es? - ut dicis; sic sum.: HIST. Apoll. 24
ergo, ut spero, prope diem te videbo.: CIC. Att. 6,2,6; → te videbo
erigere oculos et vivere: CIC. Sest. 68
erigite animos, retinete vestram dignitatem!: CIC.Att. 1,16,9
eripe me de luto, ut non infigar; libera me ab iis, qui oderunt me, et de profundis aquarum.: VVLG. Psalm. 68(69),15;→ vide humilitatem meam, et eripe me
eripe me, et erue me de manu filiorum alienorum, quorum os locutum est vanitatem.: VVLG. Psalm. 143(144), 11
eripere telum, non dare irato decet.: PVBLIL. sent. E 11
eripit se aufertque ex oculis perfecta virtus.: SEN. dial. 6,23,3
erit enim tempus, cum sanam doctrinam non sustinebunt, sed ad sua desideria coacervabunt sibi magistros prurientes auribus, / et a veritate quidem auditum avertent, ad fabulas autem convertentur.: VVLG. 2 Tim. 4,3 s.
erit id mihi gratissimum.: CIC.fam. 12,21
erit id mihi vehementer gratum.: CIC. fam. 13,39; → id mihi vehementer gratum erit
erit ille nolus, quem per te cognoveris.: PHAEDR. 3,10,58
erit rebus ipsis par et aequalis oratio.: CIC. or. 123
eritis sicut dii, scientes bonum et malum.: VVLG. Gen. 3,5
errabant acti fatis maria omnia circum.: VERG. Aen. 1.32
errare mehercule malo cum Platone, quem tu quanti facias scio et quem ex tuo ore admiror, quam cum istis vera sentire.: CIC. Tusc. 1,39
errare mihi videntur, qui existimant ... : SEN. epist. 73,1
errare, si qui in bello omnes secundos rerum proventus exspectent.: CAES. Gall. 7,29,3
erras, [sic] me decipere non potes.: PLAVT. Merc. 928
erras, Catule.: CIC. de or. 2,77
erras, inquit, Scaure.: CIC. de or. 2,265
erras, iuvenis, nihil verum dicis.: HIST. Apoll. 5

erras, si id credis, et me ignoras, Clinia.: Ter. Haut. 105
erras.: Ter. Andr. 838
errasse humanum est et confiteri errorem prudentis.: Hier. epist. 57,12
errasti aliqua in re: Cic. Mur. 62
errat longe quidem mea sententia, / qui imperium credat gravius esse aut stabilius, / vi quod fit, quam illud quod amicitia adiungitur.: Ter. Ad. 65-67
errat, qui datum sibi, quod extortum est, putat.: Pvblil. sent. E 22
errat, si quis existimat facilem rem esse donare; plurimum ista res habet difficultalis, si modo consilio tribuitur, non casu et impetu spargitur.: sen. dial. 7,24,1
errat, si quis existimat tutum esse ibi regem, ubi nihil a rege tutum est.: ≈ sen. clem. 1,19,5
erratis. si senatum probare ea, quae dicuntur a me, putatis, populum autem esse in alia voluntate.: Cic. leg agr. 1,27
error a culpa vacat.: Sen. Herc. Oct. 983

oppidum ab nomine uxoris Lavinium appellavit ≈ Liv. 1,1,11
oppidum vacuum ab defensoribus: Caes. Gall. 2.12,2
opportune advenis.: Ter. Haut. 179
opportune advenisti mihi.: Plavt. Pers. 101
opportune, importune: Vvlg. 2 Tim. 4,2 (→ praedica verbum. insta opportune, importune)
opportunissime res accidit, quod postridie eius dici mane … Germani … ad eum in castra venerunt.: ≈ Caes. Gall. 4,13,4
opposita ad oculos manu: Svet. Aug. 78,1 (→ post cibum meridianum)
oppressum ab aquila, fletus edentem graves, / leporem obiurgabat passer: Phaedr. 1,9.3 s.
opprime os!: Plavt. Asin. 586 *(Halt den Mund!)*; cfr Ter. Phorm. 986 (os opprime inpurum)
optamus enim tibi ominamurque in proximum annum consulatum.: Plin. epist. 4.15.5
optandi copia: ≈ Ov. Pont. 2.3.95 (→ pro quibus optandi …)
optare alci alqd: ≈ Sen. epist. 32.4 s.; 60,1
optare, quod sine adversario optatur, bonam mentem: Sen. nat. 3 praef. 14 (→ quid est praecipuum? non admittere in animo mala consilia … optare. quod …)
optat ephippia bos piger. optat arare caballus.: Hor. epist 1.14,43
optatissime: Fronto epist. ad M. Caes. 1,6,9 (→ vale, disertissime, doctissime, mihi carissime, dulcissime, magister optatissime, amice desiderantissime.)
optato advenis.: Ter. Andr. 533
optatus hic mi(hi) dies datus hodie est ab dis.: Pi.avt Pers. 773 s.
optavi mihi vitam honestam.: Sen. epist. 67.7
optavit ut in currum patris tolleretur; sublatus est (Phaeton).: Cic. off. 3.94

optima coniunx: Ov. trist. 3.3.55; Stat. Theb. 3.378
optima est [mors] est, quae placet: Sen. epist. 70.12
optima et laetissima tibi eveniant! (cfr Güthling Dt.-lat. Wörterbuch. s.v. *segnen*)
optima quaeque: Sen. epist. 108,23 (quam vehementes haberent tirunculi impetus primos ad o. q., si quis exhortaretur illos); Plin. epist. 1,5,13 (→ stultissimum credo ad imitandum non optima quaeque proponere)
optima quaeque dies miseris mortalibus aevi / prima fugit; subeunt morbi tristisque senectus.: Verg. georg. 3,66 s. (cfr Sin. dial. 10,9.2; epist 108.24)
optimam doloris esse naturam. quod non potest nec qui extenditur magnus esse. nec qui est magnus extendi.: Sen. epist. 94,7 (≈ epist. 30.14; 78.7)
optimam sequi viam. non iucundissimam: Sen. dial. 7.8.1
optime coniunx: Sil. 2,678
optime facis, quod bellum Dacicum scribere paras, nam quae tam recens. tam copiosa. tam lata. quae denique tam poetica et quamquam in verissimis rebus tam fabulosa materia? Plin. epist. 8,4,1
optime Felix: Vvlg. Act. 24,3 *(Anrede)*
optime meruisti de Romanis studiis.: Sen. dial. 6.1.3
optime mihi te offers.: Ter. Andr. 686
optime natalis!: Ov. trist. 5,5.13
optime novisse: ≈ Cic. Lig. 32 (→ nosti optime homines): Sen. epist. 77.16 (→ quid sapiat ostreum ...); →optime scio
optime omnino!: Avg. soliloq. 1.19,5
optime positum est beneficium, cuius meminit qui accipit.: Pvblil. sent. O 9
optime scio: Cic. fam. 13.8,1; → optime novisse
optime virorum: → virorum optime
optime!: Cic. Brut. 52; 282; Tusc. 1.119; Quinct. 79: leg. agr. 1.14 *(adv.)*
optime inquam.: Avg. beat. vit. 19
optimi adulescentes *(voc.)*: Cic. Cato 39

optimi viri (*voc.*): Cic. Cato 33 (→ audite vero, o.v., ea, quae saepissime inter me et Scipionem de amicitia disserebantur); → virorum optime; → bone vir
optimis disciplinis atque artibus studere et in his elaborare: ≈ Cic. div. in Caec. 39
optimis ominibus prosequi alqd: ≈ Cic. fam. 3,12,2 (quam tu ipse optimis ominibus prosequeris; quam = rem)
optimis rebus fruor.: Phaedr. 4,25,15 (→ laboro nihil atque ...)
optimo cuique: Cic. Flacc. 94
optimo habitu: Cic. Cael. 59 (florere)
optimo iure: Cic. Marcell. 4 (→ merito atque o. i.); Sen. apocol. 9,5
optimorum civium vel flos vel robur: Cic. or. 10,34

optimum esse emendandi genus, si scripta in aliquod tempus reponantur: QVINT. inst. 10,4,2

optimum est pati, quod emendare non possis, et deum, quo auctore cuncta proveniunt, sine murmuratione comitari.: SEN. epist. 107,9

optimum est!: PLAVT. Capt. 696

optimum est, antequam optes, mori: SEN. rem. fort. 4,1

READING 2-I

MAVRVS PISINI

[2001 CE]

APOLLO ET HYACTHINVS

KV 38

(*in excerptis*)

HYACINTHVS

Amice! Omnia iam parata sunt. Pater meus ad sacra, quae constituit, cum dilecta sorore, ut spero, actutum aderit.

ZEPHYRVS

Ni fallor, est Apollo, quem colitis.

HYACINTHVS

Ille prorsus est.

ZEPHYRVS

Oebalus ergo tanta parat Apollini sacrificia? An alios nescis esse in caelis deos? Num Semeles quidem natus, num Venus, Diana, Mars, Vulcanus vel potens ipse Superum princeps nil ture indigent vestro?

HYACINTHVS

His quoque diis, Zephyre, litamus neque ullus eorum e templis nostris laude vacuus abit. Unus tamen Apollo fanum eiusmodi suo vindicat honori. Genitor ipse noster magnum deum veneratur et ego, patris motus exemplo, idem facio.

ZEPHYRVS

O, care, quam libenter tibi animum traderem, si tu, mi Apollo, mihi meus tantum fores!

HYACINTHVS

Quid me, Zephyre dilecte, dis protinus parem iudicas? Tanto honore indignus sum, at rem bene novi: protulit ista nimius in me prorsus amor.

(Eo temporis puncto, Oebalus et Melia superveniunt)

Nunc autem genitor ipse, sorore comite, nobis occurrit.

OEBALVS

Dic, nate: suntne et hostia et ignis ad sacrificium apparata?

HYACINTHVS

Utique, pater: omnia, quae petieras, ad nutum expedita, tuum praestolantur adventum.

OEBALVS

Bene. A flamine, igitur, excitetur ignis et ture plurimo ara cuncta gemat, immo, piantis fumus in nubes eat.

MELIA

Heu, pater! Minax imbris tempestas nobis ingruit et polus universus huc noctem tenebrasque impellit!

OEBALVS

Adeste! Longioris impatiens morae, Apollo tus et hostiam a nobis petit. Saeva autem procella ad vota nostra fugiet, dein grata solis facies in has iterum plagas remeabit. Agite, sultis, et mecum preces fundite.

CHORVS

Numen o Latonium!
Audi vota supplicum,
qui ter digno te honore
certant sancte colere:
hos benigno tu favore
subditos prosequere.

OEBALVS

O Apollo, tuere semper
tuoque dignare numine
creditam tibi caram
Oebali Laconiam.

CHORVS

Numen o Latonium, etc.

(Fulminis ictus ignem et aram diruit)
(Canticum)

MELIA

Heu me! De nobis actum est. Numen preces nostras respuit!

OEBALVS

Heu me! Num quis vestrum deum temere violavit?

MELIA

Nullius culpae, pater, me ream invenio.

HYACINTHVS

Hunc deum semper colui. O Zephyre, multum vereor ne e verbis, quae antea protuleras, ira huiusmodi sit succensa!

ZEPHYRVS

Si me diligis, Hyacinthe, rem patrem cela, et verba a nobis modo dicta tace!

OEBALVS

Exstinctus ignis, ara subversa, hostia contempta nobis grande malum monent. Heu me! Totus tremo, cum omnia hoc fulmine percussa sint.

HYACINTHVS

Tu autem, genitor, qui insontem geris animum, erige mentem! Nam, quid tibi mali a probo metuendum numine? Nihil es ab isto fulgure laesus nostrumque nemo, quotquot adsumus, periit. Vivimus et omnes pristinus vigor regit. Voluit autem deus, e sublimi caelorum aula, hoc signo nostras quatere terras, ut orbi universo illius potestas magis pateret maneretque cum fiducia in nobis timor.

OEBALVS

Vera quidem loqueris, nate: vercor tamen ne Apollo, fortuito quamquam igni, Oebalum perdat.

(Accedit Apollo)

APOLLO

Apollo, credite, preces vestras audiit opemque suam his terris pollicetur, dummodo eundem exsulem recipere velitis, quia fulminantis Iovis iram odit.

OEBALVS

Quid igitur fit? Numen, sub pastoris veste occultum, in regnum nostrum suscipi cupit?

HYACINTHVS

En, genitor! Ita fallere nos Superi solent! Iam tibi, saeva post vulnera, deus aptam medelam adfert tuamque regiam, praesens, ornat.

MELIA

O quam claro lumine haec nubila dies nos recreat, dum ipse Apollo Lares nostros, optatus hospes, visitat! Quantus decor, quae forma, quanta dignitas, vel quam dia cunctis illius corporis membris et gloria et maiestas inest!

APOLLO

Melia, quid in humili pastore tam dignum aspicis, quod animi suspensa mireris?

MELIA

Video...

APOLLO

Quidnam spectas? Loquere, quaeso!

MELIA

Video pulchrum Apollinem, cui cor meum iamdudum obtuli.

APOLLO

Quod obtulisti pectus, noli posthac revocare: hoc vero, ex vitae donis, me praeter cetera iuvat.

ZEPHYRVS

Ah, quantum, Hyacinthe, deum praesentem timeo...

HYACINTHVS

Haec tam singularis dignitas me quoque timidum facit.

APOLLO

Hyacinthe, adero tibi semper amicus, si me diligere volueris.

HYACINTHVS

O quam mirum, amare si Hyacinthum poteris!

ZEPHYRVS

[En, igitur, quomodo Apollo amatum a me puerum rapiat!]

OEBALVS

O dies protinus felix! O sanctum numen! Hic si dignaberis morari, meas ingredere sedes diuque, me rogante, nobiscum mane.

APOLLO

Habebis me, crede, deum tibi semper propitium.

OEBALVS

Nonne, filia, tu deum poteris amare, qui ter favore nostro dignus exstitit?

MELIA

Quid loqueris, pater? Numquid Apollo me, mortalem, coniugali toro cupit adiungi?

OEBALVS

Id dubitare noli: Apollo te sponsam petit eique roganti (tu autem, nata, libertate utere tua) meum adsensum dedi.

MELIA

Num me, pater, consensum negate putas? Quae virgo divinum virum tantosque honores contemnere vellet, nisi stulta omnino et animi sui parum compos esset, aut ipsi obstitisset fortunae?

OEBALVS

Prudenter, nata, hoc eligis coniugium: nam, sic, per te et frater tuus et parens, uti nepotes, egregia sorte excellent, quia domus nostra hac face diva prorsus fiet.

MELIA

Dic, quaeso: ubinam est Apollo? Utinam liceret tenero illius colloquio mihi actutum frui!

OEBALVS

Una simul cum fratre et Zephyro disco ludit in silva. At huc, ut spero, citius redibit tuumque, me praesente, consensum petet.

MELIA

Petat igitur a me omnia quae vult.

ZEPHYRVS

Rex! De filii tui salute est actum: iacet Hyacinthus!

OEBALVS

Heu me! O nimis triste nuntium! Qua sorte cecidit?

ZEPHYRVS

Disco ictus, ruit.

OEBALVS

Quis filium meum necare ausus est?

ZEPHYRVS

Apollo.

OEBALVS

Contremisco!

MELIA

Quid nunc, Superi, fit? Deus ille qui me beatam reddere voluit, num fratri meo necem machinatus est? Quis tibi ista dicenti, mente sanus, crediderit?

ZEPHYRVS

Vera loquor et ipse testis illius mortis fui. Ubi autem Hyacinthum lapsum vidi, statim aufugi, ne idem malum in me quoque saeviret.

OEBALVS

Sic ergo, Apollo, insontes plectis? Favor, quo te recepi, num mei nati morte dignus erat? Itaque, eodem modo, numen infidum, et Meliam, filiam meam, patri surripere paras?

MELIA

Id a me, genitor, absit, ut talem sponsum eligam deove, qui germani madet cruore, me manus esse porrecturam praesumam!

ZEPHYRVS

Quidnam audio? Num coniugia meditatur deus? An Meliam quoque, mihi unice dilectam, rapere cupit? Qui mihi Hyacinthum sustulit, anne et huius puellae amorem mihi auferre audet?

OEBALVS

Zephyre, quae causa eum ad hoc facinus adegit?

ZEPHYRVS

Nescio. Tuus enim filius ad amoenum Eurotae litus steterat.

TERTIA EXPERIENTIA

third experience

217

PSA

PSAL · FES
MI · TIVI

PSALMI · AD LAUDES

ps. 66

Deus misere-
atur nostri ⁊
benedicat nobis:* illumi-
net vultum suum
super nos et mise-
reatur nostri.
Ut cognoscamus
in terra viam tuā:*
in omnibus gentib
us salutare tuum.
Confiteantur t̃bi
populi deus:* confi-
teantur tibi populi
omnes.
Laetentur et exs
ultent gentes:† quo
niam iudicas popu
los in aequitate,*
et gentes in terra
dirigis.
Confiteantur t̃bi
populi deus:† confi
teantur tibi p̃puli
omnes:* terra dedit
fructum suum.

After our first taste and use of the Latin language in the First Experience and perhaps also orally in the Second Experience, we are eager not to neglect the things we have learned already, but to repeat them naturally, adding details every day, and to fill out our understanding of the Latin language in this Third Experience.

This year of our Latin training has proven in the past to be the most difficult of the five Experiences for the simple reason that it introduces many concepts about verbs and the use of verbs and expressions that are practically unknown to most vernacular language speakers and users today, but these concepts will be explained, and our development will be careful and slow, as we realize that many of these concepts are subtle and difficult at first sight.

To get warmed up for this Third Latin Experience and to make sure our newcomers and returning students are ready for the Latin encounters this year, we shall review during this Experience all we have learned about nouns and adjectives and verbs with examples from the living Latin language of every era.

We have again appended to this Experience numerous reading sheets of Latin texts from every era and from many different authors of Latin literature. Let us turn to these sheets to spot the nouns and adjectives, identifying each one according to the two Blocks or according to the other forms of nouns we saw even in the last encounter of the First Experience. We will spend time pronouncing the sentences out loud and noting the forms for to-for-from, by-with-from-in, and of-possession, as well as the object and subject forms. We will also give our attention to review the active and passive verbs of the indicative mode. Very often we will reverse the words of a sentence from singular to plural or from plural to singular. In this way we will review the entire system of nouns and adjectives and indicative verbs and command forms. We must make sure we know these things well so that we can build upon them as we progress.

As has been often indicated in our Bones-experiences, the whole course in self-teaching or classroom action is projected over a period of three academic or even calendar years. This time is calculated to allow for the realities of human learning, which obviously can be very slow, to allow for gradual absorption and constant review, and to allow for inevitable forgetting and relearning. A real practical difficulty occurs in the case of people who have had Latin training previously, who must not be forced to return and begin from nothing, who on examination are in fact ready for a more advanced program. It is allowed that they enter into the Third Experience, which is the second-level stage. This, however, presupposes something that most people coming in at that point do not have, namely a whole year of treatment in the First Experience with our own system and our own terminology and our own distribution of matter. History has shown that to accommodate these people, there must be a certain number of encounters dedicated to reviewing what was done in the First Experience and making people acquainted with the elements of our system. Consequently, the first seven encounters of this Experience will not only help the newcomer to adjust to our system, but for students already acquainted with it will provide refinement of the elements of the First Experience and new material. All the while we are reviewing and refining what we presented in the First Experience, the student or enthusiast prepares for each classroom encounter by playing with a *ludus domesticus*, "home game," to sharpen perception, discernment, and understanding of all these elements. Sample *ludi domestici*, "home games," eventually will be available in our projected volume IV.

ENCOUNTER 1 (36)

ADIECTIVORUM COMPARATIO ET VARIA SIGNIFICATIO

comparison of adjectives and their diverse meaning

Introduction

The first subject we encounter is found in daily use of every language, namely what we call the comparison of adjectives. For example, in English we say:

big	bigger	biggest
small	smaller	smallest
good	better	best
fast	faster	fastest.

Although these examples are obvious in meaning, technically speaking we are talking about three degrees of comparison. The basic adjective is called the positive degree, for example, "big," "small," "good," "fast." The comparative degree here is, "bigger," "smaller," "better," "faster," and the superlative degree is, "biggest," "smallest," "best," "fastest." First we shall see how these forms are produced in Latin, and then we shall give different meanings to them that are a little broader than those typically given in English.

1. Comparison of adjectives

We learned our adjectives in two different Blocks. Nouns of Bk.I generally end in *us*, *a*, *um*, and those of Bk.II in the various ways they appear in the dictionary, as illustrated in the First Experience.

The comparative degree, "bigger," "smaller," "better," "faster," and the superlative degree, "biggest," "smallest," "best," "fastest," are easy to learn and master in Latin, because there is only one pattern for all adjectives in the comparative degree and another universal form in the superlative degree. That is to say, even though in the dictionary there are two ways of presenting the Latin adjectives corresponding to our two Blocks, when we come to the comparative degree there is only one system, and in the superlative degree there is only one system, all of which truly simplifies things very much.

For all Latin adjectives from one Block or the other, the comparative looks like this. The masculine and feminine end in *–ior;* the examples will follow. The neuter ends in *–ius*. That is to say, if you take the positive adjective, *honestus, a, um*, "honorable," the comparative degree, "more honorable," is *honestior* and *honestius*, where *honestior* is masculine and feminine and *honestius* is neuter. Thus:

honestus, a, um
honorable (m., f., n.)

honestior
more honorable (m. & f.)

honestius
more honorable (n.).

What is already confusing is that the form *honestior* does not look feminine, but it is, and *honestius* looks masculine, but it is neuter. These are the simple facts of Latin.

If you take an adjective from the other big Block, for example, the word in the dictionary *brevis, breve,* "short," the comparative, "shorter," is *brevior, brevius,* where *brevior* is the masculine and feminine and *brevius* is the neuter. Thus, we have:

brevis, breve
short (m. & f., n.)

brevior
shorter (m. & f.)

brevius
shorter (n.).

How do you deal with these forms? It is very simple. Simply treat the comparison as a noun of our Bk.II; namely, treat *brevior* and *honestior* the same way we treated *imperator, imperatoris* and *senator, senatoris,* and treat *brevius* and *honestius* the same way we treated *corpus, corporis* and *tempus, temporis.* That is all you need to know.

As the plural of *senator* is *senatores,* so too the plural of *brevior* is *breviores,* and the plural of *honestior* is *honestiores.* The forms by-with-from-in for *brevior* and *honestior* are *breviore* and *honestiore,* which end in *–e* just as the same function of *imperator* ends in *–e* about 85% of the time, as does that of *senator;* that is just normal.

In the neuter, the plural of *honestius,* "more honest thing," and of *brevius,* "shorter thing," is formed like the plural of *corpus.* You must take the second entry in the dictionary, namely *corporis,* from which you can form the plural of *corpus,* which is *corpora.* Likewise, from the of-possession form *honestioris* you can see that the plural of *honestius* is *honestiora,* and from *brevioris* you can see how *brevius* becomes the plural *breviora.*

This pattern follows the nouns perfectly. Anything you did with *imperator* or *corpus* or *tempus* will happen here in the comparative degree.

The plural form of-possession follows the rule for 85% of the nouns such as *imperatorum, senatorum, corporum;* and the form for the comparative adjectives is *honestiorum* and *breviorum.* What is confusing here is that these forms appear to have the ending *–orum* as if they belonged to Bk.I nouns. Remember that these forms were produced from the second entry in the dictionary. So, from the noun *imperator, imperatoris* you produce the plural form of-possession as *imperatorum*; so from the comparative adjective *honestior, honestioris* you produce *honestiorum*, and from *brevior, brevioris* you produce *breviorum*. The neuter plural form of possession is the same, *honestiorum* and *breviorum*. That is the end of the comparative adjective, which follows the pattern of 85% of Bk.II nouns.

At the end of this encounter we shall point out a few minor irregularities and meanings that will solve all our problems without memorizing declensions or any foolishness.

2. Superlative of adjectives

While the comparative degree follows the pattern of Bk.II nouns and adjectives, the superlative degree for all adjectives follows the pattern of Bk.I nouns and adjectives, namely those generally ending in *us, a, um*. Everything that we learned about our nouns and adjectives will apply here. If we take the positive example, *honestus, a, um*, "honest," the superlative, "most honest," has the ending *–issimus, –a, –um*. Thus:

honestus, a, um
honest (m., f., n.)

honestissimus, a, um
most honest (m., f., n.).

If you take the other positive example, *brevis, breve*, "short," the superlative degree, "shortest," is formed in this same way, *brevissimus, a, um*. You can do this in the same way with most any adjective you want in the dictionary. That is why people say *pianissimo* to mean "very soft." This form went into other languages and is easily recognizable.

These few words are all you have to remember:

honestus, a, um honest (m., f., n.)	*brevis, breve* short (m. & f., n.)
honestior, honestius more honest (m. & f., n.)	*brevior, brevius* shorter (m. & f., n.)
honestissimus, a, um most honest (m., f., n.)	*brevissimus, a, um* shortest (m., f., n.).

These two rules will cover 90% of the adjectives in the language, and we shall see a few exceptions further on.

3. Meanings

Each of these degrees of adjectives has special meanings, which are not noticed or generally learned especially by English speakers. In the comparative degree we are accustomed to say, for example, "bigger" or "more beautiful," but Latin literature suggests about five or six different meanings for the comparative degree. These are:

more beautiful
somewhat beautiful
too beautiful (which is not the superlative degree)
quite beautiful
rather beautiful.

Some English speakers might be surprised to see that "too beautiful" is the comparative degree, not the superlative.

The superlative may be considered in two ways. One is absolute as in "very beautiful." The other is a relative superlative, that is in reference to other things as in "most beautiful," "happiest," "biggest." When reading Latin literature the relative superlative will not always fit a given use, and you will need to fall back on the absolute superlative rendering such as "very happy."

4. Reminders

A reminder is fitting here that some forms do not look like what they mean. So, for example, we may have the sentence:

Filius honestius cogitat
The son is planning a rather honest thing
The son is planning a more honest thing.

Here you have to keep in mind that *filius* is masculine and singular, but *honestius* next to it can be the neuter comparative, meaning "a more honest thing." In another encounter we shall see that this sentence can also mean, "The son is planning rather honestly."

Similarly some will take *altiora* and *honestiora* to be feminine because of that final *–a*, but we know it is the neuter plural, and the following sentence means:

Filia altiora cupit
The daughter desires higher things.

5. Irregularities

If we note a few irregular forms, as occur in every human language, we can complete our consideration of the comparative and superlative degree in the Latin language during one short encounter without memorizing declensions or any other fuss.

5.1 *Eight irregular comparatives and superlatives*

In English we have several frequently used adjectives that have irregular comparative and superlative forms, for example, "good, better, best." These forms are also irregular in Latin as in many other languages. A list of these is given in Gildersleeve and Lodge nº 90, which we reproduce here (with slight adaptations for clarity):

good	*bonus, a, um*	*melior, melius*	*optimus, a, um*
bad	*malus, a, um*	*peior, peius*	*pessimus, a, um*

great	*magnus, a, um*	*maior, maius*	*maximus, a, um*
small	*parvus, a, um*	*minor, minus*	*minimus, a, um*
much	*multus, a, um*	singular: —-, *plus* (no dat., abl.) plural: *plures, plura complures, complura* (*–ia*)	*plurimus, a, um*
worthless	*nequam* (invariable)	*nequior, nequius*	*nequissimus, a, um*
frugal	*frugi* (invariable)	*frugalior*	*frugalissimus, a, um*

In each case, you can find the irregular forms for these words in the dictionary.

5.2 *superlatives in –limus, a, um*

Another irregular form concerns only the superlative, which we noted usually ends in *–issimus, a, um*. Two small numbers of adjectives have a vowel or a consonant that produces a different ending. There are six adjectives that have an *–l* as in *similis, dissimilis, humilis, facilis, difficilis, gracilis*. Instead of the double *–ss–* sound in the superlative, these adjectives have a double *–ll–* as in *simillimus, a, um* and *humillimus, a, um* and *facillimus, a, um*, and not *similissimus* nor *humilissimus* nor *facilissimus*.

5.3 *superlatives in –rimus, a, um*

There are a few more adjectives—we might find about fifteen in the dictionary—that end in the consonant *–r*. Because of that, the superlative has a double *–rr–* in place of the double *–ss–* sound. For example, *acer, acris, acre*, "sharp," forms its superlative as *acerrimus, a, um*, "sharpest" or "very sharp," not *acerissimus*. The other famous one is *pauper, pauperis*, "poor," which has the superlative *pauperrimus, a, um*, "poorest" or "very poor." Another one is *celer, celeris, celere*, "swift," which has the superlative *celerrimus, a, um*, "swiftest" or "very swift," not *celerissimus*. There are not many of these superlative forms, and everyone seems to know how to spot them easily.

5.4 *Dictionary entries*

If you have one of these irregular comparative or superlative adjectives, then finding it in the dictionary may prove difficult. The comparative and superlative forms are supplied in the dictionary entry following the positive adjective. For example, *acerrimus* is given under *acer*, and *celerrimus* is found under *celer*. Even more difficult are the forms of the eight irregular adjectives given above, where *minimus* is under *parvus*, and, the worst of all, *peior* and *pessimus* are listed in the dictionary under *malus*.

Once again the diligent teacher is reminded that any real Latin text has examples of all these items, and it will be a challenge to the teacher to find and present such examples to the students.

ENCOUNTER 2 (37)

GRADUS ADVERBIORUM. DIFFICULTATES NEUTRIUS IN FORMIS

degrees of adverbs. difficulties in the forms of the neuter

Introduction

Adverbs, by their nature, describe adjectives, other adverbs, or especially verbs. In English they typically appear with the ending *–ly*, as in "quickly," where the adjective is "quick" and the adverb "quickly." Some adverbs do not end in *–ly* and so are not as easily recognizable as in the expression "to do something better," where the adverb "better" does not end in *–ly*.

In all languages adverbs are unchanging, as in Latin. There is no plural, no gender, no function other than as an adverb. Thus, adverbs are rather easy and consistent.

1. The positive adverb

Adverbs are built from adjectives, which means that if we know how to use adjectives well, adverbs pose no difficulty.

1.1 Block I: *probe*

The adjectives of Bk.I like *probus, a, um*, "upright," and *asper, era, erum*, "rough," form their adverbs by taking the positive degree as it appears in the dictionary and changing the ending to *–e* as in *probe*, "rightly"; or the adjective *honestus, a, um*, "honorable," gives the adverb *honeste*, "honorably"; or the adjective *sanus, a, um*, "healthy," gives the adverb *sane* meaning "in a healthy way."

For future reference, the form *honeste* when used as an adverb has a long final *–ē*, and some editions of Latin literature will indicate this with a long mark over the final letter as in *honestē*, "honorably." This will help you later to distinguish the adverb from the form of address, which ends in a short final *–ĕ*, as in *honestĕ*, "O honorable man," sometimes written without the long or short vowel mark. We shall review the form of address in the next encounter.

There is a famous line of poetry by Gaius Valerius Catullus (c. 84–c. 54 BCE) in which Catullus is talking to his late brother at the brother's tomb in Asia Minor, in which Catullus goes back and forth between the long final *–ē* of the adverb and the short final *–ĕ* of address:

> *héu miser índignē fráter adémptĕ mihí*
>
> (Cat. *Carm.* CI, 6; accents added)
>
> O unfortunate brother, you having been taken away from me undeservedly.

Only the verse will tell you whether the final *–e* is long or short, and some editions may indicate the length of the vowel. Here the *indignē* is an adverb meaning "undeservedly," and *ademptĕ* is direct address for "O [you] having been taken away."

1.2 Block II: *leniter*

The adjectives of Bk.II, such as *lenis, lene*, "mild," form their adverbs with the ending *–iter*, as in *leniter*, "mildly." Although it looks like a masculine noun, you can spot this form right away as the positive adverb of Bk.II, as when the adjective *brevis, breve*, "short," produces *breviter*, "briefly," and *nobilis, nobile*, "noble," produces *nobiliter*, "nobly."

1.3 Occasionally two forms for the adverb

A few adjectives have two forms of the adverb. Sometimes they use the neuter to produce an adjective, as *facilis, facile*, "easy," produces *facile*, "easily," but *faciliter* is also used. We find *humanus, a, um*, "humane, courteous," which produces the adverb *humane*, "humanely, courteously," but *humaniter* is also used; and we have seen *lenis, lene*, "easy," produce *leniter*, "easily," but *lene* is also found. This is all dictionary matter. Another is *dulcis, dulce*, "sweet," which produce *dulciter* and *dulce* meaning "sweetly."

In summary, adjectives of Bk.I form their adverbs with the ending *–ē*, or occasionally with *–iter*, as in *humaniter*, and adjectives of Bk.II form their adverbs with the ending *–iter*, or sometimes with the simple ending in *–ē*.

1.4 Exception

One exception might be the adjective *audax, audacis*, "bold," which theoretically produces the adverb *audaciter*, "boldly," but the Romans prefer the abbreviated form *audacter*. Likewise, for *difficilis* the adverb has three forms: *difficilē, difficulter*, and *difficiliter*. But these are small exceptions easily found in your dictionary and so not to worry about.

2. Comparative adverb

Like adjectives, adverbs also have a comparative degree as in the English examples, "in an easier way," "more quickly," or "quite eloquently."

The Romans form the comparative adverb in much the same way as in Greek. They use the neuter comparative adjective as the comparative degree of the adverb. To give a few examples, from Bk.I adjectives we have *honestus, a, um*, "honorable," with the comparative adjective *honestior, honestius*, "more honorable," where *honestius* is the neuter subject and object according to the super principle. Now here *honestius* also functions as the comparative adverb meaning "more honorably." We have already seen the positive degree *honeste*, "honorably."

From Bk.II adjectives we have *brevis, breve*, "short," with the comparative adjective, "shorter," *brevior, brevius*, where *brevius* is the neuter subject and object according to the super principle. Now *brevius* is also the form for the comparative adverb meaning "more briefly." We have already seen the positive degree *breviter*, "briefly."

Some students are relieved not to have to learn a new form for the comparative adverb, but this is no consolation, because the same form is used for both the comparative adjective neuter subject and object and the comparative adverb, and you have to think and decide which is intended in every sentence. You can have ambiguous sentences such as:

Vocabulum facilius enuntiat.

Here *facilius* can be either the comparative adverb, "more easily," as in:

He pronounces the word more easily.

Or *facilius* can be the comparative adjective describing an "easier word":

He pronounces an easier word.

Because of the super principle, both *vocabulum* and *facilius* can function as either the subject or object of the sentence, so we could also have:

The easier word speaks
The word speaks more easily.

Here you are stuck because the comparative of the adverb has the same form as the comparative neuter adjective used as a subject or object according to the super principle.

3. Superlative adverb

Like adjectives, adverbs also have a superlative degree as in the English examples, "most easily" or "very easily." These are formed from the superlative adjective in the same way that the positive adverb was formed from the positive adjective. Remember that the superlative adjective is the same for both Blocks of adjectives and follows the pattern *honestissimus, a, um* with a few exceptions such as *facillimus, a, um* or *pauperrimus, a, um.*

Like the positive adverb, the superlative adverb simply ends with the long *–ē* as in *honestissime*, "most, very honorably," or *facillime*, "most, very easily," or *pauperrime*, "most, very poorly."

This means that adjectives of Bk.II such as *similis, simile*, "similar," have the superlative degree of the adjective as *simillimus, a, um*, "most, very similar," and the superlative adverb as *simillime*, "most similarly," with a long final *–e.*

Before we summarize all that has been said, as a special favor to interested people we want to add here once and for all a list of regular and irregular adverbs in the positive, comparative, and superlative degrees from Gildersleeve and Lodge n° 93 with slight adaptations for clarity, which we reproduce here for demonstration, not memorization. This list shows the long *–ē* ending of the adverbs formed from Bk.I adjectives in the positive and superlative degree of adverbs.

Positive.		Comparative.	Superlative.
altē,	*loftily,*	altius,	altissimē.
pulchrē,	*beautifully,*	pulchrius,	pulcherrimē.
miserē,	*poorly,*	miserius,	miserrimē.
fortiter,	*bravely,*	fortius,	fortissimē.
audācter,	*boldly,*	audācius,	audācissimē.
tūtō or tūtē,	*safely,*	tūtius,	tutissimē.
facile,	*easily,*	facilius,	facillimē.
bene,	*well,*	melius,	optimē.
male,	*badly,**	pēius,	pessimē.
[parvus],	*[small],*	minus, *less,*	minimē, *least.*
[magnus],	*great,*	magis, *more,*	māximē, *most.*
multum,	*much,*	plūs, *more,*	plūrimum.
cito,	*quickly,*	citius,	citissimē.
diū,	*for a long time,**	diūtius,	diūtissimē.
saepe,	*often,*	saepius,	saepissimē.
nūper,	*recently,*	——,	nūperrimē.
satis,	*enough,*	satius,	*better.*

Two words above are given in brackets, [parvus] and [magnus]. Their adverbs, theoretically *parve* and *magne*, are not found in literature, but are substituted, the former by *paulum*, meaning, "a little," "to a little degree," and the latter by the combination *magno opere*, which is deceptive especially when written as two words and not as the more common single word, *magnopere*, "with great effort," "greatly," as presented in the dictionary. Thus, *magnopere* is not an adverb, but a substitution for a missing adverb. By the way, *parve* and *magne* do exist in Latin with a short *-ĕ*, *parvĕ*, meaning, "O little boy," and *magnĕ*, meaning, "O great man," as forms of direct address, commonly known as the vocative to be discussed in the next encounter. As a final note, the two asterisks (*) indicate changes we have made to the chart given in Gildersleeve and Lodge; where we have "*badly*," they had "*ill*," which is not an adverb, and where we have "*for a long time*," they had "*long*."

4. Summary

Adjectives and adverbs are found in practically every Latin sentence as is witnessed in reading sheets of Latin texts or in examples provided by the teacher.

From Bk.I the adjective *honestus, a, um*, "honorable," produces the positive adverb *honeste*, "honorably," the comparative *honestius*, "more honorably," and the superlative *honestissime*, "most, very honorably." From Bk.II the adjective *fortis, forte*, "brave," produces the positive adverb *fortiter*, "bravely," the comparative *fortius*, "more bravely," and the superlative adverb *fortissime*, "most, very bravely."

The main problem that students have here is that all of these forms look or are the same. If beginning students are conscious of these similarities and identical forms from the outset, then they will come to terms with this difficulty of Latin much sooner, will be more cautious, and will become more mature in their whole mind and life.

To review, then, the form *facilius* can be both the comparative neuter adjective used as a subject or object, "easier," and the comparative adjective "more easily." The form *faciliter* is the positive adverb, "easily," but we also have the adverb from the neuter adjective *facile*, "easily." The superlative *facillime* is "most, very easily."

We warned people at the start that the Latin language is full of words ending in –*e* and –*i* and –*is*. To master the Latin language requires vocabulary, care, keeping our peace and calm with these details, and holding them all in order. Someone who really knows Latin has all of this under control. Real Latinists are recognizable because they notice these subtleties. Their familiarity comes from use, reading, and continual contact with the language until it all becomes very easy.

Following this Experience we have provided reading sheets so that you can have frequent, even daily, access to Latin literature, and then it becomes a pleasure.

ENCOUNTER 3 (38)

REPETITIO EX PRIMA EXPERIENTIA NOMINUM: IS = ES; VOCATIVUS

repetition of nouns from the First Experience: is = es; function of direct address

Introduction

Let us turn to the sheets to review the entire system of nouns and adjectives, including the comparative and superlative forms we learned in our last two encounters. We must make sure we know these things well so that we can build upon them as we progress. Very often we will reverse the words of a sentence from singular to plural or from plural to singular, and in this way we will show that we understand the meaning and system of Latin words.

In this encounter we shall also point out a few odd things, with which we did not wish to burden you during the First Experience. Besides what you learned in that First Experience, there are a few variations in the forms of nouns and adjectives.

1. *Omnis*

One thing you must know is that in Bk.II nouns and especially in Bk.II adjectives there is another way of writing the object plural in the masculine and feminine. We learned that in Bk.II, the plural subject and object have the same form ending in *–es* in the masculine and feminine. There are, however, some editors, for example, those of all the books printed by Oxford and several other solid publishers like Teubner, who print the object plural of these forms in another way. For example, it can be written not only, as we learned, *omnes,* but also as *omneis,* and invariably as *omnīs.*

We already mentioned this in encounter fifteen of the First Experience. We mention it again here because this causes some trouble even for the best Latin students. You must know this to be able to read good Latin literature. The problem is that the combination *o-m-n-i-s* has seven functions in Latin. It is the singular masculine and feminine subject, it is the form of-possession for all three genders in the singular and now it functions as the masculine and feminine object in the plural.

The Romans heard this in a different way because *omnēs* has a long *–ē–* sound and this carried over into its substitute *omnīs,* which has a long *–ī–* sound. Because of this the Romans were able to distinguish this use of *omnīs* from the other forms. Another example from the dictionary is *nobilis, nobile,* where the *–ĭs* is short both in the subject form *nobilĭs* and in the form of-possession, also *nobilĭs,* except for the alternative form of the masculine and feminine object plural *nobilīs*, where the ending *–īs* is long, and the Romans heard this. You simply have to know this and figure the sentence out in spite of it.

At times when the critical text has this alternate form ending in *–īs*, other publishers of primers for learning the Latin language may do a favor for the students by giving these endings as *–es*, something which we avoid because it is not fair to shield students from the unadulterated Latin text.

2. *Omnis*, continued

We are not going to learn Latin by paradigms, as we have said, so here we wish to refer to a few lines in Gildersleeve and Lodge so that people can verify our comments typographically and see the matter printed in another book. You can go to your own copy of that grammar to confirm what we shall present below in our own way.

First we shall see the alternative spelling for the object plural in the masculine and feminine which ends in a long *–īs* as given in Gildersleeve and Lodge nº 78. There you will see the adjective *facilis*, *facile*, "easy," in all its forms. Here we wish to point out only the alternative forms for the object plural first in the masculine and feminine and next in the neuter:

facilēs (īs), facilia.

Likewise, the adjective *acer*, *acris*, *acre*, "sharp," appears in each gender:

acrēs (īs), acrēs (īs), acria.

You can also see the same phenomenon for several nouns in nº 56 of Gildersleeve and Lodge:

collīs (ēs)
turrīs (ēs)
vulpīs (ēs).

3. Direct address

We first presented the seven possible functions for nouns and adjectives and pronouns in the Latin language during the sixth encounter of the First Experience, and thereafter in that first full year of Latin instruction we presented the first five of these functions: the subject, the object, the function of-possession, the function by-with-from-in and the function to-for-from. The last two functions we present in this Third Experience. Here we present the sixth function of direct address, and in encounter 34 we shall present the seventh and final function that covers the expressions of place.

The function of direct address is really the easiest of them all and needs very little treatment. We can understand what we are dealing with here from the following English examples:

"My dear friends, let us rejoice together"
"O my beloved wife, I miss you on my trip."

In both of these examples someone is addressed directly, whether as "My dear friends" or "O my beloved wife," thus our term "direct address." The Romans use the function of direct address when they call upon someone or some thing. In the books this function is called the vocative, from the Latin verb *vocare*, "to call." The term "vocative" is abbreviated in the dictionary as *voc.*

The way the Romans express direct address can be summarized here in one basic principle, followed by a second principle with certain definite strict exceptions to the first. The basic principle is that the form of direct address in the singular and in the plural is the same as the form for the subject. The two examples above illustrate this when we put them into Latin:

"My dear friends, let us rejoice together"
Cari amici gaudeamus simul.

Here you see that "My dear friends" is rendered in Latin as *Cari amici*, which is the same form as the plural subject, except that in this sentence the subject is *nos*, "we," implied in *gaudeamus*, "let us rejoice," and *Cari amici* functions as direct address. Take the other example:

"O my beloved wife, I miss you on my trip"
O coniunx carissima, te iter faciens desidero.

Here, the direct address "O my beloved wife" is rendered in Latin as *O coniunx carissima*, which is the same form as the subject, but here the subject is *ego*, "I," implied in the verb *desidero*, "I miss," and *O coniunx carissima* functions as direct address. We might note that logically the same person is both *coniunx*, in direct address, and *te*, the object of *desidero*, something that we can see more easily in English if we make the word order, "On my trip I miss you, O my beloved wife."

The same forms can function in two different ways, as the following sentence indicates.

Pater noster venit heri

"Our father came yesterday"
"O dear father, (she) came yesterday."

Another example is the following sentence.

Omnes puellae ad saltationem venitote

"All you girls must come to the dance"
"O all you girls, you must come to the dance."

In the above sentence the second command form *venitote*, "you-all must come," is addressed directly to *Omnes puellae*, "O all you girls," which functions as direct address, where the subject is *vos*, "you-all," implied in the verb. Other examples are found on every single reading sheet following each of our encounters. as can be found by the teacher or curious students.

The second basic principle contains five small exceptions to the first principle:

A. Block I words ending in *–us, i,* form their direct address with a short final *–ĕ*. That is why many prayers in Latin have the direct address, *Domine*, "O Lord," as in the prayer, *Domine, non sum dignus*, "O Lord, I am not worthy." Another prayer begins, *Angele Dei*, "O Angel of God." This applies only in the singular. The plural is back to the principle above, where *O Domini*, is the direct address, "O Masters," "O Lords," "O Misters."

B. Adjectives of the same pattern as the nouns ending in *–us, i,* have the same phenomenon; namely, from *bonus, a, um,* we have, *bone*, "O good man," but *O bona*, "O good woman," and *bonum*, "O good thing." We can put the nouns and adjectives together, and we could even address someone offensively as, *O magne asine*, "O big jackass!"

C. Proper names of the first block that end in *–ius,* like *Iulius, Antonius,* and *Sergius*, form their direct address with only one final *–i*, as in *O Antoni*, "O Anthony," *O Iuli*, "O Julius," *O Sergi*, "O Sergius." Another example is *Gaius*, the name of Calligula, whom we might address as *Gai*, "O Gaius." A popular prayer address, *Sancte Antoni*, "O St. Anthony," where both words are in direct address: *sancte*, an adjective of Block I, and *Antoni* from the proper name *Antonius*. In all of these names, the form of-possession is normal, *Antonii, Iulii, Sergii, Gaii*, but their form of direct address ends in a single *–i*.

You may notice from these examples that in Latin as in English the expression *O* sometimes accompanies the form of direct address.

D. Certain peculiarities are hanging around in the language; for example, the form of direct address of *meus*, "my," is *mi*, as in the direct address, *O mi magne amice*, "O my great friend." Do not forget that the plural is *mei*.

The form of direct address for the noun *filius* is *fili*, "O son." The one plural form *filii* can function either as the subject or as direct address, but in the singular these functions have different forms: *filius* functions as the subject and *fili* as direct address.

There is a poignant story from Scripture where King David bewails the death of his son Absalom and cries out, according to the Vulgate edition:

> *Fili mi Absalom, fili mi, fili mi Absalom*! (Vulg. Nov. *II Sam*. 19.1)
> "O my son Absalom, my son, O my son Absalom!"

E. A final detail comes from the Christian usage where the form of direct address for *Deus*, "God," is also *Deus*, "O God," not *Dee*. That is why many prayers are addressed to, *Omnipotens et misericors Deus*, where all but the *et* are in the form of direct address, meaning, "O all-powerful and merciful God."

That is the whole story, which is not that bad. Keeping in mind these principles of direct address, we can recall that many adverbs end with a long *–ē*, but with a short *–ĕ* for the form of direct address in Bk.I words ending in *–us, i*. So, if we were to say *O honestĕ, age honestē*, it would mean, "O you upright man, act morally." The Romans heard the different length of those vowels.

An example from Virgil about a god born from a goddess includes the address, *nate dea*, "O you the one having been born from a goddess," where *nate* is a participle in the form of direct address and all alone means, "O man having been born," and *dea* is the form by-with-from-in meaning "from a goddess." It may be astonishing that participles sometimes function as direct address, such as, *O miserende*, "O you the man needing to be pitied."

Catullus has two forms of direct address in poem 101, line 6, already quoted above, where he says:

> *heu miser indigne frater adempte mihi*
> "O you my wretched brother, O you the one having been taken away from me unworthily."

In this verse both *miser* and *frater adempte*, the latter one with a short final –*ĕ*, function as direct address and mean, "wretched . . . brother having been taken away." The adverb *indigne* with a long final –*ē* means, "unworthily."

There is only one more function possible for the nouns, adjectives, and pronouns of the Latin language, which we shall see toward the end of this experience, in encounter 69.

Summary

We can repeat here what we said about the adverbs just to remind you that the adverb can look like the form of direct address of Bk.I nouns (ending in –*us*, *i*). For example, the adjectives *praeclarus* and *clarus* form the adverb with a long final –*ē*, as in *praeclarē* and *clarē*, meaning "famously," but the vocative "O famous man" is formed with a short final –*ĕ*, as in *praeclarĕ* and *clarĕ*. The Romans heard this difference, but you cannot see it unless it is printed with the marks to indicate the length of the vowel. You simply have to be warned about this.

You can see and verify this in Gildersleeve and Lodge n° 33 and n° 73. The difference between direct address in the singular ending in a short –*ĕ* and the adverbs ending in a long –*ē* is key to understanding the following sentences:

> *O medicĕ, cura teipsum!*
> O doctor, cure yourself!
>
> *O amicĕ, age amicē!*
> O friend, act in a friendly way!
>
> *O bonĕ, age probē!*
> O good man, act well!

You can see that the final –*e* is short for the singular direct address *bonĕ*, "O good man," but long for the positive adverb *probē*, "well." These details will help us to complete our review of all the adjectives and nouns that go with our readings from the First Experience.

ENCOUNTER 4 (39)

REPETITIO EX PRIMA EXPERIENTIA VERBORUM EORUMQUE CONTRACTIONES; QUATTUOR IMPERIA

repetition of verbs from the First Experience and their contractions; four command forms

Introduction

As we continue to review what we learned in the First Experience, this fourth encounter of our Third Experience provides an oversight of the verb in all six times of the indicative, both active and passive. The class can take examples of real Latin sentences from our sheets and orally review what we learned from our very first encounter. They will jump around the verb times and reverse the forms from singular to plural and plural to singular and flip them from active to passive and from passive to active until everyone can produce these forms quickly. Playing with these forms will take some time, because some people will be rusty and appreciate the opportunity to learn the material again, probably after having forgotten it.

In this encounter we shall again refine what we know and add a few details. After an explanation we shall verify what we have said by referring to accepted authorities so that you can see for yourself and feel much better about what we say.

1. Fluctuation in Time 4

The first detail to point out, we already mentioned in encounter eight of the First Experience, but we repeat it here. The historians, especially Sallustius and Livy, use a variation for the form "they" in T.4, for example *amaverunt, dixerunt, viderunt*. Instead of the ending *–erunt*, they vary this ending into *–ere*, so that *amavérunt* becomes *amavére*, and *dixérunt* is contracted to *dixére*, and *vidérunt* is shortened to *vidére*. This last example is terribly deceiving, because the infinitive form is *vidēre*, and now this form can also mean "they have seen" and "they did see." This makes Latin very challenging, because *vĭdērĕ* means "to see," but *vīdērĕ* means "they saw"; Virgil and Terentius play with this all the time.

Take the example *venire*, "to come," which has the form *venerunt*, "they came," which now can be shortened to *venére* with the same meaning. One letter makes all the difference.

You can verify this usage in Gildersleeve and Lodge nº 122, which has "amā–v–ērunt (–ēre)"; nº 123 has "dēlē–v–ērunt (–ēre)"; nº 124 has "mon–u–ērunt (–ēre)"; nº 125 has "ēm–ērunt (–ēre)"; and for the verbs on the fence between *–io* and *–ĕre* we can supply the forms "dirip–u–ērunt (–ēre)"; nº 126 has "audī–v–ērunt (–ēre)." That is what those endings in parentheses mean.

This is going to occur more often than you think, so you have to know it. Cicero and the poets use this variation, but after the third or fourth century it is difficult to find. Renaissance authors will bring this usage back. In fact, some people think that they are two distinct times; maybe *amaverunt* is T.4a, and *amavere* is T.4b, but that is not how we use these forms here.

2. Contraction because of *–v*

Let's be honest; we frequently contract words in spoken English, such as:

We've all done it
So, what ya goin' to do?

The Romans did the same thing in their spoken language, because of how they heard the words. This occurs especially in colloquial Latin; Plautus does this all the time. To understand how the Romans ended up with their contractions, we have to know the basic form of the word and how it sounded, and then we can understand the contracted form.

For example, we learned the form *dixisti*. Plautus gives us its contraction *dixti*. He recorded how the Romans swallowed the syllable, as children and adults do in all languages.

The big examples come in T.4, 5, 6 of Gp.I verbs. To understand this phenomenon, take the example *amáveram*, "I had loved." The Romans pronounced *amáueram*. The sound "*v*" was heard as a "*u*." If you say *amáueram* fast enough and often enough, the sound *–ue–* is swallowed, and you end up with *amáram*, which corresponds to nothing else in the whole pattern of the Latin verb except as a contraction of T.5 *amaveram*.

Let us take an example from Gp.IV verbs. The form *audívi* was pronounced *audíui*. Because the sound of that letter *–u–* was swallowed, your dictionary will give you the alternate form *audii*. This same verb in T.6 has the form *audíerit*, which is quite explainable if you hear how the Romans pronounced *audíuerit*. Only the *–v–* is missing in this case.

Turning to T.6 of Gp.I verbs, we have the form *amavérimus*, "we shall have loved." They heard *amauérimus* and so you will find *amárimus*; although rather rare, it is in the literature. We also find *amárint* for *amáverint*, because that *–ve–* was pronounced as a *–ue–* and then was not pronounced.

This phenomenon creates no problem for people speaking with a classical pronunciation because they hear the words as the Romans did. But for people speaking Latin with Church or Italian pronunciation, these contractions may seem a mystery or a joke, but they are neither at all.

Take the example of *nosco, noscere, novi notus*, 3, "to get to know." We shall find hundreds of examples of the form *nóram*, from *nóveram*, in T.5 meaning "I had come to know." The form *nóverant* contracts to *nórant*, "they had come to know," but *nórunt* is short for *novérunt* in T.4, "they have come to know." In T.6 the form *nóvero* was written *nóro*, "I shall have come to know." Virgil says *nórint* for *nóverint*, which, also in T.6, can mean, "they will have come to know." If you look in the Latin dictionary by Lewis and Short mentioned in the bibliography, you will find all of these strange forms listed, and, unlike others, you will not go crazy nor despair.

All of these natural contractions are due to pronunciation, not some grammatical chart. They are less frequent in Gp.II and III verbs. They occur especially in Gp.I and to some extent in Gp.IV because of the letter *–v–*.

3. Variation of *–ris*

Another contraction due to pronunciation in all four verb Groups concerns how the Romans heard the passive voice of "you" in the singular, which ends in *–ris*. For example, in T.3 we have seen the form *coronáberis*, "you will be crowned." The Romans heard that ending *–ris* as short, and so it easily contracted to *–re* as in *coronábere*. This is the reality of the spoken and written language.

This occurs only in the passive T.1, 2, 3, because the passive T.4, 5, 6 are compound forms that do not end in *–ris*. We shall see it again later on in the passive forms of the subjunctive. This contraction is quite common, especially in the poets; Cicero loves it in his letters.

Take an example in T.1, the form *timéris*, "you are feared." The Romans contracted this to *timére*. Right away this contraction causes problems because it is the same form as the infinitive-gerund and the passive imperative. Take another example, "you are being avoided," *evitaris*, which the Romans heard and shortened to *evitare*, which again looks like the infinitive. You already know the infinitives *timere* and *evitare* can also be the passive commands, and now they can be an alternative passive form for "you" in the singular. This is what makes Latin very challenging but eminently interesting and possible.

The form "you are being feared," *metúeris*, contracts to *metúere*. If you see this in the poets, the meter will tell you that with this accent it can be the contracted form of *metúeris*, as well as the infinitive-gerund and the passive command.

In T.2, Cicero likes to write *diligebare*, the contracted form of *diligebaris*, "you were being loved." There is no infinitive form that looks like *diligebare* in anything we have learned or shall learn. With the deponent verb *praestolor* Cicero likes to say, for example, *mihi prestolabare*, using the contracted form of *mihi praestolabaris*, "you were waiting for me."

The plural of these forms is regular, for example, in T.3 *amabimini*, in T.1 *timemini* and *metuimini* and *evitamini* and in T.2 *evitabamini* and *praestolabamini*.

The students will know they are not being misled, when they verify this in any Latin manual, because all manuals must point it out. For example, the book of Gildersleeve and Lodge gives these forms: nº 122 has "amā–ris (–re)" and "amā–bā–ris (–re)" and "amā–be–ris (–re); nº 124 has "monē–ris (–re)," "monē–bā–ris (–re)," monē–be–ris (–re)"; nº 125 gives you "eme–ris (–re)," "emē–bā–ris (–re)," "emē–ris (–re)"; nº 126 presents the verb Group on the fence between *–io* and *–ere* as in "cape–ris (–re)," "capiē–ris (–re)"; we can add here "capiē–bā–ris (re)," which is not given in nº 126 because it follows the pattern of Gp. IV; nº 127 gives Gp. IV as in "audī–ris (–re)," "audiē–bā–ris (–re)," "audiē–ris (–re)." That is what the ending *–re* in parentheses means.

There is no sense in memorizing schemas and paradigms, but we have to be conscious about these phenomena, because this is how the Romans spoke. The Renaissance authors, like Erasmus, showed off their classical knowledge by resurrecting all this from the classical writers.

These contractions are very difficult to spot, and they take a certain amount of concentration, which is almost super-human, but they simply must be recognized. They will be pointed out graphically on the reading sheets, especially in the poets who do this all the time. Because of the verse, the poets need a short final *–ĕ*, rather than the often long final *–īs* that occurs when the next word begins with a consonant, so they say *videbáre* or *vidébere* or *vidére*.

4. Famous four

This chapter has presented a considerable amount of material that requires attention and repetition, but students very easily learn to manage these forms, because they have already learned the basic forms well. They only have to add on a little bit more to change the sentence "you have arrived" to "you've arrived."

Now to fill up one remaining hole in our training. We learned, especially in Gp.III, that "you must love!" is *dilige*. That final –e is the sign of the "you" singular command.

There are, however, four famous commands-imperatives in Latin which from the golden age until today have lost that final *–e*. They are: *dic*, "talk!" short for *dice* from *dicere; duc*, "lead!" short for *duce* from *ducere; fac*, "do!" short for *face* from *facere; fer*, "carry!" short for *fere* from *ferre*.

These four were used so often in daily life that the Romans simply left off the final *–e*. It is like baby talk that survived into adulthood and even into our day. So, for example, the form *face* practically does not exist anymore, except in Plautus and Terentius, but appears only as *fac*, as do *duc*, *dic*, and *fer*.

If we were to say today, *Dice nomen tuum!* some smarty would correct us and say, no, it is *Dic nomen tuum!* "Say your name!" which is half-correct. The imperative *dic* is still abbreviated in Italian as *di* or *dimmi*, "Tell me!" The Italians also say *fa* or *fallo*, "Do it!"

The famous phrase *Duc in altum*, "Lead into the deep," comes from the Latin Bible, the Vulgate, account of Luke 5:4, where Jesus told Simon to put out into the deep water and cast his nets there. This phrase was often quoted in our own day by John Paul II.

Likewise, Jesus challenges the rich young man, saying *hoc fac et vives*, "do this and you will live" (Vulg. Nov. *Luke* 10.28).

The form *fer* is the basis of many Latin imperatives such as *transfer*, *confer*, *infer;* none with a final –*e*. In the old days they would say *transfere*, but by the time of Cicero until our present day it has been *transfer*.

The plural forms of these are usually normal: *ducite, dicite, facite, ferte*.

5. Summary

That concludes everything that can be said about T.1 to 6 in the indicative mode of direct discourse and question and in the imperative or command mode, in both the active and passive. In three or four encounters of the First Experience we have learned three-fourths of the Latin verb. Just now we have reviewed everything you learned in the First Experience with these refining points in the Third Experience.

The only things left are the subjunctive, participles, and infinitives. They can be presented in about five minutes. The learner should be reassured that this is not an infinite undertaking. You can learn Latin and master it. Latin is challenging, but not necessarily confusing or discouraging or disappointing.

Again, some people may want to verify everything we have said in narrative form here by turning to any manual to see these contracted forms, if they do not believe it here. This will indicate that these forms are accepted and not crazy ideas of our own.

What is needed, moreover, is repetition and familiarization with the language as found in real Latin literature and genuine examples.

ENCOUNTER 5 (40)

REPETITIO EX PRIMA EXPERIENTIA PRONOMINUM; EIS = IIS; IS, EA, ID; HIC, HAEC, HOC

repetition of pronouns from the First Experience; forms of eis = iis; meanings of is, ea, id; hic, haec, hoc

Introduction

In this encounter we continue to repeat from the First Experience all the forms and the functions we have learned of the personal pronouns, that is to say: I, we, you, you (plural), he, she, it, they. This can easily be done by examining the infinite examples available in Latin literature from every age presented in the reading sheets.

1. *Nostri, nostrum; vestri, vestrum*

We shall also add a refining element to what has already been learned. Remember that you learned two different forms that mean "of us." When you learned *nostri*, "of us," you also had in parentheses *nostrum*, "of us." The same can be said for the "you" forms in the plural when you learned *vestri*, "of you all," but also put in parentheses *vestrum*, "of you all." In each case these two forms are unchangeable.

Here, we would like to remind you that there is a difference in the usage of these two forms. The forms are different, and the ideas expressed are different.

Both *vestri* and *nostri* are used where those pronouns sound like a direct object, as in:

nostri memor
mindful *of us*

nostri amantes
fond *of us*

vestri obliviscens
forgetful *of you*

vestri diligens
interested *in you.*

The forms *nostrum* and *vestrum* are used with numbers, as in:

nemo nostrum
no one of us

pauci vestrum
few of you

multi vestrum
many of you

Quot nostrum?
How many of us?

Quis vestrum?
Who of you all?

The forms *nostrum* and *vestrum* are the rarer of each pair. They are used with numbers, whereas the forms *vestri* and *nostri* are used to express a different idea, one which sounds like the object function.

2. *Is, ea, id*

Look in the dictionary under the entry for *is, ea, id*, which you learned means "he, she, it." You also learned the various functions and the forms for the various functions. Now we would like the people interested to look again in their dictionaries to see that *is, ea, id* can also mean "this" or "that" or "such." These meanings escape many people. This second set of meanings is not rare, but rather common. For example, we might say:

Legimus eos
We read them.

But we might also say with several meanings:

Legimus eos libros
We read those books
We read these books
We read such books.

By the way, "we read their books" is *Legimus eorum libros*, where *eorum libros* means "the books of them," and *legimus eius libros* means "we read the books of him, her, it," namely "his, her, its books."

There is a whole mass of examples in your dictionary and also on your reading sheets of *is, ea, id* meaning not only "he, she, it" but also "this, that" and "such."

As far as the forms go, there is nothing further to mention or say about "I," "we," "you," "you all." Other forms to point out concern "he," "she," "it." We learned that the plural masculine subject, "they, the men," is *ei*, and the form to-for-from and the form by-with-from-in are both *eis*. But in Latin literature you will see how their pronunciation of these words influenced their forms. In the plural, we can find *ei*, "they, the men," written as *ii*, and we can find *eis*, "by, with, from, in them," and "to, for, from them" written as *iis*, and some poets would even go so far as to write simply *is* for the plural forms to-for-from and by-with-from-in. This form *is* is rather rare, but *iis* is not rare; it is very common as a variation following the pronunciation of *eis*.

Those are the diverse forms. We are not concerned here with the relative pronoun. That is for another lesson.

We have to know these variations, not because we want them that way, but because the dictionary and the literature present them in that way. If we rob the students of these bits of knowledge, we are simply cheating them and not helping them at all.

3. *Hic, haec, hoc*

The new material in this encounter concerns the easily understood and learned forms for "this" and "that." The Romans wrote "this" in the masculine as *hic*—an explanation will follow below—the feminine as *haec*, and the neuter as *hoc*.

Before we look at how these forms are manipulated for their various functions, you must look in your dictionary under the little particle –*ce*. It is given in your dictionary as an enclitic, and –*ce* means "here" or "there," or many times it means nothing at all. The Romans attached the particle –*ce* onto the end of normal adjective endings, and *hum–ce* became *hunc*, "this man," used as an object, and *ho–ce* became *hoc*, in all its functions. Thus, they produced a word that is mysterious for many people, namely *hic, haec, hoc*. In the old days the forms *hic, haec, hoc* with the particle –*ce* attached were *hice, haece, hoce*, or sometimes *hicce, haecce, hocce*. What you see hidden in these words are the forms *hi, hae, ho*. If you keep that in mind, then what happens to this word is very explainable. You will see the letter –*c*– appearing in these forms, which is a mystery to many students, but not to you.

We have said that the masculine, feminine, and neuter subject forms for "this" are *hic, haec, hoc*. The object forms are in the masculine *hunc*, whose old form was *hunce*, in the feminine *hanc*, which was *hance*, and in the neuter *hoc*, which was *hoce*, and follows the super principle.

The form for of-possession in all three genders meaning "of this one" is *huius*. In that form you see the letters –*ius* which you had in *eius* before, so it is not strange that *huius* means "of this man, woman, thing."

The form for by-with-from-in in the masculine is *hoc*, short for *hoce*, in the feminine *hac*, for *hace*, and in the neuter *hoc*, also for *hoce*.

The form for to-for-from for all three genders is *huic*, which came from *huice*, and it means "to, for, from him, her, it."

In the plural the particle –*ce* is largely lost, although some authors and writers add it. The plural of *hic* is *hi*, "these men," of *haec* is *hae*, "these women," and of *hoc* is *haec*, "these things."

The plural object form for *hunc* is *hos*, for *hanc* is *has*, for *hoc* is *haec* following the super principle.

The form of-possession in the singular is the same for all three genders, *huius*, but in the plural the masculine form is *horum*, the feminine *harum*, and the neuter *horum*. You can see the pattern in Latin right away.

All the plural forms for to-for-from and by-with-from-in in all three genders is the same: *his*. Here again you see the ending –*is*, which is scattered throughout the language.

Immediately we must add, if you read Latin literature and some authors writing Latin today, they revert to the old form of *his*, which is *hisce*. That old particle –*ce* dribbled on, so to speak, for a number of centuries. You might find *huiusce*, "of this very man, woman, thing," with the particle –*ce*. This should not alarm you, because you have learned that that –*ce* was added for emphasis way back in the past, and it held on for centuries. Some modern authors think they are very elegant and clever when they write *horumce*, but we think this is pretending.

ENCOUNTER 6 (41)

REPETITIO EX PRIMA EXPERIENTIA REFLEXIVI PRONOMINIS; ADIECTIVA: ISTE – ILLE – IPSE

repetition of the reflexive pronoun from the First Experience; adjectives: iste – ille – ipse

Introduction

By way of review, reflexive pronouns and adjectives refer to the subject of the sentence. That subject can be either the grammatical or direct subject, or sometimes it is the indirect subject, or it can even be the logical subject of the whole story. Discerning which subject the reflexive refers to is sometimes not at all easy.

If it does not refer to the subject, then it is not reflexive. For example, given the sentence, "She brought her children," we ask whose children. If the children are her own, then "her" is reflexive, but if the children belong to some other woman, then "her" is not reflexive. Such are the problems that have to be resolved in any language. Let us quickly review the reflexive pronouns and adjectives and add a few refinements.

1. *Me, nos, te, vos*; myself, ourselves, yourself, yourselves

Each of the pronouns has a reflexive form. The reflexive forms for "I" and "we" and "you" and "you all" are exactly the same as for the normal pronouns. You cannot distinguish between the forms, only between their functions in the sentence. In the following examples, the form *me* is the same, but its functions are different:

Me dirigunt	They guide me
Me dirigo	I guide myself.

The second example here contains a reflexive because the pronoun *me* refers to the subject "I" contained in the verb. You can see, then, that the reflexive of these forms poses no particular difficulty.

2. *Se, sui, sibi*

When you come to the third-person forms, "he, she, it" and "they," you have to distinguish the forms along a definite dividing line, and you have to decide whether the form is reflexive or not. On one side of this dividing line are the reflexive pronouns and adjectives. Let us consider these functions one at a time and look first at the reflexive pronouns. For each of the functions, the reflexive pronoun has one form that covers the masculine, feminine, neuter, and plural: "he, she, it; one; they."

Because the reflexive pronoun refers back to the subject, it does not have a subject form. The adjective *suus, a, um*, however, can appear as a subject in some subordinate clauses, such as:

> *Imperabat Caligula ut suae redderentur pecuniae*
> Caligula was giving orders that his monies might be returned

where *suae* in subject form refers to the subject of the main sentence, "Caligula." Here is another example:

> *Cives ut sui magnis e periculis eriperentur vehementer cupiebat Iulius*
> Julius vehemently was wishing that his citizens might be snatched from great dangers

where *sui cives* is the subject of its clause, but *sui* refers to Julius in the main sentence.

The object form of the reflexive pronoun is *se* or sometimes *sese*. Depending on the subject, *se* or *sese* means, "herself" or "himself" or "itself" or "themselves" or "oneself," in each case referring back to a subject, as in the sentence:

> *Honorat se*
> She honors herself
> He honors himself
> It [the institution] honors itself
>
> *Honorant se*
> They honor themselves.

You have to find out what the subject of the verb *honorat* or *honorant* is to know the meaning of the reflexive *se*.

The reflexive pronoun in the form of-possession is *sui*. Again, depending on the subject it may mean, "of himself" or "of herself" or "of itself" or "of themselves," or "of oneself."

The reflexive pronoun in the form by-with-from-in is *se*, or sometimes *sese* as we saw for the object form. For example, rather than the expression *cum se*, you will find the word *secum* meaning "with himself" or "with herself" or "with itself" or "with themselves."

The reflexive pronoun in the form to-for-from is *sibi*, which can mean "to-for-from himself, herself, itself, themselves," depending on the subject it refers to.

We said that on one side of the dividing line are the reflexive pronouns and adjectives, so let us turn to the reflexive adjective for "he, she, it"; the form is *suus, a, um*. Its meaning depends on the subject and can be, "his" or "her" or "its" or "their" or "one's own." You have to be very careful with these because they refer back to the subject in their meaning but they agree with the noun they describe in gender and number.

On the other side of the line, we have not forgotten the normal or non-reflexive way to express possession with *eius* and *eorum* and *earum*. These refer to someone or something other than the subject, as in:

> *Mulier secum eius portat liberos*
> The woman brings with herself her (or his) children.

The Latin is clear that the children belong to another person, but the first English rendering here, while correct, is confusing or misleading, because the confusing word "her" refers to another woman, not to the subject of the sentence. The clear distinction in the above Latin may be rendered more clearly into English if we were to say:

> The woman brings with herself the children of another.

We can change the Latin sentence to indicate that the children are the woman's own by using the possessive adjective, as in:

> *Mulier secum suos portat liberos*
> She brings her children with herself.

The English here is the same as in the first example above. The English has an ambiguity that you have to clarify for the Latin by deciding to whom the children belong. We can also say, in this context, the following:

> *Mulieres suo in corde eorum portant dilectionem*
> The women bear in their own heart the love of them (children).

Here the women have love for the other people.

The key word for the reflexive pronoun and adjective is the "subject." The key word later on when we review the meaning of *eius*, "of him, her, it" or "his, her, its," will not be the "subject," but the "story." You have to get the meaning of *eius* from the whole story, whereas the meaning of *suus, a, um*; *sibi, sui, se* comes from the subject. These are two completely different systems. If you keep this in mind, you will not get them mixed up.

Thus far we have reviewed the reflexive pronoun and adjective from the First Experience. This allows us to repeat it here, because some people come fresh into the Third Experience or come up from the First Experience, and need this to be repeated many times. Once they have it clear, they have it for ever.

3. *Iste – ille – ipse*

In our last encounter we saw the heavy pronoun for "this," *hic, haec, hoc*, and we saw how these forms developed with the addition of the ending *–ce*.

To finish off the pronouns, we now turn to what we call the three cousins. These three related words have the same endings for their functions. They are easy to remember, if we put them all together and treat them as one. They are:

> *ille illa illud*
> *iste ista istud*
> *ipse ipsa ipsum.*

Just note the above neuter forms *illud* and *istud* ending in *–d*, but *ipsum* ending in the usual *–um*. These three words are unusual because they take some of their endings from the pronoun system and some from the adjective system of Bk.I. This mixed system is very easy to remember or to notice.

First we shall see what they mean. To begin, *ille, illa, illud* refers to "that one," as if across the street. Some manuals describe it as the demonstrative pronoun for the third person, referring to "that one over there." According to your dictionary it also means "that famous one," or we might say, "that well known one." The second word, *iste, ista, istud*, really refers to "that one by you." Some manuals describe it as the demonstrative of the second person. The phrases *ista penna* or *iste calamus* suggest "that pen" which you have in your hand. Notice that the masculine of these two words is *iste* and *ille*. We shall see how they get function endings in a moment.

Cicero notes this, and it is in your dictionaries that *iste, ista, istud* can express a negative estimation, something like "that bad one," "that unlikeable one," "that crummy one." When Cicero says *iste testis*, he is referring to more than just a witness, but to "that lousy witness," "that bad witness." But *iste* does not always necessarily imply a negative estimation, because it also means without judgment "that one by you." This ambivalence, however, creates problems if used in decrees and documents such as:

Isti civitati nostram mittimus salutationem
We send our greeting to that city of yours

which, regrettably, looks like:

We send our greeting to that *stupid* city of yours.

Previously we said the pronoun *hic, haec, hoc*, means "this one," and now we may add the meaning, "this one by me." We have just seen the first of the cousins, the pronoun *ille, illa, illud*, referring to "that one over there" or "that famous one," and the second cousin, the pronoun *iste, ista, istud*, referring to "that one of yours" or "that lousy one of yours." Now we turn to the third of the cousins, the pronoun *ipse, ipsa, ipsum*.

After years of Latin many people still do not understand this pronoun, because by definition *ipse, ipsa, ipsum* is technically an intensive pronoun, not reflexive. The intensive pronoun means, for example, *ego ipse*, "I *my very self*." If we were to say, *ipsum codicem lego*, "I read the manuscript *itself*, the *very* manuscript," the intensive pronoun *ipsum* means "itself" or "the very one." Many people without thinking will translate it as "I read the same book." At this point, the students are challenged to find any dictionary in this world that indicates *ipse* as meaning "the same." If they find it, they can cut it out and post it for us to see, because you will never find a dictionary that says *ipse* means "the same," but some people insist on translating it that way. An example will help to illustrate:

Tu non curas de te
You do not care about yourself.

You can intensify this sentence by saying:

> *Tu ipsa de te non curas*
> You yourself do not care about yourself.

Thus, we have *hic* and the three cousins *ille, iste, ipse*:

hic	this one by me, this one
ille	that one over there, that famous one
iste	that one by you, that crummy one of yours
ipse	the very one, the one itself.

The various forms of these pronouns follow two different systems. The singular forms of-possession and to-for-from follow the pronoun system; the remaining functions follow the adjective system. We have already pointed out that the masculine singular of the three cousins ends in *–e: ille, iste, ipse*. We have also seen that two of the cousins have neuters that end in *–d: illud, istud*, but that *ipsum* returns to the normal pattern.

Beyond these small exceptions, these pronouns follow the pattern of the adjectives of Bk.I, namely *–us, a, um*, with two big exceptions. We have already seen the first exception in the form *huius*, "of this." Likewise, the singular form of-possession for all three cousins in masculine, feminine, neuter ends in *–íus*, as in *illíus, istíus, ipsíus*, "of that man over there," "of that woman by you," "of that thing itself." In each of these the accent is indicated on the second letter, *–í–*, in normal prose. That exception does not follow the pattern of Bk.I adjectives.

The other big exception is the form to-for-from. We have already seen the form *huic*, where the final *–c* is a remnant of the ending *–ce*. If we ignore that ending *–ce*, we can see that the three cousins have a similar form to-for-from, all ending in *–i*. They are: *illi*, "to that man, woman, thing over there"; *isti*, "to that man, woman, thing by you"; *ipsi*, "to that man, woman, thing itself." You can see that the same form is used for the masculine, feminine, neuter. By the way, these same forms also function as masculine plural subjects meaning, *illi*, "those men over there"; *isti*, "those men of yours"; *ipsi*, "the very men," or "the men themselves."

The plural forms are normal according to the pattern of the adjectives of Bk.I, for example: *illarum, ipsis, istos*.

The combination of these two systems produces some identical forms that you would not expect from either of the systems considered separately. For example, *illi* is both the singular form to-for-from meaning, "to that man, woman, thing over there," and the masculine subject plural meaning, "those people." The same happens with *isti*, which means either "to that one by you" or "those lousy men." Again the form *ipsi* means either "to the man, woman, thing itself" or "they themselves" as a plural masculine subject. These pronouns are very common, and you will find them everywhere.

One other big observation you have to make is, if you look in the Bible or even in Plautus, Erasmus, and wherever you find a certain kind of colloquial talk, the Romans use *hic* and *ille* and *iste* and *ipse* to mean simply "he, she, it." Most often you will find the original meanings "this," "that one by you," "that one over there," "the one itself," but many times the natural meaning of these pronouns is diminished and lost and ultimately sounds simply as "he, she, it."

Take, for example, the sentence, *Illam vidi.* Its natural meaning is "I saw that woman over there," but the proper meaning of *illam* may be lost or disregarded, and the sentence simply means "I saw her." This is the case with all four of these pronouns; each of them can mean simply "he, she, it, they" without any special emphasis or meaning attached.

A final comment on these pronouns is confirmed by any dictionary, namely the directional use of *ille* and *hic*, where *ille* means "the former over there" and *hic* "the latter over here by me." The comical aspect of this meaning is that it depends on where you are standing, and that is why our standard Latin dictionary by Lewis and Short says that sometimes these have the reversed meaning, where *ille* means "that one over here," and *hic* "this one over there," depending on where you are standing. But the normal geographical distinction of the two prevails; namely, *hic* is the one by me, and *ille* is the one over there.

REPETITIO EX PRIMA EXPERIENTIA RELATIVI; INTERROGATIVUM, INDEFINITUM; NOVEM ADIECTIVA UNUS . . . SOLUS

repetition of the relative pronoun from the First Experience; the interrogative, indefinite; nine adjectives unus . . . solus

Introduction

When we spoke previously about the relative pronoun, we emphasized how much the Romans loved the sound "*qu*–." This sound appears in practically every Latin sentence in this world. Today we want to look at a cluster of words that are unbelievably common and that follow this phonetic preference and cause endless trouble for sleepy people.

1. *Qui, quae, quod; quis, quid*

These pronouns have several uses in Latin. The Lewis and Short dictionary (pp. 1510, 1516) presents the different uses clearly and without confusion. There we find that both pronouns can be used as indefinite pronouns meaning "someone, something," and they both can be used as interrogative pronouns meaning "who?" or "what?" A third usage applies to the pronoun *qui, quae, quod*, which can also be used as a relative pronoun meaning "who, which." This creates in a sense a forest of pronouns that all look the same but are fundamentally different. Let us look at all three of these in reverse order.

2. *Relativum*

We have already considered the use of the relative pronoun *qui, quae, quod*, meaning "who, which" in its various functions.

3. *Interrogativum*

Both pronouns, *qui, quae, quod* and *quis, quid*, may be used to express a direct question, as already touched on in encounter 13, for example:

Heri quid effecisti?
What did you accomplish yesterday?

Quis cras veniet et cuius parentes?
Who will be coming tomorrow and whose parents?

Cuius auctoritate id facis?
By whose authority are you doing this?

Qua via venisti?
By what road did you come?

Quam heri emisti vestem?
What kind of dress did you buy yesterday?

Quam sibi elegit coronam?
What kind of crown did she select for herself?

4. *Indefinitum*

Both can also be used as indefinite pronouns. In this case they are fully written out as follows. First, for the pronoun:

aliquis, aliquis, aliquid
someone, something
anyone, anything,

next, for the adjective:

aliqui, aliqua, aliquod
some (man, woman, thing)
any (man, woman, thing).

Note here that the feminine form above, *aliqua*, ends in *–a* and not as the relative in *–ae* . Anyone can confirm this in III Encounter 5 (40), Gildersleeve and Lodge nº 107. A couple of examples make this clear:

Fortasse posthac haec (ali)quis curabit
Perhaps someone will look after these things later on

Dignissimo dabimus cui pecunias
We shall give money to someone most worthy.

5. *Si, nisi, ut, cum, num, ne*

As indicated in the dictionary, the indefinite pronoun is used by the Romans especially in a quick combination and clause after the particles:

si, if
nisi, unless
ut, so that
cum, when
num, whether
ne, that not.

In this case the pronouns appear without the prefix *ali–*, but simply as:

qui, qua, quod
quis, quid.

Again, like *aliqua*, the feminine form above is *qua*, not *quae*. The important thing for students to realize is that these indefinite pronouns look like relative pronouns, because they are not distinguished by the prefix *ali–*. Realizing that they mean, "someone, something" and not "who, what" will avoid infinite difficulties, as in the following

example:	*Si quis respondet gaudeo*
which stands for:	*Si aliquis respondet gaudeo*
and means:	If anyone answers, I am happy
not:	If who answers, I am happy.

Similarly the Romans say:

Hoc scribam ne cuius animum offendam
I shall write this lest I offend *anyone's* sensitivity.

Here, the expression *ne cuius* stands for *ne alicuius*, "lest anyone's."

Again you have ready examples on every reading sheet in this world, because this construction is very common. To remember this pattern, this little ditty can help:

After *si*, *nisi*, *ut*, *cum*, *num* and *ne*, all the *ali*-s fly away.

The ditty is based on a play of words whereby *ali*-s refers to the prefix *ali*– of the indefinite pronoun and to the Latin word *alis*, meaning "with wings."

6. *Unus – solus*: the famous 9

Up to this point in our Third Experience we have reviewed the forms for the relative, indefinite, and interrogative pronouns, and we have seen their usage. Now we want to continue our discussion in the light and spirit of the pronouns *iste*, *ille*, *ipse*, which combine two systems, and belong partly to the pronoun system and partly to the adjective system. In the remainder of this encounter we see an additional nine adjectives that combine these two systems in a similar way. Because they are nine, we call them simply "the 9." Every dictionary in this world and all the manuals have this bunch of 9:

unus, a, um	one, alone, sole, only
solus, a, um	alone, only, sole
totus, a, um	whole, entire, complete (it does not mean "all")
ullus, a, um	any, any one
uter, utra, utrum	which of two (in questions)
alter, altera, alterum	the second of two, the latter of two
neuter, neutra, neutrum	neither of two
nullus, a, um	not any, none
alius, alia, aliud	an other, another (not "the other"), any other one (of many; the neuter ends in -*d* not -*m*).

One way of remembering these 9 adjectives is the acronym *unus nauta*. You can see that the first letter of each of the words in the above list can be arranged in vertical order to produce the acronym *unus nauta*:

Ullus, Nullus, Unus, Solus *Neuter, Alter, Uter, Totus, Alius.*

The 9 pose two problems. People make terrible mistakes in their meaning, and the 9 belong partly to the adjective and partly to the pronoun system. You simply have to know the 9, what they mean and what their forms are.

The 9 follow the pattern of Bk.I adjectives *honestus, a, um* and *bonus, a, um*, with the same two big exceptions we saw in *iste* and *ille*. The singular form of-possession for all the 9 ends in *–íus* just as the personal pronouns did. Note that the accent falls on the *–í–* in *–íus*. This is a stumbling block for people who want to change *tota ecclesia*, "the whole church," to say "of the whole church"; they will begin with *totus, a, um* and produce *totae ecclesiae*, which does not exist in Latin, but should be *totíus ecclesiae*. One famous example of this form is with the adjective *nullus*, "not any, none." Some bishops are called a *praelatus nullíus*, which is short for "a prelate of not any diocese, of no diocese."

The other big exception of the 9 is in the form to-for-from, which ends in a simple *–i*. You would expect that the phrase "for the whole human being" would be *toto homini*, but it is not; it is *toti homini*. The phrase "for the whole church" is not *totae ecclesiae*, but it is *toti ecclesiae*.

So, the two big exceptions are, for example, *solius* and *soli*; these cause the problems. All the other forms of the 9 are the same as Bk.I adjectives, in the singular and plural, with the exception of that form *aliud*, "another thing," which ends in *–d*, rather than in *–m*.

The combination of these two systems produces forms that are unexpectedly the same. For example, *toti* can be the form to-for-from as in,

> *Toti viro, feminae, instituto providet medicina*
> Medicine looks out for the whole man, woman, institution.

Yet *toti* still remains the masculine subject plural, as in *toti ludi*, "whole-complete schools," that is all the boys and girls, old and young of each school, not "all the schools."

The other big problem with the 9 is their meaning, and you will be caught off guard if you are not careful. A few notes will help to clear this up. For example, the adjective *totus, a, um* means "whole, entire," and not "all." So, the phrase *toti homines* means, "whole persons" or "the whole people," but not "all the people." This is confusing if you know Italian, where *tutti gli uomini* means "all the people." The phrase *totus populus* refers to "the whole citizenry," and *toti populi* refers to "entire nations," not to "all the individuals." The money redeemed *totos homines*, "whole persons," referring to the wholeness of the person, in contrast to just the mind or just the body. It does not mean, however, the money redeemed "all humans"; that would possibly be *omnes homines*.

The meaning of another one of the 9 is also surprising to many. The adjective *unus, a, um* as a number means, "one," but it can also mean "only." People do not like to see the sentence *unos libros bonos lego*, where the plural *unos* does not mean "one" but "only," as in "I read only good books." In light of this we considered naming this book *Ossa Latinitatis Una*, "Only the Bones of Latin," but this is too difficult for most ordinary people to see.

There is a famous compound of *uter*, "which of two," namely *uterque, utraque, utrumque*, meaning, "each of two, both." That is why the form of-possession is *utriúsque*. Some people have a law degree called simply *utriusque*, meaning a degree of civil law and of church law.

There is a little ditty teachers can use: *soli soli soli*. This inscription used to be written on sundials. There are three different words here. Two are in the form to-for-from and one in the form of-possession. From the noun *sol, solis*, m., "the sun" we have the form *soli*, "to the sun." From the noun *solum, soli*, n., "the ground, earth," we have "of the earth." From the adjective *solus, a, um* we have the form *soli*, meaning "to the one (sun)." So the ditty used as a dedication of the sundial is "to the sole sun of the soil." This looks like a complete mystery unless you know what word each of those *soli* comes from; then you can decide which form of each word is used here. Vocabulary and thinking!

There is nothing to learn here, just a few refinements to remember that you have already learned in regard to *ille* and *iste*. You will remember these forms after you hear them a few times. Spotting these forms on the reading sheets will help you to become familiar with them right away.

ENCOUNTER 8 (43)

LATINA IN LINGUA "QUAM" VARIE ET DIFFICULTER

"quam" in the Latin language with various usages and difficulties

Introduction

Your dictionary will give you all of this information in full; here we want to summarize several things in a few words.

Thus far you have learned the relative pronoun *qui*, *quae*, *quod*, with the feminine object form *quam* meaning, "whom." In this encounter we present a different *quam*; this one is not a pronoun. It is, rather, an unchangeable adverb. It is very popular and very frequent and provides another *qu*– sound to the language. We simply have to learn how to use this *quam*.

1. *Tam ... quam*

The first usage of the adverb *quam* is in connection with another adverb in the expression *tam ... quam*. Your dictionary tells you this expression means "just ... as" or "so ... as" or "so much ... as much," where *quam* means "as." You will find in the dictionary literary examples showing that you can separate *tam ... quam* with twenty-five words, if you know what you are doing. You might say, for example, "I studied so [*tam*] diligently the German language, which I began last year ... as [*quam*] I study the Latin language this year." You will even find *quam* toward the end of the sentence, and it is up to you to see that this last word connects with *tam ...* way out front and means, "so much ... as much."

For a complete presentation an enthusiastic student may consult a fuller list of the more common correlatives in Gildersleeve and Lodge n° 642.

2. *Quam* with the comparative

The second usage of *quam* is connected with the comparative degree of an adjective or adverb. In this case *quam* means "than," and the two elements compared, whether noun or pronoun, are in the same function on both sides of the comparison, as in:

Leporem facilius capto quam aquilam
I catch a rabbit more easily than an eagle.

The object of the verb *capto* is *leporem*, "a rabbit," so also *aquilam* is in the object form. The two elements agree in form, but need not agree in gender or number, as in this example:

Celerius currunt quam testudo
They run faster than a turtle.

The verb *currunt* implies a plural subject, whether masculine, feminine, or neuter, *ei, eae, ea*, "they, those things"; so also *testudo* is in the subject form. We can see the correct English in another Latin expression,

Puellae velocius currunt quam ego
The girls run more quickly than I.

Because *Puellae* is the subject, the other element of comparison must also be in the subject form, here *ego*, "I." This is easier to see if you supply the implied verb, "The girls run more quickly than I run" or "The girls run more quickly than I do." The common English error "The girls run more quickly than me," becomes obvious when the implied verb is expressed, because one can not say, "The girls run more quickly than me run" or "The girls run more quickly than me do."

Other examples include:

maior quam
bigger than

minor quam
smaller than

Pauciores amici venerunt quam ante
Fewer friends came than before.

Here you see the adverb *quam* used not only with the comparative of adjectives, but also with comparative adverbs, as we have already seen it used with *tam ... quam*. If you get the meaning of *quam* wrong here, the whole sentence is lost. These little particles are essential and must be learned through familiarity with them as they are used naturally in good Latin literature.

3. *Quam* with the superlative

The next usage of *quam* is with the superlative degree of an adjective or an adverb. Here *quam* means "as possible." For example, now we can say:

Scriptores eligimus quam optimos
We select *the best possible* authors

Quam celerrime debes redire
You must come back *as fast as possible*

Omnia quam maxime age
Do all things *as much as you can*
Do all things *as much as possible*
Do all things *with as much zeal as possible.*

A famous erroneous expression in school use is *quam citius*, which has been taken to mean "as quickly as possible," but that is the meaning of *quam citissime*. In medieval Latin *quam citius* was mistaken to mean "as quickly as possible," in the comparative degree, and the error persisted.

The adverb *quam* is very useful, but the problem is that *quam* has so many different meanings: "as," "than," "as possible." *Quam* will appear in a sentence, and you have to be conscious of the temptation to take it as a relative pronoun meaning "whom." But then you have to view the whole sentence to see if *quam* is used with *tam* or with a comparative adjective or adverb or with a superlative adjective or adverb.

ENCOUNTER 9 (44)

CONIUNCTIVI MODI FORMAE: T.1S, T.2S, T.3S, T.4S ACTIVE ET PASSIVE

the forms of the subjunctive mode: T.1s, T.2s, T.3s, T.4s actively and passively

Introduction

As we study human language and human expressions, linguists have distinguished certain patterns of talking that are more or less complicated, developed, distinct in different languages. They join together certain modes of speaking based on specific patterns of thinking. We shall talk here about manners or modes of speaking, where linguists talk about the mood of speech, almost as if it were like a human emotional mood, because it sets the feeling and the force of an expression. To avoid terminology, we refer to the less technical and more readily accessible "mode of speaking."

Much of what we say or think is a direct, concrete indication of something or a direct, concrete question about something. The mode of speaking that is contained in these concrete, direct statements or questions is what we called before in the First Experience the mode of direct discourse and question, the indicative mode of speaking, the mode of indication; call it what you want.

We have also seen another way of speaking that involves a whole complex of commands that we called the command mode of speaking. Distinguishing between the command mode and the mode of direct discourse and question is just a matter of considering the entire process of human thought and speech and then distinguishing these different modes of human speaking.

In addition to expressions of direct discourse such as, "I do this," "you have done this"; in addition to direct questions such as, "What will he do?"; beyond direct commands such as "Do this!" "Thou shalt not do this!"; we also have a whole host of expressions such as "to do this," "to have done this," and other expressions such as "doing this," "for doing it." These different modes of expressions signify different ways of speaking.

Latin has five different modes of speaking; that is, all human ways of thinking and expressing ourselves are divided into five different categories in Latin. Other languages have more or fewer, but Latin has five.

In this encounter we begin to discuss a third mode of speaking, in addition to what we have already learned. We use the first mode of speaking in direct discourse and questions, and the second mode in commands to communicate direct, concrete reality. In this encounter we begin to speak about human intentions, wishes, light commands, conditions, and possibilities. All of these human ways of thinking and speaking are gathered together in a large collection of feelings or ideas, and the mode of speaking about these ideas is called by one or two words depending on the country you come from. In the English-speaking world we call this mode of speaking the "subjunctive." In the German-speaking world or the world of the romance languages it is called by some form of the word "conjunctive."

The words "subjunctive" and "conjunctive" are very clear indicators of this mode of human speech. We use the term "subjunctive" because the idea of possibility, of intention, of wishing, of condition is usually attached to another idea or depends on another idea. That attachment or dependence is called in Latin *subiunctio*, "joining under," or you have the English word "subjoining." This mode of speaking, then, was given the title of subjoining, because most of the time it is added on to and connected with something else in the sentence. Although it can stand alone, most of the time it is not going to stand alone, but is going to be *subjoined* to something else, and that is why this mode of speaking is called "subjunctive."

Other languages call this mode of speaking "conjunctive" to mean it is connected with (*con*) something else, rather than underneath (*sub*) something else; the difference is but a turn of phrase. You must be ready for both words, however, depending on the book you are reading.

A few examples of this mode of speaking in English may help indicate what we are talking about. Generally speaking, in English the subjunctive of verbs will sound like "may, might, would, could, should," but there are other ways to express this mode of speaking according to its many usages. We may make a polite request such as, "Would you pass the potatoes?" We may state a wish such as, "May we go?" We may express encouragement, for example, "Let us pray." Even dogs understand the subjunctive invitation, "Let's go!"

We express our intentions using the subjunctive in English, such as, "He did this so that she might learn Latin well," or even, "He is doing this so that she learn Latin well," or we could say, "I ask that she be on time." Sometimes the subjunctive is the same as other English forms, as in, "The conductor makes an effort that they sing beautifully."

We express the possibility of some action when we state, "I might try," or when we ask the question, "Might we stay on topic?"

In English we can express an uncertain future such as, "Should the protest turn against us . . . ," or "Could we ever agree on the fundamental values here?" A parent would speak to a child only in the subjunctive, when saying, "If you be good, you may play outside." We can also describe unreality as in, "I wish you were here," or "If I were in charge of this mess . . . ," or even, "If only he had known . . . ."

When we are exasperated we can use the subjunctive and say, "Would that I could!" and "If only it were so!" Hopefully this list will help English speakers to realize that they already use the subjunctive regularly and naturally in everyday conversation.

In this encounter we shall learn an extremely small number of Latin verbal forms in the subjunctive mode. At first sight, by the way, students are relieved that there are only a few forms to learn in Latin, especially in comparison to Greek, which has twelve forms of the subjunctive-optative to learn. Do not be deceived, however, because many times the small number of forms leads to endless ambiguity in the language and a lot of headaches, because after we have learned everything, we must also think. The numerous forms in Greek, each with its own force and meaning, prohibits the ambiguity inherent in super-spare Latin.

In our next encounter we shall begin to talk about the various uses of this mode of speaking in the Latin language. Latin has basically two big modes of speaking: one the mode of direct address and discourse and the other the subjunctive mode of speaking. Again at first sight, these appear much easier and simpler than in Greek, because Greek has a whole complication of different modes. That initial complication, however, leads to easier precision and clarity, whereas the simplicity of Latin requires that you figure it all out.

It would have been better in Latin to have added another mode or several other modes of speaking and to have given these other modes special formulations. That would have clarified the thought in Latin, but as the language is given to us, you have one form expressing a dozen different ideas. What causes trouble in Latin is the limited number of forms to work with to express the vast breadth of human thought and speech.

In our system we, disappointing most beginners, do present the verbal forms without assigning any definite meaning to them for a certain, solid reason, and we shall begin to talk about the usages of this mode of speaking only in the next encounter. We approach the subjunctive mode of speaking with the idea that the forms are few, simple, and easily distinguishable, but their usage absolutely infinite. This will prepare us for our whole Latin language adventure. Because the verbal forms are very simple, they are most misleading. As we shall see in many other encounters and readings, the usage of the subjunctive is without end and infinite and extremely subtle. The easiest thing to do is to dispense with the forms themselves with a flip of the wrist in this encounter, and then begin to concentrate on their usage. We shall start with the forms in the active and the passive and of course the deponents. This is all very simple.

Just to warn people of the difficulties of Latin, as mentioned countless times already: there are too few forms, not too many. Many ordinary people do not realize this at first, but soon come to understand.

For the past 2,300 years the Latin subjunctive has had only four times or tenses. We shall not even give them names, but use only numbers to identify them: T.1s, T.2s, T.3s, T.4s, where the small "s" means "subjunctive"; and in our own book from now on we will refer to the indicative times as T.1i, T.2i, T.3i, T.4ai, T.4bi, T.5i, T.6i. For a long time do not ask to translate the subjunctive, because we shall learn its meanings by using it. Otherwise you will have to give about twelve different meanings for the subjunctive, and you will go crazy. It is much better to learn the uses of the subjunctive, and then the meanings will come more or less naturally.

We can present the forms for the entire subjunctive system in one encounter because from learning the indicative mode you already know the four verb Groups, based as they are on the four prominent vowel sounds. Now Gp.I has verbs whose infinitives end in *–āre;* those of Gp.II end in *–ēre* with a long *–ē–*; of Gp.III in *–ĕre* with a short *–ĕ–*; of Gp.IV in *–īre* with a long *–ī–*; and you also have the Group on the fence between Gp.III and IV, namely the *–io* verbs of Gp.III, *–ĕre.*

From our first encounter of the First Experience you also have all the personal endings of the verbs, and you have learned how to reverse the singular endings to the plural and the plural endings to the singular. You have also learned how to flip the verbs from their active forms to their passive forms. All of this you already know, and it all will be used to permit us to learn the forms of the entire subjunctive system in one encounter and a few minutes, as if with a flick of the wrist.

1. Time 1 subjunctive

With T.1s it is necessary to know the Group a verb belongs to. To discover why, let us look at an example from Gp.I verbs:

numero, numerare, numeravi, numeratum, 1, to number.

Without writing out paradigms and without memorizing charts you can apply what you have already learned from the First Experience to produce all the active and passive forms of T.1s.

T.1s in Gp.I has the characteristic letter *–e–*, where the "I" form is *numerem.* In that ending, *–em,* you can see the *–e–*, which is characteristic of T.1s of Gp.I verbs in *–are,* and you can see the personal ending *–m,* which you learned in the first encounter of the First Experience.

The word *numerem* is all you need to know, because all the other forms in the singular and plural have the same personal endings as we saw in the first encounter of our First Experience. That is why we write simply "*numerem ...*" with three dots following to mean that you already know the forms for the other persons in both the singular and plural.

Because you already know these forms, *numerent, numeretis, numeret, numeremus, numeres,* we even hesitate to add them here. Without learning anything new other than that the vowel is *–e–*, you have learned T.1s of Gp.I verbs. We shall point out several difficulties in a moment.

Once you have that active form, because of our flip system you can also produce the passive immediately. For example, *numerent* flips into the passive as *numerentur;* the passive "we" form is *numeremur;* for "he, she, it" the form is *numeretur;* and you also have the forms *numeremini* or in the singular *numereris;* the active form for "I," *numerem,* flips to *numerer.*

Because you already know how to work your way around the active and passive verbs, and through the personal endings, all of this is included in those three dots (*numerem ...*) without memorizing any charts or parroting a single paradigm. In regard to the forms, T.1s is simpler than the indicative, because there are no exceptions.

In Gp.II verbs, we have the example:

moneo, monēre, monui, monitum, 2, to admonish.

T.1s of this Group of verbs with a long *–ēre* has the characteristic sound *–ea–*. Here we remember that the form for "we admonish" is *monemus*, and its subjunctive counterpart is *moneamus*—but we do not give its meanings yet. The Romans saw this difference of one letter and understood the difference in meaning and mode of speaking. Once you have *moneamus* . . . , then those three dots indicate that you can already work your way through all the other forms, for example, "they" ending in *–nt*, "he, she, it" in *–t*, "you all" in *–tis*, "you" in *–s*, and the form for "I" is *moneam* . . . After that you also have all the passive forms because of the flip system.

For Gp.III verbs with a short *–ĕre*, the characteristic vowel indicating the subjunctive is the simple letter *–a–*. We have the example:

rego, regĕre, rexi, rectum, 3, to rule.

To say "she reigns" is *regit*, and its comparable form in T.1s is *regat*—to which we do not yet attach any specific meaning. Once you have *regat*, then you can easily play around and form *regamus*, *regant*, and the "I" form, which is *regam*. You have again the three dots that indicate what you already know about the remaining forms.

For Gp.IV verbs in *–ire* the characteristic vowels *–ia–* indicate the subjunctive. Our example is:

aperio, aperire, aperuit, apertum, 4, to open.

You say "I open" as *aperio*, and its subjunctive component is *aperiam* . . . The rest you know, such as the form for "they," *aperiant*. The passives are the same as always with our flip system.

By the way, the mixed Group of verbs like *rapio, rápere* follows Gp.IV verbs. So we have *rapiam* . . . Just put the three dots there, and then you know what we are talking about.

In one page of narration, without charts or any nonsense, you now know all the forms of T.1s for all four verb Groups, both active and passive, and, what is more, you can produce these forms and reverse them from singular to plural and from plural to singular and flip them from passive to active and from active to passive. You can now walk your way through or just play around with all these verbs in T.1s.

What has to be pointed out right away are several difficulties that will never go away even after years and years of Latin experience. If you do not know your vocabulary and where the verbs come from, you will make terrible mistakes because the verbs from different Groups look the same way.

For example we have T.1s *aedificemus* from *aedificare*. But remember! The ending *–emus* is the same ending as we find in *movemus*, "we do move," and *timemus*, "we are afraid." The difference is that these latter examples are from Gp.II verbs *movēre* and *timēre*, where that same ending *–emus* indicates T.1i. The endings are identical, but the meanings are completely different because one indicates the subjunctive mode of speaking and the other the indicative.

Furthermore, you have learned that verbs from Gp.III like *scrībĕre* and verbs from Gp.IV like *audire* form T.3i with the letter *–e–* as in *scribemus*, "we shall write," and *audiemus*, "we shall hear." Now you have learned that verbs of Gp.I such as *aedificare* form T.1s with the letter *–e–* as in *aedificemus*—to which we do not yet assign a meaning. The key to knowing what the ending *–emus* means is remembering to which Group the verb belongs.

Let us take another example, now from Gp.III verbs. The verb *scribo, scribere*, "to write," gives us T.1s *scribamus*. The ending *–amus* we also find in the word *amamus*, "we are loving," from the verb *amare* of Gp.I where the same ending indicates the indicative mode of speaking. Their meanings are completely different because the first is in the subjunctive mode of speaking and the second in the indicative. The only way to understand this is to know your vocabulary.

Another example comes from Gp.IV verbs where *aperio, aperire*, "to open," produces the T.1s verb *aperiat*. Those same two last letters *–at* are also found in the word *illuminat*, "she illuminates," which is T.1i from the Gp.I verb, *illumino, illuminare*, "to illuminate." Again, the prior form is in the subjunctive mode of speaking, the latter in the indicative. The verb *aperio* also gives us the form *aperiam*, which is the same form both for T.3i meaning "I shall open," and for T.1s to which we do not yet assign a meaning. Students struggle with this for many years trying to guess the meaning of words and getting it wrong, until they learn their vocabulary and know where they stand.

This may look infinitely confusing, but it is not, if you keep your head on and everything else in order. The endings of these verb forms are identical, but for different reasons. So, we come back to the principle learned in our first encounter: you have to know your vocabulary, because if you do not, you are totally lost, and guessing does not help you.

Another little note here will help you to be aware of a disaster in verb Gp.III and IV between T.1s and T.3i. Just so we know what we are talking about, that form *scribam* can be reversed to the plural form *scribemus*, meaning, " we shall write," if you understand *scribam* as T.3i meaning "I shall write." But now you know that *scribam* can also be T.1s, and its reverse to the plural is *scribamus*. Thus, the form *scribam* can function both as T.3i and as T.1s. This has been a cause of infinite arguments and discussion and desperation for centuries until our present day, and we still cannot avoid this ambiguity. People should be told these things right in the beginning.

That is why, to give another example, *faciam* can function as T.3i meaning "I shall do," or as T.1s meaning, we could say, "I should, could, may, would do," and others, as we shall learn later.

This also shows how helpful reversing the verbs from singular to plural or from plural to singular can be. When a student reverses the verb *audiam* to the plural and produces *audiemus*, "we shall hear," then the teacher knows that the student is taking *audiam* as T.3i. If the student says *audiamus*, then the teacher knows the student understands *audiam* to be T.1s. Then the teacher can help the student understand how the verb is functioning in its sentence.

2. Time 2 subjunctive

T.2s, 3s, 4s are very easy to learn. Only T.1s causes problems; the others do not.

T.2s of all verbs is formed from the active infinitive, as it appears in the dictionary. Take the examples, *cantare*, *timēre*, *dirigĕre*, *sentire* and add to those infinitives the personal endings you learned in our first encounter, and then flip them to the passive endings you have also learned, and that is the end of T.2s.

Namely, the "I" form for *cantare* is *cantarem* ... You can put the three dots there because you know the rest. This brings us back to our first encounter, and now you can produce *cantaret* and flip it to the passive *cantaretur*. There is nothing to be learned, other than to notice how T.2s is formed.

The "I" form for *movēre* is *moverem* ... , and according to our dot system you know the rest. Flip *moverem* ... to the passive and you get *moverer* ... with an *–er* at the end and then the dots; that is the end of it. The form for "they" is *moverent*, which flips into the passive as *moverentur*, just like *monerentur*. T.2s is easy to spot, because you will always see an infinitive-gerund hidden inside.

People who are going to be Latinists must also look at the deponent verbs. We said that T.2s is formed from the active infinitive as it appears in the dictionary, but that is not at all the case for the deponents; their infinitives in the dictionary are passive in form but active in meaning. You can not find the active infinitive, which does not exist for deponents, so you have to be smart and in your mind reconstruct what the active infinitive would be if there were one. From that reconstruction, you can form T.2s, using the passive endings, which will be active in meaning.

A deponent example is:

conor, *conari*, *conatus*, 1, to undertake, endeavor, attempt.

You know that that infinitive *conari* is the sign that this verb belongs to Gp.I. You form T.2s by reconstructing what the active form of the infinitive would be if it had one, to arrive at *conare*. Then you add the passive personal endings to arrive at *conarer* ... , and the dot system tells you that the rest of the forms are like *conaretur*, *conaremini*, *conareris* ...

To give a crazy example verb:

sequor, *sequi*, *secutus*, 3, to follow.

We have seen that problematic infinitive *sequi*, which does not look like an infinitive at all, and we know it is the sign of Gp.III deponent verbs. To form T.2s, you imagine in your mind what the active form of the infinitive would be were it to exist, and you get *sequere*, to which you add the passive personal endings. This is how you form *sequerer* ... and then put your three dots to indicate you know the rest. We have *sequeremini*, *sequereris* ... This is really very simple, if you know your vocabulary.

Even the verbs on the fence are manageable. For example:

ingredior, ingredi, ingressus, 3–4, to enter.

Here the *–ior* indicates Gp.IV, but *ingredi* Gp.III. To form T.2s from *ingredi*, you have to rethink what the active infinitive would be, namely *ingredere*, and from there you start with *ingrederemur, ingrederer* . . .

3. Time 3 subjunctive

T.3s and 4s are simple, but because of their simplicity they will also cause trouble. T.3s of all verbs is identical in the active to T.6i, except for the "I" form. We learned *amavero* and *monuero* and *scripsero* and *audivero* for T.6i. To form T.3s, all you have to do is to change that ending *–ero* to *–erim* and then put your three dots for the active forms. Thus, we have *cantaverim* . . . and *monuerim* . . . and any verb you want such as *dixerim* . . . , *scripserim* . . . , *audiverim* . . . That is the news of T.3s.

If we reverse *audiverim* to the plural, we get *audiverimus*, which happens to be identical with T.6i. This has caused to our present day two and one-third millennia of total confusion and total desperation. The famous example from church history comes from decrees of earlier councils. They say: *si quis dixerit*. Immediately we are confronted with *dixerit*. You will never know with certainty whether it is T.6i indicative, meaning "If someone will have said," or T.3s—leaving its meaning suspended for the moment between "may, might, should have said." How the language went on like this all these centuries seems impossible, but it was preserved, and no one knows what it means. The story is different with the "I" form because T.6i is *dixero*, "I shall have said," and T.3s is *dixerim*—left in suspense. Otherwise the forms are the same for both times in the active.

In the passive there is no problem, because the forms are totally different. The passive forms for T.3s are composed of two elements, just as in T.6i, namely the fourth principal part of the verb as given in the dictionary and now the verbal form *sim* . . . , that is actually T.1s of the verb "to be." We shall see all of the forms of *sim* . . . in another encounter.

Take as an example the verb:

cito, citare, citavi, citatum, 1, to shake, rouse, incite.

A man might say of himself *citatus sim;* a woman, *citata sim;* a computer would say *citatum sim*. What these forms mean is determined by their usage in the sentence, as we shall see in the encounters. You can see here that the fourth principal part of the verb is *citatus, citata, citatum*, and has all the forms of the adjectives of Bk.II ending in *–us, a, um* and agreeing with the subject. We remember that the passive of T.6i was *citatus ero*, "I shall have been shaken," and now the passive of T.3s is *citatus sim*. Consequently in the passive there is no confusion.

With the verb *aedifico, aedificare, aedificavi, aedificatum*, we get the forms for "he, she, it," *aedificatus, a, um sit*, and for "they," *aedificati, ae, a sint*, but we shall see the other simple forms of *sim* . . . in two encounters from now.

4. Time 4 subjunctive

This leaves only the fourth form to complete our presentation of the entire system of the subjunctive in one encounter. The forms of T.4s are very simple, but its use, like that of the other subjunctive times, is daunting, just to be honest.

Like T.3s, T.4s also has two different ways of forming the active and the passive. We shall see the active forms first.

We formed T.4i, 5i, 6i by taking the third principal part in the dictionary and adding special endings. The same thing is true here. The active forms of T.4s are formed from the third principal part of the verb in the dictionary, just as we did for T.3s. So, for example, we start with the third principal parts *vocavi*, *auxi*, *genui*, *sensi*. The special ending for these forms in T.4s is *–issem*, namely *vocavissem* … , *auxissem* … , *genuissem* … , *sensissem* … ; then our dot system indicates that you know the rest from our first encounter. So, we have the easily recognizable forms such as *audivissemus*, *timuissent*, *timuissemus*, *venisses*. Because the verbs are extremely consistent, we can simplify the whole subjunctive system with three dots.

The passive forms of T.4s are again double forms, like the passive forms of T.4i and 5i, and like the passive forms of T.3s. The two elements consist of the fourth principal part, such as *cantatus*, *a*, *um*, and T.2s of the verb "to be," such as the "I" form *essem* … Again, we shall see the other forms of "to be" in the subjunctive in two encounters from now. Thus, we have the example, *aedificatus*, *a*, *um essem* …

Those are the four subjunctives with several things to note, but once you note them, they are very simple and consistent. Because they are simple and few, they are very demanding, and you have to have an attention that is laser-beam precise.

5. Futurity in the subjunctive

You might ask about the future time in the subjunctive, but this is precisely why we use the numbers. T.1s, 2s, 3s, 4s do not really correspond to the times of the indicative, nor do they have to correspond to the indicative. What is important at this point is that you notice that there are only four times in the subjunctive. But to answer your question, it is fair to say that the subjunctive does not have special forms for future ideas. This is contrary to Greek, which has all these forms and more. Once you learn all the forms of the subjunctive in Greek, their usages are easier and clearer by far than in Latin, where the forms are easy but the usages are many times impossible to distinguish. That is what makes Latin harder because it is more demanding in these ideas.

To be sure, Latin has both simple future and completed future ideas and concepts in the subjunctive, and the Romans had a way of using their four times of the subjunctive to express all these ideas. The ideas are there, but without special forms. We shall see that in another encounter, and in encounter 11 (46) we shall see the subjunctive forms of the verb "to be," which is the simplest thing in the world because again we have one form with three dots.

CONIUNCTIVI MODI USUS INFINITUS. PLURIMA PRINCIPIA

countless uses of the subjunctive mode. very many principles

Introduction

In our last encounter we learned all the forms of the subjunctive and a few ideas. In this encounter we present a number of principles that guide our use of the subjunctive. As we just begin to get into the subjunctive, we must consider our approach in order to begin with the right attitude and the right expectations. If we do so now, then we won't have difficulties as we progress, and the use of the subjunctive will not be mysterious or confusing at all.

Principles of the subjunctive

Here are some of the principles that guide our use of the subjunctive.

1. The forms are extremely simple and consistent and regular. There are no irregularities in the active or passive if you simply follow the three dots. The passive follows the flip system for T.1s and T.2s, but has compound forms in T.3s and T.4s similar to the passive forms of T.4i, 5i, 6i. While the forms are simple, the literary employment of the subjunctive, both active and passive, requires a long and delicate study.

2. While the forms are simple, their use is very difficult because we have only 4 times in the subjunctive: T.1s, 2s, 3s, 4s. These four times have to express and have expressed every possible human thought in all its nuances for several millennia. To get all of human thought and concepts and ideas into four miserable verb times is a real problem. The difficulties are infinite of getting a thousand uses out of only four subjunctive times.

3. A continual acquaintance with Latin literature over time is needed to learn the feel for the subjunctive and its uses. While we shall catalogue them and talk about them as we go, our discussion about the subjunctive absolutely has to be grounded in the literature, which reveals that the use of the subjunctive changed over the centuries. The classical use gave way to the use of the early and medieval Christian authors, and then the classical use was restored in the Renaissance.

4. Contrary to the desires and the expectation especially of beginners, in our system we attach no definite meaning to any subjunctive form or time, because the meanings and the uses are so vast that you would need a list of twelve meanings every time you start, and even then the choice among the possible meanings depends on the way in which the subjunctive is used in

the sentence. So here we do not attach a definite meaning to the subjunctive until we start studying its individual uses. The meaning of the subjunctive will depend on the type of sentence or clause and on the particle that introduces it. These things will be explained as we go along. Just to get ready now, we could give you one particular Latin word for "when" and some other word for "when," but the one takes the subjunctive and the other the indicative, and they both sound the same in the vernacular. This demands careful and patient study, but we can learn it, absolutely.

5. Even though the students are begging, "What does this mean?" many people are surprised to know that if we list all the subjunctives that have ever appeared in Latin literature, the greater part of them, strangely enough, do not sound subjunctive in English at all. We have to insist on this major reality from the beginning, knowing that people will protest and ask why they are in the subjunctive at all. For example in the sentence "When he had done this, she went home," the Latin verb for "he had done" could be T.4s, as in, *cum hoc fecisset*, but in English the verb is rendered in the indicative. A sign of deficient training in Latin is when students jump on every Latin subjunctive and immediately say, "may, might, would, could, should," but most will not sound subjunctive in any way. Many subjunctives are there for a certain historical reason or under the influence of Greek and Indo-European languages, which do not concern us now.

6. By way of a general overview, the subjunctive can be used in two ways. One way it can be used is independently; that is, it can stand alone, not attached to anything. As in Latin, so in other languages we have the independent subjunctive, as in, "*Let* us go" or "He *should do* this" or "If I *were* you . . . , I *would* . . ." When you find such an independent subjunctive in Latin, it must sound subjunctive in other languages as well, but we are not yet ready to assign any specific meaning in English other than to say that it must sound subjunctive in our vernacular languages. If we take the sentence, *Fur fuerit! Tamen vitam emendavit*, "So what if he was a thief! Nevertheless he bettered his life," the whole expression "So what if he was" gives the force of that T.3s, *fuerit*, which functions as an independent subjunctive.

The other way the subjunctive can be used is in connection to another clause, that is subjoined or conjoined, as you wish to define it. In this case, when expressed in English, the Latin subjunctive can sound either indicative or subjunctive. What determines the sound of those Latin subjunctives in any vernacular version is the nature or type of the subjunctive clause in Latin. To anticipate what we are going to do, and to calm some people down a bit, we can insist here that there are only three types of subjunctive clauses in Latin that sound subjunctive in English as well. They are:

1. all purpose clauses, which we shall learn later in this Experience,
2. half of all conditional clauses, which we shall see in the Fourth Experience, and
3. all independent subjunctives, which you already feel.

Other than these three, all other subjunctives in Latin—perhaps a full 80% of all subjunctive verbs in Latin literature—sound indicative in English, and you might as well get used to this now. This 80% includes all causal clauses, all temporal clauses, all result clauses, all indirect questions, and half of all conditional clauses, except in select cases where a natural subjunctive is logically demanded. Do not fall into the trap of translating every Latin subjunctive by a corresponding subjunctive in the vernacular. Only the purpose clauses sound subjunctive in English along with some conditionals and all the independent natural subjunctives. All the others sound indicative in good English.

7. The use of the times of the subjunctive is not arbitrary in Latin and does not depend on the vernacular nor on dreaming or sentimentality. We must cut out the prejudice that the subjunctive is used for uncertain things, and the indicative for certain things. Some of the most certain things in life can be expressed in the subjunctive; some of the most uncertain things can be expressed in the indicative, as in the example:

> *Cum omnes moriamur* (T.1s), *cras tamen opus faciemus* (T.3i)
>
> Although we all die (very certain but expressed in the subjunctive), still we shall work tomorrow (which is very uncertain although expressed in the indicative).

We will not use native English as our guide but will start with the Latin, because Latin existed first. The decision to use T.1s, 2s, 3s, or 4s in Latin is regulated, according to Latin literature, by a definite system that correlates the subjunctive with other verbs. This system also tells you how to understand the subjunctive in the vernacular. We shall learn this system soon. We shall also systematically go through a list of ideas and find out if they are expressed in Latin with the subjunctive or not. We shall see which particles give rise to the subjunctive. We shall learn how to express these ideas correctly and without guessing or praying. This is a whole world of concepts and expressions.

The Latin subjunctive is learnable, but we need regular experience with the literature and with the use of the subjunctive in different periods and authors, as the teacher will illustrate from concrete genuine examples. Only then will we be very sure we are close to the correct meaning.

Many times the reasons for using the subjunctive overlap, and there may even be four or five possible reasons why any given Latin verb is in the subjunctive. At times it is impossible to decide among the various reasons for the use of the subjunctive, and consequently it is impossible to know for sure how the subjunctive is to sound in English. In these cases, we shall never know why a verb is in the subjunctive until we meet the authors in another life. Perhaps we can learn how to deal with about 95% of the subjunctives we encounter, but there will always be ambiguous and mysterious uses of the subjunctive, and we cannot do anything about it. We have only 4 times of the subjunctive to express an infinity of concepts and ideas and human thought.

ENCOUNTER 11 (46)

MODUS CONIUNCTIVUS IPSIUS VERBI "ESSE"

subjunctive mode of the verb itself "to be"

Introduction

Just to finish off from yesterday, as a little appendix that we hardly need are the subjunctive forms of the verb "to be." Again this is very simple because we begin with a form followed by three dots.

Subjunctive modes of the verb "to be" itself

The forms for T.1s are *sim* ... with three dots because from our First Experience you can determine the other forms such as *sitis*, *sint*, and the rest.

T.2s is taken from the infinitive, as we mentioned yesterday, and therefore it is *essem* ... with three dots. From this the forms *esset* and *esses* come naturally.

T.3s again is what we learned yesterday, and it is very consistent. Take the third principal part of the verb, *fui*, to produce T.3s *fuerim* ... and that takes care of that. Again, the forms of T.3s are identical to those of T.6i, with that one exception. Here we see that *fuerim* is T.3s, and you have already learned that T.6i is *fuero*.

T.4s also is from the third principal part, *fui*, with the ending *–issem* to produce *fuissem*, *fuissent* ... That is the subjunctive of the verb "to be."

As in our preview above, you are now ready to use the forms of *sim* ... and *essem* ... to form the passive T.3s and T.4s. This is all very consistent and not confusing at all.

ENCOUNTER 12 (47)

"CONSECUTIO TEMPORUM" IN UNIVERSUM

"sequence of tenses" in general

Introduction

To emphasize our system again, we do not give any special meanings to the subjunctive now; they will come later.

Among the principles of the subjunctive, we mentioned that the decision to use T.1s, 2s, 3s, or 4s is not arbitrary or sentimental or according to English concepts or translations. It depends, rather, on the Latin thought or idea expressed according to a definite system, which was observed rather diligently for about 1,000 years. When people became careless and did not use this system any more—including people of today—their ability to communicate their ideas clearly diminished and their misuse of the language became confusing to others. We want to understand the verbal times and how they are used in Latin and to express ourselves carefully and understand Latin writings exactly.

This system in Latin is called *consecutio temporum*, which means "the following of the tenses-times." Many people in Europe, the Germans and Italians, simply talk about the *consecutio*. The "following of the times" is the way of determining which subjunctive time to use, and which the Romans did use, when it follows or depends on a verb in another part of the sentence. The English term is "the sequence of tenses," which refers to the subsequent following of the verb times.

1. The entire sequence of tenses

In order that we can cut through the terminology to get directly to the meanings of words and their functions in a sentence, we return to our system of numbers for verb times. It is so well known and simple that you can put the numbers of the entire sequence of tenses on your thumbnails or the palm of your hand—it is really that elementary.

We shall speak here about the second general way in which a subjunctive is used, namely when it depends on another verb. We shall limit our presentation here to a subjunctive dependent on an indicative verb, because this case is the most frequent and easiest. Afterwards we can most easily present the case of a subjunctive depending on another subjunctive or infinitive or participle or command form.

This is what we observe happening in Latin literature. It is very simple. Either the Romans considered a whole sentence to be more or less in the present or future, or they considered a sentence to be set in some past.

Sentences then develop or unfold along one of these two pathways through time—present and future on one side and past on the other side—as if our thoughts and the ideas were moving along on one of two Tracks, as on train tracks.

The first task, then, is to learn which times of the indicative verb set a sentence on the present-future Track, and which times of the indicative verb set a sentence in the past-historical Track. Once the author has chosen one of these two Tracks, and the sentence comes to a thought or an idea expressed in the subjunctive, the second task is to know which time of the subjunctive to use.

You can tell from this description that the time of the indicative verb establishes the Track and in turn indicates the time of the subjunctive verb to be used. Just as the subjunctive verb depends on the indicative verb, so too the choice of the subjunctive time is determined by the choice of the indicative time, which establishes the time sequence of the whole sentence. We start out describing the sequence of tenses this simple way, although some people never understand it well and miss the whole thing for many years.

What is left is to indicate which indicative times go with which Track and which subjunctive times depend on which indicative times. We can use our numbers very effectively and easily and on two thumb nails to communicate the entire sequence of tenses. We will use our own terminology twice for a definite reason that will become clear.

2. Track I

The Romans pondered sentences where the indicative verb is in T.1i or T.3i or T.4ai, which is considered almost present, or T.6i to be more or less in the present or in the future. This is what we call Track I, and we say that verbs in T.1i, 3i, 4ai, 6i set us on Track I.

Once the sentence is developing along Track I and comes to a thought expressed in the subjunctive, then the subjunctive verb must be or is either T.1s or T.3s.

T.1s is used if the action it describes is contemporaneous with the indicative verb on which it depends, or is ongoing, incomplete, unfinished, perpetual, eternal, or future with regard to the indicative verb on which it depends. If that is the concept or the content of the subjunctive verb, then you have to use T.1s.

When you come upon a Latin sentence where one of the four indicative times is used, T.1i, 3i, 4ai, 6i, and the subjunctive is T.1s, then you need not hesitate to express the Latin subjunctive in English using the future, because there is no future subjunctive, but you have to know this. Take an example in English, "I advise the parents that their children do this next year." The second part of this sentence is obviously a future idea, but because there is no future subjunctive, we have to use T.1s to express this future concept, which is also incomplete, unfinished. Many people do not know this and get all mixed up and miss much of what the Latin sentence expresses.

Many manuals call T.1s the "present" subjunctive. We do not do this because it is misleading and confusing, especially if T.1s has a future or even eternal meaning.

We said that when T.1i, 3i, 4ai, 6i are followed by a subjunctive, the other option is T.3s. This time is used if the action it describes is antecedent to the time of the indicative verb on which it depends or is otherwise completed, finished, past, preceding, accomplished, in regard to the indicative verb, or if it is future perfect in regard to the indicative verb; the latter often escapes Latin readers or writers.

Many manuals call T.3s the "perfect" subjunctive, which is misleading, because we shall see that it has to be used for any action that is future completed in regard to verbs in T.1i, 3i, 4ai, 6i on which it depends, no matter what it sounds like in English.

Now you can see why we emphasized the very important distinction between T.4ai, meaning, for example, "I have done this," "I have been doing this," and T.4bi, meaning "I did this," "I did do this," because T.4ai is almost a present situation and so is on Track I; T.4bi is historical past separated from the present.

3. Track II

We shall use our own terminology once again, and all we have to do is change the time numbers to talk about sentences on Track II.

If the indicative verb that is running or controlling the sentence is T.2i or 4bi, which is historical past, or T.5i, then the sentence is set in the past, and we say it is on Track II. When the sentence comes to a concept that must be expressed in the subjunctive, then without much choice T.2s or T.4s is used.

The choice of the subjunctive time follows the same terminology as above; only the time numbers are changed. T.2s is used if the action it describes is contemporaneous with the indicative verb on which it depends, or is ongoing, incomplete, unfinished, perpetual, eternal, or future with regard to the indicative verb on which it depends.

We can say, for example, "He asked us that we might visit at Thanksgiving time." The Romans will use T.2s to describe this future action, which depends on a verb set in the past. When the manuals call T.2s the "imperfect" subjunctive, the terminology is confusing and misleading, and you will never suspect that it can refer to a future action.

Again we can use the same terminology as above, changing only the numbers to describe a sentence in which T.4s is used. This time is used if the action it describes is antecedent to the time of the indicative verb on which it depends or is otherwise completed, finished, past, preceding, accomplished, in regard to the indicative verb, or if it is future perfect in regard to the indicative verb. This is where most students collapse totally because they read in the manuals that T.4s is the "pluperfect" subjunctive, but depending on the sentence it can easily describe an action that is completed futurity.

On Track I, T.1s can express the future and T.3s can express the future completed, while on Track II, T.2s can express the future and T.4s can express the future completed. This is what many people never understand after years and years of Latin, because they were not introduced on the basis of literature.

4. Thumbnail portraits

Simply put, you can write our two-Track system on two thumbnails. T.1i, 3i, 4ai, 6i establish Track I with T.1s and T.3s; T.2i, 4bi, 5i establish Track II with T.2s and T.4s. Here are two thumbnail portraits of the sequence:

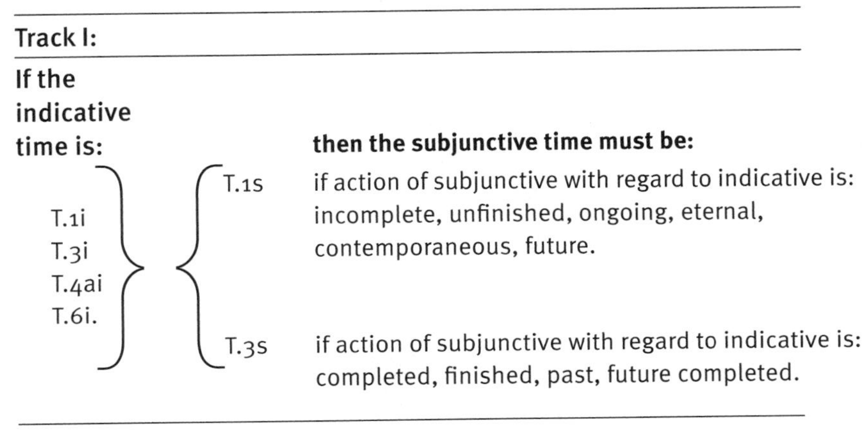

Track II:

If the indicative time is:

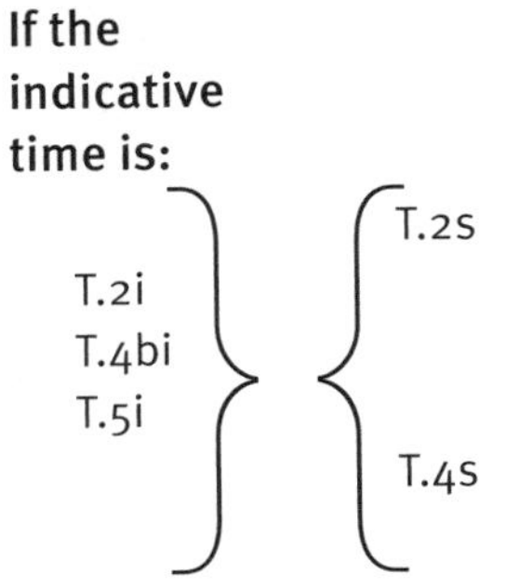

then the subjunctive time must be:

T.2s — if action of subjunctive with regard to indicative is: incomplete, unfinished, ongoing, eternal, contemporaneous, future.

T.4s — if action of subjunctive with regard to indicative is: completed, finished, past, future completed.

In passing we could say that all the imperatives we learned in previous encounters will be and must be treated as verbs of Track I. In a later encounter we shall deal separately with subjunctives depending on other subjunctives or on participles or on infinitives.

This system, however, has very few peculiarities. As you have it, this phenomenon represents 97% of Latin literature, but there is a 3% of the literature which represents special linguistic events that are explainable and excusable, but we shall not talk about that now. So this system covers 97% of the language, while the other 3% includes one or two famous occurrences that are little variations off the two-Track system as we have presented it; the students will learn this remaining 3% later.

5. Examples

At this point the teacher can provide endless examples from books or the reading sheets at the end of this book and point out how good Latinists observed this sequence of tenses very faithfully. Rather than talk about rules or regulations, we have sought to describe this literary working, so if you do not understand this system, then you are not understanding Latin correctly, either to use it actively creating your own Latin statements or passively to comprehend other people's correct Latin expressions. Take the four or five words of a simple example to help make this system concrete:

> *Cum legeretur liber gaudebamus*
> We were happy when the book was being read.

Here reading the book (T.2s) was contemporaneous with our happiness (T.2i). You can change the sentence to say:

> *Cum liber lectus esset gaudebamus*
> When the book had been read (was previously read), we were rejoicing.

Here the reading is completed (T.4s) before we would rejoice (T.2i). Take another example:

> *Nescimus quid fecerint.*

Here *nescimus* is T.1i and *fecerint* is T.3s, supported by a definite justification for the subjunctive which we shall understand later when we talk about the various reasons for the subjunctive. Many people do not believe that *fecerint* here refers to whatever in this world is antecedent to *nescimus*. In the next encounter we shall present the full range of English meanings of *fecerint* antecedent to *nescimus*. Many people would feel better and know Latin infinitely better if they would once learn these simple ideas and the functioning of the sequence of tenses.

The teacher now can show some glorious examples in accepted authors: Plautus, Augustine, the Vulgate Bible, Caesar, Erasmus, More, the Council of Trent, or Vatican II, or C. Eichenseer, or any other Latin writers of our day. They all knew Latin and represent it well. So that the students do not walk away in a cloud of unknowing, they must begin right away to read and work with and play with examples to see how the language really works.

After only three encounters with the subjunctive, the students can and now must begin immediately to reverse the real Latin examples from singular to plural and from plural to singular, and to flip them from passive to active and from active to passive and to follow those three dots to change the person of each of the verbs until they appreciate the richness of meaning that is found in these Latin verbs if you understand the sequence of tenses.

If the teacher knows what is going on with indirect questions, conditional sentences, and purpose clauses, she or he can point out the subjunctive and the relationship of the time and the action of the subjunctive to the verbs on which they depend. The teacher can say, "For now I shall translate the sentence," and then proceed to give the full range of meaning, saying that the reasons for the subjunctive will be explained one case at a time as we progress.

This will give the teacher the opportunity to explain that the meaning of the subjunctive depends on the type of its sentence or clause, but for now in this text it sounds indicative or subjunctive and its meaning is left up in the air. So much is enough, for now the students can see how approved Latin authors used a particular subjunctive time, not as a matter of imagination, barometric pressure, or the vernacular language that you are using. If you use the system, you will see the riches that are there, which are peculiar to Latin; this is not Greek or modern vernacular languages, both of which are more abundant in their expressions.

ENCOUNTER 13 (48)

CONSECUTIO MINUTATIM: LATINE ATQUE ANGLICE

sequence of tenses in detail: in Latin and English

Introduction

After having introduced in one encounter all the forms of the subjunctive and in another encounter the entire system of the sequence of tenses, saving 3% for later, immediately now we must turn to the literature to see this phenomenon in use. We feel no rush with this and would do well to spend the whole day reading any author you want—the poets, classical prose, church Latin, liturgical texts, Renaissance and neo-Latin—looking at and analyzing the sequence of tenses. At this point it is best to advance *minutatim*, "in detail, in bits," to refine our understanding of the language.

1. The sequence of tenses in detail

By way of refinement, we can point out a couple of items right away. It bears repeating that in the study of the Latin language the Latin text is our guide, not the English text. So we should not think the English is influencing the Latin; it is the opposite. We must exercise discipline in this way of thinking from the beginning.

Inasmuch as the main verb determines whether the sentence is on Track I or II, it will do so no matter where it is found in the sentence. The independent verb of a sentence does not always come geographically first. It can come last, because the word order is not essential to meaning. An entire paragraph of discourse with numerous subjunctives can all depend on the last word, which means the author had to foresee the sentence as a whole and anticipate the sequence of tenses, which unfolds until it all comes together in the last word, the indicative verb. We too have to read to the end of the sentence and understand it in its entirety, because the last word might determine the time sequence for the rest of the paragraph. It is interesting to see Cicero in one paragraph moving back and forth as he changes the main verb.

2. Latin examples and range of meaning in other languages

We shall give some examples of our own now and show how the sequence of tenses works. These examples are intended to help teachers see how they can present this material to their students without overburdening them, but by taking them one step at a time as the whole subjunctive mode of speaking opens up for them. At this point we shall limit ourselves to seeing how the sequence works in specific examples in anticipation of learning one at a time the different expressions that call for the use of the subjunctive.

One difficulty in rendering the subjunctives well and correctly is that we have to know how to express these concepts well in English. Not so long ago we used to express the Latin T.1s as, for example, "may," and the Latin T.2s as "might." What people are actually saying today is another story, but, one way or another, we have to be able to express these concepts precisely and correctly in the vernacular. We have to understand not only our Latin, but in learning Latin we often learn much about other languages as well. Take the example:

Hortantur ut proximo anno rursus veniat
They urge that he may come next year again
They urge that he come next year again.

We see in this example that there are two different ways of expressing the subjunctive in English: "he *may come*" and "he *come*." You can also see that the T.1s *veniat* is a natural way of talking about an event yet to happen in the future, where the possibility of the future comes from the nature of the sentence.

The Romans had just one verb to express this concept, but we have several ways of expressing the same concept in English, and we have to learn well the range of vernacular expressions for all of the concepts contained in the one Latin word, or we are ignorant of languages besides Latin and do not know what we are talking about. You have to be able to do all of this nicely; otherwise, you will not understand what the Latin sentence is telling you.

Take another example:

Hoc cum dixisset statim abiit
After she had said this, she went away immediately
When he had said this, he went away forthwith.

First of all, the main verb *abiit*, "she went away," is the last word in the sentence. Note that the subject of the verbs is not explicit in this sentence. Secondly, *abiit* is T.4b, establishing Track II that determines the time of the subjunctive, here T.4s *dixisset*, expressing an action antecedent to that of *abiit*. Thirdly, when you see that T.4s, you know that the sentence is on Track II and that *abiit* must be T.4b and not T.4a. Fourthly, you will learn the reason for that subjunctive in a later encounter, but for now you need to know that that subjunctive time in Latin will sound in English in the indicative, meaning, "he, she had said." Fifthly, as English is carelessly and hurriedly spoken today, some people will naturally say, "When she said this, she went away," but it is more precise and correct to keep the times and affirm, "When she *had* said this, she went away," because the sequence of tenses indicates that *dixisset* was completed before *abiit*; that is, the speaking was completed before the person went away.

We can also say:

Nescimus quid fecerint, cur nos vocaverint.

The reason for the T.3s *fecerint* is not our concern now. What is clear at this point in our treatment of the sequence of tenses is that both *fecerint* and *vocaverint* can refer to any action that occurs before *nescimus*. Any expression that is prior to *nescimus* is acceptable, for example:

Nescimus	*quid fecerint,*	*cur nos vocaverint*	(corresponding time)
We do not know	what they did	why they called us	(T.4bi)
...	what they did do	why they did call us	(T.4bi)
...	what they have done	why they have called us	(T.4ai)
...	what they have been doing	why they have been calling us	(T.4ai)
...	what they had done	why they had called	(T.5i)
...	what they had been doing	why they had been calling	(T.5i)
...	what they were doing	why they were calling	(T.2i)
...	what they used to do	why they used to call us	(T.2i)
...	what they would do	why they would call us	(T.2i)

or it can refer to completed futurity as in:

We do not know what they will have thought, why they will have called. (T.6i)

All of these expressions are contained in *fecerint* and *vocaverint* that is any time that is antecedent or complete with regard to *nescimus*. Many people are afraid or refuse to explore these possibilities. Take the sentence:

Rogavi	*quid faceret*	(corresponding time)
I asked	what she did [for a living]	(T.4bi)
...	what she was doing [for a living]	(T.2i)
...	what she would do [if she could]	(see the conditionals).

Latin is richer in that it contains all these possible expressions in the one subjunctive *faceret*, but Latin is more challenging because not all of these possibilities are evident; you have to know them. The challenge is in knowing how to manage this in the vernacular and arrive at the full range of different ways to express the relationship between *Rogavi* and *faceret*.

Catullus gives us this example:

Quare id faciam, fortasse requiris (Cat. *Carm.* LXXXV, 1)
Perhaps you ask why I am doing that.
Perhaps you ask why I do it.

The T.1s *faciam* tells the reader that we are on Track I and that the time of *faciam* is contemporaneous or subsequent to the action of another verb, which could be T.1i, 3i, 4ai, 6i. By the time we get to *requiris*, the sentence is fully understandable. We are used to thinking that the verb controlling the subjunctive has to come first geographically, but this is not true at all. We can play with the sentence of Catullus by changing the time of *requiris* to *requirebas*, and the sentence becomes:

> *Quare id facerem fortasse requirebas*
> Perhaps you were asking why I was doing that.

Because of the change to T.2i, the sentence is now on Track II, and the subjunctive has to change to T.2s. In composing this sentence you have to identify the main verb wherever it occurs in the sentence to know whether to write *facerem* or *faciam*. This does not require mental gymnastics, but you have to know what you want to say before you speak; it is interesting how that works.

In reading the sentence you first come upon that T.2s *facerem*, and you know that the sentence is on Track II and that the time of *facerem* is contemporaneous or subsequent to a verb you do not yet know until you get to the last word *requirebas*. This analysis of what is happening in a Latin sentence as it unfolds, even as we are kept in suspense until the whole idea is expressed, is one of the more interesting aspects of reading Latin literature.

Latin sharpens our ideas because we have to analyze what we want to say and make mental conclusions before we express ourselves.

Now the teacher can see how it is possible to play with these real Latin sentences to help the student to become familiar with the sequence of tenses without getting bogged down with the reason for the subjunctive and to become aware of the range of meanings possible in English. Now you can go back to the reading sheets and real Latin literature to analyze and play with the sentences. Identify the main verb, determine the Track the sentence is on and what is the time frame of the action in the subjunctive, and explore how this will be expressed in the vernacular. This takes regular practice, but the more we read, analyze, and compose, the more natural and easier it becomes for us. Most people would not recognize the difficulties here, but you, who are more enlightened, have been introduced to the sequence of tenses in a special way, in only three encounters thus far.

ENCOUNTER 14 (49)

CONSECUTIO TEMPORUM PLURIBUS IN EXEMPLIS

sequence of tenses in quite a few examples

This encounter is also dedicated to spending time on the subjunctive and especially the sequence of tenses. You can study these patterns in the reading sheets following each encounter and see how the sequence works. We are spending much time on this because it is essential. Some people think you can feel or guess your way through it, but you cannot.

ENCOUNTER 15 (50)

QUATTUOR PARTICIPIA LATINA. DIFFICULTATES ET PRINCIPIA

four Latin participles. difficulties and principles

Introduction

We shall break off our discussion of the subjunctive for now and allow ourselves to be distracted and forget what we have learned. Once we have forgotten the subjunctive, we shall come back to it and take it further. Then the students will discover that once they understand the sequence of tenses, they can easily review in a few minutes all six indicative times and the four subjunctive times naturally and without memorization or drudgery. Then the students feel better because they have already seen all ten times of the verb in Latin and can flip between active and passive and reverse between singular and plural, and they can fill in the three dots. They need only a chance to get used to all of this to do it all smoothly.

By way of general introduction to the participles, we have seen different modes of speaking. One was for indicating simple statements and questions: the indicative. Another was for giving direct commands: the imperative. In the last few encounters we have seen the subjunctive mode of speaking, which contains many concepts, including possibility and exhortation and conditionals and many other usages in the Latin language that we have to learn later on. The next mode of speaking on our list is the *participles*, which the Romans used continually to express their ideas.

Participles in Latin and in English are adjective forms of the verbs. From the verbs "to run," "to jump," "to build," we have these examples of participles:

> We see the children *running* and the dogs *jumping*.
> Do you see a new shopping center *having been built* on the same spot?

Here, "running" and "jumping" and "having been built" are all verbal forms that as adjectives describe the children, the dogs, a shopping center. From these examples we can see that a participle is an adjective form of the verb agreeing with something in the phrase. Another participle we can add is from the verb "to start:"

> They encourage the Olympic runners *about to start* the race.

The participle, "about to start," is another way of expressing the verb as an adjective that describes the runners. A different example is from the verb "to repair:"

> You see a road *needing to be repaired* immediately.

In that English expression "needing to be repaired," you may not recognize a participle, but it is a full English rendering of a one-word Latin participle. As a participle in Latin, "needing to be repaired," is a form of the verb that describes the road as would an adjective. This is what we are dealing with in English, namely forms derived from the verbs and standing as simple adjectives.

In Latin, as also in English, these participles, like adjectives, can stand alone and be used as nouns, as in:

We see the *ones running* and the *ones jumping*
I see the *one having been built* on the same spot
You see the *ones about to start* the race
They see the *one needing to be repaired.*

Each of these forms in italics is from a verb, and it is used as an adjective that stands on its own as a noun. This is not extraordinary or strange Latin to you because we have seen these things before.

Four Latin participles

The Latin language gives us, sad to say, only four participles. We have more in other languages. In Greek there are twelve, but in Latin we are restricted by the language to only four, a restriction which the Romans felt acutely. Some students are happy with only four forms to learn, but familiarity with the literature will show that the small number of participles produces headaches, because every human concept for several thousand years has been expressed with only four participles in Latin, with many more in Greek and modern languages. So four is not an advantage, it is a disadvantage. We shall give their forms in a moment.

A basic principle of our Latin training is that this verbal element will never lose its natural meaning, which we must understand and learn as soon as possible. No matter where the participle occurs, no matter how it is used, we can always reduce the forms to their natural meaning.

One of the limits of having only four participles is that there are some things that cannot be said in Latin with a participle. Even if you can say it or conceive of it in English or any vernacular language, the natural meanings of the Latin participles will have to be respected. At times when there is no possible participle that can say naturally what you want to say in Latin, either you will have to rephrase the sentence not to use a participle, or, if you still want to continue with a participle, the whole sentence has to be reworked until it admits a participle in its natural meaning. Take the example:

I see the artists *having sculpted* a beautiful statue.

If we want to put this into Latin, we might begin with the verb *sculpĕre*, "to sculpt." In Latin there exists a participle meaning, "having been sculpted," which is passive, and the verb has no active participle set in the past, but the English sentence has an active participle set in the past, "having sculpted."

The only way to preserve the natural meaning of the participle is to turn the sentence around to say: "I see a beautiful statue having been sculpted by the artists." We are limited by only four participles, and we can never violate the intrinsic meaning of the participles. These limits demand that we observe the possibilities of the Latin language, which in this case are very few. Here again is the challenge to use our heads and thoughts in working with Latin because we cannot impose on Latin what Latin does not allow.

Without resorting to paradigms, we can illustrate the natural meanings of the four participles in a graphic presentation, where we study what the available participles can say and do, and what types of expression are missing. In our little blackboard of participles we shall use the same terms we use with the subjunctive: namely, a participle is contemporaneous with the verb it depends on, or it is antecedent to the verb, or it expresses futurity with regard to the verb. After seeing these three, we shall add another participle that expresses necessity.

For us, the traditional method of naming the participles is misleading and incomplete in the sense that the traditional definitions of the participles do not correspond to the natural meaning in context. What is traditionally called a "present participle," we shall call a "contemporaneous participle," because its time is contemporaneous to the time of the verb on which it depends, no matter what time that verb is. To call this a present participle makes it sound as though its time were determined by the present of the speaker or reader, whereas it can have most any time as long as it is contemporaneous to that of the verb on which it depends.

What others call the "perfect participle," we call an "antecedent participle," because its time is antecedent to the verb on which it depends. Again, the traditional term "perfect participle" makes it sound as though its time were set in the completed past of the speaker or reader, whereas it can have most any time as long as it is completed before the time of the verb on which it depends.

What others call the "future participle" we prefer to call the "futurity participle," because its time expresses futurity relative to the verb on which it depends. Again, to call this the "future participle" is a little bit misleading because it sounds as though its time were set in the future of the speaker or reader, whereas it can have most any time as long as it expresses futurity in regard to the time of the verb on which it depends.

Even the "necessity participle," soon to be explained below, derives its time by its relationship to the verb on which it depends. Thus, the traditional terminology can be misleading and does not help people grasp the natural meaning of these participles, which must be seen in relation to the verbs on which they depend.

Just as we have learned that verbs are both active and passive, we shall also see that two of the four participles are active and two are passive. What makes the participles interesting and frustrating is the variety of options between active and passive participles that are either contemporaneous, antecedent, or subsequent, and there will always be a place for necessity. Of all the possibilities this list suggests, the Latin language gives us only four, and we cannot violate their natural meaning.

Let us arrange the blackboard according to the natural meaning of the participles. We shall not give the actual forms yet. We want, rather, just to indicate which possibilities exist and which do not.

We begin with the contemporaneous participle. The active contemporaneous participle exists, but the passive does not, as indicated below:

	active	passive
contemporaneous	*efficiens, entis*	________
antecedent		
subsequent		
necessity		

For example, Latin has a participle that means "doing" or "sculpting," but does not have a participle that means "being done" or "being sculpted." These latter two we can express in a whole clause with the indicative or the subjunctive later on, but there is no participle that means "being done"; it does not exist in Latin even though we can say it in English—which language is not our guide here.

Next, if we go to the antecedent participles, we have already said that "having sculpted" does not exist in Latin, nor does "having done." There is no antecedent active participle, but you can put a little asterisk there, and we shall talk about the deponents in the next encounter. There is, however, an antecedent passive participle in Latin, as shown here:

	active	passive
contemporaneous	*efficiens, entis*	________
antecedent	________ *	*constructus, a, um*
future		
necessity		

In Latin you can say with a participle, "having been sculpted" or "having been done," but you cannot say "having sculpted" or "having done," because the language simply does not provide for this.

Turning to the expression of futurity, Latin has a participle for "about to do," "with the intention of doing," "on the point of doing," or "about to sculpt." The futurity active participle exists, but the passive, "about to be done," does not exist, as is evident from the following:

	active	passive
contemporaneous	*efficiens, entis*	________
antecedent	________ *	*constructus, a, um*
future	*vocaturus, a, um*	________
necessity		

We can say in Latin, "I see the architects *about to build* this building," because it is active, but Latin does not permit us to say with a participle, "I see a building *about to be built*," because the natural meaning of the participles does not allow this. We can convert to a whole clause in the indicative or subjunctive, or change the sentence around to use a participle naturally.

The last participle Latin gives us means, for example, "needing to be taken up," "having to be taken up," "worthy to be taken up," "owing to be taken up," or simply "to be taken up." The necessity participle is passive, and the active form does not exist, as indicated below:

	active	passive
contemporaneous	*efficiens, entis*	________
antecedent	________ *	*constructus, a, um*
future	*vocaturus, a, um*	________
necessity	________	*defendendus, a, um*

We cannot say in Latin, "I see artists needing to sculpt this statue," so we can change the sentence to say, "I see a statue needing to be sculpted by artists."

This blackboard view of participles allows eight logical possibilities, but only four actual ones exist in Latin. Missing are the passive contemporaneous, the antecedent active, the future passive, and the necessity active.

You will see that the Romans in their conversation and writings love to use the participles in every other sentence, but that they also have to struggle with what cannot be said with the same participles. Leo the Great, Livius, Lucretius, Curtius, Thomas Aquinas, Egger, or anyone you want all struggle with what they can say or cannot say in the language, and we can see them struggling to rework their sentences to say what they want within the limits or restrictions that the language imposes on them.

In the next encounter we shall see the forms that these participles have whether they are normal verbs or deponent verbs—for both of these all the forms are really the same. The little asterisk remains to warn us about deponent verbs, which do something very odd. So we shall talk about the forms and the deponents in the next encounter.

ENCOUNTER 16 (51)

PARTICIPIORUM FORMAE

forms of the participles

Introduction

In our last encounter we introduced the four participles using the following arrangement to indicate their natural meaning, which we cannot violate. Of the eight forms possible, Latin gives us only four and leaves four possibilities blank because there is no way in the Latin language of supplying those four participles, except by filling in these gaps with a whole clause in the indicative or subjunctive. To express the concept suggested by one of those four missing possibilities requires reworking the sentence to use the existing four participles according to their natural meaning:

	active	passive
contemporaneous	*efficiens, entis*	________
antecedent	________ *	*constructus, a, um*
future	*vocaturus, a, um*	________
necessity	________	*defendendus, a, um*

The forms of the participle are very simple and follow the patterns of our Bk.I and II adjectives. You will see the Latin language is very consistent in this.

1. Participle forms

We have said that the participles are verbal forms used as adjectives. As adjectives, the participles agree with the nouns they describe. We have seen that all adjectives can be divided into two Blocks; so too the participles are divided among these two Blocks. The contemporaneous participle follows the pattern of Bk.II adjectives of one ending. The antecedent and futurity and necessity participles follow the pattern of Bk.I adjectives. The forms of the participles are extremely simple, so let us begin with some examples.

1.1 *Contemporaneous active*

Take the verb, *memoro, memorare, memoravi, memoratum*, 1, "to mention, to bring to remembrance." When this verb is used as a contemporaneous (active) participle, it is taken from the first and second principal parts in the dictionary and follows the pattern of the adjectives of Bk.II. It has the form *memorans, memorantis*, where *memorans* is the subject form and *memorantis* is the form of-possession.

You should already know how to deal with this contemporaneous active participle. The subject form *memorans* is masculine, feminine, neuter, but to produce the other forms, we work with the form *memorantis*, which also belongs to all three genders. Everything follows from there according to the pattern of the Bk.II adjectives of one ending. To give a few examples, the subject plural for the masculine and feminine is *memorantes*, which is also the form for the object plural, but you will also find the object plural form *memorantīs* where the –ī– is long, just as happened and is noted in the adjectives. The plural subject form for the neuter is *memorantia*, and then you have the neuter super principle. The object form in the singular for the masculine and feminine is *memorantem*, but because of the super principle the neuter is *memorans*. The plural form of-possession is *memorantium*. The singular form by-with-from-in is either *memorante* (85% of the time) or *memoranti* (only 15% of the time). These are the same percentages you saw for these two endings in Bk.II nouns. We shall learn when these two forms are used, but on some other day.

Its meaning in English is "mentioning, remembering"; the English form typically ends in –ing. We shall mention in the next encounter how this will sound when used as a noun.

Here are a couple of examples of the contemporaneous active participle in a full expression:

> *Vocibus delectamur puellarum canentium*
> We are delighted by the voices of the girls singing

> *Cantans versus patrios histrio magnos merebatur clausus*
> The actor singing homeland verses was meriting great applauses.

Immediately you can turn to the reading sheets and find these participles used frequently.

1.2 *Antecedent passive*

The antecedent passive participle is *memoratus, a, um*. In the First Experience you were told that its meaning as the fourth principal part in the dictionary is "having been mentioned," or, if you understand English well, "mentioned," as in the sentence, "I am talking about the authors already mentioned." That is the English of *memoratus, a, um*, nothing else. A quick example of an antecedent passive participle in a fuller thought is the following:

> *De auctoribus loquor iam memoratis*
> I am speaking about the authors already having been mentioned.

In Latin literature the teacher can assure the students that they will find such a participle in every other sentence; it is so common.

1.3 *Futurity active*

The futurity participle is active. Its form, from the fourth dictionary part, is *memoraturus, a, um*. You can put verbs of any Group into this form. For the verb *moneo, monere, monui, monitus*, the futurity participle is *moniturus, a, um*. For the Gp.IV verb, *sentio, sentire, sensi, sensum*, the futurity participle is *sensurus, a, um*. People worldwide recognize the ending *–urus, a, um* as futurity in Latin. The English word "future" has that same internal sound

–*ur*– and it refers to something "about to be." Here are its possible English meanings:

> *indicaturus, a, um*
> about to point out
> going to point out
> on the point of pointing out
> with the intention of pointing out

or, as people in the old West say:

> fixing to point out.

A couple of brief examples can help you see the futurity active participle in a fuller expression:

> *Susceperunt praesidem iusurandum pronunciaturum*
> They received the president about to pronounce the oath
>
> *Minatus est latro pecunias administro numeraturo*
> The thief threatened the functionary about to count the money.

1.4 *Passive necessity*

The last participle is *memorandus, a, um*, taken from the first two dictionary parts. It expresses passive necessity—that special idea in Latin. Possible meanings in English are:

> *memorandus, a, um*
> needing to be mentioned
> having to be mentioned
> worthy to be mentioned
> owing to be mentioned
> to be mentioned

or any other meaning you want which both is expressive of necessity and is passive. Other examples include *aedificandus, a, um* or *movendus, a, um* or *dirigendus, a, um* or *audiendus, a, um* or *rapiendus, a, um*. In our system these forms express passive necessity with meanings such as "needing to be built," "having to be moved," "owing to be directed," "worthy to be heard," or simply "to be carried off." In English we refer to a "referendum." That ending –*ndum* comes from this participle, and here it refers to something needing to be referred to the senate or people for a vote. We also refer to a "dividend," ending in –*nd*, as something to be divided among shareholders.

We are quite conscious of the confusion that exists in our textbooks and in teachers' minds about what we here call the participle of passive necessity, which by others is called the future passive participle. For us there is no future passive participle in Latin, namely "about to be crowned," because the Latin word *coronandus* for us simply means "needing to be crowned," in any time you want. The exact full meaning of the verbal form is as we have named it the participle of passive necessity. Others will call this participle the gerundive, but we separate the presentation of the passive necessity participle from our presentation of the gerundive by one full year to distinguish between these two functions with identical forms. We want to distinguish them clearly, and by a full year, lest they remain eternally ambiguous.

A quick example of the passive necessity participle in a sentence is the following:

> *Iussit nos senatrix componenda componere*
>
> The senator commanded us to put together the things needing to be put together.

These are the four participles of a normal verb. Take a verb of Gp.III: *conscribo, conscribere, conscripsi, conscriptum*, "to write up [an account]." The contemporaneous active participle is *conscribens, conscribentis*; the passive antecedent participle is *conscriptus, a, um*; the active futurity participle is *conscripturus, a, um;* the participle of passive necessity is *conscribendus, a, um*. These forms are simple and very consistent, and there are no exceptions with the forms. The meanings in English you also have.

The reading sheets are a gold mine of Latin participles. The Romans loved these participles and milked them for all they could.

2. Deponents

We have to add a note about the deponent verbs for the simple reason that they show some very interesting phenomena in their participles.

2.1 *Contemporaneous active*

Take, for example, a deponent verb of Gp.II: *confiteor, confiteri, confessum*. The active contemporaneous participle is very consistent: *confitens, confitentis*, which means "confessing," as in,

> *Testem audio magna flagitia confitentem*
> I hear the witness confessing great crimes.

What is strange here is that the participle has an active form, although by definition a deponent verb should have a passive form. Here the deponents violate their definition and take an active form and by definition an active meaning. Let's see an example right away:

> *Manibulistas gestantes viri videbantur venantes cervos et lepores*
> The men carrying rifles were seen hunting deer and hares.

You can see two participles above; *gestantes* is not from a deponent verb, but *venantes* is from a deponent verb, yet both participles have the same form. This participle and the futurity active participle are two instances in the Latin language when a deponent verb has an active form.

2.2 *Antecedent active* *

We have that asterisk to explain now. The deponents do something supremely and infinitely important when we come to the antecedent participle. Let us take the final principal parts of certain verbs: *professus*, 2; *persecutus*, 3; *elocutus*, 3; *immoratus*, 1; *elargitus*, 4. All these antecedent participles of deponent verbs are passive in form and have the natural active meaning of the deponent verbs. As you read Latin literature, this participle of the deponent verbs resolves many problems, because Latin authors wanted to have an antecedent participle that was active, and this is possible only with a deponent verb. In the sentence, "I see the workers having produced this beautiful building," the participle "having produced" is both antecedent and active. This cannot be said in Latin with a normal verb, which produces the passive antecedent participle "having been produced." The only way to say this with an active antecedent participle is with a deponent verb, if you can find one, which is not always easy. From the English sentence,

> I see the workers having produced, constructed, this beautiful building,

we can produce the Latin expression only with a deponent verb; here two are used,

> *Video oppifices pulcrum aedificium molitos, fabricatos,*

where the synonyms *molitos* from *molior* and *fabricatos* from *fabricor* are both antecedent participles that have active meaning. You will see that Latin authors are supremely conscious of this.

The opposite problem happens in this example: "I am learning the laws having been followed by few people." We cannot say "having been followed" in Latin because it is passive while all the verbs in Latin for "to follow" are deponent such as *sequor* and *sector* and so the antecedent participle will always be active in meaning. Here we have to find a different normal verb meaning more or less "to follow" in order to be able to express the passive. For example, from the following English sentence we can produce this Latin expression:

> I am learning the laws having been followed by few people
> *Leges disco a paucis servatas, custoditas.*

Both synonyms *servatas* and *custoditas* mean "having been kept."

With a deponent verb we can say, "I see few people having followed the laws," because the deponent antecedent participles are active by definition. One rendering of the English sentence is given here:

> I see few people having followed the laws
> *Paucos video leges secutos,*

where the participle *secutos* has active meaning because it is from *sequor*, a deponent verb. The antecedent participles of the deponents are very important and sought out, because this is the only way the language gives us to express an antecedent participle that is active. Latinists are totally conscious of this.

Roman authors from Horatius to Boethius to Bernardus or Pius II Piccolomini or Papa Franciscus are very well versed in this and they knew what you could or could not accomplish in Latin. Either they rework the sentence to get the participle to work passively, or they find a deponent verb to be able to use a participle in the past with active meaning. This has required a long discussion, but students love the idea once they discover it.

2.3 *Futurity active*

This participle poses no problem in the deponent verbs, except that people have to be reminded that the natural meaning of the participle ending in *–urus, a, um* is active and not passive, and you cannot force it to be passive. For example, in Latin you cannot say with a participle:

> I see a bridge about to be built.

Instead, you can say:

> I see the stone-cutters about to build the bridge
> *Lapidarios pontem video aedificaturos.*

Here you see that the futurity participle is active. Once this natural meaning is respected, then the sentence can be adapted in necessary ways. Take the example:

> *Mei me vocaverunt telephonio amici venturi*
> My friends about to come called me by phone
> ... going to come ...
> ... with the intention of coming ...
> ... on the point of coming ...
> ... fixing to come ...

2.4 *Passive necessity*

By definition deponent verbs are passive in form and active in meaning. The participle of passive necessity is a passive form with a passive meaning. When deponent verbs are expressed by this participle, they have the same form ending in *–ndus, a, um*, but they have passive meaning, which you would not expect.

Therefore, from *loquor, loqui, locutus*, the participle *loquendus* means "needing to be said." The form is passive as is the meaning, just as for the normal verbs. From *sequor, sequi, secutus*, the participle *sequendus* means "needing to be followed." It is strange that, contrary to the definition, a deponent verb should have that passive meaning, but this is how the literature gives us this form. Even *largiendus* of Gp.IV means "needing to be handed out generously," which is passive and does not conform to the idea of a deponent verb.

An example will help you to see the participle of passive necessity in context:

> *heroes exhibuerunt omnibus civibus immitandos*
> They showed off the heroes having to be imitated by all the citizens.

The participle of passive necessity is the only case in the Latin language when a deponent verb contrary to definition has a really passive meaning, whereas deponent verbs have active forms that are active in meaning for the contemporaneous active participle and the futurity active participle, and a few other forms we shall see later.

Those, then, are the four participles of both normal and deponent verbs with their natural meanings. We shall see in other encounters how these participles are used in many combinations. For now it is important to remember that no matter how or where these participles are used in the Latin language, they never lose their natural, innate, inborn meanings no matter how much you want to impose your meaning on them. This is essential for using Latin well and understanding Latin correctly, and if you are in contact with Latin literature, you will see the Latin authors struggling with the defects or the emptiness of the Latin language, Cicero among them. Greek has a much more complete system of participles, but in Latin we are stuck with only four, and you have to say anything you want to say according to their innate meaning.

ENCOUNTER 17 (52)

PARTICIPIA UT NOMINA. EXEMPLA BREVITATIS

participles as nouns. examples of brevity

Introduction

A very important usage of the participles is related to what we said about the adjectives being used as nouns. For example, the adjective *boni* can stand alone and mean, "good men," and *bona* can mean, "good things." Likewise, participles can stand alone as nouns. For example, *dicta* means, "things having been said," and *vocatas* functions as an object meaning, "women having been called."

Brevity

This usage is important, because the Romans use especially the contemporaneous active participle as a noun, in almost every sentence:

Videntes caelum laetantur
The people-ones seeing the sky are happy.

Here, *videntes* is used as a noun, although as a participle its natural meaning comes to the fore as, "the people seeing" or "the ones seeing," and as a verbal form it has its own object, "the sky." As you read Latin literature, you will find forms such as:

Quaerenti exemplum hoc igitur datur
To the one seeking an example this one therefore is given
To the person seeking this example therefore it is given
To someone seeking an example therefore this is given.

The participle *quaerenti*, has a very full meaning, "to the one seeking," or even, "to the person, the man, the woman, the individual, the thing [computer] seeking." Here the participle has an object, *exemplum*, "an example."

With the utmost emphasis and clarity it must be inculcated that in this sentence *quaerenti* does not mean simply "seeking," which in English is a gerund, as we shall see in the Fourth Experience, encounter 7 (77). But for the moment we must distinguish the participle above from the gerund in the following example:

Quaerere exemplum hoc igitur licet
Seeking this example, therefore, is allowed.

Here you see that *quaerere*, "seeking," is the noun-subject of *licet*, "[seeking] is allowed." The form *quaerere* with its function in this sentence is completely different from the participle *quaerenti*, "to the one seeking," which would produce the sentence,

> *Quaerenti exemplum hoc igitur licet*
> This, therefore, is permitted to the one seeking.

People make another terrible mistake when they see the form *quaerenti* and they imagine it to mean "for seeking," but they should know that "for seeking" is not a participle in English, rather "for seeking" also is a gerund, as in the example,

> *Quaerendo exemplum est utile lexicon*
> A dictionary is useful for seeking an example.

Here the form *quaerendo*, "for seeking," with its function is completely different from the participle *quaerenti*, "to someone seeking," which would produce the sentence,

> *Quaerenti exemplum est utile lexicon*
> A dictionary is useful to someone seeking an example.

This confusion is why we hold off from presenting the gerund until the next experience in encounter 7 (77). For now, you have the full natural meaning of the participle *quaerenti*, in the to-for-from function, meaning, "to the one seeking."

Another example is the following:

> *Quarentibus bonum invenietur*
> For people seeking a good thing it will be found.

The full, natural meaning of *quarentibus* is "to-for-from ones seeking," or "people seeking," which has an object, *bonum*, "a good thing." This sentence does not mean, "seeking good will be found," because "seeking" in this second sentence functions as a gerund, but the example requires a participle in English. Two more examples are easy to understand.

> *Quaerentis intellego desperationem*
> I understand the desperation of the one seeking

> *Utensilia geologica ab quaerentibus aurum surripui*
> I snatched the geological tools from the ones seeking gold.

Likewise, the participle *amans* means, "one loving," "a person loving," "a man loving," "a woman loving," but you must not translate *amans* as in the sentence, "loving is a great experience," because there "loving" is a gerund. We want the participle used as an adjective describing someone, something.

You had better be ready for this: knowledge of Latin contributes massively to knowledge of English, and conversely ignorance of English contributes to the ignorance of Latin. When the distinction is finally perceived between "seeking an example" and "the one seeking an example," then you are no longer lost. So the reader is encouraged to persevere through encounter 77 and beyond so that the whole picture may come into clear focus.

The participle of passive necessity can also stand alone as a noun, as in:

> *Convertendi convertentur*
> The ones needing to be changed will be changed.

The whole meaning of *convertendi* is "the ones, individuals, people, men needing to be changed." If you stick close to the full natural meaning of each participle, you will have no confusion ever.

Summary

Returning to the confusion that many people have about the participle of passive necessity, the form *amandus, a, um* can function in different ways in a sentence. We have seen here its usage as a participle of passive necessity meaning "one needing to be loved." We separate our presentation of this usage by one full year from our presentation of the other function of this form.

When we return to this discussion, we shall see that authors take this in different ways, but we shall let it go until we get to that point. To be honest with people, *amandus, a, um* for us now is a participle of passive necessity. Later on, it will have other usages, and for other people it will have other meanings. We shall keep them separate and clear and learn one thing at a time.

We have seen the forms of the four participles and what they mean naturally. We have given special attention to the deponent verbs, which are confusing, because they do not always follow the definition of a deponent verb. We have also mentioned that the participles can stand alone as verbal nouns.

ENCOUNTER 18 (53)

USUS PARTICIPIORUM: SOLUM CUM ESSE

the use of the participles: alone, with "to be"

Introduction

The four participles we have seen—and we are always conscious of those blank spaces where there are no participles—can be used in the Latin language in three general ways. First, we have already seen that they can be used alone as adjectives, which consequently can also stand alone as nouns. Second, the participles can be used in conjunction with the verb "to be," which we shall see now. Third, they can be used in a special construction we call the ablative absolute, which we shall see in our next encounter. We emphasize above all that we cannot change the natural meaning of those participles. We might have to rework our Latin or English sentence to accommodate that natural meaning.

1. Contemporaneous active participle not used with "to be"

To begin with, the contemporaneous active participle is not used with the verb "to be." This is allowed in Greek but not in Latin. Because of the influence of the Greek, in the New Testament of the Vulgate Bible, for example, you will see this Greek usage creeping over into Latin and presenting quite corrupt, unnatural Roman speech. You might see, *sunt canentes in via*, meaning "they are singing on the road." But we learned that "they are singing" is T.1i: *canunt*, which means that the contemporaneous participle with the verb "to be" is not considered an acceptable Latin usage. It represents, rather, the influence of biblical Greek as a form of colloquial jargon. In some modern languages like Italian and English it is allowed, but not in Latin. For acceptable Latin authors this usage is out of the question, because Latin has solid verbs to fulfill that same function. For example, to say *erimus venientes* for "we shall be coming" is spaghetti Latin or babble talk, but not standard Latin, which offers the verb *veniemus*.

2. Antecedent participle used with "to be"

The antecedent participle, as we said, is passive in form and meaning for a normal verb, but, if the verb is deponent, that passive form has active meaning. We have already learned in our First Experience that this participle is used with the verb "to be" to form the passive T.4i, 5i, 6i, such as *vocatus eras*, "you (man) had been called," or *vocata es*, "you (woman) have been called," or *vocatae eritis*, "you (women) will have been called." Remember that in this expression the participle agrees with the subject, masculine, feminine, neuter, singular, plural. You have also seen this participle used with the subjunctive forms of the verb "to be" to form the passive T.3s and T.4s, such as *vocatus sis* or *vocatus esses*—which we shall not render right now into English without a full sentence. With the deponent verbs, these same forms, of course, have active meanings. You already know all of this, and there is nothing new to say but to see it in action through the hand and mouth of real Latinists over the centuries. We do not have to be reminded that these two verbal parts can and often are separated by other elements in the sentence.

3. Active futurity formula

When we come to the verb "to be" used with the futurity participle or to the participle of passive necessity, we discover a beautiful part of the Latin language. The futurity active participle is coupled with the entire system of the verb "to be," which means the six times of the indicative and the four times of the subjunctive, in order to make what we call the "futurity formula." In some books you will see this called the active periphrastic, which is a mysterious and unintelligible term to many people. So we call it the active futurity formula.

To understand this formula, all you have to do is to put the two parts together, and they make sense. For example:

saltaturi sunt
they are about to dance
they are on the point of dancing
they have the intention of dancing
they are going to dance
they are fixing to dance.

The two words may be understood just as they are. Change the time of the verb "to be" in this example to T.4i, and you have, *saltaturus fuit*, "he was about to dance," "he has been on the point of dancing," or the women can say, *saltaturae fuerimus*, "we women will have been about to dance," in which the verb *fuerimus* is the same form in T.6i as in T.3s.

There is no problem here at all. You only put the entire verb "to be" with the future active participle. These two forms, by the way, are often separated by many other words or appear in reversed order, but in your mind you can put them together and see the futurity formula and say it in English as it is written in Latin.

This futurity formula has no passive because that participle is lacking in Latin. So we cannot say in Latin with this formula, "the bridge is about to be reconstructed," which is futurity passive, because there is no participle to express that. To maintain the natural meaning of the participle, once again you can rework the sentence to say, for example, "someone is about to reconstruct the bridge," *Aliquis est pontem restauraturus*. You have to learn to make this adjustment very quickly when speaking or writing Latin, because anything else will not be tolerated by the natural meaning of the participle, nor by people knowing Latin.

4. Passive necessity formula

We now come to what we call the passive necessity participle used with the verb "to be" in the "formula of passive necessity." Again the full range of six indicative times and four subjunctive times is found. Because of our way of presenting the passive necessity participle in previous encounters, now you can simply read the two parts of this construction according to their natural meaning and put them together. You can say, for example, *canticum est cantandum*, "the hymn is needing to be sung," then we can smooth out the English to say, "the hymn has to be sung," "the hymn ought to be sung," "the hymn is worthy to be sung," "the hymn must be sung." In every case the expression is both passive and expressive of necessity. We can change the form of the verb *esse*, "to be," into any time, as when and say *responsiones scribendae fuerunt* in T.4i meaning, "answers had to be written" or "answers needed to be written" or "answers have had to be written." Of course, we do not forget that "the answers have been written" is *responsiones scriptae sunt.*

In our last encounter, we mentioned that some other teachers call the participle of passive necessity by other names. Some call it the futurity passive participle or the gerundive. We have already said that in our system the futurity passive participle does not really exist, except in the minds of certain grammarians, and that we choose to keep the necessity meaning separate from the gerundive by a calendar school year, so we shall talk about those other things later on.

The great temptation is to use this construction as if the participle were active. If you want to use this participle to say, "I have to sweep the floor," and you begin your Latin sentence with *ego*, you are finished and cannot continue with this participle, because you are left with *ego verrendus sum*, "I have to be swept." The participle demands that you rephrase the statement to say, "the floor is needing to be swept by me," *pavimentum est mihi verendum.* Many students try to say, "we have to praise their voices," and begin their sentence with *nos*, "we." This will never work because the natural passive meaning of the participle requires you to rework the sentence to say, "their voices must be praised by us," *eorum nobis sunt voces laudandae.*

One final warning is needed. The form *restituti sunt* is T.4i, either T.4ai meaning, "they have been restored," or T.4bi meaning, "they were restored." The passive necessity formula *restituendi sunt* is T.1i because in this case the time comes from the verb "to be" which is coupled with the participle of passive necessity: now that takes mental discipline.

5. Dative of agent

After we presented the passive verbs, we saw in encounter 28 the expression of personal agent consisting of the preposition *a* or *ab* followed by the function to-for-from. Now we can add a detail here which is far from a mere detail. When the English sentences above are reworded to accommodate the passive necessity formula, they unexpectedly include the expression *mihi*, "by me," or *nobis*, "by us" without prepositions. In this case, that function is technically called the dative of agent. The passive necessity formula 90% of the time uses this very dative of agent. For example, the dative *matri* is clear in the sentence

> *magnum est matri Gracchorum scribendum opus,*

which 90% of the time will be the dative of agent and mean,

> "the big work is needing to be written by the mother of the Gracchi,"

but of course it does not lose its native meaning to-for-from, as in,

> "the big work is needing to be written for the mother of the Gracchi."

For example, *omnibus moriendum est*, "Dying must be done by all people," or we might say in standard English, "all people must die." Likewise, the example *nobis vivendum est* means, "living is needing to be done by us," or "we must live." Here we have smoothed out the vernacular expressions.

We have said the "dative of agent" is used 90% of the time; the other 10%, if it is even that much, is even found in Cicero, who used the other expression of agency, namely the preposition *a* or *ab* with the form by-with-from-in. For example, the expression "we have to live," can also be expressed as, *a nobis est vivendum*. This is all very clear in Gildersleeve and Lodge, numbers 354 and 355.

We have seen that the contemporaneous participle is not used with the verb "to be," and you already know how to use the antecedent participle with "to be." Now we have seen the active futurity formula and the passive necessity formula and their traps, which catch those who do not respect the natural meaning of the participles. The above is the whole story of Latin participles with the verb "to be."

ENCOUNTER 19 (54)

ABLATIVUS ABSOLUTUS

ablative absolute

Introduction

Thus far we have seen that the four participles can be used as adjectives and with the verb "to be." The participles are verbal adjectives. As adjectives, they agree with the word they modify, or they can stand alone as a noun, just as adjectives do. As verbal adjectives, the participles can have adverbs and objects. We can say, "I see the tree *having been decorated* beautifully" or "I see the beautifully *decorated* tree"; "I hear the musicians *sounding* their instruments" or "I hear *the ones sounding* their instruments," where "sounding" is a participial adjective either going with "musicians," or standing all alone as a noun, "the ones sounding."

We have also seen that three of the four participles can be combined with the verb "to be" to produce the passive or deponent forms of T.4i, 5i, 6i, or T.3s, 4s, or to produce the futurity formula and the passive necessity formula.

Now we wish to turn to the third usage of the participles. The famous "ablative absolute" is a favorite and beloved habit of the Romans in their language, and from Latin it has gone into other languages, for example, when we say in English, "*This having been said*, we can go to the next topic." The phrase "This having been said" is the English equivalent of the ablative absolute. We can say, "We were digging in the garden, *the children doing their own work*," where the second part is the ablative absolute and the first part is the main sentence.

In Latin this construction exists all over the place, and the Latins loved it because you can draw so much into a few words. It is versatile, too, in that the ablative absolute can function as a temporal clause, a causal clause, a conditional clause, almost as anything you want.

Those other clauses—temporal, causal, conditional—as we shall see beginning in encounter 23 (58) and following, have a particle, such as *ut*, *cum*, *qui*, *ne*, *dum*, and a verb in the indicative or subjunctive mode. The ablative absolute has much the same range of meaning, but does not have such a particle expressed, and its verb is expressed as a simple participle. So the concise ablative absolute stands for an expanded, complete clause that has been compressed dramatically.

Composition

The two basic elements of an ablative absolute are the subject and the verb in a participle. Both that subject and participle are expressed with what we call the form by-with-from-in, or technically the "ablative." This requires substantial reworking because indicative and subjunctive verbs have to be reformulated as ablative participles, and the subject also has to be expressed in the form by-with-from-in. The rest of the phrase can stay the same, which means that you will find prepositions, adverbs, relative clauses, whatever you want, depending on the subject and participle in the ablative.

The term "ablative absolute," then, indicates that both the subject and the participle are expressed in the ablative function, our form by-with-from-in. The term "absolute" indicates that the ablative absolute has a certain independence from the main sentence. Some people say that it is absolute because it has nothing to do with the main sentence, but this overstates the case, because it would then have no reason to be there. It is absolute, rather, for the technical reason that its subject is not and cannot be the subject or the object or the usage to-for-from of the main sentence. Thus, as absolute, it stands by itself and does not enter the main sentence in these technical ways.

So, for example, we can distinguish between the following two sentences:

> *In horto pueri ludentes magnum excitabant strepitum*
> The children playing in the garden made much noise

> *In horto pueris ludentibus, operabamur nostris in conclavibus*
> The children playing in the garden, we were working in our rooms.

The subject of the first sentence is "The children playing in the garden," and so it is not an ablative absolute. In the second sentence, the children do not enter into the main sentence, and so the phrase stands absolute, although the idea is related to the main sentence. We shall learn that the latter sentence can also be rendered into English in various ways, such as: "While, because, although the children were playing, we were working in our rooms."

Take another example:

> *In horto pueros ludentes custos ego spectabam*
> The children playing in the garden I was observing as babysitter.

Here "the children" are the object of the verb "I was observing" and therefore not an ablative absolute. Many phrases like this one sound in English almost identical to, but are quite different from, the ablative absolute.

After a while it becomes very easy to distinguish the ablative absolute, especially because we can use the ablative absolute in everyday spoken English in imitation of the Latin, for example:

> *After this had been done* and *while she was on the phone*, we were fixing the TV.

Both of the first two clauses are ablatives absolute, and you can just string them together. Julius Caesar has whole paragraphs written in this way. The above example may sound stilted in English, but more natural expressions are readily available, as in:

That said, let's turn to the next item on the agenda
All things having been said, I respectfully disagree with your remarks
That nicely done, let's move on
There being no objections, the speaker has the floor.

Certain literary writing—here I am talking about more notable examples —will use dashes to separate an absolute clause contained within another (parentheses are less in favor). While these examples place the absolute construction at the beginning of the sentence, it can be located anywhere geographically in the sentence.

The teacher will find out and discover and observe the ablatives absolute in the reading sheets in preparation for our next encounter, which will present the composition and proper rendition of this phenomenon.

ENCOUNTER 20 (55)

ABLATIVUS ABSOLUTUS ALITER PROLATUS

ablative absolute
expressed in other ways

Introduction

The formation of the ablative absolute is simple. The verb has to be one of the four participles, but practically speaking the only ones used are the contemporaneous active participle and the antecedent participle with passive meaning for normal verbs and active meaning for the deponents. You may find one solitary example using the futurity participle in perhaps twenty years of reading, like, *venturo eo nostrum sternebant triclinium*, "as he was about to come, they were preparing our banquet hall." The participle of passive necessity theoretically could be used in an ablative absolute, but is practically not going to exist, because it looks like the gerundive, as we shall see later on.

1. Composing and unfolding

The participle is given in the so-called ablative, or, as we call it, the form by-with-from-in, whether in the singular or plural. A few examples will help you to see this clearly:

Opere facto profecti sumus
The work having been done, we set out.

Here *Opere* is in the form by-with-from-in and functions as the subject of the participle *facto*, which agrees with its subject. You can see that *Opere* does not figure into the main sentence as its subject, object, or to-for-from function. That is how we render this mode of speaking into English. First, we render the participle according to its natural meaning as, "one having been done," and second we express its subject as "The work." Thus, its natural meaning is, "The work having been done ..." In the Latin expression both are in the form by-with-from-in because of this mode of speaking, but in English they do not sound as that function at all. That is why we never render the ablative absolute in English by beginning, "with ..." as if it were a simple ablative.

Another example is:

Musica effecta, plausimus
The music having been played, we applauded
After the music had been played, we applauded
Once the music had been played, we applauded.

The subject of the ablative absolute is *Musica* in the form by-with-from-in. You can see that its participle *effecta* agrees with it. We begin to render this in English by taking *Musica* as the subject of the participle *effecta*, which we render according to its natural meaning as, "The music having been played." Then we notice that the participle *effecta* is antecedent to *plausimus*, "we applauded," so we set the ablative absolute back in time to "The music had been played," and then we even interpret it temporally, as "After the music had been played."

The author Aurelius Augustinus Hipponensis (354–430 CE) has two perfect examples of what we have just explained. In his fireside chat on the psalms Augustine says:

> *Concussa terra Dominus resurrexit* (Aug. *Enar. in psal.* 63, 15)
> The earth having been shaken, the Lord rose.
>
> *Nonnullis videtur eos tantummodo peccare in Spiritum Sanctum, qui lavacro regenerationis abluti in ecclesia, et accepto Spiritu Sancto, velut tanto postea dono salvatoris ingrati, mortifero aliquo pecccato se immerserint* (Aug. *Enar. in psal.* 71, 4, 7)
>
> To some people it seems that only they sin against the Holy Spirit who, washed with the bath of regeneration in the church, and—the Holy Spirit having been received as such a great gift of the savior—afterwards they, ungrateful, have sunken themselves in some death-bringing sin.

Contrary to the punctuation, we have taken the ablative absolute to begin with *accepto Spiritu Sancto*, "the Holy Spirit having been received," and to continue with *velut tanto postea dono salvatoris*, "as such a great gift of the savior."

Here is an example given by Eusebius Hieronymus (c. 342–420 CE). In this commentary on the book of Ecclesiastes, Jerome says:

> *omnibus per paenitentiam in integrum restitutis, solus diabolus in suo permanebit errore* (Hier. *Eccles.* 1, 15)
>
> After all people have been totally restored through penance, only the devil will remain in his own error.

We have said that the contemporaneous participle in the form by-with-from-in ends with the letter *–e* 85% of the time, as in *nuntiante*. The ablative absolute is in fact part of that 85%. The subject is also placed in the form by-with-from-in, and its participle agrees with it. Here is an example with a contemporaneous active participle:

> *Musicis canentibus, dormiebamus*
> The musicians playing instruments, we were sleeping
> The musicians were playing instruments, we were sleeping
> As the musicians were playing instruments, we were sleeping.

Again, *Musicis* is in the form by-with-from-in and it functions as the subject of its participle *canentibus*, which we render according to its natural meaning as, “The musicians playing,” which is contemporaneous to *dormiebamus* in T.2i, “we were sleeping,” and thus it is set in the past as, “The musicians were playing.” Finally, the translation is smoothed out by saying “As the musicians were playing, we were sleeping.” The rendering of *canentibus* as “were playing instruments” is good proof of our insistence that *canentibus* is not any sort of “present participle,” but one contemporaneous with the ruling verb, here *dormiebamus*, “we were sleeping.”

2. Vernacular renderings

In our system we learn how to express the ablative absolute in the vernacular in three different ways, as you have seen above.

The first way is to take it as it is written, giving the participle its full natural meaning, such as:

> *Soluta hypotheca, exsultavimus*
> *The mortgage having been paid*, we had a celebration.

A second way begins with the sentence rendered according to its full natural meaning, as above. Next we discern its relationship to the main sentence and smooth it out, perhaps by making it a temporal, causal, or conditional clause, such as:

> *After the mortgage had been paid*, we had a celebration (temporal)
>
> *Because the mortgage had been paid*, we had a celebration (causal)
>
> *If the mortgage will have been paid*, we shall have a celebration (*exsultabimus*; conditional).

Or we might take the Latin sentence and say:

> *Luxuriantibus in hortis parvulis opus absolvimus domesticum*
>
> *While the children were running riot in the garden*, we completed our housework
>
> *Because the children were running riot in the garden*, we completed our housework
>
> *Although the children were running riot in the garden*, we completed our housework.

Certain sentences might suggest a conditional clause, as in:

> *Pensa in horto tranquile otiantibus pueris domestica quidem perficiemus*
>
> If the children will be at leisure and peace in the garden, we shall finish our daily home duties.

A third way to express the ablative absolute in the vernacular is based on the realization that we are dealing with modern languages. Sometimes it is best to account for all the information in the ablative absolute when writing your own story. In this case you are free to do what you want, as long as you account for all the elements of the Latin.

3. As relative, temporal, causal, or conditional clauses

The following examples show that the participles are easy to transform into a relative, temporal, causal, or conditional clause. For example, take the sentence:

> *Musica cantata, dormitabamus*
> *Musicis canentibus, dormitabamus.*

As temporal clauses we have:

> Once the music had been played ...
> After the music had been played ...
> When the musicians were singing ...
> As long as the musicians were singing ...

As causal sentences we have:

> Because the music had been played ...
> Because the musicians were singing ...

As conditional sentences we have:

> If the music was played ...
> If the musicians were singing ...

As a relative clause inside a complete sentence we have something we shall consider more fully later in this encounter.

> *Totum musica diem sonabat, qua cantata dormitabamus*
>
> All day music was sounding, which having been played, we were sleeping
> All day music was sounding, which after it had been played, we were sleeping.
>
> *Musici pessimi erant, quibus canentibus dormitabamus*
>
> The musicians were lousy, who playing, we were sleeping
> The musicians were lousy, who when they were playing, we were sleeping.

Another example of the varying interpretation is the following with a few ideas added to complete the meaning of each:

> *Operibus perfectis, laudavimus eos*
>
> We praised the people *although* the works had been finished (badly)
> We praised the people *when* the works had been finished (finally)
> We praised the people *because* the works had been finished (excellently).

All of these are possible, and sometimes there is no clue about how to do it other than to think and consider the entire statement and train of thought of the author.

Ambrose gives us this example in his work on penance:

> *Sed aiunt [Novatiani] se, exceptis gravioribus criminibus, relaxare veniam levioribus* (Ambros. *De paen.* I, 3, 10)
>
> But the [Novatiani] say that, although more serious sins have been taken out, they grant forgiveness for lighter ones.

If you pounce on that participle *exceptis* without seeing its connection to its subject *criminibus*, then you might make the mistake of saying "with the exception of."

4. Playing with the Latin

An ablative absolute can be wisely unfolded to make it into a subordinate clause with subject and verb. The subject is put in the subject form, and the participle becomes a verb in the indicative or subjunctive. The following sentence can be expanded in at least two ways:

> *Opere facto profecti sumus*
> The work having been done, we set out.

You have not yet learned about the following expressions in Latin, but as you learn them in the forthcoming encounters, you can begin to play with the ablative absolute and express it in different ways, for example:

> *Postquam opus factum est (erat), profecti sumus*
> After the work was (had been) done, we set out
>
> *Cum opus factum esset, profecti sumus*
> When (because, although) the work had been done, we set out.

You can see here that we simply unraveled the natural meaning of the participle and then rephrased the sentence according to the natural meaning of the ideas, putting them into a whole clause. Other examples are unfolded as follows:

> *Musica effecta, plausimus*
> Once the music had been played, we applauded
>
> *Postquam musica effecta est (erat), plausimus*
> After the music was (had been) played, we applauded
>
> *Cum effecta esset, plausimus*
> When (because, although) the music had been played, we applauded
>
> *Musicis canentibus, dormiebamus*
> As the musicians were playing, we were sleeping
>
> *Cum musici canebant dormiebamus*
> When the musicians were (happened to be) playing, we were sleeping

Cum musici canerent, dormiebamus
When (because, although) the musicians were playing, we were sleeping.

In this example Thascius Caecilius Cyprianus Carthaginiensis (c. 200–258 CE) speaks about believers having fallen away in practice. Cyprian says plainly:

Spretis his omnibus atque contemptis ante expiata delicta ... vis infertur corpori eius et sanguini (Cypr. *de Lapsis*, 16)

All these things having been scorned and rejected before the sins having been expiated ... violence is inflicted on his body and blood.

We can restate the ablative absolute as a temporal clause using the word *ubi*, "when":

Spreta ubi sunt haec omnia atque contempta ante delectorum expiationem ... violentia admovetur corpori eius et sanguini

When things having been scorned and rejected before the sins having been expiated ... violence is inflicted on his body and blood.

Cyprian wrote this in a letter in which he mentions a group called the "libellatici":

Placuit, frater carissime, examinatis causis singulorum libellaticos interim admitti (Cypr. *de Lapsis*, 16)

It was decided, most dear brother, the causes of the individuals having been examined, that the *libellatici* in the meanwhile be allowed in.

We can render this as a causal clause with *quandoquidem*, "seeing that," even as we jazz it up with a few words of our own:

Consenserunt ut, frater carissime, quandoquidem singulorum investigati sunt casus, libellatici interim permitterentur

Seeing that the cases of the individuals were pondered, most beloved brother, they agreed that the libellatici be given access in the meanwhile.

In these examples we are just taking that participle and unfolding it into a whole clause that is hidden there anyway.

5. Relative ablative absolute

As we saw above in number 3, here we have an ablative absolute that is expressed with a relative pronoun as its subject:

Matres, quibus liba coquentibus laetabamur, ab omnibus praecipue diligebantur

The mothers, who baking cakes we were very happy, were loved especially by all.

We may understand this expression as the joining of two sentences:

> *Matres ab omnibus praecipue diligebantur*
> The mothers were loved especially by all

and the reconstructed independent sentence that begins with an ablative absolute,

> *Matribus liba coquentibus laetabamur*
> We were very happy as the mothers were baking cakes.

The two sentences are joined by making *matribus* into a relative pronoun *quibus*, whose antecedent is *matres* in the main sentence. Thus, the subject of the ablative absolute is the relative pronoun *quibus*. It can be reformulated as a relative clause:

> *Matres quae cum liba coquerent laetabamur, praecipue ab omnibus diligebantur*
>
> The mothers, who when they were baking cakes we were happy, were loved especially by all.

Anyone who thinks such an expression is impossible to find in Latin literature can simply walk into the Pantheon in Rome and stand in awe before the tomb of Raphael and read the inscription running across the top and marvel, or see the picture of this tomb and inscription on page 456 of this volume.

At this point take your reading sheets to find the ablative absolute all over the place, in every author, poet—ancient and medieval—in laws, Galileo, Descartes. The poets love them because they are so concise, and you can say so much in one or two words. There you will see all the participles in action, and you may even realize the need to correct some erroneous ones. You can then walk your way through all we have learned and produce beautiful sentences in Latin by transferring all of these participles into relative sentences, and soon you will be able to rework them as temporal, causal sentences. Playing with authentic Latin texts in this way is another aspect of rendering our Latin training active.

ENCOUNTER 21 (56)

ABLATIVUS ABSOLUTUS IN AUCTORIBUS AC PAGINIS

ablative absolute in authors and on reading sheets

Students need regular practice spotting the ablative absolute, understanding their natural meanings and their relationship to the larger sentence, rendering them smoothly into the vernacular, and then making one's own ablatives absolute where the subject does not enter into the main clause.

The ablative absolute is limited by the possibilities and natural meanings of the participles. For example, we cannot construct an ablative absolute with an antecedent active participle unless we find a deponent verb that will have active meaning. For example, the verb *pingo, pingere, pinxi, pictum*, 3, "to paint," cannot produce the sentence "I having painted the walls, he is making lunch." The participle has to be passive as in *muris a me pictis, praeparat prandium*, "The walls having been painted by me, he is making lunch."

Latin does not allow dangling participles, but the ablative absolute requires its independence, while referring to its sentence in general.

Before you go to the reading sheets, an urgent warning is communicated in two parts to Latin readers with regard to the ablative absolute—everyone makes these mistakes. One, be careful, the essential elements of the ablative absolute, namely the participial verb and the subject both in the form by-with-from-in are most often separated in Latin sentences by one, two or even fifty words, and only your Latin eye and your scanning mind can put these two elements together. Two, again Latin literature warns us that more frequently than not the ablative absolute begins with the verbal participial form out front, whose subject may be at the far other end of the ablative absolute. The worst thing the reader can do is to pounce on the participle placed out front in the sentence and to invent some sort of meaning without regard for its subject further along in the sentence.

Now taking a deep breath, we can open up our numerous reading sheets and challenge ourselves to spot ablatives absolute and then to analyze them according to these principles and also to render them into other full-blown English expressions.

ENCOUNTER 22 (57)

ABLATIVUS ABSOLUTUS SINE PARTICIPIO "ESSE"

ablative absolute
without the participle "being"

Introduction

There is one universal use of the ablative absolute where the verb of the phrase is omitted. The only word omitted is the verb "to be," which really does not have a participle, "being," all alone in classical Latin.

The omission of "being"

The Romans put a noun with an adjective or a pronoun in the ablative and let it sit there without a participle, which is non-existent but is felt, and scholars will immediately see the ablative absolute with "being." For example:

> *Ea facietis, me invito*
> You all will do these things, I [being] unwilling.

Here the adjective *invitus, a, um* means "unwilling," and the verb "being" is not expressed, but it is felt. Or take an example like the following, inspired by Pius II Piccolomini:

> *Vixit in Etruria, patre Simone, matre vero Virginia*
> He lived in Tuscany—father being Simon, but mother Virginia

Four of the words are two ablatives absolute meaning "his father [being] Simon and his mother [being] Virginia.

The ablative absolute is distinguished from the ablative of personal agent in this example:

> *Humberto rege comprehensi sunt*
> They were arrested, when Humberto was king.

Here the ablative absolute is *Humberto rege*, "Umberto being king," or "When Umberto was king," using the Italian name of the King of Italy Umberto (1878–1900). In this sentence we do not know the link between his reign and their arrest. But if we change the sentence to:

> *Ab Humberto rege comprehensi sunt*
> They were arrested by Humberto, the king

then we have an ablative of personal agent, where *Ab Humberto rege* means that the people were arrested "by Umberto the king." This distinction is subtle to notice but changes history totally.

Our students are not allowed to render the ablative absolute in English by a clause beginning with the word "with" Some books and schools suggest using "with ..." as a simple way of translating the ablative absolute. Such a rendering, unfortunately, produces silly, ridiculous sentences because "with," as in "with a baseball bat," is instrumental, or, as in "with us," is accompaniment. The ablative absolute is more independent and does not always go that far. One example of this is in a Latin prayer when the minister says:

> *Misereatur nostri omnipotens Deus*
> *et, dimissis peccatis nostris,*
> *perducat nos ad vitam aeternam.* (*Liturgia Romana*)

If the ablative absolute *dimissis peccatis* is translated using "with ... ," then you get the following:

> May almighty God have mercy on us
> and lead us with our forgiven sins into eternal life.

Either our sins accompany us into eternal life, or they are the instrument with which God leads us to eternal life—both of which are absurd. The expression is, rather, an ablative absolute without the verb "to be," indicating that we are led into eternal life after our sins have been forgiven. However it is rendered in acceptable English, we do not permit our students to render the ablative absolute into English beginning with the word "with."

Another example is:

> *Ad venandum excesserunt elefantis occisis*
> They went on a safari, the elephants having been killed.

If you say, "They went on a safari with the elephants having been killed," then you are saying that they carried dead elephants with them on their safari, which they did not do. This practice of rendering the ablative absolute by a "with ..." clause must most diligently be avoided because it will sound silly.

Again, church law says about baptism that it is not licit to baptize anyone, *parentibus invitis*, "the parents [being] unwilling." The ablative absolute sits there, and its verb "to be" is missing, either felt or understood. Vatican documents often include the formula:

> *Quibuslibet contrariis minime obstantibus*
> Any kind of contrary things impeding in no way

meaning:

> Anything that is opposed to these provisions has no effect at all
> Any contrary ideas not causing an impediment.

In effect this means that all other agreements to the contrary are canceled.

Every page of the reading sheets following each experience has an example of this usage.

ENCOUNTER 23 (58)

USUS CONIUNCTIVI. FINALES: UT – NE – UT ... NON; FINALIS: QUI, QUAE, QUOD

uses of the subjunctive.
final clauses: ut, ne, ut ... non;
final: qui, quae, quod

Introduction

Previously in this Experience we mentioned the meaning of the subjunctive or conjunctive as well as the general approach of conditionals and wishes and potential, all of which are expressed in English by "would, could, should, may, might."

Whether a subjunctive verb in Latin will sound subjunctive or indicative in the vernacular depends on the kind or nature of the subjunctive and how the same idea is expressed in the vernacular. It may seem or sound astonishing for beginners when we say that of all the uses of the subjunctive in Latin, only three will sound subjunctive in most vernaculars. The three are as follows: a natural, independent, freestanding subjunctive; half of all conditional sentences; and purpose clauses, also called final clauses. All the other uses of the subjunctive in Latin will sound indicative in the vernacular. Considering the subjunctive in this way at the start solves all kinds of problems coming later on.

In this encounter we begin with one of the most common uses of the subjunctive in Latin, namely to express purpose or intention or, as it is sometimes called, finality.

1. final *ut, ne*

English expressions of purpose, intention, or finality are introduced by the positive ideas:

in order that ...
so that ...
that ....

or the negative ideas:

that ... not
lest ...

For example, in the indicative we say, "she comes on time." We can put this into the subjunctive and say:

I ask that she may come on time,
I ask that she come on time,

I ask that they may come on time.
I ask that they come on time.

In the first example, you can see the subjunctive "she may come." Another way to express the subjunctive here is to omit the "may" to get "she come," which you can see is subjunctive when you compare it with the indicative "she comes." The subjunctive is not as obvious in the fourth example, "I ask that they come on time," because "they come" is the same form for both the indicative and subjunctive, although some people might not notice this subjunctive mode of speaking.

Another example of the indicative is, "they are diligent in their work." We can express the verb "to be," or here "they are," in the subjunctive as "they be" or even "he be" in the following:

I am teaching them in order that they be more diligent in their work
I am teaching him in order that he be more diligent in his work.

Here "they be" and "he be" are in the subjunctive, although many people do not realize this when they see or hear it.

Another form of the subjunctive in English is the helping verb "may" in T.1s or "might" in T.2s, as in the following:

The police are there so that the citizens may have more safety
The police were put there so that the citizens might have more safety.

Each of these sentences is an example of a purpose clause introduced by the particle "that ..." or "in order that ..." or "so that ...." The ideas expressed in the subjunctive are incomplete and projected out into the future. These sentences do not need any specific expression of futurity because the nature of the purpose clause projects it into the future. You could say:

I insist they come back in five years.

Here you can still use T.1s "they come" even though the action is five years down the line, because the purpose clause naturally expresses futurity, where the final end of an action is hoped for, planned for, desired, wished for.

In Latin these ideas are expressed by the particle *ut* .... followed by the subjunctive according to the sequence of tenses. Another way of writing *ut* is *uti* (not to be confused with the infinitive of the deponent verb *utor, uti, usus*, 3, "to use").

The negative of *ut* is *ne*, which, as a type of prohibition, negates the whole clause in the subjunctive, or *ut* ... *non* to negate a particular word in the following subjunctive clause. The use of *ne* is a clear indicator of a purpose clause, because only the purpose clause forms its negative with *ne*. Another type of clause in our training will be formed with *ut* ... , but it expresses the negative with *ut non* ....

In English, purpose or final clauses sound subjunctive. The particle *ne* is usually rendered in English as, "in order that not," or as, "lest," but some people will not understand this. We shall see examples in a minute. So, in Latin we express:

ut or *uti* . . .	in order that . . . so that . . . that . . .
ne	in order that not . . . so that not . . . that not . . . lest . . .
ut . . . non . . .	in order that . . . not . . . so that . . . not . . . that . . . not . . .

Among the very first Latin Christian authors is Quintus Septimius Florens Tertullianus (c. 150/170–c. 230 CE) a pioneer who produced Latin expressions for theological terms still in use today. In his work "On the Resurrection of the Flesh," Tertullian gives us this fine examples:

> *caro abluitur, ut anima emaculetur; caro ungitur, ut anima consecretur; caro signatur, ut et anima muniatur; caro manus impositione adumbratur, ut et anima spiritu illuminetur; caro corpore et sanguine Christi vescitur, ut et anima de Deo saginetur* (Tert. *de Carnis Res*. 8)
>
> the flesh is washed off in order that the soul may be cleansed; the flesh is anointed so that the soul may be consecrated; the flesh is signed so that also the soul may be fortified; the flesh is overshadowed by the laying on of the hand so that also the soul may be illuminated with the spirit; the flesh eats the body and blood of Christ so that also the spirit may be stuffed off God.

Augustine says the following in one of his letters:

> *Nam sicut in unitate personae anima utitur corpore, ut homo sit, ita in unitate personae Deus utitur homine, ut Christus sit* (Aug. *Ep*. 137, 3)
>
> For just as in the unity of a person the soul uses the body in order that it may be a human being, thus in the unity of a person God uses the human being so that it may be Christ.

Jerome writes in his commentary on the book of Isaiah:

> *Dicam et aliud mirabilius, ne eum putes in phantasmate nasciturum: cibis utetur infantiae, butyrum comedet et lac* (Hier. *Isa*. 3, 7)
>
> I shall say also something more surprising that you may not think that he is about to be born in a fantasy: he will use the foods of infancy, he will eat butter and milk.

Tertullian writes against the man Hermogenes, saying:

> *manifestatur ex nihilo factum, et non periclitatur, ne ex aliquo factum existimetur, quando non demonstretur, ex quo sit factum*
> (Tert. *adver. Hermo.* 21)
>
> it is declared to have been made from nothingness, and it is not in danger in order that it may not be thought to have been made from something, because it is not demonstrated from what it has been made.

In his commentary on the letter to the Ephesians, Jerome says:

> *Descendit ergo in inferiora terrae, et ascendit super omnes caelos Filius Dei, ut non tantum legem prophetasque compleret, sed et alias quasdam occultas dispensationes* (Hier. *ad Eph.* 2, 4)
>
> Therefore the Son of God descended into the lower places of the earth and ascended over all the heavens, so that not only he would fulfill the law and the prophets, but also certain other hidden arrangements.

In the above quote, the *non* denies only one word, *tantum*, in the expression *ut non tantum*, "so that not only."

Returning to Tertullian, we read he following in his work on penance:

> *poenae prius magnitudinem imaginare, ut de remedii adeptione non dubites* (Tert. *Paen.* 12)
>
> You must imagine the extent of his punishment first so that you may not doubt about the attainment of the remedy.

Here again the *non* describes *dubites*, "you may not doubt."

This usage of *ut* and *uti* followed by the subjunctive as an expression of purpose is so to the fore in students that they most often forget the original meaning in your dictionary for *ut* and *uti*, is "as," "just as," "how," and in those variations the indicative is used. If you look on the reading sheets, you will find dozens of examples easily and without end of *ut* with the indicative meaning "how," something commonly overlooked by all readers.

2. final *qui, quae, quod*

We might as well mention right away, another way Romans loved to express purpose or finality is to enclose it in a relative sentence. We have the same phenomenon in English. Take the example:

> I gave them money so that they might use it on books
> *Pecuniam eis dedi ut adhiberent eam in libris.*

But instead of saying "so that they might use it," we can say, "which they might use," and so we have in English the sentence:

> I gave them money which they might use on books.

It is the same system in Latin. We can begin with the simple sentence:

Pecuniam eis dedi quam adhibebant in libris
I gave them money which they were using on books.

Here the simple relative is followed by the indicative *quam adhibebant*. But you must be warned that if this relative pronoun is followed by a subjunctive, then your mind or your training should tell you that the sentence is saying something more than the simple relative. If we change *adhibebant* from T.2i to T.2s, then we have the same thing in Latin as in the English example above:

Pecuniam eis dedi quam adhiberent in libris
I gave them money which they might use on books.

In this case, your training tells you that *quam adhiberent* is an expression of purpose, where *quam adhiberent* is a substitution for *ut eam adhiberent*, meaning "so that they might use which [money on books]."

Some people in their training are told to translate the purpose clause in Latin with the English infinitive. Philosophically this is no problem, and we can say, "I gave them money to use on books." However, seeing this English sentence, bright students will ask where the infinitive is in the Latin sentence, but it is not there. If you keep the subjunctive of a Latin purpose clause in the subjunctive in vernacular languages, then students will see the connection between the two more clearly.

The sequence of tenses is observed in purpose clauses, but it involves only T.1s on Track I and T.2s on Track II, because purpose clauses obviously have a futurity about them. The idea of a purpose clause concerns actions that are unfinished or incomplete in that they express what we want to have happen that has not happened already. The very idea of a purpose clause, then, practically precludes T.3s and 4s.

These relative sentences can be used passively or actively. For example, we can express the following sentence with the passive verb *adhiberentur* by means of a relative sentence using the same passive verb:

Nummos dedi ut ei adhiberentur in libris
I gave them coins so that they might be used for books

Nummos dedi qui adhiberentur in libris
I gave them coins which might be used for books.

You can see here that *ut ei adhiberentur*, "so that they might be used," becomes the relative sentence *qui adhiberentur*, "which might be used."

Augustine, writing in one of his letters, wraps all of this up into one fantastic sentence made just for us:

fides praecedat rationem, qua cor mundetur, ut magnae rationis capiat et perferat lucem, et hoc utique rationis est (Aug. *Ep*. 120, 1)

faith should precede reason, by which the heart may be cleansed, so that it may grasp and tolerate the light of great reason, and this indeed is a matter of reason.

It takes a certain amount of attention and intelligence to see through this and catch the nature of the purpose clause in the sentence structure. We could also add here that the Romans love to use this relative pronoun to cover for all kinds of clauses which we shall see one at a time as we progress.

A little practice with the literature will help people identify the purpose clause rather quickly, as it is one of the most common and usual expressions in the subjunctive. If we go directly to our reading sheets we shall also find a favorite element of style. The Romans like to begin the sentence with *ut* or *ne* or *qui, quae, quod* followed by the subjunctive, and only thereafter they state the main verb on which the subjunctive depends, a result of the fluid free word order to which we have become accustomed.

ENCOUNTER 24 (59)

CONIUNCTIVI USUS. CAUSALES: CUM; QUOD, QUIA, QUONIAM; QUANDO; QUI, QUAE, QUOD; QUIPPE QUI, UTPOTE QUI

uses of the subjunctive. causal sentences:
cum; quod, quia, quoniam; quando;
qui, quae, quod; quippe qui, utpote qui

Introduction

As we slowly introduce the meaning of the subjunctive, we encounter today another big mass of sentences that use both indicative and subjunctive verbs to give the reason for something. These are represented in English sentences such as:

because . . .
since . . .
seeing that . . .
inasmuch as . . .
whereas . . . .

These are called causal sentences because they give a reason or cause. The verb in Latin is in the indicative or the subjunctive mode depending on the particle used to mean "because, since," etc., as follows now below.

1. *cum* (meaning "because, since") and a subjunctive verb

If we use the word *cum* (which is also spelled *quom* or *quum*—check your dictionary) to express the word "because, since," etc., then the Latin verb is expressed in any time of the subjunctive. This is what Latin literature gives us. The subjunctive verb will follow the sequence of tenses. Although *cum* is followed by the Latin subjunctive according to the sequence of tenses, when this sentence is expressed in most languages it will sound purely indicative, not subjunctive at all. Thus, we have *cum* followed by a subjunctive verb, which means, "because, since, seeing that, inasmuch as, whereas" followed by a verb that sounds indicative. Because the subjunctive verb in Latin follows the sequence of tenses, it contains a range of meanings, which are expressed in the vernacular indicative, for example:

Celebratur hodie cum scripserit laudabiliter.

Here the subjunctive *cum scripserit* refers to any action that occurs prior to *Celebratur hodie*, according to the sequence of tenses. Thus, we have the vernacular possibilities already given in encounter 48:

		(corresponding time)
Celebratur hodie	*cum scripserit laudabiliter*	
She is celebrated today,	because she *wrote* praiseworthily	(T.4bi)
...	because she *has written* praiseworthily	(T.4ai)
...	because she *was writing* praiseworthily	(T.2i)
...	because she *had written* praiseworthily	(T.5i)
...	because she *had been writing* praiseworthily	(T.5i)
...	because she *used to write* praiseworthily	(T.2i)
...	because she *always did write* praiseworthily	(T.2i).

Here is a different example:

		(corresponding time)
laetabamini	*cum carmina audirentur*	
You all were rejoicing,	because the songs were being heard	(T.2i)
...	because the songs used to be heard	(T.2i)
...	because the songs would be heard	(see the conditionals).

What is interesting is that although *cum* takes the subjunctive in Latin, the verb sounds indicative in the vernacular and has a full range of meanings according to our already familiar sequence of tenses. At the beginning, after their experience of the indicative mode of speaking, students will beg to know what *scripserit* and *audirentur* mean in the subjunctive, and just here they can mean seven and three different things respectively, all of which are contained in the one Latin verb. This is why at the outset of our Latin course we do not attach any definite meaning to any subjunctive verb until we learn its range of meaning naturally. It takes work and practice and familiarity with the literature to understand the full range of meaning of *scripserit* and *audirentur* here.

2. *quod, quia, quoniam*

We call the three particles *quod*, *quia*, *quoniam* the "triplets," because all three mean "because, since, seeing that, in as much as, whereas" and are treated similarly expressing a reason.

Latin literature tells us that all these three without distinction are followed by the indicative when the reason given is the idea of the writer or speaker or author or historian. Examples will follow in a moment.

According to Latin literature, the same three, *quod*, *quia*, *quoniam*, are also used with the subjunctive in a special circumstance, namely when the writer or speaker or author or historian is quoting, repeating someone else's idea, whether he or she agrees with the quoted person or not. This is called reported reason or partially oblique speech and comprises one-half of indirect discourse, which we shall see at the beginning of the Fourth Experience. This does not mean that the author is negating the reason given, but simply that the reason given is the idea of someone else. For example, in English we may say simply and concretely:

> They didn't come on time because the electricity had gone out at home
>
> *Non tempore advenerunt quod* (*quia*, *quoniam*) *domi erat electrica vis intermissa.*

The Latin here uses the indicative, because the author—perhaps an historian—wishes to describe the simple fact that the electricity went out as a reason why they did not come, and that is verifiable out there in reality.

If we wish to change the sentence to indicate reported speech, quoted reason, then in Latin we must change the verb *quod erat intermissa* to the subjunctive *quod esset intermissa*. The verb in English will still sound indicative, but we have to add something to the English to account for the Latin use of the subjunctive, that is, to indicate this is a quoted reason and the reason given is the idea of someone else, even if we do not know who the other person is. That is why we say, "... because, *allegedly*, *as they said*, *as people were saying*, *as we heard*, *as people were reporting*, *as was said*, *as you may think* ...." Each of these expressions indicates indirect reporting, which is the reason for the Latin subjunctive. So our sentence becomes, for example:

> *Non tempore advenerunt quod* (*quia*, *quoniam*) *domi esset vis electrica intermissa*
>
> They didn't come on time because, *allegedly*, the electricity had gone out at home
>
> They didn't come on time because, *as they said*, the electricity had gone out at home.

This phenomenon is very common and useful for understanding Latin literature. It is usually glossed over by readers, students, and teachers with some lame excuse. We can change the whole story simply by switching from the indicative to the subjunctive. Here are a few examples:

> *Imperator factus est quia* (*quod*, *quoniam*) *sapientissimus erat*
>
> He was made the commander-in-chief because he was very wise (and that is clear from history).

Here the indicative is used to indicate that this is the author's judgment, perhaps as historian or biographer. If we change the verb *erat* to the subjunctive *esset*, according to the sequence of tenses, then we change the meaning of the sentence:

Imperator factus est quia (quod, quoniam) sapientissimus esset

He was made the commander-in-chief because, *allegedly, as people were saying, as was said*, he was very wise.

The historian or biographer is not denying what people were saying, but shifts the authority of the reported speech from the author to someone else, even if their identity is not given or known.

This distinction is crucial in official documents. When an ambassador to the Vatican retires, a document may be sent in Latin to the respective head of state, in which the author would say, for example:

Laudamus vestrum aestimamusque legatum quia opus suum laudabiliter perfecit

We praise and appreciate your ambassador because he did his work well.

This sentence indicates that the author accepts the cold fact that the ambassador had done well. The meaning of the sentence changes dramatically, however, if the verb *perfecit* were put into the subjunctive, and the document were to say:

Laudamus vestrum aestimamusque legatum quia opus suum laudabiliter perfecerit

We praise and appreciate your ambassador because, *as the rumor was, as some people were reporting, as talk had it*, he did his work well.

This sentence is an insult, because it reports the opinion of others without making the opinion the author's own, which is a slap in the face, of course: something few ambassadors or heads of state would catch or suspect.

That is the story of the triplets *quod, quia, quoniam*. You can find examples all over the place in Latin literature, which often escape understanding and appreciation.

The exemplary Latin of Rome's first real analytic historian, Gaius Sallustius Crispus (86–c. 35 BCE), illustrates for us this subtlety of Latin. Sallustius says:

Falso queritur de natura sua genus humanum, quod imbecilla atque aevi brevis forte potius quam virtute regatur (Sall. *Iug.* I)

The human race falsely complains about its own nature, for the [alleged] reason that it, weak and of short duration, is ruled by chance rather than by valor.

The subjunctive verb *regatur* following *quod*, "because" or "for the reason that," means that Sallustius is quoting the human race and not giving his own particular opinion. He distances himself from the human race complaining by calling it *falso*, "falsely." Many people will miss this subtle distinction, which we could make more explicit by saying something like the following: "because, *as the human race says, allegedly.*"

Another text of Sallustius provides this example in which Catiline is speaking:

> *publicam miserorum causam pro mea consuetudine suscepi, non quia aes alienum meis nominibus ex possessionibus solvere non possem (et alienis nominibus liberalitas Orestillae suis filiaeque copiis persolveret); sed quod non dignos homines honore honestatos videbam meque falsa suspicione alienatum esse sentiebam.* (Sall. *B. Cat.* XXXV)
>
> I undertook the public case of miserable citizens according to my custom not because I was [as was being said] not able to pay the debt from my own stocks and bonds out of my possessions (and [allegedly] that the generosity of Orestilla was paying with outside investments out of her and her daughter's resources); but because I saw unworthy people ennobled with honor and I was feeling that I had been marginalized by a false suspicion.

If we wanted to justify the use of the subjunctive verb *quia ... possem*, we would say it is because the speaker, Catiline, is quoting someone else's opinion, not his own. We have accounted for the force of this subjunctive in the English rendering by adding [as was being said] in square brackets to indicate that while these exact words are not present, the force of these words is present in that subjunctive. Likewise, we can account for the subjunctive *quia ... persolveret*, in the same way as quoted reason rather than Catiline's own. Here too we have accounted for the force of this subjunctive by adding [allegedly] to the text. After reporting the opinion of the populace of Rome twice in the subjunctive, next Catiline gives his own opinion at the end of the sentence when he says *sed quod ... videbam ... –que ... sentiebam*, "I was noticing and I was feeling," both verbs in the indicative. The distinction here is so clear it is unbelievable that you find in one nice sentence the whole story.

Returning to the account by Sallustius of the war with Iugurtha, we find this example:

> *fuere qui exercitum ... mittundum censerent et quam primum Adherbali subveniundum; de Iugurtha interim uti consuleretur, quoniam legatis non paruisset* (Sall. *Iug.* XXV)
>
> there were people who were thinking the army had to be sent and help had to be brought as soon as possible to Adherbo; in the meanwhile that a consultation should be made about Iugurtha, because [as they were saying] he had not obeyed the ambassadors.

The explanation for the subjunctive in that last phrase, *quoniam non paruisset* is that this again is not an historical expression of Sallustius, but it is the idea of those people who thought the army had to be sent to Africa, for example members of the senate. To account for the force of this subjunctive in the English rendering, you would add something like the words in square brackets, "because [as they were saying] he had not obeyed the ambassadors." This occurrence could also be justified by modal attraction as we shall see in encounter 83, in which case it would express the opinion of Sallustius and the whole meaning changes to "because he had not obeyed the ambassadors."

The subtle distinction in the use of the indicative or subjunctive, however, is characteristic of classical Latin and was recovered in the high Renaissance, when they once again felt and maintained this difference. In those eras, the hearers understood the change that is definitely there. In other later Latin literature this subtlety is lost a bit.

3. *Quando, quandoquidem, siquidem*

Look in your dictionary to find three more words for "because, since." One of them is *quando*, which many people immediately take to mean "when." But your dictionary also makes prominent the meaning "because." A second word is *quandoquidem*, written as one word, which means "because" and not "when indeed." A third word is *siquidem;* besides meaning obviously "if, indeed," *siquidem* also means "because," in the dictionary. Both *quando* and *quandoquidem* are usually used with the indicative. They are also found with the subjunctive for other reasons. An example of *quandoquidem* with the indicative meaning "because" is given by Gaius Valerius Catullus in his *Carmen* 101, composed while at his brother's tomb in modern-day, northern Turkey:

quandoquidem fortuna mihi tete abstulit ipsum,
... in perpetuum, frater, aue atque uale (Cat. *Carm.* CI, 5)

because fortune has taken away you your very self from me,
... good-bye, brother, forever and take care.

For scholars or tourists, there is an inscription in the Vatican over the arch leading to the parking lot and Library; inscribed with letters about a foot tall, it begins:

QVANDOQVIDEM IN THEATRO VATICANO
PRAESTITE MARIA MATRE SAPIENTIAE
PIVS XI PONTIFEX MAXIMVS
DIGNAM STVDIORVM SEDEM CONSTITVIT
AD BIBLIOTHECAM AD TABVLARIVM
AD PONTIFICIVM SOPHORVM COLLEGIVM
HAC PATET ADITVS

Because the Supreme Pontiff Pius XI
instituted a worthy seat of studies
in the Vatican theater
—Mary the Mother of Wisdom being the protectoress—
by this road access lies open
to the library to the archive
to the pontifical college of the wise.

The inscription explains that the Pope wanted the Vatican Library to be open to scholars. Many people will take *Quandoquidem* here to mean, "when indeed," but it means, "because." Over-confident students tend to believe this only when they see it bold and clear in the dictionary. It is on the rare side in Latin literature, but it is there. You can see an image of this inscription on p. 411 of this volume.

4. *Qui, quae, quod*

The last way to compose causal clauses is with the relative pronoun. The gasping and moaning among students is already audible because of yet another use of the relative pronoun. We warned you how the Romans loved the relative pronoun.

We have already seen that *qui, quae, quod* followed by the indicative are used in straight discourse. We have seen the interrogative *quis, quis, quid* and also the relative *qui, quae, quod* used with the indicative to express a direct question. We have seen how *qui, quae, quod* followed by the subjunctive can cover for *ut is, ea, id* followed by the subjunctive to express purpose. Now *qui, quae, quod* followed by the subjunctive can cover for the causal clause *quia* or *quoniam is, ea, id* followed by the subjunctive and meaning "because he, she, it ...." Like all the other causal clauses, this one also sounds indicative in the vernacular. Take the example:

> *Laudavi eam quae ita cecinisset.*

If you take it as a simple relative sentence meaning, "I praised her who had sung so well," then there is no reason in your interpretation for the subjunctive *cecinisset*. The Latinist will recognize the subjunctive here and say that there is something more being said here than the simple direct statement. Here the relative clause *quae cecinisset* stands in for the causal sentence *quia* or *quoniam ea cecinerat*, and means:

> *Laudavi eam quae ita cecinisset*
> I praised her *inasmuch as she* had sung so well.

Here, the relative pronoun *quae* stands in for "inasmuch as, because, seeing that she." We warned people that there must be a reason for the subjunctive in these relative sentences.

This way of speaking is very nice and quite common. Cornelius Nepos (c. 100–c. 25 BCE) does this all the time in his lives of Greek leaders. For example, Nepos describes a Greek named Cimon who became very famous because he had conquered enemies. In a two-line sentence that illustrates all we have done in this Experience, he says:

> *multos locupletavit, complures pauperes mortuos, qui unde efferrentur non reliquissent, suo sumptu extulit* (Nep. *Vitae*, V, 4)

> he enriched many people, at his own expense, he brought out to burial very many dead poor people because they [who, *qui*] had not left something from which they might be buried.

Here the relative clause *qui non reliquissent*, "because who had not left," stands for the causal sentence *quia* or *quoniam ii non reliquerant*, "because they had not left." The *unde efferrentur*, "from which they might be buried," is a purpose clause where *unde* followed by the subjunctive stands for *ut eo*, "so that from there," as in, "so that from there they might be buried." Look how much is said and meant in five Latin words!

We now have three uses for the relative clause. We have seen *qui, quae, quod* followed by the indicative to express direct speech, or followed by the subjunctive to express either purpose or now reason. We are not done with the relative clause and will see more uses for it as the use of the subjunctive expands.

5. *Quippe qui, utpote qui*

Look in your dictionary once again for particles that emphasize this causal nature of the relative pronoun. One is *quippe*. Your dictionary tells you that *quippe qui, quae, quod* means "inasmuch as who," or more clearly, "since I; inasmuch as you; since he, she, it," etc. The Latin *quippe qui, quae, quod* is followed usually by the subjunctive, but in other languages it will sound indicative.

Another is *utpote*, which also introduces an explanation. Your dictionary tells you that *utpote qui, quae, quod* means "seeing that who; inasmuch as who; since who," or more clearly, "seeing that I; inasmuch as you; since he, she, it." The first example comes from Cicero who begins by quoting an opposing lawyer and then gives his own response:

> "*Convivia cum patre non inibat.*" *Quippe, qui ne in oppidum quidem nisi perraro veniret.... Nec mirum, qui neque in urbe viveret neque revocaturus esset* (Cic. *Rosc. Am.* XVIII, 52)
>
> "He was not accustomed to enter into banquets with his father." Certainly as someone who was coming only very rarely indeed into the village.... No wonder inasmuch as [he] who did not live in the city nor was about to recall [anyone to his house].

Here you see that *quippe, qui* means, "because as someone who" or simply "certainly as." The second *qui* also follows from the same *Quippe* at the beginning of the sentence, which together mean, "inasmuch as who." Here is a further example:

> *Celebramini hodie utpote quae docte sitis locutae*
>
> You women are celebrated today inasmuch as you spoke learnedly.

Summary

Latin literature gives us numerous ways to express the reason for something. The verb in Latin will be subjunctive or indicative, depending on the initial particle, but all of these are rendered in the vernacular in the indicative. The first causal clause begins with *cum* and is followed by the subjunctive according to the sequence of tenses and contains the full range of meaning already given twice above:

Celebrantur hodie cum efficaciter docuerint

They are celebrated today, because they effectively *taught*, *have taught* (etc.).

The three cousins *quod*, *quia*, *quoniam* are followed by the indicative to indicate the view of the author or speaker:

Celebratur hodie quod, quia, quoniam laudabiliter scripsit

He is celebrated today because he praiseworthily *wrote*.

The three—*quod*, *quia*, *quoniam*—are also followed by the subjunctive to indicate the view of others or reported reason:

Celebratur hodie quod, quia, quoniam bene scripserit

He is celebrated today because, *allegedly*, he wrote well.

Quando and *quandoquidem* are usually followed by the indicative meaning "because, since," not always "when" and not "when indeed," as our consideration of time clauses will reveal. They are followed by the subjunctive when reporting the reasons of others. Again the full range of meaning of the subjunctive according to the sequence of tenses as given above also applies here:

Celebratur hodie quando bene scripserit

He is celebrated today because, *as was said*, he wrote well.

The relative clauses *qui*, *quae*, *quod* ... followed by the subjunctive stand in for *quia* or *quoniam is*, *ea*, *id* ... followed by the subjunctive. Again, the full range of meaning of the subjunctive according to the sequence of tenses as given above also applies here:

Colitur hodie quae tam bene partes egerit

She is celebrated today inasmuch as she acted the parts so well.

Other particles accompany the relative pronoun, such as *quippe qui* and *utpote qui*, which mean "inasmuch as I, you, he, she, it":

Celebratur hodie quippe qui tam bene scribat

He is celebrated today inasmuch as he writes so well.

You see the variety and richness of these causal clauses, which open with "because, since." In Latin literature you will see all this, and it is quite satisfying when you know this and can manage it confidently and comfortably in concrete examples, teaching others or yourself.

ENCOUNTER 25 (60)

USUS CONIUNCTIVI: QUAESTIO INDIRECTA NON RELATIVA

the uses of the subjunctive: indirect question, not relative

Introduction

We have arrived at our third giant use of the subjunctive in Latin. We continue to present the most common uses, and this one occurs very often. In the first encounter of our First Experience, we began to explore the mode of speaking of direct address and question. In this encounter we wish to pick up once again the direct question and develop our understanding further by considering the indirect question.

The Romans, as do we in every vernacular, asked direct questions such as, "Who did this?" "When did you come?" "Which do they want?" "Why was this built?" "How shall we be coming?" "Whom have they chosen?" "Whose decision is it?" Each of these is introduced by an interrogatory participle such as "who, when, which, why, how, whom, whose," and there is nothing special about them.

Indirect questions

The Romans also attached these real questions as subordinate to another verb, in this case a verb of thinking or saying. As it turns out, these verbs of thinking or saying are about half of human language. There are perhaps 100 of them, such as "to say," "to report," "to proclaim," "to write," "to believe," "to judge," "to surmise," "to suspect," "to hear," "to guess," "to deny," "to think," and many others of this type; they are extremely common. These verbs are called *verba dicendi et cogitandi*, "verbs of speaking and thinking." In our system we call them "M & M" verbs because they are verbs of Mouth and Mind.

The phenomenon of indirect question was carefully observed for about 500 years and again after the Renaissance until today, but often less in very early Latin like Plautus or in late Latin authors of the fifth century and beyond. It was picked up again in the Renaissance. To write Latin well in our own day this usage is essential. Most students spot this phenomenon right away.

A direct question is made to depend on a verb of M & M, as in the example:

What did you write?
Tell me what you wrote.

Here the M & M verb and its object are "Tell me . . . ," producing the indirect question ". . . what you wrote." From this you can reconstruct the direct question: "What did you write?" Even the punctuation in the vernacular indicates that the first one is a direct question and the second one is indirect, depending on the imperative sentence "Tell me."

In Latin the indirect question is expressed in the subjunctive, according to the sequence of tenses. To take the above example, we say:

Quid scripsisti?
Dic mihi quid scripseris.

The verb of the direct question, *scripsisti* in T.4bi, is in the mode of direct question. When it is made to depend on the M & M verb *Dic mihi*, "Tell me . . . ," then it is put in T.3s *scripseris*, according to the sequence of tenses.

The Latin indirect question will sound indicative in English and other vernaculars 90% of the time. A clear sign of deficient Latin training is to make the indirect question sound subjunctive, as in "might, may, would, should"; all teachers know that this happens. Take the example:

Quis hoc reminiscitur?
Who remembers this?

Nescio quis hoc reminiscatur
I do not know who remembers this.

You can see the Latin change from the indicative for the direct question to the subjunctive mode for the indirect question, while in the vernacular you really cannot hear that subjunctive, because of the indirect nature of the reporting.

This time let us begin with a sentence with an indirect question and reconstruct the direct question:

Audivimus quid Confucius hac parabola doceat
We have heard what Confucius teaches by this parable

Quid docet Confucius hac parabola?
What does Confucius teach by this parable?

If the indirect question were to be expressed in the Latin indicative, it would be considered today erroneous or bad Latin.

We have seen the causal clauses and now indirect questions expressed in the subjunctive, but this whole mass of subjunctives in the Latin language will sound indicative in English. It also confirms what we said before, that most of the subjunctives in Latin are not going to sound subjunctive in the vernacular, but simply indicative. In Italian and German and even in older English, indirect questions used to appear in the subjunctive as in Latin, but that subjunctive is now fast disappearing in those languages.

Qua aedificatis pecunia pontem?
With what money are you all building the bridge?

Intelligunt qua aedificetis pecunia pontem
They understand with what money you all are building a bridge.

The indirect question "... with what money ..." depends on a direct statement here, and it is put into the subjunctive. Let's take the simple line, already used above, of a love verse of Catullus:

> *Odi et amo. Quare id faciam fortasse requiris* (Cat. *Carm.* LXXXV, 1)
> I love and hate. Perhaps you ask why I do this.

From the verse of Catullus we can reconstruct the direct question:

> *Quare id facio*?
> Why am I doing this?

You can flip *facio* over into the subjunctive *faciam* to make an indirect question, but you will not hear this subjunctive in the indicative vernacular, as in the following:

> *Quare id faciam nescio*
> I do not know why am I doing this.

The worst thing you can do with the subjunctive in this indirect question is to translate it as "Why I may be doing this ...." As a reminder let us take the example of a causal clause:

> *Cum essent haec manifesto verissima non ea defendebam*
> Because these things were evidently very true, I was not defending them.

The above example has the causal clause *Cum essent haec manifesto verissima*, "Because these things were evidently very true." The worst thing would be to translate it as, "since they may be ... ," because this would be a disaster and confirm little understanding of what the subjunctive is doing in its clause.

Let us conclude this presentation of the indirect question with Jerome who gives us these incredible statements about divine providence in his commentary on Habacuc:

> *Ceterum absurdum est ad hoc Dei deducere maiestatem, ut sciat per momenta singula quot nascantur culices, quotve moriantur, quae cimicum et pulicum et muscarum sit in terra multitudo, quanti pisces in aqua natent, et qui de minoribus maiorum praedae cedere debeant. Non simus tam fatui adulatores Dei, ut, dum potentiam eius etiam ad ima detrahimus, in nos ipsos iniuriosi simus, eamdem rationabilium quam irrationabilium providentiam esse dicentes* (Hier. *Hab.* 1, 1)
>
> Besides it is absurd to drag down the majesty of God to this point that he know from minute to minute how many gnats are being born or how many are dying, what the multitude on earth is of bugs and fleas and flies, what big fish swim in the water and which of the smaller ones ought to give in for prey of the bigger ones. Let us not be such foolish flatterers of God that, while we pull his power down even to the bottom, we are offensive toward our very selves saying that the same providence exists of rational as of irrational things.

ENCOUNTER 26 (61)

TEMPUS IN CONIUNCTIVO FUTURUM

futurity in the subjunctive

Introduction

Contrary to Greek, Latin does not have special forms of the subjunctive to express the simple future comparable to T.3i or the completed future comparable to T.6i. The Romans, however, had all the concepts of futurity in the subjunctive, but, because there are no special verbal forms, the question arises how they expressed futurity in the subjunctive. You can solve the whole question in three little steps: the nature of the subjunctive, adverbs, active futurity formula.

1. The subjunctive

Sometimes the idea of futurity in the subjunctive depends on the very nature of the subjunctive sentence. Here we recall specifically the purpose clause, also called a final clause, where the clause itself projects the whole idea of purpose or finality into the future, and that is enough to get the future idea. Take the first example on Track I and the second on Track II:

Ut tempore veniant hortor
I exhort them that they may come on time

Ut tempestive venirent sum hortatus
I exhorted them that they might come on time.

These examples apply to their coming on time on the day after and for the next 1,000 years and more. There is enough futurity in the purpose clause to carry the idea, and we need no further word to express futurity.

Not only is futurity contained in the T.1s and 2s, but we have also said previously that the concept of completed futurity is contained in T.3s and 4s, for example:

Quam pecuniam requisivissem, eos rogavi ut mihi concederent

I asked them that they contribute the money, which I had demanded

I asked them that they contribute the money, which I would (might, could, shall) have demanded.

The use of a calendar will immediately clarify the succession of times and events in any Latin sentence. Our home-style example above is also mapped out in the calendar below. Here the main verb *rogavi* is T.4bi and establishes the action let us say during the month of June. It sets the sentence on Track II. The purpose clause *ut concederent* is T.2s and describes futurity, an action yet to occur let us say the following December. The relative expression *quam requisivissem* is T.4s and could be placed in the anterior past as an equivalent to T.5i let us say in the previous February. But in this example *requisivissem* probably has completed futurity meaning already built into the type of clause and the use of the subjunctive, so it is set in the intervening September.

Kalendarium

February	June	September	December
	rogavi		*ut concederent*
		quam requisivissem	
quam requisivissem			

This means that I asked them in June that they give the money to me in December, money which I had asked for either in the previous February or that I would have asked for in the meantime in September. The problem is that both times for *requisivissem* are possible and the Latin doesn't help you because you could take it strictly as *requisivissem* coming before *rogavi* in February (in the traditional term as a pluperfect), or you can take it as coming before *concederent* in September (in the traditional term future perfect). This is an aspect that must be seen and analyzed by examples and which many students and teachers simply do not grasp because they falsely call T.4s the pluperfect subjunctive, even when it functions as the future completed.

If we want a simple and clear classical example of the ambiguity, this example can help us from the biographer Nepos speaking about the Athenian leader Alcibiades:

> *eum amicum sibi cupiebat adiungi neque dubitabat facile se consecuturum, si modo eius conveniundi habuisset potestatem*
>
> (Nep. *Vitae*, VII, 9)
>
> he desired him to be joined to himself as a friend nor was he doubting that he would attain this easily, if only he would have had the possibility of meeting him.

All the verbs here will shine out clearly in their meaning, if we ingeniously convert the whole sentence into direct speech. This would produce the following sentence, if Alcibiades were speaking in the present moment:

> *eum amicum mihi cupio adiungi neque dubito: facile ego consequar, si modo eius conveniundi habuero potestatem*
>
> I desire him to be joined to myself as a friend nor am I doubting that I shall attain this easily, if only I shall have had the possibility of meeting him.

We can see the corresponding verbs in the two forms of discourse. Above *consecuturum* corresponds to *consequar* in T.3i below. We changed *cupiebat* and *dubitabat* above to *cupio* and *dubito* in T.1i so that we can hear Alcibiades speaking in the present moment for our ease in understanding this sentence. The real revelation here is that above *habuisset* expresses completed futurity, which is sucked into the subjunctive on Track II because of its involvement in the infinitive complex or indirect statement, and so corresponds to *consequar* in T.3i also expressing futurity.

Kalendarium

May	August	October
cupiebat		
dubitabat	*habuisset*	*consecuturum*

We can also map the sentence in direct discourse:

May	August	October
cupio		
dubito:	*habuero*	*consequar*

2. Adverbs

If the futurity of the subjunctive clause is not clear because of the content of the sentence, if for example the subjunctive clause is an indirect question, a result clause, a temporal clause, then the addition of an adverb like "then, soon, next year, in the future" can help to express futurity. Thus, an adverb of futurity, such as *mox*, *brevi*, *mature*, "soon," with a simple subjunctive is enough to express futurity. Still, the Romans felt the absence of a form expressing the future subjunctive.

Turning to a good dictionary like Lewis and Short, the teacher can find numerous examples under an entry such as *mox*. Just reading down the examples, and then turning to the books in a good library, the teacher can teach directly from the dictionary and original sources and teach the student to rely upon the dictionary as well. We find this example by Cicero:

Exspecto quam mox Chaerea hac oratione utatur

(Cic. *Rosc. Com.* I)

I am waiting how soon Chaerea is using this discourse
I am waiting how soon Chaerea may use this discourse
I am waiting how soon Chaerea will use this discourse.

An indirect question is expressed in the indicative in English, unless there is an underlying reason for the subjunctive as in the second English rendering above. Because of the natural time frame of the T.1s, with the adverb *mox*, "soon," you can easily render *utatur*, in T.1s, into English as "will use," in T.3i.

All of these same possibilities are seen in the following examples. This one comes from Plautus's work *Menaechmi*, the twin brothers:

Ma. prouisam quam mox uir meus redeat domum sed eccum uideo

(Plaut. *Men.* 704–705)

MATRONA: I shall look out how soon my husband is returning home, but, behold him, I see

MATRONA: I shall look out how soon my husband may return home, but, behold him, I see

MATRONA: I shall look out how soon my husband will return home, but, behold him, I see.

You can see here that *redeat* in T.1s can easily be rendered in English as "he will return" in T.3i.

This example comes from Livy:

Exspectabant quam mox consulibus creandis comitia edicerentur
(Liv. III, 37)

They were waiting how soon election assemblies would be announced for appointing consuls

They were waiting how soon election assemblies might be announced for appointing consuls.

You can see here that *edicerentur* in T.2s can easily be rendered in English as an expression of futurity in regard to a moment in the past. You can do the same thing with the other adverbs in the dictionary, and let a good dictionary be your guide.

3. Futurity formula

In the absence of these two above possibilities, the Romans did have a workable but not beloved solution for when it is absolutely necessary that futurity be expressed. We have called this the "futurity formula," but it applies only to the active, and not to the passive. Traditionally this is called the "future active periphrastic," if anyone understands what that means; still it will not be a helpful term for students to gain direct access to the meaning of the language. As explained, the futurity formula is composed of two parts. The first part is the futurity participle ending in *–urus, a, um*, as in *venturus, a, um; facturus, a, um; nasciturus, a, um*. The second part is any subjunctive form of the verb "esse," such as, *sit* … , *essent* … , *fuerim* … , *fuisses* …. The futurity formula is on the rare side, but acceptable or necessary in certain indirect questions. Let us start with a simple indirect question:

Non constabat quando veniret

It was not clear when she used to come (to the office every day)
It was not clear when she would come (to the office).

Here T.2s *veniret* has no perceptible indication of futurity because of the nature of the indirect question. In that case to express futurity the Latin author uses most necessarily the futurity formula:

Non constabat quando ventura esset

It was not clear when she was about to come (to the office)
It was not clear when she would be coming (to the office).

Without the futurity formula, the future time of the indirect question is totally guesswork, dreaming, erring.

We shall remind people that because of the natural meaning of the participle, the futurity formula—*venturus sit*—is active. Because there is no corresponding form in the passive, the Romans had to rework the sentence. For example, we cannot say in Latin:

> We do not know how this citadel will be built

so we have to say something like:

> *Quomodo hanc sint aedificaturi arcem nescimus*
>
> We do not know how they will be building this citadel.

The Romans do not like to use the futurity formula, except when they have to fall back on it as a matter of necessity. Because Latin does not have subjunctive forms specifically dedicated to express futurity, Latin has a severe limitation in comparison to Greek, which does in fact have these forms.

Thus, we have 3 steps to make futurity and completed futurity clear in the subjunctive. We have the nature of the subjunctive itself, specific adverbs of time, and the futurity formula in the active. The literature is waiting to confirm and inculcate this abundantly.

ENCOUNTER 27 (62)

CONSECUTIO MODO IN CONIUNCTIVO ALIA POST TEMPORA

sequence in the subjunctive mode after other verb times

Introduction

When we first presented the sequence of tenses, we limited our attention to the case where a subjunctive depends on an indicative. If we remember what we learned then, we will have no difficulty with a refinement of the sequence of tenses we wish to learn now.

1. Sequence of tenses of a subjunctive depending on a subjunctive

Let us begin with an example of a subjunctive depending on a subjunctive:

> *Accidebat ut rogaremus quid iam fecissetis et ut hoc faceretis nunc*
>
> It was the case that we asked what you all had already done and that you all now do this.

The sequence of tenses that you already learned applies here. First, the main verb *accidebat* is T.2i, which places the sequence on Track II, resulting in either T.2s or 4s; here T.2s *rogaremus* is contemporaneous. The next sequence is established by that T.2s *rogaremus*, which places the subsequent sequence on Track II, which produces either T.2s or 4s; here T.4s *fecissetis* is antecedent and T.2s *faceretis* extends into the future.

If we change the verb *accidebat* to T.4ai or T.1i, then the following sentence results:

> *Accidit ut rogemus quid iam feceritis et ut hoc faciatis nunc*
>
> It happens (has happened) that we ask what you all already did and that you all do this now
>
> It happens (has happened) that we ask what you all have already done and that you all do this now.

Here the main verb *accidit* is T.1i or T.4ai, which places the sequence on Track I, resulting in either T.1s or 3s; here T.1s *rogemus* is contemporaneous. The next sequence is established by that T.1s *rogemus*, which keeps the subsequent sequence on Track I, which produces either T.1s or 3s; here T.3s *feceritis* is antecedent, and T.1s *faciatis* extends into the future. It is very simple; each verb establishes the sequence of tenses for the verbs depending on it. It is important to notice that the *et* joins the two complements of *rogemus*, that is the indirect question *quid iam feceritis* and the expression of purpose *ut hoc faciatis nunc*.

Just as in the indicative, where the same form is used for both T.4ai establishing Track I and T.4bi establishing Track II, so likewise in the subjunctive T.3s can sound either like T.4ai, as in "he has done this; he has been doing this," or T.4bi, as in "he did this; he did do this." Consequently, T.3s can establish a following sentence on Track I or II. The first of these alternatives, "he has done this; he has been doing this," establishes Track I; and the second alternative, "he did this; he did do this," establishes Track II. This is rare, but occurs often enough in the historians. Let's take the example:

> *Miror cur Milvauchiam venerit ut Latine disceret*
> I am wondering why he came to Milwaukee that he might learn Latin.

Here you start out with T.1i *miror* and end with T.2s, which shouldn't be the case following the two-Track system. Here *miror* puts the sentence on Track I and produces T.3s *venerit*, which here has the force of T.4bi "he came," which puts the rest of the sentence on Track II and produces T.2s *disceret*. Cicero does this all the time and people must understand this.

If a T.4s produces another subjunctive, then the sequence is on Track II, as in:

> *Nescivimus quando Romam venisset ut illa Latinae studeret linguae*
> We did not know when she had come to Rome in order that she might study Latin.

You can see here that T.4s *venissent* establishes Track II and produces T.2s *studeret*, which is incomplete, future.

2. Sequence of tenses of a subjunctive depending on a participle

When a subjunctive depends on a contemporaneous participle, then the subjunctive takes its Track I or II from the main verb; namely, the contemporaneous participle transmits the time of the main verb. That is why it is contemporaneous. The subjunctive goes through that verbal participle and gets its time according to the Track I or II established by the main verb.

> *Cursantes nostrates ut victores demum evadant laetus hinc conspicor*
> From here I, a happy one, catch sight of our people running so that finally they may turn out to be champions

> *Cursantes nostrates ut victores demum evaderent laetus illinc conspicabar*
> From there I, a happy one, was watching our people running so that finally they might turn out to be champions.

You can see the purpose clause depending on the contemporaneous participle *cursantes* in both examples above, giving the intention of the athletes in training. The main verb changed from *conspicor* in T.1i to *conspicabar* in T.2i, with a corresponding change from Track I to Track II, which is transmitted through the participle and ending up with a different sequence in the subjunctive, from *evadant* in T.1s to *evaderent* in T.2s.

If the participle on which the subjunctive depends is the antecedent participle, then most of the time it is taken as producing Track II, although it can also produce Track I, if it means "having been done" or "having done." This is because the antecedent participle substitutes for verbs that otherwise would be T.4ai, 4bi, or even T.2i, T.5i, or T.6i.

> *Proximum laetantur cives circummunitum carcerem ne exlegum quis enatet*
>
> The citizens are happy that the nearby prison has been reinforced lest anyone of the outlaws escape
>
> *Proximum laetantur cives circummunitum carcerem ne exlegum quis enataret*
>
> The citizens are happy that the nearby prison had been reinforced lest anyone of the outlaws might escape.

Although the main verb is the same, the participle changes in meaning from "having been reinforced," the equivalent of T.4ai continuing Track I, to "had been reinforced," the equivalent of T.4bi or T.5i, thus shifting the sentence to Track II. Here it is clear that the Latin subjunctive verb depends on the time of the participle, not on the same main verb, which is the only way to account for the change in the sequence of tenses in the subjunctive verb.

If a subjunctive depends on the futurity participle ending in, *–urus, a, um*, then again the main verb will establish the Track I or II that continues through the futurity participle to the subjunctive. So, as with the contemporaneous participle, the subjunctive will take its time from the main verb.

> *Suffragaturis sibi suadebat senator honestatem maximam unde magis suffragia ipsa valerent*
>
> The senator was proposing to people about to vote for him the greatest possible uprightness so that from there the votes themselves might have more efficacy
>
> *Suffragaturis sibi suadet senator honestatem maximam unde magis suffragia ipsa valeant*
>
> The senator is proposing to people about to vote for him the greatest possible uprightness whence the votes themselves may be more efficacious.

Here the participle *suffragaturis* remains, but the whole sentence switches from the progressive past *suadebat*, in T.2i establishing Track II, to the present *suadet*, in T.1i establishing Track I, and therefore the different time is transmitted to the end of the sentence.

The participle of passive necessity demands a sequence depending on the main verb because necessity can be any time you want.

> *Latrunculis parcendum censebamus inutiles carceres ne ultra modum confercirentur*
>
> We were thinking that small thieves had to be spared lest useless prisons might be crammed beyond reason

> *Latrunculis parcendum censemus inutiles carceres ne ultra modum confercientur*
>
> We are thinking that small thieves must be spared lest useless prisons be crammed beyond reason.

The teacher can supply here that, *parco, parcere* is one of the 65, therefore, *latrunculis* remains in the form to-for-from, and *latrunculis parcendum* means, "sparing must be made to the petty thieves." These examples above of ours are given to point out how the whole sentence is affected or not by the participle having been used: contemporaneous-not; futurity-not; antecedent-yes; necessity-not.

That is how the sequence of tenses works when a subjunctive depends on another subjunctive or on a participle. It is very simple once you know the basic system that we learned with Tracks I and II a long time ago. We once said that the sequence of tenses can be placed on our thumbnails, which is true, because these refinements are really no problem. We shall leave the sequence of tenses arising from the infinitives to a brief mention in one or two lines when we get to the infinitives.

ENCOUNTER 28 (63)

REFLEXIVUM PRONOMEN IN CONIUNCTIVO: AMBIGUITATES

the reflexive pronoun in the subjunctive: uncertainties

Introduction

When dealing with the reflexive pronoun and possessive adjective, we already mentioned that by definition it refers back to the subject. Although the rule is clear, Latin literature tells us that it may sometimes be difficult to decide to what subject exactly the reflexive refers. The reflexive pronoun or adjective normally refers to the grammatical subject of its own clause. We have already warned people, however, that sometimes it refers to the logical subject of the sentence and sometimes in a complex construction it refers even more broadly to the subject of the whole story, outside of its own clause.

1. Reflexive pronoun and adjective in the subjunctive

In encounter 31 of the First Experience we pointed out that there are three kinds of reflexives: direct and indirect and logical. The examples we gave there concerned simple indicative sentences. Here we wish to apply this distinction more specifically to reflexive pronouns or adjectives that are hidden in a subordinate subjunctive or even indicative clause.

Again, a direct reflexive refers to the subject of its own clause, whether its clause is in the indicative or in the subjunctive. Not grammar books, but Latin literature shows us that, when the reflexive is buried in a subordinate subjunctive or even indicative clause dependent on the main clause of the sentence, many times the reflexive in that dependent clause logically reflects or refers to the subject of the principal main clause. In this case, it is called an indirect reflexive. Here the reflexive goes through the subject of its own clause to the subject of the main sentence, which is controlling the whole sentence or the whole idea, and logically you are forced to use a reflexive pronoun or adjective because the idea refers to the main controlling subject, even though this is not the grammatical subject of the dependent clause in which the reflexive is found.

This idea of an indirect use of the reflexive may seem to contradict our definition, but, if you present the reflexive as referring to a subject, then the next question is to which subject: to the subject of its own clause or to the subject of the main sentence which contains the dependent clause in which the reflexive occurs. The idea here is not the physical but the logical subject of the sentence. Presented in this way, then, the indirect use of the reflexive pronoun or adjective does not appear as much of an exception or an extraordinary thing.

2. Uncertainties

The problem, however, is the hopeless uncertainty that comes about when you try to decide to which subject a reflexive refers. Latin literature gives us complex sentences in which you will never know what the author is talking about. A perfect example can be:

> *Caesar militem iussit ut se interficeret et abiceret gladium suum*
> Caesar ordered the soldier that he might kill him and throw away his sword.

Even in English this sentence is doubtful, because you do not know who is being killed and whose sword it is. According to the definition of the reflexive, *se* and *suum* should refer to the soldier and the soldier's sword as direct reflexives. But, in as much as Caesar is giving the command and controlling the whole sentence—as well as the world!—*se* and *suum* may refer all the way back to the main subject, Caesar, as indirect reflexives.

This occurs very often and reminds us again that in Latin we have to think continuously, use our head, and follow what works in the sentence, because there is no other way to resolve this ambiguity.

We could change the sentence to say, for example:

> *Militem rogavi ut abiceret gladium suum*
> I asked the soldier that he might throw away his sword.

Here it is clear that the *suum* refers to the soldier and not to "me" and "my sword." You could say, "my sword," but that would be *gladium meum*.

Let us say:

> *Milites Caesarem obsecravere sibi ut parceret.*

If you notice the word order here where *sibi* depends on *parceret*, but is eloquently placed geographically in the sentence out in front of the *ut*, then you can see that this sentence can mean either of the following:

> The soldiers begged Caesar that he spare them
> The soldiers begged Caesar that he spare himself [and take the day off].

Turning to more pleasant thoughts, we propose this example:

> *Imperat Remus ut suum canem pascat miles*
> Remus gives command that the soldier feed his dog.

Whose dog is it here? If it is the soldier's dog, then *suus* refers directly to the subject of the verb *pascat*, that is to the soldier. But Latin literature—not some grammarians—also tells us that *suus* can refer back to the main subject controlling the whole sentence and thus to Remus. In this case, the soldier feeds the dog of Remus.

In these particular sentences there is no way around the ambiguity. You just have to know that this suspense exists between the direct and indirect reflexive and work out in your head what the story is, what the thought is, what is best. That is the only way you can attempt to resolve the ambiguity.

In an involved sentence the use of a reflexive in a subordinate statement would theoretically speaking refer to the reporting or writing or announcing verb producing the indirect discourse, but many times the reflexive refers to something within its own sentence. Here is an example from *Germania* written by Gaius Publius Cornelius Tacitus (c. 55–c. 119 CE), in which Tacitus says:

> *Ipse eorum opinionibus accedo qui Germaniae populos nullis aliis aliarum nationum conubiis infectos propriam et sinceram et tantum sui similem gentem extitisse arbitrantur* (Tac. *Germ.* 4)
>
> I myself come close to the opinions of those who believe that the peoples of Germany tainted by no other marriages of other nations have stood out both as their own untainted people and only like itself.

Theoretically speaking the *sui* should refer to the subject of *qui arbitrantur* which produces the indirect statement, namely to the people who think in this way. Here, rather, Tacitus says that the Germans are only like themselves. The reflexive *sui similem* refers to the nearest word, *gentem*.

Another example is given in the same work by Tacitus and illustrates the natural ambiguity:

> *magnaque et comitum aemulatio quibus primus apud principem suum locus* (Tac. *Germ.* 13)
>
> and [there is] a great rivalry even of the counts for whom [there is] the first place in the sight of their leader.

Logically the *principem suum* refers to the *comitum*, which is not the subject of any sentence.

We have hinted at this phenomenon before, so there is nothing new here. Only the application is more specific to reflexive pronouns or adjectives that are hidden in a subordinate subjunctive or even indicative clause that reflects or refers to the subject of the main clause, which controls the whole sentence. When the reflexive refers to a subject outside of its own clause, it is acting as an indirect reflexive.

To repeat the reflexive teaching again in such a specific way in this encounter with examples by or from the teacher is most helpful to the students; otherwise, the whole idea becomes hazy, and people forget how it works unless they are reminded repeatedly.

ENCOUNTER 29 (64)

CONIUNCTIVI USUS: CONCESSIVAE SENTENTIAE CUM PARTICULIS

uses of the subjunctive: concessive sentences with their particles

Introduction

Concessive sentences, of course, grant an exception or make a concession. They are introduced in English by the words:

although ...
even though ...
even if ...
granted that ...
albeit ....

The last one, "albeit," is older English and understood by fewer people today.

Concessive sentences and their particles

In Latin there are many words that express this idea of "although" or "even if." We shall make a list of eight of them and notice that some take the indicative, others the subjunctive, others either one. The list is easy to give, but there will be ambiguities here too.

The first is *quamquam*, "although," which is usually followed by the indicative in the grammar book, but, as your dictionary will show you, sometimes one will see the subjunctive used in concrete Latin literature.

The second is *quamvis*, "however much you wish," which is usually followed by the subjunctive. Very close to this is a third, *quantumvis*, "no matter how much you want," "even though," which is followed by the subjunctive.

The fourth is *cum* followed by the subjunctive. We have already seen that *cum* with the subjunctive can mean "because," and now it means "although," which is more or less the opposite in meaning. The difficulty is to figure out logically which meaning fits the sentence, and many times it is impossible to decide.

The fifth is *licet*, followed by the subjunctive. In other cases *licet* is a verb meaning "it is allowed," but as a concessive conjunction it means "granted that," namely "although," and even as a verb it now acts as such a connective particle.

The sixth is *ut* followed by the subjunctive. Again, the particle *ut* has about a hundred meanings, and in this case it means "although." This use is rather rare, but can be found in the literature. Publius Ovidius Naso (43 BCE–17 CE) gives us this example. Ovid says:

ut desint vires, tamen est laudanda voluntas (Ov. *Pont.* III, 4, 79)
although the powers be lacking, still good will has to be praised.

Ovid begins his sentence with this concessive clause, and the main verb *est* comes later on.

The seventh are again three conditional kinfolk taken together: *etsi*, *tametsi*, and *etiamsi*, each usually written as one word. They all mean "even if" or "even though." Because each one contains the ending –*si*, their sentences will follow the rules for conditional sentences, to be seen later. Most of the time they are followed by the indicative, but sometimes by the subjunctive, as happens in all conditionals.

The eighth and last one is again no consolation. The Romans use the relative pronoun *qui, quae, quod* followed by the subjunctive to mean "although." In this case, the relative pronoun stands in for, let's say, *cum ego, tu, is, ea, id* and means "although I, you, he, she, it," followed by the subjunctive. For example:

Magni discipulam eam existimo quae talia edat

Here the *quae* covers for *cum ea* and means:

I highly regard the student, although she publishes such things.

Be careful! We have already seen that, when the relative pronoun is followed by the subjunctive, and there is no other reason for the subjunctive, then it could substitute for a purpose clause. In that case, returning to the above sentence, we see that *quae* could stand for *ut ea*, meaning "in order that she" followed by the subjunctive, meaning therefore:

I highly esteem the student so that she may publish such things.

We have also seen that a relative clause could substitute for a causal clause, and *quae* could stand for *quod ea*, meaning, "because she," which in the vernacular sounds indicative, as in:

I highly esteem the student, because she publishes such things.

Or now it could substitute for a concessive clause and stand in for *cum ego, tu, is, ea, id*, meaning, "although I, you, he, she, it," followed by the indicative. This last use is on the rare side, but it does exist.

By the way, in the above example, the adjective *magni* may connect with the verb, *existimo*, which takes the form of-possession to express value, meaning, "I highly regard," or in the extreme it may connect with *discipulam*, meaning "[the student] of a great man." The reader may judge which of the two is more reasonable here.

ENCOUNTER 30 (65)

USUS CONIUNCTIVI. TEMPORALES: POSTQUAM, UT, DONEC, PRIUSQUAM, ANTEQUAM ANTE ... QUAM, PRIUS ... QUAM, POST ... QUAM

uses of the subjunctive. temporal clauses: after, when, until, before

Introduction

Another big area of subjunctive and indicative uses is taken up by temporal clauses beginning with words such as:

before ...
when ...
while ...
after ....

Again the use of the subjunctive or indicative depends very much on the introductory particle we use, as the literature shows us.

1. After: *postquam, post ... quam*

We start out with the expression of "after." The conjunction which the Romans use is *postquam*. Sometimes it is separated as *post ... quam* .... The *postquam* is usually followed by T.4bi, even though in English we would use T.5i, for example:

Postquam hoc fecerunt, nuntium miserunt
After they had done this, they sent the message.

You can see that *postquam* goes with the dependent sentence *hoc fecerunt*, which depends on the main verb *miserunt*, "they sent [the message]." You also see that *fecerunt* in T.4bi is rendered into good English as T.5i, "they had done." Note carefully that *postquam* means "after," but is placed with the earlier action. We do this in the English rendering above when we place the word "after" with the earlier action. First they had done this, and next they sent the message, or "after they had done this, they sent the message." This is why Gildersleeve and Lodge begin their description of antecedent action with a presentation of *postquam* (nº 561).

Another sentence will reinforce our understanding:

Postquam sunt libri diligenter conscripti, victoriam auctores reportaverunt magnam
After the books had been written carefully, the authors claimed a great victory.

Likewise, *postquam* goes with the dependent sentence *sunt libri diligenter conscripti*, which depends on the main verb *reportaverunt*, "they claimed." Again, *postquam* means "after," but it is put with the prior action of the two both in Latin and in English. First the books were written carefully, and next the authors claimed a great victory.

When the two parts are separated, the *quam* ... remains stable with the dependent sentence and thus with the earlier action, whereas and the *post* is placed in another part of the sentence. This may cause problems in logical understanding, so let us begin with *postquam* as one word:

> *Cecinerunt laeti postquam nuntium exceperunt*
> After they had received the news, the happy ones sang.

Here the *postquam* means "after" and goes with the earlier action. When we separate the two parts of *postquam*, however, the *quam* stays with the dependent sentence describing the earlier action and the *post* is placed somewhere else, as in:

> *Post cecinerunt laeti quam nuntium exceperunt.*

Everyone will be tempted to think this says: "After the happy ones sang, they received the news," which is wrong. They will reason that here *post* means "after." Rather, the one word *postquam* means "after," but, when its two parts are separated, we can account for their separate meanings by saying, *post* ... *quam* ... "later ... than ..." or "afterwards ... than ..." or even "subsequently ... than ...." You can also mentally bring the *post* back to the immovable *quam* and say ... *postquam* ... , "... after ...." Note that the *quam* does not move to join the *post*. Thus, we can say in sometimes barely admissible English:

> *Post cecinerunt laeti quam nuntium exceperunt*
>
> Afterwards (*post*) the happy ones sang, than (*quam*) they had received the news
>
> Later (*post*) the happy ones sang, than (*quam*) they had received the news
>
> The happy ones sang later than (*postquam*) they had received the news
>
> After (*postquam*) they had received the news, the happy ones sang.

Here you see that *postquam* means "after" and goes with the earlier action. You also see that *quam* stays with the earlier action when the *post* is placed elsewhere in the sentence with the meaning "afterwards" or "later." The use of T.5i in the English verb "they had received" also confirms the sequence of events.

We can summarize this by saying that *postquam* means "after" but goes with the earlier action, as in English. When the words are separated the *quam* stays with the earlier action and means "than," whereas the *post* goes with the subsequent action and means "afterwards" or "later," but not simply "after." If you understand this, then you can remember this super-logical mental process by this phrase: *post* moves to the *quam*, not *quam* to the *post*.

Here are two more examples:

> *Post auctores victoriam reportaverunt magnam quam sunt libri diligenter conscripti*
>
> Afterwards the authors celebrated a great victory, than the books had been carefully written
>
> The authors celebrated a great victory later than (*postquam*) the books had been carefully written
>
> After the books had been written carefully, the authors celebrated a great victory.

The Latin sentence looks as if the authors' victory was celebrated before they had written their books. But when the dependent sentence beginning with *quam* is expressed in good English, the T.4bi *sunt conscripti* is given in T.5i "had been written," something which helps you to see and understand what is going on.

Take another example:

> *Post profecti sunt quam cenaverunt*
> Afterwards they took off, than they had eaten.

Here, you can see that *post* means "afterwards" or "later" and goes with the latter of two actions, and that *quam* means "than" and goes with the earlier action used as the point of comparison. If you follow the rule and move the *post* so that it joins the stable *quam*, then you have "they took off later than (*postquam*) they ate," and then you might say this more smoothly in a couple of ways:

> They took off later than they had eaten
> They took off after they had eaten
> After they had eaten, they left.

2. While, as long as, until: *dum, donec, quoad*

To express time "while" or "as long as [something is happening]" or "until," Latin literature gives us three particles: *dum*, *donec*, and *quoad*. With these meanings, these particles are usually used with the indicative of any time you want, such as:

> While they were singing, we were writing letters.

This is expressed with *dum*, *donec*, or *quoad*, with the indicative:

> *dum cantabant, epistolas scribebamus.*

2.1 *Vivid present*

One phenomenon to note is that Latin literature gives us *dum* with T.1i, even when its meaning is clearly past. This is done to make a past event very vivid in the present. In English we would set the action at the appropriate time in the past, for example:

While these things were being done, Caesar crossed the Rhine River.

Here the English uses T.2i and 4bi respectively to describe actions in the past. These are brought into a vivid present by using T.1i with *dum*, as in:

Dum haec fiunt, Caesar fluvium transgressus est Rhenum

which literally means:

While these things are being done (in your sight), Caesar crossed the Rhine River.

This use of T.1i, when you would expect a past tense, occurs especially with the particle *dum*, "while, as long as."

2.2 *Until: expectation, suspense, uncertainty*

In Latin literature the particles *dum*, *donec* and *quoad* meaning "until" are used at times with the indicative and at times with the subjunctive, according to the sequence of tenses. The theory is that when simple time—clock-consultation—is involved, you use the indicative, but when expectation, suspense, or uncertainty is involved, then the subjunctive. While this is the theory, some examples are very hard to differentiate or discern, because the reality or the expectation is dubious, for example:

Custos expectabat donec tintinnabulum sonuit
The guard was waiting until the bell rang.

Here *donec* is used with the indicative *sonuit* to indicate simply the time at which the guard stopped waiting. But if I say:

Custos expectabat donec substitutus veniret
The guard was waiting until a substitute would come

then in this case you would probably use the subjunctive *veniret*, because the idea does not refer to a moment in time but to the expectation involved and perhaps the suspense in waiting until a substitute might or might not come. In many examples this distinction is hard to see.

3. Before: *antequam, ante . . . quam . . . ; priusquam, prius . . . quam . . .*

In your dictionary the expressions meaning "before" can be written as one word, *priusquam* and *antequam*, or as two words, *ante . . . quam* and *prius . . . quam*, each going with a different part of the sentence, just as we already saw with *post . . . quam . . . .* These can be followed by any combination of times you want.

3.1 *prius . . . quam; ante . . . quam . . .*

The same rule and super-logical operation we observed for *post . . . quam . . .* is also observed here: As an example take:

Responderint discipuli antequam interrogabo
The students will have responded, before I shall be asking.

You can see that *antequam* goes with the subordinate verb *interrogabo* in T.3i, which depends on the main verb *responderint*, "[the students] will have responded," in T.6i. Note carefully that *antequam* means "before," but it is placed with the later action. This may seem counterintuitive, but we do this in English as well, as in the rendering above when we place the word "before" with the later action. First the students will have responded, and next I shall be asking, or "Before I shall be asking, the students will have responded." This is why Gildersleeve and Lodge begin their description of subsequent action with a presentation of *priusquam* and *antequam* (nº 574).

We have seen that *antequam* means "before" and goes with the later action. When the two parts are separated, the *quam* … remains stable with the dependent sentence and thus with the later action, whereas the *ante* or the *prius* is placed in another part of the sentence, as in:

Ante responderint discipuli quam interrogabo.

It is tempting to think that this means, "Before the students will have responded, I shall be asking," but that is wrong. People will pounce on the word *ante* here and think it means "before." Rather, the one word *antequam* or *priusquam* means "before," but, when their two parts are separated, we can account for their separate meanings by saying, *ante* … *quam* … or *prius* … *quam* … meaning "sooner … than …" or "previously … than … " You can also mentally bring the two parts back together by moving *ante* and *prius* to join the immutable *quam*, to say "… before … ." Note that the *quam* does not move to join the *ante* or *prius*. Thus, we can say in somewhat admissible English:

Ante responderint discipuli quam interrogabo

Sooner (*ante*) the students will have answered than (*quam*) I shall be asking

The students will have answered sooner than (*antequam*) I shall be asking

Previously (*ante*) the students will have answered, than (*quam*) I shall be asking

The students will have answered before (*antequam*) I shall be asking.

You can see that *antequam* means "before" and goes with the later action. You can also see that *quam* stays with the later action when the *ante* is placed elsewhere in the sentence with the meaning "sooner" or "previously," but here not meaning "before."

Take the example:

Prius cenaverunt quam profecti sunt
Previously they ate, than they took off.

Here, you can see that *prius* means "previously" or "sooner," and goes with the earlier of the two actions *cenaverunt* in T.4bi, and *quam* means "than" and goes with the later action used as the point of comparison, *profecti sunt*, also in T.4bi. We might say this more smoothly in several ways:

They ate sooner than (*antequam*) they took off
Before they left, they ate
They ate before they left.

When the sentence is long, sometimes people do not see the connection between the *post* or *ante* or *prius* and the *quam*, and this causes terrible confusion, if you pounce on the word and say that *ante* means "before" rather than seeing its connection with *quam* and their meaning "later .... than ..." or if you pounce on the word *post* in one part of the sentence and say that it means "after" without seeing its connection to *quam* in another part of the sentence and their meaning "sooner ... than ...." It is helpful for students to see this phenomenon in the dictionary with examples from the literature, and then they will understand.

3.2 *Used with the indicative*

The times of the indicative are used with the expressions *antequam* and *priusquam* to indicate the simple fact that one event occurred before another, as the several examples above and the following example all indicate a clock-time sequence:

Hora septima matutina vocavit priusquam potui barbam abradere
He called at 7:00 A.M., before I could finish shaving.

Here we see *priusquam* followed by the indicative *potui* in T.4bi to indicate the factual occurrence of one action, here "calling," before the other, "I could finish shaving."

3.3 *Before: prohibition, uncertainty, impossibility*

Let us return to our simple example to see the fact that one event happened before the other, which is expressed using the indicative, as here where both verbs are in T.1i:

Antequam interrogo respondent discipuli
Ante respondent discipuli quam interrogo

Before I ask, the students in fact answer

But now the times of the subjunctive are used almost as prohibition or uncertainty or impossibility. That is the theory given in manuals concerning the distinction between the indicative and the subjunctive with these two expressions, a theory sometimes very difficult to see in the examples from Latin literature. In the above example, we can change the sentence by putting the verb that goes with the *antequam* or just the *quam* into the subjunctive because of either the uncertainty about whether the speaker is going to ask or the impossibility of asking. In that case we could say in Latin:

Antequam interrogem respondent discipuli
Ante respondent discipuli quam interrogem

According to our presentation of prohibitions, this sentence can mean something like:

The students answer before I can even ask
Before I may even ask, the students answer
The students answer before, keeping me from even asking
They answer sooner than I may ask.

That is the general idea. When the expression refers to simple time or concrete fact, then the indicative is used, but if anticipation, uncertainty, or doubt enters into the expression, then the subjunctive comes in naturally, both into the Latin and the modern vernacular; for example, Italians will say, *prima che io interroghi, tu respondi*, "Before I even ask, you answer." You will find examples in Latin literature that will help you, or not, because this distinction is not always observed or clear in specific examples.

4. Observation

A concern is to be expressed here and in the Fourth Experience in regard to conditionals. There are definite uses or times for the subjunctive in Latin, but as Latin turns into the Romance languages the use of the subjunctive expands. For example, certain expressions in Italian have the subjunctive, where the Latins would definitely have the indicative. In general the abuse of the subjunctive is a sign of failing or corrupted or later or spoiled Latin.

One general example concerns the use of the conditionals, which follow definite rules as we shall learn in the Fourth Experience. The clear rationale for using the subjunctive in Latin conditionals with the passage of time simply blows up, and for vastly different reasons the whole system simply becomes subjunctive. In Italian, while it is possible to find a conditional sentence in the indicative, the use of the subjunctive predominates so much that the whole phenomenon ends up in the subjunctive. This abuse or excessive use of the subjunctive suggests that anything and everything is doubtful, suspended, might not happen, and thus goes in the subjunctive. This mentality spoils both the active and the passive use of the Latin language. Publius Vergilius Maro (70–19 BCE) gives an example that can help us track this development. Virgil says in the indicative, presented here with the form *ferentis* for *ferentes:*

quidquid id est timeo Danaos et dona ferentis (Verg. *Aen.* II, 49)
whatever that is, I fear the Greeks even bringing gifts.

Later Latin authors put the uncertain part of the sentence into the subjunctive, *sit:*

Quidquid id sit timeo Danaos et dona ferentes
Whatever it be, I am afraid of the Greeks even bringing gifts.

Italians also put it into the subjunctive, for example:

Qualunque sia la cosa, non mi piace
Whatever the thing may be, it is not pleasing to me.

If you go to solid classical texts, you can almost always find out why Cicero used the subjunctive, but in medieval Latin texts the subjunctive is used so excessively that you really do not know what they are doing any more.

ENCOUNTER 31 (66)

CONIUNCTIVI USUS: TEMPORALES SENTENTIAE ET "CUM"

uses of the subjunctive: temporal sentences and "cum"

Introduction

Many grammar books, including some stuffy ones, have a long, special treatment of *cum* because it takes in a lot of the Latin language; in any case, you have to know how to deal with it. We can make a simple list, and you will recognize some things you already know and will learn new elements.

1. Because

As you know, *cum* followed by all times of the subjunctive according to the sequence of tenses can mean "because," for example:

> *Cum hoc dicat, ridemus*
> Because she says this, we are laughing

> *Haec cum carmina recitarent, oblectabamur*
> Because they were reciting these songs, we were being delighted.

2. Although

Likewise, *cum* followed by all times of the subjunctive according to the sequence of tenses can mean "although," for example:

> *Cum absurda essent effati, nos tamen consolati sumus*
>
> Although they had pronounced foolish things, nevertheless we consoled ourselves.

3. When

Cum followed by all times of the indicative must always mean "when." In a sentence set in the present or future times, *cum* with the subjunctive does not mean "when." When a sentence is set in the past-historical times, namely on Track II, then there is a big distinction in meaning where *cum* followed by the indicative means "when" and indicates simple clock-time, but *cum* followed by the subjunctive can also mean "when" and describes a circumstance. Let us look at these three different uses of *cum* meaning "when," because this is a big surprise for most people. You must know this because examples are galore, especially in the historians. Let's look first at simple historical time in the indicative.

3.1 *Historical simple time*

When the story, idea, or concept is past, then *cum* with T.2i, 4bi, 5i means "when," because here the indicative indicates simple time calculation when an action occurred, without indicating any special, logical, or causal connection between two events. For example:

> *Cum hoc in schola carmen decantabamus, in colle quirinali tintinabulum resonabat*
>
> When we were singing this hymn in class, the bell was ringing on the Quirinal Hill.

This example indicates the simple time when two actions occurred, singing a hymn in the classroom and a bell ringing at the president's palace nearby on the Quirinal. There is no logical connection between the two events, besides the clock. Take the example:

> *Cum hoc dicebat, clamor est auditus*
> When he was saying this (at 9:00 A.M.), a screech was heard
>
> *Cum autovehiculum adveniebat, canis praeter nos cucurrit*
> When the bus was approaching (at 11:00), a dog ran by us.

Because of the indicative *dicebat* or *adveniebat* in these examples, *cum* has to mean "when" and indicates a mere point of time and that there is no real connection between the two actions.

3.2 *Historical circumstances in time*

Continuing our discussion, if we wish to indicate an influence, effect, or result as the connection between the two actions in the past, then we use *cum* with the subjunctive to describe the historical circumstances when an action happened.

Now we can add a third meaning to the following example:

> *Cum hoc ridiculum-luctuosum diceret, ridebamus*
>
> Because he was saying this funny-sad thing, we were laughing
> Although he was saying this funny-sad thing, we were laughing.

Now we can say:

> When—on that occasion—he was saying this funny-sad thing, we were laughing.

Here the sentence is understood to describe the circumstances for our laughter, and this meaning comes very close to saying "because he was saying this."

3.3 *Present or future*

When the story, idea, or concept is present or future (not historical past narration), then *cum* with the indicative means "when." For example:

Cum publici accedent custodes, in cubile confugiemus
When the police will come, we'll run into the bedroom.

Here we have two verbs in T.3i. Or, take the example:

Cum hoc dicit, ridemus

When he says this, we laugh
Whenever he says this, we laugh.

Because *dicit* is T.1i, *cum* has to mean "when" inasmuch as "although" and "because" would have a subjunctive here.

There is a famous verse by Cicero:

Cum rosam viderat, tum incipere ver arbitrabatur
Whenever he had seen a rose, he thought spring was beginning.

Because of the T.5i *viderat*, Cicero here treated this as a simple measure of repeated time, for example on every 10 April. In T.2i, 4bi, 5i repeated action in the past is considered clock time and so expressed in the indicative. While this may sound circumstantial, and the reader may prefer the subjunctive, the way to understand Cicero's expression as he said it in the indicative is as simple repeated time meaning "whenever." This could easily have been placed in the subjunctive to indicate a causal link as in:

Cum rosam vidisset, tum adesse ver arbitrabatur
When (because) he had seen a rose, he thought spring was present.

All of these language possibilities require logical thought, comprehension of the story, common sense.

ENCOUNTER 32 (67)

USUS CONIUNCTIVI. CONSECUTIVAE PURAE: UT, UT NON

uses of the subjunctive. pure result: ut, ut non

Introduction

The last big use of the subjunctive in the Latin language merits our attention. This study again involves the well-known particle *ut* and in our next encounter *qui, quae, quod*, which is no consolation, because we have already seen that *ut* means half a dozen things and the uses of *qui, quae, quod* are just about infinite.

Now we wish to add result clauses, which are technically called consecutive clauses, because they contain an effect that follows from something else. For example, we say in English:

It was so hot *that we took off our hats*
It was so hot *that as a result the candle wax was melting.*

The Latin particles used in result clauses are *ut* or *uti* followed by the subjunctive, which means that they may look very much like purpose or final clauses. The particle *ut non* is a clear indication of a negative result clause in correct or standard Latin, whereas the negative of a purpose clause is expressed with the particle *ne*, as learned above, which contains a prohibitive effect. Students are going to jump on the subjunctive in the Latin and produce an English sentence sounding subjunctive, but in English, Italian, French, German, and other vernaculars, real result clauses sound indicative, because they describe the concrete outcome and effects of a situation.

Result sentences are divided into two types according to a fundamental distinction. The first type we shall see are pure result clauses, and the other type are complementary sentences of result. This distinction will prove important later on when we talk about the special exception in the sequence of tenses according to our 97%–3% rule. Here we present the pure result clause, and in the next encounter the complementary sentence of result.

1. Pure result clauses

Pure result clauses are normally preceded in the main sentence by an expression or word that prepares for the result clause. Some of these particles are:

talis ... ut ...	such ... that ...
tantum ...	so much ...
tot ...	so many ...
tam (magnus) ...	so (great) ...

tam (multi) ...	so (many) ...
sic ...	so ...
ita ...	thus ...
adeo ... *ut* ...	to such an extent ... that ....

For all the particles above, the first and the last ones indicate that for each of these the preparatory word or words are connected to a real result sentence often beginning with *ut* ... , as in the examples:

> *Tot furta patrabantur ut fores semper obserarentur*
> *So many* robberies were being committed *that the doors were always locked*

> *Tam amoenum erat caelum ut omnes in hortis inambularent*
> The weather was *so* beautiful *that all were walking around in the park.*

In these sentences the particles "so many" and "so [beautiful]" give rise to the result clauses beginning with *ut* ... that give the explanation.

2. Difference of perspective

In encounter 23 (58) of this Experience, we considered final clauses, also called purpose clauses. In this encounter we consider pure result clauses, and in the next encounter we shall see the other two types of result clauses. The distinction between purpose and result clauses can be rather fine. In some instances they have the same construction, and it can be difficult to distinguish one from the other. Concerning this distinction, Gildersleeve and Lodge brilliantly adds in minute print an essential remark:

> It is to be remarked that the difference between Final [purpose] and Consecutive [result] often consists only in the point of view. What is final [purpose] from the point of view of the doer is consecutive [result] from the point of view of the spectator (nº 543 note 2; our terminology added in brackets).

For example, we can say:

> *Loquitur magister voce tam alta ut discipuli audiant omnes.*

If taken as a purpose clause, it describes the intent of the teacher. In English the subjunctive is then employed:

> The teacher speaks with such a loud voice in order that all the students may hear.

If taken as a result clause, it describes the result of the teacher's speech, without regard to the intent of the teacher. In English the indicative is employed:

> The teacher speaks with such a loud voice with the result that all the students do hear.

While the difference between the result and the purpose clause in the Latin sentence may consist only in one's point of view, in English one must choose between the subjunctive, which expresses purpose, and the indicative, which expresses result, as is clear in another example:

Ut tribus diebus ad lunam perveniat, potentissimis sic propellitur navicula siderea machinimentis igneis

The space ship is so driven by very powerful fiery motors that it arrives at the moon within three days

The space ship is so driven by very powerful fiery motors that it may arrive at the moon within three days.

Two different meanings are hidden in the same Latin text, but in the English you have to choose between them. While we first take it as a result clause expressed with the English indicative, "the space ship is driven *in such a way that as a result* it *arrives* in three days," we can also take it as a purpose clause in the subjunctive, "it is so driven *in order that* it *may arrive* in three days."

We have given a couple of examples of our own, but the important thing is to see this in action in Latin literature. It remains to the teacher or student to find examples of these in the pages of reading sheets that we provide.

3. Negative purpose and result clauses

The distinction mentioned above might escape some people, because we are dealing with the little particle *ut*, used to express both purpose and result. Positive statements of both result and purpose are introduced by *ut*, which means the distinction between them can slip away fast.

There is, however, a completely different system and view of things in the negative, where the negative purpose clearly suggests a prohibition or a negative wish, and a negative result emphasizes the negative factual outcome. The difference between negative purpose and negative result clauses is noted in Gildersleeve and Lodge (nº 543, 4): "They differ in the kind of Subjunctive employed." We can explain this in our own terms as follows: a purpose (final) clause takes a subjunctive that expresses a wish or a command. A result (consecutive) clause takes a subjunctive that expresses possibility and resulting fact. This becomes more evident in the type of negative used with each, as Gildersleeve and Lodge continue, with our slight adaptation:

Final [purpose]:	**Consecutive [result]:**
ne (ut ne),	*ut non,* that not.
ne quis,	*ut nemo,* that no one.
ne ullus,	*ut nullus,* that no.
ne umquam, (ne quando,)	*ut numquam,* that never.
ne usquam, (nēcubi,)	*ut nusquam,* that nowhere.
ne aut—aut, (ut neve—neve,)	*ut neque—neque,* that neither—nor.

If the reader reads through the double lists you can feel the force of the prohibition in *ne* and the eventual fact in *ut non*. This is illustrated by the following classical example. The first one is by Lucius Annaeus Seneca (c. 4 BCE–65 CE). Seneca says:

Itaque negant posse voluptatem a virtute diduci et aiunt nec honeste quemquam vivere ut non iucunde vivat, nec iucunde ut non honeste quoque (Sen. *Vit. Beat.* 6, 2)

Thus, they deny that pleasure is able to be drawn away from virtue, and they say that neither does anyone live uprightly that as a result he is not living happily, nor happily that he is not also living uprightly.

Note that *ut non ... nec* open expressions of negative result. Seneca wrote the above work, *De vita beata ad Gallionem*, to his brother Gallio, who ended up the governor of Achaia, Greece, and the arbiter of the cause of Paul of Tarsus and his community, as mentioned in the biblical book of the Acts of the Apostles 18:12–17: *Gallione proconsule Achaiae ... incipiente autem Paulo aperire, os dixit Gallio ad Iudaeos ... nihil horum Gallioni curae erat*, "Gallio being the proconsul of Achaia ... as Paul was beginning to open his mouth, Gallio said to the Jews ... nothing of these things was for a care to Gallio."

Here is another text, this time from Cicero.

Non enim possunt una in civitate multi rem ac fortunas amittere ut non pluris secum in eandem trahant calamitatem: a quo periculo prohibete rem publicam (Cic. *Imp. Pomp.* 7, 19)

For many people are not able in one city to lose their resources and fortunes that as a result they do not drag more people with themselves into the same calamity: from which danger you must keep the [Roman] state far away.

Note that *ut non* introduces an expression of negative result, and that *pluris* is another form of *plures*.

Livy adds for our good:

Tempus ac necessitas belli ac discrimen summae rerum faciebant ne quis aut exemplum exquireret aut suspectum cupiditatis imperii consulem haberet (Liv. XXIV, 9)

The circumstance and the necessity of war and the crisis of the totality of things were demanding that not anyone either look for a precedent or have a consul suspected of a grab of supreme authority.

Note that *ne quis*, "lest anyone" or "that not anyone," begins a negative purpose clause. Strictly and theoretically speaking *faciebant*, "they were bringing it about," should produce an expression of negative result properly written as *ut nemo*, "so that no one," but maybe Livy either disregarded this or nodded off to sleep as he was writing.

Caesar provides this contribution:

Diviciacus multis cum lacrimis Caesarem complexus obsecrare coepit ne quid gravius in fratrem statueret (Caes., *B. G.* I, 20)

Diviciacus with many tears, having embraced Caesar, began to beg that he not decide anything more severe against his brother.

Here *ne quid*, "lest anything" or "that ... not ... anything," is an expression of negative purpose.

These verses are given by Publius Terentius Afer (195/185–c. 159 BCE). Terentius says:

> *sed heus tu, vide sis nequid inprudens ruas!*
> *patrem novisti ad has res quam sit perspicax* (Ter. *Heaut.* 369–370)
>
> but, hey you, watch out if you don't mind that you not rush as an imprudent man to anything!
>
> you know daddy how perceptive he is with regard to these things.

Rather than a beautiful indirect question, *novisti quam sit pater perspicax*, "you know how perceptive Daddy is," Terentius psychologically does what children do to this day, when he takes the subject of the subjunctive and makes it the object of the main verb, saying, "you know Daddy, how perceptive he is." This is very common in Plautus and Terentius, some of the best Latin we have. The contraction *sis* is well known to be *si vis*, "if you wish" or here "if you don't mind." Here *nequid*, "lest anything" or "that ... not anything" is an expression of negative purpose.

ENCOUNTER 33 (68)

USUS CONIUNCTIVI. CONSECUTIVAE COMPLEMENTARIAE; DESCRIPTIVAE; QUI

uses of the subjunctive. complementary result; characteristic; qui

Introduction

Coming on the same line as pure result clauses in our last encounter, two other related types of sentences present themselves for our consideration.

1. Complementary result clauses

In distinction from pure result clauses, complementary result clauses are not necessarily anticipated by explicit particles or preparatory words. Rather, they are called complementary result clauses because they complement or complete an idea suggested in the main element on which they depend. Verbs that naturally produce such result clauses belong to several concepts. They may be verbs of "happening," such as:

fit . . .	it is done, happens . . .
evenit . . .	it turns out . . .
contingit . . .	it comes about . . .
accidit . . .	it happens, has happened, happened . . .
usu venit . . . ut . . .	it occurs . . . that . . . .

The last one indicates that for each of these the preparatory word or words are connected to a real result sentence often beginning with *ut* . . . . They may be verbs of "bringing it about that," such as:

facere . . .	to see to it . . .
efficere . . .	to bring it about . . .
perficere . . . ut . . .	to accomplish . . . that, to realize . . . that . . . .

Here is such an idea:

Praefectus effecit ut folia colligerentur
The Mayor brought it about that the leaves were collected.

Another Group of verbs expresses the idea "to grant that," "to allow that":

tribuere . . .	to grant . . .
concedere . . .	to concede . . .
dare . . .	to give . . .
permittere . . .	to allow . . .
sinere . . .	to permit . . .
pati . . . ut . . .	to suffer, allow . . . that . . . .

Other verbal expressions are completed by a result clause, for example:

lex est ...	it is the law ...
consuetudo est ...	it is a custom ...
mos est ut ...	it is the habit that ...

Here the clause beginning with *ut* gives the result, the explanation, the development of the noun.

We said that one difference between purpose and result clauses is the negative particle used. Purpose clauses use *ne*, and result clauses use *ut non*, because purpose clauses in *ne* are a type of prohibition where something is not wanted to happen, whereas result clauses with *ut non* indicate solid results that do not happen, without any idea of impeding or prohibiting them. We can use this difference to help us see and understand the distance between the two types of clauses in the following examples: first of purpose, then of result:

Optavit mater ne quisquam veniret nobiscum
Mother wished that no one come with us

Casu accidit ut non ullus veniret miles
It happened by chance that not any soldier came.

Itaque ut plura non dicam neque aliorum exemplis confirmem quantum auctoritas valeat in bello, ab eodem Cn. Pompeio omnium rerum egregiarium exempla sumantur (Cic. *Imp. Pomp.* 15, 44)

Therefore, examples of all outstanding deeds should be taken up from the same Gnaeus Pompeius so that I not say too many things nor confirm with the examples of others how much authority is effective in war.

The use of the negative particle *non*, denying one particular element in the result clause, is quite faithfully observed in standard Latin.

2. Characteristic result clauses

The last group of result clauses, while important, is too often superficially invoked by many people who cannot otherwise justify a subjunctive. We are speaking about a clause of characteristic result. This type of result clause is produced by a reference in the main sentence to a type of people or a type of person or a nature of something that carries with it a certain result. This type of result clause then describes the characteristic effect of that people, person, thing.

2.1 *Qui, quae, quod*

Normally a preparatory word—one of the particles *talis ...*, *tantum ...*, and the rest, or one of the verbs *fit ...*, *evenit ...*, and many others—is used in the main sentence; however, sometimes it is simply felt or understood in the flow of the discourse. In these latter cases of omission you will see the relative pronoun *qui, quae, quod* in any function followed by the subjunctive.

We have already learned that such relative clauses can serve as relative clauses of purpose or of result, or of concession meaning "although," or of cause meaning "because." Now we learn that relative clauses with the subjunctive also cover for specifically characteristic result clauses.

In this case, the relative *qui, quae, quod* followed by the subjunctive stands in place of a *talis ut is*, "such that he" or *talis ut ea*, "of such a type that she" or *tale ut id*, "such that it" ... where *talis, talis, tale* belongs to the thought of the main sentence and *ut is, ut ea, ut id* belong to the characteristic result and go with the subjunctive. Pedagogically you can test whether a relative sentence with the subjunctive is an expression of characteristic result by adding the *talis ut is* ... to see if it works. Let us turn to an example:

> *Inveniuntur qui hoc faciant*
> (Such) people are found who do this.

What is felt or understood here is *tales ut ii* as in:

> *Inveniuntur tales ut ii hoc faciant*
> There are people found of such a type that they do this.

Understood in the following example is *tales ut nos*:

> *In senatu eramus qui hoc diceremus*
> In the senate we were those people who were saying this.

Take the example from Cicero and innumerable other authors:

> *sunt qui verum numquam dicant*
> there are people [out there] who never say the truth.

Here the subjunctive *dicant* describes a characteristic of a certain type of people with its result, namely "there are such people who say ... ," that is, "there are people such that as a result they say ... ."

It is another thing to state a simple fact in the indicative:

> *Hac sunt quinque in schola qui numquam dicunt verum*
> There are five people in this class who in fact never say the truth.

A word of caution is due because some classicists get carried away and explain all mysterious, inexplicable subjunctives by saying that they must describe a characteristic of a person or group of people, even where that is not the case. We have seen that the relative pronoun with the subjunctive can mean just about anything in the language, so we advise not jumping too quickly on just this one possibility of a characteristic result as a universal remedy.

Another example of a sentence that is not characteristic and that needs to be identified as a normal relative is this:

> *Erant qui dormiebant dum praedicabat*
> They were the ones who were sleeping while he was preaching.

The above two examples have a verb in the indicative, not the subjunctive: *qui ... dicunt; qui dormiebant.* Rather than describing a characteristic of a type or a group, the sentences describe a specific, identifiable group of a certain number of people and the fact of their sleeping. If we change the verb *dormiebant* from T.2i to T.2s, then we no longer describe the concrete action of a specific group of people, but describe the nature of a type, as in:

Erant qui dormirent dum praedicabat

There were people (such by nature) who were sleeping while he was preaching.

The Roman author Seneca revolutionized Latin style with his here short, telegraphic, modern style, which is quite distant from the creamy abundance of Cicero. Seneca is more like *The New York Times* and so much more accessible today. He guides us here with this example:

Multi inveniuntur qui ignem inferant urbibus, qui inexpugnabilia saeculis et per aliquot aetates tuta prosternant, qui aequum arcibus aggerem attollant et muros in miram altitudinem eductos arietibus ac machinis quassent (Sen. *Ep.* XCIV, 61)

Many people are found such who bring fire upon cities, who lay flat the things unassailable for centuries and safe for some ages, who lift up a rampart equal to citadels and shake to pieces with battering rams and military machines walls having been drawn up into a marvelous height.

Seneca describes these many people by giving three relative clauses of characteristic result. The first is *qui ignem inferant urbibus*, "such who bring fire upon cities," where the *qui* stands for *tales ut ii*, "such that they [bring fire upon cities]." Other than the characteristic result, there is no reason for the subjunctive here, so the verb here *inferant* in T.1s stands for *inferunt* in T.1i, and this verb describes the historical, tragic realities of their actions. The second is *qui … prosternant*, "who lay flat [the things]," where *qui* stands for *tales ut ii*, "such that they [lay flat the things]." Again, Seneca is describing the destructive accomplishments of these people, so the verb *prosternant* in T.1s stands for the indicative verb *prosternunt* in T.1i. The third one is *qui … attollant et … quassent*, "who lift up … and shake to pieces," where *qui* once again stands for *tales ut ii*, "such that they [lift up and shake to pieces]," and both verbs describe the engineering feats of these people, so likewise *attollant* in T.1s stands for the indicative verb *attollunt* in T.1i and *quassent* also in T.1s stands for *quassant* in T.1i.

Two sentences of our own also illustrate this:

Birota quidam decertant quibus praemia tribuantur

Some people compete with a bicycle to whom rewards are granted
Some people compete with a bicycle such that to them rewards are granted.

Here the relative pronoun *quibus* followed by *tribuantur* in T.1s stands for *tales ut iis praemia tribuantur*, "such that rewards are assigned to them." The subjunctive verb describes the real-world limits of human virtue of these people and so *tribuantur* in T.1s stands for *tribuuntur* in T.1i. Take another example of ours:

> *Sunt a quibus pompam ducentibus pax civilis haud perturbetur*
>
> There are some people by whom leading a parade civil peace is not disturbed
>
> There are some people such that by them leading a parade civil peace is not disturbed.

Once again the *a quibus* stands for *tales ut ab iis* followed by *perturbetur* in T.1s which stands for the indicative verb *perturbatur* in T.1i, because the subjunctive verb is describing the verifiable condition of the peace, that in fact peace is not disturbed by such people.

Another example from Seneca will round out this illustration and develop matters a bit further:

> *Nihil habere ad quod exciteris, ad quod te concites, cuius denuntiatione et incursu firmitatem animi tui temptes, sed in otio inconcusso iacere non est tranquillitas: malacia est* (Sen. *Ep.* LXVII, 14)
>
> Having nothing toward which you are driven, toward which you do move yourself, by whose announcing and attack you do test the constancy of your own spirit, is not tranquility, but it is lying in unshaken idleness: it is a dead sea.

The subject of *est*, "it is," in the first part of the sentence is the gerund *habere*, as in "having nothing is not tranquility" or "to have nothing is not tranquility." This condition is then defined with three relatives clauses of characteristic result. The first is *ad quod exciteris*, a passive verb in T.1s where *ad quod* stands for *tale ut ad id*, "[having nothing] such that toward it you are driven." The second also begins with *ad quod* which stands for *tale ut ad id concites*, again in T.1s meaning, "[having nothing] such that toward it you do move yourself." The third characterization of this condition consists of the relative *cuius*, which stands for *tale ut eius*, followed by the verb *temptes*, "such that you do test the constancy of your own spirit."

Clauses of characteristic result are in the subjunctive in Latin, but in English they sound indicative, unless there is an underlying reason for the subjunctive. For example, the clauses here are also able to describe possible circumstances rather than actual circumstances. In this case the three clauses would end up sounding like the following: the first, "such that toward it you may be driven"; the second, "such that toward it you may move yourself"; the third, "such that you may test the constancy of your own spirit." Thus, underlying these three subjunctive verbs of characteristic result may be natural subjunctive verbs, which are rendered in the subjunctive in the following English revision of the whole sentence:

Having nothing toward which you may be driven, toward which you may move yourself, by whose announcing and attack you may test the constancy of your own spirit, is not tranquility, but it is lying in unshaken idleness: it is a dead sea.

2.2 *Dignus, idoneus, indignus qui*

Other expressions that produce a characteristic result are:

dignus qui	worthy who
indignus qui	unworthy who
idoneus qui	suitable who.

Each is followed by the subjunctive, to indicate that one is not doing something at present, but is suitable or worthy that some day one may do it, for example:

Dignus erat qui (*ut is*) *hoc faceret*
He was worthy who might do this
He was worthy that he might do this

Idonea erat quam (*ut eam*) *praesidem crearent*
She was suitable whom they might make president
She was suitable that they might make her president

Indignum eum iudicant qui (*ut is*) *has scholas explicet*
They consider him unworthy who may conduct these classes.
They consider him unworthy that he conduct these classes.

To complete our Third Experience, the next two encounters will treat two rather light Latin usages that are namely indications of place and time.

ENCOUNTER 34 (69)

USUS LOCI: QUO, UNDE, UBI + CASUS LOCATIVUS

expressions of place: to where, from where, where and the locative function

Introduction

Two final considerations of our Third Experience concern in this encounter expressions of place and of time in the next encounter. Latin has a whole system of place designations, which can be illustrated easily from Latin literature of a historical nature, where one is always talking about movements and places in daily life.

1. *Quo*

The adverb *quo* means "whither, to what place, where to," as in the expression *quo vadis*, "whither goest thou?" or "to where are you going?" It is also used in an indirect question, for example, *Quo vaderes rogaverunt*, "they asked to where you were going."

1.1 *Normally*

The normal, common expression for place "to where" is either the preposition *in* with the object form to indicate motion "to" or "toward" the place itself, or the preposition *ad* with the object form to indicate motion or "to the vicinity of."

1.2 *Names of cities and small islands*

The above usage is applied to the names themselves of cities and small islands, which are put in the object form while the preposition is omitted. Thus:

> *Romam redibo*
> I shall return to Rome
>
> *Melitam cras volabimus*
> We shall fly to Malta tomorrow (Malta is considered a small island)
>
> *Athenas confugit*
> She fled to Athens.

1.3 *Isolated, common expressions*

Some isolated but very common expressions imitate the above practice. All the following nouns are in the object form. These expressions are:

rus	to the country
domum	to home (home)
humum	to, toward the ground
foras	to the outside.

For example:

Rus ibunt agricolae
The farmers will go to the country

Domum recucurrit filius familias
The family son ran back home

Humum decidit bos
The cow fell to the ground

Foras festinavit canis
The dog hastened outside (= to the outside).

The omission of the preposition is colloquial, and in standard Latin the added preposition with these three things, *ad domum* or *ad Romam* will mean "to the vicinity of home," "to the walls of Rome," not "to the place itself."

2. *Unde*

In the same threefold way we are going to treat the idea of "from where." The adverb *unde* means "whence, from what place, where from." It is also used in indirect questions, for example, *Unde veneris quaero*, "I am asking from where you have come."

2.1 *Normally*

The normal, common expression for place "from where" is one of three possibilities. First, the preposition *a* or *ab* or *abs* is used with the form by-with-from-in. Second, sometimes the form by-with-from-in is used alone, as a form of separation, that is as the "from" in by-with-from-in. Third is the preposition *ex* with the form by-with-from-in to mean "out of, from."

2.2 *Names of cities and small islands*

The above usage is adapted for the names of cities and small islands, which are put in the form by-with-from-in without a preposition. This construction is based on the natural meaning of the form by-with-from-in and a verb of motion that indicates separation. Thus:

Quando Roma es profectus?
When did you take off from Rome?

Berolino discessere
They departed from Berlin

Athenis recessimus
We retired from Athens.

2.3 *Isolated, common expressions*

Some isolated but very common expressions imitate the above practice. All the following nouns are in the form by-with-from-in. These expressions are:

rure	from the country
domo	from home
humo	from the ground
(*foris*	does not have this meaning. See 3.3 below).

For example:

Rure redibunt
They will return from the country

Domo recucurrit
He ran back from home

Humo surrexit cervus
The deer got up from the ground.

3. *Ubi*

Likewise, we shall meet the idea of "place where." The adverb *ubi* means "where, in what place, wherein." It is also used in indirect questions, for example, *Ubi futura sis scio*, "I know where you (woman) are about to be."

3.1 *Normally*

The normal, common expression for place "where" or "in which"—something that many people do not know, remember, or recognize—is the preposition *in* with the form by-with-from-in. For example:

Ego iacebam in balnei labro
I was lying in the tub of the bathroom

Epistulae diplomatico in saculo inveniebantur
The letters were always found in the diplomatic pouch.

Many people do not realize that the use of the preposition *in* here is normal and correct and common and not some exception. This construction contrasts with the construction of *in* followed by the object form, which expresses movement to or toward the place itself.

3.2 *Names of cities and small islands*

Here and until the end of this lesson we shall talk about a special usage, "the place form." The Latins call it the *casus locativus*, from *locus* meaning "place, situation," and so it is commonly called the "locative." We presented this in the sixth encounter of the First Experience, as the final function, number seven, of the possible uses of nouns and adjectives in the Latin language. Again this is used only with proper names of towns and small islands and does not detract from the normal usage above. Remember, there is no locative for "in the train," "in the plane," "in the outhouse," "in the courtroom."

In the singular.

If the name of the place is singular in form in the dictionary, then to the surprise of people studying grammar books, the ending of the form for place is not simply the old ditty "just use the genitive," our form of-possession, but rather the ending –*i*, which in many cases looks like the form of-possession. For example, *Novi Eboraci* is not only the form of-possessive meaning, "of New York"; following this rule, it is also properly the place form or locative, meaning, "in New York." It looks like the same form, but it is not. Other examples include:

Horti florent Tiburi nostri
Our gardens are flourishing in Tivoli

Graecae statuae Corinthi servabuntur
The Greek statues will be kept in Corinth.

The Latin name of the modern town Tivoli is *Tibur*, and its form of-possession is *Tiburis*, but the locative is *Tiburi*, thus its present name. This same rule explains the following, which is not an exception:

Diu vixit Lutetiae
She lived a long time in Paris.

The original form was *Lutetiai*, ending in –*i*, but this changed phonetically to *Lutetiae*. Similarly, what looks like the form of-possession *Chicagiae* is a phonetic substitution for *Chicagiai*, as is *Milvauchiae* for *Milvauchiai*, as in these expressions:

Argentariae Chicagiae vacillant
The banks are tottering in Chicago

Quae legis, scripsit Milvauchiae
He wrote the stuff, which you are reading, in Milwaukee.

In the plural.

We have seen that the singular locative ends only in –*i* (or in the altered form –*ai*, written today as –*ae*). If the name of the place is plural in the dictionary, then the only way to give the place form is to use the plural form by-with-from-in. For example from the dictionary entry *Athenae, arum,* f., Athens, we have:

Athenis mortuus est
He died in Athens.

From the dictionary entry *Parisii, orum,* m., Parisians, we have:

Floruit Parisiis
She flourished in Paris.

The city *Lutetia Parisiorum* is really the town *Lutetia* of the Parisians, so sometimes you will see *liber impressus est Lutetiae*, or *Parisiis*, or *Lutetiae Parisiorum*. Examples can be gathered from Latin historical narrative writings where the names of towns and small islands come up naturally, as in Cicero's letters (See: *Ossium Carnes Multae*, the projected companion volume to the present one). Also in innumerable books presented in Latin whose frontispiece exhibits printing in different cities. For example, some of the books on the shelves of the authors of this book were published in these cities, all given in the locative:

> *Apud Seb. Gryphium Lugduni, 1539*,
>
> "at the printing press of Sebastian Gryphius, Lyon, 1539"
>
> *Venetiis, Apud Hieronymum Polum M D LXXVIII*,
>
> "In Venice, At Girolamo Polo, 1578"
>
> *Amstelodami, Apud Ioannem Ianßonium, Aº 1633*,
>
> "In Amsterdam, At the press of John Janson, in the year 1633"
>
> *Romae MDCCLIV, Typis Generosi Salomoni in Foro S. Ignatii*
>
> "At Rome 1754, With the type-letters of Generoso Salomone in the square of St. Ignatius."

These authors are imitating Cicero's use in a letter written in the month of February during the year of his assassination, 43 BCE:

> *et Aquini et Fabrateriae consilia sunt inita de me quae te video inaudisse* (Cic. *Fam*. IX, 24, 1)
>
> decisions were made at both Aquinum and Fabrateria about me which I see you did overhear.

3.3 Isolated, common expressions

Related to the place form and not related to the names of towns and small islands are:

ruri	in the country
domi	at home
humi	on the ground

and in the plural:

foris	outside.

4. Summary: Expressions of place

quo: place to where

normally:	*in* + object form
	ad + object form

names of cities and small islands:
object form (without preposition)

expressions: *rus*
domum
humum
foras.

unde: place from where

normally: *a*, *ab*, *abs*, *ex* + form by-with-from-in
form by-with-from-in (alone expressing separation)

names of cities and small islands:
form by-with-from-in (without a preposition)

expressions: *rure*
domo
humo.

ubi: place in where

normally: *in* + form by-with-from-in

names of cities and small islands:
place form [locative]
Singular: ends in –*i* (phonetic correction to –*ae*)
Plural: form by-with-from-in, as a necessary substitution

expressions: *ruri* (place form)
domi
humi
foris (plural).

ENCOUNTER 35 (70)

TEMPORIS USUS LATINI: QUO, PER QUOD, INTRA QUOD

Latin expressions of time: at which, through which, within which

Introduction

In this encounter, the final one of our Third Experience, we present the companion to the previous encounter on expressions of place, by turning to the various expressions of time in Latin given in one brief but thorough study.

1. Time at which

Time "at which" is expressed by the form by-with-from-in without a preposition, as in:

hora quarta	at the fourth hour
die Veneris	on Friday (on the day of Venus)
hoc tempore	at this time
illis annis	in those years
	at those years
quot mensibus	in how many months.

Some people take *illis annis* to mean "during those years" and *quot mensibus*, "during how many months," both expressing extent of time.

Expressions like the medical term *bid*, which stands for *bis in die*, or the expression *tia*, standing for *ter in anno*, are really more an indication of place where on the calendar than time when. They mean:

bis in die	twice within the circle of the day
ter in anno	three times within the course of the year.

To satisfy the demands of the purists who want the preposition *in* followed by the form *by-with-from-in* to expresses "place where," they justify the expression *in die* by making it geographic, as in "in the circle of the day," as they also do with *in anno*, "in the course of the year."

2. Time during which, through which

Expressions of the duration of time, such as "during which" or "through which," are given in the object form without a preposition. For example:

tres annos regnavit	he ruled for three years
plurimos menses abscondebatur	it was being hidden for many months
longum tempus dormiebamus	we were sleeping for a long time

ibi mensem mansi	there I stayed for a month
tres annos quos nobiscum erat	three years for which length of time he was with us.

In the above expression, both *tres annos* and *quos* are in the object form to express extent of time meaning, "time over three years" or "time through three years" and "over which time" or "through which time." To be realistic we must say that this usage of the object form to express extent of time was diluted or diminished very early in Latin literature as an expression of time at which, and the idea of extent of time in the object form was lost in favor of the form by-with-from-in. We can see this shift in the following expressions:

Adfui tres annos quos aedificata est aedes
I was present for the three years during which the church was built.

The object forms are used to express extent of time in normal, standard, conservative Latin.

Adfui tribus annis quibus aedificata est aedes
I was present in the three years in which the church was built.

Here the form by-with-from-in expresses time within which, or as the purist would want it, it expresses temporal place where.

The addition of the preposition *per* adds to the expression by hinting at an arc of time or a entire cycle of time. For example:

per illud tempus	throughout that period of time
per tres annos	over a period of three years not: "for three years," which is *tres annos*.

3. Time within which

For expressions of time "within which," the form by-with-from-in is used without a preposition. For example:

Brevi tempore te conveniam
I shall meet you within a short time

Quattuor horis opus absolutum est
Within four hours the work was finished off.

The use of the preposition *intra* is undeniably found, and refers to time "within with," the same as the simple ablative (by-with-from-in), as in the thoughts:

Spatium temporis quo faciendum est
A space of time within which it has to be done

Spatium est temporis intra quod faciendum est
There is a space of time within which it must be done.

We have accomplished much in this Third Experience, dedicating ourselves to the most difficult element of the Latin language, the many overlapping, mysterious usages of the subjunctive. We have also seen the four participles in their natural meanings and many usages.

The reading sheets give you vast material with which you can confront most Latin literature. Now, instead of one or two examples or sentences here and there, your reading sheets following each experience will allow you to understand complete bodies of Latin texts using all the information and skills that you have learned in your First, Second, and now completed Third Experiences. The Fourth Experience offers high refinement of all these phenomena and continual naturalization of this teaching about the Bones of the Latin language.

Many people might laugh or be angry because there are so many Bones of the language and such a complicated skeleton, but we cannot change the nature of a beautiful body.

QVANDOQVIDEM IN THEATRO VATICANO
PRAESTITE MARIA MATRE SAPIENTIAE
PIVS XI PONTIFEX MAXIMVS
DIGNAM STVDIORVM SEDEM CONSTITVIT
AD BIBLIOTHECAM AD TABVLARIVM
AD PONTIFICIVM SOPHORVM COLLEGIVM
HAC PATET ADITVS
PONT MAX

TERTIAE EXPERIENTIAE
LECTIONUM PAGINULAE

Reading Sheets—Third Experience

READING 3-A

GAIVS IVLIVS CAESAR

[102–44 BCE]

DE BELLO GALLICO LIB. V

12 Britanniae pars interior ab eis incolitur quos natos in insula ipsi memoria proditum dicunt, maritima pars ab eis qui praedae ac belli inferendi causa ex Belgio transierant, qui omnes fere eis nominibus civitatum appellantur quibus orti ex civitatibus eo pervenerunt, et bello inlato ibi permanserunt atque agros colere coeperunt Hominum est infinita multitudo creberrimaque aedificia fere Gallicis consimilia, pecorum magnus numerus. Utuntur aut aere aut nummo aureo aut taleis ferreis ad certum pondus examinatis pro nummo. Nascitur ibi plumbum album in mediterraneis regionibus, in maritimis ferrum, sed eius exigua est copia; aere utuntur importato. Materia cuiusque generis ut in Gallia est, praeter fagum atque abietem. Leporem et gallinam et anserem gustare fas non putant; haec tamen alunt animi voluptatisque causa. Loca sunt temperatiora quam in Gallia, remissioribus frigoribus.

13 Insula natura triquetra, cuius unum latus est contra Galliam. Huius lateris alter angulus, qui est ad Cantium, quo fere omnes ex Gallia naves appelluntur, ad orientem solem, inferior ad meridiem spectat. Hoc pertinet circiter milia passuum quingenta. Alterum vergit ad Hispaniam atque occidentem solem; qua ex parte est Hibernia, dimidio minor, ut existimatur, quam Britannia, sed pari spatio transmissus atque ex Gallia est in Britanniam. In hoc medio cursu est insula quae appellatur Mona: complures praeterea minores subiectae insulae existimantur, de quibus insulis non nulli scripserunt dies continuos xxx sub bruma esse noctem. Nos nihil de eo percontationibus reperiebamus nisi certis ex aqua mensuris breviores esse quam in continenti noctes videbamus. Huius est longitudo lateris, ut fert illorum opinio, septingentorum milium. Tertium est contra septentriones, cui parti nulla est obiecta terra; sed eius angulus lateris maxime ad Germaniam spectat. Hoc milia passuum octingenta in longitudinem esse existimatur. Ita omnis insula est in circuitu vicies centum milium passuum.

14 Ex eis omnibus longe sunt humanissimi qui Cantium incolunt, quae regio est maritima omnis, neque multum a Gallica differunt consuetudine. Interiores plerique frumenta non serunt, sed lacte et carne vivunt pellibusque sunt vestiti. Omnes vero se Britanni vitro inficiunt, quod caeruleum efficit colorem, atque hoc horridiores sunt in pugna aspectu; capilloque sunt promisso atque omni parte corporis rasa, praeter caput et labrum superius. Uxores habent deni duodenique inter se communis, et maxime fratres cum fratribus parentesque cum liberis; sed qui sunt ex eis nati eorum habentur liberi quo primum virgo quaeque deducta est.

DE BELLO GALLICO LIB. VI

[...] Eo tum statu res erat ut longe principes haberentur Aedui, secundum locum dignitatis Remi obtinerent.

13 In omni Gallia eorum hominum qui aliquo sunt numero atque honore genera sunt duo. Nam plebes paene servorum habetur loco, quae nihil audet per se, nullo adhibetur consilio. Plerique, cum aut aere alieno aut magnitudine tributorum aut iniuria potentiorum premuntur, sese in servitutem dicant nobilibus, *quibus* in hos eadem omnia sunt iura quae dominis in servos. Sed de his duobus generibus alterum est druidum, alterum equitum. Illi rebus divinis intersunt, sacrificia publica ac privata procurant, religiones interpretantur: ad hos magnus adulescentium numerus disciplinae causa concurrit, magnoque hi sunt apud eos honore. Nam fere de omnibus controversiis publicis privatisque constituunt et, si quod est admissum facinus, si caedes facta, si de hereditate, de finibus controversia est, idem decernunt, praemia poenasque constituunt; si qui aut privatus aut populus eorum decreto noti stetit, sacrificiis interdicunt. Haec poena apud eos est gravissima. Quibus ita est interdictum, hi numero impiorum ac sceleratorum habentur, his omnes decedunt, aditum sermonemque defugiunt, ne quid ex contagione incommodi accipiant, neque his petentibus ius redditur, neque honos ullus communicatur. His autem omnibus druidibus praeest unus, qui summam inter eos habet auctoritatem. Hoc mortuo, aut si qui ex reliquis excellit dignitate succedit, aut, si sunt plures pares, suffragio druidum, non numquam etiam armis de principatu contendunt. Hi certo anni tempore in finibus Carnutum, quae regio totius Galliae media habetur, considunt in loco consecrato. Huc omnes undique qui controversias habent conveniunt eorumque decretis iudiciisque parent. Disciplina in Britannia reperta atque inde in Galliam translata esse existimatur, et nunc qui diligentius eam rem cognoscere volunt plerumque illo discendi causa proficiscuntur.

14 Druides a bello abesse consuerunt, neque tributa una cum reliquis pendunt; militiae vacationem omniumque rerum habent immunitatem.

Tantis excitati praemiis et sua sponte multi in disciplinam conveniunt et a parentibus propinquisque mittuntur. Magnum ibi numerum versuum ediscere dicuntur. Itaque annos non nulli xx in disciplina permanent. Neque fas esse existimant ea litteris mandare, cum in reliquis fere rebus, publicis privatisque rationibus, Graecis litteris utantur. Id mihi duabus de causis instituisse videntur, quod neque in vulgum disciplinam efferri velint neque eos qui discunt litteris confisos minus memoriae studere; quod fere plerisque accidit ut praesidio litterarum diligentiam in perdiscendo ac memoriam remittant. In primis hoc volunt persuadere, non interire animas sed ab aliis post mortem transire ad alios, atque hoc maxime ad virtutem excitari putant, metu mortis neglecto. Multa praeterea de sideribus atque eorum motu, de mundi ac terrarum magnitudine, de rerum natura, de deorum immortalium vi ac potestate disputant et iuventuti tradunt.

15 Alterum genus est equitum. Hi, cum est usus atque aliquod bellum incidit (quod fere ante Caesaris adventum quot annis accidere solebat, uti aut ipsi iniurias inferrent aut inlatas propulsarent), omnes in bello versantur; atque eorum ut quisque est genere copiisque amplissimus, ita plurimos circum se ambactos clientisque habet. Hanc unam gratiam potentiamque noverunt.

16 Natio est omnium Gallorum admodum dedita religionibus, atque ob earn causam qui sunt adfecti gravioribus morbis quique in proeliis periculisque versantur aut pro victimis homines immolant aut se immolaturos vovent, administrisque ad ea sacrificia druidibus utuntur; quod, pro vita hominis nisi hominis vita reddatur, non posse deorum immortalium numen placari arbitrantur, publiceque eiusdem generis habent instituta sacrificia. Alii immani magnitudine simulacra habent, quorum contexta viminibus membra vivis hominibus complent; quibus succensis circumventi flamma exanimantur homines. Supplicia eorum qui in furto aut in latrocinio aut altqua noxia sint comprehensi gratiora dis immortalibus esse arbitrantur, sed, cum eius generis copia deficit, etiam ad innocentium supplicia descendunt.

17 Deum maxime Mercurium colunt. Huius sunt plurima simulacra, hunc omnium inventorem artium ferunt, hunc viarum atque itinerum ducem, hunc ad quaestus pecuniae mercaturasque habere vim maximam arbitrantur. Post hunc Apollinem et Martem et Iovem et Minervam. De his eandem fere quam reliquae gentes habent opinionem: Apollinem morbos depellere, Minervam operum atque artificiorum initia tradere, Iovem imperium caelestium tenere, Martem bella regere. Huic, cum proelio dimicare constituerunt, ea quae bello ceperint plerumque devovent: quae superaverint, animalia capta immolant, reliquasque res in unum locum conferunt. Multis in civitatibus harum rerum exstructos tumulos locis consecratis conspicari licet, neque saepe accidit ut neglecta quispiam religione aut capta apud se occultare aut posita tollere auderet, gravissimumque ei ret supplicium cum cruciatu constitutum est.

18 Galli se omnes ab Dite patre prognatos praedicant, idque ab Druidibus proditum dicunt. Ob cam causam spatia omnis temporis non numero dierum sed noctium finiunt; dies natalis et mensum et annorum initia sic observant ut noctem dies subsequatur. In reliquis vitae institutis hoc fere ab reliquis differunt quod suos liberos, nisi cum adoleverunt ut munus militiae sustinere possint, palam ad se adire non patiuntur filiumque puerili aetate in publico in conspectu patris adsistere turpe ducunt.

19 Viri quantas pecunias ab uxoribus dotis nomine acceperunt tantas ex suis bonis aestimatione facta cum dotibus communicant. Huius omnis pecuniae coniunctim ratio habetur fructusque servantur: uter eorum vita superarit, ad eum pars utriusque cum fructibus superiorum temporum pervenit. Viri in uxores, sicuti in liberos, vitae necisque habent potestatem; et cum pater familiae inlustriore loco natus decessit, eius propinqui conveniunt et, de morte si res in suspicionem venit, de uxoribus in servilem modum quaestionem habent et, si compertum est, igni atque omnibus tormentis excruciatas interficiunt.

READING 3-B

PVBLILIVS SYRVS

[65–5 BCE]

PVBLILII SYRI MIMI SENTENTIAE

Discipulus est prioris posterior dies.
Damnare est obiurgare cum auxilio est opus.
Diu apparandum est bellum ut vineas celerius.
Dixeris male dicta cuncta cum ingratum hominem dixeris.
De inimico non loquaris male sed cogites.
Deliberare utilia mora tutissima est.
Dolor decrescit ubi quo crescat non habet.
Didicere flere feminae in mendacium.
Discordia fit carior concordia.
Deliberandum est saepe: statuendum est semel.
Difficilem habere oportet aurem ad crimina.
Dum est vita grata, mortis conditio optima est.
Damnum appellandum est cum mala fama luorum.
Ducis in consilio posita est virtus militum.
Dies quod donat timeas: cito raptum venit.
Dimissum quod nescitur non amittitur.
Deliberando discitur sapientia.
Deliberando saepe perit occasio.
Duplex fit bonitas simul accessit celeritas.
Damnati lingua vocem habet, vim non habet.
Dolor animi <nimio> gravior est quam corporis.
Dulce etiam fugias fieri quod amarum potest.
Difficile est dolori convenire cum patientia.
Deos ridere credo cum felix vovet.
Durum est negare superior cum supplicat.
Dissolvitur lex cum fit iudex misericors.
Dominari ex parte est cum superior supplicat.
Decima hora amicos plures quam prima invenit.
Etiam innocentes cogit mentiri dolor.
Etiam in peccato recte praestatur fides.
Etiam celeritas in desiderio mora est.
Ex vitio alterius sapiens emendat suum.
Et deest et superest miseris cogitatio.
Etiam oblivisci quid sis interdum expedit.
Ex hominum questu facta Fortuna est dea.
Effugere cupiditatem regnum est vincere.

Exsul ubi ei nusquam domus est sine sepulcro est mortuus.
Etiam qui faciunt oderunt iniuriam.
Eripere telum non dare irato decet.
Exsilium patitur patriae qui se denegat.
Etiam capillus unus habet umbram suam.
Eheu quam miserum est fieri metuendo senem!
Etiam hosti est aequus qui habet in consilio fidem.
Excelsis multo facilius casus nocet.
Extrema semper de ante factis iudicant.
Ex lite multa gratia fit formosior.
Etiam bonis malum saepe est adsuescere.
Est utique profunda ignorantia nescire quod pecces.
Etiam sine lege poena est conscientia.
Errat datum qui sibi quod extortum est putat.
Fidem qui perdit quo rem servat relicuam?
Fortuna cum blanditur captatum venit.
Fortunam citius reperias quam retineas.
Formosa facies muta commendatio est.
Frustra rogatur qui misereri non potest.
Fortuna unde aliquid fregit cassumst <reficere>.
Fraus est accipere quod non possis reddere.
Fortuna nimium quem fovet stultum facit.
Fatetur facinus is qui iudicium fugit.
Felix improbitas optimorum est calamitas.
Feras non culpes quod mutari non potest.
Futura pugnant ne se superari sinant.
Furor fit laesa saepius patientia.
Fidem qui perdit nihil pote ultra perdere.
Facilitas animi ad partem stultitiae rapit.
Fides in animum unde abiit <vix> umquam redit.
Fidem nemo umquam perdit nisi qui non habet.
Fortuna obesse nulli contenta est semel.
Fulmen est ubi cum potestate habitat iracundia.
Frustra, cum ad senectam ventum est, repetas adulescentiam.
Falsum maledictum malevolum mendacium est.
Feminae naturam regere desperare est otium.
Feras difficilia ut facilia perferas.
Fortuna vitrea est: tum cum splendet frangitur.
Feras quod laedit ut quod prodest perferas.
Facit gradum Fortuna quem nemo videt.
Fortuna plus homini quam consilium valet.
Frugalitas miseria est rumoris boni.
Famulatur dominus ubi timet quibus imperat.
Facile invenies qui bene faciant cum qui fecerunt coles.
Frenos imponit linguae conscientia.

Felicitatem in dubiis virtus impetrat.
Falsum etiam est verum quod constituit superior.
Grave praeiudicium est quod iudicium non habet.
Gravissima est probi hominis iracundia.
Gravis animi poena est quem post facti paenitet.
Gravis animus dubiam non habet sententiam.
Gravius malum omne est quod sub adspectu latet.
Gravius nocet quodcumque inexpertum accidit.
Gravis est inimicus is qui latet in pectore.
Gravissimum est imperium consuetudinis.
Grave crimen, etiam leviter cum est dictum, nocet.
Grave est quod laetus dederis tristem recipere.
(Geminat peccatum quem delicti non pudet.)
Heu quam difficilis gloriae custodia est!
Homo extra corpus est suum cum irascitur.
Heu quam est timendus qui mori tutum putat!
Homo qui in homine calamitoso est misericors meminit sui.
Honesta turpitudo est pro causa bona.
Habet in adversis auxilia qui in secundis commodat.
Heu quam miserum est ab eo laedi de quo non possis queri!
Hominem experiri multa paupertas iubet.
Heu dolor quam miser est qui in tormento vocem non habet!
Heu quam multa paenitenda incurrunt vivendo diu!
Heu quam miserum est discere servire † ubi sis doctus dominari!
Habet suum venenum blanda oratio.
Homo totiens moritur quotiens amittit suos.
Homo semper aliud, Fortuna aliud cogitat,
Honestus rumor alterum est patrimonium.
Homo ne sit sine dolore fortunam invenit.
Secunda in paupertate fortuna est fides.
Si nihil velis timere, metuas omnia.
Summissum imperium non tenet vires suas.
Secundus est a matre nutricis dolor.
Sibi supplicium ipse dat quem admissi paenitet.
Suum sequitur lumen semper innocentia.
Stultum est ulcisci velle alium poena sua.
Sibi primum auxilium eripere est leges tollere.
Suis qui nescit parcere inimicis favet.
Sine dolore est vulnus quod ferendum est cum victoria.
Semper metuendo sapiens evitat malum.
Stultum est queri de adversis, ubi culpa est tua.
Solet hora quod multi anni abstulerunt reddere.
Spina etiam grata est ex qua spectatur rosa.
Suspicio probatis tacita iniuria est.
Superari a superiore pars est gloriae.

Supplicem hominem opprimere virtus non est sed crudelitas.
Sat est disertus e quo loquitur veritas.
Thesaurum in sepulcro ponit qui senem herederem facit.
Taciturnitas stulto homini pro sapientia est.
Tam deest avaro quod habet quam quod non habet.
Tarde sed graviter sapiens <mens> irascitur.
Tuti sunt omnes unus ubi defenditur.
Temptando cuncta caeci quoque tuto ambulant.
Tam de se iudex iudicat quam de reo.
Ubi fata peccant, hominum consilia excidunt.
Voluptas e difficili data dulcissima est.
Ubi omnis vitae metus est, mors est optima.
Unus deus poenam affert, multi cogitant.
Voluptas tacita metus est mage quam gaudium.
Viri boni est nescire facere iniuriam.
Vultu an natura sapiens sis, multum interest.
Virtuti amorem nemo honeste denegat.
Ubi libertas cecidit, audet libere nemo loqui.
Vita otiosa regnum est et curae minus.
Ubi omnes peccant, spes querelae tollitur.
Ut plures corrigantur, † rite pauci eliduntur.
Virtutis omnis impedimentum est timor.
Ubi iudicat qui accusat, vis non lex valet.
Ubi emas aliena, caveas ne vendas tua.
Ubi peccatum cito corrigitur, fama solet ignoscere.
Ubi innocens damnatur, pars patriae exsulat.
Vincere est honestum, opprimere acerbum, pulchrum ignoscere.
(Velox consilium sequitur paenitentia.)

READING 3-C

QVINTVS CVRTIVS RVFVS

[27–75 CE]

HISTORIAE ALEXANDRI

LIBER IX

[**I**, 1] Alexander tam memorabili victoria laetus, qua sibi Orientis finis apertos esse censebat, Soli victimis caesis milites quoque, quo promptioribus animis reliqua belli obirent, pro contione laudatos docuit, quidquid Indis virium fuisset, illa dimicatione prostratum: [2] cetera opimam praedam fore celebratasque opes in ea regione eminere, quam peterent. Proinde iam vilia et obsoleta esse spolia de Persis; gemmis margaritisque et auro atque ebore Macedoniam Graeciamque, non suas tantum domos repleturos. [3] Avidi milites et pecuniae et gloriae, simul quia numquam eos adfirmatio eius fefellerat, pollicentur operam; dimissique cum bona spe navigia exaedificari iubet, ut, cum totam Asiam percucurrisset, finem terrarum mare inviseret. [4] Multa materia navalis in proximis montibus erat; quam caedere adgressi magnitudinis invisitatae repperere serpentes; [5] rhinocerotes quoque, rarum alibi animal, in isdem montibus erant: ceterum hoc nomen beluis inditum a Graecis; sermonis eius ignari aliud lingua sua usurpant. [6] Rex, duabus urbibus conditis in utraque fluminis, quod superaverat, ripa copiarum duces coronis et mille aureis singulos donat. Ceteris quoque pro portione aut gradus, quem in amicitia obtinebant, aut navatae operae honos habitus est. [7] Abisares, qui, priusquam cum Poro dimicaretur, legatos ad Alexandrum miserat, rursus alios misit pollicentes omnia facturum quae imperasset, modo ne cogeretur corpus suum dedere: neque enim aut sine regio imperio victurum aut regnaturum esse captivum. [8] Cui Alexander nuntiari iussit, si gravaretur ad se venire, ipsum ad eum esse venturum.

Hinc porro amne superato ad interiora Indiae processit. [9] Silvae erant prope in inmensum spatium diffusae procerisque et in eximiam altitudinem editis arboribus umbrosae. [10] Plerique rami instar ingentium stipitum flexi in humum rursus, qua se curvaverant, erigebantur, adeo ut species esset non rami resurgentis, sed arboris ex sua radice generatae. [11] Caeli temperies salubris, quippe et vim solis umbrae levant, et aquae large manant e fontibus. [12] Ceterum hic quoque serpentium magna vis erat, squamis fulgorem auri reddentibus; virus haud ullum magis noxium est: quippe morsum praesens mors sequebatur, donec ab incolis remedium oblatum est. [13] Hinc per deserta ventum est ad flumen Hiarotim. Iunctum erat flumini nemus opacum arboribus alibi invisitatis agrestiumque pavonum multitudine frequens. [14] Castris inde motis oppidum haud procul positum corona capit, obsidibusque acceptis stipendium inponit.

Ad magnam deinde, ut in ea regione, urbem pervenit, non muro solum, sed etiam palude munitam. [15] Ceterum barbari vehiculis inter se iunctis dimicaturi occurrerunt; tela aliis hastae, aliis secures erant, transiliebantque in vehicula strenuo saltu, cum succurrere laborantibus suis vellent. [16] Ac primo insolitum genus pugnae Macedonas terruit, cum eminus vulnerarentur. Deinde, spreto tam incondito auxilio, ab utroque latere vehiculis circumfusi repugnantes fodere coeperunt. [17] Et vincula, quis conserta erant, iussit incidi, quo facilius singula circumvenirentur; itaque, octo milibus suorum amissis in oppidum refugerunt. [18] Postero die, scalis undique admotis muri occupantur. Paucis pernicitas saluti fuit, qui cognito urbis excidio paludem transnavere et in vicina oppida ingentem intulere terrorem, invictum exercitum et deorum profecto advenisse memorantes.

[19] Alexander ad vastandam eam regionem Perdicca cum expedita manu misso partem copiarum Eumeni tradidit, ut is quoque barbaros ad deditionem conpelleret; ipse ceteros ad urbem validam, in quam aliarum quoque confugerant incolae, duxit. [20] Oppidani missis, qui regem deprecarentur, nihilo minus bellum parabant. Quippe orta seditio in diversa consilia diduxerat vulgum; alii omnia deditione potiora, quidam nullam opem in ipsis esse ducebant. [21] Sed dum nihil in commune consulitur, qui deditioni inminebant, apertis portis hostem recipiunt. [22] Alexander, quamquam belli auctoribus iure poterat irasci, tamen omnibus venia data et obsidibus acceptis ad proximam deinde urbem castra movit. [23] Obsides ducebantur ante agmen. Quos, cum ex muris agnovissent, utpote gentis eiusdem, in colloquium convocaverunt. Illi clementiam regis simulque vim commemorando ad deditionem eos conpulere; ceterasque urbes simili modo domitas in fidem accepit. [24] Hinc in regnum Sophites perventum est. Gens, ut barbari credunt, sapientia excellet bonisque moribus regitur. [25] Genitos liberos non parentum arbitrio tollunt aluntque, sed eorum, quibus spectandi infantum habitum cura mandata est. Si quos insignes aut aliqua parte membrorum inutiles notaverunt, necari iubent. [26] Nuptiis coeunt non genere ac nobilitate coniunctis, sed electa corporum specie, quia eadem aestimatur in liberis. [27] Huius gentis oppidum, cui Alexander admoverat copias, ab ipso Sophite obtinebatur. Clausae erant portae, sed nulli in muris turribusque se armati ostendebant, dubitabantque Macedones deseruissent urbem incolae, an fraude se occulerent, [28] cum subito patefacta porta rex Indus cum duobus adultis filiis occurrit multum inter omnes barbaros eminens corporis specie. [29] Vestis erat auro purpuraque distincta, quae etiam crura velabat; aureis soleis inseruerat gemmas; lacerti quoque et brachia margaritis ornata erant. [30] Pendebant ex auribus insignes candore ac magnitudine lapilli. Baculum aureum berylli distinguebant. Quo tradito precatus, ut sospes acciperet, se liberosque et gentem suam dedidit.

[31] Nobiles ad venandum canes in ea regione sunt; latratu abstinere dicuntur cum viderunt feram, leonibus maxime infesti. [32] Horum vim ut ostenderet Alexandro in conspectu leonem eximiae magnitudinis

iussit emitti, et quattuor omnino admoveri canes, qui celeriter feram occupaverunt. Tum ex his, qui adsueverant talibus ministeriis, unus canis leoni cum aliis inhaerentis crus avellere et, quia non sequebatur, ferro amputare coepit. [33] Ne sic quidem pertinacia victa rursus aliam partem secare institit, et inde non segnius inhaerentem ferro subinde caedebat. Ille in vulnere ferae dentes moribundus quoque infixerat: tantam in illis animalibus ad venandum cupiditatem ingenerasse naturam memoriae proditum est! [34] Equidem plura transcribo quam credo: nam nec adfirmare sustineo, de quibus dubito, nec subducere, quae accepi. [35] Relicto igitur Sophite in suo regno ad fluvium Hypasin processit Hephaestione, qui diversam regionem subegerat, coniuncto. [36] Phegeus erat gentis proximae rex, qui popularibus suis colere agros, ut adsueverant, iussis Alexandro cum donis occurrit, nihil quod imperaret detrectans.

[**II**, 2] Biduum apud eum substitit rex; tertio die amnem superare decreverat, transitu difficilem non spatio solum aquarum, sed etiam saxis inpeditum. [2] Percontatus igitur Phegea, quae noscenda erant, duodecim dierum ultra flumen per vastas solitudines iter esse cognoscit: [3] excipere deinde Gangen, maximum totius Indiae fluminum: ulteriorem ripam colere gentes Gangaridas et Prasios eorumque regemesse Aggrammen viginti, milibus equitum ducentisque peditum obsidentem vias; [4] ad hoc quadrigarum duo milia trahere, et, praecipuum terrorem, elephantos, quos trium milium numerum e plere dicebat. [5] Incredibilia regi omnia videbantur. Igitur Porum — nam cum eo erat — percontatur an vera essent, quae dicerentur. [6] Ille vires quidem gentis et regni haud falso iactari adfirmat: ceterum, qui regnaret, non modo ignobilem esse, sed etiam ultimae sortis; quippe patrem eius, tonsorem vix diurno quaestu propulsantem famem, propter habitum haud indecorum cordi fuisse reginae. [7] Ab ea in propiorem eius, qui tum regnasset, amicitiae locum admotum, interfecto eo per insidias sub specie tutelae liberum eius invasisse regnum; necatisque pueris hunc, qui nunc regnat, generasse, invisum vilemque popularibus, magis paternae fortunae quam suae memorem. [8] Adfirmatio Pori multiplicem animo regis iniecerat curam. Hostem beluasque spernebat, situm locorum et vim fluminum extimescebat. [9] Relegatos in ultimum paene rerum humanarum persequi terminum et eruere arduum videbatur. Rursus avaritia gloriae et insatiabilis cupido famae nihil invium, nihil remotum videri sinebat. [10] Et interdum dubitabat an Macedones tot emensi spatia terrarum, in acie et in castris senes facti per obiecta flumina, per tot naturae obstantes difficultates secuturi essent: abundantes onustosque praeda magis parta frui velle, quam adquirenda fatigari. [11] Non idem sibi et militibus animi. Sese totius orbis imperium mente conplexum adhuc in operum suorum primordio stare, militem labore defetigatum proximum quemque fructum finito tandem periculo expetere.

[12] Vicit ergo cupido rationem, et ad contionem vocatis militibus ad hunc maxime modum disseruit: « Non ignoro, milites, multa, quae

terrere vos possent, ab incolis Indiae per hos dies de industria esse iactata. [13] Sed non est inprovisa vobis mentientium vanitas. Sic Ciliciae fauces, sic Mesopotamiae campos, Tigrim et Euphraten, quorum alterum vado transiimus, alterum ponte, terribilem fecerant Persae. [14] Numquam ad liquidum fama perducitur; omnia illa tradente maiora sunt vero. Nostra quoque gloria, cum sit ex solido, plus tamen habet nominis quam operis.

READING 3-D

SENTENTIARVM STRVCTVRA LATINARVM

structure of Latin sentences

[200 BCE–2001 CE]

(Post recessum ex Tuderto Pii) Iacobo Picinino, [qui ex troiano conflictu cum paucis hisque prorsus inermibus ac nudis in Aprutios profugerat nec suis rebus, (qua consulere posset) ullam inuenerat uiam] ex insperato *fortuna* oblata est, (que miserum subleuaret.) Rogerottus comitisse Celani filius, [qui preter uoluntatem matris Gallicis militasset ac propterea minus gratie apud eam inuenisset.] Picininum adiens iudicium in se matris iniquum dicit: feminam Ferdinando parentem atque aduersam Gallis eiiciendam fore, sibique tradendum imperium, [qui nunquam Aragonenses aut Cathalonos amauerit]; habere amicos (qui sibi matrem tradant cum exercitu profecturo.) petit ut secum pergat cum his (que sibi remanserant) copiis opulenta spolia relaturus.

PONTIFEX PIVS II (AENEAS SYLVIVS PICCOLOMINI) [1458–1464 CE]

Angelum pacis Míchael ad istam,
(Christe) demítti rogitámus aulam,
cuncta [quo crebro veniénte] crescant
próspera nobis.
Angelus fortis Gábriel, [ut hostem
pellat antíquum] vólitet supérne,
sáepius templum cúpiens favéndo
vísere nostrum.
Angelum nobis médicum salútis
mitte de caelis Ráphael, [ut omnes
sanet aegrótos paritérque nostros
dírigat actus.]
(Christe sanctórum decus angelórum)
adsit illórum chorus usque nobis,
[ut simul tandem Tríadi per aevum
cármina demus.] Amen.

LITVRGIA HORARVM PAVLI VI [1972 CE]

KEY:
Subjects
Objects
Verbs
Distant connections
[Larger clauses]
(Lesser clauses)
et and -que

Ac [dum prima novis adolescit frondibus aetas,]
parcendum teneris et [dum se laetus ad auras
palmes agit laxis per purum immissus habenis]
ipsa acie nondum falcis temptanda, sed uncis
carpendae manibus frondes interque legendae.
inde (ubi iam validis amplexae stirpibus ulmos
exierint) tum stringe comas, tum bracchia tonde
(ante reformidant ferrum,) tum denique dura
exerce imperia et ramos compesce fluentis.

PVBLIVS VERGILIVS MARO [70–19 BCE]

Non sum itaque tibi illa monstraturus (quibus usos esse multos scio: ut peregrinatione te uel longa detineas uel amoena delectes, ut rationum accipiendarum diligentia, patrimonii administratione multum occupes temporis, ut semper nouo te aliquo negotio inplices: omnia ista ad exiguum momentum prosunt nec remedia doloris sed inpedimenta sunt; ego autem malo illum desinere quam decipi. Itaque illo te duco quo omnibus (qui fortunam fugiunt) confugiendum est, ad liberalia studia: illa sanabunt uulnus tuum, illa omnem tristitiam tibi euellent.

LVCIVS ANNAEVS SENECA [4 BCE–65 CE]

Postulat optima civilis societatis ratio, [ut populares scholae, (quae patent omnibus cuiusque e populo classis pueris,) ac publica universim instituta, (quae litteris severioribusque disciplinis tradendis et educationi iuventutis curandae sunt destinata.) eximantur ab omni Ecclesiae auctoritate, moderatrice vi et ingerentia, plenoque civilis ac politicae auctoritatis arbitrio subiciantur ad imperantium placita et ad communium aetatis opinionum amussim (31').

PONTIFEX PIVS IX [1864 CE]

KEY:
Subjects
Objects
Verbs
Distant connections
[Larger clauses]
(Lesser clauses)
et and -que

Age nunc: omnes [ecclesiae] erraverint; deceptus sit apostolus de testimonio reddendo quibusdam; nullam respexerit Spiritus Sanctus, [uti eam in veritatem deduceret] ad hoc missus a Christo, ad hoc postulatus de Patre, [ut esset doctor veritatis;] neglexerit officium Dei villicus, Christi vicarius, sinens ecclesias aliter interim intellegere aliter credere, (quam ipse per apostolos praedicabat:) ecquid verisimile est, [ut tot ac tantae in unam fidem erraverint?]

SEPTIMIVS FLORENS TERTVLLIANVS [c. 150/170–c. 230 CE]

ludite [ut lubet] et breui
liberos date. non decet
tam uetus sine liberis
nomen esse sed indidem
semper ingenerari.

Torquatus [uolo] paruulus
matris e gremio suae
porrigens teneras manus
dulce rideat ad patrem
(semihiante labello.)

GAIVS VALERIVS CATVLLVS [84–54 BCE]

KEY: Subjects are underlined with a solid line.
Objects are underlined with a broken line.
Verbs are underlined with a line of dots.
Distant connections of words and phrases are underlined with a wavey line.
[Larger clauses are in square brackets,] (lesser ones in rounded parentheses.)
The words et and -que are placed in boxes.
Note: This code is used to illustrate the functions and connections of words as an aid to teaching, and is not intended to appear in absolutely every instance.

READING 3-E

AMBROSIVS MEDIOLANENSIS

[339–397 CE]

EXAMERON VI

Inhaereamus igitur propheticis dictis nec spiritus sancti quasi uilia despectui habeamus adloquia. producat inquit terra animam uiuentem pecorum et bestiarum et reptilium. quid argumentamur alia, ubi euidenter creaturarum terrestrium natura formatur? currit enim in constitutione mundi per omnem creaturam dei uerbum, ut subito de terris omnia quae statuit deus animantium genera producantur et in futurum lege praescripta secundum genus sibi similitudinemque uniuersa succedant, ut leo leonem generet, tigris tigridem, bos bouem, cygnus cygnum, aquila aquilam. semel praeceptum in perpetuum inoleuit naturae, et ideo ministerii sui obsequium praebere terra non desinit, ut priscae animantium species reparabili generis successione in nouas reparentur aetates. sed uis ad usum hominis deriuare quae genita sunt? noli ueritatem unicuique generi naturae propriae denegare, et multo magia ea ad gratiam aptabis humanam, primura quia omnia genera pecorum, bestiarum ac piscium in aluum natura prostrauit, ut alia uentre repant, alia quae pedibus sustinentur demersa magis quadripedi corporis gressu et uelut adfixa terris uideas esse quam libera, siquidem, cum erigendi se non habeant facultatem, de terra uictum requirunt et uentris, in quem deflectuntur, solas sequuntur uoluptates. caue, o homo, pecorum more curuari, caue in aluum te non tam corpore quam cupiditate deflectas. respice corporis tui formam et speciem congruentem celsi uigoris adsume, sine sola animalia prona pascantur. cur te in edendo sternis ipse, quem natura non strauit? cur eo delectaris in quo naturae iniuria est? cur noctes et dies cibo intentus pecorum more terrena depasceris? cur inlecebris corporalibus deditus ipsum te inhonoras, dum uentri atque eius passionibus seruis? cur intellectum tibi adimis, quem tibi creator adtribuit? cur te iumentis comparas, a quibus te uoluit deus segregare dicens: nolite fieri sicut equus et mulus, in quibus non est intellectus? aut si te edacitas equi intemperantiaque delectate et adhinnire ad feminas uoluptati est, delectet in freno maxillas tuas camoque constringi. si crudelitas pascit — ferarum haec rabies est, quae propter saeuitiam trucidantur —, uide ne in te quoque crudelitatis tuae uertatur inmanitas.

Piger asinus et expositus ad praedam sensuque tardior quid aliud docet nisi nos uiuaciores esse debere nec desidia corporis animique pigrescere, confugere ad fidem, quae onera grauia ableuare consuerit? fraudulenta uulpes foueis se latibulisque demergens nonne indicium est infructuosum esse animal odioque dignum propter rapinam, despectui propter infirmitatem et ideo suae incautam salutis, dum insidiatur alienis? perdicem astutam, quae aliena oua diripiat, hoc est perdicis alterius, et corpore foueat suo, sed fraudis suae fructum habere non posse, quia, cum eduxerit pullos suos, amittit eos, quia, ubi uocem eius audierint quae oua generauit relicta ea ad illam se naturali quodam munere et amore conferunt quam ueram sibi matrem ouorum generatione cognouerint significantes hanc nutricis fungi officio, illam parentis. itaque incassum proprios fundit labores ac fraudis suae pretio multatur. unde et Hieremias ait: clamauit perdix et congregauit quae non peperit, id est oua congregauit et clamauit quasi ouans suae fraudis effectu, sed ludit operam, quia inpenso labore alii educit quos ipsa diuturnae fotu sedulitatis animauerit. huius imitator est diabolus, qui generationes creatoris aeterni rapere contendit, et si quos insipientes et sensus proprii carentes uigore potuerit congregare fouens eos inlecebris corporalibus, ubi primum uox Christi paruolis fuerit infusa, discedunt atque ad earn se conferunt matrem, quae pullos suos sicut auis materno amore conplectitur. Congregauit enim diabolus gentiles, quos non creauerat; sed ubi in euangelio suo uocem Christus emisit, ad eum se potissimum contulerunt quos sub umbra alarum suarum ipse suscepit et matri dedit ecclesiae nutriendos. leo naturae suae superbus ferocia aliarum ferarum generibus miscere se nescit, sed quasi rex quidam plurimorum dedignatur consortium, qui etiam cibura fastidit hesternum, etiam ipsas suae escae reliquias auersatur. quae autem ei se sociare fera audeat, cuius uoci tantus naturaliter inest terror, ut multa animantium, quae per celeritatem possent impetum eius euadere, rugientis eius sonitu uelut quadam ui adtonita atque icta deficiant? nam de pardi specie nec scriptura siluit quod uarietate coloris motus uarios animae suae prodat. dicit enim Hieremias: si mutabit Aethiops pellem suam et pardus uarietatem suam. non solum enim de figura, sed etiam de mobilitate furoris istud accipitur, eo quod tenebrosis et inquietis ac mobilibus infidae mentis atque animi mutationibus decoloratus populus Iudaeorum boni propositi gratiam iam tenere non possit nec ad emendationem ullam correctionemque remeare, qui semel ferinam induerit immanitatem.

Est tamen etiam in natura quadrupedum quod imitari nos sermo adhortetur propheticus, quo exemplo caueamus desidiam et exiguitate uel infirmitate corporis a uirtutis studio non reflectamur neque reuocemur ab illius propositi magnitudine. exigua est enim formica, quae maiora suis audet uiribus neque seruitio ad operandum cogitur, sed spontaneae proposito prospicientiae futura alimentorum subsidia sibi praestruit. cuius ut imiteris industriam scriptura te commonet dicens: confer te ad formicam, o piger, et imitare uias eius et esto illa sapientior. illa enim nullam culturam possidet: neque eum qui se cogat habens neque sub domino agens quemadmodum praeparat escam, quae de tuis laboribus sibi messem recondit! et cum tu plerumque egeas, illa non indiget. nulla sunt ei clausa horrea, nullae inpenetrabiles custodiae, nulli inuiolabiles acerui.

spectat custos: furtaque prohibere non audet, aspicit sua damna possessor nec uindicat. nigro conuectatur agmine praeda per campos, feruent semitae comitatu uiantum et quae conprehendi angusto ore non possunt umeris grandia frumenta truduntur. spectat haec dominus messis et erubescit tam parca piae industriae negare conpendia. quid autem de canibus loquar, quibus insitum est natura quadam referre gratiam et sollicitas excubias pro dominorum salute praetendere? unde ad inmemores beneficii et desides atque ignauos clamat scriptura: canes muti, nescientes latrare. canes ergo sunt, qui nouerint latrare pro dominis, nouerint sua tecta defendere. unde et tu disce uocem tuam exercere pro Christo, quando ouile Christi incursant lupi graues, disce in ore tuo uerbum tenere, ne quasi mutus canis commissam tibi fidei custodiam quodam praeuaricationis silentio deseruisse uidearis. talis canis uiator et comes angeli est, quem Raphahel in libro prophetico non otiose sibi et Tobis filio adiungendum putauit, quando perrexit, uti Asmodaeum fugaret, firmaret copulam; memoris enim affectus gratia pellitur daemonium, stabilitur coniugium. mutae itaque specie bestiae sanctus Raphahel angelus Tobiae iuuenis quem tuendum receperat ad relationem gratiae erudibat adfectum. quis enim non erubescat gratiam bene de se merentibus non referre, cum uideat etiam bestias refugere crimen ingrati? et illae inpertitae alimoniae seruant memoriam, tu non seruas salutis acceptae ?

Ursa insidians licet, ut scriptura ait — est enim plena fraudis fera —, tamen fertur informes utero partus edere, sed natos lingua fingere atque in speciem sui similitudinemque formare. non miraris in fera tam pii oris officia, cuius pietas naturam exprimit? ursa igitur partus suos ad sui effingit similitudinem, tu filios tuos instituere similes tibi non potes? quid quod etiam medendi industriam non praetermisit? siquidem graui adfecta caede et consauciata uulneribus mederi sibi nouit herbae, cui nomen est flomus, ut Graeci adpellant, ulcera subiciens sua, ut solo curentur adtactu. serpens quoque pastu fenuculi caecitatem repellit exceptam. itaque ubi oculos obduci sibi senserit, nota remedia petit nec fraudatur effectu. testudo uisceribus pasta serpentis, cum uenenum aduerterit sibi serpere, origano medicinam suae salutis exercet et, cum sit uolutabris palustribus mersa, curare se tamen proprio nouit antidoto certoque auxilio sanitatis potestates herbarum etiam ipsa scire se conprobat. uideas etiam uulpem lacrimola pinus medentem sibi et tali remedio inminentis mortis spatial proferentem. clamat ipse dominus in Hieremiae libro: turtur et hirundo, agri passeres custodierunt tempora introitus sui, populus autem meus non cognouit iudicia domini. nouit hirundo quando ueniat, quando etiam reuertatur, nouit etiam pia auis adnuntiare aduentus sui testimonio ueris indicium, nouit etiam formica explorare serenitatis tempora; nam cum aduerterit madidatos imbre fructus suos umescere, explorato diligentius aere quando iugem possit seruare temperiem, aceruos reserat suos et de cauernis foras suis umeris exportat, ut iugi sole propria frumenta siccentur.

READING 3-F

PAVLINVS NOLANVS

[353–431 CE]

CARMINA

II.

Pauperis ut placeat carum tibi munus amici,
munera ne reputes quae mittis ditia nobis.
nam tibi quid dignum referam pro piscibus illis,
quos tibi uicinum locupleti gurgite litus
suppeditat miros specie formaque diremptos.
at mihi uix alto uada per saxosa profundo
rarus in obscura generatur sphondylus alga.
hinc te participans bis quinque et bis tibi ternas
transmisi aequoreo redolentes nectare testas,
quas uiscus praedulce replet bicolore medulla,
oro libens sumas nec uilia dedigneris,
quae sunt parua modo magno metitus amore.

XIII.

Felix, hoc merito quod nomine, nomine et idem
qui merito, redit alma dies, qua te sibi summas
adsciuit patriam confessum Christus in aulam,
tempus adest plenis grates tibi fundere uotis.
o pater, o domine, indignis licet optime seruis,
tandem exoratum est inter tua limina nobis
natalem celebrare tuum. tria tempore longo
lustra cucurrerunt, ex quo sollemibus istis
coram uota tibi, coram mea corda dicaui.
ex illo qui me terraque marique labores
distulerint a sede tua procul orbe remoto,
nouisti; nam te mihi semper ubique propinquum
inter dura uiae uitaeque incerta uocaui.
et maria intraui duce te, quia cura pericli
cessit amore tui, nec te sine; nam tua sensi
praesidia in domino superans maris aspera Christo;
semper eo et terris te propter tutus et undis.
hunc, precor, aeterna pietate et pace serenum
posce tuis, cuius magno stas nomine, Felix.
nunc iuuat effusas in gaudia soluere mentes,
cara dies tandem quoniam hic praesentibus orta est,

semper et externum nobis celebrata per orbem,
quae te sacrauit terris et contulit astris.
ecce uias uario plebs discolor agmine pingit,
urbes innumeras una miramur in urbe.
o felix Felice tuo tibi praesule Nola,
inclita ciue sacro, caelesti firma patrono
postque ipsam titulos Romam sortita secundos,
quae prius imperio tantum et uictricibus armis,
nunc et apostolicis terrarum est prima sepulchris!
sis bonus o felixque tuis dominumque potentem
exores, liceat placati munere Christi
post pelagi fluctus mundi quoque fluctibus actis
in statione tua placido consistere portu.
hoc bene subductam religaui litore classem,
in te, conpositae mihi fixa sit anchora uitae.

VI.

LAVS SANCTI IOHANNIS.

Summe pater rerum caelique aeterna potestas,
cum quo nostra salus, sanctorum gloria, Christe,
spiritus et patri pariter natoque cohaerens,
qui mentes linguasque regis uiresque ministras,
promeruit quas sola fides, cui plena potestas
brutis ingenium uocemque infundere mutis,
praesta euangelico ductum de fonte Iohannem
in nostra arenti decurrere carmina riuo.
ille quidem tantus, quantum potuit dare mundo
qui nasci talem noua per miracula iussit . . .

XII.

Inclite confessor, meritis et nomine Felix,
mens pietate potens, summi mens accola caeli
nec minus in totis experta potentia terris,
qui dominum Christum non uincta uoce professus
contemnendo truces meruisti euadere poenas,
deuotamque animam tormenta per omnia Christo
sponte tua iussus laxatis reddere membris
liquisti uacuos rabidis lictoribus artus . . .

VIII.

Cur gentes fremuere et inania cur meditati
sunt populi? adstiterunt proceres cum regibus acti
aduersum dominum et Christum uesana frementes:

uincula rumpamus, iuga discutiamus eorum.
qui manet aeterno totis moderamine caelis,
inridebit eos iustaque loquetur in ira
terribilique minax uerbo turbabit iniquos:
ast ego rex ab eo parili dicione creatus,
praeceptum domini super almum praedico Sion.
ipse ad me dominus, meus, inquit, filius es tu,
teque hodie genui. pete; sis mihi gentibus heres,
et tua fundatur totis possessio terris.
ferrea uirga tibi est, ualido quia iure tumentes
orbe regis toto populos, ceu uasa recocto
ficta luto frangens corda, ut meliora reforme;
et nunc ecce, omnes, stratis aduertite, reges,
mentibus et quicumque hominum famulantia corda
iudicio regitis rerumque tenetis habenas,
deseruite deo trepidi mixtoque fideles
exultate metu; fiat discordia concors
dissimiles socians affectus pectore in uno,
ne timor adfligat mentes uel gaudia soluant,
si careant laeto pauidi formidine leti.
dicite iustitiam rectosque capessite mores
et iusto trepidate deo, gaudete benigno,
ne quando meritum deus irascatur in orbem
uosque uia iusta iuste pereatis abacti.
amodo iam resilire uia properetis iniqua;
ecce breui cum magna potentis inarserit ira,
uentilet ut totum diuino examine mundum
segreget et paleas igni, frumenta saluti,
tunc omnes, quibus est in eo spes fida, beati.

XXX.

(BASILICAE VETERIS INSCRIPTIONES.)

Felicis penetral prisco uenerabile cultu
lux noua diffusis nunc aperit spatiis.
angusti memores solii gaudete uidentes
praesulis ad laudem quam nitet hoc solium.

Paruus erat locus ante sacris angustus agendis
supplicibusque negans pandere posse manus,
nunc populo spatiosa sacris altaria praebet
officiis medii martyris in gremio.
cuncta deo renouata placent, nouat omnia semper
Christus et in cumulum luminis amplificat.
sic et dilecti solium Felicis honorans
et splendore simul protulit et spatio.

IIII.

ORATIO.

Omnipotens genitor rerum, cui summa potestas,
exaudi si iusta precor: ne sit mihi tristis
ulla dies, placidam nox rumpat nulla quietem.
nec placeant aliena mihi, quin et mea prosint
supplicibus nullusque habeat mihi uota nocendi
aut habeat nocitura nihil. male uelle facultas
nulla sit ac bene posse adsit tranquilla potestas.
mens contenta suo nec turpi dedita lucro
uincat corporeas casto bene conscia lecto
inlecebras, turpesque iocos obscenaque dicta
oderit illa nocens et multum grata malignis
auribus effuso semper rea lingua ueneno.
non obitu adfligar cuiusquam aut funere crescam.
inuideam numquam cuiquam nec mentiar umquam.
adsit laeta domus epulisque adludat inemptis
uerna satur fidusque comes nitidusque minister,
morigera et coniunx caraque ex coniuge nati.
moribus haec castis tribuit deus, hi sibi mores
perpetuam spondent uentura in saecula uitam.

READING 3-G

BEDA VENERABILIS

[673–735 CE]

HISTORIA ECCLESIASTICA

CAPUT IX.

Ut Ecgberct vir sanctus ad prædicandum in Germaniam venire voluerit, nec valuerit: porro Uictberct aduenerit [Al. adierit] quidem; sed quia nec ipse aliquid profecisset, rursum in Hiberniam unde venerat, redierit.

Eo tempore [DCLXXXIX] venerabilis, et cum omni honorificentia nominandus famulus Christi et sacerdos Ecgberct, quem in Hibernia insula peregrinam ducere vitam pro adipiscenda in cælis patria retulimus, proposuit animo pluribus prodesse; id est, into opere apostolico, verbum Dei aliquibus earum « quæ nondumaudierant, gentibus evangelizando committere: quarum in Germania plurimas noverat esse nationes, a quibus Angli vel Saxones qui nunc Britanniam incolunt, genus et originem duxisse noscuntur; unde haetenus a vicina gente Brittonum corrupte Garmani [*Al.*, Germani] noncupantur. Sunt autem Fresones, Rugini, Danai, Hunni [*Al.* Dani, Huni], antiqui Saxones Boructuari [*Al.*, Boructuarii] : sunt [*Al. add.* etiam] alii perplures hisdem in partibus populi paganis adhuc ritibus servientes, ad quos venire prafatus Christi miles circumnavigata Brittania disposuit, si quos forte ex illis ereptos Satanae ad Christum transferre valeret, vel si hoc fieri non posset, Romam venire ad videnda atque adoranda beatorum apostolorum ac martyrum Christi limina cogitavit.

Sed ne aliquid horum perficeret, superna illi oracula simul et opera restiterunt. Siquidem electis sociis strenuissimis et ad prædicandum verbum idoneis, utpote actione simul el eruditione præclaris, praeparatisque omnibus quae navigantibus esse necessaria videbantur, venit die quadam mane prima ad eum unus de fratribus, discipulus quondum in Brittania, et minister Deo dilecti sacerdotis Boisili, cum esset idem Boisil præpositus monasterii Mailrosensis sub abbate Eata, ut supra narravimus, referens ei visionem quæ sibi eadem nocte apparuisset : « Cum expletis, inquiens, hymnis matutinalibus in lectulo [*Al.* lecto] membra posuissem [*Al.* deposuissem], ac levis mihi somnus obrepisset, apparuit magister quondam meus et nutritor amantissimus Boisil, interrogavitque me, an eum cognoscere possem. Aio : Etiam, tu es enim Boisil. At ille: Ad hoc inquit, veni, ut responsum Domini Salvatoris Ecgbercto adferam, quod te tamen referente oportet ad illum venire. Dic ergo illi quia non valet iter quod proposuit implere: Dei enim voluntatis est ut ad Columbae monasteria magis pergat docenda. » Erat autem Columba primus doctor fidei Christianae transmontanis Pictis ad aquilonem, primusque fundator monasterii quod in Hii insula multis diu Scotorum Pictorumque populis venerabile mansit. Qui videlicet Columba nunc, a nonnullis composito a Cella et Columba nomine, Columcelli vocatur. Audiens autem verba visionis Ecgberct, præcepit fratri qui retulerat ne cuiquam haec alteri referret, ne forte inlusoria esset visio. Ipse autem tacitus rem considerans, veram [*Al.*, veracem] esse timebat: nec tamen a praeparando [*Al.*, parando] itinere, quo ad gentes docendas iret, cessare volebat.

At post dies paucos rursum venit ad cum præfatus frater, dicens quia et ea nocte sibi post expletos Matutinos [*Al.*, expletas Matutinas] Boisil per visum apparuerit, dicens : « Quare tam negligenter ac tepide dixisti Ecgbercto quæ tibi dicenda præcepi? At nunc vade, et dic illi quia, velit nolit, debet ad monasteria Coıumbæ venire, quia aratra eorum non recte incedunt: oportet autem eum ad rectum haec tramitem revocare. » Qui hæc audiens denuo præcepit fratri, ne hæc cui [*Al.*, cuiquam] patefaceret. Ipse vero, tametsi certus est factus de visione, nihilominus tentavit iter dispositum cum fratribus memoratis incipere. Cumque jam navi imposuissent quæ tanti itineris necessitas poscebat, atque opportunos aliquot dies [*Al.*, diebus] ventos exspectarent, facta est nocte quadam tam saeva tempestas, quæ perditis nonnulla ex parte his quae in navi erant rebus, ipsam in littus [*Al.*, latus] jacentem inter undas relinqueret: salvata sunt tamen omnia quæ erant Ecgbercti, et sociorum ejus. Tum ipse [*Al.*, ille] quasi propheticum illud dicens, « Quia propter me est tempestas hæc, subtraxit se illi profectioni, et remanere domi passus est. »

At vero unus de sociis ejus, vocabulo Uictberct, cum esset et ipse contemptu mundi ac doctrinae scientia insignis, nam multos annos in Hibernia peregrinus anachoreticam in magna perfectione vitam egerat [DCXC], ascendit navem, et Fresiam perveniens duobus annis continuis genti illi ac regi ejus Rathbedo [*Al.*, Radhbedo] *verbum salutis prædicabat, neque aliquem tanti laboris fructum apud barbaros invenit auditores. Tunc reversus ad dilectæ locum peregrinationis* [DCXCI], *solito in silentio vacare Domino cœpit; et quoniam externis* [*Al., exterius*] *prodesse ad fidem non poterat, suis amplius ex virtutum exemplis prodesse curabat.*

CAPUT X.

Ut Uilbrord [Al., *Wilbrord*] *in Fresia prædicans, multos ad Christum converterit; et ut socii ejus Hewaldi* [Al., *Ewaldi*] *sint martyrium passi.*

Ut autem vidit vir Domini Ecgberct, quia nec ipse ad prædicandum gentibus venire permittebatur, retentus [*Al. add. et*] ob aliam sanctæ Ecclesiæ utilitatem de qua oraculo fuerat præmonitus, nec Uictberct illas deveniens in partes, quicquam profíciebat, tentavit adhuc in opus verbi mittere viros sanctos et industrios, in quibus eximius Uilbrord presbyterii gradu et merito praefulgebat. Qui cum illo advenissent, erant autem numero duodecim, divertentes ad Pippinum ducem Francorum, gratanter ab illo suscepti sunt: et quia nuper citeriorem Fresiam, expulso inde Rathbedo [*Al.*, Radhbedo] rege, ceperat, illo eos ad praedicandum misit; ipse quoque imperiali auctoritate juvans, ne qui [*Al.*, quis] prædicantibus quicquam molestiæ inferret; multisque eos qui fidem suscipere vellent beneficiis adtollens: unde factum est, opitulante gratia divina, ut multos in brevi ab idolatria ad fidem converterent Christi [DCXCII].

Horum secuti exempla duo quidam presbyteri de natione Anglorum, qui in Hibernia multo tempore pro æterna patria exulaverant, venerunt ad provinciam antiquorum Saxonum, si forte aliquos ibidem prædicando Christo adquirere possent. Erant autem unius ambo, sicut devotionis, sic etiam vocabuli: nam uterque eorum appellabatur Hewald ; ea tamen distinctione, ut pro diversa capillorum specie unus Niger Hewald, alter Albus Hewald diceretur : quorum uterque pietate religionis imbutus, sed Niger Hewald magis sacrarum litterarum erat scientia institutus [*Al.*, instructus]. Qui venientes in provinciam, intraverunt hospitum cujusdam villici, petieruntque ab eo, ut transmitterentur ad satrapam qui super eum [*Al.*, eos] erat, eo quod haberent aliquid legationis et causæ utilis [*Al.*, utilitatis], quod deberent ad illum perferre. Non enim habent regem iidem antiqui Saxones, sed satrapas plurimos suae genti præpositos, qui ingruente belli articulo mittunt æqualiler sortes, et quemcumque sors ostenderit, hunc tempore belli ducem omnes sequuntur, huic obtemperant; peracto autem bello, rursum æqualis potentiæ omnes fiunt satrapæ. Suscepit ergo eos villicus, et promittens se mittere eos ad satrapam qui super se erat, ut petebant, aliquot diebus secum retinuit.

Qui cum cogniti essent a barbaris quod essent alterius religionis, nam [*Al., add.* hymnis] et psalmis semper atque orationibus vacabant, et quotidie sacrificium Deo victimæ salutaris offerebant habentes secum vascula sacra et tabulam altaris vice dedicatam, suspecti sunt habiti, quia si pervenirent ad satrapam et loquerentur cum illo, averterent illum a diis sui et ad novam Christianae fidei religionem transferrent, sicque paulatim omnis eorum provincia veterem cogeretur nova [*Al.*, in novam] mutare culturam. Itaque rapuerunt eos subito, et interemerunt: Album quidem Hewaldum veloci occisione gladii, Nigellum autem longo suppliciorum cruciate et horrenda membrorum omnium discerptione: quos interemptos in Rheno [*Al.*, Rhenum] projecerunt. Quod cum satrapa ille quem videre volebant audisset, iratus est valde quod ad se venire volentes peregrini non permitterentur; et mittens occidit vicanos illos omnes, vicumque incendio consumpsit. Passi sunt autem præfati sacerdotes et famuli Christi quinto Nonarum Octobrium die.

Nec martyrio eorum cælestia defuere miracula.

[Editors' note: *Al.* is an abbreviation for *Alius*, "Other," or *Alii*, "Others," referring to another or other manuscripts.]

READING 3-H

VILLELMVS TYRENSIS

[1130–1185 CE]

CHRONICON

1. Quod tempore Eraclii Augusti Homar, filius Cathab, tercius post Mahumet dux Arabum, universam occupaverit Syriam.

Docent veteres Historie, et idipsum etiam habent Orientalium traditiones, quod tempore quo Eraclius Augustus Romanum administrabat imperium, Mahumet primogeniti Sathane, qui se prophetam a domino missum mentiendo Orientalium regiones et maxime Arabiam seduxerat, ita invaluerat doctrina pestilens et disseminatus langor ita universas occupaverat provincias, ut eius successores non iam exhortationibus vel predicatione, sed gladiis et violentia in suum errorem populos descendere compellerent invitos. Cum enim predictus Augustus, victor reversus de Perside, unde crucem dominicam cum gloria reportaverat, adhuc in Syria moram faceret et per Modestum virum venerabilem, quem Ierosolimis ordinaverat episcopum, ecclesiarum ruinas, quas Cosdroe, Persarum satrapa nequissimus, hostiliter deiecerat, in priorem statum, datis sumptibus necessariis, reformari precepisset, Homar, filius Catap, a predicto seductore tercius erroris et regni successor, cum infinitis Arabum copiis egregiam Palestinorum urbem Gazam iam occupaverat violenter, unde postmodum Damascenorum fines cum suis legionibus et infinita multitudine, quam secum trahebat, ingressus Damascum expugnaverat, predicto imperatore adhuc in Cilicia rei exitum expectante. Quod cum ei nuntiaretur quod Arabes, in tantam elati superbiam et de sua multitudine presumentes, Romanorum fines invadere et eorum urbes sibi vendicare non vererentur, videns quod vires ei non suppeterent ad occurrendum tante multitudini et ut eorum comprimeret insolentiam, maluit ad propria sospes redire quam viribus imparibus bellorum se dubiis committere casibus: sic igitur eo discedente qui afflictis civibus tenebatur patrocinium ministrare, Arabum invaluit violentia, ita ut subito et infra tempus modicum a Laodicia Syrie usque in Egyptum universas occupaverint regiones.

Quis autem fuerit predictus Mahumet et unde et quomodo ad hanc proruperit insaniam ut se prophetam mentiri et a deo missum dicere presumeret, cuius porro vite et conversationis quam diu regnaverit et ubi et quos demum habuerit successors et quomodo pene orbem universum pestiferis eius repleverint dogmatibus qui eum in eodem errore sequuti sunt, alibi disseruimus diligenter, sicut ex subsequentibus datur intelligi manifeste.

2. Que fuit occasio que oportunitatem prestitit quod ita subito Orientem occupavit et quod idem Ierosolimam veniens Templum Domini reedificari precepit.

Cooperabatur sane ad eorum propositum quod paucis ante annis predictus Cosdroe, eandem Syriam violenter ingressus, urbes deiecerat, concenderat suburbana et ecclesias subvertens populum captivaverat, et urbe sancta effracta hostiliter in ea triginta sex civium milia gladio perimens crucem dominicam et loci eiusdem episcopum Zachariam cum residuo populi tam urbis quam regionis universe secum transtulit in Persidem. Hic enim rex Persarum potentissimus domini Mauricii Augusti, cuius adeo familiaris fuit beatus papa Gregorius ut unum de liberis eius de sacro fonte susciperet, filiam nomine Mariam uxorem duxit, cuius gratia coniugii lavacrum regenerationis adeptus est fuitque Romanorum amicissimus quamdiu predictus vixit imperator. Quo demum a Foca Cesare, qui eidem postmodum in imperio successit, proditiose interfecto, abhominatus eorum perfidiam qui tam nefarium hominem et adhuc domini sui cede cruentatum super se regnare passi fuerant, quasi occulte societatis reos et illius sceleris habentes conscientiam, imperii fines violenter ingressus est, in res eorum violenter deseviens, soceri necem uxore stimulante ultum iri desiderans, subactisque ceteris regionibus que Romanorum suberant dicioni, novissime Syriam, ut premisimus, obtinuit, populis eius aut peremptis gladio aut secum in Persidem deductis. Ingressi ergo Arabes terram habitatoribus reperientes vacuam, maiorem subiciendi eam sibi reppererunt oportunitatem. Sic ergo urbem deo amabilem, Ierosolimam videlicet, paribus calamitatibus involutam comprehendentes, populo, qui in ea erat modico, ut eis factus tributarius extremis conditionibus deserviret pepercerunt, permittentes eis suum habere pontificem, ecclesiam etiam, que ut predictum est deiecta fuerat, reparare et religionem libere conservare christianam. Dum autem in eadem civitate princeps supranominatus moram faceret, cepit diligenter a civibus percunctari, et maxime a viro venerabili Sophronio, eiusdem loci episcopo qui Modesto, pie memorie, iam defuncto successerat, ubinam esset locus in quo templum domini fuerat, quod a Tito Romano principe cum ipsa urbe dirutum fuisse legitur. Qui ostendentes ei locum designaverunt, aliqua vetusti operis adhuc extantia vestigia demonstrantes; ubi sumptibus qui sufficere possent ad impensam designatis et convocatis artificibus, subiecta pro votis materia tam ex marmorum diversitate quam ex lignorum differentia multiplici, Templum edificari precepit. Quo postea infra modicum tempus iuxta conceptum mentis feliciter consummato quale hodie Ierosolimis esse dinoscitur, multis et infinitis ditavit possessionibus, unde suppeterent facultates ad habenda perpetuo eiusdem sarta tecta et vetera renovanda et concinnanda luminaria per manum eorum, qui in eodem Templo deservirent. Que autem sit illius forma et que operis elegantia, quoniam pene omnibus notum est non est presentis tractare negocii. Extant porro in eodem Templi edificio intus et extra ex opere musaico Arabici idiomatis litterarum vetustissima monimenta que illius temporis esse creduntur, quibus et auctor et impensarum quantitas et quo tempore opus inceptum quoque consummatum fuerit evidenter declaratur.

3. Quanto tempore sub alternis dominiis Syria iugum passa est servitutis et quomodo fidelibus, qui sub infidelium dicione degebant, utilis fuit amicitia magnifici imperatoris Karoli cum Aarum rege Persarum contracta.

Sic igitur civitate deo amabili et sanctarum sancta peccatis nostris exigentibus infidelium subiecta hostium dicioni, iugum indebite servitutis continuis passa est laboribus per annos quadringentos nonaginta, conditionibus tamen alternis. Nam frequenti rerum mutatione dominos mutavit frequentius, secundum quorum dispositionem plerumque lucida, plerumque nubila recepit intervalla et egrotantis more temporum presentium gravabatur aut respirabat qualitate, plenius tamen convalescere non poterat que infidelium principum et populi sine deo dominatione premebatur violenta. Diebus tamen illius admirabilis et predicandi viri, Aarum videlicet qui cognominatus est Ressith, qui universo prefuit Orienti, cuius liberalitatem et urbanitatem precipuam et mores singulariter commendabiles universus etiam usque hodie Oriens admiratur et preconiis attollit immortalibus, interventu piissimi et inmortalis memorie viri, domini videlicet imperatoris Karoli, qui mutuam intercurrentibus nuntiis frequentibus inter se gratiam et mirabili subnixam federe conciliaverant, plebi dei tranquillitas prestita est et favor principis clementer indultus ad multam consolationem, ita ut magis sub imperatore Karolo quam sub dicto principe degere viderentur. De quo ita legitur in Vita predicti viri gloriosi: *Cum Aarum rege Persarum, qui excepta India totum pene tenebat Orientem, talem habuit in amicitia concordiam, ut is gratiam eius omnium qui in toto orbe terrarum erant regum ac principum amicitie preponeret solumque illum honore ac magnificentia sibi colendum iudicaret. Ac proinde cum legati eius, quos cum donariis ad sacratissimum domini ac Salvatoris nostri sepulchrum locumque resurrectionis miserat, ad eum venissent et ei domini sui voluntatem indicassent, non solum que petebantur fieri permisit, sed etiam sacrum illum et salutarem locum ut illius potestati ascriberetur concessit, et revertentibus legalis suos adiungens inter vestes et aromata et ceteras Orientalium terrarum opes ingentia illi dona direxit, cum ei ante annos paucos eum, quem tunc solum habebat, roganti mitteret elephantum.* Nec solum his qui Ierosolimis habitabant sub infidelium potestate fidelibus, verum et his qui in Egypto et in Affrica sub impietate degebant Sarracenorum, suarum largitionum frequenter dirigebat solatia et pietatis opera porrigebat, sicut in eius Vita legitur, que habet ita: *Circa pauperes sustentandos et gratuitam liberalitatem, quam Greci elemosinam vocant, devotissimus, ut non in patria solum et in suo regno id facere curaverit, verum trans maria in Syriam et Egyptum atque Affricam, Ierosolimis, Alexandrie atque Cartagini, ubi Christianos in paupertate vivere compererat, penurie eorum compatiens pecuniam mittere solebat, ob hoc maxime transmarinorum regum amicitias expetens, ut Christianis sub eorum dominatu degentibus refrigerium aliquod ac relevatio proveniret.* Quot autem et quantis rerum, temporum et dominiorum variis permutationibus hoc medio tempore flagellata fuerit tam predicta dei cultrix civitas quam universa ei adiacens regio siquis scire desiderat, earn relegat Historiam, quam nos de gestis Orientalium principum a tempore predicti seductoris Mahumet usque in hunc presentem diem, qui est nobis ab incarnatione domini millesimus centesimus octuagesimus secundus, per annos quingentos septuaginta rerum seriem complexam cum multo labore confecimus.

4. Quomodo in potestatem devenit Egyptii caliphe et quomodo Hequen nequissimo regnante servitutis iugum super fideles factum sit intolerabilius, et de ruina ecclesie Ierosolimitane.

Porro per idem tempus inter Egyptios et Persas emula nimis et pertinax erat de monarchia contentio. Ministrabat autem odiorum fomitem et incentivum maius contradictoriarum observantia traditionum, qua usque hodie uterque populus contentionibus reciprocis sacrilegos se appellant, sibi non communicantes invicem, ita ut etiam in nominibus velint habere differentiam. Qui enim Orientalium supersticionem sequuntur, lingua eorum Sunni dicuntur, qui vero Egyptiorum traditiones preterunt appellantur Ssiha, qui nostre fidei magis consentire videntur: que autem sit inter eos erroris differentia non est presentis temporis edocere. Hac igitur occasione contendebant adinvicem et nunc his, nunc illis factis superioribus multa circa subditos erat mutatio. Tandem vero Egyptiorum regno invalescente et usque Antiochiam provincias et regiones occupante, cum ceteris in eius urbs sancta legibus communibus descendit potestatem. Sub quo principatu, sicuti captivis aliquando solent tempora indulgentiora concedi, a suis anxietatibus cepit aliquantulum esse remissius, quousque consummata hominum nequicia exigente eidem regno Hequen calipha prefectus est. Hic et predecessorum suorum et successorum pariter longe vincens maliciam, factus est posteris et eius insaniam legentibus sollempnis fabula: adeo enim in omni impietate et nequicia singularis extitit, ut eius vita deo et hominibus odibilis speciales exigat tractatus. Hic inter cetera, que perniciose plurima preceperat. ecclesiam Dominice Resurrectionis, que per venerabilem virum Maximum, eiusdem loci episcopum, precipiente domino Constantino Augusto edificata fuerat, postea per reverentissimum Modestum tempore domini Eraclii reparata, funditus deici mandavit.

READING 3-1

LATINARVM STRVCTVRA SENTENTIARVM

structure of Latin sentences

[200 BCE–2001 CE]

... Recte ergo fermentum domino conparatur, [qui (cum esset specie homo humilitate paruus inbecillitate deiectus) tanta intrinsecus sapientiae virtute pollebat, [ut doctrinam ipsius mundus ipse vix caperet;] [qui (cum se coepit per totum orbem divinitatis suae vigore diffundere) statim omne hominum genus in substantiam suam sui potestate pertaxit, (ut et sucum spiritus sui sanctis infundens omnibus hoc christianos cunctos faceret esse (quod Christus est.)]

MAXIMUS TAURINENSIS [died 408–423 CE]

... Interea Iugurtha, [ubi (quae Metellus agebat) ex nuntiis accepit, simul de innocentia eius certior Roma factus] diffidere suis rebus ac tum demum veram deditionem facere conatus est. Igitur legatos ad consulem cum suppliciis mittit, [qui tantum modo ipsi liberisque vitam peterent, alia omnia dederent populo Romano.]

GAIVS SALLVSTIVS CRISPVS [86–35 BCE]

Ordo socialis igitur eiusque progressus in bonum personarum indesinenter cedere debent, siquidem rerum ordinatio ordini personarum subiicienda est et non e converso, [ipso Domino id innuente (cum dixerit sabbatum propter hominem factum esse et non hominem propter sabbatum.)] Ordo ille in dies evolvendus, in veritate fundandus, in iustitia aedificandus, amore vivificandus est; in libertate autem aequilibrium in dies humanius invenire debet.

CONCILIVM OECVMENICVM VATICANVM II [1965 CE]

KEY:

Subjects

Objects

Verbs

Distant connections

[Larger clauses]

(Lesser clauses)

et and -que

De mundi statu

Mundus est in varium sepe variatus
et a status ordine sui degradatus:
ordo mundi penitus est inordinatus,
mundus nomine tenus stat, sed est prostratus.

Transierunt vetera, perit mos antiquus;
inolevit nequior mos est plus iniquus.
nemo meus, quilibet suus est amicus;
non Saturnus regnat nunc, immo Ludowicus.

Sperabamus, quod adhuc quisquam remaneret,
mundum qui precipitem dando sustineret,
pleno cornu copie munera preberet,
nomen largi, sed et rem, quod plus est, haberet.

CARMEN BVRANVM–48 [SAECVLI XIII]

Deum Patrem omnipotèntem magnis láudibus extol-
ámus, (qui Maríam matrem Fílii sui ab ómnibus
generatiónibus celebrári vóluit) et ab eo súppli-
ces petámus: Plenam grátia intuére, et exáudi nos.
Deus, mirabílium patrátor, (qui immaculátam Vírgi-
nem Maríam córpore et ánima cæléstis glóriæ
Christi fecísti consórtem)
— filórum tuórum corda ad eándem glóriam dírige.
(Qui Maríam dedísti nobis matrem) [ipsa intercedénte,]
concéde medélam lánguidis, solámen mæréntibus, véniam peccatóribus,
— et ómnibus salútem et pacem.
(Qui Maríam plenam grátia fecísti)
— lætam grátiæ tuæ cópiam ómnibus concéde.

LITVRGIA HORARVM PAVLI VI [1972 CE]

KEY:
Subjects
Objects
Verbs
Distant connections
[Larger clauses]
(Lesser clauses)
et and -que

Quaerimus etiam (quid iste in ultima Phrygia, quid in extremis Pamphyliae partibus fecerit,) [qualis in bello praedonum praedo ipse fuerit qui in foro populi Romani pirata nefarius reperiatur]? Dubitamus [quid iste in hostium praeda molitus sit, (qui manubias sibi tantas ex L. Metelli manubiis fecerit, qui maiore pecunia quattuor columnas dealbandas quam ille omnis aedificandas locaverit?)] Exspectemus [quid dicant ex Sicilia testes]? Quis umquam templum illud aspexit (quin avaritiae tuae, quin iniuriae, quin audaciae testis esset?) quis a signo Vortumni in circum Maximum venit (quin is uno quoque gradu de avaritia tua commoneretur)?

MARCVS TVLLIVS CICERO [106–43 BCE]

KEY: Subjects are underlined with a solid line.

Objects are underlined with a broken line.

Verbs are underlined with a line of dots.

Distant connections of words and phrases are underlined with a wavey line.

[Larger clauses are in square brackets,] (lesser ones in rounded parentheses.)

The words et and -que are placed in boxes.

Note: This code is used to illustrate the functions and connections of words as an aid to teaching, and is not intended to appear in absolutely every instance.

READING 3-K

POGGIVS BRACCIOLINI

[1380–1459 CE]

EPISTOLAE

II

Poggius suo Leonardo Arretino sal. dicit.

Cum pluribus diebus ad balnea fuissem, scripsi ad Nicolaum nostrum ex ipsis balneis epistolam quam existimo te lecturum. Deinde cum Constantiam revertissem, paucis post diebus coepta est agi causa Hieronymi, quem haereticum ferunt, et quidem publice. Hanc vero tibi recensere institui, tum propter rei gravitatem, tum maxime propter eloquentiam hominis ac doctrinam. Fateor me neminem vidisse unquam, qui in causa dicenda praesertim capitis magis accederet ad facundiam priscorum, quos tantopere admiramur. Mirum est vidisse quibus verbis, qua facundia, quibus argumentis, quo vultu, quo ore, qua fiducia responderit adversariis ac demum causam perorarit, ut dolendum sit tam nobile ingenium, tam excellens, ad illa haeresis studia divertisse, si tamen vera sunt quae sibi obiciuntur. Non enim mea est tantam rem diiudicare. Acquiesco eorum sententiis qui sapientiores habentur. Neque tamen existimato in morem oratoris me singulatim hanc causam referre; longum id esset et multorum dierum opus: pertingam quosdam locos illustriores quibus viri doctrinam possis perspicere.

Cum multa in hunc Hieronymum congesta essent, quibus arguebatur haeresis, tandem placuit ut publice singulis quae obicerentur responderet. Ita in concionem deductus, cum iuberent ad illa respondere, diutius recusavit, asserens se debere prius causam suam agere, quam adversariorum respondere maledictis. Itaque se prius pro se dicentem audiendum esse asseverabat; tum ad aemulorum suorum probra in eum congesta veniendum. Sed cum haec conditio sibi denegaretur, tum surgens in medio concionis: « Quaenam est haec iniquitas, inquit, ut cum tercentum quinquaginta diebus quibus in durissimis carceribus fui, in sordibus, in squalore, in stercore, in compedibus, in rerum omnium inopia, adversarios atque obrectatores meos semper audieritis, me unam horam nolitis audire? Hinc est, ut cum illis singulorum aures patuerint atque in tam longo tempore vobis persuaserint, me haereticum, hostem fidei Dei, ecclesiasticorum persecutorem, mihi autem mei defendendi causa nulla facultas detur; vos prius mentibus vestris me tamquam improbum hominem iudicaveritis quam qui fuerim potueritis agnoscere. At qui, inquit, homines estis, non dii; non perpetui sed mortales, errare, falli, decipi, seduci potestis. Hic mundi lumina, hic orbis terrarum prudentiores esse dicuntur. Maxime vos decet elaborare, ne quid temere, ne quid insulse, ne quid praeter iustitiam faciatis. Equidem ego homuncio sum, cuius de capite agitur; nec pro me haec loquor, qui mortalis existo; verum indignum mihi videtur sapientia tot virorum aliquid adversus me statuere praeter aequitatem, non tantum re quantum exemplo nociturum. »

Haec et multa praeterea ornate cum disseruisset, strepitu et murmure plurimorum sermonem eius interpellante, tandem decretum est ut primum ad errores qui in eum conferebantur responderet, deinde loquendi quae vellet facultas daretur. Legebantur ergo ex pulpito singula capita accusationis, tum rogabatur an quid veliet obicere, deinde testimoniis confirmabantur. Incredibile est dictu quam callide responderet, quibus se tueretur argumentis. Nihil unquam protulit indignum bono viro, adeo ut si id in fide sentiebat quod verbis profitebatur, nulla in eum nedum mortis causa inveniri iusta posset, sed ne quidem levissimae offensionis. Omnia falsa esse dicebat; omnia crimina conficta ab aemulis suis. Inter cetera cum recitaretur illum sedis apostolicae detractorem, oppugnatorem Romani Pontificis, cardinalium hostem, persecutorem praelatorum et cleri Christianae religionis inimicum, tum surgens queribunda voce et manibus porrectis: « Quo nunc me vertam, patres conscripti? Quorum auxilium implorem? Quos deprecer? Quos obtester? Vosne? At isti persecutores mei vestras mentes ab mea salute abalienaverunt, cum universorum hostem me esse dixerunt eorum qui sunt iudicaturi. Nempe arbitrati sunt si haec quae in me confinxerunt levia viderentur, tamen vos vestris sententiis oppressuros communem omnium hostem atque oppugnatorem, qualem isti me falsissime sunt mentiti. Itaque si eorum verbis fidem dabitis, nihil est quod de mea salute sperandum sit. »

Multos salibus perstrinxit, multos loedoriis, multos persaepe in re moesta ridere coegit iocando in illorum obiurgationes. Cum rogaretur quid sentiret de Sacramento, inquit: « antea panem, in consecratione, et post, verum Christi corpus; » et reliqua secundum fidem. Tum quidam: « atqui aiunt te dixisse post consecrationem remanere panem; » tum ille: « apud pistorem remanet panis, » inquit. Cuidam ex ordine Praedicatorum acrius invehenti: « tace, inquit, hypocrita, » alteri per conscientiam suam contra se iuranti: « haec, inquit, tutissima est ad fallendum via. »

Cum vero propter criminum multitudinem ac pondus res eo die transigi nequiret, in diem tertium dilata est; quo die cum singulorum criminum argumenta recitata essent ac subinde pluribus testibus confirmarentur, tum surgens ille: « Quoniam, inquit, adversarios meos tam diligenter audistis, consequens est ut me quoque dicentem aequis animis audiatis. »

Data tandem, licet multis perstrepentibus, dicendi facultate, a Deo exorsus deprecatus est eam sibi dari mentem, eam dicendi facultatem, quae in commodum ac salutem suae animae verteretur. Deinde: « Scio, inquit, viri doctissimi, plures fuisse excellentes viros indigna suis virtutibus perpessos, falsis testibus oppressos, iniquissimis iudiciis condemnatos. » Incipiens autem a Socrate, iniuste a suis damnatum rettulit, neque cum posset evadere voluisse, ut duorum quae asperrima hominibus viderentur, metum demeret carceris atque mortis. Tum Platonis captivitatem, Anaxagorae et Zenonis tormenta, multorum praeterea Gentilium iniquas damnationes, Rutilii exitium, Boethii simul et aliorum quos Boethius refert indigna morte oppressos commemoravit. Deinceps ad Hebraeorum exempla transiit, et primum Moysem illum liberatorem populi, legum latorem saepissime a suis calumniatum esse dixit, tamquam seductor esset et contemptor populi; Ioseph insuper a fratribus venditum ob invidiam, post ob stupri suspicionem in vincula coniectum. Recensuit praeter hos Isaiam, Danielem et fere prophetas omnes, tamquam contemptores Dei, tamquam seditiosos iniquis circumventos sententiis. Hic etiam subiecit Susannae iudicium, multorumque praeterea qui, cum viri sanctissimi extitissent, iniustis tamen sententiis et iudiciis perierunt. Postea ad Ioannem Baptistam, deinde ad Salvatorem nostrum descendens, falsis testibus, falsis iudicum sententiis condemnatos, inquit, omnibus constare; deinde Stephanum a sacerdotum collegio interfectum, Apostolos autem omnes morti damnatos, non tamquam bonos, sed seditiosos populorum concitatores, contemptores deorum et malorum operum effectores. Iniquum esse rettulit, iniuste damnari sacerdotem a sacerdote; at id factum fuisse docuit; iniquius a sacerdotum collegio; et id quoque exemplo probavit; iniquissimum vero a concilio sacerdotum, et id etiam accidisse monstravit.

Haec diserte et cum magna omnium expectatione disseruit. At cum omne causae pondus in testibus situm esset, multis rationibus docuit nullam his testibus fidem adhibendam, praesertim cum non ex veritate, sed ex odio, malivolentia et invidia omnia dixissent. Tum odii causas ita explicavit, ut haud procul fuerit a persuadendo. Ita enim erant verisimiles ut, excepta fidei causa, parva illis testimoniis fides adhibenda esset. Commotae erant omnium mentes et ad misericordiam flectebantur. Addiderat insuper se sponte venisse ad concilium ad se purgandum. Vitam suam et studia exposuerat, officii plena et virtutis; dixerat hunc morem priscis doctissimis viris ac sanctissimis fuisse, ut in rebus fidei invicem sententiis discreparent, non ad pessundandam fidem, sed ad veritatem fidei reperiendam. Ita Augustinum et Hieronymun dissensisse, neque solum diversa sensisse, sed etiam contraria, nulla haeresis suspicione.

Expectabant omnes ut se purgaret rectractando obiecta, vel erratorum veniam postularet; at ille neque se errasse asseverans, neque se velle retractare aliorum falsa crimina, tandem descendit in laudationes Ioannis Hus dudum ad ignem damnati, virum illum bonum, iustum, sanctum appellans et illa morte indignum; se quoque paratum quodvis supplicium adire forti animo et constanti; seque inimicis suis cedere, et testibus illis tam impudenter mentientibus, qui tamen quandoque coram Deo, quem fallere non poterant, essent rationem eorum quae dixissent reddituri. Magnus erat circumstantium animi dolor; cupiebant enim virum tam egregium salvari, si bona mens affuisset. Ille autem in sententia perseverans mortem appetere videbatur, laudansque Iohannem Hus ait nihil illum adversus Ecclesiae Dei statum sensisse, sed adversus abusus clericorum, adversus superbiam, fastum et pompam praelatorum. Nam cum ecclesiarum patrimonia deberentur primum pauperibus, tum hospitibus, deinde ecclesiarum fabricis, indignum illi bono viro videri, disperdi illa meretricibus, conviviis, equorum, canumque saginae, cultui vestimentorum, et aliis rebus indignis religione Christi. Hoc autem maximi ingenii fuit, cum interrumperetur saepius oratio sua variis rumoribus, lacesseretur que a nonnullis eius sententias captantibus, neminem eorum intactum reliquit pariterque omnes ulciscens vel erubescere coegit vel tacere. Surgente murmure silebat turbam quandoque increpans, postea orationem prosequebatur, orans atque obtestans, ut eum loqui paterentur, cum se non essent amplius audituri. Nunquam ad hos rumores expavit, mente firma atque intrepida. Illud vero admirabile memoriae argumentum, tercentum quadraginta diebus fuerat in fundo turris foetidae atque obscurae, cuius asperitatem ipsemet questus est, asserens se, ut virum fortem decet, non propterea ingemuisse; ingemiscere quod se indigna perpessus est; sed mirari hominum adversus se inhumanitatem, quo in loco nedum legendi, sed ne videndi ullam habuit facultatem. Mitto anxietatem mentis qua oportuit illum quotidie agitari, quae omnem memoriam excutere debuisset; tamen tot doctissimos ac sapientissimos viros in testes suarum opinionum allegavit; tot doctores ecclesiasticos in medium protulit in sententiam suam, ut satis superque fuisset, si toto hoc tempore summo in otio, summa in quiete, sapientiae studiis operam dedisset.

READING 3-L

IOANNES PETRVS MAFFEIVS
[1536–1603 CE]

SINARUM REGIO AC MORES DESCRIBUNTUR.

Sinarum regio, quam hodie *Cinam* vulgus appellat, ultima terrarum Asiae, ab Oriente, et a Meridie, alluitur Oceano quem Sericum, vel Eoum prisci dixere: ab Occidente Indiam ulteriorem attingit: a Septentrione cingitur Massagetarum, Scytharumque limitibus. Multo latius quondam imperasse gentem, annales ipsorum, ac literae, et veterum aedificiorum illustria monumenta, et complures, in India praesertim ab iis denominatae nationes, haud obscure testantur. Sed cum sua ipsi mole viribusque fatigarentur (quod a Carthaginiensibus in re simili factum legimus) sponte misso veluti sanguine, et castigate luxuria, intra hosce fines recepere sese; gravi proposito edicto, ne quis injussu magistratuum excederet. Regna, seu provincias vastae magnitudinis, numerant quindecim cum sua cujusque metropoli: ad mare sex, mediterranea reliqua. Tellus, quod maxima ex parte intra temperatae plagae terminos continetur; radiosque Solis, suapte natura vitales puro ac patenti excipit sinu, sic fit, ut saluberrimo caelo, et purioris aurae dulcedine perfruatur; ac simul inclytae fertilitatis gleba, frugum omnis generis fundat copiam bifero triferoque proventu. Accedit ad eximiam soli fecunditatem, summa cultorum industria. Et infinita est multitudo, quippe subolescente in dies prole, et in alienas regiones migrationibus interdictis. Neque in tanta mortalium turba cessare cuipiam licet: non privato dedecore tantum, et proximi cujusque probris ac jurgiis; verum etiam publicis moribus legibusque desidia plectitur. Itaque rustici homines nullam agri partem incuria squalere patiuntur.

Saltus et colles, pinu vitibusque; campi et planities, oryza, hordeo, frumento, ceterisque segetibus nitent. Quamquam e vitibus more nostro non exprimunt merum: uvas quodam condimenti genere in hiemem adservare mos est. Ceterum ex herba quadam expressus liquor admodum salutaris, nomine *Chia,* calidus hauritur, ut apud Japonios; cujus maxime beneficio, pituitam, gravedinem, lippitudinem nesciunt; vitamque bene longam, sine ullo ferme languore traducunt. Oleis alicubi carent, sed earum vice non desunt plantae, quae humorem unctui praebeant. Pascua sunt etiam gregibus alendis uberrima; et in hortis egregie cultis cum alia nostri orbis poma, tum sapidissimos melopepones, suavissima et optima pruna ficusque, et medica citreaque variae formae ac saporis, apprime generosa mala conspicias. Ad haec, perspicui fontes, et miro colorum decore odorumque fragrantia flores ac rosae perennant. Flumina vero, quae magnas quoque patiantur naves, piscosa et amoena, viridissimo riparum vestitu, pinguibus arvis interfluunt. Quin, et ora maritima pluribus introrsum aestuariis ad omnium rerum copiam invehendam evehendamque, facili patet accessu. Ingentem praeterea volucrum et ferarurn vim, ad aucupium ac venatum, paludes, luci, saltusque suppeditant. Metalla auri, et argenti, et ferri probatissimi, et alia, incolae effodiunt. Margaritas, et praecipuae nobilitatis vasa fictilia, quae vulgo *porcellana* dicuntur; pretiosas pelles ad frigus arcendum; itemque gossipii, lini, lanae, bombycisque, et serici fila, vestemque omnis generis mittunt innumerabilem. Saccari, et mellis, rhabarbari, cafurae, minii, glastique tingendis vestibus expetiti, proventus ingens. Odoramentis cum aliis abundant; tum praecipue *mosco* (cujus nullam apud Latinos Graecosve scriptores mentionem invenio) e feris quibusdam, vulpecularum effigie, crebro verbere enectis, dein putrefactis. Denique, nihil aliunde, non ad victum modo cultumve; sed ne ad delicias quidem ac voluptates requirunt. Ac proinde nulla sub Sole gens est, apud quam aliarum gentium opes aeque consistant. Quippe vendentibus cuncta Sinis, nihil invicem redimentibus, nisi forte in usum tectorii cujusdam odorati piper ex India. Neque erat externo commercio locus; ni Sinam infinita quaedam teneret argenti cupiditas. Id praeferunt auro; et cum indidem effossum, tum e remotis regionibus illatum, avidissime accumulant. Jam de aedificiis, privatisque ac publicis operibus explicare, infinitum sit.

Urbes praecipuae magnitudinis celebrant ferme ducentas: inferioris autem ordinis, longe plurimas. Porro castella et pagi, quorum nonnulli tribus familiarum millibus incoluntur; vicique passim ita multi sese offerunt, ut summe iniri vix possit. Sunt autem egregio situ plerique: scatent aquis, procera circumdati silva; ex qua turritae praedivitum aratorum eminent domus. Porro, dispersae in aestivos maxime secessus nobilium villae, opere in primis eleganti; vel ad opacas amnium ripas garrulos avium concentus, et fugientis aquae lene murmur excipiunt: vel e montium jugis verticibusque, subjectos vallium anfractus, et vasta maris ac terrarum spatia, longe lateque despectant. Sed ipsarum praecipue urbium pulchritudo mira. Navigabilibus impositae fluviis, admodum profunda et lata fossa, moenibusque cinguntur quadrati ab imo lapidis, lateritiae ad summum structurae. Lateres autem, ex eodem argillae genere quo porcellana vasa, confecti, et calce optima interliti, in eam duritiem ac firmitatem brevi tempore coalescunt, ut ferramentis postmodum labefactari vix possint. Crassitudo moenium, quattuor, et alicubi sex capit homines: additis ad prospectum pergulis, ac moenianis, et occultis ambulationibus, qua praefecti oblectationis caussa pererrent: pomoerium, intro extraque, libero ad circuitum spatio, senis in ordinem equitibus patet. Ad obliquos autem ictus, modico intervallo, turres et propugnacula prominent, artificiosis contecta fastigiis, et podiis elegantibus adornata. Ex iis moenibus cum quaedam ante bis mille annos constet exstructa; nullam tamen in eis rimam, aut sinum, aut labem aspicias. Adeo severe acriterque sarta tecta ab regiis curatoribus exigentur. Urbis vero totius, ea ferme dimensio est. Latissimae viae duae se intersecantes, perpetuo tractu qui oculis lustrari possit, praecipuas quattuor portas aperiunt, praeferratas, ornatu magnifico, adituque ad aspectum praeclaro. Ab hisce rectis viis, aliae dein aliaeque transversae, privata et publica aedificia, vicosque distinguunt. Et ab utroque latere viarum, excurrunt porticus, quae commeantem plebem, et fabrum atque institutorum apothecas ac tabernas, a tempestatum injuria vindicent. Iam vero e lapide trifores ut plurimum, et quidem summo artificio perfecti cum inscriptionibus fornices passim visuntur. Quae monumenta, magistratu abeuntes, regii praefecti relinquunt. Magistratibus autem ipsis, celeberrimo loco stant ampla et operosa praetoria, cultissimis hortis, capacibus piscinis, fontibusque pellucidis, et variis aquarum derivationibus ad omnem animi remissionem instructa. Nec desunt aviaria, et ferarum septa, et operis topiarii tonsiles silvae, lucique densissimi, et distincta floribus prata: ut singulae praefectorum domus oppidi propemodum instar obtineant. Privatorum aedes, circa maritimam oram humiles; mediterraneis vero locis, multiplici contignatione tolluntur, vel pictura decoratae, vel opere albario candoris eximii. A primo ingressu panditur atrium, armariis circumquaque dispositis: in quibus inanium Deorum statuae collocantur. Accedunt lacus pleni piscium, ac pensiles horti. Materia in aedificationes utuntur mire laevigata, et certo lenocinii genere in auri colorem ac splendorem adducta. Pari laevore tegulum est, celce spissatum atque commissum ad pluvias arcendas: durantque seculis tecta talia, extremis imbricibus e marmorato pereleganter elaboratis. Ad singulas vero januas, viridi opacitate arbores ad lineam directae consurgunt: quarum gratissimo aspectu, quasi pabulo quodam, oculorum acies quamlibet fatigata reficitur. Porro urbes, praeterquam quod magnis, ut dixi, fluminibus pleraeque alluuntur; sunt etiam quae, ad subvectionis evectionisque commoditatem, canales navium capaces introrsum admittant. Quales multis locis apud Belgas, et alicubi etiam in Italia cernimus; marginatis utrinque semitis ad terrestre iter adstructis. Lapidei quoque pontes egregie facti non ad oppida solum, sed etiam in agris plurimi. Quae flumina propter altitudinem pilas arcusque rejiciunt; ea, consertis et contabulatis navibus pro ponte junguntur. Sin ex imbri vehementius intumuerint; solutis interim ordinibus, viatorem, gratuitate cymbae, Regis impensa transmittunt. Jam, voraginibus, et hiatibus terrae, et stagnantibus aquis, quaeque alia ad iter impedimento sunt, publice occurritur; quin etiam, asperrimis locis ad montium latera excisis cautibus, viae patescunt, ea molitione sumtuque, ut Romanam in eo genere magnificentiam non requiras. Templa etiam cum turribus, culminibusque spectantur (licet alioqui Deos contemnant Sinae) pulcherrima, et maxima. Trans pomoerium dein, praesertim ad mare, suburbia, eodem ornatu, et laxitate viarum, advenas ferme ac negotiatores frequentissimis diversoriis, et cauponis accipiunt; in quibus, praeter delicatas de gentis more potiones, omnium etiam generum cocti, crudique prostant cibi, et exquisita cupedia.

Sunt autem Sinarum populi (quemadmodum ejusdem plagae alii) prout ad Septentrionem, vel ad Meridiem vergunt, magis aut minus aeneo colore, vel candido: simis naribus, exiguis admodum ocellis, rara barba, longis crinibus, quos accurate comtos, et in verticem coactos illaqueant, et oblongum ex argento clavum in laqueum inserunt. Neque tamen una est omnibus capillamenti ratio: quippe, caelibes, comam a fronte discriminant; mariti, confundunt; atque haec praecipue nota, ordinem utrumque distinguit. Primarii, ac divites, quique militiam exercent, versicolore serico: plebeii ac pauperes, lino, seu gossipio tegunt corpora. Nam apud Sinas lana, cum maxime suppetat, minime texitur. Sagis ad veterem Hispaniae consuetudinem utuntur, media sui parte crispis ac rugosis; ceterum fusa et explicata lacinia, et laxis manicis: ipsum vero sagum, ab laeva parte confibulant. Accedit talaris tunica, quam qui e regia sunt stirpe, vel superiore aliquo magistratu funguntur, circa baltheum maxime; ceteri limbo tenus acu pingunt. Caput operiunt praecelso ac rotundo pileo, e tenuissimis virgulis atro filo praetextis.

READING 3-M

PONTIFEX IOANNES PAVLVS II

[1981 CE]

LITTERAE ENCYCLICAE

LABOREM EXERCENS homo panem cotidianum sibi comparet oportet et insimul ad perennem technicarum artium scientiarumque profectum conferat, praesertim vero ad assiduam morum humanique cultus progressionem societatis, in qua una vitam cum fratribus degit. Quo quidem verbo « laboris » omne opus ab eodem patratum significatur, nulla habita ratione eius indolis et adiunctorum; id est quaevis actio humana eo nomine appellatur, quae pro labore habetur estve habenda tot inter multiplices industriae formas, quarum homo est capax et ad quas, humanitatis suae virtute, est natura sua proclivis. Ad Dei ipsius imaginem et similitudinem factus in visibili mundi universitate ibique constitutus ut terram subiciat, homo ab ipso suo initio *ad suscipiendum laborem vocatur. Qui quidem labor est una e notis, quibus homo a ceteris animantibus* distinguitur, quorum actio, ad vitam pertinens alendam, labor nequit nuncupari. Solus enim homo ad eum est habilis, solus homo eum exsequitur, eo simul vitam suam terrenam adimplens. Quocirca labor peculiari signo hominis et humanitatis notatur, signo dicimus personae intra personarum communitatem operantis. Quod signum declarat qualis ipse sit interius et quadamtenus ipsam eius naturam constituit.

I

1. Quoniam die xv mensis Maii hoc anno nonagesimus expletus est *annus* ex quo Litterae Encyclicae, praegrande momentum habentes et a verbis *Rerum Novarum* incipientes, a praeclaro illo Summo Pontifice, « quaestionis socialis » insigni tractatore, Leone XIII, editae sunt, hoc documentum *labori humano,* quin potius *ipsi homini* cupimus dedicare, in amplo illo campo operis faciendi, ut revera esse cognoscitur, constituto. Quodsi, ut in Encyclicis Litteris, *Redemptor Hominis* inscriptis, diximus, quas in exordio ministerii nostri apud Romanam Petri Sedem emisimus, homo « est prima et praecipua via Ecclesiae » idque propter inscrutabile mysterium Redemptionis a Christo peractae, oportet ad hanc viam indesinenter redire eamque novo percurrere studio secundum varias rationes, quibus ea nobis totam plenitudinem simulque omnem fatigationem humanae vitae in terra ostendit.

Labor est quidem una ex illis rationibus, perennis et primaria, semper ad tempus, quod transigitur, proxime pertinens, atque huiusmodi, ut novam continenter postulet animi attentionem certamque testificationem. Quia novae iugiter *interrogationes* et *problemata* oriuntur, novae semper spes concipiuntur, sed etiam timores terrent et minae, quae cum primaria hac vitae humanae ratione sunt conexae; qua quidem ratione vita hominis struitur cotidie; ex qua ea sibi propriam et peculiarem haurit dignitatem; in ea pariter continetur constans veluti mensura humanae fatigationis, doloris necnon iacturae et iniustitae, quae altius pervadunt vitam socialem sive intra fines cuiusque nationis sive in gradu internationali. Si verum est hominem labores manuum suarum manducare, id est non solum panem illum cotidianum, quo corporis vita sustentatur, sed etiam panem scientiae et progressionis, civilis vitae humanitatis et ingenii culturae, verum est etiam in omne tempus hominem hoc pane vesci « *in sudore vultus sui,* » id est non solum nisu et fatigatione sui ipsius, sed etiam tot inter contentiones, conflictationes, discrimina, quae, ad laborem, ut reapse est, spectantia, vitam singularum societatum et etiam totius generis humani perturbant.

Nonagesimam anniversariam memoriam Litterarum Encyclicarum, quae verbis *Rerum Novarum* solent appellari, celebramus, dum novae progressiones in re technologica, oeconomica, politica instant, quae, ut multi asserunt periti, ad totum ambitum operis faciendi et bonorum gignendorum non minus habebunt momentum quam conversio illa et commutatio, qua ob inductam quaestuosam industriam saeculum praeteritum fuit insigne. Varia sunt, ad hoc quod attinet, elementa, quibus pondus inest generale: increbrescens inductio automatismi in multos campos effectionis bonorum; exardescens pretium energiae et materiarum praecipuarum; augescens persuasio angustiae et intolerabilis inquinamenti rerum naturae; ille veluti adventus in publicum populorum, qui, per saecula aliis subiecti, locum legitimum inter nationes et in negotiis internationalibus deliberandis sibi vindicant. Hae novae condiciones et postulationes novam ordinationem et rei accommodatam compagem structurarum oeconomiae hodiernae et distributionis laboris requirent. Quae quidem mutationes fortasse pro ingenti multitudine opificum, speciali peritia praeditorum, pro dolor, coactam cessationem ab opere, saltem ad tempus, aut necessitatem in novo se exercendi genere laboris inferent, causa erunt, quemadmodum valde probabile esse videtur, ut in regionibus locupletioribus rerum materialium abundantia celerve auctus imminuantur; verum tamen etiam levationem et spem ingerere poterunt pluries centenis milibus hominum, qui aetate nostra in ignominiosa et indigna versantur miseria.

Ecclesiae non est, ad reconditae doctrinae rationem, investigare eventus, qui fieri poterunt, eiusmodi mutationum in hominum convictu. Aestimat tamen Ecclesia sui muneris esse dignitatem et iura hominum labori deditorum semper in lumine ponere atque condiciones exprobrare, in quibus ea violantur, necnon operam conferre ad eiusmodi mutationes ita dirigendas, ut vera progressio hominis et societatis obtineatur.

2. Labor, quatenus est quaestio ad hominem pertinens, sine dubio in media illa vertitur « quaestione sociali, » ad quam per hos fere centum

annos, ex quo memoratae Litterae Encyclicae sunt editae, Ecclesiae doctrina atque multimoda incepta, cum munere eius apostolico coniuncta, peculiari ratione diriguntur. Quodsi in ipsum laborem hanc considerationem nostram intendimus, id facere nolumus modo disparili, sed potius aptum nexum servando cum tota traditione eiusdem doctrinae eorundemque inceptorum. Simul vero id agimus, secundum directoriam normam Evangelii, ea mente ut de *eiusdem Evangelii thesauro proferamus « nova et vetera. »*

. . . « . . . Exspectatio tamen novae terrae extenuare non debet, sed potius excitare, sollicitudinem hanc terram excolendi, ubi Corpus illud novae familiae humanae crescit quod aliqualem novi saeculi adumbrationem iam praebere valet. Ideo, licet progressus terrenus a Regni Christi augmento sedulo distinguendus sit, in quantum tamen ad societatem humanam melius ordinandam conferre potest, Regni Dei magnopere interest. »

Hisce in meditationibus humani laboris studuimus nos ea omnia extollere, quae sunt necessaria visa, cum per laborem debeant in terris duplicari non tantum « industriae nostrae fructus, » verum etiam « humana dignitas, communio fraterna et libertas. » Quicumque verbum Dei viventis audit christianus sociatque cum precibus opus, necesse est ipse sciat quem denique obtineat locum opus suum non in sola *progressione terrestri* rerum sed etiam *in Regni Dei incremento,* ad quod universi nos Spiritus Sancti virtute verbisque Evangelii vocamur.

Huic denique considerationi finem imponentibus gratum est nobis Benedictionem Apostolicam, caelestium donorum auxiliorumque auspicem, Vobis, Venerabiles Fratres, ac dilecti filii et filiae, amantissime in Domino impertire.

Hae Litterae, quas apparaveramus ut praeteritis Idibus Maiis foras darentur, nonagesimo anno expleto ab editis Encyclicis Litteris *Rerum Novarum,* potuerunt a nobis tunc solummodo terminali ratione recognosci, postquam valetudinarium reliquimus.

Datum ex Arce Gandulfi, die XIVmensis Septembris, in festo Exaltationis Sanctae Crucis, anno MDCCCCLXXXI, Pontificatus nostri tertio.

IOANNES PAULUS PP. II

QVARTA EXPERIENTIA

fourth experience

ILLE HIC EST RAPHAEL

TIMVIT QVO SOSPITE VINCI

RERVM MAGNA PARENS

ET MORIENTE MORI

After the First and Third Experiences, we come out on top in the Fourth Experience to refine some elements already learned and to add a number of important things. We shall add instructions about some verbal usages including the conditionals and give several special usages of the other noun and adjective functions. We shall present in the last two encounters of this Experience a brief introduction to poetic meter and a few insights into how the Latin language changed first under the influence of the Scriptures and then in a later age of its magnificent history.

With this Fourth Experience we shall finish the Bones of the Latin language. This is quite an accomplishment, because some people spend half their lives coming to clarity about how the Latin language functions. We hope to have achieved this without reverting to memory or charts, but by describing how the language works in a narrative format suitable for reading and learning on the beach or as a teacher's preparation for the classroom event, with the help of reading texts and of a following volume, number II of the *Latinitatis Corpus*, "The Body of Latin," consisting of Cicero's letters in which his expressions are cross-listed with these 105 encounters.

We begin this experience directly with the presentation of indirect discourse, in contrast to the way we began the Third Experience with seven encounters that repeated and so consolidated elements learned in the First Experience with the addition of a few refinements. This difference is due to the reality that students of Latin for many years already have requested to join us to continue learning the Latin language. Even if they have had many years of instruction, they are not encouraged to begin with the Fourth Experience, because they are new to our system and must learn a new way of thinking about the language. If at all possible they are encouraged to begin at the beginning, but if they cannot be convinced of this, the more advanced may be given entry into the Third Experience. Thus, we begin the Fourth Experience with the fresh presentation of new material.

When each encounter recorded here was presented in the classroom in Rome, we also assigned a *ludus domesticus* so that the students might play with the material in preparation for our next encounter. These are being collected for the forthcoming publication of volume four of this Body of Latin.

By the way, up to this point we have used a terminology that discloses the nature and essence of things, and we have avoided distracting and misleading terms. We want to know and learn what things mean, not what they are called. While we begin our Fourth Experience as mature Latin experts and scholars, we may use dictionary or "manual" abbreviations employed by very many people so that we may not alienate ourselves from the Latin realities of others; but we will much rather employ the essential functions of the language without mysterious terminology. Consequently, we may at times refer to the function of-possession as the genitive or simply "gen."; the function to-for-from as the dative or "dat."; the function by-with-from-in as the ablative or "abl."; and the direct object function as the accusative or "acc."; and "nom." for the nominative or subject function, as is done in a complete dictionary. For the ablative absolute we use "abl. abs." In anticipation of elements soon to be presented, we shall use the abbreviation MA for Modal Attraction. In our discussion of indirect discourse, called by its Latin name *Oratio Obliqua* and abbreviated as OO, we shall use the abbreviation M & M to refer to verbs of Mind and Mouth, along with the German abbreviation "ACI" for *Accusativus Cum Infinitivo* to refer to the accusative with the infinitive, which we present in our first encounter of this experience.

ORATIO OBLIQUA

reported speech

Introduction

We begin our Fourth Experience of the Latin language with a daily Roman way of speaking and an almost every-sentence usage of all Latin authors from the beginning to our present time. Thus far in our encounter with the Latin language we have worked with direct discourse or questions, as in the statement, "Healthy children play and jump." Now, the Latin people take this straight declaratory sentence and attach it to another verb, namely a verb of thinking or speaking, such as, "we notice," producing the sentence, "We notice healthy children to be playing and jumping." The clause "... healthy children to be playing and jumping" is what we call reported speech because it depends on the verb "we notice ..." and tells you the content of that observation.

To ensure we know what we are talking about, take another example, "These things are true." Now attach it to another verb of thinking or speaking such as, "they confess," and produce the sentence, "They confess these things to be true." The clause "... these things to be true" is what we call reported speech because it depends on the verb "They confess ..." and tells you the content of their admission.

In reported speech someone's thoughts or ideas or words are quoted as depending on a certain speaker or writer. In Latin manuals you will see the term *oratio obliqua* (sometimes written as "o.o."), which means "speech on an angle." The term "indirect discourse" is another technical way of speaking about this reported speech.

A vast class of verbs of thinking or speaking gives rise to this phenomenon. We have called these the verbs of mind and mouth or simply "M & M" verbs. These are, for example, verbs of thinking, believing, denying, suspecting, understanding, doubting, saying, writing, declaring, showing, and many others. When you take a sentence in direct speech and make it dependent on one of these words of thinking or speaking, it is expressed according to this phenomenon of indirect speech.

Immediately we might add that this usage is still current in English, perhaps less in other languages. German and Italian do not have this same phenomenon because they put reported speech into their subjunctive. For example, in English, if we start with a sentence in direct discourse such as:

The teachers are reliable. The students are all wonderful

and make them dependent on the mental operation of knowing, then it goes into indirect discourse, and we might say:

> Witnesses testify the teachers to be reliable; the students to be all wonderful.

Another example is:

Direct discourse:	They-the senators do these things well
Indirect discourse:	All have experienced them-the senators to be doing these things well.

Here the sentence "... them to be doing these things well" is made to depend on the mental operation "All have experienced ... ," and so is expressed in indirect discourse.

If you use a pronoun, sometimes you can see the indirect discourse better, for example:

Direct discourse:	She finished a good work
Indirect discourse:	E-mails announce her to have finished a good work.

Here you can clearly see that the subject "She" has been put into the object form "her" and the independent verb "finished" has become an infinitive "to have finished." Take another example:

Direct discourse:	He will call us
Indirect discourse:	You suspect him to be about to call us.

In each of these examples, the Latin phenomenon of indirect discourse generated the same phenomena still tolerable in the English phrase. Let us turn now to see how the Romans expressed reported speech.

Oratio obliqua

The phenomenon of indirect discourse in Latin is extremely simple. It is not the most difficult aspect of the language, but among the easier things to learn and use. The figure is simple. To make direct discourse into indirect discourse you first need a governing M & M verb that gives rise to the indirect discourse. The verb of M & M can be expressed or presumed or felt in the story and placed anywhere in the Latin sentence. Then, to form the indirect discourse, you put the subject of the reported sentence in the object or so-called acc. form and make the independent verb an infinitive. Thus:

1. A verb of mind or mouth introduces a reported statement.
2. Then you put the subject of the reported statement in the object form and likewise any predicate word, that is a noun or an adjective agreeing with the subject,
3. and make its verb an infinitive.

Immediately this is disturbing for many students because we always learned that the object form is used as the object of a verb or a preposition, but now it is also used as the subject of an infinitive verb in indirect discourse. This is why people sometimes speak of an "accusative subject." This whole phenomenon is also called "the accusative with the infinitive," or among the Germans "ACI," meaning *Accusativus Cum Infinitivo*, a term we shall sometimes use hereafter.

Several difficulties with reported speech are present in the following example:

> *Musicos probat modulator*
> The director tests musicians
>
> *Musicos modulatorem probare suspicamur*
> We suspect that the director is testing the musicians
> We feel that the musicians are trying the director.

First, when the sentence begins with two words in the object form, you do not know if they are objects or subjects of reported speech. Only when we come to that infinitive *probare* do we see that *modulatorem* may be its subject and its object may be *musicos*, but the opposite is also possible. Incidentally, just because *Musicos* is given first does not mean that it is the subject. Finally, the independent verb of the sentence comes last, and everything before it depends upon it. Only when you get to the last word does the expression make sense.

You will also notice that reported speech no longer uses the indicative or subjunctive, but another mode of speaking that we call the infinitive mode. The reported verb is put into one of six infinitives, active or passive, which are not difficult to deal with or manage according to our system. We shall talk about the system of infinitives in encounter 72.

This usage is all over the place in Latin literature and is still in full use today. It is standard Latin, and anything else is an error. We can look at a speech given by Alexander the Great which begins, according to Curtius, with an expression of declaring, *docuit*, "he taught them," and the entire contents of the whole passage over several pages is given with the subjects in the object form and the verbs as infinitives. This is not hard, but you have to see it, as you will. The teacher has to be ready to point out examples of reported speech in every page of reading we come across, because it is universal.

In a later encounter of this Fourth Experience we shall talk about how this phenomenon changed over time, but the important thing to note at this point is that this phenomenon exists in every age and monument of Latin for the past 2,300 years.

ENCOUNTER 2 (72)

ORATIO OBLIQUA. VERBA – INFINITIVI

reported speech. verbs – infinitives

Introduction

In this encounter we continue the previous "ACI" chapter of the Latin story and present as promised the Latin infinitives, because they are essential Bones of Latin. The infinitives are only six in number and very simple and consistent in their construction. We shall give the six infinitive forms both passive and active, and give our terminology and proven system for using and understanding them, exactly as we did with the participles and the subjunctive.

1. *Oratio obliqua*

We must understand the time forms and vernacular meanings of the six Latin infinitives strictly in relation to the verbs on which they depend. Hence, we will never call them, as most other manuals and teachers, the present infinitive or the perfect infinitive or the future infinitive, which is in fact harmfully misleading. Rather, we determine whether the reported infinitive action is contemporaneous in time with the main verb of thinking and saying on which it depends or is antecedent in time to the M & M verb or expresses some futurity with regard to the verb on which it depends. Thus, the infinitives are:

antecedent	previous to the M & M verb
contemporaneous	along with the M & M verb
futurity	subsequent to the M & M verb.

We use this special terminology here to give people direct access to the idea expressed and to liberate them from misleading terminology and linguistic difficulties.

1.1 *The forms*

The contemporaneous active infinitive you already know from the dictionary's second verbal part, called the infinitive or gerund. They are, according to the vowel groups:

honorare	to honor
delēre	to destroy
instruĕre	to set up
lenire	to mitigate
esse	to be, exist.

These active infinitives are contemporaneous with the action of the M & M verb on which they depend and will sound accordingly.

The antecedent active infinitive is the third dictionary part with the ending –*ISSE:*

honora(vi)sse (syncopated as *honorasse*)	to have honored
delevisse	to have destroyed
instruxisse	to have set up
leni(vi)sse (syncopated as *lenisse*)	to have mitigated
fuisse	to have been.

These infinitives indicate that the action is completed prior to the time of the verb of mind and mouth upon which the infinitive depends, and the interpretation will have to correspond in translation.

The active forms of the *subsequent* infinitive are composed of the futurity active participle and the infinitive *esse*, which again may be and often is omitted by all Latin authors. In a moment we shall explain their meanings, but first we present the forms:

honoraturus, a, um (esse)	going to be honoring
deleturus, a, um (esse)	with the intention to destroy
instructurus, a, um (esse)	fixing to set up
leniturus, a, um (esse)	on the point of mitigating
futurus, a, um (esse), frequently found as *fore*	about to be, exist.

The endings –*us, a, um* agree with the subject of the infinitive verb. In indirect speech this typically means that the subject and the participle are in the object form. In each of these compound forms the *esse* is very often omitted by Caesar, Livy, Sallustius, and other classical authors, including us; so there should be no panic for Latinists. Again, the action of the futurity infinitive will be subsequent to the action of the verb on which it depends, with extraordinary vernacular results.

2. Possibilities in English

The whole object-accusative and infinitive expression in Latin can be rendered according to our system in English through three acceptable, convenient interpretations, for example with futurity:

Eos audis librum scripturos esse

can be expressed with the acc. and infinitive in English:

You hear them to be about to write a book.

The reported speech can be expressed with the particle "that" with a subject and finite verb, as in:

You hear that they are about to write a book
You hear that they will write a book.

Or the reported speech may stand on its own as a subject and finite verb without the use of the particle "that," as in:

> You hear they are about to write a book
> You hear they will be writing a book.

All this must be noted, learned, actuated, and naturalized by all students and experts of the Latin language and literature.

We also have in correct, although not often heard English, the acc. with the infinitive in the following response when answering a phone:

> Whom should I say to be calling?

This same reported speech can be expressed as a subject with a finite verb, without the use of the particle "that," as in:

> Who, should I say, is calling?

A few simple examples will help you to become accustomed to these forms and our terminology and precise way of thinking about these infinitives. We can see this clearly in the example with contemporaneous action:

> *Reginam-eam muros aedificare colligo*
>
> I gather the queen-her to be building walls
> I gather that the queen-she is building walls
> I gather the queen-she is building walls.

The range of meanings here in the vernacular includes any expression that is contemporaneous with the verb *accipio*. The first option given in English retains the object form "the queen-her" and the infinitive "to be building." The second introduces the connection "that" and then renders the indirect discourse as a finite clause with the subject "she" and the finite verb "is." The third simply omits the connection "that" from the second option, and the indirect discourse remains as a finite clause. One or two of these English possibilities may express the thought more naturally than the other.

If you change the main verb to another time, say T.2i, then you have another sentence:

> *Eas credebamus pulchre puellas cantare*
>
> We used to believe them-young ladies to be singing beautifully
> We used to believe that those young ladies were singing beautifully
> We used to believe the young ladies were singing beautifully.

You can see in the first English rendering that the infinitive "to be singing" is contemporaneous with the mental operation of believing, and both actions are now set in the past tense. The T.2i verb *credebam* sets the sentence in the past, and *eas cantare* means "they were singing," but these same words mean "they are singing" when the sentence is set in the present and depends on *credo* in T.1i. Remember! To say "I know those women were singing" is, *Eas scio cantavisse.*

When people are taught that *cantare* is the *present* infinitive, then they are thrown off when the main verb changes from *credo* to *credebam*, from T.1i to T.2i with the resulting change in meaning of *eos cantare* from "they are singing" to "they were singing." They rightly ask how "they were singing" can be called "present," and the answer is that in essence it cannot. This is why we do not use the terminology of past, present, and future infinitives, but antecedent, contemporaneous, and futurity infinitives.

Strange things also happen in the English rendering of the futurity formula in reported speech, which totally demolishes many people. Take the example:

> *Milites excitaturos* (*esse*) *tentoria dubitamus*
>
> We doubt the soldiers to be about to set up tents
> ... that the soldiers are about to set up tents
> ... that the soldiers will set up tents
> ... the soldiers will be setting up tents.

Notice that *excitaturos* agrees with its subject *milites*, which is in the object form. If I change *dubito* to *intellexi*, then the meaning of the infinitive changes accordingly, as in this homey sentence:

> *Matres intellexi ornaturas* (*esse*) *cunabula*
>
> I understood the mothers to be about to decorate the cradles
> ... that the mothers were about to decorate the cradles
> ... mothers will decorate the cradles
> ... that the mothers would decorate the cradles.

The Latin infinitives all stay the same in the above examples, but when the M & M verb is placed in the past tense, then the futurity infinitive in Latin produces the English verb "would decorate," or "were about to decorate," to indicate something that was going to happen subsequent to a point in the past. Also, we have already seen that the Latin accusative with the infinitive can possibly be rendered in English by an infinitive, as in the top examples above, or with finite verbs with the word "that" or not, as in the other examples.

Thus, the vernacular rendering of the reported speech changes in interesting ways, all the while the Latin infinitive stays the same. If you understand these infinitives in relation to the verb on which they depend as either antecedent, contemporaneous, or futurity, then you will have no problem understanding Latin literature, which is regular and clear and simple.

Take finally an example with the antecedent infinitive:

> *Discunt Hadrianum Pantheon reformavisse.*

The antecedent infinitive *reformavisse* can stand for anything that occurred prior to the action of *Discunt*, T.1i, such as:

		(corresponding time)
Discunt Hadrianum	*Pantheon reformavisse*	
People learn Hadrian	has rebuilt the Pantheon	(T.4ai)
...	has been rebuilding ...	(T.4ai)
...	rebuilt ...	(T.4bi)
...	did rebuild ...	(T.4bi)
...	was rebuilding ...	(T.2i)
...	used to rebuild ...	(T.2i)
...	had rebuilt ...	(T.5i).

Again, the range of meaning in the vernacular of the infinitive includes any expression that is prior to the action of the main verb, *discunt*. If you change the main verb to a past tense, for example to *discebam* T.2i, or *cogitavisti* T.4bi, then you have:

	(corresponding time)
Formicas discebam domicilia aedificavisse	
I was learning the ants had built homes	(T.5i)
I was learning that the ants had been building homes	(T.5i).

Today it is common but theoretically less correct to say here, "I was learning the ants built homes," because in Latin the time for building the homes occurred before "I was learning."

	(corresponding time)
Cogitavisti Franciscum cantavisse (*cantasse*) *mirabiliter*	
You thought that Frank had sung wonderfully	(T.5i)
You thought that Frank had been singing wonderfully	(T.5i).

There are limited possibilities in correct English, because the expression requires a time previous to a past event. In addition to the last possibilities above, as people speak in 2016, we might add a few other possibilities that do not represent the best English:

	(corresponding time)
Cogitavisti Franciscum mirabiliter cantavisse (*cantasse*)	
You thought Frank sang wonderfully	(T.4bi)
You thought Frank did sing wonderfully	(T.4bi).

If you translate it in this way, your well-trained students will ask why "Frank sang" and "Frank did sing" are roughly contemporaneous with "you thought," when *cantavisse* is clearly antecedent to *cogitavisti*, and they will be right, because in the Latin the singing is clearly before the thinking. Maybe we are demanding too much of contemporary English.

Again, the strange thing is that the infinitives do not change, because they are contemporaneous, antecedent, or futurity with regard to the main verb, but the vernacular is adjusted to make sense in that way.

3. Passive forms

When we studied the deponent verbs, you already unconsciously saw the really passive forms of the infinitives of Gp.I, II, III, IV verbs. Deponent examples that have active meaning are:

laetari	to rejoice
fatēri	to confess
sequi	to follow
sortiri	to obtain.

Normal, real passive infinitives, not deponent, include these examples:

nominari	to be named
timēri	to be feared
pelli	to be driven
finiri	to be terminated.

We note the same old story that the form *pelli* does not look like the passive infinitive of *pellĕre*, which it is, and the form *pelleri* does not exist at all in the Latin language.

As for the active infinitives, these passive infinitives are contemporaneous with the main verb on which they depend, as in:

Istos recordor	*hymnos cotidie cantari*
I remember those	hymns to be sung daily
. . .	that those hymns are sung daily
. . .	those hymns are sung daily.

The passive forms of the *antecedent* infinitive are composed of two elements: the fourth principal part of the verb, already learned, together with the infinitive *esse:*

consecratus, a, um (esse)	to have been consecrated
amotus, a, um (esse)	to have been removed
derelictus, a, um (esse)	to have been abandoned
definitus, a, um (esse)	to have been determined.

The endings *–us, a, um* agree with the subject of the infinitive verb. In indirect speech this typically means that the subject and the participle are in the object case. The *esse* is often omitted in all authors and ages, leaving only the participial half of this infinitive form, and let us remember also that the two elements may sometimes be separated at a distance in the same sentence.

The antecedent passive infinitive is used for any action that precedes the action of the verb on which it depends, as in:

		(corresponding time)
Haec renunciatur	*audita (esse)*	
It is reported	that these things have been heard	(T.4ai)
. . .	that these things were heard	(T.4bi)
. . .	that these things used to be heard	(T.2i)

... that these things had been heard (T.5i).
[before something else
occurred]

If you put the main verb in the past tense, then the action of the antecedent infinitive is set even further in the past, as in correct English:

Est renunciatum haec audita (*esse*)
It was reported that these things had been heard (T.5i).

The expression is equivalent to T.5i, "had been heard." Wow!

To finish off the natural progression of our presentation of concepts would demand at this point that we express futurity in the passive infinitive. However, inasmuch as this requires the acquaintance with a special Latin formula which is most often misunderstood or memorized blindly, we shall present both together in encounter 81.

We can affirm the three possible ways of expressing reported speech in English, when the Latin uses passive infinitives. Sometimes one or another of the three will not flow well in English, as in the first English example below:

Indicant archaeologi cloacas Romae esse ab Etruscis factas

Archaeologists point out the sewers to have been made in Rome by the Etruscans

Archaeologists point out that the sewers in Rome were made by the Etruscans

Archaeologists point out in Rome the sewers were made by the Etruscans.

Conversely, all three of the following English sentences are expressed in the same way in Latin:

I know them to be honest
I know that they are honest
I know they are honest
Eos probos (*esse*) *novi*.

This is the schema. We would say to sum up this encounter: it is very rich in meaning with a few simple forms. I have to read the entire sentence to understand what is being said. English has the same phenomenon of the accusative with the infinitive, as well as two other ways in which to express this same Latin phenomenon. These other ways of expressing reported speech will change dramatically from one time frame to another.

A little bit of practice will make this clear. Students will be consoled and at ease when reported speech is presented in this way, because it is not difficult. The many overlapping, mysterious usages of the subjunctive are the most difficult element of the Latin language, not indirect discourse.

The reading sheets give you vast material with which you can confront most Latin literature. Now instead of one or two examples or sentences here and there, your Appendix sheets will allow you to understand complete bodies of Latin texts using all the information and skills that you have learned.

ENCOUNTER 3 (73)

OBLIQUA ORATIO: PLURIMA ALIA SPECIMINA

indirect, reported speech: very many concrete examples

Introduction

The third encounter on this subject will consist of additional examples provided by the teacher and/or found on the reading sheets at random, where the fluid word order will be pointed out and the elements of this construction will be seen as dispersed throughout the sentence in order to get the individuals used to this way of speaking. As a concession here we shall add one-line examples of indirect speech as a warm-up exercise followed by some longer sentences and a particular case to note. We must warn people that the antecedent passive and subsequent infinitives have two parts. They are not necessarily found together but can be separated by any number of words.

1. One-liner warm-ups

These short sentences will serve as a warm-up. Our first author is Gaius Plinius Caecilius Secundus (minor; 61/62–113 CE). Pliny wrote the following line in a letter:

> *Librum quem nouissime tibi misi, ex omnibus meis uel maxime placere significas* (Plin. *Ep.* VIII, 3, 1)
>
> You indicate that of all my writings the book which I sent to you most recently is pleasing even to the greatest degree.

It is interesting to see that Pliny the Younger places the main verb, *significas*, as the last word, which produces the whole indirect statement that precedes it. Here *librum* is the subject of *placere*, meaning, "the book to be pleasing." The class can play with the sentence by changing the time of the infinitive to say *librum placuisse*, "the book has been pleasing, was pleasing," or to express futurity as in, *librum placiturum*, "the book will be pleasing." We also see here that *vel* means "even"; check your dictionary.

Our second author is Livy, who says in his history of Rome:

> *"Credo ego vos audisse, milites," inquit, "quemadmodum praesidia Romana ab Siculis circumuenta et oppressa sint ..."* (Liv. XXIII, 38)
>
> He said, "I believe, soldiers, that you have heard how the Roman garrisons were surrounded and squashed by the Sicilians."

First, *inquit* stands on its own, outside the sentence in this expression of Livy. The controlling verb is *Credo*, and the content of his belief is expressed in indirect speech, *vos audisse*. We have said that the antecedent infinitive can refer to any time prior to the time of the verb on which it depends, here *credo*, but in this sentence *audisse* is followed by an indirect question *quemadmodum circumuenta et oppressa sint*, "how they were surrounded and squashed," in T.3s, which indicates that the sentence is on Track I and that *audisse* has to correspond to T.4ai to put the sentence on Track I, and consequently that *circumuenta et oppressa sint* corresponds to any time previous to *audisse*.

In his treatise on forgiveness Ambrose gives us this quick line about the beliefs of the Novatiani:

> *aiunt se, exceptis gravioribus criminibus, relaxare veniam levioribus* (Ambros. *de Paen*. I, 3, 10)

> They say that they are opening forgiveness for lighter sins, the more serious ones having been set aside.

Ambrose makes the controlling M & M verb *aiunt*, which introduces the content of their speech, *se relaxare*. The *se* refers to the subject of *aiunt*, whereas an *eos* would refer to "they," some other people. There is a beautiful ablative absolute in the middle of the whole idea, *exceptis gravioribus criminibus*. Energetic Latinists can say that *se relaxaturos* would mean, "that they are going to open," and *se relaxavisse*, "that they have opened" forgiveness for lighter sins.

A further one-liner comes from the etymologies of Isidorus Hispalensis (560–636 CE). Isidore says:

> *Ferunt autem sub Tiberio Caesare quendam artificem excogitasse vitri temperamentum, ut flexibile esset et ductile* (Isid. *Etym*. XVI, 16)

> They report, however, that under Tiberius Caesar a certain artisan thought up a mixture of glass so that it might be flexible and malleable.

Here Isidore of Seville begins with the main verb *ferunt*, "they report," in T.1i, which produces a sentence whose subject is in the object form *quendam artificem* and whose verb is an infinitive *excogitavisse*, which in turn is followed by another object, *temperamentum*, and the reader has to decide which object is serving as the subject of the infinitive. We see that *ut esset* is T.2s on Track II, and so depends on the antecedent idea of *excogitasse*, which must be the equivalent of T.4bi to produce Track II, and that *esset* is not directly dependent on the contemporaneous or eternal idea of *ferunt* in T.1i, which starts the sentence out on Track I. Jumping tracks like this will be considered carefully in a later encounter. The clause *ut esset* obviously expresses the intention, purpose, plan of the artisan. If these sentences have warmed us up sufficiently, let us turn the heat up some more.

2. Impressing reported speech

To confirm our memories about indirect discourse, we can turn to a million examples in any book, and in a moment we shall see how this phenomenon changed with time. Although Augustine is considered a later Latin author, he provides examples of perfectly normal, standard Latin so that we may refresh our minds in what we have learned. In his work on grace and free will, Augustine says:

> Certum est nos mandata servare, si volumus; [...] Certum est nos velle cum volumus; sed ille facit ut velimus bonum.... Certum est nos facere cum facimus; sed ille facit ut faciamus, praebendo vires efficacissimas voluntati. (Aug. *de Gratia*, V, 16, 32; first ellipsis by author)
>
> It is certain that we are keeping the commandments, if we wish; [...] It is certain that we wish when we wish; but he brings it about that we wish the good thing.... It is certain that we are doing this when we do this; but he brings it about that we do it, by offering most effective forces-powers to the will.

The governing verb of each sentence is T.1i, *Certum est*, "It is certain." As an M & M expression, it produces three corresponding sentences in indirect speech. All three of these have a subject in the object form, *nos*, and one of several contemporaneous infinitive verbs: *servare, velle, facere*. Just to recall, there are three standard ways to render these ACI sentences in English, and these meet with various success depending on the thought expressed:

Certum est nos servare	It is certain	us to keep
		... that we keep; that we are keeping
		... we keep; we are keeping
Certum est nos velle	It is certain	us to wish
		... that we wish; that we are wishing
		... we wish; we are wishing
Certum est nos facere	It is certain	us to do
		... that we do; that we are doing
		... we do; we are doing.

We also notice that Augustine says *cum volumus* and *cum facimus*. Both verbs are in T.1i, and so *cum* must mean "when," and cannot mean "because" or "although," which require the subjunctive.

Augustine says here, *facit ut velimus* and *facit ut faciamus*. Now *facit* is one of the verbs that give rise to a result clause; the first one here is *ut velimus* and next is *ut faciamus*, both in T.1s. In both cases, because these subjunctive verbs express a concrete result in Latin, they will sound indicative in English, as in, "that we wish" and "that we do it."

We also note that *praebendo* means "by offering," which we shall afterwards see as a gerund of instrument; its subject may not be immediately clear, but the logical statement of Augustine suggests the same subject of the controlling verb on which it depends, namely *facit*, "he brings it about ... by offering."

The teacher can play around with the infinitives to make them antecedent, *servavisse, voluisse, fecisse*, or subsequent and thus expressive of futurity, *servaturos esse, volituros esse, facturos esse*. The self-learner can change the controlling verb to T.2i, *Certum erat* … , "It was certain … ," and *facit* also to T.2i *faciebat*, with all the corresponding changes required. The infinitives remain the same in Latin, and their meaning in English will remain contemporaneous to the verb, now set in the past, and so will sound like, "It was certain that we were keeping … we were wishing … we were doing." The *cum*-clauses accordingly have to change to *cum volebamus* and *cum faciebamus*, or something like that. The result clauses also change to *ut vellemus* and *ut faceremus*, now on Track II. A new rendering of the entire citation could be:

> It was certain that we were keeping the commandments, if we were wanting; […] It was certain that we were wishing when we were wishing; but he brought it about that we were wishing the good thing.… It was certain that we were doing this when we would do this; but he brought it about that we were doing it, by offering most effective forces-powers to the will.

Our explanation of Augustine's expression was prolonged, as are the examples that follow, so that these may serve as examples of how to play with a Latin sentence in many ways so that our Latin composition may be based on authentic examples. Such play occurs in the encounter between teacher and students in class; and in the curious musings of a self-teacher; and in the domestic games or *ludi domestici* we mentioned in the introduction of this book. May our musings here serve as an inspiration to the teacher desiring to compose *ludi* on the spot for each Latin encounter from any sentence of authentic Latin you wish.

Once again Pliny gives an example from classical antiquity when he says in a letter:

> *Etenim omnes homines arbitror oportere aut immortalitatem suam aut mortalitatem cogitare, et illos quidem contendere eniti, hos quiescere remitti* (Plin. *Ep.* IX, 3, 2)
>
> For I believe that it is necessary that all people think of either their immortality or mortality, and that the former indeed are struggling, making an effort, the latter are resting, being relaxed.

Here you have indirect statements on top of each other. The controlling verb is *arbitror*, "I believe." This is an M & M verb producing the indirect statement *oportere*, which is impersonal and means variously, "it to be necessary, that it is necessary, it is necessary." What is necessary—the subject of the verb *oportere*—is expressed in three indirect statements; the first of these is *homines cogitare*, "that people think of." The second is *illos contendere, eniti*, "that the former are struggling, making an effort," using two infinitives that are synonyms. The third is *hos quiescere, remitti*, "the latter are resting, being relaxed," again using synonym infinitives.

A third example will help us to remember all that we have forgotten and prepare us for things yet to come. Our example is by Cyprian, who wrote in a letter:

> Neminem putamus a fructu satisfactionis et spe pacis arcendum, cum sciamus iuxta scripturarum divinarum fidem, auctore et hortatore ipso Deo, et ad agendam paenitentiam peccatores redigi et veniam atque indulgentiam paenitentibus non denegari. (Cypr. *Ep.* LV, 27)

> We believe no one is to be kept away from the fruit of satisfaction and the hope of reconciliation, since we know according to the trustworthiness of the divine scriptures—God himself being the author and instigator—that sinners are being driven to doing penance and that forgiveness and indulgence are not being denied to those doing penance.

The controlling verb of the whole text by Cyprian of Carthage is *putamus*, "we think," which by the way is not the first word, but lies inside the indirect statement. The sentence begins, *neminem … arcendum* (*esse*), meaning, "no one … is to be kept away." The expression *cum sciamus* in T.1s could mean "because we know" or "although we know," but cannot mean "when we know," as we have said before; here we take it as causal meaning "because we know." The content of our knowledge is then given in reported speech, *peccatores redigi*, with a passive infinitive meaning, "that sinners are being driven," and *veniam atque indulgentiam non denegari*, with another passive infinitive meaning, "that forgiveness and indulgence are not being denied." You will readily recognize the abl. abs. *auctore et hortatore ipso Deo*, whose verb is understood and means "God himself being the author and instigator." We shall see the meaning of *ad agendam paenitentiam* in several encounters, but for now it means, "to doing penance."

If we change the controlling verb to *putabamus*, nothing would change in Latin except *sciamus* to *sciremus*, but the whole translation will change:

> We were thinking that no one was to be kept away from the fruit of satisfaction and the hope of reconciliation, since we knew according to the trustworthiness of the divine scriptures—God himself being the author and instigator—that sinners were being driven to do penance and that forgiveness and indulgence were not being denied to those doing penance.

In a later encounter we shall see how this phenomenon changed with time.

The perceptive reader will notice that we do not resort to grammatical analysis in the above commentaries, but clarify the meaning of a Latin expression and how its larger ideas are put together into a complete thought. When a student or teacher in the classroom fully accounts for all the elements of a Latin expression without adding anything extraneous or changing the mode of expression to something else, then everyone can readily hear and enjoyably understand without the often cumbersome filter of grammatical analysis.

3. Nominative with the infinitive

So far in our consideration of indirect speech, we have seen limitless examples of an M & M verb causing reported discourse given with an accusative subject and an infinitive verb. We wish to point out a phenomenon that was often preferred by the Romans as stylistically better. There is a short list of verbs in Latin that take their subject from the indirect statement. The most common example is with the verb *video, videre, visi, visum*, 2, "I see," in its passive use, such as *videor*, meaning, "I am seen" or "I seem." Instead of using the impersonal expression:

It seems that the students are tired today

the Romans preferred to say this personally,

The students seem to be tired today.

In this way of speaking you can hear that the phrase "the students" is no longer the accusative subject of an infinitive, but it functions as the subject of the M & M verb. This is what people call the "nominative with the infinitive."

In inferior Latin people might say:

Videtur discipulos esse aegrotos
It seems the students to be sick

but the Romans would prefer:

Videntur discipuli aegroti esse
The students appear-seem to be sick.

The other famous verb is *dico, dicere, dixi, dictum*, 3, "to say," also used in the passive to mean, for example, *dicitur*, "it is said." Maybe the scholastics and medieval people would use it impersonally in the sentence:

Dicitur vos pulchre scribere
It is said that you write beautifully

but the Romans in standard, beautiful Latin would prefer the personal construction as in:

Vos dicimini pulchre scribere
You people are said to write beautifully.

We can summarize this phenomenon in this way: instead of the accusative subject of an infinitive verb depending on an impersonal M & M verb, the M & M verb becomes personal and takes its subject from the indirect statement.

To give another example, the impersonal verb *traditur*, "it is handed down," produces an indirect statement in the accusative with the infinitive in this sentence:

Traditur Homerum caecum fuisse
It is handed down that Homer was blind

but the Romans would prefer to make it personal and say:

Traditur Homerus caecus fuisse
Homer is said to have been blind.

Here *traditur* is personal, and its subject is *Homerus*.

Desiderius Erasmus Roterodamus (1466–1536) knew and understood this preference of the Romans, when in his *Praise of Folly* Erasmus said:

> *si cui videor haec audacius quam verius dicere, agedum paulisper ipsas hominum vitas inspiciamus* (Eras. *Stult. laus* 48)
>
> If I seem to someone to be saying these things more boldly than truthfully, come on then, let us study the very lives of people for a little time.

Here *videor* is the personal expression, where someone using poorer Latin would say, *si videtur me dicere*, "If it seems that I am saying," but the Romans and Erasmus of Rotterdam say, "I seem to be saying."

In Gildersleeve and Lodge n° 528 you can find a list of passive verbs of thinking or saying, about 6 or 7 of them, that employ the nom. with the infinitive.

ENCOUNTER 4 (74)

VERBA REMINISCENDI - OBLIVISCENDI + GENITIVUS, ETIAM ACCUSATIVUS

verbs of remembering – forgetting with the genitive function and even the accusative

Introduction

We shall take a brief pause in our treatment of indirect speech so that you may forget and relearn everything you now know. This and the next encounter consider two specific classes of verbs and their Latin uses. In line with other Indo-European languages, Latin also uses verbs of remembering and forgetting with the natural function meaning "of," as we shall see in this encounter.

Verbs of remembering – forgetting with the genitive

The dictionary will give you these verbs of remembering and forgetting:

> *reminiscor, reminisci*, 3, to remember
> *recordor, recordari, recordatus*, 1, to be mindful of
> *obliviscor, oblivisci, oblitus*, 3, to forget.

The apparent objects of these Latin verbs is in the form of-possession. This special function of the gen. can also be heard in English if we say, for example, "to be mindful of someone or something" and "to be forgetful of something or someone"; then you can hear the gen. as in the following examples:

> *Perpetuo vestrorum reminiscemur beneficiorum*
> We shall be forever mindful of your kindnesses.

It should also be noted, lest we get carried away with rules and regulations, that these verbs also can take an acc. object; consult your dictionary. It depends on the author and the contents. Again, examples have to be found and pointed out in Latin literature.

ENCOUNTER 5 (75)

PRETII ET MERCATURAE ABLATIVUS AC GENITIVUS; "OPUS EST" PECULIARIAQUE VERBA: TAEDET, PAENITET, PUDET, MISERET, PIGET

ablative of definite price
and the genitive of indefinite price; "opus est"
and special verbs

Introduction

The functions of our Latin language are also used in daily speech in evaluating and measuring things. Here the Romans used the function by-with-from-in to designate a definite price, as in *Librum emi tribus nummis* "I bought the book for-with three dollars," and then they use the function of-possession to designate indefinite price or general evaluation such as, *Tanti constat*, "It is selling for such a great price," or *Quanti aestimatur*? "How much is it valued at?"

1. Ablative of definite price

The abl. is used in commercial terms to signify definite price, for example:

Quinque centesimis coemimus libellum
We bought the pamphlet for five cents

Decem euris id venibat
It was being sold for ten euros.

2. Genitive of indefinite price

Verbs of evaluating or judging or esteeming will use the gen. of price. These verbs are not so much of a commercial nature, but a moral judgment, as these words indicate:

ducĕre	to think, judge (a meaning from the dictionary that will be a surprise and shock to most "vocabulary-list" scholars)
aestimare	to evaluate, esteem
existimare	to recon, judge
iudicare	to judge
censēre	to calculate
habēre	to consider

These verbs of evaluating are very many, and often they are misunderstood.

Once again our master leader, Terentius, writing in *Eunuchus*, sums up these last two uses of the genitive of rating but ablative of definite price in one fantastic turn of phrase. Parmeno is speaking with an old man, *Senex:*

> *PA.... emit quendam Phaedria eunuchum quem dono huic daret.*
> *SE. quoi?*
> *PA. Thaidi.*
> *SE. emit? perii hercle. quanti?*
> *PA. viginti minis. Se. actumst.*
>
> (Ter. *Eun*. 982–985; line breaks by author)

PARMENO: Phaedria bought a certain eunuch whom he might give as a gift to this one here.
OLD MAN: to whom?
PARMENO: Thais.
OLD MAN: He purchased?
For heaven's sakes I have perished. For how much?
PARMENO: for twenty dollars.
OLD MAN: it is all over with.

Here *quem ... daret* is a purpose clause where the relative *quem* stands for *ut eum* and is followed by *daret* in T.2s, meaning, "so that he might give him." We would call *dono huic* a double use of the dative in which the goal is *dono*, "for a gift" and the person is *huic*, "to this person." The form *quoi* is older Latin for *cui* "to whom." The form to-for-from *Thaidi* is the name Thais, a famous woman in Latin and Greek plays. The expression *perii hercle* means, "I have perished, by george." To the point here, *quanti*, "for how much," is the genitive of indefinite price, and the answer was *viginti minis* in the ablative of definite price, "for twenty dollars." The final word is *actumst* is a contraction of *actum est*, "it has been done," "it has been finished," "it is all over with."

Besides *quanti*, we shall also find as a trap for many readers other genitives of indefinite price as listed by Gildersleeve and Lodge in n^0 380.1. These are:

magni	much
parvi	little
tanti, tantidem	so much
pluris	more
minoris	less
quanti (and compounds)	how much
plurimi, maximi	most
minimi	least
nihili	naught

3. *Opus est*

Be careful! In the dictionary the expression *opus est* does not mean only "it is the work," but also "there is need," and, strange to say, the thing needed can be in the form of-possession or by-with-from-in or in the subject form, as in these examples indicate respectively:

Opus est margaritis nobis
There is for us a need for pearls
We need pearls

Summae indocentibus opus est patientiae
There is need of the greatest patience in people teaching
People teaching need the greatest patience

Nostro opus sunt praetiosi lapides instituto
Jewels are a need for our institution.

This is pointed out in every Latin dictionary. Just remember not to take it for what it looks like, but understand it for what it can be: "there is need."

4. The special verbs

There are five famous blood-related verbs. These all have the same construction and phenomenon.

These five verbs in Gp.II are famous cousins; here we are referring only to their impersonal use:

paenitet	to cause regret
miseret	to cause pity
pudet	to cause shame
taedet	to cause annoyance or disgust
piget	to disgust.

The phenomenon works in this way. Each verb describes an emotion. The person or thing affected with these emotions is given in the object form. The thing that is causing the emotion is given in the form of-possession. That is why we say:

Paenitet me totius vitae meae
It causes me regret of my whole life
I regret my whole life

Eos propriae pudet levitatis
It causes them shame of their own fickleness
They are ashamed of their own fickleness

Hi sunt hostes quorum senatum miserebat
These are the enemies of whom it causes the senate pity
These are the enemies for whom the senate had pity

Huius me taedet putridae scholae
It causes me disgust of this rotten school
I am sick and tired of this rotten school.

Examples of these can be found all over the place in literature or the dictionary. The verb *piget* is rather rare, but *pudet* is common.

ENCOUNTER 6 (76)

ORATIONIS OBLIQUAE EXERCITATIO ET DEMONSTRATIO SERIORE AETATE

impressing reported speech and showing it in a later age

Introduction

We have experienced thoroughly the Romans' manner of quoted or indirect speech in the ACI combination. Apart from perhaps a few isolated or disputed examples, this system of indirect speech was observed for hundreds of years. Thereafter a tendency prevailed to simplify classical languages, to speak more directly to students in school, to render the Latin uses and constructions more accessible to the general public in the emerging national languages. This occurred in classical languages, as we have the *koine* Greek of the Bible and in our field the developments of later Latin. A similar process occurred in the birth and development of other contemporary languages from, for example, Old English and High German.

Reported speech in a later age

To illustrate this development in later Latin it is our custom in class to present on one page the entries of three Latin words from a complete Latin dictionary like Lewis and Short. The entries of these *three words* point to the use of certain particles or conjunctions in Latin, whose original meaning is maintained even as they take over the function of indirect quoted speech. They are simpler and more accessible. Anyone can consult these entries in such a complete dictionary, but these developments in later Latin are not found in less-than-full Latin dictionaries or in dictionaries limited to the classical era, as is the *Oxford Latin Dictionary*. If you do not know this, you do not understand or appreciate medieval Latin, and you miss approximately 1,000 years of Latin literature; that is all!

Look in your complete dictionary under the word *quia*. You will find that it naturally means "because, since, whereas," just as we have said a hundred times. At the very end of the whole entry for *quia* in a dictionary like Lewis and Short, you will see that *quia* is used in a so-called "object clause" to mean "that ..."

An example from the Latin Vulgate Bible comes to mind, where Jesus said to Peter, *ego dico tibi quia tu es Petrus* (Vulg. *Matt.* 16.18), which is written in letters two meters tall inside the basilica of St. Peter, at the Vatican. A classicist might read this to say, "I am speaking to you because you are the rock." This use of *quia*, however, to introduce reported speech and meaning "that ..." is confirmed in a full dictionary by a number of quotations from early Christian writers and in the Vulgate Latin Bible. The New Vulgate edition omits the word *quia* here, because it is such poor Latin. It takes over in most scholastic or late patristic texts. It is not understood or appreciated by strict, closed, classicists, although it was the normal expression for 1,000 years.

The same phenomenon can be discovered in the dictionary entry for the word *quoniam*, meaning "because." In later Latin *quoniam* also was used to introduce a sentence of reported speech with the meaning "that ...." This is something that confuses strict classicists who do not realize that *quoniam* took on this second function in later Latin. Lewis and Short refers to this later usage in various ways such as, "post-Aug.," meaning, "after Augustus (17 CE)," or "freq. in the Christian writers," or "post-class.," or "eccl. Lat." referring to "ecclesiastical Latin."

Of course the most common substitution is *quod*, which also took on this function meaning "that ...." This form went into our contemporary languages as "that," "daß," "che." The examples are innumerable where the meaning of *quod* simply slips into meaning "that ...."

We might mention here that the *Oxford Latin Dictionary* is limited to Latin usage up to about 160 CE. This phenomenon, consequently, is not clearly included under the entries for *quoniam* or *quod*. Under the entry for *quia*, at the end of the second column, two lines report the rare occurrence of this phenomenon in classical language, and yet it explodes in patristic and scholastic Latin, in which for example Thomas Aquinas says 1,000 times *dicendum quod*, meaning "it must be said that."

All three, *quia*, *quoniam*, *quod*, are normally followed by the indicative, but, depending on the author, the subjunctive may appear with indicative meaning, especially with *quod*. This is extremely important because many try to read early and medieval Christian Latin who are not conscious of this and end up completely alienated from their text.

Take the example using the accusative with the infinitive:

> *Amicos confido heri advenisse tuos*
> I am sure your friends arrived yesterday.

Now, 600 years afterwards, you could say:

> *Quod amici tui heri advenerunt, omnino confido*
> I am completely confident that your friends arrived yesterday.

Even the New Latin Vulgate edition of the Bible of 1979 says in 1 Corinthians 6:9:

> *An nescitis quia iniqui regnum Dei non possidebunt*?
> Do you not know that the wicked will not possess the kingdom of God?

If you translate these as causal sentences meaning "because ... ," the whole thing is destroyed.

Another example comes from Ambrose, who says in a commentary on the Gospel of Luke:

> *Vides utique quia ubique Domini virtus studiis cooperatur humanis*
> (Ambros. *in Luc.* II, 84)

> You see certainly that the power of the Lord works together with human efforts everywhere.

The M & M verb *Vides* gives rise to the later construction, ... *quia virtus cooperatur*, in place of the classical way of speaking, ... *virtutem cooperari.* Ambrose uses the indicative mode of speaking.

A contemporary of the scholastic theologian Thomas Aquinas (c. 1225–1274), the Italian poet Dantes Alagherius (1265–1321), uses the language of the scholastics in his own philosophical work on politics, where Dante says:

> *Satis igitur declaratum est quod proprium opus humani generis, totaliter accepti, est actuare semper totam potentiam intellectus possibilis* (Dante, *de Mon.* IV)

> It has been stated enough therefore that the special work of the human race, taken in its entirety, is to actuate always the full power of the possible intellect.

Again, *declaratum est quod opus est*, is a substitute for *declaratum est opus esse.* In the place of that second *est*, Dante Alighieri uses the indicative, as did Ambrose above; it depends on the author.

A final example comes to us from the biblical scholar Jerome. In a work against the teachings of Vigilantius, Jerome says:

> *Dicis in libello tuo quod, dum vivimus, mutuo pro nobis orare possumus*
> (Hier. *contra Vigil.* 6)

> You say in your pamphlet that, as long as we live, we are able to pray mutually for each other.

Again in the indicative, Jerome's statement *Dicis quod possumus* stands for the more classical way of speaking: *Dicis nos posse.*

ENCOUNTER 7 (77)

GERUNDIUM ET GERUNDIVUM

gerund and gerundive

Introduction

We remember what was said in another Experience about the four Latin participles. One of them is going to return now for a detailed explanation. Suffice it to say that we have met the participle *cantandus –a –um*, meaning, "needing to be sung; having to be sung; owing to be sung; worthy to be sung; to be sung." What follows here is the same basic word, but with a completely different meaning.

1. Gerund

To understand the use of gerunds and gerundives, let us first look at how they are formed, beginning with the gerund. A few principles will help you to understand this phenomenon. A gerund is a verbal singular neuter noun. Thus, it is not plural. As a noun, a gerund has functions. Words that agree with a gerund are accordingly singular and neuter and follow the function of the gerund.

The subject form of the gerund is the same as the contemporaneous active infinitive, as we have emphasized. For example, *cantare* means either "singing" or "to sing," as in:

Hymnos est cantare iucundum
Singing hymns is pleasant
To sing hymns is pleasant.

Note here that *iucundum* is neuter and singular to agree with *cantare*.

The object form of the gerund has one of two possibilities. Following the super principle for neuter nouns, the object form can look like the subject form, for example, *cantare* in the sentence:

Volo cantare
I want singing
I want to sing.

The other object expression is composed of a preposition like *ad*, *inter*, *in*, which take the object form, and the gerund such as *cantandum*, *gaudendum*, *gignendum*, *adoriendum*, *pariendum*. You will notice that these gerunds are nothing else but the neuter singular objects of, for example, *cantandus, a, um*. Take the sentence:

Sumus parati ad cantandum, gaudendum, gignendum, adoriendum
We are ready for singing, rejoicing, generating, attacking.

Note that the form *cantandum* is invariable because the gerund is neuter, singular, and here the object of the preposition *ad*. Other prepositions that take the object form are also possible such as *in* or even *inter*.

The decision to use the object form *cantare* or the form *ad cantandum* is determined by the verb and sentence structure on which it depends. A complementary infinitive *cantare* is required after certain verbs such as *volo*, "I wish"; *cogito*, "I plan"; *statuo*, "I decide"; *iubeo*, "I command, order"; and many others, but if the sentence structure demands the use of the finality preposition *ad*, meaning "for, to," then the form *ad cantandum* is used.

The form of-possession is again the neuter singular of this function, namely *cantandi*, *gaudendi*, *pariendi*, as in:

Facultatem habet cantandi, gaudendi, pariendi
She has the ability of singing, rejoicing, giving birth.

The form by-with-from-in is the same as the form to-for-from because the neuter singular of these functions has the same form, as in *cantando:*

Operam dabant cantando
They were giving effort to singing

Vivimus saltando
We live by dancing.

2. Gerundive

Gerunds and gerundives have no difference in their verbal meaning; only their forms are different; one is a noun, the other an adjective. A few principles will help you to understand gerundives easily. A gerundive is a gerund used as an adjective, when an object is involved. The ancient Romans prefer the gerundive by 95% and use the gerund only 5% of the time with an object. The gerundive is preferred, stylistically better and usual. As an adjective, the gerundive will agree with its own object.

The form of the gerundive is, for example:

restaurandus, a, um
monendus, a, um
eloquendus, a, um
circumveniendus, a, um

The rule for forming a gerundive from a gerund is:

Put the object of the gerund in the function of the gerund and make the gerundive agree with it.

We begin with the above example of a gerund:

Ad cantandum hymnos sumus parati
We are ready for singing hymns.

Here we begin with the object gerund *ad cantandum* and its object *hymnos*. First we put the object of the gerund in the function of the gerund. In this case *hymnos* is already in the object form. Then, make the gerundive agree with it. So, *cantandum* becomes plural and masculine, *cantandos*, to agree with *hymnos*. The resulting sentence with a gerundive has the exact same meaning:

Hymnos sumus ad cantandos parati
We are ready for singing hymns.

Here we see that *cantandos* is in the gender and number of its own object.

Another example is:

Habet ea cantandi carmina facultatem
She has the ability of singing songs.

The noun *facultatem* is complemented by the gerund in the form of-possession, *cantandi*, and its object is *hymnos*. To form the gerundive, first, *carmina* takes the form of-possession to become *carminum*. Next *cantandi* is changed to agree with *carminum* and so becomes *cantandorum*. The resulting sentence with the stylistically preferable gerundive is:

Habet ea cantandorum carminum facultatem
She has the ability of singing hymns.

Again, the gerund contributes the form, here of-possession, and then is made to agree with its own object.

Now let us see both the gerund and the gerundive in each of their functions in the Latin sentence, first in genuine reading sheets, then in the following thumb-nail vision.

Subject

Gerund	Gerundive
Cantare hymnos est iucundum. Singing hymns is pleasant.	———

Object

Gerund	Gerundive
Hymnos cupimus cantare. We wish to sing hymns.	———
Colligebatur ad pauperes adiuvandum pecunia. *... in adiuvandum pauperes.* *... inter pauperes adiuvandum.*	*Colligebatur ad pauperes adiuvandos pecunia.* *... in adiuvandos pauperes.* *... inter pauperes adiuvandos.*

Money was being collected for helping the poor.
... unto helping the poor.
... in the midst of helping the poor.

Of, possession

Gerund	Gerundive
Habetis libros legendi occasionem.	*Habetis librorum legendorum occasionem.*

You all have an occasion of reading books.

By, with, from, in

Gerund	Gerundive
Opes fraudendo cives cumulat.	*Opes fraudendis civibus cumulat.*

It heaps up riches by defrauding citizens.

To, for, from

Gerund	Gerundive
Exercendo lacertos sudorem impendit.	*Exercendis sudorem impendit lacertis.*

He/she expends sweat for exercising the muscles.

In each example of the gerundive, one cannot easily see that the nouns *pauperes*, *librorum*, and *civibus* are still the objects of their respective gerunds, *adiuvandos*, *legendorum*, and *fraudendis*. Of course, when the object of the gerund is a masculine or neuter singular noun, the gerund and gerundive constructions are going to be identical.

3. Modern example

On page 652 of this volume you can see an image of an inscription composed for the renovation and expansion of the Vatican print shop in 1991. A fuller explanation of that inscription is found in the appendix to this book, so right here we shall limit ourselves to examining the two gerundives of this contemporary expression in Latin:

... LIBRARIAE OPIFICINAE VATICANAE
RATIONIBVS APTANDAE RECENTIBVS
NOVIS ROBORANDAE MACHINIS
IOANNES PAVLVS II PONTIFEX MAXIMVS
ALTERAS ... AEDES STRVI ...
... IVNGI ALTERAS
VOLVIT IPSE CENSVIT ...

for adapting the Vatican printing shop with recent systems
strengthening it with new machines,
Pope John Paul II
himself resolved, decreed that,
the one building be constructed ...
the other ... be joined ...

The two main verbs act in tandem, *volvit ... censuit*, "[Pope John Paul II] resolved, decreed." As verbs of M & M, these two give rise to a statement in indirect discourse. In both cases *aedes* in the object form functions as the subject of two infinitives *strui* and *iungi*. The purpose for which the Pope decreed that these two actions be accomplished is given in two gerundives where *aptandae*, "for adapting," and *roborandae*, "for strengthening," both have the same object, *opificinae*, as in, "for adapting ... for strengthening the shop." Both gerundives are in the form to-for-from as an expression of purpose.

These do not function here as participles of passive necessity, which would result in the statement that the Pope decreed that these two actions be accomplished for "the shop needing to be adapted, having to be strengthened." Rather than describe the poor conditions prior to the building project, the inscription envisions the intended improved conditions with these two gerundives.

4. Note

A quick review of various manuals, texts, and grammars reveals a serious and extensive confusion of terminology and usage. What is called here a gerundive, by other people is called a "future passive participle," something that is very hard to find in Latin literature, found once every five years of reading Latin.

The confusion of terminology remains, but the facts are certain that the participle *cantandus, a, um* has two distinct meanings and usages. The first meaning is as a gerund or gerundive and means, "singing." The second expresses passive necessity, namely, "needing to be sung, owing to be sung, worthy to be sung, having to be sung, to be sung," which we already saw in the previous Experience. The distinction between the participle of passive necessity, on the one hand, and the gerund and gerundive, on the other, is so difficult for students to understand that they are presented by us in two separate Experiences, separated by one full academic year.

This natural, essential distinction, not terminology, is important because of their different natural meanings; namely, both the gerund and gerundive are active verbal forms, but the participle of passive necessity is passive, as its title says. The gerund and gerundive are counted among the fourteen ways to express purpose, as given in a later encounter, but the participle of passive necessity does not express purpose.

ENCOUNTER 8 (78)

VERBA CUM ABLATIVO; IN VERNACULIS MAIOR DIFFICULTAS

verbs with the ablative;
a rather big difficulty in their vernacular translations

Introduction

So far we have seen the objects of verbs put in the object form. In Latin, however, as in many other languages, certain groups of verbs have their apparent objects in another form. This phenomenon in Latin is not necessarily the same as you might expect from English usage. As an example, the German word "to believe," *glauben*, is used with the function to-for-from as in *Ich glaube dir*, literally, "I believe [to] you." When we say this in English, we use the object form, "I believe you." Another German phrase is *Ich gehorche ihnen nicht*, "I do not obey [to] them," where in English we use the object form, "I do not obey them." Latin works in the same way as German here. We have recently seen the groups of verbs in Latin that for a certain reason take the form of-possession, where in English we use the simple object form. We have already seen the 65 Latin verbs whose complement is in the form to-for-from, and the compound verbs in Latin which follow this same pattern, all quite different from our common English expressions. People have difficulty in English because they cannot hear in their own language the natural meaning of those functions in Latin. Today we begin with a number of verbs that take the object form in English, but in Latin they take the form by-with-from-in for a certain definite reason.

1. Verbs with the ablative

Five famous deponent verbs in Latin, as has been seen, are representative of the Greek middle voice, where something is happening for the good of the subject. The five verbs are:

utor, uti, usus sum	to procure usefulness for one's self	= to use
fruor, frui, fructus sum	to get enjoyment for one's self	= to enjoy
fungor, fungi, functus sum	to carry out or fulfill for one's self	= to perform
potior, potiri, potitus sum	to get control of something for one's self	= to take over
vescor, vesci,—	to nourish one's self	= to eat

2. A rather big difficulty in their vernacular expressions

In English the object of these verbs will sound simply like a direct object, for example: "to perform a duty," "to enjoy the music," "to take over the government," "to use pencils," "to eat pizza." What looks like the direct object of these verbs in English is expressed in Latin by the form by-with-from-in. This can easily be understood as a kind of instrumentality connected to the middle-voice meanings given above. That is to say, for example:

to procure usefulness for one's self *by means of something*
to use a thing.

Consequently, the action of these verbs is completed in the abl. These complements are really not direct objects but oblique-indirect objects and here instruments. This creates difficulties in understanding the Latin and in expressing it in English. These verbs are obviously very common in everyday writing and speaking, as the Appendix readings confirm.

3. Other verbs with the abl.

Some books and authors add a few other verbs that from the dictionary have a similar use and phenomenon, like:

careo, carēre, carui, caritum	to be without (A manuscript *caret* does not have a given reading.)	= to lack
egeo, egēre, egui, egitum	to be in need of (used with abl. or gen.)	= to need
indigeo, indigēre, indigui, —	to be in need of (used with abl. or gen.)	= to need

Latin literature abounds in examples of these verbs, as they happen to be some of the more common activities in life: to use, to enjoy, to eat, to need.

ENCOUNTER 9 (79)

QUI, QUAE, QUOD; QUIS, QUID: VARII USUS DECEM

qui, quae, quod; quis, quid:
ten different usages

Ten ways to use *qui, quae, quod* and *quis, quid*

1. Indefinite: *qui, qua, quod* stand for the indefinite *aliqui, aliqua, aliquod* (encounter 42):

   Quaero num quis hoc fecerit
   I am asking whether anyone has done this

   Rei sunt si quibus pravis utuntur instrumentis
   They are guilty if they use some bad means.

2. *qui, quae, quod* begin a relative sentence (encounters 10–11). Examples abound.
3. Direct question: *qui, quae, quod* and *quis, quid* ask a question (encounters 13, 42):

   Qui hoc fecerunt?
   What people did this?

   Praesidem quem sunt nominaturi?
   Whom are they about to name as president?

4. Indirect question: *qui, quae, quod* and *quis, quid* + subjunctive ask an indirect question (encounter 60):

   Qui hoc fecerint quaeritur
   It is asked what people did this

   Praesidem interest quem sint nominaturi
   It is of concern whom they are about to name as president.

5. Purpose: *qui, quae, quod* and *quis, quid* + subjunctive = *ut is, ut ea, ut id* and *ut quis, ut quid* as an expression of purpose (encounter 58):

   Qui mea ne abutantur benevolentia etiam moneo amicos

   I advise even friends lest who abuse my kindness
   I advise even friends lest they abuse my kindness.

   Note: *Qui ... ne* stand for *Ne mea abutantur benevolentia ...*, "Lest they abuse my kindness."

Certam ad metam quam feliciter attingas serius ocius erit magno opere tibi enitendum

Sooner or later a great effort will have to be made by you toward a goal which you may successfully reach

Sooner or later a great effort will have to be made by you toward a goal so that you may successfully touch on it.

Canes condocefacio quae fures nostro a praedio arceant

I train female dogs who may keep thieves away from our estate

I train female dogs so that they may keep thieves away from our estate.

6. Result: *qui, quae, quod* and *quis, quid* + subjunctive = *ut is, ut ea, ut id* and *ut quis, ut quid* as an expression of result, in English sounding indicative (encounter 67):

   Nobis normae tam aspere imponebantur qui perpetuo conquereremur

   Such hard rules were being imposed on us who as a result were complaining continually

   Such hard rules were being imposed on us that as a result we were complaining continually.

   CL. Nulla mihi res posthac potest iam intervenire tanta
   quae mi aegritudinem adferat: tanta haec laetitia obortast
   (Ter. *Heaut.* 679–680)

   CLINIA. No thing so great is able any more to happen to me in the future which (as a result) brings me grief; this so great joy has risen up.

   Pubilici tam strenue cives defenderunt qui fatigatione sint prolapsi

   The police defended the citizens so energetically who collapsed with exhaustion.

   The police defended the citizens so energetically that as a result they collapsed with exhaustion.

   Note: here *qui* stands for *ut is*, "so that they," followed by the subjunctive expressing pure result in an exceptional sequence of tenses which will be explained in encounter 97.

7. Causal: *qui, quae, quod* and *quis, quid* + subjunctive = *cum is, cum ea, cum id* and *cum quis, cum quid* as a relative expression of cause, in English sounding indicative (encounter 59):

   GE. et quidem, ere, nos iamdudum hic te absentem incusamu' qui abieris
   (Ter. *Phorm.* 471)

   GETA. and indeed, master, we here are accusing you already for a long time being absent who have gone away

   GETA. and indeed, master, we here are accusing you already for a long time being absent because you have gone away

sati' nequam sum, utpote qui hodie amare inceperim

(Plaut. *Rud.* 462)

I am worthless enough as who began to be in love today

I am worthless enough as in as much as I began to be in love today

facis adeo indigne iniuriam illi qui non abstineas manum.
nam istaec quidem contumeliast (Ter. *Heaut.* 465–66)

to that extent you are making unworthily an injury for her who are not keeping your hand off.

for that indeed is an insult

to that extent you are making unworthily an injury for her because you are not keeping your hand off.

for that indeed is an insult

8. Concession: *qui, quae, quod* and *quis, quid* + subjunctive = *cum is, cum ea, cum id* and *cum quis, cum quid* as a relative expression of concession, in English sounding indicative (encounter 64):

Vectus aeronavigio in Californiam integer sum cuius volatus incommodissimus esset

I was brought by a plane to California in one piece, [although] whose flight was most uncomfortable,

I was brought by a plane to California in one piece, although its flight was most uncomfortable.

Acu salubriter depletur sanguis qui maximum vulnus infligat

Blood is taken in a healthy way by a needle which inflicts a very big wound.

Blood is taken in a healthy way by a needle although it inflicts a very big wound.

9. Characteristic result: *qui, quae, quod* and *quis, quid* + subjunctive = *talis ut is, talis ut ea, tale ut id* and *talis ut quis, tale ut quid* as a relative expression of characteristic result, in English sounding indicative (encounter 68):

Sunt qui officia lucis noctisque perverterint nec ante diducant oculos hesterna graves crapula quam adpetere nox coepit

(Sen. *Ep.* CXXII, 2)

There are some people such who have reversed the duties of day and night nor do they crack open eyes heavy with yesterday's hangover sooner than the night has begun to approach.

Note: *perverterint* stands for *perverterunt*; *diducant* for *diducunt*

Nihil umquam mihi incidet quod tristis excipiam, quod malo vultu; nullum tributum invitus conferam (Sen. *Ep.* XCVI, 2)

Nothing will ever happen to me such which I take in as a sad man, which I take in with a bad face; no tax shall I contribute as an unwilling person.

10. Modal attraction: *qui, quae, quod* and *quis, quid* + the verb in the subjunctive by modal attraction. Rather than give any examples here, refer to encounter 83 for very many examples.

How to think this through

When a reader comes across a clause consisting of *qui, quae, quod* or *quis, quid* followed by the subjunctive, many times the possibilities for the subjunctive are multiple, two, three, four reasons. The following sentences are given to show the possibilities. In the mind of the author the sentences have meaning without any further accounting for the subjunctive. The difficulty arises when we desire to account for the use of the subjunctive among the competing possibilities. For some of these examples we were able to state a preference for one possible explanation over another, but for other examples we have left the English renderings intentionally as ambiguous as the Latin relatives. Were we to ask the author to account for the use of the subjunctive we might have been given a clear response, but until we have the opportunity of asking the author someday, it is important for us to distinguish the different possible reasons for the subjunctive.

One final note is due here. In encounter 83 we shall present the tendency of an otherwise indicative verb being attracted into the subjunctive when it is an integral part of a larger statement in indirect discourse or in the subjunctive. For the purpose of a complete review here, we mention this phenomenon in anticipation of its presentation there.

Gaius Iulius Caesar (c. 100–44 BCE) will be our guide in his following sentences. Here Caesar is speaking and reporting the understanding of someone else:

cognoscit ... arcem captam esse excludendi sui causa nuntiosque dimissos ad eos qui se ex fuga in finitimas civitates recepisse dicerentur, ne Antiochiam adirent (Caes. *B. C.* III, 102)

he knows that the citadel was taken for the sake of excluding himself and messengers were sent to those who were being reported as having transferred themselves from flight into the nearby cities, that they not approach Antioch.

The controlling verb is *cognoscit*, "he knows," in T.1i and setting the sentence on Track I. As a verb of M&M, *cognoscit* produces two sentences in indirect discourse. The first subject *arcem* is in the object form and its verb *captam esse* is an infinitive. The second subject *nuntios* is in the object form and its verb *dimissos* [*esse*] is an infinitive with "esse" implied. Both of these infinitives describe antecedent action, equivalent to T.4bi, and so the sentence shifts from Track I to Track II. This latter sentence in indirect discourse comprises a relative sentence consisting of *qui* followed by the verb *dicerentur* in T.2s.

One serious possibility for the use of the subjunctive in the verb *dicerentur* is causal, where *qui* stands for *cum ii*, and the whole statement means "because they were being reported." Some people might prefer to consider this as modal attraction as we shall see in encounter 83. While other possibilities include with some difficulty a result, concessive or characteristic clause; the English rendering in each of these possibilities sounds indicative. The English rendering above is as ambiguous as the Latin by simply rendering *qui* followed by the Latin subjunctive *dicerentur*, as "who" followed by the English indicative "were being reported," which gives no hint to the Latin subjunctive in the original.

By the way, the verb *dicerentur* is a verb of M&M and also gives rise to a sentence in indirect discourse in which *se* is a reflexive pronoun in the object form functioning as the subject of *recepisse*, an infinitive verb describing an antecedent action.

Here is another example in which Julius Caesar recounts the actions and makes a request of Quintilius:

> *Quintilius circumire aciem Curionis atque obsecrare milites coepit ne primam sacramenti quod apud Domitium atque apud se quaestorem dixissent memoriam deponerent, neu contra eos arma ferrent qui eadem essent usi fortuna eademque in obsidione perpessi* (Caes. *B. C.* II, 28)
>
> Quintilius began to surround the battle line of Curio and to beg the soldiers that they not put away the first memory of the oath which they had pronounced in front of Domitius and in front of himself as a quaestor, and that they not bear arms against those who had experienced the same fortune and suffered in the same siege.

The main sentence comprises the subject *Quintilius* and the verb *coepit*, "Quintilius began," in T.4bi establishing the sentence on Track II. The verb *coepit* has two complementary infinitives, *circumire*, "to surround," and *obsecrare*, "to beg," both continuing the sentence on Track II. The intent of Quintilius in begging the soldiers is expressed in two negative purpose clauses. The first negative purpose clause consists of *ne* followed by the verb *deponerent*, "lest they put away," or "that they not put away," in T.2s; it also includes the relative clause consisting of *quod* followed by the verb *dixissent*, "which they had pronounced," in T.4s. One way to account for the use of the subjunctive in *dixissent* is causal, meaning, "because they had pronounced it [in his sight]."

By the way, the reflexive pronoun *se* does not refer directly to the subject of its immediate verb *dixissent*, "they." Rather, it refers to *Quintilius*, the subject of the main verb *coepit* and of the sentence as a whole. The noun *quaestorem* is in the object form because it stands in apposition to *se*, the object of the preposition *apud*, "in front of himself as a quaestor," even though logically it also refers to the subject of the sentence as a whole, again *Quintilius*.

The second negative purpose clause consists of *neu*, an alternative form of *neve*, followed by the verb *ferrent*, "and that they not bear" or "and lest they bear," in T.2s, continuing the sentence on Track II. The sentence continues, *contra eos arma*, "[and that they not bear] arms against those," and next the sentence describes "those [people]" in the relative clause comprising *qui* followed by two verbs, *essent usi*, "who had experienced," and *essent ... perpessi*, "who had suffered." We can account for both of these verbs by a certain well-founded suspicion that they are in the subjunctive as concessive expressions, meaning, "although they had experienced the same fortune and suffered in the same siege" or even as causal "because they had experienced the same fortune and suffered in the same siege." The other possibilities remain both here as with *dixissent* including modal attraction, result or characteristic clauses with the English rendering sounding indicative. We left our English rendering just as ambivalent as its Latin original.

Here is another sentence in which Caesar is reporting his own promises:

> *Caesar ... se frumentum daturum pollicetur. Addit etiam ut, quod quisque eorum in bello amiserit, quae sint penes milites suos eis qui amiserint restituatur* (Caes. *B. C.* I, 87)
>
> Caesar promises he is going to provide grain. He adds also that, that which each one of them had lost in war, which things are under the control of his soldiers, be restored to those who have lost [them].

The main verb *addit*, "He adds," in T.1i sets the sentence on Track I. Caesar's intention expressed in this additional remark is given in a purpose clause consisting of *ut* followed by *restituatur*, "that [it] be restored," in T.1s thus keeping the sentence on Track I. The implied antecedent of the relative *quod*, namely *id quod*, "that which," is the subject of that singular verb *restituatur*, as is also the antecedent of the relative *quae*, namely *ea quae*, "the things which"; Caesar simply gave the singular verb and implied both subjects without adding a connecting word such as "and."

Three relative sentences follow in a row, each with a verb in the subjunctive. The first two, we have said, describe the implied subjects of *restituatur*. The first of these is, *quod quisque eorum in bello amiserit*, "that which each one of them had lost in war" where *amiserit* is T.3s describing antecedent action on Track I. We can account for this subjunctive as an expression of cause, where *quod* stands for *cum id*, meaning, "because each one of them had lost [it] in war."

The second relative sentence is, *quae sint penes milites suos*, "the things which are under the control of his soldiers" where *sint* in T.1s describes ongoing action on Track I. The preposition *penes*, "in the power of," "in the possession of," takes the object form as here. This can be taken as a relative clause of characteristic result, where *quae* stands for *talia ut ea*, "such things that they," and the whole clause means, "such things that they are under the control of his soldiers."

Returning to the purpose clause *ut … restituatur*, the complement of the verb is *eis*, "[that it be restored] to those," who are then described by the relative clause *qui amiserint*, "who have lost them" in T.3s describing antecedent action on Track I. The use of the subjunctive here could be concessive where *qui* stands for *cum ii*, and the relative clause means, "although they have lost [them]."

The four subjunctive verbs here present almost a merry-go-round of usages. The only subjunctive here whose use is certainly indisputable is the purpose clause, *ut … restituatur*, which is also the only one that will sound subjunctive in English. Hopefully without forcing the matter excessively, we have suggested that the others could be taken as relative clauses of cause, characteristic result and concession. The various possibilities have to be considered for these, and modal attraction besides. While a translator may choose the most likely from among these options, it is not necessary, and the sentence may be expressed in an English rendering just as ambivalent as its Latin original, as we have done in our rendering above. Look at how demanding Latin is, if all of these linguistic phenomena are found in six or seven Latin words.

One last sentence from the master writer, who is recounting the behavior of a statue of Victory:

> *Item constabat … quo die proelium secundum Caesar fecisset, simulacrum Victoriae quod ante ipsam Minervam collocatum esset et ante ad simulacrum Minervae spectavisset ad valvas se templi limenque convertisse* (Caes. *B. C.* III, 105)
>
> Likewise it was clear that on which day Caesar had made the second battle, the statue of Victory which had been located before Minerva herself and previously had looked toward the statue of Minerva had turned itself to the doors and threshold of the temple.

The main verb *constabat*, "it was clear," in T.2i establishes the sentence on Track II. As a verb of M&M, *constabat* gives rise to a sentence in indirect discourse whose subject is *simulacrum* in the object form and verb *convertisse* an infinitive describing antecedent action, thereby shifting the sentence to Track II.

The arrangement of the statue of Victory in the temple is described by a relative clause comprising *quod* with two verbs, first the passive *collocatum esset*, "which had been located," and second the active *spectavisset*, "had looked," both in T.4s and thus on Track II. We may account for the use here of the two subjunctive verbs as a possible expression of concession where *quod* stands for *cum id*, and the relative clause means, "although it had been located … and previously had looked." However, because these two subjunctive verbs appear inside the larger expression of indirect discourse they could also be in the subjunctive by modal attraction.

Likewise depending on the sentence *simulacrum … convertisse* in indirect discourse, a second relative pronoun gives rise to another relative clause, namely *quo die*, "on which day," or more fully "on the day on which," followed by *fecisset*, "[on which day Caesar] had made" in T.4s and thus on Track II. In this case it seems most likely that *fecisset* would otherwise be an indicative verb such as *fecerat* in T.5i, but it is in the subjunctive by modal attraction as part of the larger sentence in indirect discourse, as we shall see in encounter 83.

Every time the reader approaches a relative clause with its verb in the subjunctive, these possibilities can be a helpful guide to discerning the subtleties of difference in meaning even if sometimes several competing reasons for the use of the subjunctive overlap. Sometimes the reason for the subjunctive is not all that subtle, but is demanded by the story itself, even though it remains hidden in the relative clause.

ENCOUNTER 10 (80)

GERUNDIVUM QUIBUSDAM CUM VERBIS CURANDI, TRADENDI, SUSCIPIENDI

the gerundive with certain verbs
of taking care, handing over, undertaking

Introduction

As a parallel to our discussion of the gerundive, we can point out a frequent and cherished expression of the Romans.

The gerundive with certain verbs

This expression begins with one of several groups of verbs, especially, *curare*, "to take care"; *tradere*, "to hand over"; *suscipere*, "to undertake"; and *concedere*, "to grant"; others can be found in Gildersleeve and Lodge nº 430, note 1. When each of these verbs is followed by an object in the gerundive, the meaning of this construction as a whole is given for each of these verbs as follows:

curare	+	the object in the gerundive = *to take care* (of) doing something
tradere	+	the object in the gerundive = `*to hand over* doing something
suscipere	+	the object in the gerundive = *to undertake* doing something
concedere	+	the object in the gerundive = *to grant* something for doing.

Examples are:

Viam curaverunt sternendam
They took care (of) paving the road

Liberos magistro tradidit instruendos
He handed over instructing the children to the teacher
He handed over the children to the teacher for instructing

Suscepit Redemptor homines servandos
The Redeemer undertook saving people

Dedit munera largienda
She gave gifts for distributing.

This construction is very common with the verb *curare*, for example:

Curavistis pecunias solvendas
You all had the money paid.

The famous example is often abbreviated on monuments as MFC, an abbreviation of *monumentum faciendum curavit*, meaning:

> ... he took care (of) building the monument.

Another example is:

> *Tradidit pueros mihi educandos*
> He entrusted to me educating the children
> He gave his children over to me for educating.

A final example is:

> *Tonsor adolescentem tondendum suscepit*
> The barber undertook shearing the young man.

The teacher can find many similar examples.

ENCOUNTER 11 (81)

SUPINUM DUPLEX, ETIAM IN ORATIONE OBLIQUA FORMAE PASSIVAE FUTURAE

the double supine, also in indirect discourse of the future passive

Introduction

One last element of the Latin verb, which we have intentionally left to this point, is actually a remnant of a previous verbal noun which is going to sound like a gerund-infinitive and will function as one. Its use is very restricted and very well defined by all the examples we have in Latin literature. It is very popular and useful and can be learned very easily and is easily recognizable.

This verbal noun technically is called the "supine," from the Latin term *supinus, a, um*, "lying on the back," because it rests back or relies on another word in the sentence, as in a supine position. Only two forms of this old verbal noun remain: the object form and the form by-with-from-in.

1. The object form in *-um*

The object form is formed from the fourth part of the verb and ends in the unchangeable ending *–um*, for example:

petitum
visum
exploratum.

This form is used to express purpose in combination with some verb of motion in a phrase such as, "to seek, to come, to go, to see, to explore." Examples include:

Milites salutatum venimus
We have come to greet the soldiers

Filiam Marcello nuptum tradidit
He handed over his daughter to Marcellus to marry.

By the way, deponent verbs also have both supine forms. In this case they are both active in form and meaning, as we have already seen when they are used as contemporaneous participles, futurity participles, gerunds, and gerundives. Here is a nice example from Livy:

infestus aderat, ut non uagos tantum procul a castris lignatum pabulatumque progressos exciperet sed ipsis obequitaret castris
(Liv. XXV, 34)

He was present in a hostile mood in order that he might not only cut off wanderers having gone far from the camps to collect wood and to forage, but that he might ride up to the camps themselves with his horse.

Both supines are from deponent verbs, *lignor*, "to collect wood," and *pabulor*, "to forage" or "to seek for food."

2. The form by-with-from-in ends in *–u*

The form by-with-from-in ending in *–u* is used with only a select number of adjectives to complement the idea as an infinitive. Specific examples are:

Res est iucundissima visu
The thing is very pleasant to see

mirabile dictu
a thing marvelous to say

facile factu
a thing easy to do

facile dictu, difficile factu
something easy to say, hard to do

Difficiles sunt affectus narratu
Sentiments are difficult to explain.

Inasmuch as we have already seen the noun groups, you will see immediately that the two supine forms originally were nouns in *–us, us*, and these are the relics of them. Any observant and thinking student—self-taught or in the classroom—will be able to find a few examples of this supine usage. Cicero's letters in a subsequent volume of this series will confirm all this instruction with the real thing.

3. Use of the supine with the futurity passive infinitive

Our treatment of the infinitives in encounter 72 left one form and usage for this later date. The infinitive of passive futurity provides an interesting opportunity to notice and learn special forms and meanings for the supine. Because for the Romans the Latin language ran out of forms, and they did not know what to do, they logically made up a verbal form that acts as a substitute expression of passive futurity.

This formula combines an infinitive and the supine. From the verb *eo, ire, ivi, itum*, meaning, "to go; move" we get the contemporaneous passive infinitive *iri*, meaning "motion is being made." Because it is a verb of motion *iri* can be complemented by a supine of purpose, such as *cantatum*, meaning "to sing," *motum* "to move," *factum* "to do," *obsonatum* "to buy groceries." This combination is taken as an expression of futurity. Remember, the supines are invariable, unchangeable forms that look like neuter participles, such as *cantatum, motum, directum, auditum*, but in fact are not such things.

The formula is this:

Carmina cantatum iri disces

You will learn that motion is being made to sing the songs
You will learn that the songs are about to be sung
You will learn the songs will be sung.

This example points out one Latin trap that people often fall into if they are not attentive. Here *carmina* is the object of the supine *cantatum*. Because it is not a participle, *cantatum* does not agree with *Carmina*. The form *cantatum* is the supine and thus is invariable. Here is another example with several ways to express it in English:

Negant motum iri autocineta

They deny motion is being made to move the automobile
... that the automobiles are going to be moved
... the automobiles will be moved.

You can see that *motum* does not agree with *autocineta*, because it is not a participle and that *autocineta* is the object of the supine *motum*. As a supine, *motum* is invariable. Take the example:

Statuas intellego translatum iri

I understand that motion is being made to transfer the statues.

Here we see that *statuas* is the object of the supine *translatum*, as in "to transfer the statues." This way of speaking is clumsy and awful, but it is the only way that Latin has to express the passive futurity, because the language was exhausted in forms. In English, we can restate this last example much more simply as:

I think the statues are going to be moved.

Take another couple of examples:

Suspicantur effectum iri miracula
They suspect motion is being made to produce miracles
They suspect miracles will be produced

Amicitias conciliatum iri suspicabamini
You all were suspecting that motion was being made to form friendships
You all were suspecting friendships would be formed.

This last English sentence uses the form "would" to indicate futurity from a point in the past.

4. Two examples

A letter written by Cicero to his secretary Atticus on around 9 February 49 BCE gives us an example of this expression of futurity in indirect discourse:

Pedem in Italia video nullum esse qui non in istius potestate sit. De Pompeio scio nihil, eumque, nisi in navim se contulerit, exceptum

> *iri puto. O celeritatem incredibilem! huius autem nostri—sed non possum sine dolore accusare eum de quo angor et crucior. Tu caedem non sine causa times, non quo minus quidquam Caesari expediat ad diuturnitatem victoriae et dominationis, sed video quorum arbitrio sit acturus. Recte sit; sed censeo cedendum* (Cic. *Att.* VII, 22, 1)
>
> I see there is no foot [twelve inches] in Italy which is not in the control of that guy [Caesar]. I know nothing about Pompeius, and I think that, unless he will have gotten himself onto a ship, he will be cut off. O unbelievable swiftness [of Caesar]! but of this our man [Pompeius]—but I am not able without grief to accuse him [Pompeius] about whom I am worried and tormented. Not without a reason do you fear a slaughter, not because anything is supposedly less advantageous to Caesar for the durability of victory and of domination, but I see by whose judgment he is going to be acting. Let it be all right; but I believe a concession has to be made.

Limiting our attention to the second sentence, here the main verb is the last word, *puto*, "I know," in T.1i. As a verb of M & M, *puto* gives rise to an expression in indirect discourse, whose action is future and passive. This is expressed here in OO where *iri* is the passive infinitive of a verb of motion and means, "motion is being made." Connected with *iri* is the supine of purpose *exceptum*, "to intercept" or "to cut off," which looks like a participle, but as a supine is unchangeable. The object of *exceptum* is *eum*, "him." If you pounce on *eum … exceptum*, and say "him having been cut off" or "that he has been cut off," then you will never be able to account for the passive infinitive *iri*, nor understand the function of the supine with its object. Thus, the phrase *eum exceptum iri* may be understood to say, "[I think] that motion is being made to cut him off." Its plural is *eosque exceptum iri putamus*, "we think they will be intercepted." This construction is used in a letter to Atticus where his thought skips along almost faster than he can write it.

As Cicero continues his same letter to Atticus, we run across a use of the abl. supine:

> *De Oppiis egeo consili. Quod optimum factu videbitur facies. Cum Philotimo loquere, atque adeo Terentiam habebis Idibus. Ego quid agam? qua aut terra aut mari persequar eum qui ubi sit nescio? Etsi terra quidem qui possum? mari quo? Tradam igitur isti me? Fac posse tuto—multi enim hortantur—num etiam honeste? Nullo modo quidem. A te petam consilium, ut soleo? Explicari res non potest. Sed tamen si quid in mentem venit velim scribas et ipse quid sis acturus*
> (Cic. *Att.* VII, 22, 2)
>
> As to the Oppii [people], I need advice. You will do what will appear the best thing to do. You will speak with Philotimus, and so you will have Terentia there on the Ides. What shall I do? by what either land or sea shall I follow him who I do not know where he is? Even if by land, indeed, how can I do it? by sea to what place? Therefore shall I hand

> myself over to that guy? Imagine that I can do this safely—for many are encouraging—you don't mean even honorably? In no way, indeed. Shall I ask advice of you, as I am accustomed? The matter is not able to be resolved. But nevertheless if anything comes to mind, I would like that you write also what you yourself are going to do.

Cicero's expression here, *optimum factu*, "the best thing to do," includes the form *factu*, "to do," a supine in the abl. that is used with a number of adjectives in almost set phrases.

ENCOUNTER 12 (82)

TRADITARUM EXERCITIA RERUM. VERBA INREGULARIA: FERO, EO, VOLO . . .

exercises of matters already taught.
irregular verbs: I carry, I go, I wish . . .

Introduction

Go back to the reading sheets and look around and get examples of all we have done so far to repeat them and to exercise everything that has been learned. This encounter will calmly reinforce what has been shared in the previous encounters and will also present some special verbs and verb forms needing to be seen.

Some of the most common words in every language are the most irregular in their forms and that is also true of Latin. Therefore we want to spend a little time on some very common words that are theoretically irregular in their appearance and marvelous in their usages.

These so-called "irregular verbs" can be presented in a few minutes, and the whole subject can be closed with a few shortcuts and tricks. As in all languages, the most common and ordinary and most used verbs turn out to be the most irregular. For example, we say in English:

I am, you are, she is
I teach, I taught
they catch, they caught
you swim, you swam.

The same is true in natural, human Latin.

1. *eo*

The first word is:

eo, *ire*, *ivi*, *itus*, 4, to go.

It has very, very many compounds, for example:

adeo, *ineo*, *transeo*, *intereo*, *exeo*, *abeo*, *pereo*.

This verb is basically regular, and nothing of course has changed with regard to T.4i, 5i, 6i, and T.2s, 3s, 4s, as is obvious from the principal parts. What should be pointed out especially as irregular is the setup of T.1i, 2i, 3i, and T.1s, and the rest will come very easily.

T.1i is:

ego eo
eunt
imus
itis
it
is.

From these forms you can point out all the derivations like *transit*, *intereunt*, *initis.*

T.3i is:

ibo
ibunt
ibimus
ibis
ibit
ibitis.

T.2i is:

ibam ... and the rest just as you expect.

T.1s is:

eam ... and the rest.

Note: in Plautus you may find things like:

Eas ad eas	May you go to those ladies
Contra eam eam	I may go against her.

2. *fero*

Another verb is:

fero, ferre, tuli, latus, 3, to bear, carry, bring.

The key to understanding the forms of this verb is to see in that second principal part, *ferre*, a contraction for *fer(e)re*, from verb Gp.III where the syllable *–re–* is short, and the pronunciation is quick, and this word is pronounced very often. This contraction helps to explain the other contractions. T.1i is obviously the most irregular:

fero
ferimus
ferunt
fers
fert
fertis.

Once you know the reason for this contraction, the other times of this verb are regular.

T.2i is:

ferebam ... and the rest as you expect.

T.3i is:

feram ... and the rest you know.

T.2s, do not forget, is a contraction of *fer(er)em*:

ferrem ... and the rest.

It bears noting that the verb *transferre* in T.3i is *tránsfĕret* with one *–r–* and the accent on the *tráns–*, whereas in T.2s the form is *transfĕrret* with a double *–rr–* and the accent on that second-to-last syllable, and the infinitive contraction is clearly visible.

3. *Volo, nolo, malo*

In the last set of irregular verbs, are again three cousins:

volo, velle, volui, 3, to wish
nolo, nolle, nolui, 3, not to wish, to refuse
malo, malle, malui, 3, to prefer.

They are verbs of the *–ĕre* verb Gp.III with all the regular things about them, but not foolish or irrational.

T.1i is the most irregular:

volo	*nolo*	*malo*
volumus	*nolumus*	*malumus*
vis	*non vis*	*mavis*
vultis	*non vultis*	*mavultis*
volunt	*nolunt*	*malunt*
vult	*non vult*	*mavult.*

You can see that:

nolo	is from	*non volo*
malo	is from	*magis volo.*

The comparative adverb *magis* means "to a greater degree." Thus, "to want to a greater degree" is "to prefer": *malo.*

The use of T.1s should be noted because it is very similar to other forms. T.1s is:

velim ... *nolim* ... *malim* ... and the rest as you expect.

But T.3i is:

volam ... *nolam* ... *malam* ...

You already know the special continuation of the vowel:

volemus ... *nolemus* ... *malemus* ....

T.2s, taken from the infinitive, looks much the same:

vellem ... *nollem* ... *mallem* ... and the rest.

That is the end forever of the irregular verbs. From the principal parts and obviously your training, you can form the rest successfully and happily.

ENCOUNTER 13 (83)

MODI CONIUNCTIVI ATTRACTIO: NORMAE ET EXEMPLA IN PAGINIS

attraction of the subjunctive: principles and examples on the reading pages

Introduction

Among the frequent and mysterious uses of the Latin subjunctive, one occurs that is more frequent than most people think and adds to the mountain of meanings and applications of the subjunctive. This is a phenomenon especially in the historians. It is not a law but a certain choice or preference of Latin authors, so it can be applied or not applied freely as the author wants to express his or her ideas.

The idea of attraction means that a verb normally and naturally in the indicative is attracted or "magnetically pulled" or "swallowed" into the subjunctive when the subordinate verb is part of an integral clause that is itself part of a bigger passage either in indirect discourse or in the subjunctive. This is sometimes called "modal attraction" because the otherwise indicative mode of speaking by attraction is expressed in the subjunctive mode.

The indirect discourse will be in the accusative or nominative with the infinitive. In such discourse there is a tendency to put subordinated clauses into the subjunctive according to the sequence of tenses, if the subordinate clause forms an integral or substantial part of the whole thought. Gildersleeve and Lodge nº 662 calls this "INVOLVED ORATIO OBLIQUA. ATTRACTION OF MODE." Parenthetical remarks or geographical, historical indications that do not really affect the story are left in the indicative.

This usage pertains to standard or classical Latinity. It is used many times even by Cicero, Caesar, and Sallustius; and other authors do or do not apply this phenomenon for their own reasons. Later authors, such as the scholastic authors, will avoid it completely, because it is not conducive to clear teaching and just confuses matters. The Renaissance authors will bring it back because it is characteristic of standard classical Latin. Papal documents of our present age will use this or not according to the tastes and judgment of the papal Latinist at the time!

The subjunctive here will sound indicative in English and remains one of the weakest subjunctive uses in Latin. We would say that the verb is subjunctive "just for kicks" or by attraction, because of the indirect speech, or even because of the presence of another subjunctive.

Some people see this use everywhere, even in cases where another motivation for the subjunctive is much stronger. So attraction is only one popular and common use of the subjunctive, but not the only one and not the most important one. The attraction is very weak and is not the most cogent or common reason for the subjunctive in Latin.

Examples

An example of this construction is:

> *Ciceronem narrant opus philosophicum de officiis filio proprio dedicavisse qui studiis eo tempore in grecia vacaret.*

The main verb here, *narrant*, establishes the indirect discourse, *Ciceronem ... dedicavisse.* Within this indirect discourse and integral to the whole thought is the subordinated clause *qui ... vacaret.* Here the verb *vacaret* would normally and naturally be in the indicative, but is pulled into the subjunctive in Latin. It will sound indicative in English, however:

> They say that Cicero dedicated his philosophical work on moral duties to his son, who was studying in Greece at that time.

Examples are found in the works of any author who writes at greater length, such as in Cicero's orations or philosophical writings, Caesar's commentaries, the monograms of Sallustius; of course, Livius is full of this use. Gildersleeve and Lodge n° 661 has examples of entire narrations which are first given in direct discourse. Then each narration is recast in indirect discourse. In this process the independent verbs are recast in indirect discourse with the accusative and the infinitive, and the subordinates become subjunctive by attraction.

Let us begin with one that we shall see later when we discuss another use of the abl.; for now we shall put it into indirect discourse:

> *Quo sublimior es, eo gravius cadis*
>
> The higher you are, the harder you fall.

> *Vetus adagium adseverat quo sublimior sis, eo te gravius cadere*
>
> An old adage asserts that the higher you stand the harder you fall.

Because of *adserverat* the main clause *eo gravius cadis* goes into ACI and *cadis* becomes *te cadere*; the dependent clause *Quo sublimior es* goes into the subjunctive and the verb *es* becomes *sis* on Track I. If we put the expression in a past time, it turns out to be:

> *Vetus adagium adseverabat quo sublimior esses, eo te gravius cadere*
>
> An old adage was asserting that the higher you were, the harder you were falling.

In the future we have:

> *Vetus adagium adseverat quo sublimior sis futurus, eo te gravius esse casurum*
>
> An old adage asserts that the higher you are going to be, the heavier you are going to be falling.

In this one-line example in the *Institutio oratoria*, Marcus Fabius Quintilianus (c. 35–c. 95 CE) speaks about the teacher. Quintilian says:

> *succedere se in eorum locum, a quibus sibi liberi tradantur, existimet*
> (Quint. *Inst.* II, 2, 4)
>
> He [the teacher] should think that he is following into the place of those people by whom children are entrusted to him.

The only plausible reason for Quintilian's use of the T.1s *tradantur* is because it is within the whole indirect statement *succedere se*, depending on the M & M verb *existimet*. Many other authors would simply write *traduntur* because the attraction into the subjunctive does not add meaning, except that it is a part of this bigger complex sentence. Today it would just generate confusion, because people do not realize the purpose of that subjunctive there just for kicks.

Depending on the Latin author, this phenomenon is found in every age of Latin literature; many times it is a matter of "feeling" or judgment whether to use this construction or not. Today, for example in Vatican documents, we will avoid modal attraction because it does not mean anything to most people and just causes confusion by adding yet another mysterious subjunctive, but here we will list a few more rather clear examples of this phenomenon.

The comedy writer Terentius in his play *Andria* says of himself, the poet:

> *id sibi negoti credidit solum dari,*
> *populo ut placerent quas fecisset fabulas* (Ter. *And.* 2–3)
>
> he believed that only this kind of business was being given to him, that stories, which he should have made, might be pleasing to the people.

Note that these two lines contain the matter of many of our previous encounters. The M & M verb is *credidit*, which produces the indirect statement *id dari*; the gen. of part is [*id*] *negotii*; the indirect reflexive is *sibi*, referring not to the subject of its own sentence, *id dari*, but to the subject of *credidit*, namely the poet; a purpose-final clause is *ut placerent*. The subject of *placerent* is a hidden *fabulae*, which turns up as *fabulas*, the object of *fecisset*, namely that those "stories, which stories he should have made, might be pleasing to the people." The attraction is *fecisset* in T.4s, which expresses completed futurity, because he has not yet done it. The verb depends on the idea of *dari ut placerent* and is expressed in the subjunctive because of the involved *oratio obliqua*, according to our definition. It may be a consolation to see how much Latin is contained in two lines in a play from the second century BCE We have to know everything before we know anything!

An author from just about our present day, Achille Ambrogio Damiano Ratti, who became the Pontiff Pius XI (1922–1939), gives us this example from an encyclical letter of 31 December 1929:

> *Ex his sequitur educationem non eodem modo ad societatem civilem, quo ad Ecclesiam familiamve, pertinere, sed alio plane, qui scilicet fini eius proprio respondeat* (Pius XI, *Divini illius magistri*, 62)

> From these things it follows that education belongs not in the same way to civil society, in which it belongs to the church or the family, but totally in another way, which namely corresponds to its special objective.

The M & M word is *sequitur*, "it follows [mentally,]" producing *educationem* as the subject of *pertinere*, "education belongs." One of the simplest reasons for that T.1s verb *respondeat* would be because of the whole involved sentence in the indirect statement *educationem pertinere.*

In between Terentius and Pius XI we might find Angelus Politianus (1454–1494), a Renaissance Italian poet and scholar. In one of Angelo's letters, he writes:

> *Caeterum nunc demum intellego quantum iacturae fecerim, quod te prius haud cognoverim, cum tanta mihi te cognito voluptas arriserit*
>
> (Polit. *Ep.* III, 11, 3)
>
> For the rest, now finally I understand how much of a loss I suffered, that I had absolutely not come to know you previously, because so much pleasure has smiled on me, once you had been known.

Depending on *intellego*, we see the indirect statement *quod cognoverim*, which is a characteristic substitution in later Latin for the more classical *me cognovisse.* You can see the Italian emerging even in this super Latin sentence. Dependent on the indirect statement is the indirect question *quantum fecerim.* We see [*quantum*] *iacturae*, again a gen. of part. Then we have *quod cognoverim*, which simply means, "the fact that I did not know you," or "because I did not know you"; no other reason exists for this subjunctive except for the fact that it is sandwiched between two other subjunctives *fecerim* and *arriserit*, and is part of the involved indirect speech. We also see that *cum arriserit* expresses the cause.

A teacher in this Fourth Experience could also point out that there are three subjunctives in this sentence, and not one of them will sound subjunctive in English because of the nature of the clauses in which they lie. There is a definite reason for the subjunctive in *fecerim* and *arriserit*; the former is an indirect question and the latter a causal clause. The *quod cognoverim* in-between could just as easily be expressed in the indicative, as *cognovi* or *cognoveram*, meaning "I did not get . . ." or "I had not gotten to know you."

And just for kicks, another letter of the same Angelo has:

> *Vulgare est ut qui serius paulo ad amicorum litteras respondeant nimias suas occupationes excusent* (Polit. *Ep.* IV, 2, 1)
>
> It is a common phenomenon that those who reply a little later to the letters of friends excuse their excessive occupations.

We have seen before that *Vulgare est ut excusent* is an example of a result clause. The *qui* refers to the subject of *excusent* which is an understood *ii* or *ei*, "they," and what follows is a simple example of attraction because it is part of this involved result clause. There is no other reason for that subjunctive, and he could have written *respondent* with no hesitation.

An incredible example from Iulius Caesar in his treatise on the civil war will help us understand this and much, much more:

> *haec erat summa: Caesar in Galliam reverteretur, Arimino excederet, exercitus dimitteret; quae si fecisset, Pompeium in Hispanias iturum. Interea, quoad fides esset data Caesarem facturum quae polliceretur, non intermissuros consules Pompeiumque dilectus* (Caes. *B. C.* I, 10)
>
> This was the sum substance, [they agreed that] Caesar should return to Gaul, should retreat from Rimini, should dismiss the armies; which if he would have done, Pompey would go into Spain. In the meanwhile, until a word of honor would have been given that Caesar would be doing the things he was promising, the consuls and Pompeius would not suspend the military conscriptions.

Here Caesar presumes a meeting between the parties of the civil war. The sentence describes "the sum substance" of the result of the meeting. The governing verb is *erat*, "it was," T.2i establishing the sentence on Track II. That colon was placed there by a later editor to indicate that an implied *ut* goes with the three subjunctives *reverteretur, excederet, dimitteret*, expressing the intention, decision, plan, resolution coming out of their meeting. The force of these three resolutions is felt rather strongly, as commands, a decisive plan of action. When such commands are expressed in indirect discourse, as here describing the resolution of the meeting, they are expressed in the subjunctive usually without the *ut*, something which is confirmed in Gildersleeve and Lodge nº 652.

The sentence continues to list the decisions reached at the meeting, giving them in indirect speech, rather than as command forms as the three above. A fourth resolution of their summit was that Pompey would go into Spain. This is expressed in indirect speech with the futurity formula *Pompeium iturum* (*esse*). His going into Spain, however, was conditioned on the three previous actions that in the interim Caesar would have accomplished. Because this condition depends on the indirect speech *Pompeium iturum*, it is expressed in the subjunctive, *quae si fecisset*, which is T.4s expressing a future completed action. In this case the action is future because it follows the meeting and completed because it is the condition for Pompey's going into Spain.

It was decided that the consuls and Pompey would not suspend the military conscriptions, expressed with the futurity formula *intermissuros* (*esse*) *consules Pompeiumque*. Again this future action is preceded in this case by an intermediate action that is also expressed in the subjunctive, *quoad fides esset data*, "until a word of honor would have been given," again T.4s describing an action future in regard to the meeting and completed in regard to suspending the military subscriptions. The content of the promise given, moreover, concerns what Caesar is going to do, which is itself a future action expressed in indirect speech *Caesarem facturum* (*esse*), describing an action subsequent to the promise.

The disaster here for many people is that *fecisset* and *esset data* are not so-called "pluperfect" subjunctives, but in fact are future completed subjunctives, which must be expressed in this way because Latin has no other forms.

A calendar reconstruction of our explanation would give us this view of his statement:

Calendarium:

May	June	August	September	October	November
erat		*reverteretur*			
		excederet			
		dimitteret			
			fecisset	*iturum*	
			data esset	*facturum*	
polliceretur					
					intermissuros

This example by Nepos comes from his account of the life of Eumenes:

> *Eumenes intellegebat, si copiae suae cognossent, adversus quos ducerentur, non modo non ituras, sed simul cum nuntio dilapsuras* (Nep. *Vitae*, XVIII, 3)
>
> Eumenes was realizing that, if his troops should have found out against whom they were being led, not only would they not be about to go, but that they would disperse together with the messenger.

The main verb here is T.2i *intellegebat*, establishing Track II and producing the indirect statement [*copias*] *non ituras* [*esse*] … *dilapsuras* [*esse*] expressing futurity: "the troops would not be about to go … would disperse." Those future actions were conditioned on a previous action that on is expressed in the subjunctive by attraction, *si copiae cognossent*, in T.4s, meaning, "if (in the meanwhile) the troops should have found out," which is a future completed action with regard to Eumenes realizing and completed in regard to their decision not to go but to disperse. Finally, *adversus quos ducerentur* is an indirect question that expresses incomplete action on Track II and so is in T.2s.

Calendarium:

May	June	August	September	October	November
intellegebat		*cognossent*			
		ducerentur		*non ituras*	
				dilapsuras	

Another example comes from the account of the life of Agesilaus by Nepos:

> *vidit, si, quo esset iter facturus, palam pronuntiasset, hostis non credituros aliasque regiones praesidiis occupaturos*
>
> (Nep. *Vitae*, XVII, 3)

He saw that if he should have announced openly, to what place he was about to lead the march, the enemies would not believe it and would occupy other regions with their garrisons.

You already know that *hostīs* here with a long –*ī*– is the object plural standing in for *hostes*. The M & M verb *vidit*, "he saw," in T.4bi sets the sentence on Track II and produces the indirect statements *hostes credituros* (*esse*) and –*que occupaturos* (*esse*), both expressive of futurity. The condition given for those future actions is *si pronuntiasset*, "if [in the meanwhile] he should have announced openly" in T.4s. This is a future completed action because it occurs in the future, if at all, and only after he will have announced the plan openly will they not believe it. This is why we do not call T.4s the "pluperfect," because it can have future completed meaning, as in this brief example. The clause *quo esset iter facturus* is an indirect question that depends on that future completed time. Because the sentence is on Track II, T.2s is used here with future meaning, which is why we do not call it the imperfect.

Calendarium:

May	June	August	September	October	November
vidit		*pronuntiasset*			
			esset facturus		*non credituros*
					occupaturos

In encounter 79 we gave a summary of eleven ways in which you may possibly understand both *qui, quae, quod* and *quis, quid* when followed by a subjunctive. A number of examples were included there in anticipation of the presentation of modal attraction in this encounter. To complete our presentation, then, we wish to give several examples of relative sentences whose verbs are in the subjunctive by modal attraction. In the following, Caesar is the historian recounting the events of the Gallic War:

equites ... venerunt qui nuntiarent ... omnis navis adflictas atque in litore eiectas esse, quod neque ancorae funesque subsisterent neque nautae gubernatoresque vim tempestatis pati possent

(Caes. *B. G.* V, 10)

Lieutenants came who might announce that all the ships had been smashed and cast off on the shore, because neither were the anchors and ropes holding up nor were the sailors and pilots able to suffer the force of the storm.

The main sentence is *equites venerunt*, "Lieutenants came," in T.4b setting the sentence on Track II. The Lieutenants' intention in coming is given in the relative clause of purpose, *qui nuntiarent*, "who might announce," in T.2s, where *qui* stands for *ut ii*, meaning "[Lieutenants came] in order that they [might announce]." The verb of M&M *nuntiarent* produces a statement in indirect discourse whose subject *omnis navis* is the alternative spelling for the object form *omnes naves*, and whose two infinitive verbs are *adflictas atque eiectas esse*, "that all the ships had been smashed and cast off" describing antecedent and passive action.

The reason given for this shipwreck then follows. Here *quod* means "because," and it is followed by two verbs in T.2s, *subsisterent* and *possent*, continuing Track II. The use of the subjunctive here may be due to modal attraction because the whole causal clause is involved in the indirect discourse. If so, then these two verbs stand for indicative verbs such as, *subsistebant* and *poterant*, and these two verbs describe the historical, engineering fact that the anchors and ropes were inadequate and the fact of human reality that the sailors and pilots were unable to withstand the storm. If this is the case, then the whole clause presents the author's own account of the events and conditions surrounding the shipwreck. Otherwise, the use of the subjunctive here may be due to quoted reason, if Cicero is quoting the ambassadors who themselves recounted these events concerning the anchors and ropes, sailors and pilots. The difference between these two possible explanations for the use of the subjunctive here has the consequence of shifting the story from Cicero's own account to his quoting the account of the ambassadors, and you really do not know which of these two possibilities was intended.

Another example comes from the account by Sallustius of the war with Jugurtha:

> *res ... Marium ... contra Metellum vehementer accenderat. Ita cupidine atque ira, pessumis consultoribus, grassari neque facto ullo neque dicto abstinere, quod modo ambitiosum foret* (Sall. *Iug*. LXIV)
>
> the matter had inflamed Marius against Metellus vehemently. Thus with ambition and anger—the counsellors being the worst—he was devastating far and wide nor abstaining from any deed or expression which was in keeping with [his] ambition.

The first of two sentences has as its main verb *accenderat*, "the matter had inflamed," in T.5i. The second sentence has no finite verb, but perhaps the two infinitives *grassari* and *abstinere* are historical infinitives standing for T.2i, *grassabatur* and *abstinebat*, where their subject is *Marius*, but they are written as infinitives so that the sentence skips along quickly and lightly, as indicated in Gildersleeve and Lodge nº 647.

The clause *quod modo ambitiosum foret* is not an example of *quod* followed by the subjunctive expressing quoted reason. Rather, *quod* functions as a relative pronoun here whose antecedent is *facto ullo ... dicto*, "from any deed or expression." The verb *foret* is an alternative form of *esset*, in T.2s. It easily could have been written in the indicative as *erat*, in T.2i, but perhaps, because the clause is integrally involved in the infinitive complex, this verb is written in the subjunctive by modal attraction. Here *modo* means "only." Here *ambitiosum* is an adjective meaning directly "ambitious like"; it is a neuter agreeing with *quod* and its antecedent is *facto ullo ... dicto*. The difficulty lies in translating *ambitiosum* into good English, which we have rendered as "in keeping with his ambition."

Another example is from Titus Livius:

Hernici nuntiant Volscos et Aequos, etsi abscisae res sint, reficere exercitus (Liv. III, 10)

The Hernici announce that the Volsci and the Aequi are restoring the armies even though things had been cut to pieces.

The main sentence is *Hernici nuntiant*, "The Hernici announce," in T.1i establishing the sentence on Track I. As a verb of M & M, *nuntiant* produces a sentence of indirect discourse in which *Volscos* and *Aequos* are in the object form functioning as subjects of the infinitive *reficere*. Depending on the statement in indirect discourse is the concessive condition, *etsi abscisae res sint*, "even though things had been cut to pieces," where the verb *abscisae sint* is T.3s on Track I describing antecedent action. As a concrete condition, there is no reason for the use of the subjunctive here other than possibly by modal attraction because this clause is so closely involved in the indirect discourse.

For one final example we turn once again to the account by Sallustius of the war with Jugurtha who is giving a speech:

senatus a praefecto urbis Q. Fabio vocatur ... illi non licere, si quid consules superbe in aliquem ciuium aut crudeliter fecerint, diem dicere, accusare iis ipsis iudicibus quorum in aliquem saeuitum sit? (Sall. *Iug.* XXV)

the senate is called together by Quintus Fabius, the prefect of the city ... Is it not permitted to him, if the consuls have done something proudly and cruelly against someone of the citizens, to call to court, to accuse—those very people being judges—against someone of whom savagery was committed?

The sentence narrates the content of a speech given in the senate by Iugurtha, and so this part is given in indirect discourse, where the subject of the infinitive *licere* is both accusative gerunds *diem dicere* and *accusare*, as in, "is calling to court, accusing, not permitted to him?" The expression *diem dicere* is a legal idiom meaning "to lay an accusation against" or "to impeach." Depending on this statement in indirect discourse is a factual condition *si quid consules ... fecerint*, "if the consuls have done something," in T.3s. As a factual condition one would expect the verb in T.4a, *fecerunt*, but it is in the subjunctive by modal attraction because this condition is an integral part of the indirect discourse on which it depends. The accusation is described as being made against one of the judges in the relative, *quorum in aliquem saeuitum sit*, "against someone of whom savagery was committed," in T.3s. Likewise the factual situation suggests the use of the indicative *saevitum est*, but because the relative sentence is closely involved in the indirect discourse, it is in the subjunctive by modal attraction. You may also note the ablative absolute, *iis ipsis iudicibus*, "those very people being the judges," whose verb is felt but not given. The antecedent of *quorum*, is *iis ipsis*,"those very people [being judges]," but the relative *quorum* depends on *accusare ... in aliquem*, "to accuse against someone of whom." The idea is that someone of the victims is among the judges.

ENCOUNTER 14 (84)

FINALES QUATTUORDECIM RATIONES

fourteen ways to express purpose

Fourteen ways to express purpose

The fourteen ways to express purpose in Latin are demonstrated using two basic sentences:

a. deponent: using the deponent verb: *venor, venari, venatus sum,* 1 to say "they called, invited us to hunt boars."
b. active: using the active verb: *comedo comedere, comedi, comesum,* 3 to say "they invited us to eat boars."

The main sentence is:

Nos revocaverunt . . . (T.4b)
They called us back . . .

1. *ut* + subjunctive (encounter 58):

a. dep.: *Nos revocaverunt ut venaremur apros.*
They called us back so that we might hunt boars.
b. act.: *Nos revocaverunt ut comederemus apros.*
They called us back so that we might eat boars.

2. *qui, quae, quod* + subjunctive = *ut is, ea, id* + subjunctive (a relative sentence of purpose: encounter 58):

a. dep.: *Nos revocaverunt qui apros venaremur.* (*qui = ut nos*)
They called us back who might hunt boars.
They called us back so that we might hunt boars.
b. act.: *Nos revocaverunt qui comederemus apros.* (*qui = ut nos*)
They called us back who might eat boars.
They called us back so that we might eat boars.

3. *ut* + passive subjunctive (encounter 58):

a. dep.: ——
b. pass.: *Nos revocaverunt ut a nobis comederentur apri.*
They called us back so that boars might be eaten by us.

4. *qui, quae, quod* + passive subjunctive = *ut is, ea, id* + subjunctive (a relative sentence of purpose: encounters 58, 79):

a. dep.: ——
b. pass.: *Nos revocaverunt a quibus apri comederentur.*
(*a quibus* = *ut a nobis*)
They called us back by whom boars might be eaten.
They called us back so that boars might be eaten by us.

5. Futurity active participle (as done by Livius especially: encounters 51, 52):

a. dep.: *Nos revocaverunt venaturas apros.*
They called us back women on the point of hunting boars.
b. act.: *Nos revocaverunt comesuras apros.*
They called us back women on the point of eating boars
They called us back women fixing to eat boars.

6. Supine (accusative: encounter 81):

a. dep.: *Nos revocaverunt apros venatum.*
They called us back to hunt boars.
b. act.: *Nos revocaverunt comesum apros.*
They called us back to eat boars.

7. *Ad* + gerund (encounter 77):

a. dep.: *Nos revocaverunt ad venandum apros.*
They called us back for hunting boars.
b. act.: *Nos revocaverunt ad comedendum apros.*
They called us back for eating boars.

8. *Ad* + gerundive (encounter 77):

a. dep.: *Nos revocaverunt ad apros venandos.*
They called us back for hunting boars.
b. act.: *Nos revocaverunt apros ad comedendos.*
They called us back for eating boars

9. Genitive gerund + *gratia, causa, ergo* (see dictionary):

a. dep.: *Nos revocaverunt venandi apros gratia, causa, ergo.*
They called us back for the sake of hunting boars.
b. act.: *Nos revocaverunt comedendi apros gratia, causa, ergo.*
They called us back for the sake of eating boars.

10. Genitive gerundive + *gratia, causa, ergo* (see dictionary):

a. dep.: *Nos revocaverunt venandorum gratia-causa-ergo aprorum.*
They called us back for the sake of hunting boars.
b. act.: *Nos revocaverunt aprorum comedendorum gratia-causa-ergo.*
They called us back for the sake of eating boars.

11. Dative function of the gerund (encounter 77):

(Note: Because a verb of motion as a general rule in Latin is not attached to the dat. function, we will add *idoneas*, "suitable ones, women," to the sentence in order to accommodate a dat.):

a. dep.: *Nos revocaverunt idoneas apros venando.*
They called back us women suitable ones for hunting boars.

b. act.: *Nos revocaverunt comedendo apros idoneas.*
They called back us women suitable for eating boars.

12. Dative function of the gerundive (encounter 77):

(because of the verb of motion, *idoneos*, "suitable ones," is added):

a. dep.: *Nos revocaverunt venandis apris idoneos.*

They called back us suitable ones for hunting boars.

a. act.: *Nos idoneos revocaverunt comedendis apris.*

They called back us suitable ones for eating boars.

13. *quo* + comparative + subjunctive = *ut eo* + comparative + subjunctive (a relative sentence of purpose: see dictionary):

a. dep.: *Nos revocaverunt quo apros facilius venaremur.* (*quo facilius* = *ut eo facilius*)

Literal rendering: They called us back so that by that much more easily we might hunt boars.

Smoother rendering: called us back so that all the more easily we might hunt boars.

b. act.: *Nos revocaverunt quo promptius comederemus apros.* (*quo promptius* = *ut eo promptius*)

Literal rendering: They called us back so that by that much more enthusiastically we might eat boars.

Smoother rendering: They called us back so that all the more enthusiastically we might eat boars.

14. *quo* + comparative + passive subjunctive = *ut eo* + comparative + passive subjunctive (a relative sentence of purpose: see dictionary):

a. dep.: ——

b. pass.: *Nos revocaverunt quo promptius comederentur apri a nobis.*

(*quo promptius* = *ut eo promptius* = "*so that* wild boars *by that much more enthusiastically* might be eaten . . . ,"

which is rendered "*so that* wild boars *all the more* enthusiastically might be eaten . . .")

Literal rendering: They called us back so that wild boars might be eaten by us by that much more enthusiastically.

Smoother rendering: They called us back so that wild boars might be eaten by us all the more enthusiastically.

The above fourteen constructions all express purpose. There is one final construction, which we do not use because it is poor Latin prose. Virgil and the poets use this for the conveniences and necessities of Latin poetry meter. This construction is used from the Augustan period and following. Modern languages use this construction as well. This is a final infinitive.

15. (The infinitive. In our personal Latin creations we do not do this!)

a. (dep.: *Nos revocaverunt venari apros.*
They called us back to hunt boars.)

b. (act.: *Nos revocaverunt comedere apros.*
They called us back to eat boars.)

This is the whole Latin language in its *OSSA*. It is consoling to teach it all, to learn it all, to master it all. This is almost the end of Latin phenomena, if we see them all together. Every Latin author in any library will confirm all these usages in every other sentence. Some other summaries will be given in the following to terminate our Experiences.

ENCOUNTER 15 (85)

FORMULAE IMPERATIVI UNIVERSAE: AFFIRMANTIS ET NEGANTIS

the general formulae of the command expression: affirming and negating

Introduction

As we approach the end of our Latin encounters, here we offer a useful and brief summary of the whole command or imperative system, with every possibility in the language. The command form is based on the Greek pattern. This command form can appear in the so-called imperative "mode" or in the subjunctive or in certain paraphrases. Note that there is no command form in Latin for the first person, "we" or "I," although the subjunctive may be used in a certain substitute role of exhortation.

1. Affirming expression

The entire command mode of speaking is simpler than in Greek and is articulated in two usages. One as a source of immediate, on-the-spot command, generally called by grammarians the present imperative, and another one in laws, decrees, and very colloquial, living conversation, generally called the future imperative. For example, for the verb *audio, audire, audivi, auditum*, 4, "to hear," we have the following.

1.1 *First or present imperative mode*

audi	Hear you!
audite	Hear you all!

The passive or deponent is much more challenging, because of its similarities to other functions:

audire	Be heard!
audimini	Be you all heard!

1.2 *Second or future imperative mode*

audito	You shall-must hear!
	he, she, it shall-must hear!

The plural is:

auditote	You all shall-must hear!
audiunto	They shall-must hear!

The passive or deponent forms are respectively:

auditor	You shall-must be heard! He, she, it shall-must be heard!
audiuntor	They shall-must be heard!
——	(*vos:* "you-all" form does not exist, as far as we know from literature)

1.3 *Time 1 subjunctive*

The following three subjunctive forms are sometimes called iussive, from *iussum*, meaning "command." These three subjunctives are used instead of the imperative form. In T.1s the forms are:

audias	May you hear! You should hear!
audiat	May he hear! She should hear!

The plurals of course you already know.

1.4 *Time 2 subjunctive*

A real command given on the spot, when reported in the past, as Cicero and other historians do, has to be in T.2s. It is really not a command, but the report of a command given:

Respondit desisterent scuta fabricari
He answered that they should cease making shields.

You already know the other forms.

1.5 *Time 3 subjunctive*

The use of T.3s is very rare in the affirmative expression, but it does exist with a certain frequency in every kind of classical and ecclesiastical literature such as Plautus and the *Vulgata Biblia*, and it turns out to be:

audiveris	May you hear! You should hear!
audiverit	May he hear! She should hear!

The plurals are normal.

This is very frequently rendered as "May you hear!" as above, or also as "You should hear!"

1.6 *Time 3 indicative*

A light command which is extremely common in Latin literature and not recognized by many will be given in T.3i with its corresponding classical English version:

cantabis	You shall sing!
scribes	You shall write!

This is super-correct English, where "You will sing, write" is the simple future. Consequently, "I shall; we shall; you will; you all will; they will; he, she, it will" all express a future action, whereas "I will; we will; you shall; you all shall; they shall; he, she, it shall" all express a light command. We find a contemporary example of this usage in the matter of appointing judges to the U.S. Supreme Court, where the Constitution says that the president "shall appoint . . . Judges of the Supreme Court" (Article II, section 2), where "shall appoint" has the feeling of a command expressing the intention of the document, rather than being a mere description of a future action. But what authority can say whether this is still valid today?

1.7 *Other expressions*

A number of more lengthy paraphrases in themselves have the same practical force as a command form, and they are found everywhere in the literature. They are constructed in this way:

facere, curare, videre + (*ut*) subjunctive

for example:

Fac, Cura, Vide ut quam primum revertaris
make sure, take care, see to it that you return as soon as possible.

Another expression:

Velim quam primum remigres
I would like that you return as soon as possible

Rescribas his litteris cito velim
I would like that you quickly write back to these letters

Velim tandem intelligas
I would like that you finally understand.

These expressions are very favored ones of Cicero, as will be seen through his letters in the *Carnes* book already in preparation. The *ut* is often omitted in strong, lively commands, something mentioned in all manuals like Gildersleeve and Lodge nº 546, remark 2.

2. Negating expression

Now that you have the forms up above, you just need the list of forms.

2.1 *First or present imperative mode*

ne audi	Do not listen!
ne audite	Do not you all listen!

Examples for a passive and a deponent are:

ne audire	Do not be heard!
ne audimini	Do not be heard, you people!
ne hortare	Do not exhort!
ne hortamini	You people, do not exhort!

2.2 *Second or future imperative mode*

ne audito	You shall-must not hear! He, She, It shall-must not hear!

The plural is:

ne auditote	You all shall-must not hear!
ne audiunto	They shall-must not hear!

The passive or deponent forms are respectively:

ne auditor	You shall-must not be heard! He, She, It shall-must not be heard!
ne audiuntor	They shall-must not be heard!
——	(*vos*: you all form does not exist, as far as we know)

2.3 *Time 1 subjunctive*

Ne audias!	May you not hear!
Ne audiat!	May he, she, it not hear!

The plurals of course you already know.

2.4 *Time 2 subjunctive*

The following statement from Livius provides two examples of the use of T.2s to render first a positive and second a negative command in reported speech:

> *... ibi fama est in quiete visum ab eo iuvenem divina specie, qui se ab Iove diceret ducem in Italiam Hannibali missum: proinde sequeretur neque usquam a se deflecteret oculos* (Liv. XXI, 22)
>
> ... the report is that there was seen by him in sleep a young man with divine appearance, who would say that he was sent as a leader by Jupiter into Italy to Hannibal: therefore he should follow and should not ever turn away his eyes from him.

From this indirect discourse, we may reconstruct the direct commands. First the positive command is,

> *sequeretur*
> he should-must follow

which we reconstruct as a direct command given by Jupiter:

> *Tu sequere!*
> You must follow!

Second, the negative command,

> *neque ... a se deflecteret oculos*
> he should-must not turn away his eyes from him

from which we reconstruct the direct command given by Jupiter:

> *Tu ne . . . a me deflectas oculos!*
> You should-must not turn away your eyes from me!

Note that, controlling this sentence, is the idea of M&M expressed in *fama est*, "the report is," in T.1i, setting the sentence on Track I. The content of that report is given in indirect discourse where *visum* [*esse*] is an antecedent infinitive whose subject is the object form *iuvenem*, "that a young man was seen," which sets the rest of the sentence on Track II. The young man was sent so that he might say a message to Hannibal, which is stated in the relative clause of purpose, *qui . . . diceret*, where the qui stands for *ut* is, "that he," as in, "that he would say." The content of the young man's message is given in indirect discourse where *missum* [*esse*] is an antecedent infinitive whose subject is the reflexive pronoun *se*, referring to the young man, who is also described as *ducem*, "as a leader." The commands of Jupiter are finally given to the young man-leader, that he was to go ahead to Hannibal and not turn his eyes away from Jupiter. These commands are given in T.2s, continuing the narration on Track II.

2.5 *Time 3 subjunctive*

Ne auscultaveris!	You, do not listen! (This is extremely common and popular especially in familiar colloquial speech, Plautus, Patronius, Erasmus, and the Latin Vulgate Bible. It is all over the place in the Psalms and other Renaissance authors. We used to say "Ne dixeris!" "Don't mention it!" "Don't even say that!")
Ne auscultaverit!	He, She, It should not listen! (You know the plurals.)

2.6 *Time 3 indicative*

Corresponding to the future indicative is:

> *Non audies radiophonium noctu*
> You shall not listen to the radio at night.

Here we see the only time *non* is used for a command in the language, with a T.3i negative command, as we are reminded here that the negative prohibition in the subjunctive is with *ne*.

2.7 *Circumlocutions*

The first circumlocution is composed of *noli*, the command form of *nolo, nolle, nolui*, and means here "you be unwilling. . .!" or "you refuse to. . .!" This is followed by the infinitive:

noli audire	Be unwilling to listen! Refuse to listen! Don't listen!

and in the plural:

nolíte audire You all, do not listen!

The second circumlocution we have seen before:

fac, cura, vide + *ne* + subjunctive

for example:

Facite, Curate, Videte ne cadatis
Make sure, Take care, See to it that you all do not fall! (Watch your step!)

The third expression is composed of a subjunctive, the potential form of *nolo*, "I do not want," written as T.1s *nolim*, "I would not want" followed by T.1s without *ut*, for example:

Nolim aegrotes scholas ob latinas
I would not want you to be sick because of Latin classes.

3. The irregular verbs

Of the irregular verbs, the one to note is, *fero, ferre, tuli, latus*, 3, "to bear, carry, bring" (see encounter 39).

The first or present imperatives are:

fer	Carry!
ferte	Carry, you all!

The second or future imperatives are:

ferto	You, he, she, it shall-must carry!
ferunto	They shall-must carry!
fertote	You-all shall-must carry!

These apply to the compounds such as *transfer, infer, confer, refer*.

4. Other expressions

There are other expressions available in Latin which are really not imperatives but indicate a certain necessity of action such as:

Debes audire	You ought to listen
Oportet te audire	It is fitting for you to listen
Oportet tu audias	It is necessary that you hear (*ut* is omitted)
Necesse est tibi audire	It is necessary for you to listen
Tibi audiendum est	Hearing must be done by you You must hear.

Again, these are really not imperatives but convey a sort of obligation.

We must read the Latin comedians Plautus, Terentius; the poets Martialis, Horatius; and Latin colloquial speech in every age to see all of this language functioning naturally.

ENCOUNTER 16 (86)

CONDITIONALES LATINAE SENTENTIAE TRIBUS MODIS

Latin conditional sentences in three ways

Introduction

For interested people, the conditionals are much easier in Latin than in Greek. Any author has only three conditional ideas to choose from in the Latin language, as it comes to us from the literature. Each of these is expressed in one of three specific ways according to a definite Latin system that is not dependent on a modern vernacular. No end of confusion is caused when authors begin with an expression in a modern language and render its words directly into Latin, without regard for the Latin system of expressing these three possible ideas. The only way to articulate a conditional correctly and to communicate clearly in Latin is to begin with one of the three conditional ideas in Latin and then express that idea simply and directly.

Conditionals have two parts:

the condition	"if . . ."	called the protasis
the conclusion	"then . . ."	called the apodosis.

The condition or protasis contains the positive word:

si if

or the negative:

nisi unless (where a whole clause or idea is denied)
si non if not (where an individual element is specifically denied).

Accordingly, there are three general ideas which can be expressed in Latin in conditional sentences depending on the view and will of the author.

1. Real or Factual or Logical conditions

Examples of logical or real conditional sentences are simply:

If this is so, then that is so
Unless this will happen, we shall do that
If she has not done this, she is wise.

Here the whole situation is expressed as a simple concrete fact, even though it has the uncertainty of an "if" idea. In Latin this is very easily expressed in any time of the indicative or the imperative and with any combination of any of the indicative times or of the command forms; you can mix them any way you want. The uncertainty of the "if . . . ," which affects all human life, is not the determining factor, for example:

Si recte respondebis, gaudebimus omnes

If you will answer correctly, we shall all be happy

Heri vesperi suam si orationem comparabat, sapienter agebat

If she was preparing her speech yesterday evening, she was acting wisely

Veni nobiscum, si vis

Come with us, if in fact you want

Venito nobiscum, si volueris

You must come with us, if you will have wanted so.

Innumerable other examples are found in Latin literature, as in the reading sheets after each experience.

Many people impressed by modern languages, such as Italian, French, Spanish, are falsely convinced that all conditionals are automatically put in the subjunctive because of their inherent "if . . ." uncertainty. This is false, as statistics show that the majority of conditions in Latin are expressed by the indicative, relying on the author's idea.

2. Foggy future

The second type is often called the ideal or hypothetical conditional, or it is called as in Greek the future less vivid. We call it the "suspended future" conditional or the "foggy future." An author uses this type of conditional to test the concrete facts of the case, but more or less raises it off the ground and suspends it untested and projected into an uncertain future. Many people designate this second type in English with the coordinates:

should . . . would . . .

You can hear how it is foggy or indefinite when you say:

Si non veniat magister, gaudeant discipuli

If perhaps the teacher should not come some day, the students would then be happy.

This example is not relating the definite, concrete facts expressed by the following two statements: "If the teacher does not come, the students will be happy" or "If the teacher will come, the students will be sad." Rather, the above expression leaves the cases untested, suspended, foggy.

This second type of conditional is usually expressed in Latin by T.1s in both parts, that is in both the condition and its consequence. The use of two verbs both in T.1s shows that this is an imagined case and not a concrete affirmation, for example:

Hoc si praeses dicat, operarii laetentur

If perhaps the president should say this, the workers would be very happy.

Some examples do exist of this conditional in T.3s, but they are extremely rare and always have the possibility of being interpreted as T.6i. It is hard to find such pure foggy conditionals in Latin literature. They are confined especially in philosophical writings to theoretical, philosophical cases such as, "If some intoxicated person should ask you for a gun, you probably would not hand one over."

3. Contrary-to-fact conditionals

The third type is also clear and definite, but of a negative nature, namely describing a situation that is impossible, unchangeable now, or had been impossible in the past. This is called an unreal or impossible or contrary-to-fact conditional. It is contrary to fact, because implied or hidden in the conditional itself is the fact that it is not true.

The conditional is expressed in T.2s if the unreality is now, or in T.4s if the impossibility was in the past. So you have the example:

> *Si pecuniam petivissent, libenter eis concessissem*
>
> If they had asked for the money, I would have given it to them willingly.

You can test whether the above conditional is a real fact or not by stating its contrary:

> If they had asked for the money, but they did not, I would have given it to them willingly, but I did not.

If the sentence passes this test, it means that it does not correspond to reality and is unreal, and thus is a contrary-to-fact conditional.

In these two examples above, the formula, "If they had asked," is the proper English expression for the contrary-to-fact condition, which some students may confuse with T.5i. To avoid this confusion, it might be permissible to say once or twice in class, "If they would have," so that this improper use might help the students distinguish the two time frames. Take another example:

> *Si plueret, flores crescerent*
>
> If it were raining, the flowers would be growing.
>
> The test is: it is not raining, and the flowers are not growing.

We can mix the two times of the contrary-to-fact conditional, but it is all extremely regular, for example:

> *Si Cicero non habuisset praeclaras orationes, hodie ut orator non coleretur*
>
> If Cicero had not given famous orations, today he would not be honored as a great orator.
>
> The test is to say: Cicero did indeed have famous orations, and he is currently honored as a great orator.

4. Historical variations

Those are the essential three types of conditionals. To be honest, it must be said that very soon in the development of literature people started mixing the first and the second type in the sense that they considered the "if" condition as uncertain, but the conclusion as certain. This mixture has produced examples in scholastic philosophy, patristic literature, historical writings, medieval documents, and even Renaissance and modern literature. Authors of these periods instinctively put the condition, the "if" part, for example, in T.1s and the conclusion in the indicative. This is clearly a sign of later Latin usage, which we will try to avoid, although the pressure to mix these types is great, because many people think that every conditional is uncertain and therefore in the subjunctive, which is not the case.

The inferior Latin in the Roman Catholic *Code of Canon Law*, the *Codex iuris canonici* of 1983, valid for the western church, has every single present conditional sentence expressed in the subjunctive, which is total madness. The better Latin of the eastern Code of 1990 has them all in the indicative. It is rather interesting to study certain canons that appear in both codes with the indicative conditionals expressed in the indicative in one, but in the other in the subjunctive. Scholars can only hope the original Latin text is sound.

ENCOUNTER 17 (87)

IN EXEMPLIS CONDITIONALES

conditionals in examples

The reading sheets will provide examples. They are all over the place in Latin literature and merit attention, analysis, precision, and imitation.

PLURA DE CONDITIONALIBUS: "UTINAM"

more practice with the conditionals: the particle "utinam"

Introduction

The teacher provides yet more examples from Latin literature of the conditionals, and time is provided so that the students may discern patiently and according to the gradual thought process of the human mind these thought patterns.

The particle utinam

The particle *utinam*, meaning "if only," "would that," really follows the same rules as the foggy future and the contrary-to-fact conditionals, but is not used with the first type of real conditional. If the case is possible, then *utinam* is followed by T.1s, for example:

> *Utinam aliquando intelligas*
>
> Would that you may some day understand
> I hope that you may some day understand.

The idea expressed in this example is still possible, and I still hope that it may happen. When *utinam* is followed by T.2s, then the case is impossible, irreversible, unreal in the present, as in:

> *Utinam pecunias haberemus*
>
> Would that we had monies now
> I wish that we had monies now.
> This is tested by stating the fact: "But we don't have monies now."

Likewise T.4s is used to indicate an unreal case in the past, as in:

> *Utinam Romam nobiscum venisses*
>
> Would that you had come with us to Rome
> I wish that you had come with us to Rome.
> This is tested by stating the fact: "... but you did not come to Rome with us."

ENCOUNTER 19 (89)

PASSIVA FORMULA OBLIQUIS CUM VERBIS

the passive expression of verbs with genitive, dative, ablative

Introduction

At its own time our encounter 33 presented us with an extensive treatment of forms and usages of the function to-for-from in Latin. Prudence and pedagogy suggested making a certain ending to the discussion at that time, although we were quite conscious of the fact that other important teachings and details had to be further developed with regard to that same and other similar usages of the Latin language, considering their frequency and complex nature. Therefore, this encounter in the Fourth Experience has been reserved for the continuing discussion of the function to-for-from, and to be more precise at the outset, we want to talk about the passive application of especially the 65 famous verbs and the compound verbs connected with the Latin form to-for-from. Likewise we shall also consider the passive forms of verbs complemented by the form by-with-from-in or the form of-possession. To be very honest, this requires a lot of structural or philological experience, for which we shall not turn to any sort of a grammar book. Rather the language, we insist, is presented in dictionary entries and examples, which is going to take up our time and energies right now.

1. Transitive and Intransitive verbs

It would be desirable that students of Latin have a background in human languages and the structure of the English language. To begin by giving a limited background here, we distinguish two different usages in English. We can say, "I destroy the building," or we can say "I fall onto the ice." In the first example, the verb "to destroy" is completed or complemented by an object, "[I destroy] the building." The verb "to destroy" is considered a transitive verb because its action crosses over to its object. In the second example, the verb "to fall" does not take an object because its action does not cross over to an object, but rather its action stays with its own subject and so is considered an intransitive verb.

Technically speaking, in Latin only verbs with an accusative object, that is a *direct* object, in the object form, are by definition "transitive verbs"—from the Latin *transire*, "to cross over"—whose action "goes over" into an object, expressed in the object form. Transitive verbs, whether deponent or not, are indicated in the dictionary as, "v. a." where "v." means the entry is a "verb" and "a." means the verb is "active," which is to say, "transitive." The word "active" is used in this way in the dictionary to refer not to the opposite of passive, rather this is an accepted designation for a "transitive" verb.

2. Intransitive with oblique complements

In encounter 78 we saw the verbs whose complement is in the form by-with-from-in. We explained that these verbs are the closest to the Greek middle-voice where an action is happening for the good of the subject by means of an instrument given in the form by-with-from-in. Now we can say that these verbs, whose action refers back to their subject, are intransitive. They do not take an accusative object, that is, a *direct* object, in the object form. Rather they are completed or complemented by words expressing instrumentality in the form by-with-from-in, which form is called by the technical term an "oblique case," because this form is not the direct or accusative object.

In encounter 33 we saw the 65 verbs whose complement is in the form to-for-from. We also saw a group of verbs which are compounded by adding a preposition to the verb as a prefix and the original object of that preposition becomes the complement of the verb in the form to-for-from. Now we can say that both the 65 verbs and the compound verbs are intransitive verbs; that is, their action does not cross over to an accusative object, but stays with its subject. In this case, these verbs are complemented by a word in the form to-for-from, a second oblique case.

In encounter 74 we saw verbs of remembering and forgetting whose complement is in the form of-possession. Likewise we can now say these are intransitive verbs whose complement is in the form of-possession, a third oblique case.

Intransitive verbs, both normal and deponent, are indicated in the dictionary as, "v. n.," where "v." means the entry is a verb and "n." means the verb is "neuter," which is to say, "intransitive." Here we are concerned with the intransitive verbs, which are completed or modified or complemented by words in one of the oblique forms, namely to-for-from or by-with-from-in or of-possession. Their English renderings may sound as a direct object, leading to endless confusion until the nature of the Latin language is understood.

This distinction is fine yet clearly seen between the English verbs "to exalt" and "to exult," based on their Latin sources. From the Latin *exaltare*, "to raise something up," the English verb "to exalt" is transitive, as in "to exalt virtue" or "to exalt a courageous person." From the Latin *exsultare*, "to jump up," the English verb "to exult" is intransitive, as in "to rejoice exceedingly" or "to gambol about."

Some verbs can be used in both ways as in the sentence, "leave your keys and leave," where the first use of "leave" has an object "[leave] your keys" and so is transitive, whereas the second use of "leave" means "get out of here" and cannot take an object. Another example is the sentence "you move over there, and I'll move the box," where the action of the first use of "move" stays with the subject and does not have an object and so is intransitive, whereas the second use of "move" has an object, "[I'll move] the box," and so is transitive.

Returning to our original two English sentences, we wish to present here and in this encounter their passive forms and their difficulties. We have already learned how to make the sentence "I destroy the building," passive by saying "the building was destroyed by me." We did this by taking the verb's object, "the building," and making it the subject of the passive verb "was destroyed." Next we took the original subject, "I," and made it the agent, "by me." There is nothing new here.

What is new here in our presentation of the Latin language is how to make intransitive verbs passive. Returning to our sentence, "I fell on the ice," English does not produce a clear and full passive equivalent of this expression with its intransitive verb, but Latin allows us to do so as we shall see now.

3. The passive form of verbs with the genitive, dative, ablative

Because intransitive verbs do not take an accusative object, their passive will be formed differently than for transitive verbs.

3.1 *Review: forming the passive of transitive verbs*

According to our system, we change transitive verbs from the active to the passive by changing the object of the active verb to the subject of the passive verb and by expressing the subject of the active as the agent of the passive verb, as in this example:

Fabulas meas numquam perleges
You will never read through my stories

Fabulae meae a te numquam perlegentur
My stories will never be read through by you.

3.2 *Forming the passive of intransitive verbs*

We can express our previous example, "I fell on the ice," in Latin: *Occidi in glaciem*. To construct the passive in Latin the verb must become impersonal, *occassum est*. Next, the subject of *occidi* is *ego*, which is expressed as an agent of the passive verb, *a me*, as in *occassum a me est*. The prepositional phrase *in glaciem* must remain as it is, producing: *Occasum a me in glaciem est*. We can force a direct rendering into English and say, "It was fallen by me onto the ice," which is bad English but good Latin. Or we might wish to draw a subject out of that impersonal verb and say in English, "A fall was made by me onto the ice." Still you can see that "onto the ice" remains, the subject becomes the agent "by me" and the verb becomes both impersonal and passive.

By such a transformation intransitive verbs with the oblique cases in Latin are expressed in the passive. If the active form of a normal or deponent verb takes its complement in the abl., gen., or dat., these complements must remain in the abl., gen., or dat. also with the passive form of the verb. The subject of the active verb becomes the agent of the verb's passive form. Because the active form has no direct object to become the subject of the passive form, its new subject has to be "it," neuter and impersonal, and the passive verb also has to become impersonal. This takes a bit of mental gymnastics, but it is workable and especially must be recognized in literature.

3.3 *The passive of intransitive verbs with the dative*

The use of the dat. with intransitive verbs is much more common because there are more of them, the 65 and the compound verbs. We use for example the verb *adsisto*, which takes the dat. to mean, "I stand by or near someone or something; I assist someone or something." In the active I can say:

> *Ego adsistam discipulis*
> I shall be near the students
> I shall assist the students.

To form the passive, the verb becomes impersonal, the subject becomes an agent, and the dat. remains:

> *Adsistetur discipulis a me.*

This impersonal verb can not really be expressed directly in English, as if to say:

> It will be assisted to the students by me.

But we can render this in acceptable English by drawing a subject out of the verb itself, as in:

> Assistance will be given to the students by me.

English allows the possibility of expressing the passive form with this transitive verb:

> The students will be assisted by me.

Even if we can say this in English, in the Latin we cannot say, *adsistentur discipuli a me* because *discipulis* was not the direct object of the active verb and therefore cannot become the subject of the passive verb.

We can do the same with one of the 65 verbs, if we take *parco, parcere, peperci, parsum*, 3, v. n. and *a.*, which means that this verb is typically used as an intransitive verb with a dat. complement. We say:

> *Parcet magister benevolus discipulis ipsis*
> The benevolent teacher will spare the students themselves.

The temptation is to flip the active verb into the passive and make *discipulis ipsis* the subject of the passive verb in an attempt to say, *parcentur a benevelo magistro discipuli ipsi*, as if it meant, "the students themselves will be spared by the teacher," which is impossible, because *discipulis ipsis* was not the direct object and therefore cannot become the new subject. Rather, the Romans made the verb impersonal, as in *parcetur*, literally, "it will be spared," and they left untouched *discipulis ipsis* as a complement in the form to-for-from. They also made the subject of the active verb, *magister benevolus* into the agent of the passive verb, *a benevolo magistro*. This produces the impersonal expression in the passive:

> *Parcetur a magistro benevolo discipulis ipsis.*

This cannot be expressed in the same way in English without either teasing a subject out of the impersonal verb, if possible, or using the passive form of a transitive verb, as in:

> Forbearance will have to be made to the students themselves by a benevolent teacher
>
> The students will be spared by a benevolent teacher.

Again we come back to the broken record: I must know my vocabulary, because otherwise I shall make horrific mistakes. I have to know which verbs are among the 65, which are compound, in fact the whole dictionary—well, yes.

Other examples are given first in the active and then in the passive:

> *Filiis suis periclitantibus consulebant diligenter parentes*
>
> The parents were diligently looking out for their children being in danger
>
> *Filiis eorum periclitantibus consulebatur diligenter a parentibus*
>
> Provision was being made diligently by the parents for their children being in danger
>
> *Peregrinis interdixerunt ne in urbem ingrederentur*
>
> They prohibited the foreigners that they not come into the city
>
> *Peregrinis interdictum est ab eis ne in urbem ingrederentur*
>
> Prohibition was made by them to the foreigners that the foreigners not come into the city
>
> *Subveniebamus naufragis*
>
> We were helping the shipwrecked people
> We gave assistance to the shipwrecked people
>
> *Subveniebatur a nobis naufragis*
>
> Assistance was being made by us for the shipwrecked people
> The shipwrecked people were being helped by us.

3.4 *The passive of intransitive verbs with the ablative*

The famous five verbs with abl. complements given in encounter 78 are all deponent, so they are made passive in the following way. We begin with the active idea:

> *Utimur quotidie cultris et furcis*
> Daily we use knives and forks.

Likewise, the verb is made impersonal and passive, but for a deponent verb the only form with passive meaning is the passive necessity formula, which in this case is used impersonally: *utendum est*. The subject of *utimur* is the implied pronoun *nos*, which is put in the dat. of agent *nobis*, following the

90% pattern for the passive necessity formula emphasized above. Both *cultris* and *furcis* must remain in the abl. The passive sentence is:

> *Cultris et furcis utendum est nobis*
>
> Use must be made by us of knives and forks
> Knives and forks must be used by us.

Another example begins in the active:

> *Dum vivimus fruimur vita*
> While we live, we enjoy life.

Similarly, forming the passive of this verb requires the impersonal necessity formula; the subject becomes a dat. of agent; and *vita* remains in the abl. as in:

> *Fruendum est nobis vita dum vivimus*
>
> Enjoyment of life must be made by us while we live
> Life must be enjoyed by us while we live.

In this case, *vita* cannot become the subject of the passive sentence because it never was the direct object; it must remain in the abl. with this verb. These examples may suffice here, as the teacher finds others.

3.4 *The passive of deponent intransitive verbs with the dative*

Now that we have seen how the famous five deponent verbs with an abl. complement are expressed in the passive, we can return to the intransitive verbs with the dat. and produce the passive form of deponent verbs with dat. complements in this same way. The dictionary says that the verb *medeor, mederi*, "to cure," is used with the dat., which we call one of the 65 verbs whose complement is in the form to-for-from. We begin with the active statement:

> *Medici infirmis medebimur*
> We doctors shall cure the sick.

The intransitive verb *medebimur*, "we shall cure," does not have a direct object to refashion into the subject of the passive form. Rather, *infirmis* is an oblique object which must remain in the form to-for-from when the verb is made passive. The only passive form of the deponent verb *medebimur* is the passive necessity formula, *medendum est*, which is both neuter and impersonal. The subject of *medebimur* is both an implied *nos*, "we," and the expressed *medici*, "physicians," which is made the agent of the passive verb *nobis medicis*, "by us physicians" in the form to-for-from following the 90% pattern with the passive necessity formula. So, in the passive we can say:

> *Erit infirmis medendum nobis medicis.*

We might render this literally into barely recognizable English, as:

> It will have to be cured for the infirm by us physicians.

We can refashion this into recognizable English by drawing a subject out of that impersonal verb and saying:

Cure for the infirm will have to be made by us physicians.

But, because the English verb "to cure" is transitive, we can express its passive form in the usual way, much to the benefit of the reader:

The infirm will have to be cured by us physicians.

This same Latin sentence, however, is ambiguous and only the ongoing story will tell the reader whether it tragically means rather:

The infirm will have to cure us physicians.

This ambiguity will be more common for the passive expression of deponent verbs whose complement is in the form to-for-from, because the agent is also in the form to-for-from with the passive necessity formula, following the 90% pattern.

By the way, the Latin verb *sano, sanavi, sanatum*, 1, v. a. "to cure" is transitive, and so we can produce with ease the following sentences:

active: *sanabant medici infirmos*
physicians were curing the infirm

passive: *sanabantur infirmi a medicis*
the sick were being cured by physicians

passive necessity: *sanandi erant infirmi medicis*
the sick were needing to be cured by physicians.

3.5 *The passive of intransitive verbs with the genitive*

The same rules for normal and deponent forms also apply here. When forming the passive of these verbs, the active verb becomes impersonal in the passive, the subject becomes an agent and the gen. remains. Examples are:

Recordabantur rex et regina nostri nostrorumque amicorum
The king and the queen were mindful of us and of our friends

Regi ac reginae recordandum erat nostri nostrorumque amicorum
Memory had to be made by the king and queen of us and of our friends

Numquam obliviscar beneficiorum tuorum
I will never forget your kindnesses

Mihi numquam erit obliviscendum beneficiorum tuorum
Forgetfulness will never have to be made by me of your kindnesses.

Note the dative of agent with necessity in the forms *Regi* and *reginae* and *mihi*. These examples may suffice here, as the teacher finds other examples in reading sheets or Latin literature.

In Gildersleeve and Lodge n° 346, before the presentation of the 65 there is a minute Remark 1, which almost in jest has the following ten words: "Of course, the passive of these verbs is used impersonally." This understatement of the season is a little bomb that covers much of the language. We can take consolation from the following words and then put this understatement into practice with a few words of our own:

Iam his non nobis amplius nocebitur verbis

We shall not be hurt any more by these verbs

Nobis, quibus moniti eius semper est reminiscendum, numquam amplius his sexaginta quinque verbis nocebitur

We shall no longer be hurt by these 65 verbs, who must remember his advice.

3.6. *Creating gerunds with verbs with oblique complements*

As a little side note, as a response to certain grammarians wishing to fill out an almost fictitious schema, we have simply to review what you already know regarding gerunds and gerundives. Now you know that the dat., abl., gen. complement of intransitive verbs must remain in these oblique forms. This is true even when the verb is expressed as a gerund. As a result, the complement of these intransitive gerunds must remain in the dat., abl., gen. form, which practically prohibits the production of gerundives with these intransitive verbs and their oblique complements.

If we want to say, for example, "By forgetting injuries we shall create peace," using the deponent verb *obliviscor* whose complement is in the form of-possession, you can use the gerund *obliviscendo*, "by forgetting" with its complement *iniuriarum*, "injuries" in the form of-possession, as in:

Iniuriarum obliviscendo pacem faciemus
By forgetting injuries we shall create peace.

Practically speaking, you may not find in the literature a gerundive such as *obliviscendis iniuriis*. We can do the same with verbs among the 65:

Maximam est gloriam imperator noster assecutus victis parcendo hostibus
Our general attained the greatest glory by sparing conquered enemies.

We can do the same with the famous five verbs whose complement is in the abl.:

Plures conciliabimus amicitias utendo patientia
We shall win over many friends by using patience.

There is a fine note in Gildersleeve and Lodge nº 427, note 5, indicating that in Latin literature there are a few examples of these famous five verbs used as gerundives; whether good or poor Latin, literature remains our guide. Thus, we hesitate to make absolute pronouncements, because we are dealing with human language, so on the basis of a couple of disputable examples, we hesitate to say:

Plures conciliabimus amicas patientia utenda
We shall win over many friends by using patience.

ENCOUNTER 20 (90)

COMPARATIONIS ABLATIVUS ET MENSURAE. ALIAE COMPARATIONES CORRELATIVAE. USUS CORRELATIVI ORATIONE IN OBLIQUA

the ablative of comparison and of measure.
other correlative comparisons.
correlative uses in indirect discourse

Introduction

Previously in our review of the seven noun and adjective functions in the Latin language, the fourth one on our list was that of the basic function of separation, which we call the function by-with-from-in, also known as the ablative, abbreviated abl. At that time it was also hinted that as its name suggests this function by-with-from-in serves as a whole dragnet of concepts and ideas under that general four-fold heading. Our considerations of these are spread over different encounters of our several Latin Experiences. This function surprisingly does not exist in Greek or many other languages, but in Latin it is over-used with perhaps as many as fifteen distinct applications of the form by-with-from-in including very different but somewhat related ones. Now on our journey seems the best time to talk about one of the fifteen, the technical function of the ablative of comparison, which we first define and see in various ways, and then almost by necessity we see how this use of the comparison and measure literally explodes into a mass of Latin language applications and subtleties and demanding usages. Exactly as happened with the function to-for-from, the natural meaning of the abl. corresponds to the idea of separation and is rendered by the English prepositions by-with-from-in. But, besides that natural force of the abl., we shall indicate two very common and beloved uses of it employed by the Romans in their language and literature, that of comparison and measure or degree, which introduce us to a whole world of language niceties in Latin.

1. Comparison with *quam*

In encounter 43.2 we saw *quam* meaning "than" and used as an element of comparison. For the sake of completeness we give a few more examples here that prepare us to develop this presentation further. We begin with the English sentences:

They run *faster than* a pony
She is *smaller than* her sister
They cultivate potatoes *more than* strawberries
He is *bigger than* I.

There are two components that make this comparison. First, all of these sentences have a comparative degree such as "faster," "smaller," "more," "bigger." Second, in these sentences the word "than" can be expressed in two ways in Latin. One is by the word *quam*, with the same function before as after, whether noun or pronoun. The above examples may be expressed in this way:

> *Celerius currunt quam hinnulus (equuleus)*
> *Ipsa minor est quam soror*
> *Solana amplius colunt quam fraga*
> *Maior est quam ego.*

In the first sentence you see that *hinnulus* or *equuleus*, "a pony," has the same form as the subject *ei*, "they," contained in that verb *currunt*, "they run." In the second sentence *ipsa* and *soror* share the same subject function. In the third sentence *solana* and *fraga* are both objects. In the fourth sentence, both *maior* and *ego* are subjects. Regarding this last example, in the commonly spoken English of our day, people say, "He is bigger than me." The problem with this expression in English becomes clear if you supply the missing verb, because no one says "He is bigger than me [am]," rather, people say in correct English "He is bigger than I am." The Latin here, *maior est quam ego*, clearly indicates that the English should also be, "He is bigger than I."

2. Ablative of comparison

The other way the comparison "than" is expressed in Latin is with the abl. of comparison, still combined with the comparative degree in the sentence. To form it, the object of the word *quam* is placed in the abl. and *quam* is omitted, as in:

> *Celerius currunt hinnulo (equuleo)*
> *Ipsa minor est sua sorore*
> *Solana amplius colunt fragis*
> *Maior est me.*

Take a more complex example:

> *Haec musica est et numquam excelsiorem audivi quam eam*
> This is music and I have never heard a more sublime piece than it.

This other way of expressing "than" also appears as a relative pronoun, which does not allow the *quam*. The previous example can be expressed with the relative pronoun *qua* in the abl. meaning, "than which":

> *Haec musica est qua numquam excelsiorem audivi*
> This is music than which I have never heard a more sublime piece.

It cannot be stressed enough how common this function appears. Among all the ablatives in a sentence, this one is going to appear alone, but there will always be a comparative expression or idea nearby.

3. Ablative of measure

Another usage of the abl., similar although distinct, gives the degree of difference, of distance or of comparison between things. When I say:

> The dog is three years older than the cat

the Romans are going to understand:

> The dog is older by three years than the cat.

This sentence ends up with the possibility of two abl. forms in a row, as in:

> *Canis vetustior tribus annis est fele.*

In this case *tribus annis* is an abl. of degree meaning, "by three years," and *fele* is an abl. of comparison meaning, "than the cat."

In another example, instead of saying:

> This is much better beer

the Romans will say:

> *Haec cervisia multo melior est*
> This is much better beer.

In the above example, *multo* is an abl. of measure meaning "by much."

Cicero on one occasion well before the time of Galileo says:

> *Quid potest sole maius, quem mathematici amplius duodeviginti partibus confirmant maiorem esse quam terram: quantulus nobis videtur; mihi quidem quasi pedalis; Epicurus autem posse putat etiam minorem esse eum quam videatur, sed non multo* (*Cic. Ac.* II, 26, 82)
>
> What can be bigger than the sun, which the mathematicians assert to be larger than the earth by eighteen times more: how small does it look to us; to me indeed it looks one foot long; but Epicurus thinks that it could be smaller than it appears, but not by much.

In the above citation, the noun *sole* is an ablative of comparison accompanied by the comparative *maius*, "bigger than the sun." Also, *duodeviginti partibus* is an ablative of measure or degree accompanied by the comparative *amplius*, "by eighteen times more." The comparative *maiorem* goes with *quam terram*, "larger than the earth." The final word, *multo*, is an ablative of measure or degree, "by much." Here we have three abl. uses in Latin, but students should be warned that in the vernacular translation into current English you often cannot hear "by" in any of the three, unless they are clearly expressed as above.

4. Coordinating comparatives

The function of this abl. is especially elegant and characteristic of Latin literature, but causes problems where you have coordinating comparatives. This is seen in English by the conjunction "the . . . , the . . . ," each with a comparative degree. We have already seen this above in the sentence:

The higher you are, *the* harder you fall.

In this example, the two instances of the word "the" will be expressed in Latin in this way:

> By what degree you are higher, by that degree you do fall more heavily
> *Quo sublimior es, eo gravius cadis.*

The hinges that unite the two parts of this sentence are the *quo* ... , *eo* .... They function as corresponding relatives, also called correlatives. These coordinating comparatives *quo* ... , *eo* ... , mean exactly, "by what degree ... , by that degree ... ," but are more easily rendered into English as, "the more ... , the more ... " again each with a comparative degree. This doctrine is illustrated not in the grammar books, but in the examples from literature given in Lewis and Short under the entry for *eo* on page 649 column B under the sub-heading "C. of measure or degree," where it is balanced by *quo*.

Another example involves the coordinating comparatives *quanto* ... , *tanto* ... , meaning "by how great a degree ... , by so great a degree ..." Each is followed by the comparative degree, as here:

> *Quanto plus clamaveris, tanto minus auscultaberis*
>
> By how much more you will have screeched, by so much less will you be heard.

This may also be expressed more simply in English using the coordinating comparatives "the ... , the ... ," as in:

> The more you will have screeched, the less you will be heard.

Here are several examples from literature. The first turns on the hinges, *quo pluris ... eo maiore* ..., where *pluris* is a genitive of indefinite price or value:

> *Sed mihi contra ea videtur. Nam quo pluris est univorsa res publica quam consulatus aut praetura, eo maiore cura illam administrari quam haec peti debere* (Sall. *Iug.* LXXXV)
>
> But to me the opposite seems good. For the more valuable the entire common good is than the consulship or the praetorship, the former ought to be administered by all the greater care than these latter things ought to be sought.

The next one turns on *Quanto* ..., *tanto* ... , which is synonymous with *quo* ..., *eo* ....

> *Quanto erat in dies gravior atque asperior oppugnatio ... tanto crebriores litterae nuntiique ad Caesarem mittebantur*
> (Caes. *B. G.* V, 45)
>
> The heavier and rougher the siege was from day to day ... the more frequent letters and messages were being sent to Caesar.

The last one turns on the hinges *eo gravior* ..., *quo* ... *maior:*

Quarum rerum eo gravior est dolor quo culpa maior (Cic. *Att.* XI, 11, 2)
The grief about which things is all the greater, the greater the guilt.

As a footnote aside, the teacher could make up a silly sentence for the students that indicates all of the different functions of the Latin word *eo*, such as:

Eo eo eo eo eo celerius
I go to that place with that intention with that vehicle all the faster.

For each instance of *eo* you have to look up a different word in the dictionary! Know your vocabulary.

5. Correlatives

The very mention of the correlatives or corresponding relatives, if you wish, in Latin suggests a more thorough discussion of this phenomenon, which is essentially bound up with the native music of the Latin language. The Romans preferred sentences that sounded good, or you could say that had a musical like rhythm to them. One way of attaining this linguistic effect was precisely the use of the correlatives, where you would have in a sense a singsong give and take between two parts of a sentence.

It will undoubtedly profit our Latin learning and appreciation of the music of a Latin sentence if we consider visually corresponding lists of correlative elements in Latin. To simplify matters we shall recognize due honor to Gildersleeve and Lodge and their visual presentation, and we shall obtain profit for ourselves if we present once their almost definitive list of correlatives. After that we shall discuss how these correlatives work in subordinate sentences and indirect discourse. We offer here their beautiful presentation from n° 642 without the long or short vowel marks and with the full forms of *toties* and *quoties:*

1. Adjective correlatives:

tot, totidem	*quot,*	(so)	as many	
tantus	*quantus,*	(so)	as great	as.
talis	*qualis,*		such as.	
idem	*qui,*		the same	

2. Adverbial correlatives:

tam	*quam,*	(so)	as much	
tantopere	*quantopere,*	(so)	as much	as.
totiens (toties)	*quotiens (quoties),*		as often	
tamdiu	*quamdiu,*		as long	
ita, sic				
	ut, uti, sicut, tamquam		(rare),	
	quasi (rare),			so (as.)
item, itidem	*quemadmodum,*			= as.
	quomodo,			

As we look at these two vertical lists of adjective and adverbial correlatives, our problems will be solved in writing and understanding Latin, if we take the left hand column which starts up on the top with *tot, totidem* ... and continues with *tam, tantopere* ... and ends with *item, itidem* as indicating the main principle expression or clause or verb in the entire sentence. At the same time we shall never be misled if we take the list on the right hand side, namely *quot* ... *quam* ... *quomodo* as indicating the dependent or subordinate or second level expression, or the measure of comparison. It is easy to note that many of the words in the left column begin with the letter "*t*," as in *tantus, totiens*, a few begin with the letter "*i*," namely *ita, item, itidem*, and the remaining one is *sic*. Many of the words in the right column begin with the letter "*q*," such as *quantus, quantopere*, two begin with the letter "*u*," namely *ut, uti*, and the corresponding one remaining is *sicut*.

No matter which pair I take, I can make sentences with, for example, *talis* on the left and *qualis* on the right, such as the famous saying in Latin:

> *talis filius qualis pater*
> the son is of such a nature, of what nature is the father

where the *talis* indicates the principal sentence is *talis filius*, and *qualis* indicates the subordinate sentence *qualis pater*, where the verbs are understood.

Take the pair *tamdiu* on the left, which indicates the main verb, and *quamdiu* on the right, which indicates the idea subjected or subordinated to the other, and we can say:

> *Tamdiu ignorantia omnium rerum laborabis, quamdiu linguam latinam litterasque latinas ignorabis*
>
> You will be suffering so long from the ignorance of all things, as long as you will not know the Latin language and Latin letters.

You see right away that the main sentence is "you will be suffering so long ...," and the measure or ruler of comparison is "as long as you will not know the Latin language ...." If we keep the two columns distinct, then whether the sentence is of 10 or 100 words, we shall hear the musical comparison. This balanced rhythm will save our understanding of Latin because sometimes, for example, *tam* ... and *quam* .... are divided by many other words, yet still the sentence will turn on these two hinges where *tam* ... indicates the main hinge and *quam* ... the secondary hinge, even in their reversed order *quamdiu* ..., *tamdiu* .... The learner, however, is warned to keep the principal idea in the right place, which is *tamdiu*, and the subordinate one is *quamdiu*, even if it comes first.

6. Correlatives in indirect discourse or reported speech, and subjunctive clauses

If we put any correlative expression into indirect discourse or reported speech or into one of the subordinate subjunctive clauses, then to understand and create the Latin expression all we have to remember is that the words on the left-hand side indicate the main sentence of the correlative, and the words on the right-hand side indicate the clause subordinated to the other. So, if we put the correlative *quantum* ..., *tantum* ... into indirect discourse and make it depend on a verb of M & M, then *tantum* indicates the main part of the correlative and its sentence is put into the accusative with the infinitive, while the *quantum* indicates the subordinate part of the correlative which is often put into the subjunctive by modal attraction.

A simple example would be:

> How much you study, so much you forget.

The main sentence here is "you forget so much," and the subordinate sentence "how much you study." So we can say:

> *Quantum studes, tantum oblivisceris.*

Both Latin verbs are in the indicative. Note that *tantum* is with the main verb and *quantum* is with the subordinate one, logically.

If I put this sentence into indirect discourse, I could say in a present time frame on Track I:

> *Novimus omnes tantum te oblivisci, quantum studeas*
> We all know that you do forget so much, as much as you are studying.

You can see that the main verb *novimus*, "we know," in T.1i establishes the sentence on Track I. The word from the left column, beginning with the letter "*t*," *tantum*, goes with the main sentence of the correlative and so is given with an accusative subject, *te*, and an infinitive verb, *oblivisci*, and the word from the right column, beginning with the letter "*q*," *quantum*, goes with the subordinate verb that is put into the subjunctive by modal attraction *studeas* in T.1s. We can say this on Track II, in a past time frame:

> *Noveramus omnes tantum te oblivisci, quantum studeres*
>
> We all knew that you were forgetting so much, as much as you were studying.

Immediately here we can interject a similar sentence expressed with the coordinating comparatives "the more ..., the more ...":

> *Plus quo studes, eo oblivisceris plus*
> The more you study, the more you forget.

We can express this in indirect discourse in a similar way first on Track I, then on Track II:

> *Novimus omnes plus quo studeas, eo te oblivisci plus*
> We all know that the more you are studying, the more you forget
>
> *Noveramus omnes plus quo studeres, eo te oblivisci plus*
> We all knew that the more you were studying, the more you were forgetting.

We shall take another sentence a step further:

The faster you will have run, the sooner you will arrive at the end.

The main verb here is "you will arrive at the end sooner," and the measure of comparison is "the faster you will have run." We shall express the comparatives, "faster" and "sooner," in Latin with the ablatives of degree, *quanto* ..., *tanto* ...:

> *Quanto celerius cucurreris, tanto maturius ad metam pervenies*
>
> By how much more quickly you will have run, by that much sooner you will arrive at the end.

Note that both verbs are in the indicative, Specifically the main verb going with *tanto* is *pervenies* is T.3i, and the subordinate verb going with *quanto* is *cucurreris* is T.6i.

If I put that expression into indirect discourse, then the main part, *tanto* ... *pervenies*, is expressed with an accusative subjective *te*, and corresponding to T.6i a futurity infinitive *perventuram esse*, assuming the athlete is a woman. Because the subordinate clause *quanto* ... *cucurreris*, is closely involved with the whole sentence in indirect discourse, it is put into the subjunctive by modal attraction, *quanto* ... *cucurreris*, in T.3s, which is by accident the same form as *cucurreris*, "you will have run," in T.6i. So, we can now say:

> *Bene cognoscis quanto celerius cucurreris, tanto maturius te ad metam perventuram esse*
>
> You know well that the faster you will have run, the sooner you will arrive at the end.

We can play with this sentence a bit further by setting the main verb in the historical past:

> *Tibi plane persuasisti quanto celerius cucurrisses, tanto maturius te ad metam perventuram esse*
>
> You had convinced yourself that the faster you would have run, the sooner you would arrive at the end.

The main verb here, *persuasisti*, "you had convinced," in T.4bi sets the sentence on Track II. The main part of the comparison remains the same, *tanto* ... *perventuram esse*, presuming a woman athlete. The subordinate part of the comparison, however, *cucurrisses*, "you will have run," is in T.4s to express completed action in the future. This will not surprise you, if you remember our original thumbnail presentation of the sequence of tenses when we said that T.4s is used to express completed futurity on Track II, just as T.3s is used to express completed futurity on Track I, whose example we saw just above, *quanto* ... *cucurreris*.

To play just a bit more, we can refashion the sentence as an expression of purpose:

Iam quinque annos exerceris ut quanto celerius cucurreris, tanto maturius ad metam pervenias

You already are being trained for 5 years so that the faster you will have run, the sooner you may arrive at the end.

Here, the main verb *exerceris*, "you are being trained," in T.1i sets the sentence on Track I. The main comparative sentence is expressed in the subjunctive *tanto ... pervenias*, in T.1s, and once again its subordinate clause, *quanto ... cucurreris*, in T.3s is in the subjunctive by attraction because it is closely part of the whole involved sentence.

One may be curious to see how the three classical authors would have expressed their beautiful correlative sentences presented previously in this encounter in easy and flowing indirect discourse on two different tracks:

Liquet quo pluris sit univorsa res publica quam consulatus aut praetura, eo maiore cura illam administrari quam haec peti debere
Constabat quo pluris esset univorsa res publica quam consulatus aut praetura, eo maiore cura illam administrari quam haec peti debere
(*cf. Sallustius, Iug.* LXXXV)

Liquet quanto fuerit in dies gravior atque asperior oppugnatio ... tanto crebriores litteras nuntiosque ad Caesarem missa esse
Constabat quanto esset in dies gravior atque asperior oppugnatio ... tanto crebriores litteras nuntiosque ad Caesarem mitti
(*cf. Caesar, B.G.* V, 45)

Quarum rerum liquet eo graviorem esse dolorem quo culpa maior [*sit*]
Quarum rerum constabat eo graviorem esse dolorem quo culpa maior [*esset*] (*cf. Cicero, Att.* XI, 11, 2)

The key here is to remember that the main sentences of each correlative, *eo ... administrari* and *tanto crebriores litteras ... missa esse* (*mitti*) and *eo graviorem esse dolorem* are given in the accusative with the infinitive depending on the main verb *liquet*, "it is clear," or *constabat*, "it was a confirmed fact"; and to remember that *quo* and *quanto* and *quo* introduce subordinate subjunctives because of modal attraction. Lest the student be confused *missa esse* is in the neuter plural because *litteras* is feminine and *nuntios* is masculine. This is just about as far as you can go in Latin; there is not much more to do from this perspective on the top of the mountain. Congratulations to all of you who have arrived at this point!

We are mindful that there may be many overlapping reasons for these subjunctive forms. Eventually the subtle refinement of modal attraction was no longer felt and those clauses were put in the indicative by many authors until the Renaissance.

Again, examples from Latin literature provided on our appended reading sheets are to be discovered, noted and shared and varied by the teacher with the learners or by the self-teacher.

Just to vary the matter, we return to the correlatives with a mixed expression:

Quantopere agriculturae disciplinis vacaveris, talis denique agricola institueris

With how much effort you will have kept yourself free for the sciences of agriculture, you will be trained as such a farmer

Persuasum habes quantopere agriculturae disciplinis vacaveris, talem denique te agricolam institutum iri

You are convinced that with how much effort you will have kept yourself free for the sciences of agriculture, you will be trained as such a farmer

Persuasum habebas quantopere agriculturae disciplinis vacavisses, talem denique te agricolam institutum iri

You used to be convinced that with how much effort you would have kept yourself free for the sciences of agriculture, you would be trained as such a farmer.

ENCOUNTER 21 (91)

POSSESSIONIS DATIVUS AC FINALIS

dative of possession and of purpose

Introduction

Continuing with the various functions in Latin, we can next point out two further usages of the function to-for-from that are very easy to understand and close to the natural meaning of that form.

1. Dative of possession

One is where the form to-for-from is used to express possession, as it does in many languages. This occurs especially with the verb *esse*, "to be," and similar verbs such as *videri*, "to appear," and *manere*, *restare*, "to remain." Take the example:

Mihi nulla est pecunia

No money is *for me*
No money exists *for me*
There is no money *for me*.

This sentence may be rendered into English by simply expressing the concept of "possession" contained there, as in:

I have no money.

Other examples are:

Homines quibus sunt libri felices sunt

People to whom there are books are fortunate
People who have books are fortunate

Communitati nostrae plurimi exsistunt honores

To our community there exist many honors
For our community there exist many honors
Our community has many honors.

Between the dat. of possession and the gen. of possession there is a distinction. The gen. of possession points out, if you wish, legal or legitimate possession, whereas the dat. points out an actual physical holding or possession. This distinction can be seen in the following two sentences:

Magistrorum multi libri in bibliotheca invienuntur (Magistrorum: gen. of possession)

Many books are found in the library belonging to teachers

Magistris multi libri apud eos sunt (*Magistris*: dat. of possession)
The teachers have many books at their homes.

In the first example *Magistrorum* is a genitive of possession; in the second *Magistris* is a dative of possession.

2. Dative of purpose

The dat. of purpose or end or effect is a bit clumsy in English, but the concept and idea come across very clearly if I say:

These studies are for a great consolation to me
These studies serve for a great consolation to me.

This English example is expressed in Latin with a double dat.:

Haec studia magno mihi solacio sunt.

In this case, *mihi*, "to me," is natural, as we have already seen, and *solacio*, "for a consolation," is a dat. of purpose, expressing the end or result of an action, which is almost natural to that function. This is a very common use of the dat. function.

The Romans say:

Magno mihi est honori vos salutare
It is for a great honor to me to greet you all.

In this example once again *mihi*, "to me," is natural, and *Magno honori*, "for a great honor," is the end result of the action of meeting someone. The above example means also the following in clear English:

It is a great honor for me to greet you.

The distinction between the above example and the following one is a matter of emphasis:

Magnus mihi honor est

A great honor exists to me
I have the great honor
It is a great honor for me.

This last example has the natural dat. *mihi*, but does not have the dat. of purpose, which would say more about the purpose or end of an action. Other examples of the double dat. include:

vobis dignitati est	it serves as a distinction for you all
ei gaudio est	it serves as a joy to her
eis voluptati est	it serves as or for a pleasure to them.

ENCOUNTER 22 (92)

FORE + UT

substitute for the future infinitive

Introduction

Our acquaintance with the functions and forms of Latin and especially with the phenomenon of indirect discourse (*oratio obliqua*) has introduced us to the futurity infinitive of normal and deponent and passive verbs. A problem arose for the Romans from the fact that some verbs do not have a fourth principal part and consequently cannot construct or allow to be constructed their futurity infinitive, either active or passive. Also, a problem of style was felt by particular authors, who do not willingly tolerate heavy infinitives, difficult-to-manage and at times extremely awkward.

Fore + ut: Substitute for the future infinitive

For both of these above-mentioned problems of form and style, the solution used by the Romans entails a formula that includes a subjunctive verb, which is easier to manage than infinitives, and is always available where there are not verbal forms for the infinitive. The formula requires a main verb of mind and mouth (M & M) which gives rise to the use of indirect discourse. Then, instead of a future infinitive, either the formula *futurum esse*, "to be about to be," or its equivalent with the same meaning, *fore*, is used, followed by *ut* or *ut non* and a subjunctive verb according to the sequence of tenses, depending on the main M & M verb. Thus, instead of this construction:

verb of M & M	+ accusative	+ future infinitive

either of these two equivalent constructions are used:

verb of M & M	+ *futurum esse*	+ *ut* + subjunctive verb (using the subject form)
verb of M & M	+ *fore*	+ *ut* + subjunctive verb (using the subject form).

Consequently, we could say:

Promittunt se lecturos esse haec volumina
They promise they will read these books

but to get around the heavy infinitive *lecturos esse*, "to be about to read," they can also say the following with no difference in meaning, and Caesar loves to do this very often:

Futurum (esse) promittunt ut haec volumina legant
Fore promittunt ut legant haec volumina.

The easier nature of the phrase is evident. In the passive the sentence could be:

Promittunt hos libros lectum iri a se

To avoid this construction, however, we could also say:

Promittunt futurum esse ut haec volumina a se legantur
Fore promittunt ut haec legantur a se volumina

They promise that these books will be read by themselves.

You can see here the future passive infinitive *iri* from the verb of motion *eo, ire*, "to go" and its object, the invariable supine *lectum*, "to read," whose object in turn is *hos libros*, "these books," as we saw in encounter 81.

In the historical times you will see how the sequence of tenses works:

Munera se delaturos esse promiserunt
They promised they would bring in gifts

Promiserunt futurum esse ut munera deferrent
Promiserunt fore ut munera deferrent

They promised it would happen that they would bring in gifts

and in the passive:

Promiserant opes naufragis datum iri

They had promised that resources would be given to the shipwrecked people

Promiserant futurum esse ut opes naufragis darentur
Promiserant fore ut opes naufragis darentur.

The meaning is the same for all three constructions; the desire to avoid heavy, unsightly, or rare infinitives is obvious, and the easier use of the subjunctive is also clear and very popular.

ENCOUNTER 23 (93)

DUBITARE + INFINITIVUM + NUM – QUIN

dubitare + infinitive + num – quin

Introduction

A glance at the dictionary will give you all the various uses of the word *dubito, dubitare, dubitavi, dubitatum*, 1, "to doubt, to hesitate, to be in doubt." Many people are familiar with the use of this verb with the particle *quin*. Before we see that use, we shall first consider three other uses that many people do not know about. They are:

dubitare	+ complementary infinitive
dubitare	+ indirect statement in accusative with the infinitive
positive *dubitare*	+ *num* + subjunctive
negative *dubitare*	+ *quin* + subjunctive

1. *Dubitare* with the infinitive

The first use is with the infinitive alone. Textbooks call the infinitive here a complementary infinitive because it completes the action of the verb. We understand the infinitive here as a gerund in the object function, which has the form of the infinitive as we have seen. For example:

Cur dubitas urinari in piscinam?
Why do you hesitate to dive into the pool?

You can hear the object gerund in English if you say:

Why do you hesitate diving into the pool?

Other examples are:

Non dubitavit alienas silvas incendere
He did not hesitate to put on fire other peoples' forests
He did not hesitate burning other peoples' forests

Quid dubitatis traicere pilam?
Why do you all hesitate to toss the ball over?
Why do you all hesitate tossing the ball over?

2. *Dubitare* with the accusative and infinitive

A second usage is in indirect discourse, called by us *oratio obliqua*, namely with a substantive clause also called a noun clause composed of a subject in the object form and an infinitive verb. It is called a substantive clause because the entire sentence functions as a noun. As such a sentence, the English may be rendered in several ways as we have already seen. Take this example, recalling that the infinitive is often omitted:

> *Dubitabant se tempestive adventuros* (*esse*). (The infinitive is often omitted.)
>
> They were doubting that they would arrive in time
>
> *Libros meos misisse eam per cursum publicum non dubito*
>
> I do not doubt that she has sent my books through the mail.

3. *Dubitare* + *num* + subjunctive

Other uses of *dubito* are a little more complicated but must be remembered and recognized in literature. When the verb *dubito* is used in a positive sentence, not a negative one, it may be followed by an indirect question composed of the adverb *num* with the subjunctive, where in Latin *num* means "whether." The indirect question will be expressed in English as "that, whether" with the indicative, for example:

> *Dubito num opus suum perfecerint* (T.3s)
>
> I doubt that they have done their work
>
> *Dubitavisti num te adiuvarem*
>
> You doubted whether I was helping you.

4. Negative *dubitare* + *quin* + subjunctive

The far more common usage, which everyone in the world is expecting of us and wants you to know and use, begins with a statement of negative doubt followed by a result clause composed of the particle *quin* and the subjunctive. As a result clause, the *quin* will be expressed in English as "that" and the subjunctive will be rendered in the indicative, for example:

> *Non dubitabas quin ventura esset*
>
> You were not doubting that she was going to come
>
> *Numquam dubitabo quin ipse optimus sis omnium*
>
> I shall never doubt that you yourself are the best of all
>
> *Non est dubitandum quin lingua Latina ab omnibus disci funditus possit*
>
> It must not be doubted that Latin can be learned thoroughly by all.

The common use of *dubito* with *quin* does not need to limit your knowledge and use of the first three constructions. A good, complete dictionary gives even more possible uses and examples under *dubito*.

ENCOUNTER 24 (94)

3% IN TEMPORUM CONSECUTIONE: IN CONSECUTIVIS, CONDITIONALIBUS, ET USIBUS ORIGINALIBUS

3% in the sequence of tenses: in result sentences, conditionals, and original subjunctives

Introduction

This is a very delicate matter. You have learned previously the general or universal pattern of the sequence of tenses, with its two Tracks and verb times. Then you were warned that the general pattern does not in fact cover all cases, but only 97%. So there are a few exceptions, the 3% if you will, or special cases of the sequence of tenses that will contradict the pattern you have learned. If the general pattern covers 97% of all occurrences of the sequence of tenses in Latin literature, we shall now see the remaining 3%.

1. In result clauses

The most common and well-known exception to the 97% pattern occurs in pure result clauses as given in our Third Experience. Pure result clauses are written, for example, in the pattern:

tantum ... ut	so great ... that
sic ... ut	in such a way ... that
tales ... ut	of such a nature ... that
tantos ... ut non	so great ... that not.

What is not intended as a pure result clause is the construction *accidit ut veniret*, "it happened that he came." Although expressive of result, this is not a pure result clause and does not fall into this exception.

This exception to the sequence of tenses occurs only on Track II when a past time verb, that is to say T.2i, 4bi, or even 5i, is followed by a pure result clause in T.1s or 3s, where the general rule would have produced T.2s or 4s.

This means that you can have a past verb where the effect or the result of the sentence comes up to the present time of the speaker or writer, and therefore human logic simply demands that a different sequence according to the new situation be allowed. For example, you would say:

Scripsit carmina Virgilius undevicesimo ante Christum tam pulchra ut etiam hodie bismillesimo duodecimo anno eius carmina legantur studiosissime

Virgil wrote such beautiful poems in the year 19 before Christ that as a result they are being read today most enthusiastically in the year 2012.

The above example shows how the logic simply demands that T.1s be used because the result is felt today in the year 2012.

The same pure result clause can end up with T.3s, which again does not appear in the 97% schema after indicative verbs in T.2i, 4bi, or 5i. This happens when the result is one concrete solid fact in the past, like a photograph. For example:

> *Tam robustus et fortis erat ut eo die sustulerit onus quingentarum librarum*
>
> He was so solid and strong that on that day he lifted a weight of 500 pounds.

In the above example, lifting the weight was one concrete result of his strength.

The difference in meaning that this exception to the rule makes is clear by contrasting the above example with the following, which follows the 97% rule.

> *Tam robustus et fortis erat ut quotidie tolleret onus quingentarum librarum*
>
> He was so solid and strong that daily he was lifting a weight of 500 pounds.

The use of the T.2s here comes up rather rarely and indicates a continual resulting action, in this case lifting the weight repeatedly over time. Another example may be a better one:

> *Sic vulnerati sunt in casu autoredarum ut mortui sint*
>
> They were so injured in the crash of cars that they died.

In the above example their death is the one concrete result of the car wreck, and it is given in T.3s. In contrast, this sentence may be rephrased to follow the 97% sequence of tenses, with the consequence that the result describes a continual action, as in:

> *Sic vulnerati sunt ut atrociter morerentur*
>
> They were so hurt that they were dying in a terrible way.

This last example does not indicate one concrete final result but an ongoing result. This is very common in the historians. Another example is:

> *Alcibiades ita clarus erat (=fuit) Athenis ut unus sapiens habitus sit ab historicis*
>
> *Alcibiades was so great in Athens that he was considered the only wise man by historians.*

2. In conditionals

Another logical and necessary exception to the 97% schema occurs when the sequence of tenses is combined with contrary-to-fact, unreal, impossible conditions. Only these are concerned, not logical conditionals or the foggy future. Because there are only four times of the subjunctive with which to express all of the conditionals, the logic of the contrary-to-fact conditionals simply exceeds any kind of sequence of tenses or grammatical structure or rules. This means that even if the sequence of tenses is on Track I (e.g., *nescio*), a contrary-to-fact conditional will keep the T.2s if impossible in the present and T.4s if impossible in the past. If the sequence of tenses is on Track II (e.g., *nesciebam*), the contrary-to-fact condition will again keep T.2s or 4s. For example:

> *Nescimus quid faceret si ea adesset*
>
> We do not know what she would do if she were here
>
> *Nesciebam superiore anno quid ante dictum esset si licuisset*
> *I did not know last year what would have been said previously, if it had been permitted.*

In the first example above, the independent verb *nescimus* establishes the sequence of tenses on Track I. The indirect question would normally produce T.1s or T.3s, but, because it is a contrary-to-fact conditional, the whole indirect question is placed in T.2s.

In the second example above, the conditional sentence is set in the past. The independent verb *nesciebam*, in T.2i establishes the sequence of tenses on Track II. The indirect question would normally produce T.2s or T.4s, as it does here. But the reason for both instances of T.4s is due to the underlying contrary to fact condition, which is sometimes difficult to distinguish.

Take another example:

> *Tam pudica est et verecunda ut esset honor ab ipsa recusatus, ei si talem obtulissemus*
>
> *She is so modest and shy that the honor would have been refused by her, if we had given such to her.*

In this case the independent verb establishes the sequence of tenses on Track I, but the result clause is a contrary-to-fact conditional set in the past, and thus uses T.4s. So, the contrary-to-fact conditional has to stay in the conditional formula and stand outside the sequence of tenses. The other abnormalities of contrary-to-fact conditions in indirect discourse are put forth in encounter 33 (103).

3. In original subjunctives

The last instance of the special 3% sequence of tenses is represented by natural or essential subjunctives. We begin with the natural subjunctive in the following example:

> *Quid facerem?*
>
> What should I have done?

This subjunctive is more or less potential or deliberative in the past, as mentioned in Gildersleeve and Lodge n° 265. When the above direct question becomes an indirect question in the following sentence, the natural function of the subjunctive remains, as in the following:

> *Nesciunt quid facerem.*

Although this sentence could be translated as:

> They do not know what I would do,

when the underlying question is in the subjunctive, its force comes through, as in the rendering:

> They do not know what I was supposed to do.

In this example above, the *facerem* stays as a deliberative subjunctive. The difference in meaning between the above exception and the normal use of the sequence of tenses is clear if you compare it with the following, which follows the general pattern:

> *Nesciunt quid fecerim*
> They do not know what I did.

In the above example, the subjunctive has lost the function it had in the original direct question, *Quid facerem*? "What should I have done?" Likewise, the examples:

> *Nescis quid faceret*?
> Do you not know what she was supposed to do?

> *Nescis quid fecerit*
> You do not know what she did

> *Quisnam ita stultus esset*? (contrary to fact)
> Who would be so stupid? (obviously, nobody!)

> *Nescit quisnam sic stultus esset* (indirect question contrary to fact)
> He does not know who would be so stupid

> *Nescio quisnam ita stultus fuerit* (indirect question of fact)
> I do not know who was so stupid.

This function of the subjunctive is very rare, and you have to have special instances of the original subjunctive there. This demands the usual attention, precision, and reflective consideration as always in Latin.

These three sentences comprise what we think is 3% of the language. Maybe the percentage should be higher, perhaps up to about 10%, because the second one regarding the concrete result in T.3s is very common; but we shall leave that to computer calculations, very easy to come by.

ENCOUNTER 25 (95)

TIMENDI VERBA + "PERICULUM . . . EST"

verbs of fearing and the phrase "periculum . . . est"

Introduction

Again, a study of the dictionary will show you the interesting variety of uses with Latin verbs of fearing.

1. Verbs of fearing

The verbs we are dealing with are generally:

timeo, timere, timui, 2	to fear, to be afraid of
metuo, metuere, metui, 3	"
vereor, vereri, veritus sum, 2	"
paveo, pavere, pavi, 2	to be struck with fear or terror
formido, formidare, formidavi, 1	to fear very greatly.

1.1 *With the complementary infinitive*

Like other verbs we have already seen, these can be used with the complementary infinitive, which functions as a gerund in the object form. Used in this way, verbs of fearing have a slightly different meaning, namely not simply "to fear" but "to hesitate to do something," as in:

Haec timeo tibi dicere
I hesitate to say these things to you
I fear to tell you these things.

This use of these verbs is natural and normal and does not concern us here.

1.2 *With substantive clauses*

Our main concern is what phenomenon these words have when used with entire substantive-noun clauses composed of an accusative subject and an infinitive verb, which, as we have seen, function as a noun. For example, in the English sentences:

I am afraid they do not understand
They were afraid I would not come on time.

The verbs of fearing are "I am afraid" and "they were afraid," and the dependent clauses are the sentences "they don't understand" and "I would not come on time," respectively.

The phenomenon in Latin is usually explained by saying that verbs of fearing take the opposite particle of other verbs of prohibition, as here:

ne means "that"
ut means "that not"
ne non means "that not."

The difference here is easily explainable, after we see some examples in a dictionary or the reading sheets. If I want to say:

They are afraid that the rain may impede them

we are going to say:

Timent ne se pluvia impediat.

Here *ne* takes on a positive force, meaning "that." Another example is:

Verebamini ne leones invaderent
You were afraid that the lions would attack.

A positive doubt is expressed by the opposite particle, as in the example that Cicero writes to his wife Terentia:

Timeo ut sustineas [*labores*]
I am afraid that you may not sustain [the hardships]

where the particle *ut* appears to have a negative force, meaning "that … not." Take the example:

Timebant ut tempore elephanti advenirent
They were afraid that the elephants would not come on time.

The phenomenon is easily explained, because in the old days you had two completely different sentences. The first of these sentences is a wish, either positive or negative, and the second is a verb of fearing. Take for example:

Ne pluvia nos impediat. Timemus [*contrarium*]
May the rain not block us. We are afraid [of the opposite].

In this example, the first sentence is a negative wish, *Ne pluvia nos impediat*, "may the rain not block us," and the second is the verb of fearing, "*Timemus*," which implied that we fear that the opposite of the wish may happen. In the next stage of development, these two sentences were combined into one:

Ne pluvia nos impediat timemus
May the rain not block us, we are afraid [*it will*]
We are afraid that the rain may impede us.

This same development happened for a positive wish. First it stood independently of a verb of fearing, as in:

Ut labores sustineas. Timeo
May you sustain hardships. I am afraid [*you won't*].

Likewise, these two sentences were then combined into one to say:

Ut labores sustineas timeo
That you may sustain hardships, I am afraid [*you won't*]
I am afraid you may not sustain hardships

Ut tempore advenirent. Timebant

Oh, that they might come on time. They were afraid [*of the opposite*]

Timebant ut angues tempore in circum adferrentur

They were afraid that the snakes would not be delivered on time for the circus.

2. *Periculum est*

The phrase *periculum est* works the same way as *timeo* above, as in the examples:

Periculum est ut discipuli furentem intellegant magistrum

There is a danger that the students may not understand the raving teacher

Parvuli periculum erat ne Latini sermonis subtilitatibus obruerentur

There was a danger that the little ones might be smothered by the subtleties of the Latin language.

ENCOUNTER 26 (96)

QUALITATIS DECLARATIO TRIPLEX: GENITIVO, ABLATIVO, ET DEFINITIONE ADIECTIVI

triple statement of quality:
by the genitive, ablative, and with definition of the adjective

Introduction

Qualities or descriptions in Latin are expressed in the three following ways:

by the gen. form of-possession describing mostly transient qualities, such as emotions, feelings, wishes, desires,
by the abl. form by-with-from-in describing normally permanent qualities, such as physical, geographical descriptions,
by an adjective defined by a noun in the abl. form by-with-from-in.

1. With the genitive form of-possession

Many people say that transient qualities are in the gen. function. Examples include:

Optimi sunt discipulae ingenii
The girl students are of excellent talent

Morum agricolae erant sanorum
They were farmers of healthy manners

Magni rex honoris
A king of great honor (although he may lose the honor)

Magnae laetitiae dies
Days of great joy (that might pass or be lost).

2. With the ablative form by-with-from-in

Another way of expressing quality is with the abl. function, and observers will say that most of the time it refers to physical characteristics and thus to permanent or stable qualities, for example:

Est vir rutilis capillis magno naso flaccis auribus
He is a man with blond hair, a big nose, and floppy ears.

3. With an adjective defined by a noun in the ablative

We have seen above the combination of two words either in the gen. form of-possession or in the abl. form by-with-from-in. A third way of expressing quality is to use an adjective followed by a defining noun in the abl. To form this construction a word is needed on which the adjective depends. To this adjective is joined what some books call an abl. of specification or limitation. Examples include:

> *Est sacerdos rutilus capillis,*
> *magnus naso,*
> *flaccus auribus*
>
> He is a priest blond in hair,
> big in nose,
> floppy in ears
>
> *Magister est preclarus non doctrinis sed iocis*
>
> The teacher is a famous man not with regard to his teachings but with regard to his jokes
>
> The teacher is famous in jokes and not in teachings.

This third construction tends to be common, as reading Latin daily will convince anyone.

ENCOUNTER 27 (97)

REPETITIONES ANTE ACTORUM

repetition of things done before

At is point of our systematic presentation of the Latin language and of our thorough immersion into its workings and beauties, it may be prudent and effective just to sit back and relax, not push or pressure, do nothing new for two encounters, perhaps a week, but just review calmly and pleasantly many things that we have presented of late so that the mind may have time to assimilate all that we have said. Consequently, this encounter and the next are intended to be as demanding as all the others, but present nothing new or unheard-of. Rather they go back and slowly absorb the things that were done in ten recent encounters.

We do not wish to give the impression that we are cramming all of the material in before some deadline or fixed date. At the same time we are conscious of how much time, energy, attention the Latin language requires of interested, studious, curious people, and how a little pause can help the reader consolidate what has been said in recent encounters. We are also aware of the approaching Fifth Experience in which there really is no end to learning the Latin language from texts of real literature from every age. So, we have no need to rush, but only to spare a little time for the mind to assimilate this material.

In this encounter we suggest conducting a review of these heavy uses of the by-with-from-in, to-for-from and of-possession presented in the preceding numbered encounters listed below:

Encounter 19 (89). the passive expression of intransitive verbs with:
- genitive,
- ablative,
- dative.

Encounter 20 (90). Abl. of comparison and of measure

Encounter 21 (91). Dat. of possession and of purpose

Encounter 26 (96). Statements of quality with the:
- genitive,
- ablative,
- definition by an ablative.

The interested student may read our presentations of these chapters again and review the examples provided. This breather may allow questions to arise and for people learning together to discuss this material. We encourage you to find other examples in the reading sheets and any text of Latin literature. This is also recreational time to play with the Latin texts and to create your own immortal Latin expressions.

ENCOUNTER 28 (98)

RESPICIUNTUR ITERUM MODI CONIUNCTIVI USUS QUIDAM

certain uses of the subjunctive are considered again

Like the previous encounter, this one is also intended to give some fresh air moving in and out of our learning experiences. Likewise this encounter has no particular emphasis other than a general focus on the encounters dealing with the uses of the subjunctive that we have learned since our last summary of its many usages with the relatives *qui, quae, quod* and *quis, quid* in encounter 79 and since the presentation of the attraction of mood in encounter 83. The self-learner is encouraged to read again the following presentations:

Encounter 16 (86). Conditional sentences:
- logical conditionals in the indicative and imperative
- foggy future conditionals in T.1s
- contrary-to-fact conditionals in T.2s and 4s.

Encounter 18 (88). *Utinam* + the foggy future conditional
Utinam + contrary-to-fact conditionals

Encounter 22 (92). *Fore (futurum esse)* + *ut* + subjunctive

Encounter 23 (93). *Dubitare*
- *dubitare* + infinitive
- *dubitare* + accusative + infinitive
- *dubitare* (positive) + *num* + subjunctive
- *dubitare* (negative) + *quin* + subjunctive

Encounter 24 (94). 3% exceptions to the sequence of tenses
- in expressions of pure result on Track II to state
  - one concrete result in T.3s
  - or an effect up to the present in T.1s,
- contrary-to-fact conditionals.

Encounter 25 (95). Verbs of fearing and *periculum … est* with

ne	+ subjunctive	= that
ut	+ subjunctive	= that not
ne non	+ subjunctive	= that not.

During this recreational pause, we suggest that abundant use be made of the reading sheets in whole readings as much as possible. We encourage teacher and student to discuss these many different usages of the subjunctive and to practice spotting them and above all to understand the often overlapping reasons for the use of the subjunctive. Questions may emerge prompting discussion. Time is allowed to play with the language, where the teacher will provoke the students to create their own Latin expressions based on the literature. This encounter is intended to give some breathing room so that students may develop their enjoyment of the language and satisfaction from working with it actively and passively

ENCOUNTER 29 (99)

GENITIVUS PARTITIVUS

genitive of part

Introduction

The gen. of part, also called the "partitive genitive," is found in many languages to indicate simply a designation not of a whole but of a section of something. Most examples in Latin literature are obvious and can be translated directly in English.

Genitive of part

The following examples exhibit a natural gen. of part:

plurimi militum
very many of the soldiers

nemo nostrum
no one of us

pars maior civium
the greater part, majority of the citizens.

Sometimes you will see an alternative expression such as:

nemo ex nobis
no one out of us.

Another use of the gen. of part demands a little more attention. It consists of a neuter noun or pronoun in the singular with a following gen. somewhere in the whole sentence. A few of the neuter nouns or pronouns used in this construction are:

tantum	*quantum*
nihil	*aliquid*
multum	*plus*
plurimum	*non nihil*
aliquantum	*paulum*
parum	*minus.*

The Romans loved to separate that neuter from the gen. by about five or six words, which requires the reader to make the mental connection between them and to read the whole sentence as people were taught to do years ago in these encounters, as you will see in the examples below. The first rendering in English tries to preserve the sound of the Latin, and the second is a smoother English expression of the Latin. In the first example *nihil* goes with *criminis:*

Nihil in eis invenimus criminis

Nothing of accusation do we find in them
No bit of accusation do we find in them.

In the following example *aliquantum* goes with *pecuniae:*

Mihi aliquantum heri dedit amicus meus pecuniae
Yesterday my friend gave me a little bit of money.

The Romans loved such talk, its rhythm and cleverness. We insist that the gen. can be rendered in English by a gen., but sometimes it may require careful adaptation, for example:

Plurimum habet hic liber iucunditatis

This book has very much of pleasure
This book has a big amount of pleasure.

It is very popular, but hard to see, when the two elements, the neuter and the gen., are separated by several words. Romans use this as often as they can. Cicero says, for example, in one of his letters to Atticus:

Ego si quid hic hodie novi cognoro, scies (Cic. *Att.* VII, 20)
You will know if I shall have come to know something of news here today.

Here Cicero says *quid novi* meaning "something of what is new" or simply "something new."

In English we use the equivalent of the neuter noun when we say, "Give me *some* water," but in French and Italian the gen. of part is used in their requests: "Give me *of water.*" The Romans maintain both the neuter and the gen., in saying:

Da mihi aquae aliquid
... aliquantum aquae
... aquae non nihil
Give me some bit of water

Aliquid admove mihi licopersici, quaeso, liquaminis
Pass me, please, something of tomato goo
Please, pass me the ketchup.

ENCOUNTER 30 (100)

POSSESSIONIS IN PRAEDICATO GENITIVUS: ITEM IUDICIS; MEUM – TUUM, EIUS . . .

genitive of possession in the predicate:
likewise: of a judge; mine – yours, his . . .

Introduction

In this encounter we concentrate on a use of the gen. beloved in all authors and types and times of Latin. This is not a gen. of quality or description but a gen. of-possession, meaning "of" or "belonging to." The Romans like to use this as a predicate much as we do in English.

1. *Iudicis*: it belongs to the judge

Take, for example, the English sentences:

> To be silent is the mark, duty of a wise man
> To defend the innocent belongs to a judge, is a judge's business.

The subject of these sentences is the gerund in the form of an infinitive. This is clearer if we give the Latin versions:

> *Sapientis silere est*
> *Insontes est iudicis tueri.*

Many books give a number of good English expressions for the function of this gen.: "it belongs to," "it is of," "it is the mark of," "it is the prerogative of," "it is the duty of," "it is the characteristic of."

Thus, in our examples above, the entire expression "it belongs to a judge" and "it is the mark of a wise man" are the English equivalents of this function of the gen. in Latin. As expressions of possession the above two examples are saying:

> Being silent is the thing of a wise man
> Defending innocent people is in the possession of a judge.

Where English requires the use of all of these words, the Latin is spare. All of a sudden the gen. will be used to do all of those tasks.

This construction is going to be all over the place in Latin literature, as you can imagine. It is used in phrases like this church talk of our day:

> *Romanorum pontificum est ecclesiae unitatis promotio*
>
> The promotion of the unity of the church is of the Roman pontiffs
> The promotion of the unity of the church is a job of Roman pontiffs
> The promotion of the unity of the church belongs to Roman pontiffs

Familiae humanae est pacis tutela
The protection of peace is the responsibility of the human family.

The teacher will find or provide examples of this usage, which is everywhere.

2. *Meum – tuum, eius*

Inasmuch as this gen. signifies possession, adjectives of possession are going to do the same thing. These include:

est eius	it is his business
est eorum	it is their business
est meum	it is my business
tuum est	it is your business.

As in the above examples, most of the time the adjectives of possession are neuter to agree with the subject gerund, as in:

Nostrum est docere et vestrum est discere

Teaching is our thing, and your thing is learning
It is our job to teach; it belongs to you to learn.

PROHIBENDI VOCABULA: NE – QUOMINUS – QUIN. USUS "QUIN"

verbs of prohibiting: ne – quominus – quin. the uses of quin

Introduction

Another important use of the subjunctive is with verbs of forbidding, impeding, and prohibiting in general. Examples of these verbs include:

prohibere	to hold back, prevent
impedire	to entangle, hinder
vetare	to forbid
interdicere	to forbid.

1. *Ne – quominus – quin*

These verbs are used with one of three particles:

ne	= *ut ne*	so that not
quominus	= *ut eo minus*	that all the less
quin	= *qui ne*; *ut ne*	that not

and with the subjunctive according to the sequence of tenses. The use of *ut* is hard to find here because prohibitions are negative.

These verbs of prohibiting give rise to negative final clauses. A few examples will point this out simply and easily, where we say:

Lex prohibet ne hic ambulemus

The law prohibits that we should walk here
The law prohibits us (from) walking here

Vetuistis ne hic tentoria erigeremus

You all forbade that we should set up tents here
You all forbade us (from) setting up tents here

Quaedam leges vetant quominus religio publice exerceatur

The laws forbid that the religion be practiced publicly
The laws forbid the religion (from) being practiced publicly

Leges vetant ne cives religionem profiteantur

The laws forbid that citizens exercise religion
The laws keep people (from) professing religion.

If the prohibition is positive, then the particles used are *ne* and *quominus*. If the prohibition is negative, then *quin* is usually used:

quin = ut ne that … not

For example:

> *Nihil me impediet quin eas consalutem*
> Nothing will impede that I not greet them (women)
> Nothing will impede me (from) greeting them (women).

In contrast to the Latin, a smoother rendering in English is achieved by using a gerund, as in the phrase "from doing some action." This is so, especially with the use of the negative *quin*, but learners must be reminded of the natural-original Latin expression, which does not correspond to the smooth English, which we shall see immediately.

2. The use of *quin*!!!

Besides the prohibitive sentences, the use of *quin* is very broad, at least in ten ways, as seen in the Lewis and Short dictionary. The particle *quin* always comes down to the idea of "that not" in a negative result clause, not a purpose clause (see Gildersleeve and Lodge nº 632). *Quin* is a composite that stands for *quī ne*. We may add to what the dictionary indicates, that this *quī*, with a long –*i*-, is an old ablative standing for *quo, qua, quibus*, meaning variously, "how, by which, why." The composite form *quin* means, "[someone, something prohibits] lest who," that is, "lest he, she, it," where *quin* stands for *qui, quae, quod … non* which may be expressed more fully as *ut is … non, ut ea … non, ut id … non, ut ego … non, ut tu … non*, and so forth, where the subject is expressed in the relative pronoun, meaning, "[someone, something prohibits] that he … not, that she … not, that it … not, that I … not, that you … not," and so forth. That is why you will see examples like:

> *Studuit linguae Latinae quin pretium solveret*
> She studied the Latin language in such a way that who did not pay tuition
> She studied the Latin language in such a way that she did not pay tuition
> She studied the Latin language without paying tuition

> *Respondes quin interrogem*
> You are answering that who not ask
> You are answering so that I do not ask
> You are answering without my asking.

In the first example above, *quin* stands for *quae non*, "that who not," or more fully *ut ea … non*, "that she … not." The force of that result clause is seen in the English expression, "in such a way that … " In the second example the *quin* stands for *qui non*, if the subject is a man, but if the subject is a woman, *quae non*, both meaning, "that who not," or "that I not," or more fully *ut ego … non*, "that I … not." A good dictionary also indicates that both of these phrases often may be rendered into more idiomatic English by saying "without" followed by a participial clause, as in the first example, "without paying tuition" and in the second, "without my asking."

INTEREST + REFERT EX LEXICO IPSO

verbs interest and refert from the dictionary itself

Introduction

Our Latin adventure brings us to a totally new and fascinating aspect of the language. This concerns verbs of interest and attention with some very remarkable linguistic phenomena. The verbs we are talking about are *refert* and *interest*, and a good dictionary will present the whole matter for our study.

1. *Refert*

The first thing is to point out that in the dictionary there are two entries for the verb *refert*.

1.1 *rĕfert*

One is *rĕfero, rĕferre, rettuli, rĕlatum*, 3, with a short vowel *rĕ–*. That entry means "to bring back, to carry back, to transport back." It does *not* concern us at this time in any special way.

1.2 *rēfert*

The second, *rēfero, rēferre, rēttuli, rēlatum*, 3, has a long *rē–* and is sometimes written as two separate words, *rē fert*. The reason for that semi-independent word *rē* is its origin as the abl. of *res, rei, f.* Consequently, this second entry means "it has bearing out of the thing" or "it imports something because of the thing." That is what is clearly indicated in the two words *rē fert* and explained in the elaborate dictionary entry. That long abl. in *ē* is the key to unlocking the whole problem we are going to confront.

The examples given in the dictionary for *rē fert* have the meaning, "it befits, it matters, it concerns, it is of importance, it is of consequence." We shall emphasize the force of that *rē–*, so that *rē fert* means, "it is of importance *rē:* out of, because of the matter." Consequently:

if I want to say:	it has importance out of my matter; it concerns me
I shall say:	*rē fert mea.*

In this case, the word *mea* agrees with the *rē–* in *rē fert*. In a different expression the word *tua* agrees with the *rē–* in *rē fert*:

tua rē fert
it has importance out of your matter; it concerns you.

In another example, *eius*, "of her," depends on the *rē–* in *rē fert*:

> *eius rē fert*
> it has importance out of her matter; it concerns her.

Again, *eorum*, "of them," depends on the *rē–* in *rē fert*, in the following:

> *eorum rē fert*
> it has importance out of their matter; it concerns them.

Finally, the possessive gen. *omnium*, "of all," depends on the *rē–* in *rē fert*, as in:

> *omnium rē fert*
> it concerns all people.

All these examples mean the same thing. In Lewis and Short a column and a half is dedicated to presenting terrific, exciting examples of how the Romans use this verb. There will be no difficulty or mystery in the use of this verb, if you are mindful of the *rē–* in the abl., meaning, "out of the matter, by the thing, due to the thing." To this abl. *rē–* you will join the possessive noun or pronoun in the gen. or the adjective in the abl. to indicate the person concerned:

Nostra refert	It concerns us
Infirmorum et pauperum refert	It concerns the sick and poor.

The teacher has an infinity of examples in our dictionary one better than the other for illustrating the use of this particular verb. Only Lewis and Short and the *Oxford Classical Dictionary* will give a sufficient number of examples to show how this works. Time is well spent, with supreme intellectual delight in studying carefully this entry and the examples given.

2. *Interest*

The next step is to talk about the verb *interest* in its various meanings and to come to the conclusion that amid its many applications, one of its meanings happens to be identical with the meaning of *rē fert*. The dictionary entry is *intersum, interesse, interfui*. By the way, the Latin word *interest* is not English, but Latin!

2.1 *to stand between*

The first meaning is "to stand between," whether it is geographical or temporal, as in:

> *Inter duos hos annos eius interest magistratus*
> His administration sits between these two years

> *Duos inter fluvios mons interest*
> The mountain stands between two rivers.

Closely attached to this meaning is one that is based on the compound nature of the verb *inter-sum*, prompting the use of the dat., as we have seen before. This use with the function to-for-from, has spatial, almost geographical meaning, as in, "one is in the middle of things," "involved in things." In the following example the words *omnibus rebus* are in the dat. function:

> *Interest omnibus rebus*
> He is involved in all affairs
> He is present at all affairs.

This use of *interest* does not concern us now, although it is confused with a later, more important usage by many unprepared people who will say *interest nobis*, thinking it means "it concerns us," which is totally erroneous.

2.2 *distance between*

In the dictionary, the second meaning of *interesse* is "to be different" or "to mark a distance." For example:

> *Multum interest inter . . .*
> Much distance is there between . . .

This meaning is developed only a little from the first meaning of the verb. Again, the many examples in the dictionary are marvelous and instructive in every way.

Before we look at the third meaning of *interest*, we have to warn students. Many people think that the meaning, "it concerns me" or "it is of interest to me," is expressed with the dat. function, as in *mihi interest*, but that is totally wrong and nonsensical, because of what we are going to say right now. Because of the compound verb, *mihi interest* means "it is inside of me"! Similarly, *eis interest* means, "it is present among them," which is not what we intend to say: a daily mistake especially from Italian influence.

2.3 *It concerns*

Then, we come down to the third meaning of *interest* indicated in the Lewis and Short dictionary by the Roman numeral III. The meaning given is "it makes a difference, it interests, it concerns, it is of interest or importance." What is strange about this use of the verb *interest* is that the Romans transferred this use and meaning of *rē fert* to this third meaning of *interest*. The examples given in the dictionary show this. But the strangest thing in the world, and very few people ever understand why, is the following:

If I want to say:	It concerns me
I have to say:	*Mea interest.*
But to say:	It concerns the families
is to say:	*Familiarum interest.*

Here *mea* does not mean "me," and *familiarum* does not refer to "families" alone; rather, each agrees with the *rē–* of *rē fert*, and the whole expression means:

> It has concern out of my affair
> It has concern out of the affair of families.

That is how you get *mea interest* where *mea* has nothing to do with *interest*, but is still modifying the *rē–* on *rē fert* in another part of the dictionary.

If I want to say:	It concerns the beetles,
just as I said up above:	*eorum rē fert*,
now we are going to say:	*Scarabaeorum interest.*

In the above example *scarabaeorum* has nothing to do with *interest* but is still modifying the *rē–* on *rē fert*. For example:

Vestra et rei publicae interest

It has reference from your concern and from the thing of the republic.

It concerns you all and the republic.

That is how you get the two possessives; first, *vestra* agrees with the *rē–* on *rē fert*, and then *rei publici* is the gen. of possession depending on that same *rē–*.

The examples given in the dictionary have to be studied very carefully, and a wealth of Latin and marvels will come out of them.

ENCOUNTER 33 (103)

ORATIONE IN OBLIQUA CONDICIONALES

conditionals in indirect discourse

Introduction

If we want to add icing on the cake and provide the last bit of heavy-duty material of the Latin language, here at the end of our Fourth Experience, we can present the topic of conditional sentences in reported speech or indirect discourse. As we shall see immediately, this encounter is really an extension of encounter 83, involving modal attraction within a broader sentence of reported speech. All that will be necessary is the logical application of those principles and the learning of one or two new formulae to accommodate the conditionals. This task is not superhuman or endless, but requires much logic and attention.

In every normal conditional, we have seen the condition "if … ," called the protasis, and the conclusion "then … ," called the apodosis. In simple terms, when these two elements are made to depend on one of the M & M verbs. The procedures of the three different types of conditional sentences are superimposed on the sequence of tenses and *oratio obliqua* in such a way that the condition "if … ," is expressed in the subjunctive by attraction, and the conclusion "then …" will be the accusative subject and infinitive. The varying concepts in the three types of conditionals will affect especially the accusative and infinitive part.

The incredible phenomenon and nightmare is that many of the following formulae are identical, because Latin has only four times of the subjunctive and three times of the infinitive, and it simply runs out of verb forms. Therefore, in this indirect discourse the three kinds of conditionals are going to disappear partially or totally, and some of the formulae barely exist.

Gildersleeve and Lodge say, among many other things, "In **Ōratio obliqua** the difference between Ideal and Logical Future is necessarily effaced, so far as the mood is concerned" (n° 596 remark 5), and, "In the transfer of Conditions to **Ō.O.**, the difference between many forms disappears" (n° 656. 3). That means that we cannot distinguish between the many possible meanings in what we are saying, or what is said, and also that grammarians are going to make up formulae to express this. Gildersleeve and Lodge present this in an enlightening and scary fashion in n° 656.2, where eleven formulae are reduced to only three possibilities in indirect discourse. Fantastic examples from Caesar, Livius, and Sallustius illustrating these possibilities of the Latin language and their rendition in direct speech are given in n° 657–659.

So, we can go right to examples and show this feature with logical conclusions from the sequence of tenses and encounter 83.

1. Real or Factual or Logical conditions in indirect discourse

Take one simple sentence in all six times, which we shall connect to the M & M verb *Adfirmant* in T.1i, which sets the sentence on Track I:

Si investigas, intellegis	*Adfirmant, si investiges, te intellegere*
Si investigabas, intellegebas	*. . . si investigares, te intellexisse*
	or . . . *si investiges, te intellecturum (esse)*
Si investigabis, intelleges	. . . *si investigaturus sis, te intellecturum (esse)*
Si investigavisti, intellexisti	. . . *si investigares, te intellexisse*
	or . . . *si investigavisses, te intellexisse*
Si investigaveras, intellexeras	. . . *si investigavisses, te intellexisse*
Si investigaveris, intellexeris	. . . *si investigaveris, futurum esse ut intellegas*
	or . . . *si investigaveris, fore ut intellegas.*

In the second example above, *Adfirmant, si investigares, te intellexisse*, you can see that the M & M verb *Adfirmant* in T.1i sets the sentence on Track I, and produces the accusative subject of the antecedent infinitive *te intellexisse*, which in turn sets the remainder of the sentence on Track II and produces *si investigares* in T.2s, which is in the subjunctive by attraction.

In the third example above, *Si investigabis, intelleges*, the expression *investigaturus sis* would be used in indirect discourse, if the indicative futurity of *investigabis* was not sufficiently evident or clear in the subjunctive rendition of *investiges*.

In the fourth example above, *Si investigavisti, intellexisti*, both verbs are in T.4i. Two possibilities are given for the indirect statement, and you have to leave open both possibilities because you may never know when *investigavisti* occurred. Because T.4bi signifies a past completed action, but you may not know when it happened on the calendar, each T.4bi verb in a series provides its own snapshot. For example, if you write the biography of someone, the birth and the death may both be given in T.4b, but they did not occur at the same time. Much of history is written in T.4b even though actions happened before and after one another. Thus, here you cannot know whether *investigavisti* stands for T.4bi, occurring at the same time as *intellexisti*, and thus rendered in T.2s as *investigares*, or whether *investigavisti* actually happened on the calendar prior to *intellexisti*, and so is the equivalent of T.5i, and thus rendered an antecedent action in T.4s as *investigavisses.*

In the fifth example above, *Si investigaveras, intellexeras*, both verbs are in T.5i. By nature *investigaveras* should have come first on the calendar, and so as an antecedent action is rendered in T.4s as *investigavisses.*

In the last example above, there is a difficulty with expressing the future completed *intellexeris* in T.6i with an infinitive, because the future completed infinitive does not exist in Latin. Here, *Adfirmant* establishes Track I and produces a future expression *futurum esse*, shortened to *fore*, to indicate a completed future time. By the way, in the expression *fore ut intellegas*, the *fore* means "it will be that," "it will happen that," and functions to introduce a complementary result clause *ut intellegas*. The T.1s *intellegas* continues the sentence on Track I and produces by attraction *si investigaveris* in T.3s, which expresses a past action from a completed point in the future.

When we change the M & M verb to *Adfirmaverunt* in T.4bi, then the sentence continues with similar phenomena as above, but beginning on Track II:

Si investigas, intellegis	*Adfirmaverunt, si investigares, te intellegere*
Si investigabas, intellegebas	... *si investigares, te intellexisse*
	or ... *si investigares, te intellecturum (esse)*
Si investigabis, intelleges	... *si investigaturus esses, te intellecturum (esse)*
Si investigavisti, intellexisti	... *si investigares, te intellexisse*
	or ... *si investigavisses, te intellexisse*
Si investigaveras, intellexeras	... *si investigavisses, te intellexisse*
Si investigaveris, intellexeris	... *si investigavisses, futurum ut intellegeres*
	or ... *si investigavisses, fore ut intellegeres.*

2. Foggy future in indirect discourse

Similarly, in the foggy future we begin with two verbs in T.1s to produce the following:

Si saltes, gaudeas	*Adfirmant,*	*si saltes, te gavisurum*
Si saltes, gaudeas	*Adfirmaverunt,*	*si saltares, te gavisurum.*

3. Unreal, Impossible, Contrary-to-fact conditionals in indirect discourse

Remember that in encounter 24 (94) of this Experience we said that one of the 3% exceptions of the sequence of tenses is contrary-to-fact conditions. Because unreal conditionals are outside the normal sequence of tenses, when they are expressed in indirect discourse, the time of the M & M verb practically does not matter. In the following examples, the top two are conditionals contrary to present reality. They are expressed in indirect discourse in the same way regardless of the M & M verb, as we just said. The second two are conditionals contrary to historical reality, and again they stand outside the sequence of tenses established by M & M verbs of whatever time:

Si valerent, venirent	*Adfirmant,*	*si valerent, eos venturos (esse)*
Si valerent, venirent	*Adfirmaverunt,*	*si valerent, eos venturos (esse)*
Si valuissent, venissent	*Adfirmant*	*si (elapso anno) valuissent, eos venturos fuisse*
Si valuissent, venissent	*Adfirmaverunt*	*si (elapso anno) valuissent, eos venturos fuisse.*

The above expressions in indirect discourse are fixed formulae supported by a mere one or two clear, sure examples in all of Latin literature. So we must be patient and realistic. Again, the Latin language runs out of forms to express these concepts. The bottom two examples start with a sentence that includes *venissent* in T.4s, meaning "they would have come." No infinitive form in Latin corresponds to this T.4s. Consequently, a certain roundabout way of expressing this concept was developed, but is seldom found in Latin literature. One might have expected the bottom two examples to use the same form as the top two, namely *venturos* (*esse*), where *esse* is a contemporaneous infinitive and the participle *venturos* expresses futurity, meaning "to be about to come," or "they would come." But in the bottom two sentences, an historical time frame is clearly intended, and so the infinitive was changed from *esse* to *fuisse* to accommodate this idea, by saying something like, "they affirm them to have been about to come." Even then, this forced substitution creates an almost non-existent Latin infinitive, because Latin does not have an infinitive equivalent to *venissent*.

4. Two examples

This simple and clear, classical example comes from the biographer Cornelius Nepos in his work *Eumenes:*

> *intellegebat prius adversarios rescituros de suo adventu, quam ipse tertiam partem confecisset itineris; sin per loca sola contenderet, sperabat se imprudentem hostem oppressurum* (Nep. *Vitae*, XVIII, 8)
>
> *He understood that the adversaries would find out about his arrival before he himself would (might) have finished a third of his journey; but if he would be pushing ahead over the [deserted] places alone, he was hoping that he would be taking the unawares enemy by surprise.*

Here Nepos speaks clearly without ambiguity, which we can see with the help of the following calendar. We can locate the main verb *intellegabat*, "He understood," in T.2i setting the sentence on Track II, as happening, say, in February. As a verb of M & M, *intellegebat* gives rise to a sentence that tells the content of his understanding, where *adversarios* in the object form functions as the subject of the futurity infinitive *rescituros* [*esse*], an action we can locate in the following June.

The expression *prius ... quam*, "sooner ... than ..." or "earlier ... than ..." or "previously ... than ..." can also be written as one word where the *prius* is moved in the sentence to join the immovable *quam* to make *priusquam*, meaning "before" and prefacing the later action. Of these two, the main element, here associated with *prius*, is given in indirect discourse, where *adversarios*, in the object form, functions as the subject of the futurity infinitive *rescituros* [*esse*], which we assign to the following June. The subordinated element, associated with the *quam*, includes the verb *confecisset*, in T.4s, in the subjunctive by modal attraction. As the story goes, the adversaries first find out, before he could even complete a third of his journey, but as the verb times go, it may seem counterintuitive that the futurity infinitive *rescituros* [*esse*] occurs before *confecisset* in T.4s, the last action in this sequence.

The second half of this full expression has as its main verb *sperabat*, "he was hoping," in T.2i, putting the sentence on Track II, which we can also assign to February. As a verb of M & M, *sperabat* gives rise to a statement in ACI which gives the content of his hope, where *se*, in the object form, functions as the subject of the futurity infinitive *oppressurum* [*esse*], which we assign to November. This statement in indirect discourse is itself the consequence of a conditional whose premise is given first in this half of the expression starting with *sin*, "but if" or "if however" followed by *contenderet*, "but if he would be pushing," in T2s due to modal attraction on Track II; you can see the full time frame of T.2s which begins in February and continues until its consequence occurs in November.

Kalendarium

February	June	September	November
intellegebat	*rescituros [esse]*	*confecisset*	
contenderet ►····►	···············	►···············	►
sperabat			*oppressurum*

To help us understand this sentence clearly, we can take its temporal clause out of indirect discourse to recreate the statement said by the original speaker:

> *Intellego prius adversarios rescituros de meo adventu, quam ipse tertiam partem confecero itineris; sin per loca sola contendam, spero me imprudentem hostem oppressurum*
>
> *I understand that the adversaries are going to find out about my arrival before I myself shall have finished a third of my journey; but if I push ahead over the [deserted] places alone, I am hoping that I shall be taking the unawares enemy by surprise.*

One possible explanation for *confecisset*, "he would have finished," in T.4s, and its equivalent in direct discourse, *confecero*, "I shall have finished," in T.6i, is given by Walter Hullihen in his dissertation *Antequam and Priusquam*, where he explains that T.6i, or in modal attraction T.4s, are used here where the previous action, *rescituros*, interrupts the ongoing, subsequent action of *confecero* and *confecisset* while in progress (*v.* p. 28, 61, 98). As the story goes, the speaker is imagining his journey in progress, but before he can complete one-third of his journey, the adversaries find out about his expected arrival.

In another example, Sallustius reports a speech given by Jugurtha:

> *Iugurtha accepta oratione respondit... Ceterum quo plura bene atque strenue fecisset, eo animum suum iniuriam minus tolerare. Adherbalem dolis vitae suae insidiatum; quod ubi comperisset, sceleri eius obviam isse. Populum Romanum neque recte neque pro bono facturum, si ab iure gentium sese prohibuerit* (*Sall. Iug. XXII*)

the speech having been heard, Iugurtha answered ... Besides, the more things that he had done well and energetically, the less did his spirit tolerate insult. Adherbal plotted against his life with deceits; which thing when [Iugurtha] had discovered, [Iugurtha] confronted his [Adherbal's] crime. The Roman people will be acting neither correctly nor for the common good if it will have excluded him [Iugurtha] from the law of the nations.

Standing at the beginning of our sentence is an ablative absolute *accepta oratione*, "the speech having been heard." The main sentence is *Iugurtha respondit*, "Iugurtha answered," in T.4b setting the sentence on Track II. As a verb of M&M *respondit* produces several sentences in indirect discourse, that is, *oratio obliqua*.

In the first of these, the object form *animum suum* functions as the subject of the infinitive *tolerare*, "did his spirit tolerate." The reflexive *suum* refers indirectly to Iugurtha whose experience Sallustius is recounting. This statement in *oratio obliqua* is the main part of a sentence coordinated by two correlatives each with a comparative degree, *quo plura ... eo ... minus ...*, literally, "by how much more ... by so much less ..." Often these correlatives are difficult to express in English, here we might more easily say, "the more ... the less ..." The subordinate, relative part of this correlative sentence is *quo plura bene atque strenue fecisset*, "the more things that he had done well and energetically," where the verb *fecisset* is in T.4s describing antecedent action on Track II; the verb is in the subjunctive by modal attraction because this relative sentence is an integral part of the statement in *oratio obliqua*. Thus, the subjunctive verb is describing the actual events in Iugurtha's life, and so stands for *fecerat* in T.5i.

The *oratio obliqua* continues with another sentence where *Adherbalem* in the object form functions as the subject of the infinitive *insidiatum* [*esse*]," which is one of the 65 verbs whose complement is in the form to-for-from, here *vitae suae* and meaning "against his life." Again the reflexive *suae* refers indirectly to Iugurtha, the subject of the whole account given by Sallustius.

The *oratio obliqua* continues with a sentence whose subject is only implied, perhaps *eum* or *Iugurtham* in the object form functioning as the subject of the infinitive *isse*, whose meanings include the possibility of hostility, as in "[Iugurtha] confronted." The pronoun *eius* refers to Adherbalis. The subordinate part of this relative sentence is *quod ubi comperisset*, where the pronoun *quod* is the object of *comperisset*, and the statement *ubi comperisset*, "which thing he had discovered," where *comperisset* describes an historical event, expressed in the subjunctive T.4s by modal attraction because the statement is closely associated with and so swept up into the oblique discourse. The subject of *comperisset* is once again Iugurtha, who discovered the historical plot against his own life.

Yet another statement in *oratio obliqua* consists of *Populum Romanum* in the object form functioning as the subject of the futurity infinitive *facturum* [*esse*], "is about to act" or "will be acting." Depending on this oblique statement is the conditional sentence *si ab iure gentium sese prohibuerit*, "if it will have excluded him from the law of the nations" where *prohibuerit* describes a factual condition in T.3s by modal attraction because the condition is closely involved in the oblique discourse. The pronoun *sese* likewise refers indirectly to Iugurtha about whom Sallustius narrates this story. Here *prohibuerit* as a verb in T.3s has the natural meaning of completed futurity and describes an action that occurs before the futurity infinitive *facturum* [*esse*].

Thus, this running response of Iugurtha includes three subjunctives *fecisset, comperisset, prohibuerit*, each a part of a subordinate clause, respectively a correlative, a relative and a conditional clause. Each subordinate clause in turn depends on and is integrally involved in its respective statement in *oratio obliqua*. Thus, they are in the subjunctive by modal attraction, even though they otherwise describe verifiable, concrete facts and so could have been given in the indicative. We can now place these actions on the following calendar:

Calendarium:

May	June	August	September	October	November
			accepta		
			respondit		
fecisset▸·······	▸··········	▸*tolerare*········	▸		
	insidiatum [*esse*]				
		comperisset			
		isse			
				prohibuerit	*facturum* [*esse*]

4. A crowning, triumphant, all-comprehensive sentence

We can conclude this schematic presentation of possible formulae for conditionals in indirect discourse with a symphonic, heavenly sentence of Cicero, which we believe to be one of the best things he ever wrote. It includes all the super elements that we have studied in all our encounters and demands a few years of Latin studies to be understood and enjoyed and treasured. Cicero is speaking after the assassination of Caesar. Cicero is trying to show in this work, *De divinatione*, that it is better that we can not foresee the course of our lives, because, if we knew it, we would die of grief. The sentence is:

> *quid vero Caesarem putamus, si divinasset fore ut in eo senatu, quem maiore ex parte ipse cooptasset, in curia Pompeia ante ipsius Pompeii simulacrum tot centurionibus suis inspectantibus a nobilissumis civibus partim etiam a se omnibus rebus ornatis trucidatus ita iaceret, ut ad eius corpus non modo amicorum sed ne servorum quidem quisquam accederet, quo cruciatu animi vitam acturum fuisse?*
>
> *(De Div. II, 9, 23)*
>
> *but what do we think Caesar, if he had foreseen that it would happen that in that senate, which he himself had appointed for the greater part,*

in the Pompeian senate house before the statue of Pompeius himself—as were looking on so many of his own centurions—he would lie, cut down by the most noble citizens even partly having been decorated by him with all things, in such a way that toward his body not only not any one of his friends but not even of the slaves would approach, with what torment of spirit [do we think Caesar] would he have lived his life?

We can arrange the members of the sentence in this way, with an explanation to follow.

quid vero Caesarem	contrary to fact consequence in OO 1A
putamus,	main sentence
{ *si divinasset*	contrary to fact condition; T.4s
[*fore*	OO 2
ut in eo senatu,	result 1 begins
(*quem maiore ex parte ipse cooptasset*)	relative MA/concessive; T.4s
in curia Pompeia ante ipsius Pompeii simulacrum	result 1 continues
—tot centurionibus suis inspectantibus—	ablative absolute
a nobilissumis civibus partim etiam a se omnibus rebus ornatis	agent of *trucidatus*
trucidatus ita iaceret,	result 1 concludes; T.2s
« *ut ad eius corpus non modo amicorum*	
sed ne servorum quidem quisquam accederet »] },	result 2; T.2s
quo cruciatu animi vitam acturum fuisse?	contrary-to-fact consequence in OO 1B

The main sentence is one M & M verb, *putamus*, in T.1i which sets the entire question on Track I and produces a direct question in indirect discourse (OO) where *Caesarem* in the object form functions as the subject of the infinitive *acturum fuisse* describing the consequence of a contrary-to-fact conditional set in the past, and thus T.4s. The two parts of this consequence are so separated in the sentence, by 46 words, that Cicero changes the sentence mid-way. He begins by saying something like *quid Caesarem putamus … acturum fuisse*, "What do we think Caesar would have done," a direct question. Although Cicero begins his thought in this way, by the time he gets to the end of the sentence, he forgot what he had said above and changed the object of the infinitive *acturum fuisse* from *quid* to *vitam* for a sentence something like, *quo cruciatu animi Caesarem putamus … vitam acturum fuisse*, "With what torment of spirit do we think Caesar would have lived his life," also a direct question. Had Cicero foreseen all the way to the end of his sentence, he could have begun by saying something like: *quo animi cruciatu Caesarem putamus, si divinasset … vitam acturum fuisse*, "with what torment of spirit do we think that Caesar, if he had foreseen … would have lived his life?"

The indirect discourse presents a direct question *quid* (*quo*) Caesarem … *acturum fuisse?* that functions as a contrary-to-fact consequence, the "then …" clause, whose contrary-to-fact condition, the "if …" clause, begins with its verb up front, *si divinasset* in T.4s. This confirms our formula given above, *Adfirmant si valuissent, eos venturos fuisse*. We can reconstruct the contrary-to-fact conditional, which takes the form of a direct question: *si Caesar divinasset ... quo cruciatu animi vitam egisset*? "If Caesar would have guessed ... with what torment of spirit would he have lived life."

What we said above also holds true here, namely that *egisset* in T.4s has no equivalent infinitive form to express contrary-to-fact condition. The antecedent infinitive here, *egisse* "to have lived," is not the equivalent of "he would have lived." One might have expected to express this concept with the infinitive *acturum esse* "to be about to live [his life]" or "he would live his life," but because the time frame is historical, the contemporaneous infinitive *esse* is replaced by the antecedent one, *fuisse*. This creation imposed by necessity, *acturum fuisse*, says something such as, "with what torment of spirit do we think Caesar to have been about to live his life," or more simply, "with what torment of spirit do we think Caesar would have lived his life." In all of Latinity there are extremely few examples of this.

The M & M verb, *divinasset*, produces its own indirect statement, where it would produce the accusative subject of an infinitive, *se iaciturum esse*, expressing futurity, but because the form *iaciturum* is so rare as effectively not to exist (mentioned once in Lewis and Short), Cicero used the circumlocution *fore ut iaceret* in T.2s. As we have seen recently, here on Track II the *fore* means, "it would happen that," and functions as a statement in indirect discourse which produces a complementary result clause, *ut iaceret*, in T.2s. By the way that entire result clause *ut ... accederet* is the subject of *fore*.

The relative sentence *quem ... cooptasset* in T.4s is in the subjunctive either by modal attraction (MA) meaning "which he had appointed," or it is a concessive sentence meaning "even though, although he had appointed," which naturally appears in the subjunctive in Latin, but in the English indicative.

The abl. absolute is *centurionibus suis inspectantibus*. The reflexive *suis* refers not to the subject of the abl. absolute in which it lies, but to the subject of *divinasset*, that is to Caesar.

The participle *trucidatus* agrees with the subject of *iaceret*, that is Caesar, and as a passive participle its personal agent is expressed by *a ... civibus*, who are described by their own participial clause *partim ... ornatis*. The *se* refers to Caesar.

The complementary result clause *ut ... ita iaceret*, produces its own pure result clause indicated by the preparatory word *ita* and the clause *ut ... accederet*, and the verb *accederet* is the last word of its own clause, and its clause is the last word of everything from *fore ut*—the ablative absolute excepted—and thereafter the indirect discourse takes up again.

ENCOUNTER 34 (104)

RES METRICA BREVITER

poetic meter briefly

Introduction

As far as Roman verse and poetry goes, for many centuries the rhythm and measures of the verses were determined by the length of the vowels, which were much more acutely perceived than they are today. Classical Latin poetry, accordingly, has rhythms that depend on a succession of long and short vowels in, say, 100 different patterns. In later Latin, as the length of the vowel was lost, the verses began to be formed according to the accent or the stress of the accents in the words, as in the famous *Carmina Burana*. So classical verse presents special difficulties because you must know the length of the syllables, which are given in the dictionary. Later verse and including some modern liturgical or sacred verse depend more on the accent and are easier to write and to execute and to hear.

1. Dactylic hexameter

The most common verse rhythm is found, for example, in all of Virgil, in Horace's satires, in all of Ovid's *Metamorphoses*, and in all of Lucretius and Lucanus. This rhythm is called dactylic hexameters. This rhythm is called a hexameter because of the six feet or six measures in every verse. It is called dactylic because the basic foot or measure consists of one long and two short syllables, like the human finger, which is composed of one long and two short parts. The term is taken from the Greek word for "a finger," δάκτυλος (*daktylos*). The long and two short syllables are at times put together into two long syllables. This variation back and forth of a long and two short syllables or of two long syllables in each foot varies the rhythm of words in a kind of sing-song repetition.

The succession of long and short syllables as well as the poetic pulse or accent for the dactylic or heroic hexameter is presented in Gildersleeve and Lodge nº 784; we write it in this way here.

Dactylic, Heroic Hexameter:

´´ —　　´´ —　　´´ —　　´´ —　　´´ —　　´´ —
—˘˘ |　　—˘˘ |　　—˘˘ |　　—˘˘ |　　—˘˘ |　　— —

Take an example from the work of Titus Lucretius Carus (c. 99–c. 55 BCE) *On the Nature of Things*, which was discovered by Poggio Bracciolini around 1417 and effectively shook the world into the Renaissance. We have indicated the stressed syllables in these examples of verse. Lucretius says:

Núnc age quáe moveánt animúm res áccipe, et únde
quáe veniúnt veniánt in méntem pércipe páucis (Lucr. IV, 722–23)

Now ok, learn which things move the spirit and understand
in a few words from where the things which come into the mind come into the mind.

Another example comes from Quintus Horatius Flaccus (65–8 BCE) in his letters where Horace mentions his Sabine villa in this way:

háe latebráe dulcés, etiám, si crédis, amóenae,
íncolumém tibi mé praestánt Septémbribus hóris. (Hor. *Ep.* I, 16, 15–16)

These sweet hiding places, if you believe, even attractive,
guarantee me healthy to you in September hours.

In honor of Virgil, these verses are from his didactic poem on bees, where he says:

túm trepidae ínter sé coeúnt pennísque corúscant
spículaque éxacuúnt rostrís aptántque lacértos
ét circá regem átque ipsa ád praetória dénsae
míscentúr magnísque vocánt clamóribus hóstem (Verg. *Georg.* IV, 73–76)

then [the bees] excited meet among themselves and shine with their wings
and sharpen their stingers with their beaks and ready their muscles
and are in crowds mixed together around the king and at the command post themselves
and call forth the enemy with great cries.

2. Elegiac Pentameter

The pentameter has the same rhythm as a hexameter but is divided into two members, each with two-and-one-half feet to make a total of five. The pentameter is used in connection with the hexameter to produce elegiac distich used especially in love poetry.

The figure of the elegiac pentameter is given in Gildersleeve and Lodge n° 785; we write it in this way here.

Elegiac Pentameter:

’— / –⏑⏑ | ’— / –⏑⏑ | ’ – || ’— / –⏑⏑ | ’— / –⏑⏑ | ’ –

The combination of the hexameter and pentameter is called an "elegiac distich," or "couplet."

A two-line example from the love letters of Ovid begins with the hexameter, and the pentameter follows. You can see the two members of Ovid's pentameter, which are divided between *paucí* and *qúod*.

quídquid séruatúr, cupimús magis, ípsaque fúrem
cúra vocát; paucí, qúod sinit álter, amánt (Ov. *Am.* III, 25–26)

we desire more, whatever is guarded, and the watchfulness itself
invites a thief; few people love that which the other person is allowing.

You can see here that the two members of the pentameter end with an accented syllable: *–cí* and *–mánt*. Some people say that the second half of the foot is missing, producing two members of two-and-one-half feet each.

Thomas Morus (1477–1535) in his *Epigrams* gives us first the hexameter and then the pentameter, whose two members are divided between *longó* and *fáta*. Thomas More says:

> Nón ego qúos rapuít mors, défleo. Défleo úiuos,
> Qúos urúnt longó fáta futúra metú (Morus, *Epigram*. 55)

> I do not mourn those whom death has snatched away. I cry over the living,
> whom future fates torment with long fear.

Here is a second poem from Thomas More's *Epigrammata*, whose pentameter has a division between *faciát* and *Sórs:*

> Trístia qúi paterís perfér, Sors trístia sóluet.
> Qúod si nón faciát Sórs, tibi mórs faciét (Morus *Epigram*. 74)

> You who are suffering sad things, stick it out, Fate will dissolve sad things.
> But if Fate may not do that, death will do it for you.

The following inscription was written by Albius Tibullus (c. 60–19 BCE) for his own tomb. Tibullus records this in one of his lyric poems, saying:

> híc iacet ímmití consúmptvs mórte tibv́llvs,
> méssallám terrá dúm seqvitúrqve marí *(Tib. Carm. I, 3, 55–56)*

> here lies Tibullus having been destroyed by merciless death
> while he is following Messalla on land and sea.

Again we can see here that the two members of Tibullus's pentameter end with accented syllables: *–rá* and *–rí*, and they are divided by *terrá* and *dúm*.

We are quite conscious of the varying opinions on how to read these verses, as simple prose and letting the poetic pulse come out below, or with more emphasis on the poetic accent without exaggerating it or breaking sentences up foolishly. Here you have a few examples of poetic meter, which is contained in many books in dozens of pages.

For the sake of our Latin teaching in this encounter, we have chosen to illustrate only the hexameter and pentameter. There are a few other lyric meters found in Catullus, Horatius, and Martialis that are neither of these. These are presented patiently and in scholarly detail in Gildersleeve and Lodge nº 729–827.

ENCOUNTER 35 (105)

SERIORIS LATINITATIS PROPRIETATES

characteristics of later Latin literature

Introduction

After the classic Latin authors, succeeding Latin authors—called by some patristic, medieval, or scholastic—varied in the way they wrote Latin and used Latin due to definite influences. In this encounter we present several ways in which later Latin literature developed beyond the classical forms and modes. If these ways and phenomena are not fully understood and appreciated even by classical scholars in spite of all their expertise, they will miss and misunderstand a good 1,000 years of Latin speech. Later, patristic, medieval, scholastic, and Renaissance Latin belong as much to the knowledge and beauty of Latin as anything in the classical period.

1. Biblical influences

The influence of the Latin Vulgate Bible on Latin usage cannot be over-emphasized. If you are a super classicist and not aware of the influence the Bible had on the Latin-speaking world, you will not understand the Latin language as it departs from the classical era, because that religious movement changed everything radically, especially the mentality and consequently the terminology of the Latin language and its structures. This is the most challenging aspect of ancient religious literature in Latin.

We are dealing with Scripture in Latin from the third century CE through patristic Latin until about the year 800 CE, and on to the Renaissance from the fourteenth century.

The theological, biblical vocabulary is profoundly different, and people are sorely mistaken who think that they are going to understand ancient Christian literature and then scholastic literature 900 years later without a thorough knowledge of the Bible and theology and terminology and mentality, because the vocabulary comes from a completely new world, which is biblical and scriptural and very colloquial.

2. Characteristics of style

There are many changes in Latin style that tend toward simplification of classical usages in many idioms and constructions. The tendency to simplify happens in every language from Shakespeare to *The New York Times* in 2012. Latin fluid word order still flourishes, but sentence structures are simplified.

One difference concerns the use of indirect discourse. Instead of the classical construction of the object form with the infinitive (as it is called, the accusative with the infinitive), later authors start using *quod, quia, quoniam,* meaning "that," followed by a finite verb in the indicative mode or the subjunctive mode. Examples are to be found in the reading sheets of the Christian authors, or in the examples already given in encounter 6 (76) of this Experience Four.

Some ablatives absolute are really not so absolute, and there is a little mixture between the absolute and non-absolute. Examples come from the reading sheets, as in the sentence:

> *Urbe Hierosolimitana deleta, occupaverunt eam cruciferi*
> The city of Jerusalem having been destroyed, the crusaders occupied it.

The abl. is less than absolute in that its subject, *urbe* is the same thing as the object of the main sentence, *eam*—which you should not do. The sentence can be adjusted by simply making *urbe* agree with *eam*, as in:

> *Urbem Hierosolimitanam deletam occupaverunt cruciferi*
> The crusaders occupied the city of Jerusalem having been destroyed.

At this time also the subjunctive begins to lose its force in several ways. The sequence of tenses begins to be ruled more by feeling or philosophy or the ear than by sentence and language norms and logical analysis. Frequently indirect questions are in the indicative rather than the subjunctive.

The conditionals in a present or future time frame are frequently expressed in the subjunctive for no good reason other than a change in mentality. People came to consider all conditionals as expressive of possibility or doubt or uncertainty and therefore to be expressed in the subjunctive. Even great authors like Augustine (354–430 CE) or Jerome (c. 342–420 CE) consistently put the present and future conditionals in the subjunctive. Classical students flounder around looking for a reason to explain these subjunctives, but it comes from the changing mentality or from carelessness or negligence or watering down.

Many of the refined usages, such as verbs that take certain functions and other phenomena like *interest* and *refert,* were avoided or cut down because these subtleties were being lost. The dat. of agent, for example, was almost forgotten or avoided. They might say:

> *A me vendenda pictura est*
> The picture must be sold by me.

The agent here selling the picture is given as *a me* instead of the accepted and usual *mihi,* the dat. of agent used with this expression.

Many classical texts are not understandable to the ancient Christian authors. What is worse is that just about everything that the ancient Christian authors or the scholastics wrote would appear as gibberish or nonsense or strange talk to Cicero. This is because of the change of vocabulary as is noted in Lewis and Short, who point out clearly the normal, classical usage of words and then, further down in the dictionary entries, the biblical, patristic, and ecclesiastical Latin usages. For example, the noun *sacramentum* in classical usage refers to a military oath of fidelity, but this word was used by Tertullian to translate the Greek word for "mystery," and it eventually came to name the sacraments for the Christian writers, for example, baptism and Eucharist.

Another example is the phrase *signum crucis*, which to a classical author would mean "the flag of the cross," but for Christian writers this comes to refer to "the sign of the cross" that Christians still refer to today. The classical authors would not understand the Christian use of *signum crucis* or of *sacramentum* at all.

Most people do not realize at all how different the world of classical Latin was from that of later Latin, and therefore how different their words and discourse were. People gradually lost the understanding or the habit of classical Latin and slipped into biblical, church, and medieval Latin.

3. Renaissance

In the Renaissance from about 1350 to 1650, the discovery of the ancient authors in Greek and Latin manuscripts from England to Syria reawakened the consciousness of the ancient world and the classical forms of speaking Greek and Latin. As a result, Renaissance authors strove to imitate the newly discovered classical authors, if they wanted to be considered an accepted writer in this Renaissance period. People began to imitate verbatim Cicero in everything they wrote and to use only Ciceronian vocabulary and terminology in their own productions. This caused even Erasmus to write his famous *Ciceronianus*, where he attacks some of his contemporaries as being apes of Cicero and not having the courage to expand their own vision even in the new classical environment.

Many people rightly say that the super-classical Renaissance in effect killed the living Latin of the patristic and middle ages because it raised it so high as to be unattainable and it suppressed every other kind of Latin as worthless or reprehensible.

4. Modern Latin

After the Renaissance we had modern Latin, where the classical form was still used but new vocabulary was introduced with the Industrial Revolution, the revolution in medicine, biology, psychology, and other sciences. During this era Latin was still functioning as a general language for teaching, but in a semi-classical and moderate way. That brings us up to our present day.

Examples of later—that is, patristic, medieval, and modern—Latin must be presented to any serious student of Latin because, whether we like it or not, later Latin represents one-half of the history of Latin on planet earth.

SAPIENTIS AEGYPTI
INSCVLPTAS OBELISCO FIGVRAS
AB ELEPHANTO
BELLVARVM FORTISSIMA

QUARTAE EXPERIENTIAE
LECTIONUM PAGINULAE

Reading Sheets—Fourth Experience

READING 4-A

CORNELIVS NEPOS
[100–25 BCE]

DE EXCELLENTIBVS DVCIBVS

1 MILTIADES, Cimonis filius, Atheniensis, cum et antiquitate generis et gloria maiorum et sua modestia unus omnium maxime floreret eaque esset aetate, ut non iam solum de eo bene sperare, sed etiam confidere cives possent sui, talem eum futurum, qualem cognitum iudicarunt, accidit ut Athenienses Chersonesum colonos vellent mittere. cuius generis cum magnus numerus esset et multi eius demigrationis peterent societatem, ex his delecti Delphos deliberatum missi sunt qui consulerent Apollinem, quo potissimum duce uterentur. namque tum Thraeces eas regiones tenebant cum quibus armis erat dimicandum. his consulentibus nominatim Pythia praecepit, ut Miltiadem imperatorem sibi sumerent: id si fecissent, incepta prospera futura. hoc oraculi responso Miltiades cum delecta manu classe Chersonesum profectus cum accessisset Lemnum et incolas eius insulae sub potestatem redigere vellet Atheniensium, idque Lemnii sua sponte facerent postulasset, illi irridentes responderunt tum id se facturos, cum ille domo navibus proficiscens vento aquilone venisset Lemnum. hic enim ventus ab septentrionibus oriens adversum tenet Athenis proficiscentibus. Miltiades morandi tempus non habens cursum direxit, quo tendebat, pervenitque Chersonesum.

2 Ibi brevi tempore barbarum copiis disiectis, tota regione, quam petierat, potitus, loca castellis idonea communiit, multitudinem, quam secum duxerat, in agris collocavit crebrisque excursionibus locupletavit. neque minus in ea re prudentia quam felicitate adiutus est. nam cum virtute militum devicisset hostium exercitus, summa aequitate res constituit atque ipse ibidem manere decrevit. erat enim, inter eos dignitate regia, quamvis carebat nomine, neque id magis imperio quam iustitia consecutus. neque eo setius Atheniensibus, a quibus erat profectus, officia praestabat. quibus rebus fiebat ut non minus eorum voluntate perpetuo imperium obtineret, qui miserant, quam illorum, cum quibus erat profectus. Chersoneso tali modo constituta Lemnum revertitur et ex pacto postulat ut sibi urbem tradant. illi enim dixerant, cum vento borea domo profectus eo pervenisset, sese dedituros: se autem domum Chersonesi habere. Cares, qui turn Lemnum incolebant, etsi praeter opinionem res ceciderat, tamen non dicto, sed secunda fortuna adversariorum capti resistere ausi non sunt atque ex insula demigrarunt. pari felicitate ceteras insulas, quae Cyclades nominantur, sub Atheniensium redegit potestatem.

3 Eisdem temporibus Persarum rex Darius ex Asia in Europam exercitu traiecto Scythis bellum inferre decrevit. pontem fecit in Histro flumine, qua copias traduceret. Eius pontis, dum ipse abesset, custodes reliquit principes, quos secum ex Ionia et Aeolide duxerat, quibus singulis ipsarum urbium perpetua dederat imperia. sic enim facillime putavit se Graeca lingua loquentes, qui Asiam incolerent, sub sua retenturum potestate, si amicis suis oppida tuenda tradidisset, quibus se oppresso nulla spes salutis relinqueretur. in hoc fuit tum numero Miltiades cui illa custodia crederetur. hic cum crebri afferrent nuntii male rem gerere Darium premique a Scythis, Miltiades hortatus est pontis custodes, ne a fortuna datam occasionem liberandae Graeciae dimitterent. nam si cum iis copiis, quas secum transportarat, interisset Darius, non solum Europam fore tutam, sed etiam eos, qui Asiam incolerent Graeci genere, liberos a Persarum futuros dominatione et periculo: et facile effici posse, ponte enim rescisso regem vel hostium ferro vel inopia paucis diebus interiturum. ad hoc consilium cum plerique accederent, Hestiaeus Milesius, ne res conficeretur, obstitit, dicens non idem ipsis, qui summas imperii tenerent, expedire et multitudini, quod Darii regno ipsorum niteretur dominatio: quo exstincto ipsos potestate expulsos civibus suis poenas daturos. itaque adeo se abhorrere a ceterorum consilio, ut nihil putet ipsis utilius quam confirmari regnum Persarum. huius cum sententiam plurimi essent secuti, Miltiades non dubitans tam multis consciis ad regis aures consilia sua perventura, Chersonesum reliquit ac rursus Athenas demigravit. cuius ratio etsi non valuit, tamen magnopere est laudanda, cum amicior omnium libertati quam suae fuerit dominationi.

4 Darius autem, cum ex Europa in Asiam redisset, hortantibus amicis, ut Graeciam redigeret in suam potestatem, classem quingentarum navium comparavit eique Datim praefecit et Artaphernem hisque ducenta peditum, decem milia equitum dedit, causam interserens se hostem esse Atheniensibus, quod eorum auxilio Iones Sardis expugnassent suaque praesidia interfecissent. illi praefecti regii classe ad Euboeam appulsa celeriter Eretriam ceperunt omnesque eius gentis cives abreptos in Asiam ad regem miserunt. inde ad Atticam accesserunt ac suas copias in campum Marathona deduxerunt. is est ab oppido circiter milia passuum decem. hoc tumultu Athenienses tam propinquo tamque magno permoti auxilium nusquam nisi a Lacedaemoniis petiverunt Phidippumque cursorem eius generis, qui hemerodromoe vocantur, Lacedaemonem miserunt, ut nuntiaret quam celeri opus esset auxilio. domi autem creant decem praetores, qui exercitui praeessent, in eis Miltiadem. inter quos magna fuit contentio, utrum moenibus *se* defenderent an obviam irent hostibus acieque

decernerent. unus Miltiades maxime nitebatur, ut primo quoque tempore castra fierent: id si factum esset, et civibus animum accessurum, cum viderent de eorum virtute non desperari, et hostes eadem re fore tardtores, si animadverterent auderi adversus se tam exiguis copiis dimicari.

5 Hoc in tempore nulla civitas Atheniensibus auxilio fuit praeter Plataeenses. ea mille misit militum. itaque horum adventu decem milia armatorum completa sunt, quae manus mirabili flagrabat pugnandi cupiditate. quo factum est ut plus quam collegae Miltiades valeret. eius ergo auctoritate impulsi Athenienses copias ex urbe eduxerunt locoque idoneo castra fecerunt. dein postero die sub montis radicibus acie regione instructa non apertissuma proelium commiserunt (namque arbores multis locis erant rarae) hoc consilio, ut et montium altitudine tegerentur et arborum tractu equitatus hostium impediretur ne multitudine clauderentur. Datis etsi non aequum locum videbat suis, tamen fretus numero copiarum suarum confligere cupiebat, eoque magis, quod, priusquam Lacedaemonii subsidio venirent, dimicare utile arbitrabatur. itaque in aciem peditum centum, equitum decem milia produxit proeliumque commisit. in quo tanto plus virtute valuerunt Athenienses, ut decemplicem numerum hostium profligarint, adeoque perterruerint, ut Persae non castra, sed naves petierint. qua pugna nihil adhuc exstitit nobilius: nulla enim umquam tam exigua manus tantas opes prostravit.

6 Cuius victoriae non alienum videtur quale praemium Miltiadi sit tributum docere, quo facilius intellegi possit eandem omnium civitatum esse naturam. ut enim populi Romani honores quondam fuerunt rari et tenues ob eamque causam gloriosi, nunc autem effusi atque obsoleti, sic olim apud Athenienses fuisse reperimus. namque huic Miltiadi, quia Athenas totamque Graeciam liberarat, talis honos tributus est, in porticu, quae Poecile vocatur, cum pugna depingeretur Marathonia, ut in decem praetorum numero prima eius imago poneretur isque hortaretur milites proeliumque committeret. idem ille populus, posteaquam maius imperium est nactus et largitione magistratuum corruptus est, trecentas statuas Demetrio Phalereo decrevit.

7 Post hoc proelium classem LXX navium Athenienses eidem Miltiadi dederunt, ut insulas, quae barbaros adiuverant, bello persequeretur. quo imperio plerasque ad officium redire coegit, nonnullas vi expugnavit. ex his Parum insulam opibus elatam cum oratione reconciliare non posset, copias e navibus eduxit, urbem operibus clausit omnique commeatu privavit, dein vineis ac testudinibus constitutes propius muros accessit. cum iam in eo esset, ut oppido potiretur, procul in continenti lucus, qui ex insula conspiciebatur, nescio quo casu nocturno tempore incensus est. cuius flamma ut ab oppidanis et oppugnatoribus est visa, utrisque venit in opinionem signum a classiariis regis datum. quo factum est ut et Parii a deditione deterrerentur et Miltiades, timens ne classis regia adventaret, incensis operibus, quae statuerat, cum totidem navibus atque erat profectus Athenas magna cum offensione civium suorum rediret. accusatus ergo est proditionis, quod, cum Parum expugnare posset, a rege corruptus infectis rebus discessisset. eo tempore aeger erat vulneribus, quae in oppugnando oppido acceperat. itaque quoniam ipse pro se dicere non posset, verba fecit frater eius Stesagoras. causa cognita capitis absolutus pecunia multatus est, eaque lis quinquaginta talentis aestimata est, quantus in classem sumptus factus erat. hanc pecuniam quod solvere in praesentia non poterat, in vincla publica coniectus est ibique diem obiit supremum.

8 Hic etsi crimine Pario est accusatus, tamen alia causa fuit damnationis. namque Athenienses propter Pisistrati tyrannidem, quae paucis annis ante fuerat, omnium civium suorum potentiam extimescebant. Miltiades, multum in imperiis magnisque versatus, non videbatur posse esse privatus, praesertim cum consuetudine ad imperii cupiditatem trahi videretur. nam Chersonesi omnes illos quos habitarat annos perpetuam obtinuerat dominationem tyrannusque fuerat appellatus, sed iustus. non erat enim vi consecutus, sed suorum voluntate, eamque potestatem bonitate retinebat. omnes autem et dicuntur et habentur tyranni, qui potestate sunt perpetua in ea civitate, quae libertate usa est. sed in Miltiade erat cum summa humanitas turn mira communitas, ut nemo tam humilis esset, cui non ad eum aditus pateret; magna auctoritas apud omnis civitatis, nobile nomen, laus rei militaris maxima, haec populus respiciens maluit illum innoxium plecti quam se diutius esse in timore.

READING 4-B

PVBLIVS VERGILIVS MARO

[70–19 BCE]

follows on the next seven pages

195 Talibus insidiis, perjurique arte Sinonis,
Credita res: captique dolis, lacrymisque coacti;
Quos neque Tydides, nec Larissæus Achilles,
Non anni domuere decem, non mille carinæ.
Hic aliud majus miseris multoque tremendum
200 Objicitur magis, atque improvida pectora turbat.
Laocoon, ductus Neptuno sorte sacerdos,
Solemnes taurum ingentem mactabat ad aras.
Ecce autem gemini à Tenedo tranquilla per alta
(Horresco referens) immensis orbibus angues
205 Incumbunt pelago, pariterque ad litora tendunt:
Pectora quorum inter fluctus arrecta, jubæque
Sanguineæ exuperant undas; pars cætera pontum
Pone legit, sinuatque immensa volumine terga.

INTERPRETATIO.

Talibus dolis, & vafritie perjuri Sinonis, res credita est; *& decepti fraudibus, ejusque fletu subacti* sunt ii, *quos neque Diomedes, nec Achilles Larissæus, nec decem anni, nec mille naves subegerant. Tunc aliud majus & longe magis terribile* portentum *objicitur miseris* Trojanis, *& turbat incautas mentes Laocoon sorte electus sacerdos Neptuno; sacrificabat magnum taurum ad solemnia altaria. Ecce autem (horresco narrans) duo serpentes immensis spiris à Tenedo* emissi *per mare sedatum, innatant undis, & simul accedunt ad litus: quorum pars anterior sublata è fluctibus, & cristæ sanguinolentæ excedunt undas; pars reliqua propiùs radit mare, & curvat volvendo immanes caudas.*

NOTÆ.

dentalis: inter pontum Euxinum; & eam mediterranei maris partem, quæ Issico sinu terminatur: nunc *Natolie*: de hac sermo hic est, quia in ea erat *Troas*.

193. *Pelopeia ad mœnia.*] Vel *Argos* ubi præcipue regnavit Pelops: vel totam peninsulam isthmo Corinthiaco Græciæ annexam; quæ cum *Apia* diceretur, *Peloponnesus* deinde, id est, *insula Pelopis*, vocata est a *Pelope*; qui e Phrygia, ubi Tantalus ejus pater regnaverat, coloniam eo deduxit. *Pelops* a Tantalo patre dicitur appositus fuisse Diis ad epulas, cumque humerum avidior Ceres comedisset, eburneo humero donatus a Jove. Oenomaum deinde regem Elidis curuli certamine vicit, fraude aurigæ Myrtili, qui vectem axi subduxerat: atque ita Hippodamiam Oenomai filiam solus e procis obtinuit, aliis tredecim ab Oenomao jam ante victis & occisis: eam enim is posuerat legem, ut victus moreretur, victori filia nuberet, monitus oraculis a genero sibi mortem imminere. Pelops ex Hippodamia *Atreum* ac *Thyestem* suscepit: Atreus *Menelaum* & *Agamemnona*. *Pelopeia*, quatuor syllabis, Græca diphthongo, *Pelopeia*.

197. *Tydides, &c.*] Diomedes Tydei filius, Æn. 1. 101. *Larissæus Achilles.*] Phthius potius, quia Phthiæ natus est; cum ejus pater Peleus, ex Ægina insula propter fratris sui Phoci cædem profugus, ab Eurytione Phthiæ rege in tertiam regni partem adscitus esset. Sed *Phthia* & *Larissa* vicinæ sunt Thessaliæ urbes.

198. *Mille carinæ.*] Homerus in catalogo numerat mille centum & octoginta sex. *Carina* proprie est trabs ima, quæ fundamentum est totius navis: vulgo pro tota navi usurpatur.

201. *Neptuno sorte, &c.*] De *Laocoonte* supra, v. 41. De *Neptuno*, Æ. 1. 129. Sorte ductus est sacerdos Laocoon, quia ubi non erant certi Deo sacerdotes, sorte duci mos erat: non erant autem apud Trojanos Neptuno, vel ex quo Laomedon Neptunum contempserat; vel ex quo Trojani

Fit sonitus spumante salo: jamque arva tenebant,
210 Ardentesque oculos suffecti sanguine & igni,
Sibila lambebant linguis vibrantibus ora.
Diffugimus visu exangues: illi agmine certo
Laocoonta petunt: & primum parva duorum
Corpora natorum serpens amplexus uterque
215 Implicat, & miseros morsu depascitur artus.
Post, ipsum auxilio subeuntem ac tela ferentem
Corripiunt, spirisque ligant ingentibus: & jam
Bis medium amplexi, bis collo squamea circum
Terga dati, superant capite & cervicibus altis.
220 Ille simul manibus tendit divellere nodos,
Perfusus sanie vittas atroque veneno;
Clamores simul horrendos ad sidera tollit:
Quales mugitus, fugit cum saucius aram
Taurus, & incertam excussit cervice securim.
225 At gemini lapsu delubra ad summa dracones
Effugiunt, sævæque petunt Tritonidis arcem:
Sub pedibusque Deæ, clypeique sub orbe teguntur.

INTERPRETATIO.

Fit strepitus, mari spumante: & jam attigerant litus, & suffusi sanguine & igne circa *coruscantes oculos, lambebant linguis mobilibus ora sibilantia. Fugimus exanimati aspectu: illi certo impetu currunt ad Laocoonta: & primo serpens uterque amplectendo constringit parva corpora duorum filiorum* Laocoontis, *& morsu devorat misera membra: deinde invadunt* patrem *ipsum venientem in auxilium & arma attollentem, spirisque grandibus involvunt: & jam bis complexi medium, bis circumdantes* ejus *collo dorsa squamosa, excedunt capite & collis altis. Ille simul conatur manibus disrumpere nexus, infectus* circa *tænias tabo & nigro veneno; simul emittit ad astra clamores horrendos* tales, *quales mugitus* emittit *taurus, cum vulneratus fugit altaria, & excussit è collo securim dubio* ictu impactam. *At gemini angues serpendo fugiunt ad summa templa, & abeunt in ædem sævæ Minervæ: & occultantur sub pedibus simulacri, & sub orbe clypei.*

NOTÆ.

ejus sacerdotem interfecerant, quia sacrificiis adventum Græcorum non vetuerat. Nunc itaque rati Græcos abiisse, sacra Neptuno facienda putaverunt ipso in litore; & sors in Laocoonta cecidit, jam antea sacerdotem Apollinis. De *Tenedo*, insula Hellesponti, supra, v. 21.

209. *Salo.*] Mari, Æ. 1. 541.

212. *Agmine certo.*] Certo & ordinato motu: sic G. 3. 423. *Extrem æque agmina caudæ*: locum vide.

221. *Sanie Vittas*] Sanies est sanguis mutatus ac fere corruptus, atro colore permixtus. De *vittis*, supra, v. 133.

225. *Delubra.*] Templa sic dicta, a *deluo*: quia plerumque ante templa fontes erant, aut lacus; ubi templa ingressuri deluebantur.

226. *Tritonidis arcem.*) Minervæ Tritoniæ, de qua supra, v. 171. *Arcem.*] Vel Trojanæ urbis, in qua templum illud erat, & v. 41. *Laocoon ardens summa decurrit ab arce.* Vel arcem dixit, pro templo & æde Minervæ, quocumque loco sita fuerit.

227. *Clypeique sub orbe.*] Serpentes a Pal-

Tum vero tremefacta novus per pectora cunctis
Insinuat pavor: & scelus expendisse merentem
230 Laocoonta ferunt; sacrum qui cuspide robur
Læserit, & tergo sceleratam intorserit hastam.
Ducendum ad sedes simulacrum, orandaque Divæ
Numina conclamant.
Dividimus muros, & mœnia pandimus urbis.
235 Accingunt omnes operi: pedibusque rotarum
Subjiciunt lapsus, & stupea vincula collo
Intendunt: scandit fatalis machina muros,
Fœta armis: pueri circum innuptæque puellæ
Sacra canunt, funemque manu contingere gaudent.
240 Illa subit, mediæque minans illabitur urbi.
O patria, ô Divûm domus Ilium, & inclyta bello
Mœnia Dardanidûm! quater ipso in limine portæ
Substitit, atque utero sonitum quater arma dedere.
Instamus tamen immemores, cæcique furore,

Interpretatio.

Tunc vero novus timor omnibus illabitur in corda attonita: aiuntque Laocoonta dignum fuisse pœnâ quam *persolvit; qui vulnerarit telo sacrum lignum, & immiserit tergo hastam impiam. Clamant invehendum* esse *in urbem equum, & orandam Deæ devinitatem. Evertimus muros, & aperimus munimenta urbis. Omnes præpararant se ad opus: & pedibus* equi, *rotarum supponunt orbes, & injiciunt collo funes è stupa: fatalis machina intrat muros, plena armatis: circum pueri & virgines puellæ canunt sacra carmina, & gaudent tangere manu funes. Machina progreditur, & minans inducitur in mediam urbem. O patria: ô Troja sedes Deorum, & muri Trojanorum nobiles bello! restitit quater in ipso aditu portæ, & quater arma in* ejus *alvo ediderunt strepitum. Urgemus tamen improvidi & occæcati insaniâ,*

Notæ.

lade excitatos in hujus perniciem non mirabitur, qui sciet ex Plutarchi libro de Iside, draconem sacrum fuisse Minervæ, & a Phidia Minervæ simulacro esse appositum: qui Politianum legerit, scribentem, se vidisse Romæ Palladis clypeum, squamoso draconis corio contextum, & dracunculis fimbriatum.

229. *Insinuat.*) Supple *se*: ut Æ. 1. 108. *Tum prora avertit.*

229. *Scelus expendisse merentem*] Quidam dicunt supplicium luisse tum quidem Laocoonta, non ob læsum equum, iramque Palladis; sed ob violatam alio scelere sanctitatem Appollinei templi, cujus erat sacerdos: & serpentes aufugisse in idem illud templum, quod erat in urbis arce.

230. *Robur.*] Lignum quodvis durius, G. 1. 162.

231. *Tergo.*] Dixit v. 51. *In latus, inque alvum.* Ergo a *tergo* equum aggressus, ictum in eamimpegit *lateris* partem, quæ *alvo* contermina est.

234. *Muros, &c. Mœnia, &c.*] Ita distinguit Germanus, ut *muros* velit esse, lapideum ambitum, quo urbs cingitur *mœnia*, munitiones, turres & id genus cætera, quibus muri defenduntur.

235. *Accingunt.* Supple *se*, ut v. 229. *Insinuat pavor.*

241.) *Divûm domus Ilium.*) Quia murorum structores habuit Neptunum & Apollinem: quia Ganymedem Jovis, Tithonum Auroræ delicias, e stirpe regia protulit. De *Ilio*, Troja, Æ. 1. 5. De *Dardanidis*, Trojanis, Ibid 239.

245 Et monstrum infelix sacratâ sistimus arce.
Tunc etiam fatis aperit Cassandra futuris
Ora, Dei jussu non unquam credita Teucris.
Nos delubra Deum miseri, quibus ultimus esset
Ille dies, festâ velamus fronde per urbem.
250 Vertitur interea cœlum, & ruit Oceano nox,
Involvens umbrâ magnâ terramque polumque,
Myrmidonumque dolos: fusi per mœnia Teucri
Conticuere: sopor fessos complectitur artus.
Et jam Argiva phalanx instructis navibus ibat
255 A Tenedo, tacitæ per amica silentia Lunæ,
Litora nota petens: flammas cum regia puppis
Extulerat; fatisque Deûm defensus iniquis,
Inclusos utero Danaos & pinea furtim
Laxat claustra Sinon: illos patefactus ad auras
260 Reddit equus, lætique cavo se robore promunt.

INTERPRETATIO.

& locamus funestum portentum in sacra arce. Tunc etiam Cassandra solvit in vaticinia futuræ ruinæ *vocem, Phœbi voluntate nunquam creditam à Trojanis. Nos miseri per urbem tegimus festivis ramis templa Deorum, quibus dies ille* futurus *erat extremus. Interim cœlum mutatur: &* nox cadit in Oceanum,*tegens magnis umbris & terram & cœlum, & fraudes Græcorum: Trojani sparsi per urbem, siluerunt: somnus tenet lassa membra. Et jam exercitus Græcus armatis navibus proficiscebatur è Tenedo, per opportuna silentia Lunæ tacitæ, accedens ad litora cognita: cum navis regia sustulisset facem; Sinon quoque, protectus voluntate Deorum* nobis *infestâ, aperuit clam lignea claustra, & Græcos* in *alvo clausos: equus apertus effundit eos in aërem: & hilares emittunt se è cavo ligno duces....*

NOTÆ.

246. *Cassandra.*) Priami & Hecubæ filia, quæ cum ab amatore Apolline artem accepisset vaticinandi, nec ei tamen gratiam amoris mutui retulisset: indignatus Deus effecit, ut a Trojanis fides ipsius vaticiniis non haberetur. Nupsit sub extremis illius belli temporibus Chorœbo: captâ urbe, vitiata est ab Ajace Oileï, in ipso Mivervæ templo, & in prædam Agamemnoni cessit; quem cum admoneret sæpe de cavendis Clytemnæstræ insidiis, nec dicto haberet audientem; cum ipso deinde, Ægisthi & Clytemnestræ scelere, in convivio obtruncata est. De *delubris*, supra, v. 225. De *Myrmidonibus*, Achilli subditis, v. 7.

250. *Ruit Oceano nox.*) Sole nimirum in Oceanum, ut fingitur, cadente; consequitur statim nox & post eum præcipitat, *Oceano*, id est, *in Oceanum.* Sicut *it clamor cœlo*, id est, *ad cœlum.*

254. *Argiva phalanx.*) *Phalanx* proprie, Macedonum est agmen pedestre, perpetuo umbonum textu consertum, atque ita juncto impetu in hostes incurrens; unde nomen habet juxta Suidam, a πελάζειν ἄγχι accedere prope. Ex Vegetio habebat hominum octo millia. *Argiva.*] Græca ab *Argis* urbe Peloponnesi, de qua Æ. 1. 289. De *Tenedo*, Hellesponti insula, supra, v. 21.

225. *Silentia Lunæ.*) Ne explices de Luna cum Sole conjuncta, quæ tum dicitur *silens*, quia minime lucet; sed intellige de media & silente nocte, ut explicabimus, v. 340.

Tiſandrus Sthenelusque duces, & dirus Ulyſſes,
Demiſſum lapſi per funem; Athamasque, Thoasque,
Pelidesque Neoptolemus, primusque Machaon,
Et Menelaus, & ipſe doli fabricator Epeus.
265 Invadunt urbem ſumno vinoque ſepultam:
Cæduntur vigiles: portisque patentibus omnes
Accipiunt ſocios, atque agmina conſcia jungunt.
Tempus erat, quo prima quies mortalibus ægris
Incipit, & dono Divum gratiſſima ſerpit.
270 In ſomnis ecce ante oculos mœſtiſſimus Hector
Viſus adeſſe mihi, largosque effundere fletus:

INTERPRETATIO.

Tiſandrus & Sthenelus, & improbus Ulyſſes, deſcendentes per funem dejectum; & Athamas, & Thoas, & Neoptolemus Pelei nepos, & primus Machaon, & Menelaus, & ipſe Epeus architectus doloſi equi. Aggrediuntur urbem impeditam vino ac ſomno: occiduntur excubitores: & apertis portis admittunt omnes ſocios, & conjungunt turmas ejuſdem conſilii participes. Tempus erat, quo primus ſomnus feſſis hominibus ſubit, & Deorum munere gratiſſimus illabitur. Ecce per ſomnum Hector triſtiſſimus viſus eſt mihi adſtare præ oculis, & emittere copioſas lacrymas:

NOTÆ.

261. *Tiſandrus.*] Servius ait eum fuiſſe filium Polynicis, illius, qui de regno Thebano cum fratre Eteocle confligens occidit: ſed hunc Polynicis filium vulgo *Therſandum*, non Tiſandrum vocant. At Servius, *Tiſſandrus* hic legit; Pomponius; *Theſſandrus.*

261. *Stenelus.*] Filius illius Capanei Argivi, qui eodem Thebano bello Polynicem ſecutus occiderat, vel Jovis fulmine, vel Thebanorum lapidatione obrutus.

261. *Duces.*] Non ad Tiſandrum, & Sthenelum dumtaxat, vox illa pertinet; ſed ad Ulyſſem etiam, & Neoptolemum, & alios quos hic appellat

263. *Pelidesque Neoptolemus.*] *Pyrrhus*, Achillis & Deidamiæ filius: *Pyrrhus* dictus a colore capillorum, nam πυῤῥὸς *rufus* eſt: *Neoptolemus*, a νέος *novus*, & πόλεμος *bellum*; quia admodum adoleſcens, ad belli Trojani reliquias perductus eſt: erat enim in fatis abſque aliquo Æacidarum capi Trojam non poſſe. Trojâ captâ Priamum interfecit, Polyxenam Priami filiam ſub Achillis tumulo immolavit, Andromachen Hectoris uxorem ex præda captivam habuit, Moloſſum ex ea ſuſcepit; & cum eam deinde matrimonio junxiſſet Heleno Priami filio, ducturus Hermionem Menelai & Helenæ filiam; ab Oreſte Agamemnonis filio, cui Hermione deſponſata fuerat, in Delphico Apollinis templo interfectus eſt. *Pelides* vocatur, quia *Pelei* nepos, qui Æaci fuit filius, regis in Ægina inſula, & Thetidis maritus.

263. *Primusque Machaon.*) Æſculapii filius, Podalirii frater: uterque medicus inſignis fuit, præcipue ſanandis vulneribus. *Primus*: id eſt, primo loco delapſus per funem: nec obſtat quod Tiſandrus & reliqui ſupra vocati ſint *duces*; erant enim *duces* dignitate ac munere, non deſcendendi ordine.

264. *Menelaus.*] Atrei filius, Agamemnonis frater, Tyndarei Spartani regis gener, ac deinde ſucceſſor; maritus Helenæ, quam cum raptam a Paride fruſtra legationibus a Priamo repetiiſſet, ſociali totius Græciæ bello repetiit, recepitque tandem everſo Trojano regno: & conſcenſâ navi, poſt octavum erroris annum domum rediit.

264. *Epeus.*) Ideo equi lignei fabricator dicitur, quia muralem reperit machinam

Raptatus bigis, ut quondam, aterque cruento
Pulvere, perque pedes trajectus lora tumentes.
Hei mihi, qualis erat! quantum mutatus ab illo
275 Hectore, qui redit exuvias indutus Achillis,
Vel Danaûm Phrygios jaculatus puppibus ignes!
Squalentem barbam, & concretos sanguine crines,
Vulneraque illa gerens, quæ circum plurima muros
Accepit patrios: ultro flens ipse videbar
280 Compellare virum, & mœstas expromere voces:
O lux Dardaniæ! spes ô fidissima Teucrûm!
Quæ tantæ tenuere moræ? quibus Hector ab oris
Expectate venis? ut te post multa tuorum
Funera, post varios hominumque urbisque labores
285 Defessi aspicimus? quæ causa indigna serenos
Fœdavit vultus? aut cur hæc vulnera cerno?
Ille nihil: nec me quærentem vana moratur;
Sed graviter gemitus imo de pectore ducens:
Heu fuge, nate Dea, teque his (ait) eripe flammis.
290 Hostis habet muros, ruit alto à culmine Troja:
Sat patriæ Priamoque datum: si Pergama dextrâ

INTERPRETATIO.

tractus equis, ut olim, & niger sanguineo pulvere, & transfossus loris per pedes tumidos. Hei mihi, qualis erat! quam diversus ab illo Hectore, qui rediit ornatus spoliis Achillis, vel cum injecisset ignes Trojanos in naves Græcorum! habens barbam sordidam, & capillos cohærentes sanguine, & plagas illas, quas multas accepit circa muros patriæ. Ego plorans videbar primus alloqui virum, & emittere hæc *tristia verba*: O *lumen Trojæ! ô spes firmissima Trojanorum! quæ tam longa mora te detinuit? ô Hector optate, quibus e regionibus venis? quomodo te videmus lassi, post multas neces tuorum, post diversos & urbis & civium labores? quæ causa indigna maculavit pulchram faciem? aut quare video has plagas? Ille nihil* ad hæc dixit, *nec* responsis *detinet me petentem inutilia: sed ægre trahens gemitus ex intimo pectore: Heu! fuge, fili Veneris, & te, inquit, subtrahe huic incendio. Hostis tenet urbem, cadit ab alto vertice Troja: satisfecimus patriæ & Priamo: Si Troja manu* aliquâ....

NOTÆ.

quæ vocatur etiam *aries*, ex Plin. lib. 7. 56.

272. *Raptatus bigis.*] De *Hectore* bigis raptato, Æn. 1. 487. De *bigis*, & quadrigis, duobus & quatuor equis, sub eodem jugo conjunctis, G. 1. 512.

275. *Exuvias Achillis, &c.*] Cum nempe Achilles è Græcorum castris recessisset, offensus Agamemnoni ob ereptam sibi Briseïda: territi navium incendio Græci, frustra precibus Achillem tentaverunt. Patroclus imprimis, ipsi carissimus; qui cum ad reditum impellere eum non posset, rogavit, sua sibi saltem arma militesque suos concederet, quibus, Trojanis metum incuteret. Concessit Achilles: at Patroclus, Achillis armis indutus, ab Hectore occisus est. Igitur per *Achillis exuvias*, Achillis arma intellige; non Achilli quidem, sed Patroclo direpta. Ita Homerus Iliad. 15. sub finem, & 16.

291. *Pergama, orum.*] Arx Trojæ. Æ. 1. 470.

Defendi possent, etiam hac defensa fuissent.
Sacra suosque tibi commendat Troja Penates:
Hos cape fatorum comites: his mœnia quære,
295 Magna pererrato statues quæ denique ponto.
Sic ait, & manibus vittas, Vestamque potentem,
Æternumque adytis effert penetralibus ignem.
Diverso interea miscentur mœnia luctu:
Et magis atque magis (quanquam secreta parentis
300 Anchisæ domus, arboribusque obtecta recessit)
Clarescunt sonitus, armorumque ingruit horror.
Excutior somno, & summi fastigia tecti
Ascensu supero, atque arrectis auribus asto.
In segetem veluti cum flamma furentibus Austris
305 Incidit; aut rapidus montano flumine torrens
Sternit agros, sternit sata læta boumque labores,
Præcipitesque trahit sylvas: stupet inscius alto
Accipiens sonitum saxi de vertice pastor.
Tum vero manifesta fides, Danaûmque patescunt
310 Insidiæ: jam Deiphobi dedit ampla ruinam,

INTERPRETATIO.

servari posset, hac meâ etiam fuisset servata. Troja committit tibi sua *sacra, & suos Deos: accipe hos casuum* tuorum *socios, quære illis urbem, quam tandem magnam condes pererrato mari. Sic locutus est; & manibus exportat ex adytis intimis infulas, & potentem Vestam, & ignem inextinctum. Interim urbs turbatur variis miseriis: & quamvis domus patris Anchisæ separata, & cincta arboribus submoveatur; magis & magis auditur sonus, & horror armorum imminet. Excitor è somno, & ascendens supergredior summum culmen tecti, & sto attentis auribus. Sicut quando ignis ventis sævientibus cecidit in segetem; aut* quando *præceps torrens montanis undis vastat agros, vastat segetes fertiles & labores boum, & rapit arbores in præceps: tunc pastor ignarus obstupescit audiens sonum ex alto cacumine rupis. Tunc vero clara* fuit *veritas* verborum Hectoris, *& apparent fraudes Græcorum. Jam domus magna Deiphobi fecit ruinam.*

NOTÆ.

293. *Sacra, suosque, &c.*] Per *sacra*, res eas intelligit, quæ ad ceremonias Deorum pertinebant; ut vittæ, infulæ, de quibus supra, v. 133. Pepla, de quibus Æ. 1. 484. Per *Penates*, Deorum domesticorum simulacra, de quibus infra, v. 717. Per *Vestam*, vel unum ex illis Penatium simulacris, vel ignem ipsum æternum: ait enim Ovid. Fast. 6. 291. *Nec tu aliud Vestam, quam vivam intellige flammam.* Per *ignem perpetuum*, ignem inextinctum: qui, si aliquando extingueretur; non alio igne, sed admotis Soli fomitibus ipso Solis calore excitandus erat. De hoc, deque *Vesta*, Georgicorum 1. 498.

297. *Adytis effert.*] Vel reipsa effert, vel in somnis videtur efferre. Effert autem in Æneæ domum, è templo quod erat in arce; & cum iis imperium a Priamo in Æneam transfert. Cultum porro ignis acceperant Phryges & Græci ab orientalibus populis, præcipue Persis; quibus ob usus maximos dignus Divinitate visus est, & perpetuâ custodiâ. *Adyta.*] Sunt intimæ partes domorum templorumque, in quas intrare nefas est, ab α privativo, & δύω ingredior. De *penetralibus*, in voce *penus*, Æ. 1. 708. De *Austris*, ventis meridionalibus. Ecl. 2. 58.

310. *Deiphobi.*] Priami filius fuit, qui

READING 4-C

GAIVS IVRISPERITVS
[110–180 CE]

INSTITUTIONES

[I. De ivre civili et natvrali.] 1. *Omnes populi qui legibus et moribus reguntur, partim suo proprio, partim communi omnium hominum iure utuntur; nam quod quisque* populus ipse sibi ius constituit, id ipsius proprium est uocaturque ius ciuile, quasi ius proprium ciuitatis; quod uero naturalis ratio inter omnes homines constituit, id apud omnes populos peraeque custoditur uocaturque ius gentium, quasi quo iure omnes gentes utuntur. Populus itaque Romanus partim suo proprio, partim communi omnium hominum iure utitur. Quae singula qualia sint, suis locis proponemus.

2. Constant autem iura populi Romani ex legibus, plebiscitis, senatusconsultis, constitutionibus principum, edictis eorum qui ius edicendi habent, responsis prudentium.

3. Lex est quod populus iubet atque constituit. Plebiscitum est quod plebs iubet atque constituit. Plebs autem a populo eo distat, quod populi appellatione uniuersi ciues significantur connumeratis etiam patriciis; plebis autem appellatione sine patriciis ceteri ciues significantur; unde olim patricii dicebant plebiscitis se non teneri, quia sine auctoritate eorum facta essent; sed postea lex Hortensia lata est, qua cautum est ut plebiscita uniuersum populum tenerent; itaque eo modo legibus exaequata sunt. 4. Senatusconsultum est quod senatus iubet atque constituit, idque legis uicem optinet, quamuis fuerit quaesitum. 5. Constitutio principis est quod imperator decreto uel edicto uel epistula constituit. Nec umquam dubitatum est, quin id legis uicem optineat, cum ipse imperator per legem imperium accipiat. 6. <*Edicta sunt praecepta eorum, qui ius edicenti habent*>. Ius autem edicendi habent magistratus populi Romani; sed amplissimum ius est in edictis duorum praetorum, urbani et peregrini, quorum in prouinciis iurisdictionem praesides earum habent; item in edictis aedilium curulium, quorum iurisdictionem in prouinciis populi Romani quaestores habent; nam in prouincias Caesaris omnino quaestores non mittuntur, et ob id hoc edictum in his prouinciis non proponitur. 7. Responsa prudentium sunt sententiae et opiniones eorum, quibus permissum est iura condere. Quorum omnium si in unum sententiae concurrunt, id quod ita sentiunt, legis uicem optinet; si uero dissentiunt, iudici licet quam uelit sententiam sequi; idque rescripto diui Hadriani significatur.

[II. De ivris divisione.] 8. Omne autem ius quo utimur, uel ad personas pertinet uel ad res uel ad actiones. Et prius uideamus de personis.

[III. DE CONDICIONE HOMINVM.] 9. Et quidem summa diuisio de iure personarum haec est, quod omnes homines aut liberi sunt aut serui. 10. Rursus liberorum hominum alii ingenui sunt, alii libertini. 11. Ingenui sunt qui liberi nati sunt; libertini, qui ex iusta seruitute manumissi sunt. 12. Rursus libertinorum <*tria sunt genera; nam aut ciues Romani aut Latini aut dediticiorum*> numero sunt. De quibus singulis dispiciamus; ac prius de dediticiis.

[IV. DE DEDITICIIS VEL LEGE AELIA SENTIA.] 13. Lege itaque Aelia Sentia cauetur, ut qui serui a dominis poenae nomine uincti sint, quibusue stigmata inscripta sint, deue quibus ob noxam quacstio tormentis habita sit et in ea noxa fuisse conuicti sint, quiue ut ferro aut cum bestiis depugnarent traditi sint, inue ludum custodiamue coniecti fuerint, et postea uel ab eodem domino uel ab alio manumissi, eiusdem condicionis liberi fiant, cuius condicionis sunt peregrini dediticii.

[...]

58. *Non tamen omnes nobis uxores ducere licet;* nam a quarundam nuptiis abstinere debemus. 59. Inter eas enim personas quae parentum liberorumue locum inter se optinent, nuptiae contrahi non possunt, nec inter eas conubium est, ueluti inter patrem et filiam, uel inter matrem et filium, uel inter auum et neptem; et si tales personae inter se coierint, nefarias et incestas nuptias contraxisse dicuntur. Et haec adeo ita sunt, ut quamuis per adoptionem parentum liberorumue loco sibi esse coeperint, non possint inter se matrimonio coniungi, in tantum, ut etiam dissoluta adoptione idem iuris maneat; itaque eam, quae mihi per adoptionem filiae aut neptis loco esse coeperit, non potero uxorem ducere, quamuis eam emancipauerim. 60. Inter eas quoque personas quae ex transuerso gradu cognatione iunguntur, est quaedam similis obseruatio, sed non tanta. 61. Sane inter fratrem et sororem prohibitae sunt nuptiae, siue eodem patre eademque matre nati fuerint, siue alterutro eorum: sed si qua per adoptionem soror mihi esse coeperit, quamdiu quidem constat adoptio, sane inter me et eam nuptiae non possunt consistere; cum uero per emancipationem adoptio dissoluta sit, potero eam uxorem ducere; sed et si ego emancipatus fuero, nihil inpedimento erit nuptiis. 62. Fratris filiam uxorem ducere licet, idque primum in usum uenit, cum diuus Claudius Agrippinam fratris sui filiam uxorem duxisset; sororis uero filiam uxorem ducere non licet. Et haec ita principalibus constitutionibus significantur. 63. Item amitam et materteram uxorem ducere non licet. Item eam quae mihi quondam socrus aut nurus aut priuigna aut nouerca fuit. Ideo autem diximus « quondam», quia si adhuc constant eae nuptiae, per quas talis adfinitas quaesita est, alia ratione mihi nupta esse non potest, quia neque eadem duobus nupta esse potest, neque idem duas uxores habere. 64. Ergo si quis nefarias atque incestas nuptias contraxerit, neque uxorem habere uidetur neque liberos; itaque hi qui ex eo coitu nascuntur matrem quidem habere uidentur, patrem uero non utique: nec ob id in potestate eius <*sunt, sed tales*> sunt quales sunt hi, quos mater uulgo concepit; nam et hi patrem habere non intelleguntur,

cum is *etiam* incertus sit; unde solent spurii filii appellari, uel a Graeca uoce qausi σποράδην concepti, uel quasi sine patre filii.

65. *Aliquando autem euenit, ut liberi qui statim ut nati* sunt parentum in potestate non fiant, ii postea tamen redigantur in potestatem. 66. *Veluti si Latinus* ex lege Aelia Sentia uxore ducta filium procreauerit aut Latinum ex Latina aut ciuem Romanum ex ciue Romana, non habebit eum in potestate; *sed si postea causa probata ius <Quritium> consecutus fuerit,* simul eum in potestate sua habere incipit. 67. Item si ciuis Romanus Latinam aut peregrinam uxorem duxerit per ignorantiam, cum earn ciuem Romanam esse crederet, et filium procreauerit, hic non est in potestate eius, quia ne quidem ciuis Romanus est, sed aut Latinus aut peregrinus, id est eius condicionis cuius et mater fuerit, quia non aliter quisque ad patris condicionem accedit, quam si inter patrem et matrem eius conubium sit; sed ex senatusconsulto permittitur causam erroris probare, et ita uxor quoque et filius ad ciuitatem Romanam perueniunt, et ex eo tempore incipit filius in potestate patris esse. Idem iuris est, si earn per ignorantiam uxorem duxerit quae dediticiorum numero est, nisi quod uxor non fit ciuis Romana. 68. Item si ciuis Romana per errorem nupta sit peregrino tamquam ciui Romano, permittitur ei causam erroris probare, et ita filius quoque eius et maritus ad ciuitatem Romanam perueniunt, et aeque simul incipit filius in potestate patris esse. Idem iuris est, si peregrino tamquam Latino ex lege Aelia Sentia nupta sit; nam et de hoc specialiter senatusconsulto cauetur. Idem iuris est aliquatenus, si ei qui dediticiorum numero est tamquam ciui Romano aut Latino e lege Aelia Sentia nupta sit; nisi quod scilicet qui dediticiorum numero est, in sua condicione permanet, et ideo filius, quamuis fiat ciuis Romanus, in potestatem patris non redigitur. 69. Item si Latina peregrino, cum eum Latinum esse crederet, *<e lege Aelia Sentia>* nupserit, potest ex senatusconsulto filio nato causam erroris probare, *et ita* omnes fiunt ciues Romani, et filius in potestate patris esse incipit. 70. Idem constitutum est, si Latinus per errorem peregrinam quasi Latinam aut ciuem Romanam e lege Aelia Sentia uxorem duxerit. 71. Praeterea si ciuis Romanus, qui se credidisset Latinum esse, ob id Latinam *<uxorem duxerit>*, permittitur *ei* filio nato erroris causam probare, tamquam *<si>* e lege Aelia Sentia uxorem duxisset. Item his, qui cum ciues Romani essent, peregrinos se esse credidissent et peregrinas uxores duxissent, permittitur ex senatusconsulto filio nato causam erroris probare; quo facto fiet uxor ciuis Romana et filius non solum ad ciuitatem Romanam peruenit, sed etiam in potestatem patris redigitur. 72. Quaecumque de filio esse diximus, eadem et de filia dicta intellegemus.

[...]

183. Furtorum autem genera Ser. Sulpicius et Masurius Sabinus IIII esse dixerunt, manifestum et nec manifestum, conceptum et oblatum; Labeo duo, manifestum *<et>* nec manifestum; nam conceptum et oblatum species potius actionis esse furto cohaerentes quam genera furtorum; quod sane uerius uidetur, sicut inferius apparebit. 184. Manifestum furtum quidam

id esse dixerunt, quod dum fit deprehenditur. Alii uero ulterius, quod eo loco deprehenditur, ubi fit, ueluti si in oliueto oliuarum, in uineto uuarum furtum factum est, quamdiu in eo oliueto aut uineto fur sit; aut si in domo furtum factum sit, quamdiu in ea domo fur sit. Alii adhuc ulterius eo usque manifestum furtum esse dixerunt, donec perferret eo, quo perferre fur destinasset. Alii adhuc ulterius, quandoque eam rem fur tenens uisus fuerit; quae sententia non optinuit. Sed et illorum sententia, qui existimauerunt, donec perferret eo quo fur destinasset, deprehensum furtum manifestum esse, ideo non uidetur probari, quia magnam recipit dubitationem, utrum unius diei an etiam plurium dierum spatio id terminandum sit. Quod eo pertinet, quia saepe in aliis ciuitatibus subreptas res in alias ciuitates uel in alias prouincias destinant fures perferre. Ex duabus itaque superioribus opinionibus alterutra adprobatur; magis tamen plerique posteriorem probant. 185. Nec manifestum furtum quid sit, ex iis quae diximus intellegitur. Nam *quod* manifestum non est, id nec manifestum est. 186. Conceptum furtum dicitur, cum apud aliquem testibus praesentibus furtiva res quaesita et inuenta sit. Nam in eum propria actio constituta est, quamuis fur non sit, quae appellatur concepti. 187. Oblatum furtum dicitur, cum res furtiua tibi ab aliquo oblata sit eaque apud te concepta sit; utique si ea mente data tibi fuerit, ut apud te potius quam apud eum qui dederit conciperetur. Nam tibi, apud quem concepta est, propria aduersus eum qui optulit, quamuis fur non sit, constituta est actio, <*quae*> appellatur oblati. 188. Est etiam prohibiti furti <*actio*> aduersus eum qui furtum quaerere uolentem prohibuerit.

READING 4-D

LATINARVM COMPOSITIO SCRIPTIONVM

arranging of Latin sentences

[200 BCE–2001 CE]

... novum nexuísti cum tuo pópulo testaméntum,
ut, quem mortis et resurrectiónis redemísses mystério,
divínæ in Christo fáceres natúræ consórtem
eiúsque in cælis glóriæ coherédem.
Cuius piíssimam grátiæ largitátem
in viri mulierísque significásti connúbio,
ut ad ineffábile tui amóris consílium
nos revocáret quod ágitur sacraméntum.

MISSALE ROMANVM PAVLI VI [1977 CE]

Sancta mater, istud agas,
Crucifíxi fige plagas
cordi meo válide.

Tui Nati vulneráti
tam dignáti pro me pati
pœnas mecum dívide.

Fac me vere tecum flere
Crucifíxo condolére,
donec ego víxero.

Iuxta crucem tecum stare,
ac me tibi sociáre
in planctu desídero.

Virgo vírginum præclára,
mihi iam non sis amára,
fac me tecum plángere.

Fac ut portem Christi mortem,
passiónis fac me sortem
et plagas recólere.

IACOPVS TVDERTINVS [1230–1306 CE]

KEY:
Subjects
Objects
Verbs
Distant connections
[Larger clauses]
(Lesser clauses)
et and -que

Ne hoc quidem negaverim, sequi plerumque hanc opinionem, ut fortius dicere videantur indocti, primum vitio male iudicantium, [qui maiorem habere vim credunt ea, (quae non habent artem,) ut effringere quam aperire, rumpere quam solvere, trahere quam ducere putant robustius]. [nam et gladiator, (qui armorum inscius in rixam ruit, et luctator, qui totius corporis nisu in id, quod semel invasit, incumbit,) fortior ab his vocatur, (cum interim et hic frequenter suis viribus ipse prosternitur et illum vehementis impetus excipit adversarii mollis articulus). sed sunt in hac parte, quae imperitos etiam naturaliter fallant]; nam et divisio, cum plurimum valeat in causis, speciem virium minuit, et rudia politis maiora et sparsa compositis numerosiora creduntur. [est praeterea quaedam virtutum vitiorumque vicinia, qua maledicus pro libero, temerarius pro forti, effusus pro copioso accipitur].

MARCVS FABIVS QVINTILIANVS [35–95 CE]

... Quid igitur? Solitariam vitam reprehendimus? Minime; quippe quam saepe laudavimus. Sed de ludo monasteriorum huiuscemodi volumus egredi milites, quos rudimenta non terreant; qui specimen conversationis suae multo tempore dederint; qui omnium fuerunt minimi, ut primi omnium fierent; quos nec esuries nec saturitas aliquando superavit; qui paupertate laetantur; quorum habitus, sermo, vultus, incessus doctrina virtutum est; qui nesciunt, secundum quosdam ineptos homines, daemonum oppugnantium contra se portenta confingere, ut apud imperitos et vulgi homines miraculum sui faciant et exinde sectantur lucra.

EVSEBIVS HIERONYMVS [342–420 CE]

Non est cogitatu impossibile, divina potentia fieri posse, ut a corpore animato dividatur anima intellectiva, et ipsum adhuc maneat animale; maneret nempe in ipso, tamquam basis puri animalis, principium animale, quod antea in eo erat veluti appendix.

PONTIFEX LEO XIII; S. CONGR. S.R.V. INQVISITIONIS [1887 CE]

KEY:

Subjects	[Larger clauses]
Objects	(Lesser clauses)
Verbs	et and -que
Distant connections	

MVLTA prius dominae delicta queraris oportet,
saepe roges aliquid, saepe repulsus eas,
et saepe immeritos corrumpas dentibus unguis,
et crepitum dubio suscitet ira pede!
nequiquam perfusa meis unguenta capillis,
ibat et expenso planta morata gradu.

SEXTVS PROPERTIVS [50–16 BCE]

Multa ad fidem catholicam pertinentia, dum haereticorum cal[l]ida inquietudine exagitantur, ut adversus eos defendi possint, et considerantur diligentius et intelleguntur clarius et instantius praedicantur et ab adversario mota quaestio discendi exsistit occasio.

AVRELIVS AVGVSTINVS [354–430 CE]

KEY: Subjects are underlined with a solid line.
Objects are underlined with a broken line.
Verbs are underlined with a line of dots.
Distant connections of words and phrases are underlined with a wavey line.
[Larger clauses are in square brackets,] (lesser ones in rounded parentheses.)
The words et and -que are placed in boxes.
Note: This code is used to illustrate the functions and connections of words as an aid to teaching, and is not intended to appear in absolutely every instance.

READING 4-E

MAXIMVS TAVRINENSIS
[died 408–423 CE]

SERMONES

DE SANCTA EPYFANIA.

(Dies natalis domini cum epiphania comparatur)
1. Intellegere possumus, quantam gratiam Christo domino debeamus, quia uota uotis adcumulat gaudiis gaudia nostra multiplicat. Ecce enim adhuc exultamus natum saluatorem, et iam eum laetamur renatum; necdum ortus eius est expleta festiuitas, et iam eius baptismatis est celebranda solemnitas; uix natus est hominibus, et iam renatus est sacramentis. Hodie enim — licet post multa annorum curricula — consecratus est in Iordane. Ita ergo disposuit dominus, ut uotis uota subiungeret, hoc est ut uno eodemque tempore et ederetur per uirginem et per mysterium gigneretur, essetque natiuitatum continuata festiuitas carnis atque baptismatis, ut quemadmodum tunc mirabamur eum inpolluta matre conceptum, ita et nunc suspiciamus illum pura unda submersum, et gloriemur in utroque facto, quia filium genuit mater et casta est, quia Christum unda lauit et sancta est. Nam sicut post partum glorificata est Mariae castificatio, ita et post baptismum aquae est purificatio conprobata, nisi quod maiore munere quam Maria unda ditata est. Illa enim sibi tantum meruit castitatem, ista etiam nobis contulit sanctitatem; illa meruit ne peccaret, ista ut peccata purgaret; illa propria delicta a se repulit, ista in se aliena condonat ; illi est conlata uirginitas, isti donata fecunditas; illa unum procreauit et pura est, ista generat plures et uirgo est; illa praeter Christum filium nescit, ista cum Christo mater est populorum.

(Epiphania alter natalis est domini)
2. Natalis ergo hodie alter est quodammodo saluatoris. Nam isdem eum signis isdem miraculis uidemus genitum sed maiore mysterio. Denique spiritus sanctus, qui tunc adfuit illi in utero, modo eum circumfulsit in gurgite ; qui tunc castificauit illi Mariam, modo illi fluenta sanctificat. Pater qui tunc obumbrauit in uirtute, nunc clamat in uoce; et quasi maturiore consilio qui tunc umbram praestitit natiuitati, modo testimonium perhibet ueritati. Ait enim deus: *Hic est filius meus dilectus, in quo bene conplacui; ipsum audite.* Praeclarior plane est secunda quam prima natiuitas. Illa enim sine teste silentio Christum genuit, ista cum diuinitatis professione gloriose dominum baptizauit; ab illa se Ioseph qui pater putabatur excusat, in hac se deus pater qui non credebatur insinuat; ibi laborat suspicionibus mater

quia professioni deerat pater, hic honoratur genetrix quia diuinitas filium protestatur. Honoratior, inquam, secunda quam prima natiuitas, siquidem pater hic deus maiestatis inscribitur, illic Ioseph artifex aestimatur; et licet in utraque dominus per spiritum sanctum et natus sit et baptizatus, tamen honoratior est quae de caelis clamat quam quae in terris laborat. Ioseph ergo faber pater putabatur esse domini, nec ab hoc deus, qui uere est pater saluatoris, excluditur; nam est et ipse faber. Ipse enim artifex huius mundi machinam fabricatus est, tamquam sapiens architectus caelum sublimitate suspendit terram mole fundauit maria calculis alligauit. Ipse est artifex qui ad mensuram quandam superbiae deponit fastigia humilitatis extrema sublimat; ipse est artifex qui in nostris moribus recidit superflua opera utilia quaeque conservat; ipse est artifex cuius securim ad radicem nostram positam Iohannes baptista conminatur, ut arbor quae normam iustam excesserit excisa radicitus tradatur incendio, quae autem mensuram ueritatis habuerit caelesti fabricae deputetur.

(Cum saluator in aqua mersit, omnes fontes consecrauit).
3. Hodie ergo baptizatur in Iordane. Quale hoc est baptismum, ubi purior ipso est fonte ille qui mergitur? ubi dum susceptum aqua diluit, non sordibus inficitur sed benedictionibus honoratur? Quale, inquam, saluatoris baptismum est, in quo purgantur magis fluenta quam purgant? Nouo enim sanctificationis genere Christum non tam lauit unda quam lota est. Nam ex quo saluator in aqua mersit, ex eo omnium gurgitum tractus cunctorum fontium uenas mysterio baptismatis consecrauit, ut quisque, ubi in nomine domini baptizari uoluerit, non illum mundi aqua diluat sed Christi unda purificet. Saluator autem ideo baptizari uoluit, non ut sibi munditiam adquireret, sed ut nobis fluenta mundaret.

DE HOSPITALITATE IN EVANGELIO.

(Quid dominus de hospilitate præscripserit.)
1. Aduertit sanctitas uestra, fratres, euangelicam lectionem, quemadmodum dominus discipulis suis inter ceteras exsequendas uirtutes etiam hospitalitatis iura praescripserit; ait enim: *In quacumque ciuitate introieritis, interrogate quis in ea dignus est, et ibi manete donec exeatis* et reliqua. Sancta plane et diuina sententia, quae et discipulis eligendi optionem primitus detulit et facilitatem penitus amputauit. Prouidit enim modum statuendo, ne uir sanctus aut citus esset in iudicando aut leuis in hospite conmutando. Sicut enim nobis permisit arbitrium, ita et uoluit nos tenere constantiam. Quam enim repraehensibile est, ut uir qui euangelium adnuntiat et docet errandum non esse ipse per diuersos incipiat oberrare, et domum cui pacem dixerit deserere, hospitem cui benedictionem intulerat contristare. Magna enim hospitalitatis est gratia nec facile uiolanda; omnibus aperta est, omnibus parata est, et sanctos libenter suscipit et peccatores tolerat patienter.

(Hospes et domus in mysterio Christus et ecclesia sunt)
2. Sed repetamus sanctam ipsam diuinamque sententiam! Si enim in littera placet, in mysterio forsitan plus placebit. Ait igitur, ut cum intramus in ciuitatem, interrogemus quis in ea uel hospes dignus uel idonea domus sit, et ibi maneamus, donec dies profectionis adueniat. Quae sententia altiorem nobis tribuit intellectum. Non enim mihi uidetur de huius saeculi hospite uel domo iussisse nos tam diligenter inquirere, sed de illo magis qui nos usque ad diem exitus nostri possit inoffensus hospes inlaesusque seruare. Nam huius saeculi hospitem cito laedimus cito offendimus, interdum ei et post triduum displicemus. Fidelis igitur domus et dignus hospes inquiri iussus est. Quae domus fidelior ecclesiae? Quis hospes dignior saluatore? Iste peregrinos ut filios suscipit, illa susceptos refouet ut infantes; iste hospitibus, sicut experti sumus, pedes lauare gestit, illa mensam parare festinat. Quos enim saluator uiua aqua refrigerat, hos reficit caelestibus cibis ecclesia. Hunc igitur hospitem euangelista inquiri iussit, et usque ad diem exitus nostri cum hoc habitare praecepit, ne [si] aliqua leuitate medio tempore aliorsum forsitan emigremus; hoc est ut qui semel in Christum credidimus, non iterum uelut transgressores ad idola recurramus. Scriptum est enim: *Nemo potest duobus dominis seruire.* Dum enim uni placer gestit, alterum sentit iratum. Christum igitur hospitem deserere non debemus, quemadmodum et Petrus apostolus cum suis similibus deserentibus aliis dominum non reliquit, sed dicamus quod ille ad saluatorem dixit: *Domine, ad quem ibimus? Verba uitae aeternae tu habes et nos credimus.* Ecce exsecutorem caelestium praeceptorum, qui quoniam Christi non mutauit hospitium, meruit cum Christo regni caelestis habere consortium!

DE MARGARITA EVANGELII.

(Margarita Christus est dominus)
1. Satis ad correptionem uestram arbitror posse sufficere, fratres dilecti, quod anteriori dominica profecturus nulla uobis sacrarum litterarum spiritalia dona largitus sim, sed tantum uos increpans et arguens pro peccato sine aliqua praedicationis consolatione dimiserim. Volui enim uos hoc ipsum intellegere, quam grauiter peccaueritis, cum diuina eloquia audire minime meruistis. Haec enim sacerdotum uehemens et copiosa uindicta est indignis quibusque scripturarum caelestium sacramenta non credere, nec, sicut ait dominus, dare sanctum canibus neque margaritas proicere porcorum pedibus inculcandas. Perdit enim caelestis margaritae gratiam, quisque eam foedissimo peccatori circumdare conatur. Gemma enim, sicut ipsi scitis, nisi auro non conuenit; margarita nisi pretiosis monilibus non aptatur. Estote ergo aurum optimum! Estote monile pretiosum, ut possit in uobis margarita spiritalis includi! Margarita enim Christus est dominus, quam negotiator ille diues in euangelio uenditis omnibus bonis suis emere festinauit; et maluit omnes quas habebat saeculi gemmas amittere, tantum ut unam Christi emeret margaritam.

(Increpantur ei, qui natalem Petri et Pauli celebrare noluerunt)
2. Vnde et ego, fratres, pro magnitudine quod admiseratis delicti nolui uobis pandere euangelicae refectionis eloquia, sed magis ingerere animosae indignationis iniuriam; et prius uos uerberibus spiritalibus emendare, ac sic margaritae ditare muneribus. Malui, inquam, peccatum uestrum incusando acriter increpare quam leniter dissimulando nutrire. Quisque enim fratrem non arguit peccantem quodammodo hortatur ut peccet. Nolo autem putetis quod non de amore faciam uos saepius uerberando; filius enim qui castigatione dignus est plus amatur, sicut ait scriptura: *Quem enim diligit dominus corripit; castigat autem omnem filium quem recipit.* Dicite enim mihi, si non dolendum fuerit hoc peccatum sic uos salutis uestrae inmemores tunc fuisse, ut beatissimis apostolis Petro et Paulo honorificentiam minime redderetis, cum ipsos esse sciatis doctores gentium auctores martyrum principes sacerdotum, nec uolueritis eorum natalem nobiscum festiuissimum celebrare atque illi caelesti interesse conuiuio, in quo pro martyrum suorum tanta laetitia substantiam uitae ipse nobis dominus ministrauit! Vultis autem scire, quantis bonis fraudati fueritis? Interrogate fratres qui tunc temporis mecum pariter adfuerunt, quam refecti a dominica mensa discesserint, uel quales secum domum spiritales diuitias reportarint! Vnum scio quod, si quis illa die honoratus et diues ob natalem filii sui ad decimum usque miliarium ad prandium rogauisset, propter accuratas epulas et inaequales mensuras absque dubio uos ituros fuisse.

(admonentur, martyrum memoriam celebrent)
3. Igitur, fratres, quotienscumque martyrum memoriam celebramus, praetermissis omnibus saeculi actibus sine aliqua dilatione concurrere debemus, reddere illis honorificentiam qui nobis salutem profusione sui sanguinis pepererunt; qui tamquam sacrata hostia pro nostra propitiatione domino sunt oblati, praesertim cum dicat ad sanctos suos omnipotens deus: *Qui uos honorat, me honorat; et qui uos spernit, me spernit.* Quisque ergo honorat martyres, honorat et Christum; et qui spernit sanctos, spernit et deum.

DE PASCHA.

1. Non inmerito, fratres, hodierna die psalmus hic legitur, in quo propheta exultandum praecipit et laetandum; omnes enim creaturas ad huius diei festiuitatem Dauid sanctus inuitat. Nam in hac die per resurrectionem Christi aperitur tartarum, per neophytos ecclesiae innouatur terra, caelum per sanctum spiritum reseratur; apertum enim tartarum reddit mortuos, innouata terra germinat resurgentes, caelum reseratum suscipit ascendentes. Denique ascendit latro in paradysum, sanctorum corpora ingrediuntur in sanctam ciuitatem, ad uiuos mortui reuertuntur; et profectu quodam in resurrectione Christi ad altiora cuncta elementa se

tollunt. Tartarum quos habet reddit ad superos, terra quos sepelit mittit ad caelum, caelum quos suscipit repraesentat ad dominum; et una eademque operatione saluatoris passio eleuat de imis suscitat de terrenis collocat in excelsis. Resurrectio enim Christi defunctis est uita peccatoribus uenia sanctis est gloria. Omnem ergo creaturam ad festiuitatem resurrectionis Christi Dauid sanctus inuitat; ait enim exultandum in hac die quam fecit dominus et laetandum.

2. Sed dicit aliquis: 'Si in die gratulandum est, his utique gratulandum est quos dies ipsa conplectitur; caelum autem et tartarum extra huius mundi diem sunt constituta. Quomodo igitur possunt ea aelementa ad festiuitatem huius diei uocari, cuius diei ambitu non tenentur?' Sed hic dies quem fecit dominus penetrat omnia uniuersa continet caelum terram tartarumque conplectitur. Lux enim Christi non parietibus obstruitur non aelementis diuiditur non tenebris obscuratur. Lux, inquam, Christi dies est sine nocte dies sine fine; ubique splendet ubique radiat ubique non deficit. Quod autem iste dies Christus sit, apostolus dicit: *Nox praecessit, dies autem appropinquauit.*

READING 4-F

ANSELMVS CANTVARIENSIS

[1033–1109 CE]

EPISTOLAE

AD MONIALEM M. FILIAM RICARDI

Anselmus, vocatus archiepiscopus: filiae suae carissimae M., filiae Ricardi, sponso suo Christo corde semper adhaerere et operibus oboedire.

Dulce mihi est, filia dulcissima, aliquid specialiter sanctae dulcedini tuae paterno affectu scribere, quia, quamvis te inter alias sanctas sorores tuas ut ancillam et sponsam domini mei diligam, cognosco tamen quod aliquid tibi propter amicitiam parentum tuorum plus debeam.

Legisti, carissima, quia « multi sunt vocati, pauci vero electi. » Tene igitur hanc parvam admonitionem patris tui in deo te vere diligentis, filia, ut numquam confidas te certissime esse in numero electorum, nisi certissime videris ad tantam sanctitatem profecisse, ut vere sis in numero paucorum; et cum te videris in numero paucorum, nondum secura sis, quia adhuc nescis si de illis paucis qui electi sunt sis. Qui enim dicit quia « pauci » sunt « electi », non dicit quam pauci sint. Numquam ergo secura sis, donec te videas de illis paucis, de quibus nulla est dubitatio, qualis fuit beata Agnes vel Scholastica et alii sancti viri et mulieres, quos iam in caelo cum Christo gaudere cognoscimus. Nullus igitur, filia dulcissima, virtutum profectus cordi tuo sufficiat, quin semper ad maiora proficere studeat. Nullus enim potest vitare defectum, nisi qui se semper extendit ad profectum.

Omnipotens dominus sic te sua gratia repleat, ut ad firmissimum culmen virtutum te provehat et in thalamum suae gloriae introducat. Ora pro me, dilectore tuo, filia dilectissima, ut me deus dirigat et consoletur.

AD MATHILDAM REGINAM ANGLORUM

Mathildae, gloriosae reginae Anglorum, reverendae dominae, filiae carissimae: Anselmus archiepiscopus, debitum honorem, servitium, orationes et benedictionem dei et suam, quantum potest.

Gratias magnas ago vestrae largitioni, sed multo maiores, de qua munera procedunt, sanctae dilectioni. Quae etiam mihi pia sollicitudine instat, ut in alimentis sumendis corpori largius indulgeam, ne vox et vires ad curam iniunctam mihi deficiant. Nam quoniam auditis me pro ieiunio totius diei, etiam si cotidie fieret, famem non sentire, timetis raucitatem et imbecillitatem mihi corporis evenire. Sed utinam tantum mihi sapientia et potestas quae competit suppeterent, quantum vox et vires quas habeo, ad opus mihi iniunctum sufficerent! Licet enim sic possim sine famis molestia ieiunare, satis tamen possum et volo, cum debeo, quantum expedit corpus alimentis recreare.

Memor est benigna vestra dignatio in epistola sua quod per me sit vestra celsitudo in coniugium legitimum desponsata et ad regni sublimitatem me sacrante coronata. Verum cum de me, qui huius rei minister tantum fidelis, quantum in me fuit, exstiti, hoc tam benigne, tanta gratia recolitis: satis aestimari potest quantas Christo, qui huius doni auctor et largitor est, grates in mente persolvitis.

Quas si recte, si bene, si efficaciter ipso actu vultis reddere: considerate reginam illam, quam de hoc mundo sponsam sibi illi placuit eligere. Haec est quam « pulchram » et « amicam » et « columbam » suam vocat in scripturis, et de qua illi dicitur: « astitit regina a dextris tuis. » Haec est, cui de eodem sponso suo Christo dicitur: « Audi, filia, et vide et inclina aurem tuam, et obliviscere populum tuum et domum patris tui, et concupiscet rex decorem tuum. » Quanto enim saecularium conversationem et patris sui, huius scilicet mundi, habitationem contemnendo obliviscitur, tanto pulchrior conspectui sponsi sui et amabilior cognoscitur. Hanc quantum dilexerit ipse probavit, cum se ipsum morti sponte tradere pro eius amore non dubitavit. Hanc, inquam, considerate quomodo exsul et peregrina et quasi vidua ad virum suum cum veris filiis suis gemit et suspirat, exspectans, donec ille de regione longinquua, ad quam abiit « accipere sibi regnum, » veniat, et eam ad regnum suum transferendo omnibus qui eidem amicae bona vel mala fecerint, prout quisque gessit, retribuat. Qui hanc honorant, cum illa et in illa honorabuntur; qui hanc conculcant, extra illam conculcabuntur. Qui hanc exaltant, cum angelis exaltabuntur; qui hanc deprimunt, cum daemonibus deprimentur. Hanc exaltate, honorate, defendite, ut cum illa et in illa sponso deo placeatis et in aeterna beatitudine cum illa regnando vivatis. Amen. Fiat.

AD ATHELITS ABBATISSAM ET MONIALES DE RUMESEI

Anselmus archiepiscopus: filiae carissimae, domnae abbatissae Athelits, et sanctimonialibus sub ea Christo famulantibus salutem et benedictionem.

Si vos multum non amarem, multum vos increparem, quia, postquam vos ipsae ad me nuntium vestrum misistis et de illo mortuo, quem quidam volunt pro sancto haberi, quid vobis faciendum esset nostrum consilium requisistis, in consilio nostro non stetistis, sed insuper praecepto nostro inoboedientes exstitistis. Quapropter mandans praecipio vobis ut, si a divino officio suspendi non vultis, omnem amodo honorem cuivis sancto debitum illi mortuo auferatis, et ei nec oblationem faciatis nec factam ad opus vestrum suscipiatis. Filium autem eius, qui ad tumbam ipsius decumbit et ibi moratur, a villa depellite, nec ei amplius aliquam inibi facultatem manendi relinquite. Valete.

AD RICHEZAM SOROREM SUAM

Anselmus, archiepiscopus Cantuariae: sorori suae carissimae Richezae salutem et dei in omnibus tribulationibus eius consolationem.

Scio, soror dilectissima, quia excepto viro vestro non est homo in mundo, cuius salutem et prosperitatem tantum nosse et audire desideretis, quantum meam et filii vestri Anselmi, qui mecum est. Ego enim sum unicus frater vester, et ille unicus filius vester. De iis quae erga nos sunt, legati vestri plenius vos docere poterunt viva voce quam ego per litteras. Sciatis tamen quia filius vester, nepos meus carissimus, postquam a vobis discessit, longam et gravem aegritudinem passus, tandem deo miserante integram sanitatem recepit. De me vero dico quia sanus corpore sum, sed in magnis tribulationibus versatur cor meum, ita ut nec Angliam audeam propter timorem dei fugere, nec in ea possim in ulla pace aut tranquillitate aut quiete vivere. Cotidie ita est cor meum suspensum, velut in proximo sim exiturus.

Sed quomodocumque sit de me, de vobis gaudeo, quia nuntii vestri mihi retulerunt vestram salutem et prosperitatem. Quoniam autem et prosperitas et adversitas huius vitae breves sunt et transitoriae, istas contemnamus et aeternam adversitatem fugere et perpetuam prosperitatem mereri bene vivendo contendamus. Cum ergo, soror carissima, in hac vita non habeatis in quo cor vestrum possit delectari: convertite illud totum ad deum, ut in futura vita de illo possit laetari. Vale.

Si vir vester redierit et ad me venire voluerit, mando ut nullo modo veniat.

AD ERMENGARDAM

Dominae in deo dilectae Ermengardae: frater Anselmus, abbas Becci, salutem et fideles orationes.

Quamvis vos non cognoscam visu, tamen, quia eius ordinis sum, qui omnibus hominibus debet bene velle et salubriter consulere, nulli mirum videri debet, si vestram reverentiam secundum quod audio expedire commoneo.

Audivi, carissima domina, qualiter sit inter virum vestrum et vos, quoniam nobilitas vestra non hoc patitur occultari, sed longe lateque facit publicari. In qua re primum gratias ago deo, a quo est omne bonum, qui eidem viro vestro dedit tanta constantia temporalem gloriam pro aeterna contemnere, et vobis concessit tot tribulationes pro tuenda castitate tam viriliter sufferre; ita tamen ut ille in ipso mundi contemptu non plus diligat se ipsum quam vos, nec vobis aliquid in hoc mundo sit carius illo. Certe in hoc ambo deo et bonis hominibus amabiles, ambo estis laudabiles. Utique in tanta et tam vera mutua vestra dilectione non tam corpora vestra diligere credendi estis quam animas. Corpora namque vestra nulla cura, nullo mutuo amore potestis a morte temporali eripere; animabus vero vestris, si ipsum vestrum amorem regere scitis, vitam aeternam potestis acquirere.

Quid ergo est, femina reverenda, femina probatae castitatis, quid est quod te cogit impedire virum tuum, ne perfecte quaerat salutem animae suae, quam non minus diligis quam tuam? Nullatenus enim vel cogitandum est, ut hoc facias propter vilem carnis delectationem, quam tantum, postquam ipse a te discessit, contempsisti, ut, ne virum alterum susciperes, cum hunc habere non posses, multas passa sis tribulationes, multas respueris persuasiones. Quod si detines animam eius a salutis suae profectu propter gloriam et commoda temporalia, quae amas et quae te per illum speras posse retinere: quomodo diligis animam illam, cuius certo et aeterno commodo dubia, vilia et transitoria tua praeponis commoda? Aut qua ratione potes ab eo exigere, ut ipse aeterna bona animae suae postponat temporalibus bonis corporis tui, si tu bona corporis tui praeponis bonis animae illius? Vide ergo, carissima domina, vide, fortis et prudens mulier, vide, si hoc facis, quam non bene regas amorem tuum, quam non recte diligas diligentem te virum tuum. Quid si illum cogis ut deserat consilium animae suae pro voluntate tua, et tunc morte tua vel illius occurrente, aut alio casu, sicut solet, irruente, ille non prosit tibi et tu noceas illi? Utique si noces animae illius, noces animae tuae.

O quanto melius, reverenda domina, quanto laudabilius ostenditis vos diligere virum vestrum, si non solum permittitis, sed etiam consulitis et iuvatis, ut quod incepit deo inspirante, hoc conetur perficere ipso adiuvante; si bonum illius amando vestrum facitis; si certissime creditis quia, quanto fortius propter amorem dei et proximi humanum auxilium dimittitis, tanto familiarius et securius vos divinae protectioni committitis. Confidat ergo in deo prudens vestra fortitudo et fortis prudentia; et sicut, si mortuus esset vir ille, absentiam eius sufferretis nolendo sine ullo eius et vestro proficuo, ita dum vivit, sponte illam tolerate pro magno eius et vestro praemio. Concedite ut libere faciat quod desiderat, quatenus cum illo participetis mercedem. Si enim deus curam gerit de viduis, quae non propter illum sunt viduae: multo carius illam fovebit, quam pro suo amore sponte videbit viduam. Quod si contigerit—quod forsitan non erit—ut terrenum perdatis honorem: nolite dolere, quia in caelo recipietis meliorem. Et certe quod a melioribus et sapientioribus multum contemnitur, non est multum dolendum, si perditur.

Plus aliquid vellem consulere, sed non audeo; orare tamen non timeo: Omnipotens et misericors deus ita det tibi mundi contemptum, sicut dedit viro tuo, ut in caelesti regno par sis viro tuo, soror et domina in deo dilecta.

AD IDAM COMITISSAM BONONIAE

Anselmus, servus servorum dei, vocatus archiepiscopus: reverendae et diligendae vitae merito comitissae Idae sic in hac vita deo servire, ut in futura mereatur cum deo regnare.

Scio et certus sum, domina mihi in deo carissima, soror dilectissima, filia dulcissima, quia sancta tua dilectio, qua me semper in corde tuo praesentem quasi patrem spiritualem reverenter et delectabiliter amplecteris, incessanter desiderat ea quae de me et erga me sunt cognoscere et ex mea parte aliquid audire aut legere, quatenus mihi secundum verae caritatis regulam congaudeat aut compatiatur. Cui tuae dilectioni cor meum utique simili respondet affectu. Quoniam ergo et per epistolam congruum non est narrare nunc, quae de me facta sunt hoc anno sive qualiter cor meum illa sustineat, et domnus Rainerius, dilectus amicus noster, clericus vester, multa per se vidit et plura me narrare didicit: illum precatus sum, ut ea quae de me interius et exterius cognovit, sicut qui ad hoc ipsum se a vestra reverentia missum fatetur, viva voce vivis vocibus notificet. Et quoniam iam olim certissime expertus sum, filia in deo mihi dilectissima, monita mea cor tuum delectabiliter suscipere atque animam tuam te curae meae penitus commisisse memini, aliquid necesse est quod ad exhortationem tuam pertineat subiungere.

Amica carissima in deo, dominus dicit: « Multi sunt vocati, pauci vero electi. » Numquam ergo secura sis te inter electos debere computari, donec ita vivas ut pauci sint, quibus vita tua debeat comparari. Et cum te in numero paucorum esse cognoveris, adhuc time, quia adhuc dubium erit si inter paucos electos fueris, donec te de illis paucis videas, de quorum electione nulla manet dubietas. Qui enim dixit: « pauci » sunt « electi, » non utique dixit quam pauci, ut quantumcumque nobis videamur profecisse, semper iudicemus nos nondum nisi ad initium proficiendi pervenisse. Hortor igitur et consulo filiae meae, quae se meo commisit consilio, ut bene vivendi studium, quod olim incepit, nullatenus languescat, sed, quasi cotidie incipiat, per singulos dies fervescat.

READING 4-G

VALTHERVS CHATILLON
[1135–1170 CE]

SATIRE AGAINST THE CURIA

MISSUS sum in vineam   circa horam nonam,
suam quisque nititur   vendere personam;
ergo quia cursitant   omnes ad coronam.
semper ego auditor tantum, nunquamne reponam?

Rithmis dum lascivio,   versus dum propino,
rodit forsan aliquis   dente me canino,
quia nec afflatus sum   pneumate divino
neque libra prolui   fonte caballino.

Licet autem proferam   verba parum culta
et a mente prodeant   satis inconsulta,
licet enigmatica   non sint vel occulta,
est quodam prodire tenus, si non datur ultra.

Cur sequi vestigia   veterum refutem,
adipisci rimulis   corporis salutem,
impleri divitiis   et curare cutem?
quod decuit magnos, cur michi turpe putem?

Qui virtutes appetit,   labitur in imum,
querens sapientiam   irruit in limum;
imitemur igitur   hec dicentem mimum:
o cives, cives, querenda pecunia primum

Hec est, que in sinodis   confidendo tonat,
in electionibus   prima grande sonat;
intronizat presules,   dites impersonat:
et genus et formam regina pecunia donat.

Adora pecuniam,   qui deos adoras:
cur struis armaria,   cur libros honoras?
longas fac Parisius   vel Athenis moras:
si nichil attuleris, ibis, Homere, foras.

Disputet philosophus vacuo cratere,
sciat, quia minus est scire quam habere;
nam si pauper fueris, foras expellere,
ipse licet venias musis comitatus, Homere.

Sciat artes aliquis, sit auctorum plenus,
quid prodest si vixerit pauper et egenus?
illinc cogit nuditas vacuumque penus,
hinc usura vorax avidumque in tempore fenus.

Si Ioseph in vinculis Christum prefigurat,
si tot plagis Pharao durum cor indurat,
si filiis Israel exitus obturat:
quid valet hec genesis, si paupertas iecur urat?

Quid ad rem, si populus sitit ante flumen,
si montis ascenderit Moÿses cacumen
et si archam federis obumbravit numen?
malo saginatas carnes quam triste legumen.

Illud est, cur odiens studium repellam
paupertatem fugiens vitamque misellam;
quis ferret vigilias frigidamque cellam?
tutius est iacuisse thoro, tenuisse puellam.

Quidam de scientia tantum gloriantur
et de pede Socratis semper cornicantur
et dicunt, quod opes his qui philosophantur
non bene conveniunt nec in una sede morantur.

Idcirco divitias forsan non amatis,
ut eternam postmodum vitam capiatis.
heü mentes perdite! numquid ignoratis,
quod semper multum nocuit differre paratis?

Si pauper Diogenes fuit huius sortis,
si Socrates legitur sic fuisse fortis,
Iuvenalis extitit magister cohortis
marmoreisque satur iacuit Lucanus in hortis.

Heu quid confert pauperi nobilis propago?
quid Tityrus patula recubans sub fago?
ego magis approbo rem de qua nunc ago;
nam sine divitiis vita est quasi mortis imago.

Semper habet comitem paupertas merorem,
perdit fructum Veneris et amoris florem,
quia iuxta nobilem versificatorem
non habet unde suum paupertas pascat amorem.

Adde quod superbia sequitur doctores:
inflati scientia respuunt minores;
ergo sic impletum est quod dicunt auctores:
inquinat egregios adiuncta superbia mores.

Sit pauper de nobili genere gigantum,
sciat quantum currat sol et Saturnus quantum,
per se solus habeat totum fame cantum:
gloria quantalibet quid erit si gloria tantum?

Audi, qui de Socrate disputas et scribis:
miser, vaca potius potibus et cibis;
quod si dives fieri noles vel nequibis,
inter utrumque tene, medio tutissimus ibis.

HIS SONG IN HIS LAST SICKNESS

Versa est in luctum
cythara Waltheri,
non quia se ductum
extra gregem cleri
vel eiectum doleat
aut abiecti lugeat
vilitatem morbi,
sed quia considerat,
quod finis accelerat
improvisus orbi.
Libet intueri
iudices ecclesie,
quorum status hodie
peior est quam heri.

Umbra cum videmus
valles operiri,
proximo debemus
noctem experiri;
sed cum montes videris
et colles cum ceteris
rebus obscurari,

nec fallis nec falleris,
si mundo tunc asseris
noctem dominari.

Per convalles nota
laicos exleges,
notos turpi nota
principes et reges,
quos pari iudicio
luxus et ambitio
quasi nox obscurat,
quos celestis ulcio
bisacuto gladio
perdere maturat.

Restat, ut per montes
figurate notes
scripturarum fontes:
Christi sacerdotes
colles dicti mystice,
eo quod in vertice
Syon constituti
mundo sunt pro speculo,
si legis oraculo
vellent non abuti.

Iubent nostri colles
dari cunctis fenum
et preferri molles
sanctitati senum;
fit hereditarium
Dei sanctuarium,
et ad Christi dotes
preponuntur hodie
expertes scientie
presulum nepotes.
Si rem bene notes,
succedunt in vicium
et in beneficium
terreni nepotes.

Veniat in brevi,
Iesu bone Deus,
finis huius evi,
annus iubileus!

moriar, ne videam
Antichristi frameam,
cuius precessores
iam non sani dogmatis
stant in monte crismatis
censuum censores.

THE POET HAS A DAUGHTER BORN TO HIM

Verna redit temperies
prata depingens floribus,
telluris superficies
nostris arridet moribus,
quibus amor est requies,
cybus esurientibus.

Duo quasi contraria
miscent vires effectuum:
augendo seminaria
reddit natura mutuum,
ex discordi concordia
prodit fetura fetuum.

Letentur ergo ceteri,
quibus Cupido faverit,
sed cum de plaga veteri
male michi contigerit,
vita solius miseri
amore quassa deperit.

Ille nefastus merito
dies vocari debuit,
qui sub nature debito
natam michi constituit,
dies, qui me tam subito
relativum instituit.

Cresce tamen, puellula,
patris futura baculus;
in senectute querula,
dum caligabit oculus,
mente ministrans sedula
plus proderis quam masculus.

HIS SONG OF REPENTANCE

Hactenus inmerito
militavi creaturae,
cum ex evi debito
lusi satis immature;
sed nunc, quia cogito
legem carnis moriturae,
creatori milito,
renovatus novo iure,

Iuventutis levia
redimo per seria.

Quinta pars relinquitur
intervalli iubilei,
necdum quicquam oritur
quod inclinet aurem Dei;
nil egi, nil agitur
quod relaxet vincla rei:
defecerunt igitur
sicut fumus dies mei.

Iuventutis levia
redimo per seria.

Vanitates varias
vito vitae praecedentis,
fugiens delicias;
fugit par iuventa ventis.
cum carnis blandicias
ut sentinam mundi sentis,
clipeum obicias
contra blandimenta mentis.

Iuventutis levia
redimo per seria.

Clipeus est ratio,
qua, pacienter et expresse
probans, palam facio
bona mundi nichil esse
in tam brevi spacio;
cum nos mori sit necesse,
nulla prodest satio,
nisi Christus sit in messe.

Iuventutis levia
redimo per seria.

DE CLERICIS

LICET eger cum egrotis
et ignotus cum ignotis,
fungar tamen vice cotis,
ius usurpans sacerdotis.
flete, Syon filie:
presides ecclesie
imitantur hodie
Christum a remotis.

Si privata degens vita
vel sacerdos vel levita
sibi dari vult petita
ac incedit via trita,
previa fit pactio
Symonis auspicio,
cui succedit datio,
et sic fit Giezita.

Iacet ordo clericalis
in respectu laicalis,
sponsa Christi fit mercalis,
generosa generalis;
veneunt altaria,
venit eucharistia
cum sit nugatoria
gratia venalis.

Donum Dei non donatur,
nisi gratis conferatur;
quod qui vendit vel mercatur,
lepra Syri vulneratur.
quem sic ambit ambitus,
idolorum servitus,
templo sancti spiritus
non compaginatur.

Si quis tenet hunc tenorem,
frustra dicit se pastorem
nec se regit ut rectorem,
renum mersus in ardorem.

hec est enim alia
sanguisuge filia,
quam venalis curia
duxit in uxorem.

In diebus iuventutis
timent annos senectutis,
ne fortuna destitutis
desit eis splendor cutis.
et dum querunt medium,
vergunt in contrarium,
fallit enim vitium
specie virtutis.

Ut iam loquar inamenum,
sanctum crisma datur venum,
iuvenantur corda senum
nec refrenant motus renum.
senes et decrepiti
quasi modo geniti
nectaris illiciti
hauriunt venenum.

Ergo nemo vivit purus:
castitatis perit murus,
commendatur Epicurus
nec spectatur moriturus.
grata sunt convivia;
auro vel pecunia
cuncta facit pervia
pontifex futurus.

THE LOVER IN WINTER

IMPORTUNA Veneri
redit brume glacies,
redit equo celeri
Iovis intemperies:
cicatrice veteri
squalet mea facies:
amor est in pectore,
nullo frigens frigore.

Iam cutis contrahitur,
dum flammis exerceor;

nox insomnis agitur
et in die torqueor;
si sic diu vivitur,
graviora vereor:
amor est in pectore,
nullo frigens frigore.

Tu qui colla superum,
Cupido, suppeditas,
cur tuis me miserum
facibus sollicitas?
non te fugat asperum
frigoris asperitas:
amor est in pectore,
nullo frigens frigore.

Elementa vicibus
qualitates variant,
dum nunc pigrant nivibus,
nunc calorem sentiant;
sed mea singultibus
colla semper inhiant:
amor est in pectore,
nullo frigens frigore.

READING 4-H

IOANNES BOCCACCIO
[1313–1375 CE]

DE MULIERIBUS CLARIS

XCII:
De Agrippina Neronis Cesaris matre

Agrippina Neronis Cesaris mater genere, consanguinitate, imperio et monstruositate filii ac sua non minus quam claris facinoribus emicuit.

Hec etenim Germanici Cesaris, optimi atque laudande indolis iuvenis, ex Agrippina superiori filia fuit, vocata Iulia Agrippina et Gaii Caligule principis soror nupsitque Gneo Domitio, homini ex Enobardorum familia fastidiosissimo atque gravi, ex quo Neronem, insignem toto orbi beluam, premissis ex materno utero pedibus, peperit.

Verum Domitio intercutis morbo assumpto, Nerone adhuc parvulo, cum formosissima esset, Gaius frater eius, homo spurcissimus, turpi stupro ea abusus est; et sublimatus in principem, seu minus eius mores approbans, eo quod se Lepido dominii spe miscuerit, seu emuli alicuius inpulsu, eam fere bonis omnibus privatam, relegavit in insulam. Quo tandem a multibus suis trucidato eique Claudio substituto, ab eodem revocata est.

Que tractu temporis, cum audisset Valeriam Messalinam, variis agentibus meritis, confossam, spem evestigio intravit sibi natoque potiundi orbis imperii; et celibem principem, esto Germanici patris sui fuisset frater, decora pulchritudine sua, adversus Lolliam Paulinam, opitulante Calixto liberto, et Eliam Petinam, Narcisso favente, opere Pallantis, Claudium in pregrande nuptiarum suarum desiderium traxit. Sed obstare voto videbatur honestas eo quod illi neptis esset ex fratre. Verum oratione Vitellii subornati, actum est ut in desiderium suum cogeretur precibus senatorum, eoque orante fieret a senatu decretum quo prestaretur patruos posse neptes inducere.

Et sic Agrippina, volente Claudio et orante senatu, eius venit in nuptias. Que tandem Augusta dicta est et carpento in Capitolium ferebatur, solis sacerdotibus ante concessum, et in adversos sibi sevire cepit suppliciis. Demum cum astutissima esset mulier, tempore captato, quanquam utriusque sexus filii essent Claudio, eum induxit, suadente illi Memmio Pollione, tunc consule, et urgente plurimum Pallante liberto, qui ob stuprum Agrippine summe fautor erat, ut Neronem privignum in filium adoptaret, quod ante in familia Claudiorum factum nemo meminerat; eique Octaviam, quam ex Messalina susceperat, et que Lucio Sylano nobili iuveni desponsata fuerat, sponderet in coniugem.

Quibus obtentis, rata in casses beluam incidisse, non tantum Claudii assiduarum ingurgitationum affecta tedio, quantum ne ante patris mortem Britannicus Claudii filius in etatem solidam deveniret exterrita, Narcisso etiam pro Britannico multa perorante, quasi proposito suo futurum obicem arbitrata, in mortem Claudii facinus exitiale commenta est.

Delectabatur quidem Claudius boletis plurimum illosque cibum dicebat deorum et ideo absque semine sua nasci sponte. Quod cum advertisset Agrippina, studiose coctos infecit veneno eosque, secundum quosdam, ipsa apposuit temulento. Alii vero dicunt epulanti in arce cum sacerdotibus per Alotum spadonem pregustatorem suum ab Agrippina corruptum appositos. Verum cum vomitu et alvi solutione videretur salus Claudii secutura, opera Xenophontis medici illitis veneno pennis ad vomitum continuandum porrectis, eo itum est quo cupiebat uxor.

Ipse tandem in cubiculum reductus, ignaris omnibus preter Agrippinam, mortuus est. Cuius quidem mors non ante ab Agrippina palam nuntiata est quam, amicorum suffragio, omisso Britannico tanquam iuniore, Nero iam pubescens sublimaretur in principem. Quod adeo gratum fuit Neroni ut matrem illico, tanquam bene meritam, in cunctis, tam publicis quam privatis, preponeret videreturque sibi titulum, matri vero principatum sumpsisse.

Et sic e specula romani principatus Agrippina toto effulsit orbi. Ceterum splendor iste tam grandis turpi macula labefactatus est; nam cede plurium atque exiliis aliquandiu debachata est. Preterea creditum fuit, ea patiente, preter naturalem et debitam dilectionem in matrem, amore illecebri a filio fuisse dilectam, cum is meretricem ei persimilem inter pellices assumpsisset et concubitum testarentur persepe macule vestibus iniecte, quotiens cum eo lectica delata est; dato velint alii eam in facinus hoc filium attraxisse, desiderio recuperandi dominii a quo deiecta videbatur, eo quod in Neronem quibusdam ex causis multum oblocuta fuerat; quod firmari volunt ob id quod de cetero Nero sit assuetus fugere eius contubernium et solitudines collocutionum.

Attamen que patruum in coniugium suum allexerat, boleto peremerat, ineptum iuvenem fraudibus et violentia sublimarat imperio, in detestabilem, quanquam meritam, mortem deducta est. Nam cum in multis filio gravis esset, eius meruit odium ex quo omni honore et augustali maiestate ab eo privata est. Que indignans et femineo irritata furore, eidem, uti procuraverat, sic se subrepturam imperium minata est. Quibus exterritus Nero, cum eam et oculatam nimium nosceret et ob memoriam Germanici patris amicorum subsidiis plenam, veneno ter illam surripere conatus est. Sed discreta mulier antidotis offensam vitavit.

Demum cum et laqueos ceteros, quos in necem eius tetenderat, vitasset, intellexit Nero cautiori fraude agendum fore eique exposcenti ab Aniceto prefecto classis apud Misenum olim a pueritia nutritore suo, ostensum est navim posse componi fragilem in qua suscepta Agrippina doli ignara periclitari posset.

Quod cum Neroni placuisset, eam ab Ancio venientem, quasi preteritorum odiorum penitens, ficta filiali affectione, suscepit in ulnis et usque domum prosecutus est. Inde apparata navi in suam pernitiem, ad cenam itura illam conscendit, comitantibus Creperio Gallo et Acerronia libertis; eisque per noctem navigantibus dato signo a consciis, cecidit tectum navis plurimo plumbo grave et oppressit Creperium. Deinde nautis agentibus ut tranquillo mari navis verteretur in latus, auxilia Acerronia invocante, contis remisque occisa est et Agrippina, humero saucia et in mare tandem deiecta, a litoralibus suffragantibus in Lucrinum lacum villamque suam deducta est.

Inde, ea iubente, ab Agerino liberto Neroni quoniam evasisset nuntiatum est; qui detineri illum iussit, quasi saluti sue insidiaturus venisset, missique sunt Anicetus et Herculius tetrarcus et Obarius centurio classiarius ut illam perimerent. Et cum esset ab Aniceto circundata domus et ancillula, qua sola sotiata erat Agrippina, fugisset, introgressi ministri ad eam, primus Herculeus caput eius fuste percussit; inde cum ipsa cerneret centurionem ferrum in mortem eius expedientem, protenso utero clamavit ut ventrem ferirent.

Et sic occisa nocte eadem cremata est et vilibus obsequiis terra contecta, levem demum tumulum sui<s> in via prope Misenum et Cesaris Iulii villam eidem apponentibus.

Alii volunt a Nerone conspectam post cedem et ex membris aliqua ab eodem damnata, aliqua laudata, et demum sepultam.

LXXXVIII:
De Cleopatra regina Egyptiorum

Cleopatra egyptia femina, totius orbis fabula, etsi per multos medios reges a Ptholomeo macedone rege et Lagi filio, originem traheret et Ptholomei Dyonisii seu—ut aliis placet—Minei regis filia, ad imperandum, per nephas tamen, ipsi regno pervenerit, nulla fere, ***nisi*** hac et oris formositate, vere claritatis nota refulsit, cum e contrario avaritia crudelitate atque luxuria omni mundo conspicua facta sit.

Nam, ut placet aliquibus, ut ab eiusdem dominii initio summamus exordium, Dyonisius seu Mineus, romani populi amicissimus, Iulii Cesaris consulatu primo in mortem veniens, signatis tabulis liquit ut filiorum natu maior, quem aliqui Lysaniam nominatum arbitrantur, sumpta in coniuge Cleopatra, ex filiabus etiam natu maiore, una, se mortuo, regnarent. Quod, eo quod familiarissima esset apud Egyptios turpitudo matres filiasque tantum a coniugiis exclusisse, executum est. Porro exurente Cleopatra regni libidine, ut nonnullis visum est, innocuum adolescentulum eundemque fratrem et virum suum, quindecimum etatis annum agentem, veneno assumpsit et sola regno potita est.

Hinc asserunt, cum iam Pompeius magnus Asyam fere omnem occupasset armis, in Egyptum tendens, superstitem puerum mortuo subrogasse fratri eumque regem fecisse Egypti. Ex quo indignata Cleopatra adversus eum arma corripuit et, sic se rebus habentibus, fuso apud Thesaliam Pompeio et a puero, rege a se facto, litore in egyptiaco ceso, adveniente post eum Cesare, ibidem bellum inter se gerentes invenit.

READING 4-I

LATINARVM COMPOSITIO SCRIPTIONVM

arranging of Latin sentences

[200 BCE–2001 CE]

Itaque consules, qui eum annum secuti sunt, C. Iunius Bubulcus tertium et Q. Aemilius Barbula iterum, initio anni questi apud populum deformatum ordinem praua lectione senatus, qua potiores aliquot lectis praeteriti essent, negauerunt eam lectionem se, quae sine recti prauique discrimine ad gratiam ac libidinem facta esset, obseruaturos et senatum extemplo citauerunt eo ordine qui ante censores Ap. Claudium et C. Plautium fuerat.

TITVS LIVIVS [59 ANTE–17 CE]

KEY:

Provide your own markup.

Subjects

Objects

Verbs

Distant connections

[Larger clauses]

(Lesser clauses)

et and -que

Dicamus bona uerba: uenit Natalis ad aras:
quisquis ades, lingua, uir mulierque, faue.
urantur pia tura focis, urantur odores
quos tener e terra diuite mittit Arabs.
ipse suos Genius adsit uisurus honores,
cui decorent sanctas mollia serta comas.
illius puro destillent tempora nardo,
atque satur libo sit madeatque mero,
adnuat et, Cornute, tibi, quodcumque rogabis.

ALBIVS TIBVLLVS [60–19 BCE]

Non pro his autem rogo tantum, sed pro his qui credituri sunt in me per uerbum ipsorum, ut omnes unum sint, sicut tu Pater in me, et ego in te, ut et ipsi in nobis unum sint.

7. Cuius unitatis nullum poterunt habere consortium, qui in Dei Filio Deo uero humanam negant manere naturam, inpugnatores salutiferi sacramenti, et paschalis exules festi, quod, quia ab euangelio dissentiunt et symbolo contradicunt, nobiscum celebrare non possunt, quia etsi audent sibi christianum nomen adsumere, ab omni tamen creatura, cui Christus caput est, repelluntur, uobis in hac sollemnitate merito exultantibus pieque gaudentibus, qui nullum recipientes in ueritate mendacium, nec de natiuitate Christi secundum carnem, nec de passione ac morte, nec de corporali resurrectione eius ambigitis, quoniam sine ulla separatione Deitatis, uerum Christum ab utero Virginis, uerum in ligno crucis, uerum in sepulchro carnis, uerum in gloria resurrectionis, uerum in dextera paternae maiestatis agnoscitis.

PONTIFEX LEO MAGNVS [440–461 CE]

Ipsa inde ab exordiis codificationis canonicae orientalium Ecclesiarum constans Romanorum Pontificum voluntas duos Codices, alterum pro latina Ecclesia alterum pro Ecclesiis orientalibus catholicis, promulgandi, admodum manifesto ostendit velle eosdem servare id quod in Ecclesia, Deo providente, evenit, ut ipsa unico Spiritu congregata quasi duobus pulmonibus Orientis et Occidentis respiret atque uno corde quasi duos ventriculos habente in caritate Christi ardeat.

PONTIFEX IOANNES PAVLVS II [1990 CE]

Plaudite porcelli porcorum pigra propago.
Progreditur, plures porci pingvedine pleni.
Pugnantes purgent, pecudum pars prodigioſa,
Perturbat pede potroſas plerumqve plateas,
Pars portentoſa populorum prata profanat,
Pars pungit populando potens, pars plurima plagis.
Prætendit punire pares, proſternere parvos,
Primò porcorum præfecti pectore planô.
Piſtorum porci proſtant pingvedine pulchri
Pugnantes prohibent porcellos, ponere pœnas
Praeſumunt pravis: porro plebs peſſima pergit
Protervire prius, poſt profligare potentes.
(*a*) Proconſul paſtus pomorum pulte perorat.
Pvælia pro pecude prava prodeſſe, proinde
Protervire parum patres perſæpè probâſſe
Porcorum populo pacem pridem placuiſſe:
Perpetuam, pacis promptæ præconia paſſim.
Pro præcone piè pácis per pondera plura
Proponente preces, prudens pro plebe patronus
Porcus prægrandis profert placidiſſima pacta.
(b) Paciſci placeat porcis, per prælia prorſum.
Plurima priſcorum perierunt paſcua patrum.
Praeſtat porcellis potiori pace potiri,
Præſtet prælatis primam præbere palæſtram,
Porro proclivis pugnæ plebeia poteſtas
(c) Prœlia portendit, per privilegia priſca
Proponens pugnæ porcos potuiſſe patenti
Proſtraviſſe pates, per plebiſcita probari.
Porcum pugnacem pecudem, præclara poteſtas.
Pendet per porcos pugnaces, pergite paſſim
Perdere præfectos, porci properare puſilli
(d) Perdere pingviculos, præfectos præcipitare,
Pigritia pollent prælati perpetuati,
Poſtqvam plebs pertæſa potentatus penetravit
Præcipiti pede, porcelli petière puſilli.
Pugnando properare prius, peſſundare patres.

KEY:

Provide your own markup.

Subjects

Objects

Verbs

Distant connections

[Larger clauses]

(Lesser clauses)

et and -que

Præſtituunt perſonatos præcurrere porcos.
Propugiles, porro plenum pingvedine putri.
Præclarum porcum piſtrino pinſere panem
Præcipiunt, per poſticam, per pervia portant
(e) Propterea properans proconſul poplite.

PETRVS PORCELLI [1530 CE]

Secundum principale quod est causa erroris in studio sapientiae his temporibus est quod a quadraginta annis surrexerunt quidam in studio qui se ipsos creaverunt in magistros et doctores studii theologiae et philosophiae, cum tamen numquam didicerunt aliquid dignum, nec volunt nec possunt propter statum suum, ut in sequentibus longe lateque manifestare curabo, per sententias quas inducam; de quibus licet doleam quantum possum et compatior, tamen quia veritas praevalet omnibus ideo exponam hic aliqua saltem quae publice aguntur et patent omnibus hominibus, licet pauci ponant cor suum ad haec consideranda, sicut nec ad aliqua utilia propter causas erroris, quas hic prosequor, quibus fere omnes homines turpiter excaecantur.

ROGERVS BACONIVS [1214–1292 CE]

KEY: Provide your own markup.

Subjects are underlined with a solid line.

Objects are underlined with a broken line.

Verbs are underlined with a line of dots.

Distant connections of words and phrases are underlined with a wavey line.

[Larger clauses are in square brackets,] (lesser ones in rounded parentheses.)

The words et and -que are placed in boxes.

Note: This code is used to illustrate the functions and connections of words as an aid to teaching, and is not intended to appear in absolutely every instance.

READING 4-K

IOANNES KEPLER

[1571–1630 CE]

DISSERTATIO KEPLERI

IN NUNCIUM SIDEREUM

Jampridem domi meae consederam ociosus, nihil nisi te cogitans, Galilaee praestantissime, tuasque literas. Emisso enim superioribus nundinis in publicum libro meo *Commentaria de motibus Martis* inscripto, multorum annorum labore; exque eo tempore, quasi quid difficilima expeditione bellica gloriae satis peperissem, vacatione nonnulla studiis meis interposita, fore putabam, ut inter caeteros et Galilaeus, maxime omnium idoneus, mecum, de novo astronomiae seu physicae coelestis genere promulgato, per literas conferret, intermissumque ab annis duodecim institutum resumeret.

Ecce vero tibi ex inopinato circa Idus Martias celerum ope nunciatum in Germaniam, Galilaei mei, pro lectione alieni amoris, ut qui hoc mihi honoris impertitus sis, ut per tantum virum potissimum me, et transmisso exemplari et addita commonefactione, provocandum ad scribendum censueris: quod et praestitit in tui gratiam per quam humaniter, et me in clientelam suam suscepit benevolentissime.

Quod igitur mihi propria animi propensione, quod amicis placet, quod diligenter ipse rogas, id faciam: nonnulla spe inductus, me hac epistola id tibi profuturum, si eam censueris ostendendam, ut contra morosos novitatum censores, quibus incredibile quicquid incognitum, profanum et nefandum quicquid ultra consuetas aristotelicae angustiae metas, uno proaspiste sis processurus instructior.

Temerarius forte videri possim qui tuis assertionibus, nulla propria experientia suffultus, tam facile credam. At qui non credam Mathematico doctissimo, cujus vel ausus judicii rectitudinem arguit, qui tantum abest ut sese vanitati dedat, seseque vidisse dictitet quae non viderit, popularem auram captans: ut vel receptissimis opinionibus veritatis amore non dubitet repugnare, vulgique vituperia susque deque ferre? Quid quod publice scribit, probrumque, si quod committeretur, clam habere nequaquam posset? Ego ne ut patricio Florentino fidem derogem de iis quae vidit? perspicaci lusciosus? instrumentis ocularibus instructo, ipse nudus et ab supellectili inops? Ego non credam omnes ad eadem spectacula invitati, et quod caput est, vel ipsum suum instrumentum, ad faciendam fidem oculis offerenti.

An parum hoc fuerit magnorum Hetruriae Ducum familiam ludificari, Mediceumque nomen figmentis suis praefigere, planetas interim veros pollicentem?

Quid quod propriis experimentis, quod et aliorum asseverationibus in parte libri deprehendo veracissimum? Quid causae sit, cur solum de quatuor planetis deludendum sibi putaverit orbem?

Tres sunt menses cum augustissimus Imperator super Lunae maculis varia ex me quaesivit, in ea costitutus opinione, terrarum et continentium simulacra in Luna ceu in speculo resplendescere. Allegabat hoc potissimum, sibi videri expressam Italiae cum duabus adiacentibus insulis effigiem. Specillum etiam suum ad eadem contemplanda offerebat in dies sequentes, quod omissum tamen est. Adeo eodem tempore, Galilaee Christi Domini patriam vocabulo praeferens, christiani orbis monarcham (ejusdem irrequieti spiritus instinctu, qui naturam defectum ibat) deliciis tuis aemulatus es.

Sed et antiquissima est haec de maculis Lunae narratio, fulta authoritate Pythagorae et Plutarchi summi philosophi, et qui, si hoc ad rem facit, proconsulari imperio Epirum tenuit sub Caesaribus. Ut Maestlinum adeoque et mea optica ante annos sex edita praeteream, inque suum locum inferius differam.

Haec igitur cum consentientibus testimoniis etiam alii de Lunae corpore asseverent, consentanea iis, quae tu de eodem longe dilucidissima affers experimenta: tantum abest, ut fidem tibi in reliquo libro et de quatuor circumjovialibus planetis derogem, ut potius optem mihi in parato jam esse perspicillum, quo te in deprehendendis circum-Martialibus (ut mihi proportio videtur requirere) duobus, et circum-Saturniis sex vel octo praevertam, uno forsan el altero circum- Venerio et circum-Mercuriali accessuro.

Quam ad venaturam, quod Martem attinet, tempus erit maxime idoneum October venturus, qui Martem in opposito Solis exhibet, terris (praeterquam anno 1608) omnium proximum, errore calculi trium amplius graduum.

Age igitur, ut de rebus certissimis, meisque oculis, ut omnino spero, videndis, tecum Galilaee sermonem conferam; tui quidem libri methodum secuturus, omnes vero philosophiae partes, quae vel ex hoc tuo Nuncio ruinam minantur vel confirmantur vel explicantur, juxta pervagaturus: ut nihil supersit, quod lectorem Philosophiae deditum suspensum teneat, et vel a fide tibi perhibenda prohibeat, vel ad contemnendam quae hactenus erat in precio, philosophiam impellat.

Primum libelli tui caput in fabrica perspicilli versatur, tantae quidem efficaciae, ut rem spectanti millies exhibeat majori planitie, quod tum fit si diameter tricies bis repraesentetur longior. Quod si facultas aestimatoria manet in sententia consuetae magnitudinis, necesse est ei tunc rem videri tricies bis propiorem. Distantiam enim oculus non videt sed conjicit, ut docent Optici. Da enim hominem aliquem abesse tribus millibus et ducentis passibus, videri vero sub angulo tricies bis majorem, ut videtur alius sine perspicillo centum passibus absens: cum certum habeat oculus, hominem illum remotum habere consuetam magnitudinem, censebit non pluribus centum abesse passibus, adjuvante el clarificatione visionis perspicillo procurata.

Incredibile multis videtur epichirema tam efficacis perspicilli; at impossibile aut novum nequaquam est; nec nuper a Belgio prodiit, sed tot jam annis antea proditum a Jo. Baptista Porta, Magiae naturalis lib. XVII, cap. X de crystallinae lentis affectibus. Utque appareat ne compositionam quidem cavae et convexae lentis esse novam; age verba Portae producamus. Sic ille:

> « Posito oculo in centro, retro lentem, quae remota fuerint adeo propinqua videbis, ut quasi manu ea tangere videaris, ut valde remotos cognoscas amicos: literas epistolae in debita distantia collocatae. adeo magnas videbis, ut perspicue legas. Si lentem inclinabis, ut per obliquum epistolam inspicias, literas satis majusculas videbis, ut etiam per viginti passus remotas legas. Et si lentes multiplicare noveris, non vereor quin per centum passus minimum literam conspiceris; ut ex una in alterum majores reddantur caracteres. Debilis visus ex visus qualitate specillis utatur. Qui id rectae sciverit accomodare, non parvum nanciscetur secretum. Concavae lentes, quae longe sunt, clarissime cernere faciunt convexae propinqua; unde ex visus comoditate his frui poteris. Concavo longe parva vides sed perspicua, convexo propinqua majora sed turbida. Si utrumque recte componere noveris, et longinqua et proxima majora et clara videbis. Non parum multis amicis auxilii praestitimus, qui longinqua obsoleta, proxima turbida conspiciebant, ut omnia perfectissime contuerentur. » Haec capite X.

Capite XI novum titulum facit de specillis, quibus supra omnem cogitatum longissime quis conspicere queat: sed demonstrationem de industria (quod et profitetur) sic involvit, ut nescias quid dicat, an de lentibus perlucidis agat ut hactenus, an vero speculum adjungat opacum laevigatum, cujusmodi unum et ipse in animo habeo, quod res remotas, nullo discrimine absentiae, in maxima quantitate ideoque ut propinquas, et praeterea proportionaliter auctas exhibet: tanta claritate, quanta ex speculo (quod necessario coloris fusci est) sperari potest.

Huic loco libri Portae, cum viderem praefixam quaerelam initio capitis X: *Cavarum et convexarum lentium et specillorum, tantopere humanis usibus necessariorum, neque effectum neque rationes adhuc a nemine allatas:* eam operam sumpsi ante annos sex *in astronomiae parte optica;* ut quid in simplicibus perspicillis accideret, luculenta demonstratione geometrica redderem expeditum.

Videre est ibi capite V, ubi demonstro illa quae pertinent ad modum videndi, fol. 202 conjunctas in schemate effigies cavi et convexi perspicilli, plane ad eum modum, quo solent hodie in vulgatis tubis inter se jungi. Quod si non lectio Magiae Portae, occasionem dedit huic machinamento; aut si non aliquis Belgarum ex ipsius Portae instructione fabrefactum instrumentum solutis silentii legibus morte Portae (1) multiplicavit in plura exempla, ut mercem venalem faceret: haec certe effigies ipsa fol. 202 Libri mei potuit curiosum lectorem admonere de structura, praesertim si lectionem demonstrationum mearum cum textu Portae conjunxit.

READING 4-L

PONTIFEX CLEMENS XIV
[1773 CE]

Suppressio, et extinctio Societatis Jesu.

Clemens PP. XIV.
Ad perpetuam rei memoriam.

§. 1. Dominus ac Redemptor noster Jesus Christus princips pacis a propheta prænunciatus quod hunc in mundum veniens per angelos primum pastoribus significavit, ac demum per se ipsum antequam in cœlos ascenderet semel et iterum suis reliquit discipulis, ubi omnia Deo patri reconciliavisset, pacificans per sanguinem crucis suæ, sive quae in terris, sive quæ in cœlis sunt, apostolis etiam reconciliationis tradidit ministerium, posuitque in eis verbum reconciliationis, ut legatione fungentes pro Christo, qui non est dissentionis Deus, sed pacis, et dilectionis, universo orbi pacem annuntiarent, et ad id potissimum sua studia conferrent ac labores, ut omnes in Christo geniti solliciti essent servare unitatem spiritus in vinculo pacis, unum corpus et unus spiritus, sicut vocati sunt in una spe vocationis, ad quam nequaquam pertingitur, ut inquit sanctus Gregorius Magnus, si non ad eam unita cum proximis mente curratur.

§. 15. His igitur, aliisque maximi apud omnes ponderis et auctoritatis exemplis Nobis ante oculos propositis, vehementique simul flagrantes cupiditate, ut in ea quam infra aperiemus, deliberatione fidenti animo, tutoque pede incedamus, nihil diligentiæ omisimus et inquisitionis, ut quidquid ad regularis ordinis, qui Societatis Jesu vulgo dicitur, originem pertinet, progressum, hodiernumque statum perscrutaremur, et compertum inde habuimus, eum ad animarum salutem, ad hæreticorum, et maxime infidelium conversionem, ad majus denique pietatis, et religionis incrementum a sancto suo conditore fuisse institutum, atque ad optatissimum hujusmodi finem facilius, feliciusque consequendum, arctissimo evangelicæ paupertatis voto tam in communi, quam in particulari fuisse Deo consecratum, exceptis tantummodo studiorum, seu literarum collegiis, quibus possidendi redditus ita facta est vis, et potestas, ut nihil tamen ex iis redditibus in ipsius societatis commodum, utilitatem, ac usum impendi unquam posset, atque converti.

§. l8. Multæ hinc ortæ adversus Societatem quærimoniæ, quæ nonnullorum etiam principum auctoritate munitæ, ac relationibus ad recolendæ memoriæ Paulum IV, PiumV, et Sixtum V, prædecessores

Nostros delatæ fuerunt. In his fuit claræ memoriæ Philippus II. Hispaniarum rex catholicus, qui tum gravissimas, quibus ille vehementer impellebatur, rationes, tum etiam eos, quos ab Hispaniarum inquisitoribus adversus immoderata Societatis privilegia, ac regiminis formam acceperat, clamores, et contentionum capita a nonnullis ejusdem etiam societatis viris doctrina, et pietate spectatissimis confirmata eidem Sixto V. prædecessori exponenda curavit, apud eumdemque egit, ut apostolicam Societatis visitationem decerneret, atque committeret.

§. 26. Tot itaque, ac tam necessariis adhibitis mediis, divini Spiritus, ut confidimus, adjuti præsentia, et afflatu, nec non muneris Nostri compulsi necessitate, quo et ad christianæ reipublicæ quietem, et tranquillitatem conciliandam, fovendam, roborandam, et ad illa omnia penitus de medio tollenda, quæ eidem detrimento vel minimo esse possunt, quantum vires sinunt, arctissime adigimur; cumque præterea animadverterimus prædictam Soc. Jesu uberrimos illos, amplissimosque fructus, et utilitates afferre amplius non posse, ad quos instituta fuit, a tot prædecessoribus Nostris approbata, ac plurimis ornata privilegiis imo fieri aut vix, aut nullo modo posse ut ea incolume manente, vera pax, ac diuturna Ecclesiæ restituatur. His propter gravissimis adducti causis, aliisque pressi rationibus, quos et prudentiæ leges, et optimum universalis Ecclesiæ regimen nobis suppeditant, altaque mente repositas servamus, vestigiis inhærentes eorumdem prædecessorum Nostrorum, et præsertim memorati Gregorii X. prædecessoris in generali concilio Lugdunensi, cum et nunc de Societate agatur tum instituti sui, tum privilegiorum etiam suorum ratione mendicantium ordinum numero adscripta, maturo consilio, ex certa scientia, et plenitudine potestatis apostolicæ sæpedictam Societatem extinguimus, et supprimimus: tollimus et abrogamus omnia, et singula ejus officia, ministeria, et administrationes, domus, scholas, collegia, hospitia, et loca quæcumque quavis in provincia, regno, et ditione existentia, et modo quolibet ad eam pertinentia: ejus statuta, mores, consuetudines, decreta, constitutiones, etiam juramento, confirmatione apostolica, aut alias roboratas; omnia item, et singula privilegia, et indulta generalia, vel specialia, quorum tenores præsentibus, ac si de verbo ad verbum essent inserta, ac etiamsi quibusvis formulis, clausulis irritantibus, et quibuscumque vinculis, et decretis sint concepta pro plene, et sufficienter expressis haberi volumus. Ideoque declaramus cassatam perpetuo manere, ac penitus extinctam omnem, et quamcumque auctoritatem præpositi generalis, provincialium, visitatorum, aliorumque quorumlibet dictæ Societatis superiorum tam in spiritualibus, quam in temporalibus, eamdemque jurisdictionem et auctoritatem in locorum ordinarios totaliter, et omnimode transferimus juxta modum, casus, et personas, et iis sub conditionibus, quas infra explicabimus, prohibentes, quemadmodum per præsentes prohibemus, ne ullus amplius in dictam Societatem excipiatur, et ad habitum, ac novitiatum admittatur; qui vero hactenus fuerunt excepti ad professionem votorum simplicium, vel solemnium sub pœna nullitatis admissionis, et professionis, aliisque arbitrio Nostro, nullo modo admitti possint, et valeant. Quinimo volumus, præcipimus, et mandamus, ut qui nunc tyrocinio actu vacant, statim, illico, et immediate, et cum effectu dimittantur; ac similiter vetamus, ne qui votorum simplicium professionem emiserunt, nulloque sacro ordine sunt usque adhuc initiati, possint ad majores ipsos ordines promoveri prætextu, aut titulo vel jam emissæ in Societate professionis, vel privilegiorum contra concilii Tridentini decreta eidem Societati collatorum.

§. 40. Volumus autem, ut præsentium literarum transumptis etiam impressis manu alicujus notari publici subscriptis, et sigillo alicujus personæ in dignitate ecclesiastica constitutæ munitis, eadem prorsus fides adhibeatur quæ adhiberetur ipsis præsentibus, si forent exhibitæ, vel ostensæ. Datum Romæ apud sanctam Mariam majorem sub annulo piscatoris die vicesima prima julii millesimo septingentesimo septuagesimo tertio pontificatus nostri anno quinto.

READING 4-M

HVBERTVS JEDIN

[1962 CE]

CONCILIORUM OECUMENICORUM DECRETA

PRAEFATIO

Ad conciliorum oecumenicorum decreta edenda neminem fugere potest occasionem inde oblatam esse, quod S. S. Ioannes papa XXIII concilium Vaticanum II indixit et convocavit: quo factum est ut in hoc triennio plurima opera in lucem venirent tum omnem conciliorum historiam complectentia tum alia atque alia quae ad concilia attinerent ponderantia. Illud vero admirationem movit, cum ea decreta maximi sint momenti ad ecclesiae doctrinam et disciplinam quod attinet, nullam tamen omnium oecumenicorum conciliorum decretorum collectionem uno volumine comprehensam inveniri. Nam, si excipias maioris momenti definitiones et declarationes de rebus fidei quae in Henrici Denzinger *Enchiridion symbolorum* sunt insertae, antiquorum canones conciliorum ex editionibus Bruns, Lauchert, aliorum sunt eruendi, Tridentini autem ex Pauli Manutii editione publica auctoritate facta — quae saepius deinde, nec semper sine mendis, excusa est —, multorum denique conciliorum vel ex collectionibus antiquis — Romana dico praesertim editione, Hardouin, Mansi — vel ex nostrorum temporum criticis editionibus, exempli gratia Eduardi Schwartz.

Cum nullus igitur usque ad hunc diem exstet liber qui omnia omnium conciliorum oecumenicorum decreta et de rebus fidei et de ecclesiastica disciplina contineat, ei rei hoc volumine occurrere visum est, in quo non monumenta ad historiam conciliorum componendam colliguntur, verum tamen viginti conciliorum, quae Romana catholica ecclesia agnoscit, canones et decreta quam accuratissima nunc fieri potest textus forma proponuntur. Hic autem nonnulla sunt quae desiderant explicationem quandam: etenim, si de viginti tantum conciliis agitur quae oecumenica vocantur, non ignorant qui editionem paraverunt appellationem illam magis consuetudine quam vera ecclesiae magisterii declaratione natam esse. Praeterea antiquis christianis temporibus non solum symbola et canones quae a conciliis prolata sunt ubique vim obligandi habere existimata esse, verum etiam alia scripta nonnulla, quae utrum in librum hunc essent recipienda necne non semper facile fuit diiudicare. In quorum numero decreta particularia ad forum vel administrationem pertinentia, quae non raro et antiqua Christiana aetate et ea quae dicitur media prodierunt, non sunt reponenda, quapropter omittenda existimavimus. Plane igitur cum huius editionis curators conscii sint de modo eligendi et colligendi textus alios aliter posse sentire, libenter se animadversiones accepturos profitentur, id nunc affirmare satis habentes, locos ex optimis quae sunt hodie editionibus esse descriptos, codices manuscriptos raro — exempli gratia ad concilia Lugdunensia quod attinet — esse adhibitos; criticum apparatum et rerum explicationes ea tantum complecti, quae maxime sunt necessaria; prolegomena conspectum maioris tantum momenti librorum praebere; disputationes de vi et pondere textuum, de theologicis et iuridicis quaestionibus, omnino esse omissas: librum esse denique fontium collectionem, non dogmatum et legum quae conciliis oecumenicis prodita sunt expositionem.

Restat ut dicamus esse nobis spem librum hunc et iis qui concilio Vaticano II intererunt utilitati futurum et iis qui theologiae, historiae, iuri canonico dant operam, eaque de causa conciliorum oecumenicorum decreta probe nosse debent et saepius inspicere debebunt.

Huius edendi libri consilium ab Instituto studiis religiosis promovendis, vulgo *Centro di Documentazione* dicto, initum est: huius bibliothecae et Instituti clarissimus patronus Em. mus Iacobus cardinalis Lercaro Bononiensium archiepiscopus susceptum opus et verbis et re fovit atque adiuvit, quapropter ei gratias agimus quam maximas. Rationibus editionis determinandis et singulis operis sociis muneri adsignando qui scribit interfuit. Instituti secretarius Ioseph Alberigo Universitatis Studiorum Florentinae professor et totius voluminis partes in ordinem redegit et concilia Basileense-Ferrariense-Florentinum-Romanum, Lateranense V, Vaticanum I ipse edenda curavit. Perikles-P. Joannou Universitatis Monacensis professor prioribus octo conciliis edendis operam dedit, Claudius Leonardi Bibliothecae Apostolicae Vaticanae scriptor mediae aetatis — a Lateranensi I ad Viennense — Paulus Prodi Universitatis Bononiensis professor conciliis Constantiensi et Tridentino. Pro singulis operis partibus unusquisque quattuor collaboratorum responsabilis est.

Ut absolvam, id mihi liceat commemorare, in aulae conciliaris s. Ioannis in Laterano — quae iam non extat, in qua quinque Lateranensia concilia sedem habuerunt — abside maiore Christum musivo pictum una cum Matre Dei et apostolis Petro et Paulo fuisse, reliquos vero apostolos in absidibus minoribus: quibus imaginibus Romana ecclesia id significavit, concilia eo collecta traditionem adnuntiare apostolicam ac summam illam docendi habere potestatem cuius fundamentum et radix iis verbis continetur quae in primo ecclesiae concilio ab apostolis in unum collectis, Petro agnorum et ovium pastore moderante, sunt prolata: « Visum est Spiritui sancto et nobis ... » (Ac 15, 28).

Hubertus Jedin

INTRODUCTIO

Quod Ioannes XXIII — a. 1959 ineunte — concilium Vaticanum II indicendum renuntiavit, id omnium mentes monuit quantum magnorum conciliorum historiae esset pondus, eorum decretorum maxime, quae fontes christianae doctrinae atque traditionis extant praecipui. Aliud his pondus addit mirus studii progressus ad christianorum unitatem restaurandam, quo magis magisque collustratur conciliorum vis in augenda universalis ecclesiae conscientia.

Hisce potissimum fretum Institutum, cui « Centro di Documentazione » nomen est, investigationes et studia promovit ut quae hoc volumine continentur in lucem proderet. Ipsum Institutum, iam inde a primo ortu, decem ante annos, eam delegerat peculiarem rationem voluntatemque ut in scientiis religiosis provehendis, conciliorum doctrinam et historiam penitus inquireret, ut quae magis magisque ecclesiae vitam foveret inlustraretque.

Statutorum auctoritas oecumenicorum conciliorum haud funditus omni tempore perpensa est. Quanta enim vis statutorum horum fuit, praeteritis saeculis maximeque his proximis annis, in doctrinis, in legislationibus praesertim institutisque ecclesiasticis, atque in ipsis christianorum conscientiis? Parva sane, neque ea recta, sed obliqua potius via. Etiamsi in medii aevi collectis monumentis canonicis pleraque erant statutorum excerpta conciliorum, tamen iam in iis praesentiebantur quae mox essent futura. Etenim editiones Tridentinorum decretorum eorumque auctoritas, et in legislatione et in ecclesiastica praxi et in theologica doctrina, effecerunt ut venerabilis conciliorum antecedentium traditio in dies neglegeretur. Denique, secundum hanc rationem, codex iuris canonici sua ipsius structura videtur oblivione paene obruisse quae, per alias maxime formas, ab ecclesia ante annum 1917 constituta erant.

Historici tantum, in his rebus proprie versati, studia pertinentia ad criticas editiones actuum singulorum conciliorum satis coluerunt (Schwartz, Concilium Constanciense, Concilium Basiliense, Concilium Florentinum, Concilium Tridentinum). Attamen de studiis agitur paene stantibus aut iam conclusis, adeo ut fontium conciliorum recentissima editio impressio sit anastatica, ceterum laudabilis, *Amplissimae Collectionis* Ioanni Dominici Mansi.

Haec ipsa ad historiam conciliorum plane convenire videntur in qua opus Caroli Iosephi Hefele, quod gallice edidit, auxit, persecutus est Henricus Leclercq, egregium sane extat subsidium neque tamen horum temporum necessitatibus accommodatum. Nuper, post luculentas fontium editiones, quaedam in lucem prodita sunt, veluti Huberti Jedin historia concilii Tridentini, gravissimi opus ponderis, vel Iosephi Gill historia concilii Florentini, qui ad conciliorum memoriam inlustrandam recentiores historiam interpretandi leges in suam rem converterunt.

Proximis autem decem annorum spatiis maxime viguerunt scripta monographica quae in peculiares multiplicesque rationes exarata sunt, theologicam, historicam, canonicam, quaeque aut singula historiae momenta respiciunt aut conciliorum singula statuta pertractant. Omnia haec magnum quidem studiis proventum attulerunt, sed eruditorum conatus atque etiam omnium mentes in eam partem promoverunt ubi singula et minuta densantur, non in eam unde conciliorum traditio quam late pateat cogitatione et mente complecti possit.

Ipsi horum annorum eventus novum quoddam studium novamque propensionem admoverunt cum historiae Conciliorum tum loco quo ecclesiae concilia habenda sunt. Cuius historiae compluria summaria prodierunt, in his praecipua et singularia Huberti Jedin, Francisci Dvornik et Petri Meinhold opera videntur, quibus addenda sunt nonnulla collectanea scripta, interdum ratione ac disciplina exarata, saepius docendi modo causa suscepta.

Quo quidem tempore studia haec revirescunt emittitur volumen istud quod integra editione omnia conciliorum generalium decreta complectitur, a Nicaeno I usque ad Vaticanum I. Hoc volumine Institutum nostrum id potissimum spectavit ut doctis viris opus et adiumentum afferret ad investigandum simul et meditandum, in quo textus ipsi loquerentur, curatoribus tam modice ac scienter intervenientibus ut non possent minus. Huiusmodi editio visa est non solum lacunam prope conspicuam bibliographicam explere, sed praesertim posse certam et expressam efficere illam in concilia propensionem, quae multis ex partibus apparet atque extat. Sed illud vel maxime consideravimus, hanc collectionem decretorum, textuum nempe quibus sollemniter auctoritas conciliorum oecumenicorum exprimitur quique suapte natura temporum et locorum condicionibus superstites erant futuri, posse patribus opitulari qui instanti concilio operam navabunt. Nam expedita et apta consultatio decretorum conciliorum antecedentium efficere potest ut et singulae cognitiones in promptu habeantur, et per illas quae vis sit ecclesiae traditionis conciliaris penitus intelligatur.

Nimirum huius generis liber nullo pacto poterat componi quin antea quaestiones nonnullae expedirentur, optiones quaedam certae fierent. Quisquis enim memoriam conciliorum perdidicit, non fugiet eum quantum inter hoc vel illud concilium intersit, unde iis qui hoc opus curarunt persaepe concedendum fuit summis dissimilitudinibus quae inter concilia sunt quamvis tempore contigua.

QVINTA EXPERIENTIA

fifth experience

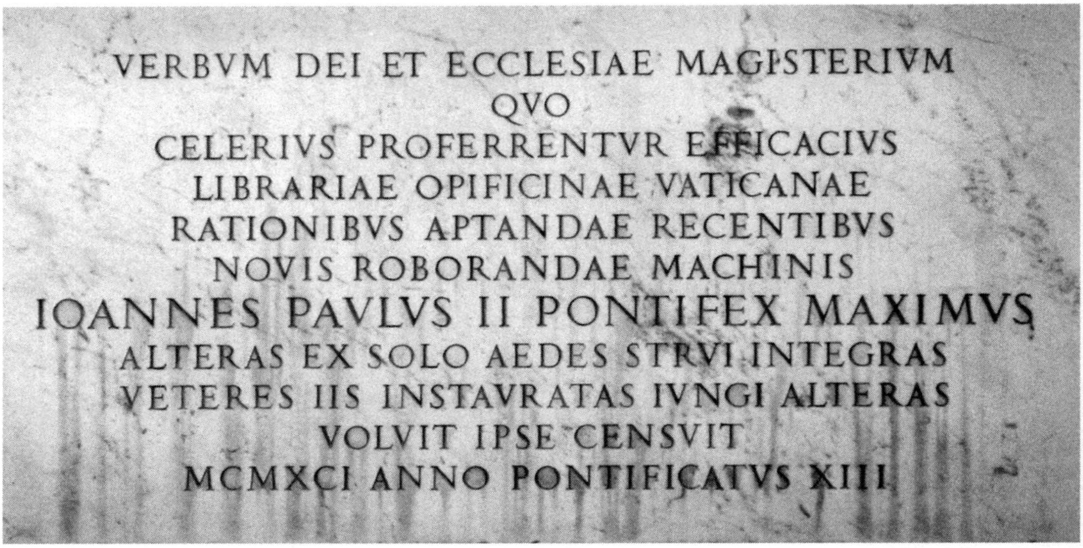

VERBVM DEI ET ECCLESIAE MAGISTERIVM
QVO
CELERIVS PROFERRENTVR EFFICACIVS
LIBRARIAE OPIFICINAE VATICANAE
RATIONIBVS APTANDAE RECENTIBVS
NOVIS ROBORANDAE MACHINIS
IOANNES PAVLVS II PONTIFEX MAXIMVS
ALTERAS EX SOLO AEDES STRVI INTEGRAS
VETERES IIS INSTAVRATAS IVNGI ALTERAS
VOLVIT IPSE CENSVIT
MCMXCI ANNO PONTIFICATVS XIII

THE FIFTH EXPERIENCE SHOULD theoretically include no new material of the Latin language inasmuch as this has been covered in the First, Third, and Fourth Experiences. In this Fifth Experience, the pleasure of the teacher and of the students will be the daily encounter with every phrase and element of the Latin language and every kind of Latin literature and the daily development of their own oral practice, with the help of a complete Latin dictionary like Lewis and Short.

Spoken Latin will accompany the readings, as the students' own contribution to Latin creativity. The vocabulary will increase with the help of a good dictionary. Constant reference to the dictionary is necessary until every meaning of a word is understood.

Regular exercise is provided in the *ludi domestici* or "home games" prepared by the teacher for every encounter. Our own collection of *ludi* produced new each year while teaching in Rome is in preparation for the fourth volume of this *Latinitatis Corpus, Latin's Body*. It is entitled *Ossibus Ludi Exercendis: Games for Exercising the Bones.*

The instructor is encouraged to provide a new collection of reading sheets each year photocopied from published sources by authors of every age and type of Latin literature, as provided in this volume. Instructors may prefer to compile specialized collections of reading sheets covering the work of one author, genre, era, topic, such as we have done with the letters of Cicero that comprise our second planned volume, entitled *Ossium Carnes Multae ex M. T. Ciceronis Epistulis: The Bones' Meats Abundant from the Letters of M. T. Cicero*, along with its audio accompaniment, entitled *Os Praesens Ciceronis Epistularis: The Immediate Mouth of Cicero in his Letters*, our third publication. Another example is the compilation of reading sheets prepared for the many tours conducted in Rome and environs, which comprise our fifth projected volume, entitled *Ossibus Revisenda Migrantibus: As Bones Roam About, Things—Places—Events to be Revisited.* With such collections of reading sheets, the door will be wide open to everything you have ever heard about Latin from 200 BCE to 2016 CE and beyond. Amen.

QVANDOQVIDEM IN THEATRO VATICANO
PRAESTITE MARIA MATRE SAPIENTIAE
PIVS XI PONTIFEX MAXIMVS
DIGNAM STVDIORVM SEDEM CONSTITVIT
AD BIBLIOTHECAM AD TABVLARIVM
AD PONTIFICIVM SOPHORVM COLLEGIVM
HAC PATET ADITVS
PONT MAX

QUINTAE EXPERIENTIAE LECTIONUM PAGINULAE

Reading Sheets—Fifth Experience

READING 5-A

MARCVS TVLLIVS CICERO [106–43 BCE]

LAELIUS DE AMICITIA

Hoc sermone, quem Cicero fingit habitum esse paucis diebus post Africani mortem anno 129 a. Chr. n., Laelius docet quid sentiat de amicitia. Quae persona loquatur, significatur nomine verbis quae facit, anteposito.

1 Q. Mucius augur multa narrare de C. Laelio socero suo memoriter et iucunde solebat nec dubitare illum in omni sermone appellare sapientem; ego autem a patre ita eram deductus ad Scaevolam sumpta virili toga, ut quoad possem et liceret, a senis latere numquam discederem; itaque multa ab eo prudenter disputata, multa etiam breviter et commode dicta memoriae mandabam fierique studebam eius prudentia doctior. quo mortuo me ad pontificem Scaevolam contuli, quem unum nostrae civitatis et ingenio et iustitia praestantissimum audeo dicere. sed de hoc alias; nunc redeo ad augurem.

Cum saepe multa tum memini domi in hemicyclio sedentem ut solebat, cum et ego essem una et pauci admodum familiares, in eum sermonem illum incidere qui tum fere multis erat in ore. meministi enim profecto Attice et eo magis, quod P. Sulpicio utebare multum, cum is tribunus pl. capitali odio a Q. Pompeio qui tum erat consul, dissideret, quocum coniunctissime et amantissime vixerat, quanta esset hominum vel admiratio vel querella. itaque tum Scaevola cum in eam ipsam mentionem incidisset, exposuit nobis sermonem Laeli de amicitia habitum ab illo secum et cum altero genero C. Fannio Marci filio paucis diebus post mortem Africani. eius disputationis sententias memoriae mandavi, quas hoc libro exposui arbitratu meo; quasi enim ipsos induxi loquentes, ne « inquam » et « inquit » saepius interponeretur atque ut tamquam a praesentibus coram haberi sermo videretur.

Cum enim saepe mecum ageres ut de amicitia scriberem aliquid, digna mihi res cum omnium cognitione tum nostra familiaritate visa est. itaque feci non invitus, ut prodessem multis rogatu tuo. sed ut in Catone Maiore qui est scriptus ad te de senectute, Catonem induxi senem disputantem, quia nulla videbatur aptior persona quae de illa aetate loqueretur quam eius, qui et diutissime senex fuisset et in ipsa senectute praeter ceteros floruisset, sic cum accepissemus a patribus maxime memorabilem C. Laeli et P. Scipionis familiaritatem fuisse, idonea mihi Laeli persona visa est quae de amicitia ea ipsa dissereret, quae disputata ab eo meminisset Scaevola. genus autem hoc sermonum positum in hominum veterum auctoritate et eorum inlustrium plus nescio quo pacto videtur habere gravitatis; itaque ipse mea legens sic adficior interdum ut Catonem, non me loqui existimem. sed ut tum ad senem senex de senectute sic hoc libro ad amicum amicissimus scripsi de amicitia. tum est Cato locutus quo erat nemo fere senior temporibus illis, nemo prudentior; nunc Laelius et sapiens (sic enim est habitus) et amicitiae gloria excellens de amicitia loquetur. Tu velim a me animum parumper avertas, Laelium loqui ipsum putes. C. Fannius et Q. Mucius ad socerum veniunt post mortem Africani; ab his sermo oritur, respondet Laelius cuius tota disputatio est de amicitia, quam legens te ipse cognosces.

[...]

FANNIUS. Istuc quidem Laeli ita necesse est. sed quoniam amicitiae mentionem fecisti et sumus otiosi, pergratum mihi feceris, spero item Scaevolae, si quem ad modum soles de ceteris rebus quom ex te quaeruntur, sic de amicitia disputaris quid sentias, qualem existumes, quae praecepta des.

SCAEVOLA. Mihi vero erit gratum; atque id ipsum cum tecum agere conarer, Fannius antevortit. quam ob rem utrique nostrum gratum admodum feceris.

5 LAELIUS. Ego vero non gravarer, si mihi ipse confiderem; nam et praeclara res est et sumus ut dixit Fannius, otiosi. sed quis ego sum? aut quae est in me facultas? doctorum est ista consuetudo eaque Graecorum, ut iis ponatur de quo disputent quamvis subito; magnum opus est egetque exercitatione non parva. quam ob rem quae disputari de amicitia possunt, ab eis censeo petatis qui ista profitentur; ego vos hortari tantum possum ut amicitiam omnibus rebus humanis anteponatis; nihil est enim tam naturae aptum, tam conveniens ad res vel secundas vel adversas. sed hoc primum sentio nisi in bonis amicitiam esse non posse; neque id ad vivum reseco ut illi qui haec subtilius disserunt, fortasse vere, sed ad communem utilitatem parum; negant enim quemquam esse virum bonum nisi sapientem. sit ita sane; sed eam sapientiam interpretantur quam adhuc mortalis nemo est consecutus, nos autem ea quae sunt in usu vitaque communi, non ea quae finguntur aut optantur, spectare debemus. numquam ego dicam C. Fabricium M.Curium Ti. Coruncanium, quos sapientes sapientes. quare sibi habeant sapientiae nomen et invidiosum et obscurum, concedant ut

viri boni fuerint. ne id quidem facient, negabunt id nisi sapienti posse concedi. agamus igitur pingui ut aiunt Minerva, qui ita se gerunt, ita vivunt ut eorum probetur fides integritas aequalitas liberalitas, nec sit in eis ulla cupiditas libido audacia, sintque magna constantia ut ii fuerunt, modo quos nominavi, hos viros bonos ut habiti sunt sic etiam appellandos putemus, quia sequantur quantum homines possunt, naturam optimam bene vivendi ducem. sic enim mihi perspicere videor ita natos esse nos ut inter omnes esset societas quaedam, maior autem, ut quisque proxume accederet. Itaque cives potiores quam peregrini, propinqui quam alieni; cum his enim amicitiam natura ipsa peperit; sed ea non satis habet firmitatis. namque hoc praestat amicitia propinquitati, quod ex propinquitate benivolentia tolli potest, ex amicitia non potest; sublata enim benivolentia amicitiae nomen tollitur, propinquitatis manet. quanta autem vis amicitiae sit, ex hoc intellegi maxime potest quod ex infinita societate generis humani quam conciliavit ipsa natura, ita contracta res est et adducta in angustum, ut omnis caritas aut inter duos aut inter paucos iungeretur.

6 Est enim amicitia nihil aliud nisi omnium divinarum humanarumque rerum cum benivolentia et caritate consensio; qua quidem haut scio an excepta sapientia nihil melius homini sit a dis inmortalibus datum. divitias alii praeponunt, bonam alii valitudinem, alii potentiam, alii honores, multi etiam voluptates. beluarum hoc quidem extremum, illa autem superiora caduca et incerta, posita non tam in consiliis nostris quam in fortunae temeritate. qui autem in virtute summum bonum ponunt, praeclare illi quidem, sed haec ipsa virtus amicitiam et gignit et continet nec sine virtute amicitia esse ullo pacto potest. iam virtutem ex consuetudine vitae sermonisque nostri interpretemur nec eam ut quidam docti verborum magnificentia metiamur virosque bonos eos qui habentur, numeremus, Paulos Catones Galos Scipiones Philos; his communis vita contenta est; eos autem omittamus qui omnino nusquam reperiuntur. talis igitur inter viros amicitia tantas oportunitates habet quantas vix queo dicere. principio qui potest esse vita 'vitalis' ut ait Ennius, quae non in amici mutua benivolentia conquiescit? quid dulcius quam habere quicum omnia audeas sic loqui ut tecum! qui esset tantus fructus in prosperis rebus, nisi haberes qui illis aeque ac tu ipse gauderet? adversas vero ferre difficile esset sine eo qui illas gravius etiam quam tu ferret. denique ceterae res quae expetuntur, oportunae sunt singulae rebus fere singulis, divitiae ut utare, opes ut colare, honores ut laudere, voluptates ut gaudeas, valitudo ut dolore careas et muneribus fungare corporis; amicitia res plurimas continet; quoquo te verteris, praesto est, nullo loco excluditur, numquam intempestiva, numquam molesta est; itaque non aqua, non igni ut aiunt locis pluribus utimur quam amicitia. neque ego nunc de vulgari aut de mediocri, quae tamen ipsa et delectat et prodest, sed de vera et perfecta loquor, qualis eorum qui pauci nominantur, fuit. nam et secundas res splendidiores facit amicitia et adversas partiens communicansque leviores.

[...]

Saepissime igitur mihi de amicitia cogitanti maxime illud considerandum videri solet utrum propter inbecillitatem atque inopiam desiderata sit amicitia, ut dandis recipiendisque meritis, quod quisque minus per se ipse posset, id acciperet ab alio vicissimque redderet, an esset hoc quidem proprium amicitiae, sed antiquior et pulchrior et magis a natura ipsa profecta alia causa. amor enim, ex quo amicitia nominata est, princeps est ad benivolentiam coniungendam. nam utilitates quidem etiam ab iis percipiuntur saepe qui simulatione amicitiae coluntur et observantur temporis causa, in amicitia autem nihil fictum est, nihil simulatum et quidquid est, id est verum et voluntarium. quapropter a natura mihi videtur potius quam ab indigentia orta amicitia, adplicatione magis animi cum quodam sensu amandi quam cogitatione, quantum illa res utilitatis esset habitura. quod quidem quale sit, etiam in bestiis quibusdam animadverti potest, quae ex se natos ita amant ad quoddam tempus et ab eis ita amantur ut facile earum sensus appareat. quod in homine multo est evidentius, primum ex ea caritate quae est inter natos et parentes, quae dirimi nisi detestabili scelere non potest; deinde cum similis sensus extitit amoris, si aliquem nacti sumus cuius cum moribus et natura congruamus, quod in eo quasi lumen aliquod probitatis et virtutis perspicere videamur. nihil est enim virtute amabilius, nihil quod magis adliciat ad diligendum, quippe cum propter virtutem et probitatem etiam eos quos numquam vidimus, quodam modo diligamus. quis est qui C. Fabrici M'. Curi non cum caritate aliqua benivola memoriam usurpet, quos numquam viderit? quis autem est qui Tarquinium Superbum, qui Sp.Cassium Sp. Maelium non oderit? cum duobus ducibus de imperio in Italia est decertatum, Pyrrho et Hannibale; ab altero propter probitatem eius non nimis alienos animos habemus, alterum propter crudelitatem semper haec civitas oderit.

9 Quodsi tanta vis probitatis est ut eam vel in eis quos numquam vidimus, vel quod maius est, in hoste etiam diligamus, quid mirum est, si animi hominum moveantur, cum eorum quibuscum usu coniuncti esse possunt, virtutem et bonitatem perspicere videantur? quamquam confirmatur amor et beneficio accepto et studio perspecto et consuetudine adiuncta, quibus rebus ad illum primum motum animi et amoris adhibitis admirabilis quaedam exardescit benivolentiae magnitudo. quam si qui putant ab inbecillitate proficisci, ut sit per quem adsequatur quod quisque desideret, humilem sane relinquunt et minime generosum ut ita dicam ortum amicitiae, quam ex inopia atque indigentia natam volunt. quod si ita esset, ut quisque minimum esse in se arbitraretur, ita ad amicitiam esset aptissimus; quod longe secus est. ut enim quisque sibi plurimum confidit et ut quisque maxime virtute et sapientia sic munitus est ut nullo egeat suaque omnia in se ipso posita iudicet, ita in amicitiis expetendis colendisque maxime excellit. quid enim? Africanus indigens mei? minime hercule! ac ne ego quidem illius; sed ego admiratione quadam virtutis eius, ille vicissim opinione fortasse non nulla quam de meis moribus habebat, me dilexit; auxit benivolentiam consuetudo. sed quamquam utilitates multae et magnae consecutae sunt, non sunt tamen ab earum spe causae diligendi profectae.

ut enim benefici liberalesque sumus, non ut exigamus gratiam (neque enim beneficium faeneramur, sed natura propensi ad liberalitatem sumus), sic amicitiam non spe mercedis adducti, sed quod omnis eius fructus in ipso amore inest, expetendam putamus. ab his qui pecudum ritu ad voluptatem omnia referunt, longe dissentiunt nec mirum; nihil enim altum, nihil magnificum ac divinum suspicere possunt qui suas omnes cogitationes abiecerunt in rem tam humilem tamque contemptam, quam ob rem hos quidem ab hoc sermone removeamus, ipsi autem intellegamus natura gigni sensum diligendi et benivolentiae caritatem facta significatione probitatis. quam qui adpetiverunt, adplicant se et propius admovent, ut et usu eius quem diligere coeperunt, fruantur et moribus sintque pares in amore et aequales propensioresque ad bene merendum quam ad reposcendum atque haec inter eos sit honesta certatio. sic et utilitates ex amicitia maximae capientur et erit eius ortus a natura quam ab inbecillitate gravior et verior. nam si utilitas amicitias conglutinaret,eadem commutata dissolveret; sed quia natura mutari non potest, idcirco verae amicitiae sempiternae sunt.

[...]

12 Haec igitur lex in amicitia sanciatur ut neque rogemus res turpes nec faciamus rogati. turpis enim excusatio est et minime accipienda cum in ceteris peccatis tum si quis contra rem publicam se amici causa fecisse fateatur. etenim eo loco Fanni et Scaevola locati sumus, ut nos longe prospicere oporteat futuros casus rei publicae. deflexit iam aliquantum de spatio curriculoque consuetudo maiorum. Tib. Gracchus regnum occupare conatus est vel regnavit is quidem paucos menses. num quid simile populus Romanus audierat aut viderat? hunc etiam post mortem secuti amici et propinqui quid in P. Scipione effecerint, sine lacrimis non queo dicere. nam Carbonem quocumque modo potuimus propter recentem poenamTib.Gracchi sustinuimus; de C. Gracchi autem tribunatu quid expectem, non lubet augurari. serpit deinde res, quae proclivis ad perniciem cum semel coepit, labitur. videtis in tabella iam ante quanta sit facta labes, primo Gabinia lege, biennio autem post Cassia. videre iam videor populum a senatu disiunctum, multitudinis arbitrio res maximas agi. plures enim discent quem ad modum haec fiant quam quem ad modum his resistatur. quorsum haec? quia sine sociis nemo quicquam tale conatur. praecipiendum est igitur bonis, ut si in eius modi amicitias ignari casu aliquo inciderint, ne existiment ita se alligatos ut ab amicis in magna aliqua re publica peccantibus non discedant;

13 Haec igitur prima lex amicitiae sanciatur ut ab amicis honesta petamus, amicorum causa honesta faciamus, ne exspectemus quidem dum rogemur; studium semper adsit, cunctatio absit; consilium vero dare audeamus libere. plurimum in amicitia amicorum bene suadentium valeat auctoritas eaque et adhibeatur ad monendum non modo aperte, sed etiam acriter, si res postulabit, et adhibitae pareatur. nam quibusdam quos audio sapientes habitos in Graecia, placuisse opinor mirabilia quaedam (sed nihil est quod illi non persequantur argutiis): partim fugiendas esse nimias amicitias, ne necesse sit unum sollicitum esse pro pluribus; satis superque esse sibi suarum cuique rerum, alienis nimis implicari molestum esse; commodissimum esse quam laxissimas habenas habere amicitiae, quas vel adducas cum velis, vel remittas; caput enim esse ad beate vivendum securitatem qua frui non possit animus, si tamquam parturiat unus pro pluribus. alios autem dicere aiunt multo etiam inhumanius (quem locum breviter paulo ante perstrinxi) praesidii adiumentique causa, non benivolentiae neque caritatis amicitias esse expetendas; itaque ut quisque minimum firmitatis haberet minimumque virium, ita amicitias adpetere maxime; ex eo fieri ut mulierculae magis amicitiarum praesidia quaerant quam viri et inopes quam opulenti et calamitosi quam ii qui putentur beati. o praeclaram sapientiam! solem enim e mundo tollere videntur qui amicitiam e vita tollunt, qua nihil a dis inmortalibus melius habemus, nihil iucundius. quae est enim ista securitas? specie quidem blanda, sed reapse multis locis repudianda. neque enim est consentaneum ullam honestam rem actionemve, ne sollicitus sis, aut non suscipere aut susceptam deponere. quodsi curam fugimus, virtus fugienda est quae necesse est cum aliqua cura res sibi contrarias aspernetur atque oderit, ut bonitas malitiam, temperantia lubidinem, ignaviam fortitudo; itaque videas rebus iniustis iustos maxime dolere, inbellibus fortes, flagitiosis modestos. ergo hoc proprium est animi bene constituti et laetari bonis rebus et dolere contrariis. quam ob rem, si cadit in sapientem animi dolor, qui profecto cadit, nisi ex eius animo extirpatam humanitatem arbitramur, quae causa est cur amicitiam funditus tollamus e vita, ne aliquas propter eam suscipiamus molestias? quid enim interest motu animi sublato non dico inter pecudem et hominem, sed inter hominem et truncum aut saxum aut quidvis generis eiusdem? neque enim sunt isti audiendi qui virtutem duram et quasi ferream esse quandam volunt; quae quidem est cum multis in rebus tum in amicitia tenera atque tractabilis, ut et bonis amici quasi diffundatur et incommodis contrahatur. quam ob rem angor iste qui pro amico saepe capiendus est, non tantum valet ut tollat e vita amicitiam, non plus quam ut virtutes, quia non nullas curas et molestias adferunt, repudientur.

14 Cum autem contrahat amicitiam ut supra dixi, si qua significatio virtutis eluceat, ad quam se similis animus adplicet et adiungat, id cum contigit, amor exoriatur necesse est. quid enim tam absurdum quam delectari multis inanibus rebus ut honore ut gloria ut aedificio ut vestitu cultuque corporis, animante virtute praedito, eo qui vel amare vel ut ita dicam, redamare possit, non admodum delectari? nihil est enim remuneratione benivolentiae, nihil vicissitudine studiorum officiorumque iucundius. quid si illud etiam addimus quod recte addi potest, nihil esse quod ad se rem ullam tam alliciat et attrahat quam ad amicitiam similitudo? concedetur profecto verum esse, ut bonos boni diligant adsciscantque sibi quasi propinquitate coniunctos atque natura. nihil est enim appetentius similium sui nec rapacius quam natura. quam ob rem hoc quidem Fanni et Scaevola constet ut opinor bonis inter bonos quasi necessariam benivolentiam, qui est amicitiae fons a natura constitutus.

READING 5-B

QVINTVS HORATIVS FLACCVS

[65–8 BCE]

CARMINVM

LIBER TERTIVS

I

Odi profanum vulgus et arceo;
favete linguis: carmina non prius
audita Musarum sacerdos
virginibus puerisque canto.
regum timendorum in proprios greges, 5
reges in ipsos imperium est Iovis,
clari Giganteo triumpho,
cuncta supercilio moventis.
est ut viro vir latius ordinet
arbusta sulcis, hic generosior 10
descendat in Campum petitor,
moribus hic meliorque fama
contendat, illi turba clientium
sit maior: aequa lege Necessitas
sortitur insignis et imos; 15
omne capax movet urna nomen.
destrictus ensis cui super impia
cervice pendet, non Siculae dapes
dulcem elaborabunt saporem,
non avium citharaeque cantus 20
somnum reducent: somnus agrestium
lenis virorum non humilis domos
fastidit umbrosamque ripam,
non Zephyris agitata Tempe.
desiderantem quod satis est neque 25
tumultuosum sollicitat mare
nec saevus Arcturi cadentis
impetus aut orientis Haedi,
non verberatae grandine vineae
fundusque mendax, arbore nunc aquas 30
culpante, nunc torrentia agros
sidera, nunc hiemes iniquas.

contracta pisces aequora sentiunt
iactis in altum molibus; huc frequens
caementa demittit redemptor 35
cum famulis dominusque terrae
fastidiosus: sed Timor et Minae
scandunt eodem quo dominus, neque
decedit aerata triremi et
post equitem sedet atra Cura. 40
quodsi dolentem nec Phrygius lapis
nec purpurarum sidere clarior
delenit usus nec Falerna
vitis Achaemeniumque costum,
cur invidendis postibus et novo 45
sublime ritu moliar atrium?
cur valle permutem Sabina
divitias operosiores?

II

ANGVSTAM amice pauperiem pati
robustus acri militia puer
condiscat et Parthos feroces
vexet eques metuendus hasta
vitamque sub divo et trepidis agat 5
in rebus, illum ex moenibus hosticis
matrona bellantis tyranni
prospiciens et adulta virgo
suspiret, eheu, ne rudis agminum
sponsus lacessat regius asperum 10
tactu leonem, quem cruenta
per medias rapit ira caedis.
dulce et decorum est pro patria mori:
mors et fugacem persequitur virum,
nec parcit imbellis iuventae 15
poplitibus timidove tergo.
Virtus repulsae nescia sordidae
intaminatis fulget honoribus,
nec sumit aut ponit securis
arbitrio popularis aurae. 20
Virtus, recludens immeritis mori
caelum, negata temptat iter via,
coetusque vulgaris et udam
spernit humum fugiente penna.
est et fideli tuta silentio 25
merces: vetabo, qui Cereris sacrum
vulgarit arcanae, sub isdem
sit trabibus fragilemque mecum

solvat phaselon: saepe Diespiter
neglectus incesto addidit integrum: 30
raro antecedentem scelestum
deseruit pede Poena claudo.

VIII

MARTIIS caelebs quid agam Kalendis,
quid velint flores et acerra turis
plena miraris positusque carbo in
caespite vivo,
docte sermones utriusque linguae? 5
voveram dulcis epulas et album
Libero caprum prope funeratus
arboris ictu.
hic dies anno redeunte festus
corticem adstrictum pice dimovebit 10
amphorae fumum bibere institutae
consule Tullo.
sume, Maecenas, cyathos amici
sospitis centum et vigiles lucernas
perfer in lucem: procul omnis esto 15
clamor et ira.
mitte civilis super urbe curas:
occidit Daci Cotisonis agmen,
Medus infestus sibi luctuosis
dissidet armis, 20
servit Hispanae vetus hostis orae
Cantaber sera domitus catena,
iam Scythae laxo meditantur arcu
cedere campis.
neglegens ne qua populus laboret 25
parce privatus nimium cavere et
dona praesentis cape laetus horae ac
linque severa.

IX

DONEC gratus eram tibi
nec quisquam potior bracchia candidae
cervici iuvenis dabat,
Persarum vigui rege beatior.
'donec non alia magis 5
arsisti neque erat Lydia post Chloen,
multi Lydia nominis
Romana vigui clarior Ilia.'
me nunc Thraessa Chloe regit,

dulcis docta modos et citharae sciens, 10
pro qua non metuam mori,
si parcent animae fata superstiti.
'me torret face mutua
Thurini Calais filius Ornyti,
pro quo bis patiar mori, 15
si parcent puero fata superstiti.'
quid si prisca redit Venus
diductosque iugo cogit aeneo,
si flava excutitur Chloe
reiectaeque patet ianua Lydiae? 20
'quamquam sidere pulchrior
ille est, tu levior cortice et improbo
iracundior Hadria,
tecum vivere amem, tecum obeam libens.

X

EXTREMVM Tanain si biberes, Lyce,
saevo nupta viro, me tamen asperas
porrectum ante foris obicere incolis
plorares Aquilonibus.
audis quo strepitu ianua, quo nemus 5
inter pulchra satum tecta remugiat
ventis, et positas ut glaciet nives
puro numine Iuppiter?
ingratam Veneri pone superbiam,
ne currente retro funis eat rota. 10
non te Penelopen difficilem procis
Tyrrhenus genuit parens.
o quamvis neque te munera nec preces
nec tinctus viola pallor amantium
nec vir Pieria paelice saucius 15
curvat, supplicibus tuis
parcas, nec rigida mollior aesculo
nec Mauris animum mitior anguibus.
non hoc semper erit liminis aut aquae
caelestis patiens latus. 20

XIII

O FONS Bandusiae splendidior vitro
dulci digne mero non sine floribus,
cras donaberis haedo,
cui frons turgida cornibus
primis et venerem et proelia destinat; 5

frustra: nam gelidos inficiet tibi
rubro sanguine rivos
lascivi suboles gregis.
te flagrantis atrox hora Caniculae
nescit tangere, tu frigus amabile 10
fessis vomere tauris
praebes et pecori vago.
fies nobilium tu quoque fontium,
me dicente cavis impositam ilicem
saxis, unde loquaces 15
lymphae desiliunt tuae.

XVIII

FAVNE, Nympharum fugientum amator,
per meos finis et aprica rura
lenis incedas abeasque parvis
aequus alumnis,
si tener pleno cadit haedus anno, 5
larga nec desunt Veneris sodali
vina craterae, vetus ara multo
fumat odore.
ludit herboso pecus omne campo,
cum tibi Nonae redeunt Decembres; 10
festus in pratis vacat otioso
cum bove pagus;
inter audaces lupus errat agnos;
spargit agrestis tibi silva frondis;
gaudet invisam pepulisse fossor 15
ter pede terram.

XXI

O NATA mecum consule Manlio,
seu tu querelas sive geris iocos
seu rixam et insanos amores
seu facilem, pia testa, somnum,
quocumque lectum nomine Massicum 5
servas, moveri digna bono die,
descende, Corvino iubente
promere languidiora vina.
non ille, quamquam Socraticis madet
sermonibus, te negleget horridus: 10
narratur et prisci Catonis
saepe mero caluisse virtus.
tu lene tormentum ingenio admoves

plerumque duro; tu sapientium
curas et arcanum iocoso 15
consilium retegis Lyaeo;
tu spem reducis mentibus anxiis,
virisque et addis cornua pauperi
post te neque iratos trementi
regum apices neque militum arma. 20
te Liber et, si laeta aderit, Venus
segnesque nodum solvere Gratiae
vivaeque producent lucernae,
dum rediens fugat astra Phoebus.

XXII

MONTIVM custos nemorumque, Virgo,
quae laborantis utero puellas
ter vocata audis adimisque leto,
diva triformis,
imminens villae tua pinus esto, 5
quam per exactos ego laetus annos
verris obliquum meditantis ictum
sanguine donem.

XXIII

CAELO supinas si tuleris manus
nascente Luna, rustica Phidyle
si ture placaris et horna
fruge Lares avidaque porca,
nec pestilentem sentiet Africum 5
fecunda vitis nec sterilem seges
robiginem aut dulces alumni
pomifero grave tempus anno.
nam quae nivali pascitur Algido
devota quercus inter et ilices 10
aut crescit Albanis in herbis
victima pontificum securis
cervice tinget: te nihil attinet
temptare multa caede bidentium
parvos coronantem marino 15
rore deos fragilique myrto.
immunis aram si tetigit manus,
non sumptuosa blandior hostia
mollivit aversos Penatis
farre pio et saliente mica. 20

XXVI

VIXI puellis nuper idoneus
et militavi non sine gloria;
nunc arma defunctumque bello
barbiton hic paries habebit,
laevum marinae qui Veneris latus 5
custodit. hic, hic ponite lucida
funalia et vectis et arcus
oppositis foribus minaces.
o quae beatam diva tenes Cyprum et
Memphin carentem Sithonia nive, 10
regina, sublimi flagello
tange Chloen semel arrogantem.

XXX

EXEGI monumentum aere perennius
regalique situ pyramidum altius,
quod non imber edax, non Aquilo impotens
possit diruere aut innumerabilis
annorum series et fuga temporum. 5
non omnis moriar, multaque pars mei
vitabit Libitinam: usque ego postera
crescam laude recens, dum Capitolium
scandet cum tacita virgine pontifex.
dicar, qua violens obstrepit Aufidus 10
et qua pauper aquae Daunus agrestium
regnavit populorum, ex humili potens
princeps Aeolium carmen ad Italos
deduxisse modos. sume superbiam
quaesitam meritis et mihi Delphica 15
lauro cinge volens, Melpomene, comam.

READING 5-C

PVBLIVS CORNELIVS TACITVS
[55–117 CE]

DE ORIGINE ET SITV GERMANORVM LIBER

1 GERMANIA omnis a Gallis Raetisque et Pannoniis Rheno et Danuvio fluminibus, a Sarmatis Dacisque mutuo metu aut montibus separatur; cetera Oceanus ambit, latos sinus et insularum inmensa spatia complectens, nuper cognitis quibusdam gentibus ac regibus, quos bellum aperuit. Rhenus, Raeticarum Alpium inaccesso ac praecipiti vertice ortus, modico flexu in occidentem versus septentrionali Oceano miscetur. Danuvius, molli et clementer edito montis Abnobae iugo effusus, pluris populos adit donec in Ponticum mare sex meatibus erumpat; septimum os paludibus hauritur.

2 Ipsos Germanos indigenas crediderim minimeque aliarum gentium adventibus et hospitiis mixtos, quia nec terra olim sed classibus advehebantur qui mutare sedes quaerebant, et inmensus ultra utque sic dixerim adversus Oceanus raris ab orbe nostro navibus aditur. quis porro, praeter periculum horridi et ignoti maris, Asia aut Africa aut Italia relicta Germaniam peteret, informem terris, asperam caelo, tristem cultu aspectuque nisi si patria sit?

Celebrant carminibus antiquis, quod unum apud illos memoriae et annalium genus est, Tuistonem deum terra editum. ei filium Mannum, originem gentis conditoremque, Manno tris filios adsignant, e quorum nominibus proximi Oceano Ingaevones, medii Hermiones, ceteri Istaevones vocentur. quidam, ut in licentia vetustatis, pluris deo ortos pluresque gentis appellationes, Marsos Gambrivios Suebos Vandilios, adfirmant, eaque vera et antiqua nomina; ceterum Germaniae vocabulum recens et nuper additum, quoniam qui primi Rhenum transgressi Gallos expulerint ac nunc Tungri, tunc Germani vocati sint: ita nationis nomen, non gentis, evaluisse paulatim, ut omnes primum a victore ob metum, mox et a se ipsis invento nomine Germani vocarentur.

3 Fuisse apud eos et Herculem memorant, primumque omnium virorum fortium ituri in proelia canunt. sunt illis

haec quoque carmina, quorum relatu, quem barritum vocant, accendunt animos futuraeque pugnae fortunam ipso cantu augurantur: terrent enim trepidantve prout sonuit acies, nec tam voces illae quam virtutis concentus videntur. adfectatur praecipue asperitas soni et fractum murmur, obiectis ad os scutis quo plenior et gravior vox repercussu intumescat. ceterum et Ulixem quidam opinantur longo illo et fabuloso errore in hunc Oceanum delatum adisse Germaniae terras, Asciburgiumque, quod in ripa Rheni situm hodieque incolitur, ab illo constitutum nominatumque [*ΑΣΚΙΠΥΡΓΙΟΝ*]; aram quin etiam Ulixi consecratam, adiecto Laertae patris nomine, eodem loco olim repertam, monumentaque et tumulos quosdam Graecis litteris inscriptos in confinio Germaniae Raetiaeque adhuc extare. quae neque confirmare argumentis neque refellere in animo est: ex ingenio suo quisque demat vel addat fidem.

4 Ipse eorum opinionibus accedo qui Germaniae populos nullis aliis aliarum nationum conubiis infectos propriam et sinceram et tantum sui similem gentem extitisse arbitrantur. unde habitus quoque corporum, tamquam in tanto hominum numero, idem omnibus: truces et caerulei oculi, rutilae comae, magna corpora et tantum ad impetum valida. laboris atque operum non eadem patientia, minimeque sitim aestumque tolerare, frigora atque inediam caelo solove adsueverunt.

5 Terra, etsi aliquanto specie differt, in universum tamen aut silvis horrida aut paludibus foeda, humidior qua Gallias, ventosior qua Noricum ac Pannoniam aspicit; satis ferax, frugiferarum arborum inpatiens, pecorum fecunda, sed plerumque inprocera. ne armentis quidem suus honor aut gloria frontis; numero gaudent, eaeque solae et gratissimae opes sunt. argentum et aurum propitiine an irati di negaverint dubito. nec tamen adfirmaverim nullam Germaniae venam argentum aurumve gignere: quis enim scrutatus est? possessione et usu haud perinde adficiuntur; est videre apud illos argentea vasa, legatis et principibus eorum muneri data, non in alia vilitate quam quae humo finguntur. quamquam proximi ob usum commerciorum aurum et argentum in pretio habent formasque quasdam nostrae pecuniae agnoscunt atque eligunt; interiores simplicius et antiquius permutatione mercium utuntur. pecuniam probant veterem et diu notam, serratos bigatosque; argentum quoque magis quam aurum sequuntur, nulla adfectione animi sed quia numerus argenteorum facilior usui est promiscua ac vilia mercantibus.

6 Ne ferrum quidem superest, sicut ex genere telorum colligitur. rari gladiis aut maioribus lanceis utuntur; hastas vel ipsorum vocabulo frameas gerunt angusto et brevi ferro, sed ita acri et ad usum habili ut eodem telo, prout ratio poscit, vel comminus vel eminus pugnent. et eques quidem scuto frameaque contentus est, pedites et missilia spargunt, pluraque singuli, atque in inmensum vibrant, nudi aut sagulo leves. nulla cultus iactatio; scuta tantum lectissimis coloribus distingunt. paucis loricae, vix uni alterive cassis aut galea. equi non forma, non velocitate conspicui; sed nec variare gyros in morem nostrum docentur: in rectum aut uno flexu dextros agunt, ita coniuncto orbe ut nemo posterior sit. in universum aestimanti plus penes peditem roboris; eoque mixti proeliantur, apta et congruente ad equestrem pugnam velocitate peditum, quos ex omni iuventute delectos ante aciem locant. definitur et numerus: centeni ex singulis pagis sunt, idque ipsum inter suos vocantur, et quod primo numerus fuit, iam nomen et honor est. acies per cuneos componitur. cedere loco, dummodo rursus instes, consilii quam formidinis arbitrantur. corpora suorum etiam in dubiis proeliis referunt. scutum reliquisse praecipuum flagitium, nec aut sacris adesse aut concilium inire ignominioso fas, multique superstites bellorum infamiam laqueo finierunt.

7 Reges ex nobilitate, duces ex virtute sumunt. nec regibus infinita ac libera potestas, et duces exemplo potius quam imperio, si prompti, si conspicui, si ante aciem agant admiratione praesunt. ceterum neque animadvertere neque vincire, ne verberare quidem nisi sacerdotibus permissum, non quasi in poenam nec ducis iussu sed velut deo imperante, quem adesse bellantibus credunt: effigiesque et signa quaedam detracta lucis in proelium ferunt. quodque praecipuum fortitudinis incitamentum est, non casus nec fortuita conglobatio turmam aut cuneum facit sed familiae et propinquitates, et in proximo pignora, unde feminarum ululatus audiri, unde vagitus infantium. hi cuique sanctissimi testes, hi maximi laudatores; ad matres, ad coniuges vulnera ferunt: nec illae numerare et exigere plagas pavent, cibosque et hortamina pugnantibus gestant.

8 Memoriae proditur quasdam acies inclinatas iam et labantes a feminis restitutas constantia precum et obiectu pectorum et monstrata comminus captivitate, quam longe inpatientius feminarum suarum nomine timent, adeo ut efficacius obligentur animi civitatum quibus inter obsides puellae quoque nobiles imperantur. inesse quin etiam sanctum aliquid et providum putant, nec aut consilia earum aspernantur aut responsa neglegunt. vidimus sub divo Vespasiano Veledam diu apud plerosque numinis loco habitam; sed et olim Auriniam et compluris alias venerati sunt, non adulatione nec tamquam facerent deas.

9 Deorum maxime Mercurium colunt, cui certis diebus humanis quoque hostiis litare fas habent. Herculem ac Martem concessis animalibus placant. pars Sueborum et Isidi sacrificat; unde causa et origo peregrino sacro parum comperi nisi quod signum ipsum in modum liburnae figuratum docet advectam religionem. ceterum nec cohibere parietibus deos neque in ullam humani oris speciem adsimulare ex magnitudine caelestium arbitrantur; lucos ac nemora consecrant, deorumque nominibus appellant secretum illud quod sola reverentia vident.

10 Auspicia sortesque ut qui maxime observant, sortium consuetudo simplex, virgam frugiferae arbori decisam in surculos amputant eosque notis quibusdam discretos super candidam vestem temere ac fortuito spargunt. mox, si publice consultetur, sacerdos civitatis, sin privatim, ipse pater familiae, precatus deos caelumque suspiciens ter singulos tollit, sublatos secundum inpressam ante notam interpretatur. si prohibuerunt, nulla de eadem re in eundem diem consultatio; sin permissum, auspiciorum adhuc fides exigitur. et illud quidem etiam hic notum, avium voces volatusque interrogare; proprium gentis equorum quoque praesagia ac monitus experiri: publice aluntur isdem nemoribus ac lucis candidi et nullo mortali opere contacti, quos pressos sacro curru sacerdos ac rex vel princeps civitatis comitantur hinnitusque ac fremitus observant. nec ulli auspicio maior fides, non solum apud plebem sed apud proceres, apud sacerdotes: se enim ministros deorum, illos conscios putant. est et alia observatio auspiciorum, qua gravium bellorum eventus explorant. eius gentis cum qua bellum est captivum quoquo modo interceptum cum electo popularium suorum, patriis quemque armis, committunt; victoria huius vel illius pro praeiudicio accipitur.

11 De minoribus rebus principes consultant, de maioribus omnes, ita tamen ut ea quoque quorum penes plebem arbitrium est apud principes praetractentur. coeunt, nisi quid fortuitum et subitum incidit, certis diebus, cum aut incohatur luna aut impletur; nam agendis rebus hoc auspicatissimum initium credunt. nec dierum numerum ut nos sed noctium computant; sic constituunt, sic condicunt: nox ducere diem videtur. illud ex libertate vitium, quod non simul nec ut iussi conveniunt, sed et alter et tertius dies cunctatione coeuntium absumitur. ut turbae placuit, considunt armati. silentium per sacerdotes, quibus tum et coercendi ius est, imperatur. mox rex vel princeps, prout aetas cuique, prout nobilitas, prout decus bellorum, prout facundia est, audiuntur auctoritate suadendi magis quam iubendi potestate. si displicuit sententia, fremitu aspernantur, sin placuit, frameas concutiunt: honoratissimum adsensus genus est armis laudare.

12 Licet apud concilium accusare quoque et discrimen capitis intendere. distinctio poenarum ex delicto: proditores et transfugas arboribus suspendunt, ignavos et inbelles et corpore infames caeno ac palude, iniecta insuper crate, mergunt. diversitas supplicii illuc respicit, tamquam scelera ostendi oporteat dum puniuntur, flagitia abscondi. sed et levioribus delictis pro modo poena: equorum pecorumque numero convicti multantur. pars multae regi vel civitati, pars ipsi qui vindicatur vel propinquis eius exsolvitur. eliguntur in isdem conciliis et principes qui iura per pagos vicosque reddunt; centeni singulis ex plebe comites consilium simul et auctoritas adsunt.

13 Nihil autem neque publicae neque privatae rei nisi armati agunt. sed arma sumere non ante cuiquam moris quam civitas suffecturum probaverit. tum in ipso concilio vel principum aliquis vel pater vel propinqui scuto frameaque iuvenem ornant: haec apud illos toga, hic primus iuventae honos; ante hoc domus pars videntur, mox rei publicae. insignis nobilitas aut magna patrum merita principis dignationem etiam adulescentulis adsignant; ceteris robustioribus ac iam pridem probatis adgregantur, nec rubor inter comites aspici. gradus quin etiam ipse comitatus habet, iudicio eius quem sectantur; magnaque et comitum aemulatio quibus primus apud principem suum locus, et principum cui plurimi et acerrimi comites. haec dignitas, hae vires magno semper electorum iuvenum globo circumdari, in pace decus, in bello praesidium. nec solum in sua gente cuique sed apud finitimas quoque civitates id nomen, ea gloria est, si numero ac virtute comitatus emineat; expetuntur enim legationibus et muneribus ornantur et ipsa plerumque fama bella profligant.

14 Cum ventum in aciem, turpe principi virtute vinci, turpe comitatui virtutem principis non adaequare. iam vero infame in omnem vitam ac probrosum superstitem principi suo ex acie recessisse; illum defendere tueri, sua quoque fortia facta gloriae eius adsignare praecipuum sacramentum est: principes pro victoria pugnant, comites pro principe. si civitas in qua orti sunt longa pace et otio torpeat, plerique nobilium adulescentium petunt ultro eas nationes quae tum bellum aliquod gerunt, quia et ingrata genti quies et facilius inter ancipitia clarescunt magnumque comitatum non nisi vi belloque tueare. exigunt enim principis sui liberalitate illum bellatorem equum, illam cruentam victricemque frameam: nam epulae et quamquam incompti largi tamen apparatus pro stipendio cedunt. materia munificentiae per bella et raptus, nec arare terram aut expectare annum tam facile persuaseris quam vocare hostem et vulnera mereri; pigrum quin immo et iners videtur sudore adquirere quod possis sanguine parare.

15 Quotiens bella non ineunt, non multum venatibus, plus per otium transigunt, dediti somno ciboque; fortissimus quisque ac bellicosissimus nihil agens, delegata domus et penatium et agrorum cura feminis senibusque et infirmissimo cuique ex familia, ipsi hebent, mira diversitate naturae cum idem homines sic ament inertiam et oderint quietem. mos est civitatibus ultro ac viritim conferre principibus vel armentorum vel frugum quod pro honore acceptum etiam necessitatibus subvenit. gaudent praecipue finitimarum gentium donis, quae non modo a singulis sed et publice mittuntur, electi equi, magnifica arma, phalerae torquesque; iam et pecuniam accipere docuimus.

16 Nullas Germanorum populis urbes habitari satis notum est, ne pati quidem inter se iunctas sedes. colunt discreti ac diversi, ut fons, ut campus, ut nemus placuit. vicos locant non in nostrum morem conexis et cohaerentibus aedificiis; suam quisque domum spatio circumdat, sive adversus casus ignis remedium sive inscitia aedificandi. ne caementorum quidem apud illos aut tegularum usus; materia ad omnia utuntur informi et citra speciem aut delectationem. quaedam loca diligentius inlinunt terra ita pura ac splendente ut picturam ac liniamenta colorum imitetur. solent et subterraneos specus aperire eosque multo insuper fimo onerant, suffugium hiemis et receptaculum frugibus, quia rigorem frigorum eius modi loci molliunt, et si quando hostis advenit aperta populatur, abdita autem et defossa aut ignorantur aut eo ipso fallunt quod quaerenda sunt.

17 Tegumen omnibus sagum fibula aut, si desit, spina consertum; cetera intecti totos dies iuxta focum atque ignem agunt. locupletissimi veste distinguntur non fluitante, sicut Sarmatae ac Parthi, sed stricta et singulos artus exprimente. gerunt et ferarum pelles, proximi ripae neglegenter, ulteriores

exquisitius ut quibus nullus per commercia cultus:
eligunt feras et detracta velamina spargunt maculis pellibusque
beluarum quas exterior Oceanus atque ignotum mare
gignit. nec alius feminis quam viris habitus, nisi quod
feminae saepius lineis amictibus velantur eosque purpura
variant, partemque vestitus superioris in manicas non ex-
tendunt, nudae bracchia ac lacertos; sed et proxima pars
pectoris patet.

18 Quamquam severa illic matrimonia, nec ullam morum
partem magis laudaveris. nam prope soli barbarorum
singulis uxoribus contenti sunt, exceptis admodum paucis
qui non libidine sed ob nobilitatem plurimis nuptiis ambiuntur.
dotem non uxor marito sed uxori maritus offert.
intersunt parentes et propinqui, ac munera probant, munera
non ad delicias muliebres quaesita nec quibus nova nupta
comatur, sed boves et frenatum equum et scutum cum
framea gladioque. in haec munera uxor accipitur, atque in
vicem ipsa armorum aliquid viro adfert: hoc maximum
vinculum, haec arcana sacra, hos coniugales deos arbitrantur. ne se mulier extra virtutum cogitationes extraque
bellorum casus putet, ipsis incipientis matrimonii auspiciis
admonetur venire se laborum periculorumque sociam,
idem in pace, idem in proelio passuram ausuramque;
hoc iuncti boves, hoc paratus equus, hoc data arma
denuntiant. sic vivendum, sic pariendum; accipere se quae
liberis inviolata ac digna reddat, quae nurus accipiant
rursusque ad nepotes referantur.

19 Ergo saepta pudicitia agunt, nullis spectaculorum inlecebris, nullis conviviorum inritationibus corruptae. litterarum
secreta viri pariter ac feminae ignorant. paucissima
in tam numerosa gente adulteria, quorum poena praesens
et maritis permissa: adcisis crinibus nudatam coram propinquis expellit domo maritus ac per omnem vicum verbere
agit. publicatae enim pudicitiae nulla venia: non forma,
non aetate, non opibus maritum invenerit. nemo enim illic
vitia ridet, nec corrumpere et corrumpi saeculum vocatur.
melius quidem adhuc eae civitates in quibus tantum virgines nubunt et cum spe votoque uxoris semel transigitur.
sic unum accipiunt maritum quo modo unum corpus
unamque vitam, ne ulla cogitatio ultra, ne longior cupiditas,
ne tamquam maritum sed tamquam matrimonium ament.
numerum liberorum finire aut quemquam ex agnatis necare
flagitium habetur, plusque ibi boni mores valent quam alibi
bonae leges.

20 In omni domo nudi ac sordidi in hos artus, in haec corpora quae miramur excrescunt. sua quemque mater uberibus alit, nec ancillis ac nutricibus delegantur. dominum ac servum nullis educationis deliciis dinoscas; inter eadem pecora, in eadem humo degunt, donec aetas separet ingenuos, virtus agnoscat. sera iuvenum venus, eoque inexhausta pubertas. nec virgines festinantur; eadem iuventa, similis proceritas; pares validaeque miscentur, ac robora parentum liberi referunt. sororum filiis idem apud avunculum qui apud patrem honor. quidam sanctiorem artioremque hunc nexum sanguinis arbitrantur et in accipiendis obsidibus magis exigunt, tamquam et animum firmius et domum latius teneant. heredes tamen successoresque sui cuique liberi, et nullum testamentum. si liberi non sunt, proximus gradus in possessione fratres patrui avunculi. quanto plus propinquorum, quanto maior adfinium numerus, tanto gratiosior senectus; nec ulla orbitatis pretia.

21 Suscipere tam inimicitias seu patris seu propinqui quam amicitias necesse est. nec inplacabiles durant; luitur enim etiam homicidium certo armentorum ac pecorum numero recipitque satisfactionem universa domus, utiliter in publicum, quia periculosiores sunt inimicitiae iuxta libertatem.

Convictibus et hospitiis non alia gens effusius indulget. quemcumque mortalium arcere tecto nefas habetur; pro fortuna quisque apparatis epulis excipit. cum defecere, qui modo hospes fuerat monstrator hospitii et comes; proximam domum non invitati adeunt. nec interest: pari humanitate accipiuntur; notum ignotumque quantum ad ius hospitis nemo discernit. abeunti, si quid poposcerit, concedere moris, et poscendi in vicem eadem facilitas. gaudent muneribus, sed nec data inputant nec acceptis obligantur. [victus inter hospites comis.]

22 Statim e somno, quem plerumque in diem extrahunt, lavantur, saepius calida, ut apud quos plurimum hiems occupat. lauti cibum capiunt; separatae singulis sedes et sua cuique mensa. tum ad negotia nec minus saepe ad convivia procedunt armati. diem noctemque continuare potando nulli probrum. crebrae, ut inter vinolentos, rixae raro conviciis, saepius caede et vulneribus transiguntur.

READING 5-D

CAECILIVS FIRMIANVS LACTANTIVS
[240–320 CE]

DE OPIFICIO DEI

1. Quam minime sim quietus etiam in summis necessitatibus, ex hoc libello poteris aestimare, quem ad te rudibus paene uerbis prout ingenii mediocritas tulit, Demetriane, perscripsi, ut et cotidianum studium meum nosses et non deessem tibi praecepter etiam nunc, sed honestioris rei meliorisque doctrinae. nam si te in litteris nihil aliud quam linguam instruentibus auditorem satis strenuum praebuisti, quanto magis in his ueris et ad uitam pertinentibus docilior esse debebis? apud quem nunc profiteor nulla me necessitate uel rei uel temporis inpediri, quominus aliquid extundam quo philosophi sectae nostrae quam tuemur instructiores doctioresque in posterum fiant, quamuis nunc male audiant castigenturque uulgo, quod aliter quam sapientibus conuenit uiuant et uitia sub obtentu nominis celent: quibus illos aut mederi oportuit aut ea prorsus effugere, ut beatum atque incorruptum sapientiae nomen uita ipsa cum praeceptis congruente praestarent. ego tamen ut nos ipsos simul et ceteros instruam, laborem nullum recuso. neque enim possum obliuisci mei tum praesertim, cum maxime opus sit meminisse, sicut ne tu quidem tui, ut spero et opto. nam licet te publicae rei necessitas a ueris et iustis operibus auertat, tamen fieri non potest quin subinde in caelum aspiciat mens sibi conscia recti. et quidem laetor omnia tibi quae pro bonis habentur prospere fluere, sed ita, si nihil de statu mentis inmutent. uereor enim ne paulatim consuetudo et iucunditas earum rerum sicut fieri solet in animum tuum inrepat, ideoque te moneo et repetens iterum(que) iterumque monebo, ne oblectamenta ista terrae pro magnis aut ueris bonis habere te credas, quae sunt non tantum fallacia, quia dubia, uerum etiam insidiosa, quia dulcia. nam ille conluctator et aduersarius noster scis quam sit astutus et idem saepe uiolentus, sicuti nunc uidemus. is haec omnia quae inlicere possunt, pro laqueis habet et quidem tam subtilibus, ut oculos mentis effugiant, ne possint hominis prouisione uitari. summa ergo prudentia est pedetemptim procedere, quoniam utrubique saltus insidet et offensacula pedibus latenter opponit. itaque res tuas prosperas in quibus nunc agis suadeo ut pro tua uirtute aut contemnas, si potes, aut non magno opere mireris. memento et ueri parentis tui et in qua ciuitate nomen dederis et cuius ordinis fueris: intellegis profecto quid loquar. nec enim te superbiae arguo, cuius in te ne suspicio quidem ulla est, sed ea quae dico, ad mentem referenda sunt, non ad corpus: cuius omnis ratio ideo conparata est, ut animo tamquam domino seruiat et regatur nutu eius. uas est enim quodammodo fictile quo animus id est homo ipse uerus continetur, et quidem non a Prometheo fictum, ut poetae locuntur, sed a summo illo rerum conditore atque artifice deo, cuius diuinam prouidentiam perfectissimamque uirtutem nec sensu conprehendere nec uerbo enarrare possibile est. temptabo tamen, quoniam corporis et animi facta mentio est, utriusque rationem quantum pusillitas intellegentiae meae peruidet, explicare. quod officium hac de causa maxime suscipiendum puto, quod Marcus Tullius uir ingenii singularis in quarto De re publica libro, cura id facere temptasset, materiam late patentem angustis finibus terminauit leuiter summa quaeque decerpens. ac ne ulla esset excusatio cur eum locum non fuerit exsecutus, ipse testatus est nec uoluntatem sibi defuisse nec curam. in libro enim De legibus primo cum hoc idem summatim stringeret, sic ait: hunc locum satis, ut mihi uidetur, in iis libris quos legistis expressit Scipio. postea tamen in libro De natura deorum secundo hoc idem latius exsequi conatus est. sed quoniam ne ibi quidem satis expressit, adgrediar hoc munus et sumam mihi audaciter explicandum quod homo disertissimus paene omisit intactum. forsitan reprehendas quod in rebus obscuris coner aliquid disputare, cum uideas tanta temeritate homines extitisse, qui uulgo philosophi nominantur, ut ea quae abstrusa prorsus atque abdita deus esse uoluit, scrutarentur ac naturam rerum caelestium terrenarumque conquirerent, quae a nobis longe remotae neque oculis contrectari neque tangi manu neque percipi sensibus possunt: et tamen de illarum omnium ratione sic disputant, ut ea quae adferunt probata et cognita uideri uelint. quid est tandem cur nobis inuidiosum quisquam putet, si rationem corporis nostri dispicere et contemplari uelimus? quae plane obscura non est, quia ex ipsis membrorum officiis et usibus partium singularum quanta ui prouidentiae quidque factum sit, intellegere nobis licet.

2. Dedit enim homini artifex ille noster ac parens deus sensum atque rationem, ut ex eo appareret nos ab eo esse generatos, quia ipse intellegentia, ipse sensus ac ratio est. ceteris animantibus quoniam rationalem istam uim non at-tribuit, quemadmodum tamen uita earum tutior esset, ante prouidit. omnes enim suis ex se pellibus texit, quo facilius possent uim pruinarum ac frigorum sustinere. Singulis autem generibus ad propulsandos impetus externos sua propria munimenta constituit, ut aut naturalibus telis repugnent fortioribus aut quae sunt inbecilliora, subtrahant se periculis pernicitate fugiendi aut quae simul et uiribus et celeritate indigent, astu se protegant aut latibulis saepiant. itaque alia eorum uel plumis leuibus in sublime suspensa sunt uel suffulta ungulis uel instructa cornibus, quibusdam in ore arma sunt dentes aut in pedibus adunci ungues: nulli munimentum ad tutelam sui deest. si qua uero in praedam maioribus cedunt, ne tamen stirps eorum funditus interiret, aut in ea sunt religata regione, ubi maiora esse non possunt, aut acceperunt uberem generandi fecunditatem, ut et bestiis quae sanguine aluntur, uictus suppeteret ex illis et inlatam tamen cladem ad conseruationem generis multitudo ipsa superaret. hominem autem ratione concessa et uirtute sentiendi atque eloquendi data eorum quae ceteris animalibus attributa sunt, fecit expertem, quia sapientia reddere poterat quae illi naturae condicio denegasset: statuit enim nudum et inermem, quia et ingenio poterat armari et ratione uestiri. Ea uero ipsa quae mutis data et homini denegata sunt, quam mirabiliter in homine ad pulchritudinem faciant, exprimi non potest. nam si homini ferinos dentes aut cornua aut ungues aut ungulas aut caudam aut uarii coloris pilos addidisset, quis non sentiat quam turpe animal esset futurum, sicut et muta, si nuda et inermia fingerentur? quibus si detrahas uel naturalem sui corporis uestem uel ea quibus ex se armantur, nec speciosa poterunt esse nec tuta, ut mirabiliter, si utilitatem cogites, instructa, si speciem, ornata uideantur: adeo miro modo consentit utilitas cum decore. hominem uero quoniam aeternum animal atque inmortale fingebat, non forinsecus ut cetera, sed interius armauit nec munimentum eius in corpore, sed in animo posuit, quoniam superuacuum fuit, cum illi quod erat maximum tribuisset, corporalibus eum tegere munimentis, cum praesertim pulchritudinem humani corporis inpedirent. unde ego philosophorum qui Epicurum secuntur amentiam soleo mirari, qui naturae opera reprehendunt, ut ostendant nulla prouidentia instructum esse ac regi mundum, sed originem rerum insecabilibus ac solidis corporibus adsignant, quorum fortuitis concursionibus uniuersa nascantur et nata sint. praetereo quae ad ipsum mundum pertinentia uitio dant, in quo ridicule insaniunt: id sumo, quod ad rem de qua nunc agimus pertinet.

3. Queruntur hominem nimis inbecillum et fragilem nasci quam cetera nascantur animalia: quae ut sunt edita ex utero, protinus in pedes suos erigi et gestire discursibus statimque aeri tolerando idonea esse, quod in lucem naturalibus indumentis munita processerint, hominem contra nudum et inermem tamquam ex naufragio in huius uitae miserias proici et expelli, qui neque mouere se loco ubi effusus est possit nec alimentum lactis adpetere nec iniuriam temporis ferre. itaque naturam non matrem esse humani generis, sed nouercam, quae cum mutis tam liberaliter gesserit, hominem uero sic effuderit, ut inops et infirmus et omni auxilio indigens nihil aliud possit quam fragilitatis suae condicionem ploratu ac fletibus ominari, scilicet

cui tantum in uita restet transire malorum.

quae cum dicunt, uehementer sapere creduntur, propterea quod unus quisque inconsiderate suae condicionis ingratus est, ego uero illos numquam tam desipere contendo quam cum haec locuntur. considerans enim condicionem rerum intellego nihil fieri aliter debuisse, ut non dicam potuisse, quia deus potest omnia, sed necesse est ut prouidentissima illa maiestas id effecerit quod erat melius et rectius. libet igitur interrogare istos diuinorum operum reprehensores quid in homine deesse, quia inbecillior nascitur, credant, num idcirco minus educentur homines, num minus ad summum robur aetatis prouehantur, num inbecillitas aut incrementum inpediat aut salutem, quoniam quae desunt ratio rependit? 'at hominis' inquiunt 'educatio maximis laboribus constat, pecudum scilicet condicio melior, quod eae cum fetum ediderint, non nisi pastus sui curam gerunt: ex quo efficitur ut uberibus sua sponte distentis alimentum lactis fetibus ministretur et id cogente natura sine matrum sollicitudine adpetant'. quid? aues, quarum ratio diuersa est, nonne maximos suscipiunt in educando labores, ut interdum aliquid humanae intellegentiae habere uideantur? nidos enim aut luto aedificant aut uirgultis et frondibus construunt, etiam ciborum expertes incubant ouis et quoniam fetus de suis corporibus alere non datum est, cibos conuehunt et totos dies in huiusmodi discursatione consumunt, noctibus uero defendunt fouent protegunt. quid amplius homines facere possint nisi hoc solum fortasse, quod non expellunt adultos, sed perpetua necessitudine ac uinculo caritatis adiunctos habent? quid quod auium fetus multo fragilior est quam hominis, quia non ipsum animal edunt, sed id quod materni corporis fotu et calore tepefactum animal efficiat? quod tamen cum spiritu fuerit animatum, id uero inplume ac tenerum non modo uolandi, sed ambulandi quoque usu caret. non ergo ineptissimus sit si quis putet male cum

uolucribus egisse naturam primum quod bis nascantur, deinde
quod tam infirmae, ut sint quaesitis per laborem cibis a
parentibus nutriendae? sed illi fortiora eligunt, inbecilliora
praetereunt. quaero igitur ab iis qui condicionem pecudum
suae praeferunt, quid eligant, si deus iis deferat optionem,
utrum malint, humanamne sapientiam cum inbecillitate an
pecudum firmitatem cum illarum natura. scilicet non tam
pecudes sunt, ut non malint uel fragiliorem multo quam nunc
est dummodo humanam quam illam inrationabilem firmitatem.
sed uidelicet prudentes uiri neque hominis rationem uolunt
cum fragilitate neque mutorum firmitatem sine ratione. ⟨quid⟩
quod nihil est tam repugnans tamque contrarium, quod unum
quodque animal aut ratio instruat necesse est aut condicio
naturae? si naturalibus munimentis instruatur, superuacua
ratio est. quid enim excogitabit? quid faciet? quid molietur?
aut in quo lumen illud ingenii ostendet, cum ea quae possint
esse rationis, ultro natura concedat? si autem ratione sit
praeditum, quid opus erit saepimentis corporis, cum semel
concessa ratio naturae munus possit inplere? quae quidem
tantum ualet ad ornandum tuendumque hominem, ut nihil
potuerit maius ac melius a deo dari. denique cum et corporis non magni homo et exiguarum uirium et ualitudinis
sit infirmae, tamen quoniam id quod est maius accepit, et
instructior est ceteris animalibus et ornatior. nam cum fra-
gilis inbecillusque nascatur, tamen et a mutis omnibus tutus
est et ea omnia quae firmiora nascuntur, etiamsi uim caeli
fortiter patiuntur, ab homine tamen tuta esse non possunt. ita
fit ut plus homini conferat ratio quam natura mutis, quoniam
in illis neque magnitudo uirium neque firmitas corporis efficere
potest quominus aut opprimantur a nobis aut nostrae subiecta
sint potestati. potestne igitur aliquis cum uideat etiam boues
lucas cum inmanissimis corporibus ac uiribus seruire homini,
queri de opifice rerum deo, quod modicas uires, quod paruum
corpus acceperit, nec beneficia in se diuina pro merito aestimat?
quod est ingrati aut ut uerius loquamur, insani. Plato
ut hos credo ingratos refelleret, naturae gratias egit,
quod homo natus esset. quanto magis melius et sanius,
qui sensit condicionem hominis esse meliorem, quam isti qui
se pecudes natos maluerunt! quos si deus in ea forte conuerterit
animalia quorum sortem praeferunt suae, iam profecto
cupiant remigrare magnisque clamoribus condicionem pristinam
flagitent, quia non est tanti robur ac firmitas corporis, ut
officio linguae careas, aut auium per aerem libera discursatio,
ut manibus indigeas. plus enim manus praestant quam
leuitas ususque pinnarum, plus lingua quam totius corporis

fortitudo. quae igitur amentia est ea praeferre quae si data sint, accipere detrectes?

4. Idem queruntur hominem morbis et inmaturae morti esse subiectum. indignantur uidelicet non deos esse se natos. 'minime', inquiunt 'sed ex hoc ostendimus hominem nulla prouidentia esse factum, quod aliter fieri debuit'. quid si ostendo id ipsum magna ratione prouisum esse, ut morbis uexari posset et uita saepe in medio cursus sui spatio rumperetur? cum enim deus animal quod fecerat sua sponte ad mortem transire cognouisset, ut mortem ipsam, quae est dissolutio naturae, capere posset, dedit ei fragilitatem, quae morti aditum ad dissoluendum animal inueniret. nam si eius roboris fieret, ut ad eum morbus et aegritudo adire non posset, ne mors quidem posset, quoniam mors sequella morborum est. inmatura uero mors quomodo abesset ab eo cui esset constituta matura? nempe nullum hominem mori uolunt nisi cum centesimum aetatis conpleuerit annum. quomodo illis in tanta repugnantia rerum poterit ratio constare? ut enim ante annos centum mori quisque non possit, aliquid illi roboris quod sit inmortale tribuendum est: quo concesso necesse est condicionem mortis excludi. id autem ipsum cuiusmodi potest esse quod hominem contra morbos et ictus extrarios solidum atque inexpugnabilem faciat ? cum enim constet ex ossibus et neruis et uisceribus et sanguine, quid horum potest esse tam firmum, ut fragilitatem repellat ac mortem? ut igitur homo indissolubilis sit ante id tempus quod illi putant oportuisse constitui, ex qua ei materia corpus attribuent? fragilia sunt omnia quae uideri ac tangi possunt. superest ut aliquid ex caelo petant, quoniam in terra nihil est quod non sit infirmum. cum ergo sic homo formandus esset a deo ut mortalis esset aliquando, res ipsa exigebat ut terreno et fragili corpore fingeretur. necesse est igitur ut mortem recipiat quandolibet, quoniam corporalis est; corpus enim quodlibet solubile atque mortale est. stultissimi ergo, qui de morte inmatura queruntur, quoniam naturae condicio locum illi facit. ita consequens erit ut morbis quoque subiectus sit: neque enim patitur natura ut abesse possit infirmitas ab eo corpore quod aliquando soluendum est. sed putemus fieri posse quemadmodum uolunt, ut homines ea condicione nascantur, ne quis morbo mortiue subiectus sit, nisi peracto aetatis suae spatio ad ultimam processerit senectutem: non igitur uident, si ita sit constitutum, quid sequatur, omni utique cetero tempore mori nullo modo posse? sed si prohiberi ab altero uictu potest, mori poterit. res igitur exigit ut homini qui ante certam diem mori non potest, ciborum alimentis, quia subtrahi possunt,

opus non sit. ⟨sed⟩ si opus cibo non erit, iam non homo
ille, sed deus fiet. ergo, ut superius dixi, qui de fragilitate
hominis queruntur, id potissimum queruntur, quod non inmortales
sempiternique sint nati. 'nemo nisi senex mori
debet'. atquin mortalitas non potest cum inmortalitate coniungi.
si enim mortalis est in senectute, inmortalis esse in
adulescentia non potest nec est ab eo condicio mortis aliena
qui quandoque moriturus est, nec ulla inmortalitas est cui sit
terminus constitutus. ita fit ut et inmortalitas exclusa in
perpetuum et ad tempus recepta mortalitas hominem constituat
in ea condicione, ut sit in qualibet aetate mortalis.
quadrat igitur necessitas undique nec debuisse fieri aliter nec
fas fuisse. sed isti rationem sequentium non uident, quia
semel errauerunt in ipsa summa. exclusa enim de rebus humanis diuina prouidentia necessario sequebatur ut omnia sua
sponte sint nata. hinc inuenerunt illas minutorum seminum
plagas et concursiones fortuitas, quia rerum originem non
uidebant. in quas se angustias cum coniecissent, iam cogebat
eos necessitas existimare animas cum corporibus nasci et item
cum corporibus extingui: adsumpserant enim nihil fieri mente
diuina. quod ipsum non aliter probare poterant quam si
ostenderent esse aliqua in quibus uideretur prouidentiae ratio
claudicare. reprehenderunt igitur ea in quibus uel maxime
diuinitatem suam prouidentia mirabiliter expressit, ut illa quae
rettuli de morbis et inmatura morte, cum debuerint cogitare
his adsumptis quid necessario sequeretur. secuntur autem
illa quae dixi: si morbum non reciperet, neque tectis neque
uestibus indigeret. quid enim uentos aut imbres aut frigora
metueret, quorum uis in eo est ut morbos adferant? idcirco
enim accepit sapientiam, ut aduersus nocentia fragilitatem
suam muniat. sequitur ⟨quod⟩ necesse est, ut quoniam retinendae rationis causa morbos capit, etiam mortem semper
accipiat, quia is ad quem mors non uenit, firmus sit necesse
est. infirmitas autem habet in se mortis condicionem, firmitas
uero ubi fuerit, nec senectus locum potest habere nec mors,
quae sequitur senectutem. praeterea si mors certae constituta
esset aetati, fieret homo insolentissimus et humanitate omni
careret. nam fere iura omnia humanitatis, quibus inter nos
cohaeremus, ex metu et conscientia fragilitatis oriuntur. denique
inbecilliora et timidiora quaeque animalia congregantur,
ut quoniam uiribus tueri se nequeunt, multitudine tueantur,
fortiora uero solitudines adpetunt, quoniam robore uiribusque
confidunt. homo quoque si eodem modo haberet ad propulsanda
pericula suppetens robur nec ullius alterius auxilio
indigeret, quae societas esset, quae reuerentia inter se, quis

ordo, quae ratio, quae humanitas? aut quid esset tetrius homine, quid efferatius, quid inmanius? sed quoniam inbecillus est nec per se potest sine homine uiuere, societatem adpetit, ut uita communis et ornatior fiat et tutior. uides igitur omnem hominis rationem in eo uel maxime stare, quod nudus fragilisque nascitur, quod morbis adficitur, quod inmatura morte multatur. quae si homini detrahantur, rationem quoque ac sapientiam detrahi necesse est. sed nimis diu de rebus apertissimis disputo, cum sit liquidum nihil sine prouidentia nec factum esse umquam nec fieri potuisse. de cuius operibus uniuersis si nunc libeat disputare per ordinem, infinita materia est. sed ego de uno corpore hominis tantum institui dicere, ut in eo diuinae prouidentiae potestatem quanta fuerit ostendam, his dumtaxat in rebus, quae sunt conprehensibiles et apertae: nam illa quae sunt animi, nec subici oculis nec conprehendi queunt. nunc de ipso uase hominis loquimur quod uidemus.

5. In principio cum deus fingeret animalia, noluit ea in rotundam formae speciem conglobare atque colligere, ut et moueri ad ambulandum et flectere se in quamlibet partem facile possent, sed ex ipsa corporis summa produxit caput. item produxit quaedam membra longius, quae uocantur pedes, ut alternis motibus solo fixa perducerent animal quo mens tulisset aut quo petendi cibi necessitas prouocasset.

READING 5-E

AMBROSIVS MEDIOLANENSIS

[339–397 CE]

EPISTVLAE

Ambrosius Antonio

1. Numquam es tacitus mihi nec umquam tuo me transmissum silentio querar, qui sciam quod tuo non desim pectori. Nam cum id pendas quod pluris est, qui potes etiam id negare quod saepe etiam in multos defluit, non tam amoris usu quam officii vicissitudine? **2.** Ego vero etiam ex meo animo tuam vicem aestimo, ut numquam me tibi et te mihi absentem putem, quoniam semper animis haeremus, numquam tuas litteras mihi deesse opiner aut meas tibi, cum te cottidie coram alloquar, in te oculos studia atque omnia officia mea dirigam. **3.** His tecum delectat congredi; nam litterae tuae, ut aperte cum individuo pectoris mei loquar, verecundari me faciunt. Unde peto ut supersedeas gratiarum relatu; mihi enim mei in vos officii summa merces est, si me debito erga vos muneri non defuisse arbitrere.

Vale et nos dilige, quia ego quoque te diligo.

Ambrosius Romulo

1. Cum sis in agro, miror qua ratione de me quaerendum putaveris, cur dixerit deus: *Ponam caelum aereum et terram ferream.* Nam species ipsa agri et praesens fertilitas docere nos potest, quanta clementia sit aeris et caeli indulgentia, quando dignatur deus ubertatem dare; quando autem sterilitas, quemadmodum clausa omnia, spissus aer, ut in rigorem aeris solidatus putetur. Unde alibi habes quia *in diebus Heliae clausum est caelum annis tribus et mensibus sex.* **2.** Significatur igitur clausum *caelum aereum* esse usum sui terris negare. Terra quoque ferrea est, cum proventus abnuit et iacta sibi semina tamquam hostili duritia genitali excludit arvo, quae gremio solet blandae matris fovere. Quando enim ferrum fructificat, quando aes imbres relaxat?

3. His igitur miserandam famem minatur impiis, ut qui pietatem filiorum communi ⟨omni⟩um domino et patri exhibere nesciunt, careant nutrimento paternae indulgentiae, sit illis *caelum aereum* concreto aere et solidato in metalli rigorem, sit illis terra ferrea partus suos nesciens et, quod plerumque in⟨o⟩pia habeat, discordias serens. Rapto enim utuntur qui victu indigent, ut alienis dispendiis famem suam ablevent.

4. Iam si et offensa inhabitantium huiusmodi sit, ut divina commotione his inferantur proelia, vere terra est ferrea, telorum segetibus inhorrens et suis nuda fructibus, fecunda ad poenam, sterilis ad alimoniam. Ubi autem abundantia? *Ecce ego pluo vobis panes* dicit dominus.

Vale et nos dilige, quia nos te diligimus.

Ambrosius Titiano

1. Venit tibi innocens victoria, ut sine voti amaritudine potiaris victoriae securitate. Rufinus enim ex magistro officiorum factus est in consulatu praefectus praetorio ac per hoc plus posse coepit, sed tibi iam nihil obesse; est enim aliarum praefectus partium. Quam gaudeo vel illi ut amico, quia honore auctus invidia levatus est, vel tibi ut filio, quia liberatus es ab eo, quem tibi graviorem iudicem arbitrabare, ut si de negotio definiveris cum tua nepte, pietatis tuae sit non formidinis.

2. Ideoque promptior esto decisioni, cuius et spes potior et fructus est: Spes quia pater neptis tuae, qui de illi⟨u⟩s sent⟨ent⟩ia sibi plurimum blandiebatur, iam quod de eo speret non habet; ille enim alia curat, praeterita neglegit, vel cum illo quod tunc gerebat deposuit officio, iste negotii sui meritum, non sententiae patronum considerat. Et fructus iucundior est, ut tibi referatur decisionis gratia, qui potueris iam spernere et non spreveris pietatem spectans necessitudinis, non stimulum offensionis.

Vale et nos dilige ut filius, quia nos te ut parentes diligimus.

Ambrosius Eusebio

1. Apparitor praefecturae, qui propter operas portuenses offensam contraxerat, iam in portu navigat. Oportune autem advenit; nam simul ut accepi litteras tuas, vidi praefectum. Rogavi pro eo, ignovit ilico, iussit retrahi epistulam, quam de facultatibus eius publicandis dictaverat. Quod si tardius venisset, nemo magis probasset inexplicabile illud opus esse portus reformandi, quam iste qui illic naufragium fecerat, nisi te habuisset gubernatorem, ut aliter non posset inde nisi nudus exire.

2. Faustinus parvulus tussi laborat. Ad sanctam sororem curatum venit, et venit sponte; expertus enim est melius sibi ventrem curari. Denique et me medicum putat, expectat prandium. Itaque hic bis ad diem curatur et coeperat pulchre valere; sed dum eum nimio amore abstinere gestiunt, tussire de ventre plus coepit; et laborabit adhuc, nisi ad medicamenta sua revertatur. Vale, et nos dilige, quia nos te diligimus.

Ambrosius Sisinnio

1. Quod filio nostro remisisti meo rogatu, quia te inconsulto uxorem acceperat, pietati magis tribuo quam nostro amori; plus est enim pietatem ipsam de te impetravisse quam cuiusce petitionem. Certe sacerdos tunc magis impetrat, cum virtus praevalet; sacerdotis enim petitio doctrina pietatis est. Impetravit igitur natura, impetravit filius eo plenius, quia postulati contemplatio temporalis solet esse, virtutis autem diuturnus habitus et iugis animorum inductio.

2. Pulchre itaque gestum, ut te patrem recognosceres, simul quia iusta indignatio fuit. Malo enim culpam fateri, ut plus laudetur paterna indulgentia. Sed et ipsa paterna offensio fuit, quoniam venturam in locum filiae tuo debuisti eligere iudicio, cui fieres pater. Namque aut natura filios suscipimus aut electione. In natura casus est, in electione iudicium,

magisque offendimus in adoptatis quam in genitalibus filiis, quia genitales filios esse degeneres ad naturam refertur, adscitos vel adoptione vel copula dedecores esse nostro errori adscribitur. Fuit ergo quod suscenseres filio. Sed fuit etiam quod remitteres quia sibi uxorem elegit: adquisisti filiam sine electionis periculo. Si bonam duxit, tibi adquisivit gratiam, si erravit, recipiendo meliores facies, refutando deteriores. **3.** Maturiore quidem consilio puella filio a patre traditur, sed maiore obsequii proposito a filio ad patrem ducitur et a viro lecta ingreditur soceri domum, dum metuit et filius displicere iudicium suum et nurus ministerium. Illam paternae electionis praerogativa adtollit adque erigit, istam offensionis humiliat metus, inclinat verecundia. Non habebit filius quod in uxorem referat quasi exsors culpae, si quid fortasse offensum sit, quod habet usus. Immo amplius elaborabit, ut in utroque suum possit probari et in uxore iudicium et in se obsequium.

4. Fecisti igitur quod boni parentes, ut cito ignosceres, sed obsecratus. Nam antequam rogareris, non erat ignoscere, sed factum probare. Deinde diutius differre veniam et tibi acerbum et illis inutile; neque enim paterna viscera diutius tolerare possent. **5.** Summae devotionis proposito Abraham filium suum secundum oraculum dei offerebat in holocaustum et quasi exsors naturae exerebat gladium, ne mora sacrificium decoloreret. **6.** Tamen ubi abstinere a filio iussus est, gladium libenter recondit, et qui immolare unigenitum fidei intentione properabat, maiore pietatis studio festinavit ovem subrogare sacrificio. **7.** Ioseph quoque ut fratrem iuniorem teneret, simulabat iracundiam fratribus et conpositam furti fraudem. Indignatus tamen, cum advolveretur genua eius unus ex fratribus, Iudas, flerent alii, fraterno victus et conpassus adfectu diutius tenere non potuit simulationem severitatis remotisque arbitris aperuit fratribus quod germani sui essent et ipse esset Ioseph, quem vendidissent, nec se memorem suae esse iniuriae et fraternae venditionis acerbitatem fraterne excusare adque id, quod posset arguere, ad altiores causas referre, eo quod ita oportuisset fieri procurante deo, ut transiret in Aegyptum, qui gentem suam frugis externae egentem pasceret, ut sterilitatis tempore alendis patri et filiis subsidio foret. **8.** Quid autem de sancto David loquar, qui degenerem filium et fraterno oblitum sanguine ad unius mulieris petitionem paternis visceribus mentem emollitus domo recepit?

9. Ipse ille evangelicus pater adulescentiorem filium, qui prodegerat omnem *substantiam* a patre acceptam *vivendo luxuriose,* regredientem tamen unius sermonis inflexus humilitate, quod in patrem peccasse se fatebatur, occursu pio fovit, supra collum eius cecidit, primam illam stolam anulum et calciamenta deferri iussit adque honoratum osculo, donatum munere, admirabili suscepit convivio.

10. Horum te imitatorem praebuisti pietete patria, qua proximo ad deum accedimus. Et ideo ego prompte filiam nostram adhortatus sum, ut etiam hiemali tempore viae laborem exciperet, commodius hibernatura non solum in hospitio, sed etiam in adfectu paterno, cum iam successerit indignationi gratia, quandoquidem, ut plene te ad similitudinem adque imitationem sanctorum referres, eos accusavisti, qui conpositis mendaciis animum tuum adversum filios excitandum arbitrati sunt.

Vale et nos dilige, quia nos te diligimus.

Ambrosius Candidiano Fratri

Summus quidem splendor in sermone est tuo, sed magis in affectu elucet mihi; nam in epistulis mentis tuae aspicio fulgorem, dilectissime frater ac beatissime. Dominus te benedicat et det tibi sui gratiam. Nam et ipse in epistulis tuis vota magis quam mea merita recognosco. Quae enim merita mea tantis tuis aequentur sermonibus?

Dilige nos, frater, quia ego te diligo.

Ambrosio Siricio

1. Gratum est mihi, cum litteras accipio tuas. At cum de conservitio nostro aliquos dirigis, ut fratrem nostrum et conpresbyterum Syrum tuis es prosecutus litteris, geminatur laetitia. Sed utinam fructus fuisset iste diuturnior! Nam statim ut venit, recurrendum putavit; quod quidem ad desiderium meum plurimum minuit, ad sui gratiam multum addidit.

2. Nam ego diligo eos vel presbyteros vel diaconos, qui cum aliquo processerint, nequaquam se patiuntur a suo diutius abesse munere; dicit enim propheta: *Non laborari sequens post te.* Quis autem potest laborare sequens Iesum, cum ipse dicat: *Venite ad me omnes qui laboratis et onerati estis, et ego vos reficiam?*

Sequamur ergo Iesum semper nec desinamus! Quodsi semper sequamur, numquam deficimus; dat enim vires sequentibus se. Itaque quo propior virtuti fueris, eo fortior eris.

3. Plerumque, cum sequimur, dicitur nobis ab adversariis: *Ubi est verbum domini? veniat!* Sed nos non fatigemur sequendo, non avertamur subdolae interrogationis impedimento. Dicebatur hoc prophetae cum mitteretur in carcerem, cum demergeretur in voraginem luti: *Ubi est verbum domini? veniat!* Sed ille multo magis secutus est et ideo ad bravium pervenit, ideo accepit coronam, quia non laboravit qui sequebatur Iesum. *Non* est enim *labor in Iacob nec dolor videbitur in lsrahel.*

Vale et nos dilige, quia et nos amantem nostri et parentem diligimus.

Ambrosius Sabino

1. Quoniam tibi quoque conplacuit nostrarum usus epistularum, in quibus quidam inter absentes praesentium sermo est, pergam frequentius te in meis scriptis, et cum solus sum, adloqui. Numquam enim minus solus sum, quam cum solus esse videor, nec minus otiosus, quam cum otiosus. Certe pro arbitrio accersio, quos volo, adque adiungo mihi, quos magis diligo aut quos aptiores arbitror; nemo interpellat, nemo interpolat. Tunc ergo te magis teneo et de scripturis confero et prolixiorem simul sermonem caedimus.

2. Sola erat Maria et loquebatur cum angelo. Sola erat, quando supervenit in eam *spiritus sanctus et virtus altissimi* obumbravit eam. Sola erat et operata est mundi salutem et concepit redemptionem universorum. Solus erat Petrus et totum per orbem consecrandarum gentium cognovit mysteria. Solus erat Adam at non est praevaricatus, quia mens eius adhaerebat deo. Postquam vero ei mulier adiuncta est, non potuit inhaerere mandatis caelestibus et ideo se abscondebat, quando deus deambulabat *in paradiso.* **3.** Et nunc deambulat in paradiso deus, quando divinas scripturas lego. Paradisus est Genesis liber, in quo virtutes pullulant patriarcharum, paradisus Deuteronomium, in quo germinant legis praecepta, paradisus Evangelium, in quo arbor vitae *bonos fructus facit* et aeternae spei mandata diffundit per universos populos.

4. Audiens itaque *diligite inimicos,* audiens dimitte omnia tua *et sequere me,* audiens *qui te percutit in maxilla, praebe ei et alteram* at haec non faciens et vi diligens eum qui me diligat, non dimittens quae habeo, iniuriam acceptam ulcisci volens et sublatum mihi extorquere, cum scriptura dicat etiam aliud, id est plus quam petitum aut ereptum est, concedendum, video me contra mandata dei facere et aperiens oculos conscientiae 'deambulare mihi deum' praesentem recognosco; cupio me abdere, cupio velare, sed nudus sum deo, apud quem *nuda et intecta sunt omnia.* Erubescens itaque tegere pudenda facinorum desidero quasi membra mei corporis. Sed quia deus omnia videt, quia foliis obumbratus, latebris tectus appareo, puto me abscondi, quia corpore amictus sum. Ipsa est 'tunica pellicia', cum qua Adam de paradiso eiectus est nec a frigore tutus nec tectus ab obprobrio, sed et iniuriae et culpae patens.

5. Liquet igitur ex his quia soli cum sumus, tunc nos offerimus deo, tunc mentem ei nostram aperimus, tunc amictum fraudis exuimus. Solus erat Adam, quando in paradiso constitutus est, solus erat et quando *ad imaginem dei* factus est, sed non erat solus, quando de paradiso eiectus est. Solus erat dominus Iesus, quando mundum redemit; *non* enim *legatus neque nuntius, sed ipse dominus* solus *salvum fecit populum suum,* etsi numquam solus est ille, in quo pater est semper. Unde et nos soli simus, ut dominus nobiscum sit.

Vale et nos dilige, quia nos te diligimus.

Ambrosius Siricio

Prisco, amico aequaevo meo, dedisti advenienti litteras. Ego quoque revertenti reddidi, quas et pro officio et pro amore debui. Utrumque igitur nostrum suo officio remuneratus est, quod et mihi tuas et meas tibi restituit. Ideo eius officii pretium incremento debet adipisci gratiae.

Vale et nos, frater, dilige, quia nos te diligimus.

Ambrosius Attico

Prisco meo dedisti litteras. Priscus meus mihi reddidit et ego Prisco. Tu Priscum ut soles dilige et plus etiam quam soles. Quod eo suadeo, quia et ipse Priscum meum facio plurimi. Est enim erga eum priscus hic noster amor, qui a pueritia iam inde nobiscum aetate accrevit simul. Sed eum multo post vidi tempore, ut vere mihi non solum nomine, sed etiam tanti intervallo temporis priscus advenerit.

Vale et amantes tui dilige, quia nos te diligimus.

Ambrosius Felici

1. Misisti mihi tubera et quidem mirae magnitudinis, ut stupori forent. Ea tam grandia nolui in sinu, ut aiunt, abscondere, sed aliis quoque demonstrare malui. Itaque partem direxi amicis, partem mihi reservavi.

2. Suave munus, non tamen ita praepotens, ut comprimeret querelam meam iure excitatam, quod nos tamdiu amantes tui nequaquam revisas. Et cave posthac, ne maiora invenias doloris tubera. Nam huius nominis diversa ratio; ut enim grata in munere, ita in corpore atque in affectu molesta sunt. De te impetra, quominus te abesse doleam; nam causa commotionis meae desiderium est tui. Effice, si potes, ut minus gratus sis.

3. Rem exposui, causam probavi. Intorquenda est amentata illa non manipularis sententia. Metuisti certe, sed vide quam movear, ut delectet iocari. Postea tamen ne excusaveris. Etenim quamvis tua haec vectigalis mihi sit excusatio, male de te iudicat nec de me melius, si aut tuam absentiam muneribus compensandam aut me muneribus redimendum putes.

Vale et nos amantes tui dilige.

Ambrosius Alypio

Antiochus, vir consulates, reddidit mihi eximietatis tuae litteras. Nec supersedi respondendi munere; nam per meos homines dedi litteras et, ni fallor, alia oborta copia geminavi epistulam. Sed quia non tam remetienda amicitiae munia quam cumulanda arbitror, oportuit ipso praesertim regrediente qui me tanto litterarum tuarum affecit nomine, referri aliquod officium sermonis mei, ut ego utrique vestrum et ille tibi absolveretur, qui debebat referre quod acceperat.

Vale et diligentes te dilige.

Ambrosius Felici Salutem

1. Etsi habitu corporis minus valebam, tamen ubi sermonem unanimi mihi pectoris tui legi, non mediocrem sumpsi ad convalescendum gratiam, quasi quodam tui adloquii poleio refotus, simul quia celebrem utrique nostrum adnuntiasti diem adfore, quo suscepisti summi gubernacula sacerdotii, de quo ante momentum cum fratre nostro Bassiano loquebar. Ortus enim sermo de basilicae, quam condidit apostolorum nomine dedicatione, dedit huic sermoni viam; siquidem significabat quod sedulo tuae quaereret sanctitatis praesentiam. **2.** Tum ego nostris fabulis intexui diem natalis tui, qui foret in exordio ipso Kalendaram Novembrium, eumque, si non fallerer, adpropinquasse et crastina celebrandum die, unde posthac non excusaturum. Promisi ergo de te, quoniam et tibi id de me licet, promisi illi, exegi mihi; praesumptum enim habeo quod adfuturus sis, quia debes adesse. Non ergo te magis meum promissum tenebit quam tuum institutum, qui id in animum indueris, ut quod oportet facias. Advertis itaque quia non tam promissi audax quam tui conscius fratri spopondi. Veni igitur, ne duos sacerdotes redarguas, te qui non adfueris, me qui tam facile promiserim.

3. Natalem autem tuum prosequemur nostris orationibus, et tu nostri in tuis votis non obliviscaris. Te noster spiritus comitabitur, tu quoque cum ingredieris *secundum tabernaculum, quod dicitur sancta sanctorum,* facito nostro more, ut nos quoque tecum inducas. Cum spiri**tu** adoles *aureum* illud *thymiamaterium,* nos ne intermiseris. Ipsum est enim quod in secundo tabernaculo est, de quo plena sapientiae *oratio* tua *sicut incensum dirigitur* ad caelestia. **4.** Ibi 'arca *testamenti undique auro tecta'*, id est doctrina Christi, doctrina 'sapientiae dei'. Ibi *dolium aureum habens manna, r*eceptaculum scilicet spiritalis alimonias et divinae promptuarium cognitionis. Ibi *virga Aaron,* insigne sacerdotalis gratiae: aruerat ante, sed in Christo refloruit. Ibi '*cherubin* super tabulas testamenti', lectionis cognitio sacrae. Ibi *propitiatorium,* supra quod in excelsis deus verbum est, *imago invisibilis dei,* quod tibi dicit: *Loquar tecum de super propitiatorium de medio duorum cherubin.* Sic enim loquitur nobiscum, ut nos eius sermonem intellegamus, vel quia non mundana, sed intellegibilia loquitur, sicut ait: *Aperiam in parabolis os meum.* Ubi enim Christus, ibi omnia, ibi doctrina eius, ibi peccatorum remissio, ibi gratia, ibi separatio mortuorum ac viventium ...

READING 5-F

RAIMVNDVS LVLLI

[1235–1315 CE]

LIBER NATALIS PVERI PARVVLI CHRISTI IESV

Deus, cum tua gratia
Incipit Liber natalis pueri paruuli Christi Iesu.

Epistola ad magnificum dominum regem Franciae.

| Gloriosissimo et sincerissima caritate uenerando domino, Philippo illustrissimo, magnifico Dei gratia Francorum regi, Puer nobis datus paruulus (*cf. Is.* 9, 6), quem inuenire cupimus, homo Christus Iesus, bonum regimen tribuat, teque totum dirigat ad sui gloriam et honorem.

O rex clementissime, hoc opusculum suscipe, in quo benedictum puerum aliqualiter contemplari poteris ut uiator, ut tandem ad ipsius utriusque naturae contemplationem peruenire te faciat, qui una cum Patre et Sancto Spiritu regnat in trinitate persona, Deus benedictus. Amen.

INCIPIT PROHEMIVM

Da, Domine, in te credentibus affectum actumque tibi placendi consimilem atque in te perseuerandi destinationem irreuocabilem et nullam cum infidelibus portionem, legisque tuae praeceptum geminum adimplere.

Fac nos, Domine, sine elatione ueraces, | sine fictione humiles, sine dissolutione hilares, sine errore iustos, sine iactantia mites, sine penuria pauperes, sine auaritia diuites, doctos studere fieri, non arroganter uelle uideri. Explicit prohemium.

INCIPIT TRACTATVS

Accidit pridie Parisius dominas sex in loco amoenissimo sibi ad inuicem obuiasse, uidelicet: Laus, Oratio, Caritas, Contritio, Confessio et Satisfactio.

I

[Lamentiones sex dominarum]

1. PRIMA DOMINA [LAVS]

| Laus primo conqueritur de hominibus huius saeculi in hunc modum:

Non laudant | Deum in se, propter se, et in aliis propter se ordinate, cum ipse sit essentia nobilis, dignitate incomparabilis et insuperabilis potestate, communicata tribus suppositis relatiuis, quae sola propter se laude digna.

Sed laudant eum extrinsece propter bona plurima, quae largitur. Quibus laudibus non contentor; immo tristis dolensque audio pluries et frequenter Deum aliquos blasphemare et eius minuere potestatem, dicen|tes Deum per se non posse | omnia sine causa media, puta caelo. Et si semel ab aliquibus audio laudem ueram, saepe tamen audio deterius.

Ideo esset mihi melius inhabitare eremum, ut talia non audirem.

2. SECVNDA DOMINA [ORATIO]

Post ait Oratio:

Heu, quam tristis doleo, quoniam Deum uerum, qui de se super omnia adorandus existit, altissimus bonitate, magnitudine et potestate, sine mutatione aeternus, in ueritate sapientissimus, uoluntate uirtuosus, iustissimus cum misericordia, | et perfectissimus in gloria, requiror a gentibus adorari, ut eis bona terrena tribuat potius quam gloriam sempiternam.

Vnde res admiratione est digna, quo modo haec Deus ualeat | sustinere de me, et quo modo queam uiuere. Vtinam tales in meo sensu uel memoria nunquam essent, nec de ipsis audiuissem fieri mentionem.

3. TERTIA DOMINA [CARITAS]

Ait postmodum Caritas:

Ego sum uirtus nobilissima a Deo data hominum uoluntati, ut per me Deum super omnia diligant, et sicut se ipsos quemlibet pro|ximum, ordine semper saluo, ut bona terrena omnia bonis essent communia eis data, taliter ut pax et concordia uniuersaliter conregnarent. Sed non sic est: immo oppositum. Quod uidetur | turbare ordinem uniuersi, quoniam fame pauperes moriuntur, nudi sunt et neglecti, petunt et non inueniunt, et diuites superbiunt bonorum superfluitate, a qua oriuntur gula et | auaritia et | alia multa mala. Et de me hodie parum curant, immo totaliter me dimittunt.

Quid ergo peccatores putant sine me facere? Quoniam si quis in regnum introierit, mecum ibit. | Nec extremum iudicium aeterni iudicis aliquis poterit impedire, neque eum decipere, cum sit sapientissimus, et uideat aperta omnia et occulta (*cf. Hebr.* 4, 13.)

Heu, quam plurimum doleo, quia subiectum non inuenio, in quo actionem habeam ac in melius perficiam. Et si quandoque quis me habeat, otiose me te|neat, est naturae meae contrarius, et sibi ipsi quam plurimum est nocivus.

4. QVARTA DOMINA [CONTRITIO]

Deinde ait Contritio:

Quando recordor, quot mala in mundo sunt et fuerunt, uidens male disponi entia, ut eidem ueniant et peiora, miror quo modo possim uiuere, nec in uoluntate existere per actum positum uel priuatum.

Volun|tas etiam hominum mihi contrariatur, quia quando deberem in ipsa actum ponere, ut haberet displicentiam decommissis, uertit se ad actum contrarium nec ueretur diuinum iudicium, quod exspectat. Quapropter tota difformis sum et infirma, a meaque natura penitus aliena. Voluntas autem huiusmodi sic peruersa, aeternis suppliciis affligetur.

5. QVINTA DOMINA [CONFESSIO]

Consequenter ait Confessio:

Ego sum uirtus, per quam sciant de commissis homines confiteri, taliter ut assit mentis uera contritio, quae dicta est soror mea, et uerbum | menti nostrae respondeat, nihilque | occultum remaneat, quin exterius reseretur, recordetur memoria, uideat intellectus, quid fecit, et quo modo Deum uel proximum offendendo, per uisum, auditum, odoratum, tactum, gustum et loquendi modum, modisque aliis, quibuscumque satisfactionem cogitet sibi possibilem | et condignam, et toto animo peccata displiceant, et pro eis iniuncta paenitentia impleatur.

Raro sum in hominibus, quando confitentur. Quid dicam, quid faciam, ubi stabo, cum amicum nequeam inuenire? Et nouit Deus, quod cotidie tristor ualde et nunquam laetabor in | posterum, quousque in hominibus habeam uerum esse.

6. SEXTA DOMINA [SATISFACTIO]

Ait sic Satisfactio:

Ego sum ancilla Iustitiae, uere oboediens et deuota.

Iustitia praecipit, ut de omni actu hominis fiat satisfactio, quo Deus uel proximus est offensus. Si uisu committitur, uigiliis, lacrimis et cordis suspiriis satisfaciam, a uanitate huius saeculi auertendo. Si auribus, audiendo illicita, conuertam ad Dei laudes et diuina officia audiendum. Quod etiam satisfaciam quoad gustum, ieiuniis sapores cibosque superfluos dimittendo, quibus humana fragilitas nata est lasciuire. Tactu satisfaciam, leuibus | et mollibus praetermissis; dura et aspera eligam, castitatis uirtute polleam, prout suadet religio christiana. Praecipit etiam, ut Deo satisfaciam de imaginatione, membris, potentiis, actibus hominis quibuscumque, et uniuersaliter quod di|mit|tam uitia, amplectendo uirtutes. Electione praeuia iudicet intellectus, secundum mensuram delicti satisfactionis modum, ut tandem sequatur contritio, laus et | oratio, caritateque inflammetur affectus.

Sed quid prodest tale praeceptum, a Iustitia mihi datum, cum iniuria regnet in omnibus? Ipsa enim, cum uitiis aliis sociata, uidelicet auaritia, gula, luxuria, superbia, accidia, inuid|ia et ira, totaliter me impedit et

Iustitiam, matrem meam. Et homines magis uitiis seruiunt quam uirtuti; et ex hoc mundus tenebrosus fit et obscurus.

| Dum autem quaelibet domina fuerit sic locuta, habuerunt consilium, ut mundum dimitterent et per deserta uagarent, ne uiderent ulterius homines uitiis induratos.

Vsquequo, ait Oratio: Non est bonum consilium, quod mundum et genus dimittamus humanum, quae nobis sunt tradita a Domino Deo nostro; nam esset magnum scandalum, et ma|iora mala et plurima sequerentur.

Sed nuper nobis dictum est, quod puer mundo natus est ex Virgine gloriosa. Qui pauper et paruulus iacet in praesepio, pannis | paucis et pauperculis inuolutus (*cf. Luc.* 2, 12). Et ideo, cum Filius Dei in tantum humiliatus est, quod puer paruus natus est, in quantum est homo factus, adeamus ipsum cum audacia, reclamemus cum fiducia. Qui tantum humiliatus est, ipse nos exaltet (*cf. Phil.* 2, 8-9; *Luc.*14, 11; 18, 14; *Matth.* 23, 12), ut a cordibus hominum extirpemus uitia et inseramus uirtutes.
Et quaelibet nostrum suo utatur | officio, et habeat plenarie actum suum

Quod dixit Oratio, aliis placuit dominabus. Et ierunt ad puerum paruulum adorandum.

II

DE INVENTIONE PVERI

Diu iuerunt praedictae dominae, de puero | sic loquentes; habentes desiderium, ut adorarent puerum, quaelibet suo modo.

Et cum uenissent ad puerum in praesepio positum, Iustitia et Misericordia ianitrices ipsas accedere propius non permittunt, donec intentionem explicant, quod uolunt puerum adorare et contemplari, quaelibet suo modo, et ab ipso habere gratiam, ut in mundo ualeant agere multum fructum.

[Explicatio intentionis sex dominarum]

I. DE LAVDE

| Laus primo ait: Dignum et iustum est puerum laudari, in quantum bonus et magnus est, quia in ipso huma|na et diuina actio est coniuncta. Nec ad huius laudes sufficio ego, nec aliqua creatura.

Sed uolo dicere, quantum mea uirtus sustinet aut natura, quod puer est Filius Dei, existens summa bonitas, magnitudo, ueritas et alia attributa, et est homo, creata bonitas, magnitudo. Ex quibus est suppositum altius in tota uniuersi natura, per quod facta sunt omnia et sua conseruatione permanent uniuersa. Ipse puer est Deus et homo, et utriusque praedicatio de utroque, qui in se continet tres naturas, | uidelicet corporis, animae rationalis et diuinam, quae personat illas duas.

In isto puero est exaltatio totius uniuersi, quia homo participat cum omnibus creaturis, et Deus est homo factus. Deus Pater misit Filium, ut genus humanum moriendo redimeret, et cum omnibus uirtutibus ageret, quae habuerunt in benedicto puero summum gradum.

Praeterea ait Misericordia: In me non est quan|titas, eo quia sum infinita; et ideo meum agere non finitum est. Et ideo, quando dimitto peccata uel infundo gratiam, simpliciter ago; peccator cum sit finitus, finite agit. Et ideo peccatores non debent de me desperare, quia plus possum | parcere, quam ipsi peccare.

Vltimo | ait Misericordia: Puer, qui | iacet in praese|pio, est uerus Deus et homo; et ipse in quantum homo est, rogat me, qui sum Deus, ut dimittam peccata hominibus, et eis gratiam faciam.

Beata Virgo Maria, mater pueri, mater subalternata est misericordiae. Ipsa rogat me continue, ut parcam peccatoribus, eo quia naturaliter sunt de suo genere et genere sui Filii, pueri Christi Iesu. Et | angeli, archangeli et omnes sancti non cessant rogare pro peccatoribus. Et omnes bene faciunt cum sciant, quod delectationes paradisi sint inaestimabiles; et angustiae inferni inaestimabiles sunt; et ipsi diligant bona et odiant mala. Verum est, quod propter preces eorum multas facio gratias, et multa peccata dimitto.

Item dico, et uerum est, quod plures uolo gratias facere et peccata dimittere, quam uolo rogari. Et hoc dignum et iustum est, cum preces sint inferius et ego superius. Quid ergo plus dicerem? Disponant se peccatores ad gratiam cum contritione, confessione et satisfactione, caritatiue laudando et me adorando, et eis peccata dimittam et me | habebunt gratiosam, abundantem, in omnibus fructuosam. Et si ipsi me rogant, quod talis sim erga ipsos, ego uolo, quod ipsi sint tales erga me, quales | dixi.

Hi sunt sermones, quos dixerunt diuinae rationes.

IV

[Laudes et preces sex dominarum]

1. DE PRECIBVS SEX DOMINARVM

Cum praedictae sex dominae uerba audiuerunt, quae reginae duodecim seu imperatrices diuinae locutae fuerunt, admirantes prae nimia rerum altitudine et profunditate, amoenitate et pulchritudine, ad inuicem | loquebantur, dicentes, quod si gentes audirent, et intelligerent talia uerba ardua et amoena, in toto mundo non esset nisi unus populus christianus. Et tunc suspirantes prae magno gaudio atque flentes, flexis genibus et ele|uatis manibus, cantauerunt et alta uoce, quaelibet suo modo.

Prima cantabat hanc cantilenam: Ave, consurgens ut aurora (*cf. Cant.* 6, 9), in te portans toti mundo praeoptatum gaudium.

Secunda dixit: Salve regina, mater pia, dulcis uita, spes et uia, ferens Dei Filium.

Alia sic: Aue regina caelorum, mater regis angelorum, nobile triclinium. Dixit sic alia domina: Aue gloriosa uirginum regina, caeli, terrae, marium.

Alia sic: Aue maris stella, Dei mater alma, paradisi ostium.

Alia sic: Aue Virgo Maria, Dei mater pia et sancti Spiritus sacrarium.

Finitis autem cantilenis, sanctam Mariam matrem, Virginem | rogauerunt, quod apud suum | benedictum Filium intercederet, ut ipsas in cordibus hominum exaltaret, et specialiter in domino Philippo, rege Franciae. In quo prae ceteris mundi rectoribus singulariter pollent hodie iustitia, ueritas, fides, caritas, recta spes in beatitudine, pulchritudo cum fortitudine, magnanimitas cum temperantia, largitas cum prudentia, humilitas et deuotio et christiana religio, pietas, benignitas, | sapientia, castitas, et breuiter | dona plurima, naturalia, gratuita et infusa, quatenus, cum ipse sit pugil ecclesiae et | defensor fidei christianae, libros et dicta Auerrois expelleret et extrahi | faceret de Parisiensi studio, taliter quod nullus de cetero auderet allegare, legere uel audire; quia multos errores turpissimos continent contra fidem, et, quod est deterius et periculosius, dictos errores frequenter generant in pluribus et diuersis. Et est turpe et dedecus dicere christianis, quod fides magis est improbabilis, quam probabilis uel apparens; quod dicunt et asserunt Auerroim haereticum imitantes.

Et etiam, quod dominus rex, magnificus atque potens, cum papa et cardinalibus ordinaret, quod Parisius et alibi essent loca et studia, in quibus diuersa linguagia fidelium et infidelium docerentur, ut uiri deuoti, sapientes et | litterati ad | exaltationem fidei per mundum uniuersum euangelium praedicarent, et per Dei gratiam inuenirentur plurimi, qui uellent propter Christum martyres fieri, sicut apostoli et eorum discipuli uoluerunt. Et quod talis ordinatio sic firmaretur, quod duraret, usquequo infidelis populus fideli populo uniretur, et esset *unum ouile et unus pastor (Ioh.* 10,16), sicut est prophetatum; et omnes laudarent et cognoscendo diligerent istum puerum benedictum, quem modo negligunt, uituperant et ignorant.

Vlterius dixerunt praedictae sex dominae, quod dominus rex Francorum cum affectu et desiderio dominum papam rogaret et requireret cardinales, quod de omnibus | religiosis militibus fieret unus ordo, | qui debellantes contra turpem populum infidelem acquirerent Terram sanctam; et quod ecclesia tribueret decimas et alia auxilia copiose. Nam contra talem Christi militiam, Saracenus populus nullatenus posset stare.

Et quia rex est defensor fidei, tenetur ad honorem pueri talem petitionem facere et attentus dictum negotium promouere. Et quod dominus papa et omnes cardinales sunt ad hoc specialiter obligati, quia praedicto puero subditi, super quo ecclesia catholica est fundata, ut per totum | mundum puer Iesus | uniuersaliter adoretur; et obstructa uia descensus ad inferos totus caelestis exercitus plenitudine iocundetur.

2. [RESPONSIO PVERI PER MARIAM ET MISSIO SEX DOMINARVM]

Verba, quae prae|dictae dominae sex dixerunt, multum beatae Mariae Virgini placuerunt. Et dixit, quod hoc erat altius et melius negotium ad laudandum puerum et ad salutem hominum, quam posset fieri uel ab homine cogitari. Et praecepit eis, quod irent ad regem Franciae et ei dicerent uerba illa, et quod praedictum negotium sanctum et arduum uiriliter et benigne cum tota sua regali potentia acceptaret, et ad istud negotium exequendum et promouendum Philippum, filium regis Maioricarum, clericum, consanguineum suum, induceret, qui est illustris, deuotus et humilis, paratus et bene dispositus, ut cum papa et cardinalibus suis tamen assensu et consilio habitis, sanctum prae|dictum negotium promoueret.

| Et ulterius Maria Virgo, mater pueri dixit eis, quod si rex Francorum hoc faciat et deuote suis uiribus exequatur, pro certo sciat, quod Filius meus eum iuuabit, custodiet et defendet; et ego eum rogabo et rogare non cessabo cum tota multitudine beatorum. Et si dictum negotium ueniat ad effectum, heu quanta laetitia, quanto gaudio, suauitate | et dulcedine in aeterna beatitudine anima regis | perfouetur, et etiam illorum omnium, qui dabunt consilium et iuuamen.

Beatae Mariae Virginis finito sermone, ei sex dominae promiserunt, quod ad | dominum regem Francorum uenirent, et ei supra dicta exponerent, uel Raimundum mitterent, qui dicto regi omnia per ordinem explicaret.

Et | hoc facto praedictae sex dominae cum reuerentia et magno gaudio a benedicto puero et eius matre Virgine recesserunt, dicentes, quod sciebant de cetero, quo modo esset ad honorandum puerum et eius matrem Virginem procedendum, et quod de omnibus hominibus uniuersi non fiat nisi ouile unicum christianum.

V
[Missio Raimundi]

1. DE LAMENTATIONE RAIMVNDI

Dum sex dominae ad dominum regem Francorum ueniebant, loquentes de his, quae audiuerant et a matre pueri habuerant in praeceptis, inuenerunt Parisius Raimundum, longam barbam habentem, clamantem et dicentem: Heu mihi! In quanta angustia sum positus, tristis, flens et dol|orosus, solus, impotens et antiquus, et quasi | ab omnibus uilipensus.

Laboraui diu, quantum potui, cum summis pontificibus, pluribus praelatis et principibus, ut puer nobis natus, Iesus, in terris a gentibus laudaretur, et gentes salutem reciperent animarum.

Cum Sara|cenis fui pluries, de fide cum ipsis disputans, captus, percussus et a terra eorum expulsus, perlustrans postmodum multas terras; et adhuc, quod desidero, non inueni. Dico et gentes moneo, ut honorem puero faciant. Quae dicunt, quod bene facio et bonam intentionem habeo; sed | in eis meum desiderium minime operatur.

Iterum ait senex Raimundus: Sum tristis et languidus et multo languore plenus, quia quod scio philosophicum uel theologicum, altum et sublime, ad confundendum errores infidelium et soluendum dicta erronea contra fidem per Artem generalem, quam habeo Dei gratia mediante, nullum quasi inuenio, qui ipsam Artem uelit uel possit complete discere uel habere. Et quia dies iam ueniunt, ut funis argenteus dirumpatur, doleo, quod talis Ars | nobilis, nulli thesauro comparabilis, omnino perdatur.

2. [RESPONSIO SEX DOMINARVM]

Dum sic Raimundus existebat in sua lamentatione, tristitia et dolore, sex praedictae dominae transeuntes per locum, audientes eundem lamentari et dolere quam plurimum, quia ita parua deuotio erga puerum in gentibus reperitur, simul conuenerunt, quod ad dominum regem secum Raimundum ducerent, ut una cum ipsis domino regi supplicaret et expo|neret de negotio nati pueri Iesu Christi. Cui dixerunt, | quae uiderant et audiuerant et praeceptum a beata Virgine eis factum.

Tunc dictus Raimundus, surgens a fletu et tristitia, de magno gaudio exultauit; et cum dominabus iocundus iuit ad supplicandum domino regi de ne|gotio ante dicto, sperans in
Domino, quod adhuc suum desiderium ueniat ad effectum.

Et cantauit laudes et gratias altissimae trinitati.

3. CANTILENA RAIMVNDI

Laus et honor Dei essentiae, diuinisque personis et dignitatibus earum. Recordemur et amemus Iesum Nazarenum et Mariam Virginem, matrem eius. Exspectemus et desideremus carnis resurrectionem, et in caelis coram Deo magnam et sempiternam glorificationem.

Et dum sic cantat, ter signo crucis | fronte se signat dicens: Age Maria Virgo cum tuo Filio benedicto in negotio supra dicto propter Filii amorem et totius trinitatis honorem.

Liber iste fuit in nocte Natalis conceptus. Et fu|it factus et finitus Parisius, ad honorem Dei mense Ianuarii, anno 1310 incarnationis Domini nostri Iesu Christi.

|Haec est uisio, quam ego Raimundus, barba floridus, ui|di Parisius, non est diu. Quam scribere uolui ad utilitatem christiani populi et ad honorem nati pueri, Iesu Christi, qui regnat cum Patre et sancto Spiritu, unus Deus.

READING 5-G

IOANNES BOCCACCIO

[1313–1375 CE]

DE MULIERIBUS CLARIS

Iohannes Boccaccius de Certaldo
mulieri clarissime Andree de Acciarolis de Florentia
Alteville comitisse

Pridie, mulierum egregia, paululum ab inerti vulgo semotus et a ceteris fere solutus curis, in eximiam muliebris sexus laudem ac amicorum solatium, potius quam in magnum rei publice commodum, libellum scripsi. Verum, dum mecum animo versarem cuinam illum primum transmicterem, ne penes me marceret ocio et ut, alieno fultus favore, securior iret in publicum, adverteremque satis non principi viro, sed potius, cum de mulieribus loqueretur, alicui insigni femine destinandum fore, exquirenti digniorem, ante alias venit in mentem ytalicum iubar illud prefulgidum ac singularis, non tantum feminarum, sed regum gloria, Iohanna, serenissima Ierusalem et Sicilie regina.

Cuius pensatis, tam inclite prosapie et avorum fulgoribus, quam novis a se forti pectore quesitis laudibus, in desiderium mictendi illum humilem devotumque ante solium sue celsitudinis incidi. Tandem, quia adeo ingens regius fulgor est et opusculi tenuis et fere semisopita favillula, timens ne a potiori lumine minor omnino fugaretur in tenebras, sensim retraxi consilium; et, nova indagine multis aliis perquisitis, ad extremum ab illustri regina in te votum deflexi meum; nec inmerito. Nam, dum mites ac celebres mores tuos, dum honestatem eximiam, summum matronarum decus, dumque verborum elegantiam mente revolverem, et cum his animi tui generositatem et ingenii vires, quibus longe femineas excedis, adverterem videremque quod sexui <in>firmiori natura detraxerit, id tuo pectori Deus sua liberalitate miris virtutibus superinfuserit atque suppleverit, et eo, quo insignita es nomine, designari voluerit —cum *andres* Greci quod latine dicimus *homines* nuncupent — te equiparandam probissimis quibuscunque, etiam vetustissimis, arbitratus sum.

Et ideo, cum tempestate nostra multis atque splendidis facinoribus agentibus clarissimum vetustatis specimen sis, tanquam benemerito tuo fulgori huius libelli tituli munus adiecisse velim, existimans non minus apud posteros tuo nomini addidisse decoris quam fecerit, olim Montisodorisii et nunc Alteville comitatus, quibus te fortuna fecit illustrem.

Ad te igitur micto et tuo nomini dedico quod hactenus a me de mulieribus claris scriptum est; precorque, inclita mulier, per sanctum pudicitie nomen, quo inter mortales plurimum emines, grato animo munusculum scolastici hominis suscipias; et, si michi aliquid creditura es, aliquando legas suadeo; suis quippe suffragiis tuis blandietur ociis, dum feminea virtute et historiarum lepiditate letaberis. Nec incassum, arbitror, agitabitur lectio si, facinorum preteritarum mulierum emula, egregium animum tuum concitabis in melius.

Et esto nonnunquam lasciva comperias immixta sacris —quod ut facerem recitandorum coegit oportunitas — ne omiseris vel horrescas; quin imo perseverans, uti viridarium intrans, eburneas manus, semotis spinarum aculeis, extendis in florem, sic, obscenis sepositis, collige laudanda; et quotiens in gentili muliere quid dignum, christianam religionem professa legeris, quod in te fore non senseris, ruborem mentis excita et te ipsam redargue quod, Christi delinita crismate, honestate aut pudicitia vel virtute supereris ab extera; et, provocato in vires ingenio, quo plurimum vales, non solum ne supereris patiare, sed ut superes quascunque egregia virtute coneris; ut, uti corpore leta iuventute ac florida venustate conspicua es, sic pre ceteris, non tantum coevis tuis, sed priscis etiam, animi integritate prestantior fias: memor non pigmentis — ut plereque facitis mulieres — decoranda formositas est, sed exornanda honestate sanctitate et primis operibus; ut, dum eidem qui tribuit gratam feceris, non solum hac in peritura mortalitate inter fulgidas una sis, sed ab eodem gratiarum Largitore, hominem exuens, in claritatem suscipiaris perpetuam.

Preterea si dignum duxeris, mulierum prestantissima, eidem procedendi in medium audaciam prebeas. Ibit quidem, ut reor, tuo emissus auspicio, ab insultibus malignantium tutus; nomenque tuum, cum ceteris illustrium mulierum, per ora virum splendidum deferet, teque tuis cum meritis — cum minime possis ubique efferri presentia — presentibus cognitam faciet, et posteritati servabit eternam. Vale.

XLVII
De Sapho puella lesbia et poeta

Saphos lesbia ex Mitilena urbe puella fuit, nec amplius sue originis posteritati relictum est. Sane, si studium inspexerimus, quod annositas abstulit pro parte restitutum videbimus, eam scilicet ex honestis atque claris parentibus genitam; non enim illud unquam degener animus potuit desiderasse vel actigisse plebeius.

Hec etenim, etsi quibus temporibus claruerit ignoremus, adeo generose fuit mentis ut, etate florens et forma, non contenta solum literas iungere novisse, ampliori fervore animi et ingenii suasa vivacitate, conscenso studio vigili per abruta Parnasi vertice celso, se felici ausu, Musis non renuentibus, immiscuit; et laureo pervagato nemore in antrum usque Apollinis evasit et, Castalio proluta latice, Phebi sumpto plectro, sacris nynphis choream traentibus, sonore cithare fides tangere et expromere modulos puella non dubitavit; que quidem etiam studiosissimis viris difficilia plurimum visa sunt.

Quid multa? Eo studio devenit suo ut usque in hodiernum clarissimum suum carmen testimonio veterum lucens sit, et erecta illi fuerit statua enea et suo dicata nomini, et ipsa inter poetas celebres numerata; quo splendore profecto, non clariora sunt regum dyademata, non pontificum infule, nec etiam triunphantium lauree.

Verum — si danda fides est— uti feliciter studuit, sic infelici amore capta est. Nam, seu facetia seu decore seu alia gratia, cuiusdam iuvenis dilectione, imo intolerabili occupata peste, cum ille desiderio suo non esset accomodus, ingemiscens in eius obstinatam duritiem, dicunt versus flebiles cecinisse; quos ego elegos fuisse putassem, cum tali sint elegi attributi materie, ni legissem ab ea, quasi preteritorum carminum formis spretis, novum adinventum genus, diversis a ceteris incedens pedibus, quod adhuc ex eius nomine saphycum appellatur.

Sed quid? Accusande videntur Pyerides que, tangente Anphyone liram, ogygia saxa movisse potuerunt et adolescentis cor, Sapho canente, mollisse noluerunt.

LXXXI
De Iulia Gaii Cesaris dictatoris filia

Iulia et genere et coniugio forsan totius orbis fuit clarissima mulierum; sed longe clarior amore sanctissimo et fato repentino.

Nam a Gaio Iulio Cesare ex Cornelia coniuge, Cynne quater consulis filia, unica progenita est. Qui Iulius ab Enea, inclito Troianorum duce, per multos reges et alios medios paternam duxit originem, maternam vero ab Anco, quondam Romanorum rege; gloria bellorum atque triunphorum et dictatura perpetua insignis plurimum homo fuit.

Nupsit preterea Pompeio magno, ea tempestate Romanorum clarissimo viro, qui in vincendis regibus, deponendis eisque de novo faciendis, nationibus subigendis, pyrratis extinguendis, favorem romane plebis obtinendo, et regum orbis totius clientelas acquirendo, non terras tantum, sed celum omne fatigavit diu. Quem adeo illustris mulier, esto iuvencula et ille provectus etate, ardenter amavit, ut ob id immaturam mortem quesierit.

Nam cum Pompeius in comitiis edilitiis sacrificaturus ab hostia, quam tenebat, ex suscepto vulnere se in varia agitante, plurimo respergeretur sanguine, et ob id, vestibus illis exutus, domum alias induturus remicteret, contigit ut deferens ante alios Iuliam pregnantem haberet obviam. Que cum vidisset viri cruentas vestes, ante quam causam exquireret, suspicata non forsan Pompeio fuisset violenta manus iniecta, quasi non illi dilectissimo sibi viro occiso supervivendum foret, in sinistrum repente delapsa timorem, oculis in tenebras revolutis, manibus clausis, concidit et evestigio expiravit: non solum viri atque civium romanorum, sed maximo totius orbis ea etate incomodo.

CI
De Iohanna anglica papa

Iohannes, esto vir nomine videatur, sexu tamen femina fuit. Cuius inaudita temeritas ut orbi toto notissima fieret et in posterum noscerecur effecit.

Huius etsi patriam Maguntium quidam fuisse dicant, quod proprium fuerit nomen vix cognitum est, esto sint qui dicant, ante pontificatus assumptionem, fuisse Gilibertum. Hoc constat, assertione quorundam, eam virginem a scolastico iuvene dilectam, quem adeo dilexisse ferunt ut, posita verecundia virginali atque pavore femineo, clam e domo patris effugeret, et amasium adolescentis in habitu et mutato sequeretur nomine; apud quem, in Anglia studentem, clericus ex<is>timatus ab omnibus et Veneri et literarum militavit studiis.

Inde iuvene morte subtracto, cum se cognosceret ingenio valere et dulcedine traheretur scientie, retento habitu nec adherere voluit alteri, nec se feminam profiteri, quin imo studiis vigilanter insistens, adeo in liberalibus et sacris literis profecit ut pre ceteris excellens haberetur.

Et sic, scientia mirabili predita, iam etate provecta, ex Anglia se Romam contulit; et ibidem aliquibus annis in trivio legens insignes habuit auditores; et cum, preter scientiam, singulari honestate ac sanctitate polleret, homo ab omnibus creditus. Et ideo notus a multis, solvente Leone quinto pontifice summo carnis debitum, a venerandissimis patribus comuni consensu premortuo in papatu suffectus est nominatusque Iohannes; cui, si vir fuisset, ut octavus esset in numero contigisset.

Que tamen non verita ascendere Piscatoris cathedram et sacra ministeria omnia, nulli mulierum a christiana religione concessum, tractare agere et aliis exhibere, apostolatus culmen aliquibus annis obtinuit Christique vicariatum femina gessit in terris. Sane ex alto Deus, plebi sue misertus, tam insignem locum teneri, tanto presideri populo tanque infausto errore decipi a femina passus non est et illam indebita audentem nec sinentem suis in manibus liquit.

Quam ob rem suadente diabolo qui eam in tam scelestam deduxerat atque detinebat audaciam, <actum est> ut, que privata precipuam honestatem servaverat, in tam sublimi evecta pontificatu in ardorem deveniret libidinis. Nec ei, que sexum diu fingere noverat, artes ad explendam defuere lasciviam. Nam adinvento qui clam Petri successorem conscenderet et exurentem pruriginem defricaret, actum est ut papa conciperet.

O scelus indignum, o invicta patientia Dei! Quid tandem? Ei que fascinare diu oculos potuerat hominum, ad incestuosum partum occultandum defecit ingenium. Nam cum is preter spem propinquior esset termino, dum ex Ianiculo, amburbale sacrum celebrans, Lateranum peteret inter Coloseum et Clementis pontificis edem, obstetrice non vocata, enixa publice patuit qua fraude tam diu, preter amasium, ceteros decepisset homines. Et hinc a patribus in tenebras exteriores abiecta, cum fetu misella abiit.

Ad cuius detestandam spurcitiem et nominis continuandam memoriam, in hodiernum usque summi pontifices rogationum cum clero et populo sacrum agentes, cum locum partus, medio eius in itinere positum, abominentur, eo omisso, declinant per diverticula vicosque et sic, loco detestabili postergato, reintrantes iter perficiunt quod cepere.

I

De Eva parente prima

Scripturus igitur quibus fulgoribus mulieres claruerint insignes, a matre omnium sumpsisse exordium non apparebit indignum: ea quippe vetustissima parens, uti prima, sic magnificis fuit insignis splendoribus. Nam, non in hac erumnosa miseriarum valle, in qua ad laborem ceteri mortales nascimur, producta est, nec eodem malleo aut incude etiam fabrefacta, seu eiulans nascendi crimen deflens, aut invalida, ceterorum ritu, venit in vitam; quin imo — quod nemini unquam alteri contigisse auditum est — cum iam ex limo terre rerum omnium Faber optimus Adam manu compegisset propria, et ex agro, cui postea Damascenus nomen inditum est, in orto delitiarum transtulisset eumque in soporem solvisset placidum, artificio sibi tantum cognito ex dormientis latere eduxit eandem, sui compotem et maturam viro et loci amenitate atque sui Factoris letabundam intuitu, immortalem et rerum dominam atque vigilantis iam viri sociam, et ab eodem Evam etiam nominatam.

Quid maius, quid splendidius potuit unquam contigisse nascenti? Preterea hanc arbitrari possumus corporea formositate mirabilem. Quid enim Dei digito factum est quod cetera non excedat pulchritudine? Et quamvis formositas hec annositate peritura sit aut, medio in etatis flore, parvo egritudinis inpulsu, lapsura, tamen, quia inter precipuas dotes suas mulieres numerant, et plurimum ex ea glorie, mortalium indiscreto iudicio, iam consecute sunt, non superflue inter claritates earum, tanquam fulgor precipuus, et apposita est et in sequentibus apponenda veniet.

Hec insuper, tam iure originis quam incolatus, paradisi civis facta et amicta splendore nobis incognito, dum una cum viro loci delitiis frueretur avide, invidus sue felicitatis hostis nepharia illi suasione ingessit animo, si adversus unicam sibi legem a Deo impositam iret, in ampliorem gloriam iri posse. Cui dum levitate feminea, magis quam illi nobisque oportuerit, crederet seque stolide ad altiora conscensuram arbitraretur, ante alia, blanda quadam suggestione, virum flexibilem in sententiam suam traxit; et in legem agentes, arboris boni et mali poma dum gustassent, temerario ausu seque genusque suum omne futurum ex quiete et eternitate in labores anxios et miseram mortem et ex delectabili patria inter vepres glebas et scopulos deduxere.

Nam, cum lux corusca, qua incedebant amicti, abiisset, a turbato Creatore suo obiurgati, perizomatibus cincti, ex delitiarum loco in agros Hebron pulsi exulesque venere. Ibi egregia mulier, his facinoribus clara, cum prima —ut a nonnullis creditum est — vertente terram ligonibus viro, colo nere adinvenisset, sepius dolores partus experta est; et, quibus ob mortem filiorum atque nepotum angustiis angeretur animus, eque misere passa; et, ut algores estusque sinam et incomoda cetera, fessa laboribus moritura devenit in senium.

CONCLUSIO

In nostras usque feminas, ut satis apparet, devenimus, quas inter adeo perrarus rutilantium numerus est, ut dare ceptis finem honestius credam quam, his ducentibus hodiernis, ad ulteriora progredi; et potissime dum tam preclara regina concluserit quod Eva, prima omnium parens, inchoavit.

Scio tamen non defuturos qui dicant multas omissas fore; et hos super, alios qui alia obiciant, que forsan merito redargui possint.

Ego autem—<ut> primis cum humilitate respondeam — omisisse multas fatebor ultro; non enim ante alia omnes attigisse poteram, quia plurimas fame triunphator tempus assumpsit. Nec michi, ex superstitibus, omnes videre potuisse datum est; et ex cognitis, non semper omnes volenti ministrat memoria. Sane, ne me omnino immemorem putent, credant volo quia non me inadvertente plurime, tam barbare quam grece atque latine et Augustorum coniuges atque regum, preterierint. Vidi equidem innumeras et carum facinora novi, sed non michi, arripienti in hoc calamum, animus fuit omnes velle describere; quin imo — ut ab initio opusculi huius testatus sum —ex multitudine quasdam elicere et apponere. Quod cum satis congrue factum rear, supervacanea restat obiectio.

Reliquis vero sic dictum sit: possibile esse et contigisse facile credam nonnulla minus recte consistere. Decipit enim persepe non solum ignorantia rerum, sed circa opus suum nimia laborantis affectio. Quod si factum sit, doleo quesoque, per venerabile honestorum studiorum decus, equo animo quod minus bene factum est prudentiores ferant; et si quis illis pie caritatis spiritus est, minus debite scripta augentes minuentesque corrigant et emendent, ut potius alicuius in bonum vigeat opus, quam in nullius commodum laceratum dentibus invidorum depereat.

READING 5-H

POLYDORVS VERGILIVS

[1470–1550 CE]

DE RERVM INVENTORIBVS

CAP. XIIII.

Quis primus musicam repererit, & quantum ea valeat ad tolerandos humanæ vitæ labores.

Musicen antiquissimam esse, poëtæ clarissimi testimonio sunt: nam Orpheus & Linus ambo diis geniti, musici insignes fuerunt, cùm alter eorum rudes atque agrestes hominum animos demulceret, cantusq; suavitate non feras modò, sed saxa etiam, ut fabulæ tradunt, sylvasq; duceret. Horatius in poëtica arte:

Sylvestres homines sacer interpresq; deorum
Cædibus & victu fœdo deterruit Orpheus,
Dictus ob hoc lenire tigres, rapidosq; leones.

Vergilius in Ecloga quarta:

Non me carminibus vincet, nec Thracius Orpheus,
Nec Linus, huic mater quamvis, atque huic pater adsit,
Orphei Calliopeia, Lino formosus Apollo.

Apud quoque eosdem autores, inter regalia convivia, laudes deorum atque heroum ad citharam canuntur, ut Iopas ille Vergilianus canit errantem lunam, solisq; lobores. Musices autem repertor, teste Plinio lib. 7, Amphion ex Antiopa, Iovis filius fuisse dicitur, propter quod poëta in Bucolicis ait:

Canto, quæ solitus, si quando armenta vocabat,
Amphion Dircæus in Actæo Aracyntho.

Ipse quoque saxa movisse fertur. Horatius in Poëtica,

Dictus & Amphion Thebanæ conditor urbis

Saxa

Saxa movêre sono testudinis.
Et Statius in primo Thebaidos :
Penitusque sequar quo carmine muris
Iusserit Amphion Tyrios accedere montes.
Sed Græci *teste Eusebio, de præparat. Euangel. lib. 2.* Musicæ harmoniæ inventionem Dionysio attribuunt. Ipse verò *in 10. ejusdem operis* Zethum & Amphionem fratres, qui Cadmi temporibus fuerunt, Musicæ repertores vocat. At Solinus hujus artis studium ex Creta manasse sentit, qui inquit Studium musicum inde cœptum, cum Iudæi Dactyli modulos crepitu ac tinnitu æris deprehensos in versificum ordinem transtulissent. Polybius tamen *in 4.* hoc Arcadum majoribus assignat, quippe qui hujus rei semper studiosi fuerint. Vocum harmonias Mercurium adinvenisse, Diodorus est auctor in primo, ἁρμονίαν Græci vocant, quàm nos dissimilium concordiam appellamus. Verum Amphionem & cæteros post hac hujus rei auctores fuisse ratio poscit, cum Iubal Hebræum Lamech filium, qui multis ætatibus præcesserat omnes illos qui Musicæ inventores produntur, Iosephus *in primo antiquitatum* dicat musicam studiosè, coluisse & psalterio citharâque cecinisse. Hæc hactenus. Sed artis origo nihilominus in dubio versari videtur : igitur expedit, ut quæstio ejusmodi tandem aliquando plana fiat. Itaque natura jam inde à principio mortalibus musicam velut muneri dedisse videtur, quando id ad tolerandos humanæ vitæ labores plurimum valet. Siquidem homo statim natus cum in cunabulis vagire incipit continuò nutriculæ cantitantis voce sopitus dormitat : quippe infantes statim plorant, quod crurum brachiorumque rectè producendorum causâ, fasciis colligantur ac ita à supplicio miseram vitam vivere incipiunt. Deinde in omnibus fermè ope-

ribus modulatio aliqua rudis hominum defatigationem semper consolatur, Vergilius:

Hinc alta sub rupe canet frondator ad auras.

Sic remiges incitantur, sic arator, auriga, mulio, longo inter laborem viamque sibilo reficitur. Quid, quod non modo ii, verùmetiam eorum sarcinaria jumenta eo cantu simul labore levantur? Nam assiduo usu compertum est, mulos valdè delectari tintinnabulorum sonitu: quapropter muliones multijugia tintinnabula ad illorum colla suspendere solent, quo facilius sarcinarum labores perferant. Eandem vim in cætera similiter animalia Musicam habere inter omnes constat: ita equi in bello tubarum clangore arrecti stare loco nesciunt, ac jam jam in certamen ruere ardent: ita leones stridore ferri maximè territantur. Sed quæso, undè ille avium concentus, quo omnis ager suo tempore resonat? ecquis docuit lusciniam varios canendi modos? hæc enim avicula sonum edit perfectâ musicæ scientiâ modalatum, qui nunc continuo spiritu trahitur in longum, nunc variatur inflexo, nunc distinguitur conciso, copulatur intorto, promittitur, revocatur, infuscatur ex inopinato: interdum & secum ipsa murmurat: plenus, gravis, acutus, creber, extentus: & breviter, audire licet omnia tàm parvulis in faucibus concini, quæ tot exquisitis tibiarum tormentis, ut ait Plinius: ars hominum excogitavit. Hujus harmoniæ natura magistra est, quæ vel ab initio alias animantes, quibus ad sonum quempiam vox apta est, musicam docuit, quemadmodum ostendimus. Atque hæc vera artis origo. Cæterùm Musicam, quàm Ægyptii, *ut Diodorus testis est*, tanquam virorum effœminatricem prohibebant juvenes perdiscere, & Ephorus, auctore Polybio in procœmio suarum historiarum ad deludendos ac fallendos ſendos homines inventam tradidit, magno olim pretio æſtimatam teſtatur Fabius, qui dicit Socratem, jam ſenem inſtitui lyrâ non erubuiſſe : & Cicero, qui *libro Tuſculanarum primo* ait Themiſtoclem, quòd in epulis recuſaſſet lyram, eſſe habitum indoctiorem : & Salii, apud Romanos, qui per urbem verſus canebant : ſed in primis David ille magnus vates, qui divino carmine Dei myſteria canit : illud quoque Græcorum adagium, Indoctos à Muſis atque Gratiis abeſſe, quod in noſtris proverbiis explanavi. Tria præterea genera ſunt ex quibus muſica conſtat : unum genus eſt, quod inſtrumentis agitur, de quo infrà dicetur : alterum, quod fingit carmina, ex quo ut poëſis pars ſit muſices, neceſſe eſt : tertium, quod inſtrumentorum opus carmenque dijudicat. Ex quo rectè ait Cicero *de Oratore, lib.* I. Muſicam verſari in numeris, & vocibus, & modis.

CAPVT VII.

Qui primi Libros ediderint, & de prima Bibliotheca: & à quo, aut ubi usus imprimendarum literarum primo inventus.

CVm in dies magis magisque hominum ingenia solâ librorum copiâ vigeant, & ad capessendas disciplinarum liberalium artes facilius omnes alliciantur, ipsaque literarum studia mirum in modum ubique gentium floreant, peccare hercle me ducerem, si tale inventum silentio præteritem, cujus nos etiam, quantum exiguum tulerit ingenium, augendi gratiâ, hunc nempe laborem suscepimus præsertim cum hujusmodi scriptorum libri, *uti divus Hier. ad Marcellam ait*, ingeniorum effigies & vera & æterna monumenta sint. Quapropter Agesilaus, *auctore Plut.* cum benè multi vellent ejus corporis simulachrum gratis effingere, nunquam id fieri passus est, animi tantum monumenta posteris relinquere studens: illud enim sculptorum, hoc suum: illud divitum, hoc bonorum opus esse dicebat. Omnium igitur primus Anaxagoras, *teste Laërtio volumine 2.* librum ab se scriptum edidit. Gellium verò *lib. 6.* scribit Pisistratum tyrannum omnium primum libros publicè legendos præbuisse. Sed perfecto quis non videt perperam Græcos hominum genus in sui laude effusissimum, hanc sibi gloriam vendicare? qui *ut Iosephus contra Appionem perspicue demonstrat* recentissimi sunt. Ex quo haud dubie multò ante Græcos, antiquissimi Hebræorum, qui Sacram historiam scripserunt, & Ægyptiorum sacerdotes

tes vel Chaldæi libros ediderunt: atq; ita Anaxagoram & Piſiſtratum apud Græcos tantum primos foras dandos libros curaſſe credere par eſt. Deinde autem, *ut idem Gellius teſtatur*, ipſi Athenienſes numerum librorũ ſtudioſius accuratiuſque auxerunt. Verùm omnem illam poſtea librorum copiam Xerxes Athenarum potitus abſtulit, aſportavitque in Perſas. Eos porrò libros univerſos multis poſt tempeſtatibus, Seleucus Macedoniæ Rex, qui Nicanor appellatus eſt, referendos Athenas curavit. Ingens poſtea numerus librorum in Ægypto à Ptolemæis regibus confectus eſt, ad millia fermè voluminum DCC. ſed ea omnia priore bello Alexandrino incenſa ſunt. Cæterum Strabo *lib.* 13. *Geographiæ*, ſcribit Ariſtotelem omnium primum Bibliothecam inſtituiſſe, ait enim: è Scepſi fuere philoſophi Socratici, Eraſtus & Coriſcus, Nereus Coriſci filius, qui Ariſtotelem & Theophraſtum audivit, & ſucceſſor fuit Bibliothecæ Theophraſti, in qua Ariſtotelica inerat: nam Ariſtoteles & Bibliothecam & ſcholam reliquit Theophraſto, & primus omnium quos ſcimus, libros congregavit, & Ægyptii reges Bibliothecæ ordinem docuit. Theophraſtus verò eam tradidit Neleo, Neleus eam Scepſim detulit, ac poſteris tradidit. *Hæc ille.* Fuit & Pergami Bibliotheca præclariſſima auctor Plin. *l.* 35. *ſtatim in principio*, ubi inquit: An priores cœperint Alexandriæ & Pergami reges, qui Bibliothecas magno certamine inſtituêre, non facile dixerim. Romę bibliothecam Aſinium Pollionem primum feciſſe, teſtatur idem *in prænotato lib.* ſcribens: Non eſt prætereundum & novitium inventum, ſiquidem non ſolum ex auro argentove, aut certè ex ære in Bibliothecis dicantur illi, quorũ immortales animæ iiſdem locis ibi loquuntur, quinimò etiã quæ non ſunt, finguntur, pariuntq; deſideria

non

non traditi vultus, ſicut in Homero evenit, quo
magis, ut equidem arbitror, nullum eſt felicitatis
ſpecimen, quam ſemper omnes ſcire cupere, qualis fuerit aliquis. Aſinii Pollionis hoc Romæ inventum, qui primus bibliothecam dicando, ingenia hominum rempublicam fecit. Sunt etiam
plures hodie in Italia bibliothecæ, ſed illa in primis omnium judicio longè celeberrima, quam
divus Federicus Feltrius dux Vrbini condidit,
quam poſtea Guido princeps ejus filius, omnis
doctrinæ decus, ac doctiſſimorum hominum prę-
ſidium, cum auro & argento, tum librorum copiâ adauxit, ornavitque. Fuit illud igitur omni-
nò magnum mortalibus munus, ſed nequaquam
conferendum cum hoc, quod noſtro tempore
adepti ſumus, reperto novo ſcribendi genere:
tantum enim uno die ab uno homine literarum
inprimitur, quantum vix toto anno à pluribus
ſcribi poſſet. Ex quo adeò diſciplinarum omnium
magna librorum copia ad nos manavit, ut nullum amplius ſuperfuturum ſit opus, quod ab homine quamvis egeno deſiderari poſſit. Illud in-
ſuper adde, quod auctores quoque plurimos, tam
Græcos quam Latinos ab omni prorſus interitus
periculo vindicavit. Quare tantæ rei auctor non
eſt ſua laude fraudandus, preſertim ut poſteritas
ſciat, cui divinum beneficium acceptum referre
debeat. Itaque Ioannes Gutenbergus natione
Theutonicus, equeſtri vir dignitate, ut ab ejus civibus accepimus, primus omnium in oppido Ger-
maniæ, quam Moguntiam vocant, hanc impri-
mendarum literarum artem excogitavit, primumque ibi ea exerceri cœpit: non minore induſtria reperto ab eodem, prout ferunt, auctore,
novo atramenti genere, quo nunc literarum
impreſſores tantùm utuntur. Decimoſexto deinde anno qui fuit ſalutis humanæ MCCCCLVIII.
quidam

quidam nomine Conradus, homo itidem Germanus, Romam primò in Italiam attulit, quam dein Nicolaus Ienſon Gallicus, primus mirum in modum illuſtravit, quæ paſſim hac tempeſtate per totum ferè terrarum orbem floret, de qua plura loquendi labore ſuperſedeo, ejus inventorem ac ſimul unde ad nos delata fuerit, prodidiſſe, haud me parum feciſſe ratus, cum ea omnibus longè notiſſima ſit: quæ propterea ut ab initio non minore quæſtu, quàm hominum admiratione vulgari cœpit, ſic paulatim, velut auguror, futura eſt vilior.

CAPVT IX.

Quis primus Memoriæ artem monſtraverit, aut qui ejuſdem gloriam adepti ſint.

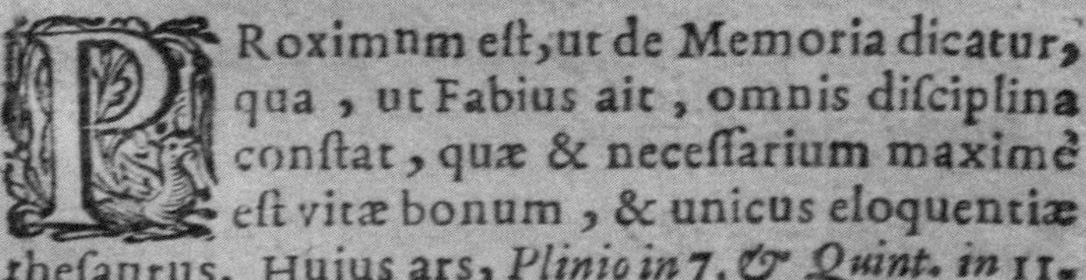

PRoximum eſt, ut de Memoria dicatur, qua, ut Fabius ait, omnis diſciplina conſtat, quæ & neceſſarium maximè eſt vitæ bonum, & unicus eloquentiæ theſaurus. Hujus ars, *Plinio in 7. & Quint. in 11.* aucto-

auctoribus , à Simonide Melico primum inventa est, qua in re multum valuit. Nam cum aliquando in Thessalia , *teste Cicer. de Orat.* epularetur apud Scopam nobilem virum,& nuntiatum esset ei, ut prodiret ad duos juvenes ante januam stantes, contigit ut hoc interim spatio conclave corruerit , ac eâ ruinâ adeò convivæ omnes contriti fuerint, ut non possent internosci à suis, qui humare, eos vellent. Tum dicitur Simonides, ex eo quod meminisset , quo eorum loco quisque cubuisset , demonstrator uniuscujusque sepeliendi fuisse. Ac ita videtur memoriâ valdè juvari signatis animo sedibus , aut mutato annulo , qui nos moneat , cur id fecerimus , quod ipse Fabius latè prosequitur. Memoria autem plurimis præcipua fuit, ut Plinius & Solinus auctores sunt. Cyrus enim Rex Persarum omnibus in exercitu suo militibus nomina reddidit : Cineas Pyrrhi regis legatus , postero die quam Romam advenerat, utriusque ordinis viros nominatim appellavit. Mithridati regi duæ & viginti linguæ (tot enim nationibus imperavit) traduntur notæ fuisse. Cæsarem verò scribere & legere simul , dictare & audire solitum accepimus. Idem etiam , *teste Spartiano*, Hadrianus Imperator facere consuevit.

CAPVT I.

A quibus primum inventa Agricultura & quot ea redundet bonis.

NON ſum equidem neſcius quoſdam fore, qui vehementer demirabuntur, nos poſtremo ferè loco de inventoribus agriculturæ aliquid tradere diſtuliſſe, cum præſertim uti Cicero *in Officiorum libris* inquit, omnium rerum ex quibus aliquid exquiritur, nihil ſit agriculturâ melius, nil uberius, nihil homine libero dignius. Verum nec eò mihi ſuccenſeant, quatenus hoc ipſum conſultò, vel, ut verius dicam, ex induſtria fecimus, ut longo legentes itinere defatigati, novum tandem paſtum, ſive, ut ita dixerim, nectar offenderent, quo vires recreare, & veluti diutinam famem explere poſſent. De hujuſce igitur rei initiis hîc commode dicemus, poſtquam demonſtravero, quantis eam laudibus jure ac meritiò præſtantiſſimi auctores efferant, utpote quę multis abundat

dat bonis. Columella itaque *in* 1. *de Re rustica* conquerens sui temporis mollitiem, ait: At me herclè vera illa proles Romuli assiduis venationibus, nec minus agrestibus operibus exercitata, firmissimis prævaluit corporibus, ac militiam belli, cum res postulavit, facilè sustinuit, duratam pacis laboribus, semperque rusticam plebem urbanæ præposuit. Cato itidem de Agricultura inquit: Fortissimi viri & milites strenuissimi ex agricolis gignuntur, minimeque malè cogitantes. Ex quo, *teste Cicerone de Senectute*, in agris senatores erant, ut L. Quintius Cincinnatus, qui dum agrum arabat, renuntiatus est dictator: ut Curius, & cæteri senes. Quare qui eos accersebant, viatores nominati sunt. Quid, quod etiam *teste Plinio lib.* 18. agrum malè colere, censorium probrum judicabatur? atque *ut inquit Cato* quem virum bonum colonum dixissent, amplissimè laudasse existimabant: Et id sanè quia, *quemadmodum Cicero pro Roscio Amerino docet*, rustica vita parsimoniæ, diligentiæ, justitiæ magistra est, at urbana non item, quam luxuries facilè inficit: ex luxuria necesse est existat avaritia, ex avaritia erumpat audacia, inde omnia maleficia gignantur. Sed ne putes hoc tantum in Romana Republica contigisse: de cultu agri præcipere, principale etiam, *ut Plinius dicit*, fuit apud exteros, siquidem & Reges fecere, Hiero, Philometor, Attalus, Archelaus. Vnde non injuria Xenophonti, *quemadmodum testis est M. Tullius in Catone*, nihil tam regale videbatur, quàm studium agri colendi. De laudibus hactenus. Agriculturam primum omnium *teste Diodoro in* 1. Osirim, qui & Dionysius dicitur, reperisse ferunt. Affirmat item Tibullus, ita scribens:

READING 5-1

CONCILIVM OECVMENICVM TRIDENTINVM

[1545–1563 CE]

SESSIO XXIV
11 NOV. 1563

[Doctrina de sacramento matrimonii]

Matrimonii perpetuum indissotubilemque nexum primus humani generis parens divini Spiritus instinctu pronuntiavit, cum dixit: *Hoc nunc os ex ossibus meis, et caro de carne mea. Quamobrem relinquet homo patrem suum et matrem, et adhaerebit uxori suae, et erunt duo in carne una.*

Hoc autem vinculo duos tantummodo copulari et coniungi, Christus dominus apertius docuit, cum postrema illa verba, tamquam a Deo prolata, referens dixit: *Itaque iam non sunt duo, sed una caro,* statimque eiusdem nexus firmitatem, ab Adamo tanto ante pronuntiatam, his verbis confirmavit: *Quod ergo Deus coniunxit, homo non separet.*

Gratiam vero, quae naturalem illum amorem perficeret, et indissolubilem unitatem confirmaret, coniugesque sanctificaret: ipse Christus, venerabilium sacramentorum institutor atque perfector, sua nobis passione promeruit. Quod Paulus apostolus innuit, dicens: *Viri, diligite uxores vestras, sicut Christus dilexit ecclesiam, et se ipsum tradidit pro ea,* mox subiungens: *Sacramentum hoc magnum est; ego autem dico, in Christo et in ecclesia.*

Cum igitur matrimonium in lege evangelica veteribus connubiis per Christum gratia praestet: merito inter novae legis sacramenta annumerandum sancti patres nostri, concilia et universalis ecclesiae traditio semper docuerunt; adversus quam impii homines huius saeculi insanientes, non solum perperam de hoc venerabili sacramento senserunt, sed de more suo, praetextu evangelii libertatem carnis introducentes, multa ab ecclesiae catholicae sensu et ab apostolorum temporibus probata consuetudine aliena, scripto et verbo asseruerunt, non sine magna christifidelium iactura. Quorum temeritati sancta et universalis synodus cupiens occurrere, insigniores praedictorum schismaticorum haereses et errores, ne plures ad se trahat perniciosa eorum contagio, exterminandos duxit, hos in ipsos haereticos eorumque errores decernens anathematismos.

Canones de sacramento matrimonii

1. Si quis dixerit, matrimonium non esse vere et proprie unum ex septem legis evangelicae sacramentis, a Christo domino institutum, sed ab hominibus in ecclesia inventum, neque gratiam conferre: a. s.

2. Si quis dixerit, licere christianis plures simul habere uxores, et hoc nulla lege divina esse prohibitum: a. s.

3. Si quis dixerit, eos tantum consanguinitatis et affinitatis gradus, qui Levitico exprimuntur, posse impedire matrimonium contrahendum, et dirimere contractum; nec posse ecclesiam in nonnullis illorum dispensare, aut constituere, ut plures impediant et dirimant: a. s.

4. Si quis dixerit, ecclesiam non potuisse constituere impedimenta matrimonium dirimentia, vel in iis constituendis errasse: a. s.

5. Si quis dixerit, propter haeresim, aut molestam cohabitationem, aut affectatam absentiam a coniuge dissolvi posse matrimonii vinculum: a. s.

6. Si quis dixerit, matrimonium ratum, non consummatum, per solemnem religionis professionem alterius coniugum non dirimi: a. s.

7. Si quis dixerit, ecclesiam errare, cum docuit et docet, iuxta evangelicam et apostolicam doctrinam, propter adulterium alterius coniugum matrimonii vinculum non posse dissolvi, et utrumque, vel etiam innocentem, qui causam adulterio non dedit, non posse, altero coniuge vivente, aliud matrimonium contrahere, moecharique eum, qui dimissa adultera aliam duxerit, et eam, quae dimisso adultero alii nupserit, a. s.

8. Si quis dixerit, ecclesiam errare, cum ob multas causas separationem inter coniuges quoad thorum, seu quoad cohabitationem, ad certum incertumve tempus, fieri posse decernit: a. s.

9. Si quis dixerit, clericos in sacris ordinibus constitutos, vel regulares, castitatem solemniter professos, posse matrimonium contrahere, contractumque validum esse, non obstante lege ecclesiastica vel voto, et oppositum nil aliud esse, quam damnare matrimonium; posseque omnes contrahere matrimonium, qui non sentiunt se castitatis (etiam si eam voverint) habere donum: a. s. Cum Deus id recte petentibus non deneget, nec patiatur, nos supra id, quod possumus, tentari.

10. Si quis dixerit, statum coniugalem anteponendum esse statui virginitatis vel coelibatus, et non esse melius ac beatius, manere in virginitate aut coelibatu, quam iungi matrimonio: a. s.

11. Si quis dixerit, prohibitionem solemnitatis nuptiarum certis anni temporibus superstitionem esse tyrannicam, ab ethnicorum superstitione profectam; aut benedictiones et alias caeremonias, quibus ecclesia in illis utitur, damnaverit: a. s.

12. Si quis dixerit, causas matrimoniales non spectare ad iudices ecclesiasticos: a. s.

Canones Super Reformatione Circa Matrimonium

Caput I

Tametsi dubitandum non est, clandestina matrimonia, libero contrahentium consensu facta, rata et vera esse matrimonia, quamdiu ecclesia ea irrita non fecit, et proinde iure damnandi sint illi, ut eos sancta synodus anathemate damnat, qui ea vera ac rata esse negant quique falso affirmant, matrimonia, a filiis familias sine consensu parentum contracta, irrita esse, et parentes ea rata vel irrita facere posse: nihilominus sancta Dei ecclesia ex iustissimis causis illa semper detestata est atque prohibuit. Verum cum sancta synodus animadvertat, prohibitiones illas propter hominum inobedientiam iam non prodesse, et gravia peccata perpendat, quae ex eisdem clandestinis coniugiis ortum habent, praesertim vero eorum, qui in statu damnationis permanent, dum, priore uxore, cum qua clam contraxerant, relicta, cum alia palam contrahunt et cum ea in perpetuo adulterio vivunt; cui malo cum ab ecclesia, quae de occultis non iudicat, succurri non possit, nisi efficacius aliquod remedium adhibeatur: idcirco sacri Lateranensis concilii, sub Innocentio III celebrati, vestigiis inhaerendo praecipit, ut in posterum, antequam matrimonium contrahatur, ter a proprio contrahentium parocho tribus continuis diebus festivis in ecclesia inter missarum solemnia publice denuntietur, inter quos matrimonium sit contrahendum; quibus denuntiationibus factis, si nullum legitimum opponatur impedimentum, ad celebrationem matrimonii in facie ecclesiae procedatur, ubi parochus, viro et muliere interrogatis, et eorum mutuo consensu intellecto, vel dicat: *Ego vos in matrimonium coniungo, in nomine Patris et Filii et Spiritus sancti,* vel aliis utatur verbis, iuxta receptum uniuscuiusque provinciae ritum. Quodsi aliquando probabilis fuerit suspicio, matrimonium malitiose impediri posse, si tot praecesserint denuntiationes: tunc vel una tantum denuntiatio fiat, vel saltem parocho et duobus vel tribus testibus praesentibus matrimonium celebretur; deinde ante illius consummationem denuntiationes in ecclesia fiant, ut si aliqua subsunt impedimenta, facilius detegantur, nisi ordinarius ipse expedire iudicaverit, ut praedictae denuntiationes remittantur, quod illius prudentiae et iudicio sancta synodus relinquit. Qui aliter, quam praesente parocho vel alio sacerdote, de ipsius parochi seu ordinarii licentia, et duobus vel tribus testibus matrimonium contrahere attentabunt: eos sancta synodus ad sic contrahendum omnino inhabiles reddit, et huiusmodi contractus irritos et nullos esse decernit, prout eos praesenti decreto irritos facit et annullat. Insuper parochum vel alium sacerdotem, qui cum minori testium numero, et testes, qui sine parocho vel sacerdote huiusmodi contractui interfuerint, necnon ipsos contrahentes graviter arbitrio ordinarii puniri praecipit. Praeterea eadem sancta synodus hortatur, ut coniuges ante benedictionem sacerdotalem, in templo suscipiendam, in eadem domo non cohabitent. Statuitque, benedictionem a proprio parocho fieri, neque a quoquam, nisi ab ipso parocho, vel ab ordinario licentiam ad praedictam benedictionem faciendam alii sacerdoti concedi posse, quacumque consuetudine, etiam immemorabili, quae potius corruptela dicenda est, vel privilegio non obstante. Quodsi quis parochus vel alius sacerdos, sive regularis sive saecularis sit, etiam si id sibi ex privilegio vel immemorabili consuetudine licere contendat, alterius parochiae sponsos sine illorum parochi licentia matrimonio coniungere, aut benedicere ausus fuerit: ipso iure tamdiu suspensus maneat, quamdiu ab ordinario eius parochi, qui matrimonio interesse debebat seu a quo benedictio suscipienda erat, absolvatur. Habeat parochus librum, in quo coniugum et testium nomina, diemque et locum contracti matrimonii describat, quem diligenter apud se custodiat.

Postremo sancta synodus coniuges hortatur, ut, antequam contrahant, vel saltem triduo ante matrimonii consummationem, sua peccata diligenter confiteantur et ad sanctissimum eucharistiae sacramentum pie accedant. Si quae provinciae aliis, ultra praedictas, laudabilibus consuetudinibus et caeremoniis hac in re utuntur, eas omnino retineri sancta synodus vehementer optat. Ne vero haec tam salubria praecepta quemquam lateant, ordinariis omnibus praecipit, ut, cum primum potuerint, curent hoc decretum populo publicari ac explicari in singulis suarum dioecesum parochialibus ecclesiis, idque in primo anno quam saepissime fiat, deinde vero quoties expedire viderint.

Decernit insuper, ut huiusmodi decretum in unaquaque parochia suum robur post triginta dies habere incipiat, a die primae publicationis in eadem parochia factae numerandos.

Caput II

Docet experientia, propter multitudinem prohibitionum multoties in casibus prohibitis ignoranter contrahi matrimonia, in quibus vel non sine magno peccato perseveratur, vel ea non sine magno scandalo dirimuntur. Volens itaque sancta synodus huic incommodo providere, et a cognationis spiritualis impedimento incipiens, statuit, ut unus tantum, sive vir sive mulier, iuxta sacrorum canonum instituta, vel ad summum unus et una baptizatum de baptismo suscipiant, inter quos ac baptizatum ipsum et illius patrem et matrem, necnon inter baptizantem et baptizatum baptizatique patrem ac matrem tantum spiritualis cognatio contrahatur.

Parochus, antequam ad baptismum conferendum accedat, diligenter ab iis, ad quos spectabit, sciscitetur, quem vel quos elegerint, ut baptizatum de sacro fonte suscipiant, et eum vel eos tantum ad illum suscipiendum admittat, et in libro eorum nomina describat, doceatque eos, quam cognationem contraxerint, ne ignorantia ulla excusari valeant. Quodsi alii ultra designatos baptizatum tetigerint, cognationem spiritualem nullo pacto contrahant; constitutionibus in contrarium facientibus non obstantibus. Si parochi culpa vel negligentia secus factum fuerit, arbitrio ordinarii puniatur. Ea quoque cognatio, quae ex confirmatione contrahitur, confirmantem et confirmatum illiusque patrem et matrem ac tenentem non egrediatur; omnibus inter alias personas huius spiritualis cognationis impedimentis omnino sublatis.

Caput III

Iustitiae publicae honestatis impedimentum, ubi sponsalia quacumque ratione valida non erunt, sancta synodus prorsus tollit; ubi autem valida fuerint, primum gradum non excedat, quoniam in ulterioribus gradibus iam non potest huiusmodi prohibitio absque dispendio observari.

Caput IV

Praeterea sancta synodus, eisdem et aliis gravissimis de causis adducta, impedimentum, quod propter affinitatem ex fornicatione contractam inducitur et matrimonium postea factum dirimit, ad eos tantum, qui in primo et secundo gradu coniunguntur, restringit. In ulterioribus vero gradibus statuit, huiusmodi affinitatem matrimonium postea contractum non dirimere.

Caput V

Si quis intra gradus prohibitos scienter matrimonium contrahere praesumpserit, separetur ac spe dispensationis consequendae careat, idque in eo multo magis locum habeat, qui non tantum matrimonium contrahere, sed etiam consummare ausus fuerit. Quodsi ignoranter id fecerit, siquidem solemnitates requisitas in contrahendo matrimonio neglexerit, eisdem subiiciatur poenis. Non enim dignus est, qui ecclesiae benignitatem facile experiatur, cuius salubria praecepta temere contempsit. Si vero solemnitatibus adhibitis impedimentum aliquod postea subesse cognoscatur, cuius ille probabilem ignorantiam habuit, tunc facilius cum eo, et gratis, dispensari poterit. In contrahendis matrimoniis vel nulla omnino detur dispensatio, vel raro, idque ex causa et gratis concedatur. In secundo gradu numquam dispensetur nisi inter magnos principes et ob publicam causam.

Caput VI

Decernit sancta synodus, inter raptorem et raptam, quamdiu ipsa in potestate raptoris manserit, nullum posse consistere matrimonium. Quodsi rapta, a raptore separata et in loco tuto et libero constituta, illum in virum habere consenserit: eam raptor in uxorem habeat; et nihilominus raptor ipse, ac omnes illi consilium, auxilium et favorem praebentes, sint ipso iure excommunicati ac perpetuo infames omniumque dignitatum incapaces. Et si clerici fuerint, de proprio gradu decidant. Teneatur praeterea raptor, mulierem raptam, sive eam in uxorem duxerit sive non duxerit, decenter arbitrio iudicis dotare.

Caput VII

Multi sunt, qui vagantur et incertas habent sedes, et, ut improbi sunt ingenii, prima uxore relicta, aliam, et plerumque plures, illa vivente, diversis in locis ducunt; cui morbo cupiens sancta synodus occurrere, omnes, ad quos spectat, paterne monet, ne hoc genus hominum vagantium ad matrimonium facile recipiant. Magistratus etiam saeculares hortatur, ut eos severe coerceant; parochis autem praecipit, ne illorum matrimoniis intersint, nisi prius diligentem inquisitionem fecerint et, re ad ordinarium delata, ab eo licentiam id faciendi obtinuerint.

Caput VIII

Grave peccatum est, homines solutos concubinas habere, gravissimum vero et in huius magni sacramenti singularem contemptum admissum, uxoratos quoque in hoc damnationis statu vivere, ac audere, eas quandoque domi, etiam cum uxoribus, alere et retinere. Quare ut huic tanto malo sancta synodus opportunis remediis provideat, statuit, huiusmodi concubinarios, tam solutos quam uxoratos, cuiuscumque status, dignitatis et conditionis exsistant, si, postquam ab ordinario, etiam ex officio, ter admoniti ea de re fuerint, concubinas non eiecerint, seque ab earum consuetudine non seiunxerint, excommunicatione feriendos esse, a qua non absolvantur, donec re ipsa admonitioni factae paruerint. Quodsi in concubinatu per annum, censuris neglectis, permanserint, contra eos ab ordinario severe pro qualitate criminis procedatur. Mulieres, sive coniugatae sive solutae, quae cum adulteris seu concubinariis publice vivunt, si ter admonitae non paruerint, ab ordinariis locorum, nullo etiam requirente, ex officio graviter pro modo culpae puniantur et extra oppidum vel dioecesim, si id eisdem ordinariis videbitur, invocato, si opus fuerit, brachio saeculari, eiiciantur; aliis poenis, contra adulteros et concubinarios inflictis, in suo robore permanentibus.

Caput IX

Ita plerumque temporalium dominorum ac magistratuum mentis oculos terreni affectus atque cupiditates excaecant, ut viros et mulieres sub eorum iurisdictione degentes, maxime divites vel spem magnae haereditatis habentes, minis et poenis adigant, cum iis matrimonium invitos contrahere, quos ipsi domini vel magistratus illis praescripserint. Quare cum maxime nefarium sit, matrimonii libertatem violare, et ab eis iniurias nasci, a quibus iura exspectantur: praecipit sancta synodus omnibus, cuiuscumque gradus, dignitatis et conditionis exsistant, sub anathematis poena, quam ipso facto incurrant, ne quovis modo, directe vel indirecte, subditos suos vel quoscumque alios cogant, quominus libere matrimonia contrahant.

Caput X

Ab adventu domini nostri Iesu Christi usque in diem epiphaniae, et a feria quarta cinerum usque in octavam paschatis inclusive, antiquas solemnium nuptiarum prohibitiones diligenter ab omnibus observari, sancta synodus praecipit. In aliis vero temporibus nuptias solemniter celebrari permittit, quas episcopi, ut ea qua decet modestia et honestate fiant, curabunt. Sancta enim res est matrimonium, et sancte tractandum.

Decretum de Reformatione

Eadem sacrosancta synodus, reformationis materiam prosequens, haec in praesenti sessione statuenda decernit.

Canon I

Si in quibuslibet ecclesiae gradibus providenter scienterque curandum est, ut in Domini domo nihil sit inordinatum nihilque praeposterum: multo magis elaborandum est, ut in electione eius, qui supra omnes gradus constituitur, non erretur. Nam totius familiae Domini status et ordo mutabit, si, quod requiritur in corpore, non inveniatur in capite; unde, etsi alias sancta synodus de promovendis ad cathedrales et superiores ecclesias nonnulla utiliter decrevit: hoc tamen munus huiusmodi esse censet, ut, si pro rei magnitudine expendatur, numquam satis cautum de eo videri possit. Itaque statuit, ut, cum primum ecclesia vacaverit, supplicationes ac preces publice privatimque habeantur, atque a capitulo per civitatem et dioecesim indicantur, quibus clerus populusque bonum a Deo pastorem valeat impetrare. Omnes vero et singulos, qui ad promotionem praeficiendorum quodcumque ius quacumque ratione a sede apostolica habent, aut alioquin operam suam praestant: nihil in his pro praesenti temporum ratione innovando, hortatur et monet, ut in primis meminerint, nihil se ad Dei gloriam et populorum salutem utilius posse facere, quam si bonos pastures et ecclesiae gubernandae idoneos promoveri studeant, eosque, alienis peccatis communicantes, mortaliter peccare, nisi quos digniores et ecclesiae magis utiles ipsi iudicaverint, non quidem precibus vel humano affectu aut ambientium suggestionibus, sed eorum exigentibus meritis praefici diligenter curaverint, et quos ex legitimo matrimonio natos et vita, aetate, doctrina atque aliis omnibus qualitatibus praeditos sciant, quae iuxta sacros canones et Tridentinae huius synodi decreta requiruntur. Quoniam vero in sumendo de praedictis omnibus qualitatibus gravi idoneoque bonorum et doctorum virorum testimonio non uniformis ratio ubique, ex nationum, populorum ac morum varietate, potest adhiberi: mandat sancta synodus, ut in provinciali synodo, per metropolitanum habenda, praescribatur quibusque locis et provinciis propria examinis seu inquisitionis aut instructionis faciendae forma, sanctissimi Romani pontificis arbitrio approbanda, quae magis eisdem locis utilis atque opportuna esse videbitur, ita tamen, ut cum deinde hoc examen seu inquisitio de persona promovenda perfecta fuerit, ea in instrumentum publicum redacta, cum toto testimonio, ac professione fidei ab eo facta, quamprimum ad sanctissimum Romanum pontificem omnino transmittatur, ut ipse summus pontifex, plena totius negotii ac personarum notitia habita, pro gregis dominici commodo de illis, si idonei per examen seu per inquisitionem factam reperti fuerint, ecclesiis possit utilius providere. Omnes vero inquisitiones, informationes, testimonia ac probationes quaecumque de promovendi qualitatibus et ecclesiae statu, a quibuscumque, etiam in Romana curia, habitae, per cardinalem, qui relationem facturus erit in consistorio, et alios tres cardinales diligenter examinentur, ac relatio ipsa cardinalis relatoris et trium cardinalium subscriptione roboretur, in qua ipsi singuli quatuor cardinales affirment, se, adhibita accurata diligentia, invenisse promovendos qualitatibus a iure et ab hac sancta synodo requisitis praeditos, ac certo existimare sub periculo salutis aeternae, idoneos esse, qui ecclesiis praeficiantur: ita ut, relatione in uno consistorio facta, quo maturius interea de ipsa inquisitione cognosci possit, in aliud consistorium iudicium differatur, nisi aliud beatissimo pontifici videbitur expedire. Ea vero omnia et singula, quae de episcoporum praeficiendorum vita, aetate, doctrina et ceteris qualitatibus alias in eadem synodo constituta sunt, decernit eadem, etiam in creatione sanctae Romanae ecclesiae cardinalium, etiam si diaconi sint, exigenda, quos sanctissimus Romanus pontifex ex omnibus christianitatis nationibus, quantum commode fieri poterit, prout idoneos repererit, assumet. Postremo eadem sancta synodus, tot gravissimis ecclesiae incommodis commota, non potest non commemorare, nihil magis ecclesiae Dei esse necessarium, quam ut beatissimus Romanus pontifex, quam sollicitudinem universae ecclesiae ex muneris sui officio debet, eam hic potissimum impendat, ut lectissimos tantum sibi cardinales adsciscat, et bonos maxime atque idoneos pastores singulis ecclesiis praeficiat; idque eo magis, quod ovium Christi sanguinem, quae ex malo negligentium et sui officii immemorum pastorum regimine peribunt, dominus noster Iesus Christus de manibus eius sit requisiturus.

Canon II

Provincialia concilia, sicubi omissa sunt, pro moderandis moribus, corrigendis excessibus, controversiis componendis, aliisque ex sacris canonibus permissis renoventur. Quare metropolitani per se ipsos, seu, illis legitime impeditis, coepiscopus antiquior intra annum ad minus a fine praesentis concilii, et deinde quolibet saltem triennio, post octavam paschae resurrectionis domini nostri Iesu Christi, seu alio commodiori tempore pro more provinciae, non praetermittat synodum in provincia sua cogere, quo episcopi omnes et alii, qui de iure vel consuetudine interesse debent, exceptis iis, quibus cum imminenti periculo transfretandum esset, convenire omnino teneantur. Nec episcopi comprovinciales, praetextu cuiuslibet consuetudinis, ad metropolitanam ecclesiam in posterum accedere inviti compellantur. Itidem episcopi, qui nulli archiepiscopo subiiciuntur, aliquem vicinum metropolitanum semel eligant, in cuius synodo provinciali cum aliis interesse debeant et, quae ibi ordinata fuerint, observent ac observari faciant. In reliquis omnibus eorum exemptio et privilegia salva atque integra maneant. Synodi quoque dioecesanae quotannis celebrentur, ad quas exempti etiam omnes, qui alias, cessante exemptione, interesse deberent nec capitulis generalibus subduntur, accedere teneantur; ratione tamen parochialium aut aliarum saecularium ecclesiarum, etiam annexarum, debeant ii, qui illarum curam gerunt, quicumque illi sint, synodo interesse. Quodsi in his tam metropolitani quam episcopi et alii suprascripti negligentes fuerint, poenas sacris canonibus sancitas incurrant.

Canon III

Patriarchae, primates, metropolitani et episcopi propriam dioecesim per se ipsos aut, si legitime impediti fuerint, per suum generalem vicarium aut visitatorem, si quotannis totam propter eius latitudinem visitare non poterunt, saltem maiorem eius partem, ita tamen, ut tota biennio per se vel visitatores suos compleatur, visitare non praetermittant. A metropolitanis vero, etiam post plene visitatam propriam dioecesim, non visitentur cathedrales ecclesiae neque dioeceses suorum comprovincialium, nisi causa cognita et probata in concilio provinciali. Archidiaconi autem, decani et alii inferiores in iis ecclesiis, ubi hactenus visitationem exercere legitime consueverunt, debeant quidem, assumpto notario de consensu episcopi, deinceps per se ipsos tantum ibidem visitare. Visitatores etiam a capitulo deputandi, ubi capitulum ius visitandi habet, prius ab episcopo approbentur; sed non ideo episcopus vel, eo impedito, eius visitator easdem ecclesias seorsum ab his visitare prohibeatur; cui ipsi archidiaconi vel alii inferiores visitationis factae infra mensem rationem reddere et depositiones testium ac integra acta ei exhibere teneantur. Non obstantibus quacumque consuetudine, etiam immemorabili, atque exemptionibus et privilegiis quibuscumque. Visitationum autem omnium istarum praecipuus sit scopus, sanam orthodoxamque doctrinam, expulsis haeresibus, inducere, bonos mores tueri, pravos corrigere, populum cohortationibus et admonitionibus ad religionem, pacem innocentiamque accendere, cetera, prout locus, tempus et occasio feret, ex visitantium prudentia ad fidelium fructum constituere. Quae ut facilius feliciusque succedant, monentur praedicti omnes et singuli, ad quos visitatio spectat, ut paterna charitate christianoque zelo omnes amplectantur, ideoque, modesto contenti equitatu famulatuque, studeant, quam celerrime, debita tamen cum diligentia, visitationem ipsam absolvere. Interimque caveant, ne inutilibus sumptibus cuiquam graves onerosive sint, neve ipsi aut quispiam suorum quidquam procurationis causa, pro visitatione etiam testamentorum ad pios usus, praeter id, quod ex relictis piis iure debetur, aut alio quovis nomine, nec pecuniam nec munus, quodcumque sit, etiam qualitercumque offeratur, accipiant; non obstante quacumque consuetudine, etiam immemorabili. Exceptis tamen victualibus, quae sibi ac suis frugaliter moderateque pro temporis tantum necessitate et non ultra erunt ministranda. Sit tamen in optione eorum, qui visitantur, si malint solvere id, quod erat ab ipsis antea solvi, certa pecunia taxata, consuetum, an vero praedicta victualia subministrare, salvo item iure conventionum antiquarum, cum monasteriis aliisque piis locis aut ecclesiis non parochialibus inito, quod illaesum permaneat. In iis vero locis seu provinciis, ubi consuetudo est, ut nec victualia nec pecunia nec quidquam aliud a visitatoribus accipiatur, sed omnia gratis fiant: ibi id observetur. Quodsi quisquam (quod absit) aliquid amplius in supradictis omnibus casibus accipere praesumpserit: is praeter dupli restitutionem intra mensem faciendam aliis etiam poenis iuxta constitutionem concilii generalis Lugdunensis, quae incipit *Exigit,* necnon et aliis poenis in synodo provinciali arbitrio synodi, absque ulla spe veniae, mulctetur.

READING 5-K

ROBERTVS BELLARMINVS

[1542–1621 CE]

SECUNDA CONTROVERSIA GENERALIS

DE MEMBRIS ECCLESIAE MILITANTIS

CAPUT XIV.

Licere Christianis aliquando bella gerere.

Sequitur quaestio quarta, quae est de bello. Continet autem haec disputatio partes tres. Primum enim demonstrandum erit, licita esse aliquando Christianis bella. Secundo, explicandae caussae justi belli. Tertio, propter Lutherum, probandum erit recte Christianos adversus Turcas arma sumere.

Ac ut a primo incipiamus, antiqua haeresis fuit Manichaeorum, qui bellum ex natura sua illicitum asserebant, et ideo Moysem, Josue, Davidem et caeteros veteris Testamenti Patres, qui bella gesserunt, tamquam impios accusabant, ut b. Augustinus refert lib. 22. cont. Faustum, cap. 74. et seq. Eandem haeresim nostro saeculo aliqui excitarunt; ac in primis Erasmus cum alibi, tum praecipue in annotationibus ad cap. 3. et 22. Luc. prolixa disputatione contendit bellum esse unum ex malis, quae tolerantur, et veteribus Judaeis a Deo permissum, Christianis autem a Christo et apostolis interdictum.

Cornelius quoque Agrippa in libro de vanitate scientiarum, cap. 79. artem bellandi a Christo prohibitam esse affirmat. Idem etiam sequutus est Joannes Ferus lib. 4. commentariorum in Matthaeum, exponens illud 26. cap. *Qui acceperit gladium, gladio peribit.* Idem docent Anabaptistae, ut testatur Melanchthon in locis theologicis, capite de magistratu. Idem etiam tribuit Joanni Oecolampadio Alphonsus a Castro, verbo *Bellum,* quod mirum mihi videtur, cum Zwinglius ejus collega adeo probarit bellum, ut in praelio pugnans perierit, et similiter Calvinus lib. 4 institut. cap. 20. et Melanchthon, ubi supra, et caeteri haeretici hujus temporis, verbo et opere doceant esse bellandum.

Nos autem, ut semper docuit Ecclesia tota et verbis et exemplis, dicimus bellum ex natura sua non esse illicitum, et non solum Judaeis, sed etiam Christianis fas esse bellum gerere, modo conditiones serventur, de quibus postea dicemus. Id quod probatur Scripturae testimonio, Judicum 3. *Hae sunt gentes, quas Dominus dereliquit, ut erudiret in eis Isräelem, et omnes qui non noverant bella Chananaeorum, et postea discerent filii eorum certare cum hostibus, et habere consuetudinem praeliandi.* Haec sane verba non permissionem, sed absolutam Dei voluntatem ostendunt. Item 1. Reg. 15. *Haec dicit Dominus exercituum, recensui quaecumque fecit Amalech Isräeli; nunc ergo vade et percute Amalech, et demolire universa ejus. Non parcas ei etc.* Hic etiam non permissionem, sed praeceptum videmus, et similium plenum est Testamentum vetus. Item Luc. 3. *Interrogabant eum et milites, dicentes; Quid faciemus et nos? Et ait illis: Neminem concutiatis, neque calumniam faciatis, et contenti estote stipendiis vestris.* Anabaptistae apud Melanchthonem dicunt Joannem permisisse bellum Judaeis, ut imperfectis: Christum autem longe aliter docuisse.

At contra; nam Joannes praeparabat viam Domino, non ergo debuit permittere id quod Christus mox ablaturus erat; nam nec illi potuissent uti ea concessione, cum eodem anno venerit Christus, et prohibuerit bellum, ut ipsi volunt; et praeterea poterant suspicari homines Christum et Joannem non convenire inter se, quod absurdissimum fuisset. Respondet aliter Erasmus: Haec dici militibus, non ut ea servantes bene viverent, sed ut minus male viverent, ut videtur etiam explicare Theophylactus.

At contra; nam Joannes praemiserat: *Facite fructus dignos poenitentiae, et omnis arbor non faciens fructum bonum, in ignem mittetur etc.* Inde compuncti publicani et milites petierunt, quis esset fructus bonus, quem facere deberent: vel ergo Joannes eos decepit, vel possunt milites salvari, si servent quod Joannes illis praecepit.

Ad Theophylactum dico duo. Primo, eum non dicere bellum esse malum, sed solum dicere Joannem hortatum esse turbas, quae erant innocentes, ad opera bona, idest, ad communicanda bona sua cum aliis: Publicanos autem et milites, qui non erant capaces hujus perfectionis, et non poterant facere bonum supererogationis, hortatum esse ut desisterent a malo. Putavit enim Theophylactus dare tunicam non habenti, ei qui habet duas, esse opus consilii et supererogationis, alioqui non vocaret turbas, quibus hoc dicitur, innocentes, nec distingueret hoc opus tamquam bonum a malo, nam si praeceptum sit non retinere duas tunicas, retinere erit malum.

Dico secundo, Theophylactum non recte exponere hunc locum; nam vocat turbas innocentes, quibus Joannes dicit: *Genimina viperarum;* Et: *Facite fructus dignos poenitentiae.* Et praeterea habere duas tunicas, est retinere superflua, ut Hieronymus dicit quaest. 1. ad Hedibiam, peccatum autem est retinere superflua. Praeterea Matth. 22. Dominus docuit tributum Caesari esse solvendum; at certum est tributum non deberi regibus, nisi ut possint alere milites in defensionem reipub. quod exponit apostolus Rom. 13. *Ideo*, inquit, *et tributa praestatis, ministri enim Dei sunt in hoc ipsum servientes*, nimirum, ut gladio puniant perturbatores publicae pacis, id enim praemiserat: *Non sine caussa gladium portat, Dei enim minister est, vindex in iram.*

Probatur secundo exemplis sanctorum, qui bella gesserunt; nam si bellum esset malum, certe a sanctis non gereretur. In veteri Testamento Abraham, Moysem, Josue, Gedeonem, Samsonem, Davidem, Josiam,

Machabaeos magna cum laude bella gessisse legimus. In novo Testamento Matth. 8. Centurio cum diceret Christo: *Habeo sub me milites, et dico huic, vade, et vadit etc.* ejus fidem Dominus laudavit, non ut militiam desereret praecepit. Actor. 10. Cornelius item Centurio dicitur, *Vir justus et timens Deum.* Ita ut etiam angelum videre meruerit, nec postea cum a s. Petro viam salutis doceretur, dictum est ei, ut militiam desereret.

Deinde post Christi in coelum ascensionem semper fuisse Christianos, aliquos vere sanctos et Deo gratos in militia, etiam sub ethnicis principibus, docet Tertullianus in apologet. c. 5. ubi refert miraculum insigne a Christianis militibus factum, cum sub M. Aurelio in Germania bellum gererent; qui certe vel non militassent, si hoc esset malum, vel si militassent non ita Deo grati fuissent, ut etiam miracula facere possent. Vide histor. Eusebii lib. 8. cap. 4. et lib. 9. cap. 10. Docet etiam Basilius in oratione de laudibus 40. militum martyrum, fuisse multos sanctorum in castris gentilium imperatorum, et similiter Gregorius nazianzenus orat. 1. in Julianum ultra medium. Denique Constantinum, Theodosium, Valentianum, Carolum Magnum, s. Ludovicum regem Galliae, s. Mauritium cum sua legione Thebaeorum, aliosque plurimos sanctos christianos bella gessisse constat, quos s. episcopi numquam reprehenderunt, immo Theodosius consulebat de eventu belli Joannem abbatem, ut Augustin. refert lib. 5. de Civit. Dei, cap. 26.

Tertio probatur, quia Deus saepe justa bella adjuvat, quod nullo modo faceret, si bellum esset illicitum; nam mala permitti possunt, sed non etiam ad ea facienda auxilium dari. Gen. 14. Abrahae, cum debellasset quatuor reges cum solis 318. famulis suis, dictum est a Melchisedech: *Benedictus Deus excelsus, quo protegente hostes in manibus tuis sunt.* Exod. 17. ad preces Moysis Deus dedit victoriam Hebraeis contra Amalech. Josue 10. pugnante Josue sol stetit, et Dominus pluebat de coelo lapides magnos, et plures occidit Deus lapidibus grandinis, quam filii Isräel hastis et gladiis. 2. Machab. 10. *Angeli in specie equitum pro Machabaeis pugnabant*, et cap. 15. legimus Deum non secundum armorum potentiam, sed prout ipsi placet, dare dignis victoriam.

Constantinum Dei auxilio miraculis evidenter ostensis, vicisse in bellis testatur. Eusebius in vita Constantini, et lib. 9. hist. c. 9. Cum Theodosio s. Joannem et s. Philippum apostolos palam pugnasse contra hostes ejus testatur Theodoretus lib. 5. hist. c. 24. pro Thedosio juniores pugnasse angelos contra Saracenos scribit Socrates lib. 7. cap. 18. De Clodoveo vide Gregorium Turonicum, lib. 2. hist. Francorum, cap. 30. Honorii exercitum divino miraculo victoriam incredibilem de Gothis retulisse, scribit b. Augustinus lib. 5. de Civit. Dei, cap. 23. innumerabilia exempla similia referri possent.

Probatur quarto ratione; Licet reipub. defendere cives suos ab internis hostibus pacis, eos necando variis generibus suppliciorum, ergo etiam licebit bello atque armis, quando alia via non potest, defendere eosdem suos cives ab hostibus externis: quia ut possint conservari respublicae, necessarium est ut omnes hostes tam internos, quam externos arcere possint; et cum hoc sit jus naturae, nullo modo credibile est, per evangelium esse sublatum.

Probatur ultimo testimoniis Patrum. Tertullianus in apolog. cap. 42. *Navigamus,* inquit, *et nos vobiscum, et militamus, et rusticamur, et mercamur.*

S. Gregorius nazianzenus orat. 3. de pace: *Licet,* inquit, *utriusque temporis habenda sit ratio, quandoquidem juxta illius legem, atque auctoritatem praeclare interdum bellum suscipitur, quamdiu tamen licet, propensiores ad* pacem esse *debemus, hoc enim sublimius est et divinius.*

S. Joannes Chrysostomus homil. in evang. de nuptiis, Joan. 2. ex variis: *Militiam,* inquit, *praetexis, et dicis, non possum esse pius: Centurio nonne miles erat, nihilque nocuit illum sua militia?*

B. Ambrosius serm. 7. *Non militare, delictum est, sed propter praedam militare, peccatum est.* Et lib. 1. de officiis, cap. 40. et 41. numerat inter virtutes, bellicam fortitudinem, et eam nostris non defuisse multis exemplis probat. Item in oratione de obitu Theodosii, vehementer Theodosium a laude bellica commendat.

B. Augustinus epist. 5. ad Marcellinum: *Nam si christiana disciplina,* inquit, *omnia bella culparet, hoc potius militibus consilium salutis petentibus in evangelio diceretur, ut abjicerent arma, seque militiae omnino subtraherent: dictum est autem, neminem concusseritis, nulli calumniam feceritis, sufficiat vobis stipendium vestrum. Quibus proprium stipendium sufficere debere praecepit, militare utique non prohibuit.* [...]

CAPUT XVI.

Licere bellum gerere Christianis contra Turcas.

Jam vero quaestio de bello contra Turcas omitti potuisset, nisi Lutherus inter alia sua paradoxa etiam hoc protulisset, ac defendere conatus esset, non licere Christianis contra Turcas bellum gerere, ut patet ex art. 34. in Bulla Leonis damnato. Luthero videtur assentiri Theodorus Bibliander in chronologia tabul. 13. ubi sic ait: *Urbanus, seu potius turbo saevissimus, a spiritu malo homicidiis gaudente impulsus, bellum pro recuperanda Judaea commovit.*

Est autem observandum, Lutherum non negare bellum contra Turcas esse licitum, quia putet in genere omne bellum esse illicitum; nam in assertione ejusdem articuli suadet bellum contra pontificem, quem Turcissimum Turcam esse dicit; neque quia existimet non habere Christianos justam caussam; constat enim omnibus Turcas nullo jure occupasse regna Christianorum, et quotidie plura occupare velle. Constat etiam eum extinguere cupere omnem religionem, et dare omnem operam, ut homines ex Christianis fiant Mahumetani. Denique constat et antiquos pontifices, ut Urbanum II. Paschalem II. Eugenium III. et alios multos, necnon generalia concilia, ut lateranense, lugdunense, viennense, et alia, generale bellum indixisse Mahumetanis, et s. Bernardum, aliosque sanctos viros concionibus publicis excitasse populos ad hoc bellum, et sermonem miraculis confirmasse, ut ipsemet b. Bernardus modeste indicat initio libri 2. de consideratione, nec aliquid horum Lutherus negat; sed sunt aliae tres caussae cur senserit non licere contra Turcas bellare.

Prima, quia voluntas Dei esse videtur, ut a Turca, tamquam flagello quodam puniamur, neque licet nobis Dei voluntati resistere, quod autem ista sit voluntas Dei, probat in assertione art. 34. ab experientia, quae docuit hactenus nihil Christianis profuisse bellum contra Turcas.

Sed haec prima caussa parum valet, nam etsi voluntas Dei sit ut peccata nostra per Turcam puniantur, tamen non est voluntas Dei, ut Turcae non resistamus, immo voluntas ejus est ut resistamus; id quod ex fine probatur. Non enim Deus permittit Turcam in nos saevire ut pereamus, sed ut convertamur, tunc autem ad conversionem perducimur, cum Turcae nos oppugnanti resistere conamur, resistendo laboramus, laborando nostram infirmitatem agnoscimus, atque inde ad Deum toto corde revertimur, et ejus auxilium imploramus. Itaque ex fine, quo Deus permittit Turcam in nos saevire, sequitur manifeste ipsum velle ut Turcae resistamus. Praeterea, ita flagellum Dei est bellum Turcae, sicut pestis, fames, haeresis, fomes peccati, et similia; nemo autem tam est stultus, qui ideo putet non esse quaerenda medicamenta contra pestem, neque terram colendam, ne moriamur fame, neque haeresi et fomiti resistendum.

Neque verum est quod Lutherus dicit, experientiam docere nihil nobis prodesse bellum contra Turcas; nam ut omittam plurimas victorias de Turcis relatas, certe cum primum arma illata sunt in terram promissionis, felicissimo eventu Hierusalem a nostris recuperata fuit, et regnaverunt Christiani annis 88. et super plura, et plura recuperabant, donec oriri coeperunt inter ipsos christianos principes contentiones, quemadmodum et nunc Turca plura occupat ob discordiam nostrorum, quam sua virtute, et harum discordiam potissima caussa fuit Lutherus ipse. Nam ut ex Joanne Cochlaeo patet in actis Lutheri anni 1526. Hungaria periit, quia Germani a rege Hungariae vocati in auxilium, maluerunt Luthero parere tunc concionanti contra bellum in Turcas, quam cogitare quid bonum commune postularet. Saltem hoc boni habet bellum, quod impeditur Turca ne tantum noceat quantum vellet. Nisi enim hactenus cum eo pugnatum esset, jamdudum ille omnia obtineret.

Secunda caussa ejus est, quia Ecclesiae utilior est tribulatio et persequutio, quam victoria et tranquillitas; unde in sermone de matrimonio reprehendit Ecclesiae consuetudinem, qua orat pro pace et quiete, cum potius pro tribulationibus orandum esset. Sed respondemus, tribulationem et persequutionem esse quidem utilem, sed periculosam, et ideo non expetendam, sed tolerandam, cum aliter fieri non potest. Unde Matth. 6. jubemur orare. *Et ne nos inducas in tentationem.* Et 1.Tim. 2. apostolus jubet orare pro regibus, ut quietam et tranquillam vitam agamus. Et b. Augustinus lib. 10. Confessionis, cap. 28. dicit: Miserias tolerandas, non amandas, nec desiderandas et petendas.

Tertia caussa, eaque praecipua fuisse videtur, odium pontificis, tanto enim odio pontificem aliquando Lutherus persequebatur, ut plane optaret videre Turcam occupantem omnia regna Christianorum, ut saltem eo modo nomen pontificis extingueretur. Neque hoc fuisse votum ac desiderium ejus nos divinamus, sed ex verbis ejus colligimus, nam in libro ad nobililatem Germaniae, cap. 25. dicit, nullum esse pulchrius regimen usquam, quam apud Turcas, qui legibus Alcorani gubernantur, nullum autem turpius, quam apud Christianos, qui jure canonico et civili reguntur. Et in assertione articuli 34. dicit, pontificem, et pontificios esse multo pejores, et truculentiores Turcis, et stultum esse pugnare pro pejoribus Turcis contra meliores, et in epistola quadam contra duo mandata imperialia: *Oro,* inquit, *cunctos pios Christianos, ne ullo modo sequamur, vel in militiam ire, vel dare aliquid contra Turcas, quandoquidem Turca decies prudentior, probiorque est, quam sunt principes nostri.* Quibus verbis quid aliud suadere conatus est, quam esse juvandos Turcas contra Christianos?

Sed haec sententia tantam absurditatem et impietatem continet, ut ipse idem Lutherus postea, cum ille ardor nonnihil deferbuisset, plane contrarium scripserit. Sic enim ait in libro de visitatione Saxonica? *Clamant,* inquit, *aliqui praedicatores temerarie, non resistendum esse Turca. Hic sermo seditiosus est, qui neque ferri, neque permitti debet. Tenenter igitur potestates resistere Turcis, qui non solum cupiunt provincias devastare, uxores ac liberos violare, et interficere, verum etiam jura provinciae, cultum Dei, omnemque ordinationem bonam abrogare ac tollere. Idcirco debent principes ob id praecipue belligerare etc.* Et ibidem: *Multo,* inquit, *tolerabilius foret viro bono videre filiorum suorum interitum, quam Turcicis eos moribus imbui; Turcae enim nullam prorsus honestatem vel sciunt, vel curant.* Haec ille.

CAPUT XV.

Quot sint, et quae justi belli conditiones.

Belli justi conditiones quatuor numerare solent, qui haec tractant. Auctoritatem legitimam, caussam justam, intentionem bonam, et modum convenientem. Sed de singulis seorsim dicendum est.

Prima igitur conditio est auctoritas legitima, dicit enim s. Augustinus lib. 22. contra Faustum, cap. 75. *Ordo ille naturalis mortalium paci accommodatus hoc poscit, ut suscipiendi belli auctoritas, atque consilium penes principem sit, exequendi autem jussa bellica ministerium milites debeant paci, salutique communi.* Et ratio idem probat; nam privati homines, et qui superiorem habent, si ab aliquo injurias accipiant, possunt ad superiorem confugere, atque ab eo judicium petere. At principes si ab aliis principibus aliquid patiantur, non habent commune aliquod tribunal, ad quod illos accusent, et ideo licet ei bello injurias publicas propulsare.

Residet autem haec auctoritas indicendi belli, secundum communem sententiam, in omnibus, principibus et populis, qui in temporalibus superiorem non habent, quales sunt reges omnes; item respub. Venetorum et similes etc. Item nonnulli duces et comites, qui nulli subsunt in temporalibus, non autem duces et comites, qui subsunt regibus immediate, qui enim subsunt aliis, non sunt per se capita reipub. sed potius membra. Nota tamen hanc auctoritatem non requiri ad bellum defensivum, sed solum ad offensivum; nam defendere se unicuique licet, non solum principi, sed etiam privato, at indicere bellum et invadere hostem, solius est supremi capitis.

Secunda conditio est caussa justa, non enim sine caussa bellum indici potest, nec etiam propter quodcumque peccatum, sed tantum propter injuriam propulsandam. Ita b. Augustin. quaest. 10. in Josue: *Justa bella,* inquit, *definiri solent, quae ulciscuntur injurias, si qua gens vel civitas, quae bello petenda est, vel vindicare neglexit, quod a suis improbe factum est, vel reddere, quod per injuriam ablatum est.* Ratio autem hujus est, quia princeps non est judex, nisi hominum sibi subditorum, ergo non potest quaecumque peccata aliorum hominum punire, sed solum ea, quae caedunt in detrimentum populi sibi subjecti; nam etsi non est judex ordinarius aliorum, est tamen defensor suorum et oratione hujus necessitatis efficitur etiam quodammodo judex eorum, qui suis injuriam fecerunt, ita ut possit eos gladio punire.

Est vero observandum caussam belli debere esse non levem, neque dubiam, sed magnam et certam, ne forte plus incommodi bellum afferrat, quam sit utilitas, quae inde speratur. Si autem dubia sit distinguendum est de principe et militibus; nam princeps ipse sine dubio peccat; nam bellum est actus justitiae punitivae, injustum est autem punire aliquem caussa nondum probata: milites autem non peccant nisi constaret certo bellum esse illicitum, debent enim subditi parere superiori, nec debent discutere imperia ejus, sed potius praesumere debent principem suum bonam caussam habere, nisi manifeste contrarium noverint; sicut etiam cum dubia est culpa alicujus particularis, peccat judex, qui eum damnat, non carnifex, qui damnatum occidit; non enim tenetur carnifex discutere sententiam judicis, ita docet Bonifacius papa in Sexto, de regulis juris, regula 25. *Quod quis,* inquit, *mandato facit judicis, dolo facere non videtur, cum habeat parere necesse.* Et b. Augustinus lib. 22. contra Faustum, cap. 75. *Hoc etiam,* inquit, *fit ut vir justus, si forte sub rege sacrilego militet, recte possit illo jubente bellare, civicae pacis ordinem servans, cui quod jubetur, vel non esse contra Dei praeceptum, certum est, vel utrum sit, certum non est, ita ut fortasse reum regem faciat iniquitas imperandi, innocentem autem militem ostendat ordo serviendi.* [...]

READING 5-L

NVNTIVS SIGNORIELLO
[1931 CE]

LEXICON PERIPATETICUM PHILOSOPHICO – THEOLOGICUM
IN QUO SCHOLASTICORUM DISTINCTIONES ET EFFATA PRAECIPUA EXPLICANTUR

EFFATA

1. VELLE RERUM MUTATIONES, AUT CONTRARIA SUCCESSIVE FIERI, NON EST MUTARE VOLUNTATEM. Aliud nempe est mutare voluntatem, aliud velle aliquarum rerum mutationes. Tunc enim voluntas mutatur, cum incipit velle, quod prius non voluit, vel desinit velle, quod voluit. At potest aliquis, eadem voluntate immobiliter permanente, vello quod prius fiat hoc, et postea eius contrarium. Quocirca, ex eo quod Deus fieri alternis vicibus diversa, immo opposita velit, nihil contra Eius immutabilitatem argui potest, siquidem illa successio et varietas non quidem ipsum actum voluntatis Dei spectat, sed effectus Divinae voluntatis.

2. VERITAS RERUM NATURALIUM EST POSTERIOR INTELLECTU DIVINO: PRIOR INTELLECTU CREATO. Intellectus enim Divinus est mensura entitatis et veritatis rerum, quippe quae dicuntur verae, quatenus consentiunt cum Ideis Divinis. Ergo veritas rerum naturalium posterior est Intellectu Divino. At res naturales sunt mensura veritatis nostrorum conceptuum, quippe qui dicuntur veri, quatenus consentiunt cum ipsis rebus. Ergo veritas rerum est prior, quam veritas nostri intellectus. Iam ex hoc ipso, quod res ipsae sint mensura intellectus nostri, atque earum mensura sint exemplaria Divini Intellectus, consequitur veritatem logicam, quae est obiectum nostri intellectus, ab ipsius intellectus aestimatione non pendere, sed in ipsa realitate rerum, et ideo in immutabilibus exemplaribus Divini Intellectus fundamentum habere.

Hoc unum satis est, ut refellantur tum veteres Sophistae, qui veritatem logicam non esse absolutam, sed relativam, tum recentes progressus assertores, qui illam mutari et progredi contendunt: « Non enim ita ideo est in re, quia videtur nobis; sed magis quia ita est in re, verum est quod videtur nobis. »

3. VERITAS NON SUSCIPIT MAGIS ET MINUS. Nempe, si accipiatur veritas prout est *adaequatio* rei et intellectus, non datur una veritas altera maior; nam ratio aequalitatis non suscipit magis et minus.

Attamen si consideretur ipsum *esse* rei, in quo veritas fundatur, existit una veritas altera maior; quae enim sunt magis entia, sunt magis vera: « Cum veritas consistat in adaequatione intellectus et rei, si consideretur veritas secundum rationem aequalitatis, quae non recipit magis et minus, sic non contingit esse aliquid magis et minus verum; sed si consideretur ipsum esse rei, quod est ratio veritatis, eadem est depositio rerum in esse et veritate; unde quae sunt magis entia, sunt magis vera; et propter hoc etiam in scientiis demonstrativis magis creduntur principia, quam conclusiones. »

4. VERUM ET BONUM CONVERTUNTUR. Tum enim bonum, tum verum convertitur cum ente. Ergo ipsum bonum convertitur cum vero, seu bonum et verum idem sunt *secundum rem.* Ea tamen differre *ratione* patet ex eo quod *bonum* respicit appetitum, *verum* autem cognitionem. Hinc sequitur ut verum *secundum rationem* sit prius quam bonum; cognitio enim naturaliter praecedit appetitum. Circa hoc effatum s. Bonaventura advertit ipsum intelligendum esse *circa idem.* « Unde si res vera, est bona; et si signum sit verum, est bonum; sed tamen non sequitur quod, si signum sit verum, signatum, sive res sit bona; et ideo hic est fallacia accidentis: omne verum est bonum; sed illud furari est verum; ergo illud furari est bonum: ex variatione minoris extremitatis. Verum enim praedicatur de illo dicto ratione compositionis, cum sit dictio modalis, bonum verum ratione attributionis. »

5. VERUM NON EST VERO CONTRARIUM. Nempe solum falsum repugnat vero. Ex hoc effato, quod evidens ex se est, Theologi, duce s. Thoma, evincunt veritatem Fidei contrariam esse non posse illis principiis, quae ratio naturaliter cognoscit. Ex eodem effato etiam consequitur, ut id, quod *simpliciter* est verum, numquam falsum esse possit; alioquin verum sibimetipsi repugnaret.

6. VERITATE UNA VERA SUNT OMNIA. Quod effatum hoc modo explicandum est: Omnia quae sunt, si ad intellectum Divinum referantur, una veritate Divina vera sunt. Unus enim et simplicissimus est intellectus Divinus. At si veritas accipiatur prout ad intellectum creatum refertur, perspicuum est non omnia esse vera una veritate, quia intellectus creati sunt diversi, et unus intellectus pluribus actibus plures veritates cognoscit. Si denique veritas *improprie* dicta consideretur, nempe si inspiciantur res, quae dicuntur verae, tunc statuendum est plurium rerum plures esse veritates, et unius rei unam esse veritatem. Res enim diversae sunt invicem, et unaquaeque earum est una: Ratio veritatis in duobus consistit, in esse rei, et in apprehensione virtutis cognoscitivae proportionata ad esse rei. Utrumque autem horum, quamvis reducatur in Deum, sicut in causam efficientem et exemplarem, nihilominus tamen quaelibet res participat suum esse creatum, quo formaliter est, et unusquisque intellectus participat lumen, per quod recte de re iudicat, quod quidem est exemplatum a lumine increato. Habet etiam intellectus suam operationem in se, ex qua completur ratio veritatis. Unde dico, quod sicut est unum Esse Divinum, quo omnia sunt sicut a principio effectivo

exemplari, nihilominus tamen in rebus diversis est diversum esse, quo formaliter res est; ita etiam est una veritas, scilicet Divina, qua omnia vera sunt, sicut principio effectivo exemplari; nihilominus sunt plures veritates in rebus creatis, quibus dicuntur verae formaliter.

7. Ex vero numquam sequitur falsum, et ex falso non potest per se sequi verum. Siquidem quoad primum, verum non potest connecti, nisi cum vero; unde quidquid iure infertur ex vero etiam verum esse debet. Ea, enim, quae sunt eadem uni tertio, necesse est ut sint eadem inter se. Hinc si in praemissis extrema cum veritate comparantur cum medio, in consequenti cum veritate secum connectenda sunt; ideoque si praemissae sunt verae, consequens necessario erit verum. Quoad alterum, ex falso non potest *per se* sequi verum, seu falsum non potest esse causa veri; falsum enim est nihil, et ideo non potest producere veritatem. Attamen *per accidens* ex falso aliquando sequitur verum, quatenus nempe id, quod infertur ex falso, possit esse verum aliunde, non propter ipsum falsum; sive sequitur verum ex falso, non prout est huiusmodi, sed prout conceditur tamquam verum, ita ut ex concesso falso sequatur verum, non quidem tamquam ex causa veritatis, sed illationis; nempe, ut loquitur s. Augustinus, *non ex veritate sententiarum, quae, cum falsae sint, nullae sunt, sed ex veritate connexionis.* E. g., in hoc syllogismo: Omnis lapis est animal; sed homo est lapis; ergo homo est animal; consequens est verum, et tamen praemissae sunt falsae. Cuius ratio est, quia ea, quae sunt eadem inter se, non debent esse eadem cum omni tertio; unde licet falsum sit duo extrema conclusionis esse eadem cuidam uni tertio, poterunt tamen esse eadem inter se.

8. Violentum non est perpetuum. *Violentum* dupliciter dicitur, primo, ex parte termini; secundo, non solum ex parte termini, sed ex parte principii, quod illum terminum producere potest. Primo modo violentum vocatur illud, quod caret aliquo bono, ad quod naturalem inclinationem habet, sed in tota natura non est aliquod principium, cuius virtute possit obtinere illud bonum. Hoc sensu dicitur caecus violenter detineri sine potentia videndi, et anima separata detineri sine corpore. Et hoc violentum, quatenus ipsae vires naturae considerantur, semper est perpetuum. Secundo modo dicitur violentum illud, quod caret aliquo bono ad quod habet naturalem inclinationem, et simul est in ipsa natura aliquod principium, per quod possit illud obtinere; sicut cum ignis per violentiam detinetur deorsum, aut lapis sursum. Iam de hoc genere *violenti* dicitur *violentum numquam esse perpetuum.*

9. Virtus consistit in medio. « Hoc, quod vult Philosophus, virtutem esse in medio, intelligendum est de virtutibus moralibus, non autem est verum de virtutibus theologicis. » Et sane, virtus moralis consistit in medio *inter superabundantiam et defectum.* Nam « virtutes morales sunt circa passiones et operationes, quas oportet dirigere secundum regulam rationis. In omnibus autem regulatis consistit rectum, secundum quod regulae aequantur; aequalitas autem media est inter maius et minus; et ideo oportet quod rectum virtutis consistat in medio eius, quod superabundat,

et eius, quod deficit a mensura rationis recta. » Virtutis autem *theologicae* « mensura et regula est ipse Deus. Fides enim nostra regulatur secundum veritatem Divinam . . .

1. BONA NON SUNT FACIENDA, UT VENIANT MALA. Huius explicatio perspicue traditur a s. Thoma iis verbis: « Si illud *ut* teneatur causaliter, est omnino verum; peccaret enim si quis ea intentione aliquem ad intrandam religionem induceret, ut apostataret. Si vero illud *ut* teneatur consecutive, sic ab omnibus bonis esset abstinendum, quia vix sunt aliqua humana bona, ex quibus occasionaliter non possent sequi aliqua mala... Tunc autem solum aliquod bonum esset praetermittendum propter consequens malum, quando malum consequens esset multo maius, quam bonum, et ut frequentius accideret. »

2. BONITAS ESSENTIALIS REI MELIOR ESSE NON POTEST; ACCIDENTALIS VERO SIC. Bonitas essentialis unius rei melior, quam bonitas alterius rei esse potest; naturas enim rerum alias aliis perfectiores esse non repugnat. Quocirca *effatum* de bonitate essentiali cuiusque rei intelligendum est. Nempe si bonitas, quae ad alicuius rei essentiam spectat, puta, esse praeditum ratione in homine, melior esse posset, non amplius illa res, sed alia prorsus diversae speciei existeret; sicut si quaternario numero alia unitas adderetur, alius numerus, non quaternarius existeret. Idem de bonitate accidentali intelligi nequit, quippe quae est extra essentiam rei.

Ex hoc effato infertur: 1° Deum unicuique rei maiorem bonitatem accidentalem conferre potuisse; 2° quoad bonitatem essentialem, Deum qualibet re creata meliorem aliam rem facere potuisse; non tamen ut haec, vel illa res maioris sit bonitatis.

3. BONUM ADDITUM BONO FACIT MAIUS. Intelligendum est, prout quodlibet bonum per participationem ex additione alterius fit melius; e.g., si quid calidum alii calido addatur, fit magis calidum. At bonum per essentiam ex additione boni per participationem non fit melius, siquidem bonitas huius in bonitate illius continetur: « Quando unum illorum bonorum est improportionatum ad aliud, tunc non addit, ut faciat illud melius. » Quocirca Deus, qui est ipsa essentia bonitatis, ex nullius boni creati additione fit magis bonus. Et sane « tota ratio omnium bonorum est in Deo; unde et Ipse dicitur omne bonum; unde non potest sibi fieri additio alicuius boni, quod in Ipso non sit. » In *moralibus* autem bonum additum bono facit maius bonum, dummodo, quemadmodum monuit s. Bonaventura, illa additio fiat, « salvo ordine; cum enim bonitas necessario ponat ordinem, si additio boni ad bonum tollat ordinem, bonum non auget, sed potius perimit. » Qua ratione ostenditur vi huius axiomatis illud minime consequi, voluntatem eo meliorem esse, quo plures sibi praestituit bonos fines principales. Nam « pluralitas finium principalium ordinem non servat, quia secundum rectum ordinem status debet esse in uno, et unicum debet esse ultimum; hinc est quod pluralitas finium principalium bonitatem

voluntatis non auget, sed potius ipsam voluntatem depravat, quia dum vult placere uni, displicet alteri, et dum vult assequi unum, perdit reliquum. »

4. Bonum commune melius est bono privato. Ratio est, quia bonum particulare ordinatur in bonum commune, sicut in finem, siquidem « esse partis est propter esse totius, unde et bonum gentis est divinius, quam bonum unius hominis. » Iam hoc effatum intelligendum est, quatenus bonum commune, et privatum ad idem spectant genus, secus enim fieri potest, ut bonum privatum sit melius secundum genus suum, e. g., « virginitas Deo dicata praefertur foecunditati carnali. »

5. Bonum quanto communius, tanto divinius. Hoc effatum « veritatem habet de communi secundum participationem unius et eiusdem rei secundum numerum. Quod enim est communius isto modo, est divinius; sicut divina Natura est communis omnibus, in quantum omnes ipsam secundum aliquam similitudinem participant. Non autem habet veritatem de communi secundum praedicationem; quomodo bonum corporis est communius, quam bonum spirituale hominis. » Hac ratione cavillatio illa dissolvitur, qua felicitatem hominis in bono corporeo, potius quam in spirituali sitam esse ita arguitur: *Bonum, quo communius, eo divinius. Ergo si bonum corporis est communius quam quodcumque aliud bonum spirituale hominis,* sequitur quod sit divinius; et *sic magis in ipso consistit felicitas, quam in bono spirituali.*

6. Bonum cuiuslibet creaturae consistit in modo, specie, et ordine. Hoc effatum oritur ex eo, quod bonum fundamentum habet in perfectione; siquidem bonum dicitur ens, prout est appetibile, appetibile autem non nisi, quod perfectum est, esse potest. Porro, quoniam rei perfectae nihil deest eorum, quae ad eius integritatem requiruntur, necesse est ut ipsa habeat propriam formam, per quam est, nec non ea, quae formam antecedant, vel consequantur oportet. Iam illud, quod formae constitutionem antecedit, est determinatio, seu mensura principiorum, ex quibus efficitur; nam res creata quidquid recipit, secundum naturam suam, hoc est naturae suae *commensuratum* recipit. Huiusmodi commensuratio significatur per *modum,* siquidem *mensura,* aiente s. Augustino; *omni rei modum praefigit.* Ipsa forma est species, quia per formam unumquodque in sua specie constituitur. Denique illud, quod formam consequitur, est inclinatio in aliquid sibi conveniens, et ad illam pertinet *ordo.* Itaque bonum eo ipso, quod in perfectione fundamentum habet, consistit in *modo, specie,* et *ordine.* Dicitur autem *bonum cuiuslibet creaturae,* quia, ut s. Thomas advertit, « habere modum, speciem, et ordinem pertinet ad rationem boni causati; sed bonum in Deo est sicut in causa; unde ad Eum pertinet imponere aliis modum, speciem, et ordinem. »

7. Bonum est diffusivum sui. Idest ad rationem boni pertinet, ut se cum aliis communicet, eodem modo, quo ad rationem finis pertinet movere. Id patet ex naturali inclinatione, qua res in se mutuo agunt, et alias, sibi assimilare nituntur, ita ut cum non possint suam individuam bonitatem cum aliis communicare, saltem bonitatem eiusdem speciei cum

eis participent. Ita ignis in ignem alia corpora convertere nititur. Atque « quanto aliquid invenitur melius, tanto ad remotiora bonitatem suam diffundit. » Monente autem s. Bonaventura, « diffusio dupliciter potest esse a bono, aut per modum multiplicationis, sicut calor vel lumen dicitur se diffundere; aut per modum utilis operationis, per quem modum dicitur bonus homo bonitatem suam diffundere, dum adhuc operatur, et laborat, ut alii bonitatem non ab ipso sed a Deo suscipiant. » Cave tamen, ne ab illo effato inferas Deum, qui est ipsa bonitas necessario debuisse producere creaturas, in quas bonitatis suae divitias effunderet; « cum enim, apposite inquit Sylvius, dicitur, quod bonum sit sui diffusivum, non significatur, quod actu se debeat alii communicare, sed quod possit: » siquidem exercitium illius communicationis a Dei sapientia et voluntate regitur. Hinc s. Bonaventura: « Bonum summum summe se diffundit; dicendum, quod verum est de diffusione naturali, sed de voluntaria, sive a proposito non est verum. Primo modo est diffusio in processione Personarum, secundo modo in productione creaturarum. »

8. BONUM EST EX INTEGRA CAUSA, MALUM EX QUOVIS DEFECTU. Seu, ut a s. Thoma exponitur: *Quilibet singularis defectus causat malum; bonum autem causatur ex integra causa.* Etenim « aliqua operatio non perficitur, nisi omnibus causis concurrentibus; impeditur autem operatio, si quodcumque eorum, quae sunt ad operationem necessaria, impeditur. » Sane actio voluntatis morali bonitate non pollet, nisi et eius obiectum, et adiuncta, et finis bona sint; e contrario absolute mala est, cum una tantum ex parte bonitas deest. Hinc idem actus voluntatis non potest simul diversam induere speciem moralitatis, e. g., esse bonus ex obiecto, et malus ex fine: « Cum aliquis vult dare eleemosynam propter inanem gloriam, hic est unus actus voluntatis, et hic actus totus malus est, licet non ab omni eo, quod in eo est, malitiam habeat; » item non potest esse malus ex obiecto, et bonus ex fine, ut cum quis furatur ad dandam eleemosynam; malitia enim desumpta ex fine operantis totum actum inficit, et eius bonitatem destruit. Hinc idem s. Thomas: « Sive voluntas sit eius, quod est secundum se malum, et sub ratione boni, sive sit boni sub ratione mali, semper voluntas erit mala. » Itaque cum « malum sit omnifarie, et bonum uno modo, non sequitur quod, si defectus alicuius rei (e. g., *bonae intentionis)* sufficit ad faciendum malum, positio eius sufficiat ad faciendum bonum. » Quod effatum etiam in naturalibus obtinet. Sic iure dicitur sanus, qui nullo prorsus corporis vitio laborat; contra, insalubris, qui vel unius humoris perturbationem patitur.

Ex hoc effato aliud sequitur, nempe: BONUM DIFFICILIUS CONSTITUITUR, QUAM MALUM. Nam « malum ex pluribus causis contingere potest, quam bonum; non enim bonum consistit, nisi omnia, quae ad perfectionem rei exiguntur, conveniant; quodcumque autem eorum subtrahatur, ratio mali incidit. »

1. Natura determinatur ad unum. *Naturae* nomine hic intelliguntur causae naturales. Porro hae dicuntur determinatae ad unum, non quidem quatenus hunc *numero* actum vel effectum possunt tantum producere, sed quatenus circa unum ex oppositis, non ad utrumque versari possunt, et quatenus uno modo plures effectus producunt. Ratio autem huius effati ex alio iam explicato colligitur, nempe, *Modus operandi sequitur modum essendi;* cum enim unumquodque *similiter habeat esse et operationem,* cumque causae naturales eiusmodi sint, ut electionis vi haud fruantur, sequitur ut in ipsis, secundum verba s. Thomae, *virtus operativa sit determinata ad unum.* Iamvero, « in illis, quae sunt determinata ad unum, semper sequitur actus naturalis, nisi impediatur, et impedimentum contingit in minore parte. » Hinc causae naturales, quoties in eadem conditione versantur, toties eosdem effectus producunt; et si aliquando ipsae suum effectum non attingunt, id non ex eo fit, quod vi illum producendi destituuntur, sed quod illarum actiones aliae causae frustrantur: ita morbus, quo hydropicus laborat, impedit, quin aqua sitim extinguat: quod impedimentum ex immediata Dei actione interdum oritur, cum nempe facta supernaturalia eveniunt. Inde est, ut Peripatetici, cum aiebant *naturam semper eodem modo operari,* adderent, *nisi impediatur.*

Ex hoc effato illud consequitur, *Natura causat quia est,* idest ex essentiae suae determinatione; nam effectus assimilatur formae agentis, per quam agit; atqui unius rei non est nisi una forma naturalis, per quam habet *esse;* ergo res naturalis effectum talem producit, qualis ipsa est. E contrario, *voluntas causat quia vult,* idest non ex natura, sed ex proprio consilio; forma enim, per quam voluntas agit, non est una tantum, sed sunt plures, prout sunt plures notiones intellectae; quocirca illud, quod voluntate agitur, non est tale, quale est agens, sed quale vult, et illud intelligit esse. Ubi tamen illud adnotandum censemus cum s. Thoma, etiam voluntatem, quippe quae *in aliqua natura fundatur,* esse *determinatam ad unum sibi proportionatum,* nempe bonum commune, licet dein circa bona particularia libere versari possit.

2. Naturae opus est opus intelligentiae. Sane res naturales, cum ad determinatum effectum producendum spectent, operantur propter finem. « Operationes naturae inveniuntur ordinate procedere in finem, sicut operationes sapientis. » Et quoniam omni vi cognoscendi illae destituuntur, ideoque non cognoscunt finem, ob quem agunt, nequeunt ad finem assequendum moveri ex seipsis, sed necesse est ut ab aliqua causa intelligente moveantur. Iam « effectus principalius attribuitur primo moventi dirigenti in finem, quam instrumentis ab eo directis. »

READING 5-M

ANTONIVS BACCI

[1957 CE]

LITTERAE ENCYCLICAE

Pius PP. XII

VENERABILES FRATRES

SALUTEM ET APOSTOLICAM BENEDICTIONEM

Miranda prorsus technicae artis inventa, quibus nostrorum temporum homines gloriantur, quamquam ex humano ingenio laboreque oriuntur, dona sunt tamen Dei Creatoris nostri, ex quo omnia opera bona procedunt: « non enim solum protulit creaturam, verum etiam prolatam tuetur et fovet. »

Ex quibus inventis alia hominum vires potentiamque adaugent atque multiplicant; alia eorum vitae condiciones meliores efficiunt; alia denique, cum animum potissimum respiciant, vel per se, vel per artificiosas imagines ac voces multitudines ipsas attingunt, et cum iisdem cuiusvis generis nuntios, cogitata et praecepta facilitate summa communicant, quibus veluti mentis pabulo enutriantur per requietis etiam ac relaxationis horas.

Ad quae postrema inventa quod attinet, maximum aetate hac nostra incrementum acceperunt cinematographicae, radiophonicae ac televisificae artes.

Quas quidem artes, vixdum in usum invectae sunt, non modo summo cum gaudio Ecclesia excepit, sed materna etiam cura sollicitudineque vigilanti, eo consilio permota, ut filios suos, progredientis aetatis iter ingressos, a periculis omnibus tueretur.

Haec cura evigilans ex ipso a Divino Redemptore accepto munere oritur; quandoquidem, ut patet omnibus, hae novi generis artes multum multumque conferunt ad peculiarem singulorum universaeque hominum communitatis cogitandi agendique modum. . . .

E progressionibus mirandis prorsus, quas nostris hisce diebus technicae disciplinae, ad cinematographicam, radiophonicam et televisificam artem quod attinet, fecerunt, ut maximae utilitates, ita maxima quoque pericula oriri possunt.

Hae enim novae opes novaque instrumenta, quae fere omnibus ad manum sunt, vim exserunt in animos potentissimam, cum idcirco quod eos luce collustrare possunt, nobilitate evehere, pulchritudine decorare; tum ex eo etiam quod eos tenebrarum obscuratione foedare, depravatione dehonestare, effrenatisque subicere queunt motibus, prouti eiusmodi spectacula res aut pravas aut honestas nostris sensibus proponunt.

Quemadmodum superiore saeculo, cum progrediens ars technica, ad ea, quae quaestus causa tractantur, pertinens, id saepenumero effecit, ut machinae in usum inductae, quae hominibus servire debent, eos potius in servitutem aerumnoso cum detrimento redigerent, ita pariter hodie increscentia eiusdem technicae artis incrementa, ad imagines, ad sonos, ad cogitata propaganda quod attinet, nisi suavi iugo legis Christi subiciantur, innumerabilium malorum fons esse possunt, quae eo vel gravia evadunt, cum non modo materiae, sed animi etiam vires misere subigantur, atque adeo humana inventa salutaribus illis utilitatibus priventur, quas ex providentis Dei consilio primum quaerere oportet.

Quapropter, cum gravem eiusmodi causam maiore cotidie paterni animi Nostri sollicitudine prosecuti simus, cumque salutares consideraverimus fructus, qui — ad cinematographica spectacula quod pertinet — ex Encyclica Epistula, quae *Vigilanti cura* inscribitur, per plus quam decennia duo iam orti sunt, Nos precibus sacrorum Pastorum laicorumque hominum harum artium studiosorum concedentes, cupimus per Encyclicas has Litteras normas et praecepta impertire, quae ad radiophonicas etiam auditiones atque ad televisionem attineant.

Postquam igitur instantes supplicationes Deo admovimus, ac Deiparae Virginis auxilium impetravimus, vos, Venerabiles Fratres, quorum pastoralem sollertemque curam perspectam habemus, eo consilio compellamus, ut non modo christiana hac de re doctrina in plena luce ponatur, sed ut etiam opportuna suscipiantur proposita et incepta; ideoque omni ope, qua possumus, vos commonere cupimus, ut grex, unicuique vestrum creditus, adversus quoslibet errores quaelibetque detrimenta muniatur, quae memoratarum artium usus in christianae vitae mores, non sine gravi discrimine, inducere possit.

I

Antequam de singulis quaestionibus agimus, quae ad has artes tres pertinent, ad cinematographicam dicimus, radiophonicam, et televisificam — novimus enim unamquamque earum ad mentis animique cultum fovendum peculiares causas solvendas proponere cum in liberalium, tum in technicarum et oeconomicarum disciplinarum campo — opportunum ducimus ea breviter enucleare principia, quae ad bona, hominum communitati et singulis civibus destinata, quam latissime fieri possit, propaganda pertineant....

Inter varias technicas artes, quae cogitata hominum propagant, illae hodie peculiarem locum occupant, ut diximus, quae cum auribus unaque simul cum oculis, per voces nempe imaginesque, omne genus nuntios quam latissime communicant.

Hic imagines vocesque propagandi modus, ad res etiam spirituales quod spectat, aptissimus est naturae hominum, secundum Aquinatis sententiam:

« Est autem naturale homini, ut per sensibilia ad intelligibilia veniat; quia omnis nostra cognitio a sensu initium habet. » Quin immo videndi facultas, cum nobilior et dignior sit ceteris sensibus, facilius ad spiritualium rerum cognitionem conducit.

Quamobrem praecipuae tres technicae artes, quibus auribus voces, oculis autem rerum imagines ex longinquo proponuntur, hoc est cinematographica, radiophonica ac televisifica ars, non ad homines tantummodo recreandos relaxandosque pertinent, quamvis non pauci hoc solum requirant auditores spectatoresque, sed ad ea potissimum propaganda, quae cum ad animi culturam, ad virtutemque alendam attineant, non parum possunt ad civilem nostrorum temporum societatem recte instituendam conformandumque conferre. . . .

Atqui eo primum spectent oportet cinematographicae, radiophonicae, televisificae artes: ut scilicet veritati virtutique inserviant.

Veritati autem propagandae ea ratione inserviant, ut vincula inter populos artiora cotidie fiant; ut iidem mutua rerum aestimatione se intellegant; ut in quovis rerum discrimine se adiuvent; ut denique inter publicae rei moderatores singulosque cives adiutrix intercedat opera.

Veritati inservire non modo postulat, ut omnes ab errore, a mendacio, a fraude omnino abstineant, sed ut etiam ea omnia devitent, quae vel falsam, vel mancam, vel alicui parti obnoxiam fovere possunt vivendi agendique rationem.

Imprimis autem veritates, Deo revelante traditae, ut res sacrae inviolabilesque habeantur. Quin immo, cur ad hoc potissimum non contendant hae nobiles artes, ut nempe Dei eiusque Filii Iesu Christi doctrinam propagent, « christianamque fidem illam mentibus inculcent, quae una potest hominum multitudinibus supernam praebere vim, qua adiutae sereno animo virtuteque consentanea queant superare discrimina, angores vero tolerare praesentis huius aetatis nostrae? »

Ac praeterea non modo veritati inserviant hae novae artes oportet, sed morali etiam humanae vitae perfectioni. Quod quidem tribus hisce modis, de quibus scripturi sumus, conferre enitantur: hoc est datis nuntiis, impertitis praeceptis, praebitisque spectaculis.

Cuiusvis rei notitia, etiamsi nihil aliud nisi veritatem reapse referat, aliquam tamen rationem in se habet, quae ad hominum pertinet aliquo modo conformandos mores. « Quae ratio, ad humanos mores attinens, numquam est neglegenda; nam quivis nuntius mentis iudicium provocat ac voluntatem movet. Nuntiator, qui suo munere fungatur digne, neminem suis dictis opprimat, sed conetur potius relatas iacturas, vel perpetrata crimina aptiore quo potest modo intellegere et explicare; quod tamen eadem excusare vel probare minime significat, sed innuere remedia ac praestare lenimenta, atque adeo ad animorum restituendam probitatem aliquid conferre. »

II

Cinematographeum, quod sexaginta circiter abhinc annis in usum invectum est, hodie maximis est instrumentis annumerandum, quibus cogitata et inventa nostrorum temporum propagari queunt.

De variis eius processibus deque eius fascinatoria vi, occasione data, iam verba fecimus. Ex hoc eius incremento, ad pellicularum series praesertim quod spectat, quae peculiarem narrationem imaginibus et vocibus expressam vivido quodam modo repraesentant, magna succrevit et negotiosa ars, cui sociam operam praestant non modo artifices, opifices et technici, sed coetus etiam de re oeconomica; quandoquidem singuli cives haud facile possunt tam gravem atque implexam operam exsequi. Quamobrem, ut cinematographeum nobile exsistat instrumentum, quo homines salutariter educentur, ad excelsa erigantur, ac meliores revera fiant, omnino necesse est, ut ii singuli universi, de quibus supra diximus, recta animati conscientia voluntateque adiutricem sibi invicem navitatem praestent, qua probandae taeniolarum cinematographei series effingantur ac propagentur.

Iis omnibus, qui ad cinematographica spectacula vigilem mentem animumque convertunt, iam huius causae gravitatem non semel patefecimus, eos adhortantes ad earum praesertim imaginum series procurandas, quae ad tam nobilem pulchritudinis speciem pertineant, ut quodam modo sanae educationis munus obire queant.

III

Nec minus diligenter exponere volumus Vobis, Venerabiles Fratres, qua urgeamur sollicitudine circa aliud instrumentum ad nuntios dimittendos aptum et eadem, qua cinematographeum, invectum aetate, radiophonium dicimus.

Quamquam tot tantisque subsidiis scaenicis et percommodis locorum rerumque adiunctis, quibus cinematographeum fruitur, non est praeditum, radiophonium tamen alias habet utilitates, quarum non omnes adhuc quaesitae sunt.

« Illius enim — quemadmodum societatis cuiusdam radiophonicae sodalibus et administris diximus — haec est condicio, ut a locorum temporisque adiunctis quasi dissociatum sit et immune, quae cetera omnia praepediunt et retardant instrumenta, quibus homines inter se communicant. Volucri enim quasi cursu multo ociore quam undae sonorae motu, citissimum ut lucis fluxus, fines omnes momento temporis transgrediens, nuntios perfert, qui ei crediti sunt. »

Novis inventis ad perfectionem paene absolutionemque perductum, radiophonium artibus technicis eximias affert utilitates, cum etiam machinae eiusmodi radiante vi ad praestituta loca sine gubernatore dirigantur. Nos autem non immerito arbitramur praeclarissimum munus, quo radiophonium spectare debeat, hoc esse: mentes hominum illuminare et erudire, eorumque ingenia et animos ad superna et incorporalia magis magisque erigere.

Intima autem animi humani studia eo pertinent, ut quis, licet domesticis contineatur parietibus, alios audiat homines, eventus cognoscat, qui procul fiunt, et socialis vitae rationem et ingenii cultum participet.

Nihil mirum igitur, si permultae domus celerrime fuerint undisonis scriniis instructae, quibus efficitur, ut inde quasi quaedam arcana fenestella pateat in orbem terrarum, qua diu noctuque actuosa vita hominum diversi cultus ingenii, diversi sermonis et generis attingatur; hoc fit per innumerabiles radiophonicas transmissiones certa ratione propositas, quibus comprehenduntur novi eventus, colloquia, sermones, res ad cognoscendum utiles et iucundae, artificia, cantus, modi musici.

IV

Reliquum est, Venerabiles Fratres, ut breviter de televisione quoque vobiscum agamus, quae quidem per Pontificatus Nostri decursum in quibusdam Nationibus mira suscepit incrementa, in aliis autem pedetemptim iam in usum inducitur.

Invalescentem huius artis consuetudinem, quae procul dubio in humani generis fastis magni ponderis est eventus, studioso animo, alacri spe gravibusque affecti sollicitudinibus prosecuti sumus, atque dum ex una parte inde ab initio saluberrimam eius vim novasque obortas utilitates extulimus, ex altera vero pericula ac male utentium intemperantiam prospeximus atque indicavimus.

Televisioni plura sunt cum cinematographica arte communia, quandoquidem eius spectationes ipsam vitae actionem agitationemque oculis exhibent; haud raro enim cinematographici ludi eidem materiam praebent. Praeterea ipsam quoque indolem atque vim radiophonicae artis propriam quodammodo participat, quippe quae potius quam in theatris, intra domesticos parietes ad homines convertatur.

Supervacaneum ducimus hoc loco Nostra iterare monita, quae de cinematographicis ludis deque radiophonicis transmissionibus iam habuimus; de officiis scilicet, quibus hac in re spectatores, auditores, auctores necnon publicae rei Moderatores tenentur. Neque est, cur iterum commemoremus curam atque diligentiam necessario adhibendam, ut varia religiosarum spectationum genera rite parentur atque promoveantur. . . .

Televisio autem praeter id, quod cum duobus ad res evulgandas artis inventis, de quibus iam diximus, commune habet, sua quoque pollet vi suaque efficacitate. Televisificae enim artis ope efficitur, ut longinquos eventus auribus oculisque subiectos eodem puncto temporis, quo contingant, spectatores conspiciant, atque ita alliciantur, ut quasi praesentes eosdem participent; ipsa autem intima domesticae vitae consuetudine eiusmodi propinquitas valde adaugetur.

Peculiaris haec oblectandi vis, qua inter sacra familiae penetralia televisio pollet, permagni quidem facienda est, quippe quae plurimum conferat ad religiosam vitam, ad humanitatem atque ad mores eorum, ex quibus familia constat, filiorum praesertim, quos recentioris huiusce inventi fascinatio procul dubio afficiet ac tenebit. Quodsi illud: « Modicum fermentum totam massam corrumpit » veritati omnino respondet, atque in adulescentibus vita corporis, quodam contagionis germine infecta, impediri potest, quominus ad plenam virium maturitatem perveniat, multo magis pravum aliquod educationis elementum religiosae vitae nervos valet elidere, ac debitam morum conformationem remorari. Ceterum quis ignorat saepissime pueros extra domum morbi vim repentem vitare posse, latentem intra domum effugere non posse?

Domestici convictus sanctitatem quoquo modo in discrimen adducere nefas est; Ecclesia igitur, prout eius ius et officium postulant, omnibus viribus semper contendit, ne pravis televisificis spectationibus sacra eiusmodi limina ullo pacto violentur.

Cum televisio inter cetera hoc quoque salutiferum sane commodum pariat, ut minores ac maiores natu domi facilius remaneant, ea profecto plurimum valet ad amoris fideique vinculum intra saepta domestica roborandum, dummodo nihil proferat, quod iisdem fidei et casti amoris virtutibus minus consentiat....

Quandoquidem autem hanc Dei causam triumphaturam firmiter confidimus, minime dubitamus quin Nostra haec praescripta ac mandata — quae quidem ad rem diligenter deducenda Pontificio Consilio de re cinematographica, radiophonica et televisifica committimus — nova apostolatus studia excitare valeant in hoc campo, qui tam laetam tamque uberem segetem pollicetur.

Hac spe suffulti, quam vestra pastoralis alacritas Nobis sane exploratissima valde confirmat, Apostolicam Benedictionem, caelestium gratiarum conciliatricem, vobis, Venerabiles Fratres, itemque clero populoque unicuique vestrum concreditis, iis nominatim, qui ad vota ac mandata Nostra adimplenda actuosam conferent operam, effusa caritate impertimus.

Datum Romae, apud Sanctum Petrum, die VIII mensis Septembris, in Festo Nativitatis Beatae Mariae Virginis, anno MDCCCCLVII, Pontificatus Nostri undevicesimo.

APPENDICES

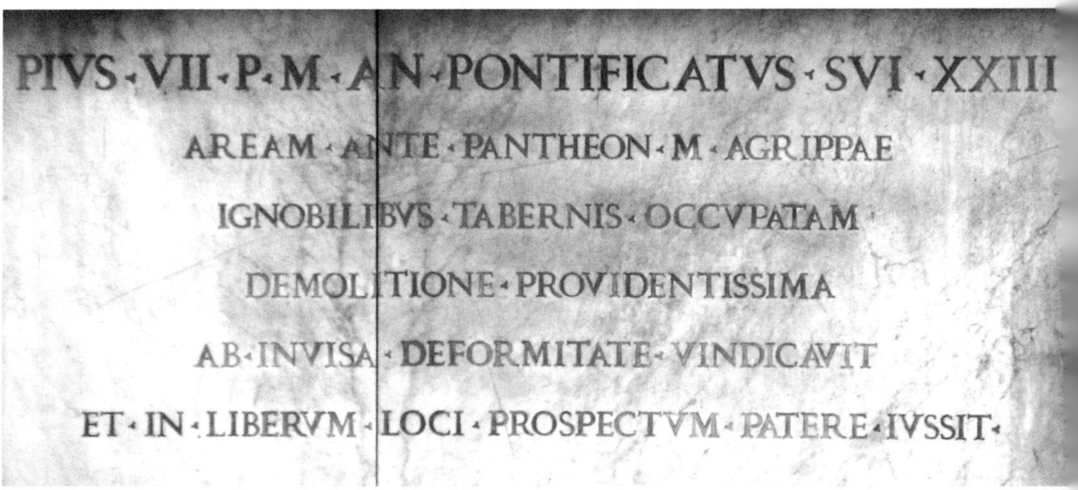

PIVS · VII · P · M · AN · PONTIFICATVS · SVI · XXIII

AREAM · ANTE · PANTHEON · M · AGRIPPAE

IGNOBILIBVS · TABERNIS · OCCVPATAM

DEMOLITIONE · PROVIDENTISSIMA

AB · INVISA · DEFORMITATE · VINDICAVIT

ET · IN · LIBERVM · LOCI · PROSPECTVM · PATERE · IVSSIT ·

ADNOTATIO DE TITULIS

a note on the inscriptions

It is clear from the contents and development of our book that our objective is educational in teaching and learning the Latin language thoroughly and at the same time making that experience enjoyable, entertaining, accessible.

The examples to illustrate the various elements of the Latin language were composed partially by the authors of this book and to a greater extent found in the reading sheets supplied for the teachers so that they have somewhere from which to begin drawing their own material.

These examples provided within the body of each experience are preceded on introductory pages by numerous images of Living Latin from various ages in Rome and elsewhere in order to spice up the text and learning experience. The images presented in this book provide real Latin texts, some lesser-known, that exist inscribed in stone, woven into a tapestry, handwritten on the page, which people do see and appreciate in this world. This book also includes three original, monumental compositions: its dedication, the expression of gratitude at the beginning of the acknowledgments, the draft dedication of a new Vatican fountain. Each text provides an opportunity to understand the expression of the author preserved and available for us.

Far separated from the images and texts themselves, a little commentary on each text is given so that these may also become learning experiences and personal encounters. The APPENDIX CUM TITULORUM EXPLICATIONIBUS "appendix with explanations of the inscriptions" begins with a list of these images and texts. Next, for each image we transcribe the Latin text followed by our own rendering of it in English. A commentary follows in which the Latin expressions are explained patiently. Each line in the commentary begins with a direct reproduction of specific Latin words of the inscription given in italics, followed by their English rendering given in quotation marks. Next a colon separates the text itself and its rendering from the commentary explaining the Latin expression.

For the convenience of the reader, we have included a VOCABULORUM COMPENDIA, "abbreviations of words," beginning on p. XLV, which includes the technical abbreviations we use in our text and in the commentary on these inscriptions.

The commentaries are presented in the hope that these Latin texts may provide a personal encounter with the expression of the authors and an opportunity for students and teachers today to appreciate even more the Latin language.

And so, the images scattered throughout the book are accompanied by a commentary in this appendix as another tool for teaching and learning so that these also may become learning experiences and personal encounters and another source of the conviction that Latin is living and attractive and teachable and learnable.

APPENDIX CUM TITULORUM EXPLICATIONIBUS

appendix with explanations of the inscriptions

LIST OF INSCRIPTIONS AND ILLUSTRATIONS

FLAGRANTI PAVLATIM EXORTA PRIVS
EX AVDIENTIVM PARTICIPVM STVDENTIVM LATINE
CONSORTIO ET AVXILIO IPSA HAEC
"LATINITATIS CORPORIS" VOLVMINA
FERVENTEM DEHINC ALIORVM SIMILIVM
AD SODALIVM AFFINIVM SECTANTIVM LATINE
ERVDITIONEM ATQVE CONFORMATIONEM
OPTATO SANE AVSPICATO
PROFICIVNTO VALENTOQVE
XVIII KAL. DEC. MMXIV

these very books "of the body of latinity"
having gradually arisen previously
from the fervent association and help
of classroom-listeners, participants
and people zealous about latin,
as is wished of course under a good omen
must profit and be effective in the future
for the ardent education and preparation
of other similar associates, companions
and ones pursuing latin
14 november 2014

This is the text of the dedication of our book on page VII.

This dedication was composed in Latin by Reginald Foster for this book series. The date corresponds to his 75th anniversary of birth. Through the coordination of Daniel Gallagher, the Latin text was written out in calligraphy by Roberto Bravi, a Vatican calligrapher, and a photograph was sent to the publisher for use in this book.

COMMENTARY

volumina . . . dehinc . . . proficiunto valentoque,
"books . . . must profit and be effective in the future": both verbs are the second, sometimes called future command forms. They mean variously, "they must profit!" or also "they shall profit!"—which is the command form in standard English in contrast to the simple future, "they will profit." The adverb *dehinc*, "in the future" is well separated geographically in the sentence from the verbs it describes. The verbs' subject is sixteen words previous in the sentence, the plural *volumina*, "books." A sentence in Latin can end with *–que*, "and."

paulatim exorta prius,
"having gradually arisen previously": all alone the natural meaning of *exorta* is "[books] having . . . arisen," "[books] having been born." It is from the deponent verb *orior*, "I arise," and thus its antecedent participle has active meaning. The adverb *paulatim* means "little by little" or "by degrees." Here *prius*, "previously," functions as a comparative adverb.

flagranti . . . ex . . . consortio et auxilio,
"from the fervent association and help": note the word order. The participle *ex*, "from," has two objects *consortio et auxilio*, "association and help," which are described by the first word in the sentence as *flagranti*, "fervent."

audientium participum studentium latine,
"of classroom-listeners, participants and people zealous about Latin": note the word order. These three genitives come between the preposition and its objects, and these genitives are in front of the nouns they depend on. All alone the contemporaneous participle *audientium* means "of ones listening in the classroom" and refers here to students. Likewise, the contemporaneous participle *studentium* means "of people being zealous," and refers also to students. The Romans used the adverb *latine*, meaning "latinly," with verbs, for example, *disco latine*, "I teach in a Latin way," to mean "I teach Latin," or *loquimur latine*, "we are speaking by the Latin tongue," to mean "we are speaking Latin." Between the two participles is the adjective used as a noun here, *participum*, "of participants."

optato sane auspicato,
"as is wished of course under a good omen": the three adverbs describing the action of both verbs are: *optato*, "according to one's wish"; *sane*, "certainly"; *auspicato*, "under a good omen." Note how similar the endings of *optato* and *auspicato* are to the two command forms *proficiunto* and *valento*; only your dictionary vocabulary can help you.

ferventem . . . ad . . . eruditionem atque conformationem,
"for the ardent education and preparation": note the word order. The preposition *ad*, "for," and its two objects, *eruditonem*, "education," and *conformationem*, "preparation," which are described by *ferventem*, "ardent," are placed way out in front.

sodalium affinium sectantium latine,
"of other similar associates, companions, and ones pursuing Latin": note the word order. These three genitives come between the preposition and its objects, and these genitives are in front of the nouns they depend on. The first two words are adjectives used as nouns, and the third, *sectantium*, "of ones pursuing," is a contemporaneous participle used as a noun.

ET · HIC · EPISCOPVS CIB$\overline{\text{V}}$: ET POT$\overline{\text{V}}$: BENEDICIT ·

and here the bishop is blessing food and drink

This is the caption woven into the frame of the Bayeux Tapestry pictured on page 2.

This scene is one of many in the tapestry created c. 1077 to narrate an account of and so to commemorate the Norman invasion of England.

COMMENTARY

et hic,
"and here": this image is part of a longer narration where one scene with its text follows from another. Thus, the connecting word "and" connects this text to the flow of the rest of the narration. The form *hic* can possibly go with the subject *episcopus* to mean "the bishop" or "this bishop." Here, rather, the text comprises a caption for the woven image, and the word *hic* refers to the picture and means, "here" or "in this place" or in the case of the tapestry, "in this image." This occurs for numerous other captions and images in the narration.

episcopus . . . benedicit,
"the bishop is blessing": the verb in the singular has a subject, *episcopus*, "the bishop." The verb *benedicit*, "[the bishop] is blessing," is in T.1i, with two other possible meanings: "[the bishop] blesses," "[the bishop] does bless."

cibū et potū,
"food and drink": the form *potu* does exist in the function by-with-from-in, but that does not make sense here. The form *cibu* as such does not exist in Latin. The two words are only partially spelled out. A horizontal line visible over the final letter of the word *potū*, as in very many instances, indicates the final letter "m" to form here the word *potum*. Presumably there is a similar line over the final letter of *cibū* to indicate the word *cibum*. This second occurrence of *et*, "and," in these seven words joins two equal elements, *cibū* and *potū*.

cibū . . . benedicit,
"[the bishop] is blessing food": the later Latin of this era prefers the object forms *cibum* and *potum* with the verb *benedixit*, whereas classical Latin authors write *benedicit* as two words, *bene* and *dicit*, and then give the person or thing addressed in the form to-for-from, as the dictionary says, because they took it to mean "to speak well to someone, or something." That would produce here the forms *bene dico cibo*, "I speak well to food." In later Latin they lost the idea of "speaking well to-for-from" and took *benedicit* as a single transitive verb with the object form, as here.

potū benedicit,
"[the bishop] is blessing . . . drink": in encounter 35 of the First Experience we present the 20% of nouns like *potus, us, m,* "a drink," which produces the form to-for-from, *potui*, which the Romans would have preferred here than the form *potum*.

QVID MIRARIS APEM QVAE MEL DE FLORIBVS HAVRIT
SI TIBI MELLITAM GVTTVRE FVNDIT AQVAM

Why are you surprised at a bee who is drawing honey from flowers
if it pours out for you honey-sweet water from the throat.

This is the inscription on the Vatican bee fountain shown in the image on page 154.

If a person stands at the St. Ann's Gate and looks along the right hand side of this main road into Vatican City, past the church of St. Ann, this fountain is visible, built into the back wall of the Vatican printing shop. Like the inscription over Raphael's tomb, this two-line poem is an elogiac couplet or dystic, double verse. The inscription refers to the fountain below where sculpted bees surround the water tap, as if they were producing from their own mouths the honey-sweet water.

COMMENTARY

Quid miraris apem,
"Why are you surprised": the main verb of the couplet is the deponent verb *miraris*, which also means "[why] do you marvel at" or "[why] do you admire."

quae mel . . . haurit,
"who is drawing honey": the noun *mel*, "honey," is neuter and so can possibly function as subject or object. The antecedent of the relative *quae* is *apem*, "a bee," but the *quae* may possibly function as the singular or plural subject. The only one that makes sense is to take the bee, *quae*, "which" or "who" as the subject of *haurit*, "is drawing" and *mel*, "honey," as the object.

Si tibi . . . fundit aquam,
"if it pours out for you . . . water": a factual or logical conditional expressed with the verb *fundit*, "it pours out," in T.1i. Many people impressed by modern languages, such as Italian, French, Spanish, are falsely convinced that all conditionals are automatically put in the subjunctive because of their inherent "if . . ." uncertainty. Rather, the majority of conditions in Latin are expressed by the indicative, relying on the author's idea. The dative of interest, *tibi*, means "for you."

mel . . . Mellitam . . . aquam,
"honey . . . honey-sweet water": the Latin text plays on the words *mel*, "honey" or "sweetness," and *mellitam aquam*, "sweet-water." The antecedent passive participle *mellitam* can be heard in English if we say, "honied-water" or more simply, "water sweetened with honey," just as we say "iced tea." Thus, the rendering "honey-sweet water."

gutture,
"from the throat": the natural meaning of the ablative includes "from."

CATHEDRALEM HANC AEDEM
LITVRGICAS OMNINO AD NORMAS
VATICANO II VENIENTES EX CONCILIO
MAGNA NON SINE DIFFICVLTATE
RENOVATAM
SOLLEMNITER ATQVE FELICITER
IX DIE MENSIS FEBRVARII ANNO MMII
ARCHIEPISCOPVS IPSE ORDINARIVS
INAVGVRAVIT ITERVM DEDICAVIT
REMBERTVS GEORGIVS WEAKLAND O.S.B.

on the ninth day of the month of February
in the year 2002
the ordinary, the Archbishop himself
Rembert George Weakland O.S.B.
solemnly and happily
consecrated, dedicated for a second time
this cathedral church
having been renovated
not without great difficulty
absolutely according to the liturgical norms
coming out of the second vatican council

This is the dedication of the Milwaukee cathedral of St. John the Evangelist shown in the image on page 202.

The text was composed by Reginald Foster while working in the Vatican Secretariat of State for the dedication of the renovated cathedral of his home town, Milwaukee, Wisconsin. The plan to renovate the cathedral was developed with consultation and approved by Archbishop Rembert Weakland, former Abbot Primate, then Archbishop of Milwaukee. His plan met substantial opposition to which the dedication refers. Because a new cathedra for the bishop was constructed, the marble back of the former cathedra was inscribed with this dedication and was mounted on the wall of the vestibule of the Cathedral.

COMMENTARY

cathedralem hanc aedem . . . inauguravit . . . dedicavit . . . Rembertus,
"Rembert . . . consecrated, dedicated . . . this cathedral church": note the word order where the first line is the object of the verbs given seven lines below, and the subject is given in the last line. The verbs are given without an expressed connective, which rhetorical phenomenon is technically called asyndeton. The church is called a cathedral after the name of the chair of the bishop, a cathedra. It is fitting that *cathedralem* is the first word inscribed onto the marble back of the previous cathedra.

cathedralem . . . renovatam,
"cathedral . . . having been renovated": the first several lines are framed by this object *cathedralem*, "cathedral," and its participle *renovatam*, "having been renovated." This connection is obvious, clear and requires reading the whole text to see and appreciate.

liturgicas omnino ad normas,
"absolutely according to liturgical norms": renovation of the church is described by this phrase where the preposition *ad*, "according to," is toward the end of the line, and its object with its own adjective frame the line *liturgicas . . . normas*, "liturgical . . . norms." The adverb *omnino* is a favorite also meaning "wholly," "entirely." As an adverb, *omnino* describes the participle in the next line, *renovatam*, "having been renovated explicitly."

Vaticano II venientes ex Concilio,
"coming out of the Second Vatican Council": note the word order where the participle *venientes*, "coming," is in the middle followed by the participle *ex*, "out of," whose object with its own adjective frame the line *Vaticano II . . . Concilio*, "the Second Vatican Council."

magna non sine difficultate,
"not without great difficulty": note the word order. The preposition *sine*, "without," is in the middle and its object with its own adjective frame the line *magna difficultate*, "great difficulty."

sollemniter atque feliciter,
"solemnly and happily": these two adverbs describe the two verbs given three lines below.

IX die mensis februarii anno MMII,
"on the ninth day of the February month in the year 2002": the abbreviation *IX* stands for *nono* to agree with *die*, "on the ninth day," and *MMII*, stands for *bismillesimo altero*, "2002." The formula follows the later church pattern where the ablative of time is used for the number, and the name of the month is given as an adjective describing the word *mensis*, "of the February month."

Inauguravit . . . dedicavit,
"[Rembert] consecrated, dedicated": the two verbs stand in tandem to one another, with no conjunction, which is called asyndeton.

Archiepiscopus ipse ordinarius,
"the ordinary, the archbishop himself": this line stands in apposition to his name given in the last line.

O.S.B.
"O.S.B.": the abbreviation stands for *Ordinis Sancti Benedicti*, "of the Order of Saint Benedict," indicating that Rembert professed vows as a Benedictine monk, of St. Vincent Archabbey, Latrobe, Pennsylvania.

PSALMI FESTIVI

PSALMI AD LAUDES

psalmus 66
DEUS misereatur nostri
et benedicat nobis:
illuminet vultum suum
super nos et misereatur nostri.
Ut cognoscamus in terra viam tuam:
in omnibus gentibus salutare tuum.
Confiteantur tibi populi deus:
confiteantur tibi populi omnes.
Laetentur et exsultent gentes:
quoniam iudicas populos in aequitate,
et gentes in terra dirigis.
Confiteantur tibi populi deus:
confiteantur tibi populi omnes:
terra dedit fructum suum.

FEAST-DAY PSALMS

PSALMS AT MORNING PRAISE

psalm 66
MAY GOD have compassion on us
and bless us:
may he illuminate his face over us and be merciful to us.
So that we may come to know your way on earth:
your salvation among all the peoples.
Let the peoples, O God, confess to you:
let all the peoples confess to you.
Let the families rejoice and exsult:
because you judge the peoples in fairness,
and you direct the nations on earth.
Let the people, O God, confess to you:
let all the peoples confess to you:
the earth has given its fruit.

This is the inscription of the manuscript of Psalm 66 shown in the image on page 252.

This folio is part of the manuscript *Antiphonale Monasticum ad usum Abbatiae S. Michaelis Farnburgensis*, "Monastic Antiphonal for the use of the Farnborough Abbey of St Michael." The manuscript was written by a monk of the Abbey. The image is used here with kind acknowledgment of Abbot Cuthbert Brogan, OSB. The image is of King David playing on the harp to accompany the choir singing the psalm. This psalm is intended for use *ad laudes*, that is, for singing God's "praises" in the morning.

Of stylistic interest is the geographical arrangement of the letters on the page. In the heading, the small letter "L" in "PSALMI," the letter "I" placed inside the subsequent letter "V," in the word "FESTIVI," and the "ES" written to save space at the end of "LAUDES." Latin words are abbreviated in several ways. The word *et*, "and," is written by an ampersand in the first line. The horizontal line over the "ā" in *tuā* indicates that the word is contracted. Often the letter "n" or "m" is omitted, as here where adding the letter "m" produces *tuam* to agree with *viam*, "your way." Another common contraction is *Dns* for *Dominus*, "Lord." The two hashes above the word "t̋bi" indicates the word *tibi*, and again "p̋puli" indicates the word *populi*.

Abbot Cuthbert explains that the musical notation is simplified for plainsong. The letter "x" above the line is a stylized *asteriscus* or asterisk, meaning "little star." The *asteriscus* enables the singer to locate the point in the text at which the first half of the psalm verse ends and so adjust the musical phrasing accordingly. The cross shaped figure "†" above the text is called a *flexus*, "a bend" or "a dip," and indicates where the reciting note dips momentarily to give musical shape and proper phrasing to a psalm verse which is unusually long. A monastic familiar with the daily singing of these texts would have no problem in singing from this psalter, which is more of an aid to memory than a full text.

COMMENTARY

misereatur nostri,
"May God have compassion on us": the form *misereatur* may be the passive form of the active verb *misero*, but here it is from the deponent verb *misereor* with active meaning, "May [God] have compassion." It is used here as an independent subjunctive. This is one of the verbs of emotion which take the genitive, here *nostri*, "of us," thus, an objective genitive (see Gildersleeve and Lodge nº 377). The English expression is "on us" or "for us" or "may God pity us."

benedicat nobis,
"[May God] bless us": by imitation of the 65 words that have their complement in the dative, the independent subjunctive *benedicat*, "may [God] bless," in T.1s, is used here with the dative complement, *nobis*. The difficulty is that the dative complement cannot be heard in the English rendering, "May God bless us." In later Latin the expression *benedicat nos*, "may [God] bless us," came to predominate.

illuminet,
"may he illuminate": a third independent subjunctive in T.1s, all of which sound subjunctive in English.

Ut cognoscamus,
"So that we may come to know": these lines are arranged in couplets for singing by alternating sides of a choir, and the punctuation reflects this. Disregarding the punctuation, then, this purpose continues the thought of the previous two lines. As a purpose clause it sounds subjunctive in English.

in omnibus gentibus,
"among all the peoples": the preposition *in* can mean "in" as well as "among," as here. There is no conjunction joining this and the next line; they are simply put next to one another by asyndeton.

Confiteantur tibi populi deus,
"Let the peoples, O God, confess to you": the deponent verb *confiteor* functions here as another independent subjunctive *confiteantur*, "Let [the peoples] confess," in T.1s, is used with the natural meaning of the dative *tibi*, "to you." In Ecclesiastical writing the verb *confiteor* is often used with the object understood, such as "praise" or "glory" or "majesty." The expression is often translated in a way that supplies one of these implied objects, such as "let the peoples, O God, confess praise to you," or more simply, "Let the peoples, O God, praise you," where the implied object is assumed into the verb.

The form *Deus* looks like the subject, but it does not have a verb. Here *Deus* is direct address, "O God" or simply "God," as even in standard classical Latin. This form of direct address is called technically the vocative.

Laetentur et exsultent gentes,
"Let the families rejoice and exult": again two independent subjunctives in T.1s. The deponent verb *Laetentur* is passive in form with active meaning, "Let [the families] rejoice."

quoniam iudicas,
"because you judge": one of the three words that mean "because": *quod, quia, quoniam*, and then three more, *siquidem, quando, quandoquidem*. The verb, *iudicas*, "you judge" in T.1i, is the first indicative verb in the psalm.

gentes . . . gentes,
"families . . . nations": the same form is used first as the subject of *Laetentur et exsultent*, "Let the families rejoice and exult," and as the object of *dirigis*, "you direct the nations." Two related meanings for *gentes* are given in the English rendering.

terra dedit fructum suum,
"the earth has given its fruit": the verbal form *dedit* can be either T.4a meaning, "[the earth] has given," or T.4b, "[the earth] gave." The English rendering above uses T.4a as touching on the present expression of harvested fruit and consequently of praise and acknowledgment.

QVANDOQVIDEM IN THEATRO VATICANO
PRAESTITE MARIA MATRE SAPIENTIAE
PIVS XI PONT MAX
DIGNAM STVDIORVM SEDEM CONSTITVIT
AD BIBLIOTHECAM AD TABVLARIVM
AD PONTIFICIVM SOPHORVM COLLEGIVM
HAC PATET ADITVS

Because the Supreme Pontiff Pius XI
established a worthy seat of studies
in the Vatican theater
—Mary the Mother of Wisdom being the protectoress—
by this road the approach lies open
to the library, to the archive,
to the pontifical college of the wise.

This is the Vatican library access inscription shown in the image on page 411.

This inscription stretches across the passageway into the inner Belvedere Courtyard, which now serves as a parking lot, with access to the Vatican Library. The inscription and passageway is visible at quite a distance when a person stands at St. Ann's Gate to Vatican City. This passageway is also seen in another image that includes more of the building, found on page 654. In that photo, the open window on the uppermost story of the building and furthest to the right was Reginald's office in the Vatican Secretariat of State. His successor, Msgr. Daniel Gallagher, now enjoys this view.

The inscription explains that Pope Pius XI wanted the Vatican Library to be open for scholars. This is the giant inscription *QUANDOQUIDEM* mentioned in the Third Experience, Encounter 24 (59).

COMMENTARY

Quandoquidem,

"Because": Many people will take *Quandoquidem* here to mean, "when indeed," but it means, "because." The students tend to believe this only when they see it in the dictionary. It is on the rare side in Latin literature, but it is there.

praestite Maria matre sapientiae,

"Mary the Mother of Wisdom being the protectoress": an ablative absolute whose verb is the implied verb of being, which was not expressed by the Romans, but felt and understood. The noun *praestite*, "protector" or in this case "protectoress" is in the ablative along with *Maria*, "Mary," serving as the subject and predicate of the implied verb of being.

Pius XI . . . constituit,
"Pius XI established": the subject and verb in T.4b of this causal clause.

hac patet aditus,
"by this road the approach lies open": the subject of the sentence is *aditus*, "the approach," one of the *–us, us* nouns. The main verb controlling the expression is *patet*, "[the approach] lies open," in T.1i. Its form in T.3i is *patebit* and in T.1s *pateat*.

The adjective *hac* generally means "here." More specifically this is the feminine ablative and agrees with an implied noun, as in either *hac via*, "by this road," or *hac parte*, "by this side." The expression of course refers to the passageway directly below the inscription.

ILLE HIC EST RAPHAEL TIMVIT QVO SOSPITE VINCI
RERVM MAGNA PARENS ET MORIENTE MORI

here is that famous Raphael,
who living
the great mother of things feared to be conquered,
and [who] dying, to die.

This is the inscription shown in the image on page 456.

This inscription stretches across the top of the tomb of Raphael Sanzio da Urbino, (1483-1520), the Italian painter and architect, whose tomb is in the Pantheon, Rome. The two line stanza is in fact an elogiac couplet or dystic double verse.

COMMENTARY

Ille hic est Raphael,
"Here is that famous Raphael": the main sentence. The verb *est* can mean "to be present in a place." The form *hic* is an adverb of place meaning "in this place" or simply "here"; its old form is *heic*. This is a classic example of *Ille* meaning "that well-known one" "that famous one," in contrast to *iste* which refers to "that lousy one."

timuit . . . rerum magna parens,
"the great mother of things feared": a second finite verb is part of a clause subordinated to the first as we shall see. The image is of "Mother Nature."

timuit . . . vinci . . . et . . . mori,
"[mother . . .] feared to be conquered . . . to die": the verb *timuit*, "[mother] feared" has two complements. The first, *vinci*, "to be conquered," is a passive infinitive. The second, *mori*, "to die," is a deponent infinitive and so has active meaning.

quo sospite . . . et moriente,
"who living . . . and [who] dying": the relative *quo* begins an ablative absolute whose verb is "to be," and so not expressed. Thus *quo sospite* means "who being safe and sound" or "who living," and does not mean "by whom," which would demand the Latin expression *a quo sospite . . . a quo moriente*, "by whom living . . . by whom dying."

The *quo* is also the subject of a second ablative absolute whose participle is *moriente*, "[who] dying." The *et* joins both ablatives absolute.

The formation of both ablatives absolute is further explained in the Second Experience, Encounter 20 (55).

In this case both ablatives absolute give the temporal circumstance for the sentences on which they depend, as in the following rendering:

Here is that famous Raphael,
who while he was living,
the great mother of things feared to be conquered,
and while he was dying, [she feared] to die.

If we express the ablative absolute as a temporal clause, it would sound like this:

> Here is that famous Raphael;
> while he was living,
> the great mother of things feared to be conquered,
> and while he was dying, [she feared] to die.

Tyler Lansford treats this inscription in his book *The Latin Inscriptions of Rome* (11.3F, 384–85). He says that the couplet was composed by Pietro Cardinal Bembo (1470–1547) for this tomb. He also provides the following translation by Alexander Pope:

> "Living, great nature feared he might out vie
> Her works and, dying, fears herself may die" (385).

SAPIENTIS AEGYPTI
INSCVLPTAS OBELISCO FIGVRAS
AB ELEPHANTO
BELLVARVM FORTISSIMA
GESTARI QVISQVIS HIC VIDES
DOCVMENTVM INTELLIGE
ROBVSTAE MENTIS ESSE
SOLIDAM SAPIENTIAM SVSTINERE

you whosoever see here
the figuras of wise egypt
having been cut into the obelisk
are being carried by an elephant
the strongest animal of animals
understand that a proof
of a robust mind is
sustaining solid wisdom

This is the inscription on the Roman elephant obelisk shown in the image on page 595.

It stands in the middle of the square in front of the basilica of Santa Maria sopra Minerva and is pictured with the Pantheon in the background.

COMMENTARY

quisquis hic vides,
"you whosoever see here": the main verb is *vides*, "you see," addressed to the reader. The subject is the implied *tu*, "you," which is described as *quisquis*, "whoever." The form *hic* is an adverb of place meaning "in this place," "here."

figuras . . . gestari . . . vides,
"you . . . see . . . the figures . . . are being carried": the main verb *vides*, "you see," is a verb of M&M producing an entire sentence in OO where *figuras* is the subject in object form and *gestari* is its contemporaneous infinitive. We render such a sentence in one of three ways. We can preserve the accusative with the infinitive in a possible English expression:

You see the figures to be carried.

We can make the indirect statement into a finite sentence with a subject and finite verb with the addition of the connecting particle "that," as in:

You see that the figures are being carried.

We can replicate the above finite sentence, but without the addition of the connecting particle "that," as in:

You see the figures are being carried.

sapientis aegypti,
"of wise Egypt": the *figuras*, "figures," are described by these genitives of possession.

insculptas obelisco figuras,
"the figures ... having been cut into the obelisk": the *figuras*, "the figures," are also described by the participle *insculptas*, "having been cut into," which is both antecedent and passive. The verb *insculpo, insculpere* 3, is one of the 65 verbs that can take its complement in the dative, here *obelisco*, "the obelisk." We can remove the prefix *in—* from the verb and restore the preposition, as in, *sculptas in obelisco*, "[figures] having been cut on the obelisk."

ab elephant ... gestari,
"are being carried by an elephant": the infinitive *gestari*, "to be carried," is passive, and the elephant is the one bearing the obelisk. The elephant is considered as a personal agent because of the preposition *ab* with *elephanto*, "by an elephant." Had the author said *elephanto* alone, without the preposition *ab*, it would have conveyed the idea of impersonal agent or instrument.

ab elephanto belluarum fortissima,
"by an elephant the strongest animal of animals": the noun *elephanto*, "an elephant," is masculine. It is modified by the superlative *fortissima*, "most strong," "strongest," which is feminine to agree with the word it describes, the implied feminine word *belua*, "a beast," which, if it were expressed, would be in apposition to *elephanto*. The form *belluarum* is a variant of *beluarum* from *belua, beluae*, f., "a beast," "an animal."

documentum intellige robustae mentis esse,
"understand that a proof of a robust mind is": the second half of the sentence centers on the command form, *intellige*, "you must understand!" As a verb of M&M, *intellige* (*sic* more correctly spelled *intellege*), gives rise to an entire sentence in OO whose subject is *documentum* in the object form and whose verb is *esse*, a contemporaneous infinitive. Again, we can render this in three ways. We can keep the accusative with the infinitive construction in English expression by saying:

understand a proof ... to be.

We can make the indirect statement into a finite sentence with an accusative and finite verb with the addition of the connecting particle "that," as in the English rendering above:

understand that a proof ... is.

We can replicate the above finite sentence, but without the addition of the connecting particle "that," as in:

understand a proof ... is.

The *documentum*, "proof," is described as *robustae mentis*, "of a strong mind," in the genitive.

documentum intellige . . . esse solidam saptientiam sustinere,
"understand that a proof . . . is sustaining solid wisdom": the predicate of the verb *esse*, "is" or "to be" is the gerund *sustinere*, "sustaining," here the object form to agree with the object form *documentum* functioning as the subject of *esse*, "a proof . . . is sustaining" or "a proof . . . is to sustain." As a gerund, *sustinere*, has its own object, *solidam sapientiam*, "to sustain solid wisdom" or "sustaining solid wisdom."

The reader is left to figure out how the three objects are functioning here where *documentum* functions as the subject of *esse*, and *solidam sapientiam* as the object of the predicate *sustinere*.

VERBVM DEI ET ECCLESIAE MAGISTERIVM
QVO
CELERIVS PROFERRENTVR EFFICACIVS
LIBRARIAE OPIFICINAE VATICANAE
RATIONIBVS APTANDAE RECENTIBVS
NOVIS ROBORANDAE MACHINIS
IOANNES PAVLVS II PONTIFEX MAXIMVS
ALTERAS EX SOLO AEDES STRVI INTEGRAS
VETERES IIS INSTAVRATAS IVNGI ALTERAS
VOLVIT IPSE CENSVIT
MCMXCI ANNO PONTIFICATVS XIII

In the year 1991, the 13th of the pontificate,
Pope John Paul II
himself resolved, decreed that,
for adapting the Vatican printing shop with recent systems
strengthening it with new machines,
the one building be constructed new from the ground
the other old one having been restored be joined to it
so that
the word of God and the teaching of the Church
might be made known so much more quickly, effectively.

This is the inscription shown in the image on page 652.

The expression was composed by Reginald for the renovated building of the printing shop in Vatican City.

COMMENTARY

Ioannes Paulus II Pontifex Maximus . . . volvit . . . censuit,
"Pope John Paul II . . . resolved, decreed": beginning our analysis with the two verbs, *volvit*, "[John Paul] resolved," *censuit*, "[John Paul] decreed," coming one upon the other by asyndeton, without a connecting word. The old Latin title *Pontifex Maximus* is still used, whereas the English has the title "Pope," which may be of Alexandrian origin, where Coptic Christians still call the head of their church by this title.

opificinae . . . aptandae . . . roborandae,
"for adapting the . . . shop . . . strengthening it": two gerundives next to one another by asyndeton without a connecting word. These dative gerundives are one way of expressing purpose. Both have the same object, *opificinae*, "shop." The first gerundive is *opificinae . . . aptandae*, "for adapting the . . . shop," and the second is *opificinae . . . roborandae*, "for strengthening it [the shop]." These can be expressed as gerunds so that their object can be more clearly seen, and the whole would be: *librariam opifi-*

cinam vaticanam rationibus aptando recentibus novis roborando machinis, with no difference in meaning, but one of style.

These gerundives would have the same spelling if they were in the feminine genitive, meaning "of adapting the ... shop ... of strengthening it," but that option does not make sense here, nor does the subject plural.

The two participles *aptandae* and *roborandae* have the same form as an expression of passive necessity, but they do not function that way here. If they did, then the whole expression would mean, "the Vatican printing shop needing to be adapted with recent systems, having to be strengthened with new machines," but this possibility does not fully fit here.

None of these theoretical possibilitas are among the possible expressions of purpose which occurs in the dative gerundive or gerund, which is the only possibility that fully explains this expression here.

Note the balance of two adjectives, *librariae ... vaticanae*, "the Vatican printing [shop]," and the four ablatives framing their two gerundives, *rationibus ... recentibus novis ... machinis*, "with recent systems ... with new machines." These adjectives also form a chiasm or X pattern of words in that the first and last correspond as nouns, *rationibus ... machinis*, "systems ... machines," and the middle two correspond as adjectives, *recentibus novis*, "with recent ... with new."

alteras ... aedes ... strui ... iungi ... alteras volvit ... censuit,
"resolved, decreed the one building to be constructed ... the other ... one ... to be joined": the two verbs *volvit*, "[John Paul] resolved," *censuit*, "[John Paul] decreed," both in T.4b, are verbs of M&M and produce two sentences in OO. The first of these has *alteras ... aedes*, "the one building," in the object form functioning as the subject of the passive infinitive *strui*, "the one building to be constructed." The second begins with the same word *aedes* and adds *alteras*, "the other ... one [building]," again in the object form functioning as the subject of the passive infinitive *iungi*, "the other ... one ... to be joined." The noun *aedes* in the plural refers to a building, while *aedes* in the singular means "a church," "a temple," "a chapel." For this reason papal documents are fixed geographically by saying at the end *ex aedibus Vaticanis*, in the plural, meaning in the singular, "from the Vatican building, home, residence."

There is a chiasm or X arrangement to the words on the stone. These two lines begin and end with the word *alteras*, "the one ... the other." In the middle of the two line couplet are the antonyms *integras ... veteres*, "new ... old."

verbum Dei et ecclesiae magisterium,
"the word of God and the teaching of the church": note the word order with the nouns at the ends and the genitives in the middle. Both *verbum*, "the word," and *magisterium*, "teaching," are subjects of the verb *proferrentur*, "[the word and teaching] might be made known." Church scholars may note that the plural verb indicates two subjects considered as distinct from one another: "the word of God" is intentionally distinct from "the teaching of the church."

quo ... celerius proferrentur efficacius,
"so that [the word and teaching] might be made known so much more quickly effectively": the two main verbs *volvit* and *censuit* in T.4b set the sentence on Track II. The relative *quo* here stands for *ut eo*, "so that ... so much." The *ut* indicates a purpose clause whose verb is *proferrentur*, "[so that the word and teaching] might

made known," a passive form in T.2s on Track II, whose subjects are both *verbum*, "the word," and *magisterium*, "the teaching," placed first in the sentence, before the *quo*.

The *eo* implied in the *quo* goes with the two comparative adverbs *celerius*, meaning, "[so that] by so much more quickly" and *efficacius*, also meaning "[so that] by so much more effectively."

We shall see in the third experience the ablative of degree of difference expressed by the pair, *quo . . . eo* "by how much [more] by that much [more]." Only half of the correlative is here, *quo*, "by so much [more]."

PIVS VII P M AN PONTIFICATVS SVI XXIII
AREAM ANTE PANTHEON M AGRIPPAE
IGNOBILIBVS TABERNIS OCCVPATAM
DEMOLITIONE PROVIDENTISSIMA
AB INVISA DEFORMITATE VINDICAVIT
ET IN LIBERVM LOCI PROSPECTVM PATERE IVSSIT

Pope Pius VII in the 23rd year of his pontificate
by a most provident demolition
freed from a detestable ugliness
the open space before the Pantheon of Marcus Agrippa
having been occupied by insignificant shops
and ordered it to lie open unto the free view of the place

This is the inscription shown in the image on page 746.

This account of opening the square for a better view of the Pantheon, Rome, is posted on one of the buildings around the square. On the facade of the Pantheon is the name of Marcus Agrippa.

COMMENTARY

Pius VII P M an pontificatus sui XXIII,
"Pope Pius VII in the 23rd year of his pontificate": the abbreviations are *Pontifex Maximus*, "the High Priest," a title from Roman religion, rendered in English as "Pope." The abbreviation *an* stands for *anno*, "in the year." The form *pontificatus* is the genitive form of this *-us, us* masculine noun. The reflexive pronoun *sui* refers back to the subject, "his" referring to Pius VII.

M Agrippae,
"of Marcus Agrippa": the abbreviation is *Marci*, "of Marcus."

Pius . . . aream . . . vindicavit et . . . iussit,
"Pius . . . freed . . . the open space and ordered it": note the order of subject, object and several lines away two verbs *vindicavit*, "[Pius] freed," and *iussit*, "[Pius] ordered," both referring to the same object *aream*, "the open space."

Pius . . . aream . . . patere iussit,
"Pius . . . ordered it to lie open": the above entry explains that the verb *vindicavit*, "[Pius] freed," has as an object *aream*, "the open space." The verb *iussit*, "[Pius] ordered" is a verb of M&M producing an entire expression in OO whose subject is *aream* in the object form and whose verb is the infinitive *patere*.

This construction may be rendered with unequal success into English in three possible ways: "Pius ordered the open space to lie open," thus preserving in English the accusative with the infinitive.

The second way is with the word "that" followed by a subject and a finite verb:

"Pius ordered that the open space lie open." Because *iussit*, "he ordered," is a verb of willing and demanding, it produces an expression of purpose, which is rendered in the English in the subjunctive, as here, "[the open space] lie open." Thus, underlying that infinitive *patere*, is the intention expressed in the subjunctive.

The third way is the same as the second, but without the particle "that": "Pius ordered the open space lie open." Once you know the second way, this one is easy to spot. In fact, this same phenomenon occurs in Latin when the wish expressed in the verb is emphasized, here *iussit*, "[Pius] ordered," the subjunctive is used without the particle *ut*, "that," as mentioned in Gildersleeve and Lodge n° 546, remark 2.

FONS CVI LVSTRICVS
TVTELAREM QVONDAM CAELITEM
DIVVM ADDIDIT IOSEPHVM
ANTISTITI SVMMO IPSI
BENEDICTO XVI
EVNDEM HONORANS PATRONVM
FAMILIAE SACRAE CVSTODEM
VINDICEM VNIVERSAE ECCLESIAE
DONO DICAVIT PERPETVO
HORTORVM ECCE VATICANORVM
LIBENTER QVOS REVISIT
FAVTORVM LIBERALITAS ARTIVM
VATICANIS IN MVSEIS
FONTEM HVNC CENTESIMVM

V Kal. IVnias MMX Pont. VI

honoring the same patron
custodian of the holy family
protector of the whole church,
the generosity of the patrons of the arts
in the Vatican museums
for a perpetual gift dedicated to
Benedict XVI,
the highest bishop himself,
behold, this the hundredth fountain
of the Vatican gardens,
which he often willingly visits,
to whom the baptismal fountain
once upon a time added Saint Joseph
as heavenly patron

28 May 2010 *sixth of the pontificate*

This is a proposed draft of an unused inscription for a new fountain in the Vatican gardens. The fountain is dedicated to St. Joseph to honor the baptismal patron of Pope Benedict XVI. This is one of the last compositions by Reginald before his retirement from the office. This inscription does not correspond to any photo, and so is presented here for Latin enjoyment.

COMMENTARY

honorans ... dicavit ... liberalitas ... fontem,
"honoring ... the generosity ... dedicated ... the ... fountain": the subject is *liberalitas*, "the generosity." The verb governing the whole expression is *dicavit*, "[generosity] dedicated" in T.4b. The object of the dedication is *fontem*, "the ... font." The contemporaneous participle *honorans*, "honoring," agrees with the subject, *liberalitas.*

fautorum liberalitas artium vaticanis in museis,
"the generosity of the patrons of the arts in the Vatican museums": the subject is described by the genitives that frame it as *fautorum ... artium*, "of the patrons of the arts." The arts are located nearby *vaticanis in museis*, "in the Vatican museums."

eundem honorans patronum,
"honoring the same patron": the first object of the participle *honorans*, "honoring," frames it: *eundem ... patronum*, "the same patron," referring to *divum Iosephum*, "St. Joseph" previously in the inscription.

familiae sacrae custodem vindicem universae ecclesiae,
"custodian of the holy family protector of the whole church": note the word order where two genitives begin and end the couplet, thus framing the nouns on which they depend in a classic chiasm or X pattern. The two nouns are synonyms, *custodem vindicem*, "custodian ... protector," and they both further describe *eundem ... patronum*, "the same patron, custodian ... protector."

Benedicto XVI ... dono dicavit perpetuo,
"dedicated to Benedict XVI ... for a perpetual gift": two datives indicate the person to whom the fountain is dedicated, *Benedicto XVI*, "to Benedict XVI," and the goal of the dedication to be *dono ... perpetuo*, "for a perpetual gift."

antistiti summo ipsi Benedicto XVI,
"[dedicated] to Benedict XVI, the highest bishop himself": the term "bishop" comes from the Greek and means "overseer." It was rendered into the Latin by transliteration as *episcopus*, "bishop," or by the word *antistes*, both masculine and feminine, whose etymological meaning is *antesto*, "I stand before," and thus refers to an "overseer" or "president" or the "high-priest" of a temple, whether male or female. The emphatic *ipsi*, "himself," agrees with *Benedicto*, "to Benedict."

fons cui lustricus ... divum addidit Iosephum,
"to whom the baptismal fountain ... added ... Saint Joseph": the Romans celebrated a rite of purification and naming of a new-born on the eighth day after birth, called a *lustrum* or by the adjective here *lustricus*. It was a Roman predecessor of the Christian practice of baptizing on the eighth day. Thus, here the *fons lustricus*, is the "lustral fountain" or "baptismal font." After the new-born child of the Ratzinger family was born, in baptism he was given the name Joseph, the future Pope Benedict XVI. Thus, the inscription speaks of Benedict XVI, to whom the baptismal font added the name "St. Joseph."

tutelarem quondam caelitem,
"once upon a time ... the heavenly patron": the adverb *quondam* describes *addidit*, "[the baptismal fountain] once upon a time added," referring to Pope Benedict's

infancy. Framing the adverb, *tutelarem ... caelitem*, "the heavenly patron," agrees with and so describes, *divum Iosephum*, "Saint Joseph, the heavenly patron."

hortorum ecce vaticanorum ... fontem hunc centesimum,
"behold, this the hundredth fountain of the Vatican gardens": the font is described by these two lines that frame three intervening lines. This is *hunc centesimum*, "the hundredth [fountain]." The fountain is located in and so property *hortorum ... vaticanorum*, "of the Vatican gardens." These last two words frame *ecce*, "behold."

libenter quos revisit,
"which he often willingly visits": the antecedent of *quos*, "which," are the *hortorum vaticanorum*, "of the Vatican gardens." The subject of the verb *revisit*, "he often visits," in T.1i here, is *is*, "he," referring to an implied *Benedictus XVI*, "Benedict XVI." The adverb *libenter*, "readily" or "spontaneously" or "willingly," describes *revisit* and is placed in front of the relative pronoun *quos*.

V Kal. iunias MMX,
"28 May 2010": the full form of the Latin date is *quinto die ante Kalendas iunias bismillesimo decimo anno*, "on the fifth day before the June Kalends in the two-thousandth tenth year," that is, in 2010. Here the month *iunias*, "June," is an adjective describing *Kal.* or more fully *Kalendas*, "the Kalends," which is the object of the implied *ante*, "before." Also implied is *die*, "on the [fifth] day."

pontificatus sexto,
"sixth of the pontificate": implied is *anno*, "in the [sixth] year." The noun *pontificatus*, "of the pontificate," is an *–us, us* noun, producing this of-possession form.

BENIGNITATI HORVM IPSORVM QVANTVM
MERITO DEBETVR AC LIBERALITATI
COEPTIS NEMPE NOSTRIS STVDIISQVE PROVEHENDIS

ISTIS TANTVNDEM IMPARES VERSICVLIS
REDDERE HISCE QVIDEM ENITIMVR
GRATIIS CONGRVIS EX ANIMO REFERENDIS

How much is meritedly owed
to the kindness of these very people and generosity
by promoting namely our undertakings and studies

with these small expressions we indeed unequal to the task
are striving to render to those people the same amount
by returning suitable thanks from the heart.

This is the thank-you note given at the beginning of the acknowledgments on page 829.

It was composed by Reginald in gratitude for our partners in this undertaking.

COMMENTARY

quantum … tantundem,
"How much … the same amount": the two parts of the sentence are correlated by these two words.

quantum merito debetur,
"How much is meritedly owed": the English rendering "how much" makes this expression sound like an indirect question, but it is not, because there is not a verb of M&M and its verb is not in the subjunctive. Rather *quantum* is one of two correlative words. The adverb *merito* also means "by merit," "deservedly," "justly."

benignitati horum ipsorum … debetur … ac liberalitati,
"[How much] is … owed to the kindness of these very people and generosity": the natural use of the dative is seen here framing the first two lines of the text. The conjunction *ac* joins *benignitati*, "to the kindness," with *liberalitati*, "to the generosity." The *ipsorum* is emphatic and agrees with *horum*, "of these very people."

coeptis … nostris studiisque provehendis,
"by promoting … our undertakings and studies": their kindness and generosity has been shown in a way described by this ablative gerundive. It could be rendered as a gerund with its objects as follows: *coepta … nostra studiaque provehendo*, where *provehendo*, "by promoting," is an ablative gerund whose objects are the two neuter nouns *coepta*, "undertakings," and *studia*, "studies." To construct the gerundive, the two objects of the gerund are put into the function of the gerund. Thus *coepta nostra studiaque* are put into the ablative and become *coeptis nostris studiisque;* they remain

plural. Then the gerund is made to agree with its own objects, *provehendis*, with no change of meaning, but a significant difference in style beloved to the Romans.

impares . . . reddere hisce quidem enitimur,
"we indeed unequal to the task . . . are striving to render to those people": the main verb of the sentence is *enitimur*, "we are striving." Its complement is the gerund *reddere*, "to render," which is followed by a natural dative, *hisce*, "to those people," "to these people," the people mentioned in the first line, *horum ipsorum*, "of these very people." The adjective *impares*, "unequal to the task," agrees with the implied subject of the verb, *nos*, "we."

istis . . . versiculis,
"with these small expressions": these ablatives framing the line refer to the lines of the Latin expression of gratitude and to the text of the acknowledgments that follow.

Gratiis congruis ex animo referendis,
"by returning suitable thanks from the heart": another ablative gerundive. We may express this as a gerund to better see its objects, by saying, *gratias congruas ex animo referendo*, with no change in meaning. To construct the gerundive, the objects are put into the function of the gerund, so, *gratiis congruis*; they remain plural. Next the gerund is made to agree with its own objects, thus, *referendis*.

BIBLIOGRAPHIA

bibliography

LEXICA

FORCELLINI, A. *Totius latinitatis lexicon.* 6 vols. Padua, 1965 (anastatic copy).

GLARE, P. G. W. *Oxford Latin Dictionary.* Oxford: Oxford University Press, 1968–1982.

LEWIS, C. T., and C. SHORT. *A Latin Dictionary.* Oxford and New York: Oxford University Press, 1879. Reprinted, 1995.

The Oxford Classical Dictionary. Edited by S. Hornblower and A. Spawforth. 3rd revised edition. Oxford: Oxford University Press, 1949. Reprinted, 2003.

Thesaurus Linguae Latinae, editus auctoritate et consilio Academicarum quinque Germanicarum, Berolinensis, Gottingensis, Lipsiensis, Monacensis, Vindobonensis. Leipzig, 1903.

INSTRUMENTA

Enchiridion Patristicum: loci ss. patrum, doctorum scriptorum ecclesiasticorum. Edited by M. J. R. de Journel. Barcelona and Rome: Herder, ^{25}1981.

Enchiridion Symbolorum definitionum et declarationum de rebus fidei et morum. Edited by H. Denzinger and A. Schönmetzer. Barcelona. Freiburg, Rome: Herder, ^{36em}1976.

GILDERSLEEVE, B. L., and G. LODGE. *Gildersleeve's Latin Grammar.* Wauconda, IL: Bolchazy-Carducci, 2003. Reprint of ^{3}1895.

GOLDMAN, N. *English Grammar for Students of Latin: The Study Guide for those Learning Latin.* Ann Arbor, MI: Olivia and Hill Press, ^{3}2004.

HULLIHEN, W. *Antequam and Priusquam with Special Reference to the Historical Development of their Subjunctive Usage.* PhD. diss., Johns Hopkins University, 1900. Baltimore, MD: Lord Baltimore Press, 1903.

KÜHNER, R., and C. STEGMANN. *Ausführliche Grammatik der lateinischen Sprache.* Munich: Max Hueber Verlag, ^{4}1962.

LANSFORD, T. *The Latin Inscriptions of Rome: A Walking Guide.* Baltimore: Johns Hopkins University Press, 2009.

Medieval Latin. Edited by K. P. Harrington. Chicago and London: University of Chicago Press, 1925.

The Oxford Companion to Classical Literature. Edited by P. Harvey. Oxford: Clarendon, 1937. Corrected and reprinted, 1959.

Schwieder, G. *Latine Loquor*. Rome: Herder, 1953.
Michael, Norbertus (II, 11, p. 69).
Norbertus, Otto (II, 13, p. 71).
Robertus, Patricius (II, 15, p. 72).
Paulus, Renatus, II, 15, p. 73.
Iacobus, Iulius (III, 45, p. 185).
Paulus, Ioannes (III, 47, p. 187).
Lucas, Lambertus (III, 46, p. 186).
Norbertus, Maximilianus (III, 48, p. 187).
Praeceptor, Terentius (IV, 48, p. 244).
Praeceptor, Vincentius (IV, 49, p. 245).
Adolphus, Praeceptor (IV, 52, p. 247).
Albertus, Magister (IV, 53, p. 248).
Ludovicus, Maximilianus (II, 10, p. 68).

Signoriello, Nuntius. *Lexicon peripateticum*, "'V' Effata," "'B' Effata," "'N' Effata." In *Lexicon Peripateticum Philosophico-Theologicum in quo scholasticorum distinctiones et effata praecipua explicantur*. Edited by N. Signoriello and F. Pustet, 437–41, 52–57, 250–51. Rome, [5]1931.

OPERA ADDUCTA POTIUS SACRA: QUOTED RATHER SACRED WORKS

Ambrosius Mediolanensis. *de Paenitentia*. In *Enchiridion Patristicum*. Edited by de Journel, nº 1292–1300.

———. *Epistulae: Ambrosius Eusebio* (lib. V, epist. 26; vol. 1, p. 179); *Ambrosius Sisinnio* (VI, 35; vol. 1, pp. 238–41); *Ambrosius Romulo* (VII, 44; vol. 2, pp. 43–44); *Ambrosius Titiano* (VII, 45; vol. 2, pp. 44–45); *Ambrosius Candidiano Fratri* (VII, 53; vol. 2, p. 71); *Ambrosius Antonio* (VIII, epist. 60; vol. 2, pp. 118–19). In *Epistularum libri VII–IX*. Edited by M. Zelzer. Corpus scriptorum ecclesiasticorum latinorum 82. Opera 10, Epistulae et Acta, 3 vols. Vienna: Hoelder, Pichler, Tempsky, 1990.

———. *Exameron*. In *Sancti Ambrosii Opera*. 7 vols. Corpus scriptorum ecclesiasticorum latinorum 32. Vol. 1. Edited by C. Schenkl, 209–15. Prague, Vienna, and Leipzig: Tempsky and Freytag, 1897.

———. *Expositio euangelii secundum Lucam*. In *Enchiridion Patristicum*. Edited by de Journel, nº 1301–1310.

Augustinus Hipponensis, Aurelius. *Epistula 120, Consentio*. In *Enchiridion Patristicum*. Edited by de Journel, nº 1429.

———. *Epistula 137*. In *Enchiridion Patristicum*. Edited by de Journel, nº 1431.

———. *de Civitate Dei*. In *Enchiridion Patristicum*. Edited by de Journel, nº 1765.

———. *de Gratia et libero arbitrio*. In *Enchiridion Patristicum*. Edited by de Journel, nº 1936–1943.

———. *in Psalmum LXIII. enarratio*. In *Enchiridion Patristicum*. Edited by de Journel, nº 1471.

———. *in Psalmum LXXI. enarratio*. In *Enchiridion Patristicum*. Edited by de Journel, nº 1501.

———. *in Psalmum XCI. enarratio*. In *Sancti Aurelii Augustini Enarrationes in*

Psalmos, 3 vols. Edited by E. Dekkers and J. Fraipont. Corpus christianorum series latina 38–40, Aurelii Augustini Opera 10. Turnhout: Brepols, 1956, 2, 1278–1283, vol. 2–3 ²1990.

Beda Venerabilis. *Historia ecclesiastica*. In *Bedae Venerabilis presbyteri Anglo-saxonis Historica ecclesiastica*. Edited by J.-P. Migne. PL 95: 241A–245A. Paris, 1861.

Biblia Sacra iuxta Vulgatam versionem. 2 vols. Edited by R. Weber et al. Stuttgart: Wurttembergische Bibelanstalt, 1969.

Codex iuris canonici, auctoritate Ioannis Pauli PP. II promulgatus, Vatican City: Typis polyglottis Vaticanis, 1983.

Concilium Oecumenicum Tridentinum, Sessio XXIV (11 novembris 1563), *Doctrina de sacramento matrimonii*; *Canones de sacramento matrimonii*; *Canones super reformatione circa matrimonium*; *Decretum de reformation*. In *Conciliorum Oecumenicorum Decreta*. Edited by G. Alberigo et alii, Centro di documentazione, Istituto per le scienze religiose. Basel et alibi: Herder, ²1962, 729–734.

Concilium Oecumenicum Vaticanum II, Constitutio pastoralis de ecclesia in mundo huius temporis *Gaudium et spes* (7 decembris 1965). In *Constitutiones, decreta, declarationes*, 607–18. Edited by Secretaria generalis Concilii Oecumenici Vaticani II. Vatican City: Typis polyglotis Vaticanis, 1966.

Concilium Vaticanum I [1869–1870 ce], sessio 2, "Professio fidei." In *Conciliorum Oecumenicorum Decreta*, 778–79. Edited by G. Alberigo et alii, Centro di documentazione, Istituto per le scienze religiose. Basel et alibi: Herder, ²1962, 778–79.

Cyprianus Carthaginensis, Thascius Caecilianus. *Epistulae*. In *Enchiridion Patristicum*. Edited by de Journel, nº 568–599.

———. *De lapsis*. In *Enchiridion Patristicum*. Edited by de Journel, nº 551–554.

Hieronymus, Sophronius Eusebius. *Contra Vigilantium*. In *Enchiridion Patristicum*. Edited by de Journel, nº 1396.

———. *Dialogus adversus pelagianos*. Edited by C. Moreschini. Corpus christianorum series latina 80. S Hieronymi presbyteri opera 3, Opera polemica 2. Turnhout: Brepols, 1990.

———. *In Ecclesiasten comentarius*. In *Enchiridion Patristicum*. Edited by de Journel, nº 1373–1375.

———. *In epistulam ad Ephesios commentarii*. In *Enchiridion Patristicum*. Edited by de Journel, nº 1365–1370.

———. *In Habacuc comentarii*. In *Enchiridion Patristicum*. Edited by de Journel, nº 1377.

———. *In Isaiam comentarii*. In *Enchiridion Patristicum*. Edited by de Journel, nº 1397.

Iacobus Tudertinus. *Stabat Mater*. In *Officium divinum ex decreto Sacrosancti Oecumenicum Concilium Vaticanum II instauratum atque auctoritate Pauli PP. VI promulgatum: Liturgia horarum iuxta ritum Romanum, editio typica altera*, 4 vols. Vatican City: Typis polyglottis Vaticanis, ²1987. *Editio typica*, 1973–1974, 4, 1136–37. *Editio typica altera*, 4, 1215–16. Vatican City: Libreria editrice Vaticana, ²2000.

Iohannes XXII. Constitutio *Gloriosam Ecclesiam* (23 ianuarii 1318). In *Enchiridion Symbolorum*. Edited by Denzinger, nº 911.

Ioannes Paulus PP. II. Constitutio apostolica *Sacri Canones* (18 octobris 1990). In *Acta Apostolicae Sedis* 82 (1990): 1037.

———. Litterae encyclicae de labore humano *Laborem exercens* (14 septembrii 1981). Vatican City: Libreria Editrice Vaticana, 1981.

Isidorus Hispalensis. *Etymologiarum sive Originum libri XX*. In *Medieval Latin*. Edited by Harrington, 76–79.

Jedin, Hubertus. *Praefatio* and *Introductio*. In *Conciliorum Oecumenicorum Decreta*. Edited by G. Alberigo et alii, Centro di documentazione, Istituto per le scienze religiose, vii–ix, xi–xiii. Basel et alibi: Herder, ²1962.

Leo Magnus, PP. *Tractatus* LXXII and *Tractatus* XXI. In *Sancti Leonis Magni Romani Pontificis tractatus septem et nonaginta*, 2 vols. Edited by A. Chavasse. Corpus christianorum series latina 138, 138A. Turnhout: Brepols, 1973.

Maximus Taurinensis. *Sermones*: 13a, "De sancta epyfania"; 34, "De hospitalitate in evangelio"; 3, "De margarita evangelii"; 53, "De pascha." In *Maximi Episcopi Taurinensis: Collectionem sermonum antiquam nonnullis sermonibus extravagantibus adiectis*. Edited by A. Mutzenbecher, 133–35, 10–11, 214. Corpus christianorum series latina 23. Turnhout: Brepols, 1962.

———. *Sermones* 33, "De eo quod scriptum est: *Simile est regnum Dei ferment.*" In *Maximi Episcopi Taurinensis: Collectionem sermonum antiquam nonnullis sermonibus extravagantibus adiectis*. Edited by A. Mutzenbecher. Corpus christianorum series latina 23. Turnhout: Brepols, 1962.

Missale Romanum ex decreto Sacrosancti Oecumenici Concilii Vaticani II instauratum auctoritate Pauli PP. VI promulgatum. "Die 9 octobris, Ss. Dionysii, episcopi, et sociorum, martyrum, Collecta," p. 623. "Missae rituales. IV Pro sponsis. 1 In celebratione matrimonii. B Praefatio." "Praefatio De Sanctis virginibus et religiosis," p. 432. Vatican City: Typis Vaticanis, ²1975.

Morus, Thomas. *Epigrammata*. In *Thomas More. Tutti gli Epigrammi*. Translated by L. Firpo and L. Paglialunga. Milan: Edizioni San Paolo, Cinisello Balsamo, 1994. See also *The Complete Works of St. Thomas More*, vol. 3, 2. New Haven and London: Yale University Press, 1984.

Nova Vulgata Bibliorum Sacrorum editio: *Sacrosancti Oecumenici Concilii Vaticani II ratione habita iussu Pauli PP. VI recognita auctoritate Ioannis Pauli PP. II promulgata, editio typica altera*. Vatican City: Libreria editrice Vaticana, ²1986.

Officium divinum ex decreto Sacrosancti Oecumenicum Concilium Vaticanum II instauratum atque auctoritate Pauli PP. VI promulgatum: *Liturgia horarum iuxta ritum Romanum, editio typica*, 4 vols. "Die 15 augusti in assumptione Beatae Mariae Virginis Sollemnitas, ad I vesperas, preces." "Die 15 septembris Beatae Mariae Virginis perdolentis, Memoria. Ad Laudes matutinas. Hymnus," "Ad Vesperas. Hymnus." "Die 29 septembris Ss. Michaelis, Gabrielis et Raphaelis, Archangelorum Festum. Ad Vesperas. Hymnus." Vatican City: Typis polyglottis Vaticanis, 1973–1974.

Paulinus Nolanus. *Carmina. II, IIII, VI, VIII, XII, XIII, XXX*. In *Sancti Pontii Meropii Paulini Nolani Carmina*. Edited by G. de Hartel. Corpus scriptorum ecclesiasticorum latinorum 30. Sancti Pontii Meropii Paulini Nolani Opera 2. Prague, Vienna, Leipzig: Tempsky and Freytag, 1894.

Pius PP. II (Aeneas Syluius Piccolomini). In *Pii II Commentarii rerum memorabilium, que temporibus suis contigerunt*. 2 vols. Edited by A. van Heck. Studi e testi 312–13. Vatican City: Bibliotheca apostolica Vaticana, 1984.

Pius PP. IX. Epistola *Cum non sine* ad archiepisc. Friburgensem (14 iulii 1864). In *Enchiridion Symbolorum*. Edited by Denzinger, nº 2947.

Pius PP. XI. Litterae encyclicae de educatione christiana. *Divini illius magistri* (31 decembris 1929). In *Enchiridion Symbolorum*. Edited by Denzinger, n° 3685–698.

Pius PP. XII [papal Latinist: Antonius Bacci]. Litterae encyclicae *Miranda prorsus* (8 septembris 1957). In *Acta Apostolicae Sedis* 49 (1957): 765–805.

S. Congr. S. R. U. Inquisitionis. Decretum quod damnantur plures propositiones ex operibus nuper editis sub nomine Antonii Rosmini Serbati *Hisce adiunctum litteris* (7, 14 decembris 1887). In *Enchiridion Symbolorum*. Edited by Denzinger, n° 3222.

Tertullianus, Quintus Septimus Florens. *De praescriptione haereticorum*. In *Enchiridion Patristicum*. Edited by de Journel, n° 295.

———. *Adversus Hermogenem*. In *Enchiridion Patristicum*. Edited by de Journel, n° 321–328.

———. *De carnis resurrectione*. In *Enchiridion Patristicum*. Edited by de Journel, n° 360–365.

———. *De paenitentia*. In *Enchiridion Patristicum*. Edited by de Journel, n° 311–317.

Venantius Fortunatus. *Miscellanea*. Edited by J.-P. Migne. PL 88: 59–362 B: *De basilica* (I, 4, p. 67), *De calice* (1, 14, p. 77), *Ad eundem* (III, 15, p. 139), *Ad eundem* (III, 16, p. 139), *De pictura* (III, 17, p. 139), *Ad Hilarium* (III, 21, p. 142), *Da archidiaconum* (III, 34, p. 150), *Ad Joannem* (III, 35, p. 150), *Ad eundem* (V, 13, p. 199), *Ad conviviam* (VII, 25, p. 259), *Ad eundem* (VII, 16, p. 259), *De brevitate vitae* (VII, 17, p. 259), *Ad eundem* (VII, 28, p. 259), *Pro castaneis* (XI, 13, p. 356), *Pro ovis* (XI, 20, p. 358), *De Absentia* (XI, 21, p. 358), *De convivio* (XIII, 22, p. 358). Paris, 1862.

OPERA ADDUCTA POTIUS SAECULARIA: QUOTED RATHER SECULAR WORKS

Baconius, Rogerus. *Compendium philosophiae*. In *A Primer of Medieval Latin. An Anthology of Prose and Poetry*. Edited by C. H. Beeson, 1, 301–2. The Lake Classical Series. Chicago, Atlanta, New York: Scott, Foresman and Company, 1925.

Boccaccio, Ioannes. *De mulieribus claris*. In *Giovanni Boccaccio, Famous Women*. Edited and translated by V. Brown. The I Tatti Renaissance Library. Cambridge, MA, and London: Harvard University Press, 2001.
[Dedicatio].
I. *De Eva parente prima*.
XLVII. *De Sapho puella lesbia et poeta*.
LXXXI. *De Iulia Gaii Caesaris dictatoris filia*.
LXXXVIII. *De Cleopatra regina Egyptiorum*.
XCII. *De Agrippina Neronis Caesaris matre*.
CI. *De Iohanna anglica papa*.
Conclusio.

Boethius, Anicius Manlius Severinus. *Philosophiae consolatio*. Edited by L. Bieler, 41–48. Corpus christianorum series latina 94. Turnhout: Brepols, 1957.

Bologna, Horatius Antonius. "Animalia hominis vita potiora." In "Diarium Latinum." *Latinitas* 48 (2000): 248.

———."De Cleopatrae forma." In "Diarium Latinum." *Latinitas* 49 (2001): 181–82.

———. "Mulieres pugiles fient." In "Diarium Latinum." *Latinitas* 49 (2001): 92.

———. "Perniciosum autocinetorum certamen." In "Diarium Latinum." *Latinitas* 48 (2000): 256–57.

Bracciolini, Poggius. *Epistolae. II. Poggius suo Leonardo Arretino*. In *Prosatori Latini del Quattrocento*. Edited by E. Garin. La letteratura italiana. Storia e testi 13. Milan and Naples: Riccardo Riccardi, 1952.

Caesar, Caius Iulius. *De Bello Civili*. In *C. Ivli Caesaris Commentariorum ... Libri ... de Bello Civili*. Edited by R. du Pontet. Scriptorum classicorum bibliotheca oxoniensis. Oxford: Clarendon Press, 1908. Reprinted, 1958.

———. *De Bello Gallico*. In *Commentariorum pars prior qua continentur libri VII de Bello Gallico cum A. Hirti supplement*. Edited by R. du Pontet. Scriptorum classicorum bibliotheca oxoniensis. Oxford: Clarendon Press, repr. 1900.

———. *De divinatione*. In *M. Tulli Ciceronis scripta quae manserunt omnia*. Edited by O. Plasberg and W. Ax. Stuttgart: Teubner, 1965.

Carmina Burana. Die Lieder der Benediktbeurer Handschrift Zweisprachige Ausgabe. Munich: Deutscher taschenbuch Verlag, 1991. The Latin text is a reproduction of the edition of A. Hilka and O. Schumann, Heidelberg, 1930–1970.

Catullus, Caius Valerius. *Carmina 61, 85, 101*. In *C. Valerii Catulli Carmina*. Edited by R. A. B. Mynors. Scriptorum classicorum bibliotheca oxoniensis. Oxford: Clarendon Press, 1958. Reprinted, 1960, 49, 94, 100.

Cicero, Marcus Tullius. *Cicero Pateo s. d.* (*ad Fam* IX, 24). In *M. Tulli Ciceronis epistulae 1: Epistulae ad familiars*. Edited by L. C. Purser. Scriptorum classicorum bibliotheca oxoniensis. Oxford: Clarendon Press, 1901. Corrected, 1957.

———. *In C. Verrem orationes sex*. In *Orationes*. 6 vols. Edited by W. Peterson. Scriptorum classicorum bibliotheca oxoniensis, vol. 3. Oxford: Clarendon Press, 1907. Reprinted, 1957.

———. *Pro sex. roscio amerino oratio*. In *Orationes*. 6 vols. Edited by W. Peterson. Scriptorum classicorum bibliotheca oxoniensis, vol. 1. Oxford: Clarendon Press, 1907. Reprinted, 1957.

———. *Laelius de amicitia*. In *M. Tulli Ciceronis scripta quae manserunt omnia*. Edited by O. Plasberg and W. Ax. Stuttgart: Teubner, 1965.

———. *M. Tulli Ciceronis de imperio Cn. Pompei ad quirites oratio*. In *Orationes*. 6 vols. Edited by W. Peterson. Scriptorum classicorum bibliotheca oxoniensis, vol. 1. Oxford: Clarendon Press, 1907. Reprinted, 1957.

———. *M. Tulli Ciceronis epistulae. 2. Epistulae ad Atticum*. 2 vols. Edited by Ludovicus Claude Purser. Scriptorum classicorum bibliotheca oxoniensis. Oxford: Clarendon Press, 1903. Reprinted, 1958.

———. *The Correspondence of M. Tullius Cicero: Arranged According to its Chronological Order; with a Revision of the Text, a Commentary, and Introductory Essays*. Edited by Robert Yelverton Tyrrell and Louis Claude Purser. Dublin and London: Hodges, Figgis & Co., and Longmans, Green & Co.; 1, [3]1904; 2, [2]1906; 3, [2]1914; 4, [2]1918; 5, [2]1915; 6, [2]1933; 7, [1]1901. Reprinted, Hildesheim: Georg Olms, 1969.

Dantes Alagherius. *Monarchia*. In *Medieval Latin*. Edited by Harrington, 552–54. Boston and New York: Allyn and Bacon, 1925.

Erasmus Roterodamus, Desiderius. *Colloquia familiaria*: "Georgius, Livinus," "Syrus, Geta." In *Opera Omnia*. 10 vols. Edited by Petrus van der Aa. Lugduni Batavorum (Leiden), 1703–1706. Anastatic reprint, London: The Gregg Press, 1962.

———. *Epistolae variae*. In *Opera Omnia*. 10 vols. Petrus van der Aa, Lugduni Batavorum (Leiden), 1703–1706. Anastatic reprint, London: The Gregg Press, 1962.

———. *Stultitiae laus*. In *Medieval Latin*. Edited by Harrington, 608–12. Boston and New York: Allyn and Bacon, 1925.

Fritsch Berolinensis, Andreas. *Index sententiarum ac locutionum. Handbuch lateinischer Sätze und Redewendungen*. Saarbrücken: Verlag der Societas Latina, 1996.

Galateus, Antonius. *Eremita*. In *Prosatori Latini del Quattrocento*. Edited by E. Garin, 1065–1125. La letteratura italiana. Storia e testi 13. Milan: Riccardi, 1952.

Horatius Flaccus, Quintus. "Sermones," "Epistulae." In *Q. Horati Flacci Opera*. First edited by E. C. Wickham. Second edition, H. W. Garrod. Scriptorum classicorum bibliotheca oxoniensis. Oxford: Clarendon Press, 1901. Reprinted, 1957.

Lactantius, Caecilius Firmianus. *De opificio Dei*. In *L. Caeli Firmiani Lactanti Opera Omnia*. Edited by S. Brandt. Corpus scriptorum ecclesiasticorum latinorum 27. 2 vols. Vienna: Tempsky, 1893.

Livius, Titus. *Ab urbe condita*. In *Titi Livi Ab urbe condita*. Edited by C. F. Walters and R. S. Conway. Scriptorum classicorum bibliotheca oxoniensis. Oxford: Clarendon Press, 1929. Corrected and reprinted, 1961.

Lucretius Carus, Titus. *De rerum natura*. In *Lucreti de rerum natura libri sex*. Edited by C. Bailey. Scriptorum classicorum bibliotheca oxoniensis. Oxford: Clarendon Press, ²1922. Reprinted, 1959.

Lullius, Raimundus. *Liber natalis pueri paruuli Christi Iesu* [*opus* 169]. *Incipit Liber natalis*. In *Opera latina*, vol. 6 (opera 167–177). Edited by H. Harada, 7, 30–37. Corpus christianorum continuatio mediaevalis 32. Turnhout: Brepols, 1975.

Martialis, Marcus Valerius. *M. Val. Martialis Epigrammata*. Edited by W. M. Lindsay. Scriptorum classicorum bibliotheca oxoniensis. Oxford: Clarendon Press, ²1929.

Nepos, Cornelius. "De excellentibus ducibus," "Eumenes." In *De viris illustribus*. In *Corneli Nepotis Vitae*. Edited by E. O. Winstedt. Scriptorum classicorum bibliotheca oxoniensis. Oxford: Clarendon Press, 1904. Reprinted, 1971.

Oliver, Mary. "Sometimes." In *Red Bird*. Boston: Beacon Press, 2008.

Ovidius Naso, Publius. *Epistulae ex Ponto*. In *P. Ovidi Nasonis tristium libri quinque, Ibis, ex Ponto*. Edited by S. G. Owen. Scriptorum classicorum bibliotheca oxoniensis. Oxford: Clarendon Press, 1915. Reprinted, 1980.

———. *Amores*. In *P. Ovidi Nasonis Amores medicamina faciei femineae ars amatoria remedia amoris*. Edited by E. J. Kenney. Scriptorum classicorum bibliotheca oxoniensis. Oxford: Clarendon Press, 1961. Corrected and reprinted, 1982.

Pisini, Maurus. *Apollo et Hyacinthus*. In *Latinitas* 49 (2001): 11–13, 14–15, 17–18.

Plautus, Titus Maccius. "Asinaria," "*Menaechmi*," "Poenulus," "Rudens," "Stichus." In *T. Macci Plauti Comoediae*. 2 vols. Edited by W. M. Lindsay. Scriptorum classicorum bibliotheca oxoniensis. Oxford: Clarendon Press, 1904. Reprinted, 1951.

Plinius Caecilius Secundus, Caius. *Epistulae*. In *C. Plini Caecili Secundi epistularum libri decem*. Edited by R. A. B. Mynors. Scriptorum classicorum bibliotheca oxoniensis. Oxford: Clarendon Press, 1963.

Politianus, Angelus. *Ep*. III, 11, "XI. Angelus Politianus Lucio Phosphoro Pontifici Signino"; *Ep*. IV, 2, "II. Angelus Politianus Iacobo Antiquario suo salute." In *Angelo Poliziano. Letters*. Edited by S. Butler, 166–70, 226–51. The I Tatti Renaissance Library. Cambridge, MA, and London: Harvard University Press, 2006.

Porcelli, Petrus. "Pugna porcorum." In *Nugae venales sive thesaurus ridendi et jocandi*. Frankfurt and Leipzig, 1703.

Propertius, Sextus. *Elegiae*. In *Sexti Properti Carmina*. Edited by I. S. Phillimore. Scriptorum classicorum bibliotheca oxoniensis. Oxford: Clarendon Press, 1901.

Publilius Syrus. *Publilii Syri mimi sententiae*. In *Minor Latin Poets*. 2 vols. Edited by J. W. Duff and A. M. Duff. Cambridge, MA, and London: Harvard University Press and William Heinemann, [2]1935. Reprinted, 1982.

Quintilianus, Marcus Fabius. *Institutio oratoria*. In *M. Fabi Quintiliani institutionis oratoriae libri XII*. 2 vols. Edited by L. Radermacher. Leipzig: Teubner, 1959. Reprinted, 1971.

Sallustius Crispus, Gaius. "Bellum Catilinae," "De bello Iugurthino." In *Sallust*. Translated by J. C. Rolfe, 1–129, 131–381. Loeb Classical Library 116. London and New York: William Heinemann and G. P. Putnam's Sons, 1921, [2]1931.

Seneca, Lucius Annaeus. *Consolatio ad Helviam matrem*. In *L. Annaei Senecae Dialogorum libri XII*. Edited by L. D. Reynolds, 312. Scriptorum classicorum bibliotheca oxoniensis. Oxford: Clarendon Press, 1977. Reprinted, 1983.

———. *L. Annaei Senecae ad Lucilium epistulae morales*. 2 vols. Edited by L. D. Reynolds. Scriptorum classicorum bibliotheca oxoniensis. Oxford: Clarendon Press, 1969.

———. *De vita beata*. In *L. Annaei Senecae Dialogorum libri duodecim*. Edited by L. D. Reynolds, 167–97. Scriptorum classicorum bibliotheca oxoniensis. Oxford: Clarendon Press, 1969.

Tacitus, Publius Cornelius. *De origine et situ germanorum liber*. In *Opera minora*. Edited by R. M. Ogilvie. Scriptorum classicorum bibliotheca oxoniensis. Oxford: Clarendon Press, 1975. Reprinted, 1980.

Terentius Afer, Publius. "Andria," "Eunuchus," "Heauton," "Timorumenos," "Phormio." In *P. Terenti Afri comoediae*. Edited by R. Kauer, W. M. Lindsay, and O. Skutsch. Scriptorum classicorum bibliotheca oxoniensis. Oxford: Clarendon Press, 1926. Augmented and reprinted, 1958.

Tibullus, Albius. *Carmina*. In *Tibulli aliorumque carminum libri tres*. Edited by I. P. Postgate. Scriptorum classicorum bibliotheca oxoniensis. Oxford: Clarendon Press, [2]1915. Reprinted, 1965.

Vergilius Maro, Publius. "Aeneis," "Georgicon." In *P. Vergili Maronis opera*. Edited by F. A. Hirtzel. Scriptorum classicorum bibliotheca oxoniensis. Oxford: Clarendon Press, 1900. Reprinted, 1959.

———. *Georgicon*. In *P. Vergili Maronis Opera*. Edited by F. A. Hirtzel. Scriptorum classicorum bibliotheca oxoniensis. Oxford: Clarendon Press, 1900. Reprinted, 1959.

Vergilius, Polydorus. *De rerum inventoribus*. In *Polydori Vergilii urbinatis de Rerum Inventoribus libri VIII et de Prodigiis libri III cum indicibus locupletissimis*. Lugduni Batavorum (Leiden): Apud Franciscum, 1644.

OTHER PUBLICATIONS BY THE AUTHORS:

Foster, R. T., and D. P. McCarthy. "Collectarum latinitas." In *Appreciating the Collect: An Irenic Methodology*, edited by J. G. Leachman and D. P. McCarthy, 27–56.

Documenta rerum ecclesiasticarum instaurata. *Liturgiam aestimare: Appreciating the Liturgy* 1. Farnborough, England: St. Michael's Abbey Press, 2008.

LEACHMAN, J. G., and D. P. MCCARTHY, eds. *Appreciating the Collect: An Irenic Methodology*. Documenta rerum ecclesiasticarum instaurata. *Liturgiam aestimare: Appreciating the Liturgy* 1. Farnborough, England: St. Michael's Abbey Press, 2008. Web-page: www.liturgyinstitute.org/appreciating-the-collect

MCCARTHY, D. P "Seeing a reflection, considering appearances: The history, theology, and literary composition of the *Missale Romanum* at a time of vernacular reflection." *Questions Liturgiques / Studies in Liturgy* 94 (2013): 109-43.

MCCARTHY, D. P., and J. G. LEACHMAN. *Listen to the Word: Commentaries on Selected Opening Prayers of Sundays and Feasts with Sample Homilies, Revised from articles that appeared in The Tablet, 18 March 2006–15 September 2007.* Documenta Rerum Ecclesiasticarum Instaurata, Varia. London: The Tablet Trust, 2009. Web-page: www.liturgyinstitute.org/listen-to-the-word

———. "Listen to the Word" Commentaries on the Latin texts of the proper prayers of select Sundays and feasts. *The Tablet.* Weekly, 18 March 2006–27 November 2011.
Web-page: www.danielmccarthyosb.com/prayer-commentaries

———. *Transition in the Easter Vigil: Becoming Christians. Paschali in vigilia Christiani nominis fieri.* Documenta rerum ecclesiasticarum instaurata. *Liturgiam aestimare: Appreciating the Liturgy* 2. Farnborough, England: St. Michael's Abbey Press, 2014. Web-page: www.liturgyinstitute.org/transition-in-the-easter-vigil

———. *Come into the Light: Church Interiors for the Celebration of Liturgy*. Documenta rerum ecclesiasticarum instaurata. Liturgiam aestimare: liturgiam provehens architectura: Architecture Promoting Liturgy. *The Tablet*. Canterbury Press, forthcoming. Web-page: www.liturgyinstitute.org/come-into-the-light/

WEBSITES:

www.thelatinlanguage.org
www.indiegogo.com/at/OSSA
www.liturgyinstitute.org
www.liturgyhome.org
www.benedictine-institute.org
www.college4life.org
www.ealingmonks.org.uk
www.stbedelibrary.org
www.kansasmonks.org
www.jamesleachman.com
www.danielmccarthyosb.com

Any scholar can find a plethora of Latin books and guides to early Christian, medieval, Renaissance Latin in a number of standard books even most recently published which we do not have to quote here.

DEBITI PHOTOGRAPHIS HONORES

honors due to the photographers

Neumagen School Relief, photograph courtesy of Rheinisches Landesmuseum, Trier, second century A.D. http://www.landesmuseum-trier.de/en/home/

Msgr. Peter Dai Bui, SDB, used with permission
- Photo of the dedication manuscript, on page VII

Detail of the Bayeux Tapestry, on page 2: in the public domain

© Giuseppe Aquino, 2015, used with permission
http://www.giuseppeaquino.com/eng/home.html
http://it.wikipedia.org/wiki/Giuseppe_Aquino
- Vatican Bee fountain with its inscription, on page 154
- Inscription over the entrance to the Belvedere Court, Vatican City, with its inscription "Quandoquidem," on pages 411, 654
- Raphael's tomb with its inscription in the Pantheon, on page 456
- Vatican printing office dedication, on page 652
- Inscription in the square in front of the Pantheon "Pius VII," on page 746

© Daniel McCarthy, 2015
- Cathedral of St. John, Milwaukee, dedicatory inscription, on page 202
- Manuscript page from the *Antiphonale Monasticum ad usum Abbatiae S. Michaelis Farnburgensis* photographed with permission of Abbot Cuthbert Brogan, OSB, on page 252

© Fr. Tim Finigan, 2015, original photographs used with permission http://the-hermeneutic-of-continuity.blogspot.be/2006/04/berninis-elephant-inscription.html
- Roman elephant obelisk with its inscription, on page 595

© Department of Special Collections and University Archives, Marquette University Libraries, Milwaukee, Wisconsin, 2015
- *Aeneidos ad usum Delphini*, on pages 600–606

Daniel McCarthy, Mary Wenger, and Gabriella Pellant of St. Aloysius Parish, West Allis, Wisconsin
- Letters of Erasmus, on pages 193–195
- Polydorus Vergilius, *De rerum inventoribus*, on pages 705–715

The indexes appear on pages 787–826

SVPER FONTIBVS

about the sources

The sources presented in the reading sheets deserve a brief technical comment. Although this specific compilation of sources in the reading sheets represents one of many we could have chosen, preparing them for this book required a monumental effort. We are grateful to the publisher for reproducing so many pages of reading material in this volume at our request.

Most of these reading sheets are not presented here according to our method, which is to photocopy them directly from the library book for distribution to the students. Rather they have been typographically reformatted for publication in this book. Still every effort has been made to locate the source and the edition of each text photocopied in that original compilation of reading sheets prepared around the year 2001–2002 from books in our personal library or the library of the Teresianum or otherwise at hand in Rome.

The BIBLIOGRAPHIA, "bibliography," beginning on p. 776, contains, to the best of our ability, all of the works mentioned in the text of this book and all of the editions we confirmed to have been used in producing the original reading sheets. If we could not confirm a particular edition, no source is given in this bibliography.

The LECTIONUM FONTES, "sources of the reading sheets," beginning on p. 790, functions as a set of end-notes for the reading sheets. The sources are presented in the order in which they appear in the reading sheets with the specific citations indicated. If it was possible to determine the exact edition from which the original text was photocopied, this source is simply given, or it is indicated by the word "in" followed by the bibliographical entry of the edition. If such was not possible, this is indicated with the abbreviation *cf.*, for *confer,* meaning "compare," followed by an alternative edition. The abbreviation *v.* for *vide*, means "see." To be honest, the source for one or two texts could not be located, but if discovered it will be included in any future editions of this volume.

The LECTIONUM AUCTORES, "authors of the reading sheets," beginning on p. 802, abbreviates the same material given in full in the LECTIONUM FONTES, "sources of the reading sheets," but arranged here according to the name of the author given in alphabetical order and the titles of the cited works by that author, but without reference to any edition.

The LOCI ADLATI, "texts having been quoted," beginning on p. 808, functions as a set of end-notes for the citations that appear within our text, excluding those from the reading sheets.

The reader will quickly notice that many of the Latin texts used to illustrate the teaching within each encounter are our own invention. After considering these, the teacher or self-learner is encouraged to turn to the reading sheets to find in Latin literature from every age genuine examples of each Latin usage. We recognize naturally the essential value of examples drawn from the literature to illustrate our presentation of the Latin language, so we have included citations from very many authors, although these are clustered more in certain encounters than others. The first time an author is presented, the full name is given in Latin followed by the author's dates. Soon thereupon is given the accepted way of referring to the author whether in English or by a single Latin name. The citations in text use the abbreviations presented in the COMPENDIARIA AUCTORUM OPERUMQUE NOMINA, "abbreviated names of works and authors," found on p. XLI.

In addition to the above technical note on the sources used in this book, the following is added here as a brief guide to using the apparatus included at the end of this volume.

The AUCTORUM A NOBIS COMMEMORATORUM NOMINA, "names of authors mentioned by us," beginning on p. 810, gives the page numbers where each of these selected Latin authors are mentioned in this book.

The RECENTIORUM NOMINA, "names of more recent people," beginning on p. 812, includes the names of people mentioned in the text of our book, but does not include Latin authors, who can be found in the indices already mentioned.

The next several indices were carefully compiled by Daniel Vowles to give the student and instructor immediate and easy access to specific items of our instruction. First, the ARGUMENTA, "subject matters," beginning on page 814, arranges the material of all 105 encounters topically. From this index of subject matters, two specific indices have been developed for the ease of access. These are, second, PARTES SIVE CASUS MUNERA ATQUE QUIBUS PERFUNGI NOMINA ADIECTIVA PRONOMINA POSSUNT LATINA, "roles or cases and functions which Latin nouns, adjectives, pronouns can perform," beginning on page 823, and, third, CONIUNCTIVI DE (MULTIPLICI) USU DISCEPTATIONUM ELENCHUS, "a list of discussions about the (multiple) use of the subjunctive," beginning on page 825, both of which present in one place the dispersed presentations on the functions of nouns and adjectives and on the subjunctive and its many usages.

The people involved in the project of writing and producing this volume are the subject of its final three elements. The section DE SCRIPTORIBUS, "about the authors," on page 827, gives a brief biographical sketch of each author, Reginald Foster and Daniel McCarthy. The next section, ADIUTORES, "helpers," on page 828, consists of brief biographies of three people closely associated with this volume: Daniel Gallagher, who wrote the foreword;

James Leachman, who wrote the prologue; and Daniel Vowles, who compiled three of the indices. These three sketches are perhaps by exception presented here because we hope this book will be used by people on different continents working in different fields of Latin literature who may not all be familiar with these three people, influential in their own right. The final section of this volume is reserved for our expression of gratitude to so many who helped us along the way. This is found in the AGNOSCENDA MERITA, "acknowledgments," beginning on page 829 with our own word of thanks expressed, as we say, *Latinly*.

LECTIONVM FONTES

sources of the reading sheets

FIRST EXPERIENCE

1-A HORATIUS FLACCUS, QUINTUS [65–8 BCE]. *Epistularum lib.* I. 8–12. In *Opera.* Edited by E. C. Wickham and H. W. Garrod. Scriptorum classicorum bibliotheca oxoniensis. Oxford: Clarendon Press, 1901. Reprinted, 1957.

1-B VELLEIUS PATERCULUS, GAIUS [19 BCE–35 CE]. *Historiarum Romanarum ad Marcum Vinicium Cosulem. libri duo* LXXXI, 3–LXXXVII, 3. Cf. *Compendium of Roman History*. Trans. F. W. Shipley. Loeb Classical Library 152. Cambridge, MA, and London: Harvard University Press, 1924.

1-C FRONTO, MARCUS CORNELIUS [100–166 CE]. *Epistulae variae.* Cf. *Correspondence.* 2 vols. Trans. C. R. Haines. Loeb Classical Library 112, 113. Cambridge, MA, and London: Harvard University Press, 1919. Revised and reprinted, 1928. Citations below from *M. Cornelii Frontonis Epistulae.* Edited by M. P. J. van den Hout. Leipzig: Teubner, 1988:

Frontonis epistularum ad M. Caes. et invicem libres V:

liber 2 epist 12, *Domino meo. Meum fratrem* (p. 31 line 21).
liber 3 epist. 11, *Domino meo. Omnia nobis* (p. 43 line 22).
liber 3 epist. 12, par 1, *Domino meo. Gratia ad me* (p. 44 line 2).
liber 5 epist. 24, *Domino meo. Quom te salvom* (p. 73 line 6).
liber 5 epist 40, *Domino meo. In hortis* (p. 76 line 8).
liber 5 epist. 44, *Domino meo. Perendie, Domine* (p. 77 line 15).
liber 5 epist 45, *Domino meo. Annum novum* (p. 77 line 22).
liber 5 epist 48 par 1, *Domino meo. Quaecumque mihi* (p. 78 line 17).
liber 5 epist 49, *Domino meo. Saenius Pompeianus* (p. 79 line 2).
liber 5 epist 52, *Domino meo. Aridelus iste* (p. 79 line 25).
liber 5 epist 55, *Domino meo. Cholera usque* (p. 80 line 18).
liber 5 epist 57, par 1, *Domino meo. Plurimos natales* (p. 81 line 17).
liber 5 epist. 59, *Domino meo. Pueri dum* (p. 82 line 8).

Incipiunt M. Frontonis epistuae ad Antoninum Pium:

epist. 4 par 1, *Domino meo Caesari. Niger Censorius* (p. 164 line 8).

1-D SENTENTIARUM STRUCTURA LATINARUM [200 BCE–2001 CE]. L Auctores multiplices.

1. LUCRETIUS CARUS, TITUS [99–55 BCE]. *De rerum natura* V, 281. Cf. *Lucreti de rerum natura libri sex.* Edited by C. Bailey. Scriptorum classicorum

bibliotheca oxoniensis. Oxford: Clarendon Press, [2]1922. Reprinted, 1959.

2. Tertullianus, Quintus Septimus Florens [c. 150/170–c. 230 ce]. *Apologeticum* IX, 19. Cf. *Quinti Septimi Florentis Tertulliani Opera*. Edited by E. Dekkers et al. Corpus christianorum series latina 1. Turnhout: Brepols, 1954.
3. Pontifex Iohannes XXII [1318 ce]. Constitutio *Gloriosam Ecclesiam* 1, 14 (23 ianuarii 1318). In *Enchiridion symbolorum definitionum et declarationum de rebus fidei et morum*. Edited by H. Denzinger and A. Schönmetzer. Barcelona, Freiburg, Rome: Herder, [36 em]1976, nº 911.
4. Ovidius Naso, Publius [43 bce–18 ce]. *Tristia* IV, 10, 57–60. Cf. *Ovidi Nasonis Tristium libri quinque*. Edited by S. G. Owen. Scriptorum classicorum bibliotheca oxoniensis. Oxford: Clarendon, 1915. Reprinted, 1989.
5. Carmen Buranum [saeculi xiii]. *Carmen* 74, 1–10. Cf. *Carmina Burana. Die Lieder der Benediktbeurer Handschrift Zweisprachige Ausgabe*. Edited by A. Hilka and O. Schumann. Trans. C. Fischer and H. Kuhn. Munich: Deutscher taschenbuch Verlag, [6]1995.
6. *Missale Romanum* Pauli PP VI [1975 ce]. "Praefatio De Sanctis virginibus et religiosis." In *Missale Romanum ex decreto Sacrosancti Oecumenici Concilii Vaticani II instauratum auctoritate Pauli PP. VI promulgatum*, 432. Vatican City: Typis Vaticanis, [2]1975.
7. Cicero, Marcus Tullius [106–43 bce]. *Cicero Pateo s.d.* (*ad Fam* IX, 24). In *M. Tulli Ciceronis epistulae* 1: *Epistulae ad familiares*. Edited by L. C. Purser. Scriptorum classicorum bibliotheca oxoniensis. Oxford: Clarendon Press, 1901. Corrected, 1957.
8. Cassianus, Iohannes [360–435 ce]. *Conlationes* X, 7, 1–7. Cf. *Conlationes XXIIII*. Edited by M. Petschenig. Corpus scriptorum ecclesiasticorum latinorum 13. Vienna: Tempsky, 1886. Revised and edited by G. Kreuz. Corpus scriptorum ecclesiasticorum latinorum 13. Vienna: Verlag der Österreichischen Akademie der Wissenschaften (Austrian Academy of Sciences Press), 2004.
9. Hieronymus, Sophronius Eusebius [342–420 ce]. *Epistula*, LII, 15. Cf. *Epistulae I–LXX*. Edited by I. Hilberg. Corpus scriptorum ecclesiasticorum latinorum 54. Epistulae 1. Vienna: Verlag der Österreichischen Akademie der Wissenschaften (Austrian Academy of Sciences Press), 1910. Revised, 1996.

1-E *Nova Vulgata Bibliorum Sacrorum editio* [1979 ce]. *Liber primus Maccabaeorum* 1.1–2.37. In *Nova Vulgata Bibliorum Sacrorum editio: Sacrosancti Oecumenici Concilii Vaticani II ratione habita iussu Pauli PP. VI recognita auctoritate Ioannis Pauli PP. II promulgata, editio typica altera*. Vatican City: Libreria editrice Vaticana, [2]1986.

1-F Augustinus, Aurelius [354–430 ce]. *In Psalmum* XCI. *enarratio. sermo* 1–6. In *Sancti Aurelii Augustini Enarrationes in Psalmos*. 3 vols. Edited by E. Dekkers and J. Fraipont, 2, 1278–1283. Corpus christianorum series latina 38–40, Aurelii Augustini Opera 10. Turnhout: Brepols, 1956; vol. 2–3, [2]1990.

1-G Venantius Fortunatus [535–600 ce]. *Miscellanea*. Edited by J.-P. Migne, 59–362B. PL 88. Paris 1862. Citations:

I, 4, *de basilica* (p. 67).

I, 14, *De calice* (p. 77).
III, 15, *Ad eundem* (p. 139).
III, 16, *Ad eundem* (p. 139).
III, 17, *De pictura* (p. 139).
III, 21, *Ad Hilarium* (p. 142).
III, 34, *Da archidiaconum* (p. 150).
III, 35, *Ad Joannem* (p. 150).
V, 13, *Ad eundem* (p. 199).
VII, 25, *ad conviviam* (p. 259).
VII, 16, *ad eundem* (p. 259).
VII, 17, *De brevitate vitae* (p. 259).
VII, 28, *Ad eundem* (p. 259).
XI, 13, *Pro castaneis* (p. 356).
XI, 20, *Pro ovis* (p. 358).
XI, 21, *De Absentia* (p. 358).
XIII, 22, *De convivio* (p. 358).

1-H BERNARDUS CLARAVALLENSIS [1090–1153 CE]. *Sententiae. series prima* 1–8, 10–20. Cf. *Sancti Bernardi opera*. 8 vols. Edited by J. Leclercq and H. Rochais, 6/2, 7–255. Rome: Editiones Cistercienses, 1972.

1-I LATINARUM COMPAGES SENTENTIARUM [200 BCE–2001 CE], Auctores varii.

1. EMMERAM, OTHLOH [1010–1072 CE]. A metric rendering of the hymn *Victimae paschali*.
2. PLINIUS SECUNDUS, CAIUS [61/62–113 CE]. *Epistulae* IX, 28, 1. Cf. *Epistulae* in *C. Plini Caecili Secundi epistularum libri decem*. Edited by R. A. B. Mynors, 281. Scriptorum classicorum bibliotheca oxoniensis. Oxford: Clarendon Press, 1963.
3. *Missale Romanum* PAULI PP VI [1975 CE]. "Die 9 octobris, Ss. Dionysii, episcopi, et sociorum, martyrum, Collecta." In *Missale Romanum ex decreto Sacrosancti Oecumenici Concilii Vaticani II instauratum auctoritate Pauli PP. VI promulgatum,* 623. Vatican City: Typis Vaticanis, [2]1975.
4. PLAUTUS, TITUS MACCIUS [254–184 BCE]. *Bacchides* 172–177. Cf. *Comoediae*. Edited by W. M. Lindsay. Scriptorum classicorum bibliotheca oxoniensis. Oxford: Clarendon Press, 1904. Reprinted, 1959.
5. PONTIFEX LEO MAGNUS [440–461 CE]. *Tractatus* 58, 5. Cf. *Sancti Leonis Magni Romanis Pontificis tractatus septem et nonaginta*. Edited by A. Chavasse, p. 348, lines 167–73, mss. α. Corpus christianorum series latina 138A. Turnhout: Brepols, 1973.
6. TIBULLUS, ALBIUS [60–19 BCE]. *Elegiae* II, 5, 3–8, 17–22. Cf. *Tibulli aliorumque carminum libri tres*. Edited by I. P. Postgate. Scriptorum classicorum bibliotheca oxoniensis. Oxford: Clarendon Press, [2]1915. Reprinted, 1965.
7. CONCILIUM VATICANUM I [1869–1870 CE]. Sessio 2 "Professio fidei" (6 ianuarii 1870). In *Conciliorum Oecumenicorum Decreta*. Edited by G. Alberigo et alii, 779. Centro di documentazione. Istituto per le scienze religiose. Basel et alibi: Herder, [2]1962.
8. LUCRETIUS CARUS, TITUS [99–55 BCE]. *De rerum natura*, V, 1448–453. In *Lucreti de rerum natura libri sex*. Edited by C. Bailey. Scriptorum classicorum bibliotheca oxoniensis. Oxford: Clarendon, [2]1922. Reprinted, 1959.

1-K CONCILIUM OECUMENICUM CONSTANTIENSE [1414–1418 CE]. *Sententia condemnatoria articulorum Ioannis Wicleff* 1–45; *Articuli damnati I. Huss* 1–25. Cf. CONCILIUM OECUMENICUM CONSTANTIENSE, sessio VIII, 4 maii 1415, Decretum a papa confirmatum 22 februarii 1418, *Errores Iohannis Wyclif*; sessio XV, 6 iulii 1415, Decretum a papa confirmatum 22 februarii 1418, *Errores Iohannis Hus*. In *Enchiridion Symbolorum definitionum et declarationum de rebus fidei et morum*. Edited by H. Denzinger and A. Schönmetzer, nº 1151–1195, 1201–1225. Barcelona, Freiburg, Rome: Herder, 36 em1976.

1-L ERASMUS ROTERODAMUS, DESIDERIUS [1466–1536 CE]. *Epistolae variae*. In *Desiderii Erasmi Opera Omnia*. 10 vols. Edited by Petrus van der Aa, vol. III/1. Lugduni Batavorum (Leiden), 1703–1706. Anastatic repr., London: The Gregg Press, 1962. Citations:

Epistola XXII. Erasmus Batto suo, column 22.
Epistola L. Erasmus cuidam, column 45.
Epistola LXVII. Erasmus Fausto suo, column 57.
Epistola LXXXIX. Erasmus Rot. Antonio Lutzenburgo, column 79.
Epistola XC. Erasmus Rot. Petro Notho, column 88.
Epistola CLVII. Erasmus Roterod. Thomae Lincaro, column 136.
Epistola CCXLII. Erasmus Gonello suo, column 237.
Epistola CCXLV. Erasmus Rot. Marco Laurino, column 238.
Epistola CCXLVI. Erasmus Rot. Antonio Clavae, column 238.
Epistola CCXCVI. Erasmus Rot. Andreae Hochstrato, column 290.

1-M BOLOGNA, HORATIUS ANTONIUS [2000–2001 CE]. Citations:

"Animalia hominis vita potiora." In "Diarium Latinum." *Latinitas* 48 (2000): 248.
"De Cleopatrae forma." In "Diarium Latinum." *Latinitas* 49 (2001): 181–82.
"Mulieres pugiles fient." In "Diarium Latinum." *Latinitas* 49 (2001): 92.
"Perniciosum autocinetorum certamen." In "Diarium Latinum." *Latinitas* 48 (2000): 256–57.

SECOND EXPERIENCE

2-A PLAUTUS, TITUS MACCIUS [254–184 CE]. *ASINARIA* 373–618. In *T. Macci Plauti Comoediae*. 2 vols. Edited by W. M. Lindsay. Scriptorum classicorum bibliotheca oxoniensis. Oxford: Clarendon Press, 1904. Reprinted, 1951.

2-B HIERONYMUS, SOPHRONIUS EUSEBIUS [342–420 CE]. *Dialogus adversus pelagianos*. Edited by C. Moreschini. Corpus christianorum series latina 80. S Hieronymi presbyteri opera 3, Opera polemica 2. Turnhout: Brepols, 1990. Citations in Liber I:

nº 1, p. 6–7.
nº 3–4, p. 7–8.
nº 7–8, p. 10–11.
nº 11–12, p. 13–14.
nº 20, p. 25–26.
nº 21, p. 27.

2-C BOETHIUS, ANICIUS MANLIUS SEVERINUS [480–524 CE]. *Philosophiae consolatio* III, 3, 1–19; 4, 3–16; 5, 1–14; 7, 1–8, 1–12, viii 1–7. Edited by L. Bieler, 41–48. Corpus christianorum series latina 94. Turnhout: Brepols, 1957.

2-D CARMEN BURANUM [SAEC. XIII]. *Carmina* 196, 199–203. Cf. *Carmina Burana. Die Lieder der Benediktbeurer Handschrift Zweisprachige Ausgabe*. Edited by A. Hilka and O. Schumann. Translated by C. Fischer and H. Kuhn. Munich: Deutscher taschenbuch Verlag, [6]1995.

2-E GALATEUS, ANTONIUS [1444–1517 CE]. *Eremita*, varia. In *Prosatori Latini del Quattrocento*. Edited by E. Garin, 1065–1125. La letteratura italiana. Storia e testi 13. Milan: Riccardi, 1952. Citations: 1072, 1074; 1076, 1078; 1090; 1098.

2-F ERASMUS ROTERODAMUS, DESIDERIUS [1466–1536 CE]. *Colloquia familiaria*: "Georgius, Livinus," "Syrus, Geta." In *Desiderii Erasmi Opera Omnia*. 10 vols. Vol. 1. Edited by Petrus van der Aa. Lugduni Batavorum (Leiden), 1703–1706. Anastatic reprint, London: The Gregg Press, 1962. Citations:

Syrus, Geta, column 637.
Successus, column 638.
Gratiarum actio, column 638.
An accepisti literas? Formula, column 655.
Responsio, column 655.
Credo, Formula, column 655.
Utilitatis, Formula, column 655.
Georgius, Livinus, column 631–32.

2-G SCHWIEDER, GEORGIUS [1962 CE]. *Latine Loquor*. Rome: Herder, 1953. Citations:

II, 10, *Ludovicus, Maximilianus*, p. 68.
II, 11, *Michael, Norbertus*, p. 69.
II, 13, *Norbertus, Otto*, p. 71.
II, 15, *Robertus, Patricius*, p. 72.
II, 15, *Paulus, Renatus*, p. 73.
III, 45, *Iacobus, Iulius*, p. 185.
III, 46, *Lucas, Lambertus*, p. 186.
III, 47, *Paulus, Ioannes*, p. 187.
III, 48, *Norbertus, Maximilianus*, p. 187.
IV, 48, *Praeceptor, Terentius*, p. 244.
IV, 49, *Praeceptor, Vincentius*, p. 245.
IV, 52, *Adolphus, Praeceptor*, p. 247.
IV, 53, *Albertus, Magister*, p. 248.

2-H FRITSCH BEROLINENSIS, ANDREAS [1996 CE]. *Index sententiarum ac locutionum. Handbuch lateinischer Sätze und Redewendungen*. Saarbrücken: Verlag der Societas Latina, 1996.

2-I PISINI, MAURUS [2001 CE]. *Apollo et Hyacinthus*, excerpts from acts 1–2. In *Latinitas* 49 (2001): 11–13, 14–15, 17–18.

THIRD EXPERIENCE

3-A CAESAR, GAIUS IULIUS [102–44 BCE]. *De bello gallico* V, 12–14; VI, 12–19. In *Commentariorum pars prior qua continentur libri VII de bello gallico cum A. Hirti supplement*. Edited by R. du Pontet. Scriptorum classicorum bibliotheca oxoniensis. Oxford: Clarendon Press, repr. 1900.

3-B PUBLILIUS SYRUS [65–5 BCE]. *Publilii Syri mimi sententiae*. In *Minor Latin Poets*. 2 vols. Edited by J. W. Duff and A. M. Duff, 3–111. Cambridge, MA, and London: Harvard University Press and William Heinemann, ^{2}1935. Reprinted 1982. Citations: 34, 36, 38, 40, 42, 44, 46, 102, 106, 110.

3-C CURTIUS RUFUS, QUINTUS [25–75 CE]. *Historiae Alexandri* IX, 1, 1–2, 15. Cf. *Quintus curtius: History of Alexander*. 2 vols. Edited by J. Henderson, 368–69. Translated by J. C. Rolfe. Loeb Classical Library. Cambridge, MA, and London: Harvard University Press, 1946. Reprinted, 2006. Translation based on the edition of Hedicke. Leipzig: Teubner, 1908. Latin text based on the edition of Hedicke.

3-D SENTENTIARUM STRUCTURA LATINARUM [200 BCE–2001 CE], Scriptores plurimi.

1. PONTIFEX PIUS II (AENEAS SYLVIUS PICCOLOMINI) [1458–1474 CE]. *Commentariorum Pii II. Pont. Max.* XI, 2, 14–24, in PIUS PP. II, *Commentarii rerum memorabilium, que temporibus suis contigerunt*. 2 vols. Edited by A. van Heck. Vol. 2, 639. Studi e testi 312–13. Vatican City: Bibliotheca apostolica Vaticana, 1984.
2. *Liturgia Horarum*. PAULI PP VI [1973–74 CE]. "Die 29 septembris Ss. Michaelis, Gabrielis et Raphaelis, Archangelorum Festum. Ad Vesperas. Hymnus." In *Officium divinum ex decreto Sacrosancti Oecumenicum Concilium Vaticanum II instauratum atque auctoritate Pauli PP. VI promulgatum: Liturgia horarum iuxta ritum Romanum, editio typical*. 4 vols. Vol. 4, 1168. Vatican City: Typis polyglottis Vaticanis, 1973–1974. *Editio typica altera*. Vol. 4, 1251–52. Vatican City: Libreria editrice Vaticana, ^{2}2000.
3. VERGILIUS MARO, PUBLIUS [70–19 BCE]. *Georgicon* II, 362–369. In *P. Vergili Maronis Opera*. Edited by F. A. Hirtzel. Scriptorum classicorum bibliotheca oxoniensis. Oxford: Clarendon Press, 1900. Reprinted, 1959.
4. SENECA, LUCIUS ANNAEUS [4 BCE–65 CE]. *Consolatio ad Heluiam matrem* 17, 2. In *L. Annaei Senecae Dialogorum libri XII*. Edited by L. D. Reynolds, 312. Scriptorum classicorum bibliotheca oxoniensis. Oxford: Clarendon Press, 1977. Reprinted, 1983.
5. PONTIFEX PIUS IX [1846–1878 CE]. Epistola *Cum non sine* ad archiepisc. Friburgensem (14 iulii 1864), par. 47, of "Propositiones Syllabi. VI. Errores de societate civili tum in se tum in suis ad Ecclesiam relationibus spectate," par. 5. In *Enchiridion symbolorum definitionum et declarationum de rebus fidei et morum*. Edited by H. Denzinger and A. Schönmetzer, n° 2947. Barcelona, Freiburg, Rome: Herder, $^{36\,\text{em}}$1976.
6. TERTULLIANUS, QUINTUS SEPTIMUS FLORENS [c. 150/170–c. 230 CE]. *De praescriptione haereticorum* XXVIII, 1. In *Enchiridion Patristicum*. Edited by M. J. Rouët de Journel, n° 295. Barcelona, Freiburg, Rome: Herder, 1981.

7. Catullus, Caius Valerius [c. 84–c. 54 bce]. *Carmina*, 61, 211–221. In *C. Valerii Catulli Carmina*. Edited by R. A. B. Mynors, 49. Scriptorum classicorum bibliotheca oxoniensis. Oxford: Clarendon, 1958. Reprinted, 1960.

3-E Ambrosius Mediolanensis [339–397 ce]. *Exameron* VI, 3, 9–20. In *Sancti Ambrosii Opera*. 7 vols. Vol. 1, 209–15. Edited by C. Schenkl. Corpus scriptorum ecclesiasticorum latinorum 32, Opera 1. Prague, Vienna, Leipzig: Tempsky and Freytag, 1897.

3-F Paulinus Nolanus [353–431 ce]. *Carmina* II; IIII; VI, 1–10; VIII; XII, 1–8; XIII; XXX. In *Sancti Pontii Meropii Paulini Nolani Carmina*. Edited by G. de Hartel. Corpus scriptorum ecclesiasticorum latinorum 30. Sancti Pontii Meropii Paulini Nolani Opera 2. Prague, Vienna, Leipzig: Tempsky and Freytag, 1894. Revised edition by Kamptner. Vienna: Verlag der Österreichischen Akademie der Wissenschaften (Austrian Academy of Sciences Press), [2]1999. II, p. 2; IIII, 3; VI lines 1–10, p. 7; VIII, 20–21; XII lines 1–8, p. 42–43; XIII, 44–45; XXX, 307.

3-G Beda Venerabilis [673–735 ce]. *Historia ecclesiastica* V, 9, 1–10, 4. In *Bedae Venerabilis presbyteri Anglo-saxonis Historica ecclesiastica*. Edited by J.-P. Migne. PL 95: 241A–245A. Paris, 1861.

3-H Villelmus Tyrensis [1130–1185 ce]. *Chronicon* 1–4. Cf. Willelmus Tyrensis, *Chronicon*. 2 vols. Edited by R. B. C. Huygens, H. E. Mayer and G. Rösch. Corpus christianorum continuatio mediaevalis 63, 63A. Turnhout: Brepols, 1986.

3-I latinarum structura sententiarum [200 bce–2001 ce]

1. Maximus Taurinensis [d. 408–423 ce], *Sermo* 33. "De eo quod scriptum est: *Simile est regnum Dei fermento*," 3. In *Maximi Episcopi Taurinensis: Collectionem sermonum antiquam nonnullis sermonibus extravagantibus adiectis*. Edited by A. Mutzenbecher, 128–31, citation 129. Corpus christianorum series latina 23. Turnhout: Brepols, 1962.
2. Sallustius Crispus, Gaius [86–c. 35 bce]. *De bello Iugurthino* 46, 1. In *Sallust*. Translated by J. C. Rolfe, 232. Loeb Classical Library 116. London and New York: William Heinemann and G. P. Putnam's Sons, 1921, [2]1931.
3. Concilium Oecumenicum Vaticanum II. Constitutio pastoralis de ecclesia in mundo huius temporis *Gaudium et spes* (7 decembris 1965), 26. In *Constitutiones, decreta, declarationes*. Edited by Secretaria generalis Concilii Oecumenici Vaticani II, 716–17. Vatican City: Typis polyglotis Vaticanis, 1966. (*Acta Apostolicae Sedis* 58 [1966]: 607–18).
4. Carmen Buranum [saec.XIII]. *Carmen* 48. "De mundi statu." Cf. *Carmina Burana. Die Lieder der Benediktbeurer Handschrift Zweisprachige Ausgabe*. Edited by A. Hilka and O. Schumann. Translated by C. Fischer and H. Kuhn. Munich: Deutscher taschenbuch Verlag, [6]1995.
5. *Liturgia Horarum*. Pauli PP VI [1973–74 ce]. "Die 15 augusti in assumptione Beatae Mariae Virginis Sollemnitas, ad I vesperas, preces." In *Officium divinum ex decreto Sacrosancti Oecumenicum Concilium Vaticanum II*

instauratum atque auctoritate Pauli PP. VI promulgatum: Liturgia horarum iuxta ritum Romanum, editio typica altera. 4 vols. Vol. 2, 1133. Vatican City: Typis polyglottis Vaticanis, [2]1987. (*Editio typica*, 1973–1974, vol. 4; *Editio typica altera*, [2]2000, 4).

6. Cicero, Marcus Tullius [106–43 bce]. *In C. Verrem orationes sex*, actionis secundae, I, 59, 154. In *Orationes*. 6 vols. Edited by W. Peterson. Scriptorum classicorum bibliotheca oxoniensis. Oxford: Clarendon, 1907. Reprinted, 1957.

3-K Poggius Bracciolini [1380–1459 ce]. *Epistolae*. II. *Poggius suo Leonardo Arretino* [30 May 1416]. In *Prosatori Latini del Quattrocento*. Edited by E. Garin, 213–301. La letteratura italiana. Storia e testi 13. Milan and Naples: Riccardo Riccardi, 1952. Citation: 228, 230, 232, 234, 236, 238.

3-L Maffeius, Ioannes Petrus [1536–1603 ce]. *Sinarum regio ac mores describuntur*.

3-M Pontifex Ioannes Paulus II [1981 ce]. Litterae encyclicae de labore humano *Laborem exercens* 1–2, 27 (14 septembris 1981). Vatican City: Libreria Editrice Vaticana, 1981 (*Acta Apostolicae Sedis* 73 [1981] 577–647; citation 577–580, 647).

FOURTH EXPERIENCE

4-A Nepos, Cornelius [100–25 ce]. "De excellentibus ducibus," 1–8. In *De viris illustribus*. In *Corneli Nepotis Vitae*. Edited by E. O. Winstedt. Scriptorum classicorum bibliotheca oxoniensis. Oxford: Clarendon, 1904. Reprinted, 1971.

4-B Vergilius Maro, Publius [70–19 bce]. *Aeneidos (ad usum serenissimi Delphini) lib* II, 196–238, 260–298. Cf. *P. Virgilii Maronis Opera*. Edited by Carolus Ruaeus, apud Fratres Vaillant & N. Prevost, Hagae-Comitum 1723, 236–37, 238–40.

4-C Gaius Iurisperitus [110–180 ce]. *Institutiones* liber I, 1–13, 58–63; III, 183–188. Cf. *idem*. 2 vols. Edited by F. De Zuzuleta. Scriptorum classicorum bibliotheca oxoniensis. Oxford: Clarendon Press, 1946, 1953.

4-D latinarum compositio scriptionum [200 bce–2001 ce]. Varia.

1. *Missale Romanum* Pauli VI [1977 ce]. *Missae rituales*. IV *Pro sponsis*. 1 *In celebratione matrimonii*. B *Praefatio*. In *Missale Romanum ex decreto Sacrosanti Oecumenici Concilii Vaticani II instauratum auctoritate Pauli PP. VI promulgatum*, 750. Vatican City: Typis Vaticanis, [2]1975.
2. Quintilianus, Marcus Fabius [35–95 ce]. *Institutio oratoria* II, 12, 1–4. In *idem*. Edited by L. Radermacher and V. Buchheit. Stuttgart: Teubner, 1959. Reprinted, 1971.
3. Iacopus Tudertinus [1230–1306 ce]. *Stabat Mater*. Cf. "Die 15 septembris Beatae Mariae Virginis perdolentis, Memoria. Ad Laudes matutinas. Hymnus" stanzas 1–4; "Ad Vesperas. Hymnus," stanzas 5–6. In *Officium divinum ex decreto Sacrosancti Oecumenicum Concilium Vaticanum II instauratum atque auctoritate Pauli PP. VI promulgatum: Liturgia horarum iuxta ritum Romanum, editio typica altera*. 4 vols. Vol. 2, 1215–16. Vatican

City: Typis polyglottis Vaticanis, ²1987. (*Editio typica* 1973–1974, 4, 1136–37; *Editio typica altera*, Libreria editrice Vaticana, Città del Vaticano ²2000, 4, 1215–16).

4. Hieronymus, Sophronius Eusebius [342–420 ce]. *Epistula* 125, 9, *cf. Epistulae CXXI–CLIV*. Edited by I. Hilberg, 128. Corpus scriptorum ecclesiasticorum latinorum 56. Sancti Eusebii Hieronymi Epistulae 3. 1910–1918.
5. S. Congr. S. R. U. Inquisitionis, Decretum quod damnantur plures propositiones ex operibus nuper editis sub nomine Antonii Rosmini Serbati *Hisce adiunctum litteris*, (7, 14 decembris 1887), XXII. In *Enchiridion symbolorum definitionum et declarationum de rebus fidei et morum*. Edited by H. Denzinger and A. Schönmetzer, nº 3222. Barcelona, Freiburg, Rome: Herder, 36 em1976. (*Cf. Acta Sanctae Sedis* 20 [1887] 403, xxii).
6. Propertius, Sextus [50–16 ce], *Elegiae* II, 4, 1–6. In *Sexti Properti Carmina*. Edited by I. S. Phillimore. Scriptorum classicorum bibliotheca oxoniensis. Oxford: Clarendon Press, 1901.
7. Augustinus, Aurelius [354–430 ce]. *De civitate Dei* XVI, 2, 1. In *Enchiridion Patristicum*. Edited by M. J. Rouët de Journel, nº 1765. Barcelona and Rome: Herder, 1981.

4-E Maximus Taurinensis [d. 408–423 ce], Maximus Taurinensis. *Sermones*. In *Maximi Episcopi Taurinensis: Collectionem sermonum antiquam nonnullis sermonibus extravagantibus adiectis*. Edited by A. Mutzenbecher. Corpus christianorum series latina 23. Turnhout: Brepols, 1962. Citations:

3 “De margarita evangelii” (p. 10–11).
13a “De sancta epyfania” (p. 44–46).
34 “De hospitalitate in evangelio” (p. 133–35).
53 “De pascha” (p. 214).

4-F Anselmus Cantuariensis [1033–1109 ce]. *Epistolae* excerptae. In *Opera Omnia*. 7 vols. Edited by F. S. Schmidt (*Epistulae* vol. 3, 4, 5). Edinburgh: Thomas Nelson and Sons, 1946–1951. Citations:

epist. 134, *Ad Ermengardam* (vol. III, p. 276–78).
epist. 167, 1–30, *Ad idam comitissam Bononiae* (vol. IV, p. 41–42).
epist. 184, *Ad monialem M. filiam Ricardi* (vol. IV, p. 68–69).
epist. 237, *Ad Athletis Abbatissam et moniales de Rumesei* (vol. IV, p. 144–45).
epist. 248, *Ad Mathildam reginam Anglorum* (vol. IV, p. 153–54).
epist. 268, *Ad Richezam sororem suam* (vol. IV, p. 183).

4-G Chatillon, Valtherus [1135–1170 ce]. Cf. *Moralisch-Satirische Gedichte Walters von Chatillon*. Edited by Karl Strecker. Heidelberg, 1929. Berlin, 1925. Citations:

Satire against the Curia.
His Song in his Last Sickness.
The Lover in Winter.
The Poet has a Daughter born to him.
De clericis.
His Song of Repentance.

4-H BOCCACCIO, IOANNES [1313–1375 CE]. *De mulieribus claris.* In *Giovanni Boccaccio, Famous Women.* Edited and translated by V. Brown. The I Tatti Renaissance Library. Cambridge, MA, and London: Harvard University Press, 2001. Citations:

XCII, *De Agrippina Neronis Caesaris matre* (384, 386, 388, 390, 392).
LXXXVIII, *De Cleopatra regina Egyptiorum* (p. 360, 362).

4-I LATINARUM COMPOSITIO SCRIPTIONUM [200 BCE–2001 CE], Scriptores plurimi.

1. LIUIUS, TITUS [59 BCE–17 CE]. *Ab urbe condita* IX, 30, 1–2. In *Titi Livi Ab urbe condita.* Edited by C. Flamstead Walters and R. Seymour Conway. Oxford, 1919. Vol. 2 reprinted, 1961.
2. TIBULLUS, ALBIUS [60–19 BCE]. Elegiae II, carmen 2, 1–9. In *Albii Tibulli aliorumque carminum libri tres*, II, 2, 1–9. Edited, I. Percival Postgate. Oxford, 1905. Reprinted, 1965.
3. PONTIFEX LEO MAGNUS [440–461 CE]. Tractatus 72, 6–7. In *Sancti Leonis Magni Romani Pontificis tractatus septem et nonaginta.* 2 vols. Vol. 2, page 448, lines 149–65. Edited by A. Chavasse. Corpus christianorum series latina 138, 138A. Turnhout: Brepols, 1973.
4. PONTIFEX IOANNES PAULUS II [1978–2005 CE]. Constitutio apostolica *Sacri Canones* (18 octobris 1990). In *Acta Apostolicae Sedis* 82 (1990): 1037.
5. PORCELLI, PETRUS [1530 CE]. "Pugna porcorum." In *Nugae venales sive thesaurus ridendi et jocandi,* 241–42. Frankfurt and Leipzig, 1703.
6. BACONIUS, ROGERUS [1214–1292 CE]. *Compendium philosophiae* V. In *A Primer of Medieval Latin. An Anthology of Prose and Poetry.* Edited by C. H. Beeson, 1, 301–2. The Lake Classical Series. Chicago, Atlanta, New York: Scott, Foresman and Company, 1925.

4-K KEPLER, IOANNES [1571–1630 CE]. *Dissertatio Kepleri. In nuncium sidereum.* Cf. G. Galilei, *Il sidereus nuncius e le scritture ad esso attinenti.* Le opere di Galileo Galilei, 3,1. Florence: Barbera, 1892. Reprinted, 1968. Note: this is Kepler's commentary on Galileo's work, which is included in the works of Galileo.

4-L PONTIFEX CLEMENS XIV [1773 CE]. *Suppressio, et extinctio Societatis Jesu.*

4-M JEDIN, HUBERTUS [1962 CE]. "Praefatio," "Introductio." In *Conciliorum Oecumenicorum Decreta, Conciliorum Oecumenicorum Decreta,* vii–ix, xi–xiii. Edited by G. Alberigo et alii. Centro di documentazione. Istituto per le scienze religiose. Basel et alibi: Herder, [2]1962.

FIFTH EXPERIENCE

5-A CICERO, MARCUS TULLIUS [106–43 BCE]. *Laelius de amicitia* 1–5, 16–22, 26–32, 40–42, 44–50. In *M. Tulli Ciceronis scripta quae manserunt Omnia.* Edited by O. Plasberg and W. Ax. Stuttgart: Teubner, 1965.

5-B HORATIUS FLACCUS, QUINTUS [65–8 BCE]. *Carminum liber tertius,* 1, 2, 8–10, 13, 18, 21–23, 26, 30. Cf. *Opera.* Edited by E. C. Wickham and H. W. Garrod.

Scriptorum classicorum bibliotheca oxoniensis. Oxford: Clarendon Press, 1901. Reprinted, 1957.

5-C TACITUS, PUBLIUS CORNELIUS [15–116 CE]. *De origine et situ germanorum liber* 1–22. In *Opera minora*. Edited by R. M. Ogilvie, 37–62. Scriptorum classicorum bibliotheca oxoniensis. Oxford: Clarendon, 1975. Reprinted, 1980.

5-D LACTANTIUS, CAECILIUS FIRMIANUS [240–320 CE]. *De opificio Dei* 1, 1–5, 1. In *L. Caeli Firmiani Lactanti Opera Omnia*. Edited by S. Brandt. Corpus scriptorum ecclesiasticorum latinorum 27. 2 vols. Vol. 1, 4–19. Vienna: Tempsky, 1893.

5-E AMBROSIUS MEDIOLANENSIS [339–397 CE]. In *Epistularum libri VII–IX*. Edited by M. Zelzer. Corpus scriptorum ecclesiasticorum latinorum 82. Opera 10, Epistulae et Acta. 3 vols. Vienna: Hoelder, Pichler, Tempsky, 1990. Citations:

V, 26, *Ambrosius Eusebio* (vol. 1, p. 179).
VI, 35, *Ambrosius Sisinnio* (vol. 1, p. 238–241).
VII, 44, *Ambrosius Romulo* (vol. 2, p. 43–44).
VII, 45, *Ambrosius Titiano* (vol. 2, p. 44–45).
VII, 53, *Ambrosius Candidiano Fratri* (vol. 2, p. 71).
VIII, 60, *Ambrosius Antonio* (vol. 2, p. 118–119).

5-F LULLIUS, RAIMUNDUS [1235–1315 CE]. *Liber natalis pueri paruuli Christi Iesu* [*opus* 169]. *Incipit Liber natalis,* I–II, 1; III, 12–V. In *Opera latina*, vol. 6 (opera 167–177), 7, 30–37. Edited by H. Harada. Corpus christianorum continuatio mediaevalis 32. Turnhout: Brepols, 1975.

5-G BOCCACCIO, IOANNES [1313–1375 CE]. *De mulieribus claris*. In *Giovanni Boccaccio, Famous Women*. Edited and translated by V. Brown. The I Tatti Renaissance Library. Cambridge, MA, and London: Harvard University Press, 2001. Citations:

[Dedicatio] (p. 2, 4, 6).
I. *De Eva parente prima* (p. 14, 16).
XLVII. *De Sapho puella lesbia et poeta* (p. 192, 194).
LXXXI. *De Iulia Gaii Caesaris dictatoris filia* (p. 338, 340).
CI. *De Iohanna anglica papa* (p. 436, 438, 440).
Conclusio (p. 472, 474).

5-H VERGILIUS, POLYDORUS [1470–1555 CE]. *De rerum inventoribus*, I, 14; II, 7, 9; III, 1. In *Polydori Vergilii urbinatis de Rerum Inventoribus libri VIII et de Prodigiis libri III cum indicibus locupletissimis,* 112–15, 117–18. Lugduni Batavorum (Leiden): apud Franciscum, 1644.

5-I CONCILIUM OECUMENICUM TRIDENTINUM [1545–1563 CE]. Sessio XXIV (11 novembris 1563). Doctrina de sacramento matrimonii. In *Conciliorum Oecumenicorum Decreta*. Edited by G. Alberigo et alii, 729–34. Centro di documentazione. Istituto per le scienze religiose. Basel et alibi: Herder, [2]1962. Citations:

Canones de sacramento matrimonii, Canones 1–12.
Canones super reformatione circa matrimonium, Capita 1–10.
Decretum de reformatione, Canones 1–3.
DOCTRINA DE SACRAMENTO MATRIMONII.

5-K BELLARMINUS, ROBERTUS [1542–1621 CE]. "Secunda controversia generalis de membris ecclesiae militantis [1615]" 14, 16, 15. Cf. BELLARMINUS, ROBERTUS, *Roberti Bellarmini Politiani Opera omnia ex editione veneta: pluribus tum additis tum correctis.* 12 vols. Edited by J. Fèvre and L. Vivès. Paris, 1870–1874.

5-L SIGNORIELLO, NUNTIUS [1931 CE]. *Lexicon peripateticum* In *Lexicon Peripateticum Philosophico-Theologicum in quo scholasticorum distinctiones et effata praecipua explicantur.* Edited by N. Signoriello. Rome: Frideric Pustet, [5]1931. Citations:

'V' Effata, 1–9 (p. 437–441).
'B' Effata, 1–8 (p. 52–57).
'N' Effata, 1–2 (p. 250–51).

5-M PONTIFEX PIO XII [BACCI, ANTONIUS, *papal Latinist* 1957 CE]. Litterae encyclicae *Miranda prorsus* (8 septembris 1957). In *Acta Apostolicae Sedis* 49 (1957): 765–805, citation 765–66, 769–771, 776, 777–78, 784–85, 793–94, 799, 500–501, 805. Note: A. Bacci was the papal Latinist when this document was promulgated by Pope Pius XII.

LECTIONVM AVCTORES

authors of the reading sheets

Epistula, LII, 15. 1-D, 9
Epistula CXXV, 9. 4-D, 4
HORATIUS FLACCUS, QUINTUS [65–8 BCE],
Carminum liber tertius, 1, 2, 8–10, 13, 18, 21–23, 26, 30. 5-B
Epistularum lib. I. 8–12. 1-A

IACOBUS TUDERTINUS [1230–1306 CE], *Stabat Mater.* 4-D, 3
IOHANNES PP. XXII [1316–1334 CE],
Constitutio *Gloriosam Ecclesiam* 1, 14 (23 ianuarii 1318). 1-D, 3
IOANNES PAULUS PP. II [1978–2005 CE],
Litterae encyclicae de labore humano *Laborem exercens* (14 septembrii 1981). 3-M
Constitutio apostolica *Sacri Canones* (18 octobris 1990). 4-I, 4

JEDIN, HUBERTUS [1962 CE], "Praefatio," "Introductio" to *Conciliorum Oecumenicorum Decreta*, ed. Alberigo. 4-M

KEPLER, IOANNES [1571–1630 CE],
Dissertatio Kepleri. In nuncium sidereum. 4-K

LACTANTIUS, CAECILIUS FIRMIANUS [240–320 CE],
De opificio Dei 1, 1–5, 1. 5-D
LEO MAGNUS PP. [440–461 CE],
Tractatus 58, 5. 1-I, 5
Tractatus 72, 6–7. 4-I, 3
LIVIUS, TITUS [59 BCE–17 CE], *Ab urbe condita* IX, 30, 1–2. 4-I, 1
LUCRETIUS CARUS, TITUS [99–55 BCE],
De rerum natura V, 281. 1-D, 1
De rerum natura, V, 1448–453. 1-I, 8
LULLIUS, RAIMUNDUS [1235–1315 CE], *Liber natalis pueri paruuli Christi Iesu* [*opus* 169], *Incipit Liber natalis*, I-II, 1, III, 12-V. 5-F

MAFFEIUS, IOANNES PETRUS [1536–1603 CE],
Sinarum regio ac mores describuntur. 3-L
MAXIMUS TAURIENSIS [d. 408–423 CE], *Collectio sermonum antiqua:*
3 "De margarita evangelii." 4-E
13a "De sancta epyfania." 4-E
33. "De eo quod scriptum est: *Simile est regnum Dei fermento.*" 3-I, 1
34 "De hospitalitate in evangelio." 4-E
53 "De pascha." 4-E

NEPOS, CORNELIUS [100–25 CE],
"De excellentibus ducibus" 1-8, in *De viris illustribus.* 4-A
Nova Vulgata Bibliorum Sacrorum editio [1979 CE],
Liber primus Maccabaeorum 1.1–2.37. 1-E

OVIDIUS NASO, PUBLIUS [43 BCE–18 CE], *Tristia* IV, 10, 57–60. 1-D, 4

PAULI PP. VI [1971 CE], *Liturgia horarum iuxta ritum Romanum*
  "Die 15 augusti in assumptione Beatae Mariae Virginis Sollemnitas, ad I vesperas, preces," 3-I, 5
  "Die 15 septembris Beatae Mariae Virginis perdolentis, Memoria. Ad Laudes matutinas. Hymnus," "Ad Vesperas. Hymnus." 4-D, 3
  "Die 29 septembris Ss. Michaelis, Gabrielis et Raphaelis, Archangelorum Festum. Ad Vesperas. Hymnus." 3-D, 2

PAULI PP. VI [1975 CE], *Missale Romanum*
  "Die 9 octobris, Ss. Dionysii, episcopi, et sociorum, martyrum, Collecta." 1-I, 3
  Missae rituales. IV *Pro sponsis*. 1 *In celebratione matrimonii*. B *Praefatio*. 4-D, 1
  "Praefatio De Sanctis virginibus et religiosis." 1-D, 6

PAULINUS NOLANUS [353–431 CE],
  Carmina: II; IIII; VI, 1–10; VIII; XII, 1–8; XIII; XXX. 3-F

PISINI, MAURUS [2001 CE],
  Apollo et Hyacinthus, excerpts from acts 1–2. 2-I

PIUS PP. II (AENEAS SYLVIUS PICCOLOMINI) [1458–1464 CE],
  Commentariorum Pii II. Pont. Max. XI, 2, 14–24. 3-D, 1

PIUS PP. IX [1846–1878 CE],
  Lettera *Cum non sine* to the Archbishop of Friburg (14 July 1864). 3-D, 5

PIUS PP. XII [1939–1958 CE] [ANTONIUS BACCI, papal Latinist 1957 CE], Litterae encyclicae *Miranda prorsus* (8 septembris 1957). 5-M

PLAUTUS, TITUS MACCIUS [254–184 CE], 2-A
  Asinaria 373–618.
  Bacchides 172–177. 1-I, 4

PLINIUS SECUNDUS, CAIUS [61/62–113 CE], *Epistulae* IX, 28, 1. 1-I, 2

PORCELLI, PETRUS [1530 CE], "Pugna porcorum." 4-I, 5

PROPERTIUS, SEXTUS [50–16 CE], *Elegiae* II, 4, 1–6. 4-D, 6

PUBLILIUS SYRUS [65–5 BCE], *Publilii Syri mimi sententiae*. 3-B

QUINTILIANUS, MARCUS FABIUS [35–95 CE],
  Institutio oratoria II, 12, 1–4. 4-D, 2

S. CONGR. S.R.U. INQUISITIONIS [1887 CE], Decretum quod damnantur plures propositiones ex operibus nuper editis sub nomine Antonii Rosmini Serbati *Hisce adiunctum litteris*, (7, 14 decembris 1887), XXII. 4-D, 5

SALLUSTIUS CRISPUS, GAIUS [86-C. 35 BCE],
  De bello Iugurthino 46, 1. 3-I, 2

SCHWIEDER, GEORGIUS [1962 CE], *Latine Loquor*. 2-G
  II, 10, *Ludovicus, Maximilianus* (p. 68). 2-G
  II, 11, *Michael, Norbertus* (p. 69). 2-G
  II, 13, *Norbertus, Otto* (p. 71). 2-G
  II, 15, *Robertus, Patricius* (p. 72). 2-G
  II, 15, *Paulus, Renatus* (p. 73). 2-G
  III, 45, *Iacobus, Iulius* (p. 185). 2-G
  III, 46, *Lucas, Lambertus* (p. 186). 2-G

LOCI ADLATI

texts having been quoted

AVCTORVM A NOBIS COMMEMORATORVM NOMINA

names of authors mentioned by us

Arranged alphabetically according to their English equivalent

Ambrose: Ambrosius Mediolanensis (333–397 CE)
Aquinas: Thomas Aquinas (c. 1225–1274)
Augustine: Aurelius Augustinus Hipponensis (354–430 CE)
Bembo, Pietro (1470–1547)
Caesar: Gaius Iulius Caesar (c. 100–44 BCE)
Catullus: Gaius Valerius Catullus (c. 84–c. 54 BCE)
Cicero: Marcus Tullius Cicero (106–43 BCE)
Cyprian: Thascius Caecilius Cyprianus Carthaginiensis (c. 200–258 CE)
Dante: Dantes Alagherius (1265–1321)
Egger: Carolus Egger (1914–2003)
Eichenseer: Caelestis Eichenseer (1924–2008)
Erasmus: Desiderius Erasmus Roterodamus (1466–1536)
Jerome: Eusebius Hieronymus (c. 342–420 CE)
Horatius: Quintus Horatius Flaccus (65–8 BCE)
Isidore: Isidorus Hispalensis (560–636 CE)
Leo: Leo Magnus (Pope, 440–461 CE)
Livy: Titus Livius (59 BCE–17 CE)
Lucilius: Gaius Ennius Lucilius (c. 180–103/2 BCE)
Lucretius: Titus Lucretius Carus (c. 99–c. 55 BCE)
Martial: Marcus Valerius Martialis (c. 40–c. 103 CE)
More: Thomas Morus (1478–1535)
Nepos: Cornelius Nepos (c. 100–c. 25 BCE)
New Vulgate Bible: *Nova Vulgata Bibliorum Sacrorum editio* ²1986
Ovid: Publius Ovidius Naso (43 BCE–17 CE)
Piccolomini: Aeneas Sylvius Piccolomini (1405–1464), Pius II (458–1464)
Pius XI: Achille Ambrogio Damiano Ratti (1922–1939)
Plautus: Titus Maccius Plautus (c. 254–184 BCE)
Pliny: Gaius Plinius Caecilius Secundus (minor; 61/62–113 CE)
Politianus: Angelus Politianus (1454–1494)
Quintilian: Marcus Fabius Quintilianus (c. 35–c. 95 CE)
Sallustius: Gaius Sallustius Crispus (86–c. 35 BCE)
Seneca: Lucius Annaeus Seneca (c. 4 BCE–65 CE)

Tacitus: Gaius Publius Cornelius Tacitus (c. 55–c. 119 CE)
Terentius: Publius Terentius Afer (195/185–c. 159 BCE)
Tertullian: Quintus Septimius Florens Tertullianus (c. 150/170–c. 230 CE)
Thomas Aquinas (c. 1225–1274)
Tibullus: Albius Tibullus (c. 60–19 BCE)
Virgil: Publius Vergilius Maro (70–19 BCE)
Vulg. Nov. *Nova Vulgata Bibliorum Sacrorum editio* 1998

RECENTIORUM NOMINA

names of more recent people

ARGVMENTA

subject matters

Compiled by Daniel Vowles

Topics are followed by their respective encounters numbered from 1 to 105.

PARTES SIVE CASVS ATQVE MVNERA QVIBVS PERFVNGI NOMINA ADIECTIVA PRONOMINA POSSVNT LATINA

roles or cases and functions
which Latin nouns, adjectives, pronouns can perform

Compiled by Daniel Vowles

Topics are followed by their respective encounters numbered from 1 to 105.

CONIVNCTIVI DE (MVLTIPLICI) VSV DISCEPTATIONVM ELENCHVS

a list of discussions about the (multiple) use of the subjunctive

Compiled by Daniel Vowles

Topics are followed by their respective encounters numbered from 1 to 105.

DE SCRIPTORIBVS

about the authors

FR. REGINALDUS THOMAS FOSTER OCD is a Discalced Carmelite priest from Milwaukee, Wisconsin. For forty years a papal Latinist and professor of the Latin language, he is renowned for his unique pedagogical method and presentation of the living Latin language. His long experience of the Latin language and dedication to teaching have made his clear presentation of Latin the standard method of teaching the language directly and without jargon or confusing terminology. In 2010 the University of Notre Dame in Indiana recognized *Reginaldus Legum Doctor honoris causa* for his contribution to the field of Latin studies. Reginald continues to teach Latin for free in Milwaukee throughout the year and during summer school every June and July.

FR. DANIEL P. McCARTHY OSB is a monk of St Benedict's Abbey, Atchison, Kansas. His study of the Latin language, concurrent with his doctoral study of liturgy in Rome, led to his collaboration as assistant and eventual colleague of Reginald. He wrote weekly commentaries on the prayers of the liturgy with original English translations published in *The Tablet* of London, England, from 2006 through 2011. With Dom James Leachman he is co-founder of the project *Appreciating the Liturgy* and of the teaching and research *Institutum Liturgicum*, London, England, where he teaches the Latin language and liturgy; and serves as co-editor of the publication project *Documenta rerum ecclesiasticarum instaurata*, with the series *Liturgiam aestimare*: *Appreciating the Liturgy*. He serves as a guest professor of the Katholieke Universiteit, Leuven, Belgium, and on the editorial board *Questions Liturgiques: Studies in Liturgy*. He also serves as a liturgical consultant for building and renovating churches. In February 2016 he began to teach on the faculty of the Pontifical Institute of Liturgy, Rome, by offering courses on the Latin expression and theological meaning of short prayers of the liturgy. He also serves as an advisor to the *Vox clara* committee of the Congregation for Divine Worship and the Discipline of the Sacraments.

ADIVTORES

helpers

MSGR. DANIEL B. GALLAGHER is a priest of the Diocese of Gaylord who has succeeded his *magister*, Reginaldus, in the Latin Section of the Vatican Secretariat of State. In addition to having taught Latin for several years, he is the author of numerous articles in Thomistic philosophy, metaphysics, and aesthetics.

FR. JAMES LEACHMAN, OSB, is a monk of Ealing Abbey, London, and associate tenured professor emeritus at the Pontifical Liturgical Institute, Rome, and guest professor at the Katholieke Universiteit, Leuven, Belgium. He is co-founder of the project *Appreciating the Liturgy*. He is a founding member of the *Institutum Liturgicum*, London, England. He founded the Benedictine Study and Arts Centre, Ealing, now renamed Benedictine Institute. He serves on the editorial boards of *Ecclesia Orans* and of *Questions Liturgiques/Studies in Liturgy*. He teaches the Latin language and Liturgical Spirituality and Monastic Studies in Ealing and is training in Process Oriented Psychology.

DANIEL VOWLES knows this volume better than most, because Daniel has been using a draft edition to teach the First and Third Experiences during the *Experientiae Latinitatis aestivae*, "Latin Summer Experiences" 2009–2014 and during academic term from 2011–2015 at the Benedictine Study and Arts Centre, Ealing, London. Daniel Vowles observed the students' responses to the material presented from the draft of this book, and from these personal encounters made numerous and meaningful suggestions to the First and Third Experiences that have significantly improved the quality and usefulness of this book. A monument of this type requires a comparable index to provide thoroughgoing access to the user. The index of elements was painstakingly prepared by Daniel Vowles, which will serve this and the subsequent book, *Ossium carnes multae: The Bones' Meats Abundant.*

AGNOSCENDA MERITA

acknowledgments

BENIGNITATI HORVM IPSORVM QVANTVM
MERITO DEBETVR AC LIBERALITATI
COEPTIS NEMPE NOSTRIS STVDIISQVE PROVEHENDIS

HISCE TANTVNDEM IMPARES VERSICVLIS
REDDERE HIS EQVIDEM ENITIMVR
GRATIIS CONGRVIS EX ANIMO REFERENDIS

How much is meritedly owed
to the kindness of these very people and generosity
by promoting namely our undertakings and studies

with these small expressions we unequal to the task
are striving to render to these the same amount
by returning suitable thanks from the heart.

This contribution could not have been realized without our reliance upon the generosity and hospitality of others to whom we return heartfelt thanks.

For their welcome throughout the dictation and editing process of the manuscript, the authors wish to thank the Franciscan Sisters of St. Clare, Sr. Mary Celine Stein and Sr. Mary Patricia Reilly, along with the staff of St. Clare Terrace, Milwaukee, and its late Director Margo O'Malley and her successor, Anne Guetersohn. For providing lodging and a quiet study, we are grateful to Catholic Memorial High School, Waukesha, Wisconsin, and its President, Fr. Paul Hartmann and also to the Parish of St. Aloysius, West Allis, Wisconsin, and to their pastor Fr. Jeffrey Prasser. Also of the parish, Mary Wenger gave the use of her camera and helped with Gabriella Pellant to photograph two of the books whose images are presented on several of the reading sheets. Several of Reginald's students helped to facilitate communication across the globe by printing and presenting questions to him and relaying his responses; among these were Christine Zainer and Rita McKillip.

We are grateful to Abbot Martin Shipperlee, OSB, and the monks of Ealing Abbey, London, England, for their hospitality and encouragement when we conducted the dictation and editing process of this text from their side of the pond. For the monastic leisure and the resources necessary to bring this project to completion, we are grateful to Abbot James Albers, OSB, and his predecessor Abbot Barnabas Senecal,

OSB, and the monks of St. Benedict's Abbey, Atchison, Kansas. The final touches on this book were given while Daniel McCarthy was a grateful guest and enjoyed the personal thoughtfulness of Abbot Kris Op de Beeck and the community of Abdij Keizersberg, Leuven, Belgium.

Our gratitude is due to Fr. James Leachman, OSB, monk of Ealing Abbey, London, and recently emeritus associate tenured professor at the Pontifical Institute of Liturgy, where he taught the Latin language and the Latin structure of the prayers of the *Missale Romanum* using a draft copy of this book, courses which he also teaches at the *Institutum Liturgicum,* London, England, and at the Benedictine Institute, both of which he founded and directs at Ealing. Also at the Benedictine Institute, Daniel Vowles has for several years taught Latin using a draft copy of this book. We are grateful to Daniel Vowles for proof-reading this volume during its last stages of editing to catch the errors that authors too easily miss. From their teaching, both James Leachman and Daniel Vowles have contributed to this book's clarity and usefulness to teachers and students alike. The careful reading of Br. Thomas Cole, OSB, monk of Pluscarden Abbey, Scotland, also helped us to catch a number of oversights.

We appreciate the sustained encouragement of Msgr. Daniel Gallagher, Reginald's successor in the Latin Section of the Vatican Secretariat of State. He also coordinated the contribution of Mr. Giuseppe Aquino, by whose kind permission numerous photographs enhance this volume, and the contribution of Msgr. Peter Dai Bui, presbyter of the Diocese of Phoenix and an official at the Pontifical Council *Cor Unum*, whose photograph makes possible the presentation of the calligraphic dedication. Daniel Gallagher assisted with the contribution of Reginald's long-time associate, Roberto Bravi, the Vatican calligrapher by whose hand the dedication of this book, composed by Reginald, was given such beautiful form, as were numerous diplomas for the students of Reginald's Summer Latin School, *Schola Latinitatis Aestiva*. Reginald's Twelve Obelisk Tour is commemorated by Fr. Tim Finigan, presbyter of the Archdiocese of Southwark, England, whose photos of the Roman elephant obelisk he generously shares so that our readers may appreciate this Latin puzzle. Abbot Cuthbert Brogan, OSB, of St. Michael's Abbey, Farnborough, gave permission to photograph the *Antiphonale Monasticum ad usum Abbatiae S. Michaelis Farnburgensis*, whose illuminated image of Psalm 66 is proudly used here.

The digital photos have been prepared for publication in print by Dr. Michael McCarthy of Overland Park, Kansas, whose fine eye and technical accomplishment have elicited the original beauty of these, some now time-worn monuments of Latinity. His generous hosting of the website www.thelatinlanguage.org has helped Reginald communicate with both his alumni and other lovers of Latin. Accomplished in web and media production, Michael has helped us to produce the videos, audio recordings and flyers that have given personal form and extended the reach of this "body of Latin." With his media savvy and James Leachman's inspiration, Daniel McCarthy developed the crowd-source funding campaign *Treasures of the Latin Language* hosted at www.indiegogo.com/at/OSSA, whose investors provided the essential funds to help sustain Daniel while he and Reginald prepared this manuscript.

We could not have produced the collection of reading sheets without the personal and technical assistance of Jane Schuele, Librarian, and Miriam O'Hare, emerita librarian of Benedictine College, Atchison, Kansas. The reading sheets were completed only through the considerable effort of Kristen Schubert, research assistant of the Catholic University of America Press. We want to mention and publicly praise the professional expertise and persevering hard work of Carole C. Burnett, editor, who microscopically scrutinized the whole volume for faults, imprecisions, and errors, and to whom we the authors and reading public are endlessly grateful. Essential to our work was the access granted by Joan Sommer to the library holdings of the Raynor Memorial Libraries of Marquette University, and the high quality scans of several passages of the *Aeneidos ad usum Delphini* provided by Amy Cooper Cary of the Department of Special Collections and University Archives, Marquette University Libraries, Milwaukee, Wisconsin. The difficult task of reproducing several of the reading sheets was skillfully assisted by the generous help of the Paideia Institute for Humanistic Study, through the coordination of its President, Jason Pedicone, and by the technical competence of Claire Burgess and the Paideia 2014–2015 Rome Fellows, Christopher Cochran and Amy Garland. As we were putting the finishing touches on the last couple of translations and developing the list of citations and abbreviations of authors and works cited, both Paul-Isaac Franks, seminarian, and his confrère Fr. Joseph Wood, of St. Thomas Aquinas Seminary in Winona, Minnesota, provided their assistance and contribution which we gratefully received.

We trust that this volume will prove to be a perennial reference point and source of inspiration for those who come to appreciate the Latin language and its many authors and wish to share in turn the same with as many people as possible.

The Mere Bones of Latin According to the Thought and System of Reginald was
designed and typeset in Minion with Meta Sans by Kachergis Book Design of Pittsboro,
North Carolina. It was printed on 60-pound House White Web, and bound
by Sheridan Books of Chelsea, Michigan.